S0-FAJ-628

The cmdty Yearbook 2021

cmdty by Barchart

www.barchart.com/solutions/cmdty

Published by Barchart.com, Inc., Chicago, Illinois

For general information on our other products and services or for technical support, please contact our Customer Support Department within the United States at (800) 238-5814 outside the United States at (312) 554-8122 or fax (312) 939-4135.

ISBN 978-0-910418-09-6

Printed in the United States of America

10 9 8 7 6 5 4 3 2 1

Barchart.com
209 W. Jackson Blvd, 2nd Floor
Chicago, Illinois 60606
Phone: 800.238.5814 or 312.554.8122
Fax: 312.939.4135
Website: www.barchart.com/solutions/cmdty
Email: info@cmdtydata.com

Table of Contents

Commodity Indexes

The Refinitiv/Core Commodity CRB® Index (ticker symbol CRY) fell sharply in early 2020 on the Covid pandemic, which caused global economic shutdowns and a plunge in commodity prices. The CRY index edged to a 2-year high in early-January 2020 but then plunged by a total of -46% to a record low in March 2020.

After posting that record low in March, the CRY index then staged a partial recovery through the remainder of 2020 and closed the year down -9.7%. Commodity prices partially recovered due to the massive amount of monetary and fiscal stimulus implemented across the world. Also, commodity prices were led higher by precious metals, which rallied on safe-haven demand and fears of inflation from the monetary and fiscal stimulus. The CRY index was held back by weakness in crude oil prices and petroleum products, which took a hit from the sharp drop in global energy demand due to reduced business activity and a virtual shutdown in global travel.

Four of the six commodity sub-sectors closed higher in 2020, while two sub-sectors closed lower. The ranked returns in 2020 were as follows: Precious Metals +27.5%, Grains +26.3%, Industrials +19.5%, Softs +10.9%, Livestock -5.5%, Energy -12.2%.

Energy

The Energy sub-sector includes Crude Oil, Heating Oil, and Natural Gas. The Energy sub-sector in 2020 closed sharply lower by an average of -12.2%. On a nearest-futures basis, crude oil in 2020 closed down -20.5%, gasoline closed down -17.0%, and heating oil closed down -27.2%. However, natural gas closed higher by +16.0%. Crude oil prices and petroleum products were undercut in 2020 by the pandemic, which caused demand to plunge. However, oil prices partially recovered from their worst levels after OPEC+ implemented aggressive production cuts.

Grains

The Grains and Oilseeds sub-sector is composed of Corn, Soybeans, and Wheat. The Grains and Oilseeds sub-sector in 2020 closed sharply higher by an average of +26.3%, adding to the gains seen in the two previous years of +5.8% in 2018 and +7.1% in 2019. On a nearest-futures basis, soybeans in 2020 rose by +39.5%, corn rose by +24.8%, and wheat rose by +14.6%.

Industrials

The Industrials sub-sector includes Copper and Cotton. The Industrials sub-sector in 2020 closed sharply higher by an average of +19.5%, adding to the small +1.0% rise seen in 2019. Copper in 2020 rose by +25.8%, adding to the +6.3% gain seen in 2019. Cotton in 2020 rose by +13.1%, more than reversing the -4.4% decline seen in 2019.

Livestock

The Livestock sub-sector includes Live Cattle and Lean Hogs. The Livestock sub-sector in 2020 closed mildly lower by an average of -5.5%, giving back part of the +8.5% increase seen in 2019. On a nearest-futures basis, live cattle futures in 2020 closed -9.4%, adding to the small -0.1% decline seen in 2019. Lean hog futures in 2020 closed down -1.6%, giving back a little of the +17.1% gain seen in 2019.

Precious Metals

The Precious Metals sub-sector includes Gold, Platinum, and Silver. The Precious Metals sub-sector in 2020 closed sharply higher by an average of +27.5%, adding to the +18.7% gain seen in 2019. In 2020, gold rose by +24.4%, silver rose by +47.4%, and platinum rose by +10.7%.

Softs

The Softs sub-sector includes Cocoa, Coffee, Orange Juice, and Sugar #11. The Softs sub-sector in 2020 closed moderately higher by an average of +10.9%, adding to the +5.4% gain seen in 2019. In 2020, orange juice closed +26.8%, sugar closed +15.4%, cocoa closed +2.5%, and coffee closed -1.1%.

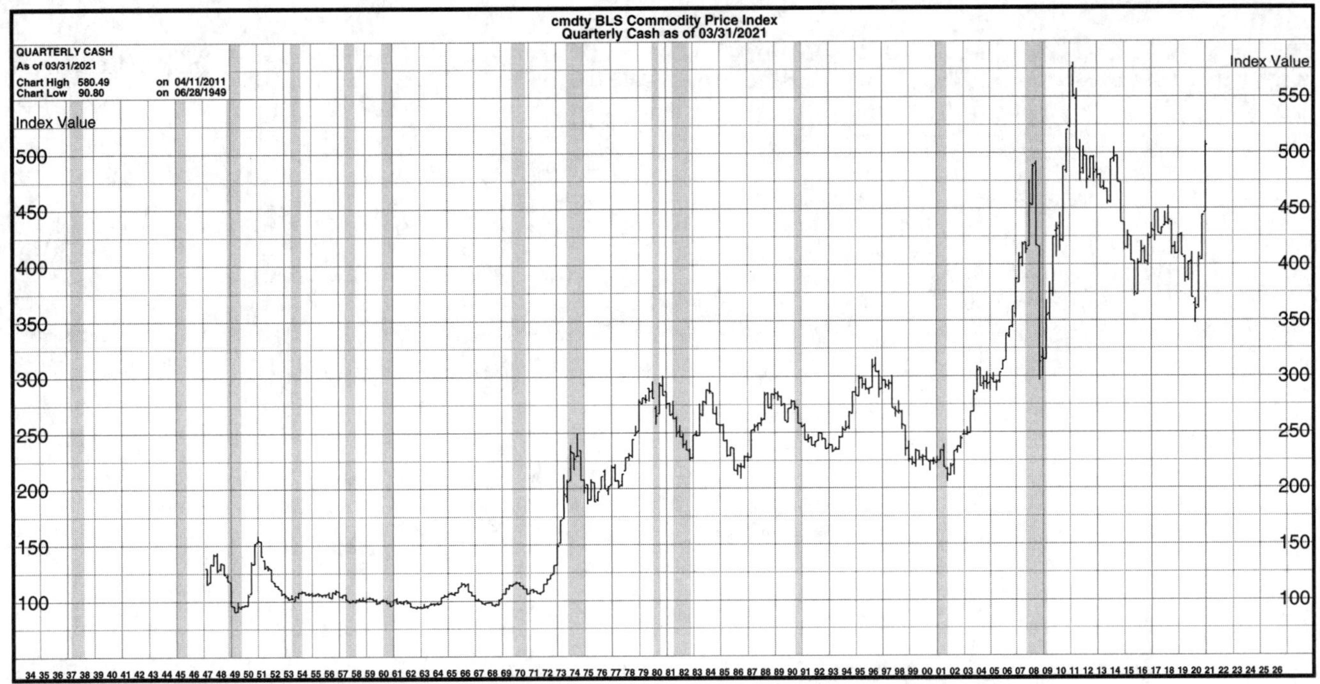

Unweighted Index of 23 Commodities: Hides, tallow, copper scrap, lead scrap, steel scrap, zinc, tin, burlap, cotton, print cloth, wool tops, rosin, rubber, hogs, steers, lard, butter, soybean oil, cocoa, corn, Kansas City wheat, Minneapolis wheat, and sugar. Shaded areas indicate US recessions.

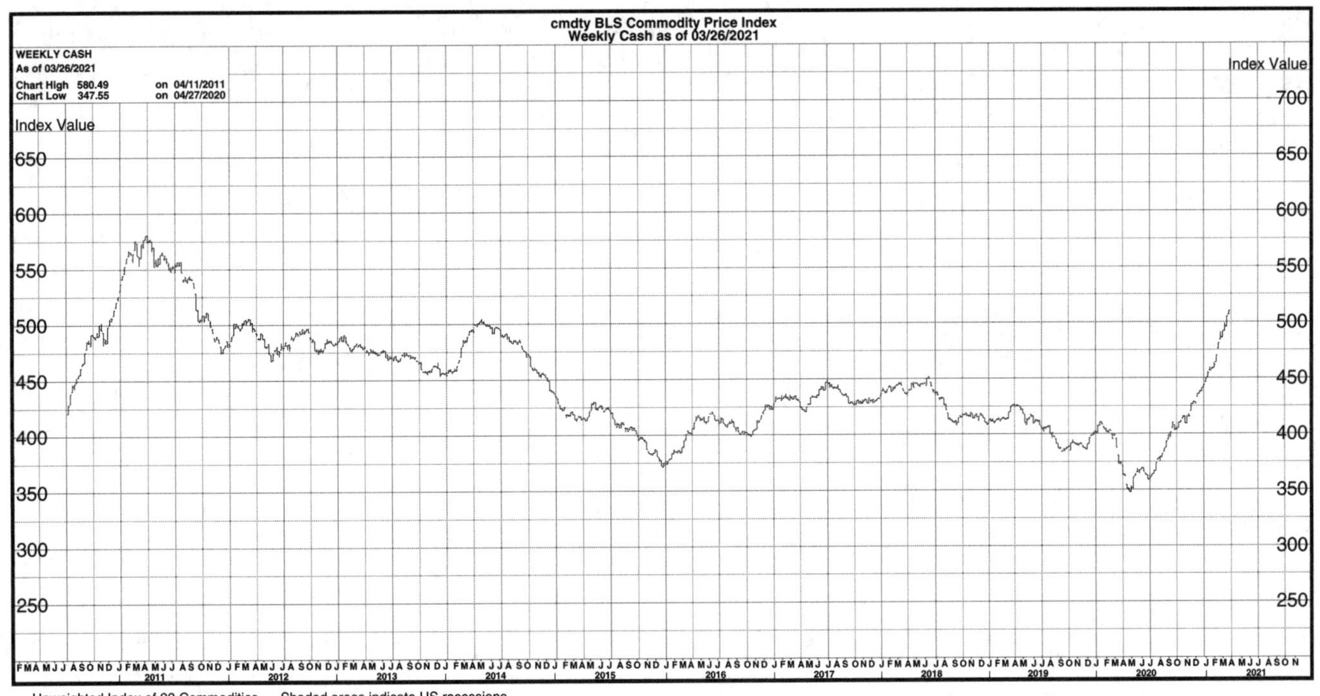

Unweighted Index of 23 Commodities. Shaded areas indicate US recessions.

cmdty BLS Commodity Price Index (1967=100)

Year	Jan.	Feb.	Mar.	Apr.	May	June	July	Aug.	Sept.	Oct.	Nov.	Dec.	Average
2011	538.09	562.60	566.40	575.61	559.14	557.32	553.30	543.59	527.83	506.85	496.08	480.93	538.98
2012	488.60	498.90	501.77	490.93	480.92	474.62	480.69	488.41	493.34	486.07	477.98	484.25	487.21
2013	485.62	481.97	481.13	477.55	474.67	474.05	469.75	471.23	470.60	462.25	458.57	459.56	472.25
2014	457.25	465.09	487.18	497.58	500.90	495.60	491.20	484.78	479.78	465.82	455.62	445.75	477.21
2015	429.10	420.06	416.96	415.41	425.99	424.32	416.08	408.18	405.50	397.38	385.58	379.17	410.31
2016	377.44	385.09	396.03	410.34	413.55	416.74	411.76	409.65	402.79	401.09	411.91	424.17	405.05
2017	431.01	433.68	433.15	423.76	431.69	440.28	444.10	439.00	430.79	428.83	430.05	430.49	433.07
2018	438.94	441.96	442.40	441.42	444.86	445.13	434.09	417.91	412.39	416.93	415.79	413.91	430.48
2019	412.09	413.25	419.52	424.52	414.57	412.09	405.07	395.48	385.93	390.23	389.27	395.16	404.77
2020	406.45	401.38	394.37	347.43	362.02	364.77	368.33	383.96	402.56	410.48	419.93	435.95	391.47

Average. *Source: cmdty by Barchart*

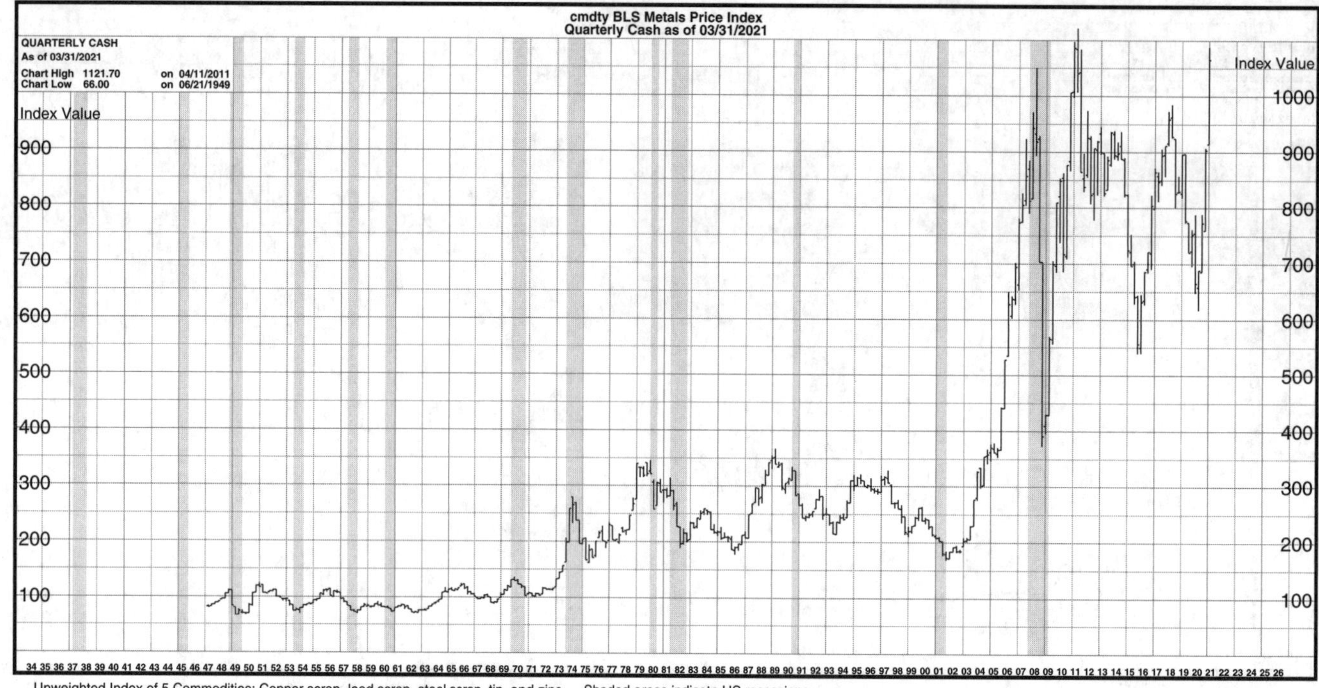

Unweighted Index of 5 Commodities: Copper scrap, lead scrap, steel scrap, tin, and zinc. Shaded areas indicate US recessions.

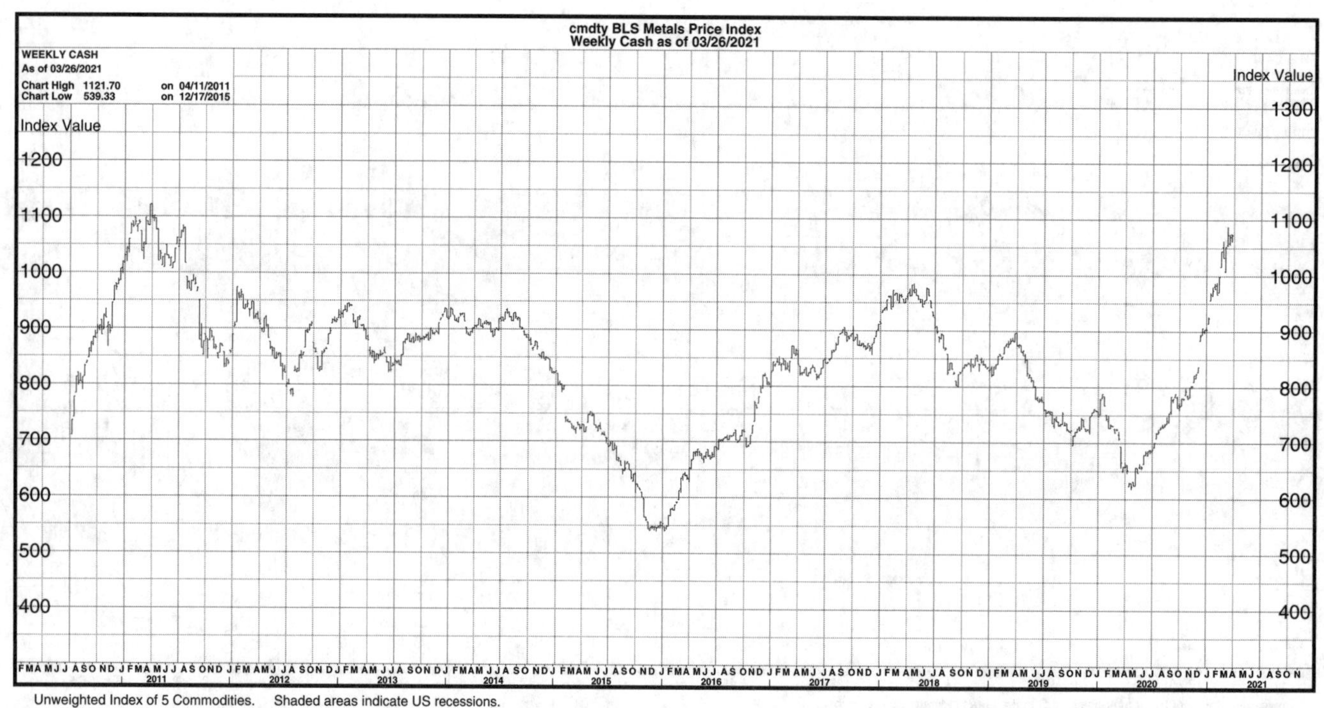

Unweighted Index of 5 Commodities. Shaded areas indicate US recessions.

cmdty BLS Metal Price Index (1967=100)

Year	Jan.	Feb.	Mar.	Apr.	May	June	July	Aug.	Sept.	Oct.	Nov.	Dec.	Average
2011	1,029.49	1,085.28	1,066.15	1,096.80	1,033.85	1,023.86	1,063.60	994.80	942.14	874.77	868.19	849.37	994.03
2012	903.04	949.99	931.85	908.47	878.62	843.33	800.76	828.46	883.07	862.76	859.31	910.40	880.01
2013	929.61	930.76	908.99	870.31	850.59	841.39	838.54	875.10	881.56	883.73	891.08	919.04	885.06
2014	925.99	920.45	900.88	905.67	908.51	897.46	921.84	922.59	903.65	876.01	856.97	836.99	898.08
2015	808.63	753.27	725.64	726.61	741.70	717.50	693.73	662.74	649.72	619.91	560.90	546.74	683.92
2016	549.39	582.24	628.81	662.38	675.30	676.25	698.07	709.14	710.14	705.02	762.46	807.03	680.52
2017	834.55	840.10	854.85	833.46	828.55	825.47	849.85	882.09	891.55	884.15	871.25	885.11	856.75
2018	938.18	960.91	957.84	970.72	955.27	954.43	896.38	848.71	816.40	837.13	842.37	840.64	901.58
2019	833.16	861.27	882.86	872.14	822.84	783.29	756.30	737.84	731.65	718.48	729.26	749.17	789.86
2020	766.00	732.19	688.18	636.00	651.04	680.58	713.15	739.13	775.25	780.54	806.50	886.86	737.95

Average. *Source: cmdty by Barchart*

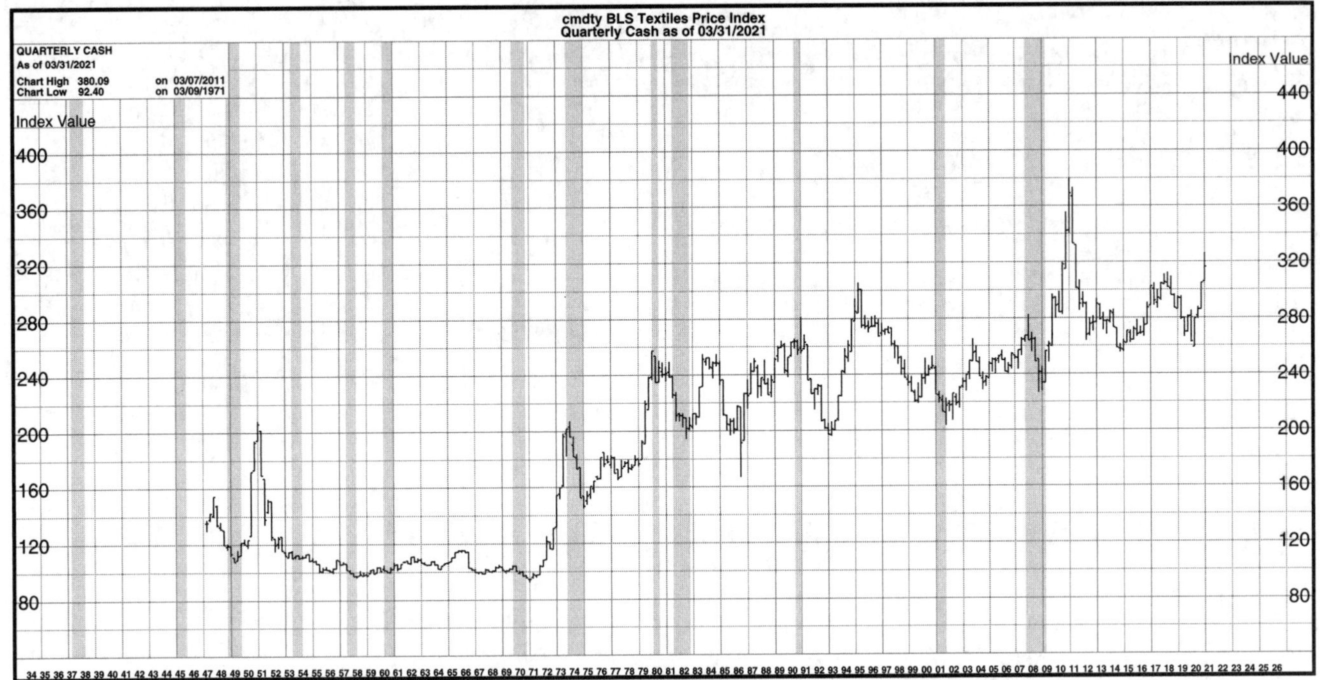

Unweighted Index of 4 Commodities: Burlap, cotton, print cloth, and wool tops. Shaded areas indicate US recessions.

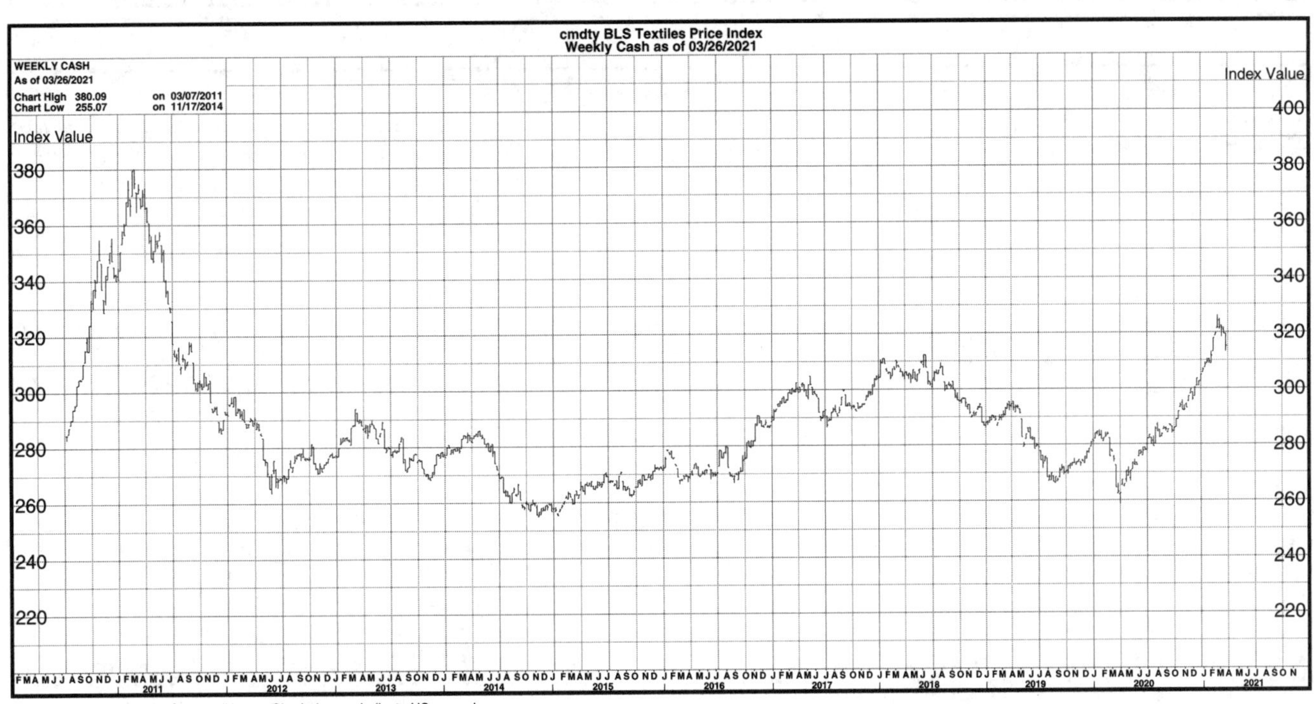

Unweighted Index of 4 Commodities. Shaded areas indicate US recessions.

cmdty BLS Textiles Price Index (1967=100)

Year	Jan.	Feb.	Mar.	Apr.	May	June	July	Aug.	Sept.	Oct.	Nov.	Dec.	Average
2011	347.26	365.82	372.19	365.44	352.18	344.70	319.66	310.92	310.19	303.37	299.19	289.50	331.70
2012	294.47	293.94	289.55	288.47	276.62	269.11	268.88	274.55	277.06	276.65	272.43	276.20	279.83
2013	279.44	283.14	289.79	286.96	286.20	283.33	278.59	278.23	275.03	274.73	269.70	275.78	280.08
2014	278.29	278.84	283.25	283.66	283.35	277.98	268.12	262.53	262.02	259.07	257.53	258.34	271.08
2015	257.16	260.85	261.80	265.21	265.95	267.24	267.42	267.46	263.78	266.74	268.72	271.68	265.33
2016	275.67	273.67	268.32	271.13	270.18	270.66	274.89	272.29	271.23	279.05	286.95	287.39	275.12
2017	292.60	296.28	299.77	300.52	299.68	293.69	290.06	292.93	295.83	293.56	295.50	301.02	295.95
2018	308.00	305.82	307.44	304.71	305.47	306.44	305.15	303.14	299.06	295.34	291.57	291.47	301.97
2019	288.81	288.83	292.65	293.47	284.62	281.83	275.44	268.15	269.65	271.96	273.52	277.23	280.51
2020	283.37	282.02	270.53	266.59	271.63	277.34	282.17	284.87	285.48	291.03	295.42	300.70	282.60

Average. *Source: cmdty by Barchart*

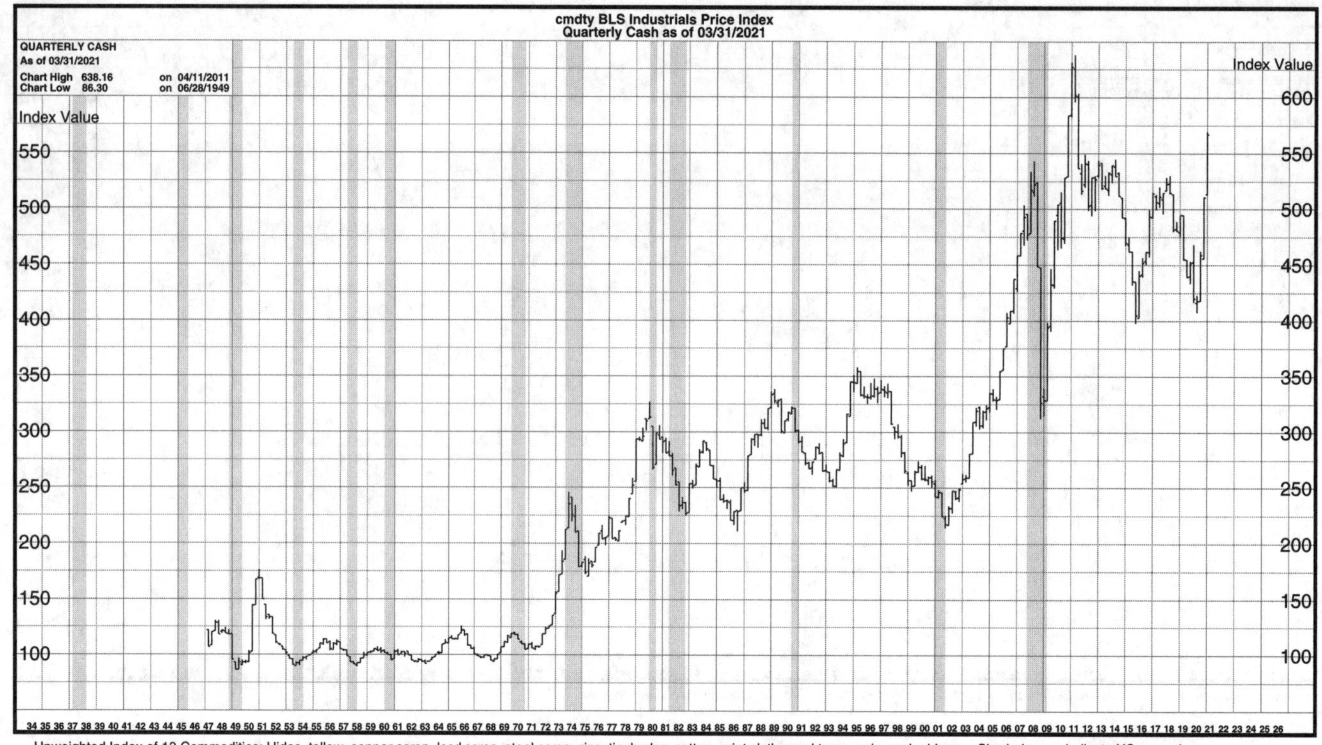

Unweighted Index of 13 Commodities: Hides, tallow, copper scrap, lead scrap, steel scrap, zinc, tin, burlap, cotton, print cloth, wool tops, rosin, and rubber. Shaded areas indicate US recessions.

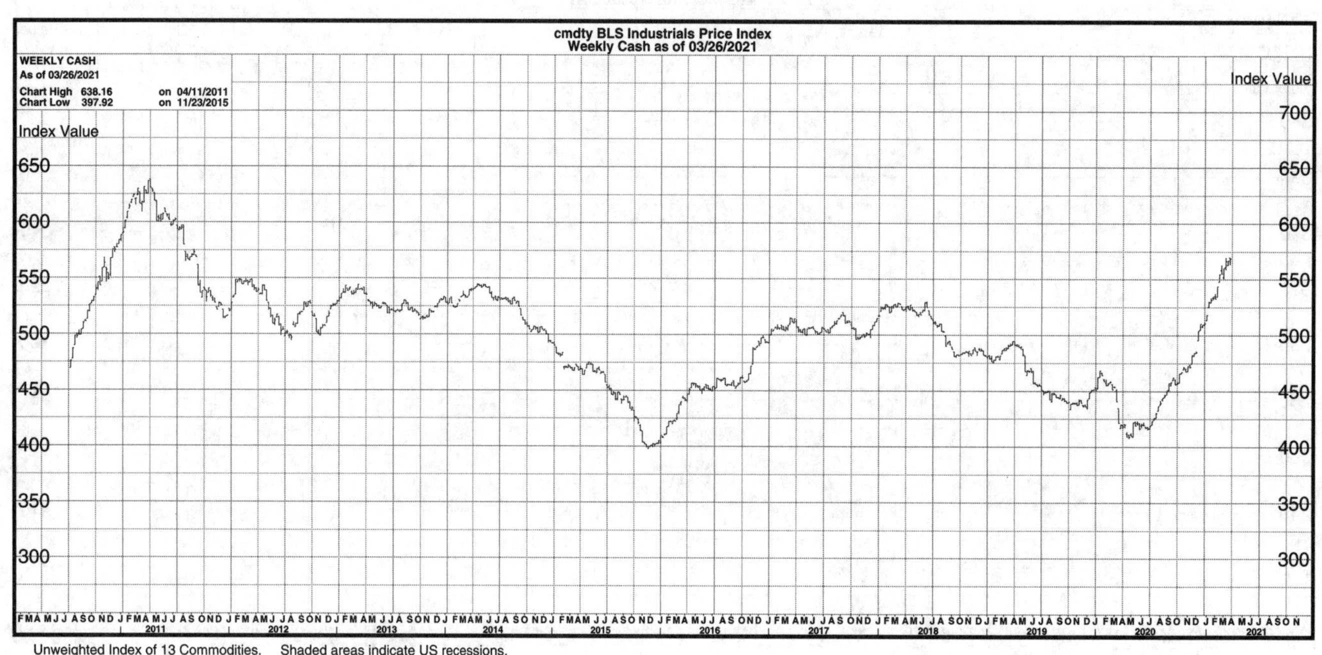

Unweighted Index of 13 Commodities. Shaded areas indicate US recessions.

cmdty BLS Industrials Price Index (1967=100)

Year	Jan.	Feb.	Mar.	Apr.	May	June	July	Aug.	Sept.	Oct.	Nov.	Dec.	Average
2011	595.51	619.22	621.89	628.72	606.29	602.99	596.81	573.01	559.74	536.77	528.95	519.49	582.45
2012	531.91	546.88	544.73	538.46	526.82	510.28	500.22	510.14	524.29	515.30	506.62	523.72	523.28
2013	534.06	538.69	539.87	532.46	524.75	523.74	520.86	525.30	521.20	514.92	519.98	529.58	527.12
2014	528.48	527.92	535.44	541.50	542.77	534.33	532.02	529.81	520.65	506.18	504.60	497.80	525.13
2015	485.52	474.22	470.13	467.83	471.58	466.96	451.80	443.96	439.86	424.27	403.04	401.58	450.06
2016	409.74	421.84	436.56	450.36	452.52	451.96	457.45	456.93	456.68	460.60	484.07	494.37	452.76
2017	503.07	506.20	510.83	505.47	504.70	502.57	504.42	511.92	513.67	502.70	499.14	506.88	505.96
2018	522.93	524.51	525.49	524.02	519.13	522.01	509.95	496.98	483.37	483.58	484.68	485.14	506.82
2019	479.23	482.58	490.35	490.65	471.54	458.61	449.63	445.49	442.17	438.31	438.36	446.51	461.12
2020	461.10	457.03	434.96	413.57	418.55	418.45	426.77	444.66	457.42	465.93	475.68	502.37	448.04

Average. *Source: cmdty by Barchart*

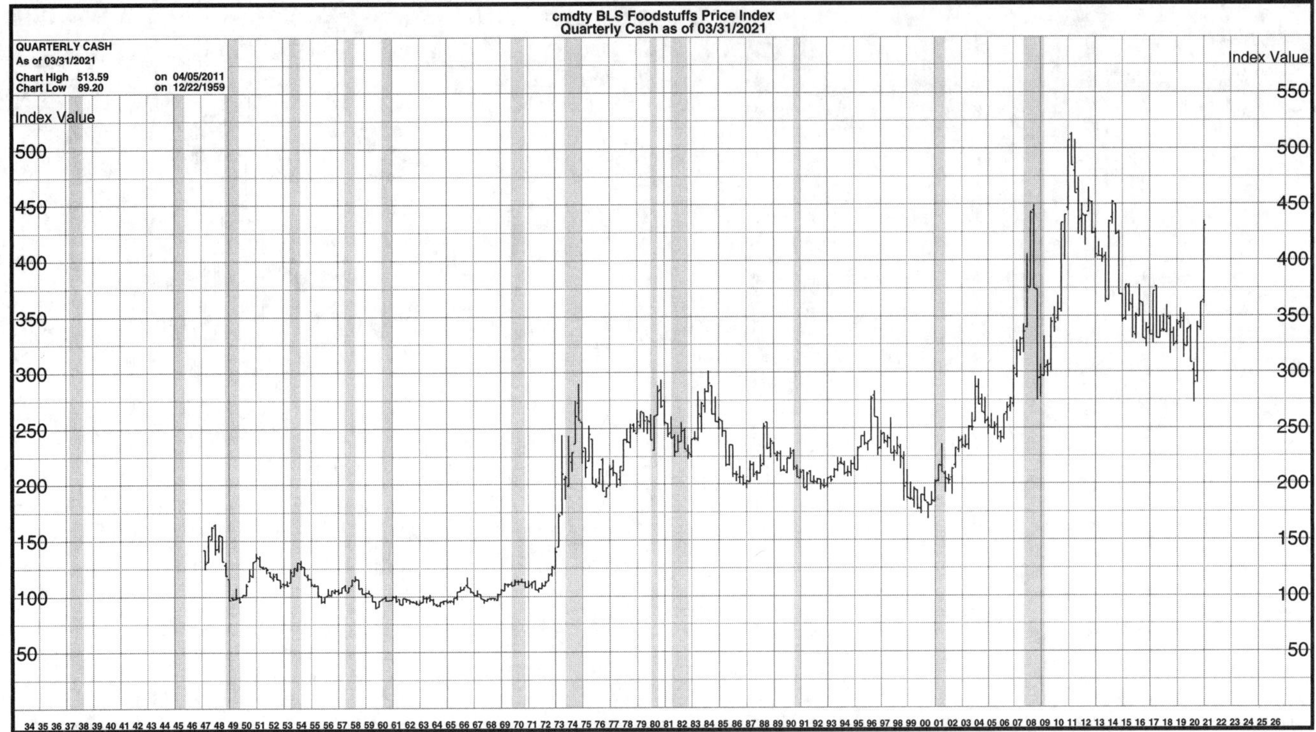

Unweighted Index of 10 Commodities: Hogs, steers, lard, butter, soybean oil, cocoa, corn, Kansas City wheat, Minneapolis wheat, and sugar. Shaded areas indicate US recessions.

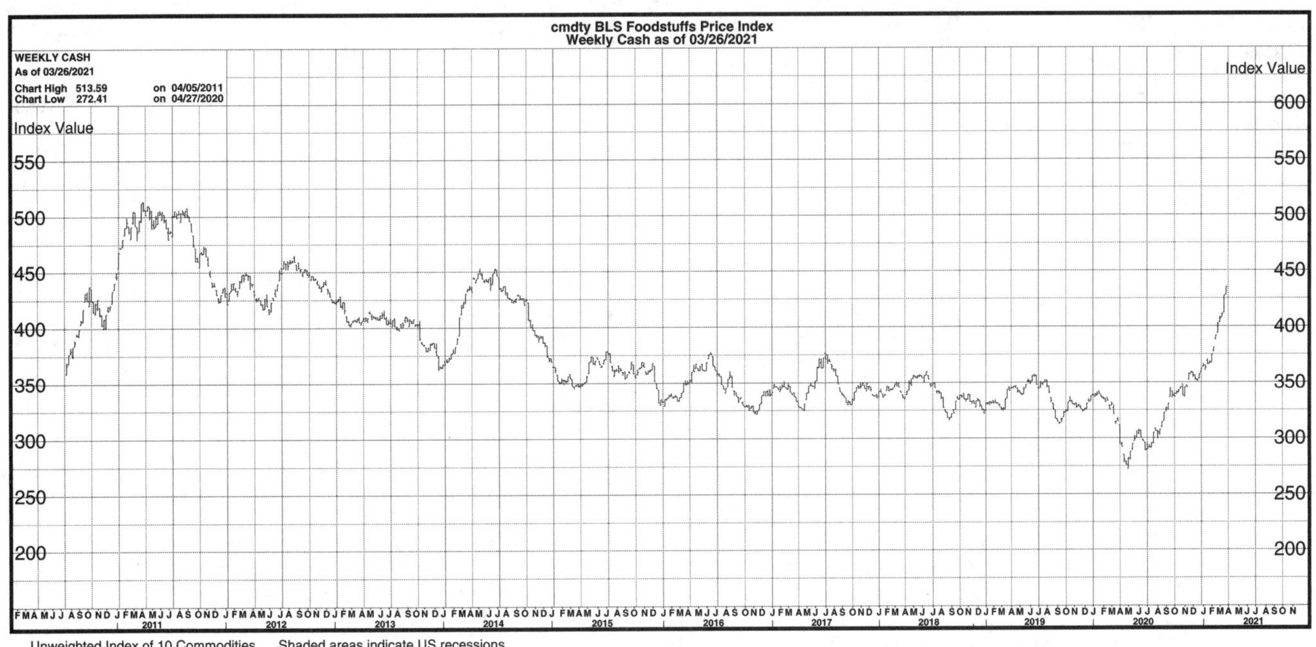

Unweighted Index of 10 Commodities. Shaded areas indicate US recessions.

cmdty BLS Foodstuffs Price Index (1967=100)

Year	Jan.	Feb.	Mar.	Apr.	May	June	July	Aug.	Sept.	Oct.	Nov.	Dec.	Average
2011	464.45	489.47	494.49	506.33	497.04	497.00	495.67	503.38	484.57	466.21	451.87	429.91	481.70
2012	431.88	436.61	445.29	429.26	421.32	427.19	453.49	458.33	451.49	446.42	439.14	432.15	439.38
2013	422.99	410.14	407.07	407.78	410.33	410.17	404.33	402.51	405.75	395.29	382.14	374.23	402.73
2014	370.69	387.03	424.76	440.01	445.70	444.24	437.38	426.08	426.02	412.87	392.84	379.75	415.61
2015	358.69	352.29	350.34	349.61	367.54	369.24	369.14	361.25	360.32	361.29	361.42	348.87	359.17
2016	334.98	337.31	343.78	358.46	362.83	370.40	353.47	349.64	335.73	328.19	326.03	339.73	345.05
2017	344.49	346.60	341.09	328.23	344.21	363.46	369.20	351.43	333.86	340.67	346.50	339.79	345.79
2018	340.59	344.84	344.76	344.32	355.67	353.36	343.73	325.14	327.65	336.27	332.96	328.82	339.84
2019	331.10	330.08	334.65	344.14	343.99	352.85	348.13	332.80	316.85	329.71	327.67	330.97	335.25
2020	338.49	332.49	320.43	284.57	293.39	298.94	297.53	310.40	334.49	341.57	350.47	354.96	321.48

Average. *Source: cmdty by Barchart*

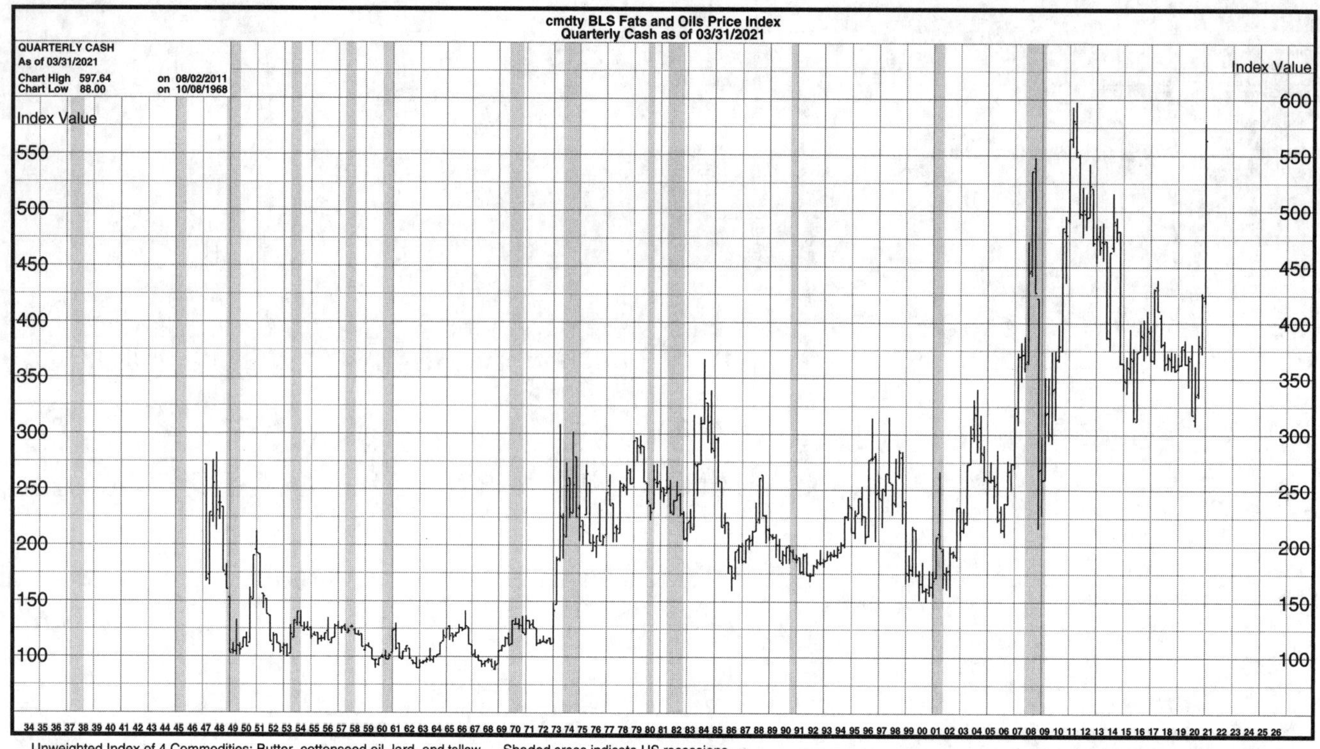

Unweighted Index of 4 Commodities: Butter, cottonseed oil, lard, and tallow. Shaded areas indicate US recessions.

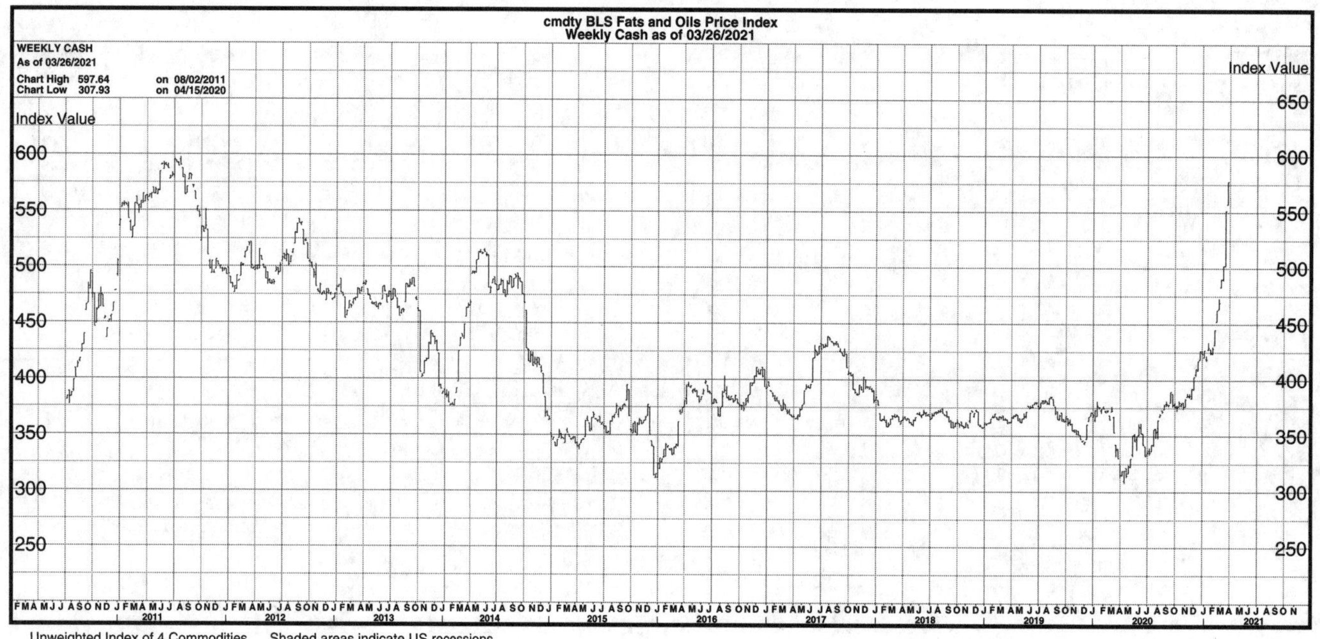

Unweighted Index of 4 Commodities. Shaded areas indicate US recessions.

cmdty BLS Fats and Oils Price Index (1967=100)

Year	Jan.	Feb.	Mar.	Apr.	May	June	July	Aug.	Sept.	Oct.	Nov.	Dec.	Average
2011	464.45	489.47	494.49	506.33	497.04	497.00	495.67	503.38	484.57	466.21	451.87	429.91	481.70
2012	431.88	436.61	445.29	429.26	421.32	427.19	453.49	458.33	451.49	446.42	439.14	432.15	439.38
2013	422.99	410.14	407.07	407.78	410.33	410.17	404.33	402.51	405.75	395.29	382.14	374.23	402.73
2014	370.69	387.03	424.76	440.01	445.70	444.24	437.38	426.08	426.02	412.87	392.84	379.75	415.61
2015	358.69	352.29	350.34	349.61	367.54	369.24	369.14	361.25	360.32	361.29	361.42	348.87	359.17
2016	334.98	337.31	343.78	358.46	362.83	370.40	353.47	349.64	335.73	328.19	326.03	339.73	345.05
2017	344.49	346.60	341.09	328.23	344.21	363.46	369.20	351.43	333.86	340.67	346.50	339.79	345.79
2018	340.59	344.84	344.76	344.32	355.67	353.36	343.73	325.14	327.65	336.27	332.96	328.82	339.84
2019	331.10	330.08	334.65	344.14	343.99	352.85	348.13	332.80	316.85	329.71	327.67	330.97	335.25
2020	338.49	332.49	320.43	284.57	293.39	298.94	297.53	310.40	334.49	341.57	350.47	354.96	321.48

Average. *Source: cmdty by Barchart*

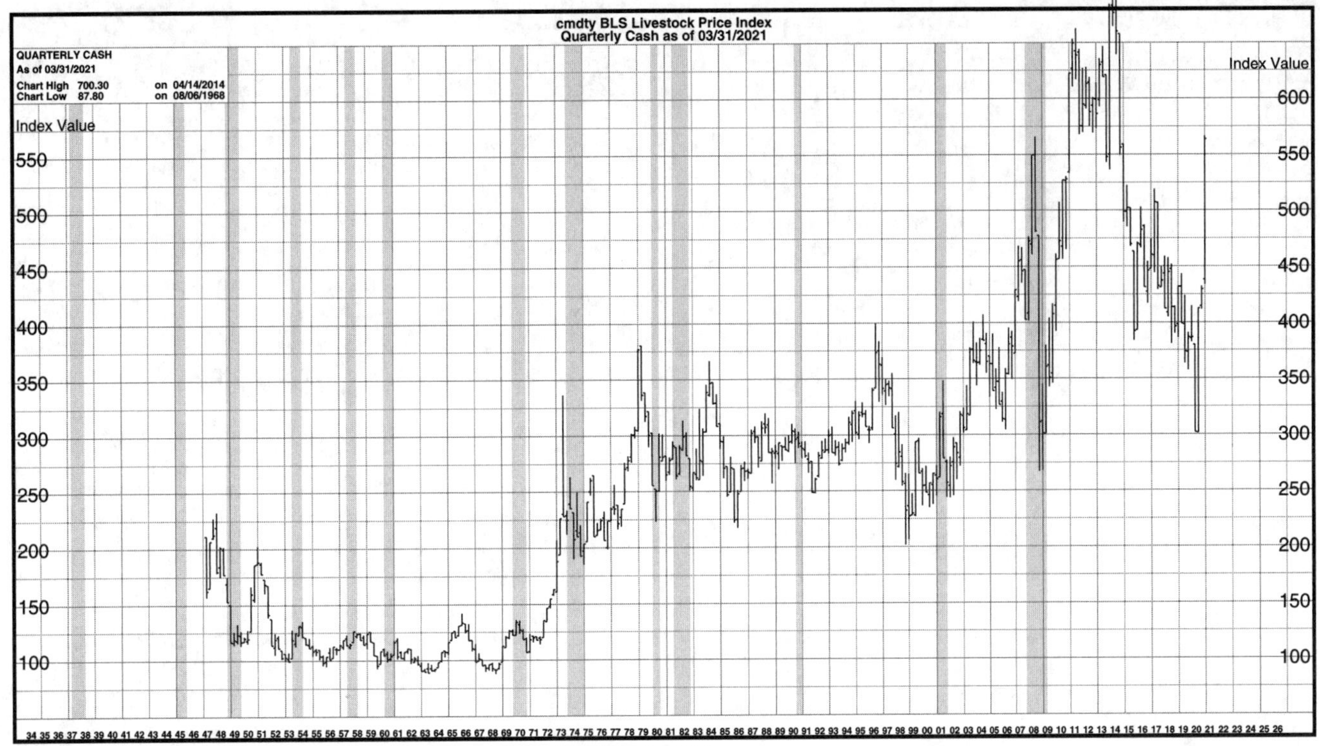

Unweighted Index of 5 Commodities: Hides, hogs, lard, steers, and tallow. Shaded areas indicate US recessions.

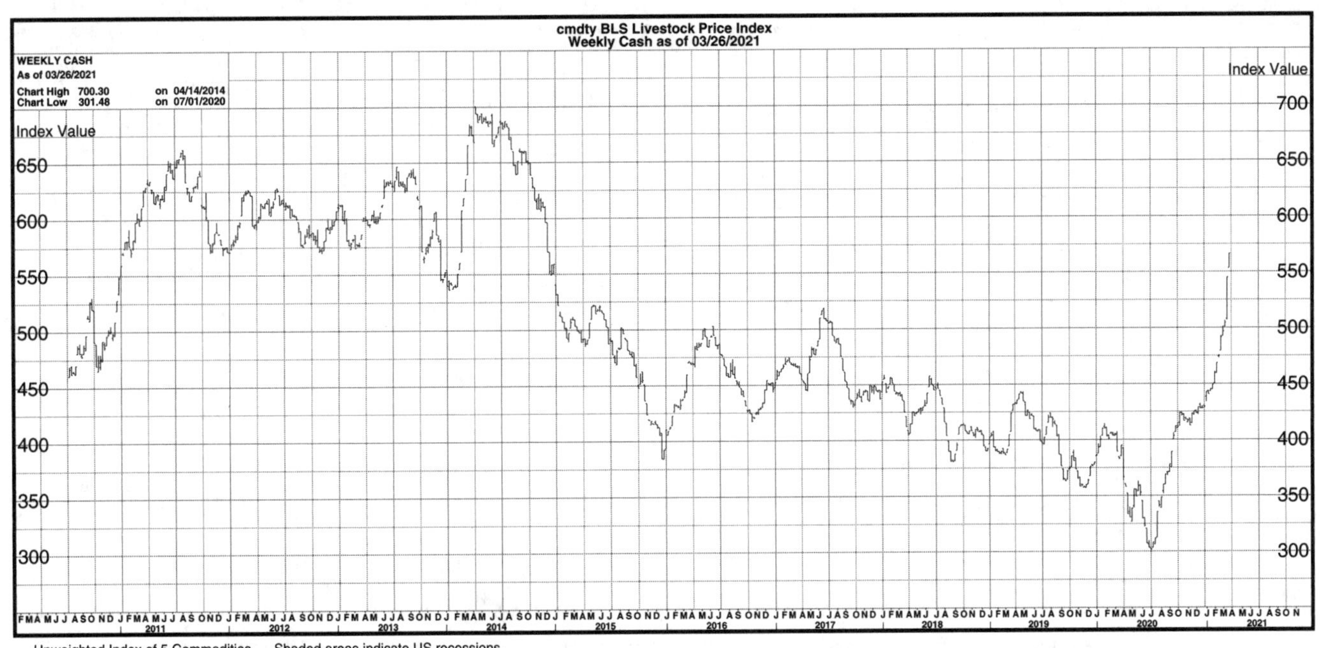

Unweighted Index of 5 Commodities. Shaded areas indicate US recessions.

cmdty BLS Livestock Price Index (1967=100)

Year	Jan.	Feb.	Mar.	Apr.	May	June	July	Aug.	Sept.	Oct.	Nov.	Dec.	Average
2011	561.16	577.76	601.55	629.36	618.46	635.68	646.41	644.21	626.64	618.26	580.65	580.02	610.01
2012	575.19	598.32	620.12	600.69	612.10	619.49	613.35	601.44	582.23	585.33	577.18	594.91	598.36
2013	606.27	584.54	580.26	598.17	601.26	626.31	634.54	630.72	637.72	591.03	583.70	571.43	603.83
2014	543.02	557.63	645.13	685.62	689.00	676.46	683.71	661.15	656.18	639.12	613.66	573.26	635.33
2015	523.85	500.96	503.91	491.27	517.22	513.03	484.28	490.90	477.86	452.68	419.99	404.96	481.74
2016	410.40	432.01	453.40	479.17	491.47	491.94	473.49	461.17	443.34	423.46	428.92	449.89	453.22
2017	459.17	470.78	466.97	452.02	478.49	506.82	500.73	478.13	439.94	438.59	442.67	443.87	464.85
2018	450.12	447.67	433.39	415.52	427.78	447.09	441.73	396.16	401.17	409.82	406.81	396.83	422.84
2019	399.14	388.75	407.21	437.39	426.55	409.36	408.37	410.57	370.18	379.01	360.20	373.81	397.55
2020	400.48	404.58	394.37	347.43	351.93	319.36	318.49	358.55	396.49	419.00	418.06	427.44	379.68

Average. *Source: cmdty by Barchart*

CMDTY INDEXES

Standard & Poor's GSCI is a registered trademark of Standard & Poor's Financial Services LLC ("S&P"), a subsidiary of The McGraw-Hill Companies, Inc.
Currently the S&P GSCI includes 24 commodity nearby futures contracts. Shaded areas indicate US recessions.

Standard & Poor's GSCI is a registered trademark of Standard & Poor's Financial Services LLC ("S&P"), a subsidiary of The McGraw-Hill Companies, Inc.
Currently the S&P GSCI includes 24 commodity nearby futures contracts. Shaded areas indicate US recessions.

S&P GSCI Index (12/31/1969=100)

Year	Jan.	Feb.	Mar.	Apr.	May	June	July	Aug.	Sept.	Oct.	Nov.	Dec.	Average
2011	634.64	661.44	707.87	744.48	695.62	679.91	689.47	651.63	638.94	625.65	653.51	642.72	668.82
2012	661.12	685.83	701.92	681.61	637.66	579.93	627.42	661.68	670.25	654.57	639.84	640.09	653.49
2013	658.10	669.41	648.20	624.14	627.04	622.56	639.34	645.98	645.31	633.40	614.88	631.12	638.29
2014	617.20	640.25	645.88	653.19	652.42	657.64	636.14	609.55	588.76	548.78	521.86	449.57	601.77
2015	388.27	412.87	403.39	423.64	443.38	436.70	402.75	360.85	362.48	364.45	345.91	315.98	388.39
2016	289.97	293.46	324.99	337.79	361.37	377.36	354.83	353.51	353.18	372.96	359.92	391.89	347.60
2017	396.61	402.05	385.28	390.60	381.04	364.63	374.75	380.46	394.88	401.99	425.01	425.39	393.56
2018	452.52	444.49	446.07	463.57	484.33	472.75	465.94	459.42	470.55	479.81	428.86	396.52	455.40
2019	401.35	417.75	430.35	449.24	434.87	412.23	421.95	398.31	410.88	405.91	417.71	428.12	419.06
2020	420.61	386.88	297.14	258.35	284.90	320.86	338.20	353.55	348.00	354.70	368.28	396.92	344.03

Average. *Source: CME Group; Chicago Mercantile Ezchange*

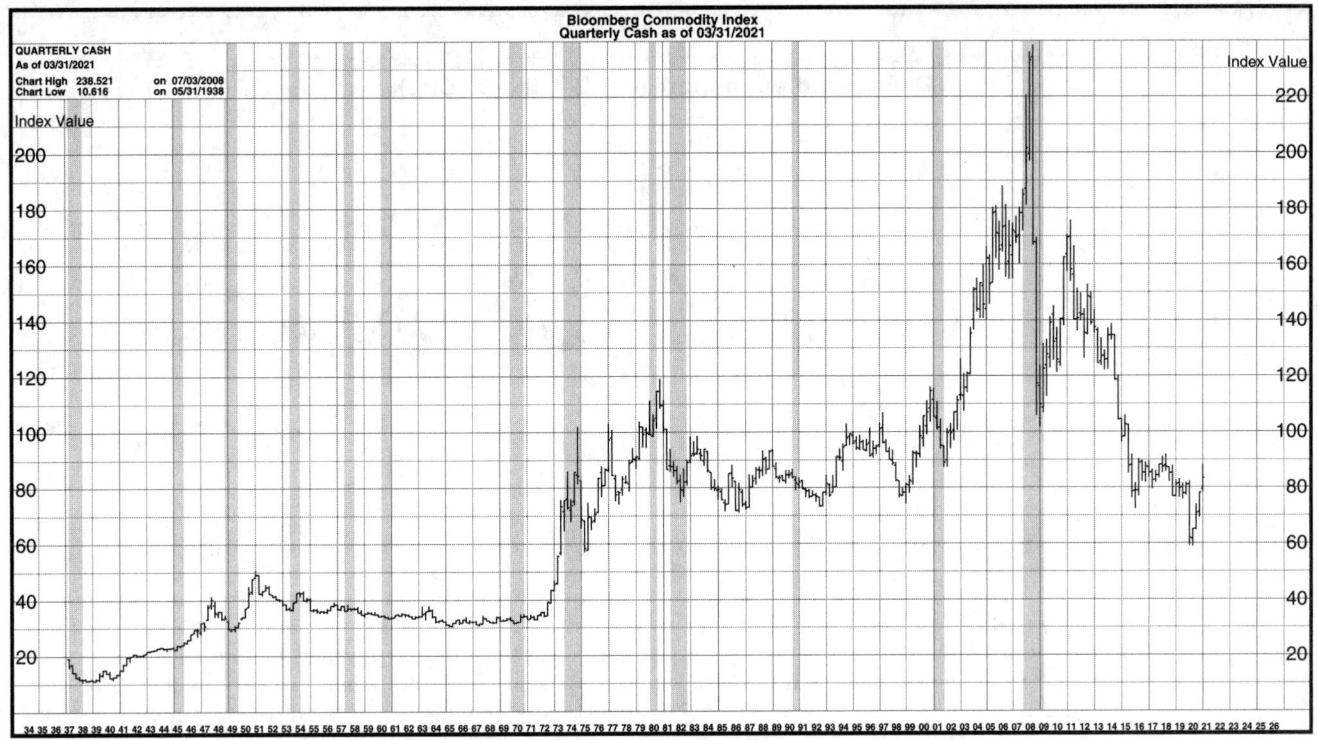

Bloomberg and Bloomberg Indices are trademarks or service marks of Bloomberg Finance L.P. 12/31/1990=100 Shaded areas indicate US recessions.

Bloomberg and Bloomberg Indices are trademarks or service marks of Bloomberg Finance L.P. 12/31/1990=100 Shaded areas indicate US recessions.

Bloomberg Commodity Index (12/31/1990=100)

Year	Jan.	Feb.	Mar.	Apr.	May	June	July	Aug.	Sept.	Oct.	Nov.	Dec.	Average
2011	160.80	163.41	165.87	171.91	163.23	161.47	162.81	159.01	154.26	145.52	146.73	141.41	158.04
2012	143.34	146.45	144.63	139.84	134.79	129.46	141.40	143.91	147.64	146.02	142.06	140.45	141.67
2013	140.01	139.55	137.44	132.99	132.04	129.38	127.65	128.32	128.98	127.48	123.20	126.25	131.11
2014	125.24	130.97	134.71	136.56	135.81	134.75	130.44	126.39	121.57	117.97	116.95	109.39	126.73
2015	102.09	102.74	99.64	100.95	103.32	100.92	96.70	89.46	88.43	88.72	83.31	78.74	94.58
2016	75.41	75.36	79.16	81.15	84.40	88.25	85.82	84.51	84.08	85.97	83.99	87.30	82.95
2017	87.80	88.15	85.30	84.99	83.53	81.21	83.04	83.40	85.03	85.16	86.78	85.14	84.96
2018	89.02	88.02	87.59	88.72	90.37	88.31	84.53	83.90	83.50	85.94	83.10	80.58	86.13
2019	79.75	80.90	81.35	81.88	79.22	78.20	79.38	76.81	78.81	78.54	79.05	79.49	79.45
2020	79.01	74.65	65.70	61.54	62.23	64.17	67.10	71.48	71.66	72.55	73.68	75.75	69.96

Average. Bloomberg and Bloomberg Indices are trademarks or service marks of Bloomberg Finance L.P. Formerly the Dow Jones-UBS Commodity Index. *Source: CME Group; Chicago Board of Trade*

COMMODITY PRICES RECOVER SHARPLY AFTER INITIAL PANDEMIC PLUNGE

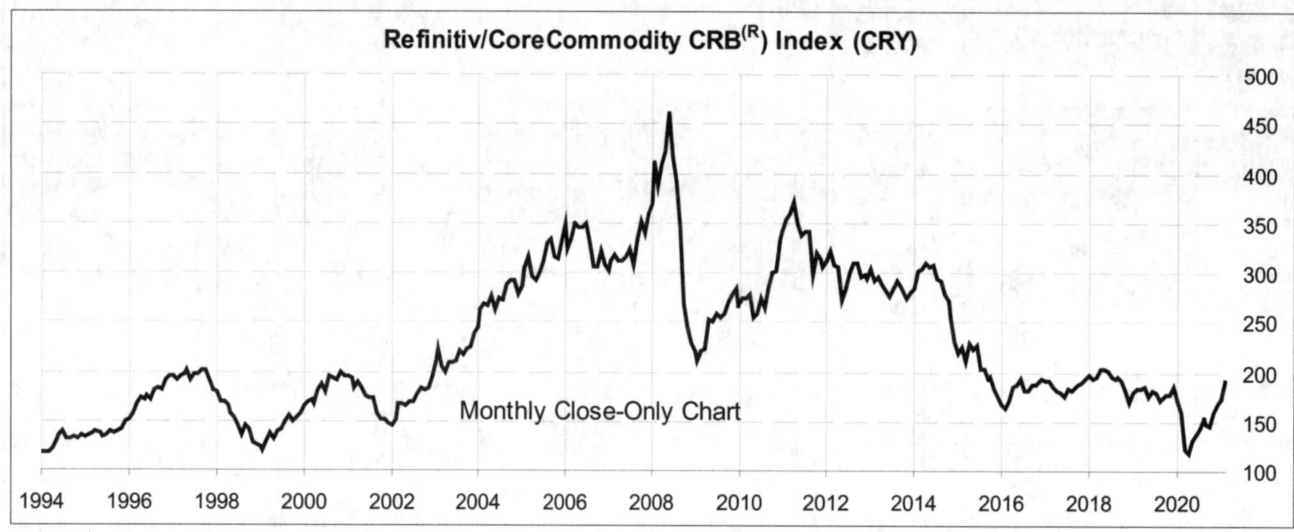

In a review of recent commodity-price history, the Refinitiv/CoreCommodity CRB(R) Index (Symbol: CRY) staged a huge bull market of +226% during the 6-1/2 year period from January 2002 to the record high in July 2008.

That 2002/08 commodity bull market was driven mainly by strong commodity demand from fast-growing emerging countries such as China, India, Brazil, and others. The fact that the rally was driven by demand, as opposed to a temporary supply disruption, accounted for its size and longevity.

Along with strong demand, the weak dollar was an important driver of the 2002/08 commodity bull market. During that time frame, the dollar plunged and provided a powerfully bullish factor for commodity prices. As the value of the dollar falls, the price of hard assets tends to rise to account for the lower value of the currency in which the hard assets are priced.

Commodity prices then plunged in the latter half of 2008 and early 2009 as the global financial crisis battered the commodity markets. Commodity demand plunged as the Great Recession sank the global economy.

Commodity prices staged a partial come-back from early 2009 to 2011 mainly because of the Federal Reserve's extremely stimulative monetary policy, which sparked investment demand for commodities and other hard assets driven by fears of an inflation outbreak.

However, commodity prices topped out in mid-2011 and then plunged by -58% to what was then a 14-year low in January 2016. Commodity prices during that period were driven lower by weak physical demand for commodities due to poor global economic growth. In addition, many investors were forced to give up on any imminent arrival of hyperinflation stemming from the Fed's extraordinarily easy monetary policy. Instead, the U.S. and global economies during that period experienced deflationary pressures in the aftermath of the 2008/09 global financial crisis and the Great Recession.

The 2011/16 slump in commodity prices was also caused by an economic slowdown in China. It is no coincidence that the massive commodity bull market began in 2002 at the same time that the Chinese economy started to show double-digit growth. China's building and investment boom produced huge demand for various types of commodities. However, commodity prices started falling after 2011 because Chinese GDP growth slid from +9.5% in 2011 to +7.7% in 2012 and then steadily fell further to a 29-year low of +6.1% by 2019.

The 2011/16 slump in commodity prices was also caused by an economic slowdown in China. It is no coincidence that the massive commodity bull market began in 2003 at the same time that the Chinese economy started to show double-digit growth. China's building and investment boom produced huge demand for various types of commodities. However, commodity prices started falling after 2011 because Chinese GDP growth slid from +9.5% in 2011 to +7.7% in 2012 and then steadily fell further to a 29-year low of +6.1% by 2019.

Ranked Commodity Bull Markets (1960-2020)

	-------- Low --------		-------- High --------		Percent Rally	Rally Duration Months	Avg CPI (yr-yr%)
2002-08	Jan 2002	145.39	Jul 2008	473.97	226.0%	78	2.8%
1971-74	Oct 1971	96.40	Feb 1974	237.80	146.7%	28	4.9%
1977-80	Aug 1977	184.70	Nov 1980	337.60	82.8%	39	10.2%
1986-88	Jul 1986	196.16	Jun 1988	272.19	38.8%	23	3.2%
1992-96	Aug 1992	198.17	Apr 1996	263.79	33.1%	44	2.8%

Note: This table uses the Refinitiv Equal Weight Commodity Index (CCI) for the bull markets from 1970-1996 because of its long history. This table then uses the Refinitiv/CoreCommodity CRB(R) Index (CRY) for the 2002-08 bull market. The CRY index has history only back to 1994. The CRY index has now replaced the CCI index, which was discontinued effective 2/1/2021.

Commodity prices in 2015 and early 2016 were also pressured by the end of the Fed's quantitative easing (QE) programs in October 2014 and the Fed's first interest rate hike in December 2015. The end of the Fed's QE programs and rising interest rates meant that there was less liquidity fuel for the commodities markets and a reduced risk of eventual hyperinflation.

However, commodity prices in early 2016 were able to rally moderately and then remained steady from 2017 through 2019. Commodity prices were helped in 2018 by the strong U.S. economy sparked by the massive 2018 tax cut. However, commodity prices in 2019 were undercut by a stronger dollar and by slower U.S. and world economic growth due to trade tensions. Commodity prices in 2019 were underpinned by the Federal Reserve's 75 basis point interest rate cut during the year.

Commodity prices in early 2020 then plunged as the global Covid pandemic emerged and caused economic shutdowns and business chaos across the globe. Commodity demand in China fell sharply in early 2020 after a major proportion of China's economy was closed from late-January through February. Petroleum demand in China, for example, plunged by some -20% on the coronavirus crisis. U.S. GDP plunged by -10% in the first half of 2020.

However, commodity prices bottomed out in April 2020 and then rallied sharply during the remainder of the year. The commodity markets were boosted by the quick monetary stimulus action from global central banks and by fiscal stimulus from governments with pandemic aid programs.

The commodity rally went into high gear in late 2020 as effective vaccines emerged and the markets started expecting the end of the pandemic and the eventual full recovery of the global economy. Also, the dollar sold off sharply starting in May 2020, which was a major supportive factor for commodity prices during 2020.

The passage by the U.S. government of a $900 billion pandemic aid plan in late December 2020 and a $1.9 trillion pandemic aid plan in March 2021 prompted expectations for very strong U.S. GDP during mid-2021. That led to an extension of the commodity rally in early 2021 to a new 2-1/2 year high.

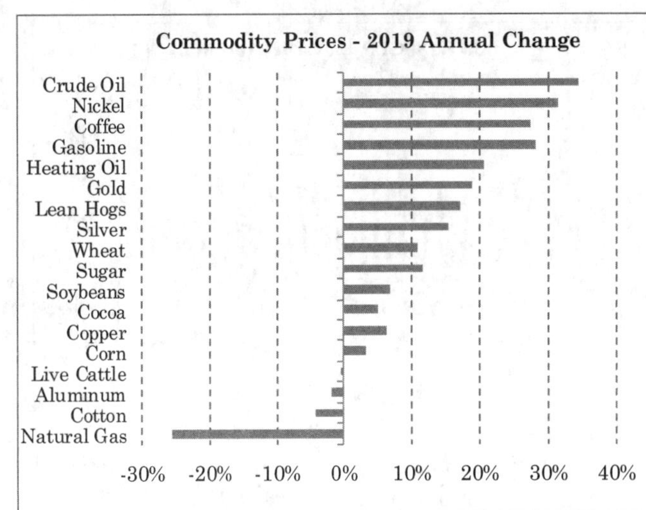

Precious metals prices saw very sharp gains in 2020 in the wake of the pandemic due to the massive monetary stimulus from most global central banks. The U.S. Federal Reserve, for example, cut interest rates nearly to zero and started a massive new quantitative easing (QE) program to buy securities and permanently inject reserves into the banking system. The European Central Bank and Bank of Japan both expanded their QE programs. The massive monetary policy stimulus caused fears of inflation and caused heavy buying of precious metals as protection.

Meanwhile, crude oil and petroleum prices were the worst commodity performers during 2020 as demand plummeted in the aftermath of the pandemic shutdowns in early 2020. Global oil demand is expected to take 2-3 years to fully recover. Meanwhile, OPEC+ in 2020 struggled to cut production fast enough to offset the plunge in demand.

Commodity prices over the long-term should see strong demand from population growth and world development. The UN forecasts that the global population will grow by about 50% to 11.2 billion people by 2100. Meanwhile, the developing world's needs continue to be enormous for food, shelter, and infrastructure, which are all sectors that utilize raw commodities. Some 80% of the world's population lives on less than $10 per day, and many of these people will be slowly integrated into the global economy.

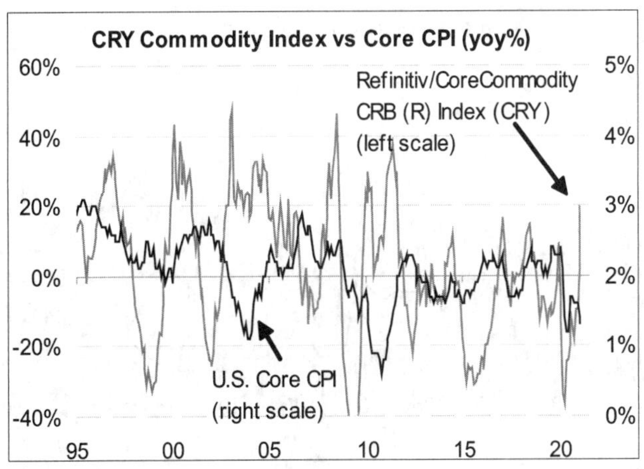

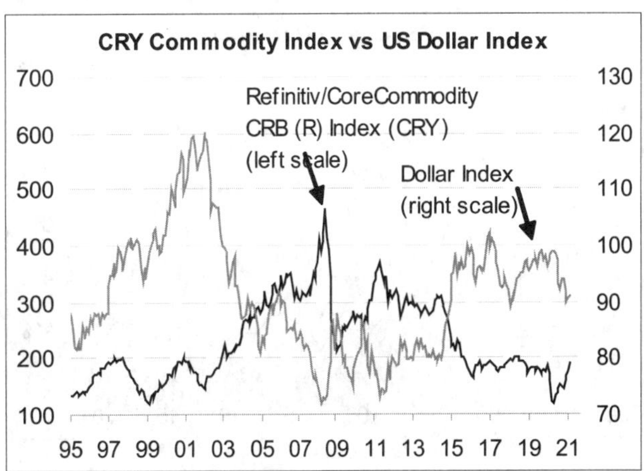

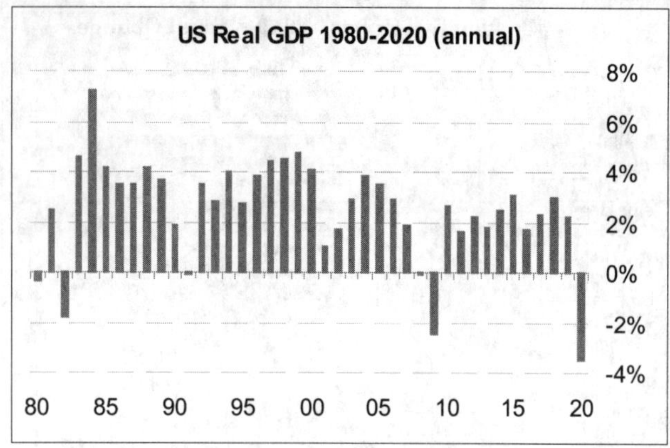

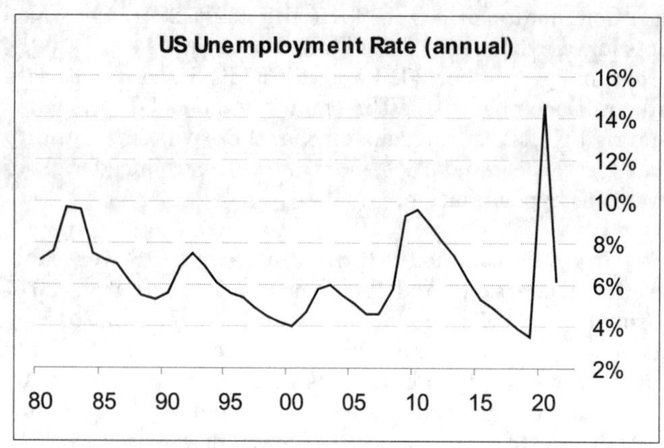

The U.S. economy has been on a roller-coaster ride in the past several years. U.S. real GDP in 2018 saw a relatively strong growth rate of +2.9%, sparked by the massive tax cut that took effect on January 1, 2018. The tax cut's economic stimulus was able to offset the negative impact from the Trump administration's trade war, which dampened global economic trade and growth.

The U.S. trade war began in January 2018 when the Trump administration slapped tariffs on imported solar cells and washing machines. In March 2018, the Trump administration then launched tariffs on imported steel and aluminum, which drew retaliatory tariffs from America's trading partners against U.S. products. The U.S./Chinese trade war ramped up during 2018 and early 2019. By September 2019, the U.S. had penalty tariffs on about $360 billion of Chinese goods, and China had retaliatory tariffs on about $110 billion of U.S. goods.

The U.S. and China in December 2019 finally reached what they called a "phase one" trade deal. That trade deal involved a partial reduction of penalty tariffs by both sides and China's agreement to buy an extra $200 billion of U.S. goods during 2020-21. The two sides left more difficult issues such as industrial subsidies to phase-two talks, but those talks never took place since Mr. Trump lost the 2020 presidential election.

U.S. GDP during 2019 showed tepid growth of +2.3% as trade tensions continued to undercut the U.S. economy. In addition, the U.S. economy started to feel the effects of the Fed's overall 2.00 percentage point rate hike that took place between December 2016 and December 2018. That rate hike left the Fed's federal funds target range at 2.25%/2.50% by the end of 2018.

By late 2018, the Fed realized that it had overdone its interest rate hikes as real GDP growth in Q4-2018 fell to a 3-year low of +1.3% and the U.S. stock market plunged in Q4-2018. The Fed during 2019, therefore, cut its funds rate target by a total of 75 basis points, leaving the funds rate target at 1.50%/1.75% by October 2019. That rate cut helped the U.S. economy to stabilize, with GDP growth of +2.5% in the second half of 2019.

The U.S. economy initially came into 2020 with a boost from the U.S./China phase-one trade deal, which was announced in December 2019 and signed on January 15, 2020. However, Covid then emerged as a major problem by late-January 2020. A major proportion of the Chinese economy was shut down from late-January through February. The coronavirus quickly spread across the world and caused major global economic disruptions.

The U.S. economy was partially shut down beginning in March as travel was halted, restaurants were forced to close, public events were canceled, and all but essential businesses were forced to either close down or have their employees work from home. U.S. GDP plunged by a total of -10.1% during the first half of 2020, meeting the definition of a depression of a GDP drop of greater than -10%. By April 2020, 22 million jobs had been lost, and the unemployment rate had soared to a record high of 14.7%.

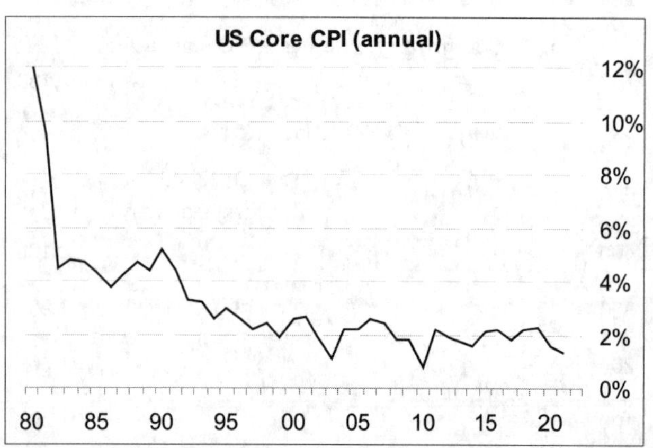

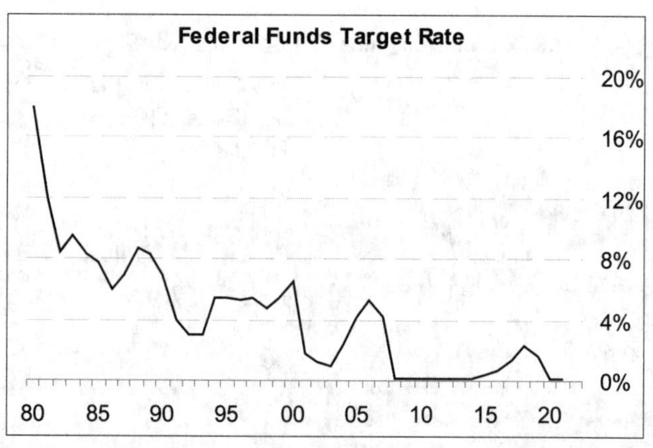

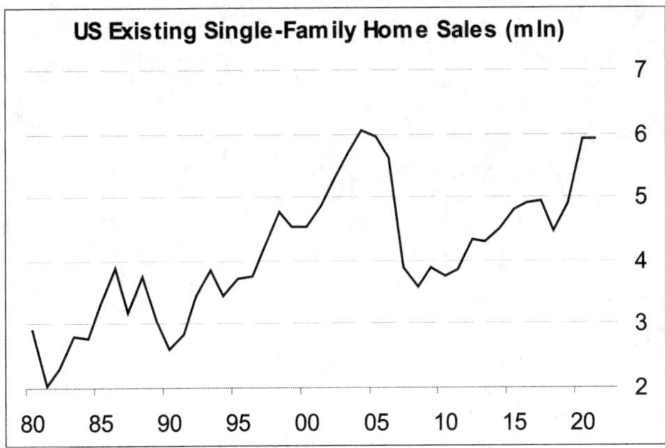

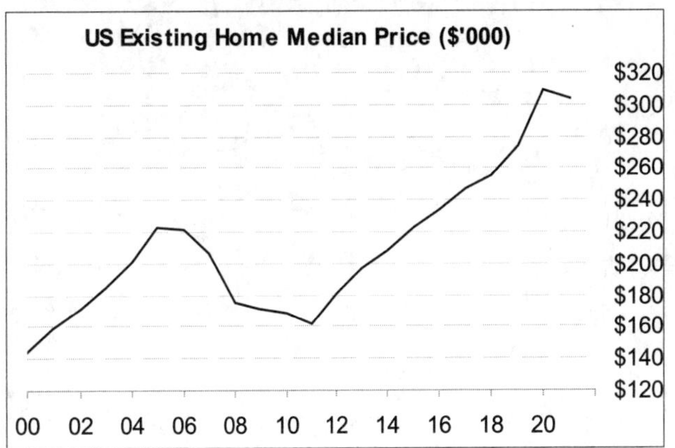

However, the U.S. economy was able to stage a partial recovery in the second half of 2020 with a GDP rise of +8.6%. The economy started to make a comeback as the country learned to live with Covid, and many businesses were allowed to reopen. The Fed also provided massive support for the economy with its monetary policy and its direct-lending programs.

Congress also swung into action with massive pandemic aid and stimulus programs. Congress first passed an $8 billion vaccine bill and then a $104 billion package with paid sick leave and unemployment benefits.

In late March 2020, the $2.2 trillion CARES Act was signed into law. That bill contained (1) $1,200 stimulus checks to many Americans, (2) an extra $600 per week of unemployment benefits for four months, (3) a $267 billion small-business loan and grant program called the Paycheck Protection Program (PPP), (4) over $130 billion in grants to the medical care system, (5) $500 billion in loans to corporate America, (6) aid for the airline and transportation industry, and (7) $150 billion in loans for state and local governments.

Congress in January 2021 then passed a $900 billion pandemic aid bill that provided an extension of unemployment benefits, $600 stimulus payments to many Americans, spending on vaccines and health care, and a host of other measures.

After President Biden took office in January 2021, Congress in March 2021 passed another $1.9 trillion pandemic aid bill that included another round of stimulus checks, unemployment benefits, aid to state and local governments, support for education and childcare, spending on vaccines and health care, and many other measures.

By March 2021, the outlook for the U.S. economy had improved significantly because the Covid infection rates plummeted from late January through mid-February. The U.S. economy started to improve as business restrictions were loosened and as people felt more at liberty to venture out into public and spend money in shops and restaurants and on travel. In addition, the two pandemic aid packages passed in early 2021, totaling $2.8 trillion, gave the U.S. economy a huge dose of fiscal stimulus.

As of March 2021, the market consensus was for very strong real GDP growth of +5.5% in 2021, which would be more than enough to overcome 2020's -3.5% drop. The consensus was for strong GDP growth of +3.8% in 2022.

The financial markets in late 2020 started to discount a strong economic recovery when it became clear that vaccines would be able to eventually end the pandemic. The markets also reacted to the massive fiscal stimulus programs. The 10-year T-note yield soared from 0.50% in mid-2020 to a 1-year high of 1.73% by March 2021. The S&P 500 index soared by 80% from a 4-year low in March 2020 to a record high in February 2021.

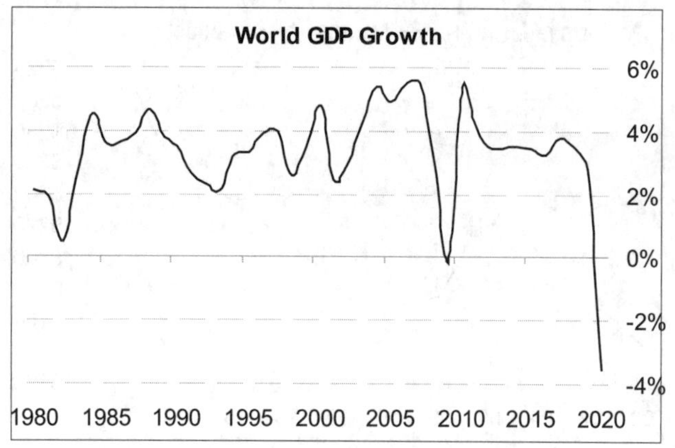

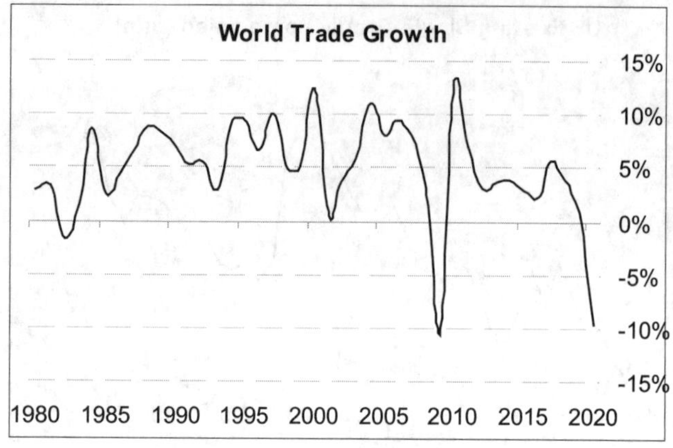

World GDP growth in 2020 fell sharply by -3.5% due to the global Covid pandemic that emerged in early 2020.

The world economy came into 2020 on a weak note due to the Trump administration's 2018-20 trade war, which disrupted global trade. By mid-2019, China and the U.S. had penalty tariffs on most of each other's products. The two sides reached a phase-one trade agreement in December 2019, but the two sides left in place most of their penalty tariffs.

The global economy in 2020 then took a heavy hit from the Covid pandemic, which started in China. China was forced to close a major proportion of its economy from late January through February as authorities tried to halt the spread of the virus.

China's real GDP in Q2-2020 plunged by -6.8% yr/yr, which was a record low for the series that has history back to 1992. However, China was able to reopen its economy fairly quickly and GDP rebounded to +6.5% yr/yr by Q4-2020. The quick rebound allowed China's GDP to still show a positive calendar-year growth rate in 2020 of +2.3%.

Meanwhile, U.S. GDP growth plunged in the first half of 2020 by a total of -10.1%, and only partially recovered by +8.6% in the second half. The pandemic recession of -10.1% was 2-1/2 times worse than the 2007/09 U.S. Great Recession, which saw a peak-to-trough decline of -4.0%. The -10.1% pandemic recession, however, was at least very brief and was much less severe than the -26% decline seen during the Great Depression in 1929-1933.

Eurozone GDP growth in 2020 plunged by -6.6%, taking a heavier hit than the U.S. economy. Europe saw tighter lockdowns than the U.S. and larger economic disruptions. The Eurozone economy at least received some good news at the end of 2020 when the EU and UK reached a post-Brexit trade agreement, allowing the UK to to exit the EU on a relatively smooth note.

Japan's GDP in 2020 also took a heavy hit of -4.9% due to the Covid pandemic and the economic lockdowns. Japan's economy barely had its head above water going into 2020 with GDP growth in 2019 of only +0.3%. Japan's economy was weak in 2019 due to trade tensions and the Japanese government's hike in the national sales tax to 10% from 8% on October 1, 2019.

Looking ahead, the world economy should see a strong recovery in 2021 as vaccinations spread and the pandemic slowly fades. The consensus is for world GDP growth in 2021 of +5.6%, which would more than recover the -3.5% decline in 2020. World GDP growth is then expected to remain relatively strong in 2022 at +4.1%.

The consensus is for strong GDP recoveries in 2021 of +8.5% in China, +5.6% in the U.S., +4.2% in the Eurozone, and +2.8% in Japan.

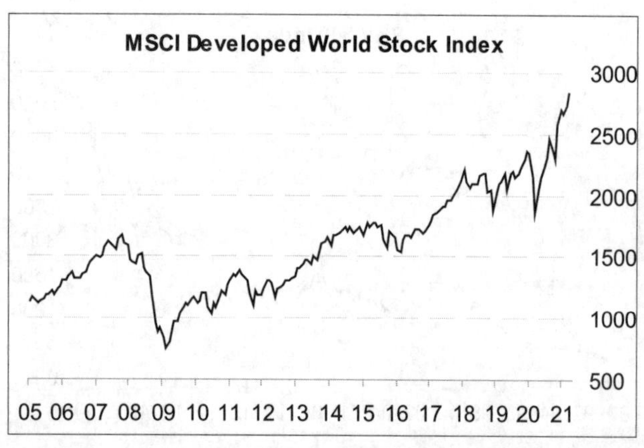

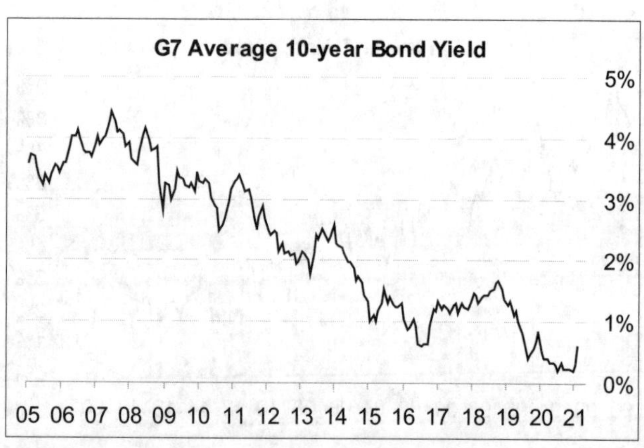

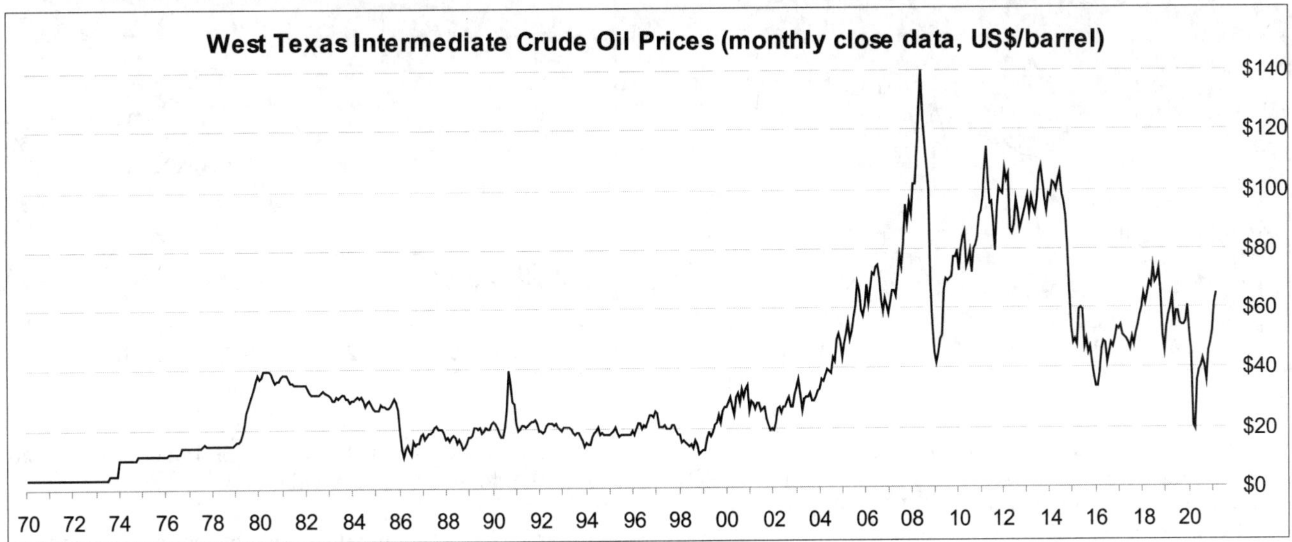

The crude oil market's long-term reality is that there are too many oil producers and too much production capacity. The only reason oil prices have not permanently crashed in recent decades is that OPEC acts as a cartel to restrict production and support oil prices.

However, Saudi Arabia has long been the only OPEC producer willing to implement sharp production cuts to support prices, thus giving other OPEC members and non-OPEC producers a free-ride on higher oil prices.

In 2014, Saudi Arabia tired of its swing-producer role and launched a price war where it boosted its production and allowed oil prices to plunge. The idea was to permanently drive the high-cost producers, including U.S. shale producers, out of business. Saudi Arabia has some of the lowest production costs in the world, meaning that Saudi Arabia, in theory, would be the last producer standing after a price war.

However, Saudi Arabia could not sustain its price war because Nymex West Texas Intermediate (WTI) crude oil futures prices plunged during 2014/15 by an extraordinary -76% from the 3-year high of $107.68 posted in mid-2014 to the 14-year low of $26.05 posted in February 2016. That plunge in oil prices devastated Saudi Arabia's government

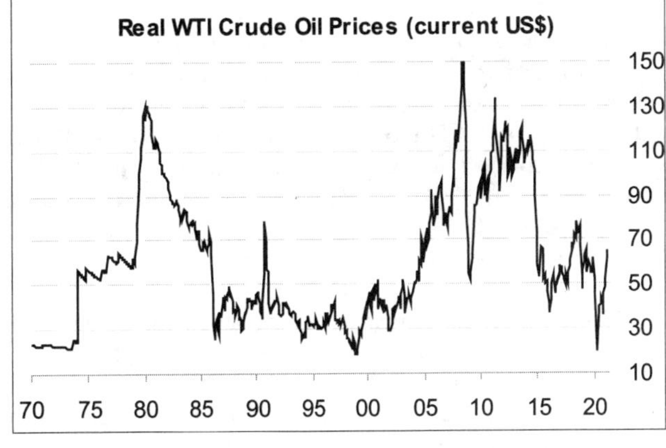

finances and forced the government to cut spending and subsidies, thus risking social unrest and perhaps even the monarchy's very existence.

Saudi Arabia was finally forced to end its failed policy and seek help in cutting world oil production. OPEC began to cooperate with non-OPEC members such as Russia in a group that became known as OPEC+. In November 2016, OPEC+ reached an agreement to cut production by 1.8 million barrels/day (bpd). The OPEC+ production

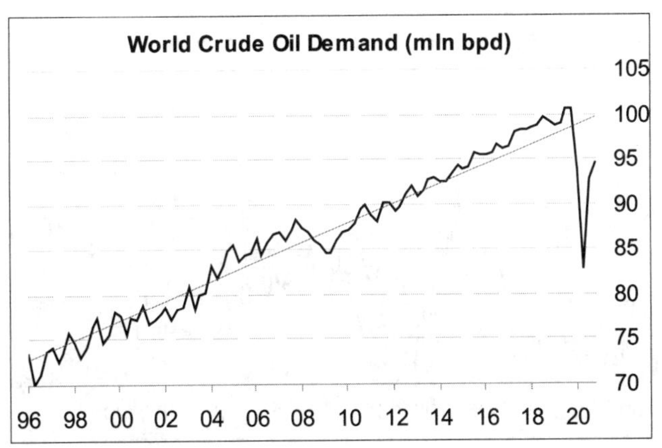

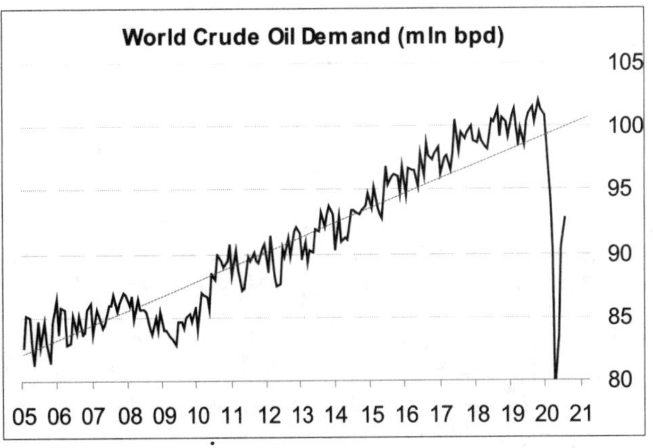

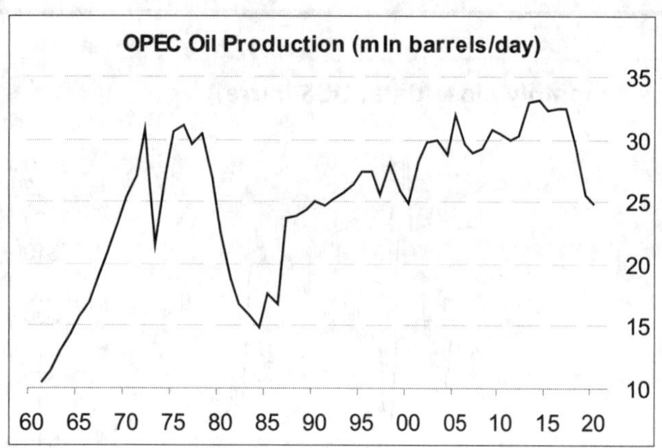

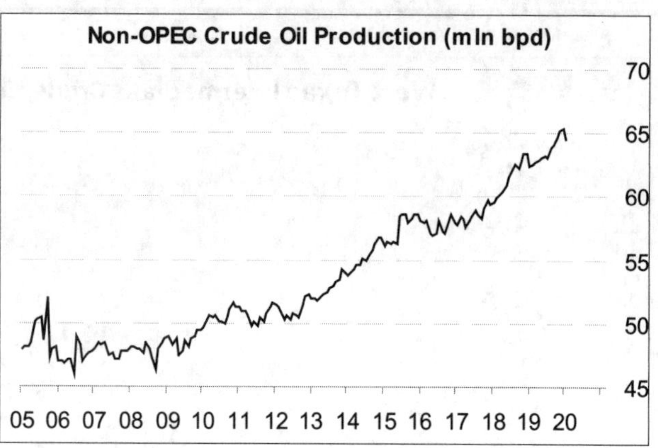

cut was successful during 2017 in bringing down excess global inventories and boosting oil prices, leading OPEC+ to extend the agreement into 2018. WTI oil prices rallied steadily from mid-2017 through mid-2018 and posted a 6-year high of $76.90 per barrel in October 2018.

The success of OPEC+ production cut agreement started to fade in mid-2018 as higher oil prices prompted U.S. oil production to soar by +23% in 2018. Also, Saudi and OPEC+ oil production rose starting in mid-2018 to offset the expected sharp decline in Iranian oil production after the U.S. in 2018 reinstated sanctions on Iran related to the nuclear deal. As a result, WTI crude oil futures prices plunged by -45% by late December 2018.

The plunge in oil prices in late 2018 forced OPEC+ to adopt a new production cut agreement totaling 1.2 million bpd for the first six months of 2019, which was later extended through the rest of 2019. The tighter supply situation in early 2019 allowed oil prices to recover to the $58 per barrel area.

Oil prices saw support in late 2019 when OPEC+ was forced to increase its production cut agreement to 1.7 million bpd for Q1-2020 because of tepid demand and a rise in U.S. oil production to a record high of 13.0 million bpd.

OPEC+ in early 2020 faced a new challenge as oil prices plunged due to the Covid pandemic that emerged in January. The pandemic shut a large proportion of China's economy in early 2020 and slashed Chinese oil demand by as much as -20%. The pandemic then moved across Europe, the U.S., and the rest of the world, leaving economic chaos and weak oil demand in its wake.

The OPEC+ Technical Committee called for a further 600,000 bpd production cut for Q2-2020, but Russia refused the larger production cut. In response, Saudi Arabia lashed out by ending the OPEC+ production cut agreement altogether, leaving in its wake a pump-at-will policy for all OPEC+ members for Q2-2020 and no production cut at all. Saudi Arabia once again embarked on a price war, except this time in the midst of a pandemic.

The result was sheer chaos in the oil markets. In April 2020, WTI crude oil futures prices plunged to a negative price of -$40.32. Sellers engaged in panic selling on the expiring WTI futures contract to avoid taking delivery on the futures contract, even to the point of paying buyers to relieve them from their delivery obligations.

OPEC+ finally responded by implementing a new production cut agreement of 7.7 million bpd for Aug-Dec 2020 to offset the plunge in oil demand seen during the global economic shutdowns caused by the pandemic. Oil prices were able to recover in the latter half of 2020 due to the OPEC+ production cut and the slow improvement in crude oil demand as the global economy recovered.

In early 2021, OPEC+ reduced its production cut to 7.2 million bpd, but Saudi Arabia agreed to an extra voluntary production cut of 1 million bpd. The result was that crude oil prices in early 2021 were able to rally above $60 per barrel.

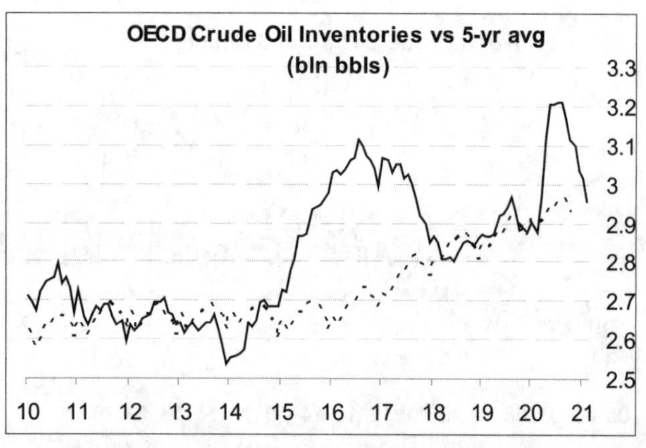

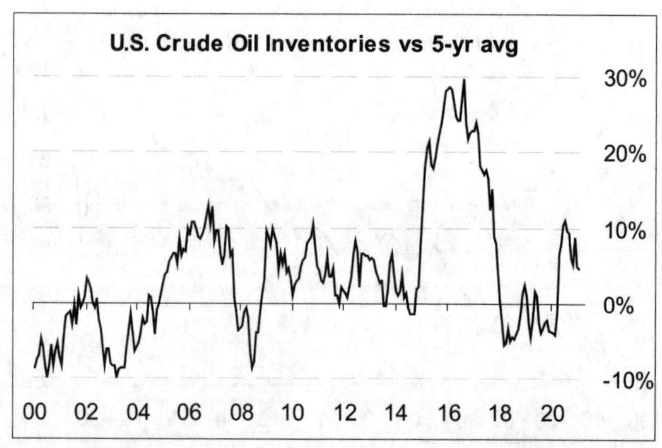

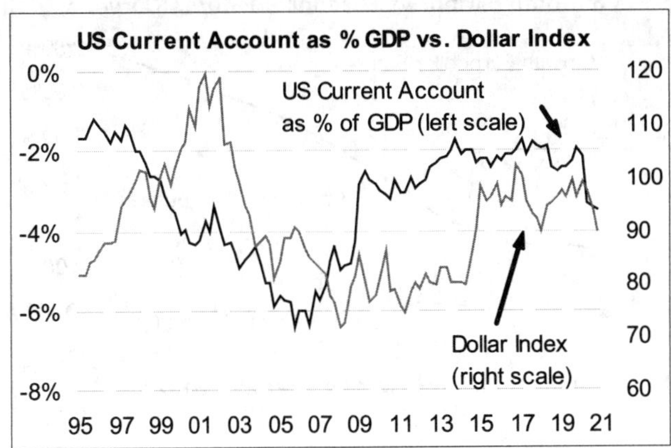

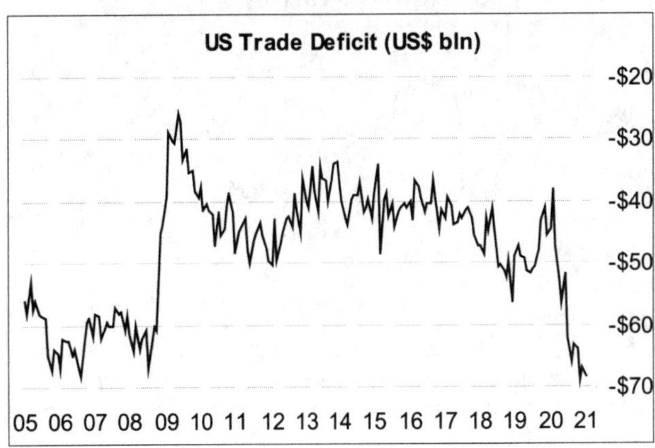

The dollar index has been generally strong since the global financial crisis and Great Recession in 2007/09. The dollar index rallied sharply in 2014 and then extended its gains to post an 18-year high in early 2017. The dollar index fell back during 2017 but then clawed its way higher in 2018 and 2019.

The dollar was generally strong in the 2016-2019 period due to the relative strength of the U.S. economy versus the European and Japanese economies. The U.S. economy received a large fiscal boost in 2018 from the massive tax cut that took effect on January 1, 2018.

The 2018 U.S. tax cut was also bullish for the dollar because the sharp cut in the minimum U.S. corporate tax rate to 21% from 35% encouraged increased direct foreign investment into the United States. Also, the new 2018 tax law imposed a tax on the $2.6 trillion of dollars that U.S. corporations earned and were holding overseas to avoid paying U.S. taxes. The new tax caused some corporations to bring their cash back to the U.S., which was bullish for the dollar since some of that overseas cash was held in foreign currencies that had to be converted into dollars.

The dollar also saw support during 2016-2019 from the Federal Reserve's interest rate hikes. Those interest rate hikes boosted the dollar by drawing more foreign capital into dollar-denominated money market investments to earn higher interest rate returns.

The Fed kept its funds rate target range near zero at 0.00%/0.25% in the aftermath of the Great Recession for the period of 2008-2015. However, the Fed then implemented its first +25 basis point (bp) rate hike to 0.25%/0.50% in December 2015. After a year-long delay, the Fed then steadily raised its funds target by a total of +200 bp from December 2016 until December 2018, providing a supportive factor for the dollar. During that time frame, the European and Japanese central banks either left their policy rates unchanged or cut their rates further. When the economy dipped in early 2019, the Fed was forced to cut interest rates by a total of -75 bp in the second half of 2019, which was a bearish factor for the dollar.

The dollar was supported by the Fed's halt of its quantitative easing (QE) programs in late 2014, which ended the Fed's spigot of liquidity injections into the banking system. After holding its balance sheet steady during 2014-18, the Fed in 2018 then started drawing down its balance sheet in a supportive move for the dollar. However, the Fed in October 2019 was forced to start boosting its balance sheet again to address a shortage of bank reserves that caused the U.S. money markets to go haywire in September 2019. Meanwhile, Europe and Japan continued their quantitative easing programs, which were bearish factors for their currencies.

Trade tensions were a bearish factor for the dollar from 2018 through 2020. The Trump administration had launched a trade war by slapping U.S. tariffs on its

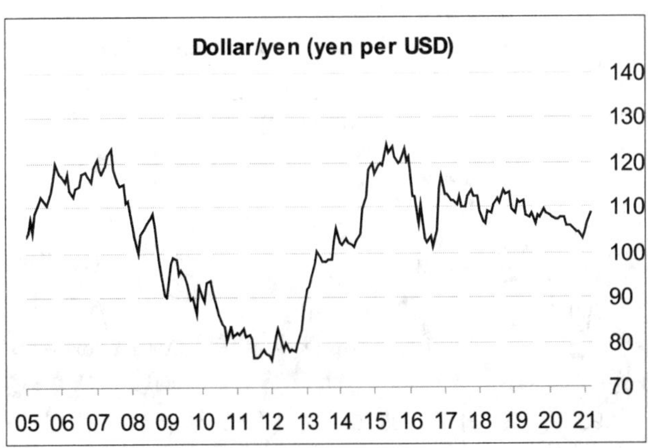

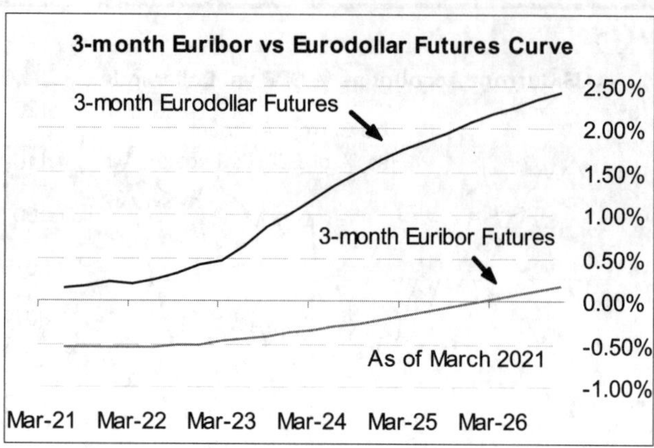

trading partners, which caused those trading partners to retaliate by slapping their own tariffs on U.S. products. The trade war caused business and consumer uncertainty and discouraged foreign business investment in the United States. The tariffs also disrupted U.S. imports and exports, as well as corporate supply chains.

The emergence of the Covid pandemic in early 2020 was initially bullish for the dollar, and the dollar index rose to a 4-year. The dollar rallied sharply on flight-to-quality as banks, investors, and corporations scrambled to obtain emergency dollar liquidity. The Federal Reserve met the emergency demand by engaging in new and expanded dollar swap lines with most major foreign central banks, allowing those central banks to obtain extra dollars that they could then use to lend out to their domestic banks.

After the pandemic panic in spring 2020 started to ease, the dollar showed weakness during the remainder of 2020 as safe-haven demand for the dollar faded and as the Fed's extremely easy monetary policy took its toll on the dollar.

The Fed in March 2020 slashed its funds rate target back to the Great Recession level of 0.00%/0.25% and adopted an unlimited quantitative easing (QE) program. The Fed in June 2020 limited that QE program to $120 billion per month. The Fed's extremely easy monetary policy during 2020 was a major bearish factor for the dollar in the latter half of 2020.

The dollar index started to stabilize in early 2021 when the U.S. Covid infection rates plunged from mid-January into March. The drop in the infection rates, partially due to the emergence of effective vaccines, raised hopes for the end of the pandemic and a full recovery of the U.S. economy. As a result, the markets started expecting the Fed to start raising interest rates much sooner than initially thought, which was a major bullish factor for the dollar.

Over the longer-term, the dollar continues to suffer from the massive U.S. current account deficit of about $500 billion, which means that about $1.4 billion of U.S. dollars flow out of the country every day. To the extent that the recipients of those trade dollars do not wish to hold and invest them in dollar-denominated assets, they sell them into the global foreign exchange markets, pushing down the value of the dollar.

The euro initially showed weakness when the pandemic started in early 2020, but then rallied during most of the rest of 2020, mainly due to dollar weakness. However, the euro was held back by bearish factors such as the European Central Bank's deposit rate of -0.50% and its two QE programs.

The yen saw some strength in the second half of 2020, mainly because of weakness in the dollar. However, the yen was undercut during 2020 by the Bank of Japan's massive QE program, its monetary policy target rate of -0.1%, and its targeting of the 10-year JGB yield near zero.

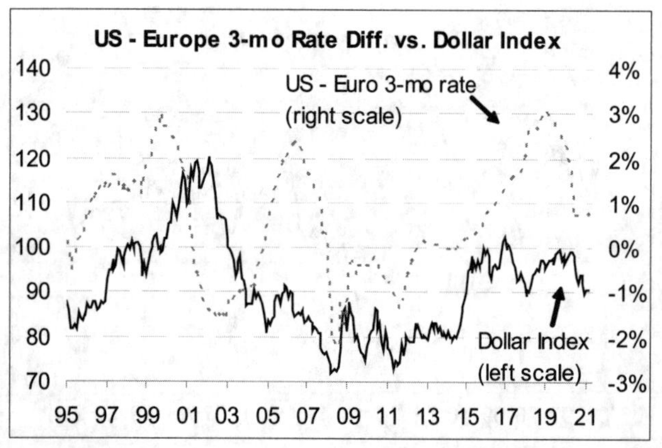

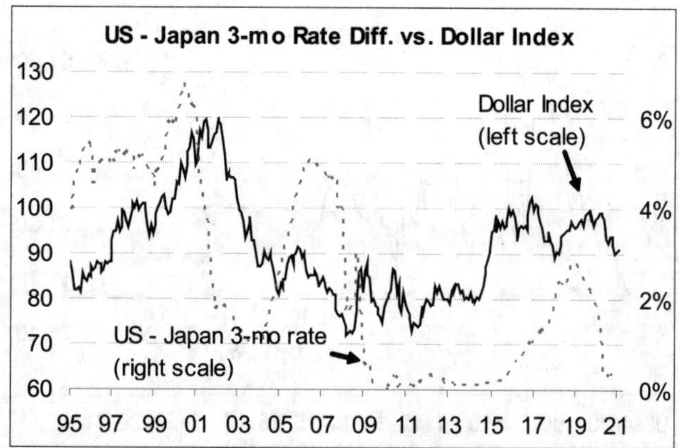

FED LAUNCHES MASSIVE STIMULUS EFFORT DUE TO PANDEMIC

The recent history of Federal Reserve policy begins with a look back at the 2008/09 global financial crisis. The Fed started cutting its federal funds rate target in October 2007 from 5.25% when the housing crisis started. By early 2009 the Fed had slashed its federal funds rate target range by 5.12 percentage points to 0.00%/0.25%.

After the financial crisis erupted into global proportions in September 2008 with the bankruptcy of Lehman Brothers, the Fed also began its so-called "quantitative easing" (QE) operations whereby it bought securities to permanently inject reserves into the banking system and thus boost liquidity.

The Fed began its first quantitative easing move (QE1) in March 2008, which involved the purchase of a total of $1.425 trillion of securities by the time the program ended in March 2010. When the economy continued to struggle in the first half of 2010, the Fed launched its QE2 program of buying another $600 billion worth of Treasury securities from November 2010 through June 2011.

The U.S. economy, beginning in the first half of 2011, faltered again due to a confluence of negative events, including high gasoline prices, the Japanese earthquake/ tsunami in March 2011, the U.S. debt ceiling debacle in early summer 2011, and the European sovereign debt crisis that began in 2011. As a result, the Fed in September 2012 began its QE3 program, which lasted until October 2014 and totaled $1.7 trillion.

By the time the Fed's QE3 program ended in October 2014, the Fed's QE programs totaled $3.7 trillion, and the Fed's balance sheet had quintupled to $4.5 trillion from the pre-crisis level of $900 billion.

The purpose of the Fed's QE programs was to (1) keep banks fully supplied with excess reserves to reduce the chance of a liquidity squeeze and to provide plenty of reserves as a base for expanded lending, (2) keep long-term Treasury yields relatively low in order to hold down private rates such as corporate bond yields and mortgage rates, and (3) provide a boost to asset prices and the stock market in order to increase household confidence and wealth.

After the Fed concluded its QE programs in October 2014, the Fed kept its balance sheet stable until late 2017 by buying new securities to replace the securities in its portfolio that matured.

In Q4-2017, the Fed began a balance sheet drawdown program in an attempt to reduce excess reserves to more normal levels and to reduce the risk of an inflation outbreak. From October 2017 through August 2019, the Fed allowed its balance sheet to decline by letting securities mature without replacement. Over that period, the Fed allowed its balance sheet to decline by $700 billion to $3.8 trillion.

The Fed ended its balance sheet drawdown program in September 2019 after the money markets went haywire because of a shortage of liquidity in the banking system. Short-term interest rates spiked higher as banks scrambled to get the liquidity they needed to meet their reserve requirements. The shortage of liquidity made it clear that the Fed had reduced its balance sheet too much and that banks did not have enough reserves for normal operations.

The Fed, in October 2019, therefore started a program of buying $60 billion of T-bills per month to provide reserves to the banking system and start pushing its balance sheet higher again. As of mid-March 2020, the Fed had boosted its balance sheet by $480 billion and had reversed nearly two-thirds of the 2017/19 decline.

Regarding interest rates, the Fed was forced by a weak U.S. economy to keep its federal funds target unchanged at the post-crisis level of 0.00%/0.25% for the six years following the global financial crisis. The Fed took its first tentative step towards raising interest rates in December 2015 with a +25 bp rate hike. However, the Fed was then forced to leave rates unchanged over the next year due to the weak U.S. economy.

In December 2016, the Fed then began a regime of progressively raising interest rates to push rates back up to more normal levels. The Fed from December 2016 through December 2018 raised interest rates eight times in +25 bp increments, for a total rate hike of 2.00 percentage points, leaving the funds rate target at 2.25%/2.50% by December 2018.

However, the U.S. stock market plunged in Q4-2018

Financial Stocks vs Financial Conditions Index

Financial Conditions Index (right scale)

S&P Diversified Financials Stock Index (left scale)

Standard Deviations

1100 1000 900 800 700 600 500 400 300 200 100 0

2 0 -2 -4 -6 -8 -10 -12 -14 -16 -18

08 09 10 11 12 13 14 15 16 17 18 19 20 21

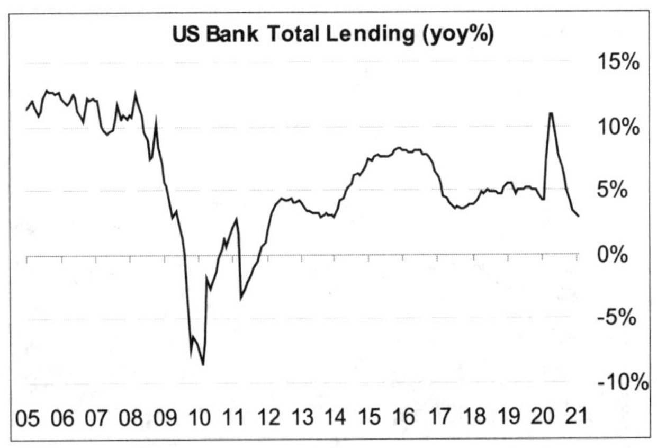

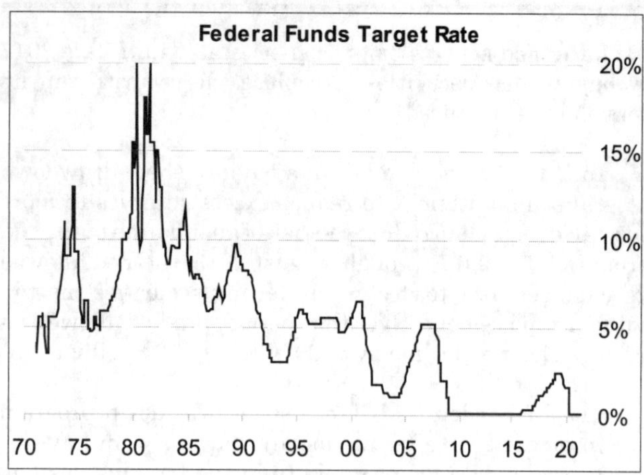

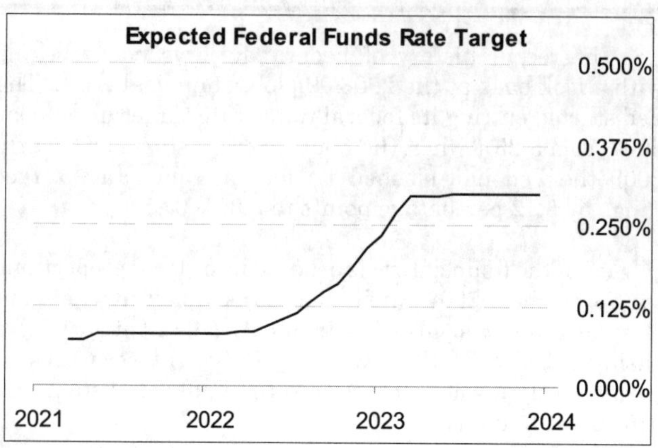

as the markets worried about the cumulative effect of the +2.25 percentage point total rate-hike seen since the post-crisis levels. That stock market plunge, combined with trade tensions and a weaker economy, forced the Fed in 2019 to cut rates three times by a total of 75 bp, leaving the funds rate target at 1.50%/1.75% by October 2019.

The global Covid pandemic then emerged in early 2020 and forced China to close a large proportion of its economy in an effort to curb the spread of the disease. U.S. Covid infection rates started rising sharply in March 2020, causing a lockdown of major sectors of the U.S. economy and a -10% plunge in U.S. GDP in the first half of 2020.

The Fed responded forcefully using all the tools at its disposal. The Fed in March 2020 slashed its funds rate target by 150 bp to 0.00%/0.25%. The Fed also announced an unlimited quantitative easing (QE) program and immediately started buying massive amounts of Treasury securities and mortgage-backed securities.

With help from new federal legislation, the Fed also turned itself into a "super-bank" with upwards of $5.5 trillion of direct lending firepower. The Fed implemented a variety of programs to provide direct loans and funds to the corporate bond market, commercial paper market, money market, asset-backed securities market, government securities dealers, and even small and medium-sized businesses.

The Fed was highly successful in preventing the worst shutdown of the U.S. economy in post-war history from turning into a long-lasting economic depression or causing a systemic global financial crisis. The Fed's aggressive action allowed the U.S. economy and financial system to absorb the body blow from the pandemic and begin to recover fairly quickly once the economy started reopening.

After the markets and the economy started to stabilize, the Fed in June 2020 announced that it would replace its unlimited QE program with a new QE program of buying $120 billion of securities per month, consisting of $80 billion of Treasury securities and $40 billion of mortgage-backed securities.

The Fed during 2020 and early 2021 made it clear that it would maintain its near-zero funds rate target and its $120 billion per month QE program for as long as necessary to meet its inflation and employment goals. The Fed said it would allow the U.S. economy to run hot in order to get back to full employment and to push inflation up to its target. The Fed in August 2020 also adopted a new and dovish "average inflation targeting" policy that explicitly provides for inflation to temporarily run above 2% so that inflation over time would average near its 2% inflation target.

As of March 2021, the markets were not fully expecting the Fed to implement its first +25 bp rate hike until late 2022. After that, the markets were expecting a slow rate hike regime of about two rate hikes per year in 2023-25 and an overall 250 bp rate hike by 2029 to 2.50%/2.75%.

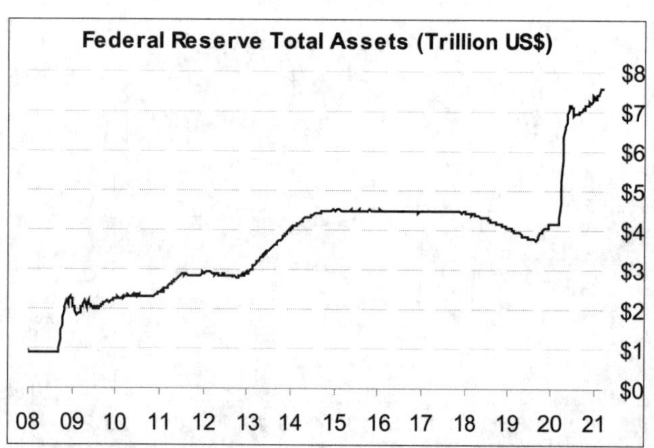

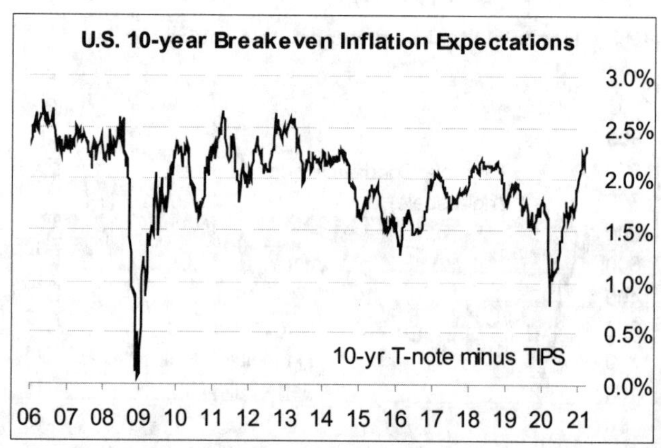

HUNDRED-YEAR PANDEMIC IS CURBED BY VACCINE SUCCESS

The seeds of a global pandemic emerged in December 2019 when a new type of coronavirus infection emerged in Wuhan, China. World health authorities named the disease "Coronavirus disease 2019" (Covid-19), and named the virus causing the disease "severe acute respiratory syndrome coronavirus 2" (SARS-CoV-2).

Other viruses seen in recent years, such as SARS (2002-03), Swine Flu (2009-2010), MERS (2012-present), and Ebola (2014-2016), stopped short of a global pandemic.

However, the Covid virus grew into a global pandemic because it is highly transmissible and sidestepped early attempts to restrict its spread. People who contract the disease can easily spread the disease to others before they know they are infected because symptoms may not emerge for up to 1-14 days.

In addition, many cases of Covid are relatively mild or even asymptomatic, meaning many people go about their normal activities and spread the disease to other people without even knowing they are infected. There is also a high likelihood that other household members will become infected due to the lag of symptoms and the lack of quarantine shelters outside their homes.

Covid turned out to be the worst global pandemic of a respiratory virus since the Spanish flu in 1918-1920 infected an estimated 500 million people and killed as many as 100 million people.

Covid spread quickly within Wuhan, China, and escaped to the rest of the world through global travel. After initially downplaying the Covid outbreak, the Chinese government took draconian measures to quarantine entire regions of China and implement widespread testing. China starting in late January shut down a large proportion of its economy in order to contain the spread of the virus.

While the Chinese government had success in curbing the spread of Covid within its borders, more open countries such as the United States and Europe were reluctant to take draconian measures and the disease quickly spread. Also, many Asian countries already had experience dealing with previous respiratory disease outbreaks and therefore had more success in curbing the spread of Covid.

By mid-March 2021, there had been 120 million Covid infections globally and 2.6 million deaths, according to Johns Hopkins Coronavirus Resource Center. In the U.S., there had been 30 million infection cases through mid-March 2021, accounting for about 9% of the total U.S. population. There were 534,000 identified deaths from Covid in the U.S. through mid-March 2021.

In the U.S., there were three distinct Covid waves. The first wave started in late March 2020. The second wave began in June 2020 and peaked in July 2020. The third wave, by far the largest, started in October 2020 and peaked in January 2021 with a 7-day average of 281,871 new daily Covid cases, according to Bloomberg data.

The number of new daily Covid cases in the U.S. then plunged from mid-January 2021 through the end of February 2021. That sharp drop was due to (1) some population immunity after at least 9% of the U.S. population recovered from the disease and had some antibodies, (2) the beginning of vaccinations in December 2020, and (3) a possible seasonal decline since Covid may have a seasonal pattern similar to that of the flu.

The Covid pandemic was the first pandemic in human history where medical researchers were able to develop and manufacture an effective vaccine on an extremely short timeline. The Pfizer and Moderna vaccines used a new technology called messenger RNA (mRNA), which gave researchers a genetic technique to design a highly-targeted vaccine for the Covid virus and provide an estimated 95% immunity for people receiving the vaccine.

The U.S. started administering vaccine doses in December 2020. The vaccination rate ramped up quickly as the vaccine production increased and vaccine-administration sites were put into place. By mid-March 2021, the U.S. had administered at least one vaccine dose to 30% of the U.S. population. Globally, 345 million vaccine doses had been given by mid-March 2021. More vaccines came online in spring 2021 from Johnson & Johnson, AstraZeneca, and many other companies.

The promising vaccine outlook raised hopes that the global Covid pandemic might soon be over, thus allowing a full global economic recovery.

U.S. Daily New Covid Cases (with 7-day avg)

Source: Bloomberg using data from Johns Hopkins, WHO, and others.

300,000
250,000
200,000
150,000
100,000
50,000
0

3/20 4/20 5/20 6/20 7/20 8/20 9/20 10/20 11/20 12/20 1/21 2/21 3/21

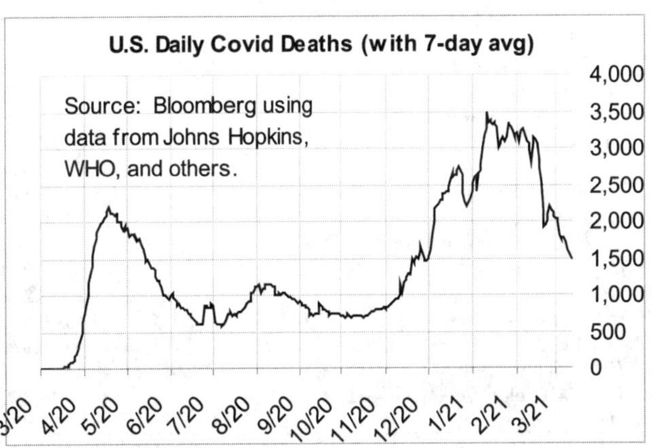

U.S. Futures Volume Highlights
2020 in Comparison with 2019

2020 Rank	EXCHANGE	2020 Contracts	%	2019 Contracts	%	2019 Rank
1	Chicago Mercantile Exchange (CME Group)	1,921,520,893	45.95%	1,589,681,093	37.38%	1
2	Chicago Board of Trade (CME Group)	1,403,666,736	33.57%	1,537,164,569	36.14%	2
3	New York Mercantile Exchange (CME Group)	542,623,678	12.98%	544,471,479	12.80%	3
4	ICE Futures U.S.	318,501,942	7.62%	291,863,849	6.86%	4
5	Commodity Exchange (CME Group)	153,950,886	3.68%	141,252,132	3.32%	5
6	CBOE Futures Exchange	50,748,204	1.21%	62,702,022	1.47%	6
7	OneChicago	3,186,854	0.08%	7,369,800	0.17%	7
8	Minneapolis Grain Exchange	2,730,936	0.07%	2,311,817	0.05%	9
	NASDAQ NFX			4,468,365	0.11%	8
	Total Futures	**4,396,930,129**	**100.00%**	**4,181,551,499**	**100.00%**	

CBOE Futures Exchange (CFE)

FUTURE	2020	2019	2018	2017	2016
CBOE S&P 500 Twelve-Month Variance (IIK)	40	65	12,212	70,343	1,290
CBOE Volatility Index (VX)	48,574,180	62,462,867	74,318,415	73,858,885	60,170,725
CBOE Volatility Index (VXM)	2,009,661				
CBOE 1 Month Ameribor (AMB1)	1,115				
CBOE 3 Month Ameribor (AMB3)	4,141	3,899			
CBOE 7 Day Ameribor (AMW)	6,041	4,727			
CBOE High Yield Corporate Bond	136,330	19,819	3,656		
CBOE Investment Grade Corporate Bond	16,696	861	18		
Total Futures	**50,748,204**	**62,710,648**	**75,555,327**	**73,991,390**	**60,177,810**

Chicago Board of Trade (CBT), division of the CME Group

FUTURE	2020	2019	2018	2017	2016
Chicago Soft Red Winter Wheat	33,365,343	30,407,143	36,805,171	33,717,805	31,059,726
Corn	89,753,068	103,189,062	97,387,154	89,876,782	85,625,219
EU Wheat	306,673	181,065	179,745	120,874	77,631
Fertilizer	35,621	24,730	13,680	5,700	
Fertilizer Products	1,415	15,215	27,360	21,700	22,842
KC Hard Red Winter Wheat	13,761,590	15,455,728	15,341,514	12,623,018	9,690,816
Mini Corn	333,329	172,423	118,883	115,646	143,840
Mini Soybeans	504,026	227,779	273,669	204,819	296,336
Mini Wheat	175,025	88,322	88,021	67,718	74,698
Oats	140,672	162,551	172,939	169,252	225,230
Rough Rice	257,363	258,873	231,294	271,183	305,045
Soybeans	61,122,980	53,333,211	58,538,591	54,504,169	61,730,753
Soybean Meal	29,914,836	29,403,484	31,838,908	25,996,399	25,953,938
Soybean Oil	32,961,867	31,694,867	31,265,884	30,232,316	29,429,298
Ethanol	12,982	79,575	112,438	149,546	172,664
S&P 500 Index	160	16,700	500		
E-micro $5 DJIA	32,643,055	7,815,787			
Mini-sized $5 Dow Jones Industrial Index	59,371,718	50,377,749	60,324,164	32,866,342	42,555,855
10-Year Treasury Note	405,990,223	449,829,752	457,719,304	375,338,442	350,762,158
10-Year Eris SOFR Swap	216				
10-Year Eris Swap	176,066	364,815	118,735	154,248	124,389
10-Year USD Deliverable Interest Rate Swap	1,042,565	599,489	516,443	601,992	631,279
1-Year Eris SOFR Swap	95,745				
2-Year Treasury Note	128,850,090	182,623,959	135,499,156	97,249,457	81,874,197
2-Year Eris SOFR Swap	15,612				
2-Year Eris Swap	319,371	564,612	161,543	24,404	27,655
3 Year Treasury Note	618,423				
30-Year Treasury Bond	95,684,575	87,795,571	92,661,809	73,337,240	70,203,290
30-Year Eris Swap	1,345	6,012	3,372	5,809	4,225
3-Year Eris SOFR Swap	8,753				
3-Year Eris Swap	49,250	192,083	39,677	32,275	9,775
4-Year Eris SOFR Swap	705				
4-Year Eris Swap	16,749	93,581	16,045	6,045	7,456
5 Year Treasury Note	244,842,677	294,399,748	287,221,081	226,441,088	201,904,771
5-Year Eris SOFR Swap	1,116				
5-Year Eris Swap	270,098	482,357	148,712	195,465	292,482
5-Year USD Deliverable Interest Rate Swap	412,582	484,142	350,138	566,751	792,880
7-Year Eris Swap	29,280	46,946	31,845	17,635	8,106
Federal Funds	52,338,248	89,714,542	65,336,892	47,978,260	33,299,445
Ultra 10-Year Treasury Note	64,579,927	57,907,848	47,350,198	29,309,367	16,979,453
Ultra T-Bond	52,401,970	47,972,662	46,632,747	33,625,955	28,430,003
DJ UBS Commodity Index	370,825	527,389	950,480	1,093,237	417,312
DJ UBS Roll Select Commodity Index	16,670	13,353	20,570	8,640	5,036
DJ US Real Estate	871,932	635,273	592,487	374,968	241,475
Total Futures	**1,403,666,736**	**1,537,164,569**	**1,468,344,802**	**1,167,503,091**	**1,073,572,475**

Chicago Mercantile Exchange (CME), division of the CME Group

FUTURE	2020	2019	2018	2017	2016
Butter	70,339	53,232	52,623	40,323	39,170
Cash Settled Cheese	166,161	133,784	136,455	128,370	117,899
Class III Milk	428,640	335,847	302,252	319,828	321,959
Class IV Milk	26,575	28,528	10,864	10,447	14,302
Dry Whey	18,683	15,013	16,852	20,786	16,042
Feeder Cattle	3,225,559	3,608,546	3,528,965	3,541,833	2,537,955
Lean Hogs	12,396,409	15,621,844	13,551,711	11,242,021	9,195,000
Live Cattle	16,138,757	16,718,841	16,440,125	16,165,210	13,122,784
Malaysian Palm Oil Calendar Swap	50,472	50,400	51,474	105,112	117,440
Nonfat Dry Milk	92,417	75,487	59,405	60,375	55,375
Pork Cutout	4,423				
USD Crude Palm Oil	38,341	17,263	8,680	6,434	3,140
Australian Dollar	25,910,300	25,229,626	28,062,547	24,054,242	25,303,506
Australian Dollar / Canadian Dollar	222	324	60	838	69
Australian Dollar / Japanese Yen	29,986	33,139	50,269	33,516	52,139
Australian Dollar / New Zealand Dollar	3,504	2,583	1,026	1,160	733
Bitcoin	2,221,723	1,603,862	923,294	9,503	
Brazilian Real	2,633,343	2,177,897	1,624,599	1,147,242	1,004,902
British Pound	27,991,765	30,542,256	32,439,027	31,167,897	29,126,002
British Pound / Japanese Yen	38,953	37,887	37,470	40,981	22,624
British Pound / Swiss Franc	5,042	4,732	3,982	1,103	479
Canadian Dollar	19,466,442	20,006,463	21,019,365	19,222,524	18,697,306
Canadian Dollar / Japanese Yen	609	230	1,489	1,490	15
Chinese Renimibi / Euro	277,829	329,142	117,420	19,826	21,091
Chinese Renimibi / US Dollar	5	10	65	345	3,803
Czech Koruna	2		75		
Czech Koruna (European)	30	42	8		
E-micro AUD/USD	2,970,125	1,202,640	1,313,037	1,012,132	1,218,358
E-micro EUR/USD	6,046,141	2,640,604	4,323,117	2,987,367	3,371,953
E-micro GBP/USD	933,208	650,407	545,675	681,701	1,038,606
E-micro INR/USD	26,073	55,850	62,787	31,089	29,960
E-mini Euro FX	1,917,534	1,101,629	1,224,546	1,142,522	949,208
E-mini Japanese Yen	232,932	203,872	163,359	318,114	393,096
Euro FX	55,419,194	52,490,124	68,785,137	56,455,834	49,455,909
Euro / Australian Dollar	85,675	61,510	33,121	40,887	21,928
Euro / British Pound	825,490	1,184,463	1,064,898	1,029,005	956,015
Euro / Canadian Dollar	55,827	42,453	45,151	57,521	33,735
Euro / Japanese Yen	692,255	895,395	1,044,615	877,007	542,332
Euro / Norwegian Krone	2,537	7,807	4,440	3,149	11
Euro / Swedish Krona	8,089	10,488	10,058	10,456	3,527
Euro / Swiss Franc	430,341	427,831	377,760	464,544	477,722
Hungarian Forint	214	70	729		
Hungarian Forint (European)	11		98		
Indian Rupee	317,569	747,029	1,089,152	472,388	160,255
Israeli Shekel	144	40	2,610	1,468	
Japanese Yen	28,945,380	32,573,773	36,979,311	41,623,449	36,588,788
Korean Won	13,713	10,354	6,846	786	207
Mexican Peso	14,804,097	15,064,180	17,081,210	13,082,141	14,074,359
Micro CAD/USD	360,021	201,285	206,791	244,321	245,995
Micro CHF/USD	62,071	42,767	18,276	11,952	21,814
Micro JPY/USD	348,677	318,376	356,863	450,068	396,958
New Zealand Dollar	7,508,683	6,974,345	7,552,938	6,352,688	5,938,492
Norwegian Krone/US Dollar	70,922	70,561	64,580	25,688	23,898
Euro / Polish Zloty	740	504	232	444	19,906
Polish Zloty	10,558	2,119	1,212	4,046	23,053
Russian Ruble	1,413,763	1,055,559	769,150	700,678	481,686
South African Rand	932,704	707,052	593,301	671,568	242,283
Swedish Krona	69,290	48,365	61,886	35,201	26,231
Swiss Franc	6,906,078	7,146,431	7,262,353	6,978,111	5,968,783
Swiss Franc/Japanese Yen	295	60	199	32	
Turkish Lira	9,330	15,069	38,992	27,812	420
E-mini Communication Services Select Sector Index	59,489	86,190	26,630		
E-mini FTSE 100 Index	4,809	26,643	54,932	33,509	20,867
E-mini NASDAQ 100 Index	146,717,097	115,080,512	124,195,504	69,559,095	65,750,522
E-mini Russell 1000 Growth Index	64,431	70,335	133,122	60,347	3,415
E-mini Russell 1000 Index	106,949	113,167	183,158	68,918	5,213
E-mini Russell 1000 Value Index	157,606	177,152	200,920	111,903	10,640
E-mini Russell 2000 Index	51,918,970	36,798,640	37,825,110	11,255,598	
E-mini S&P 500 Index	502,227,405	395,146,908	445,199,191	365,601,616	472,678,663
E-mini S&P 500 ESG Index	136,596	3,187			
E-mini S&P Consumer Discretionary Sector	125,390	106,969	237,902	95,698	150,939
E-mini S&P Consumer Staples Sector	298,942	236,144	336,374	216,011	315,638
E-mini S&P Energy Sector	426,630	230,623	459,339	200,581	141,747
E-mini S&P Financial Sector	390,959	420,726	661,070	392,947	174,419
E-mini S&P Technology Sector	190,800	490,180	137,930	81,412	60,448

Chicago Mercantile Exchange (CME), division of the CME Group (continued)

FUTURE	2020	2019	2018	2017	2016
E-mini S&P Healthcare Sector	222,608	256,116	304,283	184,740	146,804
E-mini S&P Industrial Sector	246,340	165,792	275,804	109,172	133,452
E-mini S&P Materials Sector	126,473	124,502	168,358	108,529	85,743
E-mini S&P MidCap 400 Index	4,532,446	4,108,137	4,951,100	4,332,040	5,405,757
E-mini S&P Real Estate Select Sector	104,879	90,250	116,335	73,426	14,213
E-mini S&P SmallCap 600 Index	3,504	4,446	1		
E-mini S&P Technology Sector	197,801	190,800	490,180	137,930	81,412
E-mini S&P Utilities Sector	329,203	385,556	518,335	347,959	298,401
Ibovespa Index	4,668	8,289	13,032	8,560	8,878
Micro E-mini Nasdaq 100 Index	178,531,164	31,750,965			
Micro E-mini Russell 2000 Index	23,672,428	5,004,928			
Micro E-mini S&P 500 Index	226,808,530	43,076,456			
NASDAQ Biotech	6,334	4,573	8,528	3,805	2,312
Nasdaq Water Index	94				
Nearby BTIC+ on E-mini S&P 500 Stock Price Index	1,177	34			
Nikkei 225 ($)	2,260,193	2,617,112	3,823,525	3,375,130	4,288,493
Nikkei 225 (Yen)	11,252,533	9,741,770	11,012,114	10,851,751	14,805,432
S&P 500 Annual Dividend Index	683,336	326,502	186,925		
S&P 500 Index	816,471	1,193,902	1,654,823	1,509,263	2,245,436
S&P 500 Quarterly Dividend Index	15,279	2,567	1,002		
S&P 500 Total Return Index	769,556				
Topix (Yen)	77,860	219,936	13,365		
1 Month Secured Overnight Financing Rate (SOFR)	5,224,162	3,880,376	1,096,606		
3 Month Secured Overnight Financing Rate (SOFR)	7,619,649	5,222,472	298,611		
Eurodollar (3-month)	509,912,503	687,072,595	765,208,581	639,847,185	654,947,336
MPC Sterling Overnight Index Average (SONIA)	17,761	29,609			
One Month Eurodollar	826	451	32,337	66,122	19,687
Quarterly IMM Sterling Overnight Index Average	1,990,193	2,183,171			
Asia CAT Weather	7,800				
CDD Seasonal Weather Strips	750	450	600	1,100	1,575
CDD Weather	9,650	8,975	2,150	26,250	3,375
CSI Housing Index	270	148	113	136	146
Euro HDD Weather	4,050	9,750	24,000		650
HDD Weather	40,475	15,150	14,405	9,239	6,204
Random Lumber	156,025	162,682	216,586	205,099	174,982
Goldman Sachs Commodity Index	174,903	327,866	378,542	403,424	359,987
S&P GSCI Enhanced Excess Return Swap	27,335	37,442	41,362	134,259	116,459
GSCI Excess Return Index	378,879	379,284	472,094	437,683	344,822
Tokyo CAT Weather	1,300				
Total Futures	**1,921,520,893**	**1,589,684,280**	**1,670,440,314**	**1,353,316,208**	**1,445,488,379**

Commodity Exchange (COMEX), division of the CME Group

FUTURE	2020	2019	2018	2017	2016
Alumina FOB Australia (Platts) (ALA)	1,809	1,182	5,755	6,685	60
Aluminium European Premium Duty-Paid (Metal	41,031	27,415	17,730	10,865	10,453
Aluminium European Premium Metal Bulletin (25mt-	37,909	31,620	20,068	29,963	13,573
Aluminum Futures (ALI)	43,347	15,659		5,755	8,241
Aluminum Japan Premium (Platts) (MJP)	11,870	11,560	13,155	17,399	9,103
Aluminum MW U.S. Transaction Premium Platts	108,633	81,758	98,922	85,683	68,872
Cobalt Metal (Fastmarkets) (COB)	3				
Copper (HG)	24,317,772	24,008,860	32,710,103	27,051,503	21,524,547
Copper Financial Futures (HGS)	35,352	11,165	17,294	8,988	3,881
Copper Premium Grade A CIF Shanghai (Metal	50	300	205	329	
E-mini Copper Futures (QC)	13,863	7,449	5,195	8,269	6,675
Iron Ore 62% Fe, CFR China (TSI) Futures (TIO)	23,051	54,130			
North European Hot-Rolled Coil Steel (Argus) (EHR)	6,500				
U.S. Midwest Busheling Ferrous Scrap (AMM)	26,448	12,453			
U.S. Midwest Domestic Hot-Rolled Coil Steel (CRU)	220,406	173,756			
U.S. Midwest Domestic Steel Premium (CRU) (HDG) *	180				
UxC Uranium U3O8 Futures (UX)	1,855	10,621			
E-Micro Gold Futures (MGC)	21,783,469	5,707,849	1,801,078	1,141,590	976,950
Gold (Enhanced Delivery) (4GC)	778				
Gold (GC)	78,127,531	86,508,741	80,301,590	72,802,171	57,564,840
miNY Gold Futures (QO)	386,925	241,481	96,481	92,442	130,190
miNY Silver Futures (QI)	106,315	49,552	13,401	9,704	14,985
Shanghai Gold (CNH) (SGC)	18,352	14,828			
Shanghai Gold (USD) (SGU)	60,730	27,891			
1,000-oz. Silver Futures (SIL)	2,449,936	354,422	100,519	71,118	101,937
Silver (SI)	26,126,771	24,149,148	23,987,051	23,034,989	18,218,740
Total Futures	**153,950,886**	**141,503,092**	**139,202,852**	**124,381,290**	**98,709,628**

ICE Futures U.S. (ICE) (continued)

FUTURE	2020	2019	2018	2017	2016
Canola	6,219,990	5,611,656	4,828,030	5,391,355	6,244,156
Cocoa	10,352,108	12,249,905	12,035,589	11,061,606	9,862,218
Coffee 'C'	12,557,541	15,020,918	13,387,705	9,434,122	9,856,314
Cotton #2	8,324,233	8,461,449	8,876,095	7,907,507	7,703,046
Orange Juice, Frozen Concentrate	334,456	433,636	356,854	363,499	413,904
Sugar #11	39,949,270	37,687,885	37,011,007	30,961,148	33,115,334
Sugar #16	89,714	79,289	75,141	70,679	78,410
Australian Dollar / Canadian Dollar	1,372	33	467	1,486	8,790
Australian Dollar / Japanese Yen	3,063	1,605	1,805	4,791	9,023
Australian Dollar / New Zealand Dollar	27,113	45,676	13,682	21,795	45,174
Australian Dollar / US Dollar (KAU)	8,888	11,062	13,337	17,705	14,044
Bakkt Bitcoin (USD) Daily	104	2			
Bakkt Bitcoin (USD) Monthly	827,934	85,411			
British Pound / Australian Dollar	1,093	1,715	458	1,795	9,210
British Pound / Canadian Dollar	1,417	1,140	953	1,227	6,232
British Pound / Japanese Yen	3,840	8,035	8,889	14,255	18,168
British Pound / New Zealand Dollar	1,625	457	272	1,747	4,314
British Pound / Norwegian Krone	10,605	9,701	23,600	20,036	14,881
British Pound / South Africa Rand	200	408	279	959	1,115
British Pound / Swedish Krona	292	327	815	863	1,093
British Pound / Swiss Franc	3,601	15,299	9,969	8,680	9,651
Canadian Dollar / Japanese Yen	1,120	2,382	2,262	3,500	5,508
Canadian Dollar / US Dollar (KSV)	4,117	11,411	6,651	13,445	21,408
Colombian Peso / US Dollar	0	40	866	1,950	
Euro / Australian Dollar (KRA)	6,368	32,193	11,883	10,862	23,675
Euro / British Pound (KGB)	3,435	1,614	2,608	10,714	24,116
Euro / Canadian Dollar (KEP)	575	2,888	1,796	5,191	11,088
Euro/Czech Koruna	14,527	36,121	241		
Euro / Norwegian Krone (KOL)	18,380	33,167	15,449	53,267	30,993
Euro / South African Rand	6,298	4,573	6,712	18,002	641
Euro / Swedish Krona (KRK)	15,805	33,505	37,618	32,974	41,644
Euro / Swiss Franc (KRZ)	630	1,615	364	752	10,436
Euro / US Dollar (KEO)	46,659	57,711	69,149	47,062	141,885
Euro / Czech Koruna	2,024	1,766	4,591	4,371	4,302
Euro / Hungarian Forint	153,593	163,133	124,288	144,639	84,482
Israeli Shekel / US Dollar	9,299	15,726	7,818	7,278	15,272
Japanese Yen / US Dollar (KSN)	7,334	15,205	5,944	10,779	24,463
Mexican Peso / US Dollar	1,997	1,542	954	3,162	322
New Zealand Dollar / US Dollar (KZX)	42	6	40	217	9,291
New Zealand Dollar / Japanese Yen	7,862	20,612	17,638	13,956	12,985
Norwegian Krone / Japanese Yen	420	404	370	508	658
Norwegian Krone / Swedish Koruna	31,431	84,111	74,309	78,548	77,292
Polish Zloty / Euro	19,735	43,473	44,555	66,392	24,868
Polish Zloty / US Dollar	8,625	41,628	28,662	24,331	1,727
Small British Pound / US Dollar	7,448	12,309	9,691	12,801	36,327
Swedish Krona / Japanese Yen	583	360	306	456	292
Swiss Franc / Japanese Yen (KZY)	6,972	3,258	6,256	8,479	8,097
Swiss Franc / US Dollar (KMF)	86	82	78	712	5,303
Turkish Lira / US Dollar	6,907	51,163	48,204	53,285	43,974
US Dollar Index	5,718,796	4,652,640	6,448,251	7,518,615	7,407,987
US Dollar / Czech Koruna (Half Size)	12,775	38,865	33,432	20,051	30,894
US Dollar / Hungarian Forint (Half Size)	13,317	38,899	20,412	36,922	16,744
US Dollar / Norwegian Krone (Half Size)	15,656	52,337	43,970	21,746	21,288
US Dollar / South African Rand	2,499	5,931	11,216	41,403	45,660
US Dollar / Swedish Krona (Half Size)	14,643	40,843	35,589	34,964	48,668
Global Oil Products	4,664,219	4,364,867	3,185,340		
North American Natural Gas	154,553,687	137,178,580	156,488,955	154,481,611	161,812,492
North American Natural Gas and Power	312				
North American Power	11,781,917	12,254,002	12,689,753	17,143,215	26,957,208
FANG+ Index	588,556	441,754	361,012	13,846	
MSCI ACWI NTR	467,182	342,676	303,832	376,085	383,969
Mini MSCI China Free NTR Index	18,088	915			
Mini MSCI EAFE Index	14,494,975	10,867,127	9,232,112	6,803,099	5,774,453
Mini MSCI Emerging Markets Asia NTR	46,022,840	40,475,733	35,866,309	523,135	129,558
Mini MSCI Emerging Markets	383,875	263,123	398,263	24,121,251	22,534,452
Mini MSCI Emerging Markets EMEA Index	3,800	207			
Mini MSCI Emerging Markets ESG Leaders NTR	36,292	3,600			
Mini MSCI Emerging Markets Latin America Index	14,589	12,857	11,560	7,764	11,137
Mini MSCI Emerging Markets NTR	18,480	3,467			
Mini MSCI Europe NTR Index	11	635			
Mini MSCI India NTR Index	464			50	
Mini MSCI Japan NTR Index	16,443				
Mini MSCI North America NTR Index	3,557	1,629			
Mini MSCI Pacific NTR Index	879	44			
Mini MSCI USA ESG Leaders GTR Index	236				

ICE Futures U.S. (ICE) (continued)

FUTURE	2020	2019	2018	2017	2016
Mini MSCI USA GTR Index	25,090	22			
Mini MSCI USA Index	20,500				
Mini MSCI USA Value Index	1,614	4,233	250		
Mini MSCI World ESG Leaders NTR Index	3,195				
Mini MSCI World Index	2,557	9,742	3,189	2,620	11,928
Mini MSCI World NTR Index	20,600	1,162			
Eris CDX HY Credit Index Future 5Y	5,334	6,706	6,378	7,342	10,232
Eris CDX IG Credit Index Future 5Y	13,725	6,148	6,597	20,084	26,984
100 oz. Gold	286	454	207	274	310
5,000 oz. Silver	878	292	272	730	380
Gold (Daily)	329,810	257,168	207,429	138,168	
Mini Gold	34,841	37,618	71,505	145,413	302,714
Mini Silver	42,142	40,025	58,058	79,482	138,169
Silver (Daily)	52,551	51,643	62,059	13,186	
Total Futures	**318,501,942**	**291,867,449**	**304,291,576**	**306,687,921**	**323,749,015**

Minneapolis Grain Exchange (MGE)

FUTURE	2020	2019	2018	2017	2016
Hard Red Spring Wheat	2,730,870	2,311,636	2,275,557	2,677,449	2,162,166
SPIKES Volatility Index	66	181			
Total Futures	**2,730,936**	**2,311,817**	**2,275,557**	**2,677,661**	**2,162,509**

New York Mercantile Exchange (NYMEX), division of the CME Group

FUTURE	2020	2019	2018	2017	2016
Coffee (KT)	2	2		41	169
Cotton Futures (TT)	59	39	22	20	578
No. 11 Sugar Futures (YO)	10	10	58	42	418
1% Fuel Oil Cargoes FOB NWE (Platts) vs. 3.5% Fuel	51	1,634	2,553	3,086	4,029
3.5% Fuel Oil Barges FOB Rdam (Platts) Crack Spread	403	5,351	18,153	20,260	29,875
3.5% Fuel Oil Barges FOB Rdam (Platts) Crack Spread	2,644	21,118	38,610	41,030	51,192
3.5% Fuel Oil Cargoes FOB MED (Platts) vs. 3.5% Fuel	22	198	860	4,466	9,548
3.5% Fuel Oil CIF MED (Platts) Futures (7D)	20	97	622	1,035	3,291
3.5% Fuel Oil Rdam vs. 3.5% FOB MED Spread	20	107	217	859	1,840
Argus Gasoline Eurobob Oxy Barges NWE Crack	31	53	222	127	97
Argus LLS vs. WTI (Argus) Trade Month Futures (E5)	72,825	91,454	256,755	190,327	144,567
Argus Propane (Saudi Aramco) Futures (9N)	27,087	35,928	32,923	12,890	10,114
Argus Propane Far East Index BALMO Swap (22)	1,624	2,014	2,117	1,165	592
Argus Propane Far East Index Futures (7E)	62,349	71,392	68,590	32,339	18,219
Argus Propane Far East Index vs European Propane	4,157	5,761	5,018	3,497	2,007
Argus Propane Far East Index vs Japan C&F Naphtha	34	49	51		
Argus WTI Diff vs. CMA NYMEX Trade Month (ANT)	1,330	180			
Brent Crude Oil BALMO Futures (J9)	1,706	1,960	285	578	2,293
Brent Crude Oil Futures (BB)	2,200	7,000	20,864	43,043	3,094
Brent Last Day Financial (BZ)	25,979,078	25,616,925	21,825,780	21,839,889	23,713,109
Brent Crude Oil vs. Dubai Crude Oil (Platts) Futures	34,005	65,001	106,858	119,797	33,163
Brent Financial Futures (CY)	82,520	85,595	39,825	34,990	22,091
Canadian C5+ Condensate Index (Net Energy) (CC5)	6,186	4,892	555	690	
Chicago CBOB Gasoline (Platts) vs. RBOB Gasoline	2,740	1,370	1,075		2,090
Chicago Ethanol (Platts) (CU)	874,634	1,168,154	1,133,415	1,342,798	1,322,192
Chicago ULSD (Platts) vs. NY Harbor ULSD (5C)	7,307	6,681	5,838	2,208	2,888
CIG Rockies Natural Gas (Platts IFERC) Basis	4,274	3,278	221	1,456	82,139
Coal (API 5) fob Newcastle (Argus/McCloskey) Futures	244,077	357,509	570	1,720	3,078
Coal (API2) CIF ARA (ARGUS-McCloskey) (MTF)	10,892	25,865	274,172	501,130	1,793,838
Coal (API4) FOB Richards Bay (ARGUS-McCloskey)	1,976	3,711	33,286	55,540	191,566
Columbia Gulf, Mainline Natural Gas (Platts IFERC)	22	20	214	999	22,041
Conway Natural Gasoline (OPIS) Futures (8L)	2,932	3,248	2,831	2,984	1,691
Conway Normal Butane (OPIS) BALMO Futures	90	50	80	52	30
Conway Normal Butane (OPIS) Futures (8M)	4,774	5,574	2,831	8,299	2,760
Conway Propane (OPIS) BALMO Futures (CPB)	2,024	2,708	3,608	3,532	1,482
Conway Propane (OPIS) Futures (8K)	182,933	171,286	186,616	109,794	88,313
Crude Oil Financial Futures (WS)	31,422	16,944	15,639	75,600	94,928
Crude Oil Last Day Financial Futures (26)	979				
Dakota Access Bakken (Net Energy) Monthly Index	340	540			
Dated Brent (Platts) BALMO Futures (DBB)	75				
Dated Brent (Platts) Daily Futures (7G)	640			1,400	200
Dated Brent (Platts) Financial Futures (UB)	70	1,633	5,300	2,540	26,638
Dated Brent (Platts) to Frontline Brent Futures (FY)	244	1,000	3,360	14,450	21,815
Dubai Crude Oil (Platts) BALMO Futures (BI)	300		125	50	275
Dubai Crude Oil (Platts) Financial Futures (DC)	10,650	18,592	111,582	83,846	30,297
Dutch TTF Natural Gas Calendar Month (TTF)	381,861	147,926	20,664		
East-West Gasoline Spread (Platts-Argus) Futures	4,820	23,725	58,413	32,545	22,001
East-West Naphtha: Japan C&F vs. Cargoes CIF	210	4,356	8,461	8,279	2,321
EIA Flat Tax On-Highway Diesel Futures (A5)	9,677	3,639	3,373	7,945	11,593

New York Mercantile Exchange (NYMEX), division of the CME Group (continued)

FUTURE	2020	2019	2018	2017	2016
EIA Flat Tax U.S. Retail Gasoline Futures (JE)	1,005	240	111	420	439
E-mini Crude Oil (QM)	6,834,996	5,470,936	4,692,563	3,001,906	3,380,972
E-mini Natural Gas Futures (QG)	1,612,231	439,093	433,039	311,945	338,981
E-mini NY Harbor ULSD (QH)	61	38	47	35	105
E-mini RBOB Gasoline Futures (QU)	85	73	47	51	51
Ethanol T2 FOB Rdam Including Duty (Platts)	48,990	44,366	40,167	45,681	33,306
European 3.5% Fuel Oil Barges FOB Rdam (Platts)	65	566	5,732	5,048	4,754
European 3.5% Fuel Oil Barges FOB Rdam (Platts)	2,384	11,053	78,702	85,392	91,573
European 3.5% Fuel Oil Cargoes FOB MED (Platts)	40	219	185	323	597
European 3.5% Fuel Oil Cargoes FOB MED (Platts)	37	428	1,001	1,744	4,552
European Diesel 10 ppm Barges FOB Rdam (Platts)	75	20	370	430	796
European FOB Rotterdam Marine Fuel 0.5% (Platts)	157	203			
European FOB Rotterdam Marine Fuel 0.5% (Platts)	2				
European FOB Rotterdam Marine Fuel 0.5% Barges	206	42			
European FOB Rotterdam Marine Fuel 0.5% Barges	10				
European Low Sulphur Gasoil (100mt) Bullet Futures	377	1,268	7,105	31,421	1,574,187
European Low Sulphur Gasoil Brent Crack Spread	12,428	10,730	39,294	77,557	64,857
European Low Sulphur Gasoil Financial Futures (GX)	324	305	66	244	352
European Naphtha (Platts) BALMO Futures (KZ)	86	1,463	3,087	3,923	2,257
European Naphtha (Platts) Crack Spread Futures	14,044	41,655	106,790	80,745	69,363
European Naphtha Cargoes CIF NWE (Platts)	5,746	17,896	39,775	31,941	18,916
European Propane CIF ARA (Argus) BALMO Swap	793	1,185	1,745	1,281	817
European Propane CIF ARA (Argus) Futures (PS)	18,704	21,688	21,260	15,311	15,813
European Propane CIF ARA (Argus) vs. Naphtha	4,782	6,232	10,741	6,468	3,179
Freight Route Liquid Petroleum Gas (Baltic) Future	2,299	1,633	2,533	1,797	2,557
Freight Route TC14 (Baltic) Futures (FRC)	40	1,652	600		
Freight Route TC17 (Baltic) (T7C)	290				
Freight Route TC2 (Baltic) Futures (TM)	45	2,461	1,052	220	
Freight Route TC5 (Platts) Futures (TH)	140	3,611	1,665	75	15
Freight Route TD20 (Baltic) (T2D)	2,113	6,105	4,983		
Freight Route TD20 (Baltic) BALMO (T2B)	20	15			
Freight Route TD22 (Baltic) (ACB)	735	1,140			
Freight Route TD3 (Baltic) Futures (TL)	23,464	61,189	20,671	390	
Gasoil 0.1 Barges FOB Rdam (Platts) Futures (VL)	127	149	1,506	170	30
Gasoil 0.1 Barges FOB Rdam (Platts) vs. Low Sulphur	17	21	10	354	120
Gasoline Eurobob Non-Oxy NWE Barges (Argus)	10				
Gasoline Euro-bob Oxy NWE Barges (Argus) BALMO	127	1,358	3,083	2,657	3,632
Gasoline Euro-bob Oxy NWE Barges (Argus) Crack	135	985	1,235	1,207	2,052
Gasoline Euro-bob Oxy NWE Barges (Argus) Crack	60,217	89,625	206,227	223,046	176,701
Gasoline Euro-bob Oxy NWE Barges (Argus) Futures	14,644	51,343	86,232	72,390	82,333
German Power Baseload Calendar Month (DEB)	10,066	26,696	5,441		
Group Three Sub-octane Gasoline (Platts) vs. RBOB	29,388	29,467	25,837	13,644	16,815
Group Three Sub-octane Gasoline (Platts) vs. RBOB	375				
Group Three ULSD (Platts) vs. NY Harbor ULSD	39,678	38,592	42,527	53,220	32,645
Group Three ULSD (Platts) vs. NY Harbor ULSD	1,122				
Guernsey Light Sweet Crude Oil Index (Net Energy)	2,720	296	105	200	230
Gulf Coast 3.0% Fuel Oil (Platts) BALMO Futures	2,986	9,191	14,048	16,992	9,656
Gulf Coast CBOB Gasoline A2 (Platts) vs. RBOB	3,008				
Gulf Coast CBOB Gasoline A2 (Platts) vs. RBOB	189,556	77,511	35,880	3,130	1,509
Gulf Coast Jet (Platts) Up-Down BALMO Futures	19,863	45,594	71,272	80,836	57,075
Gulf Coast Jet (Platts) Up-Down Futures (ME)	200,108	217,981	403,914	480,097	388,487
Gulf Coast Jet Fuel (Platts) Futures (GE)	3,153	429	1,606	1,270	1,923
Gulf Coast No. 2 (Platts) Up-Down Financial Futures	225	925	3,133	3,759	3,412
Gulf Coast No. 6 Fuel Oil (Platts) Crack Spread	482	3,688	18,242	19,411	15,814
Gulf Coast No.6 Fuel Oil 3.0% (Platts) Brent Crack	6,137	14,364	14,947	11,328	15,304
Gulf Coast No. 6 Fuel Oil 3.0% (Platts) Futures (MF)	121,471	258,242	608,490	629,301	681,964
Gulf Coast No. 6 Fuel Oil 3.0% (Platts) vs. European	44	527	1,005	739	1,130
Gulf Coast No. 6 Fuel Oil 3.0% (Platts) vs. European	15,803	42,072	130,251	73,204	88,311
Gulf Coast ULSD (Platts) Crack Spread Futures (GY)	1,410	360	1,655	3,870	6,981
Gulf Coast ULSD (Platts) Futures (LY)	9,985	4,053	3,950	5,953	10,572
Gulf Coast ULSD (Platts) Up-Down BALMO Futures	62,006	70,855	67,675	62,513	75,583
Gulf Coast ULSD (Platts) Up-Down Futures (LT)	531,625	409,270	383,467	551,389	619,919
Gulf Coast Unl 87 Gasoline M2 (Platts) Crack Spread	405				
Gulf Coast Unl 87 Gasoline M2 (Platts) vs. RBOB	5,006	6,749	14,760	13,553	4,760
Gulf Coast Unl 87 Gasoline M2 (Platts) vs. RBOB	62,110	150,546	187,871	181,036	109,698
Henry Hub Natural Gas (NG)	120,799,509	103,394,504	114,256,078	108,391,797	97,480,591
Henry Hub Natural Gas (Platts Gas Daily/Platts	8,392	21,170	32,088	50,542	181,858
Henry Hub Natural Gas (Platts IFERC) Basis	6,680	21,170	32,088	52,732	200,555
Henry Hub Natural Gas Last Day Financial (NN)	741,980	1,255,274	1,955,712	2,275,687	5,002,282
Henry Hub Penultimate NP (NP)	849,909	345,737	422,431	973,379	1,330,312
ISO New England Mass Hub 5 MW Peak Calendar-	768	220	12,711	17,275	45,635
ISO New England Mass Hub Day-Ahead Off-Peak	13,992	71,600	136,440	235,140	519,369
Japan C&F Naphtha (Platts) BALMO Futures (E6)	33	361	637	1,418	486
Japan C&F Naphtha (Platts) Brent Crack Spread	150	196	1,890	7,398	4,944
Japan C&F Naphtha (Platts) Futures (JA)	1,692	10,336	23,044	18,408	15,520

New York Mercantile Exchange (NYMEX), division of the CME Group (continued)

FUTURE	2020	2019	2018	2017	2016
Japan Crude Cocktail (Detailed) (JCC)	2,510	720			
Jet Fuel Cargoes CIF NWE (Platts) Crack Spread	9				
Light Sweet Oil (Net Energy) Monthly Index (LSW)	9,922	4,543	335	4,410	
LLS (Argus) vs. WTI Financial Futures (WJ)	7,900	19,989	60,624	64,990	71,223
LNG Freight Route BLNG1 (Baltic) (BF1)	15	20			
LNG Freight Route BLNG2 (Baltic) (BF2)	1,643	20			
LNG Japan/Korea Marker (Platts) Futures (JKM)	19,263	21,367	16,299	1,320	
LOOP Crude Oil Storage Futures (LPS)	4,295	33,110	53,385	46,199	57,915
LOOP Gulf Coast Sour Crude Oil (MB)	100				
Los Angeles CARB Diesel (OPIS) vs. NY Harbor	2,542	400	3,287	2,220	7,904
Los Angeles CARBOB Gasoline (OPIS) (MH)	15	10	10		
Los Angeles CARBOB Gasoline (OPIS) vs. RBOB	675	2,975	5,670	3,225	5,950
Los Angeles Jet (OPIS) vs. NY Harbor ULSD (JS)	6,625	13,784	21,774	20,120	22,112
Low Sulphur Gasoil Mini Financial Futures (QA)	6,113	6,175	2,947	1,613	2,779
Mars (Argus) vs. WTI Financial Futures (YX)	2,600	16,030	22,295	36,539	54,086
Mars (Argus) vs. WTI Trade Month Futures (YV)	188,526	215,863	233,266	260,006	140,278
Methanol FOB Houston (Argus) (MTH)	70	50			
Methanol T2 FOB Rotterdam (ICIS) (MT2)	2,278	1,455	700		
Micro European 3.5% Fuel Oil Barges FOB Rdam	1,637	3,535	1,812		
Micro European FOB Rotterdam Marine Fuel 0.5%	10,496	2,569			
Micro Gasoil 0.1% Barges FOB Rotterdam (Platts)	10,111	2,237			
Micro Singapore FOB Marine Fuel 0.5% (Platts)	8,659	861			
Micro Singapore Fuel Oil 380CST (Platts) (MAF)	2,422	23,372	4,748		
Mini 1% Fuel Oil Cargoes FOB MED (Platts) Futures	38	545	100	247	1,126
Mini 3.5% Fuel Oil Cargoes FOB MED (Platts)	70	854	260	534	1,996
Mini Argus Propane (Saudi Aramco) Futures (MAS)	3,451	2,450	2,251	405	1,010
Mini Argus Propane Far East Index Futures (MAE)	8,072	4,609	2,780	570	455
Mini Brent Financial Futures (MBC)	185	1,539	127		1,424
Mini Dated Brent (Platts) Financial Futures (MDB)	260				
Mini European 1% Fuel Oil Cargoes FOB NWE	100	577	144	163	1,605
Mini European 3.5% Fuel Oil Barges FOB Rdam	2,546	14,805	15,797	26,473	48,318
Mini European Diesel 10 ppm Barges FOB Rdam	130	140	173	910	1,301
Mini European FOB Rotterdam Marine Fuel 0.5%	4,617	1,867			
Mini European FOB Rotterdam Marine Fuel 0.5%	59				
Mini European Naphtha (Platts) BALMO Futures	598	1,862	4,846	6,653	7,596
Mini European Naphtha CIF NWE (Platts) Futures	11,410	37,392	48,644	45,730	47,818
Mini European Propane CIF ARA (Argus) (MPS)	3,829	2,774	1,462	180	
Mini Gasoline Euro-bob Oxy NWE Barges (Argus)	778	2,169	3,902	5,378	5,429
Mini Gasoline Euro-bob Oxy NWE Barges (Argus)	13,105	25,216	39,908	94,727	120,511
Mini Japan C&F Naphtha (Platts) BALMO Futures	80	168	714	242	502
Mini Japan C&F Naphtha (Platts) Futures (MJN)	7,102	14,151	22,700	20,833	16,148
Mini Middle East Naphtha FOB Arab Gulf (Platts)	160				
Mini RBOB Gasoline vs. Gasoline Euro-bob Oxy NWE	1,741	3,910	3,741	5,846	3,891
Mini RBOB Gasoline vs. Gasoline Euro-bob Oxy NWE	7,771	21,061	20,908	26,045	21,690
Mini Singapore FOB Marine Fuel 0.5% (Platts) (S5M)	17,615	2,470			
Mini Singapore FOB Marine Fuel 0.5% (Platts)	529				
Mini Singapore Fuel Oil 180 cst (Platts) BALMO	64	246	286	709	2,397
Mini Singapore Fuel Oil 180 cst (Platts) Futures (0F)	613	3,734	6,014	11,717	15,080
Mini Singapore Fuel Oil 380 cst (Platts) BALMO	72	772	615	1,559	3,116
Mini Singapore Fuel Oil 380 cst (Platts) Futures	3,810	39,136	55,855	57,540	46,049
Mini Singapore Gasoil (Platts) Futures (MSG)	8,004	3,425	5,132	3,293	651
Mini ULSD 10ppm Cargoes CIF NWE (Platts) vs.	270	540	923	1,126	1,689
Mini-Argus Butane (Saudi Aramco) (MAA)	1,325	280	50		
MISO Indiana Hub (formerly Cinergy Hub) Day-	1,346	5,312	13,630	19,513	22,142
Mont Belvieu Ethane (OPIS) BALMO Futures (8C)	4,670	1,851	1,900	3,205	1,920
Mont Belvieu Ethane (OPIS) Futures (C0)	318,159	187,794	189,923	256,776	590,762
Mont Belvieu Ethylene (PCW) BALMO Futures	50	5	321	550	84
Mont Belvieu Ethylene (PCW) Financial Futures	4,580	3,601	10,161	11,686	16,658
Mont Belvieu Iso-Butane (OPIS) Futures (8I)	9,950	8,265	6,893	7,021	3,257
Mont Belvieu LDH Iso-Butane (OPIS) Futures (MBL)	137	334	40	266	325
Mont Belvieu LDH Propane (OPIS) BALMO Futures	26,203	31,494	29,975	19,536	12,068
Mont Belvieu LDH Propane (OPIS) Futures (B0)	2,044,718	1,717,506	1,462,178	1,122,133	1,345,538
Mont Belvieu LDH Propane (OPIS) vs European CIF	29	79	23		
Mont Belvieu Mini LDH Propane (81)	60				
Mont Belvieu Natural Gasoline (OPIS) BALMO	10,720	7,781	4,191	3,667	1,981
Mont Belvieu Natural Gasoline (OPIS) Futures (7Q)	334,637	105,357	97,757	85,506	91,566
Mont Belvieu Normal Butane (OPIS) BALMO	15,851	15,312	12,905	8,436	7,211
Mont Belvieu Normal Butane (OPIS) Futures (D0)	799,900	581,603	427,121	346,469	345,287
Mont Belvieu Normal Butane LDH (OPIS) Futures	1,733	6,658	20,582	19,968	21,979
Mont Belvieu Spot Ethylene In-Well Futures (MBE)	2,640	3,975	9,160	12,370	32,365
MTBE FOB Singapore (Platts) (1NM)	1,184	913			
Naphtha Cargoes CIF NWE (Platts) Crack Spread	5	58	182	139	221
Naphtha Cargoes CIF NWE (Platts) Crack Spread	406	3,591	21,394	12,897	6,826
Natural Gas (Henry Hub) Last-day Financial (HH)	3,299,893	3,561,606	4,579,077	3,539,546	2,958,345
Natural Gas (Henry Hub) Penultimate Financial (HP)	1,850,904	1,360,246	1,438,019	1,669,023	1,574,185

New York Mercantile Exchange (NYMEX), division of the CME Group (continued)

FUTURE	2020	2019	2018	2017	2016
New York Harbor 1.0% Fuel Oil (Platts) BALMO	95	25	50	25	151
New York Harbor Residual Fuel 1.0% (Platts) Futures	8,012	10,317	12,678	28,543	39,080
NY 1% Fuel Oil (Platts) vs. Gulf Coast 3% Fuel Oil	2,718	5,447	15,373	25,857	29,944
NY 3.0% Fuel Oil (Platts) vs. Gulf Coast No. 6 Fuel	100	3,870	7,275	7,878	11,945
NY Buckeye Jet Fuel (Platts) vs. NY Harbor ULSD	7,415	25,680	35,110	44,806	63,859
NY Buckeye Jet Fuel (Platts) vs. NY Harbor ULSD	2,155	7,798	8,000	3,938	
NY Ethanol (Platts) Futures (EZ)	6,844	10,043	12,583	10,820	17,875
NY Harbor ULSD (HO)	44,003,184	43,400,809	46,277,883	43,596,206	39,389,349
NY Harbor ULSD BALMO Futures (1G)	1,517	605	243	1,057	479
NY Harbor ULSD Brent Crack Spread Futures (HOB)	9,400	19,331	9,206	35,033	38,059
NY Harbor ULSD Bullet Futures (BH)	108	96	120	340	5,578
NY Harbor ULSD Crack Spread Futures (HK)	9,951	6,585	8,636	14,244	22,662
NY Harbor ULSD Financial Futures (MP)	35,957	24,236	29,460	24,739	29,320
NY ULSD (Argus) vs. NY Harbor ULSD (7Y)	5,283	3,415	213	8,245	9,621
NY ULSD (Argus) vs. NY Harbor ULSD BALMO	415				
NY ULSD (Platts) vs. NY Harbor ULSD (UY)	700	2,000			
Panhandle Natural Gas (Platts IFERC) Basis Futures	56				
Petro European Naphtha Crack Spread BALMO	44	155	3,414	3,619	2,378
PGP Polymer Grade Propylene (PCW) Financial	12,946	8,328	5,560	6,264	5,129
PJM Western Hub Peak Calendar-Month Real-Time	15,814	59,799	63,850	223,316	657,190
Premium Unleaded Gasoline 10 ppm FOB MED	158	858	3,158	914	2,889
Propane Non-LDH Mont Belvieu (OPIS) BALMO	18,785	16,300	7,013	5,252	5,997
Propane Non-LDH Mont Belvieu (OPIS) Futures (1R)	293,277	240,228	150,843	87,065	138,706
RBOB Gasoline BALMO Futures (1D)	6,183	11,098	11,687	12,245	11,080
RBOB Gasoline Brent Crack Spread Futures (RBB)	33,794	74,208	57,935	86,718	128,539
RBOB Gasoline Bullet Futures (RT)	84	84	14,386	28,456	19,381
RBOB Gasoline Crack Spread Futures (RM)	12,610	14,130	9,658	11,362	18,804
RBOB Gasoline Financial Futures (RL)	66,794	67,785	65,352	83,819	80,700
RBOB Gasoline Physical (RB)	46,492,488	49,851,807	49,613,909	49,910,909	45,428,663
RBOB Gasoline vs. Euro-bob Oxy NWE Barges	11,398	27,974	32,982	28,899	20,434
RBOB Gasoline vs. NY Harbor ULSD (RH)	5,665	150	1,975	17,720	21,905
Singapore FOB Marine Fuel 0.5% (Platts) (S5F)	1,208	155			
Singapore FOB Marine Fuel 0.5% (Platts) BALMO	6				
Singapore FOB Marine Fuel 0.5% (Platts) vs	41	56			
Singapore Fuel Oil 180 cst (Platts) 6.35 Dubai (Platts)	375	332	539	2,480	230
Singapore Fuel Oil 180 cst (Platts) BALMO Futures	41	230	499	772	590
Singapore Fuel Oil 180 cst (Platts) Futures (UA)	215	2,511	8,683	12,108	14,209
Singapore Fuel Oil 180 cst (Platts) vs. 380 cst (Platts)	80	778	6,261	7,038	7,686
Singapore Fuel Oil 380 cst (Platts) BALMO Futures	39	937	2,454	2,693	1,933
Singapore Fuel Oil 380 cst (Platts) Futures (SE)	2,420	30,678	95,826	116,554	101,072
Singapore Fuel Oil 380 cst (Platts) vs. European 3.5%	203	6,990	21,636	29,725	24,696
Singapore Fuel Oil 380cst (Platts) Brent Crack	10	1,200	371	15	64
Singapore Gasoil (Platts) BALMO Futures (VU)	1,443	815	1,339	3,223	4,063
Singapore Gasoil (Platts) Futures (SG)	14,475	12,033	49,344	90,723	81,687
Singapore Gasoil (Platts) vs. Low Sulphur Gasoil	282	4,758	130,138	70,787	44,904
Singapore Jet Kerosene (Platts) BALMO Futures (BX)	345	50	215	536	156
Singapore Jet Kerosene (Platts) Futures (KS)	6,968	7,909	13,450	12,979	8,346
Singapore Jet Kerosene (Platts) vs. Gasoil (Platts)	575	100	35,345	18,735	14,485
Singapore Mogas 92 Unleaded (Platts) BALMO	175	1,500	6,067	2,076	5,953
Singapore Mogas 92 Unleaded (Platts) Brent Crack	3,085	11,233	20,126	13,999	19,445
Singapore Mogas 92 Unleaded (Platts) Futures (1N)	24,455	101,129	162,080	85,721	120,268
Texas Eastern Zone M-3 Natural Gas (Platts IFERC)	1,057				
UCOME Biodiesel (RED Compliant) FOB ARA (Argus)	155				
UK NBP Natural Gas (USD per MMBTU) (ICIS	75				
UK NBP Natural Gas Calendar Month (UKG)	5,975	7,445	49,382		
Urals North (Platts) vs. Dated Brent (Platts) CFD	300				
USGC Marine Fuel 0.5% Barges (Platts) (H5F)	3,413	5,396			
USGC Marine Fuel 0.5% Barges (Platts) BALMO	1,834				
USGC Marine Fuel 0.5% Barges (Platts) vs. Gulf Coast	270	1,602			
USGC to China (Platts) Dirty Freight (USC)	90	280			
USGC to UK Continent (Platts) Dirty Freight (USE)	800				
Western Canadian Select Oil (Net Energy) Monthly	29,050	43,525	73,558	88,576	
WTI BALMO Swap (42)	13,331	4,510	3,436	6,419	1,195
WTI Financial Futures (CS)	698,294	512,762	399,374	448,037	387,932
WTI Houston (Argus) vs. WTI Financial (HIL)	48,827	1,500			
WTI Houston (Argus) vs. WTI Trade Month (HTT)	871,639	716,767	555,118	245,508	30,135
WTI Houston Crude Oil (HCL)	44,752	183,174	24,641		
WTI Light Sweet Crude Oil (CL)	274,180,352	291,465,320	306,613,007	310,052,767	276,768,438
WTI Midland (Argus) vs. WTI Financial Futures (FF)	56,600	52,510	91,302	72,712	55,703
WTI Midland (Argus) vs. WTI Trade Month Futures	259,172	243,696	430,553	192,022	45,727
WTI-Brent Financial Futures (BK)	431,790	428,919	346,950	251,432	137,258
WTL Midland (Argus) vs. WTI Trade Month (WTL)	300				
WTS (Argus) vs. WTI Trade Month Futures (FH)	13,074	7,270	6,345	9,936	12,370
Palladium Futures (PA)	687,787	1,266,701	1,433,712	1,402,740	1,435,863
Platinum (PL)	4,577,531	5,862,290	5,463,799	4,852,160	3,994,072

New York Mercantile Exchange (NYMEX), division of the CME Group (continued)

FUTURE	2020	2019	2018	2017	2016
Total Futures	**542,623,678**	**544,471,479**	**572,332,919**	**571,361,340**	**536,490,550**

ONECHICAGO

FUTURE	2020	2019	2018	2017	2016
Exchange Traded Funds Futures	704,443	1,119,327	1,132,605	2,702,139	2,695,620
Single Stock Futures	2,482,411	6,250,473	5,933,687	12,227,858	9,695,835
Total Futures	**3,186,854**	**7,369,800**	**7,066,292**	**14,929,997**	**12,391,455**

Total Futures Volume

	2020	2019	2018	2017	2016
Total Futures	**4,396,930,129**	**4,181,551,499**	**4,253,091,503**	**3,656,950,204**	**3,579,554,321**
Precent Change	**5.15%**	**-1.68%**	**16.30%**	**2.16%**	**11.18%**

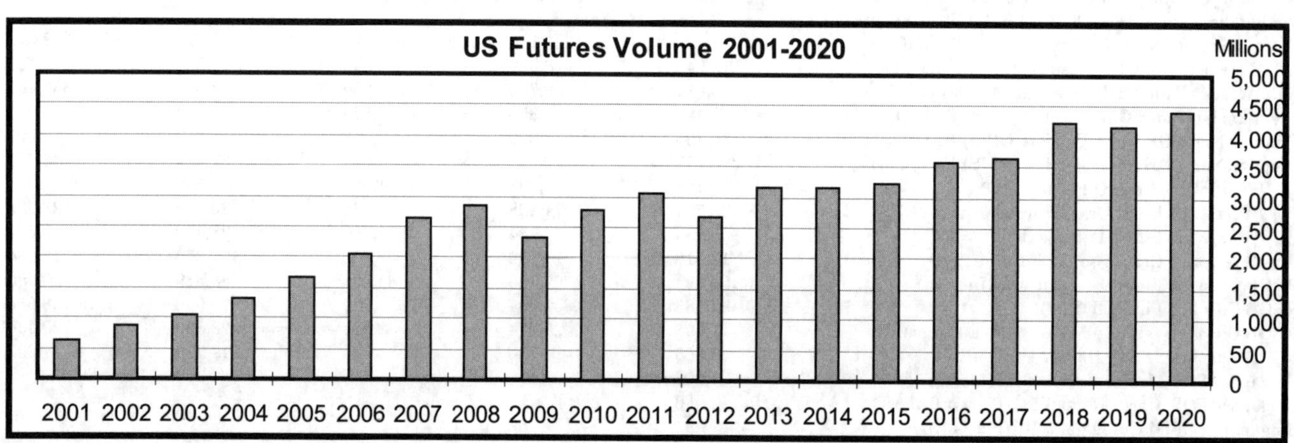

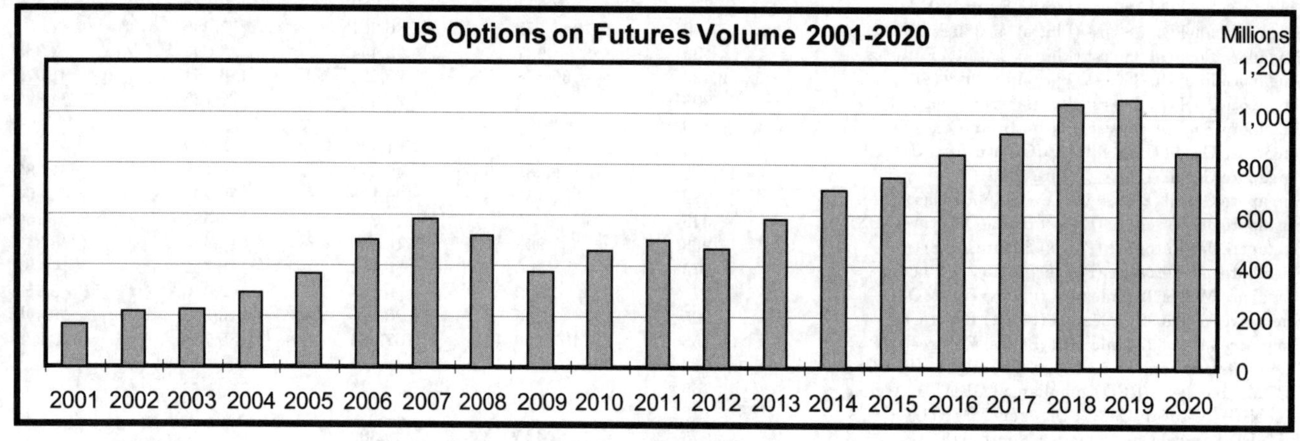

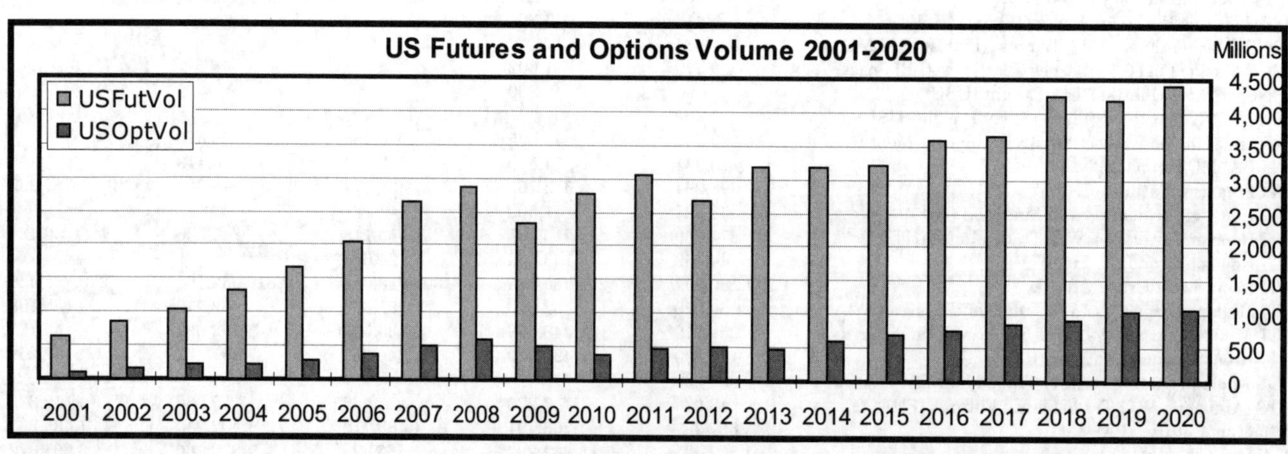

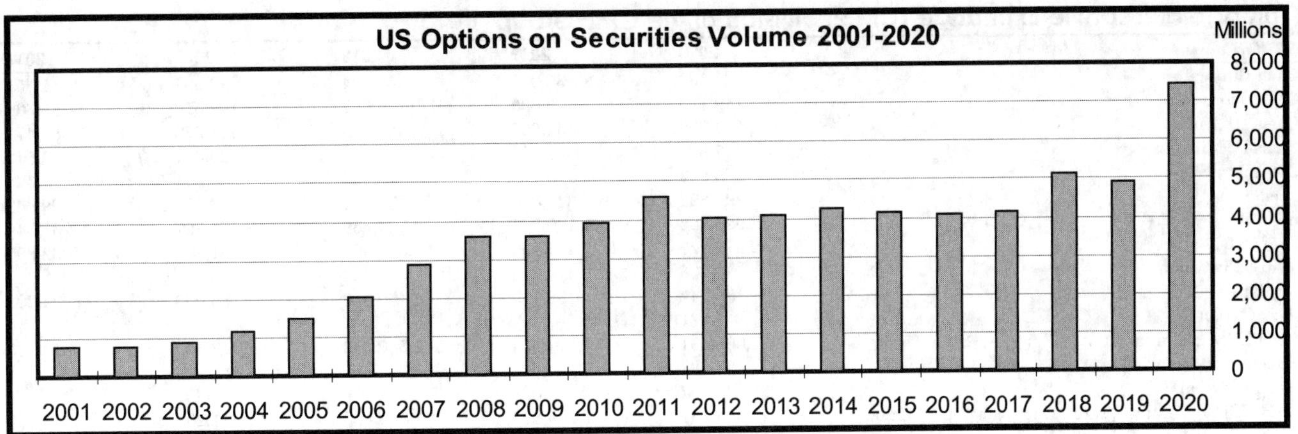

Options Traded on U.S. Futures Exchanges Volume Highlights
2020 in Comparison with 2019

2020 Rank	EXCHANGE	2020 Contracts	%	2019 Contracts	%	2019 Rank
1	Chicago Mercantile Exchange (CME Group)	464,575,401	43.89%	607,508,738	58.16%	1
2	Chicago Board of Trade (CME Group)	248,174,059	23.44%	328,957,090	31.49%	2
3	New York Mercantile Exchange (CME Group)	68,360,731	6.46%	61,279,571	5.87%	3
4	ICE Futures U.S.	53,004,312	5.01%	37,724,724	3.61%	4
5	Commodity Exchange (CME Group)	17,717,474	1.67%	19,730,697	1.89%	5
6	Minneapolis Grain Exchange	35,506	0.00%	46,179	0.00%	7
	NASDAQ NFX		0.00%	3,351,938	0.32%	6
	Total Options	**851,867,483**	**100.00%**	**1,058,598,937**	**100.00%**	

Chicago Board of Trade (CBT), division of the CME Group

OPTION	2020	2019	2018	2017	2016
Aug-Nov Soybean Calendar Spread	77			103	20
Chicago Soft Red Winter Wheat	7,692,329	7,346,623	9,403,524	7,513,694	6,977,412
Chicago SRW Wheat-Corn Intercommodity Spread	6,363	2,880	5,780	9,846	17,752
Corn	24,395,038	31,319,520	25,542,064	23,884,970	22,794,484
Corn Nearby + 2 Calendar Spread	67,529	83,045	40,753	15,940	36,758
Dec-Dec Corn Calendar Spread	3,135	18,794	20,775	12,136	18,778
Dec-July Corn Calendar Spread	3,942	28,755	19,499	39,888	26,543
Dec-July Wheat Calendar Spread	1,595	102	1,744	2,133	590
EU Wheat	22,061	67,398	7,107	486	409
Intercommodity Spread	11,286	13,620	11,463	701	4,046
Jan-March Soybean Calendar Spread	20				
July-Dec Corn Calendar Spread	25,387	31,304	11,696	17,802	36,834
July-Dec Soy Oil Calendar Spread	125				
July-Dec Wheat Calendar Spread	4,156	2,200	2,620	1,614	33,619
July-July Wheat Calendar Spread	160				493
July-Nov Soybean Calendar Spread	15,003	15,052	59,472	71,412	66,019
KC Hard Red Winter Wheat	1,109,193	1,122,351	1,009,253	530,134	346,680
March-December Corn Calendar Spread	535	384			
March-July Corn Calendar Spread	3,000	4,040			
March-July Soybean Calendar Spread	20				
March-July Wheat Calendar Spread	540	30	1,950	2,214	3,193
Nov-July Soybean Calendar Spread	2,670	3,550	1	1,696	
Nov-March Soybean Calendar Spread	1,435	20			
Nov-Nov Soybean Calendar Spread	180	2,828	118	164	2,982
Oats	3,321	4,670	6,801	14,062	18,576
Rough Rice	30,605	33,877	18,279	24,741	19,775
Soybeans	16,954,195	13,507,813	19,031,062	16,980,581	20,109,648
Soybean Crush	4,157	334	185	741	4,825
Soybean Meal	2,977,539	1,987,792	3,185,498	2,160,060	2,269,279
Soybean Nearby +2 Calendar Spread	14,060	6,425	10	1,060	1,701
Soybean Oil	2,804,226	1,599,835	1,425,379	2,050,228	2,298,191
Soymeal Nearby +2 Calendar Spread	200	490	8,415		3,785
Wheat Nearby +2 Calendar Spread	8,127	3,115	14,178	17,903	55,023
Mini $5 Dow Jones Industrial Index	33,237	53,881	125,334	74,244	127,484
10-Year Treasury Note	127,185,745	171,116,138	167,962,668	128,546,313	98,504,626
2-Year Treasury Note	2,049,411	6,189,820	5,973,549	2,292,507	1,683,900
30-Year Treasury Bond	31,868,672	37,108,236	35,397,862	27,156,898	21,244,372
5-Year Treasury Note	30,832,753	56,901,305	41,498,642	29,659,494	23,880,566
Federal Funds	10,923	79,019	19,257	16,880	94,739
Ultra 10-Year Treasury Note	16,000	34,644	128	8,487	42,788
Ultra T-Bond	15,109	267,200	120,685	40,304	86,253
Total Options	**248,174,059**	**328,957,090**	**310,928,251**	**241,151,596**	**200,815,588**

VOLUME - U.S.

Chicago Mercantile Exchange (CME), division of the CME Group

OPTION	2020	2019	2018	2017	2016
Cash Butter	33,183	36,037	49,184	22,987	15,851
Cash Settled Cheese	149,156	113,802	125,892	119,578	91,630
Class III Milk	532,056	455,653	428,200	421,226	383,472
Class IV Milk	47,971	40,192	15,501	20,321	13,873
Dry Whey	5,943	8,115	6,990	7,481	1,325
Feeder Cattle	297,898	341,888	338,741	412,553	409,638
Lean Hogs	2,928,722	4,190,367	2,769,669	2,536,927	2,208,546
Live Cattle	2,672,920	2,413,456	2,641,563	2,901,400	4,032,890
Mini BFP Milk	136	244	484	834	924
Nonfat Dry Milk	86,242	68,779	60,568	53,069	34,398
Pork Cutout	181				
AUD/USD Premium Quoted European Style Option –	1,066,131	1,177,534	1,580,352	1,312,480	170,930
Bitcoin	37,332				
Brazilian Real	707	1,821			
CAD/USD Premium Quoted European Style Option –	955,131	1,185,872	1,872,860	1,741,208	174,857
CHF/USD Premium Quoted European Style Option –	49,753	47,026	30,519	38,775	13,121
EUR/USD Premium Quoted European Style Option –	4,577,544	6,006,230	8,711,729	7,803,347	737,055
Euro/British Pound	250	74			
GBP/USD Premium Quoted European Style Option – 2	1,443,195	2,017,648	3,244,177	2,703,047	220,889
JPY/USD Premium Quoted European Style Option – 2	2,088,878	2,425,824	3,131,431	3,113,816	395,282
Mexican Peso	32,709	20,700	24,211	37,948	50,933
New Zealand Dollar	5,403	10,901	1,050		
Russian Ruble	636				1,373
E-Mini NASDAQ 100 Index	4,029,014	2,394,963	2,878,414	2,873,368	2,568,059
E-mini Russell 2000 Index (Weekly)	346,790	294,647	230,982	110,395	
E-mini Russell 2000 Index	382,617	319,866	388,874	69,951	
E-Mini S&P 500 Index	84,727,423	66,319,544	73,364,734	51,055,524	58,887,823
EOM E-Mini S&P 500 Index	23,136,877	22,735,455	31,194,081	24,790,850	20,898,070
EOM S&P 500 Index	683,589	1,392,835	2,170,861	2,347,874	2,069,567
EOW1 E-mini S&P 500 Index	12,023,282	11,898,800	14,069,450	12,669,333	11,710,684
EOW1 S&P 500 Index	524,931	927,803	1,016,605	1,092,049	706,582
EOW2 E-mini S&P 500 Index	12,873,879	12,211,898	15,832,156	12,649,778	12,992,775
EOW2 S&P 500 Index	928,442	1,610,480	2,014,974	2,097,086	1,539,741
EOW3 E-mini S&P 500 Index	27,386,900	27,486,266	43,285,692	39,320,303	27,113,276
EOW3 S&P 500 Index	799,507	1,407,823	3,081,428	4,294,574	3,156,223
EOW4 E-mini S&P 500 Index	10,270,410	10,342,681	13,910,378	11,434,439	12,923,810
EOW4 S&P 500	92,265				
Micro E-mini Nasdaq 100 Index	6,839				
Micro E-mini S&P 500 Index	86,488				
S&P 500 Index	1,644,423	2,883,033	3,974,098	3,893,439	5,674,293
3 Month Secured Overnight Financing Rate (SOFR)	9,124				
Eurodollar (3-month)	184,852,363	278,764,545	173,585,526	153,425,834	168,254,035
Eurodollar Mid-Curve	82,725,939	145,928,255	183,150,164	190,004,215	140,529,194
CDD Seasonal Strip Weather	2,000	5,000	700	2,800	29,250
Euro HDD Seasonal Strip Weather	7,000		500	2,500	2,500
HDD Seasonal Weather Strip	6,000		9,000	16,000	20,200
HDD Weather	6,225		350	1,250	2,000
HDD Weather European	500			1,500	5,500
Random Lumber	10,497	20,085	21,557	16,219	12,522
Total Options	**464,575,401**	**607,508,738**	**589,226,608**	**538,270,775**	**494,457,421**

Commodity Exchange (COMEX), division of the CME Group

OPTION	2020	2019	2018	2017	2016
Aluminum MW U.S. Transaction Premium Platts (25	150				
Copper Options (HX)	428,124	704,806	351,780	107,490	38,472
Copper Weekly Options Wk 2 (H2E)	692	1,066	154		
Copper Weekly Options Wk 3 (H3E)	742	1,133	119		
Copper Weekly Options Wk 4 (H4E)	370	361	177		
Copper Weekly Options Wk 5 (H5E)	692	603	12		
Copper Weekly Wk 1 (H1E)	1,083	764	178		
Iron Ore 62% Fe, CFR China (TSI) Average Price	10,589	10,460	1,480	44,199	72,160
U.S. Midwest Domestic Hot-Rolled Coil Steel (CRU)	1,350	1,200	300	1,530	
Gold (OG)	13,213,356	15,043,949	11,751,255	9,892,533	9,916,049
Gold Weekly Options Wk 1 (OG1)	427,573	493,369	137,349	49,292	14,995
Gold Weekly Options Wk 2 (OG2)	468,511	460,929	129,124	49,145	20,626
Gold Weekly Options Wk 3 (OG3)	392,555	389,230	144,799	48,868	12,249
Gold Weekly Options Wk 4 (OG4)	329,297	243,235	88,255	27,923	8,208
Gold Weekly Options Wk 5 (OG5)	124,762	83,447	32,861	14,976	3,625
Silver Options (SO)	2,213,958	2,208,237	1,847,187	1,438,930	1,375,636
Silver Weekly Options Wk 1 (SO1)	28,425	26,964	5,789	686	559
Silver Weekly Options Wk 2 (SO2)	26,446	26,964	5,708	262	619
Silver Weekly Options Wk 3 (SO3)	24,194	19,702	8,489	629	797
Silver Weekly Options Wk 4 (SO4)	17,061	8,859	4,486	206	472
Silver Weekly Options Wk 5 (SO5)	7,544	5,419	2,746	53	258
Total Options	**17,717,474**	**19,730,697**	**14,512,248**	**11,676,722**	**11,464,725**

ICE Futures U.S. (ICE)

OPTION	2020	2019	2018	2017	2016
Canola	148,658	102,350	102,448	154,229	177,660
Canola 1 Month CSO	2,150	1,250	1,595	295	8,630
Cocoa	1,320,582	1,320,362	1,432,751	1,360,371	1,881,082
Cocoa 1 Month	60,175	1,000			
Cocoa 2 Month	6,700				
Coffee 'C'	3,130,537	3,640,869	3,073,591	2,365,261	2,230,914
Coffee 'C' 1-month	343,794	121,581	92,950	42,934	53,187
Coffee 'C' 2-month	82,075	35,190	14,730	8,300	5,475
Cotton #2	1,277,595	1,641,029	2,402,085	1,824,315	2,074,521
Cotton #2 2-month	1,200	4,780	9,313	9,180	
Orange Juice Frozen Concentrate	62,263	87,712	60,625	86,104	71,379
Sugar #11	6,156,858	5,646,890	5,708,889	4,763,196	7,279,040
Sugar #11 1-month	84,531	77,506	33,069	16,510	38,178
Sugar #11 2-month	1,150	600		1,450	950
Bakkt Bitcoin (USD) Monthly	189	68			
US Dollar Index	3,969	9,775	5,708	10,210	22,893
Global Oil Products	505,811	428,483	329,163		
North American Natural Gas and Power	39,816,075	24,604,779	28,027,203	42,656,346	39,140,813
Total Options	**53,004,312**	**37,724,724**	**41,294,620**	**53,362,810**	**53,045,272**

Minneapolis Grain Exchange (MGE)

OPTION	2020	2019	2018	2017	2016
Hard Red Spring Wheat	35,506	46,179	59,727	121,684	22,429
Total Options	**35,506**	**46,179**	**59,727**	**121,704**	**22,589**

New York Mercantile Exchange (NYMEX), division of the CME Group

OPTION	2020	2019	2018	2017	2016
3.5% Fuel Oil Barges FOB Rdam (Platts) Crack	6	36			
Brent Crude Oil Futures-Style Margin Option (BZO)	555,154	1,088,704	1,967,269	540,735	259,439
Brent Crude Oil Last Day Financial Calendar Spread	36,675	35,890	423,088		
Brent Financial Average Price Options (BA)	7,629	4,896	16,462	5,347	15,237
Brent Last Day Financial (European) Options (BE)	411,516	372,326	469,058	38,281	43,890
Brent Last Day Financial Options (OS)	25		1,290	3,912	12,234
Chicago Ethanol (Platts) Average Price Options (CVR)	51,531	121,721	70,070	73,329	85,662
Coal (API 2) cif ARA (Argus/McCloskey) Options	11,104	555	290	1,600	9,505
Coal (API 4) fob Richards Bay (Argus/McCloskey)	475	1,125	2,145	275	2,485
Conway Propane (OPIS) Average Price Options (CPR)	126	40		18	520
Crude Oil (LO)	29,567,191	31,250,967	44,521,982	42,901,045	45,879,991
Crude Oil Calendar Strip Options (6F)	170	400	170		
Crude Oil Semi-Annual Strip (6Y)	50	150			
Crude Oil Weekly Options Wk 1 (LO1)	194,719	210,177	188,943	164,240	82,795
Crude Oil Weekly Options Wk 2 (LO2)	120,386	179,113	179,572	158,374	48,765
Crude Oil Weekly Options Wk 3 (LO3)	123,972	124,926	160,965	103,804	35,405
Crude Oil Weekly Options Wk 4 (LO4)	195,102	207,146	202,068	191,368	56,458
Crude Oil Weekly Options Wk 5 (LO5)	59,518	69,759	71,635	61,548	28,646
Dutch TTF Natural Gas Margined Calendar Month	217,820				
EIA Flat Tax On-Highway Diesel Average Price	1,540	660	792	72	
Gulf Coast Jet Fuel (Platts) Average Price Options	600	1,050	3,898	2,168	3,668
Light Sweet Crude Oil (WTI) Daily Physical Options	1,850	1,800	21,350	31,435	38,425
Light Sweet Crude Oil (WTI) Financial 1 Month	1,018,670	596,260	893,940	771,245	1,851,715
Light Sweet Crude Oil European Financial Option	120,264	138,884	149,026	258,029	344,468
Mont Belvieu Ethane (OPIS) Average Price Options	630	200	1,350	3,095	6,755
Mont Belvieu LDH Propane (OPIS) Average Price	664	4,872	6,662	8,572	11,486
Mont Belvieu Normal Butane (OPIS) Average Price	1,040	560	3,300	1,200	1,560
Natural Gas (American) (ON)	1,457,403	1,581,253	2,383,119	2,586,748	3,444,463
Natural Gas (European) (LN)	28,452,319	19,232,369	22,852,904	28,303,431	23,520,044
Natural Gas (Henry Hub) Daily Options (KD)	42,853	46,755	202,634	517,490	375,887
Natural Gas (Henry Hub) Last-day Financial 1 Month	1,125,958	1,198,305	570,809	487,016	168,709
Natural Gas (Henry Hub) Last-day Financial 2 Month	27,950	31,150	1,430	14,950	4,505
Natural Gas (Henry Hub) Last-day Financial 3 Month	500,225	251,925	44,246	159,825	228,182
Natural Gas (Henry Hub) Last-day Financial 5 Month	12,450	6,400	2,550	4,050	1,200
Natural Gas (Henry Hub) Last-day Financial 6 Month	152,000	136,025	102,850	70,320	11,275
Natural Gas (Henry Hub) Last-day Financial Options	82,335	70,896	52,503	47,791	28,902
Natural Gas Calendar Strip Options (6J)	38,580	31,440	37,282	14,670	28,068
Natural Gas Short-Term Options D01 (U01)	500	650	550	3,716	5,025
Natural Gas Short-Term Options D02 (U02)	700	675	2,798	4,258	4,800
Natural Gas Short-Term Options D03 (U03)	650	704	2,279	2,273	3,170
Natural Gas Short-Term Options D04 (U04)	1,350	1,400	1,975	2,613	5,000
Natural Gas Short-Term Options D05 (U05)	350	625	1,630	11,208	3,550
Natural Gas Short-Term Options D06 (U06)	150	605	1,500	9,148	2,905
Natural Gas Short-Term Options D07 (U07)	600	754	1,851	3,675	5,100
Natural Gas Short-Term Options D08 (U08)	400	2,650	1,477	5,637	3,522
Natural Gas Short-Term Options D09 (U09)	300	800	1,634	5,214	5,617

New York Mercantile Exchange (NYMEX), division of the CME Group (continued)

OPTION	2020	2019	2018	2017	2016
Natural Gas Short-Term Options D10 (U10)	450	1,150	1,250	6,029	4,595
Natural Gas Short-Term Options D11 (U11)	250	1,250	1,236	7,575	3,205
Natural Gas Short-Term Options D12 (U12)	600	1,530	1,900	4,740	4,450
Natural Gas Short-Term Options D13 (U13)	600	251	500	5,119	4,361
Natural Gas Short-Term Options D14 (U14)	200	150	863	3,980	5,225
Natural Gas Short-Term Options D15 (U15)	800	1,675	797	5,415	3,755
Natural Gas Short-Term Options D16 (U16)	300	250	700	7,010	4,175
Natural Gas Short-Term Options D17 (U17)	375	450	2,296	5,147	1,405
Natural Gas Short-Term Options D18 (U18)	200	325	1,622	2,565	3,055
Natural Gas Short-Term Options D19 (U19)	325	200	348	5,345	1,845
Natural Gas Short-Term Options D20 (U20)	300	500	1,425	4,330	1,680
Natural Gas Short-Term Options D21 (U21)	200	50	613	3,642	2,325
Natural Gas Short-Term Options D22 (U22)	100	1	1,271	3,527	4,205
Natural Gas Short-Term Options D23 (U23)	150	117	898	1,672	2,280
Natural Gas Short-Term Options D24 (U24)	50	250	879	3,225	2,080
Natural Gas Short-Term Options D26 (U26)	0	100	600	292	1,580
Natural Gas Short-Term Options D27 (U27)	1,150		525	2,020	1,050
Natural Gas Short-Term Options D28 (U28)	600	425	100	3,255	3,925
Natural Gas Short-Term Options D29 (U29)	950	150	510	906	3,475
Natural Gas Short-Term Options D30 (U30)	1,075	800	100	4,745	2,100
Natural Gas Short-Term Options D31 (U31)	150	1,400	477	6,250	1,125
Natural Gas Summer Strip (4D)	400				
Natural Gas Winter Strip (6I)	600	1,500	2,700		
NY Harbor ULSD Average Price Option (AT)	19,274	27,861	35,782	36,891	67,799
NY Harbor ULSD Calendar Spread Option - 1 Month	100	2,550	2,600	1,700	5,900
NY Harbor ULSD Crack Spread Average Price (3W)	3,000				
NY Harbor ULSD European Financial Option (LB)	3,527	2,374	2,767	2,813	4,789
NY Harbor ULSD Option (OH)	153,729	316,435	386,859	395,078	606,514
PJM Northern Illinois Hub Peak 50 MW Calendar-	43				
PJM WES HUB PEAK CAL MTH (6OA)	770	1,200	860	4,100	1,220
RBOB Gasoline Crack Spread (RX)	2,161	636	2		
RBOB Gasoline European Financial Option (RF)	1,043	1,624	125	1,335	60
RBOB Gasoline Physical Options (OB)	95,724	153,519	144,932	293,296	390,579
Singapore Mogas 92 Unleaded (Platts) Average Price	200				
WTI Average Price Options (AO)	686,055	639,489	534,847	640,113	409,273
WTI Crude Oil 1 Month Calendar Spread (WA)	2,221,732	2,460,664	2,410,650	2,084,297	3,005,974
WTI Midland (Argus) vs. WTI Trade Month Average	1,400				
WTI-Brent Crude Oil Spread Options (BV)	531,332	584,330	856,315	564,527	279,675
Palladium Options (PAO)	6,969	14,317	29,533	66,745	42,072
Platinum Option (PO)	28,347	41,412	45,372	36,869	53,221
Total Options	**68,360,731**	**61,279,571**	**80,135,670**	**81,888,081**	**81,861,593**

Total Options Volume

	2020	2019	2018	2017	2016
Total Options	**851,867,483**	**1,058,598,937**	**1,044,587,915**	**933,478,491**	**846,804,946**
Percent Change	**-19.53%**	**1.34%**	**11.90%**	**10.24%**	**12.90%**

Options Traded on U.S. Securities Exchanges Volume Highlights
2020 in Comparison with 2019

2020 Rank	EXCHANGE	2020 Contracts	%	2019 Contracts	%	2019 Rank
1	Chicago Board Options Exchange	1,349,799,569	33.39%	1,147,034,647	27.85%	1
2	NASDAQ PHLX	888,987,070	21.99%	702,977,046	17.07%	2
3	NYSE-ARCA	711,701,208	17.61%	424,951,742	10.32%	3
4	NASDAQ Options Market	688,942,003	17.04%	390,007,372	9.47%	6
5	BATS Exchange	687,320,373	17.00%	396,796,395	9.64%	5
6	NYSE Amex Options (formerly American Stock	578,952,684	14.32%	374,339,448	9.09%	7
7	International Securities Exchange	545,827,621	13.50%	398,331,710	9.67%	4
8	International Securities Exchange Gemini	392,674,146	9.71%	184,636,951	4.48%	9
9	Miami International Securities Exchange	330,303,726	8.17%	177,520,123	4.31%	10
10	EDGX Options Exchange	296,397,463	7.33%	133,844,192	3.25%	12
11	MIAX Pearl	293,410,388	7.26%	233,794,910	5.68%	8
12	C2 Exchange	229,842,408	5.69%	171,698,126	4.17%	11
13	Boston Options Exchange	202,168,886	5.00%	112,597,175	2.73%	13
14	International Securities Exchange Mercury	52,111,029	1.29%	10,708,978	0.26%	16
15	NASDAQ Boston	14,846,436	0.37%	11,063,646	0.27%	14
16	North American Derivative Exchange	11,737,457	0.29%	10,134,748	0.25%	15
	Total Options	**7,463,916,559**	**100.00%**	**4,898,107,661**	**100.00%**	

BATS Exchange

OPTION	2020	2019	2018	2017	2016
All Options on Exchange Traded Funds	266,752,562	142,979,604	172,060,862	168,212,740	168,150,127
Mini S&P 500 Index (XSP)	115,200				
Russell 2000 Index (RUT)	350,038	345,794	143,678		
All Options on Individual Equities	420,102,573	253,470,997	250,502,129	241,480,873	243,884,574
Total Options	**687,320,373**	**396,796,395**	**422,706,669**	**409,693,613**	**412,034,701**

Boston Options Exchange (BOX)

OPTION	2020	2019	2018	2017	2016
All Options on Exchange Traded Funds	44,691,602	28,372,667	30,130,999	25,553,513	41,356,496
All Options on Individual Equities	157,477,284	84,224,508	76,663,505	61,350,871	67,846,228
Total Options	**202,168,886**	**112,597,175**	**106,794,504**	**86,904,384**	**109,202,724**

Chicago Board of Options Exchange (CBOE)

OPTION	2020	2019	2018	2017	2016
All Options on Exchange Traded Funds	309,506,264	256,122,935	314,139,114	270,500,753	263,288,570
CBOE Volatility Index (VIX)	124,518,765	126,627,356	167,470,555	181,311,346	148,246,402
Dow Jones Industrial Index (DJX)	932,057	910,779	1,567,995	1,170,884	998,327
FTSE 100 Mini Index (UKXM)	12			1	15
Mini S&P 500 Index Options (XSP)	10,426,396	17,180,762	4,875,256	3,592,641	2,884,850
MSCI EAFE (MXEA)	167,050	149,812	112,372	73,466	15,350
MSCI Emerging Markets Index (MXEF)	328,700	265,892	150,384	52,085	41,967
NASDAQ 100 Index (NDX)	6,814		25,503	394,530	2,046,264
OEX S&P 100 Index (American) (OEX)	159,751	366,486	506,473	476,985	917,571
Russell 1000 Index (RUI)	251	53	134	82	6,619
Russell 1000 Growth Index (RLG)	269	63	100	16	
Russell 1000 Value Index (RLV)	6	20	24		
Russell 2000 Index (RUT)	7,242,142	8,275,719	11,613,303	14,291,140	15,396,172
European-style S&P 100 Index Options (XEO)	31,046	224,474	21,700	33,378	62,895
S&P 500 ESG Index (SPESG)	1,186				
S&P 500 Index (SPX)	312,949,642	318,943,920	371,345,596	292,029,953	257,953,004
S&P Financial Select Sector Index (SIXM)	2				
S&P Health Care Select Sector Index (SIXV)	3				
S&P Real Estate Select Sector Index (SIXRE)	2	1,767			
S&P Utilities Select Sector Index (SIXU)	571	35			
All Options on Individual Equities	583,528,640	417,964,483	411,439,134	367,853,258	339,332,263
Total Options	**1,349,799,569**	**1,147,034,647**	**1,283,269,272**	**1,132,457,708**	**1,033,349,820**

International Securities Exchange (ISE)

OPTION	2020	2019	2018	2017	2016
All Options on Exchange Traded Funds	256,650,192	208,728,591	209,785,242	156,110,848	238,614,905
Nasdaq 100 Reduced Value Index (NQX)	35,413	15,768	7,847		
Nasdaq 100 Index (NDX)	1,936,639	1,058,791	1,057,226	1,139,203	537,138
All Options on Individual Equities	287,205,377	188,528,560	191,654,091	177,613,092	217,936,044
Total Options	**545,827,621**	**398,331,710**	**402,504,406**	**334,888,824**	**457,206,056**

Nasdaq Options Market

OPTION	2020	2019	2018	2017	2016
All Options on Exchange Traded Funds	209,504,624	112,830,238	149,159,270	121,122,230	110,316,449
All Options on Individual Equities	479,437,379	277,177,134	279,491,687	219,730,415	173,506,188
Total Options	**688,942,003**	**390,007,372**	**428,650,957**	**340,852,645**	**283,822,637**

Nasdaq PHLX

OPTION	2020	2019	2018	2017	2016
US Dollar Settled Australian Dollar (XDA)	3,133	2,851	2,968	5,356	12,403
US Dollar Settled British pound (XDB)	6,393	4,860	5,516	7,559	35,031
US Dollar Settled Canadian Dollar (XDC)	7,901	22,668	29,618	37,066	37,604
US Dollar Settled Euro (XDE)	4,816	5,253	23,245	52,970	36,252
US Dollar Settled Japanese Yen (XDN)	2,082	795	2,172	6,969	59,432
US Dollar Settled New Zealand Dollar (XDZ)	59	11	5	29	511
US Dollar Settled Swiss Franc (XDS)	220	402	1,471	773	6,786
All Options on Exchange Traded Funds	306,323,120	267,020,181	310,961,742	275,771,318	259,774,337
Gold/Silver Index (XAU)	205,899	732,701	1,046,912	375,915	357,830
KBW Bank Index (BKX)	425	69	1,805	82,494	113,199
Nasdaq Non-Financial 100 Index (NDX)	1,077,773	1,611,297	2,395,544	2,136,456	1,804,336
PHLX Housing Sector Index (HGX)	844	917	1,649	1,322	2,322
PHLX Oil Service Index (OSX)	97	179	247	45,349	35,375
Semiconductor Index (SOX)	2,872	9,474	2,482	4,143	9,905
Utility Index (UTY)	420	443	529	714	582
All Options on Individual Equities	581,351,016	433,564,945	409,694,673	363,108,201	319,805,435
Total Options	**888,987,070**	**702,977,046**	**724,170,578**	**641,637,538**	**582,093,570**

Total Options on Securities Volume

	2020	2019	2018	2017	2016
Total Options	**7,463,916,559**	**4,898,107,661**	**5,132,099,960**	**4,175,996,435**	**4,042,097,154**
Percent Change	**52.38%**	**-4.56%**	**22.90%**	**3.31%**	**-1.84%**

Volume - Worldwide

ASX, Australia

	2020	2019	2018	2017	2016
S&P/ASX Index	1,369	5,239	7,212	25,610	8,054
All Futures on Individual Equities	2,893,184	3,117,588	2,837,126	2,921,155	4,718,169
Total Futures	**2,894,553**	**3,122,827**	**2,844,338**	**2,946,765**	**4,726,223**
S&P / ASX Index	8,012,316	9,744,177	12,720,573	10,728,593	12,138,930
All Options on Individual Equities	58,196,424	67,999,671	72,126,000	86,902,467	85,174,090
Total Options	**66,208,740**	**77,743,848**	**84,846,573**	**97,631,060**	**97,313,020**

ASX 24, Australia

(formerly Sydney Futures Exchange)	2020	2019	2018	2017	2016
Eastern Australia Feed Barley	14,141	6,670	3,413	2,510	6,490
Eastern Australia Wheat	122,953	77,261	84,217	76,374	28,931
WA Wheat	0	20			
ASX Electricity Base Load $300 CAP Quarterly NSW	11,976	11,708	12,743	8,639	9,415
ASX Electricity Base Load $300 CAP Quarterly QLD	8,095	8,959	11,507	10,109	10,146
ASX Electricity Base Load $300 CAP Quarterly SA (GS)	1,971	1,754	2,697	762	962
ASX Electricity Base Load $300 CAP Quarterly VIC	7,516	7,856	10,776	6,887	9,763
ASX Electricity Base Load $300 Cap Strip Future (RN)	316	410	1,055	572	415
ASX Electricity Base Load $300 Cap Strip Future (RQ)	40	409	832	787	323
ASX Electricity Base Load $300 Cap Strip Future (RS)	10	60	130	11	55
ASX Electricity Base Load $300 Cap Strip Future (RV)	35	152	618	147	350
ASX Electricity Base Load Monthly Futures NSW (EN)	314	220	861	91	140
ASX Electricity Base Load Monthly Futures QLD (EQ)	78	25	195	191	364
ASX Electricity Base Load Quarterly NSW	56,515	42,613	36,040	29,615	34,554
ASX Electricity Base Load Quarterly QLD	70,347	50,540	42,101	40,575	41,378
ASX Electricity Base Load Quarterly SA	2,646	3,566	3,734	2,376	3,523
ASX Electricity Base Load Quarterly VIC	66,287	60,318	50,149	46,038	52,513
ASX Electricity Base Load Strip NSW	7,050	5,963	3,757	3,210	3,167
ASX Electricity Base Load Strip QLD	10,599	7,093	3,960	3,355	3,280
ASX Electricity Base Load Strip SA	133	320	342	133	191
ASX Electricity Base Load Strip VIC	8,642	7,109	4,973	4,754	5,904
ASX Electricity Peak Load Quarterly NSW	873	2,204	1,962	1,984	2,116
ASX Electricity Peak Load Quarterly QLD	897	1,482	2,423	1,436	1,353
ASX Electricity Peak Load Quarterly SA	1	24	40	85	36
ASX Electricity Peak Load Quarterly VIC	1,289	1,432	1,658	2,049	2,417
ASX Electricity Peak Load Strip Futures NSW (DN)	6	71	163	80	79
ASX Electricity Peak Load Strip Futures QLD (DQ)	0	180	264	122	27
ASX Electricity Peak Load Strip Futures VIC (DV)	135	120	95	196	60
ASX NZ Electricity Base Load Calendar Month (ED)	100,808	35,458	56,747	53,691	26,871
ASX NZ Electricity Base Load Calendar Month (EH)	98,609	34,833	56,248	49,445	28,440
ASX NZ Electricity Base Load Quarterly (EA)	118,438	65,302	56,651	46,280	32,854
ASX NZ Electricity Base Load Quarterly (EE)	130,163	47,374	51,933	50,577	35,990
ASX NZ Electricity Base Load Strip (EF)	152				
ASX NZ Electricity Base Load Strip OTAHUHU	150	395	210	30	
ASX NZ Electricity Peak Load Quarterly (EC)	350	1,175	1,580	1,130	1,890
ASX NZ Electricity Peak Load Quarterly (EG)	280	190	440	110	270
ASX VIC Monthly Base Load Electricity	115	123	271	364	298
VIC Gas	1,119	1,256	593	10	15
VIC Gas Strip	50	100	70		
Mini-ASX SPI 200	1,807	3,505	3,008	6,949	29,059
S&P/ASX 200 A-REIT Index	60,180	76,542	162,623	103,992	97,935
S&P/ASX 200 Financials-x-A-REIT Index	228	333	8	603	1,539
S&P/ASX 200 Gross TR Index	82,177	34,258			
S&P/ASX 200 Resources Index	303	29		1,869	6,108
SPI 200	18,523,878	16,507,385	15,498,686	12,461,177	12,196,602
10 Year Treasury Bonds	61,482,878	54,525,625	51,250,531	43,578,795	40,121,694
20 Year Bonds	182,627	229,152	322,917	403,859	567,077
2yr Bundle IR Strip Futures	16	170			
3 Year Treasury Bonds	51,843,835	63,562,102	55,198,297	55,928,705	51,827,874
30 Day Interbank Cash Rate	2,993,870	6,789,536	1,604,936	1,980,701	3,762,252
5 Year Treasury Bond	45,205				
Bank Bills 90 Day	16,520,510	33,492,955	32,850,509	30,326,252	29,899,739
New Zealand 90 Day Bank Bill	2,594,669	2,459,705	1,956,974	1,478,877	1,705,915
NZ White Pack 1st Yr Bank Bill Strip	100	43	110		
Red Pack 2nd yr IR Strip Futures	202	2,975	2,009		
White Pack 1st yr IR Strip Futures	130	2,673	1,174		
Total Futures	**155,175,714**	**178,171,733**	**159,357,611**	**146,719,362**	**140,640,990**
Eastern Australia Wheat	1,595	340		275	
ASX Electricity Base Load Quarterly NSW	9,260	4,735	3,924	2,564	2,536
ASX Electricity Base Load Quarterly QLD	6,085	6,328	3,265	2,855	3,796
ASX Electricity Base Load Quarterly SA	190	24	52	192	81
ASX Electricity Base Load Quarterly VIC	7,974	7,888	6,340	4,050	4,580
ASX Electricity Base Load Strip NSW	8,877	6,224	1,455	2,256	2,164
ASX Electricity Base Load Strip QLD	22,534	9,326	5,688	4,564	4,429
ASX Electricity Base Load Strip SA	10		75	15	75
ASX Electricity Base Load Strip VIC	16,843	7,424	3,950	3,358	3,248

ASX 24, Australia (continued)

(formerly Sydney Futures Exchange)	2020	2019	2018	2017	2016
ASX NZ Electricity Base Load Quarterly (EA)	23,100	15,000	12,550	7,030	720
ASX NZ Electricity Base Load Quarterly (EE)	10,800	4,500	7,350	3,860	240
SPI 200	69,274	49,580	129,638	159,222	293,385
10 Year Treasury Bonds	34,419	1,500	30,540	13,856	14,950
10-Year Bonds Intra-Day	25,915			100	
Overnight 10 Year Treasury Bonds	5,700	600	3,550	4,900	125
3 Year Treasury Bond	27,389	289,113	109,357	84,856	337,775
3 Year Bonds Intra-Day	217,420	708,821	349,454	416,542	581,801
Overnight 3 Year Treasury Bond	87,490	328,925	288,212	441,623	524,071
Total Options	**574,875**	**1,440,328**	**955,400**	**1,152,218**	**1,779,806**

Bolsa de Mercadorias & Futuros (BM&F), Brazil

	2020	2019	2018	2017	2016
Arabica Coffee	155,833	140,331	106,901	102,474	125,904
Arabica Coffee Rollover	3,229	5,820	7,279	14,188	9,852
Corn Cash Settled	1,661,659	926,710	980,296	792,259	741,933
Cross Listing Mini-Sized Soybean CME	40,041	45,264	95,443	69,177	84,272
Hydrous Ethanol	62,342	31,358	39,064	21,476	25,524
Live Cattle	616,032	443,480	285,685	502,727	429,292
Australian Dollar	14,167	89,980	121,237	62,966	48,949
Canadian Dollar	4,245	108,175	129,140	46,408	21,659
Chilean Peso	1,519	10,027	8,495	11,356	18,196
Euro	64,800	260,320	430,075	393,680	426,920
Mexican Peso	18,865	41,164	67,522	42,697	34,173
Mini US Dollar	692,247,449	340,261,685	266,982,975	146,458,100	92,119,754
Mini US Dollar Rollover	366,867	167,742	111,815		
New Zealand Dollar	276	3,938	6,195	10,153	3,613
Pound Sterling	3,779	88,891	56,948	30,563	29,487
South African Rand	4,054	24,338	36,978	18,120	6,816
Swiss Franc	7,448	11,976	24,612	10,868	14,117
Turkish Lira	6,138	1,862	20,321	22,230	12,640
US Dollar	79,718,495	94,587,950	91,695,866	74,087,470	71,281,293
US Dollar forward points	4,195,135	5,041,235	4,556,775	5,010,115	4,966,735
US Dollar Rollover	8,088,060	8,803,720	8,076,875	14,939,854	16,838,265
Yen	7,695	44,635	93,619	62,017	33,087
Yuan (CNY)	358			1,118	
West Texas Intermediate (WTI)	5,022	24,763	34,001	60,781	18,841
Bovespa Mini Index	2,888,021,160	1,614,094,434	706,224,217	290,827,570	150,763,004
Bovespa Rollover	3,530,975	3,216,715	2,559,215	5,079,920	4,509,610
Bovespa Stock Index Futures	41,414,065	36,110,325	23,827,497	18,945,370	19,212,830
E-mini S&P 500	315,577	260,228	229,142	136,135	164,886
E-mini S&P 500 Rollover	41,849	29,147	41,657	35,954	23,745
IBrX-50	50,242	21,928	29,547	16,146	19,623
Mini Ibovespa Rollover	1,306,567	454,043	79,274		
Forward Exchange Rate	1,045	2,589	33,742	102,823	31,911
ID x IPCA Spread Futures	3,821,420	3,797,915	3,174,330	2,104,405	332,245
ID x US Dollar Spread Futures	1,460,584	1,750,578	1,471,403	1,738,831	3,201,458
DI x US Dollar Swap with reset	2,197,072	2,157,940	2,739,421	18,030	189,699
ID x US Dollar FRA	34,991,800	42,743,930	41,123,360	61,401,079	58,612,981
Interest Rate Swap	261,512	115,785	120,585	152,501	102,014
Interest Rate x Exchange Rate	1,269,141	609,603	290,057	155,750	388,062
Interest Rate x Price Index	4,878	22,872	89,469	28,876	769,807
One Day Inter-Bank Deposit	513,754,645	476,189,923	371,801,536	354,386,047	302,518,177
US T-Note	106,790	84,062	81,195	41,698	16,189
Gold Spot (250g)	34,637	12,090	8,685	8,430	7,253
Odd-lot gold spot (0.225g)	80,039	40,928	34,821	43,560	29,399
Odd-lot gold spot (10g.)	91,295	31,935	16,785	18,855	18,349
Total Futures	**4,280,048,801**	**2,632,912,334**	**1,528,367,247**	**978,038,985**	**728,583,549**
Arabica Coffee	15,125	1,972	1,453	1,983	729
Corn Cash Settled	442,714	314,406	417,450	291,191	216,628
Live Cattle on Futures	372,150	344,806	214,768	350,240	158,381
Flexible US Dollar	56,848	117,874	57,378	126,079	724,841
US Dollar	6,689,668	10,166,813	8,826,246	8,684,500	7,578,200
E-mini S&P 500	64,686	29,926	13,099		
Exchange Traded Funds	383,848,797	51,103,609	17,921,657	31,666,541	4,225,345
Flexible BOVA11 Index	2,764,697	86,412	35,233	72,103	8,003
Flexible Bovespa Stock Index	171,851	2,835,547	278,113	402,362	219,462
Ibovespa Index	22,041,644	13,086,311	848,522	1,091,642	1,416,900
All Options on Individual Equities	1,374,772,830	952,119,214	913,153,184	681,905,062	692,006,945
Flexible Spot Interest Rate Index	1,282,228	2,013,857	880,737	1,612,327	678,291
IDI Index	234,756,100	214,451,390	102,904,073	98,481,487	50,194,640
One Day Inter-Bank Deposit	234,000	1,039,760	152,490	6,596,925	1,264,615
Total Options	**2,027,513,338**	**1,247,711,949**	**1,045,705,931**	**831,319,970**	**758,722,239**

Athens Derivatives Exchange S.A. (ADEX), Greece

	2020	2019	2018	2017	2016
FTSE/Athex Large Cap	422,831	607,807	640,572	629,413	895,527
All Futures on Individual Equities	9,500,346	9,656,078	13,212,566	18,698,023	14,496,353
Total Futures	**9,923,177**	**10,263,885**	**13,853,138**	**19,327,436**	**15,391,880**
FTSE/Athex Large Cap	36,545	62,994	81,295	95,203	66,983
All Options on Individual Equities	15,538	21,083	11,679	24,572	11,853
Total Options	**52,083**	**84,077**	**92,974**	**119,775**	**78,836**

Bolsa de Valores de Colombia (BCV), Colombia

	2020	2019	2018	2017	2016
Mini US Dollar	33,073	61,396	123,606	115,348	143,230
US Dollar	279,268	438,988	600,378	292,448	456,633
COLCAP Index	85,787	42,662	9,907	1,734	474
All Futures on Individual Equities	161,653	225,107	136,291	419,785	602,897
10-year Treasury Bond	33,790	18,565	62,651	144,516	74,754
2-year Treasury Bond	52,614	59,554	35,888	44,602	62,199
5-year Treasury Bond	48,227	53,627	86,972	78,328	33,602
IBR	2,090	3,314	9,104	19,267	29,775
Total Futures	**696,502**	**903,213**	**1,064,797**	**1,116,028**	**1,403,564**
US Dollar	514	1,833	5		
Total Options	**514**	1,833	5		

Borsa Istanbul, Turkey

(formerly TurkDEX)	2020	2019	2018	2017	2016
Wheat	11	6	726	15	4
CNH/TRY	2,219	9,260	12,793	640	
EUR/USD Cross Currency	6,287,866	871,211	1,655,729	1,822,681	1,471,151
GBP/USD	145,931	30,043	42		
RUB/TRY	383	257	370	126	
TRY/EUR	1,225,073	623,727	4,250,947	2,003,497	2,432,494
TRY/USD	52,352,244	63,063,667	91,295,379	64,523,385	36,496,794
Base Load Electricity	50,217	50,006	25,805	33,428	246,169
BIST 30 Index	98,651,034	61,859,313	55,181,858	43,851,583	45,495,203
BIST Bank Index	9,083	32,566	528		
BIST Industrials Index	735	2,016	172		
BIST Liquid 10 Ex Banks	4,162	82			
BIST Liquid Banks	48,178	13			
All Futures on Individual Equities	1,196,068,823	196,631,519	54,692,782	15,949,196	7,081,902
Turkish Lira Short Term Reference Rate	128	90			
Gold	137,639,246	50,953,484	19,363,020	5,033,306	3,551,717
USD/Ounce Gold	18,630,727	6,522,961	2,644,588	2,067,576	1,227,497
Total Futures	**1,511,117,057**	**380,650,221**	**229,129,165**	**135,291,078**	**98,008,597**
TRY/USD	725,204	2,079,234	4,522,535	7,711,002	6,080,600
BIST 30 Index	305,857	241,664	148,171	218,207	290,827
All Options on Individual Equities	5,328,340	5,024,915	2,593,550	2,902,061	2,873,483
Total Options	**6,359,401**	**7,345,813**	**7,264,256**	**10,831,270**	**9,244,910**

Borsa Italiana, Italy

	2020	2019	2018	2017	2016
Electricity	440	1,066	1,475	1,172	2,891
Mini S&P/MIB Index	6,707,675	6,819,045	3,837,339	3,039,553	4,789,081
S&P/MIB Index	2,682,599	2,365,666	8,405,118	7,201,735	10,603,083
All Futures on Individual Equities	1,107,832	3,838,395	3,114,540	2,668,343	3,708,532
Single Stock Dividend Futures	126,908	39,105	17,810	76,346	41,392
Total Futures	**10,662,357**	**13,063,277**	**15,376,282**	**12,987,323**	**19,145,698**
S&P/MIB Index	2,317,553	2,979,002	3,798,540	2,645,143	5,786,699
All Options on Individual Equities	12,130,416	14,660,271	17,061,970	18,518,552	24,091,505
Total Options	**14,447,969**	**17,639,273**	**20,860,510**	**21,163,695**	**29,878,204**

Bombay Stock Exchange, India

	2020	2019	2018	2017	2016
EUR/INR	547,630	157,711	995,115	1,232,645	1,655,492
EUR/USD	2	12	332,801		
GBP/INR	572,122	234,900	686,087	1,271,200	962,629
GBP/USD	2	18	138,891		
JPY/INR	209,046	240,107	187,853	353,801	715,899
US Dollar/Indian Rupee	312,457,722	385,270,880	453,709,423	262,138,344	319,413,292
S&P Sensex Index (BSX)	81,021	82,687	393	44,102	63,932
All Futures on Individual Equities	34,048	2,910	295	3,801	3,672
91-day Government of India (GOI) Treasury Bill	2,150,242	5,836,307	7,212,166	9,338,072	6,179,322
Total Futures	**316,051,835**	**391,825,556**	**463,268,028**	**274,381,965**	**328,994,243**
US Dollar/Indian Rupee	336,417,376	597,155,819	559,489,717	334,052,119	207,386,529
S&P Sensex Index (BSX)	34,394,746	196,935			
All Options on Individual Equities	161,309,756	20,086	2	6	126,898
Total Options	**532,121,878**	**597,391,241**	**559,489,719**	**334,052,239**	**214,064,265**

Budapest Stock Exchange (BSE), Hungary

	2020	2019	2018	2017	2016
AUD/USD	5,770	10,580	10,500	1,800	3,700
CAD/HUF	100	300	3,500	5,700	300
CHF/HUF	107,950	191,750	155,950	122,000	146,305
CHF/JPY	300	400	7,600		6,400
CZK/HUF	115	181	240	50	
EUR/AUD	1,500	4,400	8,600	1,200	
EUR/CAD	800	10,800	18,600	3,200	800
EUR/CHF	28,650	52,350	36,850	13,650	23,310
EUR/GBP	27,425	11,225	24,350	25,365	66,245
EUR/HUF	2,981,695	3,083,318	2,952,475	2,134,171	2,832,411
EUR/NOK	18,100	73,900	14,900	11,150	24,450
EUR/PLN	7,100	3,750	1,900	28,900	2,900
EUR/SEK	10,600	1,900	4,500		2,600
EURO/JPY	5,320	5,930	47,550	58,150	1,000
EURO/TRY	700	1,900	90,576	72,915	102,307
EURO/USD	286,603	451,700	666,248	563,986	1,083,078
GBP/CHF	200	800	1,800		200
GBP/HUF	171,978	209,518	224,697	268,249	408,284
GBP/JPY	1,900	8,100	6,600		2,400
GBP/USD	171,537	50,410	50,900	110,900	119,565
JPY/HUF	4,160	8,000			
NOK/HUF	150	3,550	4,300		400
PLN/HUF	3,280	5,140	900	260	1,990
TRY/HUF	500	1,320	7,195	18,450	26,650
USD/CAD	4,650	1,400	4,703	13,873	46,670
USD/CHF	4,650	2,900	2,850	800	27,400
USD/HUF	1,614,641	1,695,409	1,539,878	2,819,431	2,276,697
USD/JPY	18,320	12,950	50,194	154,830	115,106
USD/NOK	7,100	41,000	20,000	8,750	4,400
USD/PLN	9,230	13,630	13,450	4,180	600
USD/TRY	100		42,210	21,940	32,000
All Futures on Individual Equities	867,267	481,622	596,858	522,503	426,501
Total Futures	**6,362,391**	**6,445,183**	**6,633,826**	**7,000,145**	**7,797,885**
EUR/HUF	11,650	72,450	64,850	1,900	2,550
EUR/USD	400	400	500		600
USD/HUF	4,000	800	1,600	14,500	1,000
Total Options	**16,050**	**73,850**	**70,150**	**21,100**	**10,550**

Dalian Commodity Exchange (DCE), China

	2020	2019	2018	2017	2016
Corn	177,715,573	99,119,054	66,812,732	127,323,949	122,362,964
Corn Starch	28,299,982	16,563,847	22,613,108	50,433,910	67,445,264
Egg	132,053,500	37,130,045	19,918,457	37,262,376	22,474,739
No. 1 Soybeans	59,445,167	18,450,462	22,111,727	26,324,058	32,570,158
No. 2 Soybeans	18,359,635	17,791,929	24,476,720	42,551	1,834
Polished Round-Grained Rice	5,160,978	413,624			
RBD Palm Olein	315,167,096	135,504,196	44,344,644	68,046,475	139,157,899
Soybean Meal	359,464,679	272,869,691	238,162,413	162,877,864	388,949,970
Soybean Oil	173,116,523	87,543,178	54,135,551	57,158,378	94,761,814
Coke	57,464,017	55,680,120	69,071,834	40,121,040	50,461,050
Hard Coking Coal	26,431,404	22,874,614	46,465,289	42,194,764	41,077,427
Liquefied Petroleum Gas	48,251,668				
Iron Ore	284,630,172	296,538,011	236,491,632	328,743,737	342,265,309
Block Board	1,910	380	689	1,286	8,157
Ethenylbenzene	52,440,684	3,958,697			
Ethylene Glycol	83,320,391	74,101,992	2,323,861		
Fibre Board	1,033,613	1,171,841	29,630	1,056	710
Linear Low Density Polyethylene (LLDPE)	95,802,284	63,438,716	36,735,543	61,420,753	100,931,133
Polypropylene	173,374,543	93,707,685	49,349,161	56,691,866	123,768,347
Polyvinyl Chloride (PVC)	58,472,901	33,792,856	36,362,787	39,000,407	11,242,993
Total Futures	**2,150,006,720**	**1,330,650,938**	**969,405,778**	**1,097,644,470**	**1,537,479,768**
Corn	10,444,550	6,760,187			
Soybean Meal	30,120,942	17,809,235	12,521,591	3,635,682	
Liquefied Petroleum Gas	1,294,634				
Iron Ore	11,599,097	363,865			
Linear Low Density Polyethylene (LLDPE)	924,492				
Polypropylene	1,598,980				
Polyvinyl Chloride (PVC)	1,338,451				
Total Options	**57,321,146**	24,933,287	12,521,591	3,635,682	

Dubai Gold & Commodities Exchange

	2020	2019	2018	2017	2016
AUD/USD Rolling	737				
Australian Dollar	267,576	5,582	12,133	19,179	8,628
Canadian Dollar	88,459	3,980	17,367	23,427	4,054
Chinese Yuan	5,762	3,110	24,128	5,433	13,039
EUR/USD Rolling	6,876				
Euro	512,869	227,886	376,991	275,723	122,150
GBP/USD Rolling	3,582				
Indian Rupee	7,639,530	11,257,041	12,509,330	10,216,672	11,670,100
Indian Rupee Weekly	45,026				
Japanese yen	90,457	8,069	35,832	50,549	21,496
Mini Indian Rupee	832,081	1,463,453	1,861,404	1,120,475	1,060,546
Rupee Quanto	2,326,547	7,731,279	3,705,241	2,647,629	5,042,013
Sterling Pound	291,918	60,406	142,024	169,056	137,457
Swiss Franc	92,635	4,826	11,144	9,940	1,879
USD/ZAR	38	1,522	5,431	5,857	8,189
Brenrt Crude Oil	7,710	24,248	21,377	4,211	39
WTI	33,085	64,635	66,847	66,426	103,486
WTI Mini	1,587	7,497	30,512	41,131	63,467
Indian Single Stock Futures	79,950	1,673,914	2,674,548	1,353,725	76,618
Copper	2,662	5,736	14,362	17,818	7,632
Gold	388,189	478,136	230,568	310,195	447,599
Gold Quanto	822	7,651	215,202	190,713	281,241
Silver	12,374	5,755	7,385	20,982	37,770
Spot Gold	1,195	35	536	14,513	4,981
Total Futures	**12,731,667**	**23,037,817**	**22,072,962**	**16,777,992**	**19,327,252**
Indian Rupee	893	28,326	187,174	661,666	342,534
Total Options	**893**	**28,326**	**187,174**	**661,666**	**342,534**

Dubai Mercantile Exchange (DME)

	2020	2019	2018	2017	2016
Brent vs. Dubai (Platts) Crude Oil	2,250	30,205	59,195	14,609	300
Dubai Crude Oil (Platts)	10,700	31,218	52,249	80,207	
Oman Crude Oil	1,163,569	1,440,465	1,125,731	1,480,511	1,949,004
Total Futures	**1,176,519**	**1,501,888**	**1,237,175**	**1,575,427**	**1,949,658**

EUREX, Frankfurt, Germany

	2020	2019	2018	2017	2016
AUD/USD (FCAU)	244	1,859	337		
AUD/USD Rolling Spot (RSAU)	115	989	321		
EUR/AUD (FCEA)	58	150			
EUR/AUD Rolling Spot (RSEA)	96	14			
EUR/CHF (FCEF)	37,411	16,059	523		
EUR/CHF Rolling Spot (RSEF)	81	558	330		
EUR/GBP (FCEP)	57,239	13,750	749		
EUR/GBP Rolling Spot (RSEP)	143	771	648		
EUR/JPY (FCEY)	4,187	616	112		
EUR/JPY Rolling Spot (RSEY)	253	275	223		
EUR/USD Futures	509,911	32,526	3,808		4
EUR/USD Rolling Spot (RSEU)	1,042	8,480	4,770		
GBP/CHF (FCPF)	304	576			
GBP/CHF Rolling Spot (RSPF)	47	39	20		
GBP/USD Futures	731	8,464	1,244		
GBP/USD Rolling Spot (RSPU)	530	4,098	965		
NZD/USD (FCNU)	97	1,297	30		
NZD/USD Rolling Spot (RSNU)	76	14	10		
USD/CHF (FCUF)	174	2,601	60		
USD/CHF Rolling Spot (RSUF)	64	140	20		
USD/JPY (FCUY)	167	608	9		
USD/JPY Rolling Spot (RSUY)	840	2,415	554		
ATX	214,248	168,901	169,647	237,373	349,325
ATX five	567	2,585	4,863	8,739	12,430
CECE EUR	3,064	9,916	14,182	15,703	20,853
Dax	25,039,383	27,798,116	26,563,806	21,547,762	27,261,861
Dax 50 ESG (FSDX)	540				
DivDAX	94,215	53,678	23,096	19,163	11,883
Euro Stoxx	275,546	418,220	436,621	321,687	169,001
Euro Stoxx 50 ESG Index (FSSX)	5,344				
Euro Stoxx 50 ex Financials Index	44,054	44,385	51,884	43,821	31,301
Euro Stoxx 50 Index	352,195,151	292,360,338	318,635,725	282,107,311	374,452,071
Euro Stoxx 50 Index Dividend	8,219,978	6,386,331	6,976,107	4,172,068	5,651,691
Euro Stoxx 50 Index Market-on-Close (FES1)	4,737	993	5,248	122	
Euro Stoxx 50 Index Total Return Futures (TESX)	9,884,445	3,668,361	1,705,583	543,845	680
Euro Stoxx 50 Low Carbon Index (FSLC)	3,312	925			

EUREX, Frankfurt, Germany (continued)

	2020	2019	2018	2017	2016
Euro Stoxx 50 Variance Index	1,223	7,724	36,696	5,722	
Euro Stoxx Automobiles & Parts	85,990	105,525	119,174	78,994	108,800
Euro Stoxx Banks	92,545,411	81,319,688	73,510,289	55,560,883	42,645,554
Euro Stoxx Banks Index Dividend	1,145,526	730,407	226,855	33,135	7,759
Euro Stoxx Basic Resources	55,047	46,901	60,182	52,451	52,230
Euro Stoxx Chemicals	8,384	11,133	26,897	11,037	11,993
Euro Stoxx Construction & Materials	12,955	12,088	18,010	12,694	38,523
Euro Stoxx Consumer Products & Services (FESK)	17				
Euro Stoxx Energy (FESJ)	80				
Euro Stoxx Financial Services	19,686	4,083	2,536	2,732	21,628
Euro Stoxx Food and Beverage	50,862	33,433	31,047	19,006	42,334
Euro Stoxx Food, Beverage & Tobacco (FESW) *	2				
Euro Stoxx Healthcare	29,217	23,723	20,253	17,919	30,016
Euro Stoxx Industrial Goods & Services	13,169	22,253	12,950	16,730	25,320
Euro Stoxx Insurance	272,118	379,728	265,011	263,284	315,050
Euro Stoxx Large	29,005	20,911	13,469	7,859	9,557
Euro Stoxx Media	10,112	15,217	10,867	9,585	55,656
Euro Stoxx Mid	299,289	236,683	368,376	392,283	84,762
Euro Stoxx Oil & Gas	175,647	204,476	236,040	302,392	436,417
Euro Stoxx Personal & Household Goods	18,100	11,844	9,271	11,248	43,646
Euro Stoxx Personal Care, Drug & Grocery Stores (FESP)	1				
Euro Stoxx Real Estate	209,993	162,137	90,951	57,069	87,141
Euro Stoxx Retail	10,061	10,237	14,151	9,575	27,410
Euro Stoxx Select Dividend 30 Index	1,531,850	1,495,020	655,339	451,157	378,281
Euro Stoxx Select Dividend 30 Index Dividend	133,644	52,158	5,900	6,090	14,715
Euro Stoxx Small	302,242	201,954	272,896	188,880	254,510
Euro Stoxx Technology	42,495	30,000	22,597	25,055	57,178
Euro Stoxx Telecommunications	167,984	287,011	246,035	143,842	184,634
Euro Stoxx Travel & Leisure	18,537	21,967	10,134	4,745	53,180
Euro Stoxx Utilities	381,614	474,081	311,713	375,938	464,788
iStoxx Europe Carry Factor Index (FXFC)	25,946	68,893	66,335	15,303	
iStoxx Europe Low Risk Factor Index (FXFR)	213,753	123,544	105,141	16,101	
iStoxx Europe Momentum Factor Index (FXFM)	12,493	77,299	86,725	41,770	
iStoxx Europe Quality Factor Index (FXFQ)	17,849	123,344	119,425	19,436	
iStoxx Europe Size Factor Index (FXFS)	26,258	47,246	49,059	20,546	
iStoxx Europe Value Factor Index (FXFV)	117,861	79,813	137,218	65,649	
iStoxx SR Atlas Copco Class B/Class A (RFAT)	121				
iStoxx SR BMW Preference/Common (RFBW)	1				
iStoxx SR Epiroc Class B/Class A (RFEP)	1				
iStoxx SR Heineken Holding/NV (RFHE)	3				
iStoxx SR Henkel Common/Preference (RFHN)	1				
iStoxx SR Industrivärden Class C/Class A (RFIN)	1				
iStoxx SR Investor AB Class A/Class B (RFIV)	1				
iStoxx SR Lindt & Sprüngli Participation/Registered	1				
iStoxx SR Maersk Class A/Class B (RFMA)	1				
iStoxx SR Roche Bearer/Participation (RFRO)	21				
iStoxx SR Royal Dutch Shell A-NL/B-LN (RFRD)	1				
iStoxx SR Schibsted Class B/Class A (RFSB)	1				
iStoxx SR Schindler Registered/Participation (RFSH)	1				
iStoxx SR Sixt Preference/Common (RFSX)	1				
iStoxx SR SSAB Class B/Class A (RFSS)	61				
iStoxx SR Swatch Registered/Bearer (RFUH)	1				
iStoxx SR Volkswagen Preference/Common Futures	11				
iStoxx SR Volvo Class B/Class A (RFVO)	1				
MDAX	160,600	163,427	201,375	172,975	249,155
Eurex Daily Futures on Mini KOSPI 200 Futures	937,059	79,748	73,112	69,905	1,701
Mini-DAX Futures	16,909,306	11,445,916	10,489,283	6,166,085	6,162,026
Mini-Futures auf VSTOXX	12,691,172	15,924,750	15,538,785	13,423,085	10,085,067
MSCI AC ASEAN (FMSE)	879	86	105		
MSCI AC Asia (FMAA)	4,559	12			
MSCI AC Asia ex Japan (FMXJ)	3,040	22,160	11,316	6,850	
MSCI AC Asia Pacific ex Japan	34,177	16,049	23,328	29,929	43,875
MSCI ACWI	149,909	111,976	29,686	1,912	8,256
MSCI ACWI (EUR / NTR) (FMAE)	64,867	34,998	607		
MSCI ACWI ex USA (USD / NTR) (FMXU)	535	1,659	125		
MSCI Australia (FMAU)	303,941	147,969	298,239	242,242	38,367
MSCI Canada (USD / GTR) (FMGC)	425,279	293,398	198,449	229,149	28,725
MSCI Canada (USD / NTR) (FMCA)	854	399	165	47	
MSCI Chile	108,511	120,971	53,505	43,576	4,910
MSCI China Free	386,459	365,233	514,489	786,979	201,279
MSCI Colombia	24,915	26,979	11,463	9,232	2,080
MSCI Czech Rep (FMCZ)	15	5	991	1,698	
MSCI Denmark Index (FMDM)	2,216				
MSCI EAFE (USD, Price) (FMFP)	95,580	214,546	69,422	16,195	
MSCI EAFE ESG Screened (FMSF)	50				

EUREX, Frankfurt, Germany (continued)

	2020	2019	2018	2017	2016
MSCI EAFE NTR (USD) (FMFA)	293				
MSCI EAFE NTR (USD) (FMFA)	60,470	222,301	101,739	31,506	
MSCI Egypt	1,614	1,345	1,731	986	169
MSCI EM Dividend Points Index (FEFD)	100				
MSCI EM EMEA ex Turkey (FMXT)	60	725	985		
MSCI EM ESG Screened (FMSM)	53,573				
MSCI EM Growth (FMMG)	185				
MSCI Emerging Markets	409,897	860,887	710,041	613,520	64,859
MSCI Emerging Markets Asia	3,641,961	3,370,812	2,115,231	1,424,180	537,034
MSCI Emerging Markets EMEA	612,107	825,362	604,205	447,480	65,195
MSCI Emerging Markets Financials Index (FMMF)	2,490				
MSCI Europe (FMEN)	254,672	272,294	50,474	28,987	37,526
MSCI Emerging Markets Latin America	708,448	613,873	467,385	346,083	59,382
MSCI Europe (FMEF)	134,738	443,529	193,156	80,736	8,029
MSCI Emerging Markets Value Index (FMMV)	205				
MSCI EMU (GTR, EUR) (FMGM)	5	729	2,656	6,414	
MSCI EMU (NTR, EUR) (FMMU)	225,372	225,482	223,704	86,676	10,688
MSCI EMU Growth (FMIG)	5,075	150			
MSCI EMU Value (FMIV)	9,625	180			
MSCI Europe	2,525,632	1,913,191	2,411,484	1,593,727	1,727,702
MSCI Europe (EUR / GTR) (FMGE)	1,138	451	547	91	
MSCI Europe (FMEP)	172,135	843,870	34,840	43,347	125,363
MSCI Europe (NTR, USD) (FMED)	598,552	441,202	357,321	475,192	47,069
MSCI Europe (USD / GTR) (FMGU)	15	117	5,640	3,772	
MSCI Europe ex Switzerland (EUR / NTR) (FMXS)	772	1,355			
MSCI Europe ex UK (FMXG)	79,902				
MSCI Europe Growth (FMEG)	21,235	20,414	23,651	17,578	2,420
MSCI Europe Small Cap (FMES)	27,543				
MSCI Europe Value (FMEV)	47,696	16,101	17,831	18,840	6,288
MSCI France (EUR / GTR) (FMGF)	40	226	147	57,950	
MSCI France (EUR, NTR) (FMFR)	733	64,150	223	40	
MSCI Hong Kong	61,563	96,396	102,126	73,262	15,372
MSCI Hungary (FMHU)	4	301	724	203	
MSCI India (FMIN)	201,189	31,635	11,914	33,094	15,285
MSCI Indonesia	82,742	72,262	184,735	179,255	33,378
MSCI Italy Index (FMIT)	79	18,670			
MSCI Japan (GTR, USD) (FMJG)	75	284	2,756	313	
MSCI Japan ESG Screened (FMSJ)	107				
MSCI Japan Index	897,615	361,961	628,502	929,911	91,140
MSCI Kokusai (FMKG)	5				
MSCI Kokusai (FMKN)	5				
MSCI Kuwait Index (FMKW)	46,456				
MSCI Malaysia	52,299	25,168	137,679	122,203	16,883
MSCI Mexico	250,502	240,707	210,517	194,750	11,912
MSCI New Zealand (FMNZ)	1,109	1,064	1,738	1,290	339
MSCI North America (USD / GTR) (FMGA)	40	8,737	5,163	46	
MSCI North America (USD / NTR) (FMNA)	13,266	101,266	338,659	223,766	941
MSCI Pacific (NTR, USD) (FMAP)	15,475	23,946	6,679	11,479	
MSCI Pacific (NTR, USD) (FMPA)	73,804	49,922	78,295	146,649	17,429
MSCI Pacific ex Japan (FMPX)	42,202	62,519	35,762	35,395	4,580
MSCI Peru (FMPE)	24,056	24,927	12,703	1,899	
MSCI Philippines	32,210	19,493	56,698	47,103	7,922
MSCI Poland	10,619	11,070	23,434	17,550	4,062
MSCI Qatar	46,213	24,354	12,829	17,451	5,467
MSCI Russia	131,313	119,709	148,040	75,415	11,717
MSCI Russia Index	2,790	5,762	12,913	12,955	8,085
MSCI Saudi Arabia (FMSA)	462,844	287,278			
MSCI Singapore (FMSI)	25,524	23,142	12,466	10,792	
MSCI South Africa	95,382	160,581	164,337	107,033	11,593
MSCI Sweden Index (FMSD)	980				
MSCI Taiwan (FMTW)	239,698	9,376	1,121	3,187	
MSCI Thailand	158,843	71,347	183,868	196,266	59,576
MSCI UAE	11,467	8,341	6,724	7,533	1,584
MSCI UK	3,559	4,585	3,440	2,209	2,104
MSCI UK (USD / NTR) (FMDK)	29,801	180,613	126,848	106,427	1,410
MSCI USA (FMUS)	6,832	57,564	85,717	42,606	7,912
MSCI USA (GTR, USD) (FMGS)	84,394	7,967	52,016	85	
MSCI USA ESG Screened Index (FMSU)	129				
MSCI USA Momentum (NTR, USD) (FMUM)	5,998				
MSCI USA Value Weighted (NTR, USD) (FMUV)	16,709	13,573	24,985	39,378	10,197
MSCI World (EUR / GTR) (FMWE)	335	352	857	1,609	
MSCI World (FMWN)	3,546,880	2,883,071	1,762,619	945,318	1,155,683
MSCI World (FMWO)	2,021,246	1,920,361	1,454,761	705,112	291,414
MSCI World (FMWP)	285,166	221,677	84,538	31,734	1,241
MSCI WORLD (NTR, GBP) (FMWB)	167				

EUREX, Frankfurt, Germany (continued)

	2020	2019	2018	2017	2016
MSCI World (USD / GTR) (FMWG)	90	151	110	101	
MSCI World Energy Index (FMWR)	8,368				
MSCI World ESG Screened Index (FMSW)	9				
MSCI World Growth (FMOG)	17,666				
MSCI World Small Cap Index (FMSC)	3,598				
MSCI World Value (FMOV)	9,751	5,483	9,026		
OMX-Helsinki 25	69,131	149,990	127,858	78,477	142,486
RDX USD Index	182,221	273,556	634,628	771,787	1,045,762
SMI Index Dividend	997	1,059	1,049	1,095	1,795
Stoxx Europe 50 Index	577,573	509,092	875,239	732,831	776,440
Stoxx Europe 600	23,501,240	19,130,411	16,668,181	11,324,758	11,707,122
Stoxx Europe 600 Automobiles & Parts	1,266,349	1,077,007	840,193	681,659	475,406
Stoxx Europe 600 Banks	4,932,301	4,041,402	4,422,463	3,445,360	3,583,783
Stoxx Europe 600 Basic Resources	1,126,601	1,237,788	1,742,841	1,443,957	1,333,904
Stoxx Europe 600 Chemicals	66,059	78,172	70,748	94,424	82,140
Stoxx Europe 600 Construction & Materials	143,041	102,074	109,575	104,813	167,898
Stoxx Europe 600 Consumer Products & Services (FSTQ)	46				
Stoxx Europe 600 Energy (FSTJ)	181				
Stoxx Europe 600 ESG-X Index (FSEG)	1,142,610	667,802			
Stoxx Europe 600 Financial Services	51,500	102,365	119,564	105,130	68,535
Stoxx Europe 600 Food & Beverage	372,399	614,213	273,901	194,096	266,973
Stoxx Europe 600 Food, Beverage & Tobacco (FSTW)	61				
Stoxx Europe 600 Healthcare	323,638	413,526	400,083	384,617	445,425
Stoxx Europe 600 Industrial Goods & Services	314,560	406,821	326,405	302,349	381,840
Stoxx Europe 600 Insurance	681,151	706,753	420,464	591,707	665,868
Stoxx Europe 600 Media	120,766	147,437	209,846	112,557	97,764
Stoxx Europe 600 Oil & Gas	2,434,807	1,965,100	2,329,873	1,841,403	1,954,186
Stoxx Europe 600 Oil & Gas Index Dividend	600				
Stoxx Europe 600 Personal & Household Goods	43,981	87,458	69,954	106,706	88,258
Stoxx Europe 600 Personal Care, Drug & Grocery Stores	110				
Stoxx Europe 600 Real Estate	340,253	298,932	294,858	170,454	162,256
Stoxx Europe 600 Retail	102,534	112,450	198,033	102,170	72,615
Stoxx Europe 600 Technology	270,294	337,929	286,387	256,900	158,332
Stoxx Europe 600 Telecom	1,192,643	998,116	995,784	650,678	477,998
Stoxx Europe 600 Travel & Leisure	319,757	130,532	131,592	103,229	108,297
Stoxx Europe 600 Utilities	804,470	753,748	693,582	844,596	508,135
Stoxx Europe ESG Leaders Select 30 Index (FSLS)	7,015	12,298			
Stoxx Europe Large 200	68,126	92,519	91,542	78,041	103,773
Stoxx Europe Mid 200	75,040	143,904	146,037	176,942	263,100
Stoxx Europe Select 50 EUR Index (FXXS)	9,418	54,529			
Stoxx Europe Small 200	701,823	553,941	694,573	527,862	682,410
STOXX Global Select Dividend 100 Index	24,134	24,708	4,080	6,061	11,856
Stoxx Europe Climate Impact index (FSCI)	897	177			
Swiss Leader Index (SLI)	23,157	28,569	21,542	19,334	32,134
Swiss Market Index (SMI)	13,449,542	12,482,456	13,548,464	11,084,756	12,745,219
Swiss Market Index Mid-Cap (SMIM)	127,801	159,075	156,082	122,353	155,951
Tecdax	97,197	79,694	124,522	96,535	98,207
All Futures on Individual Equities	77,446,301	232,348,638	176,533,099	101,528,094	101,258,985
Single Stock Dividend	6,749,735	6,780,685	6,578,908	4,080,465	2,448,326
3 Month Euribor	26,365	31,359	70,761	74,505	169,335
Euro-BOBL	106,586,687	120,893,813	138,001,817	135,394,434	130,704,593
Euro-BONO	150,509	165,573	173,450	209,596	146,360
Euro-BTP	30,074,179	28,365,361	30,283,789	28,950,808	28,339,932
Euro-BUND	174,394,697	184,787,059	202,027,816	195,580,025	186,714,728
Euro-BUXL	16,961,719	15,147,783	16,009,717	14,350,348	11,840,847
Euro-OAT	43,325,753	39,117,211	37,970,925	35,941,066	29,041,392
Euro-SCHATZ	94,630,224	89,976,582	108,326,655	86,000,890	73,660,249
Short Term Euro-BTP	17,928,094	17,117,521	18,116,789	12,186,532	6,766,913
Swiss Government Bond (CONF)	43,290	68,870	91,981	106,716	102,360
Three-Month SARON (FSO3)	8,952	7,114	948		
Bloomberg Energy Sub-Index	16,042	13,656	12,252		
Bloomberg Energy Subindex (XLEN)	249	348	3,253	27,489	10,806
Bloomberg ex-Agriculture & Livestock Index	1,362	5,396	3,020		
Bloomberg ex-Agriculture & Livestock XL Futures	6,135	9,887	8,881	8,544	9,350
Bloomberg Petroleum Sub-Index	6,627	13,108	10,292	7,949	7,518
Bloomberg Precious Metals XL (XLPR)	1,755	3,892			
Total Futures	**1,168,829,124**	**1,246,552,327**	**1,253,900,917**	**1,049,331,509**	**1,085,268,363**
ATX	163	115	1,265	1,115	7,400
DAX	23,731,926	29,386,511	25,824,668	22,215,330	27,974,560
DAX 1st Friday Weekly	856,806	1,281,143	1,007,234	652,280	653,731
DAX 2nd Friday Weekly	756,560	1,165,169	857,549	623,562	671,853
DAX 4th Friday Weekly	882,379	1,255,344	904,474	694,396	782,122
DAX 5th Friday Weekly	371,415	439,907	321,539	248,808	321,664
db x-trackers MSCI Emerg. Markets TRN	32	1	15	381	522
db x-trackers MSCI World TRN (DBXW)	3		5	4	

EUREX, Frankfurt, Germany (continued)

	2020	2019	2018	2017	2016
DivDAX	2,002	1,100			
ETFS Gold (OPHA)	1,858	3,854	80,000	6,300	
Euro STOXX 50 Index	295,157,618	270,464,560	273,634,066	263,152,091	286,250,081
Euro STOXX 50 Index - 1st Friday	7,012,095	7,902,802	6,915,517	5,010,118	4,020,370
Euro STOXX 50 Index - 2nd Friday	5,155,504	5,956,798	5,363,211	3,815,340	4,237,875
Euro STOXX 50 Index - 4th Friday	6,430,659	7,310,953	7,252,612	6,317,176	4,771,520
Euro Stoxx 50 Index Dividend	2,587,947	2,402,348	2,372,411	1,063,310	1,332,581
Euro Stoxx 50 Index Options (OESX-MEEx) (OMSX)	5,231,841	3,643,444	585,205		
Euro Stoxx Automobiles & Parts	11,325	5,374	10,804	5,343	4,052
Euro Stoxx Banks	59,314,336	58,147,059	46,613,902	33,944,306	27,694,785
Euro Stoxx Banks 1st Friday	62,182	58,331	33,631	4,368	36,197
Euro Stoxx Banks 2nd Friday	155,616	77,671	14,534	6,810	5,397
Euro Stoxx Banks 4th Friday	107,485	128,477	31,560	36,323	48,468
Euro Stoxx Banks 5th Friday	78,366	42,630	9,135	12,295	19,767
Euro Stoxx Basic Resources	4,712	123	5,850	4,142	1,343
Euro Stoxx Chemicals	844	1,158	2,772	294	1,883
Euro Stoxx Construction & Materials	1,439	3,938	673	40	190
Euro Stoxx Food and Beverage	572	7,178	2,661	886	106
Euro Stoxx Healthcare	3,965	3,025	590	634	1,870
Euro Stoxx Industrial Goods & Services	1,888	2,512	961	782	859
Euro Stoxx Insurance	66,725	83,013	52,230	35,279	68,583
Euro Stoxx Oil & Gas	42,275	9,820	17,165	19,566	28,630
Euro Stoxx Personal & Household Goods	8,004	8,177	3,009	4,457	2,086
Euro Stoxx Real Estate (OESL)	4,744	18,600	57,316	6,564	
Euro Stoxx Select Dividend 30 Index	489,881	453,892	189,924	121,100	47,480
Euro Stoxx Technology	9,763	7,858	6,877	3,146	13,310
Euro Stoxx Telecom	11,604	31,267	87,635	4,634	3,331
Euro Stoxx Utilities	39,265	240,991	313,507	50,289	106,422
iShares Core FTSE 100 UCITS (Dist) (ISF)	20,058				
iShares Core MSCI Europe UCITS ETF (IQQY)	1				
iShares Core MSCI World UCITS ETF (IWDA)	600				
iShares Core S&P 500 UCITS ETF (CSPX)	201	47			
iShares DAX® UCITS ETF (DE)	3,437	142	7,500	18,589	31,466
iShares EURO STOXX50® UCITS ETF	166,636	150,080	8,959	218,302	254,172
iShares Euro Stoxx Banks 30-15 UCITS ETF (DE) (EXX1)	14,056	11,157	2,632	4,030	
iShares J.P. Morgan USD Corporate Bond ETF (OHYG)	39,420	100			
iShares Physical Gold (IGLN)	7,631,561	8,023,753	1,311,740		
iShares Stoxx Europe 600 UCITS ETF (DE) (EXSA)	4,665	9,771	164	13	
iShares USD Corporate Bond ETF (OQDE)	100		220		
iShares USD High Yield Corporate Bond ETF (OHYU)	125,218	213,704	41,141		
iShares USD High Yield Corporate Bond UCITS (EHYU)	1,355				
iShares USD Treasury Bond 20+ Yr UCITS (ODTL)	94,650				
Kospi 200	26,046,645	35,236,582	38,604,669	26,091,710	21,328,717
MDAX	2,005	6,599	1,869	2,498	11,100
MSCI AC Asia Pacific ex Japan (OMAS)	13,574	9,729	510		
MSCI ACWI (NTR, USD) (OMAC)	19,100				
MSCI EAFE (USD, Price) (OMFP)	103,796	203,236	128,079	47,333	
MSCI EM (OMEF)	7,287	19,168	30,393	11,362	91,779
MSCI EM (OMEN)	14,620	22,606	105	16,406	36,032
MSCI Emerging Markets	75,193	73,486	222,786	224,960	186,950
MSCI Emerging Markets Asia (OMEA)	598,780	627,112	507,710	170,671	7,458
MSCI Europe	4,364	7,575		3,623	66,920
MSCI Europe (OMEP)	2,462	796			168,260
MSCI World	240,505	200,557	290,718	335,599	185,360
MSCI World (OMWN)	49,414	1,600	16,326		
MSCI World (OMWP)	490,662	484,914	199,062	16,307	15,100
RDX USD Index	69,526	118,847	692,322	576,094	614,261
Stoxx Europe 50 Index	1,364	5,734	12,407	15,394	32,578
Stoxx Europe 600	1,396,484	469,062	196,912	629,772	97,847
Stoxx Europe 600 Automobiles & Parts	281,770	275,766	219,805	97,483	124,581
Stoxx Europe 600 Banks	561,317	606,692	271,058	205,981	636,435
Stoxx Europe 600 Basic Resources	83,092	215,641	235,487	220,448	334,456
Stoxx Europe 600 Chemicals	0	3,462		2	717
Stoxx Europe 600 Construction & Materials	6,235	2,062			656
Stoxx Europe 600 ESG-X Index (OSEG)	39,300	6,000			
Stoxx Europe 600 Financial Services	1,410	1,930	30	191	1,159
Stoxx Europe 600 Food & Beverage	4,552	24,591	4,100	9,505	26,220
Stoxx Europe 600 Healthcare	15,764	24,300	20,708	24,727	35,847
Stoxx Europe 600 Industrial Goods & Services	32,426	15,432	102,256	52,666	53,080
Stoxx Europe 600 Insurance	45,918	33,627	33,707	20,032	10,805
Stoxx Europe 600 Media	2,321	4,641	2,871	93	1,248
Stoxx Europe 600 Oil & Gas	379,471	203,615	262,267	334,032	436,129
Stoxx Europe 600 Personal & Household Goods	316	643	1,630	4,322	13,539
Stoxx Europe 600 Real Estate	9,750	22,250	23,500	11,750	
Stoxx Europe 600 Technology	14,304		6		99

EUREX, Frankfurt, Germany (continued)

	2020	2019	2018	2017	2016
Stoxx Europe 600 Telecom	69,962	45,464	229,264	65,796	50,763
Stoxx Europe 600 Travel & Leisure	27,092	1,518	369	148	35,825
Stoxx Europe 600 Utilities	94,518	51,804	28,813	45,908	28,059
Stoxx Europe ESG Leaders Select 30 Index (OSLS)	5,503				
Stoxx Europe Select 50 EUR Index (OXXS)	16,500	30,000			
Stoxx Global Select Dividend 100 Index	22,116	68,590	14,880	17,716	33,110
Swiss Leader Index (SLI)	124	163	103	2,919	12,631
Swiss Market Index (SMI)	4,435,551	4,249,292	4,345,091	3,929,715	3,950,989
Swiss Market Index (SMI) - 1st Friday	34,657	18,418	4,703	5,532	3,757
Swiss Market Index (SMI) - 2nd Friday	26,478	9,488	8,403	4,002	2,015
Swiss Market Index (SMI) - 4th Friday	30,499	14,011	7,905	7,819	2,489
Swiss Market Index (SMI) - 5th Friday	9,993	8,095	1,669	1,942	1,687
Swiss Market Index Mid-Cap (SMIM)	5,669	8,681	8,715	4,195	12,039
TecDAX	6	421	196	401	12,689
VSTOXX (OVS2)	6,902,246	7,390,272	8,583,691	2,008,927	
Xtrackers MSCI Europe UCITS (DBXA)	1				
All Options on American Samoa	745	22			
All Options on Austrian Equities	726,701	329,206	378,184	572,046	488,809
All Options on Belgian Equities	752,524	961,382	1,030,297	714,267	624,172
All Options on Dutch Equities	13,093,588	14,429,438	11,550,630	13,142,352	12,238,251
All Options on Finnish Equities	7,475,002	6,916,411	6,851,910	6,952,407	9,985,076
All Options on French Equities	29,630,798	25,810,689	24,312,363	22,017,290	21,643,909
All Options on Georgian Equities	64,445	2,192			
All Options on German Equities	73,393,731	73,996,664	84,935,707	72,642,208	80,812,584
All Options on Great Britain	158,723	148,179	112,727	93,377	231,828
All Options on Ireland	403,238	56,845	10,275	43,370	10,702
All Options on Italian Equities	3,348,257	5,117,701	5,209,627	5,321,227	6,963,201
All Options on Niger Equities	2,226				
All Options on Russian Equities	279,347	114,873	1,059,310	263,758	500,913
All Options on Spanish Equities	5,584,799	5,063,637	5,305,355	5,799,277	7,976,521
All Options on Swazi Equities	85,594	19,406			
All Options on Swedish Equities	134,404	920,924	11,202	12,680	12,054
All Options on Swiss Equities	53,979,340	51,783,295	48,123,718	41,610,620	45,029,440
3-Month Euribor	1,260	439	610	2,317	5,215
Bund Weekly - Week1 (OGB1)	156,399	137,921	107,490	90,376	82,582
Bund Weekly - Week2 (OGB2)	135,871	152,090	67,033	70,284	119,226
Bund Weekly - Week3 (OGB3)	75,315	61,015	35,948	42,217	93,612
Bund Weekly - Week4 (OGB4)	55,073	17,219	22,882	10,127	23,564
Bund Weekly - Week5 (OGB5)	45,246	40,440	22,360	29,157	44,313
Euro-Bobl	3,131,576	5,617,826	12,012,901	12,918,246	9,580,664
Euro-BTP (OBTP)	1,239,870	1,304,071	1,717,815	85,678	
Euro-Bund	27,849,102	46,267,820	43,572,017	42,673,925	34,904,716
Euro-Buxl (OGBX)	128,386				
Euro-OAT	90,228	228,883	380,416	98,873	20
Euro-Schatz	11,476,974	11,268,003	19,444,653	17,319,057	14,428,689
iShares Physical Silver (ISLN)	98,138	42,829			
Xetra-Gold	161	1,252		77	567
Total Options	**692,587,460**	**700,591,869**	**697,862,164**	**626,566,801**	**641,553,408**

Euronext Derivatives Market

	2020	2019	2018	2017	2016
Corn	442,558	375,065	410,980	370,081	522,273
Milling Wheat	12,969,205	10,128,337	10,675,119	8,997,886	9,006,649
Rapeseed	2,304,362	2,146,228	2,348,117	2,790,491	2,567,941
AEX Mini	9,195	10,908	13,511	13,381	65,529
AEX Stock Index (FTI)	8,859,689	8,993,504	8,980,034	8,741,565	9,919,048
Bel 20 Index (BXF)	1,020	1,730	981	2,578	3,396
CAC 40	28,761,490	30,264,082	30,279,622	32,457,671	33,784,414
CAC 40 Dividend Index	236,850	306,912	347,000	411,963	175,085
CAC 40 Mini	7,511	20,872	25,235	5,891	15,669
CAC 40 Total Return	329,120	158,875	1,110		
Eurozone ESG Large 80 Index	181				
FTSE EPRA Europe	91,845	99,485	106,285	108,322	102,981
OBX Index	2,078,746	2,575,215	2,723,548	2,810,099	3,426,747
PSI 20 Index	69,001	120,006	130,941	170,838	197,332
Tailor Made Forwards/Futures	1,219,621	1,878,512	2,916,204	3,431,915	2,586,041
All Futures on Individual Equities	26,826,433	4,357,037	1,092,497	378,951	257,004
Single Stock Dividend Futures	271,452	39,326	12,419	10,958	13,569
Single Stock Forwards/Futures	243,399	721,480	702,393	1,032,993	1,430,965
Paris Real Estate Index	10	36			
Total Futures	**84,721,688**	**62,197,700**	**60,768,066**	**61,747,772**	**64,095,023**
Corn	51,484	38,637	39,446	34,238	71,369
Milling Wheat	1,224,892	736,633	973,588	734,663	1,222,123
Rapeseed	135,551	92,421	135,029	226,086	349,886

Euronext Derivatives Market (continued)

	2020	2019	2018	2017	2016
AEX Daily	3,758,055	3,177,912	2,918,897	1,959,405	1,386,412
AEX Mini	43,638	22,927	19,107	16,524	14,624
AEX-Index (AEX)	9,820,327	8,872,233	9,681,101	7,147,796	5,708,911
AEX Weekly	3,104,777	2,654,073	2,606,585	1,818,891	1,411,476
CAC 40 (€10)	2,495,784	3,303,787	3,811,892	3,713,089	2,282,839
CAC 40 (WEEKLY)	47,549	42,005	9,319	17,744	60,664
ISHARES EURO STOXX 50 UCITS ETF (DIST)	30,099	19,915	9,427	11,230	6,699
ISHARES MSCI EMERGING MARKETS UCITS ETF	46	4,986	12,334	3,692	370
ISHARES MSCI EUROPE UCITS ETF (DIST)	118	1,543	1,673	1,563	492
ISHARES MSCI WORLD UCITS ETF (DIST)	105	990	1,524	4,202	552
ISHARES S&P 500 UCITS ETF (DIST)	243	3,442	4,684	5,387	2,067
OBX Index	700,760	715,544	919,367	781,785	753,393
All Options on Individual Equities	69,448,101	70,133,873	74,602,767	70,084,311	57,015,075
Total Options	**90,861,529**	**91,870,122**	**97,918,193**	**89,324,257**	**73,587,263**

Hong Kong Futures Exchange (HKFE), Hong Kong

	2020	2019	2018	2017	2016
INR Currency - INR/USD	169,336	11,130			
RMB Currency - AUD/CNH	669	8,277	1,304	409	88
RMB Currency - CNH/USD	2,231	11,759	12,214	11,939	4,867
RMB Currency - EUR/CNH	425	14,656	8,956	1,750	952
RMB Currency - JPY/CNH	265	4,689	2,291	485	390
RMB Currency - USD/CNH	1,768,449	1,938,891	1,755,130	732,569	538,594
CES China 120 Index	73	111	765	1,511	642
Hang Seng Index	41,635,063	51,317,694	57,668,346	31,486,965	32,313,994
Hang Seng Mainland Banks Index Futures	1,146	22,255	22,516	8,067	285
Hang Seng Mainland Oil & Gas Index Futures	11,042	45,120	20,973	2,637	6
Hang Seng Mainland Properties Index Futures	1,224	17,261	28,456	4,744	5
Hang Seng TECH Index *	49,122				
HSCEI Dividend Point Index	448,663	531,215	413,292	472,147	589,188
HSCEI Gross Total Return Index	58	24	2		
HSCEI Net Total Return Index	6	23	2		
H-Shares Index	36,256,445	34,151,099	37,451,281	28,852,655	33,031,130
HSI Dividend Point Index	25,098	13,790	12,822	18,243	16,886
HSI Gross Total Return Index	172	165	14		
HSI Net Total Return Index	137	120	13		
HSI Volatility Index	168	159	1	68	87
Mini Hang Seng Index	27,902,077	22,170,547	24,664,381	11,487,207	12,477,552
Mini H-Shares Index	4,538,491	3,686,219	5,551,632	3,661,193	4,870,262
MSCI AC Asia ex Japan NTR Index	135,546	237,533	5,545		
MSCI Australia Net Total Return (USD) Index	45				
MSCI China Free (USD) Index	10				
MSCI China Free Net Total Return (USD) Index	19,703				
MSCI EM Asia Net Total Return (USD) Index	39,967				
MSCI Emerging Markets (USD) Index	204				
MSCI Emerging Markets Net Total Return (USD) Index	40				
MSCI India Net Total Return (USD) Index	5,948				
MSCI Indonesia (USD) Index	704				
MSCI Indonesia Net Total Return (USD) Index	14,316				
MSCI Japan Net Total Return (USD) Index	10,748				
MSCI Malaysia Net Total Return (USD) Index	3,144				
MSCI Philippines Net Total Return (USD) Index	33				
MSCI Singapore Free (SGD) Index	2,397				
MSCI Singapore Free Net Total Return (USD) Index	63				
MSCI Singapore Net Total Return (USD) Index	2				
MSCI Taiwan (USD) Index	548,214				
MSCI Taiwan 25/50 (USD) Index	5,758				
MSCI Taiwan 25/50 Net Total Return (USD) Index	3				
MSCI Taiwan Net Total Return (USD) Index	37,874				
MSCI Thailand Net Total Return (USD) Index	14,877				
All Futures on Individual Equities	1,141,729	917,358	863,027	121,532	225,978
One-Month Hibor	55	95	167	20	
Three-Month Hibor	259	175	592	568	52
Iron Ore (Monthly)	97,048	55,944	9,517	18,194	
London Aluminium Mini (USD) Futures	31,543	9,246			
London Aluminium Mini Futures	2	21	635	937	1,829
London Copper Mini (USD) Futures	88,849	19,516			
London Copper Mini Futures	1	2	124	731	3,354
London Lead Mini Futures	14	12		234	7
London Nickel Mini (USD) Futures	10,288	552			
London Zinc Mini (USD) Futures	56,267				
London Zinc Mini Futures	3	150	651	483	12,394
Gold (CNH)	6,796	81,768	25,006	110,763	
Gold (USD)	61,886	491,405	326,700	55,372	

Hong Kong Futures Exchange (HKFE), Hong Kong (continued)

	2020	2019	2018	2017	2016
Silver (USD)	1,282				
Total Futures	**115,145,978**	**115,759,091**	**128,847,222**	**77,060,327**	**84,100,129**
RMB Currency - USD/CNH	8,969	15,429	30,067	10,473	
Hang Seng Index	9,811,797	12,466,854	12,716,495	10,129,325	9,353,749
Hang Seng Index Weekly	1,191,533	246,717			
H-shares Index	20,725,642	21,563,408	24,258,084	19,777,920	19,475,726
H-shares Weekly Index	409,897	94,203			
Mini Hang Seng Index	3,345,582	3,343,429	2,461,296	1,640,881	1,424,379
Mini H-Shares Index	564,142	582,623	583,549	377,243	197,399
All Options on Individual Equities	131,021,660	108,813,894	127,279,101	105,839,179	73,582,114
Total Options	**167,079,222**	**147,126,707**	**167,335,854**	**137,785,021**	**104,050,543**

ICE Futures Europe (ICE), United Kingdom

	2020	2019	2018	2017	2016
Cocoa	8,240,073	7,732,270	7,817,955	8,378,774	6,430,848
Cocoa	6,509,645	8,240,073	7,732,270	7,817,955	8,378,774
Robusta Coffee - 10 Tonne	4,784,163	5,079,789	4,268,610	4,458,111	4,378,442
UK Feed Wheat	108,565	103,612	113,009	91,701	108,264
White Sugar	3,373,567	3,531,614	3,442,923	2,874,270	2,654,375
Belgian Power Futures	9,779	12,822	26,486	17,312	21,574
ICE Brent	231,879,831	221,331,490	235,001,152	241,544,633	210,561,053
CER Futures	16,183	11,391	20,109	11,089	30,029
Dutch Power	98,905	108,281	141,732	167,323	156,556
Dutch TTF Gas	27,315,177	18,000,903	9,317,729	7,541,880	6,909,038
EUA Futures	8,945,417	7,462,422	7,776,993	4,891,577	5,137,885
EUA Phase 3 Daily	630,198	456,796	664,929	327,280	234,444
EUA UK Auction	222,051		202,106	211,920	160,516
EUAA Futures	4,715	275	1,684	26	651
EUAA UK Auction	3,373		1,720	1,451	1,842
French Power Futures	2,106		60		
gC Newcastle Coal	84,524,207	80,009,445	82,672,960	259,626	374,545
German Natural Gas Futures	212,419	196,896	185,488	4,387	1,555
German Power Futures	10,697	12,842	3,046	288	42
ICE Gas Oil	104,478	33,196	21,677	74,686,410	66,158,348
ICE Global Oil Products	28,944,927	39,024,310	33,749,182	38,857,776	34,102,096
ICE Heating Oil	36,021,671	10,669,610	7,284,007	5,512,333	4,935,310
Italian Power Futures	40,400	29,614	1,891		
ICE Natural Gas	18,002	9,230	7,315	11,683,665	11,178,265
ICE NYH (RBOB) Gasoline (Monthly)	7,729,024	8,582,620	9,357,935	5,115,433	5,395,099
ICE Richards Bay Coal	21,064,950	7,162,351	5,192,657	56,312	84,875
ICE Rotterdam Coal	47,783	39,698	50,637	992,492	1,217,874
ICE UK Electricity Futures Peak (1MWh)	857,053	898,785	1,011,767	19,850	40,285
Spanish Power	36				
Italian PSV Natural Gas Futures	5,145	3,316	2,044	15,200	3,415
ICE WTI Crude	50,122,648	53,597,867	56,802,221	54,967,258	47,289,665
FTSE 100 Declared Dividend	1,400	3,602	3,050	510	2,800
FTSE 100 Dividend Index	1,060,525	466,274	515,653	372,215	347,063
FTSE 100 Index	37,140,466	33,659,627	36,915,549	33,318,372	37,954,717
FTSE 250 £2	489,264	478,246	432,451	470,451	507,061
MSCI AC Asia Pacific Ex Japan Futures	1,954	2,189	2,450	1,432	6,701
MSCI All Countries Asia Ex Japan Index Futures	189,899	183,018	199,615	166,770	275,561
MSCI Brazil Index Future	552,498	437,944	232,864	225,688	41,406
MSCI Emerging Markets (EM) Index Future	160,602	290,091	956,714	1,065,757	861,893
MSCI Emerging Markets Net TR EUR Index Future	67,447	143,113	171,639	112,342	153,487
MSCI EMU Energy Net Return EUR Index	431	11,861			
MSCI EMU Financials Net Return EUR Index	2,090	25,804			
MSCI EMU Health Care Net Return EUR Index	1,058	10,396			
MSCI EMU Information Technology Net Return EUR	1,027	16,472			
MSCI EMU Materials Net Return EUR Index	638	6,520			
MSCI EMU Telecommunication Services Net Return	4,790	28,238			
MSCI EMU Utilities Net Return EUR Index	1,424	8,294			
MSCI Europe Consumer Disc NTR EUR Index Future	184	7,522	14,655	5,477	6,779
MSCI Europe Consumer Stap NTR EUR Index Futures	1,294	4,072	7,474	1,280	3,032
MSCI Europe Energy NTR EUR Index Future	1,076	7,281	9,122		
MSCI Europe Ex UK Index Futures	7,904	22,500	15,634	1,067	1,856
MSCI Europe Financials NTR EUR Index Future	6,845	17,431	25,698	3,266	5,373
MSCI Europe Health Care NTR EUR Index Future	702	6,097	9,393		
MSCI Europe Index Future	432,379	212,449	284,640	405,755	472,209
MSCI Europe Industrials NTR EUR Index	700	1,350	7,992		
MSCI Europe IT NTR EUR Index Future	57	11,651	22,003		
MSCI Europe Materials NTR EUR Index	1,034	5,044	5,915	3,341	4,516
MSCI Europe Tele Services NTR EUR Index Future	135	14,162	21,291		
MSCI Europe Utilities NTR EUR Index Future	212	6,244	14,186		
MSCI India Index Futures	172,557	162,047	248,842	424,783	221,953

ICE Futures Europe (ICE), United Kingdom (continued)

	2020	2019	2018	2017	2016
MSCI Japan Index Futures	3,939	2,439	15,729	6,685	1,508
MSCI Pacific ex Japan Index Futures	93,057	259,586	456,611	384,381	344,457
MSCI Switzerland Net Total Return CHF - Standard	8,137	3,626	5,840	4,878	13,544
MSCI World Consumer Disc NTR USD Index Futures	6,959	17,253	1,564	13,081	13,199
MSCI World Consumer Stap NTR USD Index Futures	23,439	39,252	54,103	66,184	17,554
MSCI World Energy Net TR USD Index Futures	7,666	41,367	78,133	34,748	6,442
MSCI World Financials Net TR USD Index Futures	32,811	97,110	81,985	118,897	32,115
MSCI World Health Care Net TR USD Index Futures	10,512	26,254	21,799	18,925	11,420
MSCI World Index Future	409,877	411,544	944,505	1,331,516	768,871
MSCI World Industrials Net TR USD Index Futures	31,405	19,898	8,256	15,066	11,105
MSCI World IT Net TR USD Index Futures	24,898	25,793	2,911	36,917	7,667
MSCI World Materials Net TR USD Index Futures	11,001	30,666	18,215	27,002	14,575
MSCI World Min Volatility NTR USD Index	32,744	33,018	10,195	17,333	5,211
MSCI World Net Total Return EUR Index Future	3,136	22,974	11,815	61,890	71,562
MSCI World Real Estate NTR Index Future	36,160	47,074	61,052	99,117	12,113
MSCI World Telecom Net TR USD Index Futures	15,521	5,256	93,109	59,754	30,658
MSCI World Utilities Net TR USD Index Futures	25,772	74,661	134,505	71,583	29,311
Russell UK MID 150 NTR Index	62,188	100,516	199,255	322,438	134,747
All Futures on Individual Equities	11,439,230	39,181,471	102,738,810	82,062,578	41,588,169
1 Month Secured Overnight Financing Rate	350,060	277,598	50,787		
3 Month Euribor	280,792	409,940	226,441,372	197,286,277	134,881,365
3 Month Euroswiss	174,410,276	185,435,139	7,397,204	6,496,257	5,760,114
3 Month Secured Overnight Financing Rate	4,400,390	6,631,148	51,783		
3-Month Short Sterling	1,970,394	863,494	216,984,337	198,845,679	153,940,833
ERIS Standard EUR 2 Year 0.00% Interest Rate Future	161,026,815	177,433,667	11,119	12,094	8,529
ERIS Standard EUR 3 Year 0.00% Interest Rate Future	8,165,465	2,922,791	1,548	260	2,406
Short Gilt	61,065,544	57,799,640	9,141	21,024	44,788
Swapnote € - 10 Yr	61	1,278	13,759	10,844	18,386
Swapnote € - 2 Yr	342	2,975	287,410	209,775	334,860
Swapnote € - 5 Yr	92	6,133	172,105	167,587	238,512
Three Month Euro (EONIA)	14,890	68,576	712,939	803	
Total Futures	**973,287,184**	**1,127,416,373**	**1,038,826,477**	**842,507,861**	**775,161,967**
Cocoa	1,169,041	1,193,032	1,456,382	2,692,602	1,883,865
Robusta Coffee 10 Tonne	637,093	805,450	930,305	835,963	633,806
UK Feed Wheat	382	1,025	957	2,613	1,583
White Sugar	28,158	5,314	7,943	11,556	5,650
Dutch TTF Gas	25,590,449	24,943,223	704,130	527,890	339,080
EUA	3,241,443	1,121,285	728,794	522,161	433,897
gC Newcastle Coal	2,630,825	2,515,690	68,934	93,258	105,550
German Power Options	200,728	123,535			
ICE Brent Crude Oil	4,565	18,410	18,282,452	16,152,414	13,594,212
ICE Gasoil	10,085	400	193,863	254,617	279,438
ICE Global Oil Products	2,063,715	2,309,684	1,693,696	1,252,118	1,668,712
ICE Natural Gas	173,635	567,805	1,506,030	1,604,115	2,032,675
ICE Richards Bay Coal	750	150	1,050	3,500	4,800
ICE Rotterdam Coal	12,045	290,365	331,229	792,480	559,574
ICE WTI Crude	3,694,346	5,074,934	3,957,901	4,642,881	4,942,451
CAC 40 Index - Euro FLEX	150				
FTSE 100 Euro FLEX Index	39,964	44,536	39,382	55,291	21,418
FTSE 100 (ESX)	12,202,691	12,856,406	12,378,557	15,846,915	16,804,267
FTSE 250 Index FLEX	29,916	10,763	6,948	14,371	6,010
All Options on Individual Equities	12,686,408	14,955,206	15,555,053	22,437,120	25,911,090
3 Month Euribor	13,323,706	13,698,090	10,512,677	10,485,675	15,984,090
3 Month Euribor 1 Year Mid Curve	8,718,918	9,517,322	6,973,347	6,285,825	6,234,485
3 Month Euribor 2 Year Mid Curve	4,258,186	8,220,483	7,078,526	4,542,141	7,157,550
3 Month Euribor 3 Year Mid Curve	2,183,589	3,923,186	4,895,059	2,118,763	2,492,075
3 Month Sterling	46,168,361	29,350,989	23,621,519	27,132,950	15,542,252
3 Month Sterling 2 Year Mid Curve	4,537,953	7,305,315	8,191,545	3,985,856	3,135,867
3 Month Sterling 3 Year Mid Curve	117,386	243,829	215,950	213,738	177,470
3 Month Sterling Mid Curve	9,358,624	9,429,538	8,763,610	8,843,680	6,627,443
Long Gilt	144,801	148,038	22,020		
Total Options	**977,893,502**	**973,287,184**	**1,127,416,373**	**1,038,826,477**	**842,507,861**

ICE Futures Singapore (ICE), Singapore

	2020	2019	2018	2017	2016
Bakkt Bitcoin (USD) Monthly	292,137	18,946			
Malaysian Ringgit/US Dollar Futures	680,424	647,350	117,676	2,376	2
Mini US Dollar Index Futures	337,238	334,057	288,321	7,282	70
Mini US Dollar/Singapore Dollar	676,448	206,079			
Mini Brent Crude Futures (100 BBL)	30,583	136,107	1,807,071	1,767,406	1,694,092
Mini Low Sulphur Gasoil Futures (10mt)	2,205	5,764	9,663	7,615	115,536
Mini Low Sulphur Gasoil Futures (10mt)	451	2,515	334,813	503,621	187,530
Total Futures	**2,019,486**	**1,367,671**	**2,566,022**	**2,288,311**	**2,003,921**

JSE Securities Exchange of South Africa, Africa

	2020	2019	2018	2017	2016
CBOT Soybean	15,348	7,291	14,266	7,782	8,076
CBOT Soybean Meal	19,005	11,113	1,339	435	59
CBOT Soybean Oil (OILS)	20,571	4,518	993	366	19
CBOT Wheat	614	610	1,290	983	1,217
Corn	303,287	265,287	216,808	171,913	149,786
KCBT Wheat	1,523	2,980	3,406	2,557	1,446
Mini Bitter Sorghum (MSBT)	159	425			
Mini Sweet Sorghum (MSRG)	1,407	303			
Quanto Soybean (QSBN)	9,991	14,342	16,965	514	11,028
Quanto Soybean Meal Maxi (XQMX)	6				
Quantro Cocoa (QCOC)	54		20	862	
Quantro Coffee (QCFF)	1,220	1,486	830	873	1,221
Quantro Corn (QCRN)	57,216	164,578	35,677	27,180	82,335
Quantro Cotton (QCTN)	74	736	827	70	230
Quantro Sugar (QSUG)	1,572	380	531	237	272
Soya (50t) (SOYA)	341,610	415,233	423,611	306,847	222,518
Sunflower Seeds (SUNS)	269,253	215,653	265,476	269,011	196,310
Wheat (WEAT)	380,665	342,561	347,143	352,627	417,109
White Maize 100 Ton (WMAZ)	976,191	929,834	1,004,457	898,611	1,122,405
Yellow Maize 100 Ton (YMAZ)	768,914	767,505	662,397	572,696	505,944
Any-Day Expiry Dollar/Rand	3,728,268	2,192,350	3,708,259	3,394,361	1,193,224
ZAAD/Rand	454,089	260,385	324,989	475,108	292,015
British Pound/Rand	1,677,761	3,689,395	4,045,724	2,600,430	1,774,346
Canadian Dollar/Rand	15,104	23,460	21,360	50,924	31,556
Dollar/Rand	25,334,216	29,495,638	29,720,494	35,692,269	26,217,084
Euro/Rand	2,950,344	3,599,137	2,460,294	3,663,447	2,110,808
Hong Kong Dollar/Rand (ZAHK)	6,544	15,592		38,560	95,070
Japanese/Rand	91,311		199,354	41,784	205,171
Kenyan Shilling/Rand (ZAKS)	4,332	4,332	6,143	4,796	14,274
Maxi Dollar/Rand	1,495,100	1,416,100	837,114	1,123,100	2,014,700
New Zealand Dollar/Rand	4,184	3,638	1,500	308	688
Norwegian Krone/Rand	23,090			17,544	
Quanto Euro/Dollar	43,856	27,118	96,242	256,862	172,349
Quanto Sterling/Dollar (GBUS)	29,977	13,297	6,222	152,452	12,533
Swiss Franc/Rand	11,987	22,746	20,580	34,343	80,261
Turkish Lira/Rand	35,000	336,451	171,050	237,829	349
Brent Crude Oil	12,233	27,751	44,360	43,134	59,511
Crude Oil	393	1,286	4,968	6,520	17,236
Diesel	3,681	7,570	11,800	21,124	35,895
Quanto Heating Oil (QHEA)	154				
Quantro Crude Oil (QBRN)	14,051	263	546	909	24,453
Quantro Natural Gas (QNAT)	1,066	110	30	36	4
Equity Can-Do	667,291	833,286	2,013,093	2,449,191	10,366,375
FTSE/JSE Capped Shareholder Weighted 40 Index	4,699,611	3,552,552	2,997,890	1,160,400	
FTSE/JSE Capped Shareholder Weighted 40 Total	39,344				
FTSE/JSE FNDI 30 Index (FNDI)	2,385	2,556	4,052	3,605	4,129
FTSE/JSE Shareholder Weighted Top 40 Index (DTOP)	1,787,043	3,528,129	5,427,717	9,129,648	8,872,706
FTSE/JSE Shareholder Weighted Top 40 Total Return	5,191				
FTSE/JSE Top 40 Index - Mini (ALMI)	377,872	444,680	397,174	400,892	479,879
FTSE/JSE Top 40 Index (ALSI)	7,724,343	9,506,127	9,285,641	9,640,472	12,249,981
FTSE/JSE Top 40 Total Return Index (ATRI)	53,494				
MSCI South African Index (MXZA)	87	24,474	7,094	49,144	171,690
All Futures on Individual Equities	16,017,005	10,929,304	9,263,458	15,080,250	15,049,127
Dividend Futures	17,152,630	7,588,057	7,076,507	9,080,623	9,311,120
eCFD Futures	5,520,831	17,745,127	11,726,122	11,983,410	21,632,772
IDX Dividend Futures	17,294,207	11,219,885	25,165,267	110,582,896	167,213,875
IDX Futures	11,805,166	5,672,161	26,437,327	123,984,857	166,708,902
Copper	1,209	1,107	4,287	3,727	1,302
Quantro Copper (QCOP)	485	154	74	54	412
Gold	5,130	6,597	6,224	11,098	9,343
Palladium (PALL)	1,657	658	1,707	2,640	3,349
Platinum	2,431	2,190	2,423	4,376	4,356
Quantro Gold (QGLD)	2,022	1,572	1,325	1,324	2,887
Quantro Palladium (QPLD)	453	2,632	426		408
Quantro Platinum (QPLT)	1,176	4,209	1,900	1,006	896
Quantro Silver (QSIL)	1,582	1,230	557	331	735
Silver	2,979	4,116	2,726	4,360	5,131
Total Futures	**122,271,045**	**115,471,599**	**144,750,987**	**344,071,265**	**449,425,390**
Corn	274	1,308	187	375	933
Quanto Soybean (XQBN)	4				
Quanto Soybean Meal Maxi (XQMX)	2				
Quantro Soyabean (XQSB)	4	1,450	10		
Soya (50t)	23,450	8,368	12,625	26,833	35,725
Sunflower Seed (SUNS)	12,897	3,781	14,624	34,877	23,726
Wheat (WEAT)	11,841	17,029	17,923	9,520	13,009

JSE Securities Exchange of South Africa, Africa (continued)

	2020	2019	2018	2017	2016
White Maize (WMAZ)	136,076	177,574	224,535	171,160	316,144
Yellow Maize (YMAZ)	91,668	92,896	80,964	46,489	78,054
Any-Day Expiry Dollar/Rand	9,142,557	7,029,648	6,972,934	6,820,519	3,796,016
British Pound/Rand	78,243	144,420	9,000	19,000	194,563
Dollar/Rand	17,286,759	19,849,042	20,847,146	11,691,397	9,785,698
Euro/Rand	583,540	1,477,645	4,123,447	2,043,748	154,012
Equity Can-Do	190,619	890,043	822,167	4,307,492	2,359,501
FTSE/JSE African Banks Index (J835)	4,225		6,270		
FTSE/JSE Capped Shareholder Weighted 40 Index	513,456	286,102	163,267	39,792	
FTSE/JSE Shareholder Weighted Top 40 Index (DTOP)	2,471,446	2,504,060	3,027,619	2,165,411	1,800,141
FTSE/JSE Top 40 Index (ALSI)	613,648	1,131,349	1,563,611	2,215,258	2,510,109
All Options on Individual Equities	16,267,955	7,772,521	7,783,111	9,279,216	8,692,146
eCFD Options	29,015				
Total Options	**47,457,679**	**41,391,092**	**45,945,082**	**38,873,037**	**29,776,855**

Korea Futures Exchange (KFE), Korea

	2020	2019	2018	2017	2016
Euro	876,402	611,753	660,860	750,072	771,273
Japanese yen	603,817	840,461	683,645	566,382	521,657
US Dollar	105,524,538	85,556,591	74,821,050	60,882,377	64,308,611
Yuan	8,273	3,716	4,541	5,150	4,963
Euro Stoxx 50	378	2,165	1,283		
KOSDAQ 150 Futures	22,992,829	13,981,907	13,353,982	2,984,151	1,204,706
KOSPI 200	90,553,417	61,703,473	64,338,721	48,617,581	33,925,669
Kospi 200 Sector	1,063,131	454,175			
KRX 300	78,158	124,284			
Mini KOSPI 200 Futures	39,357,509	22,031,736	20,906,086	14,738,747	8,992,497
V-Kospi 200	10,287	7,727			
All Futures on Individual Equities	1,126,736,372	616,946,569	501,723,576	280,064,162	172,120,372
10 Year Treasury Bond	17,669,136	17,737,866	15,136,390	12,156,888	14,493,794
3 Year Treasury Bond	30,162,655	26,734,179	22,989,204	22,130,599	26,046,011
Total Futures	**1,435,636,902**	**846,736,604**	**714,619,338**	**442,896,109**	**322,389,553**
Kosdaq 150	358,029	185,414			
KOSPI 200	610,510,383	637,637,015	657,832,873	540,103,609	337,007,133
Kospi 200 Weekly	120,039,385	13,330,380			
Mini KOSPI 200	13,750,819	24,278,148	17,063,243	14,661,725	22,029,182
All Options on Individual Equities	4,635,451	24,549,633	18,743,585	17,674,231	11,564,672
Total Options	**749,294,067**	**699,980,590**	**693,639,701**	**572,439,565**	**370,600,987**

London Metal Exchange (LME), United Kingdom

	2020	2019	2018	2017	2016
Alumina	160	920			
Aluminium	62,019,871	66,046,920	65,574,126	51,429,383	53,073,441
Aluminium Alloy	34,024	61,856	57,478	61,723	128,006
Aluminium Premium Duty Paid US Midwest (Platts)	368	899			
Cobalt	1,331	9,595	12,932	14,261	7,894
Copper - Grade A	32,606,077	35,622,832	38,599,069	33,885,113	36,947,881
North American Special Aluminum Alloy (NASAAC)	65,093	216,972	257,996	348,578	358,797
Primary Nickel	17,583,717	24,468,858	24,011,101	21,080,612	19,947,714
Special High Grade Zinc	23,542,072	29,648,051	33,430,054	29,642,124	26,942,407
Standard Lead	11,190,170	11,864,206	13,437,086	10,920,001	10,571,590
Steel HRC FOB China (Argus)	104,714	45,884			
Steel HRC North America (Argus)	26,999	28,315			
Steel Rebar	61,569	60,050	54,297	64,430	8,637
Steel Scrap	280,599	320,587	484,843	307,532	49,099
Tin	1,242,544	1,329,569	1,272,723	1,215,432	1,353,350
Gold	1,926	269,933	732,188	639,546	
Silver	6,945	70,800	148,566	95,625	
Total Futures	**148,768,179**	**170,066,247**	**178,072,459**	**149,704,368**	**149,388,960**
Copper - Grade A	1,765,400	1,424,398	1,675,489	1,767,797	1,762,967
Copper Grade A TAPOs	20,348	25,367	50,056	30,736	28,806
High Grade Primary Aluminum	2,449,337	2,018,103	3,083,333	3,307,496	2,915,725
Lead TAPOs	805	13,630	2,399	4,934	320
Nickel TAPOs	2,096	14,176	7,950	1,776	9,942
Primary Aluminium TAPOs	51,442	73,390	162,831	50,894	93,580
Primary Nickel	554,216	717,616	606,017	912,003	732,523
Special High Grade Zinc	1,006,930	1,110,348	906,392	1,360,303	1,159,365
Special High Grade Zinc TAPOs	7,412	8,294	6,427	2,955	22,032
Standard Lead	221,948	331,974	209,498	197,451	364,451
Tin	2	560	570	130	6,660
Total Options	**6,079,936**	**5,737,976**	**6,711,092**	**7,637,225**	**7,102,541**

Malaysia Derivatives Exchange, Malaysia

	2020	2019	2018	2017	2016
Crude Palm Oil (FCPO)	14,606,684	10,704,273	10,471,357	11,919,425	10,415,755
Crude Palm Oil (USD) (FUPO)	391				
RBD Palm Olein (FPOL)	15	104,492	507,394		
KLSE Composite Index (FKLI)	3,497,416	2,281,506	2,497,513	2,034,237	2,750,951
Mini FTSE Bursa Malaysia Mid 70 Index (FM70)	56,131	353,344	173,132		
Single Stock Futures (SSF)	118				
5 Year Malaysian Government Securities (FMG5)	320				
Gold	214	792	619	2,500	8,997
Total Futures	**18,161,289**	**13,444,407**	**13,650,015**	**13,956,213**	**13,175,743**
Crude Palm Oil (OCPO)	63,626	53,100	66,066	38,866	40,120
KLSE Composite Index (OKLI)	8,873	13,243	10,486	20,285	10,171
Total Options	**72,499**	**66,343**	**76,552**	**59,151**	**50,291**

MATBA ROFEX, Argentina

MaTBA and RFE merged into MATba ROFEX in August 2019.	2020	2019	2018	2017	2016
Chicago Corn	29,312	23,843	66,104	71,980	49,041
Chicago Soybean	73,794	32,546	134,520	241,780	192,082
Corn	126,548	110,029	67,695	49,367	42,852
Corn Mini	106,090	77,104	53,827	4,980	
Novillo Index (Cattle)	72	168	1,746	2,041	
Soybean	192,396	228,001	192,993	151,427	164,779
Soybean 30 ton	1,343	4,340	825	6	11
Soybean Mini	322,801	260,439	213,239	11,758	
Ternero Index (Cattle)	7	219	440	40	
Wheat	67,176	69,724	61,569	18,034	16,381
Wheat Mini	73,930	63,887	34,665	5,285	
Chinese Yuan	9,507				
U.S. Dollar	112,821,268	206,104,436	189,223,855	148,562,920	112,242,365
Oil Crude	359,181	534,285	240,875	247,371	178,855
ROFEX 20 Index	2,195,099	2,173,099	1,359,226		
Galicia Stock Futures	793,172	85,460			
Pampa Energia Stock Futures	22,064				
YPF S.A. Stock Futures	5,208				
Goverment Bonds - BONAR 2024	17,836	38,701	26,079	33,696	30,224
Gold	127,475	128,536	73,094	65,933	51,650
Total Futures	**117,344,279**	**209,939,518**	**192,747,209**	**150,192,977**	**113,264,913**
Chicago Corn	4,456	27,896	59,515	20,488	19,856
Chicago Soybeans	8,270	7,376	68,236	68,245	256,547
Corn	24,448	23,277	13,575	33,010	39,741
Soybean Mini	18	16	42		
Sunflower	58,924	50,193	57,575	6	
Wheat	8,123	13,881	17,200	2,231	1,446
US Dollar (DLR)	18,664	25,729	45,348	72,365	32,639
Oil Crude	3,294	7,859	1,687	2,130	
ROFEX 20 Index	9,039	37,007	8,892		
Gold	5,705	2,741	9,363	426	14,512
Total Options	**140,941**	**196,005**	**306,369**	**227,904**	**378,614**

MEFF Renta Variable (RV), Spain

	2020	2019	2018	2017	2016
Ibex 35	5,905,782	5,965,905	6,342,478	6,268,290	6,836,500
Ibex 35 Dividend Impact	91,571	144,831	70,725	43,372	58,044
Mini Ibex 35	1,543,507	1,454,885	1,490,232	1,618,857	2,498,973
All Futures on Individual Equities	10,968,411	15,298,027	10,703,192	11,671,215	9,467,294
Single Stock Dividend Futures Plus	7,752		200	880	760
Stock Dividend	130,055	758,700	471,614	346,555	367,785
Total Futures	**18,647,078**	**23,622,390**	**19,081,191**	**19,956,922**	**19,231,335**
IBEX 35 Plus Index	2,436,534	3,806,355	4,183,154	4,303,701	3,222,390
All Options on Individual Equities	19,393,317	17,492,103	20,237,873	20,316,354	22,900,619
Total Options	**21,829,851**	**21,298,458**	**24,421,027**	**24,620,055**	**26,123,009**

Metropolitan Stock Exchange, India

	2020	2019	2018	2017	2016
EUR/Indian Rupee	57,787	139,910	100,465	92,975	582,240
GBP/Indian Rupee	35,183	171,841	118,633	161,143	661,589
JPY/Indian Rupee	261	1,397	3,826	65,848	333,927
US Dollar/Indian Rupee	10,175,486	4,347,615	10,060,783	19,488,001	45,178,861
Total Futures	**10,268,717**	**4,660,763**	**10,283,909**	**19,807,967**	**46,756,617**

Mexican Derivatives Exchange (MEXDER), Mexico

	2020	2019	2018	2017	2016
Mexican Peso/Euro	30	324	78	296	5,638
Mexican Peso/US Dollar	5,917,076	5,095,123	6,265,233	8,576,423	8,627,126
IPC Stock Index	590,791	900,338	915,347	864,563	988,673
Mini IPC Stock Index	4,309	8,727	20,197	160,197	513,903
All Futures on Individual Equities	31,150	38,888	15,200	277,720	8,750
DC24 Bond	51,100	293,081	444,486	544,737	1,319,848
NV42 Bond	8,651		1,500	45,876	155,012
NV47 Bond	7,880	13,500	1,600		
Total Futures	**6,610,987**	**6,377,583**	**7,841,451**	**10,613,400**	**12,528,580**
Mexican Peso/US Dollar	78,081	46,975	126,508	94,134	32,904
IPC Stock Index	7,650	11,087	10,789	22,685	56,413
All Options on Individual Equities	150,692	805,011	352,759	300,820	322,308
Total Options	**236,423**	**863,075**	**490,057**	**417,886**	**411,918**

Montreal Exchange (ME), Canada

	2020	2019	2018	2017	2016
S&P/MX International Cannabis Index (SMJ)	19				
S&P/TSX 60 Index Mini Futures (SXM)	13,344	51,559	79,938	97,432	19,930
S&P/TSX 60 Index Standard Futures (SXF)	8,177,604	7,805,301	7,623,603	6,144,651	6,090,257
S&P/TSX Composite Index Banks (Industry Group)	59,000	3,266	5,699	1,679	2,754
S&P/TSX Composite Index Mini (SCF)	21	16	51	164	143
Share Futures	11,707,465	4,406,202	1,051,667	1,145,427	608
10 Year Government of Canada Bond (CGB)	32,067,932	31,684,621	28,769,478	23,946,703	20,968,281
2 Year Government of Canada Bond Futures (CGZ)	97,912				
Bankers Acceptance 3 Months (BAX)	23,026,123	29,816,722	29,018,180	28,962,355	26,316,537
3 Month CORRA (CRA)	13,077				
5 Year Canadian Gov't Bond (CGF)	5,471,435	4,130,134	406,782	358,078	116,799
Total Futures	**80,633,932**	**77,915,152**	**66,966,714**	**60,656,540**	**53,516,409**
US Dollar (USX)	24,460	2,184	128	9,008	19,006
ETFs	9,359,748	7,985,724	14,482,523	11,417,417	11,724,768
S&P Canada 60 Index (SXO) (incl. LEAPS)	30,476	62,055	198,698	193,038	671,462
S&P/TSX Composite Index Banks (Industry Group) (SXJ)	340				4
All Options on Individual Equities	25,059,590	29,142,959	29,405,993	23,178,799	25,302,965
10 Year Government of Canada Bond Futures (OGB)	26,740	16,876	43,447	11,650	4,553
3 Month Bankers Acceptance Futures (OBX)	714,811	1,034,240	1,095,579	801,051	683,247
Total Options	**35,216,165**	**38,253,743**	**45,226,368**	**35,610,963**	**38,406,005**

Moscow Interbank Currency Exchange (MICEX), Russia

	2020	2019	2018	2017	2016
Sugar (cash settled - SA)	459	231	1,075	283	1,141
Wheat	29				
AUD/USD	771,933	386,083	539,229	461,766	614,498
CNY/RUB	18	51	405	825	2,837
EUR/RUB	44,785,761	22,255,214	23,895,450	23,140,836	23,579,817
EUR/USD	43,090,669	28,938,812	58,384,706	40,782,844	34,882,762
GBP/USD	2,550,258	2,192,563	1,214,176	2,035,835	1,900,109
USD/CAD	140,216	85,969	176,629	266,011	467,540
USD/CHF	98,565	77,805	77,234	92,989	95,846
USD/INR	12	38	7		
USD/JPY	731,708	573,911	1,423,892	3,303,245	3,652,237
USD/RUB	755,425,507	384,155,770	496,225,103	590,260,376	860,140,157
USD/TRY	47	1,398	5,289	2,380	66,637
USD/UAH	14	6	7	87	499
Brent Oil	742,813,393	616,575,153	441,379,480	451,643,376	435,468,923
Henry Hub Natural Gas	3,951,213				
Light Sweet Crude Oil	1,175,282	768,838	584,178		
MICEX Index	6,405,236	4,979,524	6,980,201	5,180,920	4,652,963
MICEX Index (mini)	9,390,393	8,775,996	13,503,373	12,939,134	25,448,910
RTS Index	156,014,870	87,273,759	118,174,805	134,467,991	204,593,580
RTS Standard Index	129	63	35	289	109
Russian Market Volatility	7,023	875	4,906	41,370	34,792
All Futures on Individual Equities	197,864,826	205,933,694	235,942,818	201,803,970	253,211,955
10 Year Federal Bond issued by Russian Federation	70,637	118,873	89,245	368,746	600,683
15 Year Federal Bond issued by Russian Federation	77,360	130,844	47,784	548,376	647,605
2-year Russian Federation Government Bond Futures	22,697	27,318	16,351	145,552	348,263
4-year Russian Federation Government Bond Futures	19,967	21,759	20,059	166,373	626,123
6-year Russian Federation Government Bond Futures	43,606	52,439	12,514	207,377	365,174
Ruble Overnight Index Average (RUONIA)	33,546	104,215	107,804	23,462	2,470
Russian Secured Funding Averge Rate (RUSFAR)	10,035	3,869			
Russian Secured Funding Averge Rate (RUSFAR) (USD)	1,089				
Aluminum	587	1			
Copper	3,775	840	449	939	31,718
Nickel	207	28			

Moscow Interbank Currency Exchange (MICEX), Russia (continued)

	2020	2019	2018	2017	2016
Zinc	102	149	6		
Gold	32,846,380	19,577,553	14,526,824	23,562,649	22,656,213
Palladium	464,871	277,634	54,499	115,908	63,397
Platinum	1,110,323	714,563	240,011	180,024	191,923
Refined Silver	67,041,637	16,981,009	13,838,317	9,155,351	3,823,058
Total Options	**2,066,964,380**	**1,402,715,767**	**1,427,803,286**	**1,500,899,284**	**1,878,174,500**
EUR/RUB	163,537	66,679	207,263	248,956	464,423
EUR/USD	114,318	14,012	13,819	7,785	22,551
GBP/USD	30	1,040	802	2,760	
USD/JPY	401	551	292	6,664	
USD/RUB	22,200,335	22,488,457	32,220,569	36,555,667	30,184,048
Brent Crude Oil	10,077,081	8,709,740	7,660,935	6,652,353	4,513,050
Light Sweet Crude Oil	482	194	69,067		
MICEX Index (mini)	4,395	11,354	9,842	50,445	2,293,439
MICEX Index	2,912	294	704	935	10,185
RTS Index	18,515,579	18,532,558	31,112,682	38,010,457	28,281,676
All Options on Individual Equities	1,770,677	2,393,960	1,230,677	2,154,952	6,146,989
Gold	94,355	29,320	26,099	26,579	35,276
Platinum	183	13	34	1	25
Refined Silver	30,368	16,512	19,186	16,127	16,643
Total Options	**52,974,653**	**52,328,165**	**72,571,971**	**83,733,681**	**71,970,718**

Nasdaq Exchanges Nordic Markets

	2020	2019	2018	2017	2016
OMX (Index)	43,195,648	39,948,069	42,008,960	38,820,112	42,405,041
OMX (Index) Mini	79,961				
All Futures on Individual Equities	1,541,341	2,550,850	2,794,528	3,431,710	3,550,905
10 Year Swedish Government Bond Future (SGB10H)	690,750	626,839	752,054	879,493	809,944
2 Year Nordea Hypotek Bond Future (NDH2YH)	34,443	64,077	53,476	23,657	72,335
2 Year Spintab Bond Future (SWH2YH)	139,142	100,011	87,581	86,203	168,943
2 Year Stadshypotek Bond Future (STH2YH)	282,349	268,828	189,666	212,128	208,338
2 Year Swedish Government Bond Future (SGB2YH)	999,097	834,882	922,069	826,965	597,913
5 Year Nordea Hypotek Bond Future (NDH5YH)	117,364	68,014	84,571	104,924	128,571
5 Year Spintab Bond Future (SWH5YH)	207,999	186,334	145,909	108,313	102,037
5 Year Stadshypotek Bond Future (STH5YH)	424,419	391,925	419,471	374,548	357,908
5 Year Swedish Government Bond Future (SGB5YH)	719,557	994,442	1,125,232	1,133,559	938,531
Danish Mortgage Bond Futures (3MBF)	1,450	4,450	18,850	17,100	9,600
Danish Mortgage Bond Futures (3YMBF)	2,900	5,950	13,400	9,920	15,500
NIBOR-FRA	14,000	173,000	240,000	626,000	792,000
Policy Rate (RIBA)	2,357,000	2,540,006	2,074,019	2,691,300	1,718,140
STIBOR-FRA	1,264,000	3,644,700	9,226,260	7,689,266	5,467,864
Total Futures	**52,071,420**	**52,403,177**	**60,164,146**	**57,435,006**	**57,846,969**
OMX Index Options	7,123,973	7,057,965	6,499,806	6,108,213	8,260,077
All Options on Individual Equities	16,869,595	19,186,998	19,691,435	22,592,140	24,950,383
STIBOR-FRA	470,000	604,500	917,500	285,000	20,000
Total Options	**24,463,568**	**26,849,463**	**27,108,741**	**28,985,353**	**33,230,460**

National Stock Exchange of India

	2020	2019	2018	2017	2016
Degummed Soy Oil	13,462				
EUR/Indian Rupee	43,707,847	19,075,483	23,507,247	17,924,752	14,993,193
EUR/US Dollar	800,463	1,636,658	5,725,331		
GBP/Indian Rupee	70,931,798	33,793,268	24,384,480	20,380,086	19,809,931
GBP/US Dollar	1,035,424	1,606,684	3,701,986		
JPY/Indian Rupee	15,012,590	10,137,877	9,331,971	7,472,207	10,465,101
US Dollar/Indian Rupee	605,182,124	551,281,470	537,847,778	312,477,915	351,162,981
US Dollar/JPY	13,980	38,142	220,697		
Brent Crude Oil	2,387	4,108			
Bank Nifty Index	76,245,807	42,384,424	27,055,983	19,362,201	26,097,774
CNX IT Index	7,408	59,075	109,503	80,572	58,977
CNX Nifty Index	54,753,338	40,741,390	41,545,725	34,779,564	48,552,800
All Futures on Individual Equities	256,437,505	254,383,777	252,190,234	201,923,887	172,712,809
Government of India Security	8,107,442	16,359,218			
Gold	36	11,123			
Gold Mini	18,483	73,761			
Total Futures	**1,132,270,094**	**971,671,954**	**925,724,006**	**614,511,019**	**644,017,804**
EUR/Indian Rupee	100,140	14,154	347,340		
EUR/US Dollar	10	16	3,331		
GBP/Indian Rupee	500,038	35,609	148,172		
GBP/US Dollar	1,518	584	418		
JPY/Indian Rupee	3,712	6,031	57,975		
US Dollar/Indian Rupee	776,695,344	648,945,670	484,853,286	371,600,526	351,632,420
Bank Nifty Index	4,295,092,542	2,994,080,115	1,587,426,222	800,401,601	319,723,806
CNX IT Index	7	1,677	35	66	136
CNX Nifty Index	2,372,865,911	1,161,043,042	622,118,790	562,315,794	715,273,610

National Stock Exchange of India (continued)

	2020	2019	2018	2017	2016
All Options on Individual Equities	272,134,027	201,388,733	169,407,341	116,497,267	88,815,026
Government of India Security	453,937	32,192			
Gold Mini	356,543				
Total Options	**7,718,203,729**	**5,005,547,823**	**2,864,366,136**	**1,850,822,486**	**1,475,445,016**

Osaka Exchange, Japan

	2020	2019	2018	2017	2016
Corn	18,628				
Red Beans	19				
Rubber (TSR20)	80				
Rubber	574,420				
Soybean	2				
FTSE China Index 50	62	3	4		
JPX-Nikkei Index 400 Futures	5,788,162	6,698,433	8,152,838	7,669,469	7,370,575
Mini-TOPIX Futures	8,223,304	4,677,733	4,480,852	3,624,850	2,955,098
Nikkei 225	27,171,013	22,527,189	26,193,823	23,054,495	26,765,460
Nikkei 225 Dividend Index	22,029	20,874	2,926	6,682	19,305
Nikkei 225 Mini	321,718,519	237,577,721	273,327,463	219,518,050	233,940,373
Nikkei VI Futures	32,056	30,503	10,020	17,006	78,088
OSE DJIA	388,464	277,986	234,893	71,194	63,800
TAIEX Index	1,004,774	796,304	338,669	306,302	204
TOPIX	791	242	224	1	22,560,705
TOPIX Banks Index	27,702,276	26,345,546	26,224,277	24,392,610	33,001
TOPIX Core30	355,926	429,600	401,396	172,701	5,440
TSE Mothers Index	1,080	2,097	3,302	2,830	54,171
10 Year Japan Government Bond	1,653,567	511,923	687,027	254,100	7,383,298
Mini 10 Year Japan Government Bond	7,148,071	9,611,513	10,304,257	8,190,265	5,742
SL-JGB 20 Year Japan Government Bond	1,648	1,957	3,434	1,602	843
Gold (Daily)	589,757				
Gold	3,588,090				
Gold Mini	950,287				
Palladium	2,129				
Platinum (Rolling Spot)	39,589				
Platinum	762,302				
Platinum Mini	97,249				
Silver	30,635				
Total Futures	**407,864,929**	**309,509,663**	**350,366,699**	**287,283,166**	**301,490,246**
Nikkei 225	28,666,550	29,763,572	35,502,311	32,594,768	33,763,728
Nikkei 225 Weekly	634,770	697,579	601,555	493,801	256,350
TOPIX Index	306,978	238,319	179,262	259,384	145,716
All Options on Individual Equities (Combined)	1,347,612	1,226,146	869,163	915,787	922,341
10 Year Japan Government Bond	323,210	631,807	783,545	861,714	958,472
Total Options	**31,279,120**	**32,568,423**	**37,981,446**	**35,125,454**	**36,047,087**

Shanghai Metal Exchange, China

	2020	2019	2018	2017	2016
Rubber	100,942,773	53,850,389	61,845,475	89,341,052	97,371,256
Woodpulp	34,362,850	36,345,367	8,975,314		
Bitumen	204,756,838	102,908,784	69,802,079	97,440,530	186,814,247
Fuel Oil	477,193,406	176,719,415	39,268,835	1,432	2,922
Aluminum	52,864,722	32,757,569	46,618,361	65,423,439	44,391,785
Copper	57,164,215	36,520,132	51,247,050	54,100,135	72,394,915
Hot Rolled Coil	82,346,338	70,411,675	86,816,386	103,131,555	43,281,751
Lead	11,211,637	7,710,171	10,203,832	12,509,166	4,561,200
Nickel	179,764,100	160,444,120	114,818,738	74,154,526	100,249,941
Stainless Steel	10,831,251	590,753			
Steel Rebar	366,043,408	465,171,782	530,976,610	702,019,499	934,148,409
Tin	13,314,333	3,246,074	2,741,587	2,083,571	3,168,348
Wire Rod	4,031	174,118	157,334	98	61
Zinc	60,330,404	71,066,468	92,348,782	91,449,266	73,065,922
Gold	52,405,455	46,208,567	16,123,891	19,478,090	34,759,523
Silver	357,232,087	142,823,743	42,250,568	53,111,169	86,501,561
Total Futures	**2,060,767,848**	**1,406,949,127**	**1,174,194,842**	**1,364,243,528**	**1,680,711,841**
Rubber	2,533,597	822,063			
Aluminium	846,355				
Copper	4,602,626	4,197,483	1,193,828		
Zinc	1,183,921				
Gold	2,347,373	40,926			
Total Options	**11,513,872**	5,060,472	1,193,828		

Singapore Exchange (SGX), Singapore

	2020	2019	2018	2017	2016
SICOM RSS3 Rubber	12,563	27,211	62,285	68,422	64,034
SICOM TSR20 Rubber	1,841,763	1,847,650	1,749,307	1,407,000	1,349,662
AUD/JPY	174	4	19	10	135
AUD/USD	58	44	3	14	838
CNY/USD	657	1,087	3,481	5,985	6,729
EUR/CNH	7,299	10,702	7,220	2,862	450
INR/USD	14,675,901	13,930,092	12,814,105	7,955,136	5,666,369
KRW/USD	360,801	428,903	139,698	64,011	32,698
KRW/USD (Full Size)	16,779				
SGD/CNH	759	290	310	78	65
TWD/USD	13,695	4,407	970	25	5
TWD/USD (Full-Sized)	2,231				
USD/CNH	10,034,485	9,069,418	5,338,643	1,902,105	514,057
USD/CNH FlexC	5,524	969			
USD/INR	41,541				
USD/JPY (Standard)	4	4	3	4,151	1,162
USD/SGD	190,023	60,530	63,997	61,757	62,895
USD/SGD (Full Size)	116,227				
USD/SGD FlexC (Full Size)	20				
Coking Coal	148,336	96,651	117,895	144,701	8,450
Electricity (Monthly)	8,732	10,590	2,424	207	
Electricity Futures	20,946	23,174	7,043	2,537	1,889
Energy Futures	6,186	6,537	4,709	8,035	12,119
Petrochemicals Futures	21,399	10,890	9,927	8,720	3,050
Thermal Coal	465,500	139,700	48,700		
CNX Nifty Banks Index Futures	120,712	4,028	219,604	726,690	120,166
CNX Nifty Index	25,649,420	21,037,813	21,378,076	21,186,591	21,273,910
FTSE Asia ex Japan NTR (USD) Index	59,143				
FTSE China A50 Index	96,578,641	97,770,859	88,028,881	67,407,030	70,107,740
FTSE China H50 Index	3,604				
FTSE Emerging Market Asia Index	2				
FTSE EPRA Nareit Asia ex Japan Index	472				
FTSE Indonesia Index	67,071				
FTSE Malaysia NTR (USD) Index	7,980				
FTSE Taiwan Index	6,068,356				
FTSE Thailand NTR (USD) Index	175,605				
iEdge S-REIT Leaders Index	634				
Mini Nikkei 225	180	1,016	620,795	244,305	3,642
MSCI Australia NTR Index	115,123	377,727	149,502		
MSCI China Index Futures	2	1,803	12,638	39,165	39,536
MSCI China NTR Index	399,410	977,754	368,978	2,391	
MSCI Emerging Markets Asia NTR Index	289,081	938,234	510,842	16,448	
MSCI Emerging Markets Index	1,789	693	3,070	46	
MSCI Emerging Markets NTR Index	772	612	411		
MSCI Hong Kong NTR Index	9,259	28,620			
MSCI India NTR Index	689,626	999,503	675,490	77,785	
MSCI Indonesia Index	106,765	184,051	317,921	249,296	289,231
MSCI Indonesia NTR Index	210,055	194,523	72,515	6,142	
MSCI Japan NTR Index	313,528	718,676	610,839		
MSCI Malaysia NTR Index	101,573	128,554	34,366		
MSCI New Zealand NTR Index	17				
MSCI Philippines NTR Index	36,626	39,169	8,345		
MSCI Singapore Index Futures	12,102,273	10,685,237	10,232,425	10,012,785	7,664,389
MSCI Singapore NTR Index (USD)	1,657	4,693			
MSCI Taiwan Index	17,214,710	21,613,830	20,952,086	19,314,868	18,146,726
MSCI Taiwan NTR Index	650,231	1,152,654	697,469	31,521	
MSCI Thailand NTR Index	186,196	177,336	37,894		
MSCI Vietnam NTR Index	40	23			
Nikkei 225	24,089,539	21,816,078	23,813,108	21,724,646	24,335,028
Nikkei 225 Total Return Index	1,300				
Nikkei Stock Average Dividend Point Index	74,067	88,035	56,270	90,946	102,048
Straits Times Index	134	54	322	1,093	734
USD Nikkei 225	3,867	58	175	1,016	3,318
All Futures on Individual Equities	2,583,072	1,882,585	390,005		
All Futures on Individual Equities (Singapore)	78,285				
Mini Japanese Government Bond	404,421	426,829	521,185	548,951	607,675
Iron Ore 62%	16,719,723	14,582,987	10,473,351	12,804,720	11,787,611
Iron Ore 65%	423,666	205,370	19,070		
Iron Ore Lump Premium Futures	180,197	292,559	202,905	133,575	33,740
Forward Freight Agreement	958,698	801,913	702,220	445,943	412,631
Total Futures	**234,669,125**	**223,904,728**	**203,261,393**	**166,824,929**	**162,855,245**
SICOM TSR20 Rubber	1,944	842			
USD_CNH FX	3,802	165	75	284	20
MSCI Singapore Index	150	3,400	426,551	293,407	940
Nikkei 225 Index	318,711	406,037	51,955	19,543	5,967,910

Singapore Exchange (SGX), Singapore

	2020	2019	2018	2017	2016
SGX S&P CNX Nifty Index	18,500	40,470	11,059,024	8,218,454	189,795
Coking Coal	8,089,583	10,602,232	4,900	4,400	
Iron Ore 62% (Futures)	3,909,271	4,771,060	2,441,426	2,958,407	3,147,236
Iron Ore 62% (Swaps)	20				
OTC Forward Freight Agreements on Futures	138,345	138,958	141,490	47,075	135,904
Total Options	**12,480,326**	**15,963,164**	**14,126,121**	**11,550,021**	**9,566,838**

Taiwan Futures Exchange, Taiwan

	2020	2019	2018	2017	2016
AUD/USD FX (XAF)	43,343	106,597	49,032		
EUR/USD FX (XEF)	41,737	128,534	77,987	94,290	33,214
GBP/USD FX (XBF)	72,976	177,547	75,468		
USD/CHN FX (RHF)	41,740	75,333	66,743	67,793	99,204
USD/CNT FX (RTF)	172,431	289,375	283,451	269,020	523,716
USD/JPY FX (XJF)	41,738	184,376	71,851	102,815	36,309
Brent Crude Oil (BRF)	37,449	28,562	27,118		
DJIA Index (UDF)	2,603,974	2,209,699	1,466,111	403,078	
ETF Futures	915,305	1,064,343	1,520,673	1,224,271	1,748,371
FTSE 100 Index (F1F)	7,254				
FTSE4Good TIP Taiwan ESG Index (E4F)	98,518				
GreTai Securities Weighted Stock Index (GTF)	16,554	15,431	7,881	8,117	3,320
Mini Taiex Futures (MTX)	60,051,670	29,744,412	37,268,930	21,552,246	23,864,953
Nasdaq 100 Index (UNF)	698,868	75,851			
S&P 500 (SPF)	256,005	233,038	125,444	38,658	
Taiex (TX)	46,324,077	34,226,802	46,946,307	34,014,500	34,534,902
Taiwan 50 Futures (T5F)	32,056	34,574	12,052	4,112	233
Taiwan Stock Exch NonFin/NonElcc SubIndx (XIF)	71,679	43,917	96,311	78,376	110,869
Taiwan Stock Exchange Electronic Sector Index Futures	868,644	840,977	992,544	792,372	889,791
Taiwan Stock Exchange Finance Sector Index Futures	415,313	374,106	539,434	673,890	862,330
TIP Taiwan BIO Index (BTF)	56,602				
TOPIX Futures (TJF)	70,037	165,075	88,285	176,841	316,578
TPEx 200 Index (G2F)	153,747	41,522			
All Futures on Individual Equities	25,837,101	19,788,425	22,812,494	18,763,068	9,954,514
Gold Futures (GDF)	62,224	26,465	20,396	12,933	10,131
NT Dollar Gold (TGF)	160,835	145,837	110,513	75,442	101,744
Total Futures	**139,151,877**	**90,042,348**	**112,731,243**	**78,408,549**	**73,102,459**
USD/CNH FX (RHO)	2,743	13,405	16,193	15,128	9,822
USD/CNT FX (RTO)	22,980	108,539	118,833	123,562	140,488
ETF Options (ETC)	136,200	156,358	153,669	165,967	330,369
Taiex (TXO)	201,733,160	170,012,273	194,438,947	186,410,859	167,342,279
Taiwan Stock Exchange Electronic Sector Index Options	85,870	125,808	229,985	180,453	155,433
Taiwan Stock Exchange Finance Sector Index Options	93,262	56,501	139,980	145,482	234,487
All Options on Individual Equities	124,732	206,166	209,341	215,425	289,101
NTD-denominated Gold (TGO)	42,522	44,076	45,385	40,075	73,749
Total Options	**202,241,469**	**170,723,134**	**195,352,333**	**187,297,120**	**168,576,097**

Tel-Aviv Stock Exchange (TASE), Israel

	2020	2019	2018	2017	2016
TA-25 Index	6	0	3,659	12,457	18,644
Total Futures	**6**	**0**	**3,659**	**12,457**	**22,104**
Shekel-Dollar Rate	13,199,641	10,512,887	13,771,524	13,120,123	12,708,033
Shekel-Euro Rate Options	439,272	573,144	588,438	394,679	428,333
TA-Banks Index	40,405	40,028	70,240	107,668	123,258
TA-100 index	177,723	135,460	125,492	97,451	80,109
TA-25 Index	27,799,863	23,571,396	32,902,984	32,183,095	37,745,708
All Options on Individual Equities	749,501	727,657	644,761	725,658	990,111
Total Options	**42,406,405**	**35,560,572**	**48,103,439**	**46,628,674**	**52,075,552**

Thailand Futures Exchange, Thailand

	2020	2019	2018	2017	2016
Japanese Rubber Futures	344				
Rubber	17,253	54,565	34,482	10,613	250
US Dollar	2,803,128	673,060	685,847	346,890	204,470
SET50	57,465,829	42,450,175	42,544,040	26,321,073	32,192,984
All Futures on Individual Equities	47,386,674	52,098,173	55,332,444	47,480,762	33,826,624
10 Baht Gold	2,605,404	3,444,577	4,102,613	3,500,669	2,721,773
50 Baht Gold	91,272	116,409	165,400	191,116	182,177
Gold (100 Grams)	3,413	33,157	106,443	57,770	
Gold Online	8,108,010	3,974,556	88,411		
Silvcer Online	13,621				
Total Futures	**118,494,948**	**102,844,672**	**103,059,680**	**77,908,893**	**69,147,354**
SET 50	1,698,625	1,677,323	1,362,520	1,081,681	428,810
Total Options	**1,698,625**	**1,677,323**	**1,362,520**	**1,081,681**	**428,810**

Tokyo Commodity Exchange (TOCOM), Japan

	2020	2019	2018	2017	2016
Corn	98,431	170,754	266,411	385,035	469,557
Corn	27,834	98,431	170,754	266,411	385,035
Red Beans	55	3,737	11,154	14,313	19,594
Rubber	519,369	1,198,789	1,681,524	2,136,254	2,366,213
Rubber (TSR20)	1,472	384,275	126,785		
Chukyo Gasoline	8,890	7,463	11,300	12,281	10,159
Chukyo Kerosene	9,186	3,670	5,285	7,779	5,744
Crude Oil	5,973,086	2,679,766	4,537,185	5,286,870	5,963,788
East Area Baseload Electricity	7,625	518			
East Area Peakload Electricity	1,518	80			
Gasoline	102,818	261,050	730,665	647,470	992,868
Gasoline (Barge Delivered)	33	2,461	3,999	4,945	
Kerosene	41,180	94,779	186,753	228,833	237,165
Kerosene (Barge Delivered)	4	2,488	3,958	4,897	
West Area Baseload Electricity	1,480	90			
West Area Peakload Electricity	632	36			
Gold	5,006,284	8,430,249	8,090,879	6,397,872	8,541,329
Gold (Daily Futures)	970,328	1,438,996	2,834,674	3,545,698	3,830,446
Gold Mini	716,062	802,260	787,036	752,050	1,224,290
Gold Physical Transaction	65	282	281	304	130
Palladium	20,725	49,063	37,731	32,745	31,621
Platinum	1,427,046	3,140,555	2,811,442	2,755,776	2,890,485
Platinum (Rolling Spot)	96,174	168,139	1,384,105	1,818,007	
Platinum Mini	155,900	185,073	141,473	157,623	233,847
Silver	17,410	22,214	19,918	22,426	61,136
Total Futures	**15,105,176**	**18,985,235**	**23,597,767**	**24,157,345**	**26,917,289**

Tokyo International Financial Futures Exchange (TIFFE), Japan

	2020	2019	2018	2017	2016
Australian Dollar/Japanese Yen	3,314,040	2,431,935	2,872,116	2,013,196	5,330,221
Australian Dollar/Japanese Yen (Large)	2,457	3,038	2,744	5,682	59,938
Australian Dollar/US Dollar	381,908	145,046	224,403	355,991	486,770
British Pound/Australian Dollar	99,897	63,514	90,171	110,176	202,394
British Pound/Japanese Yen	3,035,693	2,639,242	2,477,581	2,135,877	5,023,899
British Pound/Japanese Yen (Large)	1,153	3,705	2,550	8,301	19,839
British Pound/Swiss Franc	36,126	27,002	23,341	29,228	33,290
British Pound/US Dollar	726,209	443,803	470,655	658,807	1,078,624
Canadian Dollar/Japanese Yen	193,305	146,247	188,629	244,116	351,540
Euro/Australian Dollar	141,284	98,584	131,382	114,358	305,297
Euro/British Pound	65,852	57,841	71,368	75,466	241,636
Euro/Japanese Yen	1,513,554	1,111,614	1,787,220	1,700,235	2,365,744
Euro/Japanese Yen (Large)	951	2,699	9,190	6,335	18,816
Euro/Swiss Franc	17,806	15,434	21,565	45,366	28,369
Euro/US Dollar	770,598	495,985	1,017,450	1,213,754	2,244,455
Euro/US Dollar (Large)	704	1,296	39,347	3,527	5,103
Hong Kong Dollar/Japanese Yen	40,701	20,727	26,778	47,349	93,112
Mexican Peso/Japanese Yen	4,322,725	2,063,506	1,726,944	136,401	
New Zealand Dollar/Japanese Yen	878,651	909,964	1,081,621	1,057,673	2,026,071
New Zealand Dollar/US Dollar	89,268	75,249	92,851	142,729	213,060
Norway Krone/Japanese Yen	106,233	37,761	36,510	77,431	46,274
Polish Zloty/Japanese Yen	67,241	101,048	139,930	261,339	292,385
South African Rand/Japanese Yen	3,494,719	2,998,325	4,475,626	4,156,809	3,859,663
Sweden Krona/Japanese Yen	51,842	33,373	22,858	58,552	18,396
Swiss Franc/Japanese Yen	302,455	176,093	200,746	163,086	285,508
Turkish Lira /Japanese Yen	3,626,738	5,379,481	6,109,747	3,529,833	3,679,657
US Dollar/Japanese Yen	7,181,607	5,352,811	8,363,218	10,478,227	14,992,697
US Dollar/Canadian Dollar	73,379	39,434	44,536	86,180	138,148
US Dollar/Japanese Yen (Large)	14,634	31,274	118,431	32,827	56,820
US Dollar/Swiss Franc	49,721	34,505	40,733	46,742	95,729
DAX Margin	122,657	115,109	79,616	155,430	92,311
DAX Margin (¥100)	5,353				
DJIA Margin	5,683,235	2,202,598	1,055,650	1,874,728	601,241
DJIA Margin (¥10)	1,789,796				
FTSE 100 Margin	115,765	89,972	97,404	185,022	89,560
FTSE 100 Margin (¥100)	10,172				
Nikkei 225 Margin	10,701,148	5,254,459	4,266,773	5,722,311	5,203,500
Nikkei 225 Margin (¥100)	395,034				
3 Month Euroyen	263,657	855,250	1,423,666	1,545,861	2,506,430
Total Futures	**49,688,268**	**33,457,924**	**38,833,350**	**38,478,945**	**52,086,497**
Gold	12,610	32,146			
Total Options	**12,610**	**32,146**			

Warsaw Stock Exchange, Poland

	2020	2019	2018	2017	2016
CHFPLN	58,339	59,367	51,837	50,816	76,536
EURPLN	418,192	204,356	237,052	112,502	234,512
GBPPLN	36,121	47,969	28,666	34,916	3,392
USDPLN	1,930,020	1,021,824	1,726,908	878,169	944,883
WIG.GAMES Index	3,545	289			
WIG.MS-BAS Index	873	129			
WIG.MS-FIN Index	1,003	131			
WIG.MS-PET Index	241	55			
WIG20 Index	6,126,743	3,877,152	4,448,485	4,507,035	4,681,125
WIG40 Index	74,120	72,664	81,417	75,908	112,556
All Futures on Individual Equities	2,466,161	1,444,397	1,296,270	1,651,089	1,537,581
Total Futures	**11,115,358**	**6,728,343**	**7,870,705**	**7,318,662**	**7,597,905**
WIG20 Index	374,491	251,893	292,949	304,494	377,232
Total Options	**374,491**	**251,893**	**292,949**	**304,494**	**377,232**

Zhengzhou Commodity Exchange (ZCE), China

	2020	2019	2018	2017	2016
Apple (AP)	63,009,295	37,461,668	99,956,445	793,933	
Chinese Jujube (CJ)	6,526,230	27,734,015			
Common Wheat (PM)	757	74	301	82	173
Cotton No. 1 (CF)	108,338,363	63,971,129	58,533,251	26,068,232	80,530,129
Cotton Yarn (CY)	2,400,716	1,699,201	1,533,644	124,156	
Early Rice (RI)	1,952	2,926	38,199	1,037	2,000
Japonica Rice (JR)	11,806	2,730	12,608	261	342
Late Rice (LR)	4,464	18,792	537,759	202	334
Rapeseed (RS)	2,378	63,645	1,354	1,908	18,879
Rapeseed Meal (RM)	159,893,801	138,085,360	104,361,264	79,736,545	246,267,758
Rapeseed Oil (OI)	105,447,334	37,786,701	35,083,678	25,994,757	27,312,246
Strong Gluten Wheat (WH)	32,096	12,405	107,031	377,494	500,078
White Sugar (SR)	124,551,207	112,515,650	64,004,805	61,073,198	117,293,884
Thermal Coal (ZC)	61,174,572	27,495,364	48,874,599	30,708,183	50,299,868
Ferrosilicon	31,344,180	9,316,202	21,563,209	16,278,210	659,485
Silicon Manganese	45,290,175	11,171,963	18,856,010	24,921,207	1,364,525
Flat Glass (FG)	185,258,846	30,916,599	25,143,634	41,091,381	67,648,313
Methanol (MA)	344,876,192	265,105,646	163,897,244	137,007,280	136,739,016
Polyester Staple Fiber (PF)	16,413,948				
PTA (TA)	322,078,663	312,483,830	170,871,552	140,399,689	172,659,870
Soda Ash (SA)	68,406,084	1,564,832			
Urea (UR)	16,646,171	4,693,463			
Total Futures	**1,661,709,230**	**1,082,102,195**	**813,376,587**	**584,577,755**	**901,297,047**
Cotton No. 1 (CF)	4,982,118	3,463,533			
Rapeseed Meal (RM)	3,383,491				
White Sugar (SR)	6,254,314	6,772,677	4,593,395	1,492,393	
Thermal Coal (ZC)	3,565,955				
Methanol (MA)	10,163,945	171,444			
PTA (TA)	11,788,268	193,731			
Total Options	**40,138,091**	10,601,385	4,593,395	1,492,393	

Total Worldwide Volume

	2020	2019	2018	2017	2016
Total Futures	**15,584,098,137**	**11,366,179,855**	**10,313,364,036**	**9,498,067,932**	**10,840,432,649**
Percent Change	**51.11%**	**19.67%**	**-4.86%**	**-1.95%**	**41.33%**
Total Options	**12,891,108,555**	**9,268,575,114**	**6,938,205,944**	**5,222,802,081**	**4,409,177,613**
Percent Change	**85.80%**	**77.46%**	**57.36%**	**-3.68%**	**-6.72%**
Total Futures and Options	**28,475,206,692**	**20,634,754,969**	**17,251,569,980**	**14,720,870,013**	**15,249,610,262**
Percent Change	**65.06%**	**40.17%**	**13.13%**	**-2.57%**	**23.01%**

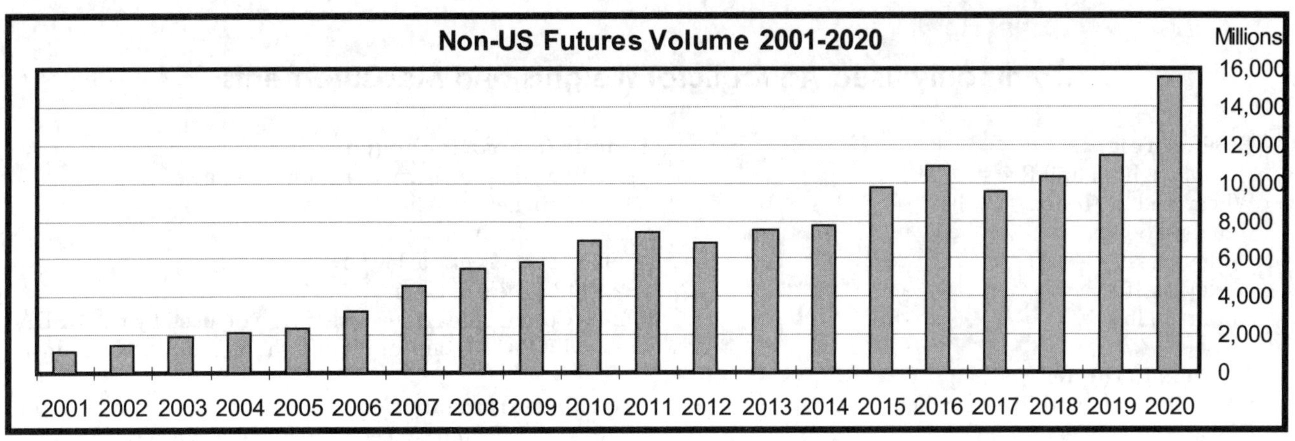
Non-US Futures Volume 2001-2020
Millions
16,000
14,000
12,000
10,000
8,000
6,000
4,000
2,000
0
2001 2002 2003 2004 2005 2006 2007 2008 2009 2010 2011 2012 2013 2014 2015 2016 2017 2018 2019 2020

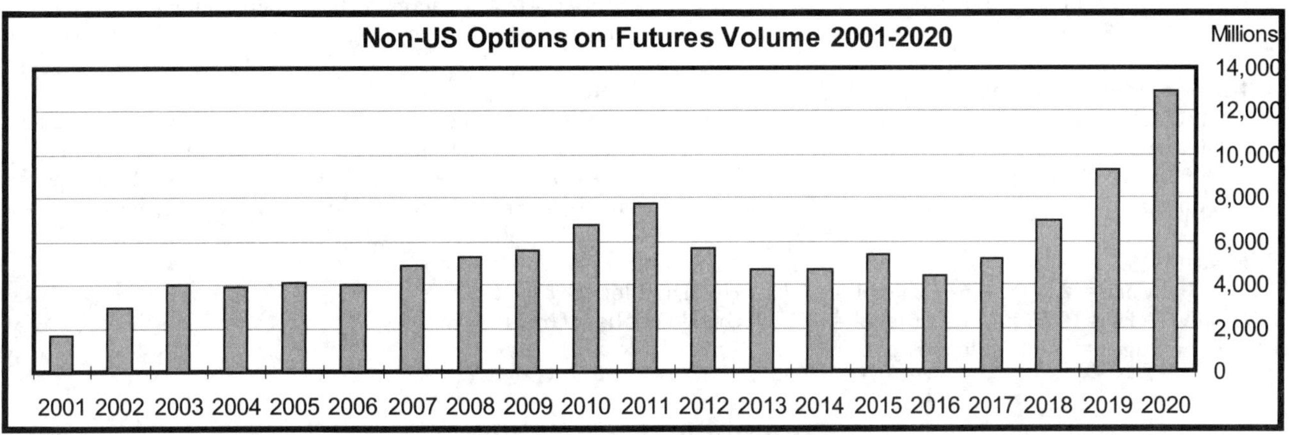
Non-US Options on Futures Volume 2001-2020
Millions
14,000
12,000
10,000
8,000
6,000
4,000
2,000
0
2001 2002 2003 2004 2005 2006 2007 2008 2009 2010 2011 2012 2013 2014 2015 2016 2017 2018 2019 2020

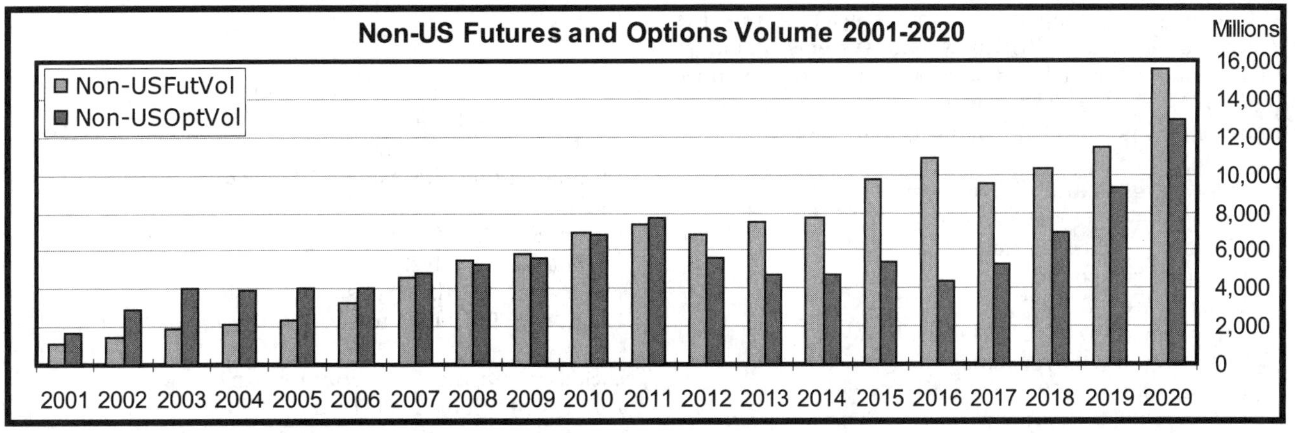
Non-US Futures and Options Volume 2001-2020
Non-USFutVol
Non-USOptVol
Millions
16,000
14,000
12,000
10,000
8,000
6,000
4,000
2,000
0
2001 2002 2003 2004 2005 2006 2007 2008 2009 2010 2011 2012 2013 2014 2015 2016 2017 2018 2019 2020

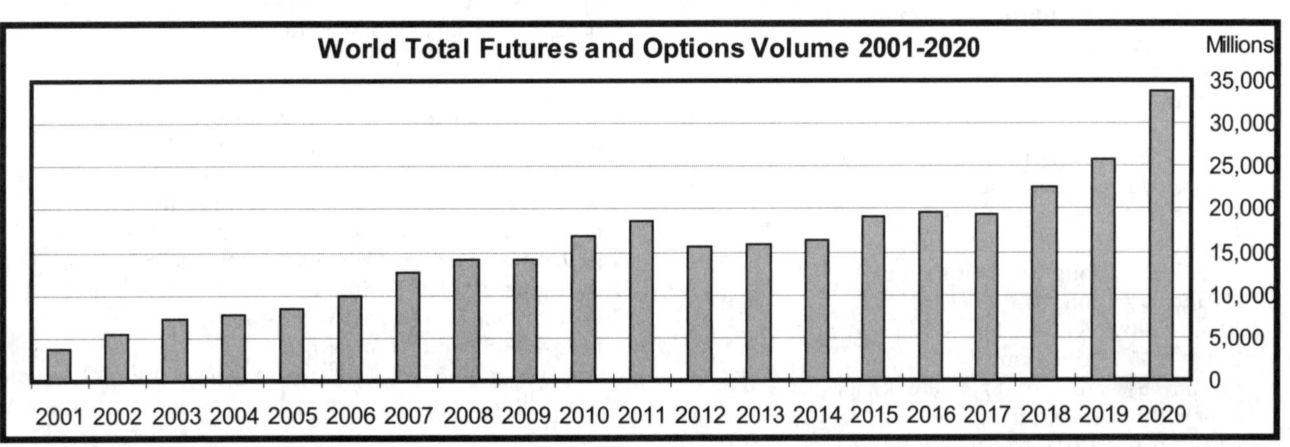
World Total Futures and Options Volume 2001-2020
Millions
35,000
30,000
25,000
20,000
15,000
10,000
5,000
0
2001 2002 2003 2004 2005 2006 2007 2008 2009 2010 2011 2012 2013 2014 2015 2016 2017 2018 2019 2020

Conversion Factors

Commonly Used Agricultural Weights and Measurements

Bushel Weights:
Corn, Sorghum and Rye = 56 lbs.
Wheat and Soybeans = 60 lbs.
Canola = 50 lbs.
Barley Grain = 48 lbs.
Barley Malt = 34 lbs.
Oats = 32 lbs.

Bushels to tonnes:
Corn, Sorghum and Rye = bushels x 0.0254
Wheat and Soybeans = bushels x 0.027216
Barley Grain = bushels x 0.021772
Oats = bushels x 0.014515

1 tonne (metric ton) equals:
2204.622 lbs.
1,000 kilograms
22.046 hundredweight
10 quintals

1 tonne (metric ton) equals:
39.3679 bushels of Corn, Sorghum or Rye
36.7437 bushels of Wheat or Soybeans
22.046 hundredweight
45.9296 bushels of Barley Grain
68.8944 bushels of Oats
4.5929 Cotton bales (the statistical bale used by the USDA and ICAC contains a net weight of 480 pounds of lint)

Area Measurements:
1 acre = 43,560 square feet = 0.040694 hectare
1 hectare = 2.4710 acres = 10,000 square meters
640 acres = 1 square mile = 259 hectares

Yields:
Rye, Corn: bushels per acre x 0.6277 = quintals per hectare
Wheat: bushels per acre x 0.6725 = quintals per hectare
Barley Grain: bushels per acre x 0.538 = quintals per hectare
Oats: bushels per acre x 0.3587 = quintals per hectare

Ethanol
1 bushel Corn = 2.75 gallons Ethanol = 18 lbs Dried Distillers Grain
1 tonne Corn = 101.0 gallons Ethanol = 661 lbs Dried Distillers Grain
1 tonne Sugar = 149.3 gallons Ethanol

Commonly Used Weights

The troy, avoirdupois and apothecaries' grains are identical in U.S. and British weight systems, equal to 0.0648 gram in the metric system. One avoirdupois ounce equals 437.5 grains. The troy and apothecaries' ounces equal 480 grains, and their pounds contain 12 ounces.

Troy weights and conversions:
24 grains = 1 pennyweigh
20 pennyweights = 1 ounce
12 ounces = 1 pound
1 troy ounce = 31.103 grams
1 troy ounce = 0.0311033 kilogram
1 troy pound = 0.37224 kilogram
1 kilogram = 32.1507 troy ounces
1 tonne = 32,151 troy ounces

Avoirdupois weights and conversions:
27 11/32 grains = 1 dram
16 drams = 1 ounce
16 ounces = 1 lb.
1 lb. = 7,000 grains
14 lbs. = 1 stone (British)
100 lbs. = 1 hundredweight (U.S.)
112 lbs. = 8 stone = 1 hundredweight (British)
2,000 lbs. = 1 short ton (U.S. ton)
2,240 lbs. = 1 long ton (British ton)
160 stone = 1 long ton
20 hundredweight = 1 ton
1 lb. = 0.4536 kilogram
1 hundredweight (cwt.) = 45.359 kilograms
1 short ton = 907.18 kilograms
1 long ton = 1,016.05 kilograms

Metric weights and conversions:
1,000 grams = 1 kilogram
100 kilograms = 1 quintal
1 tonne = 1,000 kilograms = 10 quintals
1 kilogram = 2.204622 lbs.
1 quintal = 220.462 lbs.
1 tonne = 2204.6 lbs.
1 tonne = 1.102 short tons
1 tonne = 0.9842 long ton

U.S. dry volumes and conversions:
1 pint = 33.6 cubic inches = 0.5506 liter
2 pints = 1 quart = 1.1012 liters
8 quarts = 1 peck = 8.8098 liters
4 pecks = 1 bushel = 35.2391 liters
1 cubic foot = 28.3169 liters

U.S. liquid volumes and conversions:
1 ounce = 1.8047 cubic inches = 29.6 milliliters
1 cup = 8 ounces = 0.24 liter = 237 milliliters
1 pint = 16 ounces = 0.48 liter = 473 milliliters
1 quart = 2 pints = 0.946 liter = 946 milliliters
1 gallon = 4 quarts = 231 cubic inches = 3.785 liters
1 milliliter = 0.033815 fluid ounce
1 liter = 1.0567 quarts = 1,000 milliliters
1 liter = 33.815 fluid ounces
1 imperial gallon = 277.42 cubic inches = 1.2 U.S. gallons = 4.546 liters

Energy Conversion Factors

U.S. Crude OIl (average gravity)
1 U.S. barrel = 42 U.S. gallons
1 short ton = 6.65 barrels
1 tonne = 7.33 barrels

Barrels per tonne for various origins

Abu Dhabi	7.624
Algeria	7.661
Angola	7.206
Australia	7.775
Bahrain	7.335
Brunei	7.334
Canada	7.428
Dubai	7.295
Ecuador	7.580
Gabon	7.245
Indonesia	7.348
Iran	7.370
Iraq	7.453
Kuwait	7.261
Libya	7.615
Mexico	7.104
Neutral Zone	6.825
Nigeria	7.410
Norway	7.444
Oman	7.390
Qatar	7.573
Romania	7.453
Saudi Arabia	7.338
Trinidad	6.989
Tunisia	7.709
United Arab Emirates	7.522
United Kingdom	7.279
United States	7.418
Former Soviet Union	7.350
Venezuela	7.005
Zaire	7.206

Barrels per tonne of refined products:

aviation gasoline	8.90
motor gasoline	8.50
kerosene	7.75
jet fuel	8.00
distillate, including diesel	7.46
residual fuel oil	6.45
lubricating oil	7.00
grease	6.30
white spirits	8.50
paraffin oil	7.14
paraffin wax	7.87
petrolatum	7.87
asphalt and road oil	6.06
petroleum coke	5.50
bitumen	6.06
LPG	11.6

(continued above)

Approximate heat content of refined products:
(Million Btu per barrel, 1 British thermal unit is the amount of heat required to raise the temperature of 1 pound of water 1 degree F.)

Petroleum Product	Heat Content
asphalt	6.636
aviation gasoline	5.048
butane	4.326
distillate fuel oil	5.825
ethane	3.082
isobutane	3.974
jet fuel, kerosene	5.670
jet fuel, naptha	5.355
kerosene	5.670
lubricants	6.065
motor gasoline	5.253
natural gasoline	4.620
pentanes plus	4.620

Petrochemical feedstocks:

naptha less than 401*F	5.248
other oils equal to or greater than 401*F	5.825
still gas	6.000
petroleum coke	6.024
plant condensate	5.418
propane	3.836
residual fuel oil	6.287
special napthas	5.248
unfinished oils	5.825
unfractionated steam	5.418
waxes	5.537

Source: U.S. Department of Energy

Natural Gas Conversions

Although there are approximately 1,031 Btu in a cubic foot of gas, for most applications, the following conversions are sufficient:

Cubic Feet					MMBtu
1,000	(one thousand cubic feet)	=	1 Mcf	=	1
1,000,000	(one million cubic feet)	=	1 MMcf	=	1,000
10,000,000	(ten million cubic feet)	=	10 MMcf	=	10,000
1,000,000,000	(one billion cubic feet)	=	1 Bcf	=	1,000,000
1,000,000,000,000	(one trillion cubic feet)	=	1 Tcf	=	1,000,000,000

Acknowledgments

The editors wish to thank the following for source material:

Agricultural Marketing Service (AMS)
Agricultural Research Service (ARS)
American Bureau of Metal Statistics, Inc. (ABMS)
American Metal Market (AMM)
Bureau of the Census
Bureau of Economic Analysis (BEA)
Bureau of Labor Statistics (BLS)
Chicago Board of Trade (CBT)
Chicago Mercantile Exchange (CME / IMM / IOM)
Commodity Credit Corporation (CCC)
Commodity Futures Trading Commision (CFTC)
Economic Research Service (ERS)
Farm Service Agency (FSA)
Federal Reserve Bank of St. Louis
Food and Agriculture Organization of the United Nations (FAO)
Foreign Agricultural Service (FAS)
Futures Industry Association (FIA)
ICE Futures U.S, Canada, Europe (ICE)
International Cotton Advisory Committee (ICAC)
International Cocoa Organization (ICCO)
Minneapolis Grain Exchange (MGEX)
National Agricultural Statistics Service (NASS)
New York Mercantile Exchange (NYMEX)
Oil World
The Organisation for Economic Co-Operation and Development (OECD)
The Silver Institute
United Nations (UN)
United States Department of Agriculture (USDA)
Wall Street Journal (WSJ)

Aluminum

Aluminum (atomic symbol Al) is a silvery, lightweight metal that is the most abundant metallic element in the earth's crust. Aluminum was first isolated in 1825 by a Danish chemist, Hans Christian Oersted, using a chemical process involving a potassium amalgam. A German chemist, Friedrich Woehler, improved Oersted's process by using metallic potassium in 1827. He was the first to show aluminum's lightness. In France, Henri Sainte-Claire Deville isolated the metal by reducing aluminum chloride with sodium and established a large-scale experimental plant in 1854. He displayed pure aluminum at the Paris Exposition of 1855. In 1886, Charles Martin Hall in the U.S. and Paul L.T. Heroult in France simultaneously discovered the first practical method for producing aluminum through electrolytic reduction, which is still the primary method of aluminum production today.

By volume, aluminum weighs less than a third as much as steel. This high strength-to-weight ratio makes aluminum a good choice for the construction of aircraft, railroad cars, and automobiles. Aluminum is used in cooking utensils and the pistons of internal-combustion engines because of its high heat conductivity. Aluminum foil, siding, and storm windows make excellent insulators. Because it absorbs relatively few neutrons, aluminum is used in low-temperature nuclear reactors. Aluminum is also useful in boat hulls and various marine devices due to its resistance to corrosion in saltwater.

Futures and options on Primary Aluminum and Aluminum Alloy are traded on the London Metal Exchange (LME). Aluminum futures are traded on the Multi Commodity Exchange of India, and the Shanghai Futures Exchange (SHFE). The London Metals Exchange aluminum futures contracts are priced in terms of dollars.

Supply – World production of aluminum in 2020 rose by +3.2% yr/yr to a new record high of 65.2 million metric tons. The world's largest producers of aluminum in 2020 were China with 56.7% of world production, Russia with 5.5%, Canada with 4.8%, and Australia with 2.5%. U.S. production of primary aluminum through November of 2020 fell -6.6% yr/yr to 1.020 million metric tons.

Demand – U.S. consumption of aluminum in 2020 fell -41.9% yr/yr to 2.870 million metric tons, a 5-decade low.

Trade – U.S. exports in 2020 fell -2.4% yr/yr to 2.880 million metric tons, below the 2012 record high of 3.480 million metric tons. U.S. imports of aluminum in 2020 fell -35.8% yr/yr to 3.730 million metric tons. The U.S. was a net importer in 2020 and relied on imports for 13% of its consumption.

World Production of Primary Aluminum In Thousands of Metric Tons

Year	Australia	Brazil	Canada	China	France	Germany	Norway	Russia	Spain	United Kingdom	United States	Venezuela	World Total
2011	1,945	1,440	2,988	20,000	334	432	1,389	3,993	365	213	1,986	380	46,800
2012	1,860	1,436	2,781	23,500	349	410	1,145	4,024	230	60	2,070	208	49,300
2013	1,777	1,304	2,967	26,500	346	492	1,155	3,601	235	44	1,946	186	52,100
2014	1,704	962	2,858	28,300	360	531	1,250	3,300	350	42	1,710	138	54,100
2015	1,646	772	2,880	31,400	420	541	1,225	3,529	350	47	1,590	119	57,700
2016	1,635	793	3,209	31,873	425	547	1,220	3,561	350	48	818	147	58,600
2017	1,487	802	3,212	32,273	429	550	1,230	3,583	350	48	741	144	59,500
2018	1,576	659	2,924	35,802	380	540	1,300	3,627	350	48	891	80	63,600
2019[1]	1,570		2,850	35,000			1,400	3,640			1,100		63,200
2020[2]	1,600		3,100	37,000			1,400	3,600					65,200

[1] Preliminary. [2] Estimate. *Source: U.S. Geological Survey (USGS)*

Production of Primary Aluminum (Domestic and Foreign Ores) in the U.S. In Thousands of Metric Tons

Year	Jan.	Feb.	Mar.	Apr.	May	June	July	Aug.	Sept.	Oct.	Nov.	Dec.	U.S. Total
2011	152	140	162	162	170	167	171	172	169	175	171	177	1,986
2012	178	167	179	174	179	173	177	171	164	170	166	171	2,070
2013	171	155	172	167	171	165	168	163	157	154	149	154	1,946
2014	153	139	153	143	147	140	143	143	136	137	134	141	1,710
2015	142	130	143	138	142	133	134	135	128	128	121	113	1,587
2016	106	96	77	63	64	62	64	62	61	62	61	63	841
2017	62	56	63	60	64	61	63	63	60	63	61	64	741
2018	66	61	71	71	73	63	68	76	76	84	88	95	892
2019	95	87	93	92	94	91	92	90	87	91	89	91	1,092
2020[1]	92	88	95	92	96	89	82	80	72	75	74	77	1,012

[1] Preliminary. *Source: U.S. Geological Survey (USGS)*

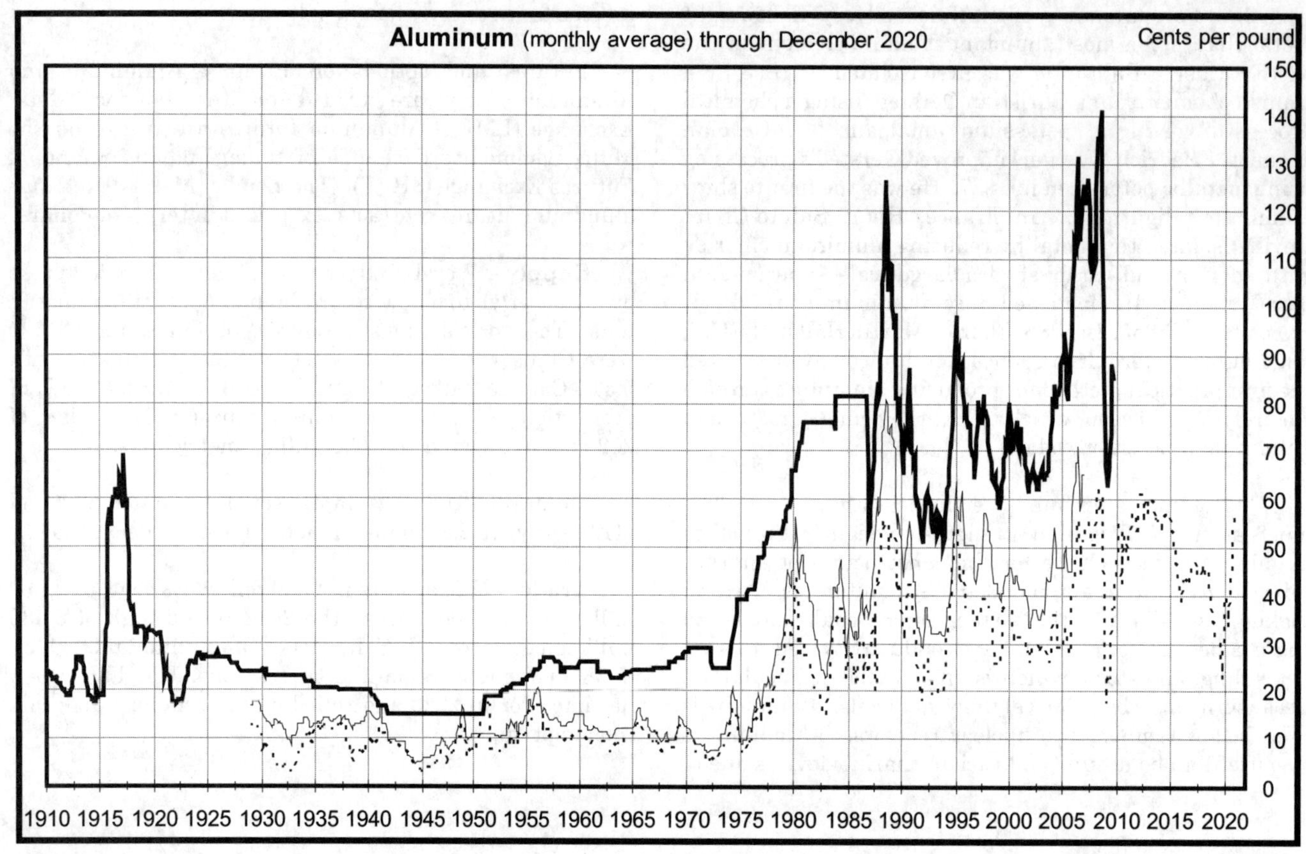

Salient Statistics of Aluminum in the United States In Thousands of Metric Tons

								Net Shipments[5] by Producers									
								Wrought Products				Castings					
	Net Import Reliance as a % of Apparent	Production		Primary Ship-	Recovery from Scrap		Apparent Con-	Plate, Sheet,	Rolled Structural	Ex- truded		Perma- nent				Total All Net Ship-
Year	Consump	Primary	Second ary	ments	Old	New	sumption	Foil	Shapes[3]	Shapes[4]	All	Mold	Die	Sand	All	ments
2011	3	1,986	3,110	8,520	1,440	1,670	3,570	4,450	703	1,530	6,683	475	949	147	1,580	8,263
2012	11	2,070	3,380	9,670	1,630	1,760	3,950	4,000	537	1,700	6,237	494	1,010	178	1,690	7,927
2013	21	1,946	3,410	9,920	1,630	1,790	4,520	4,770	915	2,130	7,815	589	1,110	127	1,860	9,675
2014	33	1,710	3,640	9,960	1,690	1,870	5,070	4,830	914	1,950	7,694	604	1,240	132	2,000	9,694
2015	41	1,587	3,380	10,400	1,560	2,000	5,300	5,020	887	2,100	8,007	563	1,330	214	2,120	10,127
2016	53	818	3,580	10,600	1,570	2,010	5,090	5,220	629	2,460	8,309	526	1,470	295	2,300	10,609
2017	59	741	3,630	11,000	1,590	2,050	5,680	5,330	626	2,490	8,446	505	1,550	284	2,350	10,796
2018	50	891	3,710	11,200	1,570	2,140	4,900	5,580	708	2,580	8,868	590	1,590	295	2,500	11,368
2019	47	1,093			1,540	1,920	4,940	5,850	777	2,720	9,347	600	1,600	300	2,530	11,877
2020[1]	13	1,000			1,500	1,700	2,870									

[1] Preliminary. [2] To domestic industry. [3] Also rod, bar & wire. [4] Also rod, bar, tube, blooms & tubing. [5] Consists of total shipments less shipments to other mills for further fabrication. *Source: U.S. Geological Survey (USGS)*

Supply and Distribution of Aluminum in the United States In Thousands of Metric Tons

						Inventories - December 31 -								Inventories - December 31 -	
	Apparent Con-	Production							Apparent Con-	Production					
Year	sumption	Primary	From Old Scrap	Imports	Exports	Private	Govern- ment[3]	Year	sumption	Primary	From Old Scrap	Imports	Exports	Private	Govern- ment[3]
2009	3,320	1,727	1,260	3,680	2,710	937	----	2015	5,300	1,587	1,560	5,081	3,010	1,350	----
2010	3,460	1,726	1,250	3,610	3,040	1,010	----	2016	5,090	818	1,570	6,019	2,820	1,400	----
2011	3,570	1,986	1,440	3,710	3,420	1,060	----	2017	5,680	741	1,590	6,920	2,900	1,470	----
2012	3,950	2,070	1,630	4,349	3,480	1,140	----	2018	4,900	891	1,570	5,945	3,070	1,570	----
2013	4,520	1,946	1,630	4,725	3,390	1,130	----	2019[1]	4,940	1,093	1,540	5,806	2,950	1,600	----
2014	5,070	1,710	1,690	4,849	3,240	1,280	----	2020[2]	2,870	1,000	1,500	3,730	2,880	1,400	----

[1] Preliminary. [2] Estimate. [3] National Defense Stockpile. *Source: U.S. Geological Survey (USGS)*

Aluminum Products Distribution of End-Use Shipments in the United States In Thousands of Metric Tons

Year	Containers & Packaging	Building & Construction	Trans-portation	Electrical	Consumer Durables	Machinery & Equipment	Other Markets	Total to Domestic Users	Exports	U.S. Total
2009	2,150	964	1,910	593	458	475	254	6,810	1,280	8,090
2010	2,200	1,030	2,390	668	547	564	318	7,720	1,460	9,180
2011	2,160	1,110	2,820	798	631	682	322	8,520	1,700	10,200
2012	2,110	1,180	3,220	861	672	696	343	9,080	1,690	10,800
2013	2,090	1,310	3,430	867	700	726	332	9,450	1,720	11,200
2014	2,090	1,390	3,810	807	748	768	343	9,960	1,620	11,600
2015	2,140	1,420	4,180	800	741	768	327	10,400	1,620	12,000
2016	2,160	1,470	4,220	836	794	784	318	10,600	1,410	12,000
2017	2,130	1,530	4,370	919	860	841	333	11,000	1,340	12,300
2018[1]	2,100	1,600	4,300	960	920	920	350	11,200	1,500	12,700

[1] Preliminary. *Source: U.S. Geological Survey (USGS)*

Salient Statistics of Recycling Aluminum in the United States

Year	Percent Recycled	New Scrap[1]	Old Scrap[2]	Recycled Metal[3]	Apparent Supply	New Scrap[1]	Old Scrap[2]	Recycled Metal[3]	Apparent Supply
		In Metric Tons				Value in Thousands of Dollars			
2008	60.0	2,130,000	1,500,000	3,630,000	6,070,000	5,660,000	3,970,000	9,640,000	16,100,000
2009	58.0	1,570,000	1,260,000	2,820,000	4,890,000	2,740,000	2,200,000	4,940,000	8,550,000
2010	56.0	1,540,000	1,250,000	2,790,000	5,000,000	3,550,000	2,880,000	6,430,000	11,500,000
2011	60.0	1,670,000	1,440,000	3,110,000	5,210,000	4,280,000	3,690,000	7,970,000	13,300,000
2012	57.0	1,750,000	1,620,000	3,380,000	5,880,000	3,900,000	3,620,000	7,510,000	13,100,000
2013	54.0	1,790,000	1,630,000	3,410,000	6,310,000	3,710,000	3,380,000	7,090,000	13,100,000
2014	51.0	1,870,000	1,690,000	3,570,000	6,940,000	4,310,000	3,900,000	8,210,000	16,000,000
2015	49.0	2,000,000	1,560,000	3,560,000	7,310,000	3,900,000	3,030,000	6,920,000	14,200,000
2016	50.0	2,010,000	1,580,000	3,580,000	7,100,000	3,560,000	2,790,000	6,350,000	12,600,000
2017	47.0	2,050,000	1,590,000	3,630,000	7,740,000	4,430,000	3,440,000	7,870,000	16,800,000

[1] Scrap that results from the manufacturing process. [2] Scrap that results from consumer products. [3] Metal recovered from new plus old scrap.
Source: U.S. Geological Survey (USGS)

Producer Prices for Aluminum Used Beverage Can Scrap In Cents Per Pound

Year	Jan.	Feb.	Mar.	Apr.	May	June	July	Aug.	Sept.	Oct.	Nov.	Dec.	Average
2011	86.78	89.11	90.98	96.08	94.72	94.05	90.95	86.54	83.69	78.07	75.25	73.18	86.62
2012	77.30	79.83	79.87	75.67	74.27	69.76	70.81	70.35	77.82	75.72	74.33	80.09	75.49
2013	79.03	79.19	75.69	76.25	75.18	73.08	71.02	72.27	68.95	69.74	68.16	68.76	73.11
2014	73.24	76.75	77.52	82.43	79.62	80.41	83.80	85.33	85.93	85.92	91.17	88.64	82.56
2015	83.85	81.13	75.14	71.00	61.70	56.09	57.86	58.00	60.24	59.30	56.84	59.89	65.09
2016	60.63	61.60	59.87	60.71	59.90	60.36	61.30	61.52	60.02	63.00	67.15	67.81	61.99
2017	70.30	72.37	73.35	71.55	68.27	67.23	67.05	70.98	73.12	74.09	72.88	69.95	70.93
2018	75.57	75.66	75.59	81.81	84.41	85.29	77.40	73.37	65.87	63.50	59.35	58.12	73.00
2019	54.98	57.58	59.60	59.48	57.00	54.12	54.00	53.18	51.50	51.59	53.24	53.12	54.95
2020	53.40	51.66	50.02	40.79	39.80	44.77	47.45	48.40	50.93	52.18	56.55	62.82	49.90

Source: American Metal Market (AMM)

Average Price of Cast Aluminum Scrap (Crank Cases) in Chicago[1] In Cents Per Pound

Year	Jan.	Feb.	Mar.	Apr.	May	June	July	Aug.	Sept.	Oct.	Nov.	Dec.	Average
2011	48.75	52.50	52.50	52.50	52.50	52.50	56.00	57.50	56.93	54.50	54.70	52.45	53.61
2012	55.05	59.60	61.50	60.93	59.23	55.93	55.50	55.50	58.55	59.50	57.00	58.67	58.08
2013	60.50	60.45	59.50	59.00	58.50	58.35	55.50	56.00	55.90	55.54	55.55	54.50	57.44
2014	54.50	53.50	53.50	55.00	56.50	56.50	56.50	56.55	57.40	56.50	56.50	55.45	55.70
2015	53.40	52.50	51.32	50.50	51.00	46.50	46.41	43.88	42.45	41.41	38.97	38.64	46.42
2016	39.97	40.50	41.50	41.50	43.45	43.05	44.05	43.46	41.93	43.50	44.50	44.50	42.66
2017	45.60	45.97	46.93	47.00	45.95	44.95	44.50	44.65	46.50	46.50	45.95	44.00	45.71
2018	45.40	46.03	44.50	44.02	45.05	44.98	41.93	39.93	37.45	36.50	34.50	34.00	41.19
2019	31.50	31.50	31.50	31.50	30.50	30.50	29.91	27.41	25.50	22.93	22.50	22.50	28.15
2020	37.07	39.24	39.95	34.17	33.80	35.77	37.20	39.60	43.60	47.00	51.76	57.50	41.39

[1] Dealer buying prices. Source: American Metal Market (AMM)

Aluminum Exports of Crude Metal and Alloys from the United States In Thousands of Metric Tons

Year	Jan.	Feb.	Mar.	Apr.	May	June	July	Aug.	Sept.	Oct.	Nov.	Dec.	U.S. Total
2011	25.5	24.2	30.2	34.6	26.1	23.1	25.7	23.2	23.2	24.3	29.5	24.4	314.0
2012	30.8	29.5	32.0	29.9	31.0	30.6	31.6	32.2	24.3	24.3	33.0	24.5	353.7
2013	27.5	29.4	31.1	32.9	30.0	29.8	26.5	33.7	31.0	32.3	32.3	25.9	362.4
2014	31.1	25.6	30.5	30.7	33.0	31.0	28.7	31.5	30.0	33.7	26.9	28.2	360.9
2015	26.5	26.0	25.2	25.0	26.9	29.5	26.7	27.2	25.2	26.1	22.9	22.8	310.0
2016	25.7	24.5	25.3	22.1	22.7	18.7	19.4	20.1	23.6	21.7	21.2	17.1	262.1
2017	24.9	20.5	23.7	22.3	22.4	24.5	22.8	27.7	21.0	23.9	22.5	18.9	275.1
2018	25.6	28.4	23.6	25.5	25.3	22.8	24.9	27.5	23.0	25.5	22.2	18.1	292.4
2019	22.2	18.6	20.9	21.8	20.9	19.0	18.3	19.2	17.4	18.6	18.4	17.5	232.8
2020[1]	16.6	19.0	20.3	10.0	9.1	15.9	14.6	14.8	16.8	15.5	15.3	14.4	182.2

[1] Preliminary. *Source: U.S. Geological Survey (USGS)*

Aluminum General Imports of Crude Metal and Alloys into the United States In Thousands of Metric Tons

Year	Jan.	Feb.	Mar.	Apr.	May	June	July	Aug.	Sept.	Oct.	Nov.	Dec.	U.S. Total
2011	211.0	212.0	232.0	220.0	285.0	263.0	220.0	241.0	263.0	243.0	192.0	245.0	2,827.0
2012	281.0	284.0	248.0	231.0	293.0	240.0	233.0	234.0	214.0	204.0	196.0	244.0	2,902.0
2013	248.0	220.0	283.0	457.0	314.0	267.0	273.0	271.0	242.0	219.0	299.0	220.0	3,313.0
2014	253.0	221.0	439.0	291.0	290.0	294.0	237.0	270.0	253.0	271.0	213.0	270.0	3,302.0
2015	273.0	245.0	312.0	322.0	299.0	301.0	301.0	251.0	283.0	270.0	267.0	259.0	3,383.0
2016	362.0	270.0	385.0	350.0	336.0	401.0	346.0	345.0	349.0	316.0	392.0	381.0	4,233.0
2017	459.0	394.0	476.0	434.0	411.0	410.0	411.0	379.0	338.0	358.0	358.0	400.0	4,828.0
2018	333.0	374.0	555.0	381.0	349.0	297.0	332.0	292.0	313.0	306.0	294.0	306.0	4,132.0
2019	298.0	284.0	312.0	314.0	287.0	315.0	91.2	73.8	53.9	65.1	302.0	317.0	2,713.0
2020[1]	347.0	208.0	246.0	338.0	316.0	262.0	253.0	270.0	214.0	231.0	241.0	229.0	3,155.0

[1] Preliminary. *Source: U.S. Geological Survey (USGS)*

Average Price of Aluminum (Cash) in London In U.S. Dollars per Metric Ton

Year	Jan.	Feb.	Mar.	Apr.	May	June	July	Aug.	Sept.	Oct.	Nov.	Dec.	Average
2011	2,441.8	2,509.0	2,556.1	2,662.8	2,595.6	2,553.7	2,525.5	2,381.0	2,293.5	2,180.7	2,080.0	2,024.4	2,400.3
2012	2,151.4	2,207.9	2,184.2	2,048.5	2,002.6	1,885.5	1,876.3	1,842.1	2,064.1	1,974.4	1,948.9	2,086.8	2,022.7
2013	2,036.5	2,053.6	1,911.3	1,861.1	1,832.6	1,814.6	1,769.6	1,816.3	1,761.3	1,814.6	1,748.0	1,739.8	1,846.6
2014	1,727.4	1,695.2	1,705.4	1,810.7	1,751.1	1,839.0	1,948.3	2,030.5	1,990.4	1,946.2	2,055.6	1,909.5	1,867.4
2015	1,814.7	1,817.8	1,773.9	1,819.2	1,804.0	1,687.7	1,639.5	1,548.1	1,589.6	1,516.5	1,467.9	1,497.2	1,664.7
2016	1,481.1	1,531.3	1,531.0	1,571.2	1,550.6	1,593.5	1,629.1	1,639.3	1,592.4	1,665.9	1,737.1	1,727.7	1,604.2
2017	1,791.2	1,860.8	1,901.5	1,921.2	1,913.0	1,885.3	1,903.0	2,030.3	2,096.5	2,131.5	2,097.4	2,080.5	1,967.7
2018	2,209.7	2,182.4	2,070.8	2,254.7	2,299.7	2,237.6	2,082.2	2,051.5	2,026.5	2,029.9	1,938.5	1,920.4	2,108.7
2019	1,853.7	1,863.0	1,871.2	1,845.5	1,781.3	1,756.0	1,797.0	1,740.7	1,753.5	1,726.0	1,774.8	1,771.4	1,794.5
2020	1,773.1	1,688.1	1,610.9	1,459.9	1,466.4	1,568.6	1,643.8	1,737.3	1,743.8	1,806.1	1,935.3	2,014.7	1,704.0

Contract Size = 25 Metric Tons *Source: London Metal Exchange (LME)*

Average Price of Aluminum (3-Month) in London In U.S. Dollars per Metric Ton

Year	Jan.	Feb.	Mar.	Apr.	May	June	July	Aug.	Sept.	Oct.	Nov.	Dec.	Average
2011	2,458.4	2,539.2	2,586.4	2,689.4	2,591.9	2,584.3	2,554.8	2,414.2	2,327.7	2,207.7	2,098.4	2,034.6	2,423.9
2012	2,182.2	2,248.6	2,225.5	2,088.3	2,042.5	1,923.7	1,907.3	1,875.4	2,077.0	2,001.1	1,966.6	2,098.1	2,053.0
2013	2,073.3	2,094.8	1,950.5	1,893.3	1,864.5	1,854.9	1,814.3	1,863.4	1,808.0	1,860.5	1,793.5	1,784.6	1,888.0
2014	1,771.7	1,738.5	1,748.5	1,848.0	1,792.4	1,873.3	1,968.9	2,040.1	2,022.0	1,962.2	2,043.7	1,927.5	1,894.7
2015	1,827.3	1,835.0	1,781.7	1,809.7	1,836.8	1,726.6	1,680.2	1,576.4	1,605.3	1,541.0	1,482.0	1,497.9	1,683.3
2016	1,481.5	1,525.0	1,537.7	1,581.1	1,564.5	1,602.1	1,641.0	1,651.6	1,606.4	1,671.3	1,735.3	1,720.4	1,609.8
2017	1,786.8	1,870.7	1,912.3	1,933.4	1,917.1	1,892.1	1,921.1	2,036.7	2,122.6	2,150.6	2,114.8	2,096.7	1,979.6
2018	2,217.8	2,171.0	2,088.9	2,251.8	2,298.7	2,233.9	2,065.6	2,074.9	2,058.1	2,040.8	1,950.8	1,922.8	2,114.6
2019	1,867.4	1,888.2	1,895.1	1,865.0	1,809.6	1,782.9	1,819.4	1,770.2	1,779.4	1,733.7	1,767.6	1,781.9	1,813.3
2020	1,792.8	1,713.2	1,633.6	1,497.1	1,498.3	1,590.6	1,677.4	1,774.5	1,781.3	1,822.6	1,948.7	2,026.6	1,729.7

Contract Size = 25 Metric Tons *Source: London Metal Exchange (LME)*

Antimony

Antimony (atomic symbol Sb) is a lustrous, extremely brittle and hard crystalline semi-metal that is silvery-white in its most common allotropic form. Antimony is a poor conductor of heat and electricity. In nature, antimony has a strong affinity for sulfur and such metals as lead, silver, and copper. Antimony is primarily a byproduct of the mining, smelting, and refining of lead, silver, and copper ores. There is no longer any mine production of antimony in the U.S.

The most common use of antimony is in antimony trioxide, a chemical that is used as a flame retardant in textiles, plastics, adhesives, and building materials. Antimony trioxide is also used in battery components, ceramics, bearings, chemicals, glass, and ammunition.

Prices – Antimony prices in 2020 fell -12.0% yr/yr to 268.55 cents per pound and remained well below the 2011 record high of 671.10 cents per pound. However, antimony prices are far above the over 3-decade low price of 66.05 cents per pound posted in 1999.

Supply – World mine production of antimony in 2020 fell -5.6% yr/yr to 153,000 metric tons and remained below the 2008 and 2011 record high of 185,000 metric tons. China accounted for 52.3% of world antimony production in 2020. After China, the only significant producers were Russia with 18.6% and Tajikistan with 18.3%. U.S. secondary production of antimony in 2020 fell -3.4% yr/yr to 4,000 metric tons.

Demand – U.S. industrial consumption of antimony in 2017 fell -7.4% yr/yr to 7,780 metric tons. Regarding consumption of antimony in the U.S. in 2017, 31.1% was used for metal products, 36% was used for flame-retardants, and 9.9% was used for non-metal products.

Trade – The gross weight of U.S. imports of antimony oxide in 2020 fell -19.1% yr/yr to 14,000 metric tons. U.S. exports of antimony oxide in 2020 fell -10.9% yr/yr to 1,400 metric tons.

World Mine Production of Antimony (Content of Ore) In Metric Tons

Year	Australia	Bolivia	Canada	China	Kyrgyzstan	Russia	South Africa	Tajikistan	Turkey	World Total
2016	3,598	2,669	----	107,525	573	8,000	1,200	14,000	1,950	144,000
2017	3,115	2,700	----	98,000	----	14,400	1,200	14,000	2,000	137,000
2018	2,170	3,110	----	89,600	----	30,000	----	15,200	2,400	147,000
2019[1]	2,030	3,000	----	89,000	----	30,000	----	28,000	2,400	162,000
2020[2]	2,000	3,000	----	80,000	----	30,000	----	28,000	2,000	153,000

[1] Preliminary. [2] Estimate. [3] Less than 1/2 unit. *Source: U.S. Geological Survey (USGS)*

Salient Statistics of Antimony in the United States In Metric Tons

	Avg. Price	Production[3]			Imports for Consumption				Industry Stocks, December 31[3]				
	Cents/lb.	Primary[2]			Ore		Oxide						
Year	C.i.F. U.S. Ports	Mine	Smelter	Secondary (Alloys)[2]	Gross Weight	Antimony Content	(Gross Weight)	Exports (Oxide)	Metallic	Oxide	Sulfide	Other	Total
2017	398.00	----	W	4,370	----	61	17,800	1,600			----		1,360
2018	388.00	----	W	4,090	----	96	19,200	1,750			----		1,400
2019[1]	390.00	----	W	4,140	----	121	17,300	1,570			----		
2020[2]	398.00	----	W	4,000	----	130	14,000	1,400			----		

[1] Preliminary. [2] Estimate. [3] Antimony content. [4] Including primary antimony residues & slag. W = Withheld proprietary data.
Source: U.S. Geological Survey (USGS)

Industrial Consumption of Primary Antimony in the United States In Metric Tons (Antimony Content)

	Metal Products						Flame Retardents		Non-Metal Products				
Year	Ammu-nition	Anti-monial Lead[3]	Sheet & Pipe[4]	Bearing Metal & Bearings	Solder	Products	Plastics	Total	Ceramics & Glass	Pigments	Plastics	Total	Grand Total
2014	W	W	W	18	46	2,440	2,440	2,820	W	877	W	3,260	8,520
2015	W	W	W	20	19	2,450	2,200	2,860	W	808	W	2,960	8,270
2016	W	W	W	9	15	2,840	2,290	2,790	W	703	W	2,770	8,400
2017[1]	W	W	W	8	14	2,410	2,420	2,810	W	769	W	2,560	7,780

[1] Preliminary. [2] Estimated coverage based on 77% of the industry. W = Withheld proprietary data. *Source: U.S. Geological Survey (USGS)*

Average Price of Antimony[1] in the United States In Cents Per Pound

Year	Jan.	Feb.	Mar.	Apr.	May	June	July	Aug.	Sept.	Oct.	Nov.	Dec.	Average
2017	343.19	358.05	393.84	406.65	408.04	397.31	364.01	379.44	384.42	370.76	366.18	370.33	378.52
2018	373.63	388.62	394.60	382.37	373.58	373.25	362.83	375.06	388.05	382.06	371.23	362.88	377.34
2019	360.51	358.34	345.38	325.66	317.62	294.82	276.95	272.52	269.13	282.44	283.66	275.56	305.22
2020	267.17	283.95	288.74	267.92	257.79	247.65	240.97	248.91	263.84	271.59	284.21	299.81	268.55

[1] Prices are for antimony metal (99.65%) merchants, minimum 18-ton containers, c.i.f. U.S. Ports. *Source: American Metal Market (AMM)*

Apples

The apple tree is the common name of trees from the rose family, Rosaceae, and the fruit that comes from them. The apple tree is a deciduous plant and grows mainly in the temperate areas of the world. The apple tree is believed to have originated in the Caspian and Black Sea area. Apples were the favorite fruit of the ancient Greeks and Romans. The early settlers brought apple seeds with them and introduced them to America. John Champman, also known as Johnny Appleseed, was responsible for the extensive planting of apple trees in the Midwestern United States.

Prices – The average monthly price of apples received by growers in the U.S. in 2020 rose +56.7% yr/yr to 60.45 cents per pound.

Supply – World apple production in the 2020-21 marketing year is expected to fall -4.1% yr/yr to 76.131 million metric tons. The world's largest apple producers in 2020/21 are expected to be China (with 53.2% of world production), the European Union (16.1%), the U.S. (6.1%), and Turkey (5.6%). U.S. apple production in 2020/21 is expected to fall -3.1% to 4.671 million metric tons and remained far above the 2-decade low of 3.798 million metric tons posted in 2002-03.

Demand – The utilization breakdown of the 2019 apple crop showed that 67.4% of apples were for fresh consumption, 12.1% for juice and cider, 10.1% for canning, 3.2% for dried apples and 1.1% for frozen apples. U.S. per capita apple consumption in 2019 was 17.5 pounds.

World Production of Apples[3], Fresh (Dessert & Cooking) In Thousands of Metric Tons

Crop Year	Argentina	Brazil	Chile	China	European Union	India	Japan	Russia	South Africa	Turkey	Ukraine	United States	World Total
2013-14	630	1,379	1,310	36,300	11,865	2,498	816	1,417	793	3,128	1,085	4,732	72,231
2014-15	650	1,265	1,210	37,350	13,636	2,498	812	1,409	920	2,480	1,180	5,112	74,712
2015-16	600	1,055	1,335	38,900	12,453	2,520	765	1,311	924	2,570	1,099	4,546	74,474
2016-17	560	1,308	1,310	40,393	12,723	2,258	735	1,509	902	2,926	1,076	5,010	76,641
2017-18	560	1,195	1,330	41,390	10,005	1,920	756	1,360	836	3,032	1,462	5,085	75,512
2018-19	550	1,195	1,210	33,000	15,029	2,300	756	1,611	894	3,600	1,462	4,479	72,524
2019-20[1]	570	1,195	1,124	42,425	11,705	2,370	756	1,779	942	3,620	1,462	4,821	79,413
2020-21[2]	570	1,195	1,170	40,500	12,227	2,300	756	1,540	960	4,300	1,462	4,671	76,131

[1] Preliminary. [2] Estimate. *Source: Foreign Agricultural Service, U.S. Department of Agriculture (FAS-USDA)*

Salient Statistics of Apples[2] in the United States

	-- Production --		- Growers Prices -		----- Utilization of Quantities Sold ----- Processed[5]								----- Foreign Trade[4] -----			
												Domestic				
Year	Total	Utilized	Fresh Cents/ lb.	Processing $/ton	Fresh	Canned	Dried	Frozen	Juice & Cider	Other[3]	Avg. Fram Price Cents/ lb.	Farm Value Million $	Exports Fresh	Dried[5]	Imports Fresh & Dried[5]	Fresh Per Capita Consumption Lbs.
	Millions of Pounds												Metric Tons			
2012	8,992	8,927	45.3	281.0	6,595	749	223	67	1,112	53	37.1	3,315.0	908.8	22.3	243.1	16.0
2013	10,523	10,432	40.5	197.0	6,919	1,264	161	239	1,520	72	30.2	3,132.9	848.7	23.7	243.9	17.4
2014	11,863	11,270	32.7	178.0	7,909	1,135	171	251	1,480	60	25.6	2,870.7	1,057.9	26.1	209.5	18.7
2015	10,103	10,023	44.1	201.0	6,928	1,110	179	188	1,329	187	33.6	3,350.1	747.3	28.0	233.6	17.5
2016	11,495	11,046	40.5	214.0	7,745	1,211	339	138	1,342	137	31.6	3,492.6	867.5	----	171.0	19.2
2017	11,554	11,210	40.7	248.0	7,816	1,162	370	123	1,395	180	32.1	3,601.4	1,007.3	----	134.3	18.1
2018	10,240	9,874	38.7	207.0	6,827	----	----	----	----	----	29.9	3,013.7	742.3	----	146.4	16.9
2019[1]	11,018	10,628	32.7	199.0	7,430	----	----	----	----	----	25.8		862.1	----	107.8	17.5

[1] Preliminary. [2] Commercial crop. [3] Mostly crushed for vinegar, jam, etc. [4] Year beginning July. [5] Fresh weight basis.
Source: Economic Research Service, U.S. Department of Agriculture (ERS-USDA)

Price of Apples Received by Growers (for Fresh Use) in the United States In Cents Per Pound

Year	Jan.	Feb.	Mar.	Apr.	May	June	July	Aug.	Sept.	Oct.	Nov.	Dec.	Average
2013	43.8	41.6	39.5	NQ	NQ	NQ	NQ	NQ	NQ	NQ	NQ	NQ	41.6
2014	NQ	NQ	NQ	39.2	37.2	34.4	33.2	38.8	46.9	40.2	35.8	31.8	37.5
2015	31.6	29.2	27.8	25.9	24.3	20.7	19.0	30.3	44.3	41.6	40.1	44.7	31.6
2016	44.7	44.7	45.9	45.1	39.1	38.0	40.6	46.1	53.0	45.2	39.9	39.6	43.5
2017	39.7	36.9	35.8	35.3	36.0	36.3	37.0	42.6	59.1	45.9	39.9	39.7	40.4
2018	37.5	35.0	33.6	32.7	29.6	28.6	31.1	29.6	45.2	39.6	38.7	40.1	35.1
2019	39.7	37.9	37.7	38.1	38.3	37.2	38.8	40.2	48.9	39.1	33.3	33.6	38.6
2020[1]	31.3	58.3	57.7	57.7	57.9	58.6	60.0	64.2	70.7	69.1	69.7	70.2	60.5

[1] Preliminary. NQ = No quote. *Source: Economic Research Service, U.S. Department of Agriculture (ERS-USDA)*

Arsenic

Arsenic (atomic symbol As) is a silver-gray, extremely poisonous, semi-metallic element. Arsenic, which is odorless and flavorless, has been known since ancient times, but it wasn't until the Middle Ages that its poisonous characteristics first became known. Metallic arsenic was first produced in the 17th century by heating arsenic with potash and soap. Arsenic is rarely found in nature in its elemental form and is typically recovered as a by-product of ore processing. Recently, small doses of arsenic have been found to put some types of cancer into remission. It can also help thin blood. Homoeopathists have successfully used undetectable amounts of arsenic to cure stomach cramps.

The U.S. does not produce any arsenic and instead imports all its consumption needs for arsenic metals and compounds. More than 95 percent of the arsenic consumed in the U.S. is in compound form, mostly as arsenic trioxide, which in turn is converted into arsenic acid. Production of chromated copper arsenate, a wood preservative, accounts for about 90% of the domestic consumption of arsenic trioxide. Three companies in the U.S. manufacture chromate copper arsenate. Another company used arsenic acid to produce an arsenical herbicide. Arsenic metal is used to produce nonferrous alloys, primarily for lead-acid batteries.

One area where there is increased consumption of arsenic is in the semiconductor industry. Very high-purity arsenic is used in the production of gallium arsenide. High-speed and high-frequency integrated circuits that use gallium arsenide have better signal reception and lower power consumption. An estimated 30 metric tons per year of high-purity arsenic is used in the production of semiconductor materials.

In the early 2000s, as much as 88% of U.S. arsenic production was used for wood preservative treatments, so the demand for arsenic was closely tied to new home construction, home renovation, and deck construction. However, the total demand for arsenic in 2004 dropped by 69% from 2003. Due to arsenic's toxicity and tighter environmental regulation, only 65% of that much smaller amount was used for wood preservative treatments.

Supply –World production of white arsenic (arsenic trioxide) in 2020 fell -0.9% yr/yr to 32,000 metric tons. The world's largest producer is China with 75.0% of world production, followed by Morocco with 17.2%, Russia with 4.7%, and Belgium with 3.1% China's production of arsenic was at its high in 2002 at about 40,000 metric tons per year but has since dropped to about 25,000 in the last fifteen years or so. The U.S. supply of arsenic in 2020 rose 40.4% yr/yr to 10,500 metric tons.

Demand – U.S. demand for arsenic in 2020 rose +40.4% to 10,500 metric tons. Arsenic is mainly used in wood preservatives, with smaller usage levels in non-ferrous alloys, electrical, and glass.

Trade – U.S. imports of trioxide arsenic in 2017 fell by -7.3% yr/yr to 7,320 metric tons, but still above the 2010 record low of 5,920 metric tons. U.S. exports of trioxide arsenic in 2020 fell -64.3% yr/yr to 20 metric tons, far below the record high of 3,270 metric tons in 2005.

World Production of White Arsenic (Arsenic Trioxide) In Metric Tons

Year	Belgium	Bolivia	Chile	China	Japan	Mexico	Morocco	Peru	Morocco	Peru	Portugal	Russia	World Total
2013	1,000	120	10,000	25,000	45	----	8,968	1,520	----	1,500	38,300	1,500	60,900
2014	1,000	52	10,000	25,000	45	----	3,863	1,520	----	1,500	33,100	1,500	53,900
2015	1,000	33	----	25,000	45	----	7,566	1,960	----	1,500	37,200	1,500	50,500
2016	1,000	38	----	25,000	45	----	6,122	1,900	----	1,500	35,700	1,500	47,600
2017	1,000	40	----	24,000	45	----	6,000	1,900	----	1,500	34,600	1,500	52,400
2018	1,000	40	----	24,000	45	----	6,000	1,900	----	1,500	33,400	1,500	45,800
2019[1]	1,000	120	----	24,000	45	----	5,500	700	----	1,500	32,300	1,500	46,700
2020[2]	1,000	100	----	24,000	40	----	5,500		----	1,500	32,000	1,500	45,000

[1] Preliminary. [2] Estimate. [3] Output of Tsumeb Corp. Ltd. only. [4] Includes low-grade dusts that were exported to the U.S. for further refining.
Source: U.S. Geological Survey (USGS)

Salient Statistics of Arsenic in the United States (In Metric Tons -- Arsenic Content)

	Supply				Distribution		Estimated Demand Pattern						Average Price			
	Imports												Trioxide	Metal		
Year	Metal	Com-pounds	Industry Stocks Jan. 1	Total	Apparent Demand	Industry Stocks Dec. 31	Agricul-tural Chem-icals	Glass	Wood Preserv-atives	Non-Ferrous Alloys & lectric	Other	Total	Mexican -- Cents/Pound --	Chinese	Imports Trioxide[3]	Exports
2013	514	6,290	----	6,804	6,810	----	----	----	----	----	----	6,810	----	2	8,310	1,630
2014	688	5,260	----	5,948	5,940	----	----	----	----	----	----	5,940	----	2	6,940	2,970
2015	514	5,920	----	6,434	6,430	----	----	----	----	----	----	6,430	----	2	7,810	1,670
2016	793	5,320	----	6,113	6,120	----	----	----	----	----	----	6,120	----	2	7,900	1,760
2017	942	5,980	----	6,922	6,920	----	----	----	----	----	----	6,920	----	2	7,320	698
2018	929	5,540	----	6,469	6,470	----	----	----	----	----	----	6,470	----	1		107
2019[1]	391	7,090	----	7,481	7,480	----	----	----	----	----	----	7,480	----	2		56
2020[2]	500	10,000	----	10,500	10,500	----	----	----	----	----	----	10,500	----	2		20

[1] Preliminary. [2] Estimate. [3] For Consumption. *Source: U.S. Geological Survey (USGS)*

Barley

Barley is the common name for the genus of cereal grass and is native to Asia and Ethiopia. Barley is an ancient crop and was grown by the Egyptians, Greek, Romans, and Chinese. Barley is now the world's fourth-largest grain crop, after wheat, rice, and corn. Barley is planted in the spring in most of Europe, Canada and the United States. The U.S. barley crop year begins June 1. It is planted in the autumn in parts of California, Arizona, and along the Mediterranean Sea. Barley is hardy and drought resistant and can be grown on marginal cropland. Salt-resistant strains are being developed for use in coastal regions. Barley grain, along with hay, straw, and several by-products are used for animal feed. Barley is used for malt beverages and for cooking. Barley, like other cereals, contains a large proportion of carbohydrate (67%) and protein (12.8%).

Barley futures are traded on ASX 24 exchange and National Commodity & Derivatives Exchange (NCDEX).

Prices – The monthly average price for all barley received by U.S. farmers in the 2019/20 marketing year rose by +0.2% yr/yr to $4.70 per bushel.

Supply – World barley production in the 2020-21 marketing year is forecasted to rise +1.3% yr/yr to 157.186 million metric tons. The world's largest barley crop of 179.038 million metric tons occurred in 1990-91. The world's largest barley producers in 2020/21 are expected to be the European Union with 40.1% of world production, Russia with 13.1%, Australia with 7.0%, Canada with 6.8%, Turkey with 5.2., and Ukraine with 5.1%,

U.S. barley production in the 2020/21 marketing year is expected to fall by -4.2% yr/yr to 165.324 million bushels, but that is still only about a quarter of the record U.S. barley crop of 608.532 million bushels seen in 1986/87. U.S. farmers are expected to harvest -4.0% yr/yr fewer acres in 202/21 at 2.133 million acres. Ending stocks for the 2020/21 marketing year are expected to fall -2.1% to 78,577 million bushels.

Demand – U.S. total barley disappearance in 2020/21 is expected to fall -6.4% yr/yr to 174.000 million bushels. About 82.3% of barley is used for food and alcoholic beverages, 15.1% for animal feed and residual, and 2.6% for seed.

Trade – World exports of barley in 2020/21 are expected to rise +5.9% yr/yr to 29.145 million metric tons. The largest world exporters of barley in 2020/21 are expected to be the European Union with 22.3% of the world's exports, Russia with 18.5%, and Ukraine with 14.4%. The largest importers of barley in 2020/21 are expected to be Saudi Arabia with 26.6% of the world's imports and China with 24.5%.

World Production of Barley In Thousands of Metric Tons

Year	Argen-tina	Australia	Canada	Ethiopia	European Union	Iran	Kazakh-stan	Morocco	Russia	Turkey	Ukraine	United States	World Total
2011-12	4,500	8,221	7,892	1,592	51,883	2,530	2,593	2,318	16,938	7,000	9,098	3,370	133,266
2012-13	5,000	7,472	8,012	1,782	54,875	2,770	1,500	1,201	13,952	5,500	6,935	4,768	129,276
2013-14	4,750	9,174	10,282	1,908	59,674	3,000	2,539	2,723	15,389	7,300	7,561	4,719	144,427
2014-15	2,900	8,646	7,117	1,953	60,609	3,200	2,412	1,638	20,026	4,000	9,450	3,953	141,663
2015-16	4,940	8,993	8,257	2,047	62,095	3,200	2,675	3,393	17,083	7,400	8,751	4,750	149,548
2016-17	3,300	13,506	8,839	2,025	59,866	3,724	3,231	620	17,547	4,750	9,874	4,353	147,083
2017-18	3,740	9,254	7,891	2,032	58,651	3,100	3,305	2,466	20,211	6,400	8,695	3,119	143,182
2018-19	5,060	8,819	8,380	2,200	55,980	2,800	3,971	2,910	16,737	7,000	7,604	3,343	139,424
2019-20[1]	3,800	9,000	10,383	2,300	63,219	3,600	3,830	1,161	19,939	7,900	9,528	3,756	156,582
2020-21[2]	3,700	11,000	10,741	2,350	63,100	3,750	3,800	640	20,600	8,100	8,000	3,600	157,186

[1] Preliminary. [2] Estimate. *Source: Foreign Agricultural Service, U.S. Department of Agriculture (FAS-USDA)*

World Exports of Barley In Thousands of Metric Tons

Year	Argen-tina	Australia	Canada	Ethiopia	European Union	Iran	Kazakh-stan	Morocco	Russia	Turkey	Ukraine	United States	World Total
2011-12	3,616	5,377	1,299	3,008	46	704	3,544	9	103	2,463	193	----	20,400
2012-13	3,581	4,484	1,432	4,966	267	164	2,237	17	----	2,134	193	107	19,630
2013-14	2,891	6,217	1,561	5,741	441	416	2,709	28	6	2,476	311	34	22,857
2014-15	1,552	5,219	1,517	9,547	431	483	5,348	21	9	4,456	311	43	29,030
2015-16	3,077	5,745	1,195	10,834	81	804	4,241	54	3	4,412	235	42	30,823
2016-17	2,556	9,190	1,546	5,667	1	682	2,951	26	129	5,354	95	114	28,461
2017-18	2,399	5,662	2,021	5,899	1	1,347	5,884	53	147	4,289	111	7	27,963
2018-19	3,237	3,687	2,296	4,886	6	1,820	4,661	68	148	3,561	107	62	24,633
2019-20[1]	2,421	3,325	2,346	8,099	1	1,366	4,470	52	2	4,984	125	45	27,534
2020-21[2]	2,500	5,000	3,000	6,500	5	1,500	5,400	75	30	4,200	174	100	29,145

[1] Preliminary. [2] Estimate. *Source: Foreign Agricultural Service, U.S. Department of Agriculture (FAS-USDA)*

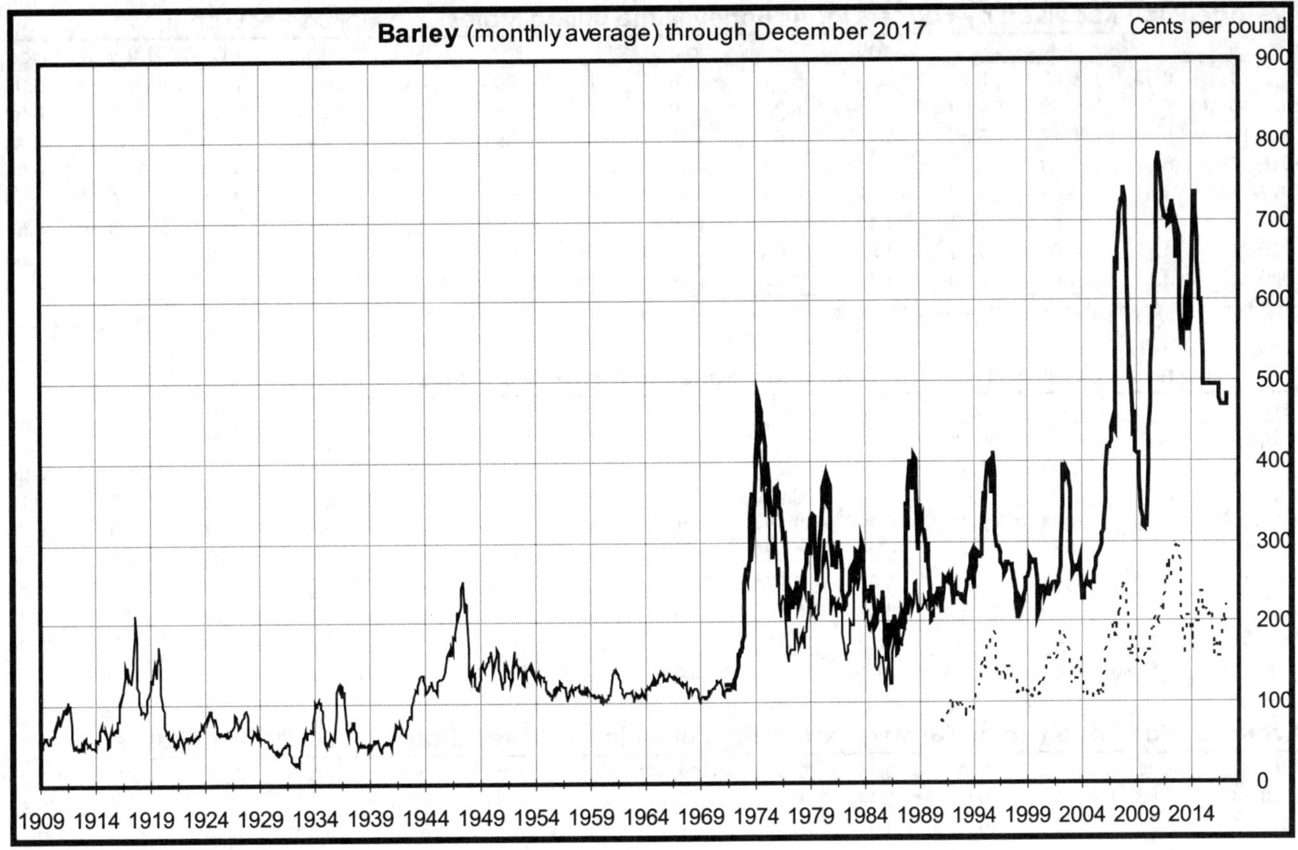

Barley Acreage and Prices in the United States

Crop Year Beginning June 1	Acreage (1,000 Acres) Planted	Acreage (1,000 Acres) Harvested for Gain	Yield Per Harvested Acre (Bushels)	Seasonal Prices: Received by Farmers[3] All	Received by Farmers[3] Feed[4]	Received by Farmers[3] Malting[4]	Portland No. 2 Western	Government Price Support Operations: National Average Loan Rate	Target Price	Put Under Support (mil. Bu.)	Percent of Production
				Dollars per Bushel							
2013-14	3,528	3,040	71.3	6.06	4.22	6.49	----	1.95	2.63	4.2	1.9
2014-15	3,031	2,497	72.7	5.22	3.20	5.77	----	1.95	4.95	3.9	2.1
2015-16	3,623	3,158	69.1	5.46	3.11	5.78	----	1.95	4.95	8.3	3.8
2016-17	3,059	2,565	77.9	4.97	2.73	5.26	----	1.95	4.95	9.3	4.6
2017-18	2,486	1,962	73.0	4.47	3.00	4.67	----	1.95	4.95	4.5	3.1
2018-19	2,548	1,982	77.5	4.64	3.25	4.80	----	1.95	4.95	5.1	3.3
2019-20[1]	2,772	2,221	77.7	4.69	3.37	4.85	----				
2020-21[2]	2,621	2,133	77.5	4.70	3.20	4.90	----				

[1] Preliminary. [2] Estimate. [3] Excludes support payments. *Source: Economic Research Service, U.S. Department of Agriculture (ERS-USDA)*

Salient Statistics of Barley in the United States In Millions of Bushels

Crop Year Beginning June 1	Supply: Beginning Stocks	Supply: Production	Supply: Imports	Supply: Total Supply	Disappearance: Domestic Use: Food & Alcohol Beverage	Domestic Use: Seed	Domestic Use: Feed & Residual	Domestic Use: Total	Exports	Total Disappearance	Ending Stocks: Gov't Owned	Ending Stocks: Privately Owned	Ending Stocks: Total Stocks
2013-14	80.4	216.7	18.7	315.9	148.3	5.1	65.9	219.4	14.3	233.6	----	82.3	82.3
2014-15	82.3	181.5	23.6	287.4	154.3	5.9	34.4	194.5	14.3	208.8	----	78.6	78.6
2015-16	78.6	218.2	18.6	315.3	153.1	5.2	44.2	202.4	10.8	213.2	----	102.1	102.1
2016-17	102.1	199.9	9.6	311.7	151.6	4.2	45.2	200.9	4.4	205.3	----	106.4	106.4
2017-18	106.4	143.3	9.1	258.8	147.5	4.3	7.4	159.2	5.1	164.3	----	94.5	94.5
2018-19	94.5	153.5	5.9	253.9	143.7	4.7	14.0	162.4	4.9	167.4	----	86.5	86.5
2019-20[1]	86.5	172.5	7.1	266.1	137.1	4.4	38.6	180.1	5.7	185.9	----	80.3	80.3
2020-21[2]	80.3	165.3	7.0	252.6	136.7	4.3	25.0	166.0	8.0	174.0	----	78.6	78.6

[1] Preliminary. [2] Estimate. [3] Uncommitted inventory. [4] Includes quantity under loan & farmer-owned reserve. [5] Included in Food & Alcohol.
Source: Economic Research Service, U.S. Department of Agriculture (ERS-USDA)

Average Price Received by Farmers for All Barley in the United States In Dollars Per Bushel

Year	June	July	Aug.	Sept.	Oct.	Nov.	Dec.	Jan.	Feb.	Mar.	Apr.	May	Average
2013-14	6.35	6.38	6.15	5.88	5.94	6.20	6.11	6.04	5.94	5.94	5.90	5.94	6.06
2014-15	6.01	5.62	5.60	5.31	5.24	5.09	5.16	4.86	5.22	4.87	4.94	4.75	5.22
2015-16	5.04	5.19	5.59	5.49	5.54	5.55	5.88	5.47	5.51	5.43	5.29	5.59	5.46
2016-17	5.39	5.00	4.89	4.54	4.85	4.97	5.12	4.91	5.08	4.97	4.87	5.05	4.97
2017-18	4.47	4.54	4.52	4.32	4.44	4.60	4.38	4.45	4.58	4.46	4.44	4.45	4.47
2018-19	4.62	4.52	4.54	4.49	4.25	4.78	4.64	4.57	4.65	4.88	4.80	4.90	4.64
2019-20	4.81	4.69	4.74	4.56	4.58	4.74	4.51	4.67	4.68	4.89	4.64	4.76	4.69
2020-21[1]	4.57	4.66	4.60	4.76	4.74	4.78	4.79	4.67					4.70

[1] Preliminary. *Source: National Agricultural Statistical Service, U.S. Department of Agriculture (NASS-USDA)*

Average Price Received by Farmers for Feed Barley in the United States In Dollars Per Bushel

Year	June	July	Aug.	Sept.	Oct.	Nov.	Dec.	Jan.	Feb.	Mar.	Apr.	May	Average
2013-14	5.75	5.17	4.42	4.25	4.10	3.63	3.65	4.21	3.77	3.81	3.77	4.15	4.22
2014-15	4.32	3.85	3.31	2.97	3.13	2.84	2.99	2.99	2.94	3.08	3.05	2.90	3.20
2015-16	3.55	2.97	3.00	3.24	2.97	3.03	3.11	3.14	3.07	2.79	2.82	3.67	3.11
2016-17	3.38	3.18	2.75	2.39	2.52	2.49	2.87	2.61	2.75	2.50	2.64	2.69	2.73
2017-18	3.47	3.04	2.97	2.62	3.07	2.80	2.85	3.01	2.83	2.90	3.08	3.33	3.00
2018-19	3.79	3.41	3.12	3.07	2.97	3.23	3.06	3.11	3.23	3.23	3.39	3.44	3.25
2019-20	4.32	3.89	3.43	3.18	3.10	2.81	3.32	3.27	3.16	3.55	3.16	3.20	3.37
2020-21[1]	3.24	3.37	3.05	3.10	3.28	3.32	3.01	3.20					3.20

[1] Preliminary. *Source: National Agricultural Statistical Service, U.S. Department of Agriculture (NASS-USDA)*

Average Price Received by Farmers for Malting Barley in the United States In Dollars Per Bushel

Year	June	July	Aug.	Sept.	Oct.	Nov.	Dec.	Jan.	Feb.	Mar.	Apr.	May	Average
2013-14	6.68	6.56	6.56	6.44	6.49	6.61	6.52	6.52	6.43	6.30	6.45	6.37	6.49
2014-15	6.30	5.90	6.11	5.91	5.76	5.69	5.63	5.47	5.67	5.39	5.75	5.62	5.77
2015-16	5.68	5.73	5.91	5.74	5.78	5.80	5.99	5.68	5.70	5.64	5.71	6.03	5.78
2016-17	5.70	5.33	5.31	5.13	5.17	5.21	5.32	5.19	5.20	5.13	5.13	5.27	5.26
2017-18	4.66	4.78	4.70	4.64	4.64	4.81	4.51	4.60	4.77	4.60	4.73	4.58	4.67
2018-19	4.88	4.79	4.68	4.72	4.42	4.85	4.78	4.71	4.75	5.02	4.92	5.03	4.80
2019-20	4.88	4.83	4.89	4.78	4.77	4.84	4.81	4.82	4.78	5.08	4.73	4.98	4.85
2020-21[1]	4.95	4.92	4.78	4.92	4.97	5.00	4.86	4.82					4.90

[1] Preliminary. *Source: National Agricultural Statistical Service, U.S. Department of Agriculture (NASS-USDA)*

Stocks of Barley in the United States In Thousands of Bushels

	On Farms				Off Farms				Total Stocks			
Year	Mar. 1	June 1	Sept. 1	Dec. 1	Mar. 1	June 1	Sept. 1	Dec. 1	Mar. 1	June 1	Sept. 1	Dec. 1
2013	35,180	15,840	105,620	81,340	81,897	64,557	90,470	88,063	117,077	80,397	196,090	169,403
2014	43,830	19,110	97,820	74,510	77,734	63,145	81,997	81,625	121,564	82,255	179,817	156,135
2015	41,990	20,940	135,840	96,670	76,247	57,639	83,132	83,738	118,237	78,579	218,972	180,408
2016	57,910	27,740	130,600	99,100	79,832	74,370	99,737	93,408	137,742	102,110	230,337	192,508
2017	56,490	27,050	90,400	74,340	88,211	79,314	89,283	84,528	144,701	106,364	179,683	158,868
2018	48,540	26,420	91,350	72,070	81,491	68,061	83,456	80,561	130,031	94,481	174,806	152,631
2019	46,180	22,870	116,720	87,630	75,216	63,653	73,112	69,756	121,396	86,523	189,832	157,386
2020[1]	51,580	25,100	108,980	84,990	63,760	55,153	70,484	60,011	115,340	80,253	179,464	145,001

[1] Preliminary. *Source: National Agricultural Statistics Service, U.S. Department of Agriculture (NASS-USDA)*

Production of Barley in the United States, by State In Thousands of Bushels

Year	Arizona	California	Colorado	Idaho	Minnesota	Montana	North Dakota	Oregon	Pennsylvania	Virginia	Washington	Wyoming	U.S. Total
2013	8,142	3,150	7,714	57,660	5,175	43,160	46,080	3,500	4,080	3,608	14,040	6,052	216,745
2014	4,000	1,825	6,696	51,700	3,120	44,660	35,845	1,900	3,550	2,212	6,300	7,276	181,542
2015	1,920	1,595	8,190	56,260	9,240	44,720	67,200	1,924	2,600	1,200	5,040	8,170	218,187
2016	2,048	4,500	9,675	62,060	5,214	46,800	42,880	2,144	2,850	804	7,161	7,872	199,914
2017	2,227	1,450	8,976	48,450	5,168	28,815	26,000	2,356	3,150	803	4,505	6,426	143,258
2018	1,100	1,794	7,685	53,530	5,092	33,600	28,490	1,378	2,079	630	4,891	5,100	153,527
2019	1,890	3,102	7,176	55,120	3,685	44,840	32,040	2,730	1,750	455	5,880	7,062	172,499
2020[1]	976	1,457	6,525	55,000	2,350	45,675	28,980	1,800	2,280	441	6,390	5,952	165,324

[1] Preliminary. *Source: National Agricultural Statistics Service, U.S. Department of Agriculture (NASS-USDA)*

Weekly Outstanding Export Sales and Cumulative Exports of U.S. Barley

In Thousands of Metric Tons

Marketing Year 2019/2020 Week Ending	Weekly Exports	Accumu-lated Exports	Net Sales	Out-standing Sales
Jun 06, 2019		42,501		18,738
Jun 06, 2019	534	534	18,738	49,964
Jun 13, 2019	621	1,155	-4	49,339
Jun 20, 2019	1,048	2,203	300	48,591
Jun 27, 2019	595	2,798	500	48,496
Jul 04, 2019	2,203	5,001	420	46,713
Jul 11, 2019	465	5,466	15	46,263
Jul 18, 2019	660	6,126		45,603
Jul 25, 2019	1,798	7,924	4,998	48,803
Aug 01, 2019	1,389	9,313		47,414
Aug 08, 2019	220	9,533	-24	47,170
Aug 15, 2019	625	10,158		46,545
Aug 22, 2019	973	11,131	180	45,752
Aug 29, 2019	229	11,360	500	46,023
Sep 05, 2019	1,380	12,740	44	44,687
Sep 12, 2019	207	12,947		44,480
Sep 19, 2019	720	13,667	73	43,833
Sep 26, 2019	1,922	15,589		41,911
Oct 03, 2019	1,177	16,766		40,734
Oct 10, 2019	1,208	17,974		39,526
Oct 17, 2019	928	18,902	2	38,600
Oct 24, 2019	578	19,480	-21	38,001
Oct 31, 2019	1,828	21,308	1,013	37,186
Nov 07, 2019	1,115	22,423	110	36,181
Nov 14, 2019	1,223	23,646		34,958
Nov 21, 2019	515	24,161	500	34,943
Nov 28, 2019	1,006	25,167		33,937
Dec 05, 2019	907	26,074	-389	32,641
Dec 12, 2019	625	26,699	227	32,243
Dec 19, 2019	732	27,431		31,511
Dec 26, 2019	1,271	28,702		30,240
Jan 02, 2020		28,702	-7	30,233
Jan 09, 2020	781	29,483	750	30,202
Jan 16, 2020	406	29,889		29,796
Jan 23, 2020	942	30,831	-10,964	17,890
Jan 30, 2020	1,202	32,033	14	16,702
Feb 06, 2020	950	32,983		15,752
Feb 13, 2020	368	33,351	80	15,464
Feb 20, 2020	299	33,650	300	15,465
Feb 27, 2020	608	34,258	-1	14,856
Mar 05, 2020		34,258		14,856
Mar 12, 2020	190	34,448		14,666
Mar 19, 2020	3,401	37,849		11,265
Mar 26, 2020	811	38,660	215	10,669
Apr 02, 2020	112	38,772	195	10,752
Apr 09, 2020		38,772		10,752
Apr 16, 2020		38,772		10,752
Apr 23, 2020		38,772	300	11,052
Apr 30, 2020	339	39,111		10,713
May 07, 2020	602	39,713	1	10,112
May 14, 2020	575	40,288	215	9,752
May 21, 2020	263	40,551	217	9,706
May 28, 2020	499	41,050		9,207
Jun 04, 2020		41,050		9,207

Marketing Year 2020/2021 Week Ending	Weekly Exports	Accumu-lated Exports	Net Sales	Out-standing Sales
Jun 04, 2020	491	491	9,207	40,226
Jun 11, 2020		491		40,226
Jun 18, 2020		491		40,226
Jun 25, 2020	832	1,323	954	40,348
Jul 02, 2020	195	1,518		40,153
Jul 09, 2020	281	1,799	-2,984	36,888
Jul 16, 2020	327	2,126		36,561
Jul 23, 2020	267	2,393		36,294
Jul 30, 2020	306	2,699	550	36,538
Aug 06, 2020	5,128	7,827	-17	31,393
Aug 13, 2020	340	8,167		31,053
Aug 20, 2020	254	8,421		30,799
Aug 27, 2020		8,421		30,799
Sep 03, 2020	19	8,440		30,780
Sep 10, 2020		8,440		30,780
Sep 17, 2020	40	8,480	2,815	33,555
Sep 24, 2020		8,480		33,555
Oct 01, 2020	225	8,705		33,330
Oct 08, 2020	160	8,865		33,170
Oct 15, 2020	227	9,092		32,943
Oct 22, 2020	1,334	10,426		31,609
Oct 29, 2020	521	10,947		31,088
Nov 05, 2020	811	11,758	750	31,027
Nov 12, 2020		11,758		31,027
Nov 19, 2020	605	12,363		30,422
Nov 26, 2020		12,363		30,422
Dec 03, 2020	1,549	13,912		28,873
Dec 10, 2020	586	14,498	-12,280	16,007
Dec 17, 2020	990	15,488		15,017
Dec 24, 2020	1,386	16,874	54	13,685
Dec 31, 2020		16,874		13,685
Jan 07, 2021		16,874		13,685
Jan 14, 2021		16,874		13,685
Jan 21, 2021	365	17,239		13,320
Jan 28, 2021	1,495	18,734	10	11,835
Feb 04, 2021	255	18,989		11,580
Feb 11, 2021	1,024	20,013	2,039	12,595
Feb 18, 2021	1,281	21,294	-239	11,075
Feb 25, 2021	435	21,729		10,640
Mar 04, 2021	249	21,978	1,136	11,527
Mar 11, 2021		21,978		11,527
Mar 18, 2021	728	22,706	-4,707	6,092
Mar 25, 2021				
Apr 01, 2021				
Apr 08, 2021				
Apr 15, 2021				
Apr 22, 2021				
Apr 29, 2021				
May 06, 2021				
May 13, 2021				
May 20, 2021				
May 27, 2021				

Source: Foreign Agricultural Service, U.S. Department of Agriculture (FAS-USDA)

Bauxite

Bauxite is a naturally occurring, heterogeneous material comprised of one or more aluminum hydroxide minerals plus various mixtures of silica, iron oxide, titanium, alumina-silicates, and other impurities in trace amounts. Bauxite is an important ore of aluminum and forms by the rapid weathering of granite rocks in warm, humid climates. It is easily purified and can be converted directly into either alum or metallic aluminum. It is a soft mineral with hardness varying from 1 to 3, and specific gravity from 2 to 2.55. Bauxite is dull in appearance and may vary in color from white to brown. It usually occurs in aggregates in pea-sized lumps.

Bauxite is the only raw material used in the production of alumina on a commercial scale in the United States. Bauxite is classified according to the intended commercial application, such as abrasive, cement, chemical, metallurgical, and refractory. Of all the bauxite mined, about 95 percent is converted to alumina to produce aluminum metal with some smaller amounts going to nonmetal uses as various forms of specialty alumina. Small amounts are used in non-metallurgical bauxite applications. Bauxite is also used to produce aluminum chemicals and is used in the steel industry.

Supply – World production of bauxite in 2020 rose +3.6% yr/yr to 371.000 million metric tons. The world's largest producer of bauxite is Australia, with 29.6% of the world's production, followed by Guinea with 22.1%, China with 16.2%, Brazil with 9.4%, India with 5.9%, and Jamaica with 2.1%. Chinese production of bauxite has almost tripled in the past 15 years. India's bauxite production has also risen rapidly and is about double the amount seen 15 years ago.

Demand – U.S. consumption of bauxite in 2019 rose by +31.1% yr/yr to 5.100 million metric tons, but still well below the record high of 15.962 million metric tons seen in 1980.

Trade – The U.S. relies on imports for almost 100% of its consumption needs. Domestic ore, which provides less than 1 percent of the U.S. requirement for bauxite, is mined by one company from surface mines in the states of Alabama and Georgia. U.S. imports of bauxite in 2019 rose +6.3% yr/yr to 3.710 million metric tons, well below the record high of 14.976 million metric tons seen in 1974. U.S. exports of bauxite in 2019 fell -27.0% yr/yr to 3.22 million metric tons.

World Production of Bauxite In Thousands of Metric Tons

Year	Australia	Brazil	China	Greece	Guinea	Guyana[3]	Hungary	India	Jamaica[3]	Russia[3]	Sierra Leone	Suriname	World Total
2011	69,976	33,625	45,000	2,324	15,696	1,818	155	13,000	10,189	5,943	1,300	3,236	254,000
2012	76,281	34,988	47,000	1,816	16,041	2,210	144	13,463	9,339	5,700	776	2,873	255,000
2013	81,119	33,896	50,400	1,844	16,887	1,649	94	20,664	9,435	6,028	616	2,706	295,000
2014	78,632	36,308	59,200	1,873	17,257	1,602	14	22,636	9,677	6,293	1,161	2,708	258,000
2015	80,910	37,057	65,000	1,832	16,303	1,500	8	27,757	9,629	5,900	1,334	1,600	299,000
2016	82,000	34,400	60,800	1,800	31,500	1,700	10	23,886	8,540	5,431	1,369	----	270,000
2017	87,900	38,500	70,000	1,800	46,200	1,500	----	22,900	8,250	5,520	----	----	309,000
2018	86,400	29,000	70,000		57,000		----	23,000	11,000	5,650	----	----	327,000
2019[1]	105,000	34,000	70,000		67,000		----	23,000	9,020	5,570	----	----	358,000
2020[2]	110,000	35,000	60,000		82,000		----	22,000	7,700	6,100	----	----	371,000

[1] Preliminary. [2] Estimate. [3] Dry Bauxite equivalent of ore processed. *Source: U.S. Geological Survey (USGS)*

Salient Statistics of Bauxite in the United States In Thousands of Metric Tons

Year	Net Import Reliance as a % of Apparent Consump	Average Price F.O.B. Mine $ per Ton	Consumtion by Industry: Total	Alumina	Abrasive	Chemical	Re-fractoty	Dry Equivalent: Imports[4]	Exports[3]	Con-sumption	Stocks, December 31: Producers & Consumers	Gov't Owned	Total
2011	100	39	8,820	8,670	----	----	----	9,540	22	8,820	W	----	W
2012	>75	36	9,560	9,330	----	----	----	10,300	11	9,560	W	----	W
2013	>75	----	10,200	9,810	----	----	----	9,830	4	10,200	W	----	W
2014	>75	----	9,840	9,600	----	----	----	10,800	3	9,840	W	----	W
2015	>75	----	9,660	9,340	----	----	----	10,400	3	9,660	W	----	W
2016	>75	----	5,360	5,080	----	----	----	4,930	5	5,360	W	----	W
2017	>75	----	3,510	3,340	----	----	----	3,430	5	3,510	W	----	W
2018	>75	----	3,890		----	----	----	3,490	4		W	----	W
2019[1]	>75	----	5,100		----	----	----	3,710	3		W	----	W
2020[2]	>75	----			----	----	----				W	----	W

[1] Preliminary. [2] Estimate. [3] Including concentrates. [4] For consumption. W = Withheld. *Source: U.S. Geological Survey (USGS)*

Bismuth

Bismuth (symbol Bi) is a rare metallic element with a pinkish tinge. Bismuth has been known since ancient times, but it was confused with lead, tin, and zinc until the middle of the 18th century. Among the elements in the earth's crust, bismuth is ranked about 73rd in natural abundance. This makes bismuth about as rare as silver. Most industrial bismuth is obtained as a by-product of ore extraction.

Bismuth is useful for castings because of the unusual way that it expands after solidifying. Some of bismuth's alloys have unusually low melting points. Bismuth is one of the most difficult of all substances to magnetize. It tends to turn at right angles to a magnetic field. Because of this property, it is used in instruments for measuring the strength of magnetic fields.

Bismuth finds a wide variety of uses such as pharmaceutical compounds, ceramic glazes, crystal ware, and chemicals and pigments. Bismuth is found in household pharmaceuticals and is used to treat stomach ulcers. Bismuth is opaque to X-rays and can be used in fluoroscopy. Bismuth has also found new use as a nontoxic substitute for lead in various applications such as brass plumbing fixtures, crystal ware, lubricating greases, pigments, and solders. There has been environmental interest in the use of bismuth as a replacement for lead used in shot for waterfowl hunting and in fishing sinkers. Another use has been for galvanizing to improve drainage characteristics of galvanizing alloys. Zinc-bismuth alloys have the same drainage properties as zinc-lead without being as hazardous.

Prices – The average price of bismuth (99.99% pure) in the U.S. in 2020 fell -14.5% yr/yr to $2.72 per pound, well below the 2007 record high of $13.32 per pound.

Supply – World mine production of bismuth in 2016 fell -1.0% yr/yr to 10,200 metric tons, down from the 2015 record high of 10,300 metric tons. The world's largest producer in 2016 was China with 72.5% of world production, followed by Mexico with 6.9%. World refinery production of Bismuth in 2020 fell -19.4% to 17,000 metric tons. China had 82.4% of production, Japan had 2.8%, and Mexico had 1.6%, and Kazakhstan had 1.4%. The U.S. does not have any significant domestic refinery production of bismuth.

Demand – U.S. consumption of bismuth in 2020 fell by -8.8% yr/yr to 500 metric tons, well below the record high of 2,630 metric tons in 2007. In 2017 the consumed uses of bismuth were 65.1% for chemicals and 13.0% for fusible alloys.

Trade – U.S. imports of bismuth in 2020 fell -13.0% yr/yr to 2,000 metric tons, well below the 2007 record high of 3,070 metric tons. In 2017, 6.2% of U.S. imports came from Mexico and 5.0% from Belgium. U.S. exports of bismuth and alloys in 2020 rose +5.9% yr/yr to 670 metric tons, well below the 2010 record high of 1,040 metric tons.

World Production of Bismuth In Metric Tons (Mine Output=Metal Content)

	Mine Output, Metal Content						Refined Metal						
Year	Canada	China	Japan	Mexico	Peru	World Total	Belgium	China	Japan	Kazak-hastan[3]	Mexico	Peru	World Total
2014	10	3	7,600	948	40	8,600	----	15,871	588	230	864	----	19,000
2015	10	3	7,500	700	40	10,300	----	16,013	632	220	603	----	19,400
2016	10	3	7,400	700	40	10,200	----	14,000	428	270	539	----	19,700
2017	----	----	----	----	----	----	----	13,500	525	270	513	----	18,500
2018							----	14,000	571	290	333	----	19,200
2019[1]							----	16,000	540	270	300	----	21,100
2020[2]							----	14,000	480	240	270	----	17,000

[1] Preliminary. [2] Estimate. *Source U.S. Geological Survey (USGS)*

Salient Statistics of Bismuth in the United States In Metric Tons

	Bismuth Consumed, By Uses							Imports from Metallic Bismuth from				
Year	Metal-lurgical Additives	Other Alloys & Uses	Fusible Alloys	Chem-icals[3]	Total Con-sumption	Consumer Stocks Dec. 31	Exports of Metal & Alloys	Belgium	Mexico	Preu	Total	Dealer Price $ Per Pound
2014	W	W	66	499	655	430	567	303.0	----	71.6	2,270	11.14
2015	W	W	84	416	621	456	519	155.0	16.4	----	1,950	6.43
2016	W	W	99	453	651	513	431	130.0	161.0	0.1	2,190	4.53
2017	W	W	99	439	694	489	392	141.0	176.0	----	2,820	4.93
2018	W	W	96	314	570	346	653	143.0	205.0	----	2,510	4.64
2019[1]	W	W			548	443	636				2,300	3.19
2020[2]	W	W			500	500	670				2,000	2.70

[1] Preliminary. [2] Estimate. [3] Includes pharmaceuticals. *Source: U.S. Geological Survey (USGS)*

Average Price of Bismuth (99.99%) in the United States In Dollars Per Pound

Year	Jan.	Feb.	Mar.	Apr.	May	June	July	Aug.	Sept.	Oct.	Nov.	Dec.	Average
2017	4.72	4.63	4.70	4.84	4.93	4.87	4.85	4.87	5.17	5.20	5.20	5.25	4.94
2018	5.22	5.21	5.28	5.22	5.04	4.68	4.55	4.35	4.27	4.17	3.80	3.69	4.62
2019	3.68	3.94	3.68	3.57	3.42	3.19	2.92	2.84	2.74	2.75	2.81	2.66	3.18
2020	2.58	2.58	2.63	2.57	2.59	2.60	2.61	2.67	2.91	2.98	2.98	2.98	2.72

Source: American Metal Market (AMM)

Broilers

Broiler chickens are raised for meat rather than for eggs. The broiler industry was started in the late 1950s when chickens were selectively bred for meat production. Broiler chickens are housed in massive flocks, mainly between 20,000 and 50,000 birds, with some flocks reaching over 100,000 birds. Broiler chicken farmers usually rear five or six batches of chickens per year.

After just six or seven weeks, broiler chickens are slaughtered (a chicken's natural lifespan is around seven years). Chickens marketed as pouissons, or spring chickens, are slaughtered after four weeks. A few are kept longer than seven weeks to be sold as the larger roasting chickens.

Prices – The average monthly price received by farmers for broilers (live weight) in 2020 fell by -24.5% yr/yr to 36.4 cents per pound. The average monthly price of wholesale broilers (ready-to-cook) in 2020 fell by -34.5% to 82.50 cents per pound, farther below the 2014 record high of 104.88 cents per pound.

Supply – Total production of broilers in 2020 rose +1.5% yr/yr to 44.550 billion pounds. The number of broilers raised for commercial production in 2020 was up +0.1% yr/yr to 9.228 billion birds, at a new record high. The average live weight per bird rose +1.4% to 6.1 pounds, which was a new record high and was about 70% heavier than the average bird weight of 3.62 pounds seen in 1970, attesting to the increased efficiency of the industry.

Demand – U.S. per capita consumption of broilers in 2020 rose by +1.8% to 94.7 pounds (ready-to-cook) per-person per-year, a new record high. U.S. consumption of chicken has more than doubled in the past two decades, up from 47.0 pounds in 1980, as consumers have increased their consumption of chicken because of the focus on low-carb diets and because chicken is a leaner and healthier meat than either beef or pork.

Broiler Supply and Prices in the United States

	Federally Inspected Slaughter					Per Capita Consumption	Prices	
Years and Quarters	Number (Million)	Average Weight (Pounds)	Liveweight Pounds (Mil. Lbs.)	Certified RTC[3] Weight (Mil. Lbs.)	Total Production RTC[3] (Mil. Lbs.)	RTC[3] Basis (Mil. Lbs.)	Farm (Cents per Pound)	Georgia Dock[4] (Cents per Pound)
2015	8,688	6.12	53,165	40,046	40,048	89.0	52.92	113.83
2016	8,768	6.16	54,037	40,692	40,696	89.7	50.38	111.93
2017	8,916	6.20	55,313	41,661	41,662	90.8	54.58	----
2018	8,984	6.25	56,185	42,328	43,905	92.4	56.83	----
2019	9,135	6.31	57,641	43,426	43,905	95.1	48.18	----
2020[1]	9,138	6.43	58,588	44,155	44,550	96.1	36.43	----
I	2,348	6.35	14,919	11,237	11,237	24.4	44.77	----
II	2,258	6.47	14,523	10,940	10,940	23.9	31.23	----
III	2,258	6.47	14,523	10,940	11,358	24.5	31.57	----
IV	2,274	6.43	14,624	11,039	11,015	23.3	38.13	----

[1] Preliminary. [2] Estimate. [3] Total production equals federal inspected slaughter plus other slaughter minus cut-up & further processing condemnation. [4] Ready-to-cook basis. *Source: Economic Research Service, U.S. Department of Agriculture (ERS-USDA)*

Salient Statistics of Broilers in the United States

	Commercial Production		Average			Total Chickens[3] Supply and Distribution							
						Production			Storage			Consumption	
Year	Number (Mil. Lbs.)	Liveweight (Mil. Lbs.)	Liveweight Per Bird (Mil. Lbs.)	Average Price (cents Lb.)	Value of Production (Mil. $)	Federally Inspected (In Millions of Pounds)	Other Chickens (In Millions of Pounds)	Total (In Millions of Pounds)	Stocks January 1 (In Millions of Pounds)	Exports (In Millions of Pounds)	Broiler Feed Ratio (pounds)	Total (Mil. Lbs.)	Per Capita[4] (Pounds)
2014	8,545	51,379	6.01	63.9	32,728	38,550		38,550	675	7,407	5.0	31,377	83.30
2015	8,689	53,376	6.14	52.9	28,716	40,046		40,046	683	6,465	5.0	33,652	88.90
2016	8,768	54,037	6.16	50.4	25,936	40,692		40,692	840	6,803	4.7	34,194	90.90
2017	8,916	55,313	6.20	54.6	30,232	41,661		41,661	786	6,910	5.4	34,895	
2018	9,032	56,518	6.26	56.8	31,746	42,583		42,583					
2019[1]	9,221	58,266	6.32	48.2		43,889		43,889					
2020[2]	9,228	59,135	6.41	36.4		44,573		44,573					

Preliminary. [2] Estimate. [3] Ready-to-cook. [4] Retail weight basis. Source: Economic Research Service, U.S. Department of Agriculture (ERS-USDA)

Average Wholesale Broiler[2] Prices RTC (Ready-to-Cook) In Cents Per Pound

Year	Jan.	Feb.	Mar.	Apr.	May	June	July	Aug.	Sept.	Oct.	Nov.	Dec.	Average
2014	96.45	92.45	106.26	110.11	117.59	113.40	107.16	99.69	107.05	106.68	103.68	98.07	104.88
2015	99.62	92.56	98.88	104.79	106.71	101.17	91.01	82.61	77.40	74.09	75.37	82.05	90.52
2016	87.90	81.52	84.46	88.41	93.72	96.93	88.62	79.71	76.68	70.73	79.28	84.04	84.33
2017	85.58	85.07	94.49	96.91	108.97	109.02	103.80	92.47	88.38	84.84	86.06	87.33	93.58
2018	94.00	91.08	101.97	108.73	117.59	118.92	110.60	87.33	83.13	83.56	86.91	89.75	97.80
2019	98.90	89.78	93.33	97.61	100.89	94.63	88.24	80.88	76.92	78.86	78.30	84.63	88.58
2020[1]	90.56	80.64	79.35	53.52	73.75	73.60	70.41	66.08	63.58	67.70	76.80	82.47	73.21

[1] Preliminary. [2] 12-city composite wholesale price. *Source: Economic Research Service, U.S. Department of Agriculture (ERS-USDA)*

Butter

Butter is a dairy product produced by churning the fat from milk, usually cow's milk, until it solidifies. In some parts of the world, butter is also made from the milk of goats, sheep, and even horses. Butter has been in use since at least 2,000 BC. Today butter is used principally as a food item, but in ancient times it was used more as an ointment, medicine, or illuminating oil. Butter was first churned in skin pouches thrown back and forth over the backs of trotting horses.

It takes about 10 quarts of milk to produce 1 pound of butter. The manufacture of butter is the third largest use of milk in the U.S. California is generally the largest producing state, followed closely by Wisconsin, with Washington as a distant third. Commercially finished butter is comprised of milk fat (80% to 85%), water (12% to 16%), and salt (about 2%). Although the price of butter is highly correlated with the price of milk, it also has its own supply and demand dynamics.

The consumption of butter has dropped in recent decades because pure butter has a high level of animal fat and cholesterol that have been linked to obesity and heart disease. The primary substitute for butter is margarine, which is produced from vegetable oil rather than milk fat. U.S. per capita consumption of margarine has risen from 2.6 pounds in 1930 to recent levels near 8.3 pounds, much higher than U.S. butter consumption.

Butter Futures and options are traded on the CME Group. The CME's butter futures contract calls for the delivery of 20,000 pounds of butter and is priced in cents per pound. Futures on butter are traded on the New Zealand Futures Exchange (NZFE).

Prices – The average monthly price of butter at the CME in 2020 fell -29.2% yr/yr to $1.5782/pound, down from the 2017 record high of $2.3278/pound.

Supply – World production of butter in 2021 is forecasted to rise +2.2% yr/yr to 11.458 million metric tons, a new record high. The world's largest producers of butter for 2021 are forecasted to be India with 55.0% of the world production, the European Union with 21.4%, the United States with 8.7%, New Zealand with 4.5%, and Russia with 2.4%. Production of creamery butter by U.S. factories in 2020 rose +7.5% yr/yr to 2.125 billion pounds, a new record high.

Demand – Total commercial use of creamery butter in the U.S. rose 2.2% yr/yr to 2.099 million pounds in 2020. That is about one-third more than the commercial use of butter back in the 1950s. Cold storage stocks of creamery butter in the U.S. on January 1, 2021, rose +5.8% yr/yr to 189.655 million pounds.

Trade – World imports of butter in 2021 are expected to rise +2.4% yr/yr to 521,000 metric tons. U.S. imports of butter in 2021 are expected to rise +4.3% to 73,000 metric tons. World exports of butter in 2021 are expected to rise +1.3% yr/yr to 931,000 metric tons. U.S exports in 2021 are expected to be unchanged yr/yr to 26,000 metric tons, which is far below the 1993 record high of 145,000 metric tons.

Supply and Distribution of Butter in the United States In Millions of Pounds

	Supply				Distribution							93 Score AA Wholesale Price	
					Domestic Disappearance			Department of Agriculture					
Year	Production	Cold Storage Stocks[3] Jan. 1	Imports	Total Supply	Total	Per Capita (Pounds)	Exports	Stocks[4] Jan. 1	Stocks[4] Dec 31	Removed by USDA Programs	Total Use	$ per Pound	
2012	1,859.5	106,856	37.478	2,002	1,746	5.5	104	----	----	----	1,850	----	1.6029
2013	1,862.5	153,027	26.455	2,041	1,724	5.5	205	----	----	----	1,929	----	1.5560
2014	1,855.3	112,467	46.297	2,015	1,746	5.5	163	----	----	----	1,909	----	2.1643
2015	1,849.5	104,728	83.775	2,039	1,834	5.6	51	----	----	----	1,885	----	2.0886
2016	1,839.4	155,082	103.616	2,097	1,872	5.7	60	----	----	----	1,931	----	2.0815
2017	1,847.5	166,043	90.389	2,103	1,870	5.7	64	----	----	----	1,933	----	2.3278
2018	1,891.0	168,787	130.071	2,191	1,905		108	----	----	----	2,013	----	2.2503
2019[1]	1,905.1	179,333	145.504	2,222	1,989		57	----	----	----	2,046	----	2.2302
2020[2]	2,289.0	189,655	141.094	2,269	2,039		55	----	----	----	2,094	----	1.8363

[1] Preliminary. [2] Estimates. [3] Includes butter-equivalent. [4] Includes butteroil. [5] Includes stocks held by USDA.
Source: Economic Research Service, U.S. Department of Agriculture (ERS-USDA)

Quarterly Commercial Disappearance of Creamery Butter in the United States In Millions of Pounds

Year	First Quarter	Second Quarter	Third Quarter	Fourth Quarter	Total	Year	First Quarter	Second Quarter	Third Quarter	Fourth Quarter	Total
2009	371.0	352.3	343.2	457.9	1,524.6	2015	417.3	403.2	468.4	509.5	1,798.4
2010	362.6	353.0	365.1	443.5	1,524.1	2016	447.6	406.3	457.7	546.4	1,857.9
2011	387.0	372.0	426.3	494.5	1,679.7	2017	412.9	428.8	463.5	550.5	1,855.8
2012	402.5	403.6	435.6	491.3	1,733.0	2018	429.0	421.6	468.5	576.2	1,895.3
2013	412.3	372.2	434.2	517.8	1,736.5	2019	442.7	427.2	472.9	594.2	1,937.0
2014	380.9	433.5	433.6	508.5	1,756.4	2020[1]	457.2	511.2	489.2	613.6	2,071.3

[1] Preliminary. *Source: Economic Research Service, U.S. Department of Agriculture (ERS-USDA)*

World Production of Butter[3] In Thousands of Metric Tons

Year	Argentina	Australia	Brazil	Canada	European Union	India	Japan	Mexico	New Zealand	Russia	Ukraine	United States	World Total
2014	52	125	85	88	2,250	4,887	61	207	580	252	115	842	9,748
2015	46	120	83	91	2,335	5,035	65	216	594	260	103	839	9,999
2016	37	110	82	93	2,345	5,200	66	217	570	246	103	834	10,119
2017	30	103	83	109	2,340	5,400	60	223	525	270	109	838	10,309
2018	33	93	85	116	2,345	5,600	60	228	550	256	106	893	10,588
2019	29	70	85	112	2,375	5,850	62	231	525	268	89	905	10,821
2020[1]	39	75	80	120	2,425	6,100	70	234	525	278	82	959	11,207
2021[2]	37	80	81	122	2,450	6,300	66	237	520	280	77	992	11,458

[1] Preliminary. [2] Forecast. [3] Factory (including creameries and dairies) & farm. NA = Not available.
Source: Foreign Agricultural Service, U.S. Department of Agriculture (FAS-USDA)

Production of Creamery Butter in Factories in the United States In Thousands of Pounds

Year	Jan.	Feb.	Mar.	Apr.	May	June	July	Aug.	Sept.	Oct.	Nov.	Dec.	Total
2013	188,037	173,335	181,421	166,658	163,785	140,124	132,746	134,370	132,232	145,886	142,192	161,730	1,862,516
2014	184,030	166,097	166,626	167,730	166,285	140,391	137,788	129,092	131,802	151,201	144,518	169,755	1,855,315
2015	173,634	155,976	167,816	165,457	169,409	143,692	135,525	128,072	133,652	148,414	152,323	175,549	1,849,519
2016	170,746	168,272	174,916	171,210	166,178	147,705	135,169	123,523	135,283	139,858	143,086	163,453	1,839,399
2017	178,060	161,013	177,021	161,956	163,397	139,200	135,625	131,152	134,552	144,671	149,721	171,105	1,847,473
2018	182,143	167,669	181,847	175,216	170,122	142,122	134,564	133,571	135,041	148,896	149,428	170,388	1,891,007
2019	189,642	164,525	180,694	172,371	170,044	154,848	150,705	141,323	144,334	162,921	161,852	183,774	1,977,033
2020[1]	193,422	188,035	195,886	217,531	177,966	150,200	154,883	151,631	151,612	165,383	173,175	205,533	2,125,257

[1] Preliminary. *Source: Economic Research Service, U.S. Department of Agriculture (ERS-USDA)*

Cold Storage Holdings of Creamery Butter in the United States, on First of Month In Millions of Pounds

Year	Jan.	Feb.	Mar.	Apr.	May	June	July	Aug.	Sept.	Oct.	Nov.	Dec.
2013	153,027	207,075	238,342	254,991	309,719	321,954	318,893	295,751	263,928	233,031	181,799	121,627
2014	112,467	143,890	171,773	191,755	186,914	209,430	199,248	180,834	172,789	152,361	147,956	107,566
2015	104,728	148,885	179,003	184,373	232,372	265,198	256,000	254,347	212,189	187,528	178,834	132,740
2016	155,082	192,101	235,559	243,134	295,771	324,942	328,149	332,848	318,774	269,125	228,158	161,203
2017	166,043	221,556	269,857	272,500	292,284	313,593	310,158	307,359	280,194	255,839	217,918	159,258
2018	168,787	226,694	265,756	273,955	307,325	338,492	336,625	318,325	209,851	282,379	231,223	154,366
2019	179,333	211,168	243,511	269,697	290,820	313,822	326,297	329,595	304,368	290,649	234,507	180,637
2020[1]	189,655	247,376	301,820	309,587	372,598	375,777	362,452	371,467	371,519	343,948	299,731	251,820

[1] Preliminary. *Source: Agricultural Statistics Board, U.S. Department of Agriculture (ASB-USDA)*

Average Price of Butter at Chicago Mercantile Exchange In Cents Per Pound

Year	Jan.	Feb.	Mar.	Apr.	May	June	July	Aug.	Sept.	Oct.	Nov.	Dec.	Average
2013	1.4933	1.5713	1.6421	1.7197	1.5997	1.5105	1.4751	1.4013	1.5233	1.5267	1.6126	1.5963	1.5560
2014	1.7756	1.8047	1.9145	1.9357	2.1713	2.2630	2.4624	2.5913	2.9740	2.3184	1.9968	1.7633	2.1643
2015	1.5714	1.7293	1.7166	1.7937	1.9309	1.9065	1.9056	2.1542	2.6690	2.4757	2.8779	2.3318	2.0886
2016	2.1214	2.0840	1.9605	2.0563	2.0554	2.2640	2.2731	2.1776	1.9950	1.8239	1.9899	2.1763	2.0815
2017	2.2393	2.1534	2.1392	2.0992	2.2684	2.5688	2.6195	2.6473	2.4370	2.3293	2.2244	2.2078	2.3278
2018	2.1587	2.1211	2.2011	2.3145	2.3751	2.3270	2.2361	2.3009	2.2545	2.2600	2.2480	2.2071	2.2503
2019	2.2481	2.2659	2.2773	2.2635	2.3366	2.3884	2.3897	2.2942	2.1690	2.1071	2.0495	1.9736	2.2302
2020	1.8813	1.7913	1.7235	1.1999	1.4710	1.8291	1.6925	1.5038	1.5163	1.4550	1.3941	1.4806	1.5782

Source: Economic Research Service, U.S. Department of Agriculture (ERS-USDA)

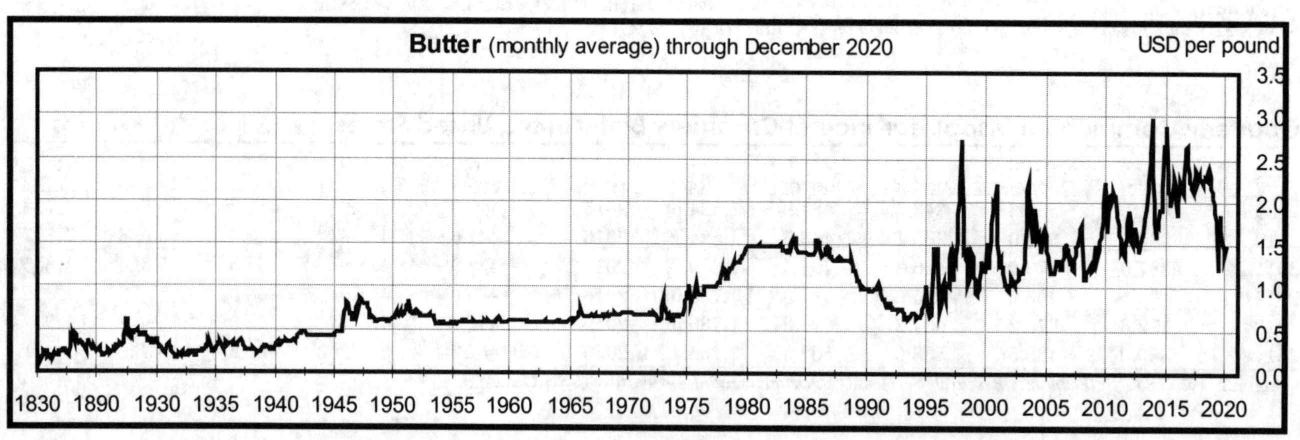

Cadmium

Cadmium (atomic symbol Cd) is a soft, bluish-white, metallic element that can easily be shaped and cut with a knife. Cadmium melts at 321 degrees Celsius and boils at 765 degrees Celsius. Cadmium burns brightly in air when heated, forming the oxide CdO. In 1871, the German chemist Friedrich Stromeyer discovered cadmium in incrustations in zinc furnaces.

Rare greenockite is the only mineral-bearing cadmium. Cadmium occurs most often in small quantities associated with zinc ores, such as sphalerite. Electrolysis or fractional distillation is used to separate the cadmium and zinc. About 80% of world cadmium output is a by-product of zinc refining. The remaining 20% comes from secondary sources and the recycling of cadmium products. Cadmium recycling is practical only from nickel-cadmium batteries and from some alloys and dust from electric-arc furnaces.

Cadmium is used primarily for metal plating and coating operations in transportation equipment, machinery, baking enamels, photography, and television phosphors. It is also used in solar modules, pigments and lasers, and in nickel-cadmium and solar batteries.

Supply – World cadmium production in 2020 fell by -5.7% yr/yr to 23,000 metric tons, down from the 2018 record high of 25,100 metric tons. The largest producer was China, with 35.7% of total world production, followed by South Korea with 13.0%, and both Japan and Canada with 7.8%.

Demand – U.S. cadmium consumption in 2010 rose by +139.7% yr/yr to 477 metric tons. Of the total apparent consumption that year, about 75% was used for batteries, 12% for pigments, 8% for coatings and plating, 4% for nonferrous alloys, and 1% for other uses.

Trade – The U.S. has been a net exporter of cadmium since 2004. In 2020 the U.S. imports fell -46.4% yr/yr to 263 metric tons. U.S. exports of cadmium in 2020 rose +265.6% yr/yr to 446 metric tons, but still well below the 2-decade high of 661 metric tons in 2009.

World Refinery Production of Cadmium In Metric Tons

Year	Australia	Canada	China	Germany	India	Japan	Kazakh-stan	Korea, South	Mexico	Nether-lands	Russia	United States[3]	World Total
2013	380	1,313	7,496	400	287	1,826	1,319	3,904	1,451	610	1,200	W	22,500
2014	350	1,187	8,201	400	116	1,829	1,633	5,645	1,409	620	1,200	W	25,100
2015	380	1,159	8,162	400	130	1,959	1,475	5,600	1,283	620	1,200	W	24,600
2016	400	2,305	8,200	400	21	1,988	1,500	5,600	1,244	620	1,200	W	25,800
2017	400	1,802	8,200	400	61	2,142	1,500	5,600	1,156	600	1,200	W	25,400
2018		1,680	8,200			1,980	1,500	5,000	1,360	1,100	1,200	W	25,100
2019[1]		1,803	8,200			2,000	1,500	4,400	1,395	1,100	900	W	24,400
2020[2]		1,800	8,200			1,800	1,500	3,000	1,300	1,100	900	W	23,000

[1] Preliminary. [2] Estimate. [3] Primary and secondary metal. *Source: U.S. Geological Survey (USGS)*

Salient Statistics of Cadmium in the United States In Metric Tons of Contained Cadmium

Year	Net import Reliance As a % of Apparent Consumption	Production (Metal)	Producer Shipments	Cadmium Sulfide Production	Production Other Compounds	Imports of Cadmium Metal[3]	Exports[4]	Apparent Consumption	Industry Stocks Dec. 31[5]	New York Dealer Price $ Per Lb.
2014	E	W	W	----	----	139	270	W	W	.88
2015	E	W	W	----	----	326	596	W	W	.67
2016	<25	W	W	----	----	292	540	W	W	.61
2017	<25	W	W	----	----	296	428	W	W	.79
2018	<50	W	W	----	----	294	140	W	W	1.31
2019[1]	<50	W	W	----	----	491	122	W	W	1.21
2020[2]	<50	W	W	----	----	263	446	W	W	1.04

[1] Preliminary. [2] Estimate. [3] For consumption. [4] Cadmium metal, alloys, dross, flue dust. [5] Metallic, Compounds, Distributors. [6] Sticks & Balls in 1 to 5 short ton lots of metal (99.95%). E = Net exporter. *Source: U.S. Geological Survey (USGS)*

Average Price of Cadmium (99.95%) in the United States In Dollars Per Pound

Year	Jan.	Feb.	Mar.	Apr.	May	June	July	Aug.	Sept.	Oct.	Nov.	Dec.	Average
2016	46.79	52.36	58.74	68.79	73.00	71.64	64.29	54.30	50.77	54.05	63.89	67.50	60.51
2017	67.50	70.75	74.20	77.90	78.35	74.32	70.69	70.50	71.64	90.86	104.55	102.14	79.45
2018	101.00	121.85	152.50	155.43	143.46	130.83	129.66	127.50	127.50	127.50	127.50	126.50	130.94
2019	125.30	135.88	138.00	137.66	131.11	123.10	113.22	109.09	108.57	110.00	108.10	116.38	121.37
2020	119.15	119.75	121.50	116.67	107.50	105.00	97.30	94.25	91.61	89.56	89.75	93.89	103.83

Source: American Metal Market (AMM)

Canola (Rapeseed)

Canola is a genetic variation of rapeseed that was developed by Canadian plant breeders specifically for its nutritional qualities and its low level of saturated fat. The term Canola is a contraction of "Canadian oil." The history of canola oil begins with the rapeseed plant, a member of the mustard family. The rape plant is grown both as feed for livestock and birdfeed. For 4,000 years, the oil from the rapeseed was used in China and India for cooking and as lamp oil. During World War II, rapeseed oil was used as a marine and industrial lubricant. After the war, the market for rapeseed oil plummeted. Rapeseed growers needed other uses for their crops, and that stimulated the research that led to the development of canola. In 1974, Canadian plant breeders from the University of Manitoba produced canola by genetically altering rapeseed. Each canola plant produces yellow flowers, which then produce pods. The tiny round seeds within each pod are crushed to produce canola oil. Each canola seed contains approximately 40% oil. Canola oil is the world's third-largest source of vegetable oil, accounting for 13% of world vegetable oils, following soybean oil at 32%, and palm oil at 28%. The rest of the seed is processed into canola meal, which is used as high-protein livestock feed.

The climate in Canada is especially suitable for canola plant growth. Today, over 13 million acres of Canadian soil are dedicated to canola production. Canola oil is Canada's leading vegetable oil. Due to strong demand from the U.S. for canola oil, approximately 70% of Canada's canola oil is exported to the U.S. Canola oil is used as a salad oil, cooking oil, and for margarine as well as in the manufacture of inks, biodegradable greases, pharmaceuticals, fuel, soap, and cosmetics.

Canola futures and options are traded on the ICE U.S. Exchange. The futures contract calls for the delivery of 20 metric tons of canola and 5 contracts are together called a "1 board lot." The futures contract is priced in Canadian dollars per metric ton.

Prices – ICE U.S. canola prices on the nearest-futures chart (Barchart.com symbol code RS) in 2020 rose steadily all year to close the year up +7.8% yr/yr at CD$637.00 per metric ton. The average monthly wholesale price of canola oil in the Midwest in 2020 rose +13.7% yr/yr to 40.79 cents per pound. The average monthly wholesale price of canola meal (delivery Pacific Northwest) in the 2020/21 crop year rose +6.7% to $292.29 per short ton.

Supply – World canola production in the 2020/21 marketing year is forecasted to fall -0.5% yr/yr to 68.896 million metric tons, down from the 2017/2018 record high. The world's largest canola producers are expected to be Canada with 27.6% of world production in 2020/21, European Union with 24.4%, China with 19.2%, and India with 11.1%. U.S. production of canola in 2020/21 is expected to rise +1.5% yr/yr to 1.576 million metric tons. U.S. production of canola oil in 2020/21 is expected to rise by +5.5% to 870,000 metric tons which is a new record high. World production of canola meal in 2020/21 is expected to fall -0.9% to 39.157 million metric tons.

Demand – World crush demand for canola in 2020/21 is expected to fall -0.8% yr/yr to 67.734 million metric tons. World consumption of canola meal in 2020/21 is expected to fall -1.2% yr/yr to 39.115 million metric tons. World consumption of canola oil in 2020/21 is expected to fall -1.4% to 27.672 million metric tons.

Trade – World canola exports in 2020/21 are expected to fall by -2.9% to 15,468 million metric tons and remain below the 2017/18 record high. World canola oil exports are expected to fall by -1.8% to 5.472 million metric tons, below last year's record high, and world canola meal exports to rise +2.6% yr/yr to 6.932 million metric tons, a new record high. World canola imports in 2020/21 are expected to fall by -0.6% to 15,140 million metric tons, world canola oil imports are expected to fall by -4.1% to 5.231 million metric tons, and world canola meal imports are expected to fall by -5.3% to 7.003 million metric tons. Regarding U.S. canola trade, U.S. canola imports in 2020/21 are expected to rise +4.4% to 590,000 metric tons, and U.S. exports are expected to fall -18.7% to 148,000 metric tons.

World Production of Canola (Rapeseed) In Thousands of Metric Tons

Year	Australia	Bangla-desh	Belarus	Canada	China	European Union	India	Kazakh-stan	Pakistan	Russia	Ukraine	United States	World Total
2011-12	3,427	262	379	14,608	13,137	19,240	6,030	148	179	956	1,437	694	61,228
2012-13	4,142	294	705	13,869	13,401	19,560	6,851	117	220	945	1,300	1,087	63,305
2013-14	3,832	230	676	18,551	13,523	21,306	6,650	242	231	1,259	2,352	1,000	70,627
2014-15	3,540	230	730	16,410	13,914	24,587	5,080	241	216	1,324	2,200	1,138	70,422
2015-16	2,775	230	382	18,377	13,859	21,997	5,920	138	194	1,001	1,744	1,305	68,735
2016-17	4,313	230	260	19,599	13,128	20,538	6,620	170	190	997	1,250	1,405	69,488
2017-18	3,893	230	603	21,458	13,274	22,184	7,100	279	260	1,497	2,217	1,394	75,154
2018-19[1]	2,366	230	456	20,724	13,281	20,061	8,000	394	270	1,989	2,850	1,644	72,987
2019-20[2]	2,330	230	578	19,607	13,485	16,880	7,700	241	410	2,040	3,465	1,553	69,222
2020-21[3]	3,600	230	550	19,000	13,200	16,800	7,650	125	460	2,500	2,500	1,576	68,896

[1] Preliminary. [2] Estimate. [3] Forecast. *Source: Economic Research Service, U.S. Department of Agriculture (ERS-USDA); The Oil World*

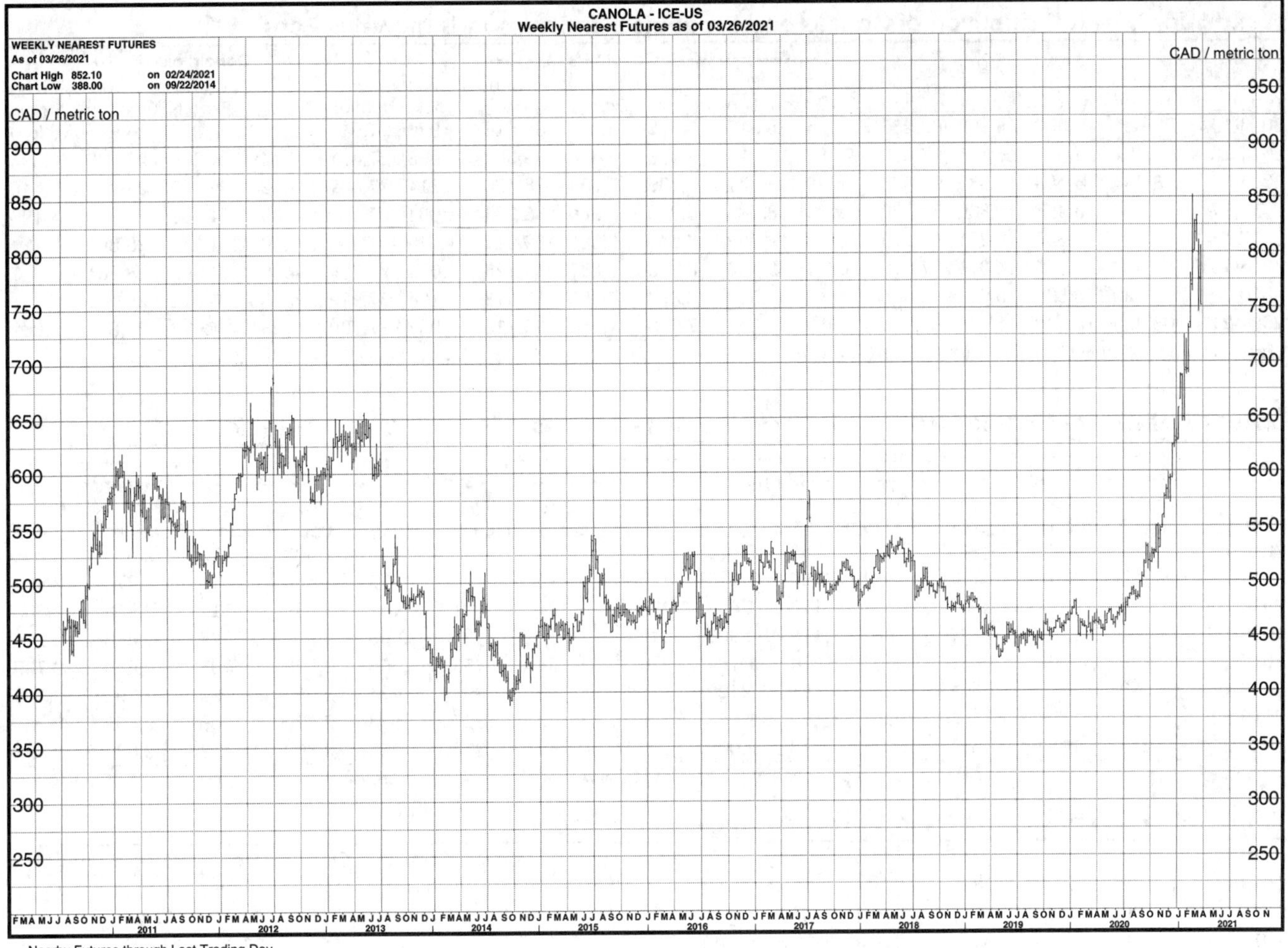

Nearby Futures through Last Trading Day.

Volume of Trading of Canola Futures in Winnipeg In 20 Metric Ton Units

Year	Jan.	Feb.	Mar.	Apr.	May	June	July	Aug.	Sept.	Oct.	Nov.	Dec.	Total
2011	345,505	483,744	342,887	417,453	326,805	436,050	268,144	331,289	490,065	443,909	361,250	406,052	4,653,153
2012	375,738	588,006	536,743	535,291	367,014	399,329	299,775	279,962	332,661	487,242	279,767	388,733	4,870,261
2013	413,545	558,269	295,056	489,741	355,341	347,609	276,608	381,094	523,431	654,471	479,983	716,539	5,491,687
2014	536,669	570,465	454,015	552,959	369,170	424,087	331,748	298,308	486,457	615,158	346,000	568,886	5,553,922
2015	489,637	486,854	400,209	447,467	327,911	644,971	335,432	365,804	447,279	624,741	403,539	585,625	5,559,469
2016	408,059	641,600	441,094	619,493	518,643	644,052	358,823	385,481	407,031	702,156	490,671	627,053	6,244,156
2017	397,507	549,415	508,671	521,424	344,251	530,093	331,900	298,854	390,755	625,937	381,367	511,181	5,391,355
2018	349,016	530,467	351,802	541,694	324,795	561,388	269,381	251,140	260,732	537,386	333,575	516,654	4,828,030
2019	368,405	516,738	415,251	588,285	438,572	513,703	275,852	296,384	435,966	767,539	323,919	671,042	5,611,656
2020	496,090	575,177	481,171	426,406	297,740	508,999	409,940	425,008	661,995	702,630	505,482	729,352	6,219,990

Contract size = 20 tonnes. *Source: ICE Futures Canada (ICE)*

Average Open Interest of Canola Futures in Winnipeg In 20 Metric Ton Units

Year	Jan.	Feb.	Mar.	Apr.	May	June	July	Aug.	Sept.	Oct.	Nov.	Dec.
2011	204,715	207,186	188,138	176,678	166,554	166,105	150,624	166,066	188,592	166,852	160,276	140,345
2012	151,192	181,837	200,941	228,092	242,231	224,287	220,919	224,646	233,085	198,147	157,664	147,883
2013	155,134	189,913	178,763	164,200	143,013	129,283	118,115	145,257	186,811	177,248	200,975	226,220
2014	230,796	224,847	230,852	219,844	168,705	165,651	147,462	165,501	173,282	159,986	142,371	139,732
2015	170,492	217,729	205,075	168,204	151,739	189,500	180,410	173,734	172,828	186,334	174,098	187,855
2016	187,904	177,999	171,820	162,225	173,204	172,984	155,301	173,698	195,884	190,086	208,329	210,792
2017	181,938	181,007	185,572	185,411	178,603	159,381	117,599	128,345	180,168	173,585	192,341	171,325
2018	171,262	180,496	184,370	210,695	207,565	200,361	172,198	173,769	178,603	147,365	168,872	175,750
2019	179,931	175,601	186,451	182,587	181,226	149,724	145,360	160,362	191,328	189,443	178,886	185,330
2020	187,307	189,665	177,355	173,681	178,525	171,799	165,281	199,313	230,858	205,153	220,330	210,429

Contract size = 20 tonnes. *Source: ICE Futures Canada (ICE)*

World Supply and Distribution of Canola and Products In Thousands of Metric Tons

Year	Canola Production	Canola Imports	Canola Exports	Canola Crush	Canola Ending Stocks	Canola Meal Production	Canola Meal Imports	Canola Meal Exports	Canola Meal Consumption	Canola Meal Ending Stocks	Canola oil Production	Canola oil Imports	Canola oil Exports	Canola oil Consumption	Canola oil Ending Stocks
2013-14	70,627	15,550	15,100	66,232	7,764	38,317	6,502	6,357	38,516	936	27,016	3,809	3,829	25,669	6,270
2014-15	70,422	14,313	15,105	67,092	7,287	38,715	6,008	6,068	38,593	998	27,411	3,948	4,066	26,930	6,633
2015-16	68,735	14,106	14,382	66,635	6,242	38,557	5,706	5,694	38,453	1,114	27,307	4,123	4,170	28,245	5,648
2016-17	69,488	15,498	15,836	67,326	5,134	38,785	5,898	5,989	38,774	1,034	27,530	4,397	4,498	28,887	4,190
2017-18	75,154	15,325	16,231	68,214	8,105	39,368	6,246	6,389	39,211	1,048	27,906	4,506	4,611	28,867	3,124
2018-19[1]	72,987	14,329	14,311	67,877	9,647	39,153	6,843	6,847	39,125	1,072	27,684	4,862	4,962	28,061	2,647
2019-20[2]	69,222	15,528	15,923	68,306	7,044	39,510	7,396	7,296	39,578	1,104	27,979	5,453	5,571	28,062	2,446
2020-21[3]	68,896	15,440	15,468	67,734	5,083	39,157	7,003	7,181	39,115	968	27,729	5,231	5,472	27,672	2,262

[1] Preliminary. [2] Estimate. [3] Forecast. *Source: Economic Research Service, U.S. Department of Agriculture (ERS-USDA); The Oil World*

Salient Statistics of Canola and Canola Oil in the United States In Thousands of Metric Tons

Year	Canola Supply: Stocks June 1	Canola Supply: Production	Canola Supply: Imports	Canola Supply: Total Supply	Canola Disappearance: Exports	Canola Disappearance: Crush	Canola Disappearance: Total[3]	Canola Oil Supply: Stocks Oct. 1	Canola Oil Supply: Production	Canola Oil Supply: Imports	Canola Oil Supply: Total Supply	Canola Oil Disappearance: Exports	Canola Oil Disappearance: Domestic	Canola Oil Disappearance: Total
2013-14	81	1,000	927	2,008	159	1,685	2,008	64	708	1,536	2,308	119	2,064	2,308
2014-15	129	1,138	777	2,044	160	1,737	2,044	125	704	1,675	2,504	110	2,273	2,504
2015-16	110	1,305	359	1,774	176	1,542	1,774	121	721	1,797	2,639	111	2,413	2,639
2016-17	161	1,405	697	2,263	118	2,003	2,263	115	798	2,000	2,913	123	2,656	2,913
2017-18	109	1,394	651	2,154	154	1,765	2,154	134	753	1,852	2,739	105	2,546	2,739
2018-19	88	1,644	564	2,296	181	1,722	2,296	88	697	1,774	2,559	90	2,397	2,559
2019-20[1]	139	1,553	565	2,257	182	1,833	2,257	72	825	1,828	2,725	106	2,559	2,725
2020-21[2]	219	1,576	590	2,385	148	2,005	2,385	60	870	1,963	2,893	112	2,675	2,893

[1] Preliminary. [2] Forecast. [3] Includes planting seed and residual. *Source: Economic Research Service, U.S. Department of Agriculture (ERS-USDA)*

Wholesale Price of Canola Oil in Midwest In Cents Per Pound

Year	Jan.	Feb.	Mar.	Apr.	May	June	July	Aug.	Sept.	Oct.	Nov.	Dec.	Average
2013	57.19	59.38	58.95	60.44	60.45	57.50	53.25	48.05	46.00	44.88	45.05	42.63	52.81
2014	39.75	42.56	45.75	47.63	47.50	46.00	43.63	40.10	38.94	39.45	38.94	39.25	42.46
2015	38.80	38.94	35.69	37.19	38.55	40.19	38.30	35.13	33.31	34.20	33.63	36.50	36.70
2016	34.06	34.63	35.55	36.80	35.06	35.10	33.55	36.94	37.25	38.94	39.25	40.20	36.44
2017	38.69	37.25	37.30	36.13	37.06	37.85	39.75	41.19	41.15	39.06	39.69	38.65	38.65
2018	38.31	37.44	37.10	37.31	38.25	37.75	38.69	38.75	38.19	38.94	37.45	36.75	37.91
2019	37.13	37.75	36.15	35.44	34.10	34.63	34.56	35.25	35.00	36.31	36.15	38.06	35.88
2020[1]	37.90	35.50	32.88	32.38	32.40	36.63	40.50	47.81	47.94	44.35	49.50	51.65	40.79

[1] Preliminary. *Source: Economic Research Service, U.S. Department of Agriculture (ERS-USDA)*

Average Price of Canola in Vancouver In Canadian Dollars Per Metric Ton

Year	Jan.	Feb.	Mar.	Apr.	May	June	July	Aug.	Sept.	Oct.	Nov.	Dec.	Average
2011	567.16	577.71	558.19	569.44	555.48	574.44	563.30	547.52	528.64	509.52	513.06	502.88	547.28
2012	512.75	539.92	591.55	626.52	624.60	629.57	657.26	632.65	644.75	627.09	594.75	601.67	606.92
2013	613.04	636.36	635.99	641.70	643.47	626.04	571.91	513.54	473.76	457.25	461.44	418.96	557.79
2014	386.37	380.71	412.23	435.66	459.42	453.37	446.33	430.27	397.71	404.23	423.82	419.92	420.84
2015	432.04	437.63	444.39	443.37	448.45	488.36	514.22	475.87	457.49	460.78	454.54	460.90	459.84
2016	466.39	454.66	450.95	482.41	508.73	502.94	461.72	437.87	426.82	457.28	484.44	488.93	468.60
2017	484.48	493.42	489.15	497.87	516.16	508.58	521.58	482.09	468.24	481.75	496.16	484.15	493.64
2018	475.97	488.09	504.44	516.61	520.50	511.14	491.80	475.69	465.45	Disc.	----	----	494.41

Source: ICE Futures Canada (ICE)

Average Wholesale Price of Canola Meal, 36% Pacific Northwest In Dollars Per Short Ton

Year	Oct.	Nov.	Dec.	Jan.	Feb.	Mar.	Apr.	May	June	July	Aug.	Sept.	Average
2013-14	334.95	342.86	373.60	365.48	384.21	383.68	398.39	407.14	387.65	317.81	303.74	316.94	359.70
2014-15	301.75	356.31	349.31	311.56	296.21	279.54	261.35	274.60	305.85	328.03	285.83	264.01	301.20
2015-16	257.69	248.98	240.64	231.76	224.34	228.87	247.53	329.01	345.14	306.03	255.35	231.00	262.20
2016-17	225.05	234.78	243.30	267.41	276.90	276.33	270.66	279.64	281.66	307.73	289.45	262.33	267.94
2017-18	257.73	255.74	266.53	270.20	315.95	334.58	332.16	336.93	302.75	279.84	274.55	266.86	291.15
2018-19	279.40	279.16	291.42	----	----	----	----	259.55	278.76	265.45	----	253.03	272.40
2019-20	267.90	----	----	----	253.67	274.75	274.53	276.25	270.03	271.11	281.09	296.60	273.99
2020-21[1]	327.24	253.75	275.00	313.18									292.29

[1] Preliminary. *Source: Economic Research Service, U.S. Department of Agriculture (ERS-USDA)*

Cattle and Calves

The beef cycle begins with the cow-calf operation, which breeds the new calves. Most ranchers breed their herds of cows in summer, thus producing the new crop of calves in spring (the gestation period is about nine months). This allows the calves to be born during the milder weather of spring and provides the calves with ample forage through the summer and early autumn. The calves are weaned from the mother after 6-8 months, and most are then moved into the "stocker" operation. The calves usually spend 6-10 months in the stocker operation, growing to near full-sized by foraging for summer grass or winter wheat. When the cattle reach 600-800 pounds, they are typically sent to a feedlot and become "feeder cattle." In the feedlot, the cattle are fed with a special food mix to encourage rapid weight gain. The mix includes grain (corn, milo, or wheat), a protein supplement (soybean, cottonseed, or linseed meal), and roughage (alfalfa, silage, prairie hay, or an agricultural by-product such as sugar beet pulp). The animal is considered "finished" when it reaches full weight and is ready for slaughter, typically at around 1,200 pounds, which produces a dressed carcass of around 745 pounds. After reaching full weight, the cattle are sold for slaughter to a meatpacking plant. Futures and options on live cattle and feeder cattle are traded at the CME Group. Both the live and feeder cattle futures contracts trade in terms of cents per pound.

Prices – CME live cattle futures prices (Barchart.com electronic symbol LE) pushed up to the high for 2020 in January at $1.2755 a pound. Cattle prices rose on expectations for increased Chinese demand for U.S. beef after China eased hormone-limit requirements for beef imports as part of the phase-one U.S./China trade deal signed in mid-January 2020. However, the gains in cattle were short-lived as cattle prices plunged in late January and trended lower into April 2020 when they posted an 11-year low of $0.8145 a pound. The spread of Covid throughout the world undercut global meat demand and boosted U.S. beef supplies. Cattle prices trended higher into year-end, though, as the spread of the pandemic in the U.S. prompted a beef buying frenzy as lockdowns forced restaurants to close and consumers stocked up on beef as they remain sheltered at home. Also, the pandemic caused a drop in U.S. meat production as many meat producers were forced to close when their workers became sick from Covid. The USDA in May 2020 cut its U.S. beef production estimate for the first time since 2015 because of the pandemic. The plunge in U.S. beef production fueled a surge in beef packer profits, which soared to a record $1,009.20/head in May. Foreign demand for U.S. beef surged in Q4 of 2020 as most Asian economies reopened from the pandemic. U.S. beef export sales in the week ended November 12, 2020, jumped to a 19-year high of 60.5 MMT, led by South Korean purchases. Cattle prices finished 2020 down -9.4% yr/yr at $1.1295 per pound.

Supply – The world's number of cattle as of January 1, 2021, rose +1.4% to 1.002 billion head. As of January 1, 2021, the number of cattle on farms in India (the world's largest herd) rose +0.8% to 305.400 million head and on Brazilian farms (the world's second-largest herd) rose by +3.32.5% to 252.250 million head. As of January 1, 2021, the number of cattle and calves on U.S. farms fell by -1.1% yr/yr to 93.793 million head. The USDA reported that U.S. commercial production of beef in 2020 was virtually unchanged at 27.158 billion pounds.

Demand – The federally-inspected slaughter of cattle in the U.S., a measure of cattle consumption, fell by -2.8% yr/yr to 32.252 million head in 2019, up from the 5-decade low of 28.296 million head in 2015.

Trade – U.S. imports of live cattle in 2020 rose by +3.5% yr/yr to 2.114 million head. U.S. exports of live cattle in 2019 rose +27.7% yr/yr to 305,800 head, the highest level since 2000's level of 481,200 head. U.S. imports of beef in 2020 rose +10.4% to 3.375 billion pounds. U.S. exports of beef in 2019 fell -3.1% yr/yr to 2.935 billion pounds.

World Cattle and Buffalo Numbers as of January 1 In Thousands of Head

Year	Argentina	Australia	Brazil	Canada	China	European Union	India	Mexico	New Zealand	Russia	United States	Uraguay	World Total
2012	50,714	28,506	197,550	12,230	93,840	87,054	300,000	20,090	10,021	19,901	91,160	11,232	968,251
2013	52,201	28,418	203,273	12,240	91,373	87,106	299,600	18,521	10,180	19,680	90,095	11,384	968,358
2014	52,396	29,291	207,959	12,050	89,858	87,619	300,200	17,760	10,183	19,273	88,243	11,903	969,055
2015	52,168	29,102	213,035	11,640	90,073	88,406	300,600	17,120	10,368	18,920	89,173	12,053	954,835
2016	53,118	27,413	219,180	11,610	90,558	89,152	301,000	16,615	10,033	18,528	91,888	12,016	963,214
2017	54,163	24,971	226,045	11,535	88,345	89,152	301,400	16,490	10,152	18,248	93,625	11,864	968,284
2018	54,793	26,176	232,350	11,565	90,388	88,819	301,900	16,584	10,146	18,195	94,298	11,744	979,441
2019	55,008	25,734	238,158	11,480	89,153	87,450	302,700	16,699	10,107	18,050	94,805	11,396	983,296
2020[1]	54,461	23,690	244,144	11,240	91,380	86,597	303,100	16,900	10,151	18,024	94,413	11,477	988,218
2021[2]	54,000	23,165	252,250	11,165	95,700	85,720	305,400	17,000	10,062	18,000	94,800	12,157	1,002,096

[1] Preliminary. [2] Forecast. *Source: Foreign Agricultural Service, U.S. Department of Agriculture (FAS-USDA)*

Cattle Supply and Distribution in the United States In Thousands of Head

Year	Cattle & Calves on Farms Jan. 1	Imports	Calves Born	Total Supply	Livestock Slaughter - Cattle and Calves: Commercial: Federally Inspected	Other[3]	All Commercial	Farm	Total Slaughter	Deaths on Farms	Exports	Total Disappearance
2011	92,887	2,107	35,357	130,352	34,394	546	34,939	169	35,108	4,017	194	39,319
2012	91,160	2,283	34,469	127,912	33,185	538	33,723	149	33,872	3,881	191	37,944
2013	90,095	2,033	33,630	125,758	32,698	526	33,224	130	33,355	3,870	161	37,385
2014	88,243	2,358	33,522	124,123	30,242	494	30,734	124	30,857	3,850	108	34,815
2015	89,173	1,985	34,087	125,244	28,742	462	29,204	116	29,320	3,880	73	33,273
2016	91,888	1,708	35,063	128,659	30,602	472	31,066	123	31,189	3,875	69	35,133
2017	96,325	1,806	35,758	133,889	32,208	494	32,702	116	32,817	3,928	195	36,940
2018	94,298	1,900	36,313	132,510	33,090	495	33,585	119	33,703	3,991	240	37,934
2019[1]	94,805	2,043	35,592	132,439	33,648	489	34,137		34,137	4,165	306	38,607
2020[2]	93,793	2,114	35,136	131,043								

[1] Preliminary. [2] Estimate. [3] Wholesale and retail. *Source: Economic Research Service, U.S. Department of Agriculture (ERS-USDA)*

Beef Supply and Utilization in the United States

Years and Quarters	Beginning Stocks	Production: Commercial	Production: Total	Imports	Total Supply	Exports	Ending Stocks	Total Disappearance	Per Capita Disappearance: Carcass Weight	Per Capita Disappearance: Retail Weight Total
2017	----	26,187	26,187	2,993	29,180	2,859	----	----	----	57.0
I	----	6,303	6,303	700	7,003	653	----	----	----	14.0
II	----	6,407	6,407	812	7,219	680	----	----	----	14.2
III	----	6,736	6,736	814	7,550	746	----	----	----	14.4
IV	----	6,742	6,742	668	7,410	781	----	----	----	14.3
2018	----	26,872	26,872	2,998	29,870	3,160	----	----	----	57.3
I	----	6,466	6,466	722	7,188	731	----	----	----	14.0
II	----	6,726	6,726	805	7,531	801	----	----	----	14.5
III	----	6,819	6,819	807	7,626	828	----	----	----	14.4
IV	----	6,862	6,862	664	7,526	799	----	----	----	14.4
2019	----	27,155	27,155	3,058	30,213	3,026	----	----	----	58.1
I	----	6,414	6,414	739	7,153	700	----	----	----	14.0
II	----	6,817	6,817	836	7,653	790	----	----	----	14.8
III	----	6,923	6,923	771	7,694	788	----	----	----	14.5
IV	----	7,001	7,001	712	7,713	749	----	----	----	14.8
2020[1]	----	27,158	27,158	3,375	30,533	2,935	----	----	----	58.6
I	----	6,929	6,929	774	7,703	769	----	----	----	14.7
II	----	6,054	6,054	848	6,902	607	----	----	----	13.6
III	----	7,110	7,110	1,028	8,138	758	----	----	----	15.6
IV	----	7,065	7,065	725	7,790	800	----	----	----	14.7
2021[2]	----	27,190	27,190	3,115	30,305	3,090	----	----	----	57.6
I	----	6,855	6,855	780	7,635	725	----	----	----	14.8
II	----	6,760	6,760	830	7,590	770	----	----	----	14.5
III	----	6,825	6,825	790	7,615	800	----	----	----	14.0
IV	----	6,750	6,750	715	7,465	795	----	----	----	14.0

[1] Preliminary. [2] Forecast. *Source: Economic Research Service, U.S. Department of Agriculture (ERS-USDA)*

United States Cattle on Feed in 13 States In Thousands of Head

Year	Number on Feed[3]	Placed on Feed	Marketings	Other Disappearance
2017	10,605	23,513	21,899	730
I	10,605	5,792	5,313	165
II	10,919	5,737	5,643	192
III	10,821	5,693	5,546	155
IV	10,813	6,291	5,397	218
2018	11,489	23,287	22,310	786
I	11,489	5,806	5,373	193
II	11,729	5,617	5,865	194
III	11,287	5,863	5,575	175
IV	11,400	6,001	5,497	224
2019[1]	11,680	23,580	22,526	776
I	11,680	5,839	5,370	196
II	11,953	5,666	5,941	198
III	11,480	5,692	5,693	191
IV	11,288	6,383	5,522	191
2020[2]	11,958	22,626	21,877	725
I	11,958	5,228	5,716	173
II	11,297	5,282	4,928	198
III	11,438	6,177	5,728	170
IV	11,717	5,939	5,505	184

[1] Preliminary. [2] Estimate. [3] Beginning of period. *Source: Economic Research Service, U.S. Department of Agriculture (ERS-USDA)*

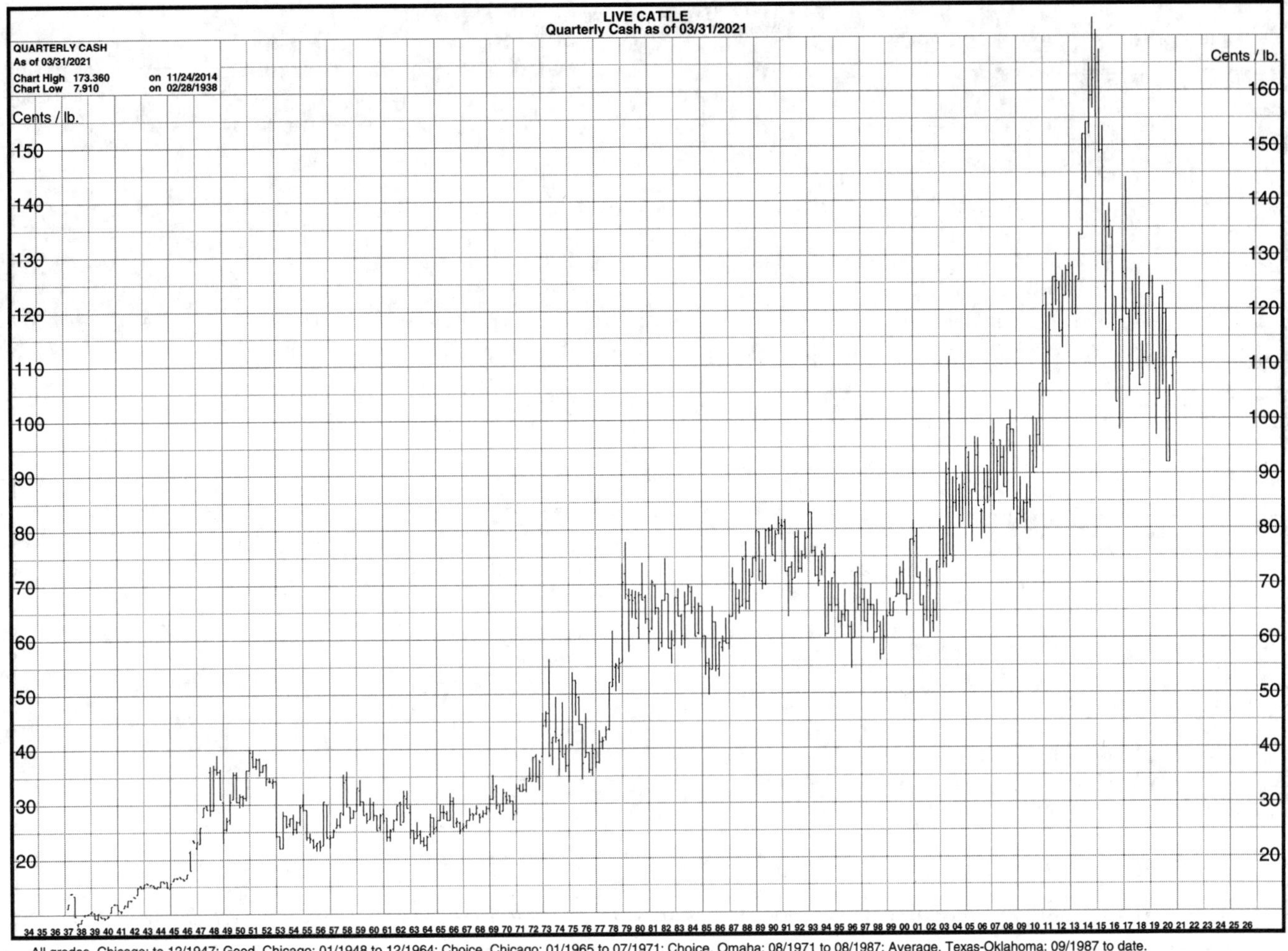

All grades, Chicago: to 12/1947; Good, Chicago: 01/1948 to 12/1964; Choice, Chicago: 01/1965 to 07/1971; Choice, Omaha: 08/1971 to 08/1987; Average, Texas-Oklahoma: 09/1987 to date.

United States Cattle on Feed, 1000+ Capacity Feedlots, on First of Month In Thousands of Head

Year	Jan.	Feb.	Mar.	Apr.	May	June	July	Aug.	Sept.	Oct.	Nov.	Dec.
2011	11,513	11,571	11,386	11,257	11,175	10,902	10,433	10,579	10,700	11,282	11,889	12,055
2012	11,861	11,811	11,677	11,482	11,110	11,077	10,710	10,656	10,647	10,989	11,254	11,348
2013	11,172	11,070	10,845	10,924	10,760	10,767	10,375	10,025	9,876	10,110	10,585	10,724
2014	10,523	10,678	10,716	10,792	10,554	10,497	10,043	9,752	9,719	9,985	10,571	10,816
2015	10,626	10,713	10,688	10,797	10,640	10,571	10,236	10,002	9,986	10,228	10,809	10,800
2016	10,575	10,709	10,770	10,853	10,783	10,804	10,356	10,165	10,135	10,256	10,665	10,652
2017	10,605	10,782	10,772	10,919	10,998	11,096	10,821	10,604	10,504	10,813	11,332	11,516
2018	11,489	11,630	11,715	11,729	11,558	11,553	11,287	11,093	11,125	11,400	11,692	11,739
2019	11,680	11,676	11,785	11,953	11,807	11,728	11,480	11,112	10,982	11,288	11,816	12,031
2020[1]	11,958	11,928	11,811	11,297	11,200	11,671	11,438	11,284	11,394	11,717	11,973	12,036

[1] Preliminary. *Source: Economic Research Service, U.S. Department of Agriculture (ERS-USDA)*

United States Cattle Placed on Feed, 1000+ Capacity Feedlots In Thousands of Head

Year	Jan.	Feb.	Mar.	Apr.	May	June	July	Aug.	Sept.	Oct.	Nov.	Dec.	Total
2011	1,889	1,667	1,914	1,785	1,810	1,695	2,135	2,246	2,469	2,492	2,037	1,673	23,812
2012	1,847	1,714	1,792	1,521	2,084	1,664	1,922	2,007	2,004	2,180	1,943	1,576	22,254
2013	1,869	1,438	1,884	1,720	2,055	1,551	1,684	1,772	1,988	2,378	1,867	1,654	21,860
2014	2,014	1,658	1,801	1,623	1,909	1,468	1,559	1,725	2,014	2,368	1,794	1,537	21,470
2015	1,789	1,551	1,809	1,548	1,719	1,481	1,547	1,632	1,941	2,286	1,602	1,527	20,432
2016	1,779	1,710	1,892	1,664	1,889	1,525	1,572	1,879	1,895	2,171	1,843	1,785	21,604
2017	1,981	1,694	2,117	1,848	2,119	1,770	1,615	1,928	2,150	2,393	2,099	1,799	23,513
2018	2,068	1,817	1,921	1,695	2,124	1,798	1,742	2,070	2,051	2,248	1,996	1,757	23,287
2019	1,967	1,858	2,014	1,842	2,063	1,761	1,705	1,884	2,103	2,462	2,093	1,828	23,580
2020[1]	1,955	1,716	1,557	1,432	2,052	1,798	1,893	2,057	2,227	2,192	1,903	1,844	22,626

[1] Preliminary. *Source: Economic Research Service, U.S. Department of Agriculture (ERS-USDA)*

Nearby Futures through Last Trading Day.

United States Cattle Marketings, 1000+ Capacity Feedlots[2] In Thousands of Head

Year	Jan.	Feb.	Mar.	Apr.	May	June	July	Aug.	Sept.	Oct.	Nov.	Dec.	Total
2011	1,774	1,791	1,990	1,807	2,002	2,092	1,918	2,053	1,813	1,787	1,774	1,776	22,577
2012	1,816	1,755	1,918	1,815	2,017	1,965	1,913	1,955	1,598	1,837	1,761	1,678	22,028
2013	1,892	1,603	1,724	1,815	1,948	1,880	1,970	1,871	1,692	1,827	1,660	1,736	21,618
2014	1,788	1,549	1,660	1,778	1,865	1,847	1,787	1,692	1,683	1,685	1,475	1,655	20,464
2015	1,625	1,516	1,631	1,639	1,711	1,747	1,725	1,588	1,642	1,630	1,532	1,674	19,660
2016	1,589	1,591	1,747	1,658	1,794	1,912	1,713	1,868	1,732	1,705	1,787	1,777	20,873
2017	1,751	1,648	1,914	1,703	1,951	1,989	1,784	1,979	1,783	1,801	1,844	1,752	21,899
2018	1,858	1,675	1,840	1,803	2,056	2,006	1,873	1,983	1,719	1,887	1,869	1,741	22,310
2019	1,910	1,683	1,777	1,928	2,070	1,943	2,002	1,953	1,738	1,875	1,813	1,834	22,526
2020[1]	1,931	1,775	2,010	1,459	1,500	1,969	1,990	1,892	1,846	1,873	1,779	1,853	21,877

[1] Preliminary. *Source: Economic Research Service, U.S. Department of Agriculture (ERS-USDA)*

Quarterly Trade of Live Cattle in the United States In Head

	Imports					Exports				
Year	First Quarter	Second Quarter	Third Quarter	Fourth Quarter	Total	First Quarter	Second Quarter	Third Quarter	Fourth Quarter	Total
2011	580,696	488,356	376,602	661,649	2,107,303	35,446	41,142	45,749	71,571	193,908
2012	672,076	650,094	326,509	634,109	2,282,788	41,379	45,837	36,427	67,241	190,884
2013	595,623	474,806	309,404	653,290	2,033,123	30,707	50,454	38,259	41,258	160,678
2014	599,440	562,937	415,409	780,581	2,358,367	27,541	25,988	25,813	28,342	107,684
2015	564,315	534,024	413,354	472,875	1,984,568	12,576	23,575	15,664	20,744	72,559
2016	490,504	459,089	288,205	470,251	1,708,049	13,498	11,733	10,219	34,035	69,485
2017	517,913	439,901	317,584	530,501	1,805,899	31,987	32,447	34,867	95,332	194,633
2018	467,307	497,270	364,205	570,731	1,899,513	37,834	47,737	62,942	90,987	239,500
2019	567,085	562,871	330,188	582,609	2,042,753	61,985	49,821	68,007	125,937	305,750
2020[1]	530,203	584,788	432,959	566,261	2,114,211	69,291	52,041	77,718	122,092	321,142

[1] Preliminary. *Source: Economic Research Service, U.S. Department of Agriculture (ERS-USDA)*

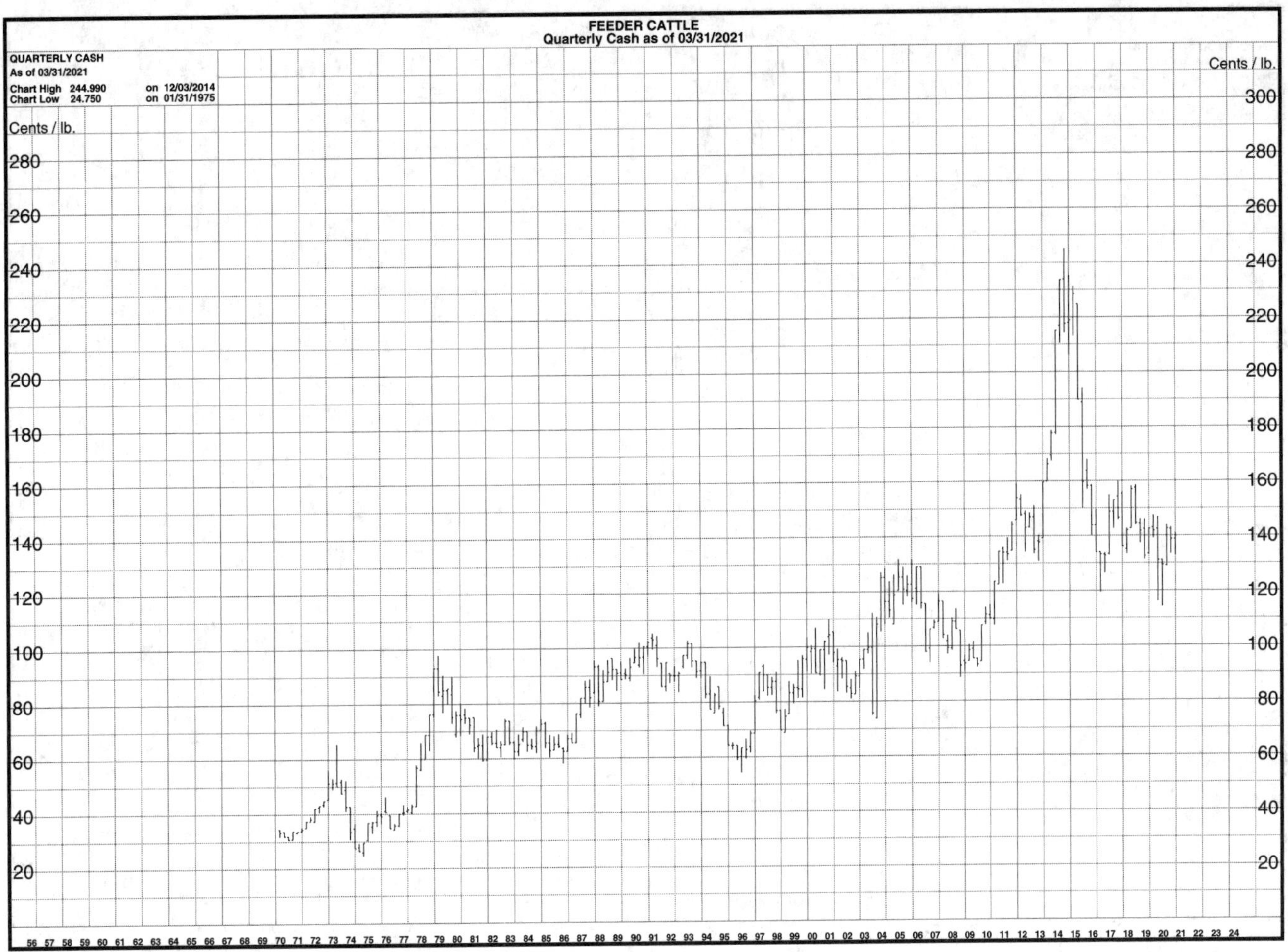

Oklahoma City: to date.

Average Slaughter Steer Price, Choice 2-4, Nebraska Direct (1100-1300 Lb.) In Dollars Per 100 Pounds

Year	Jan.	Feb.	Mar.	Apr.	May	June	July	Aug.	Sept.	Oct.	Nov.	Dec.	Average
2014	143.33	146.45	151.93	149.01	146.19	149.55	158.57	158.35	159.86	164.91	170.04	163.09	155.11
2015	165.13	160.29	163.42	162.98	160.76	151.13	149.17	149.06	136.28	132.88	126.90	125.00	148.58
2016	133.15	133.85	137.83	129.52	129.90	122.95	117.10	116.91	106.22	101.76	106.23	115.24	120.70
2017	119.92	121.83	126.91	131.18	138.42	130.10	118.08	113.01	107.73	113.40	122.49	119.73	121.90
2018	124.35	127.93	124.97	121.11	116.14	110.10	112.39	109.98	110.69	111.53	115.28	120.34	117.07
2019	123.28	124.66	127.51	125.82	118.03	113.08	112.99	111.13	103.30	109.80	115.96	120.20	117.15
2020[1]	123.86	117.31	111.06	105.18	103.14	99.98	97.72	105.51	103.28	106.36	109.39	110.00	107.73

[1] Preliminary. *Source: Economic Research Service, U.S. Department of Agriculture (ERS-USDA)*

Average Price of Feeder Steers in Oklahoma City In Dollars Per 100 Pounds

Year	Jan.	Feb.	Mar.	Apr.	May	June	July	Aug.	Sept.	Oct.	Nov.	Dec.	Average
2014	170.98	170.61	174.43	178.55	185.49	201.90	216.19	221.28	228.15	239.59	240.37	233.67	205.10
2015	224.57	210.18	212.80	218.29	219.14	226.34	219.98	215.14	200.97	188.55	181.41	159.43	206.40
2016	162.19	158.82	160.13	154.07	146.07	144.74	142.23	146.88	136.34	124.66	126.85	131.41	144.53
2017	132.65	127.78	129.29	136.04	144.23	150.36	149.39	146.20	149.54	155.21	157.93	152.81	144.29
2018	149.61	147.91	141.90	136.73	136.14	140.75	147.25	150.14	153.97	156.14	149.97	146.09	146.38
2019	144.00	141.23	139.72	143.93	135.89	132.53	138.02	139.56	138.44	144.50	146.22	144.35	140.70
2020	145.17	140.57	128.37	118.95	123.91	128.99	135.40	142.24	141.42	139.14	137.16	138.37	134.97

Source: Economic Research Service, U.S. Department of Agriculture (ERS-USDA)

Federally Inspected Slaughter of Cattle in the United States In Thousands of Head

Year	Jan.	Feb.	Mar.	Apr.	May	June	July	Aug.	Sept.	Oct.	Nov.	Dec.	Total
2014	2,634	2,204	2,413	2,556	2,597	2,568	2,562	2,463	2,490	2,591	2,210	2,398	29,684
2015	2,377	2,135	2,342	2,346	2,345	2,430	2,459	2,288	2,435	2,469	2,259	2,414	28,296
2016	2,320	2,252	2,493	2,373	2,479	2,670	2,443	2,711	2,578	2,592	2,632	2,572	30,115
2017	2,533	2,330	2,726	2,425	2,713	2,821	2,577	2,903	2,655	2,753	2,726	2,543	31,704
2018	2,714	2,378	2,661	2,599	2,868	2,842	2,729	2,937	2,577	2,908	2,762	2,544	32,518
2019	2,786	2,416	2,609	2,789	2,900	2,769	2,903	2,887	2,635	2,926	2,737	2,713	33,069
2020[1]	2,854	2,539	2,875	2,189	2,223	2,820	2,866	2,751	2,756	2,889	2,657	2,734	32,152

[1] Preliminary. *Source: National Agricultural Statistics Service, U.S. Department of Agriculture (NASS-USDA)*

Nearby Futures through Last Trading Day using Selected contract months: February, April, June, August, October and December.

Volume of Trading of Live Cattle Futures Chicago In Thousands of Contracts

Year	Jan.	Feb.	Mar.	Apr.	May	June	July	Aug.	Sept.	Oct.	Nov.	Dec.	Total
2011	1,181.8	910.9	1,531.6	928.4	1,293.3	1,097.4	1,148.8	1,034.4	1,325.4	1,067.2	1,136.1	877.4	13,532.6
2012	1,179.7	1,078.3	1,516.9	1,180.1	1,399.6	1,022.4	1,293.1	1,097.1	1,185.9	977.2	1,090.4	964.8	13,985.4
2013	1,484.1	1,069.5	1,249.3	977.9	1,189.7	831.3	1,020.8	884.5	972.5	1,040.2	986.9	756.2	12,463.0
2014	1,381.4	970.0	1,270.2	847.7	1,139.3	1,126.6	1,503.5	1,023.5	1,303.4	1,061.5	962.5	1,009.6	13,599.3
2015	1,282.2	918.7	1,163.5	959.6	1,139.1	955.3	1,166.5	901.6	1,344.2	1,222.5	1,213.9	1,173.9	13,440.9
2016	1,127.6	956.2	1,187.4	1,010.7	1,234.8	852.5	1,070.5	990.9	1,335.8	1,028.2	1,257.5	1,070.7	13,122.8
2017	1,300.9	958.4	1,552.2	1,260.5	2,164.7	1,201.2	1,487.1	1,155.8	1,364.4	1,228.1	1,501.6	990.4	16,165.2
2018	1,493.4	1,078.6	1,621.7	1,294.7	1,680.4	1,170.3	1,476.9	1,205.5	1,433.2	1,397.4	1,466.9	1,121.1	16,440.1
2019	1,657.5	1,139.7	1,778.9	1,440.6	1,760.8	1,132.9	1,321.6	1,338.6	1,539.7	1,154.9	1,488.3	965.6	16,719.1
2020	1,607.7	1,452.6	2,194.9	1,204.7	1,499.0	997.6	1,373.3	1,120.5	1,331.4	1,239.8	1,211.4	905.9	16,138.8

Contract size = 40,000 lbs. *Source: CME Group; Chicago Mercantile Exchange (CME)*

Average Open Interest of Live Cattle Futures in Chicago In Contracts

Year	Jan.	Feb.	Mar.	Apr.	May	June	July	Aug.	Sept.	Oct.	Nov.	Dec.
2011	344,671	358,852	366,250	380,138	346,614	326,592	322,313	309,147	324,714	336,225	325,195	315,700
2012	333,921	350,623	358,333	351,179	337,579	318,041	305,336	290,534	294,356	289,303	327,964	331,211
2013	329,529	330,784	335,436	325,462	315,201	290,113	275,925	289,980	295,826	314,058	333,154	323,189
2014	354,327	371,310	369,611	352,639	345,372	352,223	343,096	313,046	315,722	313,134	317,289	286,556
2015	261,167	243,091	259,858	273,309	296,935	287,815	241,553	236,485	258,984	258,122	271,979	256,669
2016	274,078	272,513	291,131	282,634	271,110	247,299	248,641	247,108	262,608	268,144	278,901	294,562
2017	333,745	332,286	360,860	404,610	421,183	403,152	372,623	320,894	327,393	334,666	380,212	341,419
2018	353,135	370,641	362,617	348,766	356,141	329,947	317,434	301,001	314,505	335,731	342,814	347,681
2019	386,607	393,106	437,825	440,940	384,191	357,676	331,025	324,793	338,349	308,578	362,444	381,270
2020	384,707	341,499	305,367	266,157	264,856	271,676	273,740	291,037	294,504	279,047	275,585	284,898

Contract size = 40,000 lbs. *Source: CME Group; Chicago Mercantile Exchange (CME)*

Beef Steer-Corn Price Ratio[1] in the United States

Year	Jan.	Feb.	Mar.	Apr.	May	June	July	Aug.	Sept.	Oct.	Nov.	Dec.	Average
2011	22.3	19.6	21.3	19.2	18.2	17.2	18.2	16.6	18.3	21.3	21.6	21.5	19.6
2012	21.4	20.9	20.8	20.2	19.7	19.5	16.4	15.7	18.1	18.7	18.3	18.6	19.0
2013	18.7	17.8	17.8	18.2	18.2	17.8	17.8	19.6	23.0	27.6	30.2	29.9	21.4
2014	31.7	33.3	33.2	31.8	31.2	32.9	38.7	43.8	45.3	45.7	46.9	43.8	38.2
2015	43.5	42.5	42.5	43.7	44.2	43.5	39.5	40.5	38.0	35.1	36.5	33.7	40.3
2016	36.1	37.4	38.5	37.4	35.1	33.2	33.3	36.8	33.9	31.0	32.7	34.0	35.0
2017	35.0	35.2	36.4	37.9	40.0	38.8	34.7	35.2	32.7	34.0	38.4	37.2	36.3
2018	37.4	37.6	36.2	34.1	33.2	31.6	32.3	33.3	32.4	32.7	33.7	33.6	34.0
2019	34.8	35.0	35.7	36.3	33.6	28.9	27.2	28.5	27.4	28.3	31.3	32.3	31.6
2020[1]	33.0	32.3	31.0	33.7	34.7	34.8	30.5	33.3	30.9	29.9	28.8	28.0	31.7

[1] Bushels of corn equal in value to 100 pounds of steers and heifers. [2] Preliminary. *Source: Economic Research Service, U.S. Department of Agriculture*

Average Price Received by Farmers for Beef Cattle in the United States In Dollars Per 100 Pounds

Year	Jan.	Feb.	Mar.	Apr.	May	June	July	Aug.	Sept.	Oct.	Nov.	Dec.	Average
2011	107.00	108.00	115.00	119.00	112.00	107.00	111.00	111.00	112.00	117.00	120.00	120.00	113.25
2012	125.00	127.00	128.00	124.00	122.00	121.00	114.00	117.00	121.00	123.00	123.00	124.00	122.42
2013	126.00	123.00	125.00	125.00	126.00	122.00	120.00	121.00	122.00	127.00	130.00	130.00	124.75
2014	138.00	144.00	148.00	148.00	146.00	147.00	156.00	158.00	157.00	161.00	167.00	164.00	152.83
2015	164.00	159.00	160.00	162.00	160.00	155.00	149.00	148.00	139.00	128.00	129.00	122.00	147.92
2016	130.00	132.00	135.00	131.00	128.00	125.00	119.00	117.00	108.00	101.00	104.00	111.00	120.08
2017	117.00	119.00	125.00	128.00	136.00	132.00	120.00	114.00	105.00	109.00	119.00	118.00	120.17
2018	120.00	125.00	125.00	119.00	120.00	112.00	110.00	110.00	108.00	110.00	113.00	117.00	115.75
2019	121.00	123.00	126.00	125.00	120.00	114.00	112.00	111.00	103.00	107.00	113.00	118.00	116.08
2020[1]	122.00	120.00	113.00	108.00	109.00	109.00	97.10	103.00	104.00	106.00	107.00	108.00	108.84

[1] Preliminary. *Source: National Agricultural Statistics Service, U.S. Department of Agriculture (NASS-USDA)*

Average Price Received by Farmers for Calves in the United States In Dollars Per 100 Pounds

Year	Jan.	Feb.	Mar.	Apr.	May	June	July	Aug.	Sept.	Oct.	Nov.	Dec.	Average
2011	136.00	139.00	148.00	147.00	137.00	133.00	138.00	134.00	132.00	145.00	153.00	157.00	141.58
2012	169.00	184.00	184.00	178.00	176.00	166.00	144.00	155.00	162.00	164.00	161.00	163.00	167.17
2013	168.00	170.00	163.00	159.00	157.00	152.00	162.00	178.00	200.00	190.00	192.00	197.00	174.00
2014	208.00	209.00	216.00	222.00	229.00	249.00	257.00	271.00	279.00	307.00	305.00	303.00	254.58
2015	288.00	277.00	290.00	288.00	288.00	292.00	275.00	273.00	241.00	234.00	217.00	193.00	263.00
2016	196.00	201.00	199.00	183.00	173.00	168.00	145.00	158.00	142.00	134.00	144.00	148.00	165.92
2017	152.00	151.00	159.00	164.00	171.00	164.00	157.00	163.00	173.00	177.00	177.00	174.00	165.17
2018	174.00	180.00	175.00	170.00	165.00	158.00	153.00	160.00	169.00	174.00	169.00	166.00	167.75
2019	169.00	170.00	170.00	174.00	148.00	149.00	144.00	142.00	144.00	154.00	158.00	159.00	156.75
2020[1]	168.00	168.00	160.00	151.00	151.00	149.00	149.00	153.00	155.00	156.00	162.00	165.00	157.25

[1] Preliminary. *Source: National Agricultural Statistics Board, U.S. Department of Agriculture (NASS-USDA)*

Federally Inspected Slaughter of Calves and Vealers in the United States In Thousands of Head

Year	Jan.	Feb.	Mar.	Apr.	May	June	July	Aug.	Sept.	Oct.	Nov.	Dec.	Total
2011	70.8	67.9	71.8	57.9	60.0	71.5	72.4	78.9	72.5	71.5	71.9	71.8	838.9
2012	66.6	59.3	58.5	55.4	58.2	55.0	66.5	71.6	63.2	71.6	69.4	64.5	759.8
2013	69.9	58.7	61.6	57.7	57.6	56.7	69.1	63.5	62.0	68.5	59.7	65.8	750.8
2014	62.0	51.5	52.9	48.0	45.9	44.6	47.8	43.0	41.8	42.6	35.2	42.2	557.5
2015	39.3	36.1	39.2	34.7	32.7	34.5	36.0	33.9	36.8	39.6	38.2	44.5	445.5
2016	41.2	37.8	41.3	34.2	34.9	37.0	37.1	40.3	41.8	47.6	46.6	48.1	487.9
2017	45.9	39.6	44.3	38.4	38.5	39.6	38.3	45.4	42.9	43.2	41.7	45.6	503.4
2018	48.4	40.4	43.0	42.1	45.7	44.6	47.0	51.6	47.8	52.9	54.9	53.0	571.4
2019	53.0	47.9	45.1	42.1	45.5	43.7	53.0	50.2	48.4	54.6	45.8	49.1	578.4
2020[1]	49.2	39.1	42.5	32.6	31.7	35.9	40.3	33.4	31.6	36.3	34.4	40.0	447.0

[1] Preliminary. *Source: Crop Reporting Board, U.S. Department of Agriculture (CRB-USDA)*

Cement

Cement is made in a wide variety of compositions and is used in many ways. The best-known cement is Portland cement, which is bound with sand and gravel to create concrete. Concrete is used to unite the surfaces of various materials and to coat surfaces to protect them from various chemicals. Portland cement is almost universally used for structural concrete. It is manufactured from lime-bearing materials, usually limestone, together with clays, blast-furnace slag containing alumina and silica or shale. The combination is usually approximately 60 percent lime, 19 percent silica, 8 percent alumina, 5 percent iron, 5 percent magnesia, and 3 percent sulfur trioxide. Gypsum is often added to slow the hardening process. In 1924, the name "Portland cement" was coined by Joseph Aspdin, a British cement maker, because of the resemblance between concrete made from his cement and Portland stone. The United States did not start producing Portland cement in any great quantity until the 20th century. Hydraulic cements are those that set and harden in water. Clinker cement is an intermediate product in cement manufacture. The production and consumption of cement is directly related to the level of activity in the construction industry.

Prices – The average value (F.O.B. mill) of Portland cement in 2020 rose by +0.8% yr/yr to $124.00 per ton, posting a new record high.

Supply – World production of hydraulic cement in 2020 was unchanged yr/yr at 4.100 billion metric tons, just below the 2014 record high of 4.190 billion. The world's largest hydraulic cement producers were China with 53.7% of world production in 2020, India with 8.3%, the U.S. with 2.2%, and Turkey with 1.6%.

U.S. production of cement in 2020 rose +1.1% yr/yr to 89.00 million metric tons, but still below the 2005 record high of 99.319 million metric tons. U.S. shipments of cement from mills in the U.S. in 2020 rose +0.6% to 100.000 million metric tons but remained below the 2005 record high of 128.000 million metric tons.

Demand – U.S. consumption of cement in 2020 fell -1.0% yr/yr at 102.000 million metric tons, still far below the 2005 record high of 128.260 million metric tons.

Trade – The U.S. relied on imports for 15% of its cement consumption in 2020. The two main suppliers of cement to the U.S. were Canada and Mexico. U.S. exports of cement in 2020 fell -0.2% yr/yr to 1.000 million metric tons.

World Production of Hydraulic Cement In Thousands of Short Tons

Year	Brazil	China	France	Germany	India	Italy	Japan	Korea, South	Russia	Spain	Turkey	United States	World Total
2013	69,975	2,411,000	18,018	31,308	231,000	23,100	57,962	47,291	66,503	13,736	71,337	77,415	4,030,000
2014	71,254	2,492,000	16,400	32,099	240,000	21,400	57,913	47,048	69,139	14,587	71,239	83,124	4,150,000
2015	65,283	2,359,000	15,600	31,150	260,000	21,000	54,827	52,044	62,104	15,000	71,419	84,940	4,070,000
2016	57,476	2,410,000	15,900	32,737	280,000	19,300	53,255	56,747	54,935	15,000	75,403	85,153	4,150,000
2017	54,004	2,331,000	16,000	33,991	281,000	20,000	55,195	56,500	54,678	14,500	80,552	86,799	4,080,000
2018	53,000	2,200,000			300,000		55,300	57,500	53,700		72,500	87,000	4,050,000
2019[1]	54,000	2,300,000			340,000		53,000	50,000	56,000		57,000	89,000	4,100,000
2020[2]	57,000	2,200,000			340,000		53,000	50,000	56,000		66,000	90,000	4,100,000

[1] Preliminary. [2] Estimate. *Source: U.S. Geological Survey (USGS)*

Salient Statistics of Cement in the United States

Year	Net Import Reliance as a % of Apparent Consump	Production: Portland	Production: Other[3]	Production: Total	Capacity Used at Portland Mills %	Shipments From Mills: Total (Mil. MT)	Shipments From Mills: Value[4] (Mil. $)	Average Value (F.O.B. Mill) $ per MT	Stocks at Mills Dec. 31	Exports	Apparent Consumption	Imports for Consumption[5] by Country: Canada	Japan	Mexico	Spain	Total
		--- 1,000 Metric tons ----							1,000 Metric Tons							
2013	7	74,689	2,115	76,804	62.6	83,187	7,760	95.00	6,570	1,670	81,800	3,615	2	308	[6]	7,095
2014	8	80,315	2,220	82,535	67.1	90,204	8,940	100.50	6,140	1,404	89,145	3,739	1	354	[6]	8,304
2015	11	82,093	2,312	84,405	68.5	93,338	9,800	106.50	7,230	1,288	92,150	4,497	2	338	270	11,255
2016	13	82,181	2,514	84,695	69.5	95,373	10,500	111.00	7,420	1,283	95,150	4,512	1	466	389	13,238
2017	13	83,963	2,393	86,356	69.8	97,935	11,300	117.00	7,870	1,035	97,160	4,352	1	686	601	13,497
2018	14			86,368		99,419		121.00	8,580	919	98,500					
2019[1]	14			88,000		103,000		123.00	7,140	1,002	103,000					
2020[2]	15			89,000		103,000		124.00	7,800	1,000	102,000					

[1] Preliminary. [2] Estimate. [3] Masonry, natural & pozzolan (slag-line). [4] Value received F.O.B. mill, excluding cost of containers. [5] Hydraulic & clinker cement for consumption. [6] Less than 1/2 unit. *Source: U.S. Geological Survey (USGS)*

Shipments of Finished Portland Cement from Mills in the United States In Thousands of Metric Tons

Year	Jan.	Feb.	Mar.	Apr.	May	June	July	Aug.	Sept.	Oct.	Nov.	Dec.	Total
2014	4,405.2	4,336.7	5,644.2	6,786.1	7,503.4	7,598.1	8,240.1	7,970.4	8,187.0	8,742.4	5,905.7	5,685.6	81,018.8
2015	4,874.8	4,288.7	5,697.8	6,890.4	6,920.1	7,977.7	8,318.2	8,169.8	9,035.5	8,311.3	6,512.3	5,930.7	82,927.4
2016	4,725.8	5,376.4	6,723.3	6,763.5	7,136.6	8,268.5	7,237.9	8,272.8	7,741.7	7,958.6	7,008.8	5,414.3	82,628.2
2017	4,869.2	5,398.2	6,687.5	6,673.6	7,738.1	8,236.3	7,507.0	8,497.2	7,606.4	8,222.6	7,253.1	5,515.0	84,204.1
2018	5,125.4	5,130.2	6,589.9	7,220.0	8,205.8	8,135.0	8,034.7	8,769.6	7,307.9	8,421.8	6,699.3	5,346.6	84,986.2
2019	5,565.0	5,013.8	6,386.3	7,550.0	7,941.0	7,791.7	8,653.3	8,910.4	8,162.9	8,656.2	6,830.7	5,809.9	87,271.2
2020[1]	5,962.4	5,447.4	6,619.9	7,128.4	7,562.4	8,734.2	8,497.4	8,298.4	8,019.8	8,602.4	7,429.4	6,480.2	88,782.4

[1] Preliminary. *Source: U.S. Geological Survey (USGS)*

Cheese

Since prehistoric times, humans have been making and eating cheese. Dating back as far as 6,000 BC, archaeologists have discovered that cheese had been made from cow and goat milk and stored in tall jars. The Romans turned cheese-making into a culinary art, mixing sheep and goat milk and adding herbs and spices for flavoring. By 300 AD, cheese was being exported regularly to countries along the Mediterranean coast.

Cheese is made from the milk of cows and other mammals such as sheep, goats, buffalo, reindeer, camels, yaks, and mares. More than 400 varieties of cheese exist. There are three basic steps common to all cheese making. First, proteins in milk are transformed into curds, or solid lumps. Second, the curds are separated from the milky liquid (or whey) and shaped or pressed into molds. Finally, the shaped curds are ripened using a variety of aging and curing techniques. Cheeses are usually grouped according to their moisture content into fresh, soft, semi-soft, hard, and very hard. Many classifications overlap due to texture changes with aging.

Cheese is a multi-billion-dollar a year industry in the U.S. Cheddar cheese is the most common natural cheese produced in the U.S., accounting for 35% of U.S. production. Cheeses originating in America include Colby, cream cheese, and Monterey Jack. Varieties other than American cheeses, mostly Italian, now have had a combined level of production that easily exceeds American cheeses.

Futures and options on cheese are traded on the CME Group. The CME's cheese futures contract calls for the delivery of 20,000 pounds of cheese and is priced in Dollars per pound.

Prices – Average monthly price of American Cheese at the CME Group in 2020 rose +12.3% yr/yr to $1.9977 per pound, but still below the 2014 record high of $2.1094 cents per pound.

Supply – World production of cheese in 2021 is expected to rise +2.2% yr/yr to 21.688 million metric tons, which would be a new record high. The European Union is expected to be the world's largest producer of cheese, with 48.2% of the total world production in 2021. U.S. production was the next largest with 28.7% of the total. U.S. production of all cheese in 2020 rose +0.6% to 13.191 billion pounds, which was a new record high.

World Production of Cheese In Thousands of Metric Tons

Year	Argentina	Australia	Brazil	Canada	European Union	Japan	Korea, South	Mexico	New Zealand	Russia	Ukraine	United States	World Total
2012	564	352	700	386	9,287	47	23	293	328	790	245	4,938	18,420
2013	549	318	722	388	9,368	49	22	316	311	713	247	5,036	18,485
2014	562	328	736	396	9,560	46	24	343	325	760	203	5,222	18,986
2015	566	343	754	419	9,740	46	23	363	355	861	190	5,367	19,525
2016	552	344	745	445	9,810	47	25	375	360	865	186	5,525	19,807
2017	514	348	771	497	10,050	46	35	396	386	951	190	5,733	20,428
2018	444	366	760	510	10,160	45	37	419	370	970	192	5,914	20,740
2019	523	364	770	515	10,210	44	40	437	365	983	187	5,959	20,981
2020[1]	488	385	750	510	10,350	45	43	455	350	1,035	180	6,000	21,222
2021[2]	537	395	760	515	10,450	47	44	460	365	1,060	175	6,218	21,688

[1] Preliminary. [2] Forecast. NA = Not available. *Source: Foreign Agricultural Service, U.S. Department of Agriculture (FAS-USDA)*

Production of Cheese in the United States In Millions of Pounds

	American			Swiss,				Crean &				Total	Cottage Cheese		
Year	Whole Milk	Part Skim	Total	Including Block	Munster	Brick	Lim-burger	Neufchatel Cheese	Italian Varieties	Blue Mond	All Other Varieties	of All Cheese[2]	Lowfat	Curd[3]	Cream-ed[4]
2011	4,227	----	4,227	329.1	146.6	11.4	[5]	714.6	4,585.3	[5]	147.5	10,595	381.5	423.7	322.1
2012	4,355	----	4,355	320.6	152.5	12.5	[5]	807.7	4,632.8	[5]	146.6	10,886	386.1	423.9	323.2
2013	4,420	----	4,420	294.5	163.2	9.3	[5]	842.3	4,735.5	[5]	151.9	11,102	370.3	389.4	307.4
2014	4,588	----	4,588	297.8	163.7	2.9	[5]	851.7	4,950.2	[5]	154.2	11,512	364.6	381.1	303.1
2015	4,694	----	4,694	312.0	177.5	3.4	[5]	876.3	5,081.8	[5]		11,831	363.0	400.6	317.5
2016	4,769	----	4,769	312.0	181.4	2.8	[5]	909.0	5,304.4	[5]		12,182	367.8	406.4	329.4
2017	5,072	----	5,072	316.7	189.2	2.4	[5]	918.1	5,395.2	[5]		12,640	344.4	390.4	330.5
2018	5,254	----	5,254	332.3	191.2	2.3	[5]	914.8	5,556.9	[5]		13,025	342.1	402.4	352.8
2019	5,211	----	5,211	338.3	196.9	2.0	[5]	931.6	5,668.1	[5]		13,107	324.9	388.0	353.5
2020[1]	5,340	----	5,340	329.2			[5]	994.1	5,600.6	[5]		13,191	319.5	392.5	376.6

[1] Preliminary. [2] Excludes full-skim cheddar and cottage cheese. [3] Includes cottage, pot, and baker's cheese with a butterfat content of less than 4%.
[4] Includes cheese with a butterfat content of 4 to 19 %. [5] Included in All Other Varieties. NA = Not available.
Source: Economic Research Service, U.S. Department of Agriculture ERS-USDA)

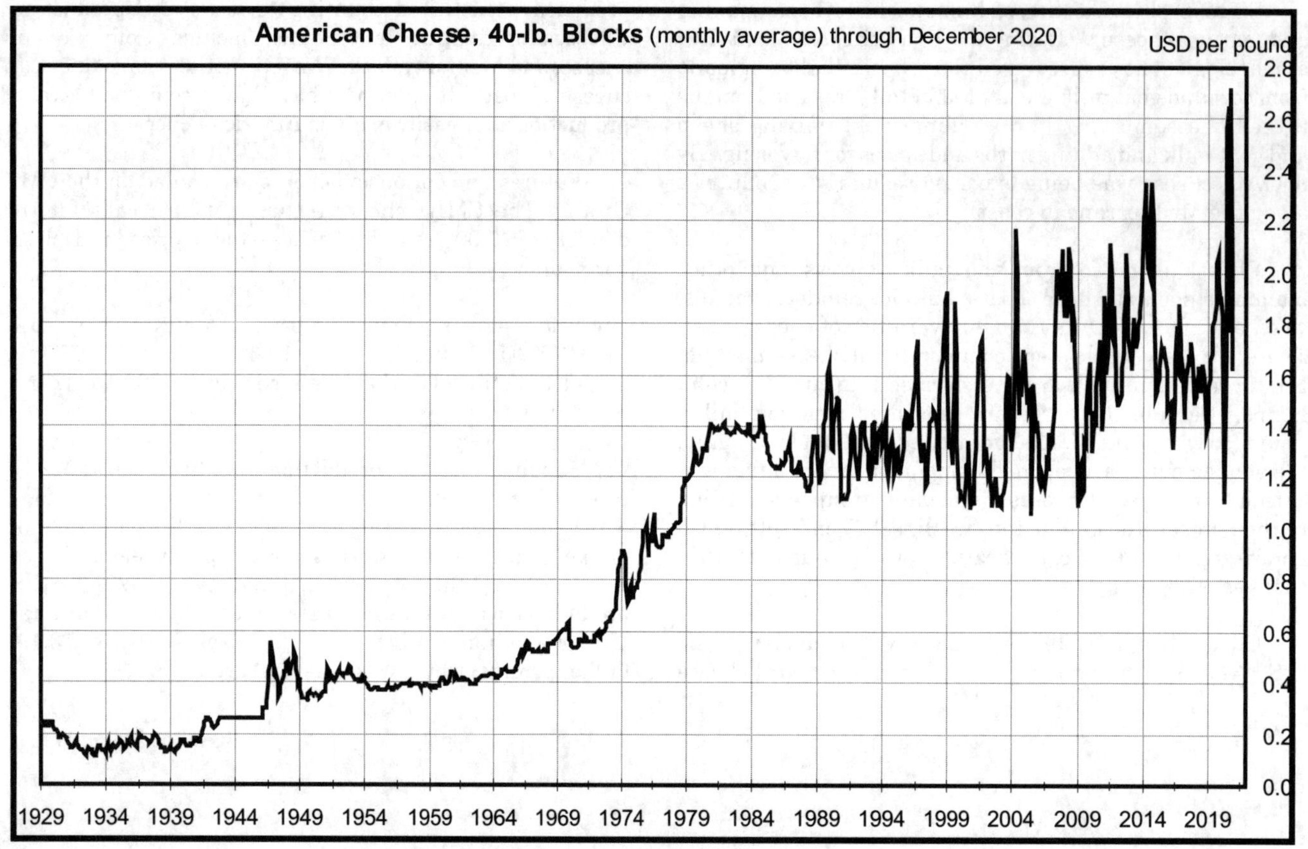

Average Price of Cheese, 40-lb. Blocks, Chicago Mercantile Exchange In U.S. Dollars Per Pound

Year	Jan.	Feb.	Mar.	Apr.	May	June	July	Aug.	Sept.	Oct.	Nov.	Dec.	Average
2011	1.5140	1.9064	1.8125	1.6036	1.6858	2.0995	2.1150	1.9725	1.7561	1.7231	1.8716	1.6170	1.8064
2012	1.5546	1.4793	1.5193	1.5039	1.5234	1.6313	1.6855	1.8262	1.9245	2.0757	1.9073	1.7448	1.6980
2013	1.6965	1.6420	1.6240	1.8225	1.8052	1.7140	1.7072	1.7493	1.7956	1.8236	1.8478	1.9431	1.7642
2014	2.2227	2.1945	2.3554	2.2439	2.0155	2.0237	1.9870	2.1820	2.3499	2.1932	1.9513	1.5938	2.1094
2015	1.5218	1.5382	1.5549	1.5890	1.6308	1.7052	1.6659	1.7111	1.6605	1.6674	1.6176	1.4616	1.6103
2016	1.4757	1.4744	1.4877	1.4194	1.3174	1.5005	1.6613	1.7826	1.6224	1.6035	1.8775	1.7335	1.5797
2017	1.6866	1.6199	1.4342	1.4976	1.6264	1.6022	1.6586	1.6852	1.6370	1.7305	1.6590	1.4900	1.6106
2018	1.4938	1.5157	1.5614	1.6062	1.6397	1.5617	1.5364	1.6341	1.6438	1.5874	1.3951	1.3764	1.5460
2019	1.4087	1.5589	1.5908	1.6619	1.6799	1.7906	1.8180	1.8791	2.0395	2.0703	1.9664	1.8764	1.7784
2020[1]	1.9142	1.8343	1.7550	1.1019	1.6704	2.5620	2.6466	1.7730	2.3277	2.7103	2.0521	1.6249	1.9977

[1] Preliminary. *Source: Economic Research Service, U.S. Department of Agriculture (ERS-USDA)*

Average Price of American Cheese, Barrels, Chicago Mercantile Exchange In U.S. Dollars Per Pound

Year	Jan.	Feb.	Mar.	Apr.	May	June	July	Aug.	Sept.	Oct.	Nov.	Dec.	Average
2011	1.4876	1.8680	4.8049	1.5756	1.6902	2.0483	2.1124	1.9571	1.7010	1.7192	1.8963	1.5839	2.0370
2012	1.5358	1.4823	1.5152	1.4524	1.4701	1.5871	1.6826	1.7889	1.8780	2.0240	1.8388	1.6634	1.6599
2013	1.6388	1.5880	1.5920	1.7124	1.7251	1.7184	1.6919	1.7425	1.7688	1.7714	1.7833	1.8651	1.7165
2014	2.1727	2.1757	2.2790	2.1842	1.9985	1.9856	1.9970	2.1961	2.3663	2.0782	1.9326	1.5305	2.0747
2015	1.4995	1.4849	1.5290	1.6135	1.6250	1.6690	1.6313	1.6689	1.5840	1.6072	1.5305	1.4638	1.5756
2016	1.4842	1.4573	1.4530	1.4231	1.3529	1.5301	1.7363	1.8110	1.5415	1.5295	1.7424	1.6132	1.5562
2017	1.5573	1.6230	1.4072	1.4307	1.4806	1.3972	1.4396	1.5993	1.5691	1.6970	1.6656	1.5426	1.5341
2018	1.3345	1.4096	1.5071	1.4721	1.5870	1.4145	1.3707	1.5835	1.4503	1.3152	1.3100	1.2829	1.4198
2019	1.2379	1.3867	1.4910	1.5925	1.6278	1.6258	1.7343	1.7081	1.7463	2.0224	2.2554	1.8410	1.6891
2020[1]	1.5721	1.5470	1.4399	1.0690	1.5980	2.3376	2.4080	1.4937	1.6401	2.2213	1.8437	1.4609	1.7193

[1] Preliminary. *Source: Economic Research Service, U.S. Department of Agriculture (ERS-USDA)*

Production of Cheese[2] in the United States In Millions of Pounds

Year	Jan.	Feb.	Mar.	Apr.	May	June	July	Aug.	Sept.	Oct.	Nov.	Dec.	Total
2011	883.5	804.6	912.2	883.3	912.3	889.0	854.9	861.9	867.9	899.1	895.6	930.6	10,595.0
2012	911.8	860.6	955.6	898.5	918.2	901.2	882.6	891.2	870.6	930.4	914.3	951.2	10,886.2
2013	931.7	848.7	954.3	929.8	943.9	912.1	893.9	931.7	899.2	954.8	922.5	979.3	11,101.7
2014	962.4	859.4	976.0	967.3	977.2	951.0	965.0	935.6	943.0	987.8	965.2	1,022.1	11,512.1
2015	994.1	896.7	1,013.0	977.3	988.2	976.1	1,002.0	979.0	965.5	1,018.0	986.4	1,035.1	11,831.4
2016	1,025.7	947.5	1,028.6	1,003.2	1,010.7	998.4	1,020.8	1,006.8	991.4	1,052.2	1,029.2	1,067.0	12,181.5
2017	1,060.9	958.4	1,069.8	1,057.1	1,074.7	1,044.0	1,052.0	1,045.3	1,026.8	1,082.4	1,065.7	1,102.8	12,640.0
2018	1,098.7	992.8	1,108.0	1,078.1	1,085.2	1,066.0	1,087.1	1,087.0	1,059.1	1,154.2	1,096.0	1,112.4	13,024.6
2019	1,098.4	991.3	1,122.4	1,085.0	1,105.9	1,067.7	1,087.6	1,113.6	1,080.5	1,138.2	1,093.4	1,122.5	13,106.7
2020[1]	1,110.5	1,031.7	1,124.0	1,063.8	1,101.0	1,111.4	1,107.6	1,085.2	1,096.7	1,131.3	1,099.6	1,127.7	13,190.5

[1] Preliminary. [2] Excludes cottage cheese. *Source: National Agricultural Statistics Service, U.S. Department of Agriculture (NASS-USDA)*

Production of American Cheese[2] in the United States In Thousands of Pounds

Year	Jan.	Feb.	Mar.	Apr.	May	June	July	Aug.	Sept.	Oct.	Nov.	Dec.	Total
2011	356,983	327,255	363,518	355,848	369,073	362,050	349,031	337,523	337,549	351,654	348,331	367,855	4,226,670
2012	366,533	343,759	378,063	363,348	367,591	360,364	356,169	353,167	347,486	370,139	364,541	384,092	4,355,252
2013	377,258	347,262	384,770	376,891	387,590	362,977	345,707	381,125	347,449	371,125	356,220	381,474	4,419,848
2014	388,420	345,464	387,071	385,322	399,239	374,373	385,175	376,203	369,843	393,414	383,500	399,999	4,588,023
2015	402,222	357,376	395,823	396,691	407,667	390,447	397,235	394,943	379,550	392,592	380,004	399,921	4,694,471
2016	402,377	368,000	402,001	398,750	403,040	392,166	401,815	393,459	379,456	403,397	400,983	423,444	4,768,888
2017	434,638	390,324	429,569	434,669	443,095	419,273	414,508	414,292	403,555	430,496	413,725	443,985	5,072,129
2018	448,124	406,189	443,185	444,287	442,968	429,076	440,937	435,388	424,032	457,122	434,185	448,340	5,253,833
2019	439,283	391,027	442,723	430,539	443,683	427,638	434,449	452,030	415,687	445,601	432,438	456,378	5,211,476
2020[1]	437,451	418,605	450,058	447,044	442,282	436,406	454,712	447,095	434,659	462,048	448,192	461,073	5,339,625

[1] Preliminary. [2] Includes Cheddar, Colby, Monterey, and Jack. *Source: National Agricultural Statistics Service, U.S. Department of Agriculture*

Production of Cheddar Cheese in the United States In Thousands of Pounds

Year	Jan.	Feb.	Mar.	Apr.	May	June	July	Aug.	Sept.	Oct.	Nov.	Dec.	Total
2011	270,755	239,469	262,728	260,547	279,567	266,254	256,667	243,255	247,264	247,636	251,795	270,413	3,096,350
2012	271,840	252,207	274,434	263,771	268,475	260,253	258,484	250,658	242,852	262,610	259,112	278,747	3,143,443
2013	280,944	251,977	284,123	279,144	281,307	259,631	246,804	269,747	241,687	268,497	252,211	273,767	3,189,839
2014	283,595	254,140	283,494	290,713	293,923	274,257	274,163	265,918	262,230	277,835	266,025	290,745	3,317,038
2015	296,767	262,602	287,042	287,350	296,447	287,956	286,435	279,379	271,551	278,915	265,947	292,720	3,393,111
2016	297,480	258,530	286,426	300,166	293,238	280,220	284,607	281,932	271,561	284,058	286,571	309,709	3,434,498
2017	327,339	291,518	323,453	329,682	327,467	302,102	298,297	298,318	291,766	307,844	296,609	327,073	3,721,468
2018	331,985	301,256	320,257	319,153	318,665	312,869	325,217	311,974	297,632	323,213	314,170	326,117	3,802,508
2019	323,210	280,816	315,229	306,510	321,122	307,403	305,911	321,190	284,142	309,584	309,223	330,369	3,714,709
2020[1]	319,240	302,408	318,292	330,891	317,737	309,012	323,991	324,030	306,953	328,957	320,161	334,193	3,835,865

[1] Preliminary. *Source: National Agricultural Statistics Service, U.S. Department of Agriculture (NASS-USDA)*

Production of Mozzarella Cheese in the United States In Thousands of Pounds

Year	Jan.	Feb.	Mar.	Apr.	May	June	July	Aug.	Sept.	Oct.	Nov.	Dec.	Total
2011	307,978	273,554	310,367	300,077	308,898	298,100	287,392	286,670	286,434	296,943	296,616	321,399	3,574,428
2012	311,892	291,441	318,710	302,550	306,314	299,675	291,932	286,230	286,444	297,141	297,676	324,843	3,614,848
2013	311,837	278,522	323,187	302,643	307,092	307,964	307,910	296,420	301,973	318,997	307,484	335,960	3,699,989
2014	333,319	300,506	335,385	332,466	331,181	328,829	327,914	311,973	319,861	326,866	326,093	350,532	3,924,925
2015	341,183	305,421	344,459	330,958	333,451	331,196	338,554	316,045	316,408	332,824	335,210	363,227	3,988,936
2016	353,001	323,713	358,081	340,584	345,063	339,993	350,089	328,118	334,808	346,013	338,728	359,555	4,117,746
2017	353,165	315,534	362,560	348,680	352,115	350,106	351,858	336,517	332,291	347,484	351,563	365,619	4,167,492
2018	365,563	328,591	372,712	358,320	359,072	355,249	367,437	357,346	358,579	381,217	370,269	377,006	4,351,361
2019	379,627	347,234	391,166	372,686	374,770	370,364	368,167	370,384	375,726	384,612	375,266	383,976	4,493,978
2020[1]	381,983	353,200	388,257	351,712	378,291	382,043	365,266	351,956	365,058	366,108	361,574	373,101	4,418,549

[1] Preliminary. *Source: National Agricultural Statistics Service, U.S. Department of Agriculture (NASS-USDA)*

Cold Storage of All Varieties of Cheese in the United States, on First of Month In Thousands of Pounds

Year	Jan.	Feb.	Mar.	Apr.	May	June	July	Aug.	Sept.	Oct.	Nov.	Dec.
2011	1,047,926	1,052,397	1,035,332	1,029,494	1,040,145	1,049,185	1,051,424	1,084,946	1,065,363	1,046,014	1,017,627	977,765
2012	991,616	1,020,057	1,026,405	1,045,473	1,072,146	1,069,086	1,094,965	1,092,617	1,049,484	1,040,006	995,363	985,871
2013	1,023,102	1,032,196	1,068,756	1,105,725	1,121,293	1,150,039	1,149,377	1,146,131	1,100,351	1,070,697	1,019,716	996,609
2014	1,009,381	1,015,053	1,010,132	1,018,290	1,037,586	1,065,540	1,055,442	1,054,892	1,041,408	1,013,782	995,666	1,017,192
2015	1,017,936	1,048,243	1,067,060	1,068,645	1,085,909	1,111,854	1,142,241	1,161,796	1,167,393	1,152,446	1,146,191	1,148,060
2016	1,146,086	1,178,194	1,182,308	1,191,394	1,209,222	1,249,382	1,250,328	1,275,546	1,241,119	1,235,452	1,222,315	1,182,646
2017	1,198,334	1,192,166	1,226,457	1,262,244	1,303,328	1,308,929	1,316,698	1,369,506	1,333,551	1,308,072	1,267,950	1,258,630
2018	1,280,484	1,278,637	1,317,731	1,324,728	1,345,280	1,384,940	1,388,638	1,412,980	1,360,489	1,379,703	1,375,149	1,352,739
2019	1,344,794	1,369,236	1,366,937	1,384,366	1,397,974	1,385,616	1,380,784	1,360,510	1,364,830	1,373,856	1,341,695	1,322,482
2020[1]	1,322,014	1,353,618	1,362,091	1,374,507	1,478,640	1,454,505	1,415,905	1,391,664	1,377,907	1,355,799	1,341,428	1,346,792

Quantities are given in "net weight." [1] Preliminary. *Source: National Agricultural Statistics Service, U.S. Department of Agriculture (NASS-USDA)*

Cold Storage of Natural American Cheese in the United States, on First of Month In Thousands of Pounds

Year	Jan.	Feb.	Mar.	Apr.	May	June	July	Aug.	Sept.	Oct.	Nov.	Dec.
2011	630,789	637,935	621,023	611,200	622,121	622,672	619,147	648,834	647,268	639,175	619,376	583,993
2012	610,998	642,204	634,614	651,005	663,532	652,052	662,387	670,734	649,397	641,685	610,931	611,687
2013	635,590	643,184	661,019	684,653	698,655	714,637	710,604	701,964	668,361	661,046	626,161	613,965
2014	618,265	630,820	628,679	639,067	648,900	656,446	655,239	660,438	648,784	631,279	623,336	635,776
2015	627,769	636,019	645,670	634,270	644,113	669,464	685,745	698,029	709,029	698,875	696,781	699,794
2016	701,073	716,370	716,357	725,837	734,121	757,530	756,950	769,705	742,497	742,804	736,017	713,231
2017	726,403	722,449	744,640	772,702	804,645	816,266	810,234	831,538	800,994	780,466	740,404	733,378
2018	746,846	741,772	762,770	766,628	780,256	804,075	800,379	823,342	787,435	803,750	811,593	798,970
2019	800,336	803,578	783,210	784,761	782,769	786,579	784,362	773,183	767,366	774,761	743,621	740,367
2020[1]	749,886	779,672	778,265	776,360	834,295	820,018	793,026	785,521	789,594	772,362	756,168	762,041

Quantities are given in "net weight." [1] Preliminary. *Source: National Agricultural Statistics Service, U.S. Department of Agriculture (NASS-USDA)*

Cold Storage of Other Natural American Cheese in the United States, on First of Month In Thousands of Lbs.

Year	Jan.	Feb.	Mar.	Apr.	May	June	July	Aug.	Sept.	Oct.	Nov.	Dec.
2011	385,645	378,142	379,698	385,737	386,597	392,811	397,914	401,944	384,518	375,535	366,010	354,919
2012	352,981	351,944	364,742	365,596	379,769	387,458	402,201	391,272	371,295	369,388	354,411	343,278
2013	355,765	358,611	377,607	390,483	394,135	406,351	407,426	411,452	399,984	379,676	365,632	356,542
2014	366,428	358,812	354,511	351,798	360,370	378,556	372,231	369,861	365,539	356,819	346,730	356,997
2015	368,885	389,813	397,035	409,802	417,810	420,966	435,655	442,176	436,161	431,534	428,006	425,601
2016	420,426	437,724	441,248	440,928	450,509	466,885	468,886	480,139	472,603	466,593	461,870	444,666
2017	447,731	445,787	454,818	463,489	471,721	466,421	480,969	510,959	505,726	502,198	503,269	500,319
2018	507,271	508,132	527,077	529,020	535,831	549,441	556,947	557,449	541,843	545,105	532,781	523,903
2019	514,683	536,305	552,680	568,118	587,029	574,352	569,005	560,148	570,124	572,703	571,930	557,575
2020[1]	547,950	551,044	559,737	574,875	618,651	609,939	598,874	585,606	567,711	562,675	565,111	564,688

Quantities are given in "net weight." [1] Preliminary. *Source: National Agricultural Statistics Service, U.S. Department of Agriculture (NASS-USDA)*

Cold Storage of Swiss Cheese in the United States, on First of Month In Thousands of Pounds

Year	Jan.	Feb.	Mar.	Apr.	May	June	July	Aug.	Sept.	Oct.	Nov.	Dec.
2011	31,492	36,320	34,611	32,557	31,427	33,702	34,363	34,168	33,577	31,304	32,241	30,073
2012	27,637	25,909	27,049	28,872	28,845	29,576	30,377	30,611	28,792	28,933	30,021	30,906
2013	31,747	30,401	30,130	30,589	28,503	29,051	31,347	32,715	32,006	29,975	27,923	26,102
2014	24,688	25,421	26,942	27,425	28,316	30,538	27,972	24,593	27,085	25,684	25,600	24,419
2015	21,282	22,411	23,587	24,573	23,986	21,424	20,841	21,591	22,203	22,037	21,404	22,665
2016	24,587	24,100	24,703	24,629	24,592	24,967	24,492	25,702	26,019	26,055	24,428	24,749
2017	24,200	23,930	26,999	26,053	26,962	26,242	25,495	27,009	26,831	25,408	24,277	24,933
2018	26,367	28,733	27,884	29,080	29,193	31,424	31,312	32,189	31,211	30,848	30,775	29,866
2019	29,775	29,353	31,047	31,487	28,176	24,685	27,417	27,179	27,340	26,392	26,144	24,540
2020[1]	24,178	22,902	24,089	23,272	25,694	24,548	24,005	20,537	20,602	20,762	20,149	20,063

Quantities are given in "net weight." [1] Preliminary. *Source: National Agricultural Statistics Service, U.S. Department of Agriculture (NASS-USDA)*

Chromium

Chromium (atomic symbol Cr) is a steel-gray, hard, and brittle, metallic element that can take on a high polish. Chromium and its compounds are toxic. Discovered in 1797 by Louis Vauquelin, chromium is named after the Greek word for color, *khroma*. Vauquelin also discovered that an emerald's green color is due to the presence of chromium. Many precious stones owe their color to the presence of chromium compounds.

Chromium is primarily found in chromite ore. The primary use of chromium is to form alloys with iron, nickel, or cobalt. Chromium improves hardness and resistance to corrosion and oxidation in iron, steel, and nonferrous alloys. It is a critical alloying ingredient in the production of stainless steel, making up 10% or more of the final composition. More than half of the chromium consumed is used in metallic products, and about one-third is used in refractories. Chromium is also used as a lustrous decorative plating agent, in pigments, leather processing, plating of metals, and catalysts.

Supply – World mine production of chromium in 2020 fell -10.7% yr/yr to 40.000 million metric tons, a record high. The world's largest producers of chromium in 2020 were South Africa with 40.0% of world production, Kazakhstan with 16.8%, and India with 10.0%. South Africa's production in 2020 fell -2.4% yr/yr to 16.000 million metric tons, which was down from the previous year's record high of 16,395. Kazakhstan's production in 2020 was unchanged at 6.7 million metric tons, a record high. Turkey has emerged as a major producer with 6.3 million metric tons, more than triple its levels in the late-1990s. India has emerged as a major producer of chromium in the past three decades. India's 2020 production level of 4.0 million metric tons was more than ten times the level of 360,000 metric tons seen 30 years earlier.

Trade – The U.S. relied on imports for 75% of its chromium consumption in 2020. That is well below the record high of 91% posted back in the 1970s. U.S. chromium imports in 2017 rose +110.9% yr/yr from 348,210 to 734,000 metric tons. U.S. exports of chromium in 2017 rose +387.8% yr/yr from 2,708 to 13,310 metric tons.

World Mine Production of Chromium In Thousands of Metric Tons (Gross Weight)

Year	Albania	Brazil	Cuba	Finland	India	Iran	Kazakhstan	Madagascar	Philippines	South Africa	Turkey	Zimbabwe	World Total[1]
2011	161	494	----	693	4,326	418	5,059	67	25	10,824	2,282	599	26,900
2012	380	425	----	425	3,255	412	5,233	112	37	11,317	3,295	408	26,900
2013	521	430	----	982	2,633	344	5,255	88	35	13,690	4,141	355	30,000
2014	679	717	----	2,285	2,374	359	5,411	124	47	14,038	10,241	408	38,200
2015	646	527	----	1,952	2,666	277	5,383	148	16	15,656	8,301	208	37,000
2016	727	550	----	2,105	3,329	342	5,543	108	26	14,708	6,066	225	34,800
2017	950	550	----	1,954	3,478	324	6,313	209	21	16,548	7,850	689	40,100
2018	960	550	----	2,211	4,300	330	6,689	100	45	17,617	8,000	895	43,100
2019[1]			----	2,415	4,139		6,700			16,395	10,000		44,800
2020[2]			----	2,400	4,000		6,700			16,000	6,300		40,000

[1] Preliminary. [2] Estimate. *Source: U.S. Geological Survey (USGS)*

Salient Statistics of Chromite in the United States In Thousands of Metric Tons (Gross Weight)

						Consumption by -- Primary Consumer Group --			- Government[5] Stocks, Dec. 31 -			--- $/Metric Ton ---	
Year	Net Import Reliance as a % of Apparent Consumpn	Production of Ferro-chromium	Exports	Imports for Consumption	Reexports	Total	Metallurgical & Chemical	Refractory	Metallurgical & Chemical	Refractory	Total Stocks	South Africa[3]	Turkish[4]
2011	67	W	25	399	----	----	----	----	----	----	----	----	----
2012	73	W	27	416	----	----	----	----	----	----	----	----	----
2013	69	W	23	355	----	----	----	----	----	----	----	----	----
2014	75	W	22	467	----	----	----	----	----	----	----	----	----
2015	64	W	10	329	----	----	----	----	----	----	----	----	----
2016	66	W	3	348	----	----	----	----	----	----	----	----	----
2017	71	W	7	399	----	----	----	----	----	----	----	----	----
2018	76	W	5	432	----	----	----	----	----	----	----	----	----
2019[1]	73	W			----	----	----	----	----	----	----	----	----
2020[2]	75	W			----	----	----	----	----	----	----	----	----

[1] Preliminary. [2] Estimate. [3] Cr_2O_3, 44% (Transvaal). [4] 48% Cr_2O_3. [5] Data through 1999 are for Consumer. W = Withheld.
Source: U.S. Geological Survey (USGS)

Coal

Coal is a sedimentary rock composed primarily of carbon, hydrogen, and oxygen. Coal is a fossil fuel formed from ancient plants buried deep in the Earth's crust over 300 million years ago. Historians believe coal was first used commercially in China for smelting copper and for casting coins around 1,000 BC. Almost 92% of all coal consumed in the U.S. is burned by electric power plants, and coal accounts for about 55% of total electricity output. Coal is also used in the manufacture of steel. The steel industry first converts coal into coke, then combines the coke with iron ore and limestone, and finally heats the mixture to produce iron. Other industries use coal to make fertilizers, solvents, medicine, pesticides, and synthetic fuels.

There are four types of mined coal: anthracite (used in high-grade steel production), bituminous (used for electricity generation and for making coke), sub-bituminous, and lignite (both used primarily for electricity generation).

Futures and options on coal are traded on ICE Futures Europe, New York Mercantile Exchange, and Singapore Exchange. Futures are traded on CME Group, Dalian Commodity Exchange, and Zhengzhou Commodity Exchange.

Price – Coal futures trade at the CME Group. The contract trades in units of 1,550 tons and is priced in terms of dollars and cents per ton. In 2019, the average mine price rose +0.2% to $36.07 per short ton.

Supply – U.S. production of bituminous coal in 2020 fell -23.7% yr/yr to 539,053 million tons, the lowest level since 1973.

Demand – U.S. consumption of coal in 2019 fell -14.8% to 586.539 million tons, the lowest level since 1975.

Trade – U.S. exports of coal in 2019 fell -19.7% yr/yr to 92.852 million tons. The major exporting destinations for the U.S. are Europe and Asia. U.S. imports in 2019 rose +12.5% yr/yr to 6.697 million tons.

World Production of Primary Coal In Thousands of Short Tons

Year	Australia	China	Colombia	Germany	India	Indonesia	Kazakhstan	Poland	Russia	South Africa	Turkey	United States	World Total
2010	467,823	3,779,212	82,021	202,286	578,216	363,343	122,278	146,257	329,258	280,403	80,908	1,084,368	8,159,180
2011	461,799	4,149,575	94,625	208,846	590,753	431,209	128,364	152,680	325,887	276,853	82,885	1,095,628	8,680,790
2012	492,786	4,348,754	98,207	217,144	600,408	460,541	132,858	158,197	363,058	285,031	77,458	1,016,458	8,918,522
2013	521,124	4,380,935	94,247	210,493	613,626	522,904	131,808	156,875	385,818	282,780	72,877	984,842	8,990,787
2014	555,812	4,270,260	97,640	205,597	629,696	504,965	125,647	150,374	393,765	288,695	71,911	1,000,049	8,894,257
2015	556,120	4,129,851	94,300	203,612	645,766	508,789	118,299	149,147	409,701	278,003	64,390	896,941	8,626,407
2016	554,764	3,708,155	99,772	193,593	661,800	502,871	113,620	143,996	423,095	281,430	80,473	728,364	8,060,191
2017	550,567	3,884,058	99,813	193,039	683,057	508,438	124,291	139,597	449,579	283,074	81,679	774,609	8,344,220
2018[1]	534,720	4,076,051	92,907	186,312	729,332	604,705	125,327	134,432	476,919	285,130	92,524	756,167	8,672,045
2019[2]	554,665	4,279,854	90,462	144,749	714,749			123,406	481,701		99,205	706,307	

[1] Preliminary. [2] Estimate. NA = Not available. *Source: United Nations*

Production of Bituminous & Lignite Coal in the United States In Thousands of Short Tons

Year	Alabama	Colorado	Illinois	Indiana	Kentucky	Montana	Ohio	Pennsylvania	Texas	West Virgina	Virgina	Wyoming	U.S. Total
2010	19,915	25,163	33,241	34,950	104,960	44,732	26,707	58,593	40,982	22,385	135,220	442,522	1,084,368
2011	19,071	26,890	37,770	37,426	108,766	42,008	28,166	59,182	45,904	22,523	134,662	438,673	1,095,628
2012	19,321	28,566	48,486	36,720	90,862	36,694	26,328	54,719	44,178	18,965	120,425	401,442	1,016,458
2013	18,620	24,236	52,147	39,102	80,380	42,231	25,113	54,009	42,851	16,619	112,786	387,924	984,842
2014	16,363	24,007	57,969	39,267	77,335	44,562	22,252	60,910	43,654	15,059	112,187	395,665	1,000,049
2015	13,191	18,879	56,101	34,295	61,425	41,864	17,041	50,031	35,918	13,914	95,633	375,773	896,941
2016	9,643	12,634	43,422	28,767	42,868	32,336	12,564	45,720	39,001	12,910	79,757	297,218	728,364
2017	12,613	15,047	48,128	31,418	42,608	35,232	9,336	49,065	36,338	13,205	92,733	316,454	774,118
2018[1]	14,783	14,026	49,482	34,598	39,740	38,610	8,993	49,968	24,823	13,012	95,510	304,188	756,167
2019[2]	14,124	12,868	45,853	31,559	36,006	34,468	7,779	50,053	23,307	12,297	93,279	276,912	703,609

[1] Preliminary. [2] Estimate. *Source: Energy Information Administration, U.S. Department of Energy (EIA-DOE)*

Production[2] of Bituminous Coal in the United States In Thousands of Short Tons

Year	Jan.	Feb.	Mar.	Apr.	May	June	July	Aug.	Sept.	Oct.	Nov.	Dec.	Total
2011	91,355	85,575	96,548	88,563	86,850	88,878	85,498	95,495	94,013	94,643	94,109	94,101	1,095,628
2012	95,102	85,914	85,849	77,514	81,717	81,816	86,321	90,816	81,818	85,239	84,147	80,205	1,016,458
2013	82,529	77,414	84,381	78,724	83,075	80,841	84,344	90,013	82,707	80,435	80,408	77,827	982,699
2014	82,835	75,177	86,794	82,835	83,645	78,929	84,275	87,167	83,410	85,286	81,587	86,163	998,102
2015	86,548	72,210	81,430	74,704	69,942	66,484	76,618	82,777	77,868	75,705	68,613	63,036	895,936
2016	60,413	57,181	55,186	48,089	52,983	59,356	61,667	68,118	64,947	68,578	67,006	63,176	726,700
2017	68,236	64,221	64,167	58,598	61,950	66,053	62,834	70,434	62,759	66,201	64,184	63,061	772,697
2018	61,827	60,129	65,351	57,892	61,048	61,408	62,817	69,160	62,289	66,355	62,690	63,305	754,271
2019	65,836	58,315	55,667	61,213	61,862	56,706	59,069	63,795	58,597	57,674	54,393	53,184	706,309
2020[1]	55,612	47,379	46,061	39,000	36,934	39,259	43,196	47,499	45,119	46,599	45,960	46,436	539,053

[1] Preliminary. [2] Includes small amount of lignite. *Source: Energy Information Administration, U.S. Department of Energy (EIA-DOE)*

Production[2] of Pennsylvania Anthracite Coal In Thousands of Short Tons

Year	Jan.	Feb.	Mar.	Apr.	May	June	July	Aug.	Sept.	Oct.	Nov.	Dec.	Total
2011	163	156	176	177	180	186	185	218	205	191	199	198	2,235
2012	198	185	193	205	213	206	210	224	195	186	179	174	2,368
2013	183	172	187	186	196	191	174	186	171	168	168	163	2,143
2014	157	143	165	147	148	140	174	180	172	176	168	177	1,947
2015	170	142	160	182	171	162	204	220	207	192	174	160	2,145
2016	156	147	142	128	141	157	117	129	123	147	144	135	1,665
2017	178	168	168	156	165	176	133	149	133	167	162	159	1,912
2018	144	140	152	155	163	164	151	166	149	177	167	169	1,896
2019	192	170	162	232	235	215	207	224	205	269	253	248	2,611
2020[1]	246	210	204	147	139	148	194	213	202				1,704

[1] Preliminary. [2] Represents production in Pennsylvania only. *Source: Energy Information Administration, U.S. Department of Energy (EIA-DOE)*

Salient Statistics of Coal in the United States In Thousands of Short Tons

				Exports						
Year	Production	Imports	Consumption	Brazil	Canada	Europe	Asia	Total	Total Ending Stocks[2]	Losses & Unaccounted For[3]
2011	1,095,628	13,088	1,002,948	8,680	6,845	53,942	27,533	107,259	231,951	11,506
2012	1,016,458	9,159	889,185	7,954	7,211	66,399	32,512	125,746	238,853	14,980
2013	984,842	8,906	924,442	8,610	7,110	60,755	27,245	117,659	200,335	1,451
2014	1,000,049	11,350	917,731	8,032	6,724	52,469	19,450	97,257	197,727	11,101
2015	896,941	11,318	798,115	6,339	5,958	37,894	17,544	73,958	238,431	5,452
2016	728,364	9,850	731,071	6,939	5,011	27,381	15,714	60,271	192,990	2,452
2017	774,609	7,803	716,856	7,563	5,286	39,561	32,841	96,945	166,956	4,596
2018	756,167	5,954	688,105	8,595	5,726	43,808	40,281	115,632	130,047	5,363
2019	706,309	6,697	586,539	7,515	5,118	33,264	32,459	92,852	158,772	5,164
2020[1]	539,053									

[1] Preliminary. [2] Producer & distributor and consumer stocks, excludes stocks held by retail dealers for consumption by the residential and commercial sector. [3] Equals production plus imports minus the change in producer & distributor and consumer stocks minus consumption minus exports.
Source: Energy Information Administraion, U.S. Department of Energy (EIA-DOE)

Consumption and Stocks of Coal in the United States In Thousands of Short Tons

	Consumption									Stocks, Dec. 31			
	Electric Utilities				Industrial					Consumer			
Year	Anthracite	Bituminous	Lignite	Total	Coke Plants	Other Industrial[2]	Residential and Commercial	Total	Electric Utilities	Coke Plants	Other Industrials	Producers and Distributors
2010	----	----	----	975,052	21,092	49,289	3,081	1,048,514	174,917	1,925	4,525	49,820
2011	----	----	----	932,484	21,434	46,238	2,793	1,002,948	172,387	2,610	4,455	51,897
2012	----	----	----	823,551	20,751	42,838	2,045	889,185	185,116	2,522	4,475	46,157
2013	----	----	----	857,962	21,474	43,055	1,951	924,442	147,884	2,200	4,097	45,652
2014	----	----	----	851,602	21,297	42,946	1,887	917,731	151,548	2,640	4,196	38,894
2015	----	----	----	738,444	19,708	38,459	1,503	798,115	195,548	2,236	4,382	35,871
2016	----	----	----	678,554	16,485	34,849	1,183	731,071	162,009	1,675	3,637	25,309
2017	----	----	----	664,993	17,538	33,264	1,061	716,856	137,687	1,718	3,242	23,999
2018	----	----	----	637,217	18,337	31,580	972	688,105	102,793	1,807	3,258	21,692
2019[1]	----	----	----	538,601	17,967	29,095	876	586,539	128,180	2,333	3,258	31,320

[1] Preliminary. [2] Including transportation. [3] Excludes stocks held at retail dealers for consumption by the residential and commercial sector.
Source: Energy Information Administration, U.S. Department of Energy (EIA-DOE)

Average Prices of Coal in the United States In Dollars Per Short Ton

	End-Use Sector				Exports				End-Use Sector				Exports		
Year	Electric Utilities	Coke Plants	Other Industrial[2]	Imports[3]	Steam	Metal-lurgical	Total Average[3]	Year	Electric Utilities	Coke Plants	Other Industrial[2]	Imports[3]	Steam	Metal-lurgical	Total Average[3]
2011	----	184.44	70.62	103.32	80.42	185.99	148.86	2016	----	----	----	65.75	48.58	71.13	73.66
2012	----	190.55	70.33	96.78	76.16	152.23	118.43	2017	----	----	----	79.53	58.29	134.55	102.09
2013	----	156.99	69.32	83.35	69.23	115.50	95.06	2018	----	----	----	82.39	64.60	138.98	104.63
2014	----	----	----	80.96	67.05	99.49	87.08	2019	----	----	----	80.04	64.62	134.09	105.34
2015	----	----	----	71.61	56.44	89.31	76.89	2020[1]	----	----	----	74.51	60.22	111.79	90.90

[1] Preliminary. [2] Manufacturing plants only. [3] Based on the free alongside ship (F.A.S.) value.
Source: Energy Information Administration, U.S. Department of Energy (EIA-DOE)

Trends in Bituminous Coal, Lignite and Pennsylvania Anthracite in the United States In Thousands of Short Tons

	Bituminous Coal and Lignite							Pennsylvania Anthracite					All Mines
	Production				Labor Productivity							Labor	Labor
					Under-							Productivity	Productivity
	Under-			Miners[1]	Ground	Surface	Average	Under-			Miners[1]	Short Tons	Short Tons
Year	Ground	Surface	Total	Employd	-Short Tons Per Miner Per Hour-			Ground	Surface	Total	Employed	Miner/Hr.	Miner/Hr.
2010	337,155	747,214	1,084,368	86,057	2.89	9.47	5.55	139	1,566	1,705	928	.98	5.55
2011	345,606	750,022	1,095,628	91,482	2.72	8.97	5.19	166	1,965	2,131	952	1.11	5.19
2012	342,387	674,072	1,016,458	89,838	2.84	8.97	5.19	120	2,215	2,335	1,146	1.02	5.19
2013	341,685	643,157	984,842	80,396	3.07	9.69	5.53	95	1,965	2,060	1,095	1.01	5.53
2014	354,704	645,345	1,000,049	74,931	3.35	10.42	5.95	93	1,740	1,833	956	.98	5.96
2015	306,821	590,119	896,941	65,971	3.45	10.95	6.28	86	1,867	1,953	1,005	.94	6.28
2016	252,106	476,258	728,364	51,795	3.83	10.73	6.61	91	1,409	1,500	952	.83	6.61
2017	273,129	501,480	774,609	53,051	3.77	10.92	6.55	79	1,788	1,867	914	1.07	6.55
2018	275,361	480,806	756,167	53,583	3.68	10.36	6.24	72	1,739	1,811	900	1.03	6.23
2019	267,373	438,936	706,309	52,804	3.60	9.88	5.95	63	2,522	2,585	916	1.43	5.94

[1] Excludes miners employed at mines producing less than 10,000 tons.
Source: Energy Information Administration, U.S. Department of Energy (EIA-DOE)

Average Mine Prices of Coal in the United States In Dollars Per Short Ton

	Average Mine Prices by Method			Average Mine Prices by Rank				Bituminous		All Coal
	Under-				Sub-			& Lignite	Anthracite	CIF[3] Electric Utility
Year	ground	Surface	Total	Lignite	bituminous	Bituminous	Anthracite[1]	FOB Mines[2]	FOB Mines[2]	Plants
2010	60.73	24.13	35.61	18.76	14.11	60.88	59.61	60.88	59.61	44.27
2011	70.47	27.00	41.01	18.77	14.07	68.50	75.70	68.50	75.70	46.29
2012	66.56	26.43	39.95	19.60	15.34	66.04	80.21	66.04	80.21	45.77
2013	60.98	24.50	37.24	19.96	14.86	60.61	87.82	60.61	87.82	45.03
2014	56.97	22.83	34.83	19.44	14.72	55.99	90.98	55.99	90.98	45.66
2015	52.20	21.47	31.83	22.36	14.63	51.57	97.91	51.57	97.91	42.58
2016	49.02	20.47	30.57	19.99	14.83	48.40	97.61	48.40	97.61	40.39
2017	56.99	20.95	33.72	19.51	14.29	55.60	93.17	55.60	93.17	33.72
2018	60.38	21.90	35.99	20.21	13.64	59.43	99.97	59.43	99.97	35.99
2019	58.68	22.47	36.07	19.86	14.01	58.93	102.22	58.93	102.22	

[1] Produced in Pennsylvania. [2] FOB = free on board. [3] *CIF = cost, insurance and freight.* W = Withheld data.
Source: Energy Information Adminstration, U.S. Department of Energy (EIA-DOE)

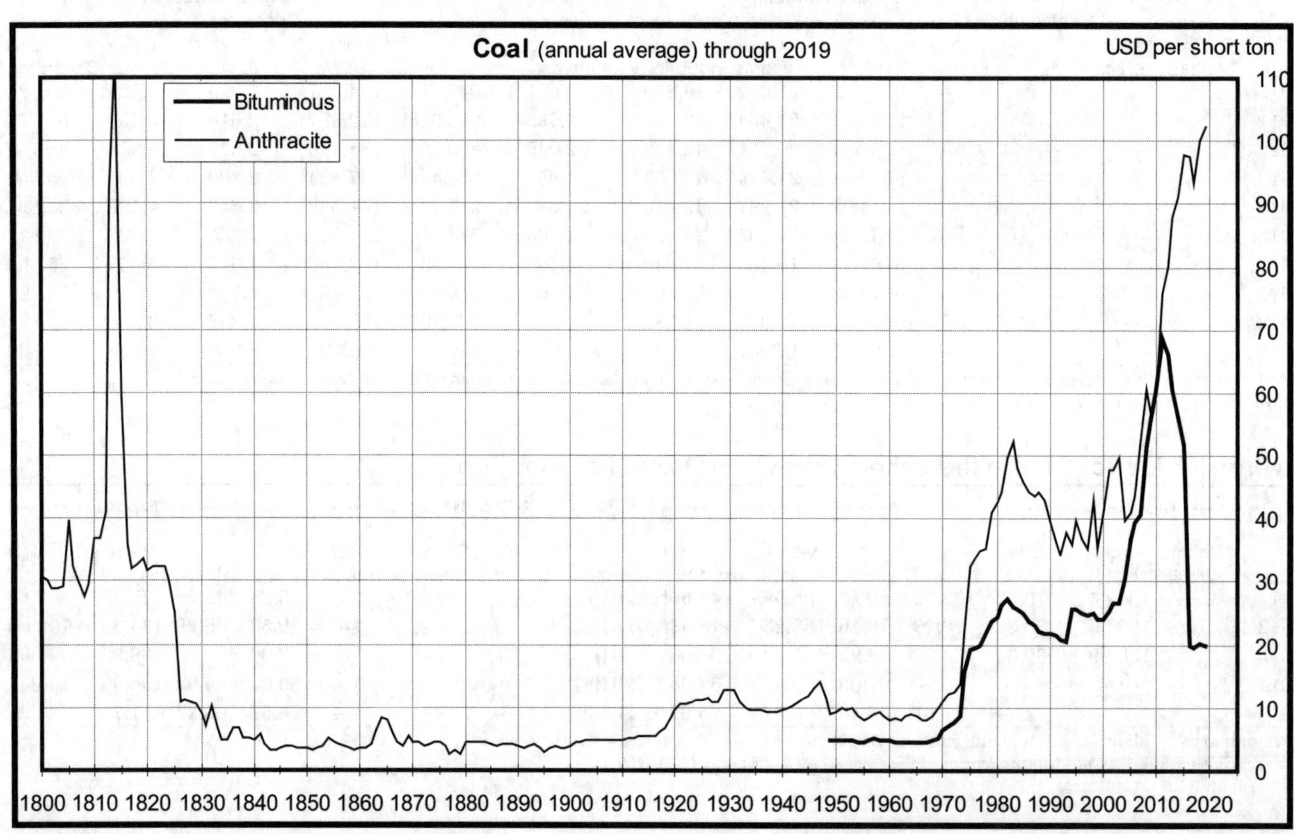

Cobalt

Cobalt (atomic symbol Co) is a lustrous, silvery-white, magnetic, metallic element used chiefly for making alloys. Cobalt was known in ancient times and used by the Persians in 2250 BC to color glass. The name *cobalt* comes from the German word *kobalt* or *kobold*, meaning evil spirit. Miners gave cobalt its name because it was poisonous and troublesome since it polluted and degraded other mined elements, like nickel. In the 1730s, George Brandt first isolated metallic cobalt and was able to show that cobalt was the source of the blue color in glasses. In 1780, it was recognized as an element. Cobalt is generally not found in nature as a free metal and is instead found in ores. Cobalt is mainly produced as a by-product of nickel and copper mining.

Cobalt is used in a variety of applications: high-temperature steel alloys; fasteners in gas turbine engines; magnets and magnetic recording media; drying agents for paints and pigments; and steel-belted radial tires. Cobalt-60, an important radioactive tracer and cancer-treatment agent, is an artificially produced radioactive isotope of cobalt.

Prices – The price of cobalt in 2020 fell by -5.6% yr/yr to $16.00 per pound, well below the 2008 record high of $39.01 per pound.

Supply – World production of cobalt in 2020 fell -2.8% yr/yr to 140,000 metric tons, down from the 2008 record high of 148,000. The world's largest cobalt mine producers in 2020 were the Congo with 67.9% of world production, Russia with 4.5%, and Australia with 4.1%.

The U.S. does not specifically mine or refine cobalt, although some cobalt is produced as a byproduct of other mining operations. Imports, stock releases, and secondary materials comprise the U.S. cobalt supply. Secondary production includes extraction from super-alloy scrap, cemented carbide scrap, and spent catalysts. In the U.S. there are two domestic producers of extra-fine cobalt powder. One company produces the powder from imported primary metal and the other from recycled materials. There are only about seven companies that produce cobalt compounds. U.S. secondary production of cobalt in 2020 was unchanged yr/yr at 2,750 metric tons, still below the record high of 3,080 metric tons seen in 1998.

Demand – U.S. consumption of cobalt in 2020 fell -30.4% yr/yr to 8,700 metric tons, a new high. In 2015, the largest use of cobalt by far was for super-alloys, with 38.4% of consumption. Other smaller-scaled applications for cobalt include cutting and wear-resistant materials at 8.1% and magnetic alloys at 3.3%. Demand for some other uses is not available as proprietary information.

Trade – U.S. imports of cobalt in 2020 fell -28.1% to 10,000 metric tons, down from the 2019 record high of 13,900. In 2017, the U.S. relied on imports for 76% of its cobalt consumption, down from the 99% level seen in the early 1970s.

World Mine Production of Cobalt In Metric Tons (Cobalt Content)

Year	Australia	Botswana	Brazil	Canada	China	Congo[3] (Kinshasa)	Cuba	Indonesia	Morocco	New Caledonia	Russia	Zambia	World Total
2011	3,848	149	3,623	6,836	6,800	59,000	5,100	1,600	2,160	3,100	6,100	7,702	111,000
2012	5,870	195	2,900	3,698	2,200	52,000	4,700	1,700	2,000	2,670	6,300	5,435	96,800
2013	6,400	248	3,500	4,005	2,600	56,000	4,000	1,700	2,000	3,190	6,300	2,500	103,000
2014	6,201	196	3,828	3,907	2,800	62,000	3,700	1,300	2,150	4,040	6,300	2,300	113,000
2015	5,721	316	2,771	4,339	3,000	66,000	4,300	1,300	2,250	3,640	6,200	1,700	117,000
2016	5,140	248	200	4,126	3,100	63,000	5,100	1,200	2,400	3,390	5,500	600	109,000
2017	5,034	----	----	3,866	3,100	73,000	5,000	1,200	2,200	2,780	5,900	1,000	120,000
2018	4,880			3,520	2,000	104,000	3,500		2,100	2,100	6,100		148,000
2019[1]	5,740			3,340	2,500	100,000	3,800		2,300	1,600	6,300		144,000
2020[2]	5,700			3,200	2,300	95,000	3,600		1,900		6,300		140,000

[1] Preliminary. [2] Estimate. [3] Formerly Zaire. *Source: U.S. Geological Survey (USGS)*

Salient Statistics of Cobalt in the United States In Metric Tons (Cobalt Content)

					Consumption by End Uses											
Year	Net Import Reliance As a % of Apparent Consump	Cobalt Secondary Production	Processor and Consumer Stocks Dec. 31	Imports for Consumption	Ground Coat Frit	Stainless & Heat Resisting	Catalysts	Super-alloys	Tool Steel	Magnetic Alloys	Pigments	Drier in Paints, etc[3]	Cutting & Wear-Resistant Material	Welding Materials	Total Apparent Uses	Price $ Per Pound[4]
2011	76	2,210	1,040	10,600	W	W	W	4,650	W	313	W	W	773	438	9,230	17.99
2012	77	2,160	980	11,100	W	W	W	4,190	W	285	W	W	774	414	9,540	14.07
2013	75	2,160	1,070	10,400	W	W	W	3,770	W	303	W	W	705	397	8,660	12.89
2014	75	2,200	1,410	11,300	----	----	----	3,930	----	328	----	----	783	573	8,710	14.48
2015	73	2,750	1,070	11,400	----	----	----	3,960	----	----	----	----	726	----	10,300	13.44
2016	76	2,750	969	12,800	----	----	----	4,080	----	----	----	----	672	----	11,500	12.01
2017	69	2,750	1,020	11,900	----	----	----	4,240	----	----	----	----	753	----	8,950	26.97
2018	64	2,750	1,060	11,900											7,700	37.43
2019[1]	78	2,750	1,090	13,900											12,500	16.95
2020[2]	76	2,750	1,000	10,000											8,700	16.00

[1] Preliminary. [2] Estimate. [3] Or related usage. [4] Annual spot for cathodes. W = Withheld. *Source: U.S. Geological Survey (USGS)*

Cocoa

Cocoa is the common name for a powder derived from the fruit seeds of the cacao tree. The Spanish called cocoa "the food of the gods" when they found it in South America 500 years ago. Today, it remains a valued commodity. Dating back to the time of the Aztecs, cocoa was mainly used as a beverage. The processing of the cacao seeds, also known as cocoa beans, begins when the harvested fruit is fermented or cured into a pulpy state for three to nine days. The cocoa beans are then dried in the sun and cleaned in special machines before they are roasted to bring out the chocolate flavor. After roasting, they are put into a crushing machine and ground into cocoa powder. Cocoa has a high food value because it contains as much as 20 percent protein, 40 percent carbohydrate, and 40 percent fat. It is also mildly stimulating because of the presence of theobromine, an alkaloid that is closely related to caffeine. Roughly two-thirds of cocoa bean production is used to make chocolate and one-third to make cocoa powder.

Four major West African cocoa producers, the Ivory Coast, Ghana, Nigeria, and Cameroon, together account for about two-thirds of world cocoa production. Outside of West Africa, the major producers of cocoa are Indonesia, Brazil, Malaysia, Ecuador, and the Dominican Republic. Cocoa producers like Ghana and Indonesia have been making efforts to increase cocoa production while producers like Malaysia have been switching to other crops. Ghana has had an ongoing problem with black pod disease and the crop's smuggling into the neighboring Ivory Coast. Brazil was once one of the largest cocoa producers but has had problems with witches' broom disease. In West Africa, the main crop harvest starts in the September-October period and can be extended into the January-March period. Cocoa trees reach maturity in 5-6 years but can live to be 50 years old or more. The cocoa tree will produce thousands of flowers during a growing season, but only a few will develop into cocoa pods.

Cocoa futures and options are traded at the ICE Futures U.S. and ICE Futures Europe exchanges. The futures contracts call for the delivery of 10 metric tons of cocoa and the contract is priced in US dollars per metric ton.

Prices – ICE cocoa futures prices (Barchart.com symbol CC) in February 2020 pushed up to a 3-1/2 year high of $2,998 per metric ton on excessive dryness in West Africa during Q1-2020, which sparked fund buying of cocoa futures. Cocoa prices then rallied as commodity funds by late-February built up the largest long position seen in six years. Long liquidation began after the International Cocoa Organization (ICCO) in March cut its 2019/20 cocoa deficit estimate to -85,000 MT from the 2018/19 deficit of -107,000 MT. Cocoa prices continued lower in Q2-2020 as the Covid pandemic spread worldwide and spurred lockdowns and travel restrictions that curbed chocolate confectionery sales in restaurants and airports. Cocoa prices posted their low for the year in July 2020 of $2,137 per metric ton on weak global cocoa demand. European cocoa processing in Q2-2020 dropped -8.9% yr/yr to 314,109 MT, the biggest decline in eight years. Weak cocoa demand prompted ICCO in August 2020 to project a 2019/20 global cocoa surplus of 42,000 MT, showing a much more plentiful supply situation than its previous estimate for a global 2019/20 cocoa deficit of -85,000 MT. Cocoa prices zigzagged higher into November when they posted a 4-1/2 year high of $3,054 per metric ton. Prices surged in November after Hershey reportedly bought a large amount of cocoa through the ICE Futures U.S. Exchange instead of buying beans in the physical market, which sparked a short squeeze in December ICE futures. Cocoa prices finished 2020 up +2.5% yr/yr at $2,603 per metric ton.

Supply – The world production of cocoa beans in the 2019/20 crop year rose +0.4% to 5.596 million metric tons. The world's largest cocoa producer by far is the Ivory Coast with 39.0% of the world's production, followed by Ghana with 14.5% and Indonesia with 14.0%. Closing stocks of cocoa in the 2019/20 crop year rose by +2.4% yr/yr to 1.760 million metric tons.

Demand – World seasonal grindings of cocoa in 2019/20 fell -3.1% yr/yr to 4.635 million metric tons, a new record high. The European Union is by far the largest global consumer of cocoa, consuming about 34.1% of the global crop.

Trade – U.S. imports of cocoa and cocoa products in 2020 fell by -0.3% yr/yr to 1.393 million metric tons, below the 2017 record high of 1.456 million metric tons.

World Supply and Demand Cocoa In Thousands of Metric Tons

Crop Year Beginning Oct. 1	Stocks Oct. 1	Net World Production[4]	Total Availability	Seasona Grindings	Closing Stocks	Stock Change	Stock/Consumption Ratio %
2010-11	1,418	4,309	5,727	3,938	1,746	328	44.3
2011-12	1,746	4,095	5,841	3,972	1,828	82	46.0
2012-13	1,828	3,943	5,771	4,180	1,552	-276	37.1
2013-14	1,552	4,370	5,922	4,335	1,543	-9	35.6
2014-15	1,543	4,252	5,795	4,152	1,600	57	38.5
2015-16	1,600	3,994	5,594	4,127	1,427	-173	34.6
2016-17	1,427	4,768	6,195	4,394	1,753	326	39.9
2017-18[1]	1,753	4,648	6,401	4,585	1,770	17	38.6
2018-19[2]	1,770	4,780	6,550	4,784	1,718	-52	35.9
2019-20[3]	1,718	4,724	6,442	4,635	1,760	42	38.0

[1] Preliminary. [2] Estimate. [3] Forecast. [4] Obtained by adjusting the gross world crop for a one percent loss in weight.
Source: International Cocoa Organization (ICO

World Production of Cocoa Beans In Metric Tons

Crop Year Beginning Oct. 1	Brazil	Cameroon	Colombia	Côte d'Ivoire	Dominican Republic	Ecuador	Ghana	Indonesia	Malaysia	Mexico	Nigeria	Papau New Guinea	World Total
2010-11	235,389	264,077	39,534	1,301,347	58,334	132,099	632,037	844,626	15,654	50,114	399,200	39,400	4,329,436
2011-12	248,524	240,000	37,202	1,511,255	54,279	224,163	700,020	712,200	4,605	42,175	391,000	47,600	4,614,869
2012-13	253,211	268,941	41,670	1,485,882	72,225	133,323	879,348	740,500	3,645	38,825	383,000	38,700	4,613,416
2013-14	256,186	275,000	46,739	1,448,992	68,021	128,446	835,466	720,900	2,809	33,284	367,000	41,200	4,484,825
2014-15	273,793	272,000	47,732	1,637,778	69,913	156,216	858,720	728,400	2,665	26,969	329,870	45,369	4,744,750
2015-16	278,299	310,000	54,798	1,796,000	75,500	180,192	858,720	593,331	1,729	28,007	302,066	46,278	4,827,752
2016-17	213,871	211,000	56,785	1,634,000	81,246	177,551	858,720	656,817	1,723	26,863	298,029	45,457	4,651,282
2017-18[1]	235,809	246,200	89,282	2,034,000	86,599	205,955	969,300	590,684	1,012	27,287	325,000	45,528	5,268,238
2018-19[2]	239,318	249,900	97,978	2,154,400	85,139	235,182	904,700	767,280	814	28,399	340,000	45,598	5,573,392
2019-20[3]	259,425	280,000	102,154	2,180,000	88,961	283,680	811,700	783,978	1,005	28,452	350,146	45,668	5,596,397

[1] Preliminary. [2] Estimate. [3] Forecast. *Source: Food and Agricultural Organization of the United Nations (FAO)*

World Consumption of Cocoa[4] In Thousands of Metric Tons

Crop Year Beginning Oct. 1	Canada	Côte d'Ivoire	Brazil	European Union	Ghana	Indonesia	Japan	Malaysia	Singapore	Turkey	United States	Russia	World Total
2010-11	62	361	239	1,492	230	190	40	305	83	70	401	61	3,938
2011-12	60	431	243	1,383	212	270	40	297	83	75	387	63	3,972
2012-13	64	471	241	1,443	225	290	40	293	77	75	429	71	4,180
2013-14	67	519	240	1,461	234	340	44	259	79	88	446	62	4,335
2014-15	62	558	224	1,432	234	335	45	195	81	86	400	46	4,152
2015-16	62	492	225	1,483	202	382	47	194	81	84	398	49	4,127
2016-17	62	577	227	1,503	250	455	49	216	82	102	390	52	4,397
2017-18[1]	62	559	231	1,575	310	483	55	236	90	99	385	55	4,596
2018-19[2]	61	605	235	1,585	320	487	54	327	89	104	400	60	4,805
2019-20[3]	58	615	222	1,560	333	512	57	360	95	111	400	60	4,861

[1] Preliminary. [2] Estimate. [3] Forecast. [4] Figures represent the "grindings" of cocoa beans in each country.
Source: International Cocoa Organization (ICO)

Imports of Cocoa Butter in Selected Countries In Metric Tons

Year	Australia	Austria	Belgium	Canada	France	Germany	Italy	Japan	Netherlands	Sweden	Switzerland	United Kingdom	United States
2011	15,081	5,155	75,003	22,463	61,948	89,511	21,988	19,475	91,297	6,010	26,813	43,440	92,572
2012	15,971	5,090	75,402	24,090	71,043	92,370	25,999	26,566	72,416	6,219	26,430	51,541	72,085
2013	17,900	5,425	75,585	25,929	65,205	109,853	30,310	24,260	92,547	6,192	28,795	50,789	80,676
2014	16,074	4,912	79,049	26,250	68,073	124,839	28,364	27,351	82,319	6,400	28,767	47,171	97,774
2015	17,527	4,119	81,283	24,950	62,998	106,110	28,406	21,305	62,409	6,284	27,548	59,164	95,125
2016	16,293	4,970	93,024	26,218	64,443	130,642	28,150	22,362	77,969	6,247	27,545	53,109	82,678
2017	17,798	5,557	95,598	25,385	78,733	145,287	28,914	23,553	86,544	6,519	29,483	53,778	111,696
2018	18,548	4,363	94,139	23,912	74,686	143,417	31,726	26,584	96,183	5,752	29,087	60,147	108,329
2019	21,013	4,973	107,047	26,702	74,322	163,171	34,426	26,668	104,785	6,405	29,005	66,526	114,707
2020[1]	21,952	6,004	118,700	23,432	91,512	129,604	37,560	21,676	99,212	7,936	24,004	66,456	126,264

[1] Preliminary. *Sources: Food and Agricultural Organization of the United Nations (FAO)*

Imports of Cocoa Liquor and Cocoa Powder in Selected Countries In Metric Tons

	Cocoa Liquor						Cocoa Powder						
Year	France	Germany	Japan	Netherlands	United Kingdom	United States	Belgium	France	Germany	Italy	Japan	Netherlands	United States
2011	84,704	79,039	9,358	82,633	12,108	22,996	18,324	58,723	54,215	27,717	17,361	53,899	162,723
2012	83,905	82,605	9,351	74,125	14,907	20,461	16,226	53,499	52,762	25,370	17,201	45,494	161,081
2013	96,205	81,726	8,487	98,497	9,934	18,379	19,336	65,479	59,576	26,630	15,897	49,255	150,266
2014	94,219	77,645	9,829	112,010	9,238	22,302	18,833	59,356	69,838	28,444	17,705	56,878	154,294
2015	69,450	74,768	11,884	76,553	10,348	14,764	47,539	56,542	69,652	33,407	19,771	28,048	137,590
2016	73,167	78,359	12,215	79,963	16,134	32,559	46,881	46,516	69,627	33,500	19,768	30,216	180,582
2017	96,669	63,007	14,719	115,370	13,957	30,067	29,992	41,469	68,300	35,693	21,258	71,285	182,884
2018	85,741	61,730	16,307	148,578	15,848	34,418	23,502	46,315	70,963	37,269	19,976	79,249	156,978
2019	92,926	62,977	16,605	137,938	20,712	45,375	27,160	49,100	70,960	39,228	17,840	98,996	163,504
2020[1]	100,056	78,620	12,572	160,004	12,708	91,412	25,972	50,395	187,478	40,161	21,244	80,228	177,571

[1] Preliminary. *Source: Food and Agricultural Organization of the United Nations (FAO)*

Imports of Cocoa and Products in the United States In Metric Tons

Year	Jan.	Feb.	Mar.	Apr.	May	June	July	Aug.	Sept.	Oct.	Nov.	Dec.	Total
2011	132,295	144,126	88,224	89,816	91,987	138,011	125,210	121,553	93,780	97,723	90,074	100,511	1,313,310
2012	147,347	152,455	115,034	99,232	82,919	90,586	91,538	95,556	83,121	91,707	88,361	99,904	1,237,761
2013	118,129	125,897	119,255	106,917	136,359	88,132	112,058	94,986	93,586	91,863	90,006	126,702	1,303,889
2014	105,743	141,186	165,373	133,870	95,607	94,784	104,583	98,192	91,016	93,453	80,532	91,672	1,296,010
2015	109,669	121,573	132,182	138,943	115,781	124,700	107,942	88,465	101,383	105,487	87,698	105,521	1,339,343
2016	123,193	144,838	122,403	125,085	99,749	95,351	97,444	109,180	100,657	114,504	105,660	129,828	1,367,892
2017	143,196	143,358	175,485	162,652	129,538	111,460	108,712	100,961	90,012	95,449	95,478	99,473	1,455,775
2018	149,657	134,349	134,869	129,987	111,950	93,772	104,645	111,269	92,118	105,331	99,051	108,658	1,375,657
2019	129,159	139,778	126,889	139,919	130,856	104,081	112,192	105,572	103,153	106,925	86,189	112,285	1,396,996
2020[1]	122,994	144,552	152,889	128,688	105,708	111,954	106,218	99,647	111,169	104,048	95,729	109,582	1,393,178

[1] Preliminary. *Source: Foreign Agricultural Service, U.S. Department of Agriculture (FAS-USDA)*

Visible Stocks of Cocoa in Port of Hampton Road Warehouses[1], at End of Month In Thousands of Bags

Year	Jan.	Feb.	Mar.	Apr.	May	June	July	Aug.	Sept.	Oct.	Nov.	Dec.
2010	13.3	12.3	12.3	12.3	12.3	12.3	12.3	12.3	12.3	12.3	12.3	12.3
2011	10.4	12.3	12.3	12.3	12.3	12.3	12.3	12.3	11.6	11.6	11.6	11.6
2012	11.6	11.6	11.6	11.6	11.6	11.6	11.6	11.6	11.6	11.3	11.3	11.3
2013	11.3	11.3	11.3	9.6	9.6	9.6	10.5	10.5	5.1	9.6	9.5	9.6
2014	9.6	9.6	9.6	9.6	9.6	9.6	9.6	9.6	9.6	9.6	9.6	9.6
2015	9.6	9.6	9.6	9.6	9.6	7.2	7.2	7.2	7.2	7.2	7.2	7.2
2016	7.2	7.2	7.2	7.2	7.2	7.2	7.2	7.2	7.2	7.2	7.2	7.2
2017	7.2	6.5	6.5	6.5	6.5	6.5	6.5	6.5	6.5	6.5	2.7	2.7
2018	2.4	2.4	2.0	2.0	1.9	1.9	1.4	1.4	----	----	----	----
2019	----	----	----	----	----	----	----	----	----	----	----	----

[1] Licensed warehouses approved by ICE. *Source: ICE Futures U.S. (ICE)*

Visible Stocks of Cocoa in Philadelphia (Del. River) Warehouses[1], at End of Month In Thousands of Bags

Year	Jan.	Feb.	Mar.	Apr.	May	June	July	Aug.	Sept.	Oct.	Nov.	Dec.
2011	2,551.7	2,900.4	2,856.1	2,633.1	2,546.0	2,971.6	3,388.2	3,089.4	3,055.1	2,758.3	2,559.1	2,856.1
2012	3,210.7	3,538.5	4,156.0	4,123.5	3,985.5	3,815.8	3,792.4	3,655.2	3,442.7	3,204.1	2,895.2	2,956.3
2013	3,070.3	3,690.7	3,924.4	3,884.4	4,110.6	4,035.9	3,945.1	3,897.9	3,583.0	3,170.0	2,921.9	3,050.1
2014	3,215.1	3,687.7	4,395.1	4,862.6	4,647.1	4,354.2	4,167.4	3,909.4	3,569.5	3,168.6	2,816.0	2,494.7
2015	2,640.6	2,953.7	3,044.0	3,700.4	3,780.4	4,166.1	4,013.1	3,788.7	3,568.2	3,286.3	3,146.1	2,956.1
2016	3,186.6	3,464.0	3,960.3	3,809.4	3,690.7	3,441.0	3,155.1	2,908.5	2,606.9	2,546.0	2,479.5	2,493.6
2017	2,961.9	3,695.8	4,460.4	5,117.8	5,394.3	5,245.8	4,992.7	4,669.1	4,318.8	3,834.3	3,462.8	3,147.5
2018	3,746.2	4,259.6	4,501.8	5,054.0	4,870.3	4,579.7	4,386.0	4,215.1	3,955.9	3,633.1	3,269.1	3,236.1
2019	3,344.6	3,701.7	3,901.5	4,104.4	4,281.1	4,171.4	3,958.4	3,706.2	3,461.9	3,112.4	2,808.2	2,550.9
2020	2,797.9	3,406.5	3,637.2	3,906.0	3,904.8	3,823.1	3,731.8	3,496.9	3,380.1	3,218.4	2,885.5	2,831.3

[1] Licensed warehouses approved by ICE. *Source: ICE Futures U.S. (ICE)*

Visible Stocks of Cocoa in New York Warehouses[1], at End of Month In Thousands of Bags

Year	Jan.	Feb.	Mar.	Apr.	May	June	July	Aug.	Sept.	Oct.	Nov.	Dec.
2011	499.4	604.9	701.2	711.1	639.3	661.5	719.8	734.1	807.6	884.8	875.5	857.6
2012	845.1	881.2	1,031.7	1,016.7	962.8	944.4	862.3	928.4	877.0	829.7	752.3	716.5
2013	679.9	619.6	621.1	708.3	779.6	779.6	717.2	660.4	589.3	529.2	451.3	475.6
2014	391.0	386.7	364.5	482.6	619.3	566.5	505.4	435.9	419.3	380.9	317.1	308.3
2015	276.6	266.0	245.3	260.4	286.9	366.0	342.2	314.5	284.7	277.7	278.0	287.8
2016	283.3	353.2	412.3	388.1	317.4	302.9	299.7	311.3	312.4	289.8	250.2	274.9
2017	336.9	318.2	344.6	388.7	424.8	399.4	367.4	331.1	291.6	252.7	244.0	232.2
2018	271.1	281.8	288.4	315.4	278.3	264.7	265.4	240.5	224.6	206.8	197.7	230.7
2019	223.0	245.5	305.6	327.8	351.3	335.2	326.5	296.8	288.6	246.5	198.2	175.7
2020	250.2	310.0	336.6	375.0	358.1	323.2	305.2	289.6	266.7	237.2	224.5	228.8

[1] Licensed warehouses approved by ICE. *Source: ICE Futures U.S. (ICE)*

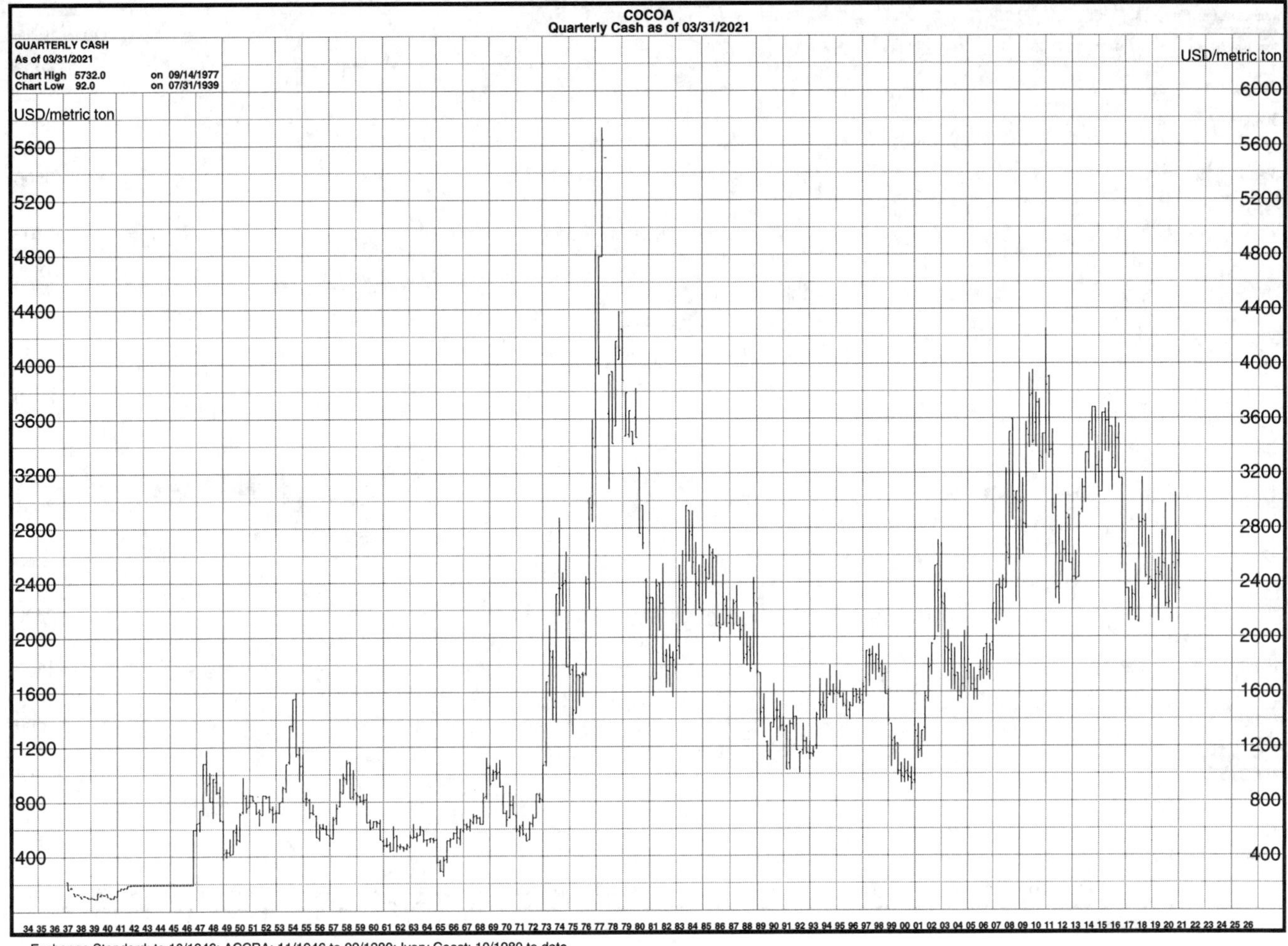

Exchange Standard: to 10/1946; ACCRA: 11/1946 to 09/1980; Ivory Coast: 10/1980 to date.

Average Cash Price of Cocoa, Ivory Coast in New York In Dollars Per Metric Ton

Year	Jan.	Feb.	Mar.	Apr.	May	June	July	Aug.	Sept.	Oct.	Nov.	Dec.	Average
2011	3,507	3,937	3,992	3,697	3,565	3,360	3,422	3,312	3,199	2,949	2,831	2,396	3,347
2012	2,448	2,621	2,647	2,553	2,605	2,506	2,595	2,759	2,956	2,787	2,745	2,724	2,662
2013	2,519	2,455	2,428	2,492	2,566	2,494	2,521	2,672	2,819	2,988	2,996	3,099	2,671
2014	3,068	3,281	3,325	3,340	3,287	3,476	3,494	3,591	3,523	3,455	3,176	3,191	3,351
2015	3,170	3,181	3,181	3,129	3,331	3,493	3,590	3,424	3,546	3,434	3,630	3,632	3,395
2016	3,297	3,124	3,327	3,333	3,412	3,439	3,482	3,434	3,288	3,070	2,800	2,620	3,219
2017	2,493	2,379	2,381	2,214	2,200	2,235	2,195	2,256	2,231	2,354	2,411	2,190	2,295
2018	2,148	2,362	2,701	2,974	2,952	2,800	2,748	2,573	2,626	2,511	2,569	2,530	2,625
2019	2,304	2,251	2,205	2,380	2,369	2,483	2,458	2,199	2,370	2,471	2,610	2,531	2,386
2020	2,669	2,870	2,433	2,326	2,400	2,404	2,211	2,508	2,607	2,421	2,624	2,581	2,505

Source: Economic Research Service, U.S. Department of Agriculture (ERS-USDA)

Total Visible Stocks of Cocoa in Warehouses[1], at End of Month In Thousands of Bags

Year	Jan.	Feb.	Mar.	Apr.	May	June	July	Aug.	Sept.	Oct.	Nov.	Dec.
2011	3,158.1	3,611.9	3,757.3	3,520.8	3,324.1	3,729.7	4,185.3	3,892.5	3,928.4	3,704.4	3,491.6	3,767.1
2012	4,108.5	4,627.0	5,393.6	5,343.0	5,149.2	4,947.6	4,834.9	4,758.7	4,483.8	4,161.4	3,753.2	3,763.1
2013	3,814.6	4,416.3	4,653.7	4,690.9	4,987.5	4,966.3	4,745.1	4,632.7	4,232.5	3,754.5	3,436.3	3,574.1
2014	3,648.9	4,117.1	4,800.1	5,384.4	5,305.6	4,960.0	4,711.8	4,384.1	4,027.5	3,588.3	3,171.9	2,824.9
2015	2,939.1	3,241.1	3,310.7	3,978.6	4,085.2	4,546.7	4,369.9	4,117.8	3,867.5	3,578.7	3,438.3	3,255.3
2016	3,481.4	3,828.6	4,384.0	4,209.0	4,019.5	3,755.4	3,465.7	3,230.7	2,930.3	2,846.7	2,740.7	2,779.4
2017	3,309.3	4,023.4	4,814.4	5,515.9	5,828.5	5,654.6	5,369.5	5,009.6	4,617.9	4,096.9	3,714.4	3,386.7
2018	4,025.4	4,549.1	4,793.7	5,372.4	5,151.2	4,847.1	4,653.5	4,457.3	4,180.9	3,840.3	3,467.2	3,467.2
2019	3,568.1	3,947.6	4,207.5	4,432.2	4,632.3	4,506.6	4,284.9	4,003.0	3,750.5	3,358.8	3,006.4	2,726.6
2020	3,048.2	3,716.5	3,973.8	4,280.9	4,262.9	4,146.3	4,037.0	3,786.5	3,646.7	3,455.6	3,110.0	3,060.1

[1] Licensed warehouses approved by ICE. *Source: ICE Futures U.S. (ICE)*

COCOA

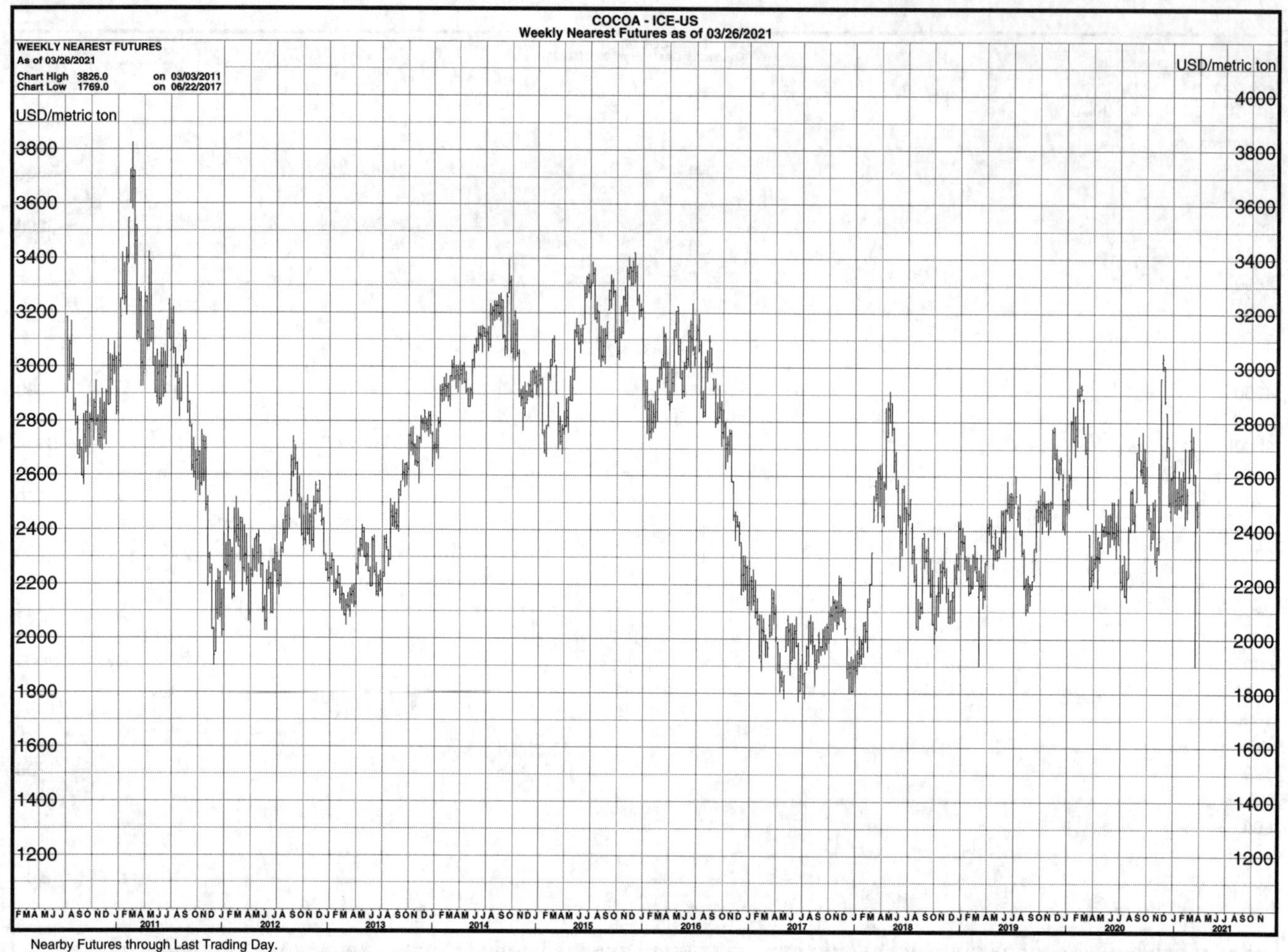

Nearby Futures through Last Trading Day.

Volume of Trading of Cocoa Futures in New York In Contracts

Year	Jan.	Feb.	Mar.	Apr.	May	June	July	Aug.	Sept.	Oct.	Nov.	Dec.	Total
2011	395,349	401,740	390,590	423,879	357,282	454,217	328,156	571,410	335,481	388,486	554,320	347,142	4,948,052
2012	395,832	586,013	474,613	605,217	459,683	620,166	457,510	627,854	346,794	467,949	651,655	306,527	5,999,813
2013	505,589	598,270	425,547	752,332	541,022	792,100	504,933	646,114	379,515	484,417	621,749	332,158	6,583,746
2014	571,906	588,461	453,219	593,071	454,372	625,401	551,959	541,132	478,549	617,492	508,452	331,778	6,315,792
2015	586,564	679,362	694,091	739,813	520,024	710,582	531,381	801,763	602,091	770,424	775,633	501,308	7,913,036
2016	940,394	950,705	667,648	927,406	857,735	778,284	712,599	987,963	730,541	856,408	829,030	623,505	9,862,218
2017	797,471	929,400	906,294	974,013	927,022	1,095,512	790,389	1,116,901	660,699	1,066,289	1,049,735	747,881	11,061,606
2018	973,387	1,122,890	1,135,854	1,266,511	972,472	1,176,038	884,333	1,090,296	707,925	1,021,630	1,077,251	607,002	12,035,589
2019	959,836	1,002,621	902,855	1,276,699	972,169	973,933	855,795	1,253,742	1,031,822	1,059,938	1,171,287	789,208	12,249,905
2020	1,103,060	1,164,829	1,236,846	704,730	636,723	846,543	698,239	916,850	661,515	791,450	996,174	595,149	10,352,108

Source: ICE Futures U.S. (ICE)

Average Open Interest of Cocoa Futures in New York In Contracts

Year	Jan.	Feb.	Mar.	Apr.	May	June	July	Aug.	Sept.	Oct.	Nov.	Dec.
2011	148,426	158,965	163,700	159,411	157,851	162,945	172,670	166,766	176,524	191,211	168,734	167,339
2012	171,138	165,555	170,143	178,362	183,549	174,848	186,439	190,328	202,142	202,142	189,765	193,643
2013	197,848	192,704	200,696	199,773	220,741	196,543	176,618	183,556	201,739	219,812	212,717	213,685
2014	210,130	216,867	215,297	206,091	204,253	216,264	214,879	213,149	208,448	199,236	177,425	186,443
2015	200,884	193,672	211,199	199,675	208,637	215,736	219,497	182,777	200,200	216,932	232,054	234,884
2016	227,549	234,056	238,732	234,122	242,073	198,093	215,818	206,006	210,888	251,984	244,643	254,911
2017	275,443	265,621	285,852	284,418	296,408	257,541	273,750	244,093	258,013	253,440	241,566	251,261
2018	275,944	263,249	296,500	289,878	304,760	266,004	247,961	240,819	242,329	264,377	241,641	235,570
2019	251,715	236,101	255,428	244,996	251,723	265,064	281,033	265,389	284,179	304,661	316,902	314,178
2020	311,242	347,493	278,299	215,335	224,401	219,668	224,055	209,904	219,811	211,501	192,405	214,734

Source: ICE Futures U.S. (ICE)

Coconut Oil and Copra

Coconut oil and copra come from the fruit of the coconut palm tree, which originated in Southeast Asia. Coconut oil has been used for thousands of years as cooking oil and is still a staple in the diets of many people living in tropical areas. Until shortages of imported oil developed during WWII, Americans also used coconut oil for cooking.

Copra is the meaty inner lining of the coconut. It is an oil-rich pulp with a light, slightly sweet, nutty flavor. Copra is used mainly as a source of coconut oil and is also used shredded for baking. High-quality copra contains about 65% to 72% oil, and oil made from the copra is called crude coconut oil. Crude coconut oil is processed from copra by expeller press and solvent extraction. It is not considered fit for human consumption until it has been refined, which consists of neutralizing, bleaching, and deodorizing it at high heat with a vacuum. The remaining oil cake obtained as a by-product is used for livestock feed.

Premium grade coconut oil, also called virgin coconut oil, is the oil made from the first pressing without the addition of any chemicals. Premium grade coconut oil is more expensive than refined or crude oil because the producers use only selected raw materials, and there is a lower production yield due to only one pressing.

Coconut oil accounts for approximately 20% of all vegetable oils used worldwide. Coconut oil is used in margarines, vegetable shortening, salad oils, confections, and sports drinks to boost energy and enhance athletic performance. It is also used in the manufacture of soaps, detergents, shampoos, cosmetics, candles, glycerin, and synthetic rubber. Coconut oil is very healthy, unless it is hydrogenated, and is easily digested.

Supply – World production of copra in 2019 fell -0.4% at 4.682 million metric tons and remained below the record high of 5.662 million metric tons posted in 2001. The world's largest producers of copra in 2019 were the Philippines with 34.6% of world production, Indonesia with 30.3%, India with 12.6%, and Mexico with 5.1%. World production of coconut oil in the 2018/19 marketing year rose +5.6% yr/yr to 2.907 million metric tons.

Demand – Virtually all the world's production of copra goes for crushing into coconut meal and oil (over 99%). World consumption of coconut oil in 2018/19 rose by +8.1% yr/yr to 2.886 million metric tons, but still below the 2009/10 record high of 3.574 million metric tons.

Trade – Copra is generally crushed in the country of origin, meaning that less than 4% of copra itself is exported; the rest is exported in the form of coconut oil. World exports of coconut oil in 2018/19 rose by +9.0% yr/yr to 1.920 million metric tons, but still below the 2009/10 record high of 2.406 million metric tons.

World Production of Copra In Thousands of Metric Tons

Year	India	Indonesia	Ivory Coast	Malaysia	Mexico	Mozambique	Papua New Guinea	Philippines	Sri Lanka	Thailand	Vanuatu	Vietnam	World Total
2010	690	1,440	46	53	211	48	102	2,680	85	48	32	57	5,816
2011	680	1,400	46	51	209	48	115	1,700	87	44	32	57	4,791
2012	670	1,550	46	58	216	49	85	2,030	90	48	32	57	5,247
2013	640	1,470	29	79	207	50	80	2,300	90	49	25	57	5,392
2014	670	1,530	27	62	203	52	72	1,740	80	49	25	57	4,881
2015	620	1,540	28	64	209	54	95	1,680	83	49	18	57	4,812
2016	580	1,290	26	58	221	50	97	1,280	95	46	28	55	4,141
2017[1]	420	1,180	28	67	231	52	114	1,370	90	46	27	56	4,001
2018[2]	530	1,460	30	65	237	52	118	1,670	90	48	21	57	4,703
2019[3]	590	1,420	30	68	239	53	110	1,620	92	50	25	60	4,682

[1] Preliminary. [2] Estimate. [3] Forecast. *Source: The Oil World*

World Supply and Distribution of Coconut Oil In Thousands of Metric Tons

	Production							Consumption						Ending Stocks		
Year	India	Indonesia	Malaysia	Philippines	World Total	World Exports	World Imports	European Union	India	Indonesia	Philippines	United States	World Total	Philippines	United States	World Total
2009-10	400	890	45	1,732	3,621	2,406	2,374	794	404	179	445	587	3,574	55	84	457
2010-11	398	847	50	1,240	3,090	1,948	1,973	730	409	153	336	474	3,237	70	62	336
2011-12	393	914	47	1,208	3,114	1,908	1,907	594	402	143	375	487	3,067	110	77	381
2012-13	380	850	51	1,654	3,471	2,078	2,086	716	381	193	564	521	3,423	80	80	436
2013-14	391	933	51	1,153	3,050	1,866	1,859	646	392	176	364	518	3,119	68	65	359
2014-15	377	937	51	1,093	2,968	1,964	1,953	537	389	161	233	531	2,893	69	61	424
2015-16	346	805	45	888	2,593	1,642	1,658	536	340	166	198	469	2,688	74	66	345
2016-17[1]	270	691	45	953	2,476	1,674	1,643	476	262	181	119	439	2,452	58	52	338
2017-18[2]	302	845	41	1,035	2,754	1,761	1,774	567	296	195	148	433	2,669	90	47	436
2018-19[3]	345	856	40	1,127	2,908	1,920	1,919	629	342	214	165	440	2,886	82	62	456

[1] Preliminary. [2] Estimate. [3] Forecast. *Source: The Oil World*

Supply and Distribution of Coconut Oil in the United States In Millions of Pounds

Year	--- Rotterdam --- Copra Tonne	Coconut Oil, CIF ------ $ U.S. ------	Imports For Consumption	Stocks Oct. 1	Total Supply	Exports	-------- Disapearance -------- Total Domestic	Edible Products	Inedible Products	------ Production of Coconut Oil (Refined) ------ Total	Oct.-Dec.	Jan.-Mar.	April-June	July-Sept.
2009-10	613	921	1,338	183	1,521	41	1,836	441	W	833.0	190.1	214.9	211.2	216.8
2010-11	1,188	1,772	1,080	186	1,266	85	1,045	467	W	808.8	202.2	NA	NA	NA
2011-12	829	1,244	1,165	169	1,334	60	1,073	NA	NA	NA	NA	NA	NA	NA
2012-13	570	858	1,214	176	1,390	56	1,149	NA	NA	NA	NA	NA	NA	NA
2013-14	854	1,278	1,173	143	1,316	64	1,142	----	----	----	----	----	----	----
2014-15	749	1,128	1,261	134	1,395	99	1,171	----	----	----	----	----	----	----
2015-16	907	1,360	1,157	146	1,302	111	1,034	----	----	----	----	----	----	----
2016-17	1,076	1,620	1,036	115	1,151	98	968	----	----	----	----	----	----	----
2017-18[1]	784	1,175	991	104	1,095	48	955	----	----	----	----	----	----	----
2018-19[2]	501	752	1,058	137	1,195	55	970	----	----	----	----	----	----	----

[1] Preliminary. [2] Forecast. *Source: Bureau of Census, U.S. Department of Commerce*

Average Price of Coconut Oil (Crude) Tank Cars in New York In Cents Per Pound

Year	Jan.	Feb.	Mar.	Apr.	May	June	July	Aug.	Sept.	Oct.	Nov.	Dec.	Average
2010	36.20	35.75	37.88	41.99	43.60	44.00	46.49	54.31	55.94	63.65	69.00	79.50	50.69
2011	87.00	92.50	85.00	91.80	95.50	96.50	87.00	81.75	74.40	57.75	57.00	61.00	80.60
2012	68.25	68.00	64.90	63.63	59.25	54.00	52.75	50.30	47.75	43.75	41.40	38.88	54.40
2013	39.38	41.25	39.30	38.00	38.20	40.75	41.50	41.50	46.00	45.00	59.30	61.00	44.26
2014	59.70	63.00	65.38	62.75	65.70	65.31	62.88	56.60	55.31	53.75	55.69	56.50	60.21
2015	56.30	54.94	52.94	49.50	52.25	53.19	52.30	51.56	50.75	51.05	50.31	52.20	52.27
2016	53.69	54.44	67.75	76.90	68.38	69.35	70.85	72.06	74.30	70.00	73.50	78.20	69.12
2017	83.63	90.00	73.90	82.81	84.00	83.60	81.00	85.88	86.63	68.50	72.25	72.10	80.36
2018	68.75	66.00	55.90	58.75	52.50	46.20	45.00	45.00	44.50	43.00	39.00	37.50	50.18
2019[1]	39.00	37.25	35.30	33.50	33.00	32.00	32.00	33.20	34.50	34.00	35.60	44.50	35.32

[1] Preliminary. *Source: Economic Research Service, U.S. Department of Agriculture (ERS-USDA)*

Consumption of Coconut Oil in End Products (Edible and Inedible) in the United States In Millions of Pounds

Year	Jan.	Feb.	Mar.	Apr.	May	June	July	Aug.	Sept.	Oct.	Nov.	Dec.	Total
2002	55.4	41.3	50.8	59.3	53.9	46.4	50.7	51.8	45.9	54.3	56.1	49.4	615.4
2003	51.2	49.3	56.8	50.6	52.3	46.7	48.9	49.6	50.3	47.8	41.8	38.5	583.7
2004	50.0	51.7	58.5	54.6	48.5	55.6	52.9	55.1	48.9	48.2	64.3	51.7	640.0
2005	46.7	52.0	47.9	48.8	51.4	55.5	47.2	58.1	49.2	52.8	53.4	58.1	621.1
2006	70.4	62.7	50.4	47.5	50.7	51.6	43.1	51.6	43.8	49.6	44.4	40.8	606.4
2007	49.8	48.5	47.0	51.2	53.7	60.3	60.3	74.2	67.5	71.8	71.3	62.7	718.3
2008	63.6	72.1	64.8	74.4	69.7	70.4	65.8	67.6	65.8	63.0	63.6	53.6	794.5
2009	67.9	62.8	60.2	66.9	66.9	27.6	36.5	28.1	29.4	32.8	32.1	30.6	541.8
2010	41.0	36.6	45.3	34.9	39.8	38.6	37.2	40.4	32.1	41.4	39.9	70.8	498.0
2011[1]	34.6	37.0	40.6	38.0	39.0	37.0	26.7	NA	NA	NA	NA	NA	433.5

[1] Preliminary. *Source: Bureau of Census, U.S. Department of Commerce*

Stocks of Coconut Oil (Crude and Refined) in the United States, on First of Month In Millions of Pounds

Year	Jan.	Feb.	Mar.	Apr.	May	June	July	Aug.	Sept.	Oct.	Nov.	Dec.
2002	245.9	238.8	249.6	251.3	233.5	231.6	303.3	301.6	245.8	226.5	273.8	264.1
2003	195.2	194.0	214.3	224.9	223.7	187.8	162.2	202.9	195.6	218.9	184.6	186.1
2004	167.2	160.3	192.6	181.7	131.4	108.7	90.6	132.8	149.2	131.3	147.7	182.5
2005	225.9	163.7	188.4	191.0	170.6	187.7	263.5	250.4	253.7	242.1	252.3	273.3
2006	268.3	236.9	224.5	227.3	260.2	229.1	213.8	214.4	204.7	224.5	179.2	180.2
2007	214.4	228.5	261.5	223.1	191.8	157.9	171.2	154.4	127.7	128.4	142.5	212.6
2008	205.6	192.9	180.9	191.9	223.9	203.9	187.8	181.5	180.4	182.2	163.3	174.6
2009	164.1	183.7	215.6	167.2	143.9	138.0	134.8	133.2	102.3	182.3	159.0	154.7
2010	220.2	204.5	172.1	144.6	119.3	120.3	172.2	179.3	197.1	185.8	166.7	167.2
2011[1]	181.5	150.2	162.7	154.6	150.0	157.6	158.4	190.9	NA	NA	NA	NA

[1] Preliminary. *Source: Bureau of Census, U.S. Department of Commerce*

Coffee

Coffee is one of the world's most important cash commodities. Coffee is the common name for any type of tree in the genus madder family. Coffee is a tropical evergreen shrub that has the potential to grow 100 feet tall. The coffee tree grows in tropical regions between the Tropics of Cancer and Capricorn in areas with abundant rainfall, year-round warm temperatures averaging about 70 degrees Fahrenheit, and no frost. In the U.S., the only places that produce any significant amount of coffee are Puerto Rico and Hawaii. The coffee plant will produce its first full crop of beans at about five years old and then be productive for about 15 years. The average coffee tree produces enough beans to make about 1 to 1 ½ pound of roasted coffee per year. It takes approximately 4,000 handpicked green coffee beans to make a pound of coffee. Wine was the first drink made from the coffee tree using coffee cherries, honey, and water. In the 17th century, the first coffee house, also known as a "penny university" because of the price per cup, opened in London. The London Stock Exchange grew from one of these first coffee houses.

Coffee is generally classified into two types of beans: arabica and robusta. The most widely produced coffee is arabica, which makes up about 70 percent of total production. It grows mainly at high altitudes of 600 to 2,000 meters, with Brazil and Colombia being the largest producers. Arabic coffee is traded at the Intercontinental Exchange (ICE). The stronger of the two types is robusta. It is grown at lower altitudes, with the largest producers being Indonesia, West Africa, Brazil, and Vietnam. Robusta coffee is traded on the LIFFE exchange.

Ninety percent of the world coffee trade is in green (unroasted) coffee beans. Seasonal factors have a significant influence on the price of coffee. There is no extreme peak in world production at any one time of the year, although coffee consumption declines by 12 percent or more below the year's average in the warm summer months. Therefore, coffee imports and roasts both tend to decline in spring and summer and pick up again in fall and winter.

Meager prices for coffee can create serious long-term problems for coffee producers. When prices fall below production costs, there is little economic incentive to produce coffee, and coffee trees may be neglected or completely abandoned. When prices are low, producers cannot afford to hire the labor needed to maintain the trees and pick the crop at harvest. The result is that trees yield less due to reduced use of fertilizer and fewer employed coffee workers. One effect is a decline in the quality of the coffee that is produced. Higher quality Arabica coffee is often produced at higher altitudes, which entails higher costs. It is this coffee that is often abandoned. Although the pressure on producers can be severe, the market eventually comes back into balance as supply declines in response to low prices.

Coffee prices are subject to upward spikes in June, July, and August due to possible freeze scares in Brazil during the winter months in the Southern Hemisphere. The Brazilian coffee crop is harvested starting in May and extending for several weeks into the winter months in Brazil. A major freeze in Brazil occurs roughly every five years on average.

Coffee futures and options are traded at the ICE Futures U.S. and ICE Futures Europe exchanges, and the B3 Exchange (formerly BM&F/BOVESPA). Coffee futures are traded on the JSE Securities Exchange (JSE).

Prices – ICE Arabica coffee futures prices (Barchart.com symbol KC) traded sideways to lower through the first half of 2020. Coffee supplies were ample in early 2020 after the International Coffee Organization (ICO) reported that 2019 global arabica coffee exports rose +6.5% yr/yr to 82.75 million bags. Demand concerns weighed on coffee prices and boosted supplies as the pandemic forced restaurants and coffee shops to close throughout the world. U.S. inventories of green coffee, or unroasted beans, surged +8.2% in April 2020, the largest monthly increase since 2012. The weak demand prompted ICO in August to project a global surplus of +952,000 bags, showing a much more plentiful supply situation than its previous estimate for a 2019/20 global coffee deficit of -486,000 bags. Also, a plunge in the Brazilian real to a record low against the dollar in May 2020 undercut coffee prices since the weak real boosted the incentive for export selling by Brazil's coffee producers. Coffee prices sank to their low for 2020 in June at 92.70 cents per pound. Coffee prices pushed higher in Q3 and posted the high for 2020 in September at 134.80 cents per pound. Shrinking coffee inventories supported coffee prices after ICE-monitored coffee inventories trended lower throughout the year and fell to a 21-year low in October 2020. Coffee prices also found support from concern that a La Nina weather pattern would bring hot and dry conditions to Brazil, which could curb coffee yields. However, weak demand kept coffee prices from rallying further and prompted ICO in October to raise its 2019/20 global coffee surplus estimate to 1.54 million bags from an August forecast of 952,000 bags. Prices finished 2020 down -1.1% yr/yr at 128.25 cents per pound.

Supply – World coffee production in the 2020/21 marketing year (July-June) is expected to rise +4.1% yr/yr to 175.480 million bags (1 bag equals 60 kilograms or 132.3 pounds) but still below the 2018/19 record of 176.764 million bags. Coffee ending stocks in the 2020/21 marketing year are expected to rise +12.8% yr/yr to 41.336 million bags which is a new record high. Brazil is the world's largest coffee producer by far with 38.7% of the world's supply followed by Vietnam with 16.5%

Demand – U.S. coffee consumption in 2020 fell -9.1% yr/yr to 26.543 million bags, down from the 2019 record high of 29.211 million bags.

Trade – World coffee exports in 2020/21 are forecasted to rise +2.4% yr/yr to 138.421 million bags, down from last year's record high of 137.924. The world's largest exporters of coffee in 2020/21 are expected to be Brazil with 29.8% of world exports, Vietnam with 19.3%, and Columbia with 9.8%. U.S. coffee imports in 2020 fell -9.2% yr/yr to 26.543 million bags, down from the 2019 record high of 28.217. The key countries from which the U.S. imported coffee in 2020 were Brazil with 29.5% of U.S. imports, Columbia with 19.1%, Mexico with 4.955, and Guatemala with 4.5%.

World Supply and Distribution of Coffee for Producing Countries In Thousands of 60 Kilogram Bags

Year	Beginning Stocks	Production	Imports	Total Supply	Total Exports	Bean Exports	Rst/Grn Exports	Soluble Exports	Domestic Use	Ending Stocks
2011-12	28,640	144,837	111,458	284,935	117,661	101,144	2,411	14,106	141,526	25,748
2012-13	25,748	158,018	116,585	300,351	122,847	104,993	2,730	15,124	142,139	35,365
2013-14	35,365	160,054	117,011	312,430	128,877	110,004	3,220	15,653	142,389	41,164
2014-15	41,164	153,816	117,444	312,424	123,643	103,734	3,523	16,386	145,677	43,104
2015-16	43,104	152,939	124,507	320,550	133,388	112,970	3,417	17,001	152,769	34,393
2016-17	34,393	161,704	126,597	322,694	133,547	113,801	3,737	16,009	153,892	35,255
2017-18	35,255	159,845	128,039	323,139	131,164	111,149	3,750	16,265	159,750	32,225
2018-19[1]	32,225	176,764	135,751	344,740	141,237	120,596	3,924	16,717	164,956	38,547
2019-20[2]	38,547	168,498	127,657	334,702	135,210	114,427	4,397	16,386	162,841	36,651
2020-21[3]	36,651	175,480	133,023	345,154	138,421	117,527	4,312	16,582	165,398	41,335

[1] Preliminary. [2] Estimate. [3] Forecast. 132.276 Lbs. Per Bag *Source: Foreign Agricultural Service, U.S. Department of Agriculture (FAS-USDA)*

World Production of Green Coffee In Thousands of 60 Kilogram Bags

Crop Year	Brazil	Colombia	Costa Rica	Cote d'Ivoire	El Salvador	Ethiopia	Guate-mala	India	Indo-nesia	Mexico	Uganda	Vietnam	World Total
2011-12	49,200	7,655	1,775	1,600	1,200	6,320	4,410	5,230	7,970	4,300	3,075	26,000	144,837
2012-13	57,600	9,927	1,675	1,750	1,250	6,500	4,010	5,303	11,900	4,650	3,600	26,500	158,018
2013-14	57,200	12,075	1,450	1,675	550	6,345	3,515	5,075	11,900	3,950	3,850	29,833	160,054
2014-15	54,300	13,300	1,400	1,400	700	6,475	3,185	5,440	10,470	3,180	3,550	27,400	153,816
2015-16	49,400	14,000	1,625	1,600	560	6,510	3,295	5,800	12,100	2,300	3,650	28,930	152,939
2016-17	56,100	14,600	1,300	1,090	600	6,943	3,570	5,200	10,600	3,300	5,200	26,700	161,704
2017-18	52,100	13,825	1,525	1,250	660	7,055	3,780	5,266	10,400	4,000	4,350	29,300	159,845
2018-19[1]	66,500	13,870	1,250	2,000	654	7,350	3,770	5,325	10,600	3,550	4,800	30,400	176,764
2019-20[2]	60,500	14,100	1,472	1,725	605	7,450	3,450	4,967	10,700	3,700	4,250	31,300	168,498
2020-21[3]	67,900	14,100	1,500	1,800	475	7,500	3,650	5,250	10,700	3,900	4,800	29,000	175,480

[1] Preliminary. [2] Estimate. [3] Forecast. 132.276 Lbs. Per Bag *Source: Foreign Agricultural Service, U.S. Department of Agriculture (FAS-USDA)*

World Exportable[4] Production of Green Coffee In Thousands of 60 Kilogram Bags

Crop Year	Brazil	Colom-bia	Cote d'Ivoire	Ethiopia	Guate-mala	Honduras	India	Indo-nesia	Mexico	Peru	Uganda	Vietnam	World Total
2011-12	29,843	7,360	1,620	3,140	3,840	5,290	5,223	7,145	3,365	5,140	3,000	24,495	117,661
2012-13	30,660	8,855	1,680	3,500	3,770	4,480	4,858	10,325	3,616	4,100	3,575	24,643	122,847
2013-14	34,146	11,040	1,570	3,285	3,175	3,940	5,013	10,380	2,725	4,100	3,600	28,289	128,877
2014-15	36,573	12,420	1,350	3,500	3,070	4,760	4,894	8,720	2,560	2,750	3,400	21,530	123,643
2015-16	35,543	12,390	1,540	3,405	3,044	5,000	5,693	9,896	2,340	3,300	3,500	29,500	133,388
2016-17	33,081	13,755	990	3,853	3,330	7,175	6,158	8,174	2,865	4,025	4,600	27,550	133,547
2017-18	30,454	12,725	1,150	3,893	3,465	7,225	6,148	8,010	3,220	4,185	4,500	27,900	131,164
2018-19[1]	41,426	13,715	1,940	4,174	3,604	6,910	5,778	6,150	2,896	4,383	4,600	27,400	141,237
2019-20[2]	40,240	13,015	1,665	4,100	3,205	4,900	5,254	7,152	2,770	4,360	4,000	26,400	135,210
2020-21[3]	41,020	13,600	1,725	4,150	3,404	5,575	5,460	7,085	3,000	4,265	4,500	26,650	138,421

[1] Preliminary. [2] Estimate. [3] Forecast. [4] Marketing year begins in October in some countries and April or July in others. Exportable production represents total harvested production minus estimated domestic consumption. 132.276 Lbs. Per Bag
Source: Foreign Agricultural Service, U.S. Department of Agriculture (FAS-USDA)

Coffee Imports in the United States In Thousands of 60 Kilogram Bags

Year	Brazil	Colombia	Costa Rica	Republic	Ecuador	El Salvador	Ethiopia	Guate-mala	Indo-nesia	Mexico	Peru	Vene-zuela	World Total
2011	6,971	3,552	707	26	73	657	283	1,576	990	1,639	1,051	0	24,912
2012	5,582	3,009	749	77	45	397	207	1,787	1,328	1,989	863	0	24,841
2013	6,090	4,241	762	34	54	427	268	1,696	1,344	1,923	869	4	25,683
2014	7,326	4,611	671	23	71	205	293	1,390	1,117	1,393	873		26,221
2015	7,817	5,376	586	4	54	287	366	1,190	1,218	1,230	776		26,415
2016	6,704	5,253	648	4	52	217	292	1,011	1,212	1,030	1,112		27,502
2017	6,218	5,767	492	9	41	273	439	1,282	1,247	1,305	1,065		27,918
2018	6,347	5,701	603	7	4	248	425	1,380	969	1,366	1,052	71	27,217
2019	7,975	5,964	511	16	3	273	430	1,404	1,039	1,306	1,051	52	29,217
2020[1]	7,839	5,063	584	10	11	200	409	1,185	930	1,291	957	0	26,543

[1] Preliminary. 132.276 Lbs. Per Bag *Source: Bureau of Census, U.S. Department of Commerce*

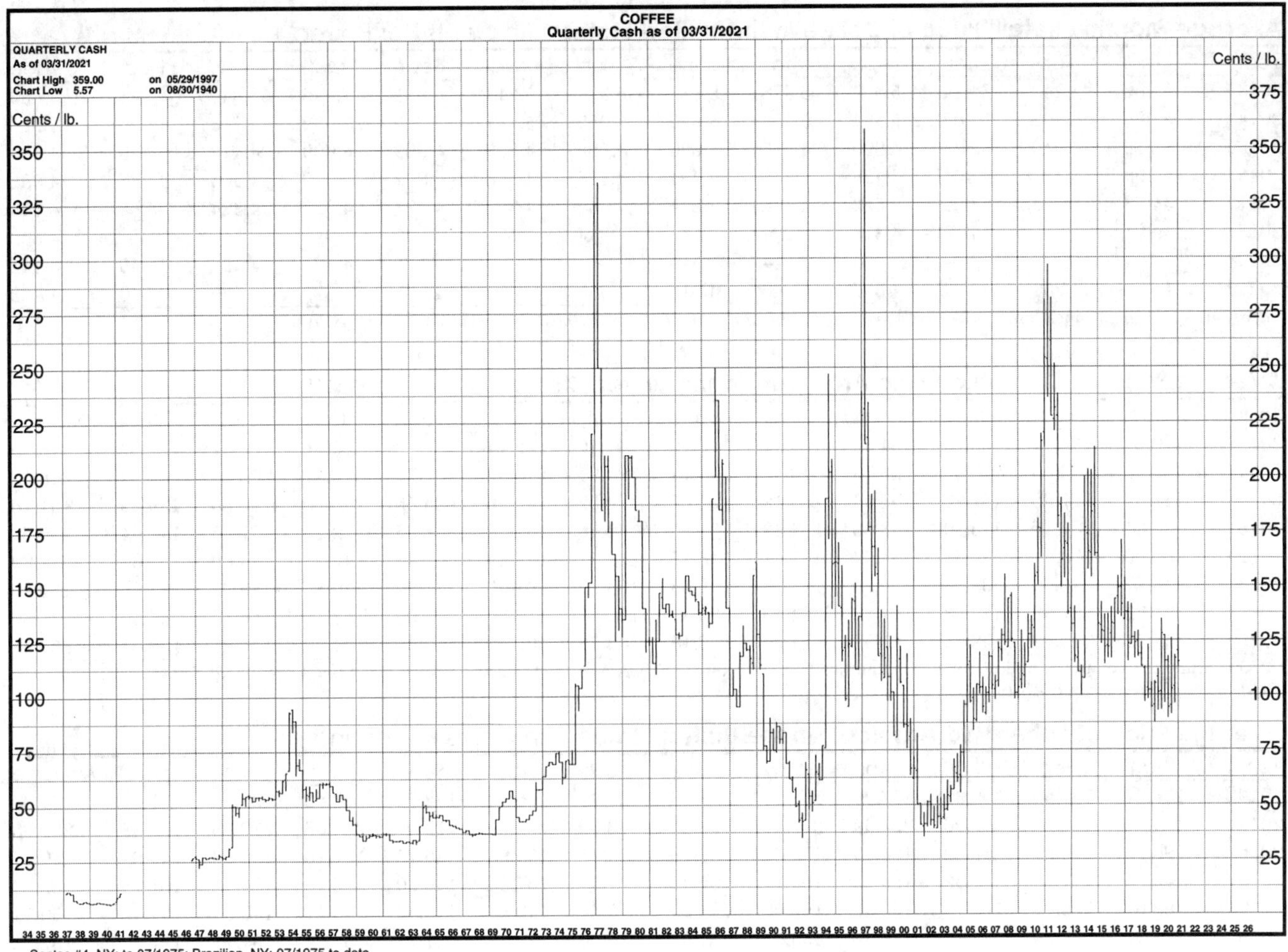

Santos #4, NY: to 07/1975; Brazilian, NY: 07/1975 to date.

Monthly Coffee Imports in the United States In Thousands of 60 Kilogram Bags (132.276 Lbs. Per Bag)

Year	Jan.	Feb.	Mar.	Apr.	May	June	July	Aug.	Sept.	Oct.	Nov.	Dec.	Total
2011	2,058	1,913	2,389	2,187	2,105	2,092	2,050	1,830	1,871	2,013	2,138	2,267	24,912
2012	2,376	1,891	2,186	1,945	2,172	2,081	2,269	2,246	2,055	1,803	1,893	1,923	24,841
2013	2,200	1,933	2,090	2,154	2,629	2,283	2,459	2,184	1,875	1,933	1,828	2,115	25,683
2014	1,919	1,895	2,407	2,489	2,545	2,468	2,356	2,357	2,174	2,019	1,640	1,943	26,213
2015	1,780	1,708	2,430	2,255	2,489	2,407	2,338	2,265	2,269	2,120	2,154	2,194	26,410
2016	2,135	2,166	2,293	2,305	2,551	2,408	2,316	2,333	2,382	2,014	2,419	2,179	27,503
2017	2,349	2,362	2,681	2,280	2,476	2,532	2,350	2,437	2,109	2,119	1,992	2,235	27,921
2018	2,090	2,220	2,420	2,382	2,542	2,225	2,274	2,186	2,013	2,260	2,266	2,349	27,225
2019	2,472	2,216	2,495	2,519	2,942	2,640	2,625	2,628	2,299	2,128	1,988	2,259	29,211
2020[1]	2,293	1,901	2,384	2,417	2,547	2,674	2,173	1,913	1,915	2,073	1,991	2,261	26,543

[1] Preliminary. *Source: Bureau of the Census, U.S. Department of Commerce*

Average Price of Brazilian[1] Coffee in New York In Cents Per Pound

Year	Jan.	Feb.	Mar.	Apr.	May	June	July	Aug.	Sept.	Oct.	Nov.	Dec.	Average
2011	209.26	237.43	257.24	271.39	266.02	247.19	242.66	251.78	251.70	230.62	233.13	225.59	243.67
2012	222.41	211.95	188.15	177.20	170.39	151.55	171.69	158.75	162.59	155.77	146.35	138.80	171.30
2013	139.36	133.37	129.74	130.11	129.82	116.91	114.89	111.97	106.33	103.58	98.82	100.48	117.95
2014	107.49	142.75	174.89	182.89	170.89	154.02	154.00	171.99	168.11	181.58	169.10	157.87	161.30
2015	151.21	143.32	127.81	129.02	123.49	124.97	119.77	121.21	113.14	118.43	122.95	123.73	126.59
2016	121.21	122.24	130.38	128.10	129.05	138.38	144.76	141.41	149.80	153.15	157.72	137.14	137.78
2017	145.70	137.68	134.07	130.39	125.40	122.39	127.26	128.24	124.46	120.01	117.26	114.00	127.24
2018	115.60	114.19	112.99	112.56	113.34	110.44	107.20	102.41	98.17	111.21	109.59	100.61	109.03
2019	101.56	100.67	97.50	94.42	93.33	99.97	103.01	96.07	97.74	97.35	107.23	117.37	100.52
2020	106.89	102.00	109.05	108.91	104.45	99.05	103.66	114.78	116.25	105.85	109.70	114.74	107.94

[1] And other Arabicas. *Source: Foreign Agricultural Service, U.S. Department of Agriculture (FAS-USDA)*

Average Monthly Retail[1] Price of Coffee in the United States In Cents Per Pound

Year	Jan.	Feb.	Mar.	Apr.	May	June	July	Aug.	Sept.	Oct.	Nov.	Dec.	Average
2013	5.902	5.742	6.014	5.674	5.678	5.588	5.394	5.214	5.091	5.149	5.040	4.948	5.453
2014	5.025	5.002	5.005	5.204	5.153	4.670	5.099	5.167	5.215	5.032	4.713	4.590	4.990
2015	4.738	4.910	4.827	4.990	4.715	4.686	4.790	4.808	4.669	4.609	4.412	4.486	4.720
2016	4.498	4.447	4.405	4.428	4.443	4.481	4.428	4.316	4.372	4.309	4.306	4.281	4.393
2017	4.468	4.583	4.650	4.622	4.597	4.545	4.335	4.373	4.323	4.327	4.324	4.285	4.453
2018	4.291	4.267	4.343	4.313	4.294	----	----	----	4.306	----	----	----	4.302
2019	----	----	----	----	----	----	----	----	----	4.174	4.197	4.053	4.141
2020	4.174	4.250	4.334	4.396	4.466	4.517	4.536	4.504	4.487	4.522	4.485	4.520	4.433

[1] Roasted in 13.1 to 20 ounce cans. *Source: Foreign Agricultural Service, U.S. Department of Agriculture (FAS-USDA)*

Average Price of Colombian Mild Arabicas[1] in the United States In Cents Per Pound

Year	Jan.	Feb.	Mar.	Apr.	May	June	July	Aug.	Sept.	Oct.	Nov.	Dec.	Average
2013	170.64	164.74	163.46	164.52	161.14	148.56	147.70	142.47	135.93	130.14	123.92	125.82	148.25
2014	133.51	173.96	213.63	223.79	213.45	196.14	194.91	210.42	202.77	219.27	203.71	191.53	198.09
2015	182.32	171.68	151.94	157.06	150.19	152.02	144.52	146.96	135.55	143.10	138.63	139.89	151.16
2016	135.21	137.17	145.20	143.66	144.49	156.86	164.46	160.78	168.85	172.28	177.85	156.64	155.29
2017	164.96	163.67	158.40	154.97	151.41	146.12	152.51	155.15	151.47	144.26	144.09	141.62	152.39
2018	143.77	141.50	139.45	139.29	140.26	138.55	133.92	129.99	125.74	140.83	139.27	127.86	136.70
2019	129.28	127.93	125.23	124.42	124.40	133.49	137.63	129.20	131.90	132.09	146.12	161.50	133.60
2020	147.52	146.43	158.99	161.92	154.96	147.16	153.38	167.22	168.36	154.28	161.21	170.44	157.66

[1] ICO monthly and composite indicator prices on the New York Market, 1979 ICA Agreement basis. *Source: Foreign Agricultural Service, U.S. Department of Agriculture (FAS-USDA)*

Average Price of Other Mild Arabicas[1] in the United States In Cents Per Pound

Year	Jan.	Feb.	Mar.	Apr.	May	June	July	Aug.	Sept.	Oct.	Nov.	Dec.	Average
2013	158.27	153.00	152.96	152.96	151.43	138.86	138.44	135.63	132.78	128.83	122.75	127.05	141.08
2014	135.03	176.28	216.06	226.99	215.24	198.91	198.59	214.50	212.01	227.06	212.93	200.59	202.85
2015	190.90	179.94	160.02	164.00	158.48	159.76	154.45	156.92	146.15	153.25	147.98	148.66	160.04
2016	145.03	147.70	157.50	154.22	155.19	165.45	171.76	167.54	176.30	178.96	184.12	161.78	163.80
2017	168.61	166.35	160.15	155.40	150.00	143.22	149.66	149.88	146.56	140.71	140.90	137.42	150.74
2018	138.81	136.28	135.03	134.34	135.61	134.03	130.60	125.21	121.18	137.34	137.11	127.10	132.72
2019	128.46	128.45	123.89	121.13	120.55	129.73	135.47	126.23	128.89	126.99	140.98	157.11	130.66
2020	142.19	135.50	148.33	154.52	149.84	141.52	146.78	163.25	166.56	152.06	150.73	157.81	150.76

[1] ICO monthly and composite indicator prices on the New York Market, 1979 ICA Agreement basis. *Source: Foreign Agricultural Service, U.S. Department of Agriculture (FAS-USDA)*

Average Price of Robustas 1976[1] in the United States In Cents Per Pound

Year	Jan.	Feb.	Mar.	Apr.	May	June	July	Aug.	Sept.	Oct.	Nov.	Dec.	Average
2013	105.79	109.70	112.47	107.58	105.76	97.05	102.41	100.73	93.48	90.01	85.67	95.30	100.50
2014	92.93	101.14	111.90	110.68	108.35	104.63	107.23	105.07	105.57	109.39	106.81	103.51	105.60
2015	102.33	103.74	98.07	92.06	87.56	90.25	87.12	85.78	81.50	82.78	81.74	79.28	89.35
2016	74.71	74.04	75.60	80.18	83.93	85.94	90.82	91.79	96.88	103.65	103.72	101.85	88.59
2017	108.32	106.49	106.73	103.58	98.36	101.95	104.94	104.52	99.18	98.39	91.33	87.59	100.95
2018	88.65	89.24	88.18	88.31	88.74	86.07	84.42	80.74	76.70	85.32	83.52	77.57	84.79
2019	78.24	78.65	76.96	73.28	71.12	74.02	73.93	70.78	70.64	68.63	73.28	73.22	73.56
2020	70.55	68.07	67.46	63.97	64.53	64.62	67.69	72.68	72.77	68.36	72.38	72.04	68.76

[1] ICO monthly and composite indicator prices on the New York Market, 1979 ICA Agreement basis. *Source: Foreign Agricultural Service, U.S. Department of Agriculture (FAS-USDA)*

Average Price of Composite 1979[1] in the United States In Cents Per Pound

Year	Jan.	Feb.	Mar.	Apr.	May	June	July	Aug.	Sept.	Oct.	Nov.	Dec.	Average
2013	135.38	131.51	131.38	129.55	126.96	117.58	118.93	116.45	111.82	107.03	100.99	106.56	119.51
2014	110.75	137.81	165.03	170.58	163.94	151.92	152.50	163.08	161.79	172.88	162.17	150.66	155.26
2015	148.24	141.10	127.04	129.02	123.49	124.97	119.77	121.21	113.14	118.43	122.95	114.63	125.33
2016	110.89	111.75	117.83	117.93	119.91	127.05	132.98	131.00	138.22	142.68	145.82	131.70	127.31
2017	139.07	145.50	139.67	136.09	131.21	123.71	129.19	131.93	129.67	124.55	124.28	121.47	131.36
2018	123.67	120.83	119.80	118.76	119.57	115.10	110.54	104.46	99.87	115.59	113.27	102.10	113.63
2019	102.94	100.06	95.81	92.47	91.95	100.69	105.43	95.85	98.73	98.10	109.94	126.36	101.53
2020	110.73	102.62	112.87	111.22	101.69	92.56	97.96	111.79	113.81	100.37	106.41	114.96	106.42

[1] ICO monthly and composite indicator prices on the New York Market, 1979 ICA Agreement basis. *Source: Foreign Agricultural Service, U.S. Department of Agriculture (FAS-USDA)*

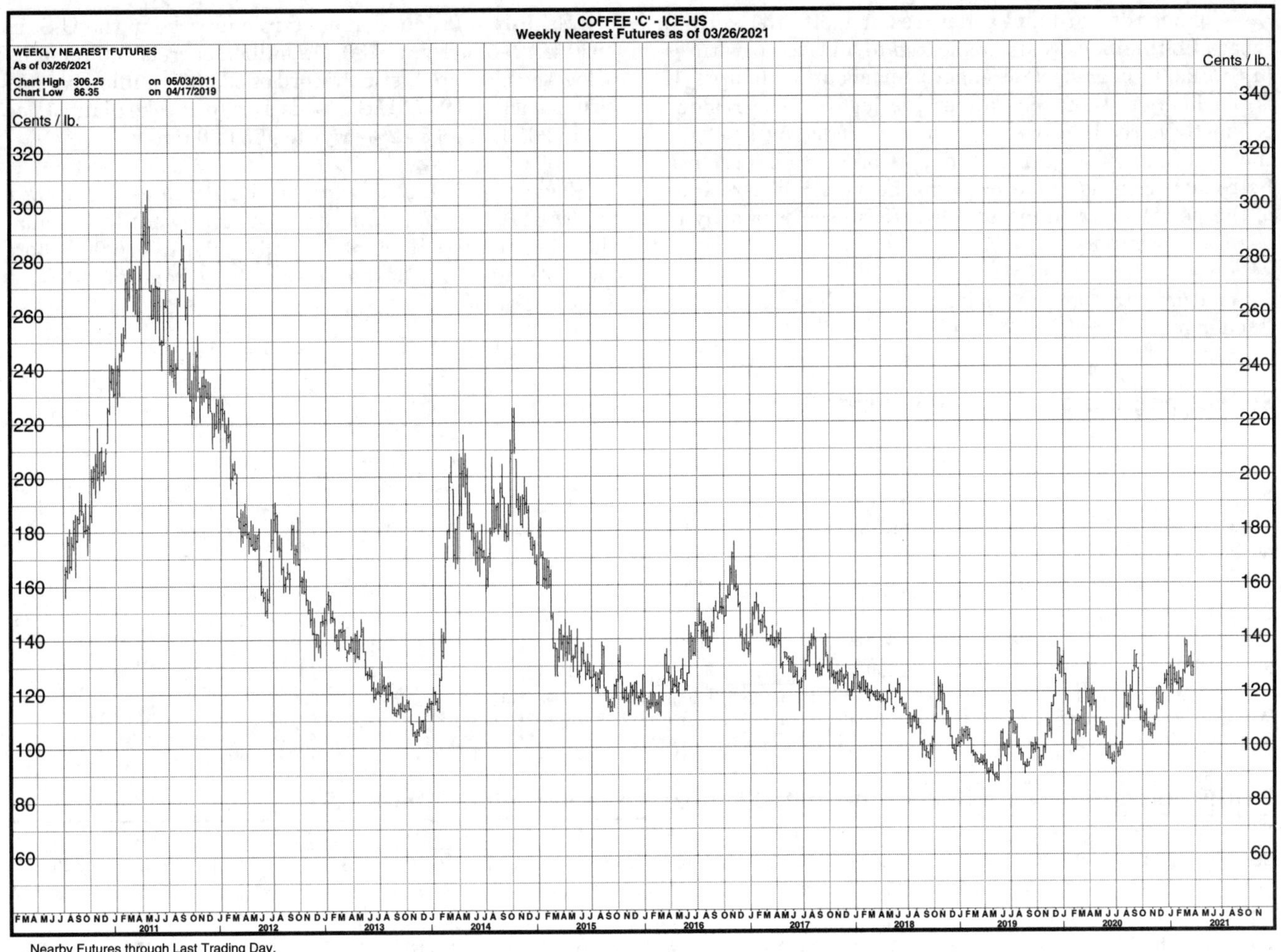

Nearby Futures through Last Trading Day.

Volume of Trading of Coffee "C" Futures in New York   In Contracts

Year	Jan.	Feb.	Mar.	Apr.	May	June	July	Aug.	Sept.	Oct.	Nov.	Dec.	Total (1,000)
2011	390,345	471,890	408,416	516,121	388,052	555,238	332,701	577,095	391,134	420,084	483,740	239,722	5,174.5
2012	401,399	578,415	541,098	628,814	494,615	642,772	466,738	581,141	406,023	503,577	603,866	277,026	6,125.5
2013	555,032	758,665	468,082	904,549	609,068	742,238	590,940	703,755	347,915	423,480	700,471	319,834	7,124.0
2014	567,574	1,140,881	596,963	736,494	458,676	596,745	404,407	619,641	394,952	583,259	610,793	341,845	7,052.2
2015	586,593	795,022	615,139	786,626	596,214	847,139	540,970	964,634	490,262	633,066	864,055	388,415	8,108.1
2016	665,155	983,217	863,904	1,009,149	777,352	1,181,746	553,988	908,304	600,690	695,422	1,092,826	524,561	9,856.3
2017	621,047	824,746	618,426	1,018,525	642,116	1,079,212	637,351	983,180	599,210	701,745	1,135,521	573,043	9,434.1
2018	931,694	1,202,836	818,537	1,357,172	937,402	1,313,761	939,824	1,698,417	734,886	1,493,016	1,342,642	617,518	13,387.7
2019	954,859	1,329,453	980,429	1,766,310	1,246,724	1,552,865	1,096,293	1,277,160	750,981	1,133,869	1,715,103	1,216,872	15,020.9
2020	1,060,249	1,555,988	1,401,056	884,553	716,071	1,157,397	916,683	1,259,794	1,001,186	829,123	1,139,719	635,722	12,557.5

Contract size = 37,500 lbs.   *Source: ICE Futures U.S. (ICE)*

Average Open Interest of Coffee "C" Futures in New York   In Contracts

Year	Jan.	Feb.	Mar.	Apr.	May	June	July	Aug.	Sept.	Oct.	Nov.	Dec.
2011	139,619	133,869	123,270	120,639	113,874	109,539	108,411	108,089	114,318	119,559	107,527	102,687
2012	113,404	131,880	149,533	151,527	148,352	147,775	137,737	137,322	141,421	147,434	141,940	141,395
2013	151,087	161,116	170,696	168,341	164,440	167,032	153,493	151,666	154,791	160,797	159,934	146,729
2014	146,800	162,005	169,201	160,266	162,103	163,163	161,218	156,931	154,752	168,847	156,410	155,382
2015	166,609	172,443	195,176	190,207	190,814	183,516	186,782	178,827	187,577	188,355	188,664	169,129
2016	193,283	190,752	194,420	190,067	190,161	182,825	182,322	175,300	180,542	194,806	205,128	187,602
2017	184,650	177,790	184,499	200,509	210,358	220,709	222,738	197,922	197,826	225,779	216,415	211,636
2018	232,027	234,405	257,968	267,133	256,291	272,561	306,898	319,784	326,360	303,193	252,010	262,406
2019	289,302	298,522	330,681	339,589	340,252	289,964	266,503	269,809	265,338	297,591	288,911	280,314
2020	288,410	297,314	257,518	231,067	243,733	269,731	270,527	263,448	271,972	275,901	269,054	258,135

Contract size = 37,500 lbs.   *Source: ICE Futures U.S. (ICE)*

Coke

Coke is the hard and porous residue left after certain types of bituminous coals are heated to high temperatures (up to 2,000 degrees Fahrenheit) for about 17 hours. It is blackish-gray and has a metallic luster. The residue is mostly carbon. Coke is used as a reducing agent in the smelting of pig iron and the production of steel. Petroleum coke is made from the heavy tar-like residue of the petroleum refining process. It is used primarily to generate electricity.

Futures on coke are traded on the Dalian Commodity Exchange.

Supply – Production of petroleum coke in the U.S. in 2020 fell -9.5% yr/yr to 280.712 million barrels and remains below the U.S. production record of 369.305 million barrels posted back in 1957. U.S. stocks of coke at coke plants (Dec 31) in 2019 rose +34,2% yr/yr to 475,000 tons.

Trade – U.S. coke exports in 2019 fell -15.9% yr/yr to 957,347 short tons, and 85.3% of that went to Canada. U.S. coke imports in 2019 fell -0.6% yr/yr to 116,000 short tons. About 31.2% of the imports were from Canada and 9.5% from Poland.

Salient Statistics of Coke in the United States In Thousands of Short Tons

Year	Total Production	Coke Total	Breeze Total	Consumption[2]	Producer and Distributor Stocks: Dec. 31	Exports	Imports
2013	16,226	15,320	906	14,351	872	840	138
2014	NA	15,154	NA	14,359	797	946	77
2015	14,470	13,755	715	13,128	707	857	140
2016	12,416	11,855	561	11,212	579	1,000	229
2017	13,554	12,948	606	11,818	558	1,209	58
2018	14,507	13,806	701	12,976	354	1,151	117
2019[1]	14,142	13,464	678	12,492	475	967	116

[1] Preliminary. [2] Equal to production plus imports minus the change in producer and distributor stocks minus exports.
W = Withheld. *Source: Energy Information Administration, U.S. Department of Energy (EIA-DOE)*

Production of Petroleum Coke in the United States In Thousands of Barrels

Year	Jan.	Feb.	Mar.	Apr.	May	June	July	Aug.	Sept.	Oct.	Nov.	Dec.	Total
2014	26,979	23,225	26,073	26,851	26,716	26,020	29,087	28,017	26,498	26,383	26,383	28,485	320,717
2015	27,131	23,655	26,744	25,434	26,722	26,531	28,090	27,341	25,749	25,858	27,078	28,384	318,717
2016	27,669	25,498	27,657	26,846	27,638	27,488	29,710	29,120	27,782	26,504	27,713	29,251	332,876
2017	28,715	24,498	26,747	27,709	29,018	28,113	29,113	28,358	24,187	26,703	27,286	28,556	329,003
2018	27,460	24,563	27,740	27,003	28,074	27,423	28,199	29,609	26,529	26,862	26,718	29,164	329,344
2019	26,971	22,775	25,638	24,593	24,422	25,582	28,008	27,677	24,694	24,956	26,196	28,599	310,111
2020[1]	28,158	25,862	25,247	21,759	22,173	22,165	24,200	23,099	21,900	22,324	21,675	22,150	280,712

[1] Preliminary. *Source: Energy Information Administration, U.S. Department of Energy (EIA-DOE)*

Coke and Breeze Production at Coke Plants in the United States In Thousands of Short Tons

Year	Middle Atlantic	East North Central	East South Central	Other	U.S. Total	Coke Total	Breeze Total
2013	W	8,864	W	7,362	16,226	15,320	906
2014	NA	NA	NA	NA	NA	15,154	NA
2015	4,722	7,562	1,270	916	14,470	13,755	715
2016	3,560	6,645	1,231	980	12,416	11,855	561
2017	4,066	7,181	1,238	1,069	13,554	12,948	606
2018	4,353	7,810	1,301	1,043	14,508	13,806	701
2019[1]	4,017	7,899	1,376	850	14,142	13,464	678

[1] Preliminary. W = Withheld. *Source: Energy Information Administration, U.S. Department of Energy (EIA-DOE)*

Coal Carbonized and Coke and Breeze Stocks at Coke Plants in the United States In Thousands of Short Tons

	Coal Carbonized at Coke Plants By Census Division					Stocks at Coke Plants, Dec. 31 By Census Division						
Year	Middle Atlantic	East North Central	East South Central	Other	Total	Middle Atlantic	East North Central	East South Central	Other	Total	Coke Total	Breeze Total
2013	W	11,948	W	9,526	21,474	W	739	W	344	1,083	872	211
2014	NA	NA	NA	NA	NA	NA	NA	NA	NA	NA	NA	NA
2015	6,219	10,584	1,204	1,701	19,708	797	1,172	197	70	2,236	----	----
2016	4,694	8,947	1,253	1,591	16,485	304	1,024	203	144	1,675	----	----
2017	5,347	9,295	1,308	1,588	17,538	355	1,042	145	176	1,718	----	----
2018	5,731	9,694	1,242	1,670	18,337	444	1,015	197	151	1,807	----	----
2019[1]	5,505	9,772	935	1,712	17,924	446	1,371	286	230	2,333	----	----

[1] Preliminary. W = Withheld. *Source: Energy Information Administration, U.S. Department of Energy (EIA-DOE)*

Copper

The word *copper* comes from the name of the Mediterranean island Cyprus that was a primary source of the metal. Dating back more than 10,000 years, copper is the oldest metal used by humans. From the Pyramid of Cheops in Egypt, archeologists recovered a portion of a water plumbing system that had copper tubing in serviceable condition after more than 5,000 years.

Copper is one of the most widely used industrial metals because it is an excellent conductor of electricity, has strong corrosion-resistance properties, and is very ductile. It is also used to produce the alloys of brass (a copper-zinc alloy) and bronze (a copper-tin alloy), both of which are far harder and stronger than pure copper. Electrical uses of copper account for about 75% of total copper usage, and building construction is the single largest market (the average U.S. home contains 400 pounds of copper). Copper is biostatic, meaning that bacteria will not grow on its surface, and it is therefore used in air-conditioning systems, food processing surfaces, and doorknobs to prevent the spread of disease.

Copper futures and options are traded on the London Metal Exchange (LME) and the CME Group. Copper futures are traded on the Shanghai Futures Exchange. The CME copper futures contract calls for the delivery of 25,000 pounds of Grade 1 electrolyte copper and is priced in terms of cents per pound.

Prices – CME copper futures prices (Barchart.com symbol HG) trended lower in Q1-2020 and sank to a 4-1/2-year low in March of $2.0595 per pound. A rally in the dollar index to a 4-year high in March undercut copper prices, as did concern that the spread of the Covid pandemic would spark a global recession and decimate copper demand. Chinese Shanghai copper inventories surged to a 4-1/2 year high in March as the economy contracted from the pandemic. After posting a 4-1/2-year low in March, however, copper prices trended higher the remainder of the year. Copper demand rebounded in the second half of 2020 as some economies emerged from lockdowns as global governments boosted stimulus measures in an attempt to spur economic growth. Also, copper supplies took a hit after copper production in Chile, the world's largest copper producer, fell as workers were stricken with Covid. Copper prices soared to an 8-year high in December at $3.6340 per pound and finished 2020 up +25.8% yr/yr at $3.5140 per pound.

Supply – World production of copper in 2020 fell -2.0% yr/yr to 20.000 million metric tons, down from the 2018 record high. The largest producer of copper was Chile with 28.5% of the world's production, followed by Peru with 11.0%, China with 8.5%, Australia with 4.4%, and the U.S. with 4.2%. U.S. production of total new copper in 2020 fell -12.7% yr/yr to 860,000 metric tons, far below the record U.S. production level of 2.140 million metric tons seen in 1998.

Demand – U.S. consumption of refined copper in 2020 fell -7.1% yr/yr to 1.700 million metric tons. The primary users of copper in the U.S. are wire rod mills, followed by brass mills.

Trade – U.S. exports of refined copper in 2020 (annualized through September) fell -67.7% yr/yr to 40,427 metric tons, down from the 2018 record high of 189,820. U.S. imports of copper in 2020 (annualized through September) rose +1.7% yr/yr to 677,333 metric tons, below the record high of 1.070 million metric tons in 2006.

World Mine Production of Copper (Content of Ore) In Thousands of Metric Tons

Year	Australia	Canada[3]	Chile	China	Indonesia	Mexico	Peru	Poland	Russia	South Africa	United States[3]	Zambia	World Total[2]
2011	957.9	569.8	5,262.8	1310	534.9	444.0	1,235.3	426.7	713	96.6	1,113	663.0	16,100
2012	914.0	579.5	5,433.9	1590	394.0	500.0	1,298.7	427.1	720	81.0	1,167	695.0	16,900
2013	1,001.0	631.9	5,776.0	1720	504.0	480.0	1,375.6	429.3	722	76.5	1,249	760.0	18,250
2014	970.0	673.0	5,749.6	1780	374.4	515.0	1,379.6	421.7	742	87.6	1,357	708.0	18,410
2015	971.0	697.0	5,764.0	1710	574.5	594.0	1,700.8	426.2	732	77.4	1,383	712.0	19,130
2016	948.0	708.0	5,500.0	1900	727.0	752.0	2,350.0		710		1,430	763.0	20,100
2017	860.0	620.0	5,500.0	1710	622.0	742.0	2,450.0		705		1,260	740.0	20,000
2018	920.0		5,830.0	1590	651.0	751.0	2,440.0		751		1,220	854.0	20,400
2019[1]	934.0		5,790.0	1680	340.0	715.0	2,460.0		801		1,260	797.0	20,400
2020[2]	870.0		5,700.0	1700		690.0	2,200.0		850		1,200	830.0	20,000

[1] Preliminary. [2] Estimate. [3] Recoverable. *Source: U.S. Geological Survey (USGS)*

Commodity Exchange Warehouse Stocks of Copper, on First of Month In Short Tons

Year	Jan. 1	Feb. 1	Mar. 1	Apr. 1	May 1	June 1	July 1	Aug. 1	Sept. 1	Oct. 1	Nov. 1	Dec. 1
2011	64,951	73,220	82,935	84,725	82,468	80,732	80,716	82,753	85,773	88,511	89,917	87,737
2012	90,055	89,703	91,159	86,523	75,051	59,070	53,335	48,129	49,757	50,336	56,551	63,632
2013	70,712	74,111	75,025	76,241	85,562	79,838	71,733	64,565	36,518	31,099	26,347	19,076
2014	13,033	19,224	13,589	19,967	18,292	16,378	19,653	23,912	27,984	34,162	29,759	28,137
2015	26,157	21,289	18,034	26,864	23,316	22,518	30,120	37,283	36,860	40,153	53,517	72,749
2016	69,753	65,615	67,502	71,991	65,495	61,044	62,445	65,416	67,282	70,575	71,961	78,310
2017	88,902	102,072	125,849	144,120	155,295	157,922	163,072	171,314	181,926	196,210	206,099	209,143
2018	210,972	221,036	230,376	233,927	248,744	231,364	223,981	200,039	189,050	172,440	157,434	135,536
2019	110,086	85,970	57,629	42,692	34,300	31,637	33,886	40,110	43,829	39,719	36,285	40,097
2020	37,550	31,415	28,617	32,253	42,268	60,505	62,206	89,049	85,425	79,843	79,945	81,592

Source: CME Group; Commodity Exchange (COMEX)

Salient Statistics of Copper in the United States   In Thousands of Metric Tons

	New Copper Produced - From Domestic Ores -						Imports[5]		Exports					Apparent Consumption	
Year	Mines	Smelters	Refineries	From Foreign Ores	Total New	Secondary Recovery	Unmanufactured	Refined	Ore, Concentrate[6]	Refined[7]	COMEX	Primary Producers (Refined)	Blister & Material in Solution	Refined Copper (Reported)	Primary & Old Copper[8]
2011	1,110	538	545	----	992	153	----	670	252	40	80	409	13	1,760	1,730
2012	1,170	485	491	----	962	164	----	630	301	169	64	236	12	1,760	1,760
2013	1,250	516	518	----	993	166	----	734	348	111	15	259	13	1,830	1,760
2014	1,360	522	535	----	1,050	173	----	620	410	127	24	190	10	1,760	1,780
2015	1,380	527	503	----	1,090	166	----	687	392	86	63	209	14	1,810	1,820
2016	1,430			----	1,180	149	----	708	331	134		223		1,800	1,880
2017	1,260			----	1,040	146	----	813	237	94		265		1,800	1,860
2018	1,220			----	1,070	149	----	778	253	190		244		1,820	1,830
2019[1]	1,260			----	985	150	----	663	363	125		111		1,830	1,810
2020[2]	1,200			----	860	150	----	680	390	40		150		1,700	1,600

[1] Preliminary. [2] Estimate. [3] Also from matte, etc., refinery reports. [4] From old scrap only. [5] For consumption. [6] Blister (copper content). [7] Ingots, bars, etc. [8] Old scrap only. W = Withheld. *Source: U.S. Geological Survey (USGS)*

Consumption of Refined Copper[3] in the United States   In Thousands of Metric Tons

	By-Products						By Class of Consumer						
Year	Cathodes	Wire Bars	Ingots and Ingot Bars	Cakes & Slabs	Billets	Other[4]	Wire Rod Mills	Brass Mills	Chemical Plants	Ingot Makers	Foundries	Miscellaneous[5]	Total Consumption
2006	1,910.0	W	30.8	37.1	W	135.0	1,570.0	490.0	1.0	4.5	21.4	24.1	2,110.0
2007	1,930.0	W	28.8	42.7	W	135.0	1,610.0	476.0	1.0	4.5	19.4	25.7	2,140.0
2008	1,820.0	W	28.6	45.0	W	130.0	1,490.0	479.0	0.3	4.5	20.4	24.7	2,020.0
2009	1,450.0	W	27.4	43.6	W	125.0	1,140.0	454.0	0.4	4.5	19.1	30.1	1,650.0
2010	1,570.0	W	22.5	44.1	W	127.0	1,250.0	459.0	0.4	4.5	18.2	34.6	1,760.0
2011	1,580.0	W	2.5	43.8	W	136.0	1,270.0	430.0	1.5	5.0	17.7	37.5	1,760.0
2012	1,610.0	W	2.3	42.8	W	102.0	1,280.0	424.0	0.3	4.5	19.9	34.3	1,760.0
2013	1,680.0	W	2.1	43.5	W	103.0	1,310.0	457.0	0.2	4.5	18.5	36.2	1,830.0
2014[1]	1,620.0	----	2.9	43.7	----	92.5	1,270.0	424.0	0.2	W	27.9	26.1	1,760.0
2015[2]	1,670.0	----	3.0	42.3	----	99.4	1,320.0	422.0	6.6	----	32.8	26.0	1,810.0

[1] Preliminary. [2] Estimate. [3] Primary & secondary. [4] Includes Wirebars and Billets. [5] Includes iron and steel plants, primary smelters producing alloys other than copper, consumers of copper powder and copper shot, and other manufacturers. W = Withheld.
Source: U.S. Geological Survey (USGS)

Salient Statistics of Recycling Copper in the United States

	New Scrap[1]	Old Scrap[2]	Recycled Metal[3]	Apparent Supply		New Scrap[1]	Old Scrap[2]	Recycled Metal[3]	Apparent Supply
Year	In Metric Tons				Percent Recycled	Value in Thousands of Dollars			
2008	700,000	159,000	859,000	2,700,000	31.8	4,930,000	1,120,000	6,050,000	18,900,000
2009	639,000	138,000	777,000	2,220,000	35.0	3,400,000	734,000	4,130,000	11,800,000
2010	642,000	143,000	785,000	2,400,000	32.7	4,930,000	1,100,000	6,030,000	18,400,000
2011	649,000	153,000	802,000	2,380,000	33.7	5,810,000	1,370,000	7,180,000	21,300,000
2012	642,000	164,000	807,000	2,400,000	34.0	5,200,000	1,330,000	6,530,000	19,400,000
2013	630,000	166,000	797,000	2,390,000	33.0	4,720,000	1,250,000	5,970,000	17,900,000
2014	672,000	173,000	845,000	2,450,000	35.0	4,710,000	1,210,000	5,930,000	17,200,000
2015	640,000	166,000	806,000	2,460,000	33.0	3,610,000	940,000	4,550,000	13,900,000
2016	690,000	149,000	839,000	2,570,000	33.0	3,420,000	740,000	4,160,000	12,700,000
2017	702,000	146,000	848,000	2,570,000	33.0	4,430,000	918,000	5,350,000	16,200,000

[1] Scrap that results from the manufacturing process. [2] Scrap that results from consumer products. [3] Metal recovered from new plus old scrap.
Source: U.S. Geological Survey (USGS)

Copper Refined from Scrap in the United States   In Metric Tons

Year	Jan.	Feb.	Mar.	Apr.	May	June	July	Aug.	Sept.	Oct.	Nov.	Dec.	Total
2011	3,830	2,970	3,240	2,970	3,240	3,060	3,030	3,200	3,010	3,110	3,010	2,630	37,300
2012	3,060	3,350	2,960	2,950	2,940	3,030	2,810	2,770	3,070	4,510	4,010	3,870	39,500
2013	3,870	3,660	4,550	4,770	4,910	4,910	4,680	3,800	3,780	3,990	3,970	4,450	46,900
2014	3,860	3,870	3,750	3,960	3,810	3,900	3,930	3,430	4,210	3,900	3,800	3,600	46,000
2015	4,030	3,810	4,150	4,180	4,360	3,310	3,570	3,890	4,200	5,010	4,250	4,050	48,800
2016	4,250	7,190	4,900	3,200	3,180	3,260	3,280	3,300	3,810	3,410	3,220	3,330	46,330
2017	3,240	4,090	3,240	3,230	3,380	3,280	3,220	3,340	3,310	3,280	3,240	3,250	40,100
2018	3,220	3,260	3,220	3,260	3,330	3,400	3,390	3,220	3,810	4,180	3,370	3,520	41,180
2019	3,770	3,330	3,950	3,600	3,470	3,480	3,860	5,860	3,360	3,220	3,240	3,240	44,380
2020[1]	3,260	3,220	3,220	4,530	4,380	3,620	3,720	3,380	3,490	3,220			43,248

[1] Preliminary. *Source: U.S. Geological Survey (USGS)*

Imports of Refined Copper into the United States In Metric Tons

Year	Jan.	Feb.	Mar.	Apr.	May	June	July	Aug.	Sept.	Oct.	Nov.	Dec.	Total
2011	57,400	50,500	66,200	73,100	65,500	45,500	69,500	32,300	64,300	46,700	50,300	48,900	670,000
2012	37,800	51,100	47,100	51,600	52,400	57,200	53,400	49,500	46,200	52,700	64,700	86,800	630,000
2013	86,800	64,600	88,200	55,600	83,600	69,200	70,000	50,200	42,800	40,300	33,900	48,500	734,000
2014	42,900	36,200	45,100	56,200	54,100	53,000	62,900	46,700	59,900	58,600	46,000	58,500	620,000
2015	70,900	50,300	68,700	60,500	56,100	64,500	78,500	47,400	47,800	51,700	44,200	45,400	686,000
2016	57,700	57,700	52,000	53,600	51,800	55,100	61,100	60,200	55,200	64,500	67,100	72,000	708,000
2017	72,600	59,600	84,800	51,900	63,500	66,100	72,500	55,200	86,800	76,500	65,200	58,400	813,100
2018	88,300	77,000	72,900	61,800	64,600	66,200	59,500	59,700	67,300	64,700	51,000	44,500	777,500
2019	57,300	37,800	40,500	65,400	52,400	55,200	68,200	50,600	60,700	69,300	49,000	59,500	665,900
2020[1]	62,300	34,400	70,500	74,300	66,200	63,300	37,300	59,800	39,900	57,300			678,360

[1] Preliminary. *Source: U.S. Geological Survey (USGS)*

Exports of Refined Copper from the United States In Metric Tons

Year	Jan.	Feb.	Mar.	Apr.	May	June	July	Aug.	Sept.	Oct.	Nov.	Dec.	Total
2011	1,640	5,010	3,130	2,120	3,500	1,930	1,850	5,140	2,140	2,350	6,870	4,690	40,400
2012	9,610	18,300	26,000	37,900	33,000	10,200	4,940	5,700	4,280	3,160	3,320	3,540	159,000
2013	3,540	5,300	5,110	5,380	5,740	4,890	8,270	17,100	14,900	10,300	15,200	17,700	113,000
2014	9,420	9,000	8,630	5,470	7,670	6,270	10,200	8,360	11,000	11,100	17,300	22,900	127,000
2015	5,860	8,490	10,100	6,620	7,190	9,400	5,870	6,430	4,490	6,110	8,690	7,270	86,500
2016	6,390	16,800	24,800	9,650	22,000	5,600	6,510	6,420	6,630	7,750	13,100	8,040	133,690
2017	12,300	9,100	9,760	12,200	9,230	6,140	7,140	6,680	7,190	5,210	4,400	4,810	94,160
2018	9,550	7,270	12,100	13,700	13,800	11,200	11,300	15,700	15,600	31,000	36,200	12,400	189,820
2019	12,600	13,100	10,200	13,500	11,000	13,800	9,810	6,960	8,410	8,530	9,510	7,830	125,250
2020[1]	4,170	2,470	4,000	1,580	540	1,220	5,300	6,470	4,570	2,930			39,900

[1] Preliminary. *Source: U.S. Geological Survey (USGS)*

Production of Refined Copper in the United States In Short Tons

Year	Jan.	Feb.	Mar.	Apr.	May	June	July	Aug.	Sept.	Oct.	Nov.	Dec.	Total
2011	86,800	76,300	84,900	79,700	82,900	86,400	79,200	79,700	93,600	89,600	95,100	96,500	1,030,000
2012	88,500	82,400	78,400	74,400	78,200	68,300	82,600	87,900	82,400	94,100	92,900	91,300	1,000,000
2013	89,300	76,200	85,700	88,500	83,000	80,300	83,800	85,300	81,100	94,800	92,800	99,200	1,040,000
2014	96,600	87,300	88,400	95,500	99,600	98,400	103,000	101,000	91,600	80,900	70,000	82,300	1,090,000
2015	83,700	85,500	93,900	90,700	86,700	91,000	94,400	93,000	97,600	104,000	107,000	113,000	1,140,000
2016	110,000	99,200	110,000	100,000	103,000	97,500	100,000	101,000	103,000	105,000	98,500	94,100	1,221,300
2017	101,000	93,900	105,000	91,000	84,800	83,000	90,600	99,400	95,700	82,400	70,900	81,200	1,078,900
2018	92,800	92,300	98,000	85,200	90,900	88,000	95,300	97,100	87,000	93,400	96,400	94,700	1,111,100
2019	83,200	68,100	76,400	83,000	86,500	90,000	96,500	94,100	97,000	95,500	W	W	1,030,000
2020[1]	66,600	74,800	78,100	69,100	72,600	71,800	78,200	77,400	74,200	80,800			892,320

Recoverable Copper Content. [1] Preliminary. *Source: U.S. Geological Survey (USGS)*

Mine Production of Recoverable Copper in the United States In Thousands of Metric Tons

	Recoverable Copper			Contained Copper		
Year	Arizona	Others[2]	Total	Electrowon	Concentrates[3]	Total
2011	751.3	361.0	1,112.5	448.9	689.7	1,138.4
2012	763.3	404.1	1,167.9	471.0	724.0	1,196.4
2013	795.0	453.0	1,250.0	475.0	804.0	1,280.0
2014	893.0	464.0	1,360.0	514.0	871.0	1,380.0
2015	985.0	419.0	1,410.0	588.0	851.0	1,440.0
2016	968.5	461.2	1,431.0	614.5	848.9	1,464.0
2017	867.7	391.1	1,257.5	557.5	729.6	1,287.0
2018	801.2	420.8	1,223.1	532.0	715.7	1,247.3
2019	860.8	398.5	1,256.6	527.6	757.7	1,285.9
2020[1]	882.7	320.5	1,204.3	542.4	687.6	1,228.9

[1] Preliminary. [2] Includes production from Alaska, Idaho, Missouri, Montana, Nevada, New Mexico, and Utah. [3] Includes copper content of precipitates and other metal concentrates. *Source: U.S. Geological Survey (USGS)*

Production of Recoverable Copper in Arizona In Thousands of Short Tons

Year	Jan.	Feb.	Mar.	Apr.	May	June	July	Aug.	Sept.	Oct.	Nov.	Dec.	Total
2011	57.3	53.0	60.8	59.3	66.5	63.9	61.9	65.0	64.4	66.5	67.1	65.6	751.3
2012	62.8	64.5	65.7	64.6	65.2	56.7	60.7	66.2	60.9	64.0	67.5	64.5	763.3
2013	65.7	57.7	66.5	64.1	70.7	64.6	68.2	65.1	66.6	68.5	65.9	71.3	795.0
2014	69.7	66.6	75.1	70.3	68.6	73.1	75.8	76.2	73.3	82.3	72.1	85.6	893.0
2015	78.4	70.5	80.5	75.9	76.5	77.2	81.3	84.1	83.9	89.3	85.7	90.3	985.0
2016	84.5	79.4	81.6	81.2	83.5	79.8	80.2	86.4	80.1	81.0	74.2	76.6	968.5
2017	71.0	64.2	77.5	72.5	75.1	71.9	73.5	71.2	75.0	66.9	72.8	76.1	867.7
2018	68.8	61.5	68.2	65.4	69.3	70.6	66.8	69.1	63.0	64.0	65.2	69.3	801.2
2019	67.9	63.6	74.0	69.7	71.5	73.4	79.2	77.3	74.0	72.3	66.0	71.9	860.8
2020[1]	65.8	65.4	73.8	76.4	75.5	77.7	79.3	78.8	72.4	70.5			882.7

[1] Preliminary. *Source: U.S. Geological Survey (USGS)*

Copper Stocks in the United States at Yearend In Metric Tons

		Refined Copper						
Year	Crude Copper[2]	Refineries[3]	Wire-rod Mills[3]	Brass Mills[3]	Other[4]	Comex	LME[5]	Total Refined
2010	21.1	10.3	19.7	6.4	4.3	58.6	284.0	384.0
2011	13.0	8.4	24.0	6.9	4.4	79.8	286.0	409.0
2012	12.3	12.9	28.1	6.5	4.3	64.1	120.0	236.0
2013	12.7	15.0	32.6	6.7	4.2	15.0	185.0	258.0
2014	9.9	9.5	42.0	6.4	4.4	24.2	102.0	189.0
2015	13.9	12.0	36.2	7.6	7.6	63.3	83.8	210.0
2016	14.4	4.2	26.7	7.4	5.7	80.1	98.9	223.0
2017	12.6	5.8	27.8	7.9	5.5	192.0	27.1	265.0
2018	9.2	3.9	21.8	8.2	5.4	99.6	104.0	243.0
2019[1]	16.4	7.0	20.0	7.5	7.1	34.1	35.0	111.0

[1] Preliminary. [2] Copper content of blister and anode. [3] Stocks of refined copper as reported; no estimates are made for nonrespondents. [4] Monthly estimates based on reported and 2011 annual data, comprising stocks at ingot makers, chemical plants, foundries, and miscellaneous manufacturers. [5] London Metal Exchange Ltd., U.S. warehouses. *Source: U.S. Geological Survey (USGS)*

Stocks of Crude Copper[2] in the United States, at End of Month In Thousands of Metric Tons

Year	Jan.	Feb.	Mar.	Apr.	May	June	July	Aug.	Sept.	Oct.	Nov.	Dec.
2011	25.2	24.8	24.7	24.9	27.2	20.1	20.1	13.0	14.3	18.5	14.5	13.0
2012	10.9	14.2	16.5	19.2	15.0	12.6	12.3	12.5	16.7	19.7	18.6	12.3
2013	8.6	20.1	17.9	21.8	28.7	11.5	12.8	10.7	11.2	14.2	15.3	12.7
2014	13.4	13.8	18.4	15.1	22.2	14.7	10.3	15.9	15.7	11.3	9.7	9.9
2015	14.2	11.3	11.3	11.3	16.6	15.4	13.2	14.3	21.2	17.9	13.5	13.9
2016	13.7	14.5	13.6	12.4	16.1	19.5	13.5	12.5	12.6	14.7	13.8	14.4
2017	11.7	13.2	13.5	26.1	11.0	11.0	11.0	7.4	12.1	13.6	16.7	12.6
2018	15.0	14.6	9.0	9.9	8.1	14.3	9.7	9.0	9.1	8.9	7.4	9.2
2019	9.6	10.2	15.0	8.9	9.2	13.6	15.5	14.5	8.3	25.4	10.2	16.4
2020[1]	9.6	17.9	7.9	7.4	11.9	11.0	11.3	15.7	13.5	15.2		

[1] Preliminary. [2] Copper content of blister and anode. *Source: U.S. Geological Survey (USGS)*

Total Stocks of Refined Copper in the United States, at End of Month In Thousands of Metric Tons

Year	Jan.	Feb.	Mar.	Apr.	May	June	July	Aug.	Sept.	Oct.	Nov.	Dec.
2011	282.0	383.0	372.0	366.0	365.0	359.0	368.0	370.0	377.0	383.0	387.0	409.0
2012	393.0	358.0	309.0	268.0	235.0	210.0	199.0	192.0	187.0	194.0	203.0	236.0
2013	261.0	275.0	308.0	325.0	318.0	314.0	306.0	292.0	273.0	260.0	250.0	258.0
2014	246.0	239.0	258.0	246.0	222.0	201.0	198.0	202.0	215.0	210.0	193.0	189.0
2015	182.0	186.0	195.0	197.0	178.0	171.0	166.0	185.0	187.0	190.0	198.0	210.0
2016	220.0	215.0	187.0	172.0	163.0	134.0	149.0	152.0	177.0	192.0	210.0	223.0
2017	241.0	242.0	248.0	243.0	218.0	219.0	222.0	246.0	256.0	268.0	266.0	265.0
2018	286.0	283.0	297.0	315.0	323.0	344.0	357.0	347.0	316.0	283.0	258.0	243.0
2019	229.0	191.0	135.0	128.0	117.0	107.0	117.0	118.0	120.0	117.0	121.0	111.0
2020[1]	93.3	107.0	114.0	120.0	139.0	158.0	165.0	153.0	159.0	140.0		

[1] Preliminary. *Source: U.S. Geological Survey (USGS)*

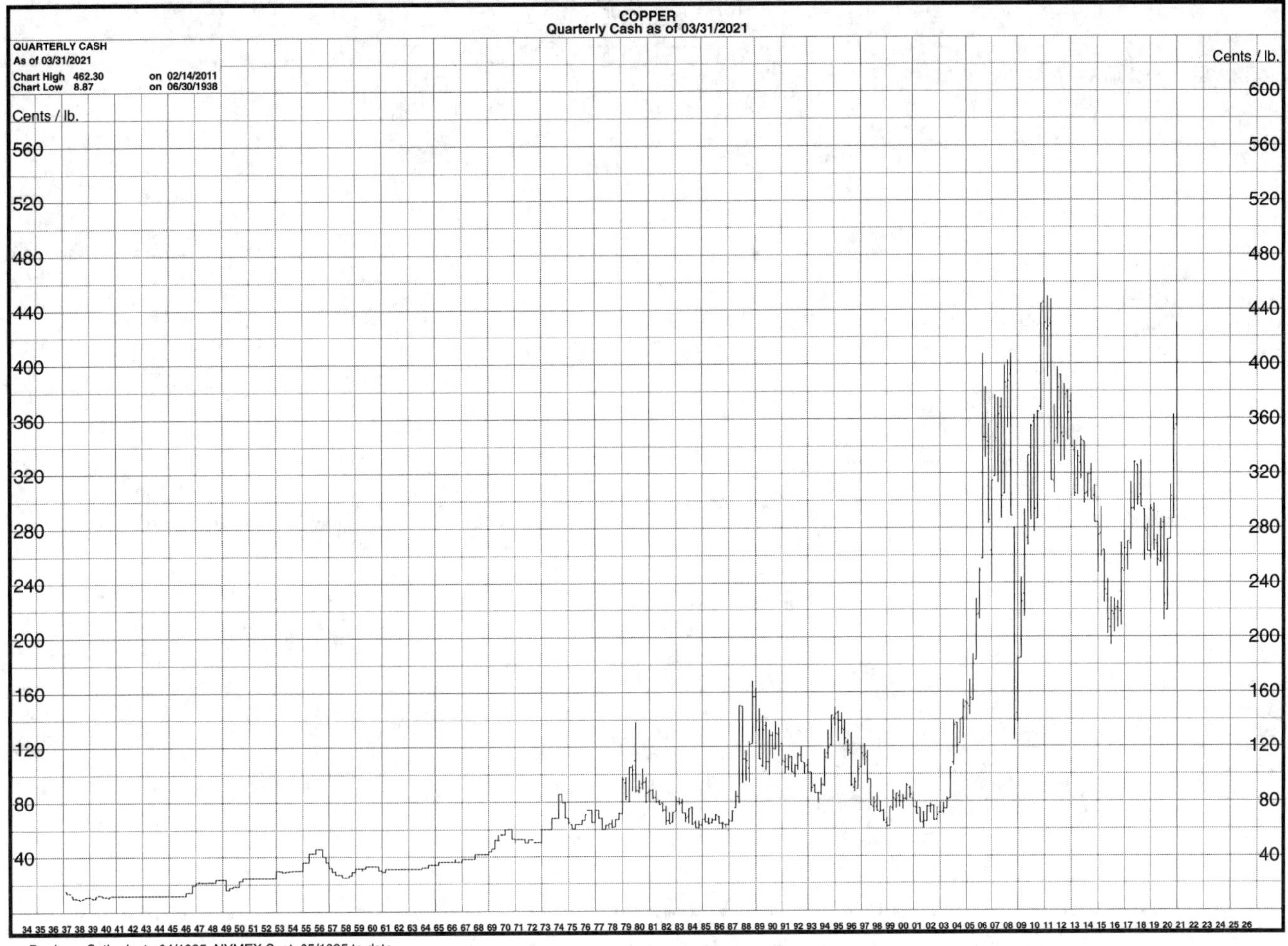

Producer Cathode: to 04/1995; NYMEX Spot: 05/1995 to date.

Producers' Price of Electrolytic (Wirebar) Copper, Delivered to U.S. Destinations In Cents Per Pound

Year	Jan.	Feb.	Mar.	Apr.	May	June	July	Aug.	Sept.	Oct.	Nov.	Dec.	Average
2011	439.85	454.13	436.70	435.63	410.49	415.91	445.11	412.86	378.78	339.15	349.89	348.73	405.60
2012	371.87	389.59	389.13	377.51	362.32	340.76	349.95	348.05	378.12	374.24	356.44	368.84	367.24
2013	372.47	371.83	351.31	332.72	337.45	325.95	321.50	335.18	334.13	334.93	328.07	339.43	340.41
2014	342.10	334.93	315.05	313.99	320.45	317.04	329.34	322.01	315.28	309.62	308.64	296.45	318.74
2015	271.73	268.95	277.04	281.50	295.59	273.57	254.27	239.79	243.31	243.04	222.34	214.01	257.10
2016	206.43	213.16	228.88	224.08	217.34	216.02	226.98	220.02	219.50	219.55	251.14	262.05	225.43
2017	267.08	274.55	269.56	264.04	260.33	265.44	278.13	301.13	303.66	314.81	314.38	315.32	285.70
2018	324.91	322.49	312.22	314.51	312.31	318.18	286.26	276.64	276.71	283.18	282.25	279.59	299.10
2019	275.49	292.82	297.25	299.38	281.88	275.57	276.24	264.69	267.12	268.29	272.78	284.49	279.67
2020	282.85	266.00	243.96	237.63	245.55	266.32	293.10	298.73	309.80	313.31	326.70	360.80	287.06

Source: American Metal Market (AMM)

Dealers' Buying Price of No. 2 Heavy Copper Scrap in Chicago In Cents Per Pound

Year	Jan.	Feb.	Mar.	Apr.	May	June	July	Aug.	Sept.	Oct.	Nov.	Dec.	Average
2011	285.00	292.50	299.13	295.00	290.72	295.23	315.00	311.41	293.69	241.55	261.50	256.97	286.48
2012	262.50	287.75	292.50	283.93	280.00	259.64	262.50	262.50	275.39	282.50	270.25	281.39	275.07
2013	287.74	292.24	287.02	272.50	263.18	269.00	255.23	260.55	265.00	274.63	272.76	277.76	273.13
2014	287.02	277.50	266.55	262.73	270.36	269.07	270.64	268.26	262.64	257.24	255.50	240.31	265.65
2015	220.60	205.08	215.50	218.86	232.50	219.77	212.86	195.79	195.12	193.91	184.97	165.64	205.05
2016	160.61	158.50	168.02	169.50	170.26	166.27	173.15	172.20	169.21	170.40	182.00	198.45	171.55
2017	194.80	202.97	199.67	195.50	193.23	191.95	195.50	205.93	213.85	218.95	222.00	220.00	204.53
2018	229.79	231.50	227.50	223.02	222.59	228.17	212.93	201.80	192.45	201.50	199.00	201.50	214.31
2019	196.50	205.87	214.50	218.50	210.32	195.00	193.32	188.68	177.50	177.50	179.50	179.12	194.69
2020	----	----	----	----	----	----	----	----	----	----	----	----	----

Source: American Metal Market (AMM)

COPPER

Nearby Futures through Last Trading Day using selected contract months: March, May, July, September and December.

Volume of Trading of Copper Futures in Chicago In Thousands of Contracts

Year	Jan.	Feb.	Mar.	Apr.	May	June	July	Aug.	Sept.	Oct.	Nov.	Dec.	Total
2011	777.6	1,079.7	931.9	1,079.4	915.2	1,170.7	765.9	1,312.5	1,142.5	1,268.8	1,234.6	812.7	12,491.5
2012	1,131.5	1,572.7	1,222.8	1,768.1	1,491.4	1,790.3	1,163.1	1,478.0	1,084.8	1,137.7	1,469.8	848.6	16,158.8
2013	1,163.8	1,547.7	1,199.1	2,262.6	1,646.6	1,760.9	1,307.1	1,696.7	913.6	1,265.4	1,443.0	920.9	17,127.4
2014	1,049.9	1,236.2	1,401.8	1,422.9	933.0	1,434.3	1,081.3	1,276.8	1,089.7	1,269.0	1,459.4	927.7	14,582.2
2015	1,376.3	1,513.4	1,327.0	1,570.8	1,078.6	1,638.6	1,410.3	1,753.1	1,197.7	1,227.4	1,843.6	1,049.2	16,986.1
2016	1,324.0	1,754.8	1,611.4	2,018.8	1,522.9	2,148.7	1,510.2	1,876.0	1,294.0	1,498.6	3,531.3	1,433.8	21,524.5
2017	1,697.3	2,348.1	1,823.1	2,266.8	1,867.4	2,297.6	1,740.5	2,945.0	2,309.5	2,410.7	2,992.4	2,353.2	27,051.5
2018	2,761.2	3,000.6	2,510.6	3,091.0	2,562.9	3,619.8	2,833.2	3,402.4	2,349.7	2,625.9	2,546.7	1,406.1	32,710.1
2019	2,015.9	2,441.6	1,748.1	2,243.5	2,082.2	2,257.1	1,875.7	2,397.1	1,491.4	1,674.0	2,116.7	1,665.7	24,008.9
2020	2,072.0	2,823.8	2,324.8	1,761.1	1,252.2	2,228.5	1,944.9	2,322.5	1,984.5	1,837.2	2,214.5	1,551.7	24,317.8

Source: CME Group; Commodity Exchange (COMEX)

Average Open Interest of Copper Futures in Chicago In Contracts

Year	Jan.	Feb.	Mar.	Apr.	May	June	July	Aug.	Sept.	Oct.	Nov.	Dec.
2011	162,325	157,918	138,261	134,959	122,036	128,861	148,876	130,312	120,015	126,973	124,770	115,634
2012	134,294	159,589	152,255	154,073	147,975	149,350	138,220	148,201	147,632	153,484	148,322	148,754
2013	160,188	174,428	166,007	179,530	162,279	180,744	165,350	160,513	149,129	150,400	162,528	160,424
2014	160,638	155,280	153,880	153,104	148,544	148,751	171,388	153,255	146,669	170,902	167,274	155,661
2015	175,389	178,359	165,403	163,159	173,340	174,453	165,716	180,019	153,941	160,277	181,603	175,301
2016	192,827	185,631	174,735	192,037	197,457	211,980	174,617	187,041	193,526	198,811	230,065	233,247
2017	253,784	288,886	266,753	273,442	249,694	258,588	280,781	328,948	300,294	297,370	283,754	254,501
2018	287,421	266,506	275,877	253,876	256,236	273,982	294,730	270,229	234,947	241,389	235,321	214,508
2019	259,860	249,458	255,711	252,487	260,544	273,779	263,606	283,002	239,479	252,253	230,046	244,905
2020	269,401	265,190	211,541	182,166	169,597	186,131	220,836	229,403	240,197	238,695	231,769	245,818

Source: CME Group; Commodity Exchange (COMEX)

Corn

Corn is a member of the grass family of plants and is a native grain of the American continents. Fossils of corn pollen that are over 80,000 years old have been found in lake sediment under Mexico City. Archaeological discoveries show that cultivated corn existed in the southwestern U.S. for at least 3,000 years, indicating that the indigenous people of the region cultivated corn as a food crop long before the Europeans reached the New World. Corn is a hardy plant that grows in many different areas of the world. It can grow at altitudes as low as sea level and as high as 12,000 feet in the South American Andes Mountains. Corn can also grow in tropical climates that receive up to 400 inches of rainfall per year, or in areas that receive only 12 inches of rainfall per year. Corn is used primarily as livestock feed in the United States and the rest of the world. Other uses for corn are alcohol additives for gasoline, adhesives, corn oil for cooking and margarine, sweeteners, and as food for humans. Corn is the largest crop in the U.S., both in terms of dollar value and the number of acres planted.

The largest futures market for corn is at the CME Group. Corn futures also trade at the Bolsa de Mercadorias & Futuros (BM&F) in Brazil, the Budapest Commodity Exchange, the Marche a Terme International de France (MATIF), the Mercado a Termino de Buenos Aires in Argentina, the Kanmon Commodity Exchange (KCE) in Korea, and the Tokyo Grain Exchange (TGE). The CME futures contract calls for the delivery of 5000 bushels of No. 2 yellow corn at par contract price, No. 1 yellow at 1-1/2 cents per bushel over the contract price, or No. 3 yellow at 1-1/2 cents per bushel below the contract price.

Prices – CME corn futures prices (Barchart.com electronic symbol code ZC) trended lower into Q2-2020 and posted an 11-year low of $3.0025 per bushel in April. The Covid pandemic forced lockdowns that reduced fuel consumption and ethanol demand. U.S. ethanol output in the week ended April 3, 2020 plunged -20% w/w to an average daily rate of 672,000 bbl, the lowest since the Energy Information Administration (EIA) began publishing weekly data in 2010. That weak demand caused U.S. ethanol inventories to climb to a record 27.689 million bbl in April. Corn prices were also under pressure as U.S. corn acreage was set to expand as farmers planned to plant 97 million acres of corn in 2020, the most since 2013. Corn prices moved sideways into August as they consolidated modestly above the 11-year low. Expectations for a bumper U.S corn crop were bearish for prices after the USDA estimated a record 181.8 bushels per acre in the August WASDE report. Corn prices then trended higher into year-end as exceptional Chinese demand for U.S. corn helped push prices higher as China attempted to fulfill its commitment to its phase one trade deal with the U.S. For example, in the week of July 24, 2020, China purchased a record 1.937 MMT of U.S. corn. Also, typhoons in China devastated its 2020 corn crop just as feed-demand for corn exploded in China as the country's hog farmers were boosting hog herds that had been devastated by the swine flu. The insatiable Chinese corn demand reduced U.S. corn supplies as the USDA's Quarterly Grain Stocks report showed that U.S. corn supplies as of September 2020 fell to 1.995 billion bushels, well below expectations of 2.266 billion bushels. China's Jan-Sep 2020 purchases of U.S. corn soared +73% yr/yr to 6.67 MMT, the highest in 15 years. The strong foreign demand prompted the USDA in its November 2020 WASDE report to raise its U.S. 2020/21 corn export estimate to a record 2.65 billion bushels. Corn prices also rallied after a La Nina weather pattern in South America curbed crop yields and prompted Argentina in December to suspend corn export licenses to maintain adequate domestic feed supply. Corn prices soared to a 6-1/2 year high in December at $4.8575 a bushel and finished 2020 up +24.8% yr/yr at $4.84 a bushel.

Supply – World production of corn in the 2020/21 marketing year is forecasted to rise +1.6% yr/yr to 1.134 billion metric tons, a new record high. The world's largest corn producers are forecasted to be the U.S. with 31.8% of world production, China with 23.0%, and Brazil with 9.6%. Production in both China and Brazil has more than tripled since 1980. Production in the U.S. over that same time frame has roughly doubled. The world area harvested with corn in 2020/21 is forecasted to rise +1.3% yr/yr to 338.4 million hectares. World ending stocks of corn and coarse grains in 2020/21 are forecasted to fall -4.6% yr/yr to 316.2 million metric tons.

U.S. corn production for the 2020/21 marketing year (Sep-Aug) is forecasted to rise +6.5% yr/yr to 14.507 billion bushels. U.S. farmers are forecasted to harvest 82.527 million acres of corn for grain usage in 2020/21, which is up +1.53% yr/yr. The U.S. corn yield in 2020/21 is forecasted to rise +5.0% yr/yr to 175.8 bushels per acre, down from the 2017/18 record high. U.S. 2020/21 ending stocks are forecasted to fall -19.1% yr/yr to 1.552 billion bushels. The largest corn-producing states in the U.S. in 2020 were Iowa with 16.1% of U.S. production, Illinois with 15.1%, Nebraska with 12.5%, Minnesota with 10.5%, and Indiana with 6.8%.

Demand – World consumption of course grains in the 2020/21 crop year is expected to rise +1.9% yr/yr to 1.454 billion metric tons, a record high. The largest category of usage in 2020/21, aside from animal feed, will be for ethanol production (alcohol fuel) with 5.200 billion bushels, which is 78.5% of total non-feed usage. That was up +7.2% yr/yr. After ethanol, the largest non-feed usage categories are for high fructose corn syrup (HFCS) with 6.4% of U.S. usage, glucose, and dextrose sugars with 5.4%, corn starch with 3.5%, cereal and other corn products with 3.2%, and alcoholic beverages with 2.6%.

Trade – U.S. exports of corn in 2020/21 are expected to rise +43.4% yr/yr to 64.773 million metric tons. Brazil's corn exports in 2020/21 are expected to rise +11.4% yr/yr to 39.000 million metric tons. Argentina's corn exports are expected to fall -4.2% yr/yr to 34.000 million metric tons.

World Production of Corn or Maize In Thousands of Metric Tons

Crop Year Beginning Oct. 1	Argentina	Brazil	Canada	China	European Union	India	Indonesia	Mexico	Russia	South Africa	Ukraine	United States	World Total
2011-12	21,000	73,000	11,359	211,316	68,316	21,759	8,850	18,726	6,962	12,759	22,838	312,789	910,293
2012-13	27,000	81,500	13,060	229,559	59,142	22,258	8,500	21,591	8,213	12,365	20,922	273,192	898,760
2013-14	26,000	80,000	14,191	248,453	64,931	24,259	9,100	22,880	11,635	14,925	30,900	351,316	1,027,295
2014-15	29,750	85,000	11,606	249,764	75,734	24,173	9,000	25,480	11,325	10,629	28,450	361,136	1,057,639
2015-16	29,500	67,000	13,680	264,992	58,748	22,567	10,500	25,971	13,168	8,214	23,333	345,506	1,015,178
2016-17	41,000	98,500	13,889	263,613	61,935	25,900	10,900	27,575	15,305	17,551	27,969	384,778	1,127,843
2017-18	32,000	82,000	14,096	259,071	62,046	28,753	11,900	27,569	13,201	13,104	24,115	371,096	1,078,557
2018-19[1]	51,000	101,000	13,885	257,174	64,376	27,715	12,000	27,600	11,415	11,824	35,805	364,262	1,123,770
2019-20[2]	51,000	102,000	13,404	260,779	66,718	28,636	12,000	26,500	14,275	16,000	35,887	345,962	1,116,414
2020-21[3]	47,500	109,000	13,563	260,670	63,600	28,500	12,000	28,000	14,000	16,000	29,500	360,252	1,133,887

[1] Preliminary. [2] Estimate. [3] Forecast. *Source: Foreign Agricultural Service, U.S. Department of Agriculture (FAS-USDA)*

World Supply and Demand of Coarse Grains In Millions of Metric Tons/Hectares

Crop Year Beginning Oct. 1	Area Harvested	Yield	Production	World Trade	Total Consumption	Ending Stocks	Stocks as % of Consumption[3]
2011-12	318.4	3.70	1,175.5	133.3	1,171.6	156.1	13.3
2012-13	320.5	3.60	1,159.1	132.3	1,139.4	175.8	15.4
2013-14	331.1	4.00	1,314.1	165.3	1,238.6	251.2	20.3
2014-15	332.8	4.00	1,346.3	174.2	1,281.6	316.0	24.7
2015-16	326.0	4.00	1,303.9	185.9	1,270.7	349.2	27.5
2016-17	338.4	4.20	1,419.5	183.1	1,382.7	386.0	27.9
2017-18	328.6	4.10	1,359.6	189.9	1,375.4	370.2	26.9
2018-19	331.1	4.20	1,398.1	204.5	1,421.2	347.1	24.4
2019-20[1]	334.0	4.20	1,411.6	212.9	1,427.2	331.5	23.2
2020-21[2]	338.4	4.30	1,438.9	226.7	1,454.2	316.2	21.7

[1] Preliminary. [2] Estimate. [3] Represents the ratio of marketing year ending stocks to total consumption. *Source: Foreign Agricultural Service, U.S. Department of Agriculture (FAS-USDA)*

Acreage and Supply of Corn in the United States In Millions of Bushels

Crop Year Beginning Sept. 1	Planted	Harvested: For Grain	Harvested: For Silage	Yield Per Harvested Acre Bushels	Carry-over, Sept. 1: On Farms	Carry-over, Sept. 1: Off Farms	Supply: Beginning Stocks	Supply: Production	Supply: Imports	Supply: Total Supply
	In Thousands of Acres									
2011-12	91,936	83,989	5,935	147.2	315	813	1,128	12,360	29	13,471
2012-13	97,291	87,365	7,419	123.1	314	675	989	10,755	160	11,904
2013-14	95,365	87,451	6,281	158.1	275	546	821	13,829	36	14,686
2014-15	90,597	83,136	6,371	171.0	462	770	1,232	14,216	32	15,479
2015-16	88,019	80,753	6,237	168.4	593	1,138	1,731	13,602	68	15,401
2016-17	94,004	86,748	6,186	174.6	627	1,110	1,737	15,148	57	16,942
2017-18	90,167	82,733	6,434	176.6	787	1,506	2,293	14,609	36	16,939
2018-19	88,871	81,276	5,061	176.4	620	1,520	2,140	14,340	28	16,509
2019-20[1]	89,745	81,337	6,615	167.5	814	1,407	2,221	13,620	42	15,883
2020-21[2]	90,978	82,527		175.8	751	1,169	1,919	14,507	25	16,127

[1] Preliminary. [2] Estimate. *Source: Economic Research Service, U.S. Department of Agriculture (ERS-USDA)*

Production of Corn (For Grain) in the United States, by State In Millions of Bushels

Year	Illinois	Indiana	Iowa	Kansas	Michigan	Minnesota	Missouri	Nebraska	Ohio	South Dakota	Texas	Wisconsin	US Total
2011	1,946.8	839.5	2,356.4	449.4	335.1	1,201.2	350.0	1,536.0	508.8	653.4	136.7	517.9	12,359.6
2012	1,286.3	597.0	1,876.9	375.3	314.2	1,374.5	247.5	1,292.2	438.0	535.3	200.0	396.0	10,755.1
2013	2,100.4	1,031.9	2,140.2	504.0	345.7	1,294.3	435.2	1,614.0	649.0	802.8	265.2	439.4	13,829.0
2014	2,350.0	1,084.8	2,367.4	566.2	355.8	1,177.8	628.7	1,602.1	610.7	787.4	294.5	485.2	14,215.5
2015	2,012.5	822.0	2,505.6	580.2	335.3	1,428.8	437.4	1,692.8	498.8	799.8	266.0	492.0	13,602.0
2016	2,255.7	946.3	2,740.5	698.6	320.3	1,544.0	570.5	1,699.9	524.7	825.9	323.9	573.2	15,148.0
2017	2,201.0	936.0	2,605.8	686.4	300.5	1,480.2	552.5	1,683.3	557.6	736.6	313.6	509.8	14,609.4
2018	2,268.0	967.7	2,499.0	642.4	289.2	1,357.7	466.2	1,785.6	617.1	777.6	189.0	545.2	14,340.4
2019	1,846.2	814.6	2,583.9	800.7	236.7	1,254.3	463.5	1,785.4	421.5	557.3	286.0	443.2	13,619.9
2020[1]	2,184.0	992.3	2,336.8	759.0	316.8	1,525.1	551.1	1,818.6	554.4	752.4	259.9	533.6	14,506.8

[1] Preliminary. *Source: National Agricultural Statistics Service, U.S. Department of Agriculture (NASS-USDA)*

Quarterly Supply and Disappearance of Corn in the United States In Millions of Bushels

Crop Year Beginning Sept. 1	Supply: Beginning Stocks	Supply: Pro-duction	Supply: Imports	Supply: Total Supply	Disapperance: Domestic Use: Food & Alcohol	Domestic Use: Seed	Domestic Use: Feed & Residual	Domestic Use: Total	Exports	Total Disap-pearance	Total Ending Stocks
2016-17	1,737	15,148	57.1	16,942	6,856	29.3	5,470	12,355	2,294	14,649	2,293.3
Sept.-Nov.	1,737	15,148	14.3	16,899	1,689	----	2,279	3,968	548	4,516	12,383.5
Dec.-Feb.	12,383	----	11.8	12,395	1,711	----	1,523	3,235	539	3,773	8,622.0
Mar.-May	8,622	----	17.3	8,639	1,714	27.3	982	2,723	687	3,410	5,229.1
June-Aug.	5,229	----	13.7	5,243	1,741	2.1	686	2,430	520	2,949	2,293.3
2017-18	2,293	14,609	36.0	16,939	7,027	29.6	5,304	12,361	2,438	14,798	2,140.3
Sept.-Nov.	2,293	14,609	10.8	16,914	1,743	----	2,256	3,998	349	4,347	12,566.5
Dec.-Feb.	12,567	----	8.4	12,575	1,739	----	1,497	3,236	447	3,683	8,892.1
Mar.-May	8,892	----	7.6	8,900	1,753	28.2	951	2,733	862	3,595	5,304.8
June-Aug.	5,305	----	9.3	5,314	1,792	1.5	600	2,394	780	3,174	2,140.3
2018-19	2,140	14,340	28.0	16,509	6,764	29.1	5,429	12,222	2,066	14,288	2,220.7
Sept.-Nov.	2,140	14,340	6.2	16,487	1,710	----	2,208	3,918	632	4,550	11,936.8
Dec.-Feb.	11,937	----	8.7	11,945	1,642	----	1,191	2,833	500	3,332	8,613.2
Mar.-May	8,613	----	6.4	8,620	1,694	18.6	1,118	2,831	586	3,417	5,202.2
June-Aug.	5,202	----	6.7	5,209	1,718	10.5	912	2,640	348	2,988	2,220.7
2019-20[1]	2,221	13,620	41.9	15,883	6,252	30.3	5,903	12,185	1,778	13,963	1,919.5
Sept.-Nov.	2,221	13,620	17.9	15,859	1,628	----	2,634	4,262	270	4,531	11,327.3
Dec.-Feb.	11,327	----	8.9	11,336	1,711	----	1,319	3,030	355	3,385	7,951.6
Mar.-May	7,952	----	9.5	7,961	1,331	28.2	993	2,352	606	2,958	5,003.0
June-Aug.	5,003	----	5.5	5,009	1,582	2.1	957	2,541	548	3,089	1,919.5
2020-21[2]	1,919	14,182	25.0	16,127	6,345	30.0	5,650	12,025	2,550	14,575	1,551.9
Sept.-Nov.	1,919	14,182	5.7	16,108	1,615	----	2,726	4,340	446	4,786	11,321.7

[1] Preliminary. [2] Estimate. *Source: Economic Research Service, U.S. Department of Agriculture (ERS-USDA)*

Corn Production Estimates and Cash Price in the United States

Year	Corn for Grain Production Estimates (In Thousands of Bushels): Aug. 1	Sept. 1	Oct. 1	Nov. 1	Final	St. Louis No. 2 Yellow (Dollars Per Bushel)	Omaha No. 2 Yellow	Gulf Ports No. 2 Yellow	Kansas City No. 2 White	Chicago No. 2 Yellow	Average Farm Price[2]	Value of Pro-duction (Mil. $)
2011-12	12,914,085	12,497,070	12,432,910	12,309,936	12,359,612	6.95	6.65	7.22	7.37	6.73	6.36	76,940
2012-13	10,778,589	10,727,364	10,705,729	10,725,191	10,755,111	6.94	7.20	7.58	7.52	7.17	6.88	74,155
2013-14	13,763,025	13,843,320	NA	13,988,720	13,828,964	4.91	4.35	5.16	4.63	4.47	4.48	61,928
2014-15	14,031,915	14,395,350	14,474,920	14,407,420	14,215,532	3.82	3.60	4.35	3.75	3.76	3.69	52,952
2015-16	13,686,063	13,584,945	13,554,923	13,653,507	13,601,964	3.80	3.49	4.18	3.75	3.75	3.61	49,339
2016-17	15,153,472	15,092,908	15,057,404	15,225,586	15,148,038	3.64	3.28	3.95	3.62	3.55	3.37	51,304
2017-18	14,152,966	14,184,466	14,280,112	14,577,502	14,609,407	3.63	3.46	4.07	3.71	3.55	3.40	49,568
2018-19	14,586,485	14,826,690	14,777,826	14,625,974	14,340,369	3.85	3.68	4.29	3.98	3.79	3.65	52,102
2019-20	13,900,651	13,799,151	13,779,335	13,661,005	13,619,928	3.74	3.26	3.93	3.65	3.65	3.52	52,911
2020-21[1]	15,278,202	14,899,557	14,721,705	14,506,795	14,506,795	4.70	4.33	5.17	4.66	4.54	3.80	

[1] Preliminary. [2] Season-average price based on monthly prices weigthed by monthly marketings.
Source: Economic Research Service, U.S. Department of Agriculture (ERS-USDA)

Distribution of Corn in the United States In Millions of Bushels

Crop Year Beginning Sept. 1	Food, Seed and Industrial Use: HFCS	Glucose & Dextrose	Starch	Alcohol: Fuel	Alcohol: Bev-rage[3]	Seed	Cereal & Other Products	Total	Livestock Feed[4]	Exports (Including Grain Equiv. of Products)	Domestic Disap-pearance	Total Utilization
2011-12	513	297	254	5,000	137	24.5	203	6,428	4,512	1,539.2	10,943	12,482
2012-13	491	292	249	4,641	140	31.0	199	6,044	4,309	730.1	10,353	11,083
2013-14	478	307	251	5,124	141	29.7	200	6,531	5,002	1,920.8	11,533	13,454
2014-15	478	298	246	5,200	142	29.3	201	6,595	5,287	1,866.9	11,883	13,750
2015-16	472	337	238	5,224	143	30.6	203	6,647	5,118	1,898.6	11,765	13,664
2016-17	467	371	235	5,432	146	29.3	204	6,885	5,470	2,294.0	12,355	14,649
2017-18	459	371	236	5,605	149	29.6	207	7,057	5,304	2,437.5	12,361	14,798
2018-19	441	355	230	5,378	150	29.1	209	6,793	5,275	2,060.0	12,080	14,140
2019-20[1]	405	355	230	4,850	170	30.1	220	6,260	5,175	2,050.0	12,055	14,105
2020-21[2]	425	355	230	5,200	170	30.0	215	6,625				

[1] Preliminary. [2] Estimate. [3] Also includes nonfuel industrial alcohol. [4] Feed and waste (residual, mostly feed).
Source: Economic Research Service, U.S. Department of Agriculture (ERS-USDA)

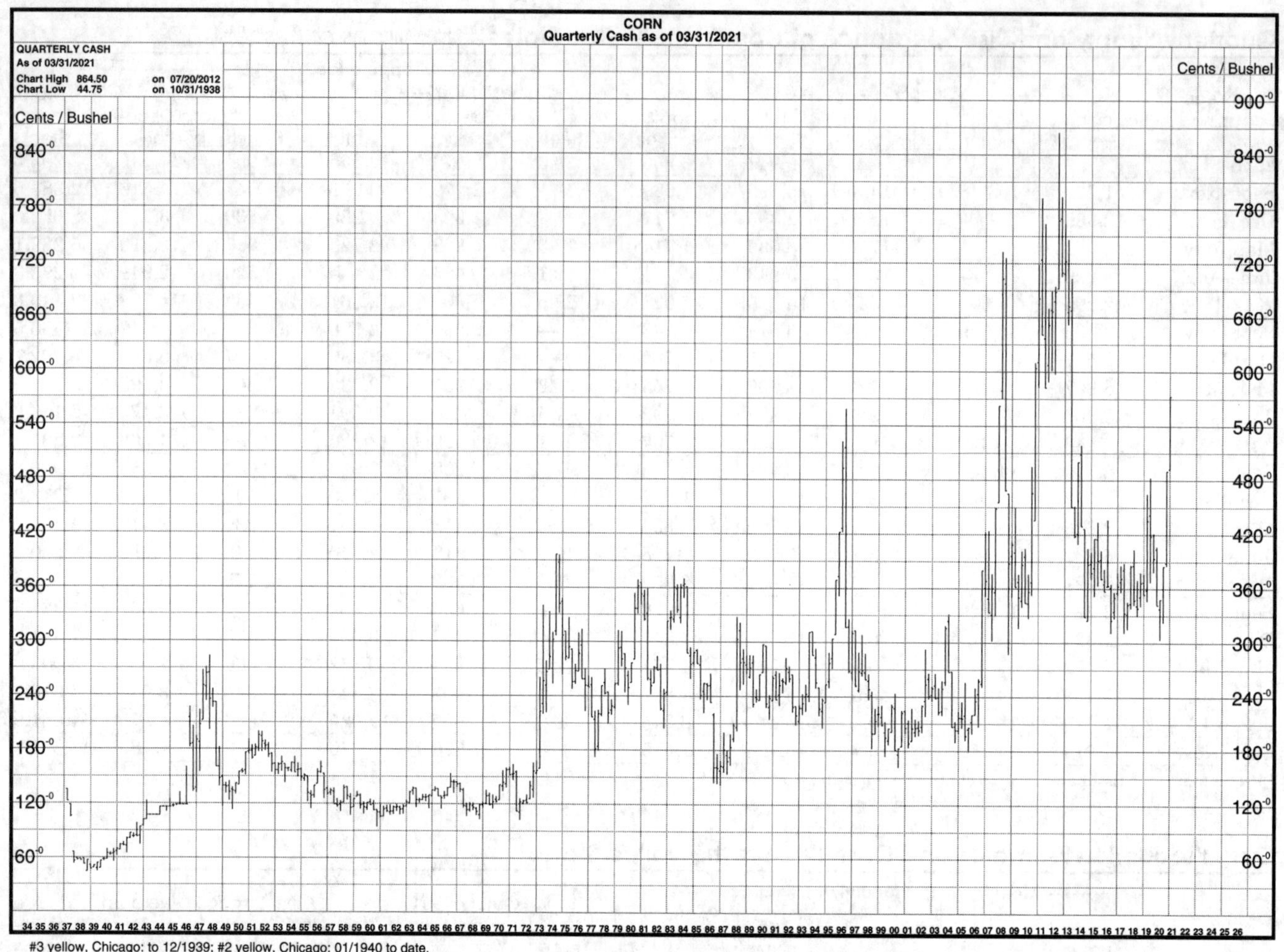

#3 yellow, Chicago: to 12/1939; #2 yellow, Chicago: 01/1940 to date.

Average Cash Price of Corn, No. 2 Yellow in Central Illinois In Dollars Per Bushel

Year	Sept.	Oct.	Nov.	Dec.	Jan.	Feb.	Mar.	Apr.	May	June	July	Aug.	Average
2011-12	6.77	6.23	6.26	5.96	6.25	6.41	6.46	6.34	6.27	6.30	7.85	8.15	6.60
2012-13	7.70	7.48	7.39	7.23	7.17	7.15	7.33	6.57	6.83	6.94	6.61	5.98	7.03
2013-14	4.78	4.20	4.10	4.13	4.13	4.33	4.64	4.98	4.72	4.37	3.74	3.59	4.31
2014-15	3.16	3.09	3.45	3.75	3.67	3.65	3.66	3.59	3.49	3.52	3.85	3.51	3.53
2015-16	3.55	3.67	3.62	3.62	3.55	3.56	3.54	3.61	3.74	3.91	3.28	3.09	3.56
2016-17	3.09	3.27	3.28	3.34	3.45	3.51	3.40	3.41	3.47	3.49	3.51	3.27	3.37
2017-18	3.15	3.15	3.14	3.21	3.29	3.45	3.52	3.54	3.73	3.38	3.22	3.24	3.34
2018-19	3.12	3.28	3.36	3.53	3.53	3.50	3.43	3.37	3.59	4.21	4.29	3.95	3.60
2019-20	3.55	3.79	3.66	3.73	3.82	3.75	3.51	3.06	2.99	3.13	3.21	3.84	3.50
2020-21[1]	3.62	3.97	4.22	4.45	5.23	5.56							4.51

[1] Preliminary. *Source: Economic Research Service, U.S. Department of Agriculture (ERS-USDA)*

Average Cash Price of Corn, No. 2 Yellow at Gulf Ports[2] In Dollars Per Bushel

Year	Sept.	Oct.	Nov.	Dec.	Jan.	Feb.	Mar.	Apr.	May	June	July	Aug.	Average
2011-12	7.50	6.98	6.97	6.57	6.94	7.10	7.13	6.96	6.84	6.79	8.46	8.44	7.22
2012-13	8.15	8.16	8.18	7.85	7.70	7.70	7.85	7.11	7.50	7.58	7.10	6.07	7.58
2013-14	5.27	5.13	5.06	5.06	5.03	5.32	5.65	5.65	5.51	5.14	4.64	4.48	5.16
2014-15	4.14	4.15	4.54	4.55	4.44	4.41	4.43	4.38	4.23	4.24	4.56	4.14	4.35
2015-16	4.22	4.36	4.22	4.17	4.09	4.06	4.05	4.17	4.30	4.62	4.11	3.82	4.18
2016-17	3.78	3.88	3.83	3.88	4.07	4.14	4.04	3.98	4.03	4.01	4.00	3.77	3.95
2017-18	3.74	3.77	3.78	3.79	3.96	4.15	4.36	4.46	4.55	4.19	3.98	4.13	4.07
2018-19	3.93	4.07	4.09	4.25	4.24	4.31	4.23	4.11	4.36	4.96	4.81	4.14	4.29
2019-20	4.00	4.25	4.23	4.24	4.36	4.29	4.12	3.73	2.66	3.76	3.88	3.65	3.93
2020-21[1]	4.23	4.74	4.85	5.06	5.89	6.24							5.17

[1] Preliminary. [2] Barge delivered to Louisiana Gulf. *Source: Economic Research Service, U.S. Department of Agriculture (ERS-USDA)*

Weekly Outstanding Export Sales and Cumulative Exports of U.S. Corn In Thousands of Metric Tons

Marketing Year 2019/2020 Week Ending	Weekly Exports	Accumulated Exports	Net Sales	Outstanding Sales	Marketing Year 2020/2021 Week Ending	Weekly Exports	Accumulated Exports	Net Sales	Outstanding Sales
Sep 05, 2019	412,243	412,243	1,232,510	6,778,106	Sep 03, 2020	245,713	245,713	3,073,677	18,601,190
Sep 12, 2019	457,306	869,549	1,464,566	7,785,366	Sep 10, 2020	901,965	1,147,678	1,609,185	19,308,410
Sep 19, 2019	278,922	1,148,471	493,966	8,000,410	Sep 17, 2020	845,178	1,992,856	2,139,002	20,602,234
Sep 26, 2019	458,330	1,606,801	562,616	8,104,696	Sep 24, 2020	750,181	2,743,037	2,027,125	21,879,178
Oct 03, 2019	474,396	2,081,197	284,456	7,914,756	Oct 01, 2020	934,785	3,677,822	1,225,651	22,170,044
Oct 10, 2019	556,585	2,637,782	368,576	7,726,747	Oct 08, 2020	815,104	4,492,926	655,165	22,010,105
Oct 17, 2019	489,040	3,126,822	491,457	7,729,164	Oct 15, 2020	898,018	5,390,944	1,831,566	22,943,653
Oct 24, 2019	494,284	3,621,106	549,138	7,784,018	Oct 22, 2020	734,183	6,125,127	2,243,739	24,453,209
Oct 31, 2019	317,879	3,938,985	487,944	7,954,083	Oct 29, 2020	728,763	6,853,890	2,610,852	26,335,298
Nov 07, 2019	602,235	4,541,220	581,568	7,933,416	Nov 05, 2020	730,922	7,584,812	978,329	26,582,705
Nov 14, 2019	673,060	5,214,280	788,022	8,048,378	Nov 12, 2020	844,630	8,429,442	1,088,575	26,826,650
Nov 21, 2019	635,334	5,849,614	806,751	8,219,795	Nov 19, 2020	871,141	9,300,583	1,665,614	27,621,123
Nov 28, 2019	494,779	6,344,393	546,115	8,271,131	Nov 26, 2020	1,072,268	10,372,851	1,371,445	27,920,300
Dec 05, 2019	531,371	6,875,764	873,525	8,613,285	Dec 03, 2020	714,971	11,087,822	1,362,192	28,567,521
Dec 12, 2019	720,062	7,595,826	1,709,368	9,602,591	Dec 10, 2020	965,375	12,053,197	1,924,488	29,526,634
Dec 19, 2019	331,735	7,927,561	624,775	9,895,631	Dec 17, 2020	835,664	12,888,861	651,102	29,342,072
Dec 26, 2019	447,466	8,375,027	531,393	9,979,558	Dec 24, 2020	1,339,613	14,228,474	964,547	28,967,006
Jan 02, 2020	514,555	8,889,582	161,888	9,626,891	Dec 31, 2020	1,027,853	15,256,327	748,910	28,688,063
Jan 09, 2020	544,677	9,434,259	784,762	9,866,976	Jan 07, 2021	1,464,289	16,720,616	1,437,743	28,661,517
Jan 16, 2020	392,060	9,826,319	1,006,873	10,481,789	Jan 14, 2021	886,650	17,607,266	1,437,562	29,212,429
Jan 23, 2020	681,932	10,508,251	1,234,660	11,034,517	Jan 21, 2021	1,413,986	19,021,252	1,850,306	29,648,749
Jan 30, 2020	599,003	11,107,254	1,247,802	11,683,316	Jan 28, 2021	995,496	20,016,748	7,436,504	36,089,757
Feb 06, 2020	782,762	11,890,016	968,815	11,869,369	Feb 04, 2021	1,565,732	21,582,480	1,448,649	35,972,674
Feb 13, 2020	760,882	12,650,898	1,248,825	12,357,312	Feb 11, 2021	1,387,132	22,969,612	999,165	35,584,707
Feb 20, 2020	844,671	13,495,569	864,635	12,377,276	Feb 18, 2021	1,190,062	24,159,674	453,281	34,847,926
Feb 27, 2020	884,613	14,380,182	769,205	12,261,868	Feb 25, 2021	2,010,177	26,169,851	115,888	32,953,637
Mar 05, 2020	851,715	15,231,897	1,471,165	12,881,318	Mar 04, 2021	1,592,851	27,762,702	395,506	31,756,292
Mar 12, 2020	970,158	16,202,055	904,524	12,815,684	Mar 11, 2021	2,199,438	29,962,140	985,890	30,542,744
Mar 19, 2020	846,016	17,048,071	1,814,255	13,783,923	Mar 18, 2021	2,035,987	31,998,127	4,481,853	32,988,610
Mar 26, 2020	1,258,536	18,306,607	1,075,436	13,600,823	Mar 25, 2021				
Apr 02, 2020	1,290,271	19,596,878	1,848,917	14,159,469	Apr 01, 2021				
Apr 09, 2020	1,222,075	20,818,953	906,618	13,844,012	Apr 08, 2021				
Apr 16, 2020	763,401	21,582,354	659,382	13,739,993	Apr 15, 2021				
Apr 23, 2020	1,051,505	22,633,859	1,356,689	14,045,177	Apr 22, 2021				
Apr 30, 2020	1,400,367	24,034,226	774,632	13,419,442	Apr 29, 2021				
May 07, 2020	1,311,073	25,345,299	1,073,237	13,181,606	May 06, 2021				
May 14, 2020	1,261,263	26,606,562	884,162	12,804,505	May 13, 2021				
May 21, 2020	1,061,193	27,667,755	427,185	12,170,497	May 20, 2021				
May 28, 2020	1,343,304	29,011,059	633,971	11,461,164	May 27, 2021				
Jun 04, 2020	1,241,155	30,252,214	660,727	10,880,736	Jun 03, 2021				
Jun 11, 2020	877,447	31,129,661	357,792	10,361,081	Jun 10, 2021				
Jun 18, 2020	1,313,026	32,442,687	461,650	9,509,705	Jun 17, 2021				
Jun 25, 2020	1,439,913	33,882,600	361,061	8,430,853	Jun 24, 2021				
Jul 02, 2020	1,084,317	34,966,917	195,242	7,541,778	Jul 01, 2021				
Jul 09, 2020	1,014,288	35,981,205	981,068	7,508,558	Jul 08, 2021				
Jul 16, 2020	1,050,923	37,032,128	220,585	6,678,220	Jul 15, 2021				
Jul 23, 2020	971,230	38,003,358	-29,321	5,677,669	Jul 22, 2021				
Jul 30, 2020	685,480	38,688,838	101,596	5,093,785	Jul 29, 2021				
Aug 06, 2020	1,333,065	40,021,903	377,188	4,137,908	Aug 05, 2021				
Aug 13, 2020	1,196,989	41,218,892	61,574	3,002,493	Aug 12, 2021				
Aug 20, 2020	939,091	42,157,983	270,350	2,333,752	Aug 19, 2021				
Aug 27, 2020	464,216	42,622,199	95,759	1,965,295	Aug 26, 2021				
Sep 03, 2020	651,592	43,273,791	-63,316	1,250,387					

Source: Foreign Agricultural Service, U.S. Department of Agriculture (FAS-USDA)

Average Price Received by Farmers for Corn in the United States In Dollars Per Bushel

Year	Sept.	Oct.	Nov.	Dec.	Jan.	Feb.	Mar.	Apr.	May	June	July	Aug.	Average
2011-12	6.38	5.73	5.83	5.86	6.07	6.28	6.35	6.34	6.34	6.37	7.14	7.63	6.36
2012-13	6.89	6.78	7.01	6.87	6.96	7.04	7.13	6.97	6.97	6.97	6.79	6.21	6.88
2013-14	5.40	4.63	4.37	4.41	4.42	4.35	4.52	4.71	4.71	4.50	4.06	3.63	4.48
2014-15	3.49	3.57	3.60	3.79	3.82	3.79	3.81	3.75	3.64	3.59	3.80	3.68	3.69
2015-16	3.68	3.67	3.59	3.65	3.66	3.58	3.56	3.56	3.68	3.82	3.60	3.21	3.61
2016-17	3.22	3.29	3.24	3.32	3.40	3.44	3.49	3.43	3.45	3.43	3.49	3.27	3.37
2017-18	3.27	3.26	3.15	3.23	3.29	3.38	3.51	3.58	3.68	3.58	3.47	3.36	3.40
2018-19	3.40	3.42	3.41	3.54	3.56	3.60	3.61	3.53	3.63	3.98	4.16	3.93	3.65
2019-20	3.80	3.85	3.68	3.71	3.79	3.78	3.68	3.29	3.20	3.16	3.21	3.12	3.52
2020-21[1]	3.40	3.61	3.79	3.97	4.24								3.80

[1] Preliminary. *Source: Economic Research Service, U.S. Department of Agriculture (ERS-USDA)*

Corn Price Support Data in the United States

Crop Year Beginning Sept. 1	National Average Loan Rate[3]	Target Price	Placed Under Loan	% of Production	Acquired by CCC	Owned by CCC Aug. 31	CCC Inventory As of Dec. 31: CCC Owned	CCC Inventory As of Dec. 31: Under CCC Loan	Quantity Pledged (Thousands of Bushels)	Face Amount (Thousands of Dollars)
	Dollars Per Bushel		Millions of Bushels							
2009-10	1.95	2.63	934	7.1	0	0	0	----	935,064	1,707,057
2010-11	1.95	2.63	801	6.4	0	0	0	----	801,131	1,455,091
2011-12	1.95	2.63	574	4.6	0	0	0	----	574,224	1,050,954
2012-13	1.95	2.63	368	3.4	0	0	0	----	367,998	675,046
2013-14	1.95	2.63	460	3.3	0	0	0	----	460,885	823,153
2014-15	1.95	3.70	574	4.0	0	0	0	----	7,822	16,432
2015-16	1.95	3.70	746	5.5	0	0	0	----	44,185	110,902
2016-17	1.95	3.70	880	5.8	0	0	0	----	59,619	116,982
2017-18[1]	1.95	3.70	980	6.7	0	0	0	----		
2018-19[2]	1.95	3.70	919	6.4	0	0	0	----		

[1] Preliminary. [2] Estimate. [3] Findley or announced loan rate. NA = Not available.
Source: National Agricultural Statistics Service, U.S. Department of Agriculture (NASS-USDA)

U.S. Exports[1] of Corn (Including Seed), By Country of Destination In Thousands of Metric Tons

Crop Year Beginning Oct. 1	Algeria	Canada	Egypt	Israel	Japan	Mexico	Korea, South	Russia	Saudi Arabia	Spain	Taiwan	Venezuela	Total
2010-11	----	962	2,939	679	13,762	6,059	7,476	----	574	330	2,731	852	45,109
2011-12	----	718	298	29	11,703	3,189	9,878	----	361	1	1,500	1,398	38,282
2012-13	----	451	----	0	6,511	296	4,861	----	345	9	514	1,079	18,176
2013-14	76	604	2,940	469	12,379	5,312	10,895	----	1,030	693	1,772	1,058	50,599
2014-15	239	1,444	1,127	26	11,832	3,645	11,220	1	1,184	66	1,830	806	46,758
2015-16	663	926	792	388	11,187	3,881	13,535	----	1,522	66	2,302	1,078	50,989
2016-17	91	650	258	107	12,579	4,762	14,297	----	2,029	205	2,663	384	55,561
2017-18	48	1,724	1,640	757	13,811	6,047	15,498	----	1,577	1,167	2,734	440	63,537
2018-19	----	2,395	225	134	12,496	3,292	15,688	----	770	1	1,685	95	49,124
2019-20[2]	43	1,711	49	497	10,040	2,893	14,564	----	850	0	781	469	46,858

[1] Excludes exports of corn by-products. [2] Preliminary. *Source: Foreign Agricultural Service, U.S. Department of Agriculture (FAS-USDA)*

Stocks of Corn (Shelled and Ear) in the United States In Millions of Bushels

Year	On Farms: Mar. 1	On Farms: June 1	On Farms: Sept. 1	On Farms: Dec. 1	Off Farms: Mar. 1	Off Farms: June 1	Off Farms: Sept. 1	Off Farms: Dec. 1	Total Stocks: Mar. 1	Total Stocks: June 1	Total Stocks: Sept. 1	Total Stocks: Dec. 1
2011	3,384,000	1,681,500	314,950	6,175,000	3,139,228	1,988,338	812,695	3,472,466	6,523,228	3,669,838	1,127,645	9,647,466
2012	3,192,000	1,482,000	313,700	4,586,000	2,831,356	1,666,204	675,327	3,446,732	6,023,356	3,148,204	989,027	8,032,732
2013	2,669,200	1,260,100	275,000	6,380,000	2,730,726	1,506,144	546,185	4,072,532	5,399,926	2,766,244	821,185	10,452,532
2014	3,860,500	1,863,200	462,000	7,087,000	3,147,623	1,988,516	769,904	4,124,380	7,008,123	3,851,716	1,231,904	11,211,380
2015	4,380,000	2,275,000	593,000	6,829,000	3,369,806	2,177,988	1,138,164	4,406,178	7,749,806	4,452,988	1,731,164	11,234,178
2016	4,335,000	2,471,400	627,400	7,611,000	3,487,233	2,239,679	1,109,658	4,774,776	7,822,233	4,711,079	1,737,058	12,385,776
2017	4,908,000	2,841,400	787,000	7,739,000	3,713,992	2,387,682	1,506,303	4,827,501	8,621,992	5,229,082	2,293,303	12,566,501
2018	5,002,000	2,750,100	620,000	7,451,000	3,890,126	2,554,704	1,520,335	4,485,798	8,892,126	5,304,804	2,140,335	11,936,798
2019	5,131,000	2,949,600	814,100	7,103,000	3,482,206	2,252,636	1,406,649	4,224,338	8,613,206	5,202,236	2,220,749	11,327,338
2020[1]	4,454,000	2,867,000	750,800	7,046,000	3,497,576	2,135,987	1,168,662	4,275,696	7,951,576	5,002,987	1,919,462	11,321,696

[1] Preliminary. *Source: National Agricultural Statistics Service, U.S. Department of Agriculture (NASS-USDA)*

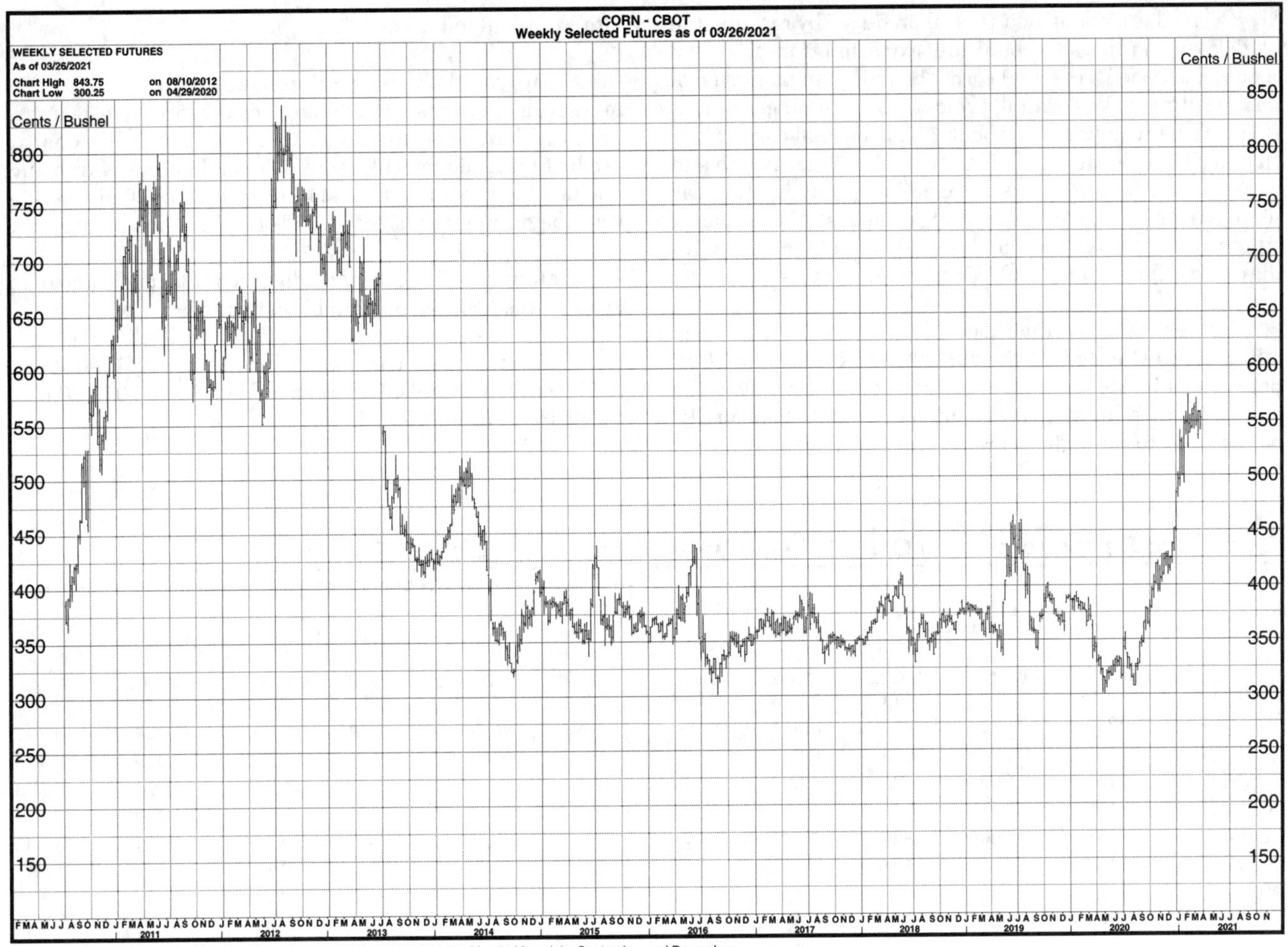

Nearby Futures through Last Trading Day using selected contract months: March, May, July, September and December.

Volume of Trading of Corn Futures in Chicago In Thousands of Contracts

Year	Jan.	Feb.	Mar.	Apr.	May	June	July	Aug.	Sept.	Oct.	Nov.	Dec.	Total
2011	5,981.0	7,473.1	7,552.4	8,715.1	5,676.9	8,639.5	5,119.3	6,834.9	5,385.7	5,568.2	8,003.4	4,055.2	79,004.8
2012	6,194.8	7,388.6	6,538.5	7,418.0	6,162.5	8,027.0	6,825.3	6,003.0	4,164.7	4,701.6	6,406.8	3,353.5	73,184.3
2013	5,151.4	6,347.6	4,929.5	7,089.9	4,937.7	5,823.6	4,824.9	6,128.2	3,436.3	4,919.5	7,695.2	3,039.0	64,322.6
2014	5,790.8	7,614.4	5,772.2	6,996.2	4,613.5	6,677.8	4,938.4	5,781.3	3,784.4	5,875.4	7,439.7	4,153.1	69,437.3
2015	5,468.9	6,810.9	6,111.2	7,860.2	5,957.5	10,795.4	8,553.2	7,835.9	4,880.3	5,708.6	8,736.5	4,375.5	83,094.3
2016	5,878.1	7,858.5	6,061.1	11,510.4	6,909.2	11,322.0	6,258.8	7,704.5	4,498.0	5,321.4	8,319.7	3,983.4	85,625.2
2017	5,911.2	8,379.3	6,001.8	8,751.1	6,167.8	11,804.7	8,516.1	9,294.9	4,606.4	5,878.6	10,685.8	3,879.2	89,876.8
2018	6,474.5	10,818.8	8,754.6	10,249.8	8,164.3	11,485.8	6,613.3	8,637.0	5,584.7	6,586.2	9,690.5	4,327.7	97,387.2
2019	6,008.6	10,270.7	7,945.3	10,348.0	13,559.8	13,195.1	8,041.4	10,317.4	5,322.1	6,103.5	8,302.7	3,774.4	103,189.1
2020	6,270.8	8,339.9	7,778.8	8,115.2	4,561.6	10,234.8	7,114.3	9,064.2	5,978.7	8,256.3	8,792.8	5,245.7	89,753.1

Contract size = 5,000 bu. *Source: CME Group; Chicago Board of Trade (CBT)*

Average Open Interest of Corn Futures in Chicago In Thousands of Contracts

Year	Jan.	Feb.	Mar.	Apr.	May	June	July	Aug.	Sept.	Oct.	Nov.	Dec.
2011	1,595.6	1,697.7	1,598.8	1,617.6	1,439.8	1,406.3	1,196.7	1,244.3	1,214.8	1,220.0	1,268.5	1,156.4
2012	1,209.5	1,289.9	1,312.4	1,330.4	1,212.9	1,125.0	1,138.0	1,211.6	1,175.6	1,247.8	1,282.1	1,168.4
2013	1,187.9	1,275.3	1,264.8	1,270.8	1,160.8	1,196.6	1,135.7	1,166.2	1,114.6	1,252.2	1,335.0	1,193.8
2014	1,284.5	1,343.4	1,318.8	1,396.1	1,338.9	1,370.7	1,332.4	1,316.6	1,254.5	1,289.5	1,298.1	1,216.6
2015	1,291.3	1,332.4	1,296.8	1,360.9	1,370.6	1,428.7	1,350.7	1,346.0	1,253.1	1,309.6	1,365.9	1,291.4
2016	1,374.6	1,372.9	1,349.8	1,432.1	1,364.2	1,438.5	1,297.8	1,353.5	1,303.9	1,322.3	1,345.3	1,227.3
2017	1,306.7	1,431.1	1,403.8	1,443.3	1,364.3	1,406.1	1,377.3	1,412.7	1,378.6	1,496.8	1,641.6	1,522.8
2018	1,623.6	1,670.6	1,821.7	1,837.2	1,852.3	1,950.0	1,850.8	1,729.7	1,693.3	1,659.4	1,702.9	1,574.6
2019	1,646.1	1,720.2	1,769.3	1,774.3	1,688.8	1,789.0	1,781.6	1,732.2	1,612.6	1,597.3	1,589.0	1,471.0
2020	1,530.9	1,576.5	1,435.7	1,441.2	1,428.9	1,564.1	1,531.9	1,525.6	1,458.9	1,601.4	1,733.7	1,684.7

Contract size = 5,000 bu. *Source: CME Group; Chicago Board of Trade (CBT)*

Corn Oil

Corn oil is a bland, odorless oil produced by refining the crude corn oil that is mechanically extracted from the germ of the plant seed. High-oil corn, the most common type of corn used to make corn oil, typically has an oil content of 7% or higher compared to about 4% for normal corn. Corn oil is widely used as cooking oil, for making margarine and mayonnaise, and for making inedible products such as soap, paints, inks, varnishes, and cosmetics. For humans, studies have shown that no vegetable oil is more effective than corn oil in lowering blood cholesterol levels.

Prices –The average monthly price of corn oil (wet mill price in Chicago) in the 2019/20 marketing year (Oct-Sep) rose +18.8% to 32.00 cents per pound, far below the 2007-08 record high of 69.40 cents per pound. Seasonally, prices tend to be highest around March/April and lowest late in the calendar year.

Supply – U.S. corn oil production in the 2019/20 marketing year rose +0.2% yr/yr to 5.775 billion pounds, but still down from the 2017/18 record high. Seasonally, production tends to peak around December and March and reaches a low in July. U.S. stocks in the 2019/20 marketing year (beginning Oct 1) fell -21.5% to 82 million pounds.

Demand – U.S. usage (domestic disappearance) in 2019/20 rose +0.1% to 5.282 billion pounds.

Exports – U.S. corn oil exports in 2019/20 fell -0.5% to 570 million pounds. U.S. corn oil imports in 2019/20 rose by +9.4% to 70 million pounds.

Supply and Disappearance of Corn Oil in the United States In Millions of Pounds

	Supply				Disappearance						
Year	Stocks Oct. 1	Pro-duction	Imports	Total Supply	Baking and Frying Fats	Salad and Cooking Oil	Marg-arine	Total Edible Products	Domestic Disap-pearance	Exports	Total Disap-pearance
2010-11	139	3,650	47.6	3,836	W	2,375	W	1,691	2,805	792	3,596
2011-12	240	3,625	45.8	3,911	NA	NA	NA	NA	2,742	1,003	3,746
2012-13	165	3,685	60.0	3,910	----	----	----	----	2,726	1,019	3,745
2013-14	165	3,890	42.1	4,097	----	----	----	----	2,928	1,004	3,932
2014-15	165	4,740	38.8	4,944	----	----	----	----	3,870	909	4,779
2015-16	165	5,300	82.8	5,548	----	----	----	----	4,289	1,094	5,383
2016-17	165	5,850	73.0	6,088	----	----	----	----	4,841	1,120	5,961
2017-18	127	6,066	62.3	6,256	----	----	----	----	5,423	728	6,151
2018-19[1]	104	5,765	64.0	5,933	----	----	----	----	5,279	573	5,852
2019-20[2]	82	5,775	70.0	5,927	----	----	----	----	5,282	570	5,852

[1] Preliminary. [2] Estimate. W = Withheld. *Source: Economic Research Service, U.S. Department of Agriculture (ERS-USDA)*

Production[2] of Crude Corn Oil in the United States In Millions of Pounds

Year	Oct.	Nov.	Dec.	Jan.	Feb.	Mar.	Apr.	May	June	July	Aug.	Sept.	Total
2004-05	208.8	187.1	191.0	205.2	182.5	206.6	217.2	188.2	211.5	206.7	198.5	189.0	2,392
2005-06	207.5	199.9	200.3	209.2	184.8	217.6	191.7	218.7	206.7	215.3	222.0	209.0	2,483
2006-07	228.7	216.0	226.1	224.7	187.9	216.4	194.1	214.4	212.7	219.8	209.5	209.4	2,560
2007-08	213.5	213.0	214.0	205.4	193.7	222.5	190.7	220.9	193.7	214.9	217.3	207.3	2,507
2008-09	206.3	210.6	198.7	200.3	199.8	218.8	189.4	202.5	189.0	186.0	201.4	215.8	2,419
2009-10	212.9	205.2	203.2	197.9	188.1	212.4	214.7	205.4	214.7	216.8	213.6	200.1	2,485
2010-11[1]	205.1	211.2	198.9	220.9	199.4	218.1	203.1	215.0	216.3	205.7			2,512

[1] Preliminary. [2] Not seasonally adjusted. *Source: Bureau of the Census, U.S. Department of Commerce*

Average Corn Oil Price, Wet Mill in Chicago In Cents Per Pound

Year	Oct.	Nov.	Dec.	Jan.	Feb.	Mar.	Apr.	May	June	July	Aug.	Sept.	Average
2011-12	54.24	53.98	53.36	54.00	56.30	59.31	60.75	58.05	52.90	54.76	57.26	58.21	56.09
2012-13	54.75	51.93	50.63	52.06	51.71	47.76	47.06	45.23	42.50	38.91	38.93	38.46	46.66
2013-14	37.85	38.79	38.31	38.79	41.07	43.19	41.94	41.02	40.01	39.02	38.00	35.17	39.43
2014-15	34.50	33.96	33.68	34.86	36.13	37.73	39.27	39.50	40.34	41.49	40.75	37.55	37.48
2015-16	36.60	36.43	38.25	39.93	40.29	41.05	42.12	40.33	39.94	38.86	39.06	38.11	39.25
2016-17	36.22	36.83	38.12	37.89	38.11	37.90	37.63	37.71	38.00	37.53	36.75	36.48	37.43
2017-18	34.96	34.46	33.96	30.68	29.72	29.66	29.50	29.65	29.54	28.76	26.80	26.46	30.35
2018-19	27.18	26.37	26.46	26.21	25.65	26.72	27.94	27.76	27.38	26.75	27.31	27.48	26.93
2019-20	28.30	30.36	31.25	33.30	36.00	36.94	44.88	47.64	51.34	45.45	44.75	43.38	39.47
2020-21[1]	43.15	42.53	41.48	44.23									42.85

[1] Preliminary. *Source: Economic Research Service, U.S. Department of Agriculture (ERS-USDA)*

Cotton

Cotton is a natural vegetable fiber that comes from small trees and shrubs of a genus belonging to the mallow family, one of which is the common American Upland cotton plant. Cotton has been used in India for at least the last 5,000 years and probably much longer, and was also used by the ancient Chinese, Egyptians, and North and South Americans. Cotton was one of the earliest crops grown by European settlers in the U.S.

Cotton requires a long growing season, plenty of sunshine and water during the growing season, and then dry weather for harvesting. In the United States, the Cotton Belt stretches from northern Florida to North Carolina and westward to California. In the U.S., planting time varies from the beginning of February in Southern Texas to the beginning of June in the northern sections of the Cotton Belt. The flower bud of the plant blossoms and develops into an oval boll that splits open at maturity. At maturity, cotton is most vulnerable to damage from wind and rain. Approximately 95% of the cotton in the U.S. is now harvested mechanically with spindle-type pickers or strippers and then sent off to cotton gins for processing. There it is dried, cleaned, separated, and packed into bales.

Cotton is used in a wide range of products, from clothing to home furnishings to medical products. The value of cotton is determined by the staple, grade, and character of each bale. Staple refers to short, medium, long, or extra-long fiber length, with medium staple accounting for about 70% of all U.S. cotton. Grade refers to the color, brightness, and amount of foreign matter and is established by the U.S. Department of Agriculture. Character refers to the fiber's diameter, strength, body, maturity (ratio of mature to immature fibers), uniformity, and smoothness. Cotton is the fifth leading cash crop in the U.S. and is one of the nation's principal agricultural exports. The weight of cotton is typically measured in terms of a "bale," which equals 480 pounds.

Cotton futures and options are traded at the ICE Futures U.S. exchange. Cotton futures are also traded on the Bolsa de Mercadorias & Futuros (BM&F). Cotton yarn futures are traded on the Central Japan Commodity Exchange (CCOM) and the Osaka Mercantile Exchange (OME). The New York Cotton Exchange's futures contract calls for the delivery of 50,000 pounds net weight (approximately 100 bales) of No. 2 cotton with a quality rating of Strict Low Middling and a staple length of 1-and-2/32 inch. Delivery points include Texas (Galveston and Houston), New Orleans, Memphis, and Greenville/ Spartanburg in South Carolina.

Prices – ICE cotton futures prices (Barchart.com symbol CT) in January 2020 climbed to a 1-1/2 year high 79.31 cents per pound as improved U.S./China trade relations prompted China's Agricultural Ministry in January to raise China's 2019/20 cotton import estimate to 1.8 MMT from a prior forecast of 1.6 MMT. However, cotton prices then trended lower through Q1-2020 as the spread of the Covid pandemic forced lockdowns that devastated China's cotton demand. The slack demand boosted cotton supplies and sent prices tumbling to an 11-1/2-year low of 48.35 cents per pound in April 2020. India's Textile Ministry forecast in April that 2019/20 cotton stockpiles in India, the world's biggest cotton producer, would surge to a 30-year high of 12 million bales as Chinese cotton demand plunged due to the pandemic. Also, the USDA, in its May WASDE report, predicted that global 2019/20 cotton consumption would fall -13% yr/yr to 105 million bales, the largest annual decline since the 19th century. In June, the International Cotton Advisory Committee predicted that global 2019/20 cotton inventories would expand to a 5-year high of 21.75 MMT on weak demand from the pandemic. Cotton prices then trended higher into year-end on the outlook for smaller U.S. output after the USDA projected U.S. cotton plantings in 2020 would fall -11.3% yr/yr to 12.185 million acres, the lowest acreage since 2017. Adverse U.S. weather in the second half of 2020 cut U.S. cotton production, and the USDA in its December WASDE report cut its U.S. 2020/21 cotton production estimate to 15.95 million bales, down -20% yr/yr and well below the consensus of 16.74 million bales. Cotton prices rallied to a 1-1/2 year high in December of 78.20 cents per pound and finished 2020 up +13.1% yr/yr at 78.12 cents a pound.

Supply – World cotton production in 2020/21 is forecasted to fall -7.6% yr/yr to 112,867 million bales (480 pounds per bale) and remain below the 2011/12 record high of 127.243 million bales. The world's largest cotton producers are forecasted to be India with 28.1% of world production in 2020/21, China with 21.4%, the U.S. with 13.2%, Brazil with 10.6%, and Pakistan with 3.8%. World ending stocks in 2020/21 are forecasted to fall -3.0% yr/yr to 96.37 million bales, down from the 2014/15 record high of 106.857.

The U.S. cotton crop in 2020/21is forecasted to fall -19.9% yr/yr to 15.949 million bales and remained below the 2005/06 record high of 23.890 million bales. U.S. farmers are forecasted to harvest 9.005 million acres of cotton in 2020/21, down -22.5% yr/yr. The U.S. cotton yield in 2020/21 is forecasted to rise +3.3% yr/yr to 850 pounds per acre, but still down from the 2017/18 record high of 905 pounds per acre. The leading U.S. producing states for cotton in 2019 were Texas with 32.9% of U.S. production, Georgia with 14.4%, Arkansas with 8.2%, Mississippi with 7.90%, Alabama with 5.0%, and Missouri with 4.60%, and California with 3.8%.

Demand – World consumption of cotton in 2020/21 is forecasted to rise +12.9% yr/yr to 115.814 million bales but remain below the 2017/18 record high of 122.878. The largest consumers of cotton in 2020/21 are expected to be China with 33.2% of the world total, India with 20.7%, and Pakistan with 8.7%. U.S. consumption of cotton cloth has fallen sharply by almost half in the past decade due to the movement of the textile industry out of the U.S. to low-wage foreign countries. U.S. consumption of cotton by mills in 2020/21 is expected to rise by +2.0% yr/yr to 2.236 million bales.

Trade – World exports of cotton in 2020/21 are expected to rise +5.6% yr/yr to 43.557 million bales, but that is still below the 2012/13 record high of 46.435 million bales. Major world cotton importers for 2020/21 are expected to be China with 24.1% of total world imports, Bangladesh with 15.8%, Vietnam with 15.4%, Pakistan with 11.3%, and Turkey with 10.3%.

COTTON

Supply and Distribution of All Cotton in the United States In Thousands of 480-Pound Bales

Crop Year Beginning Aug. 1	Acre: Planted	Acre: Harvested	Yield	Supply: Beginning Stocks[3]	Supply: Production[4]	Supply: Imports	Supply: Total	Mill Use	Exports	Total	Unaccounted	Ending Stocks	Farm Price[5]	"A" Index Price[6]	Value of Production
	--- 1,000 Acres ---		Lbs./Acre												Million USD
2011-12	14,735	9,461	790	2,600	15,573	19	18,192	3,300	11,714	15,014	172	3,350	93.5	----	6,986.0
2012-13	12,264	9,322	892	3,350	17,314	10	20,674	3,500	13,026	16,526	-348	3,800	75.7	----	6,291.8
2013-14	10,407	7,544	821	3,800	12,909	13	16,722	3,550	10,530	14,080	-292	2,350	83.8	----	5,191.5
2014-15	11,037	9,347	838	2,350	16,319	12	18,681	3,575	11,246	14,821	-210	3,650	65.7	----	5,147.2
2015-16	8,581	8,075	766	3,650	12,888	33	16,571	3,450	9,153	12,603	-168	3,800	64.5	----	3,989.0
2016-17	10,074	9,508	867	3,800	17,170	7	20,977	3,250	14,917	18,167	-60	2,750	69.7	----	5,813.8
2017-18	12,718	11,100	905	2,750	20,923	3	23,676	3,225	15,847	19,072	-304	4,200	71.0	----	7,222.5
2018-19	14,100	9,991	882	4,200	18,367	5	22,570	2,980	14,760	17,740	-113	4,850	74 - 80	----	6,375.2
2019-20[1]	13,736	11,613	810	4,636	19,913		23,863	2,135	15,021	17,156		6,868		----	6,012.7
2020-21[2]	12,116	9,005	799	6,868	15,949		21,033	2,285	14,725	17,010		4,070		----	

[1] Preliminary. [2] Estimate. [3] Excludes preseason ginnings (adjusted to 480-lb. bale net weight basis). [4] Includes preseason ginnings. [5] Marketing year average price. [6] Average of 5 cheapest types of SLM 1 3/32" staple length cotton offered on the European market.
Source: Economic Research Service, U.S. Department of Agriculture (ERS-USDA)

World Production of All Cotton In Thousands of 480-Pound Bales

Crop Year Beginning Aug. 1	Australia	Brazil	Burkina	China	Greece	India	Mexico	Pakistan	Turkey	Turkmen-istan	United States	Uzbek-istan	World Total
2011-12	5,500	8,620	795	34,000	1,330	28,700	1,180	10,600	3,440	1,525	15,573	4,000	127,244
2012-13	4,600	6,020	1,215	35,000	1,194	28,500	1,036	9,300	2,650	1,700	17,314	4,600	123,901
2013-14	4,100	7,960	1,250	32,750	1,369	31,000	933	9,500	2,300	1,550	12,909	4,100	120,359
2014-15	2,300	7,180	1,350	30,000	1,286	29,500	1,319	10,600	3,200	1,525	16,319	3,900	119,217
2015-16	2,850	5,920	1,100	22,000	1,010	25,900	943	7,000	2,650	1,450	12,888	3,800	96,163
2016-17	4,050	7,020	1,310	22,750	1,033	27,000	765	7,700	3,200	1,325	17,170	3,725	106,677
2017-18	4,800	9,220	1,200	27,500	1,222	29,000	1,560	8,200	4,000	1,340	20,923	3,860	123,959
2018-19	2,200	13,000	850	27,750	1,410	25,800	1,735	7,600	3,750	910	18,367	3,275	118,578
2019-20[1]	625	13,780	880	27,250	1,675	29,500	1,570	6,200	3,450	920	19,913	3,500	122,137
2020-21[2]	2,500	12,000	900	27,500	1,400	29,500	1,050	4,300	2,900	1,000	14,953	3,500	112,867

[1] Preliminary. [2] Estimate. *Source: Foreign Agricultural Service, U.S. Department of Agriculture (FAS-USDA)*

World Consumption of Cotton In Thousands of 480-Pound Bales

Crop Year Beginning Aug. 1	Bangla-desh	Brazil	China	India	Indonesia	Mexico	Pakistan	Thailand	Turkey	United States	Uzbek-istan	Vietnam	World Total
2011-12	3,710	4,000	38,000	19,450	2,450	1,725	10,025	1,325	5,600	3,128	1,350	1,675	103,876
2012-13	4,710	4,100	36,000	21,050	3,050	1,825	10,775	1,525	6,050	3,848	1,450	2,250	107,880
2013-14	5,310	4,200	34,500	23,050	3,050	1,875	10,425	1,550	6,300	3,842	1,600	3,200	109,978
2014-15	5,810	3,400	34,500	24,500	3,250	1,875	10,625	1,500	6,500	3,785	1,750	4,100	112,589
2015-16	6,310	3,100	36,000	24,750	3,000	1,875	10,325	1,295	6,700	3,618	1,800	4,500	113,486
2016-17	6,810	3,200	38,500	24,350	3,300	1,775	10,325	1,225	6,650	3,310	2,000	5,400	116,473
2017-18	7,510	3,400	41,000	24,150	3,500	1,925	10,925	1,150	7,550	3,195	2,500	6,600	122,993
2018-19	7,210	3,400	39,500	24,000	3,150	2,025	10,725	1,075	6,900	2,883	2,800	7,000	120,203
2019-20[1]	6,910	2,700	33,000	20,000	2,400	1,525	9,225	800	6,600	1,989	3,000	6,300	102,571
2020-21[2]	7,310	3,003	38,500	24,000	2,700	1,625	10,025	675	7,200	2,356	3,150	6,700	115,814

[1] Preliminary. [2] Estimate. *Source: Foreign Agricultural Service, U.S. Department of Agriculture (FAS-USDA)*

World Ending Stocks of Cotton In Thousands of 480-Pound Bales

Crop Year Beginning Aug. 1	Argen-tina	Australia	Bangla-desh	Brazil	China	India	Mexico	Pakistan	Turkey	Turkmen-istan	United States	Uzbek-istan	World Total
2011-12	881	3,807	768	7,863	31,081	8,319	710	2,835	1,241	2,254	3,350	1,398	72,035
2012-13	789	2,399	1,166	5,541	50,361	9,195	646	2,710	1,315	2,554	3,800	1,548	89,326
2013-14	942	1,807	1,271	7,218	62,707	8,559	584	2,475	1,399	1,879	2,350	1,748	99,946
2014-15	727	1,818	1,331	7,112	66,420	10,586	693	2,890	1,671	1,279	3,650	1,298	106,830
2015-16	632	1,880	1,515	5,709	56,698	7,044	605	2,615	1,652	829	3,800	1,098	90,282
2016-17	472	2,189	1,630	6,929	45,919	7,880	445	2,315	1,594	654	2,750	1,073	80,301
2017-18	691	3,039	1,855	8,657	37,993	9,225	655	2,830	1,950	669	4,200	1,433	81,107
2018-19	696	1,572	1,783	12,256	35,670	9,304	694	2,495	1,694	629	4,850	1,158	80,270
2019-20[1]	1,128	802	2,515	14,404	36,899	17,884	669	3,390	2,766	724	7,250	1,358	99,276
2020-21[2]	1,358	1,767	2,250	13,426	36,274	19,384	544	2,515	2,516	724	4,600	1,408	96,317

[1] Preliminary. [2] Estimate. *Source: Foreign Agricultural Service, U.S. Department of Agriculture (FAS-USDA)*

World Exports of Cotton In Thousands of 480-Pound Bales

Crop Year Beginning Aug. 1	Australia	Benin	Brazil	Burkina	Cote d'Ivoire	Greece	India	Malaysia	Mali	Turkmen-istan	United States	Uzbek-istan	World Total
2011-12	4,640	275	4,792	770	480	1,100	11,080	825	625	700	11,714	2,500	46,029
2012-13	6,168	350	4,307	1,115	620	1,092	7,761	700	800	800	13,026	3,000	46,360
2013-14	4,852	600	2,230	1,300	830	1,288	9,261	210	900	1,625	10,530	2,300	41,197
2014-15	2,404	750	3,910	1,350	860	1,165	4,199	81	850	1,500	11,246	2,600	36,224
2015-16	2,828	650	4,314	1,080	780	959	5,764	142	1,000	1,250	9,153	2,200	34,945
2016-17	3,731	825	2,789	1,155	625	1,017	4,550	111	1,100	850	14,917	1,750	38,059
2017-18	3,915	1,070	4,174	1,225	620	1,076	5,182	152	1,300	625	16,281	1,000	41,711
2018-19	3,632	1,390	6,018	800	895	1,355	3,521	313	1,350	150	14,837	750	41,642
2019-20[1]	1,360	1,200	8,937	930	625	1,467	3,200	300	1,175	100	15,527	300	41,238
2020-21[2]	1,500	1,350	10,000	800	950	1,350	5,000	300	600	200	15,250	300	43,557

[1] Preliminary. [2] Estimate. *Source: Foreign Agricultural Service, U.S. Department of Agriculture (FAS-USDA)*

World Imports of Cotton In Thousands of 480-Pound Bales

Crop Year Beginning Aug. 1	Bangla-desh	China	India	Indonesia	Korea, South	Malaysia	Mexico	Pakistan	Taiwan	Thailand	Turkey	Vietnam	World Total
2011-12	3,400	24,533	600	2,500	1,170	1,125	1,000	900	863	1,263	2,382	1,625	45,423
2012-13	5,000	20,327	1,187	3,137	1,314	900	950	1,800	941	1,511	3,692	2,410	47,630
2013-14	5,300	14,122	675	2,989	1,286	350	1,040	1,200	857	1,546	4,475	3,200	41,436
2014-15	5,750	8,284	1,226	3,345	1,321	280	830	950	873	1,475	4,074	4,275	36,480
2015-16	6,375	4,406	1,072	2,941	1,175	443	975	3,300	707	1,275	4,486	4,600	35,720
2016-17	6,800	5,032	2,736	3,391	1,025	392	1,000	2,450	644	1,226	3,851	5,500	37,874
2017-18	7,600	5,710	1,677	3,517	904	739	925	3,400	632	1,149	4,391	7,000	41,551
2018-19	7,000	9,640	1,800	3,051	781	744	850	2,850	592	1,075	3,607	6,940	42,430
2019-20[1]	7,500	7,136	2,280	2,512	571	850	590	3,975	400	700	4,672	6,480	40,678
2020-21[2]	6,900	10,500	1,000	2,600	550	850	750	4,900	390	680	4,500	6,700	43,545

[1] Preliminary. [2] Estimate. *Source: Foreign Agricultural Service, U.S. Department of Agriculture (FAS-USDA)*

Average Spot Cotton, 1-3/32", Price (SLM) at Designated U.S. Markets[2] In Cents Per Pound (Net Weight)

Year	Aug.	Sept.	Oct.	Nov.	Dec.	Jan.	Feb.	Mar.	Apr.	May	June	July	Average
2011-12	106.41	105.50	100.97	97.13	89.53	94.10	89.52	87.76	88.07	77.26	72.12	70.91	89.94
2012-13	74.76	74.19	72.87	72.06	75.42	77.99	81.37	87.28	85.39	84.29	86.63	86.07	79.86
2013-14	87.80	85.65	83.66	78.84	83.15	85.69	87.45	90.94	89.71	87.41	82.74	73.89	84.74
2014-15	68.94	68.70	67.32	63.40	63.13	62.12	66.02	64.89	67.33	67.30	67.09	66.60	66.07
2015-16	66.09	63.93	65.06	65.17	66.47	64.76	62.05	59.91	63.51	64.42	66.74	73.12	65.10
2016-17	72.48	71.58	71.93	73.41	73.31	75.24	75.92	77.10	76.91	78.55	72.72	69.05	74.02
2017-18	70.52	71.93	69.47	71.10	76.32	80.83	78.44	82.77	82.52	85.57	88.85	87.33	78.80
2018-19	84.10	80.10	77.12	77.06	76.07	72.23	70.61	73.25	75.65	67.58	64.71	61.60	73.34
2019-20	57.69	60.54	64.25	64.46	65.87	69.08	65.86	55.84	52.25	56.02	59.48	61.94	61.11
2020-21[1]	62.08	62.94	67.40	69.92	74.03	80.38	86.37						71.87

[1] Preliminary. *Source: Agricultural Marketing Service, U.S. Department of Agriculture (AMS-USDA)*

Average Producer Price Index of Gray Cotton Broadwovens Index 1982 = 100

Year	Jan.	Feb.	Mar.	Apr.	May	June	July	Aug.	Sept.	Oct.	Nov.	Dec.	Average
2009	111.0	111.0	111.0	107.2	107.2	107.2	107.2	107.5	107.5	107.5	108.9	108.9	108.5
2010	109.8	113.7	113.7	113.7	114.9	116.6	119.0	118.8	118.8	118.8	119.1	119.1	116.3
2011	144.8	145.4	147.0	153.5	154.3	154.3	162.1	162.0	161.3	148.5	148.5	141.1	151.9
2012	139.1	139.2	139.2	135.0	135.0	135.2	126.1	126.1	126.1	124.7	123.6	122.7	131.0
2013	122.6	122.3	123.3	126.9	126.4	126.4	126.4	126.4	126.4	127.7	127.7	127.7	125.9
2014	124.5	124.5	121.8	124.7	124.7	124.7	124.8	124.8	124.8	123.3	123.3	123.3	124.1
2015	118.2	121.2	121.2	121.5	121.5	121.5	123.7	123.7	123.7	123.5	123.5	123.5	122.2
2016	122.6	122.6	122.6	121.9	121.9	121.9	122.6	122.6	122.6	123.6	123.6	123.6	122.7
2017	125.2	125.3	125.3	129.2	129.2	129.2	128.5	128.5	128.5	126.4	126.4	126.4	127.3
2018[1]	127.3	127.3	127.3	133.1	133.1	133.1	133.1	----	----	----	----	----	130.6

[1] Preliminary. *Source: Bureau of Labor Statistics (0337-01), U.S. Department of Commerce*

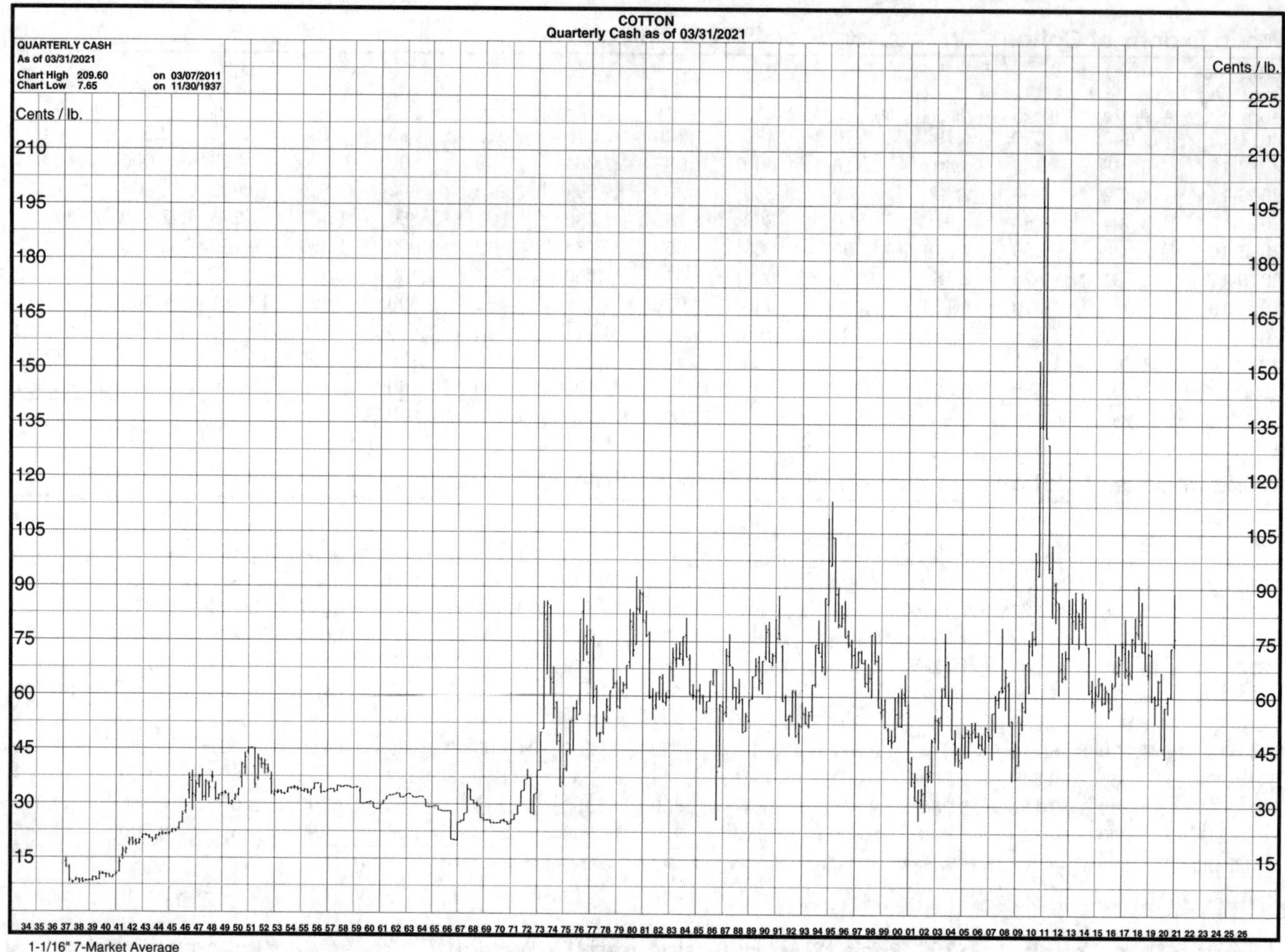

Average Price of SLM 1-1/16", Cotton/5 at Designated U.S. Markets In Cents Per Pound (Net Weight)

Year	Aug.	Sept.	Oct.	Nov.	Dec.	Jan.	Feb.	Mar.	Apr.	May	June	July	Average
2011-12	102.89	102.06	97.63	93.59	85.99	89.83	85.17	83.14	83.37	72.51	67.35	66.14	85.81
2012-13	69.97	69.38	68.03	67.34	70.61	73.33	76.87	82.80	80.94	79.84	82.18	81.62	75.24
2013-14	83.36	81.25	77.37	74.43	78.75	81.43	83.21	86.70	85.48	83.20	78.54	69.63	80.28
2014-15	64.99	64.83	63.51	59.64	59.38	58.19	61.74	60.65	63.08	63.06	62.86	62.36	62.02
2015-16	61.85	59.70	60.83	60.99	62.32	60.69	58.06	55.96	59.65	60.36	62.78	69.25	61.04
2016-17	68.57	67.65	68.04	69.42	69.69	71.81	73.02	74.33	74.13	75.75	69.85	66.24	70.71
2017-18	67.71	69.12	66.67	68.09	73.13	77.58	75.24	79.57	79.34	82.40	85.54	83.95	75.70
2018-19	80.75	76.72	73.90	73.72	72.66	68.72	67.17	69.78	72.27	64.05	61.19	58.08	69.92
2019-20	54.17	57.01	60.63	60.89	62.39	65.60	62.38	52.35	48.73	52.40	56.00	58.46	57.58
2020-21[1]	58.60	59.46	63.87	66.30	70.37	76.69	82.79						68.30

[1] Preliminary. [2] Grade 41, leaf 4, staple 34, mike 35-36 and 43-49 , strength 23.5-26.4. *Source: Agricultural Marketing Service, U.S. Department of Agriculture (AMS-USDA)*

Average Price[1] Received by Farmers for Upland Cotton in the United States In Cents Per Pound

Year	Aug.	Sept.	Oct.	Nov.	Dec.	Jan.	Feb.	Mar.	Apr.	May	June	July	Average
2011-12	94.0	93.5	92.2	92.6	88.9	90.1	92.3	90.0	90.4	84.4	77.1	76.6	88.5
2012-13	71.4	70.7	69.8	69.2	71.8	72.9	76.9	77.5	78.4	78.3	79.3	80.9	74.8
2013-14	76.9	74.6	77.8	75.9	77.2	77.5	80.2	81.7	82.7	81.7	83.9	84.7	79.6
2014-15	70.5	68.9	64.5	62.7	60.8	59.1	57.8	61.3	62.6	65.9	66.8	69.3	64.2
2015-16	58.0	60.3	57.9	60.0	61.3	60.3	59.8	58.2	58.7	63.2	67.0	74.5	61.6
2016-17	67.1	67.0	66.0	67.2	67.9	67.0	68.8	69.2	69.3	69.9	70.4	73.0	68.6
2017-18	64.7	64.1	66.5	67.3	68.6	68.9	68.1	68.3	67.7	69.6	75.7	76.4	68.8
2018-19	69.7	70.8	72.1	72.9	72.6	65.4	67.6	68.9	70.5	69.6	68.2	74.7	70.3
2019-20	56.2	59.4	59.0	59.7	61.6	59.7	60.7	57.6	54.9	55.0	56.5	60.3	58.4
2020-21[2]	57.3	59.3	60.1	63.4	65.6	69.5							62.5

[1] Weighted average by sales. [2] Preliminary. *Source: Agricultural Marketing Service, U.S. Department of Agriculture (AMS-USDA)*

Purchases Reported by Exchanges in Designated U.S. Spot Markets[1] In Running Bales

Crop Year Beginning Aug. 1	Aug.	Sept.	Oct.	Nov.	Dec.	Jan.	Feb.	Mar.	Apr.	May	June	July	Market Total
2011-12	9,762	31,213	95,360	122,388	131,642	227,089	115,427	119,698	25,990	20,764	20,687	36,712	956,732
2012-13	38,533	55,227	81,437	408,050	417,927	382,992	112,442	62,556	65,991	27,923	25,573	12,135	1,690,786
2013-14	20,398	26,066	52,042	198,579	433,317	345,007	141,663	57,669	24,792	24,878	7,569	6,815	1,338,795
2014-15	21,486	35,934	141,203	200,756	593,113	425,345	404,710	121,097	117,746	26,509	19,259	20,128	2,127,286
2015-16	18,634	24,429	56,127	220,807	424,830	297,380	196,419	128,004	61,364	28,446	16,622	56,367	1,529,429
2016-17	9,555	26,482	54,441	251,092	253,534	549,344	214,644	159,483	38,442	8,097	2,411	3,121	1,570,646
2017-18	16,659	20,322	57,282	341,259	429,829	427,512	255,750	152,678	156,773	152,630	35,949	13,783	2,060,426
2018-19	11,511	5,796	18,533	79,339	122,132	226,334	204,858	331,767	115,807	74,715	64,716	27,775	1,283,283
2019-20	35,241	71,105	103,590	199,665	455,781	350,099	108,467	49,111	77,192	46,280	47,722	----	1,544,253
2020-21	111,277	70,474	120,167	192,423	419,707	229,316	109,048						1,252,412

[1] Seven markets. *Source: Agricultural Marketing Service, U.S. Department of Agriculture (AMS-USDA)*

Production of All Cotton in the United States In Thousands of 480-Pound Bales

Year	Alabama	Arizona	Arkansas	California	Georgia	Louisiana	Mississippi	Missouri	North Carolina	South Carolina	Ten-nessee	Texas	U.S. Total
2011	685	820	1,277	1,341	2,465	511	1,200	741	1,026	519	813	3,540	15,573
2012	745	612	1,297	1,261	2,910	478	993	731	1,225	593	743	5,015	17,314
2013	590	483	720	943	2,320	326	719	496	766	360	414	4,185	12,909
2014	653	520	787	714	2,570	404	1,078	570	995	528	494	6,203	16,319
2015	554	308	471	526	2,255	189	672	400	527	155	305	5,748	12,888
2016	706	395	840	747	2,180	268	1,081	566	343	250	575	8,133	17,170
2017	808	515	1,074	865	2,225	404	1,351	750	741	471	732	9,296	20,923
2018	888	466	1,133	914	1,955	420	1,462	921	702	420	770	6,884	18,367
2019[1]	1,028	393	1,506	821	2,740	582	1,621	915	1,040	497	960	6,337	19,913
2020[2]	790	370	1,300	610	2,300	350	1,260	740	570	315	680	5,247	15,949

[1] Preliminary. [2] Forecast. *Source: Agricultural Statistics Board, U.S. Department of Agriculture (ASB-USDA)*

Cotton Production and Yield Estimates in the United States

	Forecasts of Production (1,000 Bales of 480 Lbs.[1])						Actual	Forecasts of Yield (Lbs. Per Harvested Acre)						Actual
Year	Aug.1	Sept.1	Oct. 1	Nov. 1	Dec. 1	Jan. 1	Crop	Aug.1	Sept.1	Oct. 1	Nov. 1	Dec. 1	Jan. 1	Yield
2011	16,554	16,556	16,608	16,300	15,827	----	15,573	822	807	809	794	771	----	790
2012	17,651	17,109	17,287	17,447	17,257	----	17,314	784	786	795	802	793	----	892
2013	13,053	12,899	NA	13,105	13,069	----	12,909	813	796	NA	808	806	----	821
2014	17,502	16,538	16,255	16,397	15,923	----	16,319	820	803	790	797	773	----	838
2015	13,082	13,428	13,338	13,281	13,031	----	12,888	795	789	784	782	768	----	766
2016	15,879	16,142	16,034	16,162	16,524	----	17,170	800	802	797	803	821	----	867
2017	20,545	21,758	21,115	21,377	21,440	----	20,923	892	908	889	900	902	----	905
2018	19,235	19,682	19,763	18,408	18,588	----	18,367	911	895	901	852	860	----	882
2019	22,516	21,862	21,705	20,817	20,206	----	19,913	855	839	833	799	775	----	810
2020	18,080	17,064	17,045	17,092	15,949	----	15,949	938	910	909	911	850	----	799

[1] Net weight bales. *Source: Agricultural Statistics Board, U.S. Department of Agriculture (ASB-USDA)*

Supply and Distribution of Upland Cotton in the United States In Thousands of 480-Pound Bales

Crop Year	Area			Supply				Disappearance				Farm
Beginning Aug. 1	Planted (1,000 Acres)	Harvested (1,000 Acres)	Yield Lbs./Acre	Beginning Stocks[3]	Pro-duction	Imports	Total Supply	Mill Use	Exports	Total	Ending Stocks	Price[5] Cents/ Lb.
2011-12	14,428	9,156	772	2,572	14,722	13	17,307	3,278	11,120	14,398	3,081	88.5
2012-13	12,026	9,085	874	3,081	16,534	6	19,621	3,478	12,182	15,660	3,613	74.8
2013-14	10,206	7,345	802	3,613	12,275	6	15,894	3,527	9,850	13,377	2,225	79.6
2014-15	10,845	9,157	826	2,225	15,753	9	17,987	3,550	10,836	14,386	3,391	64.2
2015-16	8,422	7,903	756	3,391	12,455	30	15,876	3,425	8,619	12,044	3,664	61.6
2016-17	9,878	9,320	855	3,664	16,601	5	20,270	3,221	14,303	17,524	2,686	68.6
2017-18	12,465	10,850	895	2,686	20,223	1	22,910	3,198	15,211	18,409	4,197	68.8
2018-19	13,850	9,742	865	4,097	17,566	5	21,663	2,953	14,092	17,045	4,636	70.3
2019-20[1]	13,507	11,389	810	4,636	19,227		23,866	2,485	14,400	16,885	7,013	58.4
2020-21[2]	13,475	8,812	839	7,013	15,395		25,853	2,780	15,325	18,105	7,743	62.5

[1] Preliminary. [2] Estimate. [3] Excludes preseason ginnings (adjusted to 480-lb. bale net weight basis). [4] Includes preseason ginnings.
[5] Marketing year average price. *Source: Economic Research Service, U.S. Department of Agriculture (ERS-USDA)*

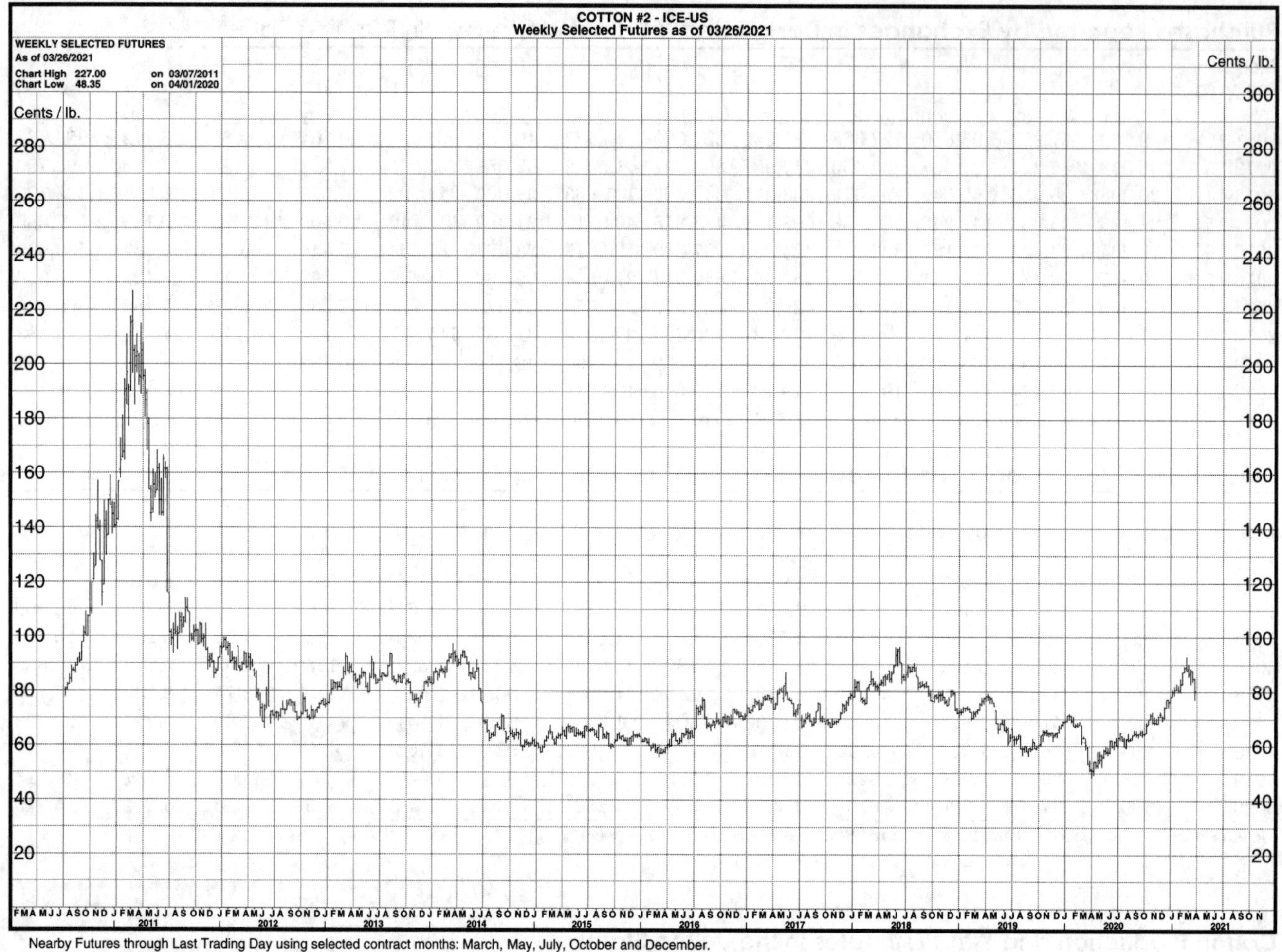

Nearby Futures through Last Trading Day using selected contract months: March, May, July, October and December.

Volume of Trading of Cotton #2 Futures in New York In Contracts

Year	Jan.	Feb.	Mar.	Apr.	May	June	July	Aug.	Sept.	Oct.	Nov.	Dec.	Total
2011	457,454	719,075	590,294	602,903	325,606	536,555	293,608	290,265	307,617	350,452	598,711	215,914	5,288,454
2012	471,729	605,161	499,276	660,539	564,011	826,818	308,028	339,672	349,649	584,358	632,610	288,501	6,130,352
2013	599,171	738,954	474,475	725,015	494,848	729,167	282,565	464,074	273,354	487,233	588,624	297,544	6,155,024
2014	544,180	602,542	446,810	568,063	399,736	611,785	362,461	338,548	460,119	477,742	625,593	350,304	5,787,883
2015	474,061	764,365	532,511	774,667	504,552	748,679	391,137	541,234	378,522	492,136	718,549	405,429	6,725,842
2016	556,311	939,909	544,144	920,712	567,195	802,595	582,169	538,811	437,283	528,534	876,713	408,670	7,703,046
2017	621,642	919,593	648,217	805,263	728,004	731,750	367,996	499,490	527,357	539,450	954,722	564,023	7,907,507
2018	908,692	1,040,986	697,571	967,537	865,014	966,955	395,024	544,209	451,364	641,924	889,009	507,810	8,876,095
2019	607,201	901,354	685,982	877,964	771,698	778,893	467,666	555,618	498,553	771,503	953,641	591,376	8,461,449
2020	803,523	1,108,447	999,072	819,599	497,631	678,605	409,570	476,008	508,333	701,383	828,278	493,784	8,324,233

Contract size = 50,000 lbs. *Source: ICE Futures U.S. (ICE)*

Average Open Interest of Cotton #2 Futures in New York In Contracts

Year	Jan.	Feb.	Mar.	Apr.	May	June	July	Aug.	Sept.	Oct.	Nov.	Dec.
2011	204,871	198,798	176,675	180,626	150,430	148,695	138,168	144,300	150,834	155,592	149,292	146,219
2012	156,940	180,632	183,618	186,859	188,255	185,629	171,383	180,207	183,282	199,026	179,969	165,382
2013	185,106	201,378	205,753	188,311	181,012	173,729	162,260	191,013	178,447	203,972	172,006	164,247
2014	180,149	171,213	178,245	178,514	190,808	169,165	152,321	167,437	181,359	190,436	181,192	175,349
2015	197,949	192,586	182,898	180,941	191,700	175,835	177,911	185,267	180,786	192,945	184,447	188,025
2016	188,149	196,230	211,958	203,691	191,903	197,043	216,925	236,332	238,644	251,736	250,363	248,786
2017	263,192	275,644	277,202	252,849	254,360	219,791	213,858	221,829	238,371	230,544	232,469	262,608
2018	301,515	271,212	272,354	270,033	290,493	289,963	257,708	260,562	253,033	259,661	241,659	217,465
2019	228,469	234,159	223,225	218,548	217,558	192,072	190,297	213,722	231,086	238,617	224,486	205,207
2020	251,311	219,080	204,701	183,388	179,296	172,208	173,848	194,284	218,706	237,465	229,699	220,397

Contract size = 50,000 lbs. *Source: ICE Futures U.S. (ICE)*

Average Spot Prices of U.S. Cotton,[2] Base Quality (SLM) at Designated Markets In Cents Per Pound

Crop Year Beginning Aug. 1	Dallas (EastTex.-Okl.)	Fresno (San Joaquin Valley)	Greenville (South-east)	Greenwood (South Delta)	Lubbock (West Texas)	Memphis (North Delta)	Phoenix Desert (Southwest)	Average
2011-12	86.95	85.73	83.30	87.75	83.31	86.74	86.91	85.81
2012-13	73.79	74.74	77.50	76.56	73.68	76.56	73.89	75.24
2013-14	79.27	78.88	82.74	81.85	79.14	81.85	78.23	80.28
2014-15	60.75	62.32	63.55	62.64	60.71	62.64	61.57	62.02
2015-16	59.29	60.88	63.32	62.44	59.16	62.44	59.73	61.04
2016-17	70.25	69.62	72.91	71.81	70.06	71.81	68.51	70.71
2017-18	74.38	74.55	78.79	77.59	73.14	77.60	73.52	76.01
2018-19	68.59	69.92	71.52	68.67	68.04	71.52	68.54	72.55
2019-20	57.06	55.16	60.53	59.40	56.90	59.47	54.66	57.58
2020-21[1]	53.28	52.00	57.18	56.00	53.28	56.00	51.50	54.17

[1] Preliminary [2] Prices are for mixed lots, net weight, uncompressed in warehouse.
Source: Agricultural Marketing Service, U.S. Department of Agriculture (AMS-USDA)

Cotton Ginnings[1] in the United States To: In Thousands of Running Bales

Crop Year	Aug. 1	Sept. 1	Sept. 15	Oct. 1	Oct. 15	Nov. 1	Nov. 15	Dec. 1	Dec. 15	Jan. 1	Jan. 15	Feb. 1	Mar. 1	Total Crop
2011-12	203	822	1,095	1,734	3,467	6,440	9,214	11,668	13,064	13,949	14,458	14,805	----	15,153
2012-13	60	473	756	1,552	2,943	6,307	9,394	12,263	14,194	15,327	16,029	16,547	----	16,834
2013-14	W	132	274	486	1,101	3,038	5,723	8,260	10,459	11,402	12,053	12,391	----	12,521
2014-15	1	367	696	1,154	2,108	4,807	7,530	10,246	12,601	14,214	15,030	15,538	----	15,876
2015-16	----	105	293	635	1,448	3,704	5,738	7,955	9,830	11,092	11,737	12,251	12,517	12,529
2016-17	35	438	701	1,167	2,308	5,016	7,584	10,296	12,261	13,858	14,840	15,881	16,559	16,710
2017-18	107	571	789	1,249	2,298	4,915	7,878	11,287	13,963	16,120	17,398	18,654	19,557	20,441
2018-19	20	489	745	1,287	2,421	4,878	7,083	10,265	12,275	NA	NA	16,651	17,473	17,909
2019-20	4	359	622	1,283	2,840	6,250	9,304	12,924	15,598	17,472	18,278	18,925	19,303	19,409
2020-21[2]	4	288	587	915	1,661	3,987	6,535	9,570	11,579	13,003	13,454	13,995	14,193	

[1] Excluding linters. [2] Preliminary. W = Withheld. *Source: National Agricultural Statistics Service, U.S. Department of Agriculture (NASS-USDA)*

Exports of All Cotton[2] from the United States In Thousands of Running Bales

Year	Aug.	Sept.	Oct.	Nov.	Dec.	Jan.	Feb.	Mar.	Apr.	May	June	July	Total
2011-12	302	303	422	776	930	1,284	1,583	1,672	1,322	1,241	942	785	11,561
2012-13	743	743	494	731	1,098	1,549	1,796	1,730	1,445	1,394	913	694	13,330
2013-14	767	533	414	606	975	1,417	1,345	1,347	1,087	873	607	446	10,418
2014-15	499	380	354	572	1,024	1,126	1,430	1,596	1,418	1,369	945	769	11,482
2015-16	560	404	370	396	643	776	918	1,083	1,083	1,077	1,042	909	9,261
2016-17	966	799	569	828	1,291	1,580	1,734	1,936	1,634	1,592	1,209	1,175	15,313
2017-18	933	577	447	727	1,399	1,647	1,980	2,329	2,198	1,989	1,428	1,088	16,741
2018-19	815	715	609	681	976	1,225	1,484	2,110	1,758	1,831	1,687	1,430	15,320
2019-20	1,034	910	732	841	1,320	1,699	1,969	2,003	1,254	1,238	1,464	1,629	16,093
2020-21[1]	1,424	924	1,195	1,329	1,425								15,110

[1] Preliminary. *Source: Foreign Agricultural Service, U.S. Department of Agriculture (FAS-USDA)*

U.S. Exports of American Cotton to Countries of Destination In Thousands of 480-Pound Bales

Crop Year Beginning Aug. 1	Canada	China	Hong Kong	Indo-nesia	Italy	Japan	Korea, South	Mexico	Philip-pines	Taiwan	Thailand	United Kingdom	Total
2010-11	10	4,863	47	889	53	186	513	1,245	37	357	712	1	14,714
2011-12	3	6,279	45	329	15	97	329	956	16	271	275	0	11,561
2012-13	2	5,615	105	533	8	120	355	979	31	419	353	0	13,330
2013-14	2	2,646	13	701	9	115	461	1,009	39	299	457	0	10,418
2014-15	2	2,709	16	978	22	114	670	950	42	349	466	7	11,460
2015-16	1	842	0	690	9	124	476	994	34	330	379	0	9,260
2016-17	1	2,310	1	1,476	9	121	598	1,007	65	422	577	1	15,314
2017-18	1	2,626	2	1,587	14	122	606	949	57	466	666	1	16,714
2018-19[1]	1	1,633	7	1,037	9	101	449	794	46	431	563	1	15,456
2019-20[2]	0	2,988	16	874	16	126	402	522	8	274	409	0	15,948

[1] Preliminary. [2] Estimate. *Source: Foreign Agricultural Service, U.S. Department of Agriculture (FAS-USDA)*

Cotton[1] Government Loan Program in the United States

Crop Year Beginning Aug. 1	Support Price (Cents Per Lb.)	Target Price (Cents Per Lb.)	Put Under Support (Ths Bales)	% of Production	Acquired (Ths. Bales)	Owned July 31 (Ths. Bales)
2009-10	52.00	71.3	8,278	70.2	0	0
2010-11	52.00	71.3	11,403	64.8	0	0
2011-12	52.00	71.3	7,268	49.3	1	0
2012-13	52.00	71.3	8,330	50.4	0	0
2013-14	52.00	71.3	3,981	32.4	0	0
2014-15	52.00	NA	7,625	48.4	0	0
2015-16	52.00	NA	6,758	54.3	0	0
2016-17	52.00	NA	9,373	56.4	0	0
2017-18	49.49	NA	9,597	46.7	0	0
2018-19[1]	52.00	NA	8,250	47.0	15	0

[1] Upland. [2] Preliminary. NA = Not applicable. *Source: Economic Research Service, U.S. Department of Agriculture (ERS-USDA)*

Weekly Outstanding Export Sales and Cumulative Exports of U.S. Cotton In Running Bales

Marketing Year 2019/2020 Week Ending	Weekly Exports	Accumulated Exports	Net Sales	Outstanding Sales
Aug 01, 2019	72,798	72,798	2,560,770	7,372,803
Aug 08, 2019	274,150	346,948	329,140	7,427,793
Aug 15, 2019	343,960	690,908	163,964	7,247,797
Aug 22, 2019	171,016	861,924	146,048	7,222,829
Aug 29, 2019	230,029	1,091,953	162,822	7,155,622
Sep 05, 2019	166,869	1,258,822	74,645	7,063,398
Sep 12, 2019	166,602	1,425,424	84,999	6,981,795
Sep 19, 2019	175,928	1,601,352	155,236	6,961,103
Sep 26, 2019	154,745	1,756,097	177,837	6,984,195
Oct 03, 2019	149,069	1,905,166	188,841	7,023,967
Oct 10, 2019	151,601	2,056,767	206,468	7,078,834
Oct 17, 2019	148,635	2,205,402	140,508	7,070,707
Oct 24, 2019	149,013	2,354,415	108,148	7,029,842
Oct 31, 2019	129,682	2,484,097	164,483	7,064,643
Nov 07, 2019	126,177	2,610,274	345,079	7,283,545
Nov 14, 2019	137,866	2,748,140	227,600	7,373,279
Nov 21, 2019	184,438	2,932,578	281,514	7,470,355
Nov 28, 2019	166,737	3,099,315	163,699	7,467,317
Dec 05, 2019	186,324	3,285,639	277,116	7,558,109
Dec 12, 2019	213,214	3,498,853	249,440	7,594,335
Dec 19, 2019	202,090	3,700,943	135,097	7,527,342
Dec 26, 2019	224,517	3,925,460	246,181	7,549,006
Jan 02, 2020	211,416	4,136,876	151,973	7,489,563
Jan 09, 2020	301,710	4,438,586	232,935	7,420,788
Jan 16, 2020	282,590	4,721,176	307,764	7,445,962
Jan 23, 2020	327,079	5,048,255	347,123	7,466,006
Jan 30, 2020	418,811	5,467,066	332,276	7,379,471
Feb 06, 2020	400,463	5,867,529	350,865	7,329,873
Feb 13, 2020	375,681	6,243,210	235,302	7,189,494
Feb 20, 2020	324,084	6,567,294	214,649	7,080,059
Feb 27, 2020	478,193	7,045,487	395,505	6,997,371
Mar 05, 2020	424,633	7,470,120	484,229	7,056,967
Mar 12, 2020	369,544	7,839,664	340,692	7,028,115
Mar 19, 2020	386,823	8,226,487	277,091	6,918,383
Mar 26, 2020	400,831	8,627,318	147,535	6,665,087
Apr 02, 2020	486,591	9,113,909	-5,167	6,173,329
Apr 09, 2020	311,951	9,425,860	-183,779	5,677,599
Apr 16, 2020	266,243	9,692,103	15,660	5,427,016
Apr 23, 2020	253,700	9,945,803	434,818	5,608,134
Apr 30, 2020	370,317	10,316,120	370,282	5,608,099
May 07, 2020	241,730	10,557,850	238,084	5,604,453
May 14, 2020	252,233	10,810,083	128,898	5,481,118
May 21, 2020	267,411	11,077,494	44,641	5,258,348
May 28, 2020	237,923	11,315,417	-10,089	5,010,336
Jun 04, 2020	294,327	11,609,744	399,621	5,115,630
Jun 11, 2020	348,300	11,958,044	97,573	4,864,903
Jun 18, 2020	316,129	12,274,173	102,725	4,651,499
Jun 25, 2020	276,959	12,551,132	67,296	4,441,836
Jul 02, 2020	329,317	12,880,449	43,772	4,156,291
Jul 09, 2020	311,657	13,192,106	-17,455	3,827,179
Jul 16, 2020	271,330	13,463,436	-13,084	3,542,765
Jul 23, 2020	320,784	13,784,220	118,698	3,340,679
Jul 30, 2020	346,759	14,130,979	-68,537	2,925,383
Aug 06, 2020	43,555	14,174,534	1,408	2,883,236

Marketing Year 2020/2021 Week Ending	Weekly Exports	Accumulated Exports	Net Sales	Outstanding Sales
Aug 06, 2020	278,612	278,612	2,890,127	6,288,532
Aug 13, 2020	421,533	700,145	128,026	5,995,025
Aug 20, 2020	277,513	977,658	156,627	5,874,139
Aug 27, 2020	273,891	1,251,549	131,458	5,731,706
Sep 03, 2020	230,526	1,482,075	126,671	5,627,851
Sep 10, 2020	187,872	1,669,947	519,604	5,959,583
Sep 17, 2020	281,948	1,951,895	92,691	5,770,326
Sep 24, 2020	218,197	2,170,092	233,751	5,785,880
Oct 01, 2020	142,334	2,312,426	178,427	5,821,973
Oct 08, 2020	192,621	2,505,047	98,870	5,728,222
Oct 15, 2020	194,093	2,699,140	227,760	5,761,889
Oct 22, 2020	228,801	2,927,941	288,693	5,821,781
Oct 29, 2020	270,048	3,197,989	115,557	5,667,290
Nov 05, 2020	292,992	3,490,981	236,760	5,611,058
Nov 12, 2020	277,325	3,768,306	131,406	5,465,139
Nov 19, 2020	183,018	3,951,324	354,689	5,636,810
Nov 26, 2020	180,818	4,132,142	277,863	5,733,855
Dec 03, 2020	323,190	4,450,336	403,042	5,813,707
Dec 10, 2020	251,260	4,701,596	420,902	5,983,349
Dec 17, 2020	276,776	4,978,372	412,309	6,118,882
Dec 24, 2020	275,075	5,253,447	287,902	6,131,709
Dec 31, 2020	269,998	5,523,445	153,052	6,014,763
Jan 07, 2021	274,554	5,797,999	326,002	6,066,211
Jan 14, 2021	322,381	6,120,380	292,355	6,036,185
Jan 21, 2021	275,268	6,395,648	322,713	6,083,630
Jan 28, 2021	318,956	6,714,604	286,695	6,051,369
Feb 04, 2021	433,629	7,148,233	275,364	5,893,104
Feb 11, 2021	311,835	7,460,068	119,515	5,700,784
Feb 18, 2021	292,374	7,752,442	247,813	5,656,223
Feb 25, 2021	377,400	8,129,842	169,041	5,447,864
Mar 04, 2021	351,610	8,481,452	211,990	5,308,244
Mar 11, 2021	351,871	8,833,323	437,726	5,394,099
Mar 18, 2021	313,514	9,146,837	271,194	5,351,779
Mar 25, 2021				
Apr 01, 2021				
Apr 08, 2021				
Apr 15, 2021				
Apr 22, 2021				
Apr 29, 2021				
May 06, 2021				
May 13, 2021				
May 20, 2021				
May 27, 2021				
Jun 03, 2021				
Jun 10, 2021				
Jun 17, 2021				
Jun 24, 2021				
Jul 01, 2021				
Jul 08, 2021				
Jul 15, 2021				
Jul 22, 2021				
Jul 29, 2021				

Source: Foreign Agricultural Service, U.S. Department of Agriculture (FAS-USDA)

Cottonseed and Products

Cottonseed is crushed to produce both oil and meal. Cottonseed oil is typically used for cooking oil, and cottonseed meal is fed to livestock. Before the cottonseed is crushed for oil and meal, it is de-linted of its linters. Linters are used for padding in furniture, absorbent cotton swabs, and for the manufacture of many cellulose products. The sediment left by cottonseed oil refining, called "foots," provides fatty acids for industrial products. The value of cottonseeds represents a substantial 18% of a cotton producer's income.

Prices – The average monthly price of cottonseed oil in 2020 rose by +28.8% yr/yr to 43.96 cents per pound, but remained far below the 2008 record high of 68.09 cents per pound. The average monthly price of cottonseed meal in 2020 rose by +24.0% yr/yr to $279.940 per short ton, farther below the 2014 record high of $368.98 per short ton.

Supply – World production of cottonseed in the 2020/21 marketing year is forecasted to fall -5.4% to 42.009 million metric tons, farther below the 2011-12 record high of 48.007. The world's largest cottonseed producers in 2020/21 are expected to be India with 29.3% of world production, China with 27.1%, the U.S. with 9.9%, and Pakistan with 4.6%. U.S. production of cottonseed in the 2020/21 marketing year is expected to fall by -22.8% yr/yr to 4.587 million tons. U.S. production of cottonseed oil in 2020/21 is expected to fall -4.4% to 460 million pounds, but far below the 20-year high of 957 million pounds posted in 2004-05.

Demand – U.S. cottonseed crushed (consumed) in the U.S. in the 2020/21 marketing year is expected to fall -3.6% to 1.650 million tons, which is far below the levels of over 4 million tons seen in the 1970s.

Trade – U.S. exports of cottonseed in 2020/21 are expected to fall -26.7% to 250 million tons. U.S. imports in 2020/21 are expected to rise by +400.0% to 5,000 short tons.

World Production of Cottonseed In Thousands of Metric Ton

Crop Year Beginning Oct. 1	Argentina	Australia	Brazil	Burkina	Burma	China	European Union	India	Mali	Pakistan	Turkey	United States	World Total
2012-13	278	1,377	2,019	335	389	13,720	484	12,100	246	4,000	870	5,140	46,348
2013-14	451	1,205	2,671	345	368	12,835	512	13,161	241	4,100	740	3,813	45,268
2014-15	407	664	2,349	373	370	11,757	526	12,524	294	4,616	1,050	4,649	44,372
2015-16	180	881	1,937	304	295	8,600	407	10,996	276	3,032	870	3,668	35,631
2016-17	163	1,250	2,298	362	285	8,800	417	11,463	351	3,336	1,050	4,871	38,978
2017-18	218	1,442	3,019	332	310	10,800	486	12,312	396	3,552	1,300	5,826	45,089
2018-19	245	661	4,254	235	289	10,875	546	10,953	359	3,292	1,224	5,108	43,104
2019-20[1]	282	187	4,575	243	299	10,679	640	12,524	382	2,686	1,126	5,393	44,420
2020-21[2]	297	781	3,984	248	301	11,365	537	12,312	81	1,949	947	4,161	42,009

[1] Preliminary. [2] Estimate. *Source: The Oil World*

Salient Statistics of Cottonseed in the United States In Thousands of Short Tons

Crop Year Beginning Aug. 1	Supply: Stocks	Supply: Production	Supply: Imports	Supply: Total Supply	Disappearance: Crush	Disappearance: Exports	Disappearance: Other	Disappearance: Total	Farm Price USD/Ton	Value of Production Mil. USD	Products Produced: Oil (Million Pounds)	Products Produced: Meal (1,000 Short Tons)
	In Thousands of Short Tons											
2012-13	430	5,666	182	6,278	2,500	191	3,094	5,786	252.0	1,456	800	1,125
2013-14	492	4,203	198	4,893	2,000	219	2,250	4,468	246.0	1,054	630	900
2014-15	425	5,125	60	5,610	1,900	228	3,045	5,173	194.0	1,016	610	855
2015-16	437	4,043	16	4,496	1,500	136	2,469	4,105	227.0	933	465	705
2016-17	391	5,369	51	5,811	1,769	342	3,300	5,411	195.0	1,056	542	805
2017-18	400	6,422	0	6,822	1,854	478	4,040	6,372	139.0	912	561	845
2018-19	451	5,631	1	6,083	1,760	387	3,458	5,606	115-155	878	456	748
2019-20[1]	477	5,945	1	6,423	1,712	341	3,914	5,967		494		
2020-21[2]	456	4,587	5	5,048	1,650	250	2,807	4,707				

[1] Preliminary. [2] Estimate. *Source: Economic Research Service, U.S. Department of Agriculture (ERS-USDA)*

Average Wholesale Price of Cottonseed Meal (41% Solvent)[2] in Memphis In Dollars Per Short Ton

Year	Jan.	Feb.	Mar.	Apr.	May	June	July	Aug.	Sept.	Oct.	Nov.	Dec.	Average
2012	213.00	190.00	225.00	240.63	270.00	294.38	350.50	407.50	393.75	343.00	376.88	345.00	304.14
2013	327.50	279.38	301.88	314.50	311.88	329.38	344.50	330.00	374.38	355.00	345.00	401.88	334.60
2014	378.34	388.75	401.25	405.50	416.88	412.50	359.50	310.00	360.63	346.88	313.13	334.38	368.98
2015	313.75	302.50	310.50	288.13	274.38	281.00	299.38	295.63	293.50	292.50	291.88	267.50	292.55
2016	248.75	238.13	216.50	207.50	242.50	284.00	280.00	280.00	285.00	241.88	221.00	217.50	246.90
2017	223.50	221.88	210.63	195.00	179.50	179.38	200.84	198.50	213.75	229.00	228.75	232.50	209.44
2018	259.00	303.13	323.13	263.13	262.50	257.50	253.13	260.00	258.75	249.00	240.00	243.75	264.42
2019	247.50	235.00	226.25	216.50	215.00	215.63	218.00	221.25	215.83	213.13	233.75	250.83	225.72
2020[1]	239.38	250.63	259.00	281.88	251.88	245.50	245.00	245.00	248.50	301.88	365.63	425.00	279.94

[1] Preliminary. *Source: Economic Research Service, U.S. Department of Agriculture (ERS-USDA)*

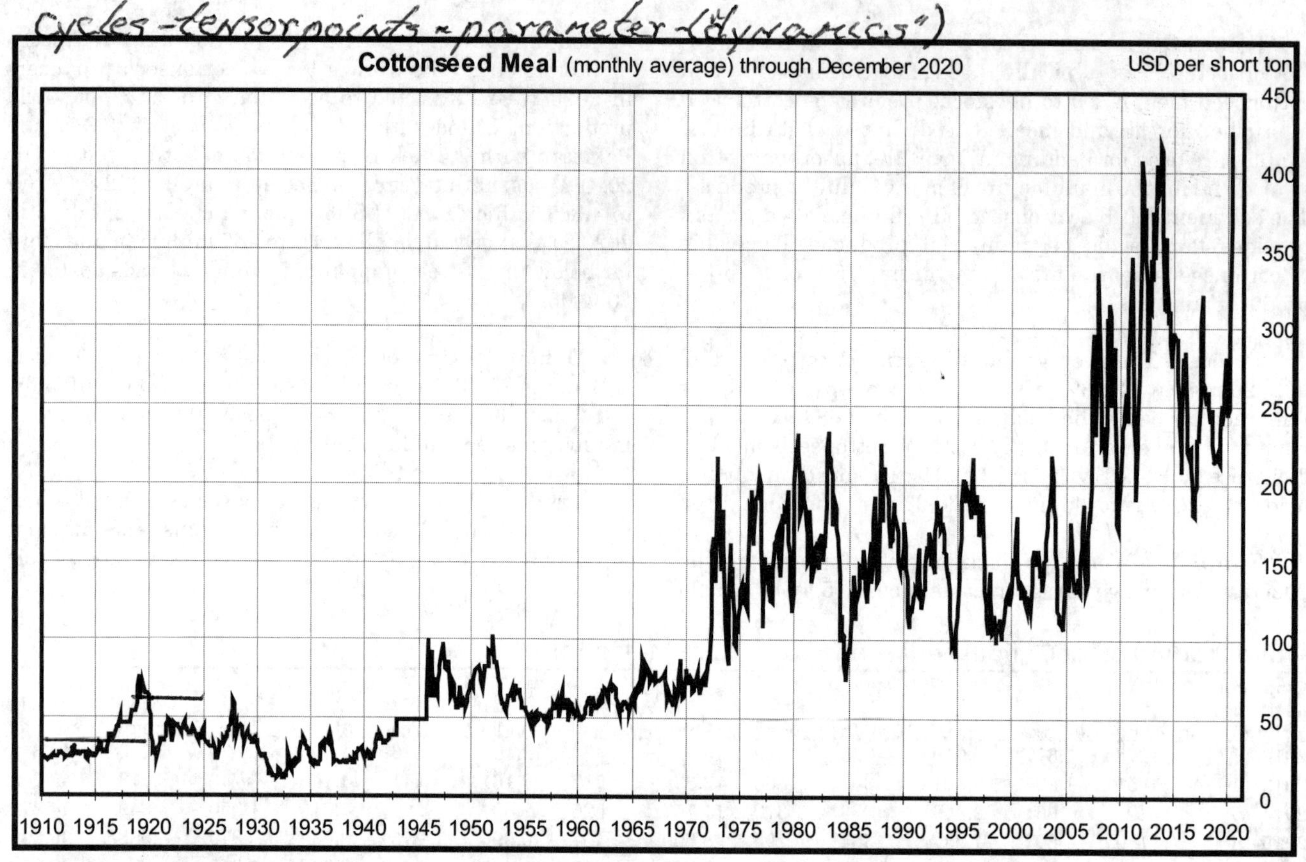

Supply and Distribution of Cottonseed Oil in the United States In Millions of Pounds

Crop Year Beginning Oct. 1	Supply: Stocks	Supply: Production	Supply: Imports	Supply: Total Supply	Disappearance: Domestic	Disappearance: Exports	Disappearance: Total	Per Capita Consumption of Salad & Cooking Oils --- In Lbs. ---	Utilization Food Uses: Shortening	Utilization Food Uses: Salad & Cooking Oils	Utilization Food Uses: Total	Prices: U.S.[3] (Crude) --- $/Metric Ton ---	Prices: Rott[4] (Cif)
2011-12	165	755	10.0	930	572	259	830	100	NA	NA	NA	1,173	1,188
2012-13	100	800	20.0	920	599	221	820	100	----	----	----	1,071	1,121
2013-14	100	630	32.0	762	514	148	662	100	----	----	----	1,337	----
2014-15	90	610	17.0	717	541	119	659	58	----	----	----	1,008	----
2015-16	58	465	7.0	530	433	55	488	42	----	----	----	1,011	----
2016-17	42	542	0	583	435	104	539	44	----	----	----	902	----
2017-18	44	561	0	605	461	112	573	32	----	----	----	703	----
2018-19	32	456	0	488	370	83	453	35	----	----	----	775	----
2019-20[1]	35	481	0	517	388	84	472	45	----	----	----	882	----
2020-21[2]	45	460	0	510	400	65	465	45	----	----	----	882	----

[1] Preliminary. [2] Estimate. [3] Valley Points FOB; Tank Cars. [4] Rotterdam; US, PBSY, fob gulf. W = Withheld.
Source: Economic Research Service, U.S. Department of Agriculture (ERS-USDA)

Exports of Cottonseed Oil (Crude and Refined) from the United States In Thousands of Pounds

Year	Jan.	Feb.	Mar.	Apr.	May	June	July	Aug.	Sept.	Oct.	Nov.	Dec.	Total
2011	8,142	11,103	19,150	17,085	15,053	9,531	11,479	14,273	13,515	25,841	31,753	18,691	195,617
2012	18,551	12,596	31,375	19,626	20,622	24,030	17,908	21,019	16,715	21,956	17,805	15,878	238,080
2013	19,609	20,389	16,582	21,550	21,218	19,340	15,042	15,886	15,406	15,674	13,338	11,094	205,128
2014	13,667	19,061	18,084	20,029	8,709	7,165	2,999	5,895	12,687	12,384	11,780	14,205	146,664
2015	19,843	8,117	10,559	11,852	6,246	6,162	4,005	8,573	4,379	8,700	4,634	6,080	99,149
2016	5,390	1,338	3,211	5,406	4,703	3,031	2,271	5,894	4,168	6,622	15,929	10,107	68,070
2017	10,899	8,438	9,269	8,538	6,577	5,865	5,385	11,003	5,265	7,084	8,038	6,769	93,130
2018	16,387	9,282	10,793	6,797	7,626	6,980	18,567	8,421	4,152	13,262	13,725	4,527	120,518
2019	10,254	5,764	12,006	4,045	3,495	8,860	3,112	3,251	9,663	6,932	13,835	6,506	87,723
2020[1]	7,387	4,120	6,094	14,813	4,922	5,424	4,624	3,120	5,917	6,340	5,883	4,765	73,409

[1] Preliminary. *Source: Economic Research Service, U.S. Department of Agriculture (ERS-USDA)*

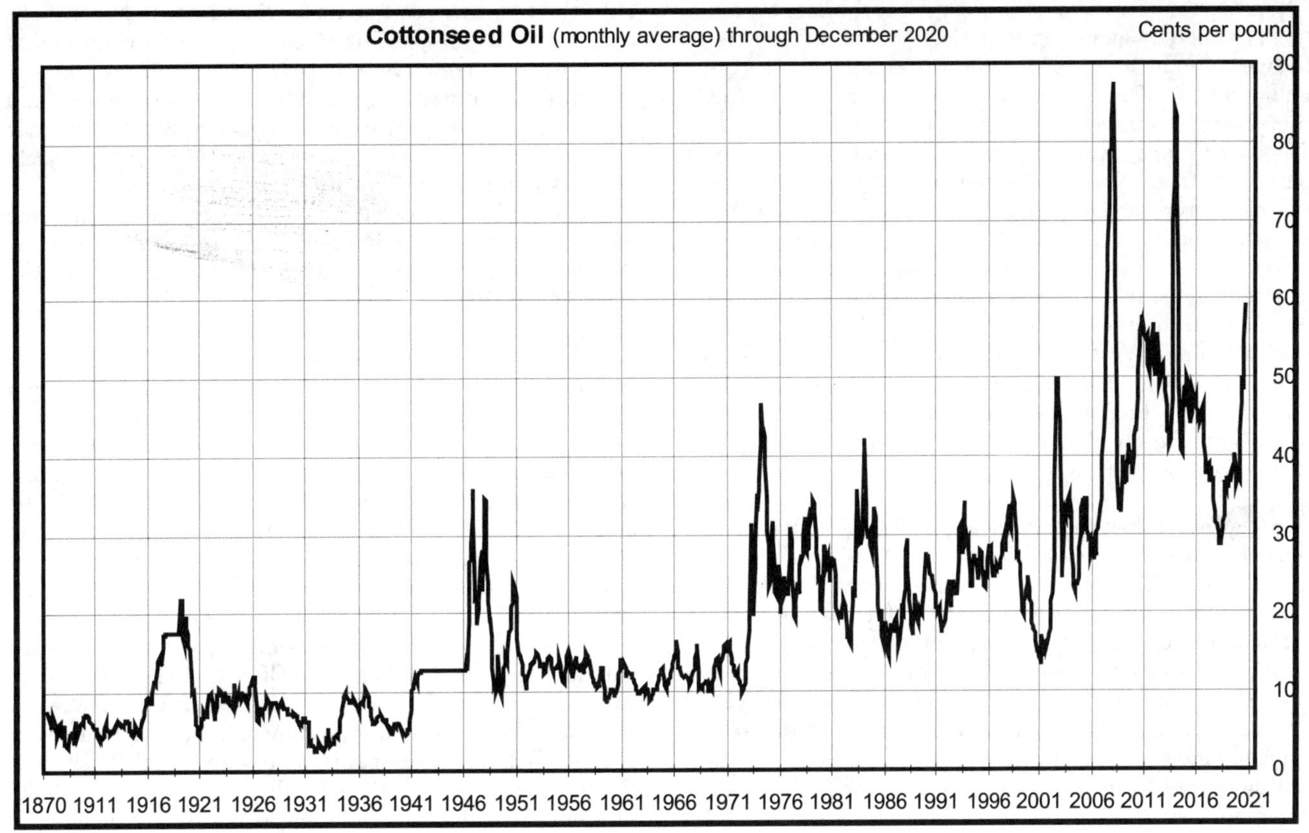

Average Price of Crude Cottonseed Oil, PBSY, Greenwood, MS.[1] in Tank Cars In Cents Per Pound

Year	Jan.	Feb.	Mar.	Apr.	May	June	July	Aug.	Sept.	Oct.	Nov.	Dec.	Average
2011	55.92	56.75	55.50	57.70	56.06	55.25	54.75	54.75	55.35	51.56	50.50	51.10	54.60
2012	52.19	54.56	55.95	56.88	52.00	50.05	53.75	54.65	55.50	51.31	49.05	50.06	53.00
2013	50.94	51.56	50.20	49.94	49.75	48.25	46.19	43.10	42.81	41.19	42.05	43.19	46.60
2014	47.10	57.81	69.94	75.00	84.25	83.31	73.15	61.25	49.63	41.45	40.75	40.31	60.33
2015	44.95	48.81	46.06	48.19	48.90	49.94	49.15	46.25	44.13	44.25	45.19	48.35	47.01
2016	47.31	46.06	46.20	47.35	46.06	45.55	44.75	45.25	44.15	44.88	45.81	46.40	45.81
2017	44.56	41.50	39.45	37.56	38.63	38.60	38.88	36.38	38.45	37.06	37.00	34.25	38.53
2018	32.75	31.44	31.35	31.19	31.25	29.90	28.75	28.60	28.88	30.56	31.45	32.06	30.68
2019	33.94	36.44	35.70	37.13	35.65	36.69	37.50	36.45	38.07	37.94	38.40	40.25	37.01
2020[1]	40.10	38.50	36.19	37.31	37.20	36.75	43.00	46.81	49.69	48.35	54.44	59.20	43.96

[1] Preliminary. *Source: Economic Research Service, U.S. Department of Agriculture (ERS-USDA)*

Exports of Cottonseed Oil to Important Countries from the United States In Metric Tons

Year	Canada	Dominican Republic	Egypt	Guate-mala	Japan	Mexico	Nether-lands	El Salvador	Korea, South	Turkey	Venez-uela	Total
2011	39,847.8	.8	----	----	----	920.0	45,845.7	----	----	2.8	----	88,730.9
2012	30,697.9	.9	----	----	510.0	----	73,891.0	226.8	----	25.9	----	107,992.2
2013	22,335.7	----	----	----	222.5	35.1	63,532.9	1,169.8	----	321.9	----	93,045.6
2014	11,934.5	----	----	----	2,118.0	----	36,433.4	925.6	----	315.9	----	66,688.9
2015	12,316.0	----	----	134.2	913.4	529.0	24,767.3	466.8	----	67.5	----	44,990.0
2016	3,473.7	----	----	311.2	473.6	512.3	19,599.3	.8	----	.6	----	30,837.0
2017	5,141.1	----	----	206.7	591.0	----	22,013.1	2.3	----	29.1	----	41,770.0
2018	6,303.6	----	3,149.7	----	1,100.6	42.7	17,088.9	----	----	20.3	----	47,319.2
2019	3,990.3	----	----	----	1,242.1	109.6	21,069.1	----	----	9.4	----	37,747.7
2020[1]	5,096.9	2.4	----	----	1,800.4	68.6	18,882.9	----	----	9.4	----	33,398.1

[1] Preliminary. *Source: Foreign Agricultural Service, U.S. Department of Agriculture (FAS-USDA)*

Currencies

A "currency" rate involves the price of the base currency (e.g., the dollar) quoted in terms of another currency (e.g., the yen), or in terms of a basket of currencies (e.g., the dollar index). The world's major currencies have traded in a floating exchange rate regime ever since the Bretton-Woods international payments system broke down in 1971 when President Nixon broke the dollar's peg to gold. The two key factors affecting a currency's value are central bank monetary policy and the trade balance. An easy monetary policy (low interest rates) is bearish for a currency because the central bank is aggressively pumping new currency reserves into the marketplace and because foreign investors are not attracted to the low interest rate returns available in the country. By contrast, a tight monetary policy (high interest rates) is bullish for a currency because of the tight supply of new currency reserves and attractive interest rate returns for foreign investors.

The other key factor driving currency values is the nation's current account balance. A current account surplus is bullish for a currency due to the net inflow of the currency, while a current account deficit is bearish for a currency due to the net outflow of the currency. Currency values are also affected by economic growth and investment opportunities in the country. A country with a strong economy and lucrative investment opportunities will typically have a strong currency because global companies and investors want to buy into that country's investment opportunities. Futures on major currencies and on cross-currency rates are traded primarily at the CME Group.

Dollar – The dollar index (Barchart.com symbol DXY00) came into 2020 on a relatively strong note as the U.S. economy in 2019 outperformed Europe and Japan. Also, the dollar had higher interest rate differentials and attracted heavy capital inflows from overseas where there were poor returns, with more than $10 trillion of global debt securities having negative yields. The dollar index then spiked higher in March 2020 when the coronavirus pandemic caused a plunge in the global stock and corporate bond markets and caused fears about a new financial crisis. The dollar index spiked higher on massive emergency demand for dollar liquidity around the world. However, the dollar index fell back after the Federal Reserve used new and expanded dollar swap lines with most major foreign central banks to meet that overseas demand for dollar liquidity. The dollar index then fell during the remainder of 2020 as the Federal Reserve's easy monetary policy took its toll. The Fed in March 2020 slashed its federal funds rate target to 0.00%/0.25% and instituted a new quantitative easing (QE) program with unlimited purchases of Treasury securities and mortgage-backed securities. The Fed in June 2020 then adopted a formal QE program with securities purchases of $120 billion per month. The dollar was able to modestly recover in early 2021 as hopes grew for a full economic recovery as U.S. Covid infections plunged and effective vaccines became available. The dollar in early 2021 received a boost as expectations grew that the Fed might start raising interest rates by late 2022 or early 2023.

Euro – EUR/USD (Barchart.com symbol ^EURUSD) in 2020 whipsawed to a 4-year low in March but then rallied through most of the rest of the year and closed the year up +8.9%. The euro initially saw weakness in March as the dollar rallied sharply on safe-haven demand when the Covid pandemic caused concern that there might be another global financial crisis. However, the euro then rallied during the remainder of 2020 as the pandemic crisis faded and safe-haven demand for the dollar ebbed. The pandemic was an underlying bearish factor for the euro after the Eurozone economy was hit hard by the pandemic with a GDP drop of -6.6%. The ECB in 2020 left its interest rates unchanged. However, in another bearish factor for the euro, the ECB in March launched a new quantitative easing (QE) program called the Pandemic Emergency Purchase Program (PEPP). By the end of 2020, the PEPP program totaled 1.85 trillion euros and was scheduled to last at least until March 2022.

Yen – USD/JPY (Barchart.com symbol ^USDJPY) during 2020 was whipsawed in March by the pandemic crisis but then showed weakness during most of the remainder of the year and closed the year down -4.9%. The yen saw support during 2020 mainly from dollar weakness and yen repatriation by Japanese institutional investors. The yen was undercut during 2020 as Japanese GDP took a sharp hit of -4.9% because of the pandemic. The Bank of Japan (BOJ) left its monetary policy largely unchanged during 2020 because the BOJ was already pumping a huge amount of extra liquidity into the banking system before the pandemic started because of weak economic growth and low inflation. Japan's GDP growth in 2019 was weak at +0.3% due to the Japanese government's hike in Japan's national sales tax to 10% from 8% that took effect on October 1, 2019. The BOJ during 2020 left its policy rate unchanged at -0.1% and left its target at zero for the 10-year JGB bond yield.

Nearby Futures through Last Trading Day.

U.S. Dollars per British Pound

Year	Jan.	Feb.	Mar.	Apr.	May	June	July	Aug.	Sept.	Oct.	Nov.	Dec.	Average
2011	1.5789	1.6137	1.6158	1.6385	1.6338	1.6219	1.6150	1.6359	1.5776	1.5773	1.5799	1.5587	1.6039
2012	1.5522	1.5806	1.5829	1.6009	1.5909	1.5556	1.5598	1.5718	1.6113	1.6073	1.5964	1.6144	1.5854
2013	1.5961	1.5468	1.5083	1.5309	1.5287	1.5498	1.5184	1.5505	1.5875	1.6089	1.6112	1.6383	1.5646
2014	1.6468	1.6566	1.6617	1.6747	1.6841	1.6916	1.7075	1.6700	1.6303	1.6077	1.5773	1.5631	1.6476
2015	1.5139	1.5334	1.4969	1.4960	1.5454	1.5586	1.5558	1.5581	1.5334	1.5335	1.5193	1.4984	1.5286
2016	1.4387	1.4309	1.4256	1.4315	1.4523	1.4210	1.3145	1.3103	1.3148	1.2336	1.2441	1.2471	1.3554
2017	1.2351	1.2487	1.2348	1.2643	1.2923	1.2812	1.2999	1.2956	1.3317	1.3202	1.3232	1.3405	1.2890
2018	1.3828	1.3962	1.3976	1.4070	1.3462	1.3285	1.3169	1.2879	1.3057	1.3011	1.2896	1.2663	1.3355
2019	1.2907	1.3012	1.3174	1.3028	1.2839	1.2674	1.2462	1.2150	1.2353	1.2656	1.2881	1.3103	1.2770
2020	1.3074	1.2951	1.2355	1.2415	1.2291	1.2525	1.2684	1.3134	1.2953	1.2973	1.3214	1.3446	1.2835

Average. *Source: FOREX*

Volume of Trading of British Pound Futures in Chicago In Thousands of Contracts

Year	Jan.	Feb.	Mar.	Apr.	May	June	July	Aug.	Sept.	Oct.	Nov.	Dec.	Total
2011	2,520.0	2,519.3	2,933.2	2,170.3	2,578.2	2,683.0	2,159.4	2,348.8	2,732.7	2,313.8	2,015.5	2,054.4	29,028.8
2012	1,688.5	2,010.0	2,445.6	2,058.2	2,510.7	2,495.4	2,189.7	2,168.2	2,372.3	2,133.3	1,941.9	2,152.6	26,166.3
2013	2,460.2	2,647.5	2,948.2	2,172.0	2,678.5	3,067.9	2,504.8	2,298.1	2,348.2	2,002.0	1,936.9	2,173.5	29,237.8
2014	2,123.0	2,139.8	2,315.4	1,415.6	1,592.2	2,547.6	1,728.8	1,781.2	3,181.2	2,283.2	1,740.6	1,988.2	24,837.0
2015	2,024.6	1,677.7	2,854.7	1,918.6	2,234.4	2,374.3	1,744.8	2,048.9	2,139.5	1,635.5	1,506.4	1,985.3	24,144.7
2016	1,919.1	2,025.0	2,574.4	1,967.0	1,953.3	4,034.0	2,337.1	1,855.1	2,559.9	2,714.9	2,678.6	2,507.8	29,126.0
2017	2,491.4	1,975.1	3,110.3	2,009.6	2,313.0	3,147.8	1,991.9	2,124.7	3,406.7	2,570.9	2,940.8	3,085.7	31,167.9
2018	2,930.4	2,739.3	3,020.1	2,256.6	2,838.9	3,023.7	2,501.4	2,318.6	2,974.4	2,407.6	2,873.0	2,555.1	32,439.0
2019	2,387.4	2,153.5	3,367.7	1,911.6	2,340.7	2,398.6	2,081.9	2,341.3	3,177.6	3,406.7	1,731.0	3,243.9	30,542.3
2020	1,979.5	2,268.4	3,581.3	1,329.0	1,635.6	2,592.6	2,052.1	1,964.1	2,959.7	2,410.4	1,893.8	3,325.5	27,991.8

Contract size = 62,500 GBP. *Source: CME Group; Chicago Mercantile Exchange (CME)*

Average Open Interest of British Pound Futures in Chicago In Contracts

Year	Jan.	Feb.	Mar.	Apr.	May	June	July	Aug.	Sept.	Oct.	Nov.	Dec.
2011	92,434	118,770	118,434	114,166	111,901	103,047	106,501	100,953	142,668	174,087	162,814	206,391
2012	198,201	190,107	167,722	159,541	191,394	150,584	115,951	115,580	166,427	165,761	156,794	188,125
2013	165,256	184,350	248,526	201,357	202,681	172,212	145,625	145,596	167,475	181,110	186,634	226,964
2014	207,609	232,142	231,703	226,479	236,374	262,034	246,579	231,599	184,224	135,955	160,534	165,669
2015	178,585	173,893	187,709	180,094	179,361	174,693	167,418	168,889	163,232	155,414	169,080	191,263
2016	252,441	261,454	274,786	240,358	242,020	225,029	231,642	245,379	247,713	259,915	250,809	229,322
2017	223,750	212,997	257,227	252,578	258,691	226,183	199,970	215,422	220,244	182,430	180,126	203,247
2018	220,399	202,010	190,552	186,782	193,666	210,213	186,764	243,357	252,436	216,670	227,938	229,210
2019	210,633	197,522	170,408	150,947	179,450	216,885	249,765	278,217	256,642	234,991	214,554	228,383
2020	200,192	213,507	194,982	157,693	175,157	183,015	177,970	180,039	169,698	150,271	140,788	150,321

Contract size = 62,500 GBP. *Source: CME Group; Chicago Mercantile Exchange (CME)*

Nearby Futures through Last Trading Day.

Canadian Dollars per U.S. Dollar

Year	Jan.	Feb.	Mar.	Apr.	May	June	July	Aug.	Sept.	Oct.	Nov.	Dec.	Average
2011	0.9939	0.9875	0.9767	0.9574	0.9682	0.9771	0.9558	0.9814	1.0023	1.0201	1.0253	1.0238	0.9891
2012	1.0132	0.9970	0.9934	0.9929	1.0106	1.0275	1.0137	0.9930	0.9788	0.9872	0.9969	0.9899	0.9995
2013	0.9919	1.0094	1.0240	1.0185	1.0206	1.0315	1.0404	1.0404	1.0354	1.0367	1.0488	1.0637	1.0301
2014	1.0947	1.1054	1.1106	1.0992	1.0890	1.0825	1.0734	1.0922	1.1007	1.1214	1.1332	1.1542	1.1047
2015	1.2128	1.2500	1.2610	1.2338	1.2183	1.2354	1.2851	1.3144	1.3270	1.3071	1.3275	1.3710	1.2786
2016	1.4229	1.3790	1.3212	1.2814	1.2949	1.2890	1.3037	1.3000	1.3091	1.3247	1.3446	1.3351	1.3255
2017	1.3206	1.3110	1.3382	1.3435	1.3597	1.3293	1.2698	1.2608	1.2295	1.2599	1.2766	1.2767	1.2980
2018	1.2432	1.2586	1.2930	1.2729	1.2867	1.3129	1.3133	1.3036	1.3033	1.3014	1.3205	1.3447	1.2962
2019	1.3296	1.3207	1.3370	1.3377	1.3459	1.3281	1.3100	1.3269	1.3242	1.3189	1.3236	1.3165	1.3266
2020	1.3084	1.3284	1.3943	1.4047	1.3969	1.3548	1.3501	1.3229	1.3221	1.3209	1.3064	1.2806	1.3409

Average. *Source: FOREX*

Volume of Trading of Canadian Dollar Futures in Chicago In Thousands of Contracts

Year	Jan.	Feb.	Mar.	Apr.	May	June	July	Aug.	Sept.	Oct.	Nov.	Dec.	Total
2011	1,477.5	1,505.0	2,143.4	1,403.3	1,943.9	2,213.2	1,557.3	2,545.8	2,479.4	2,000.8	1,624.9	1,522.3	22,416.7
2012	1,441.3	1,790.3	2,203.3	1,812.6	2,260.5	2,546.9	1,947.1	1,871.8	2,213.3	1,713.8	1,467.8	1,530.9	22,799.4
2013	1,472.2	1,439.5	1,815.4	1,502.0	1,770.9	1,891.0	1,434.3	1,327.6	1,256.7	1,077.0	986.0	1,455.2	17,427.8
2014	1,495.5	1,064.6	1,572.7	903.8	917.2	1,253.6	1,064.6	1,057.9	1,612.2	1,569.7	1,191.6	1,393.1	15,096.5
2015	1,371.7	1,298.8	1,881.8	1,394.8	1,170.1	1,595.7	1,447.1	1,477.1	1,710.6	1,283.7	1,040.4	1,630.2	17,301.9
2016	1,794.8	1,487.2	1,748.1	1,481.8	1,476.4	1,665.3	1,240.5	1,408.3	1,860.5	1,507.1	1,614.2	1,413.1	18,697.3
2017	1,405.8	1,093.9	1,726.1	1,277.3	1,559.2	2,136.4	1,641.9	1,517.9	2,143.3	1,559.1	1,420.4	1,741.3	19,222.5
2018	1,721.5	1,622.3	2,110.0	1,530.7	1,964.4	2,133.5	1,410.3	1,639.3	1,688.7	1,667.5	1,544.8	1,986.5	21,019.4
2019	1,526.4	1,255.7	1,866.9	1,538.3	1,735.1	1,939.3	1,391.6	1,651.6	1,931.9	1,886.1	1,347.5	1,936.1	20,006.5
2020	1,518.8	1,768.0	2,724.2	1,230.4	1,118.7	1,770.0	1,364.4	1,277.8	1,893.1	1,527.5	1,378.3	1,895.2	19,466.4

Contract size = 100,000 CAD. *Source: CME Group; Chicago Mercantile Exchange (CME)*

Average Open Interest of Canadian Dollar Futures in Chicago In Contracts

Year	Jan.	Feb.	Mar.	Apr.	May	June	July	Aug.	Sept.	Oct.	Nov.	Dec.
2011	123,984	139,328	141,949	141,548	124,951	108,081	118,209	111,898	102,180	118,239	127,296	143,821
2012	119,930	126,823	147,325	128,867	141,093	120,545	101,536	134,628	225,238	185,312	168,662	167,449
2013	142,358	161,037	216,418	167,325	145,528	128,346	126,955	115,698	127,754	114,266	121,783	158,005
2014	159,815	152,844	144,262	119,310	123,899	117,918	125,230	111,259	91,900	100,526	106,812	106,069
2015	108,171	115,078	124,649	120,477	120,938	101,560	143,112	167,447	148,706	121,352	137,170	164,083
2016	165,688	157,798	129,610	111,929	124,671	127,872	117,139	122,876	115,488	105,483	122,002	102,506
2017	98,335	125,839	131,989	145,292	209,032	184,268	169,578	192,761	210,929	173,057	147,137	136,029
2018	158,422	156,598	142,004	125,633	132,447	160,264	154,993	145,448	136,094	119,192	130,139	163,042
2019	158,349	145,288	150,911	150,358	146,396	148,551	175,565	162,610	152,850	156,993	180,311	171,026
2020	189,278	169,358	149,473	118,708	124,870	115,870	135,503	135,224	126,834	119,361	135,770	159,984

Contract size = 100,000 CAD. *Source: CME Group; Chicago Mercantile Exchange (CME)*

Nearby Futures through Last Trading Day.

Euro per U.S. Dollar

Year	Jan.	Feb.	Mar.	Apr.	May	June	July	Aug.	Sept.	Oct.	Nov.	Dec.	Average
2011	1.3374	1.3661	1.4018	1.4472	1.4324	1.4400	1.4289	1.4339	1.3754	1.3727	1.3551	1.3148	1.3921
2012	1.2910	1.3238	1.3213	1.3164	1.2788	1.2546	1.2293	1.2403	1.2873	1.2969	1.2837	1.3124	1.2863
2013	1.3306	1.3340	1.2956	1.3025	1.2978	1.3202	1.3090	1.3320	1.3362	1.3638	1.3496	1.3704	1.3285
2014	1.3616	1.3669	1.3827	1.3811	1.3733	1.3600	1.3538	1.3315	1.2895	1.2680	1.2474	1.2307	1.3289
2015	1.1605	1.1352	1.0830	1.0817	1.1157	1.1237	1.0997	1.1144	1.1236	1.1218	1.0728	1.0896	1.1101
2016	1.0868	1.1106	1.1143	1.1339	1.1298	1.1241	1.1065	1.1205	1.1214	1.1023	1.0786	1.0538	1.1069
2017	1.0630	1.0640	1.0688	1.0718	1.1057	1.1238	1.1531	1.1820	1.1906	1.1757	1.1745	1.1835	1.1297
2018	1.2202	1.2345	1.2339	1.2274	1.1814	1.1675	1.1686	1.1548	1.1661	1.1483	1.1363	1.1377	1.1814
2019	1.1419	1.1346	1.1300	1.1232	1.1184	1.1295	1.1212	1.1122	1.1006	1.1056	1.1046	1.1113	1.1194
2020	1.1098	1.0904	1.1060	1.0869	1.0904	1.1257	1.1473	1.1829	1.1785	1.1765	1.1836	1.2170	1.1413

Average. *Source: FOREX*

Volume of Trading of Euro FX Futures in Chicago In Thousands of Contracts

Year	Jan.	Feb.	Mar.	Apr.	May	June	July	Aug.	Sept.	Oct.	Nov.	Dec.	Total
2011	7,402.8	6,451.9	7,437.7	5,453.1	7,657.0	7,504.8	6,906.8	8,061.0	8,376.7	7,008.3	6,638.4	5,338.4	84,236.8
2012	5,611.6	5,984.0	6,055.0	4,864.4	6,510.0	7,165.7	5,311.9	5,059.1	5,927.6	5,197.0	5,281.1	4,440.5	67,407.7
2013	5,675.6	6,088.9	6,391.7	5,480.1	6,055.8	5,970.9	5,093.7	4,390.9	4,120.9	3,988.5	4,047.7	3,981.0	61,285.6
2014	4,422.1	3,733.1	4,781.4	3,046.6	3,338.3	4,261.9	3,048.4	3,507.4	6,106.3	5,900.3	4,564.9	5,497.7	52,208.3
2015	5,560.3	3,639.7	7,724.4	5,745.4	5,549.4	6,980.8	4,666.0	5,245.6	5,468.3	4,455.2	4,243.0	6,077.9	65,356.1
2016	4,077.1	4,559.6	5,453.9	3,688.1	3,192.6	4,996.0	2,734.2	2,994.6	4,677.7	3,357.0	4,596.8	5,128.3	49,455.9
2017	4,328.4	3,667.0	5,810.9	3,353.5	4,129.2	5,345.8	4,449.8	4,681.0	5,929.7	4,704.7	4,593.7	5,462.1	56,455.8
2018	6,129.6	4,985.2	6,336.2	4,410.2	7,312.1	7,459.5	4,527.2	6,009.6	6,216.1	5,419.0	4,626.7	5,353.7	68,785.1
2019	4,149.7	3,318.9	5,517.7	3,915.4	3,879.5	5,625.9	3,785.7	3,989.0	5,715.2	3,891.3	2,976.1	5,725.8	52,490.1
2020	3,592.5	4,460.3	7,943.4	2,910.0	3,047.6	5,615.9	4,709.7	4,291.7	5,891.3	3,726.3	3,359.6	5,870.9	55,419.2

Contract size = 125,000 EUR. *Source: CME Group; Chicago Mercantile Exchange (CME)*

Average Open Interest of Euro FX Futures in Chicago In Contracts

Year	Jan.	Feb.	Mar.	Apr.	May	June	July	Aug.	Sept.	Oct.	Nov.	Dec.
2011	190,755	202,950	225,190	244,014	257,695	222,331	184,688	178,500	231,100	228,018	251,778	297,070
2012	301,627	288,301	275,581	277,812	349,794	369,192	321,319	318,368	276,124	220,770	225,676	217,375
2013	214,230	236,476	211,778	220,576	242,334	232,139	217,712	237,132	250,358	270,275	239,030	258,190
2014	251,507	285,722	289,786	266,980	270,902	302,019	322,167	390,128	429,750	434,763	467,267	427,194
2015	430,963	443,172	477,046	453,055	436,488	388,813	358,550	366,585	340,638	357,347	432,251	432,591
2016	402,675	425,594	367,707	340,746	352,037	344,370	380,293	367,126	350,287	403,624	430,112	425,424
2017	413,834	410,809	414,949	414,920	429,990	435,606	439,731	464,075	459,095	444,328	467,275	505,655
2018	587,907	576,878	540,887	501,746	521,277	539,601	491,694	522,487	503,058	486,553	526,379	541,129
2019	523,488	531,388	513,724	501,896	518,852	525,286	536,433	541,997	533,735	522,478	573,113	576,176
2020	575,652	614,696	620,821	546,543	550,837	592,110	630,078	705,319	684,320	643,667	637,589	676,072

Contract size = 125,000 EUR. *Source: CME Group; Chicago Mercantile Exchange (CME)*

Nearby Futures through Last Trading Day.

Japanese Yen per U.S. Dollar

Year	Jan.	Feb.	Mar.	Apr.	May	June	July	Aug.	Sept.	Oct.	Nov.	Dec.	Average
2011	82.61	82.57	81.65	83.18	81.14	80.47	79.29	77.05	76.88	76.68	77.54	77.83	79.74
2012	76.93	78.60	82.54	81.28	79.69	79.36	78.98	78.68	78.16	79.00	81.04	83.86	79.84
2013	89.19	93.11	94.88	97.75	100.97	97.30	99.64	97.80	99.18	97.85	100.12	103.55	97.61
2014	103.80	102.12	102.34	102.51	101.83	102.07	101.75	102.97	107.37	108.03	116.37	119.42	105.88
2015	118.27	118.75	120.36	119.52	120.85	123.67	123.31	123.04	120.08	120.15	122.63	121.63	121.02
2016	118.20	114.63	112.94	109.58	109.00	105.46	104.08	101.31	101.84	103.85	108.63	116.12	108.80
2017	114.94	112.98	112.90	110.05	112.23	110.96	112.37	109.85	110.81	112.93	112.82	112.92	112.14
2018	110.89	107.87	106.09	107.62	109.69	110.13	111.48	111.04	112.04	112.77	113.35	112.25	110.43
2019	108.95	110.46	111.14	111.69	109.98	108.06	108.24	106.21	107.50	108.16	108.90	109.09	109.03
2020	109.30	110.03	107.67	107.77	107.19	107.60	106.72	106.04	105.60	105.20	104.40	103.75	106.77

Average. *Source: FOREX*

Volume of Trading of Japanese Yen Futures in Chicago In Thousands of Contracts

Year	Jan.	Feb.	Mar.	Apr.	May	June	July	Aug.	Sept.	Oct.	Nov.	Dec.	Total
2011	2,542.6	2,572.2	3,764.0	2,438.4	2,297.9	2,563.3	2,023.5	2,701.8	2,393.6	2,135.9	1,425.0	1,510.9	28,369.1
2012	1,445.7	1,772.5	2,609.4	1,752.1	1,820.9	2,037.7	1,397.4	1,721.5	2,223.2	1,912.0	2,189.4	2,638.8	23,520.6
2013	3,831.3	4,175.7	3,820.2	4,510.5	4,431.7	5,387.8	2,849.1	2,885.5	3,045.1	2,564.9	2,379.8	2,880.5	42,762.3
2014	3,335.1	2,865.2	3,324.4	2,335.1	2,285.1	2,615.9	2,143.3	2,335.6	3,904.6	4,728.3	3,791.3	4,655.9	38,319.8
2015	4,041.9	2,593.2	3,160.9	2,462.5	2,548.1	3,539.0	2,236.0	3,410.2	3,926.7	2,985.0	2,201.2	3,075.8	36,180.5
2016	3,637.8	3,997.1	3,022.3	2,736.8	2,141.9	3,547.6	2,632.9	2,225.8	3,262.3	2,343.2	3,889.4	3,151.8	36,588.8
2017	3,844.0	2,739.9	4,044.3	2,989.3	3,355.7	3,767.5	2,819.8	3,398.4	4,610.2	3,425.4	3,496.3	3,132.6	41,623.4
2018	3,479.6	3,457.9	3,574.2	2,600.7	3,248.2	3,097.7	2,775.9	2,522.3	2,585.9	3,624.0	2,707.5	3,305.4	36,979.3
2019	2,676.8	2,013.3	2,896.6	2,126.6	3,223.0	3,162.4	2,168.4	3,377.7	2,995.4	2,562.4	2,303.3	3,067.8	32,573.8
2020	2,894.9	3,621.5	4,886.9	1,517.2	1,465.3	2,354.0	1,858.3	1,849.7	2,070.0	1,762.1	2,067.2	2,597.3	28,944.4

Contract size = 12,500,000 JPY. *Source: CME Group; Chicago Mercantile Exchange (CME)*

Average Open Interest of Japanese Yen Futures in Chicago In Contracts

Year	Jan.	Feb.	Mar.	Apr.	May	June	July	Aug.	Sept.	Oct.	Nov.	Dec.
2011	112,265	119,793	118,104	123,251	102,290	101,702	121,491	128,615	135,195	151,744	147,224	168,945
2012	162,827	160,215	161,521	145,491	143,219	151,494	127,493	147,320	152,104	136,446	176,769	226,165
2013	203,930	217,961	246,456	211,493	222,136	199,960	182,942	168,128	184,355	160,423	204,490	251,937
2014	217,565	201,386	190,296	174,544	163,960	170,679	163,460	202,088	234,084	205,740	233,431	252,694
2015	218,141	204,791	206,382	190,770	217,291	275,725	249,546	259,312	213,125	181,162	237,763	217,541
2016	243,541	246,520	196,787	171,510	161,320	155,959	156,403	163,674	156,868	157,987	177,739	247,079
2017	206,164	203,979	208,760	199,364	209,490	199,979	238,520	221,773	210,652	262,262	270,180	240,954
2018	242,152	261,583	232,642	151,792	163,587	159,871	195,077	189,113	204,846	225,418	222,065	225,312
2019	218,956	188,471	182,210	186,856	183,500	150,681	136,179	154,403	149,503	155,896	185,665	189,780
2020	185,583	207,128	148,638	127,937	154,095	145,299	146,576	150,267	155,711	170,881	179,877	203,787

Contract size = 12,500,000 JPY. *Source: CME Group; Chicago Mercantile Exchange (CME)*

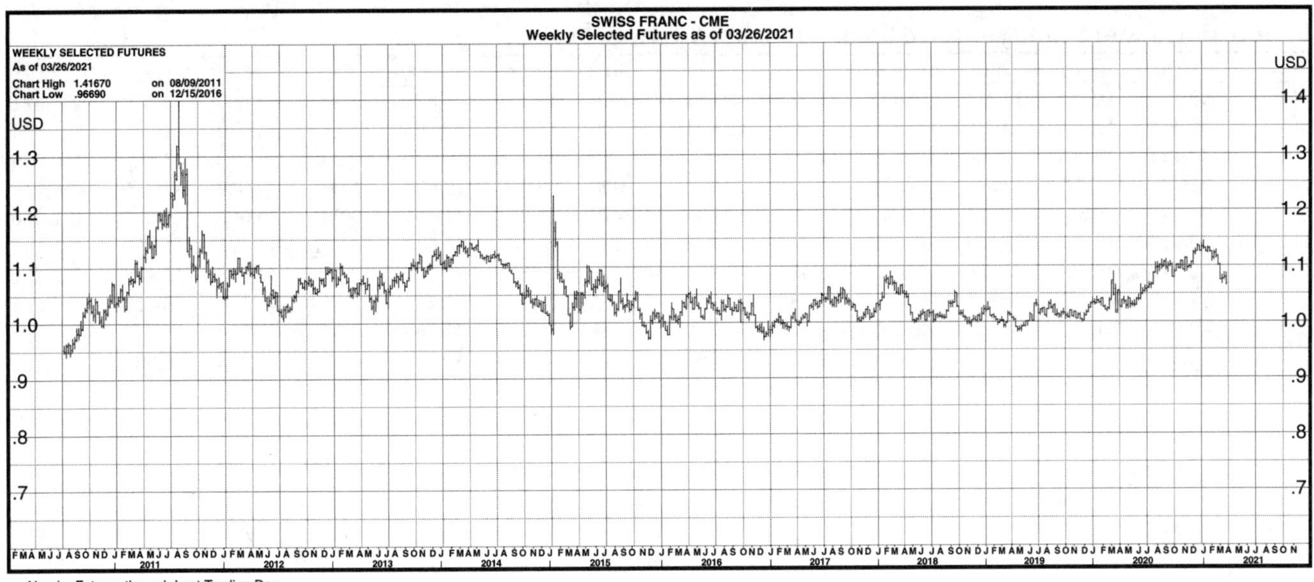

Nearby Futures through Last Trading Day.

Swiss Francs per U.S. Dollar

Year	Jan.	Feb.	Mar.	Apr.	May	June	July	Aug.	Sept.	Oct.	Nov.	Dec.	Average
2011	0.9567	0.9495	0.9187	0.8964	0.8733	0.8404	0.8221	0.7810	0.8734	0.8963	0.9086	0.9335	0.8875
2012	0.9377	0.9119	0.9129	0.9131	0.9397	0.9574	0.9771	0.9685	0.9394	0.9327	0.9388	0.9212	0.9375
2013	0.9243	0.9215	0.9465	0.9368	0.9564	0.9330	0.9446	0.9255	0.9232	0.9032	0.9126	0.8937	0.9268
2014	0.9039	0.8934	0.8805	0.8830	0.8888	0.8955	0.8977	0.9100	0.9367	0.9526	0.9641	0.9769	0.9152
2015	0.9412	0.9361	0.9796	0.9602	0.9325	0.9309	0.9544	0.9685	0.9723	0.9697	1.0099	0.9938	0.9624
2016	1.0070	0.9916	0.9809	0.9642	0.9792	0.9691	0.9820	0.9716	0.9737	0.9872	0.9969	1.0201	0.9853
2017	1.0079	1.0017	1.0022	1.0007	0.9863	0.9678	0.9602	0.9653	0.9626	0.9820	0.9913	0.9869	0.9846
2018	0.9605	0.9346	0.9478	0.9686	0.9972	0.9901	0.9945	0.9879	0.9682	0.9940	1.0009	0.9922	0.9780
2019	0.9895	1.0018	1.0003	1.0087	1.0105	0.9878	0.9878	0.9788	0.9906	0.9929	0.9931	0.9819	0.9936
2020	0.9693	0.9763	0.9578	0.9700	0.9692	0.9517	0.9334	0.9101	0.9150	0.9123	0.9107	0.8880	0.9387

Average. *Source: FOREX*

Volume of Trading of Swiss Franc Futures in Chicago In Thousands of Contracts

Year	Jan.	Feb.	Mar.	Apr.	May	June	July	Aug.	Sept.	Oct.	Nov.	Dec.	Total
2011	848.8	1,025.6	1,266.4	827.0	928.5	1,074.6	936.2	1,098.0	643.1	539.6	489.5	561.4	10,238.7
2012	552.9	773.9	1,034.3	865.2	1,140.5	1,163.6	870.0	855.3	827.8	623.8	599.5	604.6	9,911.3
2013	767.5	643.9	850.4	696.4	1,085.0	938.7	665.1	677.3	688.4	711.0	632.6	705.7	9,061.8
2014	714.1	552.0	819.7	535.8	607.3	792.8	721.4	758.5	1,121.3	1,026.6	834.4	1,154.9	9,638.9
2015	752.0	244.8	537.2	472.1	421.0	513.2	379.8	433.0	433.6	381.7	458.4	607.8	5,634.4
2016	406.6	559.6	531.2	399.3	393.9	650.6	328.1	418.4	596.9	454.4	604.0	625.8	5,968.8
2017	474.3	372.0	598.5	391.8	645.0	638.1	603.4	687.9	772.9	551.5	527.2	715.5	6,978.1
2018	712.9	521.6	651.2	504.3	626.3	699.4	502.7	633.4	709.1	564.5	483.6	653.0	7,262.1
2019	470.9	340.4	688.3	514.3	526.3	809.6	463.6	623.8	725.4	645.6	532.9	805.3	7,146.4
2020	574.8	644.6	1,190.5	379.1	399.9	578.0	517.6	510.5	646.6	408.3	436.8	619.2	6,906.0

Contract size = 125,000 CHF. *Source: CME Group; Chicago Mercantile Exchange (CME)*

Average Open Interest of Swiss Franc Futures in Chicago In Contracts

Year	Jan.	Feb.	Mar.	Apr.	May	June	July	Aug.	Sept.	Oct.	Nov.	Dec.
2011	42,658	46,656	62,300	65,373	70,315	61,349	50,716	20,516	33,972	25,587	29,848	44,100
2012	40,696	48,122	50,263	40,932	59,311	68,970	60,351	56,214	47,686	36,825	43,328	47,914
2013	42,982	44,119	58,519	49,385	59,413	47,741	36,890	38,631	39,298	51,347	45,586	53,657
2014	42,329	48,122	56,682	47,081	49,564	42,368	38,273	52,798	61,701	58,348	60,929	63,108
2015	54,230	35,769	42,525	32,785	32,615	26,518	26,717	40,075	40,143	37,866	64,828	62,677
2016	50,939	51,074	43,286	40,453	46,929	48,028	42,074	42,193	43,527	58,626	57,887	63,292
2017	48,235	47,924	48,104	45,251	49,672	45,409	40,566	40,367	41,027	56,027	80,732	88,812
2018	72,099	71,614	56,365	60,123	100,513	102,678	91,755	89,149	66,738	65,735	78,129	79,614
2019	64,926	72,668	80,612	83,816	92,633	66,089	52,993	55,459	60,491	64,391	70,885	68,183
2020	50,882	53,178	41,286	33,135	39,248	41,089	49,709	55,420	53,401	48,887	51,484	53,062

Contract size = 125,000 CHF. *Source: CME Group; Chicago Mercantile Exchange (CME)*

United States Merchandise Trade Balance[2] In Millions of Dollars

Year	Jan.	Feb.	Mar.	Apr.	May	June	July	Aug.	Sept.	Oct.	Nov.	Dec.	Total
2011	-48,123	-44,753	-44,312	-42,685	-47,725	-49,882	-46,070	-45,052	-43,477	-45,509	-47,460	-49,473	-554,521
2012	-50,126	-42,780	-49,749	-46,842	-45,106	-42,941	-42,406	-44,030	-38,794	-41,467	-45,332	-36,334	-525,907
2013	-40,127	-40,991	-34,300	-38,476	-41,693	-34,420	-36,353	-36,616	-39,920	-36,292	-33,993	-33,649	-446,830
2014	-37,448	-40,137	-42,958	-43,754	-39,594	-38,914	-38,953	-36,952	-41,688	-41,081	-39,819	-42,845	-484,143
2015	-38,871	-33,883	-48,691	-39,844	-38,562	-42,500	-40,379	-44,251	-41,691	-40,934	-40,555	-41,099	-491,260
2016	-40,026	-43,215	-36,551	-37,566	-39,342	-41,658	-40,537	-40,563	-36,545	-39,232	-44,465	-41,469	-481,169
2017	-42,918	-39,520	-40,889	-43,807	-43,588	-42,223	-42,853	-41,517	-41,165	-42,644	-45,558	-47,109	-513,791
2018	-47,247	-48,714	-42,893	-44,666	-41,160	-44,404	-50,572	-50,381	-51,453	-52,398	-49,634	-56,413	-579,935
2019	-49,023	-47,300	-48,914	-49,203	-51,258	-51,749	-51,041	-50,778	-47,839	-43,029	-41,054	-45,676	-576,864
2020[1]	-44,379	-38,008	-47,243	-52,611	-56,310	-51,766	-62,110	-66,064	-63,224	-63,978	-69,038	-66,969	-681,700

[1] Preliminary. [2] Not seasonally adjusted. *Source: Bureau of Economic Analysis, U.S. Department of Commerce (BEA)*

Index of Real Trade-Weighted Dollar Exchange Rates for Total Agriculture[3] (U.S. Markets) (2000 = 100)

Year	Jan.	Feb.	Mar.	Apr.	May	June	July	Aug.	Sept.	Oct.	Nov.	Dec.
2011	96.3	95.9	95.6	94.7	94.8	94.8	93.8	94.6	96.6	97.2	97.2	97.5
2012	97.0	95.5	96.5	96.7	97.9	99.0	97.9	97.3	96.5	96.0	96.2	95.7
2013	96.1	97.3	98.1	97.7	98.2	99.2	99.6	99.5	99.5	98.2	98.6	99.0
2014	100.2	100.4	100.5	99.8	99.5	99.7	99.5	99.9	101.0	101.9	103.1	104.7
2015	106.2	107.7	109.5	108.7	108.6	110.0	111.7	113.8	114.3	112.9	113.8	114.7
2016	117.0	115.9	113.7	112.1	113.4	113.8	114.0	113.1	113.9	114.6	117.9	120.1
2017	120.2	118.3	117.8	116.9	117.0	115.6	113.9	112.9	112.3	114.0	114.2	113.6
2018	110.2	109.7	110.2	110.1	113.0	114.8	114.9	115.2	115.7	115.9	116.7	116.1
2019[1]	114.9	114.8	115.5	115.9	117.1	116.5	115.8	117.4	117.7	117.3	117.0	116.9
2020[2]	116.8	116.5	116.4	116.4	116.0	115.4	114.9	114.5	114.1	113.7	113.3	113.0

[1] Preliminary. [2] Forecast. [3] Real indexes adjust nominal exchange rates for differences in rates of inflation, to avoid the distortion caused by high-inflation countries. A higher value means the dollar has appreciated. Federal Reserve Board Index of trade-weighted value of the U.S. dollar against 10 major currencies. Weights are based on relative importance in world financial markets.
Source: Bureau of Economic Analysis, U.S. Department of Commerce (BEA)

Index of Real Trade-Weighted Dollar Exchange Rates for Total Agriculture[3] (U.S. Competitors) (2000 = 100)

Year	Jan.	Feb.	Mar.	Apr.	May	June	July	Aug.	Sept.	Oct.	Nov.	Dec.
2011	97.1	95.9	94.7	92.5	93.1	92.8	92.7	93.0	96.6	97.2	97.6	99.1
2012	99.8	97.3	98.0	98.5	101.1	102.9	102.9	102.2	100.4	99.6	100.0	98.4
2013	97.7	97.9	99.5	98.9	99.6	100.5	101.3	101.2	101.0	98.9	100.0	99.8
2014	101.3	101.6	100.7	100.2	100.5	101.2	101.0	102.0	104.4	105.9	106.8	108.1
2015	111.8	114.0	118.0	117.6	116.0	116.9	119.0	120.1	121.5	120.5	122.8	122.9
2016	125.7	123.8	121.9	119.4	120.0	120.3	120.6	119.4	120.1	121.0	123.4	125.2
2017	124.7	123.3	122.9	122.2	120.8	119.7	117.6	116.0	115.4	116.7	117.0	115.9
2018	113.6	113.3	113.8	114.5	119.1	121.1	121.5	123.2	124.7	120.5	120.7	120.3
2019[1]	123.5	123.6	124.8	125.6	127.0	125.6	125.0	128.0	129.1	129.0	129.3	129.5
2020[2]	124.9	124.5	124.2	124.0	123.7	123.2	122.9	123.6	124.5	125.7	127.1	128.8

[1] Preliminary. [2] Forecast. [3] Real indexes adjust nominal exchange rates for differences in rates of inflation, to avoid the distortion caused by high-inflation countries. A higher value means the dollar has appreciated. Federal Reserve Board Index of trade-weighted value of the U.S. dollar against 10 major currencies. Weights are based on relative importance in world financial markets.
Source: Bureau of Economic Analysis, U.S. Department of Commerce (BEA)

Merchandise Trade and Current Account Balances[3] In Billions of Dollars

	Merchanise Trade Balance					Current Account Balance				
Year	Canada	Germany	Japan	Switzerland	United Kingdom	Canada	Germany	Japan	Switzerland	United Kingdom
2011	-49.7	229.4	128.3	54.5	-51.5	-40.7	195.3	146.5	40.7	-84.4
2012	-65.7	252.1	62.5	71.2	-101.3	-58.2	185.7	221.3	86.1	-83.0
2013	-59.4	245.9	46.4	79.7	-142.3	-49.7	226.3	128.1	54.5	-51.5
2014	-43.1	282.4	36.8	60.2	-149.3	-65.7	250.5	62.5	71.3	-101.3
2015	-55.3	289.1	136.9	76.5	-142.1	-59.4	254.7	46.3	79.7	-142.3
2016	-49.0	292.0	193.6	63.2	-139.7	-43.1	292.9	36.6	60.2	-149.3
2017	-46.5	297.7	204.4	45.2	-88.1	-56.1	302.5	136.4	75.6	-142.1
2018	-45.4	297.7	175.6	72.5	-108.5	-49.4	296.2	189.2	66.1	-139.7
2019[1]	-48.9	286.2	150.5	65.9	-157.7	-48.9	297.1	196.6	64.4	-98.6
2020[2]	-47.1	281.2	162.6	65.9	-145.7	-52.8	311.0	163.6	78.6	-94.4

[1] Estimate. [2] Projection. [3] Not seasonally adjusted. *Source: Organization for Economic Cooperation and Development (OECD)*

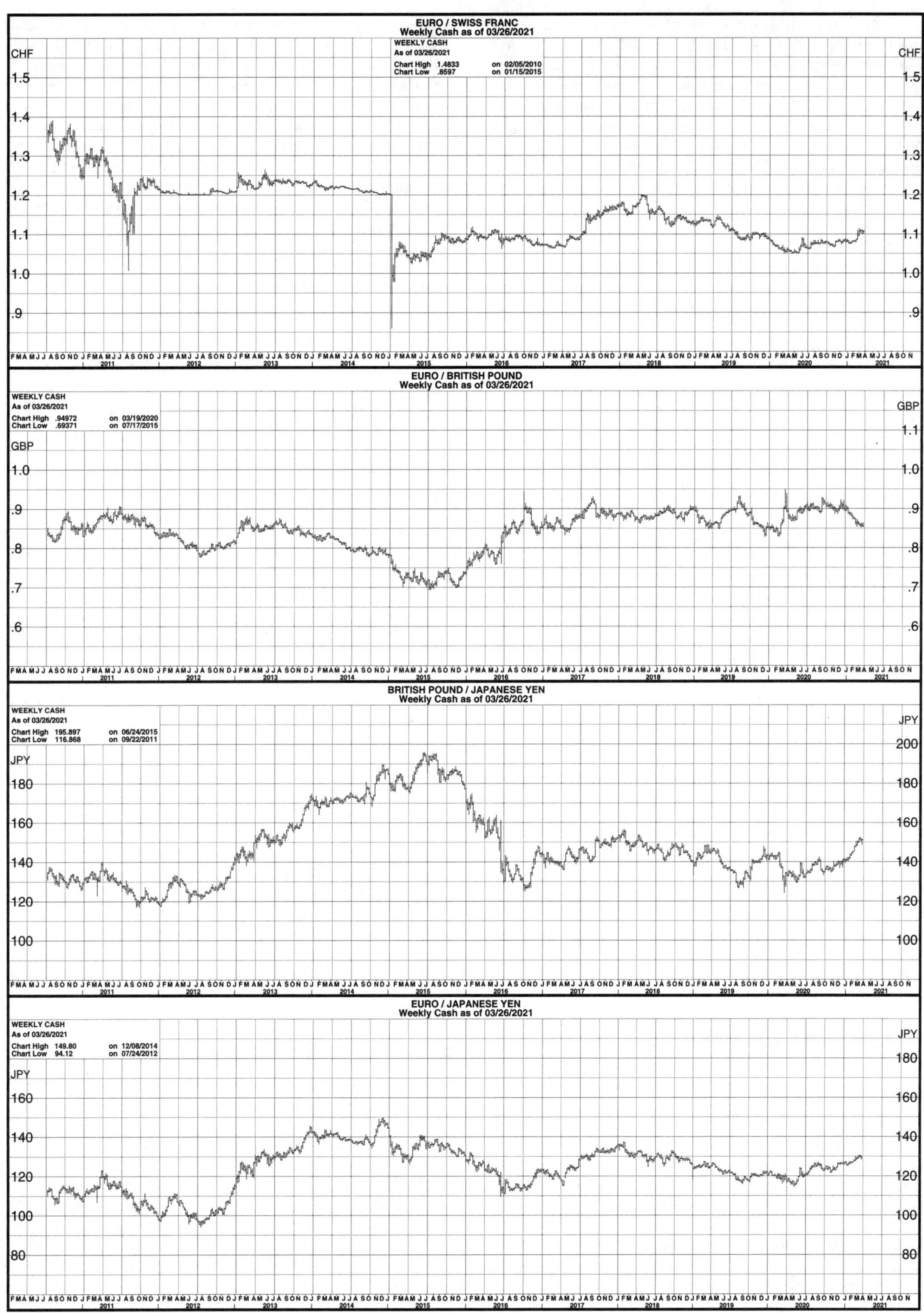
EURO / SWISS FRANC
Weekly Cash as of 03/26/2021
WEEKLY CASH
As of 03/26/2021
Chart High 1.4833 on 02/05/2010
Chart Low .8597 on 01/15/2015
CHF
EURO / BRITISH POUND
Weekly Cash as of 03/26/2021
WEEKLY CASH
As of 03/26/2021
Chart High .94972 on 03/19/2020
Chart Low .69371 on 07/17/2015
GBP
BRITISH POUND / JAPANESE YEN
Weekly Cash as of 03/26/2021
WEEKLY CASH
As of 03/26/2021
Chart High 195.897 on 06/24/2015
Chart Low 116.868 on 09/22/2011
JPY
EURO / JAPANESE YEN
Weekly Cash as of 03/26/2021
WEEKLY CASH
As of 03/26/2021
Chart High 149.80 on 12/08/2014
Chart Low 94.12 on 07/24/2012
JPY

Forex.

Diamonds

The diamond, which is the mineral form of carbon, is the hardest, strongest natural material known on earth. The name *diamond* is derived from *adamas*, the ancient Greek term meaning "invincible." Diamonds form deep within the Earth's crust and are typically billions of years old. Diamonds have also have been found in and near meteorites and their craters. Diamonds are considered precious gemstones but lower grade diamonds are used for industrial applications such as drilling, cutting, grinding and polishing.

Supply – World production of natural gem diamonds in 2020 fell by -10.2% yr/yr to 74.000 million carats, well below the 2008 record high of 114.000 million carats (one carat equals 1/5 gram or 200 milligrams). The world's largest producers of natural gem diamonds are Russia with 32.4% of world production in 2020, Botswana with 17.6%, and Angola with 10.8%. World production of natural industrial diamonds in 2020 was down -1.8% yr/yr to 54.000 million carats. The main producers of natural industrial diamonds in 2020 were Russia with 35.2% of world production, Australia with 22.2%, Congo with 22.2%, and Botswana with 19.3%. World production of synthetic diamonds in 2011 was 4.380 million carats. The main producer of synthetic diamonds that year was China, with 91.3% of world production.

Trade – The U.S. in 2020 imported 550,000 carats of natural diamonds and relied on imports for 47% of its consumption.

World Production of Natural Gem Diamonds In Thousands of Carats

Year	Angola	Australia	Botswana	Brazil, unspecified	Central African Republic	China, unspecified	Congo (Kinshasa)	Ghana, unspecified	Namibia	Russia	Sierra Leone	South Africa	World Total
2015	8,120	271	14,500	32	----	----	3,200	174	2,053	23,500	400	5,780	70,900
2016	8,120	279	14,400	184	9	[5]	4,640	142	1,718	22,600	439	6,650	73,200
2017	8,500	343	16,000	255		230	3,780		1,950	23,800	231	7,750	88,100
2018	7,570	281	17,100	251		99	3,030		2,400	24,200	590	7,930	89,000
2019[1]	8,230	260	16,600	166		100	2,670		2,020	25,400	649	5,740	82,400
2020[2]	8,000	200	13,000	100			3,000		1,900	24,000	550	4,000	74,000

[1] Preliminary. [2] Estimate. [3] Less than 1/2 unit. *Source: U.S. Geological Survey (USGS)*

World Production of Natural Industrial Diamonds[4] In Thousands of Carats

Year	Angola	Australia	Botswana	Brazil	Central African Republic	China	Congo (Kinshasa)	Ghana	Russia	Sierra Leone	South Africa	Venezuela	World Total
2015	902	13,300	6,230	----	----	----	12,800	----	18,400	100	1,440	----	56,500
2016	902	13,700	6,150	----	2	----	18,600	----	17,700	110	1,660	----	60,900
2017		17,000	7,000	----		----	15,000	----	19,000		2,000	----	63,000
2018		14,000	7,000	----		----	12,000	----	19,000		2,000	----	58,000
2019[1]		13,000	7,000	----		----	11,000	----	20,000		1,000	----	55,000
2020[2]		12,000	5,000	----		----	12,000	----	19,000		3,000	----	54,000

[1] Preliminary. [2] Estimate. [3] Formerly Zaire. *Source: U.S. Geological Survey (USGS)*

U.S. Exports of Industrial Diamonds In Thousands of Carats

Year	Belgium	France	Hong Kong	India	Israel	Mexico	Singapore	Switzerland	Thailand	United Arab Emirates	United Kingdom	Other	World Total
2011	269.0	1.2	2,320.0	768.0	293.0	604.0	6.1	190.0	168.0	131.0	492.0	12.5	5,450.0
2012	393.0	0.9	2,390.0	525.0	576.0	473.0	3.6	9.3	116.0	45.1	8.7	10.7	4,800.0
2013	90.9	10.8	2,140.0	489.0	346.0	420.0	1.9	10.8	154.0	49.1	19.7	13.2	4,060.0
2014	55.6	3.3	1,980.0	381.0	78.5	416.0	3.9	2.2	153.0	88.7	26.3	5.6	3,470.0
2015[1]	187.0	67.1	1,660.0	672.0	243.0	316.0	6.8	12.3	146.0	391.0	6.7	6.2	4,020.0
2016[2]	564.0	9.4	1,170.0	669.0	184.0	331.0	5.1	44.2	148.0	408.0	49.7	6.3	3,790.0

[1] Preliminary. [2] Estimate. *Source: U.S. Geological Survey (USGS)*

Salient Statistics of Industrial Diamonds in the United States In Millions of Carats

	Bort, Grit & Powder & Dust -- Natural and Synthetic								Stones (Natural)							Net Import Reliance
	--- Production ---															
Year	Manufactured Diamond	Secondary	Imports for Consumption	Exports & Reexports	In Manufactured Products	Gov't Sales	Apparent Consumption	Price Value of Imports $/Carat	Secondary Production	Imports for Consumption	Exports & Reexports	Gov't Sales	Apparent Consumption	Price Value of Imports $/Carat		% of Consumption
2015	----	63.5	275.0	140.0	----	----	238.0	.20	----	1.3	----	----	----	17.50		57
2016	----	66.1	216.0	134.0	----	----	190.0	.23	----	1.4	----	----	----	13.60		43
2017	----	11.0	399.0	161.0	----	----	290.0	.16	----	1.2	----	----	----	12.90		79
2018	----	32.0	574.0	39.0	----	----	651.0	.12	----	2.5	----	----	----	2.90		67
2019[1]	----	36.0	312.0	114.0	----	----	348.0	.14	----	1.6	----	----	----	3.90		57
2020[2]	----	35.0	220.0	91.0	----	----	270.0	.18	----	.6	----	----	----	7.40		47

[1] Preliminary. [2] Estimate. [3] Less than 1/2 unit. *Source: U.S. Geological Survey (USGS)*

Eggs

Eggs provide a low-priced protein source worldwide. Each commercial chicken lays between 265-280 eggs per year. In the United States, the grade and size of eggs are regulated under the federal Egg Products Inspection Act (1970). The grades of eggs are AA, A, and B, and must have sound, whole shells and must be clean. The difference among the grades of eggs is internal and mostly reflects the freshness of the egg. Table eggs vary in color and can be determined by the color of the chicken's earlobe. For example, chickens with white earlobes lay white eggs and chickens with reddish-brown earlobes lay brown eggs. In the U.S., egg size is determined by the weight of a dozen eggs, not individual eggs, and range from Peewee to Jumbo. Store-bought eggs in the shell stay fresh for 3 to 5 weeks in a home refrigerator, according to the USDA.

Eggs are primarily used as a source of food, although eggs are also widely used for medical purposes. Fertile eggs, as a source of purified proteins, are used to produce many vaccines. Flu vaccines are produced by growing single strains of the flu virus in eggs, which are then extracted to make the vaccine. Eggs are also used in biotechnology to create new drugs. The hen's genetic make-up can be altered so that the whites of the eggs are rich in tailored proteins that form the basis of medicines to fight cancer and other diseases. The U.S. biotech company Viragen and the Roslin Institute in Edinburgh have produced eggs with 100 mg or more of the easily extracted proteins used in new drugs to treat various illnesses, including ovarian and breast cancers.

Prices – The average monthly price of all eggs received by farmers in the U.S. in 2020 rose +14.4% yr/yr to 91.4 cents per dozen, well below the 2015 record high of 164.6 cents.

Supply – World egg production in 2019 rose +3.2% at 1.578 billion eggs. The world's largest egg producers were China with 36.6% of world production, the U.S. with 7.2%, Mexico and Brazil with 3.5%, and Japan and Russia with 2.8%. U.S. egg production in 2020 fell -1.9% to 111.200 billion eggs, which is down from the 2019 record high of 113. 370.The average number of hens and pullets on U.S. farms in 2019 rose by +1.3% yr/yr to 399.656 million, a new record high.

Demand – U.S. consumption of eggs in 2020 rose +1.0% yr/yr to 8.085 billion dozen eggs, a new record high. U.S. consumption of eggs is up sharply by about 30% from ten years earlier, reflecting the increased popularity of eggs in American diets. U.S. per capita egg consumption in 2021 is forecasted to rise +0.8% yr/yr to 288.3 eggs per year per person. Per capita egg consumption reached a high of 277.2 eggs in 1970, fell sharply in the 1990s to a low of 174.9 in 1995, and then began rebounding in 1997 to current levels of about 290 eggs per year.

Trade – U.S. imports of eggs in 2020 fell -0.6% yr/yr to 18.000 million dozen eggs. U.S. exports of eggs in 2020 fell -0.6% yr/yr to 280.000 million dozen eggs, down from the 2014 record high of 393.844 million dozen.

World Production of Eggs In Millions of Eggs

Year	Brazil	China	France	Germany	Italy	Japan	Mexico	Russia	Spain	Ukraine	United Kingdom	United States	World Total
2011	40,731	484,633	14,088	12,035	13,482	41,377	49,170	40,778	12,995	18,428	11,201	92,450	1,228,485
2012	41,676	493,184	14,155	12,246	13,661	41,780	46,361	41,548	11,409	18,919	10,806	94,364	1,255,761
2013	43,431	495,741	15,766	12,593	12,679	42,033	50,317	40,779	11,787	19,419	11,517	97,555	1,284,782
2014	44,811	459,063	15,935	12,685	12,749	41,699	48,438	41,313	12,498	19,391	11,653	100,879	1,275,228
2015	45,219	465,429	16,319	11,807	13,093	42,015	50,048	42,093	12,780	16,615	11,966	97,208	1,296,553
2016	46,115	465,807	13,605	11,979	13,300	42,704	51,324	43,043	13,183	14,799	12,370	102,112	1,315,073
2017	50,574	538,823	14,631	12,087	12,994	43,353	52,287	44,290	13,503	15,351	12,886	107,242	1,492,315
2018[1]	53,163	544,311	14,366	12,326	13,150	43,796	54,187	44,398	13,186	15,971	13,303	110,074	1,528,600
2019[2]	55,406	576,793	13,101	12,511	12,810	43,996	55,656	44,492	12,872	16,511	13,643	113,253	1,577,535

[1] Preliminary. [2] Forecast. [3] Selected countries. *Source: Food and Agricultural Organization of the United Nations (FAO)*

Salient Statistics of Eggs in the United States

Year	Hens & Pullets: On Farm Dec. 1[3] (Thousands)	Hens & Pullets: Average Number During Year (Thousands)	Rate of Lay Per Layer During Year[4] (Number)	Eggs: Total Produced (Millions)	Eggs: Price in cents Per Dozen	Eggs: Value of Production[5] (Million USD)	Total Egg Production (Million Dozen)	Imports[6] (Million Dozen)	Exports[6] (Million Dozen)	Used for Hatching (Million Dozen)	Consumption: Total (Million Dozen)	Consumption: Per Capita Eggs[6] (Number)
2012	346,965	341,052	274	93,533	100.1	7,929	7,930	18.5	301.7	941.4	6,666	254.6
2013	356,923	354,844	275	96,698	108.8	8,679	8,186	16.9	371.8	964.8	6,827	258.0
2014	370,637	364,707	277	101,186	125.8	10,258	8,404	34.7	393.8	980.6	7,106	267.5
2015	346,343	352,411	276	97,208	164.6	13,608	8,101	123.3	313.6	995.6	6,781	256.3
2016	377,371	365,997	279	102,112	76.6	6,514	8,579	129.5	302.8	1,009.6	7,327	272.0
2017	382,266	378,787	281	105,841	86.3	7,597	8,879	34.2	354.9	1,035.2	7,589	279.9
2018	396,870	394,361	279	109,633	115.2	10,586	9,173	17.8	333.1	1,057.5	7,751	287.5
2019[1]	403,273	399,656	283	113,370	79.9		9,438	18.1	281.8	1,076.3	8,009	293.6
2020[2]							9,440	18.0	280.0	1,090.0	8,085	292.8

[1] Preliminary. [2] Forecast. [3] All layers of laying age. [4] Number of eggs produced during the year divided by the average number of all layers of laying age on hand during the year. [5] Value of sales plus value of eggs consumed in households of producers. 6/ Shell-egg equivalent of eggs and egg products. *Source: National Agricultural Statistics Service, U.S. Department of Agriculture (NASS-USDA)*

EGGS

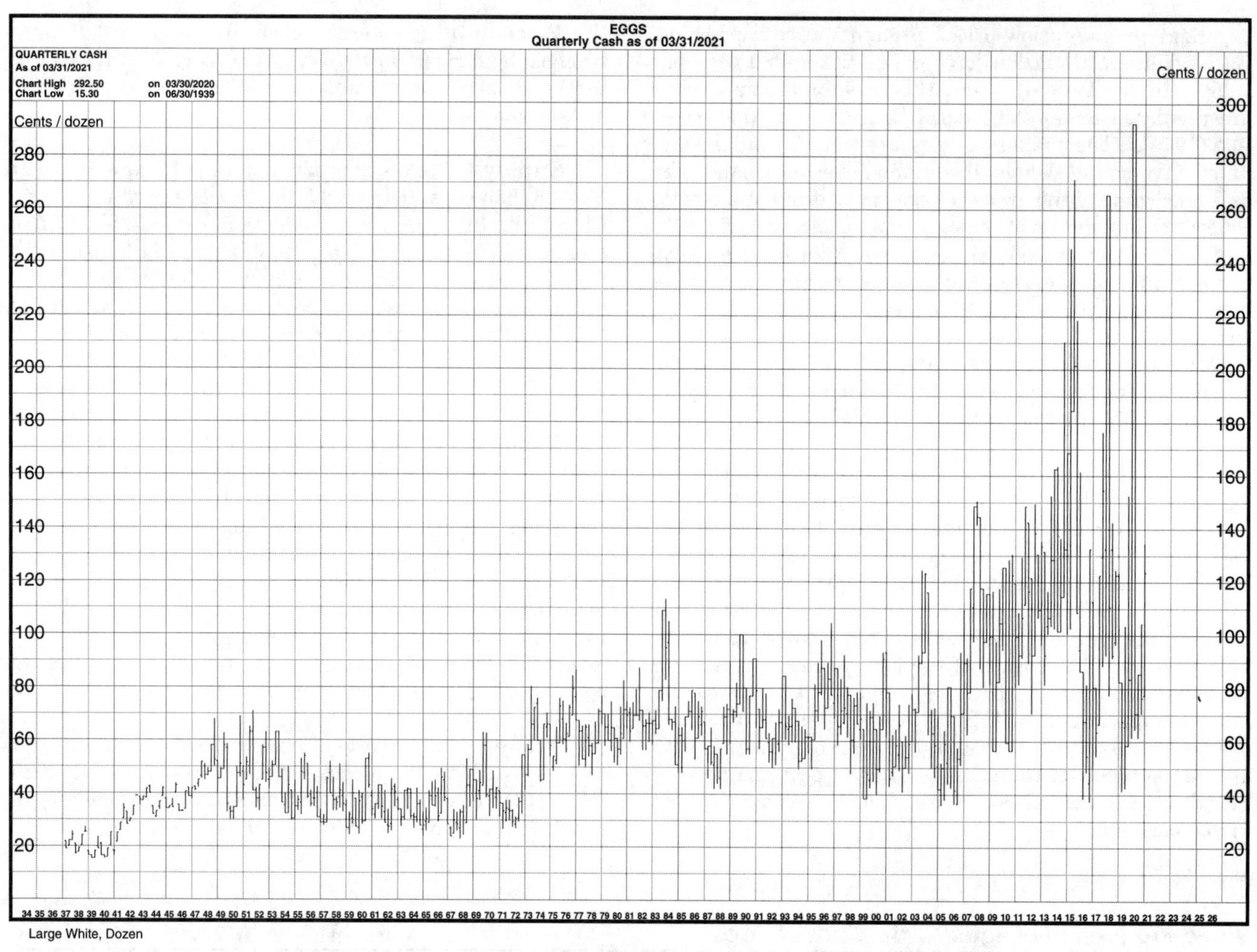

Large White, Dozen

Average Price Received by Farmers for All Eggs in the United States In Cents Per Dozen

Year	Jan.	Feb.	Mar.	Apr.	May	June	July	Aug.	Sept.	Oct.	Nov.	Dec.	Average
2011	85.0	95.4	84.9	105.0	82.2	88.6	88.0	115.0	102.0	102.0	102.0	122.0	97.7
2012	87.9	88.5	99.5	86.5	82.8	90.7	96.9	113.0	122.0	102.0	118.0	113.0	100.1
2013	106.0	99.3	115.0	88.5	117.0	93.0	104.0	108.0	103.0	104.0	132.0	136.0	108.8
2014	112.0	140.0	124.0	127.0	117.0	109.0	124.0	108.0	105.0	114.0	152.0	177.0	125.8
2015	125.0	129.0	154.0	108.0	173.0	200.0	190.0	239.0	190.0	143.0	200.0	124.0	164.6
2016	118.0	108.0	96.7	67.6	54.7	53.7	64.8	65.1	60.1	51.0	58.8	121.0	76.6
2017	79.5	62.3	78.3	63.3	61.9	63.5	82.3	74.9	109.0	90.1	138.0	133.0	86.3
2018	115.0	126.0	201.0	120.0	85.1	103.0	109.0	109.0	93.1	91.2	113.0	117.0	115.2
2019	101.0	92.3	86.6	63.3	47.5	71.4	51.1	89.1	68.0	66.3	129.0	93.1	79.9
2020[1]	75.3	89.3	172.0	104.0	77.4	71.9	76.2	77.6	83.2	99.4	96.8	73.4	91.4

[1] Preliminary. *Source: Economic Research Service, U.S. Department of Agriculture (ERS-USDA)*

Average Wholesale Price of Shell Eggs (Large) Delivered, Chicago In Cents Per Dozen

Year	Jan.	Feb.	Mar.	Apr.	May	June	July	Aug.	Sept.	Oct.	Nov.	Dec.	Average
2011	100.20	99.08	86.37	106.05	87.31	86.95	92.70	114.07	105.93	111.79	112.50	130.07	102.75
2012	106.25	91.47	98.59	96.10	76.55	92.50	105.45	131.33	119.50	114.28	123.93	123.90	106.65
2013	112.93	112.92	114.30	97.86	105.45	89.75	104.77	106.82	106.50	106.41	133.60	150.21	111.79
2014	113.10	135.97	133.93	145.98	116.21	115.83	122.16	116.02	111.93	117.11	143.18	194.45	130.49
2015	111.10	133.50	149.18	113.10	136.20	223.82	206.55	260.40	217.02	161.95	192.55	157.14	171.88
2016	106.71	131.80	93.05	62.93	55.45	46.18	69.70	57.24	64.74	44.07	58.07	94.31	73.69
2017	78.47	65.84	63.76	68.39	55.77	60.32	74.45	80.85	104.85	110.00	130.74	169.80	88.60
2018	116.40	150.24	205.07	177.93	90.95	88.93	129.55	105.22	93.45	99.54	115.26	120.80	124.45
2019	104.98	103.45	83.98	67.73	45.27	56.25	51.68	67.50	84.25	59.91	120.10	119.50	80.38
2020[1]	70.29	96.50	151.59	200.77	83.70	69.14	73.00	66.93	81.21	100.41	101.10	78.73	97.78

[1] Preliminary. *Source: National Agricultural Statistics Service, U.S. Department of Agriculture (NASS-USDA)*

Total Egg Production in the United States In Millions of Eggs

Year	Jan.	Feb.	Mar.	Apr.	May	June	July	Aug.	Sept.	Oct.	Nov.	Dec.	Total
2011	7,833	7,013	7,840	7,617	7,773	7,503	7,732	7,719	7,503	7,783	7,612	7,987	91,915
2012	7,892	7,283	7,916	7,653	7,850	7,582	7,798	7,869	7,625	7,965	7,874	8,226	93,533
2013	8,125	7,321	8,195	7,929	8,139	7,857	8,082	8,178	7,969	8,267	8,098	8,538	96,698
2014	8,490	7,636	8,522	8,298	8,523	8,242	8,597	8,591	8,289	8,632	8,521	8,845	101,186
2015	8,656	7,730	8,688	8,352	8,141	7,577	7,850	7,878	7,647	7,970	7,875	8,261	97,208
2016	8,308	7,948	8,622	8,333	8,643	8,349	8,672	8,751	8,507	8,851	8,707	9,100	102,112
2017	9,053	8,124	9,007	8,687	8,918	8,636	8,953	8,922	8,578	8,920	8,791	9,252	105,841
2018	9,132	8,278	9,243	8,932	9,252	8,966	9,239	9,305	9,052	9,370	9,171	9,693	109,633
2019	9,658	8,689	9,675	9,378	9,618	9,215	9,454	9,491	9,223	9,664	9,497	9,809	113,370
2020[1]	9,690	8,946	9,539	9,096	9,121	8,832	9,317	9,353	9,057	9,505	9,327	9,610	111,393

[1] Preliminary. *Source: National Agricultural Statistics Service, U.S. Department of Agriculture (NASS-USDA)*

Per Capita Disappearance of Eggs[4] in the United States In Number of Eggs

Year	First Quarter	Second Quarter	Third Quarter	Fourth Quarter	Total	Year	First Quarter	Second Quarter	Third Quarter	Fourth Quarter	Total
2010	61.5	61.4	62.2	62.8	247.9	2016	67.4	66.4	67.4	70.8	272.0
2011	61.3	61.5	62.8	64.3	250.0	2017	69.0	69.3	70.3	71.2	279.9
2012	63.3	62.3	63.3	65.6	254.6	2018	69.6	70.9	72.7	74.3	287.5
2013	64.2	63.3	64.5	66.0	258.0	2019[1]	73.1	73.0	72.9	74.6	293.6
2014	65.6	66.2	67.2	68.5	267.5	2020[2]	72.6	69.2	70.8	73.3	285.9
2015	65.7	62.9	61.9	65.7	256.3	2021[3]	70.8	70.7	72.7	74.1	288.3

[1] Preliminary. [2] Estimate. [3] Forecast. *Source: Economic Research Service, U.S. Department of Agriculture (ERS-USDA)*

Egg-Feed Ratio[1] in the United States

Year	Jan.	Feb.	Mar.	Apr.	May	June	July	Aug.	Sept.	Oct.	Nov.	Dec.	Average
2011	5.8	6.0	5.1	6.4	4.5	4.9	4.9	6.7	6.3	6.8	6.8	8.7	6.1
2012	5.1	5.0	5.7	4.5	5.0	4.8	4.8	5.6	7.0	5.6	6.6	6.3	5.5
2013	5.6	5.0	6.1	4.2	6.3	4.4	5.3	6.1	6.4	7.3	10.4	10.7	6.5
2014	8.0	10.9	8.9	8.9	7.9	7.3	9.6	8.6	9.0	10.5	15.1	17.7	10.2
2015	11.4	12.2	15.3	9.6	18.2	21.8	19.5	26.5	20.7	14.7	22.9	12.2	17.1
2016	11.4	10.2	8.8	4.6	2.7	2.5	4.0	4.4	3.9	2.6	3.7	12.1	5.9
2017	6.7	4.3	6.4	4.4	4.2	4.5	6.9	6.1	10.9	8.3	15.3	14.4	7.7
2018	11.6	12.8	22.2	11.3	6.8	9.3	10.5	11.0	8.7	8.5	11.7	11.8	11.4
2019	9.5	8.4	7.6	4.6	2.3	5.1	2.5	7.6	5.0	4.7	13.0	8.3	6.6
2020[1]	5.6	7.4	18.7	10.1	6.3	5.5	6.1	6.3	6.6	8.5	7.7	4.7	7.8

[1] Pounds of laying feed equivalent in value to one dozen eggs. [2] Preliminary. *Source: Economic Research Service, U.S. Department of Agriculture (ERS-USDA)*

Hens and Pullets of Laying Age (Layers) in the United States, on First of Month In Thousands

Year	Jan. 1	Feb. 1	Mar. 1	Apr. 1	May 1	June 1	July 1	Aug. 1	Sept. 1	Oct. 1	Nov. 1	Dec. 1
2011	344,255	340,247	339,296	342,237	339,520	336,232	336,559	334,997	335,794	334,826	336,909	338,472
2012	340,522	339,826	340,926	343,073	341,885	341,486	338,416	337,525	339,302	341,076	345,269	346,965
2013	344,920	344,916	347,025	348,468	344,363	345,740	343,944	349,862	351,870	349,950	352,971	356,923
2014	363,828	362,628	363,000	364,610	364,840	363,604	363,572	365,799	365,748	366,306	366,329	370,637
2015	368,380	364,996	365,857	366,022	357,858	332,788	332,422	334,040	334,912	338,273	340,554	346,343
2016	356,109	359,429	366,253	366,749	366,217	365,830	364,432	364,935	368,128	370,254	371,438	377,371
2017	377,198	376,955	375,688	376,790	374,671	372,584	372,241	372,995	374,769	376,694	379,323	382,266
2018	382,305	388,227	392,297	392,843	391,760	371,749	391,377	389,840	391,569	391,885	393,060	396,870
2019	403,274	402,220	404,853	406,457	402,890	397,289	392,406	392,182	394,418	396,565	400,204	403,273
2020[1]	403,751	399,049	394,752	396,294	388,282	384,039	380,123	378,247	381,924	385,173	387,770	391,018

[1] Preliminary. *Source: National Agricultural Statistics Service, U.S. Department of Agriculture (NASS-USDA)*

Eggs Laid Per Hundred Layers in the United States In Number of Eggs

Year	Jan.	Feb.	Mar.	Apr.	May	June	July	Aug.	Sept.	Oct.	Nov.	Dec.	Average
2011	2,289	2,064	2,301	2,234	2,300	2,230	2,303	2,301	2,238	2,317	2,254	2,351	2,265
2012	2,320	2,140	2,315	2,234	2,297	2,229	2,307	2,325	2,241	2,321	2,275	2,347	2,279
2013	2,327	2,090	2,326	2,259	2,329	2,249	2,315	2,331	2,271	2,352	2,281	2,354	2,290
2014	2,337	2,105	2,342	2,275	2,340	2,267	2,357	2,349	2,265	2,356	2,312	2,388	2,308
2015	2,349	2,103	2,360	2,292	2,339	2,258	2,334	2,332	2,247	2,319	2,261	2,335	2,294
2016	2,322	2,190	2,352	2,274	2,361	2,287	2,378	2,387	2,304	2,386	2,328	2,411	2,332
2017	2,400	2,159	2,394	2,312	2,387	2,319	2,403	2,386	2,283	2,360	2,308	2,381	2,341
2018	2,351	2,121	2,354	2,277	2,362	2,290	2,365	2,381	2,311	2,387	2,322	2,406	2,327
2019	2,398	2,153	2,385	2,317	2,404	2,334	2,410	2,413	2,332	2,426	2,364	2,427	2,364
2020[1]	2,414	2,254	2,411	2,316	2,356	2,304	2,445	2,446	2,354	2,458	2,395	2,453	2,384

[1] Preliminary. *Source: National Agricultural Statistics Service, U.S. Department of Agriculture (NASS-USDA)*

Egg-Type Chicks Hatched by Commercial Hatcheries in the United States In Thousands

Year	Jan.	Feb.	Mar.	Apr.	May	June	July	Aug.	Sept.	Oct.	Nov.	Dec.	Total
2011	40,587	37,412	43,600	42,956	42,946	38,918	36,948	41,428	39,803	37,616	37,503	38,889	478,606
2012	41,290	40,523	43,101	43,202	44,564	38,829	35,968	42,269	38,319	37,901	36,492	40,985	483,443
2013	43,831	42,236	43,584	46,031	50,154	42,252	39,936	38,794	42,166	42,506	41,845	41,144	514,479
2014	44,345	41,269	44,801	46,384	49,684	44,271	42,489	39,731	43,671	44,665	36,544	42,991	520,845
2015	43,868	43,774	50,187	50,193	48,315	47,212	42,790	47,131	49,391	50,194	45,848	46,679	565,582
2016	47,775	54,289	57,055	51,266	57,306	57,562	41,609	43,258	44,892	43,344	41,648	45,731	585,735
2017	45,367	48,127	55,919	52,762	53,506	49,722	41,862	45,861	42,725	51,495	48,363	46,697	582,406
2018	51,900	50,148	58,147	58,986	59,756	53,019	50,806	53,207	49,610	54,960	47,043	46,370	633,952
2019	56,219	52,182	55,658	60,668	60,816	51,858	50,919	46,246	50,386	50,266	48,113	46,114	629,445
2020[1]	52,825	48,169	56,065	60,931	52,790	55,537	46,140	50,007	49,989	50,597	48,042	51,765	622,857

[1] Preliminary. *Source: National Agricultural Statistics Service, U.S. Department of Agriculture (NASS-USDA)*

Cold Storage Holdings of Frozen Eggs in the United States, on First of Month In Thousands of Pounds[2]

Year	Jan.	Feb.	Mar.	Apr.	May	June	July	Aug.	Sept.	Oct.	Nov.	Dec.
2011	25,357	26,788	28,143	27,287	27,681	29,025	33,813	33,924	31,009	31,889	33,895	32,967
2012	36,491	37,415	36,326	33,669	32,528	34,498	40,191	38,654	35,856	31,375	28,971	27,251
2013	27,376	29,659	28,620	27,138	29,339	28,856	30,591	26,118	30,144	33,577	33,832	29,754
2014	30,350	34,687	34,631	29,044	27,430	28,300	30,142	31,453	29,820	31,126	31,960	30,349
2015	30,718	34,670	35,648	31,978	31,260	28,216	26,890	27,408	30,572	32,324	37,486	36,013
2016	40,896	42,158	37,400	31,741	33,670	35,961	37,960	37,209	31,725	33,084	34,344	36,490
2017	35,652	36,913	41,071	41,911	41,176	39,033	41,712	40,193	35,166	33,934	32,928	27,911
2018	30,162	31,041	32,308	28,175	27,763	30,236	30,705	29,791	31,990	28,935	30,267	29,603
2019	29,376	32,257	34,492	37,561	36,093	35,413	37,369	36,266	36,362	36,299	33,680	35,236
2020[1]	40,771	38,272	38,423	39,586	44,175	37,985	39,293	39,036	39,254	37,878	34,887	32,436

[1] Preliminary. [2] Converted on basis 39.5 pounds frozen eggs equals 1 case. *Source: National Agricultural Statistics Service, U.S. Department of Agriculture (NASS-USDA)*

Electric Power Production by Electric Utilities in the United States In Millions of Kilowatt Hours

Year	Jan.	Feb.	Mar.	Apr.	May	June	July	Aug.	Sept.	Oct.	Nov.	Dec.	Total
2011	220,900	188,700	195,148	183,567	196,994	225,535	253,142	242,540	199,144	181,359	176,515	197,306	2,460,850
2012	196,498	176,554	175,331	169,095	194,593	210,514	242,595	229,579	191,871	178,825	178,834	194,884	2,339,173
2013	207,123	180,975	189,129	173,761	190,354	213,033	232,867	229,557	198,719	182,713	181,991	207,837	2,388,059
2014	222,165	191,345	193,194	170,329	191,866	212,311	227,343	225,392	194,390	176,990	180,869	196,279	2,382,473
2015	208,073	194,871	184,609	165,379	184,165	208,270	229,212	223,696	196,273	172,561	165,247	182,965	2,315,323
2016	203,384	179,182	171,452	162,936	179,569	213,557	234,890	232,277	195,105	171,134	164,301	197,136	2,304,923
2017	199,391	164,437	179,245	164,153	183,781	205,299	233,807	220,364	185,458	174,251	168,569	195,521	2,274,276
2018	214,525	171,847	175,132	165,093	189,538	212,232	235,229	228,767	198,116	177,541	178,265	190,963	2,337,248
2019	202,052	174,633	177,458	159,490	185,133	198,468	229,082	224,601	197,147	168,516	168,594	180,830	2,266,004
2020[1]	183,402	170,842	163,598	143,947	163,895	191,989	230,003	222,622	180,793	164,866	157,591	185,116	2,158,664

[1] Preliminary. *Source: Energy Information Administration, U.S. Department of Energy (EIA-DOE)*

Electric Power

The modern electric utility industry began in the 1800s. In 1807, Humphry Davy constructed a practical battery and demonstrated both incandescent and arc light. In 1831, Michael Faraday built the first electric generator proving that rotary mechanical power could be converted into electric power. In 1879, Thomas Edison perfected a practical incandescent light bulb. The electric utility industry evolved from gas and electric carbon-arc commercial and street lighting systems. In 1882, in New York City, Thomas Edison's Pearl Street electricity generating station established the industry by displaying the four key elements of a modern electric utility system: reliable central generation, efficient distribution, successful end-use, and a competitive price.

Electricity is measured in units called watts and watt-hours. Electricity must be used when it is generated and cannot be stored to any significant degree. That means the power utilities must match the level of electricity generation to the level of demand to avoid wasteful over-production. The power industry has been deregulated to some degree in the past decade, and now major utility companies sell power back and forth across major national grids to meet supply and demand needs. The rapid changes in the supply-demand situation mean that the cost of electricity can be very volatile.

Electricity futures and options are traded on the ASX 24 exchange. Electricity futures are traded on Borsa Istanbul, Borsa Italiana (IDEM), ICE Futures Europe, Nasdaq Commodities, New York Mercantile Exchange, Singapore Exchange, and Tokyo Commodity Exchange.

Supply – U.S. electricity production in 2020 fell -4.7% yr/yr to 2.159 trillion kilowatt-hours. That was still well below the record high of 3.212 trillion kilowatt-hours in 1998 and indicates how electricity production has been reduced mainly by more efficient production and distribution systems, and to some extent by conservation of electricity by both business and residential consumers.

U.S. electricity generation in 2020 required the use of 11.988 billion cubic feet of natural gas (up +3.3% yr/yr), 428 million tons of coal (down -20.3% yr/yr), and 32 million barrels of petroleum (down -6.1% yr/yr).

In terms of kilowatt-hours, natural gas is the most widely used source of electricity production in the U.S., accounting for 37.3% of electricity production in 2019, followed by coal (24.2%), nuclear (20.4%), hydro (7.2%), and fuel oil (0.4%). Alternative sources of fuel for electricity generation that are gaining favor include geothermal, biomass, solar, wind, etc. but so far, they only account for 10.3% of total electricity production in the U.S.

Demand – Residential use of electricity accounts for the largest single category of electricity demand with usage of 1.440 trillion kilowatt-hours in 2019, accounting for 37.8% of overall usage. Business users in total use more electricity than residential users, with commercial businesses accounting for 35.7% of usage and industrial businesses accounting for 26.3% of usage.

World Net Generation of Electricity In Billions of Kilowatt Hours

Year	Brazil	Canada	China	France	Germany	India	Japan	Korea, South	Russia	Spain	United Kingdom	United States	World Total
2010	19,392	47,229	343,943	41,190	66,179	24,851	77,414	39,679	86,413	21,632	15,640	28,967	343,336
2011	NA	48,788	382,748	38,508	72,167	24,844	84,433	41,389	87,632	21,367	16,156	27,693	342,145
2012	NA	49,573	397,608	38,882	75,529	24,614	83,554	41,641	88,674	21,493	16,504	27,342	337,874
2013	19,029	47,267	430,730	38,545	78,706	23,984	75,009	41,189	87,552	21,412	16,151	26,976	338,184
2014	19,078	49,987	452,675	36,082	86,641	23,139	75,909	45,511	87,989	NA	15,156	25,048	341,142
2015	19,668	49,396	452,344	36,197	90,347	23,503	81,308	43,402	89,448	----	13,606	24,645	340,615
2016	20,458	51,951	489,532	36,036	92,129	23,870	72,109	43,622	90,590	----	13,642	24,412	339,736
2017	21,107	54,678	521,224	33,938	NA	23,720	75,768	46,095	91,170	----	13,094	23,957	336,300
2018[1]	20,488	53,456	560,008	32,293	----	23,392	75,399	47,481	92,449	----	13,244	23,446	348,151
2019[2]	20,700	52,601	584,210	31,142	----	23,951	73,205	47,247	91,121	----	12,438	21,850	349,076

[1] Preliminary. [2] Estimate. NA = Not avaliable. *Source: Energy Information Administration, U.S. Department of Energy (EIA-DOE)*

World Consumption of Electricity In Billions of Kilowatt Hours

Year	Brazil	Canada	China	France	Germany	India	Italy	Japan	Korea, South	Russia	United Kingdom	United States	World Total
2010	455.6	534.5	3,713.7	474.0	554.5	727.5	307.0	1,061.4	450.4	858.5	331.0	3,889.2	18,704.0
2011	471.5	551.7	4,178.9	451.0	547.6	803.2	311.0	1,056.7	473.0	874.8	320.5	3,886.4	19,398.5
2012	488.8	543.1	4,435.1	462.3	545.9	846.1	305.5	990.1	483.2	889.1	322.2	3,838.5	19,803.9
2013	504.7	562.2	4,845.4	463.9	545.0	935.6	296.5	996.7	488.4	881.1	322.0	3,876.5	20,459.3
2014	518.3	560.4	5,066.5	441.6	533.7	1,028.6	291.0	972.9	495.9	891.1	309.1	3,914.5	20,857.9
2015	510.0	546.4	5,251.2	450.8	538.2	1,084.9	296.2	954.9	499.8	890.1	311.1	3,914.3	21,278.5
2016	510.4	550.7	5,564.8	457.7	538.5	1,168.1	293.5	947.1	508.7	909.6	310.0	3,921.1	21,876.8
2017	516.7	553.1	5,950.9	455.2	538.8	1,225.9	299.9	948.9	511.8	918.6	306.5	3,888.5	22,486.3
2018[1]	528.6	558.8	6,453.2	449.6	533.2	1,277.2	301.6	939.8	534.6	929.2	307.3	4,032.8	23,398.4
2019[2]	597.2	549.3		449.4	524.3		297.2	902.8	527.0	965.2	300.5	3,989.6	

[1] Preliminary. [2] Estimate. NA = Not avaliable. *Source: Energy Information Administration, U.S. Department of Energy (EIA-DOE)*

ELECTRIC POWER

World Installed Capacity of Electricity In Billions of Kilowatt Hours

Year	Brazil	Canada	China	France	Germany	India	Italy	Japan	Russia	Spain	United Kingdom	United States	World Total
2010	113.7	132.3	969.7	124.1	162.9	204.8	106.6	286.9	229.3	102.1	92.9	1,039.1	5,063.9
2011	117.1	132.9	1,066.3	127.0	168.0	233.9	118.8	289.6	232.8	102.9	93.1	1,051.3	5,292.4
2012	121.4	130.7	1,151.5	130.5	178.4	258.4	124.6	294.9	231.3	105.2	95.3	1,063.0	5,509.9
2013	128.1	133.3	1,265.1	130.1	185.3	280.9	124.5	302.4	238.9	106.0	93.0	1,060.1	5,739.8
2014	134.8	136.7	1,377.0	130.1	197.5	310.0	121.7	272.9	259.5	106.1	96.1	1,075.7	5,975.7
2015	141.7	143.6	1,516.2	132.2	203.3	341.5	117.0	283.1	257.5	106.4	95.8	1,073.8	6,231.2
2016	150.8	146.1	1,660.2	133.2	208.2	369.2	114.2	296.0	265.0	105.6	97.2	1,087.1	6,539.6
2017	157.2	146.9	1,794.0	133.1	214.0	392.1	114.2	302.6	267.2	103.8	108.8	1,100.5	6,809.0
2018[1]	163.0	147.8	1,911.3	133.5	227.9	411.3	115.2	315.7	272.5	103.7	107.9	1,114.3	7,070.7
2019[2]												1,122.3	

[1] Preliminary. [2] Estimate. NA = Not avaliable. *Source: Energy Information Administration, U.S. Department of Energy (EIA-DOE)*

Electricity in the United States In Billions of Kilowatt Hours

	Net Generation				Trade				End Use		
Year	Electric Power Sector[2]	Commercial Sector[3]	Industrial Sector[4]	Total	Imports[5]	Exports[5]	Net Imports[5]	T&D Losses[6] and Unaccounted for[7]	Retail Sales[8]	Direct Use[9]	Total
2011	3,948.2	10.1	141.9	4,100.1	52.3	15.0	37.3	254.8	3,749.8	132.8	3,882.6
2012	3,890.4	11.3	146.1	4,047.8	59.3	12.0	47.3	262.7	3,694.7	137.7	3,832.3
2013	3,903.7	12.2	150.0	4,066.0	70.4	11.4	59.0	256.6	3,724.9	143.5	3,868.3
2014	3,937.0	12.5	144.1	4,093.6	66.5	13.3	53.2	243.5	3,764.7	138.6	3,903.3
2015	3,919.3	12.6	145.7	4,077.6	75.8	9.1	66.7	244.1	3,759.0	141.2	3,900.2
2016	3,918.1	12.7	145.9	4,076.7	72.7	6.2	66.5	240.9	3,762.5	139.8	3,902.3
2017	3,877.5	13.1	143.8	4,034.3	65.7	9.4	56.3	226.1	3,723.4	141.1	3,864.5
2018	4,010.8	13.3	146.8	4,170.9	58.3	13.8	44.5	211.1	3,860.1	144.1	4,004.2
2019	3,964.7	13.7	148.5	4,126.9	59.1	20.0	39.0	211.3	3,811.2	143.5	3,954.6
2020[1]	3,840.5	13.1	142.1	3,995.8	61.4	14.9	46.6	244.1	3,661.0	137.3	3,798.3

[1] Preliminary. [2] Electricity-only and combined-heat-and-power (CHP) plants within the NAICS 22 category whose primary business is to sell electricity, or electricity and heat, to the public. [3] Commercial combined-heat-and-power (CHP) and commercial electricity-only plants. [4] Industrial combined-heat-and-power (CHP) and industrial electricity-only plants. [5] Electricity transmitted across U.S. borders. Net imports equal imports minus exports. [6] Transmission and distribution losses. [7] Data collection frame differences and nonsampling error. [8] Electricity retail sales to ultimate customers by electric utilities and other energy service providers. [9] Use of electricity that is 1) self-generated, 2) produced by either the same entity that consumes the power or an affiliate, and 3) used in direct support of a service or industrial process located within the same facility or group of facilities that house the generating equipment. Direct use is exclusive of station use. *Source: U.S. Geological Survey (USGS)*

Electricity Net Generation in the United States by Sector In Millions of Kilowatt Hours

	Fossil Fuels						Renewable Energy						
Year	Coal[2]	Petro-leum[3]	Natural Gas[4]	Other Gases[5]	Nuclear electric power	Hydro- +electric Pumped Storage[6]	Conven-tional Hydro-electric Power	Biomass: Wood[7]	Biomass: Waste[8]	Geo-thermal	Solar/ PV[9]	Wind	Total
2010	1,847,290	37,061	987,697	11,313	806,968	-5,501	260,203	37,172	18,917	15,219	1,212	94,652	4,125,060
2011	1,733,430	30,182	1,013,689	11,566	790,204	-6,421	319,355	37,449	19,222	15,316	1,818	120,177	4,100,141
2012	1,514,043	23,190	1,225,894	11,898	769,331	-4,950	276,240	37,799	19,823	15,562	4,327	140,822	4,047,765
2013	1,581,115	27,164	1,124,836	12,853	789,016	-4,681	268,565	40,028	20,830	15,775	9,036	167,840	4,065,964
2014	1,581,710	30,232	1,126,609	12,022	797,166	-6,174	259,367	42,340	21,650	15,877	17,691	181,655	4,093,606
2015	1,352,398	28,249	1,333,482	13,117	797,178	-5,091	249,080	41,929	21,703	15,918	24,893	190,719	4,077,601
2016	1,239,149	24,205	1,378,307	12,807	805,694	-6,686	267,812	40,947	21,813	15,826	36,054	226,993	4,076,827
2017	1,205,835	21,390	1,296,415	12,469	804,950	-6,495	300,333	41,152	21,610	15,927	53,286	254,303	4,034,268
2018	1,145,962	25,226	1,468,727	13,463	807,084	-5,905	292,524	41,005	17,410	15,967	63,825	272,650	4,170,912
2019[1]	966,148	18,567	1,581,815	13,634	809,409	-5,261	273,707	39,851	18,561	16,011	72,234	300,071	4,118,051

[1] Preliminary. [2] Anthracite, bituminous coal, subbituminous coal, lignite, waste coal, and coal synfuel. [3] Distillate fuel oil, residual fuel oil, petroleum coke, jet fuel, kerosene, other petroleum, waste oil, and propane. [4] Natural gas, plus a small amount of supplemental gaseous fuels. [5] Blast furnace gas, and other manufactured and waste gases derived from fossil fuels. [6] Pumped storage facility production minus energy used for pumping. [7] Wood and wood-derived fuels. [8] Municipal solid waste from biogenic sources, landfill gas, sludge waste, agricultural byproducts, and other biomass. [9] Solar thermal and photovoltaic (PV) energy. *Source: U.S. Geological Survey (USGS)*

Total Electricity Net Generation in the United States In Billions of Kilowatt Hours

Year	Jan.	Feb.	Mar.	Apr.	May	June	July	Aug.	Sept.	Oct.	Nov.	Dec.	Total
2011	362.9	313.1	318.7	302.4	323.6	367.7	418.7	406.5	337.9	308.7	304.1	335.7	4,100.1
2012	339.5	309.4	309.1	295.2	336.5	360.8	414.6	395.7	334.6	311.7	306.0	334.6	4,047.8
2013	349.0	309.7	325.4	299.3	322.2	356.8	394.8	385.3	340.9	314.9	314.5	353.0	4,066.0
2014	377.3	324.3	331.8	297.6	324.7	357.8	385.8	384.3	339.9	314.5	317.5	338.0	4,093.6
2015	360.5	334.5	324.2	294.1	322.1	362.4	400.4	392.1	350.1	312.1	300.7	324.4	4,077.6
2016	352.7	313.7	304.4	292.9	316.8	367.8	411.9	409.7	351.5	312.9	297.1	345.3	4,076.7
2017	343.2	289.7	317.9	294.3	322.5	357.9	404.4	384.3	335.9	320.4	310.3	353.5	4,034.3
2018	373.2	306.9	321.5	300.7	338.0	371.0	410.3	407.3	356.2	324.9	322.3	338.5	4,170.9
2019	359.5	315.0	326.6	296.6	330.3	352.9	410.0	401.4	360.5	320.3	315.7	338.3	4,126.9
2020[1]	340.4	317.9	306.9	275.8	304.2	353.0	414.6	399.8	334.2	314.4	301.8		3,995.8

[1] Preliminary. *Source: Energy Information Administration, U.S. Department of Energy (EIA-DOE)*

Imports[2] of Electricity in the United States In Billions of Kilowatt Hours

Year	Jan.	Feb.	Mar.	Apr.	May	June	July	Aug.	Sept.	Oct.	Nov.	Dec.	Total
2011	4.3	3.7	4.0	3.8	4.9	4.5	6.0	5.6	4.0	3.7	3.5	4.3	52.3
2012	4.1	3.6	4.2	5.0	5.5	5.4	6.7	6.3	4.9	4.4	4.7	4.4	59.3
2013	5.8	5.3	5.8	5.0	5.9	6.0	6.7	6.9	5.6	5.6	6.0	5.9	70.4
2014	5.5	4.4	5.6	4.8	5.4	5.5	6.3	6.7	6.0	5.4	5.6	5.4	66.5
2015	6.0	5.6	6.6	6.5	6.6	6.7	6.9	7.2	6.6	5.3	5.8	5.9	75.8
2016	6.5	5.4	5.8	4.7	5.6	6.7	7.7	7.3	5.3	5.8	6.4	5.4	72.7
2017	7.0	5.7	6.0	5.6	5.1	6.0	5.9	6.5	5.2	4.0	3.9	4.8	65.7
2018	5.2	4.8	5.6	4.5	5.2	5.5	5.4	6.1	4.3	3.7	3.8	4.1	58.3
2019	4.8	4.6	5.0	4.4	4.7	5.2	5.6	5.9	5.3	3.7	4.8	5.2	59.1
2020[1]	4.6	4.5	5.1	4.7	5.2	5.2	6.6	6.8	4.7	4.2	4.7		61.4

[1] Preliminary. [2] Electricity transmitted across U.S. borders. Net imports equal imports minus exports. *Source: Energy Information Administration, U.S. Department of Energy (EIA-DOE)*

Exports[2] of Electricity in the United States In Billions of Kilowatt Hours

Year	Jan.	Feb.	Mar.	Apr.	May	June	July	Aug.	Sept.	Oct.	Nov.	Dec.	Total
2011	1.6	1.5	1.5	1.6	1.3	1.3	1.3	1.0	1.0	0.9	1.1	0.9	15.0
2012	0.9	0.9	1.2	1.3	1.2	1.2	1.0	0.9	0.9	0.7	0.8	1.1	12.0
2013	1.0	0.8	0.9	1.2	1.0	0.8	1.0	0.9	0.7	1.0	0.9	1.1	11.4
2014	1.3	1.3	1.9	1.3	0.8	1.0	1.0	0.9	0.8	1.0	0.9	1.1	13.3
2015	0.8	1.4	0.9	0.6	0.6	0.6	0.6	0.7	0.7	0.7	0.7	0.8	9.1
2016	0.4	0.6	0.7	0.5	0.4	0.6	0.6	0.6	0.6	0.4	0.4	0.6	6.2
2017	0.5	0.7	1.0	1.1	0.8	0.8	0.7	0.8	0.7	0.7	0.8	0.7	9.4
2018	1.1	1.3	1.2	1.6	1.1	1.2	0.9	1.1	1.1	0.9	1.3	0.9	13.8
2019	1.5	1.4	2.5	2.0	1.7	1.5	2.0	1.8	1.8	1.5	1.2	1.2	20.0
2020[1]	1.4	1.7	1.3	1.5	1.5	1.3	1.2	0.9	1.0	0.9	1.0		14.9

[1] Preliminary. [2] Electricity transmitted across U.S. borders. Net imports equal imports minus exports. *Source: Energy Information Administration, U.S. Department of Energy (EIA-DOE)*

Total End Use of Electricity in the United States In Billions of Kilowatt Hours

Year	Jan.	Feb.	Mar.	Apr.	May	June	July	Aug.	Sept.	Oct.	Nov.	Dec.	Total
2011	345.3	306.9	302.4	285.6	298.7	339.9	382.8	385.0	337.5	298.6	286.1	313.6	3,882.6
2012	322.6	298.0	294.7	281.3	308.3	336.6	383.5	377.2	329.5	301.9	289.5	309.2	3,832.3
2013	333.0	302.6	309.2	288.9	301.0	332.2	371.7	366.3	335.2	306.0	293.2	329.1	3,868.3
2014	353.3	319.6	313.8	286.7	302.6	334.2	363.9	364.3	338.5	307.9	296.7	321.8	3,903.3
2015	341.9	317.5	316.5	286.1	299.3	338.3	375.9	374.7	345.0	307.6	287.6	309.8	3,900.2
2016	332.8	307.9	297.4	280.4	296.1	341.6	384.7	393.9	348.4	308.0	288.6	322.4	3,902.3
2017	330.3	286.7	303.1	284.0	303.3	340.6	380.4	372.8	332.9	310.9	294.8	324.7	3,864.5
2018	357.0	303.8	308.6	289.6	315.1	350.2	388.1	394.3	349.4	321.1	302.6	324.7	4,004.2
2019	341.2	306.8	313.6	284.8	308.2	333.2	388.9	385.4	352.5	320.1	297.6	322.4	3,954.6
2020[1]	324.1	301.8	296.9	268.8	281.4	326.9	386.6	375.9	328.8	306.5	284.0		3,798.3

[1] Preliminary. *Source: Energy Information Administration, U.S. Department of Energy (EIA-DOE)*

Ethanol

World Production of Fuel Ethanol In Thousands of Barrels per Day

Year	Australia	Brazil	Canada	China	Colombia	France	Germany	India	Jamaica	Spain	Thailand	United States	World Total
2007	22.4	6,230.2	224.2	464.5	75.3	148.9	108.9	72.1	78.5	112.1	48.0	6,521.0	14,815.0
2008	40.0	7,463.5	240.2	544.5	70.5	256.3	160.2	80.1	102.5	96.1	91.3	9,308.8	19,459.6
2009	56.0	6,610.0	362.4	680.6	47.4	247.3	200.4	27.6	----	126.9	115.6	10,937.8	20,660.0
2010	75.9	7,112.2	378.7	684.2	54.9	268.9	212.7	13.8	----	137.7	124.5	13,297.9	23,681.2
2011	88.0	5,803.4	445.6	708.2	63.5	272.0	199.3	100.7	----	127.5	134.1	13,929.1	23,296.6
2012	95.5	6,036.6	471.1	786.6	77.9	251.5	213.5	84.2	----	105.2	130.0	13,218.0	23,864.6
2013	84.2	6,978.0	465.0	809.8	81.7	259.6	229.4	105.4	----	123.2	262.2	13,292.7	25,342.0
2014	71.6	7,128.7	472.6	814.5	84.0	262.1	241.8	96.6	----	120.8	292.0	14,312.8	26,628.5
2015[1]	68.8	7,669.3	477.1	849.5	119.8	264.0	248.1	189.1	----	129.1	324.0	14,807.2	27,824.4
2016[2]	68.8	7,374.4	486.8	868.4	122.6	249.4	247.3	306.4	26.1	102.6	352.2	15,413.2	

[1] Preliminary. [2] Estimate. *Source: Renewable Fuels Association*

Salient Statistics of Ethanol in the United States

Year	Ethanol Plants	Ethanol Production Capacity (mgy)	Plants Under Con-struction	Capacity Under Construction (mgy)	Farmer Owned Plants	Farmer Owned Capacity (mgy)	Percent of Total Capacity Farmer	Farmer Owned UC Plants	Farmers Owned UC Capacity	Percent of Total UC Capacity	States with Ethanol Plants
2011	204	14,071.4	10	560.0	----	----	----	----	----	----	29
2012	209	14,906.9	2	140.0	----	----	----	----	----	----	29
2013	211	14,837.4	2	50.0	----	----	----	----	----	----	28
2014	210	14,879.5	7	167.0	----	----	----	----	----	----	28
2015	213	15,077.0	3	100.0	----	----	----	----	----	----	29
2016	214	15,594.0	3	162.0	----	----	----	----	----	----	28
2017	213	15,998.0	3	91.0	----	----	----	----	----	----	28
2018	211	16,241.0	7	465.0	----	----	----	----	----	----	28
2019[1]	205	16,924.0	4	183.0	----	----	----	----	----	----	26
2020[2]	210	16,501.0	9	350.0	----	----	----	----	----	----	27

[1] Preliminary. [2] Estimate. *Source: Renewable Fuels Association*

Production of Fuel Ethanol in the United States In Thousands of Barrels

Year	Jan.	Feb.	Mar.	Apr.	May	June	July	Aug.	Sept.	Oct.	Nov.	Dec.	Total
2011	28,467	25,300	28,178	26,538	27,720	27,224	27,541	27,976	26,588	28,013	28,383	29,718	331,646
2012	29,038	26,647	27,548	26,346	27,616	26,513	25,236	26,092	24,376	24,976	24,744	25,582	314,714
2013	24,778	22,494	25,620	25,601	27,197	26,722	26,923	26,279	25,564	27,995	27,915	29,405	316,493
2014	28,194	25,269	28,120	27,733	28,888	28,629	29,413	28,665	27,807	28,644	28,588	30,831	340,781
2015	29,770	26,814	29,485	27,910	29,666	29,684	30,249	29,762	28,571	29,886	29,675	31,081	352,553
2016	30,452	28,810	30,957	28,208	30,346	30,443	31,469	31,856	30,048	31,006	30,706	32,680	366,981
2017	32,887	29,307	32,393	29,639	31,863	30,794	31,384	32,672	30,701	32,212	32,631	32,952	379,435
2018	32,428	29,519	32,216	30,532	32,215	31,924	33,496	33,773	30,667	32,380	31,514	31,736	382,400
2019	31,601	28,576	30,895	30,951	32,443	31,895	32,541	31,921	29,232	30,941	31,358	33,275	375,629
2020[1]	33,343	30,516	29,406	16,945	21,098	25,958	28,707	28,419	27,778	29,402	29,908	30,097	331,577

[1] Preliminary. *Source: Energy Information Administration, U.S. Department of Energy (EIA-DOE)*

Stocks of Fuel Ethanol in the United States In Thousands of Barrels

Year	Jan.	Feb.	Mar.	Apr.	May	June	July	Aug.	Sept.	Oct.	Nov.	Dec.
2011	20,826	21,016	21,593	21,065	20,609	19,217	18,788	18,123	18,465	18,038	18,308	18,238
2012	21,475	22,393	22,583	22,050	21,635	21,239	20,224	19,180	19,921	18,626	19,992	20,350
2013	19,894	19,009	18,410	17,370	16,804	16,428	17,072	16,945	15,986	15,750	15,569	16,424
2014	17,153	16,865	17,310	17,610	18,330	18,785	18,696	18,218	18,724	17,341	17,035	18,739
2015	20,647	21,057	20,878	20,854	20,154	20,128	19,701	19,390	18,944	18,984	20,099	21,596
2016	23,347	23,171	22,730	21,336	20,962	21,284	21,381	21,198	20,713	20,113	19,463	19,758
2017	22,679	23,195	23,981	23,671	22,855	21,770	21,167	21,186	21,507	21,663	23,203	23,043
2018	24,229	24,335	22,883	23,256	22,636	21,880	22,802	22,833	24,422	23,675	23,679	23,338
2019	25,026	24,448	23,311	23,218	22,818	22,573	23,235	22,721	23,036	21,784	21,641	22,349
2020[1]	24,047	24,555	27,501	26,102	22,247	19,826	19,784	20,143	20,027	21,422	23,257	24,687

[1] Preliminary. *Source: Energy Information Administration, U.S. Department of Energy (EIA-DOE)*

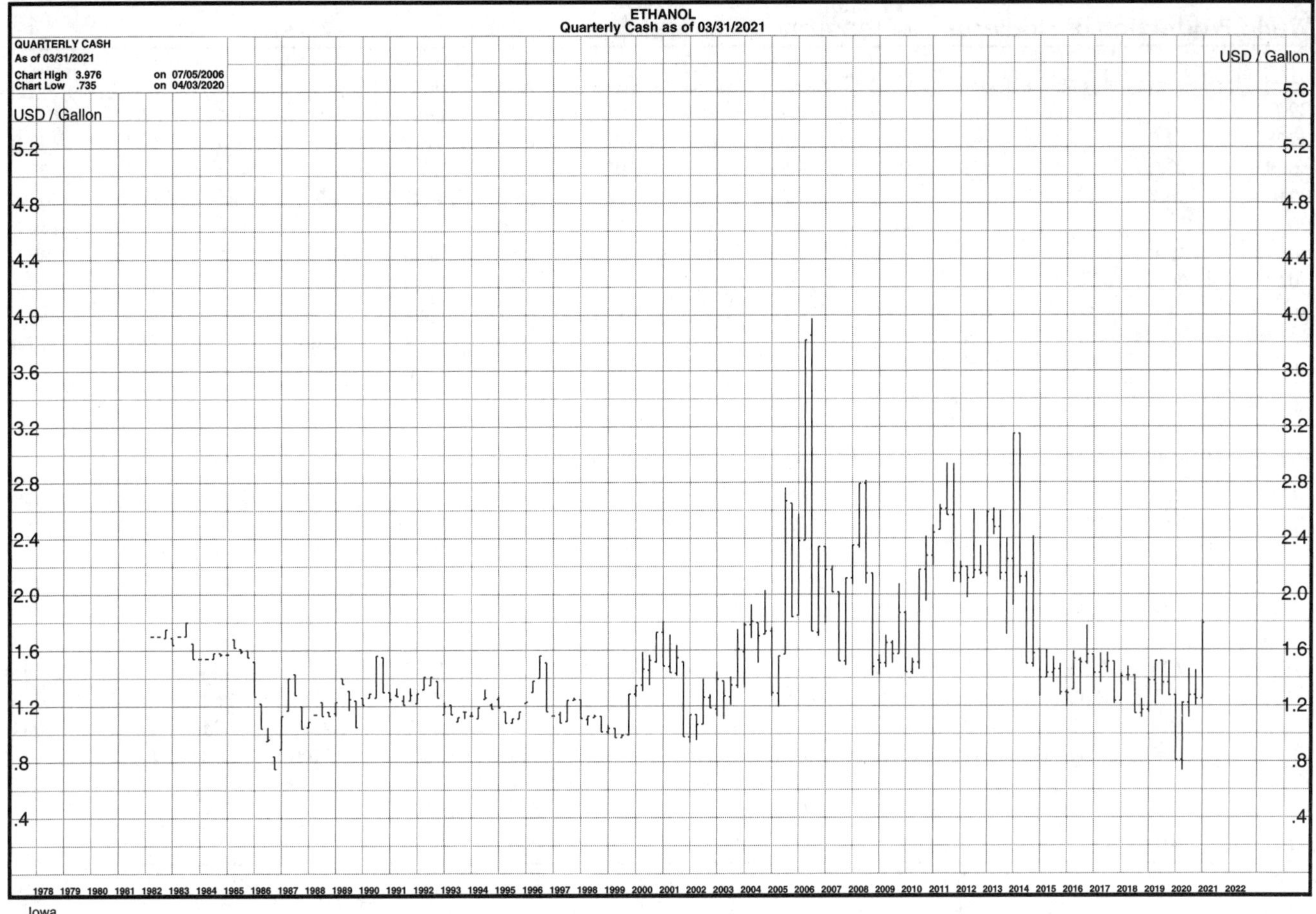

Average Price of Ethanol in the United States[1] In Dollars Per Gallon

Year	Jan.	Feb.	Mar.	Apr.	May	June	July	Aug.	Sept.	Oct.	Nov.	Dec.	Average
2012	2.128	2.089	2.177	2.152	2.107	2.002	2.399	2.532	2.397	2.296	2.301	2.265	2.237
2013	2.197	2.331	2.473	2.478	2.553	2.571	2.430	2.287	2.346	2.096	1.942	2.314	2.335
2014	2.073	1.946	2.478	2.800	2.237	2.225	2.100	2.096	1.827	1.561	2.019	1.995	2.113
2015	1.382	1.313	1.386	1.479	1.568	1.440	1.493	1.418	1.408	1.472	1.425	1.347	1.428
2016	1.235	1.304	1.273	1.417	1.466	1.562	1.480	1.333	1.430	1.519	1.545	1.649	1.434
2017	1.400	1.381	1.378	1.541	1.446	1.505	1.472	1.487	1.510	1.407	1.357	1.267	1.429
2018	1.270	1.338	1.408	1.430	1.397	1.403	1.406	1.341	1.223	1.196	1.230	1.156	1.317
2019	1.172	1.209	1.309	1.305	1.253	1.449	1.477	1.360	1.302	1.482	1.434	1.360	1.343

[1] Northeast and Northwest Iowa. *Source: Agricultural Marketing Service, U.S. Department of Agriculture (AMS-USDA)*

Volume of Trading of Ethanol Futures in Chicago In Contracts

Year	Jan.	Feb.	Mar.	Apr.	May	June	July	Aug.	Sept.	Oct.	Nov.	Dec.	Total
2015	24,040	13,103	17,508	20,055	20,013	17,466	17,981	11,506	10,947	10,938	11,211	12,893	187,661
2016	14,151	11,923	15,335	13,085	13,549	20,010	14,181	12,121	13,043	11,682	16,030	17,554	172,664
2017	18,902	15,630	18,607	16,246	17,896	9,817	6,524	9,114	6,012	10,185	9,943	10,670	149,546
2018	10,502	9,213	8,683	9,238	9,476	9,346	6,682	8,319	8,239	9,346	12,343	11,051	112,438
2019	10,629	10,252	10,627	8,269	9,526	6,965	5,391	4,336	2,770	4,506	3,618	2,686	79,575
2020	2,688	2,261	2,826	2,231	1,138	601	222	170	190	172	239	244	12,982

Contract size = 29,000 US gallons. *Source: CME Group; Chicago Board of Trade (CBT)*

Average Open Interest of Ethanol Futures in Chicago In Contracts

Year	Jan.	Feb.	Mar.	Apr.	May	June	July	Aug.	Sept.	Oct.	Nov.	Dec.
2015	6,518	6,892	7,296	6,781	7,978	7,336	6,511	5,381	4,905	5,167	5,098	4,253
2016	4,270	4,361	4,130	4,449	5,193	5,170	4,828	4,361	4,477	5,054	5,571	5,352
2017	5,783	4,991	4,743	4,849	3,660	2,551	2,062	1,742	1,501	1,674	2,011	2,332
2018	2,812	2,162	1,970	1,982	1,916	1,957	1,899	2,069	2,177	2,367	2,598	2,796
2019	2,446	1,942	1,420	1,452	1,523	986	974	658	531	555	584	633
2020	653	508	461	542	395	154	91	68	55	70	51	125

Contract size = 29,000 US gallons. *Source: CME Group; Chicago Board of Trade (CBT)*

World Production of Biodiesel In Thousands of Barrels per Day

Year	Argentina	Austria	Belgium	Brazil	China	France	Germany	Indonesia	Italy	Spain	Thailand	United States	World Total
2007	3.7	5.1	----	5.8	6.1	19.1	58.9	4.7	4.0	3.6	1.8	32.0	180.7
2008	14.6	4.9	----	19.3	9.2	35.2	49.9	10.9	13.1	4.4	7.3	44.1	265.3
2009	23.0	5.2	2.6	27.7	10.2	41.8	48.3	5.7	15.7	14.6	10.5	33.7	307.5
2010	38.7	5.4	6.9	41.1	9.8	40.0	61.2	12.8	15.7	16.9	11.4	22.4	364.4
2011	51.7	4.7	6.2	46.1	12.7	36.6	60.9	31.0	11.6	13.6	10.9	63.1	449.0
2012	52.2	4.1	6.2	46.8	15.7	43.7	55.6	37.9	5.6	9.9	15.7	64.5	482.5
2013	39.4	3.5	6.1	50.3	18.6	43.1	59.7	48.3	9.0	14.5	18.6	88.7	537.2
2014	51.3	5.2	9.0	59.0	19.5	47.0	68.1	51.7	11.4	24.0	20.2	83.4	597.7
2015[1]	35.9	6.8	5.0	67.8	9.4	48.6	61.9	20.3	11.4	22.0	21.5	82.4	547.9
2016[2]	48.3	5.7	4.7	65.5	8.6	45.1	62.4	63.0	11.0	26.8	21.4	102.0	

[1] Preliminary. [2] Estimate. *Source: Renewable Fuels Association*

Production of Biodiesel in the United States In Thousands of Barrels (mbbl)

Year	Jan.	Feb.	Mar.	Apr.	May	June	July	Aug.	Sept.	Oct.	Nov.	Dec.	Average
2012	1,751	1,887	2,251	2,237	2,428	2,223	2,127	2,176	1,949	1,792	1,363	1,406	23,588
2013	1,640	1,672	2,412	2,548	2,645	2,699	3,072	3,086	3,025	3,272	3,080	3,217	32,368
2014	1,727	1,801	2,361	2,223	2,531	2,645	2,926	2,987	2,754	2,928	2,610	2,958	30,452
2015	1,727	1,851	2,326	2,568	2,784	2,901	2,883	2,933	2,479	2,535	2,521	2,573	30,080
2016	2,490	2,504	2,861	2,856	3,222	3,205	3,331	3,385	3,206	3,433	3,408	3,425	37,327
2017	2,208	2,238	2,761	3,020	3,242	3,344	3,560	3,559	3,507	3,515	3,523	3,515	37,993
2018	2,945	2,996	3,493	3,344	3,538	3,718	3,892	4,028	3,850	4,039	3,783	3,991	43,616
2019	3,427	3,108	3,353	3,623	3,675	3,370	3,776	3,712	3,377	3,436	3,034	3,163	41,054
2020[1]	3,196	3,067	3,594	3,407	3,505	3,590	3,849	3,872	3,790	3,798	3,593	3,775	43,036

[1] Preliminary. *Source: Energy Information Administration, U.S. Department of Energy (EIA-DOE)*

Stocks of Biodiesel in the United States In Thousands of Barrels (Mbbl)

Year	Jan.	Feb.	Mar.	Apr.	May	June	July	Aug.	Sept.	Oct.	Nov.	Dec.
2014	3,708	3,726	3,604	3,402	3,135	2,798	3,089	2,786	2,293	2,641	3,084	3,131
2015	4,032	4,245	4,244	4,071	3,599	3,063	3,404	3,333	3,021	3,070	3,600	3,943
2016	4,222	4,133	4,167	4,358	4,091	4,726	4,443	4,265	4,227	4,690	5,314	6,398
2017	6,397	6,475	6,189	5,706	4,909	5,052	5,405	5,356	4,849	4,485	4,233	4,268
2018	4,557	4,924	4,916	4,681	4,257	3,845	3,583	3,412	3,360	3,647	4,056	4,684
2019	5,377	5,509	5,371	5,315	4,802	4,404	4,397	3,844	3,706	3,760	3,870	3,919
2020[1]	4,312	4,046	4,419	4,392	4,340	4,318	3,878	3,560	3,220	3,476	3,922	3,884

[1] Preliminary. *Source: Energy Information Administration, U.S. Department of Energy (EIA-DOE)*

Imports of Biodiesel in the United States In Thousands of Barrels (mbbl)

Year	Jan.	Feb.	Mar.	Apr.	May	June	July	Aug.	Sept.	Oct.	Nov.	Dec.	Average
2013	38	88	439	372	410	698	358	385	781	1,177	1,641	1,765	8,152
2014	222	161	240	135	133	235	493	571	352	507	989	540	4,578
2015	372	526	340	330	336	673	1,157	961	1,062	863	701	1,078	8,399
2016	248	287	565	969	1,117	1,630	1,681	1,873	1,835	1,822	2,184	2,668	16,879
2017	241	549	650	681	948	1,736	1,670	1,582	205	386	222	504	9,374
2018	246	146	457	308	325	296	157	281	277	468	416	536	3,913
2019	308	267	509	410	281	310	333	140	280	314	417	433	4,002
2020[1]	336	302	333	611	475	446	346	234	360	420	448	373	4,684

[1] Preliminary. *Source: Energy Information Administration, U.S. Department of Energy (EIA-DOE)*

Exports of Biodiesel in the United States In Thousands of Barrels (mbbl)

Year	Jan.	Feb.	Mar.	Apr.	May	June	July	Aug.	Sept.	Oct.	Nov.	Dec.	Average
2013	16	37	176	371	563	587	429	687	511	415	408	476	4,675
2014	134	141	91	261	208	263	320	264	136	40	65	51	1,974
2015	22	23	191	240	255	260	255	275	200	161	76	133	2,091
2016	42	49	234	246	335	220	250	235	150	114	143	80	2,098
2017	42	59	136	283	239	226	453	387	100	217	49	35	2,228
2018	102	103	255	217	382	275	259	263	190	188	156	61	2,453
2019	72	92	240	370	419	300	392	290	238	158	56	83	2,710
2020[1]	31	76	215	526	496	494	341	524	426	113	73	64	3,380

[1] Preliminary. *Source: Energy Information Administration, U.S. Department of Energy (EIA-DOE)*

Fertilizer

A fertilizer is a natural or a synthetic chemical substance, or a mixture of both, that enriches the soil to promote plant growth. The three primary nutrients that fertilizers provide are nitrogen, potassium, and phosphorus. In ancient times, and still today, many commonly used fertilizers contain one or more of the three primary ingredients: manure (containing nitrogen), bones (containing small amounts of nitrogen and large quantities of phosphorus), and potash (containing potassium).

At least fourteen different nutrients have been found essential for crops. These include three organic nutrients (carbon, hydrogen, and oxygen, which are taken directly from air and water), three primary chemical nutrients (nitrogen, phosphorus, and potassium), and three secondary chemical nutrients (magnesium, calcium, and sulfur). The others are micronutrients or trace elements and include iron, manganese, copper, zinc, boron, and molybdenum.

Prices – The average price of ammonia (Gulf Coast delivery), a key source of ingredients for fertilizers, rose by +22.9% yr/yr in 2018 to $295 per metric ton, but is still far below the 2008 record high of $590 per metric ton. The average price of potash in the U.S. in 2018 rose by +11.4% yr/yr to $490.00 per metric ton, but still below the 2009 record high of $800.00 per metric ton.

Supply – World production of ammonia (as contained in nitrogen) in 2020 rose +1.4% to 144.000 million metric tons, a new record high. The world's largest producers of ammonia in 2020 were China with 26.4% of world production, Russia with 10.4%, the U.S. with 9.7%, and India with 9.0%.

World production of phosphate rock, basic slag, and guano in 2020 fell -1.8% yr/yr to 223.000 million metric tons. The world's largest producers of phosphate rock in 2020 were China with 40.4% of world production, Morocco with 16.6%, the U.S. with 10.8%, and Russia with 5.8%. U.S. production in 2020 rose +3.0% yr/yr to 24.000 million metric tons.

World production of marketable potash in 2020 rose +4.1% yr/yr to 43.000 million metric tons. The world's largest producers of potash in 2019 were Canada with 32.6% of world production, Russia with 17/7%. Belarus with 17.0%, and China with 11.6%. U.S. production of potash in 2020 fell -7.8% to 470,000 metric tons.

Demand – U.S. consumption of phosphate rock in 2020 rose +2.0% to 26.000 million metric tons. U.S. consumption of potash in 2020 rose by +3.8% yr/yr to 5.5 million metric tons. U.S. consumption of nitrogen in 2018 fell -2.5% to 11.600 million metric tons.

Trade – U.S. imports of nitrogen in 2019 fell -20.9% yr/yr to 2.000 million metric tons, and the U.S. relied on imports for 12% of its consumption. U.S. imports of phosphate rock in 2020 rose +7.5% yr/yr to 2.300 million metric tons. U.S. imports of potash in 2020 rose +3.2% to 5.100 million metric tons, higher than the 4-decade low of 2.220 million metric tons posted in 2009. Imports accounted for 90% of U.S. consumption.

World Production of Ammonia In Thousands of Metric Tons of Contained Nitrogen

Year	Canada	China	France	Germany	India	Indonesia	Japan	Mexico	Netherlands	Poland	Russia	United States	Total
2012	3,942	45,520	2,644	2,823	10,650	5,100	867	772	2,200	2,026	11,401	8,730	139,000
2013	3,830	47,175	810	2,757	10,840	5,000	828	758	2,300	2,119	11,879	9,170	140,000
2014	3,716	46,850	760	2,540	10,780	5,000	787	714	2,200	2,200	12,030	9,330	140,000
2015	4,004	47,603	1,040	2,500	10,800	5,000	790	473	2,300	2,200	12,455	9,590	142,000
2016	4,133	46,922	1,010	2,500	10,800	5,000	725	438	2,300	2,237	13,300	10,200	144,000
2017	3,745	43,600	1,010	2,500	10,800	5,000	717	411	2,300	2,337	14,020	11,600	142,000
2018	3,832	41,000	1,000	2,600	11,400	5,000	673	124	2,400	2,170	14,900	13,100	144,000
2019[1]	3,940	38,000		2,420	12,200	5,000			2,200	2,200	15,000	13,500	142,000
2020[2]	3,900	38,000		2,400	13,000	5,000			2,200	2,200	15,000	14,000	144,000

[1] Preliminary. [2] Estimate. *Source: U.S. Geological Survey (USGS)*

Salient Statistics of Nitrogen[3] (Ammonia) in the United States In Thousands of Metric Tons

	Net Import Reliance	-- Production[3] (Fixed) ---					Nitrogen[5] -- Compounds --		- Stocks, Dec. 31 -			----- Average Price ($/Metric Ton) -----			
												------- Urea -------		Ammonium	Ammonia
Year	As a % of Apparent Consumption	Fertilizer	Non-fertilizer	Total	Imprts[4] (Fixed)	Exports	Pro-duced	Con-sumption	Am-monia	Fixed Nitrogen Com-pounds	Ammonia Con-sumption (Apparent)	FOB Gulf[6] Coast	FOB Corn Belt	Nitrate: FOB Corn Belt	FOB Gulf Coast
2012	37	7,600	1,140	8,730	5,170	31	8,579	12,300	180	180	13,900	393-410	440-480	760-820	579
2013	34	8,070	1,100	9,170	4,960	196	8,759	11,900	240	240	13,900	325-342	370-380	510-550	541
2014	30	8,210	1,120	9,330	4,150	111	8,391	11,400	280	280	13,300	322-333	360-385	570-640	531
2015	30	8,440	1,150	9,590	4,320	93	8,266	12,000	420	420	13,700	225-230	265-295	445-470	481
2016	26	8,930	1,220	10,200	3,840	183	8,918	11,700	400	400	13,800	232-242	255-275	290-405	245
2017	18	10,200	1,390	11,600	3,090	612	9,666	11,900	320	480	14,100	243-260	270-280	260-270	280-300
2018	14	11,600	1,540	13,100	2,530	224	10,087	11,600	490	450	15,300	257-264	300-320	250-280	295
2019[1]	11			13,500	2,020	338			420		15,200				
2020[2]	10			14,000	2,000	400			400		16,000				

[1] Preliminary. [2] Estimate. [3] Anhydrous ammonia, synthetic. [4] For consumption. [5] Major downstream nitrogen compounds. [6] Granular.
Source: U.S. Geological Survey (USGS)

World Production of Phosphate Rock, Basic Slag & Guano In Thousands of Metric Tons (Gross Weight)

Year	Brazil	China	Egypt	Israel	Jordan	Morocco	Russia	Senegal	Syria	Togo	Tunisia	United States	World Total
2011	6,738	81,000	4,746	3,105	7,594	28,052	10,300	1,411	3,541	866	2,479	28,100	200,000
2012	6,740	95,000	6,236	3,513	6,383	27,060	10,300	1,416	1,534	1,159	2,762	30,100	216,000
2013	6,715	111,700	5,922	3,578	5,399	26,400	10,700	909	1,000	1,214	3,283	31,200	232,000
2014	6,513	120,000	5,378	3,357	7,144	27,390	10,800	1,285	1,234	1,098	3,784	25,300	237,000
2015	5,800	142,000	5,303	3,849	8,336	26,264	11,600	2,100	538	1,150	3,240	27,400	263,000
2016	5,200	135,000	5,000	3,947	7,991	26,929	12,400	2,200	----	850	3,660	27,100	255,000
2017	5,200	144,000	4,400	3,850	8,690	30,000	13,300	1,390	----	825	4,420	27,900	269,000
2018	5,740	120,000	5,000	3,550	8,020	34,800	14,000	1,650	100	800	3,340	25,800	249,000
2019[1]	4,700	95,000	5,000	2,810	9,220	35,500	13,100	3,420	2,000	800	4,110	23,300	227,000
2020[2]	5,500	90,000	5,000	2,800	9,200	37,000	13,000	3,500	360	800	4,000	24,000	223,000

[1] Preliminary. [2] Estimate. *Source: U.S. Geological Survey (USGS)*

Salient Statistics of Phosphate Rock in the United States In Thousands of Metric Tons

Year	Mine Production	Marketable Production	Value Million Dollars	Imports for Consumption	Exports	Apparent Consumption	Producer Stocks, Dec. 31	Avg. Price FOB Mine $/Metric Ton	Avg. Price of Florida & N. Carolina - $/Met. Ton - FOB Mine (-60% to +74%) - Domestic	Export	Average
2011	129,000	28,100	2,720	3,750	----	32,000	4,580	96.64	----	----	----
2012	150,000	30,100	3,080	3,570	----	30,900	6,700	102.54	----	----	----
2013	139,000	31,200	2,850	3,170	----	31,900	9,000	91.11	----	----	----
2014	112,000	25,300	1,990	2,380	----	29,100	5,880	78.59	----	----	----
2015	127,000	27,400	1,980	1,960	----	28,100	6,730	72.41	----	----	----
2016	130,000	27,100	2,090	1,590	----	28,200	7,450	76.90	----	----	----
2017	123,000	27,900	2,060	2,470	----	28,800	8,440	73.67	----	----	----
2018	115,000	25,800	1,830	2,770	----	26,000	10,600	70.77	----	----	----
2019[1]		23,300		2,140	----	25,500	9,940	67.98	----	----	----
2020[2]		24,000		2,300	----	26,000	9,500	70.00	----	----	----

[1] Preliminary. [2] Estimate. *Source: U.S. Geological Survey (USGS)*

World Production of Marketable Potash In Thousands of Metric Tons (K_2O Equivalent)

Year	Belarus	Brazil	Canada	Chile	China	Germany	Israel	Jordan	Russia	Spain	United Kingdom	United States	World Total
2011	5,306	395	10,686	832	3,800	3,215	1,610	1,355	6,498	521	470	1,000	35,800
2012	4,840	347	8,976	1,018	3,770	3,149	1,830	1,094	5,563	632	549	900	32,800
2013	4,243	311	10,196	1,130	5,300	3,075	2,268	1,046	6,100	711	549	960	36,100
2014	6,340	311	10,818	1,200	6,110	3,130	2,213	1,255	7,439	685	610	850	41,300
2015	6,468	293	11,462	1,200	5,710	3,110	1,540	1,413	6,954	690	610	740	40,700
2016	6,180	306	10,790	1,200	5,780	2,800	2,050	1,202	6,588	670	450	500	39,000
2017	7,102	290	12,214	1,100	5,510	2,700	2,000	1,392	7,300	610	250	480	41,400
2018	7,200	200	13,800	1,200	5,000	3,200	2,200	1,480	7,170	700	190	520	43,300
2019[1]	7,350	247	12,300	840	5,000	3,000	2,040	1,520	7,340	500		510	41,300
2020[2]	7,300	250	14,000	900	5,000	3,000	2,000	1,500	7,600	470		470	43,000

[1] Preliminary. [2] Estimate. *Source: U.S. Geological Survey (USGS)*

Salient Statistics of Potash in the United States In Thousands of Metric Tons (K_2O Equivalent)

Year	Net Import Reliance As a % of Apparent Consump	Production	Sales by Producers	Value Million Dollars	Imports for Consumption	Exports	Apparent Consumption	Producer Stocks Dec. 31	----------- Dollars per Ton ----------- Avg Value of Product	Avg Value of K_2O Equiv	Avg. Price[3] (Metric Ton)
2011	83	1,000	990	740.0	4,980	175	5,800	----	320.00	745.00	730.00
2012	82	900	980	750.0	4,240	200	5,000	----	340.00	765.00	650.00
2013	82	960	880	630.0	4,650	255	5,300	----	315.00	715.00	590.00
2014	85	850	930	680.0	4,970	100	5,800	----	345.00	735.00	555.00
2015	89	740	620	550.0	5,190	106	5,700	----	360.00	880.00	570.00
2016	88	510	600	410.0	4,550	96	5,100	----	290.00	680.00	460.00
2017	92	480	490	380.0	5,870	128	6,200	----	285.00	775.00	440.00
2018	92	520	520	390.0	5,710	105	6,100	----	280.00	750.00	490.00
2019[1]	90	510	480		4,940	145	5,300	----			
2020[2]	90	470	520		5,100	140	5,500	----			

[1] Preliminary. [2] Estimate. [3] Unit of K_2O, standard 60% muriate F.O.B. mine. *Source: U.S. Geological Survey (USGS)*

Fish

Fish are the primary source of protein for a large portion of the world's population. The worldwide yearly harvest of all sea fish (including aquaculture) is between 85 and 130 million metric tons. There are approximately 20,000 species of fish, of which 9,000 are regularly caught. Only 22 fish species are harvested in large amounts. Ground-fish, which are fish that live near or on the ocean floor, account for about 10% of the world's fishery harvest and include cod, haddock, pollock, flounder, halibut, and sole. Large pelagic fish such as tuna, swordfish, marlin, and mahi-mahi, account for about 5% of world harvest. The fish eaten most often in the United States is canned tuna.

Rising global demand for fish has increased the pressure to harvest more fish to the point where all 17 of the world's major fishing areas have either reached or exceeded their limits. Atlantic stocks of cod, haddock, and blue-fin tuna are all depleted, while in the Pacific, anchovies, salmon, and halibut are all over-fished. Aquaculture, or fish farming, reduces pressure on wild stocks and now accounts for nearly 20% of world harvest.

Supply – The U.S. total of fishery products in 2018 fell by -0.7% to 22.103 billion pounds, which is down from the 2017 record high of 22.266. The U.S. total domestic catch in 2018 fell -5.4% to 9.385 billion pounds, and that comprised 42.5% of total U.S. supply. Of the U.S. total domestic catch in 2018, 68.3% of the catch was finfish for human consumption, 20.0% of the catch was a variety of fish for industrial use, and 11.6% was shellfish for human consumption. The principal species of U.S. fishery landings in 2018 were Pollock with 3.371 billion pounds, Menhaden with 1.582 billion pounds, Pacific Salmon with 576.0 million pounds, Flounder with 525.1 million pounds, and Sea Herring with 145.8 million pounds.

About 30% of the fish harvested in the world are processed directly into fishmeal and fish oil. Fishmeal is used primarily in animal feed. Fish oil is used in both animal feed and human food products. World fishmeal production in the 2018/19 marketing year rose by 1.5% to 5.113 million metric tons. Peru, the European Union, and Thailand are the world's largest producers of fish meal. World production of fish oil in the 2018/19 marketing year fell -5.6% to 941.8 thousand metric tons. Peru, Chile, and the U.S. are the world's largest producers of fish oil.

Trade – U.S. imports of fishery products in 2018 rose +3.0% yr/yr to 12.718 billion pounds, a new record high, comprising 57.5% of total U.S. supply.

					Domestic Catch					Imports				
Year	Grand Total	For Human Food - Finfish	For Human Food - Shellfish[3]	For Industrial Use[4]	Total	Percent of Grand Total	For Human Food - Finfish	For Human Food - Shellfish[3]	For Industrial Use[4]	Total	Percent of Grand Total	For Human Food - Finfish	For Human Food - Shellfish[3]	For Industrial Use[4]
2012	20,757	13,159	4,907	2,692	9,634	46.4	6,163	1,314	2,157	11,123	53.6	6,996	3,592	535
2013	20,988	13,787	4,786	2,416	9,870	47.0	6,777	1,266	1,827	11,118	53.0	7,009	3,520	589
2014	21,431	14,060	5,054	2,317	9,486	44.3	6,588	1,240	1,658	11,945	55.7	7,473	3,814	659
2015	21,426	13,862	4,986	2,579	9,718	45.4	6,621	1,129	1,968	11,709	54.6	7,241	3,857	611
2016	21,542	13,746	5,034	2,762	9,572	44.4	6,393	1,092	2,088	11,970	55.6	7,353	3,942	675
2017	22,266	14,421	5,384	2,461	9,916	44.5	7,121	1,107	1,688	12,350	55.5	7,301	4,276	773
2018[1]	22,103	13,941	5,538	2,625	9,385	42.5	6,409	1,091	1,886	12,718	57.5	7,532	4,447	739

[1] Preliminary. [2] Live weight, except percent. [3] For univalue and bivalues mollusks (conchs, clams, oysters, scallops, etc.) the weight of meats, excluding the shell is reported. [4] Fish meal and sea herring. *Source: Fisheries Statistics Division, U.S. Department of Commerce*

Fisheries -- Landings of Principal Species in the United States In Millions of Pounds

	Fish									Shellfish					
Year	Cod, Atlantic	Flounder	Halibut	Herring, Sea	Man-haden	Pollock	Salmon, Pacific	Tuna	Whiting	Clams (Meats)	Crabs	Lobsters American	Oysters (Meats)	Scallops (Meats)	Shrimp
2012	11	703	34	270	1,771	2,887	636	60	16	91	367	150	33	57	303
2013	5	717	30	298	1,467	3,014	1,069	56	14	91	332	149	35	41	283
2014	5	714	23	309	1,256	3,156	720	59	16	91	295	148	34	34	295
2015	3	555	25	247	1,618	3,269	1,066	57	14	86	326	146	28	36	327
2016	3	565	25	192	1,728	3,361	561	56	14	89	317	159	33	41	271
2017	2	545	26	180	1,413	3,396	1,008	55	12	85	275	133	32	52	283
2018[1]	2	525	22	146	1,582	3,371	576	52	11	86	289	146	30	58	289

[1] Preliminary. *Source: National Marine Fisheries Service, U.S. Department of Commerce*

U.S. Fisheries: Quantity & Value of Domestic Catch & Consumption & World Fish Oil Production

	Disposition										
Year	Fresh & Frozen	Canned	Cured	For Meal, Oil, etc.	Total	For Human Food	For Industrial Products	Ex-vessel Value[3]	Average Price	Fish Per Capita Consumption	World[2] Fish Oil Production
	Millions of Pounds							Million $	Cents /Lb.	Pounds	1,000 Tons
2012	7,541	299	82	1,712	9,634	7,477	2,157	5,103	----	14.4	933
2013	8,009	365	45	1,451	9,870	8,043	1,827	5,466	----	14.5	941
2014	7,916	196	63	1,311	9,486	7,828	1,658	5,448	----	14.6	917
2015	7,622	364	65	1,667	9,718	7,750	1,968	5,203	----	15.5	903
2016	7,509	186	57	1,820	9,572	7,484	2,088	5,312	----	14.9	865
2017	8,091	289	136	1,400	9,916	8,228	1,688	5,421	----	16.0	895
2018[1]	7,443	180	139	1,623	9,385	7,500	1,885	5,571	----	16.1	1,060

[1] Preliminary. [2] Crop years on a marketing year basis. [3] At the Dock Prices. Source: Fisheries Statistics Division, U.S. Department of Commerce

Imports of Seafood Products into the United States In Thousands of Pounds

Year	Trout, fresh and frozen	Atlantic salmon, fresh	Pacific salmon, fresh[2]	Atlantic salmon, frozen	Pacific salmon, frozen[2]	Atlantic salmon, fillets	Salmon, canned and pre-pared[3]	Tilapia[4]	Shrimp, frozen	Shrimp, fresh and prepared[5]	Oysters[6]	Mussels[6]	Clams[6]	Scallops[6]
2012	19,616	222,313	9,770	4,828	65,491	276,703	27,539	503,644	922,877	253,456	18,566	75,384	45,518	34,021
2013	18,713	190,427	12,153	5,604	71,480	317,981	37,106	504,698	865,142	248,812	19,830	70,916	48,705	60,429
2014	19,312	172,283	11,070	6,853	76,248	360,274	32,381	508,484	989,966	265,538	21,356	74,665	50,989	60,041
2015	26,708	236,674	10,051	6,112	78,790	371,476	32,387	496,083	996,935	292,139	24,498	71,002	52,969	48,365
2016	31,366	239,288	14,670	8,223	89,165	371,643	30,619	434,606	1,039,634	290,126	25,096	78,855	54,918	50,178
2017	27,929	262,441	9,658	6,367	96,676	390,807	33,582	402,947	1,139,829	325,782	25,775	78,107	51,859	40,077
2018	34,712	273,251	9,068	6,172	105,803	439,352	35,074	415,889	1,182,010	353,579	29,577	67,374	56,242	45,498
2019[1]	31,806	245,435	7,254	5,110	86,012	385,755	37,635	307,305	994,596	262,634	19,454	66,964	40,251	28,475

[1] Preliminary. [2] Includes salmon with no specific species noted. [3] Includes smoked and cured salmon. [4] Frozen whole fish plus fresh and frozen fillets. [5] Canned, breaded or otherwise prepared. [6] Fresh or prepared. *Source: Bureau of the Census, U.S. Department of Commerce*

Exports of Seafood Products From the United States In Thousands of Pounds

Year	Trout, fresh and frozen	Atlantic salmon, fresh	Pacific salmon, fresh[2]	Atlantic salmon, frozen	Pacific salmon, frozen[2]	Salmon, canned and prepared[3]	Shrimp, frozen	Shrimp, fresh and prepared[4]	Oysters[5]	Mussels[5]	Clams[5]	Scallops[5]
2012	1,779	17,234	20,934	380	222,933	92,838	14,951	9,260	7,781	931	14,056	28,756
2013	2,148	15,574	24,129	223	359,834	101,469	14,760	7,897	7,624	1,043	18,114	21,206
2014	2,232	11,868	17,704	295	310,551	94,793	15,251	12,972	8,229	1,275	17,483	20,064
2015	1,317	9,590	23,825	335	413,075	87,624	25,699	11,931	8,370	1,217	18,491	16,824
2016	2,188	23,094	33,543	1,342	272,348	82,959	11,441	13,367	7,765	1,262	19,494	18,236
2017	3,836	12,655	26,168	1,516	427,477	64,462	8,020	9,535	7,533	1,944	16,612	16,437
2018	3,460	18,181	14,641	642	280,138	56,269	8,347	11,988	7,674	1,321	15,383	14,173
2019[1]	3,468	15,596	14,784	643	296,899	37,286	4,224	10,136	6,279	1,690	11,584	11,108

[1] Preliminary. [2] Includes salmon with no specific species noted. [3] Includes smoked and cured salmon. [4] Canned, breaded, or prepared. [5] Fresh or prepared. *Source: Bureau of the Census, U.S. Department of Commerce*

World Production of Fish Meal In Thousands of Metric Tons

Year	Chile	Denmark	European Union	Iceland	Japan	Norway	Peru	Russia	South Africa	Spain	Thailand	United States	World Total
2011-12	464.5	90.0	307.2	130.3	189.8	86.0	1,413.8	76.9	96.2	30.0	489.0	278.6	5,046.2
2012-13	336.6	140.4	368.2	123.0	207.0	101.0	775.0	81.9	28.4	30.5	462.5	236.7	4,334.2
2013-14	395.9	161.8	392.3	82.0	201.0	132.7	1,070.9	75.3	74.8	30.1	460.0	227.0	4,738.5
2014-15	338.8	192.0	427.1	152.0	198.0	174.1	671.2	87.8	72.2	30.4	430.0	279.1	4,468.3
2015-16	236.9	175.0	417.4	90.0	194.8	139.0	558.7	93.4	85.1	30.0	400.0	252.5	4,261.7
2016-17[1]	313.2	222.1	469.4	117.0	192.0	156.8	1,087.0	98.8	80.3	31.0	366.0	251.3	5,049.7
2017-18[2]	349.0	192.6	446.2	133.2	189.9	145.2	1,008.0	105.0	71.8	35.0	375.0	276.8	5,038.9
2018-19[3]	345.4	175.0	434.3	101.0	192.0	123.0	1,060.0	103.0	68.0	35.0	383.0	238.4	5,113.4

[1] Preliminary. [2] Estimate. [3] Forecast. *Source: The Oil World*

World Production of Fish Oil In Thousands of Metric Tons

Year	Canada	Chile	China	Denmark	Iceland	Japan	Norway	Peru	Africa	Russia	United States	World Total	Fish Oil CIF[4] $ Per Tonne
2011-12	6.0	117.5	17.8	35.2	59.9	56.2	36.0	307.4	5.8	5.7	56.5	1,053.7	1,718
2012-13	6.2	91.1	18.7	46.8	50.5	58.4	36.0	137.6	2.2	7.3	78.1	892.9	2,190
2013-14	6.0	137.9	20.0	50.1	44.3	60.0	53.2	174.4	4.8	8.6	60.8	969.4	1,791
2014-15	6.1	110.3	24.0	50.1	48.2	62.6	58.8	85.7	7.3	8.6	64.8	867.4	1,909
2015-16	6.1	87.9	40.0	53.7	29.2	61.8	56.8	77.0	7.6	21.0	80.7	843.9	1,713
2016-17[1]	6.0	111.9	32.0	55.7	36.3	62.1	56.0	165.7	7.3	7.5	52.0	935.9	1,445
2017-18[2]	6.0	131.3	31.0	49.7	44.3	71.0	46.8	174.0	6.4	14.1	75.8	998.0	1,683
2018-19[3]	6.0	134.0	33.0	45.8	31.8	71.8	40.0	140.0	6.2	10.3	59.0	941.8	1,566

[1] Preliminary. [2] Estimate. [3] Forecast. [4] Any origin, N.W. Europe. *Source: The Oil World*

Average Price of Fish Meal, 60% protein, Domestic, East Coast In U.S. Dollars Per Ton

Year	Oct.	Nov.	Dec.	Jan.	Feb.	Mar.	Apr.	May	June	July	Aug.	Sept.	Average
2012-13	1,265.00	1,415.00	1,427.50	1,441.50	1,511.88	1,525.00	1,525.00	1,525.00	1,500.00	1,477.50	1,465.63	1,395.63	1,456.22
2013-14	1,347.00	1,335.00	1,322.50	1,328.75	1,334.38	1,333.75	1,345.00	1,345.00	1,400.00	1,479.00	1,505.00	1,512.50	1,382.32
2014-15	1,546.25	1,718.13	1,821.88	1,861.25	1,825.00	1,791.50	1,740.63	1,518.13	1,412.50	1,380.00	1,329.00	1,312.50	1,604.73
2015-16	1,353.75	1,431.25	1,437.50	1,437.50	1,437.50	1,432.50	1,398.88	1,335.00	1,377.50	1,392.50	1,381.00	1,368.75	1,398.64
2016-17	1,359.38	1,362.50	1,362.50	1,362.50	1,362.50	1,343.75	1,300.00	1,290.00	1,300.00	1,302.50	1,310.00	1,312.50	1,330.68
2017-18[1]	1,327.50	1,355.00	1,394.17	1,480.50	1,500.00	1,500.00	1,500.00	1,500.00	----	----	----	----	1,444.65
2018-19[1]	----	----	----	----	----	----	----	----	----	----	----	----	----

[1] Preliminary. *Source: Economic Research Service, U.S. Department of Agriculture (ERS-USDA)*

Catfish Sales of Foodsize Fish in the United States In Thousands of Fish

Year	Alabama	Arkansas	California	Mississippi	North Carolina	Texas	Other[2]	U.S. Total
2011	62,300	14,800	1,360	107,000	2,970	10,400	1,240	201,880
2012	64,700	11,300	1,260	117,000	2,940	7,700	1,160	206,630
2013	62,400	15,500	1,510	106,000	2,750	10,200	2,400	201,810
2014	63,400	9,980	1,340	97,900	1,990	7,050	2,940	184,600
2015	63,000	9,560	1,050	110,000	2,120	7,880	1,900	195,510
2016	62,300	10,300	1,150	105,000	1,930	8,020	1,880	190,580
2017	66,300	11,100	910	112,000	1,380	6,740	1,400	199,830
2018	63,600	10,900	1,600	121,000	1,400	8,520	1,780	208,800
2019	60,300	10,700	1,210	113,000	W	W	11,235	196,445
2020[1]	55,300	9,960	W	128,000	W	8,100	2,665	204,105

[1] Preliminary. [2] Other States include State estimates not shown and States suppressed due to disclosure.
Source: National Agricultural Statistics Service, U.S. Department of Agriculture (NASS-USDA)

Catfish Sales of Foodsize Fish in the United States In Thousands of Pounds (Live Weight)

Year	Alabama	Arkansas	California	Mississippi	North Carolina	Texas	Other[2]	U.S. Total
2011	119,200	25,500	2,850	173,900	5,200	16,900	2,200	348,000
2012	122,600	20,000	2,150	174,800	5,200	12,700	1,960	340,166
2013	109,300	25,300	2,800	175,300	4,000	15,800	3,500	337,130
2014	105,300	17,200	2,550	161,500	3,400	14,300	3,248	307,498
2015	107,500	14,500	2,200	171,700	3,250	15,600	2,694	317,444
2016	109,000	16,300	1,640	172,000	3,500	15,400	2,334	320,174
2017	112,900	16,800	1,580	180,500	2,600	14,000	2,048	330,428
2018	104,600	18,300	2,850	192,000	2,500	20,200	3,151	343,601
2019	102,500	18,600	2,400	203,500	W	W	20,990	347,990
2020[1]	94,000	15,700	W	192,100	W	17,000	4,748	323,548

[1] Preliminary. [2] Other States include State estimates not shown and States suppressed due to disclosure.
Source: National Agricultural Statistics Service, U.S. Department of Agriculture (NASS-USDA)

Trout Sales of Fish 12" or longer (Foodsize) in the United States In Thousands of Fish

Year	California	Colorado	Georgia	Idaho	Michigan	North Carolina	Pennsylvania	Virginia	Washington	West Virginia	Wisconsin	Other[2]	U.S. Total
2011	1,260	260	150	27,600	220	3,450	1,710	490	210	370	470	1,950	38,215
2012	1,120	220	W	30,900	230	3,180	1,030	460	W	420	470	3,580	41,700
2013	W	250	145	30,100	145	3,310	870	430	W	440	480	4,380	41,170
2014	1,310	210	W	36,100	105	3,310	880	480	W	420	410	4,150	48,285
2015	1,350	310	W	32,700	W	3,220	910	590	W	550	440	4,460	45,350
2016	W	380	W	33,000	W	3,960	980	460	W	630	W	6,035	46,305
2017	W	640	W	27,700	W	3,500	970	500	W	590	390	5,965	40,965
2018	W	430	W	22,200	W	3,640	1,210	460	W	450	370	6,975	35,935
2019	W	W	W	19,900	W	W	1,090	440	W	400	340	9,960	32,390
2020[1]	W	390	W	W	W	W	960	450	W	350	310	22,970	25,430

[1] Preliminary. [2] Other States include State estimates not shown and States suppressed due to disclosure. W = Withheld.
Source: National Agricultural Statistics Service, U.S. Department of Agriculture (NASS-USDA)

Trout Sales of Fish 12" or longer (Foodsize) in the United States In Thousands of Pounds (Live Weight)

Year	California	Colorado	Georgia	Idaho	Michigan	North Carolina	Pennsylvania	Virginia	Washington	West Virginia	Wisconsin	Other[2]	U.S. Total
2011	1,580	410	167	33,000	214	3,350	1,570	552	620	506	450	2,300	44,786
2012	1,370	393	W	36,600	251	3,250	1,100	525	W	515	465	10,960	55,529
2013	W	441	163	35,700	167	3,700	1,050	498	W	551	447	13,178	56,666
2014	1,550	404	W	42,200	119	4,050	1,030	489	W	518	403	9,121	60,733
2015	1,600	405	W	39,100	W	3,700	1,050	567	W	464	414	9,767	57,947
2016	W	441	W	39,700	W	4,400	1,090	427	W	569	W	11,598	59,087
2017	W	634	W	33,600	W	4,150	1,070	524	W	515	378	12,168	53,887
2018	W	591	W	27,000	W	4,000	1,200	512	W	435	357	13,261	47,548
2019	W	W	W	25,000	W	W	1,200	540	W	410	314	16,006	43,758
2020[1]	W	614	W	W	W	W	1,100	516	W	343	291	41,213	44,077

[1] Preliminary. [2] Other States include State estimates not shown and States suppressed due to disclosure. W = Withheld.
Source: National Agricultural Statistics Service, U.S. Department of Agriculture (NASS-USDA)

Flaxseed and Linseed Oil

Flaxseed, also called linseed, is an ancient crop that was cultivated by the Babylonians around 3,000 BC. Flaxseed is used for fiber in textiles and to produce oil. Flaxseeds contain approximately 35% oil, of which 60% is omega-3 fatty acid. Flaxseed or linseed oil is obtained through either the expeller extraction or solvent extraction method. Manufacturers filter the processed oil to remove some impurities and then sell it as unrefined. Unrefined oil retains its full flavor, aroma, color, and naturally occurring nutrients. Flaxseed oil is used for cooking and as a dietary supplement as well as for animal feed. Industrial linseed oil is not for internal consumption due to possible poisonous additives and is used for making putty, sealants, linoleum, wood preservation, varnishes, and oil paints.

Prices – The average monthly price received by U.S. farmers for flaxseed in the 2020/21 marketing year (through January 2020 rose by +8.7% yr/yr to $10.17 per bushel, still below the record high of $14.10 per bushel posted in the 2012/13 marketing year.

Supply – World production of flaxseed in the 2018/19 marketing year rose by +8.1% yr/yr to 2.617 million metric tons, only slightly below the 10-year high of 2.864 million metric tons in 2005/06. The world's largest producer of flaxseed in 2018/19 was Russia at 46.0% of total world production, Canada with 18.8%, China with 13.8%, and India with 5.7%. U.S. production of flaxseed in 2019 rose +43.2% to 6,395 million bushels, but still below the record level of 10.095 million bushels in 2015. North Dakota is by far the largest producing state for flaxseed and accounted for 79.1% of flaxseed production in 2019, followed by Montana with 20.9%.

World production of linseed oil in 2018/19 fell by -1.3% yr/yr to 735,700 metric tons. The world's largest producers of linseed oil were China with 30.7 of world production in 2018/19, Belgium with 16.2%, the U.S. with 10.7%, and Russia with 10.1%. U.S. production of linseed oil in 2018/19 fell by -14.1% yr/yr to 176.000 million pounds.

Demand – U.S. distribution of flaxseed in 2019/20 rose by 9.8% yr/yr to 11.034 million bushels. The breakdown of use was 88.1% for crushing into meal and oil, 6.3% for exports, 3.1% for residual, and 2.4% for seed.

Trade – U.S. exports of flaxseed in 2019/20 rose by +170.4% yr/yr to 700,000 thousand bushels. U.S. imports of flaxseed in 2019/20 fell by -14.8% yr/yr to 4.699 million bushels.

World Production of Flaxseed In Thousands of Metric Tons

Crop Year	Argentina	Australia	Bangladesh	Canada	China	Egypt	France	Hungary	India	Romania	United States	Former USSR	World Total
2009-10	52	8	7	930	318	8	21	1	154	1	189	206	2,163
2010-11	32	7	7	419	353	12	36	----	147	2	230	326	1,806
2011-12	21	7	7	399	359	5	31	1	152	3	71	802	2,136
2012-13	17	7	6	489	391	5	26	----	149	4	147	571	2,053
2013-14	20	6	6	731	399	2	16	1	140	4	85	618	2,255
2014-15	17	6	9	840	350	5	23	1	155	3	162	688	2,457
2015-16	20	6	5	943	330	5	48	1	125	4	256	873	2,835
2016-17[1]	17	6	5	591	365	8	42	1	184	3	221	1,139	2,815
2017-18[2]	14	6	4	555	362	5	55	2	150	4	98	1,133	2,604
2018-19[3]	15	6	5	493	360	6	44	2	148	3	113	1,204	2,617

[1] Preliminary. [2] Estimate. [3] Forecast. *Source: The Oil World*

Supply and Distribution of Flaxseed in the United States In Thousands of Bushels

Crop Year Beginning June 1	Planted (1,000 Acres)	Harvested (1,000 Acres)	Yield Per Acre (Bushels)	Supply: Beginning Stocks	Supply: Production	Supply: Imports	Supply: Total Supply	Distribution: Seed	Distribution: Crush	Distribution: Exports	Distribution: Residual	Distribution: Total
2011-12	178	173	16.1	2,170	2,791	8,286	13,247	279	10,500	654	694	12,127
2012-13	349	336	17.3	1,120	5,798	6,928	13,846	147	11,000	1,020	755	12,922
2013-14	181	172	19.5	924	3,356	6,759	11,039	252	8,700	599	725	10,276
2014-15	311	302	21.1	763	6,368	7,464	14,595	375	11,850	528	1,034	13,787
2015-16	463	456	22.1	808	10,095	4,436	15,339	303	10,700	870	553	12,425
2016-17	374	366	23.7	2,914	8,656	3,086	14,656	245	10,500	1,332	410	12,486
2017-18	303	272	14.1	2,170	3,842	5,451	11,463	168	9,000	480	186	9,834
2018-19[1]	208	198	22.6	1,629	4,466	5,516	11,611	303	9,300	262	-91	9,774
2019-20[2]	374	284	19.8	1,562	5,625	4,381	11,568	247	8,950	855	253	9,450
2020-21[3]	305	296	19.3	1,263	5,706	5,766	12,735	247	9,550	900	573	10,370

[1] Preliminary. [2] Estimate. [3] Forecast. NA = not avaliable. *Source: Economic Research Service, U.S. Department of Agriculture (ERS-USDA)*

Supply and Distribution of Linseed Meal in the United States In Millions of Pounds

Crop Year Beginning June 1	Supply: Stocks June 1	Supply: Production	Supply: Imports	Supply: Total Supply	Disappearance: Domestic Disappear-ance	Disappearance: Exports	Disappearance: Total Disappear ance	Ending Stocks	Average Price at Minneapolis (34% Protein) Cents/Lb.
2011-12	5	189	8	202	194	3	197	5	238.35
2012-13	5	198	6	209	199	5	204	5	320.13
2013-14	5	157	1	163	153	6	158	5	359.42
2014-15	5	213	3	221	212	4	216	5	263.90
2015-16	5	193	7	205	196	4	200	5	234.78
2016-17	5	189	6	200	190	5	195	5	313.17
2017-18	5	162	7	174	166	3	169	5	236.92
2018-19	5	165	8	178	170	2	173	5	236.37
2019-20[1]	5	161	10	176	169	2	171	5	199.50
2020-21[2]	5	172	10	187	180	2	182	5	300.00

[1] Preliminary. [2] Forecast. *Source: Economic Research Service, U.S. Department of Agriculture (ERS-USDA)*

Supply and Distribution of Linseed Oil in the United States In Millions of Pounds

Crop Year Beginning June 1	Supply: Stocks June 1	Supply: Production	Supply: Total Supply	Disappearance: Exports	Disappearance: Domestic Disappearance	Disappearance: Total Disappearance	Average Price at Minneapolis Cents/Lb.
2011-12	38	205	248	124	89	213	NA
2012-13	35	215	255	126	94	220	NA
2013-14	35	170	210	117	58	175	NA
2014-15	35	231	270	183	52	235	NA
2015-16	35	209	248	196	17	213	NA
2016-17	35	205	244	194	15	209	NA
2017-18	35	176	215	167	14	180	NA
2018-19	35	178	219	173	11	184	NA
2019-20[1]	35	175	215	155	25	180	NA
2020-21[2]	35	186	226	164	27	191	NA

[1] Preliminary. [2] Forecast. *Source: Economic Research Service, U.S. Department of Agriculture (ERS-USDA)*

World Production and Price of Linseed Oil In Thousands of Metric Tons

Year	Argen-tina	Bang-ladesh	Belgium	China	Egypt	Germany	India	Japan	United Kingdom	United States	Former USSR	World Total	Rotterdam Ex-TankUSD $/Tonne
2009-10	1.7	2.1	96.9	159.2	5.2	34.5	45.2	2.0	2.6	115.7	21.9	587.7	1,114
2010-11	1.9	2.0	107.2	120.4	4.3	40.9	41.4	1.6	5.9	103.1	25.1	538.9	1,451
2011-12	1.1	2.3	108.8	144.5	4.3	49.5	41.1	1.6	5.6	100.2	24.3	609.5	1,267
2012-13	1.6	2.0	107.2	152.0	2.9	44.8	38.6	2.0	4.9	94.3	21.4	592.5	1,217
2013-14	----	----	112.0	186.6	2.9	48.7	35.3	1.5	6.7	81.6	19.4	601.1	1,191
2014-15	----	----	123.2	219.7	3.5	49.4	38.6	2.6	6.1	108.7	20.2	679.0	1,162
2015-16	----	----	131.8	225.8	4.7	49.4	34.3	----	6.9	97.8	35.2	728.9	825
2016-17	----	----	125.4	225.7	4.7	52.6	46.2	----	8.5	89.0	47.0	786.8	828
2017-18[1]	----	----	127.6	225.8	6.3	51.9	40.8	----	8.9	78.4	61.1	743.1	837
2018-19[2]	----	----	119.0	225.8	5.6	52.6	37.9	----	9.2	78.4	74.0	735.7	826

[1] Preliminary. [2] Forecast. *Source: The Oil World*

Production of Flaxseed in the United States, by States In Thousands of Bushels

Year	Minnesota	Montana	North Dakota	South Dakota	U.S. Total
2011	45	208	2,426	112	2,791
2012	45	156	5,478	119	5,798
2013	76	240	2,920	120	3,356
2014	48	425	5,805	90	6,368
2015	42	450	9,315	288	10,095
2016	----	616	7,896	144	8,656
2017	----	342	3,435	65	3,842
2018	----	629	3,792	45	4,466
2019	----	1,335	5,060	----	5,625
2020[1]	----	----	----	----	5,706

[1] Preliminary. *Source: National Agricultural Statistics Service, U.S. Department of Agriculture (NASS-USDA)*

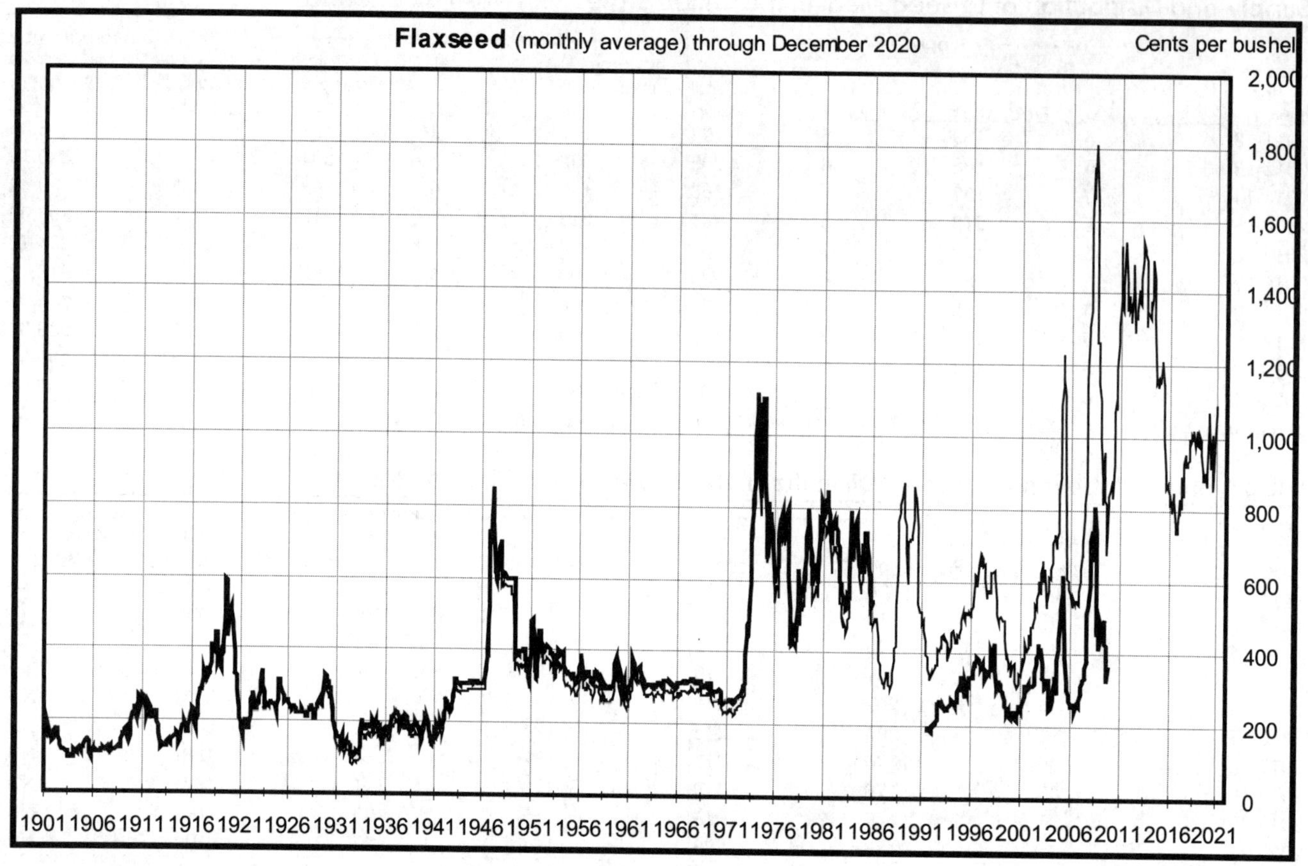

Average Price Received by Farmers for Flaxseed in the United States In Dollars Per Bushel

Year	July	Aug.	Sept.	Oct.	Nov.	Dec.	Jan.	Feb.	Mar.	Apr.	May	June	Average
2011-12	15.40	14.30	13.50	13.90	13.90	13.50	13.70	13.20	13.30	14.10	14.80	12.90	13.88
2012-13	13.30	13.30	13.30	13.50	14.10	13.80	13.70	14.30	14.40	14.90	15.40	15.20	14.10
2013-14	15.10	14.90	13.10	13.50	13.40	13.40	13.30	13.80	13.50	13.90	14.90	14.40	13.93
2014-15	14.00	13.30	11.70	11.50	11.60	11.40	11.70	11.50	11.50	12.00	12.10	11.40	11.98
2015-16	11.50	10.00	9.07	8.57	8.71	8.62	8.46	8.10	8.37	8.10	7.93	8.44	8.82
2016-17	8.48	8.25	7.61	7.37	7.36	7.59	8.26	7.86	8.34	8.03	8.96	8.52	8.05
2017-18	8.40	9.30	9.55	9.23	9.21	9.36	9.40	10.00	9.76	9.92	10.10	10.00	9.52
2018-19	9.96	10.20	9.79	9.79	10.20	9.87	9.85	9.79	10.10	9.93	9.54	9.08	9.84
2019-20	9.10	8.84	8.84	9.01	8.70	8.91	8.97	10.40	10.70	9.15	9.57	10.10	9.36
2020-21[1]	9.64	8.56	9.64	9.76	10.70	10.90	12.00						10.17

[1] Preliminary. *Source: National Agricultural Statistics Service, U.S. Department of Agriculture (NASS-USDA)*

Average Price of Linseed Meal (34% protein) at Minneapolis In Dollars Per Ton

Year	July	Aug.	Sept.	Oct.	Nov.	Dec.	Jan.	Feb.	Mar.	Apr.	May	June	Average
2011-12	260.63	247.50	239.38	243.75	239.00	221.25	209.00	193.75	216.25	256.25	279.00	287.50	241.11
2012-13	343.00	358.75	340.63	334.00	297.50	335.83	296.00	303.75	303.75	309.00	331.88	340.00	324.51
2013-14	382.50	317.50	400.00	363.75	316.25	328.75	330.00	377.50	413.75	388.00	355.00	323.75	358.06
2014-15	295.00	252.50	302.50	214.38	283.75	287.50	250.00	230.63	230.50	239.38	256.88	258.00	258.42
2015-16	284.38	287.50	256.00	215.00	209.80	200.00	195.00	197.50	195.00	218.13	301.50	375.63	244.62
2016-17	364.38	335.00	316.25	305.63	296.00	290.00	297.00	299.38	297.50	291.25	290.00	282.63	305.42
2017-18	250.63	253.00	236.88	214.00	205.00	209.17	215.50	233.13	237.50	238.13	267.50	271.25	235.97
2018-19	278.00	265.63	235.00	196.50	209.38	225.83	219.00	225.00	235.63	241.50	233.75	228.88	232.84
2019-20	232.50	235.00	226.25	226.50	226.88	231.67	248.13	262.50	263.00	260.00	257.50	245.63	242.96
2020-21[1]	250.00	251.75	227.00	239.38	253.75	275.00	313.18						258.58

[1] Preliminary. *Source: Economic Research Service, U.S. Department of Agriculture (ERS-USDA)*

Fruits

A fruit is any seed-bearing structure produced from a flowering plant. A widely used classification system divides fruit into fleshy or dry types. Fleshy fruits are juicy and include peaches, mangos, apples, and blueberries. Dry fruits include tree nuts such as almonds, walnuts, and pecans. Some foods that are commonly called vegetables, such as tomatoes, squash, peppers, and eggplant, are technically fruits because they develop from the ovary of a flower.

Worldwide, over 430 million tons of fruit are produced each year and are grown everywhere except the Arctic and the Antarctic. The tropics, because of their abundant moisture and warm temperatures, produce the most diverse and abundant fruits. Mexico and Chile produce more than half of all the fresh and frozen fruit imported into the U.S. In the U.S., the top three fruits produced are oranges, grapes, and apples. Virtually all U.S. production of almonds, pistachios, and walnuts occurs in California, which leads the U.S. in tree nut production.

Prices – Overall fruit prices were fairly strong in 2019 with the fresh fruit Consumer Price Index (CPI) falling -1.4% to 360.1, and the processed fruit CPI index rose +2.1% to 158.2. Individual fruit prices, however, were mixed in 2019: Red Delicious apples (unchanged at $1.294 per pound), bananas (unchanged 57.4 cents per pound), Anjou pears (-1.56% at $1.603 per pound), Thompson seedless grapes (-5.4% at $2.129 per pound), lemons (-5.3% at $2.129 per pound), grapefruit (-0.1% at $1.345 per pound), and navel oranges (-3.3% at $1.367 cents per pound).

Supply – U.S. commercial production of selected fruits in 2019 rose +6.2% to 24.752 million short tons. By weight, grapes accounted for 27.8% of that U.S. fruit production figure, followed by apples at 22.3%, and oranges at 21.9%. The value of U.S. fruit production in 2019 fell -1.5% yr/yr to $28.770 billion.

Demand – U.S. per capita fresh fruit consumption in 2019 rose +0.8% to 115.800 pounds per year, down from the 2017 record high of 116.750. The highest per capita consumption categories for non-citrus fruits in 2019 were bananas (27.380 pounds) and apples (17.460 pounds). Per capita consumption of citrus fruits were oranges (8.240 pounds), tangerines & tangelos (6.800 pounds), lemons (4.880 pounds), limes (4.100 pounds), and grapefruit (1.430 pounds). The utilization breakdown for 2017 shows that total U.S. non-citrus fruit was used for fresh fruit (43.2%), wine (25.5%), dried fruit (9.7%), juice (8.2%), canned fruit (6.5%), and frozen fruit (4.1%). The value of utilized non-citrus fruit production in 2018 fell -8.7% to $16.466 billion.

Commercial Production for Selected Fruits in the United States In Thousands of Short Tons

Year	Apples	Cherries[2]	Cranberries	Grapes	Grapefruit	Lemons	Nectarines	Oranges	Peaches	Pears	Pineapple[3]	Prunes & Plums	Strawberries	Tangelos	Tangerines	Total All Fruits
2013	5,262	479	448	8,632	1,204	912	162	8,268	905	877	----	364	1,524	45	682	30,118
2014	5,932	516	420	7,884	1,047	824	187	6,768	853	832	----	452	1,512	40	732	28,348
2015	5,051	462	428	7,621	910	904	160	6,353	845	817	----	441	1,533	30	863	26,801
2016	5,748	515	481	7,697	803	904	151	6,088	792	739	----	265	1,480	18	935	26,930
2017	5,777	567	420	7,384	698	882	142	5,088	701	737	----	443	1,360	7	1,029	25,586
2018	5,120	494	446	7,596	509	888	121	3,875	652	806	----	380	1,305	7	804	23,304
2019[1]	5,509	485	396	6,871	604	1,002	134	5,427	682	729	----	375	1,126	7	1,107	24,752

[1] Preliminary. [2] Sweet and tart. [3] Utilized production. *Source: Economic Research Service, U.S. Department of Agriculture (ERS-USDA)*

Utilized Production for Selected Fruits in the United States In Thousands of Short Tons

	Utilized Production (In Thousands of Short Tons)				Value of Production (In Thousands of Dollars)			
Year	Citrus[2]	Noncitrus	Tree nuts[3]	Total	Citrus[2]	Noncitrus	Tree nuts[3]	Total
2013	11,111	19,433	2,659	33,203	3,169,544	16,220,440	10,462,270	29,852,254
2014	9,411	19,151	2,567	31,129	3,704,444	16,410,049	11,816,331	31,930,824
2015	9,060	18,334	2,552	29,946	3,353,750	16,602,493	8,461,676	28,417,919
2016	8,748	18,598	3,110	30,456	3,435,675	17,571,574	8,690,836	29,698,085
2017	7,697	18,313	2,985	28,995	3,532,125	18,032,949	9,023,875	30,588,949
2018	6,076	17,487	3,226	26,789	3,330,152	16,184,328	9,690,038	29,204,518
2019[1]	8,140	16,931	3,316	28,386	3,399,879	15,446,455	9,923,969	28,770,303

[1] Preliminary. [2] Year harvest was completed. [3] Tree nuts on an in-shell equivalent.
Source: Economic Research Service, U.S. Department of Agriculture (ERS-USDA)

Annual Average Retail Prices for Selected Fruits in the United States In Dollars Per Pound

Year	Red Delicious Apples	Bananas	Anjou Pears	Thompson Seedless Grapes	Lemons	Grapefruit	Oranges: Navel	Oranges: Valencias
2013	1.386	.600	----	2.494	1.582	1.048	1.151	1.032
2014	1.354	.588	----	2.639	1.968	1.109	1.319	----
2015	1.358	.586	----	2.591	1.981	1.091	1.304	----
2016	1.442	.573	1.674	2.758	2.037	.970	1.246	----
2017	1.294	.563	1.603	2.641	2.007	1.279	1.341	----
2018	----	.574	1.579	2.584	2.249	1.346	1.413	----
2019[1]	----	.574	1.603	2.445	2.129	1.345	1.367	----

[1] Estimate. *Source: Economic Research Service, U.S. Department of Agriculture (ERS-USDA)*

Utilization of Noncitrus Fruit Production, and Value in the United States 1,000 Short Tons (Fresh Equivalent)

Year	Utilized Production	Fresh	Processed: Canned	Dried	Juice	Frozen	Wine	Other Processed	Value of Utilized Production $1,000
2009	18,021	7,514	1,394	2,148	1,235	742	4,373	269	12,232,459
2010	17,835	7,414	1,386	2,318	1,103	706	4,271	298	12,751,568
2011	18,111	7,666	1,301	2,399	1,153	737	4,155	316	13,886,156
2012	17,635	7,443	1,100	2,091	1,213	707	4,707	374	15,611,441
2013	19,433	7,824	1,396	2,321	1,636	896	5,068	406	16,220,440
2014	19,151	8,291	1,221	2,194	1,638	897	4,526	459	16,410,049
2015	18,334	7,695	1,258	2,323	1,397	877	4,255	530	16,602,493
2016	18,598	7,916	1,232	1,858	1,547	898	4,668	479	17,571,574
2017	18,313	7,909	1,186	1,778	1,498	746	4,663	534	18,032,949
2018[1]	17,618								16,466,042

[1] Preliminary. *Source: Economic Research Service, U.S. Department of Agriculture (ERS-USDA)*

Average Price Indexes for Fruits in the United States

Year	Index of all Fruit & Nut Prices Received by Growers (1990-92=100)	Producer Price Index (1982 = 100): Fresh Fruit	Dried Fruit	Canned Fruits and Juices	Frozen Fruits and Juices	Consumer Price Index (1982-84 = 100): Fresh Fruit	Processed Fruit
2010	89.0	123.8	----	187.3	148.7	322.3	141.0
2011	100.0	117.7	----	195.4	160.0	333.1	146.0
2012	112.0	119.0	----	203.8	168.9	336.6	150.4
2013	119.0	121.2	----	206.4	170.3	343.2	154.5
2014	136.0	124.5	----	208.7	172.7	359.7	154.0
2015	139.0	124.2	----	217.1	176.8	352.0	157.5
2016	138.0	138.7	----	223.2	177.0	359.8	158.2
2017	130.0	147.9	----	229.4	180.4	361.4	156.5
2018	130.0	145.1	----	227.3	180.8	365.2	154.9
2019[1]	124.0	136.3	----	223.0	179.5	360.1	158.2

[1] Estimate. NA = Not availavle. *Source: Economic Research Service, U.S. Department of Agriculture (ERS-USDA)*

Fresh Fruit: Per Capita Consumption[1] in the United States In Pounds

Year	Cutrus Fruit: Oranges	Tangerines & Tangelos	Lemons	Limes	Grape-fruit	U.S. Total	Noncitrus Fruit: Apples	Apricots	Avoc-ados	Bananas	Blue-berries	Cherries	Cran-berries
2010	9.68	3.78	2.79	2.57	2.76	21.59	15.31	.12	4.00	25.61	1.12	1.31	.06
2011	9.97	4.15	3.47	2.51	2.72	22.81	15.47	.12	5.10	25.54	1.29	1.30	.06
2012	10.47	4.18	3.95	2.57	2.37	23.54	16.05	.10	5.62	26.90	1.33	1.50	.07
2013	10.39	4.49	3.48	2.96	2.64	23.97	17.43	.11	6.11	27.99	1.41	.99	.08
2014	9.38	5.00	3.43	3.07	2.40	23.28	18.71	.12	6.98	27.86	1.51	1.17	.07
2015	8.67	5.22	3.60	3.02	2.24	22.75	17.48	.08	7.19	27.92	1.60	1.15	.12
2016	9.18	5.29	4.15	3.48	1.97	24.07	19.15	.13	6.86	27.43	1.78	1.17	.12
2017	8.03	5.86	4.26	3.75	1.92	23.82	18.06	.09	8.01	28.59	1.74	1.47	.09
2018	8.19	5.92	4.23	4.06	1.56	23.95	16.91	.12	8.47	28.26	2.00	1.28	.07
2019[1]	8.24	6.80	4.88	4.10	1.43	25.46	17.46	.15	7.81	27.38	2.33	1.25	.07

[1] All data on calendar-year basis except for citrus fruits; apples, August; grapes and pears, July; grapefruit, September; lemons, August of prior year; all other citrus, November. [2] Preliminary. *Source: Economic Research Service, U.S. Department of Agriculture (ERS-USDA)*

Fresh Fruit: Per Capita Consumption[1] in the United States In Pounds

Year	Noncitrus Fruit Continued: Grapes	Kiwifruit	Mangos	& Peaches	Pears	Pineapples	Papaya	Prunes	Straw-berries	Total Noncitrus	Total Fruit
2010	7.94	.50	2.24	4.73	2.91	5.70	1.17	.78	7.23	80.91	102.50
2011	7.36	.58	2.53	4.47	3.22	5.72	1.05	.87	7.36	82.36	105.16
2012	7.59	.55	2.49	3.86	2.76	6.42	.97	.63	7.97	85.12	108.66
2013	7.76	.46	2.87	3.02	2.84	6.74	1.12	.54	8.01	87.85	111.82
2014	7.67	.56	2.52	3.15	2.85	7.19	1.14	.53	7.96	90.73	114.01
2015	7.87	.63	2.60	2.91	2.67	6.98	1.33	.56	7.72	89.71	112.46
2016	8.09	.58	2.96	2.73	2.76	7.28	1.43	.66	7.39	91.31	115.38
2017	8.23	.61	3.22	2.66	2.69	7.75	1.36	.68	6.80	92.92	116.75
2018	8.07	.62	3.17	2.20	2.92	7.80	1.26	.60	7.14	90.91	114.86
2019[1]	8.39	.68	3.25	2.13	2.79	7.62	1.27	.61	7.14	90.34	115.80

[1] All data on calendar-year basis except for citrus fruits; apples, August; grapes and pears, July; grapefruit, September; lemons, August of prior year; all other citrus, November. [2] Preliminary. *Source: Economic Research Service, U.S. Department of Agriculture (ERS-USDA)*

Average Price Received by Growers for Grapefruit in the United States In Dollars Per Box

Year	Jan.	Feb.	Mar.	Apr.	May	June	July	Aug.	Sept.	Oct.	Nov.	Dec.	Average
2011	6.94	6.31	5.69	5.27	7.55	9.50	8.20	7.10	9.50	8.67	7.90	7.18	7.48
2012	6.83	6.79	6.91	10.20	9.62	15.43	13.23	10.33	10.13	12.49	7.68	6.87	9.71
2013	7.19	5.71	4.29	4.33	8.26	8.76	6.66	6.36	8.76	7.96	8.54	7.51	7.03
2014	7.30	5.78	5.60	5.34	7.89	7.69	7.19	8.05	13.40	12.33	9.82	8.92	8.28
2015	7.03	4.83	5.34	5.33	5.47	12.21	9.33	5.63	7.79	13.21	13.36	11.43	8.41
2016	10.70	9.13	8.86	12.77	14.81	13.82	15.26	14.08	W	19.08	13.14	12.14	13.07
2017	11.25	11.57	11.95	13.62	16.44	15.18	14.10	W	14.66	20.91	19.88	16.13	15.06
2018	15.88	15.80	16.04	18.21	17.02	14.71	13.34	9.57	15.16	20.61	20.89	18.68	16.33
2019	15.99	14.61	11.44	13.51	13.94	11.95	11.34	5.81	8.08	11.09	15.86	12.81	12.20
2020[1]	10.23	9.08	9.73	11.26	11.87	13.41	15.95	16.55	14.54	22.81	21.38	17.22	14.50

On-tree equivalent. [1]Preliminary. *Source: National Agricultural Statistics Service, U.S. Department of Agriculture (NASS-USDA)*

Average Price Received by Growers for Lemons in the United States In Dollars Per Box

Year	Jan.	Feb.	Mar.	Apr.	May	June	July	Aug.	Sept.	Oct.	Nov.	Dec.	Average
2011	8.84	3.91	5.70	8.54	10.26	12.32	16.16	21.99	17.98	12.87	14.10	14.29	12.25
2012	12.97	11.38	12.51	15.55	17.19	16.10	17.29	11.89	14.94	16.38	13.96	11.60	14.31
2013	10.65	7.28	7.08	9.18	14.77	16.35	18.98	28.45	27.85	32.77	26.65	23.52	18.63
2014	21.17	21.69	21.31	22.39	24.54	29.91	40.05	33.68	37.40	38.47	29.54	21.15	28.44
2015	18.53	13.44	16.14	21.65	31.76	38.51	37.34	29.40	31.71	36.54	30.18	24.42	27.47
2016	23.05	22.04	24.29	25.09	31.67	29.95	26.47	29.54	31.84	31.49	27.88	23.13	27.20
2017	23.44	25.12	24.65	27.10	31.30	40.90	41.85	29.79	29.58	25.49	28.32	30.84	29.87
2018	30.17	23.65	20.72	18.20	21.73	29.14	40.34	53.01	49.63	41.29	31.76	26.23	32.16
2019	22.58	15.76	15.54	13.38	16.25	19.43	22.12	27.97	29.34	30.34	29.70	22.43	22.07
2020[1]	16.14	14.98	10.64	10.91	14.21	20.07	21.01	18.85	20.88	24.74	25.45	23.20	18.42

On-tree equivalent. [1]Preliminary. *Source: National Agricultural Statistics Service, U.S. Department of Agriculture (NASS-USDA)*

Average Price Received by Growers for Grapes in the United States In Dollars Per Box

Year	Jan.	Feb.	Mar.	Apr.	May	June	July	Aug.	Sept.	Oct.	Nov.	Dec.	Average
2011	NQ	NQ	NQ	NQ	NQ	1,080	1,480	960	820	790	980	1,040	1,021
2012	NQ	NQ	NQ	NQ	NQ	1,410	1,030	980	1,130	1,540	1,770	1,780	1,377
2013	NQ	NQ	NQ	NQ	NQ	NQ	NQ	NQ	NQ	NQ	NQ	NQ	NQ
2014	NQ	NQ	NQ	NQ	NQ	1,870	1,550	1,360	1,350	1,530	1,660	1,680	1,571
2015	NQ	NQ	NQ	NQ	2,330	1,690	1,340	1,470	1,490	1,590	1,810	2,070	1,724
2016	NQ	NQ	NQ	NQ	NQ	NQ	1,480	1,330	1,360	1,460	1,520	2,310	1,577
2017	NQ	NQ	NQ	NQ	NQ	NQ	1,590	1,500	1,500	1,460	1,540	1,660	1,542
2018	NQ	NQ	NQ	NQ	NQ	2,550	1,600	1,310	1,210	1,080	1,030	1,140	1,417
2019	NQ	NQ	NQ	NQ	NQ	1,620	1,400	1,260	1,310	1,300	1,500	2,090	1,497
2020[1]	NQ	NQ	NQ	NQ	NQ	2,630	2,280	2,150	2,040	2,010	2,020	2,100	2,176

Fresh. [1]Preliminary. NQ = No quote. *Source: National Agricultural Statistics Service, U.S. Department of Agriculture (NASS-USDA)*

Average Price Received by Growers for Peaches in the United States In Dollars Per Box

Year	Jan.	Feb.	Mar.	Apr.	May	June	July	Aug.	Sept.	Oct.	Nov.	Dec.	Average
2011	NQ	NQ	NQ	NQ	1,290	705	666	704	564	NQ	NQ	NQ	786
2012	NQ	NQ	NQ	NQ	1,100	836	780	737	689	NQ	NQ	NQ	828
2013	NQ	NQ	NQ	NQ	NQ	NQ	NQ	NQ	NQ	NQ	NQ	NQ	NQ
2014	NQ	NQ	NQ	NQ	NQ	1,270	1,180	1,070	954	NQ	NQ	NQ	1,119
2015	NQ	NQ	NQ	NQ	1,480	1,110	937	1,030	835	NQ	NQ	NQ	1,078
2016	NQ	NQ	NQ	NQ	1,220	993	1,230	1,320	1,080	NQ	NQ	NQ	1,169
2017	NQ	NQ	NQ	NQ	NQ	1,530	1,710	1,400	1,310	NQ	NQ	NQ	1,488
2018	NQ	NQ	NQ	NQ	NQ	1,130	1,140	1,110	918	NQ	NQ	NQ	1,075
2019	NQ	NQ	NQ	NQ	1,720	1,180	1,090	1,150	941	NQ	NQ	NQ	1,216
2020[1]	NQ	NQ	NQ	NQ	1,500	1,190	1,310	1,680	1,810	NQ	NQ	NQ	1,498

Fresh. [1]Preliminary. NQ = No quote. *Source: National Agricultural Statistics Service, U.S. Department of Agriculture (NASS-USDA)*

Average Price Received by Growers for Pears in the United States In Dollars Per Box

Year	Jan.	Feb.	Mar.	Apr.	May	June	July	Aug.	Sept.	Oct.	Nov.	Dec.	Average
2011	639	636	625	599	571	565	561	576	490	533	512	474	565
2012	428	386	301	286	353	594	673	583	601	692	686	713	525
2013	774	778	753	NQ	NQ	NQ	NQ	NQ	NQ	NQ	NQ	NQ	768
2014	NQ	NQ	NQ	592	686	893	695	531	631	696	692	702	680
2015	725	729	652	610	619	633	635	706	690	747	778	813	695
2016	844	785	749	793	914	1,050	810	810	816	829	787	756	829
2017	782	806	722	668	694	734	631	764	829	848	832	888	767
2018	879	857	779	678	680	798	788	688	660	663	616	614	725
2019	574	561	539	545	620	731	781	696	722	693	678	721	655
2020[1]	733	1,200	1,170	1,050	1,040	1,050	1,340	1,590	1,390	1,400	1,340	1,310	1,218

Fresh. [1]Preliminary. NA = Not available. *Source: National Agricultural Statistics Service, U.S. Department of Agriculture (NASS-USDA)*

Average Price Received by Growers for Strawberries in the United States In Dollars Per Box

Year	Jan.	Feb.	Mar.	Apr.	May	June	July	Aug.	Sept.	Oct.	Nov.	Dec.	Average
2011	217.00	126.00	99.20	93.50	80.80	72.70	89.20	78.80	87.60	66.90	84.40	153.00	104.09
2012	137.00	113.00	103.00	94.40	82.70	74.40	74.00	85.00	87.60	90.10	139.00	222.00	108.52
2013	109.00	123.00	117.00	NA	NA	NA	NA	NA	NA	NA	NA	NA	116.33
2014	NA	NA	NA	87.60	96.10	91.80	89.30	92.70	133.00	112.00	152.00	209.00	118.17
2015	135.00	101.00	63.60	76.80	72.60	61.50	60.20	86.70	71.30	100.00	190.00	209.00	118.17
2016	195.00	167.00	81.00	84.30	68.60	60.50	59.40	69.40	50.90	71.00	167.00	193.00	100.98
2017	147.00	128.00	94.90	66.60	53.20	59.20	74.10	84.70	109.00	98.00	164.00	154.00	102.34
2018	169.00	125.00	118.00	105.00	55.30	52.70	66.60	50.50	84.00	67.30	99.00	W	90.22
2019	222.00	126.00	114.00	79.20	61.80	80.30	79.20	83.30	104.00	100.00	115.00	W	105.89
2020[1]	264.00	257.00	189.00	123.00	107.00	108.00	199.00	145.00	171.00	208.00	231.00	186.00	182.33

Fresh. [1]Preliminary. NA = Not available.. *Source: National Agricultural Statistics Service, U.S. Department of Agriculture (NASS-USDA)*

Cold Storage Stocks of Frozen Apples in the United States, on First of Month In Thousands of Pounds

Year	Jan.	Feb.	Mar.	Apr.	May	June	July	Aug.	Sept.	Oct.	Nov.	Dec.
2011	89,093	91,277	85,564	74,199	74,565	67,990	58,857	55,216	45,730	46,911	53,790	61,286
2012	73,898	76,390	73,470	70,943	66,459	60,688	59,358	57,905	55,178	51,344	51,748	54,843
2013	56,202	51,297	48,411	46,119	42,047	39,547	34,354	34,202	31,733	32,414	37,339	50,486
2014	49,831	56,312	60,384	61,220	60,693	58,666	56,046	55,517	52,050	49,676	53,072	52,828
2015	55,400	55,350	53,314	52,079	50,761	49,547	46,985	42,987	36,586	31,854	35,761	38,917
2016	37,596	38,707	37,994	37,761	39,147	38,682	39,040	36,171	32,361	29,104	28,198	32,407
2017	34,929	37,963	36,919	38,679	44,495	40,049	37,418	34,995	34,475	29,471	26,836	29,408
2018	32,007	34,420	35,915	36,968	35,087	32,441	33,715	30,609	24,822	22,366	21,602	23,141
2019	28,276	31,782	35,345	35,219	35,149	28,196	28,122	26,479	22,539	20,286	20,326	21,713
2020[1]	27,323	28,963	29,614	28,670	29,494	30,574	29,982	29,829	28,310	27,780	26,264	29,656

[1] Preliminary. *Source: Economic Research Service, U.S. Department of Agriculture (ERS-USDA)*

Cold Storage Stocks of Frozen Apricots in the United States, on First of Month In Thousands of Pounds

Year	Jan.	Feb.	Mar.	Apr.	May	June	July	Aug.	Sept.	Oct.	Nov.	Dec.
2011	4,833	3,519	3,517	2,944	2,034	2,192	6,003	12,132	8,630	6,564	4,982	4,643
2012	4,863	3,593	3,460	3,003	2,591	1,990	9,440	11,011	9,636	8,737	6,318	4,053
2013	4,018	3,395	2,340	1,907	1,452	1,668	11,874	7,871	7,204	6,276	4,639	4,501
2014	3,895	3,532	3,406	3,380	2,384	1,974	12,488	9,847	7,852	7,533	6,471	6,191
2015	5,941	5,246	4,720	4,162	4,051	3,390	11,760	11,058	10,059	7,931	6,128	5,640
2016	4,921	4,319	3,804	3,434	2,968	3,301	11,086	16,226	13,454	11,690	9,998	8,958
2017	8,456	6,506	4,103	3,163	2,848	2,279	11,696	11,048	8,512	7,335	6,098	5,506
2018	4,873	4,295	3,616	2,974	2,275	1,664	8,301	9,538	8,843	8,148	7,549	6,640
2019	6,458	4,762	4,248	3,432	2,770	2,082	3,760	3,819	3,528	3,237	6,689	6,054
2020[1]	5,294	4,224	3,436	3,101	2,340	2,461	8,706	6,774	6,871	4,703	3,751	3,156

[1] Preliminary. *Source: Economic Research Service, U.S. Department of Agriculture (ERS-USDA)*

Cold Storage Stocks of Frozen Blackberries[2] in the United States, on First of Month

In Thousands of Pounds

Year	Jan.	Feb.	Mar.	Apr.	May	June	July	Aug.	Sept.	Oct.	Nov.	Dec.
2011	23,857	18,649	14,941	14,603	13,864	13,113	11,946	20,833	36,913	38,718	37,111	33,876
2012	31,909	26,925	24,149	21,359	19,248	18,076	15,138	40,692	40,867	39,689	37,508	36,152
2013	35,272	33,021	25,975	24,247	21,792	17,887	18,727	40,606	39,237	37,880	33,468	32,048
2014	30,066	28,823	27,183	22,994	21,110	21,107	22,053	42,581	40,339	37,494	34,756	32,368
2015	30,925	28,843	25,499	23,071	20,892	19,931	25,158	34,001	35,240	33,078	30,553	28,366
2016	26,594	24,457	23,752	23,008	20,296	19,131	36,373	43,885	43,330	38,711	36,110	33,134
2017	31,753	29,540	26,983	24,151	23,147	20,956	22,085	36,913	34,707	31,603	28,024	26,682
2018	24,449	21,402	18,205	16,182	14,751	12,534	14,481	38,714	33,447	32,294	30,098	27,069
2019	24,639	22,803	20,594	19,569	17,377	14,258	12,664	32,157	31,509	29,664	27,854	23,989
2020[1]	21,741	18,410	16,608	13,943	14,291	12,998	14,030	34,685	33,928	28,560	23,801	23,249

[1] Preliminary. [2] Includes IQF, Pails and Tubs, Barrels (400lbs net), and Concentrate. *Source: Economic Research Service, U.S. Department of Agriculture (ERS-USDA)*

Cold Storage Stocks of Frozen Blueberries in the United States, on First of Month

In Thousands of Pounds

Year	Jan.	Feb.	Mar.	Apr.	May	June	July	Aug.	Sept.	Oct.	Nov.	Dec.
2011	116,485	104,091	93,103	80,016	65,583	50,865	57,467	76,551	167,015	174,805	160,156	147,757
2012	136,966	124,003	114,066	96,723	85,700	73,717	82,218	148,315	238,510	234,207	215,588	196,702
2013	171,296	165,932	152,187	137,358	119,814	100,876	103,559	166,382	260,094	251,279	235,007	217,393
2014	201,834	172,718	150,626	130,825	117,065	98,716	102,012	171,661	269,537	265,303	240,830	229,225
2015	208,324	187,523	166,469	152,745	133,836	119,276	132,732	236,349	273,614	280,085	259,198	245,754
2016	224,696	211,459	191,351	164,927	154,142	145,414	157,928	260,675	315,436	332,379	308,554	294,135
2017	268,895	241,947	223,211	195,417	184,367	157,140	147,915	197,723	276,632	266,423	256,727	230,843
2018	222,060	192,354	162,564	134,469	116,387	96,891	99,912	175,163	244,902	247,396	228,308	199,883
2019	182,857	178,750	148,696	129,739	112,147	92,992	93,422	174,711	280,464	290,020	278,570	262,652
2020[1]	246,625	240,304	215,903	196,198	175,610	166,842	176,415	233,701	319,296	316,717	291,261	261,142

[1] Preliminary. *Source: Economic Research Service, U.S. Department of Agriculture (ERS-USDA)*

Cold Storage Stocks of Frozen Cherries[2] in the United States, on First of Month

In Thousands of Pounds

Year	Jan.	Feb.	Mar.	Apr.	May	June	July	Aug.	Sept.	Oct.	Nov.	Dec.
2011	110,166	97,223	87,153	71,167	62,380	50,776	40,803	96,444	124,645	108,842	98,395	90,339
2012	83,622	73,371	65,185	54,211	44,684	32,532	26,924	59,120	51,815	50,514	49,966	56,135
2013	51,161	44,651	38,315	33,746	26,644	19,127	14,227	114,938	150,224	139,064	128,171	114,676
2014	112,101	99,639	91,631	82,926	71,746	58,869	50,181	103,362	178,542	164,429	153,521	144,280
2015	134,908	129,319	120,870	105,707	98,519	85,866	79,028	146,251	158,170	159,154	141,734	132,880
2016	123,378	113,844	102,584	91,204	81,431	72,293	63,925	173,739	196,001	184,839	174,878	156,973
2017	142,913	131,911	121,549	111,923	102,192	93,736	83,809	155,363	166,554	158,660	154,858	142,281
2018	134,946	125,530	115,381	108,226	98,931	88,879	74,151	167,724	184,463	169,664	156,443	145,503
2019	141,203	126,955	120,147	114,474	111,041	94,508	84,115	117,089	162,132	152,361	145,276	139,349
2020[1]	128,711	118,983	105,679	102,965	93,006	85,708	77,292	108,801	112,451	107,092	100,699	93,002

[1] Preliminary. [2] Tart (ripe tart pitted). *Source: Economic Research Service, U.S. Department of Agriculture (ERS-USDA)*

Cold Storage Stocks of Frozen Peaches in the United States, on First of Month

In Thousands of Pounds

Year	Jan.	Feb.	Mar.	Apr.	May	June	July	Aug.	Sept.	Oct.	Nov.	Dec.
2011	56,317	52,137	46,376	39,799	35,267	31,398	27,005	28,034	56,462	77,798	73,554	73,053
2012	66,344	60,950	60,096	48,374	44,074	39,734	35,430	36,517	59,775	70,173	67,100	55,085
2013	50,717	45,535	40,062	33,489	28,880	22,290	19,137	36,193	59,642	72,610	73,147	65,548
2014	61,092	53,367	47,862	39,621	32,936	25,714	19,497	34,001	54,810	63,033	57,543	52,384
2015	47,465	44,353	38,646	35,803	30,722	27,566	26,877	41,488	63,360	78,572	75,817	75,253
2016	74,308	68,463	62,266	54,489	52,746	49,601	48,346	62,290	83,003	93,794	91,530	88,731
2017	81,881	74,285	69,924	64,477	58,878	53,696	53,066	62,003	83,564	87,901	85,238	84,813
2018	76,686	68,986	60,036	54,899	46,756	40,717	35,517	37,622	47,951	69,188	69,577	64,956
2019	62,532	58,556	54,491	52,611	43,830	41,729	38,043	39,840	47,955	65,860	66,485	57,342
2020[1]	52,109	45,926	43,092	38,683	33,640	32,659	28,069	35,796	48,826	52,050	47,520	43,389

[1] Preliminary. *Source: Economic Research Service, U.S. Department of Agriculture (ERS-USDA)*

Cold Storage Stocks of Frozen Raspberries[2] in the United States, on First of Month In Thousands of Pounds

Year	Jan.	Feb.	Mar.	Apr.	May	June	July	Aug.	Sept.	Oct.	Nov.	Dec.
2011	1,694	1,669	963	322	140	175	190	814	889	751	768	701
2012	353	377	338	226	215	107	103	816	2,096	1,761	837	653
2013	716	619	543	421	320	354	763	1,518	1,395	1,121	1,050	985
2014	852	710	677	620	592	462	1,442	2,027	1,401	1,381	1,353	1,245
2015	1,145	1,089	969	944	924	867	2,152	2,555	1,828	1,655	1,625	1,444
2016	1,356	1,303	1,227	1,131	1,122	1,065	3,149	2,381	1,625	1,633	1,455	1,340
2017	1,281	1,047	960	1,012	1,021	870	911	2,015	1,995	1,905	1,584	1,590
2018	1,498	1,756	1,677	1,703	1,423	1,306	2,081	2,718	1,992	1,796	1,625	1,513
2019	1,467	1,170	1,088	904	793	822	998	1,694	1,430	1,437	1,362	1,164
2020[1]	890	707	637	828	843	721	991	1,245	1,507	1,449	1,482	1,541

[1] Preliminary. [2] Red: Includes IQF, Pails and Tubs, Barrels (400 lbs net), and Concentrate. *Source: Economic Research Service, U.S. Department of Agriculture (ERS-USDA)*

Cold Storage Stocks of Frozen Strawberries[2] in the United States, on First of Month In Thousands of Pounds

Year	Jan.	Feb.	Mar.	Apr.	May	June	July	Aug.	Sept.	Oct.	Nov.	Dec.
2011	263,147	233,644	203,393	177,108	180,773	244,433	333,190	384,184	367,425	350,563	348,285	323,160
2012	291,697	259,308	224,105	199,485	206,876	305,961	399,764	424,417	414,358	399,632	381,561	343,201
2013	302,987	265,250	240,083	218,149	334,359	397,352	421,128	463,698	428,160	392,032	345,152	320,036
2014	279,977	240,382	215,168	211,064	233,147	257,783	357,526	362,127	330,666	294,969	270,553	236,828
2015	206,841	175,520	163,599	186,817	199,290	238,106	341,295	360,045	328,775	314,350	278,860	253,146
2016	235,852	208,274	190,132	203,784	225,525	264,440	390,681	396,716	377,156	376,035	367,939	331,389
2017	304,827	289,622	274,147	255,978	266,206	312,244	357,628	411,241	402,915	363,542	333,050	309,351
2018	281,076	253,019	216,083	195,880	186,979	249,528	377,233	373,196	350,619	328,177	286,210	253,178
2019	227,433	193,851	172,444	157,833	182,594	228,838	269,490	277,960	275,315	250,277	211,085	188,847
2020[1]	157,388	129,425	115,173	127,564	159,405	231,699	265,090	268,538	263,179	216,688	186,749	157,224

[1] Preliminary. [2] Includes IQF and Poly, Pails and Tubs, Barrels and Drums, and Juice Stock. *Source: Economic Research Service, U.S. Department of Agriculture (ERS-USDA)*

Cold Storage Stocks of Other Frozen Fruit in the United States, on First of Month In Thousands of Pounds

Year	Jan.	Feb.	Mar.	Apr.	May	June	July	Aug.	Sept.	Oct.	Nov.	Dec.
2011	439,996	404,540	367,245	345,131	294,806	254,167	217,588	189,747	150,499	160,415	452,421	452,416
2012	423,367	388,229	360,867	331,923	294,833	256,890	220,723	194,871	170,723	224,022	525,515	510,323
2013	493,200	444,506	417,678	382,611	355,428	316,247	284,810	277,685	238,619	224,171	470,098	589,226
2014	575,025	528,790	475,527	440,532	389,071	341,283	305,249	286,727	264,490	293,231	542,534	576,843
2015	535,775	482,436	434,463	385,477	348,811	321,532	297,358	309,251	309,356	377,612	659,912	665,020
2016	587,967	603,399	557,741	521,065	525,633	489,438	473,450	483,812	464,629	514,081	853,189	872,413
2017	808,397	764,821	738,926	665,196	604,047	543,809	491,595	502,270	493,106	515,569	700,422	709,259
2018	666,624	595,561	554,544	487,759	462,212	399,596	404,649	395,232	361,493	398,684	741,609	710,973
2019	654,518	598,220	547,960	501,052	457,599	399,196	357,543	335,751	318,388	332,966	668,223	645,653
2020[1]	592,537	514,997	447,440	401,446	371,327	324,116	284,967	250,533	258,879	326,544	538,226	506,235

[1] Preliminary. *Source: Economic Research Service, U.S. Department of Agriculture (ERS-USDA)*

Cold Storage Stocks of Total Frozen Fruit in the United States, on First of Month In Millions of Pounds

Year	Jan.	Feb.	Mar.	Apr.	May	June	July	Aug.	Sept.	Oct.	Nov.	Dec.
2011	1,165.1	1,060.7	950.9	847.7	770.1	750.6	785.5	953.4	1,058.5	1,063.6	1,317.2	1,269.3
2012	1,189.3	1,082.2	989.1	881.4	813.3	835.1	889.5	1,077.5	1,145.4	1,178.0	1,425.6	1,342.3
2013	1,246.6	1,123.5	1,030.1	934.9	985.0	962.6	954.1	1,251.3	1,335.0	1,270.0	1,431.1	1,489.0
2014	1,405.6	1,261.1	1,140.4	1,052.0	981.1	912.1	972.2	1,176.0	1,317.9	1,286.1	1,461.4	1,426.8
2015	1,315.4	1,191.8	1,084.2	1,016.4	949.2	921.6	1,028.1	1,294.3	1,322.6	1,385.6	1,580.9	1,535.4
2016	1,398.6	1,349.4	1,240.4	1,165.4	1,163.7	1,141.0	1,309.2	1,611.2	1,658.5	1,707.9	1,993.9	1,934.0
2017	1,788.9	1,673.4	1,585.8	1,439.9	1,360.5	1,291.0	1,262.8	1,530.3	1,633.1	1,585.8	1,707.8	1,650.3
2018	1,547.8	1,390.3	1,256.2	1,119.0	1,041.0	992.9	1,117.5	1,379.1	1,417.4	1,425.1	1,677.2	1,556.3
2019	1,449.4	1,320.6	1,195.1	1,095.5	1,039.6	974.6	953.7	1,128.3	1,267.9	1,266.4	1,535.3	1,446.4
2020[1]	1,325.1	1,183.9	1,046.0	973.1	935.1	938.6	933.0	1,079.0	1,193.8	1,189.5	1,314.3	1,216.9

[1] Preliminary. *Source: Economic Research Service, U.S. Department of Agriculture (ERS-USDA)*

Gas

Natural gas is a fossil fuel that is colorless, shapeless, and odorless in its pure form. It is a mixture of hydrocarbon gases formed primarily of methane, but it can also include ethane, propane, butane, and pentane. Natural gas is combustible, clean-burning, and gives off a great deal of energy. Around 500 BC, the Chinese discovered that the energy in natural gas could be harnessed. They passed it through crude bamboo-shoot pipes and then burned it to boil sea water to create potable fresh water. Around 1785, Britain became the first country to commercially use natural gas produced from coal for streetlights and indoor lights. In 1821, William Hart dug the first well specifically intended to obtain natural gas, and he is generally regarded as the "father of natural gas" in America. There is a vast amount of natural gas estimated to still be in the ground in the U.S. Natural gas as a source of energy is significantly less expensive than electricity per Btu.

Natural gas futures and options are traded at the CME Group. The CME natural gas futures contract calls for the delivery of natural gas representing 10,000 million British thermal units (mmBtu) at the Henry Hub in Louisiana, which is the nexus of 16 intra-state and inter-state pipelines. The contract is priced in terms of U.S. Dollars per mmBtu. CME also has basic swap futures contracts available for 30 different natural gas pricing locations versus the benchmark Henry Hub location. Natural gas futures are also traded at ICE Futures Europe.

Prices – CME natural gas futures (Barchart.com symbol code NG) on the nearest-futures chart started 2020 at $2.130 per mmBtu, moved generally sideways most of the year but then hit a one-year high in November, only to moved lower again to finally close the year up +19.2% at $2.537 per mmBtu.

Supply – U.S. recovery of natural gas in 2018 rose +10.9% to a record high of 36.991 trillion cubic feet. The top U.S. producing states for natural gas in 2018 were Texas with 24.0% of U.S. production, Pennsylvania with 19.0%, Oklahoma with 9.0%, Louisiana with 8.6%, Colorado with 5.6%, Wyoming with 4.6%, and New Mexico with 4.5%. In 2019 the world's largest natural gas producers were the U.S. with 3,003,354 Terajoules and Russia with 2,051,081 Terajoules of production.

Demand – U.S. total delivered consumption of natural gas in 2018 rose +10.4% yr/yr to 27.482 trillion cubic feet, of which about 38.8% was delivered to electrical utility plants, 30.2% to industrial establishments, 18.2% to residences, and 12.7% to commercial establishments.

Trade – U.S. imports of natural gas (consumed) in 2017 rose +1.2% yr/yr to 3,042 billion cubic feet, down from the 2007 record high of 4,608 billion cubic feet. U.S. exports of natural gas in 2017 rose +35.6% yr/yr to 3,168 billion cubic feet for a new record high.

World Dry Natural Gas Production   In Billion Cubic Feet

Year	Algeria	Canada	China	Indonesia	Iran	Netherlands	Norway	Qatar	Russia	Saudi Arabia	United States	Uzbekistan	World Total
2006	3,079	6,548	2,067	2,199	3,836	2,732	3,094	1,790	21,736	2,594	18,504	2,216	101,621
2007	2,996	6,416	2,446	2,422	3,952	2,687	3,168	2,232	21,595	2,628	19,266	2,302	104,141
2008	3,055	6,046	2,685	2,472	4,107	2,957	3,503	2,719	21,515	2,841	20,159	2,387	107,858
2009	2,876	5,634	2,975	2,557	4,986	2,786	3,664	3,154	18,890	2,770	20,624	2,169	105,418
2010	2,988	5,390	3,334	2,917	5,161	3,131	3,756	4,121	20,915	2,969	21,316	2,123	112,438
2011	2,923	5,218	3,629	2,693	5,361	2,851	3,576	5,130	22,202	3,127	22,902	2,226	116,690
2012	3,053	5,070	3,666	2,619	5,640	2,843	4,052	5,546	21,764	3,439	24,033	2,222	119,302
2013	2,813	5,129	3,986	2,606	5,696	3,053	3,841	5,800	22,139	3,462	24,334	2,106	120,879
2014[1]	2,942	5,349	4,360	2,594	6,162	2,482	3,843	5,650	21,225	3,547	25,890	2,180	122,305
2015[2]	2,933	5,295	4,487	2,571	6,526	1,935	4,139	5,794	21,141	3,614	27,059	1,967	124,090

[1] Preliminary. [2] Estimate. *Source: Energy Information Administration, U.S. Department of Energy (EIA-DOE)*

Marketed Production of Natural Gas in the United States, by States   In Million Cubic Feet

Year	Alaska	Arkansas	California	Colorado	Kansas	Louisiana	New Mexico	Oklahoma	Pennsylvania	Texas	Wyoming	Total
2010	374,226	926,639	286,841	1,578,379	324,720	2,210,099	1,292,185	1,827,328	572,902	6,715,294	2,305,525	22,381,873
2011	356,225	1,072,212	250,177	1,637,576	309,124	3,029,206	1,237,303	1,888,870	1,310,592	7,112,863	2,159,422	24,036,352
2012	351,259	1,146,168	246,822	1,709,376	296,299	2,955,437	1,215,773	2,023,461	2,256,696	7,475,495	2,022,275	25,283,278
2013	338,182	1,139,654	252,310	1,604,860	292,467	2,360,202	1,171,640	1,993,754	3,259,042	7,633,618	1,858,207	25,562,232
2014	345,310	1,122,733	238,988	1,643,487	286,480	1,960,813	1,229,519	2,331,086	4,257,693	7,985,019	1,794,413	27,497,754
2015	343,625	1,010,382	236,648	1,688,733	284,184	1,805,197	1,245,145	2,499,599	4,812,983	7,890,459	1,808,519	28,772,044
2016	332,749	823,196	205,025	1,685,755	244,795	1,784,396	1,229,647	2,468,312	5,210,209	7,225,472	1,662,909	28,400,049
2017	344,385	694,676	212,458	1,706,364	219,639	2,139,830	1,299,732	2,513,897	5,453,638	7,189,566	1,590,059	29,203,550
2018	341,315	589,973	202,616	1,831,325	201,505	2,810,636	1,485,142	2,946,117	6,210,673	7,847,102	1,640,264	32,823,295
2019[1]	329,422	529,655	193,947	1,986,945	185,061	3,147,346	1,812,482	3,175,113	6,961,344	8,989,824	1,474,967	36,188,467

[1] Preliminary. *Source: Energy Information Administration, U.S. Department of Energy (EIA-DOE)*

World Production of Natural Gas Plant Liquids Thousand Barrels per Day

Year	Algeria	Canada	Mexico	Saudi Arabia	Russia	United States	Persian Gulf[2]	OAPEC[3]	OPEC-12[4]	OPEC-11[4]	World
2006	270	685	338	472	1,860	1,739	2,722	2,554	3,292	3,270	8,178
2007	260	726	328	486	1,940	1,783	2,813	2,582	3,407	3,383	8,394
2008	250	677	318	500	2,080	1,784	2,985	2,592	3,550	3,540	8,514
2009	325	640	326	539	1,980	1,910	2,922	2,744	3,562	3,552	8,641
2010	340	597	332	574	1,920	2,074	2,935	2,972	3,592	3,582	8,901
2011	322	591	334	611	1,920	2,216	3,102	2,958	3,637	3,627	9,130
2012	342	611	318	647	1,920	2,408	3,152	3,164	3,786	3,776	9,502
2013	300	639	320	684	1,920	2,606	3,141		3,685	3,673	9,636
2014[1]	300	665	320	720	1,800	2,964	3,117		3,644	3,629	10,013

Average. [1] Preliminary. [2] Bahrain, Iran, Iraq, Kuwait, Qatar, Saudi Arabia, and the United Arab Emirates. [3] Organization of Arab Petroleum Exporting Countriess: Algeria, Iraq, Kuwait, Libya, Qatar, Saudi Arabia, and the United Arab Emirates. [4] OPEC-12: Organization of the Petroleum Exporting Countries: Algeria, Angola, Indonesia, Iran, Iraq, Kuwait, Libya, Nigeria, Qatar, Saudi Arabia, the United Arab Emirates, and Venezuela. OPEC-11 does not include Angola. *Source: Energy Information Administration, U.S. Department of Energy (EIA-DOE)*

Recoverable Reserves and Deliveries of Natural Gas in the United States In Billions of Cubic Feet

Year	Gross With-drawals	Recoverable Reserves of Natural Gas Dec. 31[2]	Deliveries: Residential	Deliveries: Commercial	Deliveries: Electric Utility Plants[3]	Deliveries: Industrial	Deliveries: Total	Lease & Plant Fuel	Used as Pipline Fuel	Heating Value BTU per Cubic Foot
2010	26,816	304,625	4,782	3,103	7,387	6,826	22,127	1,286	674	1,023
2011	28,479	334,067	4,714	3,155	7,574	6,994	22,467	1,323	688	1,022
2012	29,542	308,036	4,150	2,895	9,111	7,226	23,411	1,396	731	1,024
2013	29,523	338,264	4,897	3,295	8,191	7,425	23,839	1,483	833	1,027
2014	31,405	368,704	5,087	3,466	8,146	7,646	24,381	1,512	700	1,032
2015	32,915	307,730	4,613	3,202	9,613	7,522	24,989	1,576	678	1,037
2016	32,592	322,234	4,347	3,110	9,985	7,729	25,212	1,545	687	1,037
2017	33,357	438,460	4,412	3,164	9,250	7,949	24,824	1,564	722	1,036
2018[1]	36,991		4,980	3,485	10,626	8,268	27,402	1,753	797	1,036

[1] Preliminary. [2] Estimated proved recoverable reserves of dry natural gas. [3] Figures include gas other than natural (impossible to segregate); therefore, shown separately from other consumption. *Source: Energy Information Administration, U.S. Department of Energy (EIA-DOE)*

Salient Statistics of Natural Gas in the United States

Year	Supply: Marketed Production	Supply: Extraction Loss	Supply: Dry Production	Supply: Storage Withdrawals	Supply: Imports (Consumed)	Supply: Total Supply	Disposition: Consumption	Disposition: Exports	Disposition: Added to Storage	Disposition: Total Disposition	Avg. Price: Well-head Price	Avg. Price: Imports	Avg. Price: Exports	Avg. Price: Residential	Avg. Price: Commercial	Avg. Price: Industrial	Avg. Price: Electric Utilities
	In Billions of Cubic Feet										Dollars Per Thousand Cubic Feet						
2009	21,648	1,024	20,624	2,966	3,751	28,365	22,910	1,072	3,315	27,297	3.67	4.19	4.47	12.14	10.06	5.33	4.93
2010	22,382	1,066	21,316	3,274	3,741	29,397	24,087	1,137	3,291	28,515	4.48	4.52	5.02	11.39	9.47	5.49	5.27
2011	24,036	1,134	22,902	3,074	3,469	30,579	24,477	1,506	3,422	29,405	3.95	4.24	4.64	11.03	8.91	5.13	4.89
2012	25,283	1,250	24,033	2,818	3,138	31,239	25,538	1,619	2,854	30,011	2.66	2.88	3.25	10.65	8.10	3.88	3.54
2013	25,562	1,357	24,206	3,702	2,883	32,147	26,155	1,572	3,156	30,883	----	3.83	4.08	10.32	8.08	4.64	4.49
2014	27,498	1,608	25,890	3,586	2,695	33,779	26,593	1,514	3,839	31,946	----	5.30	5.51	10.97	8.90	5.62	5.19
2015	28,772	1,707	27,065	3,100	2,718	34,590	27,244	1,784	3,638	32,666	----	2.99	3.07	10.38	7.91	3.93	3.38
2016[1]	28,400	1,808	26,592	3,325	3,006	34,731	27,444	2,335	2,977	32,756	----	2.24	2.79	10.05	7.28	3.52	2.99
2017[2]	29,197	1,906	27,291	3,559	3,042	35,798	27,126	3,168	3,308	33,601	----	2.72	3.54	10.98	7.89	4.14	3.52

[1] Preliminary. [2] Estimate. *Source: Energy Information Administration, U.S. Department of Energy (EIA-DOE)*

Average Price of Natural Gas at Henry Hub In Dollars Per MMBtu

Year	Jan.	Feb.	Mar.	Apr.	May	June	July	Aug.	Sept.	Oct.	Nov.	Dec.	Average
2011	4.49	4.09	3.97	4.24	4.31	4.54	4.42	4.06	3.90	3.57	3.24	3.17	4.00
2012	2.67	2.51	2.17	1.95	2.43	2.46	2.95	2.84	2.85	3.32	3.54	3.34	2.75
2013	3.33	3.33	3.81	4.17	4.04	3.83	3.62	3.43	3.62	3.68	3.64	4.24	3.73
2014	4.71	6.00	4.90	4.66	4.58	4.59	4.05	3.91	3.92	3.78	4.12	3.48	4.39
2015	3.00	2.88	2.83	2.61	2.85	2.78	2.84	2.77	2.66	2.34	2.09	1.94	2.63
2016	2.29	1.98	1.73	1.92	1.93	2.59	2.82	2.82	3.00	2.98	2.54	3.59	2.52
2017	3.28	2.86	2.88	3.11	3.15	2.98	2.98	2.90	2.98	2.88	3.01	2.82	2.99
2018	3.91	2.67	2.69	2.80	2.80	2.96	2.83	2.96	3.00	3.26	4.12	3.97	3.16
2019	3.11	2.69	2.89	2.65	2.64	2.40	2.36	2.22	2.56	2.33	2.65	2.22	2.56
2020	2.02	1.90	1.79	1.77	1.75	1.65	1.76	2.30	1.92	2.39	2.61	2.58	2.04

Source: Energy Information Administration, U.S. Department of Energy (EIA-DOE)

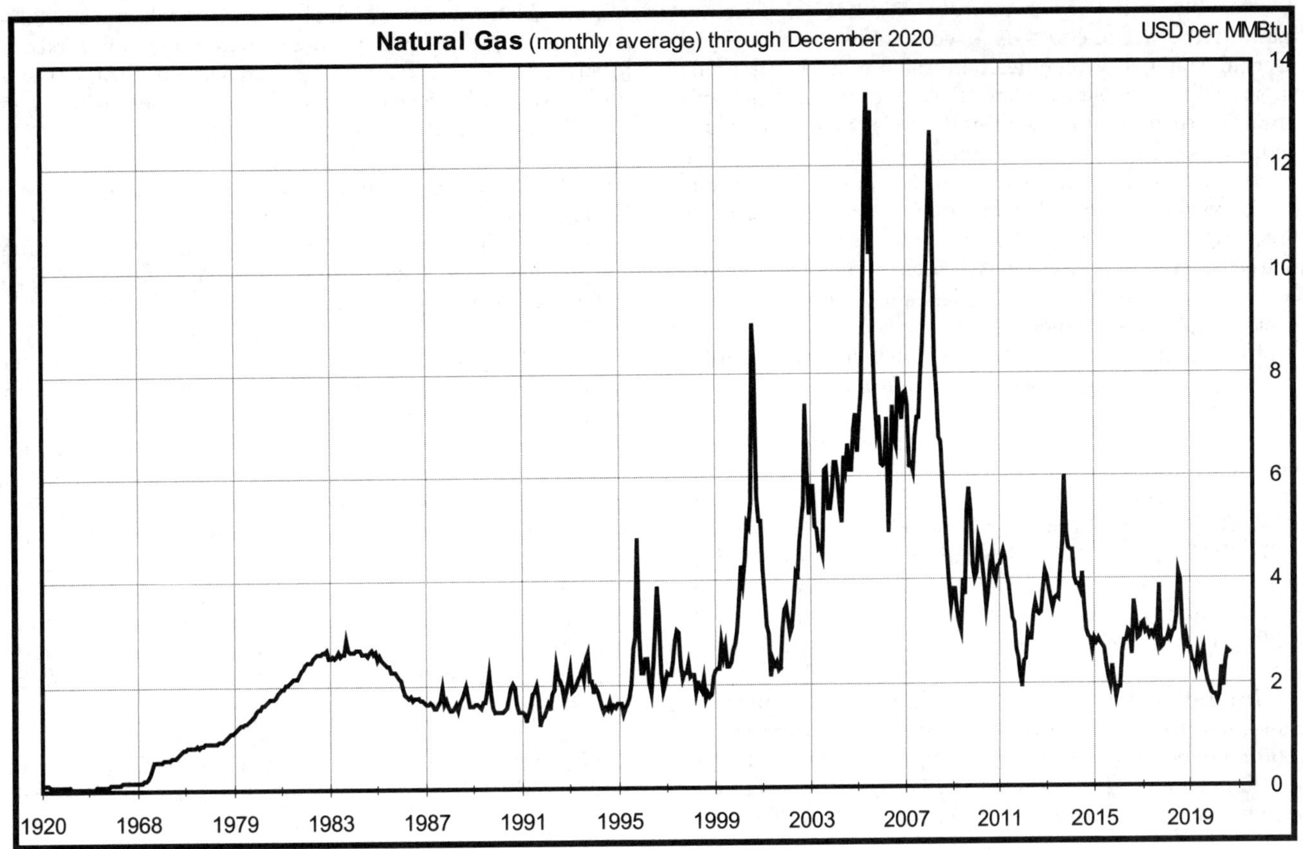

Volume of Trading of Natural Gas Futures in New York In Thousands of Contracts

Year	Jan.	Feb.	Mar.	Apr.	May	June	July	Aug.	Sept.	Oct.	Nov.	Dec.	Total
2011	6,468.6	6,123.2	7,284.0	6,432.0	6,015.2	6,759.5	5,317.9	6,904.9	6,363.8	7,199.9	6,117.1	5,878.3	76,864.3
2012	9,328.0	8,723.2	6,798.8	7,488.9	8,660.3	8,639.0	7,412.7	8,579.0	7,272.7	9,259.2	6,262.3	6,375.6	94,799.5
2013	7,329.4	6,910.3	8,343.9	9,484.9	6,796.2	6,271.5	5,626.2	6,944.2	5,741.2	6,991.3	5,618.2	8,225.0	84,282.5
2014	8,872.0	8,301.5	4,804.4	5,114.8	5,031.3	5,425.1	5,022.7	5,374.9	5,623.7	6,087.8	7,980.1	6,568.4	74,206.6
2015	7,617.0	7,014.7	6,255.0	6,141.5	6,663.2	7,705.9	6,403.9	6,458.0	5,714.9	7,578.3	6,236.2	7,984.0	81,772.5
2016	6,472.9	7,003.9	7,649.5	8,350.1	7,090.1	8,875.2	6,769.1	8,506.9	7,646.7	10,240.1	9,073.3	9,802.9	97,480.6
2017	8,858.6	8,635.1	9,138.2	7,911.2	9,389.8	9,195.0	7,515.3	8,159.4	8,498.8	10,583.3	10,006.5	10,500.6	108,391.8
2018	14,188.6	8,454.1	7,287.5	8,409.2	8,241.5	8,010.4	7,091.6	8,462.0	9,776.6	12,263.9	14,219.3	7,851.3	114,256.1
2019	9,169.8	7,329.3	6,074.7	6,944.0	7,049.8	8,344.2	9,037.2	9,283.3	9,893.3	10,971.2	9,960.5	9,337.3	103,394.5
2020	11,404.6	12,025.5	12,118.2	11,076.8	9,852.9	9,631.0	8,484.7	9,607.2	9,345.8	9,313.3	8,484.7	9,454.9	120,799.5

Contract size = 10,000 MMBtu. *Source: CME Group; New York Mercantile Exchange (NYMEX)*

Average Open Interest of Natural Gas Futures in New York In Thousands of Contracts

Year	Jan.	Feb.	Mar.	Apr.	May	June	July	Aug.	Sept.	Oct.	Nov.	Dec.
2011	820.8	917.0	922.1	948.1	956.5	980.4	977.0	990.3	952.1	969.6	977.2	981.2
2012	1,122.7	1,241.6	1,226.2	1,271.3	1,221.7	1,177.7	1,120.4	1,089.0	1,106.9	1,184.3	1,166.7	1,157.0
2013	1,172.0	1,196.1	1,315.3	1,539.1	1,511.7	1,434.8	1,389.5	1,356.6	1,306.4	1,263.8	1,271.2	1,302.4
2014	1,278.0	1,246.6	1,160.8	1,104.7	1,021.9	1,032.9	1,017.1	962.3	970.3	914.8	952.5	939.1
2015	991.0	1,004.6	979.6	1,016.3	1,015.3	1,038.6	1,001.3	957.0	918.7	977.8	1,011.8	1,007.1
2016	912.6	995.9	1,076.7	1,117.9	1,081.1	1,061.2	1,014.6	1,057.1	1,059.3	1,142.7	1,169.7	1,220.4
2017	1,195.9	1,247.4	1,364.8	1,432.0	1,537.9	1,421.3	1,337.6	1,324.8	1,317.7	1,374.0	1,377.5	1,505.8
2018	1,426.6	1,365.8	1,392.4	1,463.5	1,484.9	1,512.8	1,507.3	1,583.4	1,642.3	1,621.5	1,409.2	1,258.8
2019	1,313.6	1,253.7	1,180.5	1,226.5	1,290.5	1,317.6	1,314.3	1,337.1	1,214.9	1,235.8	1,185.8	1,297.0
2020	1,442.7	1,460.9	1,332.2	1,227.5	1,246.1	1,303.0	1,295.0	1,255.1	1,254.9	1,221.3	1,220.2	1,191.7

Contract size = 10,000 MMBtu. *Source: CME Group; New York Mercantile Exchange (NYMEX)*

Gasoline

Gasoline is a complex mixture of hundreds of lighter liquid hydrocarbons and is used chiefly as a fuel for internal-combustion engines. Petroleum crude, or crude oil, is still the most economical source of gasoline with refineries turning more than half of every barrel of crude oil into gasoline. The three main steps to all refining operations are the separation process (separating crude oil into various chemical components), conversion process (breaking the chemicals down into molecules called hydrocarbons), and treatment process (transforming and combining hydrocarbon molecules and other additives). Another process, called hydro treating, removes a significant amount of sulfur from finished gasoline, as is currently required by the state of California.

Octane is a measure of a gasoline's ability to resist pinging or knocking noise from an engine. Most gasoline stations offer three octane grades of unleaded fuel—regular at 87 (R+M)/2, mid-grade at 89 (R+M)/2, and premium at 93 (R+M)/2. Additional refining steps are needed to increase the octane, which increases the retail price. This does not make the gasoline any cleaner or better but yields a different blend of hydrocarbons that burn more slowly.

In an attempt to improve air quality and reduce harmful emissions from internal combustion engines, Congress in 1990 amended the Clean Air Act to mandate the addition of ethanol to gasoline. Some 2 billion gallons of ethanol are now added to gasoline each year in the U.S. The most common blend is E10, which contains 10% ethanol and 90% gasoline. Auto manufacturers have approved that mixture for use in all U.S. vehicles. Ethanol is an alcohol-based fuel produced by fermenting and distilling crops such as corn, barley, wheat, and sugar.

RBOB gasoline futures and options trade at the CME Group. The CME's gasoline futures contract calls for the delivery of 1,000 barrels (42,000 gallons) of RBOB gasoline in the New York harbor and is priced in terms of U.S. Dollars and cents per gallon.

Price – CME gasoline futures prices (Barchart.com symbol code RB) started 2020 at $1.6596 per gallon, spiked down to a 30-year low of $0.5927 per gallon but then rallied to finally close the year down -7.1% at $1.5423 per gallon. The average monthly retail price of regular unleaded gasoline in 2020 fell -17.5% yr/yr to $2.17 per gallon. The average monthly retail price of unleaded premium motor gasoline in the U.S. in 2020 fell -13.1% to $2.79 per gallon.

Supply – U.S. production of finished motor gasoline in 2020 fell -13.5% yr/yr to 8.724 million barrels per day. Gasoline stocks in December of 2020 were down -2.6% to 25.310 million barrels.

Demand – U.S. consumption of finished motor gasoline in 2020 fell -13.3% yr/yr to 8.037 million barrels per day, down from the 2018 record high.

World Production of Motor Gasoline In Thousands of Barrels Per Day

Year	Brazil	Canada	China	France	Germany	India	Italy	Japan	Mexico	Russia	United Kingdom	United States	World Total
2008	364.0	703.8	1,483.0	386.8	584.7	374.0	460.4	974.1	430.0	832.0	471.0	8,548.0	21,425.0
2009	374.0	717.8	1,711.0	365.8	559.9	527.0	434.0	980.0	454.5	837.0	472.3	8,786.0	22,247.9
2010	399.0	719.0	1,720.0	317.0	499.0	605.0	438.0	1,012.0	408.0	840.0	460.0	9,059.0	22,306.5
2011	425.0	670.4	1,850.0	303.5	499.3	627.0	405.3	943.4	387.2	857.0	453.3	9,058.0	22,288.5
2012	462.0	687.4	2,098.0	276.0	478.7	704.0	395.7	919.9	404.5	893.0	396.5	8,926.0	22,451.4
2013	491.0	675.3	2,298.0	250.7	473.4	708.0	357.8	934.0	422.8	920.0	406.8	9,234.0	22,882.9
2014	533.7	672.0	2,577.5	265.4	465.1	755.4	343.5	920.5	407.2	909.9	363.7	9,571.0	23,605.1
2015[1]		810.9		164.2	421.9		183.9	893.4	766.9		294.3	9,178.4	
2016[2]		847.5		169.3	420.9		181.2	896.8	795.9		289.8		
2017[2]		778.4		166.9	396.4		159.3	803.1	700.9		262.6		

[1] Preliminary. [2] Estimate. *Source: Energy Information Administration, U.S. Department of Energy (EIA-DOE)*

World Imports of Motor Gasoline In Thousands of Barrels Per Day

Year	Australia	Canada	Indo-nesia	Iran	Malaysia	Mexico	Nether-lands	Nigeria	Saudi Arabia	Singa-pore	United Kingdom	United States	World Total
2004	59.6	65.0	99.7	142.6	54.7	161.7	181.3	136.9	----	161.6	50.2	496.4	2,891.4
2005	57.5	81.7	125.2	156.0	66.3	214.2	212.2	128.1	41.1	166.6	55.1	602.7	3,242.9
2006	56.1	98.8	128.9	172.9	76.3	245.5	242.4	126.4	79.2	172.4	87.8	475.2	3,212.4
2007	46.8	75.3	145.3	119.8	73.3	284.7	170.7	135.4	75.2	200.0	75.6	412.6	3,040.0
2008	70.7	94.2	94.8	130.0	78.1	307.1	225.2	107.4	108.0	230.3	53.7	301.6	3,030.0
2009	77.1	89.1	199.3	132.5	74.0	307.6	234.1	140.0	102.9	20.2	77.8	223.4	2,943.9
2010	47.3	79.9	219.0	93.9	97.1	354.4	217.2	162.7	86.2	324.9	85.3	134.3	3,366.9
2011	57.2	90.4	268.8	31.1	104.6	386.8	240.5	142.0	51.9	323.3	88.0	104.8	3,508.0
2012[1]	57.3	62.2	307.9	9.6	134.9	374.9	276.2	137.3	92.2	305.7	111.5	44.1	3,628.2
2013[2]	63.6	54.7				319.4	225.1				108.7	45.0	

[1] Preliminary. [2] Estimate. *Source: Energy Information Administration, U.S. Department of Energy (EIA-DOE)*

World Exports of Motor Gasoline In Thousands of Barrels Per Day

Year	Canada	France	Germany	India	Italy	Nether-lands	Russia	Singa-pore	United Kingdom	United States	Vene-zuela	Virgin Islands	World Total
2004	156.2	161.7	121.5	67.5	127.6	340.4	98.3	240.4	169.3	124.3	178.0	158.9	3,358.6
2005	161.4	179.1	132.1	53.1	161.3	376.4	138.4	332.0	152.5	135.5	172.0	159.3	3,655.9
2006	138.8	160.0	128.6	86.4	161.3	400.4	147.4	330.2	161.5	141.8	132.0	131.6	3,669.6
2007	147.4	147.0	125.4	105.3	208.7	297.6	140.4	376.5	169.7	127.0	115.1	140.1	3,562.2
2008	129.3	182.6	132.2	126.8	196.6	357.1	104.3	428.7	162.6	171.7	117.0	131.9	3,635.9
2009	136.5	148.4	125.5	228.1	166.8	376.0	105.2	216.8	177.2	195.4	127.5	115.8	3,564.1
2010	149.7	133.2	112.1	318.9	192.7	382.9	69.2	525.4	208.4	295.8	9.5	107.9	3,887.4
2011	130.7	118.5	109.6	329.1	187.2	348.7	90.3	535.7	214.3	478.8	27.9	102.3	4,052.4
2012[1]	138.4	107.9	114.9	336.8	201.8	448.9	74.9	530.9	196.5	408.9	8.7	18.0	4,020.3
2013[2]	143.2	85.8	115.4		180.4	409.3			238.5	373.0			

[1] Preliminary. [2] Estimate. *Source: Energy Information Administration, U.S. Department of Energy (EIA-DOE)*

Production of Finished Motor Gasoline in the United States In Thousand Barrels per Day

Year	Jan.	Feb.	Mar.	Apr.	May	June	July	Aug.	Sept.	Oct.	Nov.	Dec.	Average
2011	8,714	8,866	8,908	8,978	9,157	9,289	9,166	9,264	9,140	8,932	9,141	9,128	9,057
2012	8,385	8,606	8,705	8,720	8,950	9,157	9,073	9,237	8,888	9,176	9,156	9,051	8,925
2013	8,718	8,926	8,971	9,042	9,299	9,472	9,374	9,340	9,190	9,484	9,476	9,495	9,232
2014	8,849	9,111	9,368	9,652	9,834	9,809	9,983	9,741	9,404	9,552	9,607	9,898	9,567
2015	9,260	9,504	9,524	9,720	9,771	9,846	9,989	9,998	9,878	9,935	9,799	9,806	9,752
2016	9,378	9,834	9,932	9,876	10,058	10,280	10,224	10,293	10,020	10,059	9,969	10,013	9,995
2017	9,281	9,507	9,802	9,855	10,126	10,270	10,164	10,176	9,778	10,129	10,220	10,104	9,951
2018	9,529	9,797	10,053	9,974	10,138	10,314	10,174	10,243	9,927	10,301	10,240	10,020	10,059
2019	9,735	9,730	10,051	10,010	10,217	10,231	10,240	10,435	9,922	10,254	10,227	9,997	10,088
2020[1]	9,626	9,742	8,575	6,352	7,477	8,745	9,026	9,312	9,090	9,252	8,882	8,607	8,724

[1] Preliminary. *Source: Energy Information Administration, U.S. Department of Energy (EIA-DOE)*

Disposition of Finished Motor Gasoline, Total Product Supplied in the United States In Thousand Barrels per Day

Year	Jan.	Feb.	Mar.	Apr.	May	June	July	Aug.	Sept.	Oct.	Nov.	Dec.	Average
2011	8,370	8,604	8,799	8,796	8,817	9,067	9,031	8,925	8,744	8,649	8,537	8,683	8,752
2012	8,190	8,598	8,582	8,741	8,979	8,996	8,810	9,154	8,561	8,701	8,483	8,389	8,682
2013	8,331	8,395	8,641	8,855	9,033	9,078	9,146	9,124	8,946	8,944	8,923	8,670	8,841
2014	8,273	8,647	8,697	8,955	9,023	9,039	9,249	9,311	8,822	9,148	8,921	8,941	8,919
2015	8,639	8,829	9,057	9,189	9,262	9,417	9,470	9,460	9,289	9,245	9,112	9,148	9,176
2016	8,653	9,221	9,373	9,176	9,417	9,608	9,578	9,687	9,484	9,093	9,233	9,283	9,317
2017	8,507	9,008	9,325	9,295	9,550	9,772	9,595	9,752	9,378	9,357	9,110	9,247	9,325
2018	8,788	8,796	9,465	9,206	9,515	9,797	9,640	9,778	9,153	9,294	9,290	9,179	9,325
2019	8,743	8,963	9,174	9,356	9,401	9,674	9,484	9,821	9,169	9,337	9,199	8,945	9,272
2020[1]	8,761	8,967	7,781	5,853	7,188	8,286	8,458	8,508	8,545	8,255	7,978	7,863	8,037

[1] Preliminary. *Source: Energy Information Administration, U.S. Department of Energy (EIA-DOE)*

Stocks of Finished Gasoline[2] on Hand in the United States, at End of Month In Thousands of Barrels

Year	Jan.	Feb.	Mar.	Apr.	May	June	July	Aug.	Sept.	Oct.	Nov.	Dec.
2011	69,617	67,835	61,206	54,636	56,353	55,521	53,335	54,546	56,308	55,052	57,573	60,631
2012	61,550	58,671	54,112	50,538	49,986	51,896	51,952	48,294	47,788	49,668	52,626	55,211
2013	55,228	53,143	47,327	45,108	46,376	48,634	49,726	47,655	39,780	37,595	37,548	38,976
2014	39,790	37,687	34,274	30,710	31,057	28,854	28,320	27,514	28,773	27,432	29,532	30,615
2015	29,923	30,558	26,891	25,898	26,580	25,678	24,418	26,048	29,028	27,638	27,805	28,453
2016	26,800	27,218	26,468	25,039	23,708	24,874	24,773	25,641	25,088	25,892	26,525	28,610
2017	28,496	25,727	21,728	21,828	21,983	22,480	23,157	24,584	21,765	23,154	23,595	24,641
2018	25,230	24,986	23,129	22,808	23,873	24,709	24,295	23,299	24,801	24,914	24,267	25,732
2019	29,517	24,197	21,652	21,544	22,559	20,979	21,872	23,073	22,997	23,320	24,816	25,974
2020[1]	27,673	25,852	22,577	22,870	24,044	23,499	24,305	25,151	22,436	25,205	25,039	25,310

[1] Preliminary. [2] Includes oxygenated and other finished. *Source: Energy Information Administration, U.S. Department of Energy (EIA-DOE)*

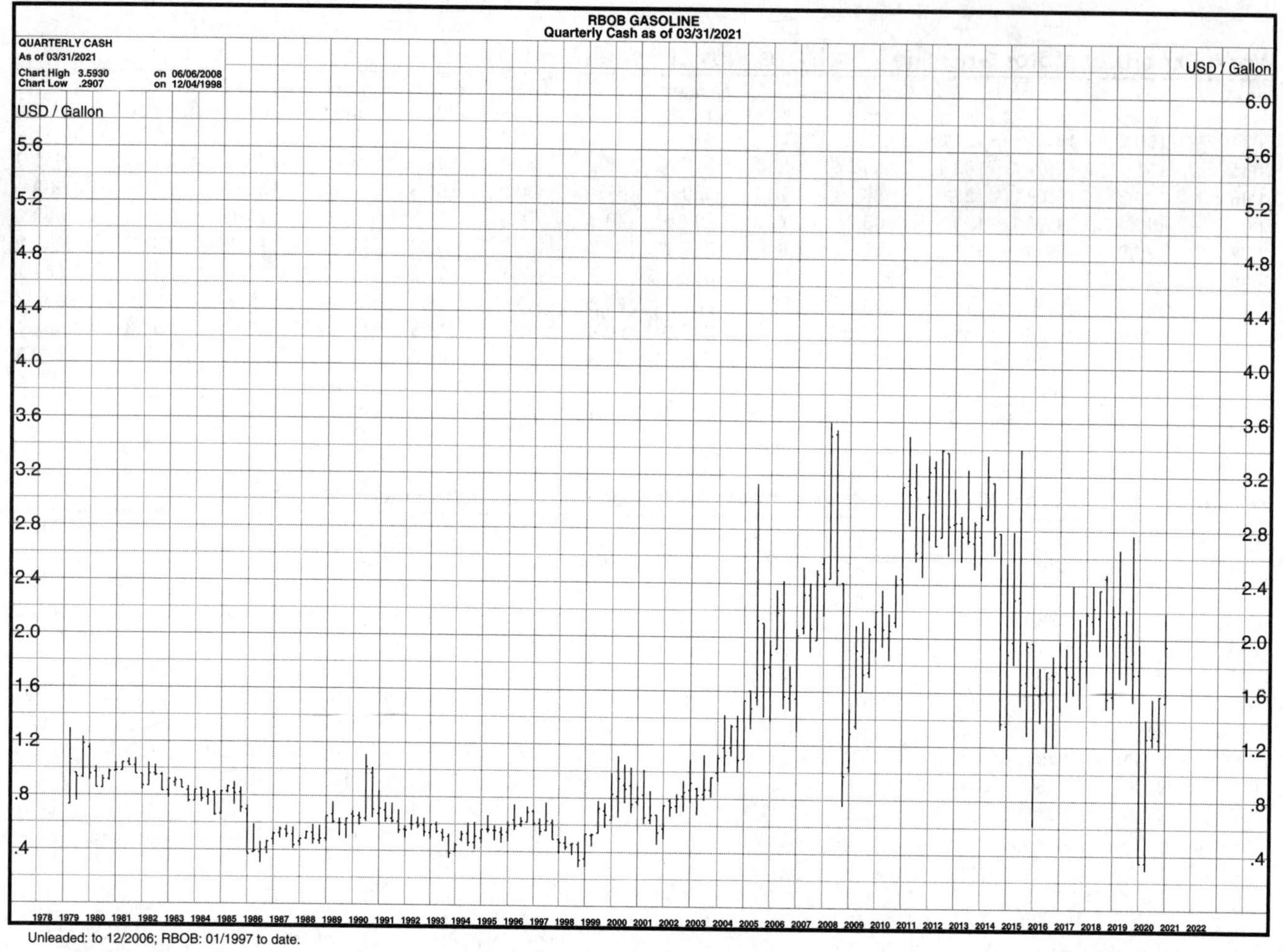

Unleaded: to 12/2006; RBOB: 01/1997 to date.

Average Spot Price of Unleaded Gasoline in New York In Dollars Per Gallon

Year	Jan.	Feb.	Mar.	Apr.	May	June	July	Aug.	Sept.	Oct.	Nov.	Dec.	Average
2011	2.4480	2.5580	2.8380	3.1780	3.0240	2.8350	3.0210	2.8350	2.7680	2.7720	2.6290	2.6340	2.7970
2012	2.8220	3.0440	3.1670	3.2060	2.8770	2.6020	2.7470	3.0220	3.2700	2.9750	2.8170	2.7270	2.9390
2013	2.8520	3.0530	2.9140	2.7060	2.7420	2.7400	2.9240	2.9330	2.7970	2.6850	2.6730	2.7360	2.8110
2014	2.6720	2.7950	2.7530	2.8960	2.8620	2.8960	2.8020	2.7050	2.7210	2.3980	2.1650	1.6830	2.6100
2015	1.3640	1.6070	1.6440	1.7930	1.9380	2.0050	1.8600	1.6200	1.4600	1.3970	1.3770	1.2760	1.6120
2016	1.1210	1.0580	1.2010	1.4480	1.5660	1.5060	1.3540	1.3790	1.4380	1.5220	1.4620	1.6340	1.3908
2017	1.6200	1.5470	1.4920	1.6110	1.5400	1.4450	1.5620	1.6880	1.8670	1.7150	1.8300	1.7570	1.6395
2018	1.8990	1.8170	1.8340	1.9950	2.1290	2.0300	2.0740	2.0770	2.0930	2.0280	1.6250	1.4490	1.9208
2019	1.4250	1.5680	1.8120	2.0420	1.9160	1.7400	1.8900	1.6940	1.7260	1.7280	1.7240	1.7130	1.7482
2020	1.6580	1.5800	0.8910	0.5930	0.8760	1.1210	1.2200	1.2480	1.2270	1.2010	1.1900	1.3590	1.1803

Source: Energy Information Administration, U.S. Department of Energy (EIA-DOE)

Average Refiner Price of Finished Motor Gasoline to End Users[2] in the United States In Dollars Per Gallon

Year	Jan.	Feb.	Mar.	Apr.	May	June	July	Aug.	Sept.	Oct.	Nov.	Dec.	Average
2011	2.615	2.712	3.072	3.340	3.419	3.184	3.172	3.134	3.090	2.980	2.922	2.808	3.050
2012	2.914	3.087	3.389	3.405	3.289	3.061	2.981	3.248	3.357	3.261	2.994	2.828	3.154
2013	2.850	3.221	3.233	3.102	3.188	3.184	3.146	3.097	3.059	2.893	2.759	2.759	3.041
2014	2.816	2.913	3.104	3.214	3.245	3.265	3.128	3.016	2.936	2.670	2.406	2.013	2.894
2015	1.673	1.858	2.054	2.058	2.322	2.374	2.338	2.218	1.920	1.849	1.711	1.604	1.998
2016	1.505	1.332	1.552	1.725	1.869	1.961	1.804	1.754	1.788	1.819	1.759	1.849	1.726
2017	1.900	1.862	1.904	1.997	1.963	1.906	1.871	1.952	2.154	2.042	2.122	2.034	1.976
2018	2.108	2.127	2.160	2.315	2.494	2.469	2.442	2.421	2.428	2.441	2.205	1.973	2.299
2019	1.854	1.949	2.137	2.487	2.520	2.366	2.375	2.252	2.242	2.289	2.229	2.182	2.240
2020[1]	2.150	2.060	1.862	1.490	1.598	1.768	1.806	1.814	1.804	1.773	1.736		1.806

[1] Preliminary. [2] Excludes aviation and taxes. *Source: Energy Information Administration, U.S. Department of Energy (EIA-DOE)*

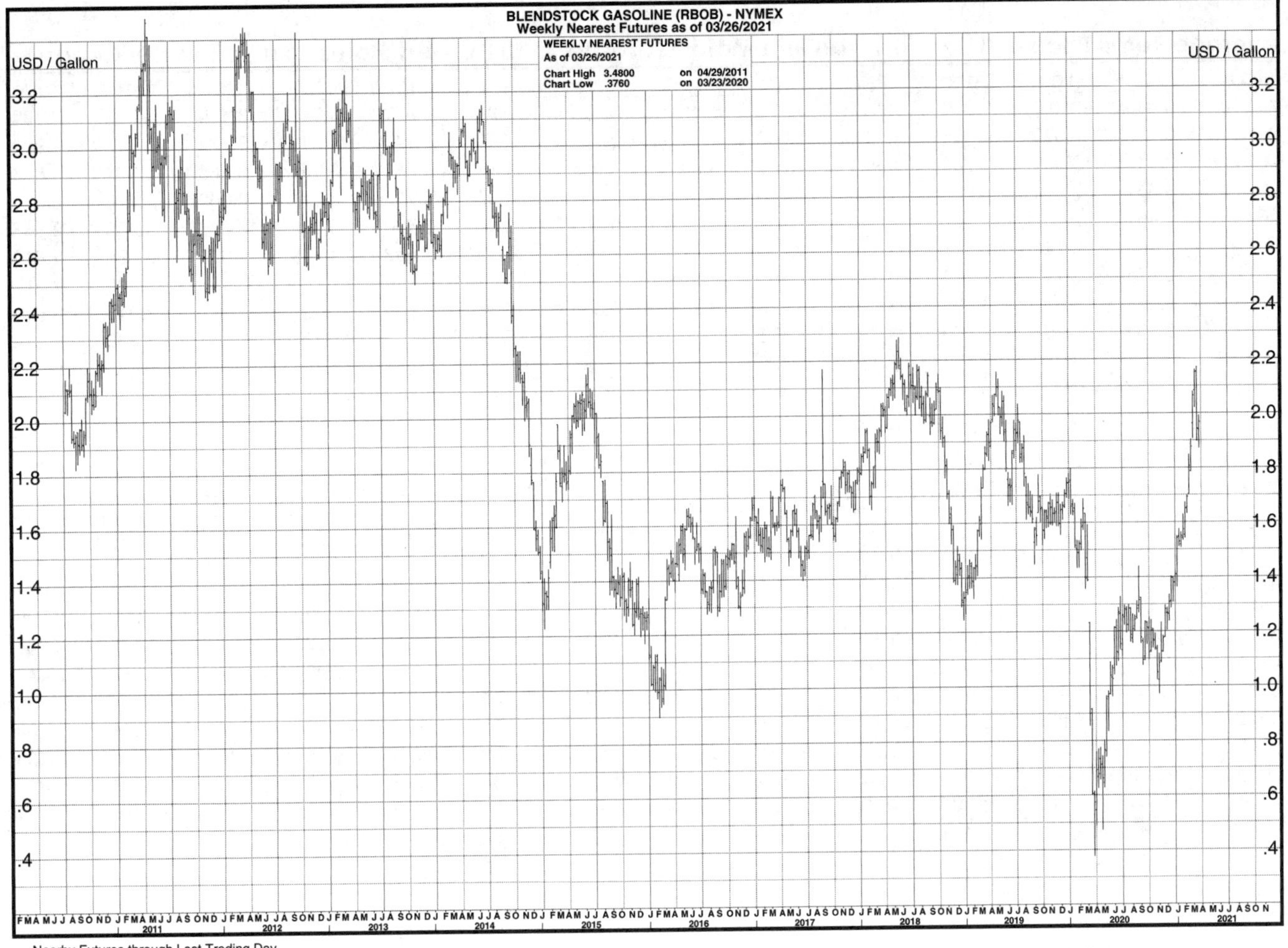

Nearby Futures through Last Trading Day.

Volume of Trading of Gasoline, RBOB[1] Futures in New York — In Thousands of Contracts

Year	Jan.	Feb.	Mar.	Apr.	May	June	July	Aug.	Sept.	Oct.	Nov.	Dec.	Total
2011	2,315.2	2,274.1	2,342.8	2,592.4	3,390.6	2,720.4	2,078.4	2,874.5	2,745.1	2,791.8	2,780.3	2,223.6	31,129.3
2012	2,899.2	2,844.2	3,480.0	3,789.4	3,257.2	3,107.9	2,844.9	3,043.1	3,015.4	3,298.3	2,674.1	2,350.2	36,603.8
2013	2,981.2	3,000.0	3,079.8	3,578.7	3,090.8	2,566.9	3,105.3	2,810.5	2,516.6	2,664.8	2,777.1	2,298.6	34,470.3
2014	2,470.9	2,417.0	2,562.7	3,316.9	3,240.6	2,679.3	3,001.7	2,894.1	3,173.3	3,170.5	2,713.5	2,781.4	34,421.9
2015	3,070.7	3,387.9	3,396.1	3,449.5	3,113.9	3,869.0	3,621.4	3,736.9	2,961.2	3,158.0	3,171.9	3,365.6	40,302.1
2016	3,362.4	3,841.7	3,723.6	3,546.6	3,874.1	4,362.3	3,427.0	4,134.4	4,677.2	3,413.1	3,844.7	3,221.5	45,428.7
2017	3,748.5	4,433.7	4,380.3	3,721.6	4,343.5	4,454.4	4,065.8	5,803.7	4,139.1	3,734.5	3,717.3	3,368.5	49,910.9
2018	4,290.5	3,815.0	3,992.9	4,067.4	4,569.1	4,175.0	3,959.4	4,858.9	3,901.0	4,626.3	3,953.8	3,404.7	49,613.9
2019	3,927.9	3,660.4	5,049.3	5,243.9	4,833.5	4,270.2	4,235.3	3,663.8	4,111.6	3,832.5	3,585.7	3,437.8	49,851.8
2020	4,556.7	4,861.5	5,625.8	3,936.0	3,244.3	3,495.7	3,338.0	3,613.2	3,361.7	3,635.1	3,386.0	3,438.6	46,492.5

[1] Data thru September 2005 are Unleaded, October 2005 thru December 2006 are Unleaded and RBOB.
Contract size = 42,000 US gallons. *Source: CME Group; New York Mercantile Exchange (NYMEX)*

Average Open Interest of Gasoline, RBOB[1] Futures in New York — In Contracts

Year	Jan.	Feb.	Mar.	Apr.	May	June	July	Aug.	Sept.	Oct.	Nov.	Dec.
2011	280,084	274,277	275,857	293,452	280,369	251,349	245,309	250,244	268,974	273,495	280,706	275,994
2012	312,848	345,884	374,449	348,606	306,453	293,802	258,931	273,299	290,070	279,312	276,945	282,942
2013	312,415	328,903	318,974	301,346	283,215	277,107	270,359	271,797	264,119	232,420	240,735	246,590
2014	252,519	274,087	283,756	310,549	332,460	314,754	307,808	274,978	283,206	310,119	334,015	349,589
2015	366,741	362,191	372,013	383,705	383,960	372,487	367,208	378,562	371,326	345,971	360,109	365,200
2016	379,473	406,615	420,305	392,100	405,314	401,323	389,932	406,922	395,691	408,750	380,734	390,804
2017	425,330	421,979	398,661	406,054	403,723	402,039	392,477	408,427	415,138	403,480	429,908	400,346
2018	437,285	434,342	424,422	450,029	479,806	461,515	441,321	459,928	438,527	406,263	406,427	406,667
2019	419,362	415,527	410,706	432,882	408,391	373,707	393,550	403,171	378,190	366,086	398,540	378,433
2020	408,399	391,038	368,635	378,558	373,104	361,741	346,636	355,345	362,771	366,985	397,811	417,834

[1] Data thru September 2005 are Unleaded, October 2005 thru December 2006 are Unleaded and RBOB.
Contract size = 42,000 US gallons. *Source: CME Group; New York Mercantile Exchange (NYMEX)*

Average Retail Price of Unleaded Premium Motor Gasoline[2] in the United States In Dollars per Gallon

Year	Jan.	Feb.	Mar.	Apr.	May	June	July	Aug.	Sept.	Oct.	Nov.	Dec.	Average
2011	3.345	3.424	3.807	4.074	4.192	3.972	3.915	3.893	3.887	3.745	3.700	3.553	3.792
2012	3.663	3.840	4.138	4.194	4.062	3.825	3.726	3.991	4.140	4.079	3.782	3.626	3.922
2013	3.646	3.990	4.038	3.901	3.936	3.957	3.951	3.919	3.881	3.702	3.585	3.604	3.843
2014	3.651	3.694	3.858	3.986	4.020	4.027	3.976	3.835	3.758	3.547	3.262	2.940	3.713
2015	2.497	2.621	2.867	2.868	3.166	3.218	3.252	3.120	2.860	2.749	2.640	2.532	2.866
2016	2.455	2.248	2.411	2.585	2.710	2.807	2.702	2.629	2.682	2.719	2.675	2.698	2.610
2017	2.815	2.793	2.827	2.909	2.894	2.859	2.800	2.883	3.120	2.996	3.056	2.985	2.911
2018	3.042	3.091	3.101	3.258	3.423	3.440	3.399	3.384	3.400	3.431	3.251	3.015	3.270
2019	2.874	2.901	3.079	3.382	3.471	3.328	3.327	3.222	3.214	3.297	3.254	3.190	3.212
2020[1]	3.157	3.071	2.893	2.527	2.490	2.673	2.783	2.795	2.810	2.782	2.727	2.778	2.791

[1] Preliminary. [2] Including taxes. *Source: Energy Information Administration, U.S. Department of Energy (EIA-DOE)*

Average Retail Price of Unleaded Regular Motor Gasoline[2] in the United States In Dollars per Gallon

Year	Jan.	Feb.	Mar.	Apr.	May	June	July	Aug.	Sept.	Oct.	Nov.	Dec.	Average
2011	3.091	3.167	3.546	3.816	3.933	3.702	3.654	3.630	3.612	3.468	3.423	3.278	3.527
2012	3.399	3.572	3.868	3.927	3.792	3.552	3.451	3.707	3.856	3.786	3.488	3.331	3.644
2013	3.351	3.693	3.735	3.590	3.623	3.633	3.628	3.600	3.556	3.375	3.251	3.277	3.526
2014	3.320	3.364	3.532	3.659	3.691	3.695	3.633	3.481	3.403	3.182	2.887	2.560	3.367
2015	2.110	2.249	2.483	2.485	2.775	2.832	2.832	2.679	2.394	2.289	2.185	2.060	2.448
2016	1.967	1.767	1.958	2.134	2.264	2.363	2.225	2.155	2.208	2.243	2.187	2.230	2.142
2017	2.351	2.299	2.323	2.418	2.386	2.337	2.281	2.374	2.630	2.484	2.548	2.459	2.408
2018	2.539	2.575	2.572	2.737	2.907	2.914	2.873	2.862	2.873	2.887	2.671	2.414	2.735
2019	2.289	2.353	2.564	2.835	2.901	2.752	2.776	2.655	2.630	2.673	2.620	2.587	2.636
2020[1]	2.567	2.465	2.267	1.876	1.879	2.076	2.176	2.177	2.193	2.159	2.090	2.168	2.174

[1] Preliminary. [2] Including taxes. *Source: Energy Information Administration, U.S. Department of Energy (EIA-DOE)*

Average Retail Price of All-Types[2] Motor Gasoline[3] in the United States In Dollars per Gallon

Year	Jan.	Feb.	Mar.	Apr.	May	June	July	Aug.	Sept.	Oct.	Nov.	Dec.	Average
2011	3.139	3.215	3.594	3.863	3.982	3.753	3.703	3.680	3.664	3.521	3.475	3.329	3.577
2012	3.447	3.622	3.918	3.976	3.839	3.602	3.502	3.759	3.908	3.839	3.542	3.386	3.695
2013	3.407	3.748	3.792	3.647	3.682	3.693	3.687	3.658	3.616	3.434	3.310	3.333	3.584
2014	3.378	3.422	3.590	3.717	3.745	3.750	3.690	3.540	3.463	3.241	2.945	2.618	3.425
2015	2.170	2.308	2.544	2.545	2.832	2.889	2.893	2.745	2.463	2.357	2.249	2.125	2.510
2016	2.034	1.833	2.021	2.196	2.324	2.422	2.287	2.218	2.269	2.304	2.246	2.289	2.204
2017	2.409	2.360	2.386	2.479	2.448	2.400	2.344	2.436	2.688	2.545	2.608	2.521	2.469
2018	2.596	2.632	2.631	2.795	2.963	2.970	2.930	2.919	2.930	2.945	2.733	2.479	2.794
2019	2.352	2.412	2.620	2.894	2.963	2.814	2.836	2.716	2.694	2.741	2.687	2.652	2.698
2020[1]	2.631	2.530	2.334	1.946	1.946	2.141	2.243	2.245	2.260	2.228	2.159	2.235	2.242

[1] Preliminary. [2] Also includes types of motor oil not shown separately. [3] Including taxes. *Source: Energy Information Administration, U.S. Department of Energy (EIA-DOE)*

Average Refiner Price of Finished Aviation Gasoline to End Users[2] in the United States In Dollars per Gallon

Year	Jan.	Feb.	Mar.	Apr.	May	June	July	Aug.	Sept.	Oct.	Nov.	Dec.	Average
2011	3.323	3.374	3.767	4.132	4.091	3.913	4.027	3.920	3.915	3.697	3.620	W	3.803
2012	3.732	W	4.133	4.313	W	W	W	4.091	4.262	4.064	3.561	3.599	3.971
2013	W	4.060	4.022	3.860	3.900	4.191	4.224	4.298	3.982	3.653	3.673	3.678	3.932
2014	W	4.142	W	W	W	W	W	W	W	W	W	W	3.986
2015	W	W	W	W	W	W	W	W	W	W	W	W	W
2016	W	W	W	W	W	W	W	W	W	W	W	W	W
2017	W	W	W	W	W	W	W	W	W	W	W	W	W
2018	W	W	W	W	W	W	W	W	W	W	W	W	W
2019	W	W	W	W	W	W	W	W	W	W	W	W	W
2020[1]	W	W	W	W	W	W	2.761	2.805	2.613	2.495	2.485		2.632

[1] Preliminary. [2] Excluding taxes. NA = Not available. W = Withheld proprietary data. *Source: Energy Information Administration, U.S. Department Energy (EIA-DOE)*

Gold

Gold is a dense, bright yellow metallic element with a high luster. Gold is an inactive substance and is unaffected by air, heat, moisture, and most solvents. Gold has been coveted for centuries for its unique blend of rarity, beauty, and near indestructibility. The Egyptians mined gold before 2,000 BC. King Croesus of Lydia created the first known, pure gold coin in the sixth century BC.

Gold is found in nature in quartz veins and secondary alluvial deposits as a free metal. Gold is produced from mines on every continent apart from Antarctica, where mining is forbidden. Because gold is virtually indestructible, much of the gold that has ever been mined still exists in one form or another. The largest producer of gold in the U.S. by far is the state of Nevada, with Alaska and California running a distant second and third.

Gold is a vital industrial commodity. Pure gold is one of the most malleable and ductile of all the metals. It is a good conductor of heat and electricity. The prime industrial use of gold is in electronics. Another important sector is dental gold, where it has been used for almost 3,000 years. Other applications for gold include decorative gold leaf, reflective glass, and jewelry.

In 1792, the United States first assigned a formal monetary role for gold when Congress put the nation's currency on a bimetallic standard, backing it with gold and silver. Under the gold standard, the U.S. government was willing to exchange its paper currency for a set amount of gold, meaning its currency was backed by gold. However, President Nixon in 1971 severed the convertibility between the U.S. dollar and gold, which led to the breakdown of the Bretton Woods international payments system. Since then, the prices of gold and paper currencies have floated freely. U.S. and other central banks now hold physical gold reserves primarily as a store of wealth.

Gold futures and options are traded at the CME Group. Gold futures are traded at the Bolsa de Mercadorias and Futuros (BM&F) and at the Tokyo Commodity Exchange (TOCOM), and the Korea Futures Exchange (KOFEX). The CME gold futures contract calls for the delivery of 100 troy ounces of gold (0.995 fineness), and the contract trades in terms of dollars and cents per troy ounce.

Prices – CME gold futures prices (Barchart.com symbol GC) posted the low for 2020 at $1,451 per ounce in March after the dollar rallied to a 3-year high. Also, a slump in global stock markets in March prompted investors to liquidate their long gold positions to raise cash to cover equity losses. Gold prices then reversed course and rallied sharply into August when they posted a record high of $2,063 per ounce. Gold saw support as the dollar index trended lower from March's 3-year high and dropped to a 2-1/2-year low in December. Gold also found support from aggressive stimulus from global central banks in an attempt to contain the economic damage from the pandemic. In addition, slumping global government bond yields sparked demand for gold as a store of value after the 10-year T-note yield dropped to a record low of 0.314% in March, and the German bund yield sank to a record low of -0.907%. Gold prices fell back into year-end, however, as massive pandemic stimulus boosted U.S. stock indexes to all-time highs and bond yields rebounded, which curbed demand for gold as a safe haven. Gold prices finished 2020 sharply higher by +24.4% yr/yr at $1,895 per troy ounce.

Supply – World mine production of gold in 2020 fell -3.0% yr/yr at 3.200 million kilograms, down from the 2018 record high (1 kilogram equals 32.1507 troy ounces). The world's largest producers of gold in 2020 were China with 11.9% of world production, followed by Australia with 10.0%, Russia with 9.4%, the U.S with 5.9%, Peru with 3.9%, and South Africa with 2.8%.

U.S. gold mine production in 2020 fell -5.0% yr/yr to 190,000 kilograms. Canada's gold mine production in 2020 fell -2.9% yr/yr to 170,000 kilograms, down from the 2018 record high of 183,000 kilograms.

U.S. refinery production of gold from domestic and foreign ore sources in 2020 fell -2.4% yr/yr to 200,000 kilograms. U.S. refinery production of gold from secondary scrap sources in 2020 rose +3.4% yr/yr to 120,000 kilograms.

Demand – U.S. consumption of gold in 2020 rose +6.0% yr/yr to 160,000 kilograms. U.S. usage of gold is mostly for jewelry.

Trade – U.S. exports of gold (excluding coinage) in 2020 fell -24.8% yr/yr to 270,000 kilograms, well below the 2012 record high of 699,000 kilograms. U.S. imports of gold for consumption in 2020 rose +206.5% yr/yr to 610,000 kilograms.

World Mine Production of Gold In Kilograms (1 Kilogram = 32.1507 Troy Ounces)

Year	Australia	Brazil	Canada	China	Ghana	Indonesia	Papua New Guinea	Peru	Russia	South Africa	United States	Uzebek-istan	World Total
2012	250,000	66,773	107,486	403,000	86,972	69,291	59,100	161,544	217,800	155,286	235,000	93,000	2,750,000
2013	267,000	79,573	133,636	428,000	89,224	59,804	54,092	156,264	231,700	160,016	230,000	98,000	2,930,000
2014	273,963	81,038	152,460	451,000	90,754	69,349	57,939	140,090	249,100	151,622	210,000	100,000	3,030,000
2015	279,000	83,280	162,504	450,000	80,325	92,339	60,046	147,110	251,210	144,504	214,000	102,000	3,090,000
2016	290,000	85,000	165,034	453,000	79,199	80,000	62,293	153,029	253,150	144,500	222,000	102,000	3,120,000
2017	301,000	80,000	164,000	426,000	128,000	75,000	64,000	151,000	270,000	137,000	237,000	104,000	3,230,000
2018	315,000	85,000	183,000	401,000	127,000	135,000	67,000	143,000	311,000	117,000	226,000	104,000	3,300,000
2019[1]	325,000	90,000	175,000	380,000	142,000	139,000	74,000	128,000	305,000	105,000	200,000	93,000	3,300,000
2020[2]	320,000	80,000	170,000	380,000	140,000	130,000	70,000	120,000	300,000	90,000	190,000	90,000	3,200,000

[1] Preliminary. [2] Estimate. *Source: U.S. Geological Survey (USGS)*

GOLD

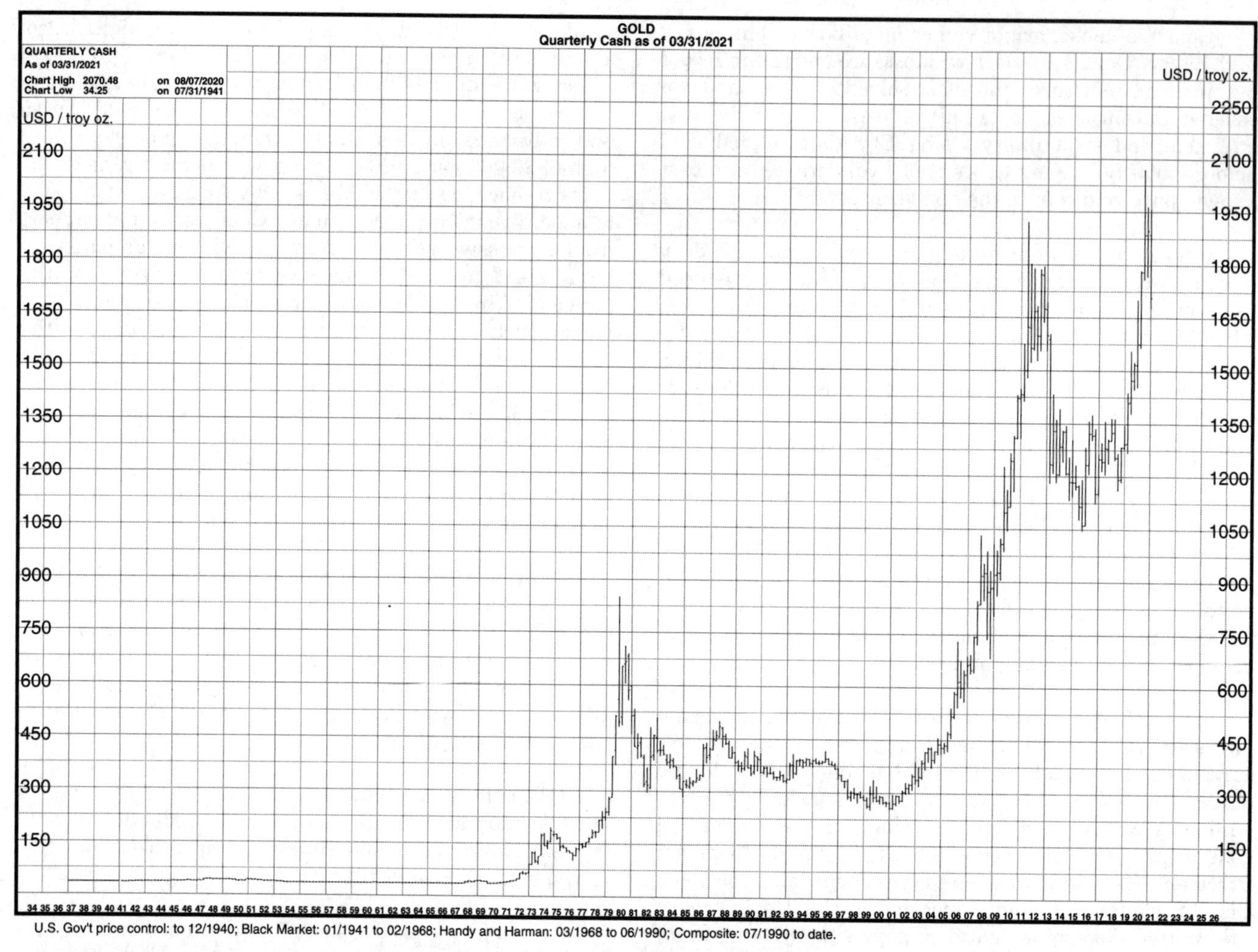

U.S. Gov't price control: to 12/1940; Black Market: 01/1941 to 02/1968; Handy and Harman: 03/1968 to 06/1990; Composite: 07/1990 to date.

Salient Statistics of Gold in the United States In Kilograms (1 Kilogram = 32.1507 Troy Ounces)

			- Refinery Production -				-------- Stocks, Dec. 31 ---------			----------- Consumption -----------				
Year	Mine Production	Value Million $	Domestic & Foreign Ores	Secondary (Old Scrap)	Exports, Excluding Coinage	Imports for Consumption	Treasury Department[3]	Futures Exchange	Industry	Official World Reserves[4]	Dental	Industrial[5]	Jewelry & Arts	Total
2011	234,000	11,800.0	220,000	263,000	664,000	550,000	8,140,000	353,000	6,470	31,100	----	----	----	168,000
2012	235,000	12,600.0	218,000	215,000	699,000	326,000	8,140,000	344,000	4,070	31,700	----	----	----	147,000
2013	230,000	10,400.0	223,000	210,000	686,000	315,000	8,140,000	243,000	5,940	31,900	----	----	----	160,000
2014	210,000	8,570.0	253,000	135,000	492,000	308,000	8,140,000	325,000	7,540	32,000	----	----	----	152,000
2015	214,000	8,000.0	244,000	238,000	478,000	265,000	8,140,000	198,000	7,330	32,700	----	----	----	165,000
2016	222,000	9,190.0	242,000	220,000	393,000	374,000	8,140,000	285,000	4,110	33,300	----	----	----	210,000
2017	237,000	9,600.0	207,000	119,000	461,000	255,000	8,140,000	284,000	1,770	33,600	----	----	----	159,000
2018	225,600		205,000	117,000	474,000	213,000	8,140,000				----	----	----	154,000
2019[1]	200,400		205,000	116,000	359,000	199,000	8,140,000				----	----	----	151,000
2020[2]	187,309		200,000	120,000	270,000	610,000	8,140,000				----	----	----	160,000

[1] Preliminary. [2] Estimate. [3] Includes gold in Exchange Stabilization Fund. [4] Held by market economy country central banks and governments and international monetary orgainzations. [5] Including space and defense. NA = Not available. *Source: U.S. Geological Survey (USGS)*

Monthly Average Gold Price (Handy & Harman) in New York Dollars Per Troy Ounce

Year	Jan.	Feb.	Mar.	Apr.	May	June	July	Aug.	Sept.	Oct.	Nov.	Dec.	Average
2011	1,359.39	1,371.13	1,424.01	1,478.55	1,511.63	1,528.66	1,576.70	1,757.21	1,765.99	1,665.36	1,743.83	1,645.50	1,569.00
2012	1,656.88	1,743.10	1,673.77	1,649.72	1,588.34	1,598.98	1,592.98	1,627.97	1,747.24	1,748.69	1,719.98	1,684.18	1,669.32
2013	1,670.17	1,628.47	1,592.85	1,490.22	1,415.91	1,342.36	1,288.31	1,349.30	1,346.63	1,316.19	1,276.94	1,220.65	1,411.50
2014	1,244.53	1,300.60	1,336.08	1,298.45	1,288.74	1,279.10	1,310.59	1,295.13	1,236.14	1,222.49	1,175.33	1,200.62	1,265.65
2015	1,250.75	1,227.08	1,178.63	1,198.93	1,198.63	1,181.50	1,128.31	1,117.93	1,124.88	1,159.25	1,086.44	1,068.25	1,160.05
2016	1,097.81	1,199.50	1,245.14	1,242.26	1,260.95	1,276.40	1,336.66	1,340.17	1,326.01	1,266.57	1,238.35	1,150.13	1,248.33
2017	1,192.10	1,234.20	1,231.09	1,266.88	1,246.04	1,260.26	1,236.84	1,283.04	1,314.07	1,279.51	1,281.90	1,264.44	1,257.53
2018	1,331.30	1,330.73	1,324.66	1,334.76	1,303.45	1,281.57	1,237.71	1,201.71	1,198.39	1,215.37	1,220.65	1,250.94	1,269.27
2019	1,291.75	1,320.06	1,300.90	1,285.91	1,283.70	1,359.04	1,412.89	1,500.41	1,510.58	1,494.81	1,470.50	1,481.23	1,392.65
2020	1,561.07	1,600.37	1,593.48	1,682.71	1,717.63	1,734.11	1,855.45	1,972.67	1,926.24	1,903.27	1,875.95		1,765.72

Source: U.S. Geological Survey (USGS)

Nearby Futures through Last Trading Day using selected contract months: February, April, June, August, October and December.

Volume of Trading of Gold Futures in Chicago In Thousands of Contracts

Year	Jan.	Feb.	Mar.	Apr.	May	June	July	Aug.	Sept.	Oct.	Nov.	Dec.	Total
2011	4,724.6	2,740.4	4,512.3	3,145.2	4,955.3	3,078.9	4,278.2	6,406.6	5,300.5	3,026.4	4,105.3	2,901.9	49,175.6
2012	4,146.5	3,506.7	4,860.6	2,834.8	4,913.7	3,479.4	3,732.7	2,793.5	3,460.8	3,147.0	4,380.3	2,637.3	43,893.3
2013	4,221.1	3,632.3	3,906.6	5,218.8	5,312.3	3,744.7	4,647.2	3,466.7	3,331.9	3,458.2	3,577.1	2,777.7	47,294.6
2014	3,754.8	2,607.5	4,200.3	2,692.9	3,631.1	2,508.1	3,848.3	2,381.8	3,205.8	3,703.7	4,676.7	3,307.7	40,518.8
2015	4,507.9	2,558.8	4,403.4	3,057.0	3,721.5	2,856.0	4,554.8	3,431.6	2,917.1	3,070.1	4,034.0	2,735.2	41,847.3
2016	4,102.0	4,369.5	5,720.2	3,902.5	5,880.1	4,936.3	5,798.5	4,387.9	4,022.6	3,815.0	7,108.7	3,521.6	57,564.8
2017	5,978.9	4,392.4	6,119.4	4,612.2	6,367.4	4,906.6	5,957.0	6,808.8	7,184.1	6,665.5	8,623.3	5,186.6	72,802.2
2018	9,161.9	6,078.6	8,036.1	6,655.1	8,676.6	5,739.0	7,231.2	6,274.2	5,495.6	6,470.2	6,351.2	4,132.0	80,301.6
2019	6,245.8	4,010.5	6,711.5	5,096.3	7,142.7	7,308.6	9,490.3	9,582.3	8,582.9	8,016.2	8,927.4	5,394.2	86,508.7
2020	9,827.2	7,936.4	10,356.4	4,285.5	5,155.4	4,427.6	7,278.5	7,735.9	6,265.9	4,645.3	6,177.1	4,035.4	78,126.5

Contract size = 100 oz. *Source: CME Group; Commodity Exchange (COMEX)*

Average Open Interest of Gold Futures in Chicago In Contracts

Year	Jan.	Feb.	Mar.	Apr.	May	June	July	Aug.	Sept.	Oct.	Nov.	Dec.
2011	556,448	479,014	507,118	522,520	513,744	504,841	522,091	517,064	494,932	438,488	453,477	424,014
2012	426,896	445,515	434,210	402,740	423,294	417,783	424,790	400,896	471,946	469,628	461,382	430,717
2013	442,707	435,425	437,300	416,489	431,460	383,314	424,302	388,278	380,768	382,216	395,583	383,980
2014	397,700	381,045	404,828	369,755	395,313	385,660	400,977	365,066	381,961	400,455	433,102	372,432
2015	415,408	399,097	415,894	397,632	411,656	417,416	451,224	430,894	416,389	448,795	425,138	398,843
2016	403,929	421,355	491,060	496,873	561,027	553,721	616,676	571,588	576,954	508,303	484,383	401,266
2017	444,716	423,037	436,599	458,759	447,814	462,182	468,238	490,304	562,694	524,694	530,233	460,378
2018	563,606	528,812	525,719	505,825	496,142	461,716	499,723	471,934	468,159	472,864	490,986	416,930
2019	489,807	488,012	503,968	439,367	485,122	530,157	602,830	604,243	628,729	626,969	697,262	720,262
2020	770,857	690,974	592,184	492,108	509,613	501,447	583,285	549,531	565,752	555,588	553,266	551,544

Contract size = 100 oz. *Source: CME Group; Commodity Exchange (COMEX)*

Commodity Exchange Warehouse Stocks of Gold, on First of Month In Thousands of Troy Ounces

Year	Jan. 1	Feb. 1	Mar. 1	Apr. 1	May 1	June 1	July 1	Aug. 1	Sept. 1	Oct. 1	Nov. 1	Dec. 1
2011	11,694.3	11,401.9	11,075.3	11,033.0	11,140.8	11,310.3	11,439.7	11,431.5	11,559.8	11,246.8	11,236.9	11,301.8
2012	11,469.4	11,434.6	11,405.2	11,350.5	10,895.2	10,978.4	10,831.7	10,806.6	10,844.5	11,009.3	11,243.3	11,151.0
2013	11,058.7	11,009.3	10,289.3	9,279.4	8,129.2	8,054.9	7,534.5	6,991.4	7,013.2	6,862.8	7,153.7	7,247.9
2014	7,828.1	7,081.3	7,177.1	7,740.8	7,935.6	8,262.7	8,298.5	8,684.3	9,927.3	9,127.3	8,056.0	7,928.7
2015	7,932.1	7,983.9	8,321.5	8,010.7	7,718.4	7,871.5	8,043.6	7,572.3	7,221.1	6,852.5	6,700.8	6,377.6
2016	6,352.5	6,427.0	6,785.0	6,851.2	7,250.3	8,452.7	9,286.6	10,718.8	10,932.9	10,702.4	10,600.9	10,002.9
2017	9,158.9	8,986.3	8,942.2	8,956.9	8,931.0	8,750.3	8,616.7	8,660.6	8,693.6	8,761.4	8,707.2	8,914.8
2018	9,142.7	9,257.9	9,132.9	9,060.6	9,049.6	9,017.2	8,564.6	8,641.4	8,388.7	8,330.7	8,066.5	8,020.7
2019	8,434.3	8,439.1	8,162.5	8,034.0	7,782.0	7,677.3	7,696.7	7,783.6	8,057.1	8,188.4	8,284.4	8,828.0
2020	8,699.0	8,712.8	8,647.4	9,245.5	10,362.6	10,423.1	12,758.9	14,820.9	16,093.3	16,718.8	17,356.2	17,326.8

Source: CME Group; Commodity Exchange (COMEX)

Central Gold Bank Reserves In Millions of Troy Ounces

Year	Belgium	Canada	France	Ger-many	Italy	Japan	Nether-lands	Switzer-land	United Kingdom	United States	World Total
2011	7.3	0.1	78.3	109.2	78.8	24.6	19.7	33.4	10.0	261.5	1,002.2
2012	7.3	0.1	78.3	109.0	78.8	24.6	19.7	33.4	10.0	261.5	1,017.5
2013	7.3	0.1	78.3	108.9	78.8	24.6	19.7	33.4	10.0	261.5	1,023.0
2014	7.3	0.1	78.3	108.8	78.8	24.6	19.7	33.4	10.0	261.5	1,028.7
2015	7.3	0.1	78.3	108.7	78.8	24.6	19.7	33.4	10.0	261.5	1,051.5
2016	7.3	----	78.3	108.6	78.8	24.6	19.7	33.4	10.0	261.5	1,080.1
2017	7.3	----	78.3	108.5	78.8	24.6	19.7	33.4	10.0	261.5	1,093.1
2018	7.3	----	78.3	108.3	78.8	24.6	19.7	33.4	10.0	261.5	1,100.6
2019	7.3	----	78.3	108.2	78.8	24.6	19.7	33.4	10.0	261.5	1,118.3
2020[1]	7.3	----	78.3	108.1	78.8	24.6	19.7	33.4	10.0	261.5	1,133.1

[1] Preliminary. [2] International Monetary Fund. *Source: American Metal Market (AMM)*

Mine Production of Recoverable Gold in the United States In Kilograms

Year	Alaska	California	Nevada	Washington	Other States[2]	Total
2011	25,800	W	172,000	W	36,100	234,000
2012	27,700	W	175,000	W	31,400	235,000
2013	32,200	W	170,000	W	27,800	230,000
2014	31,400	W	151,000	W	27,800	210,000
2015	28,000	W	162,000	W	24,200	214,000
2016	27,600	W	165,000	W	30,000	222,000
2017	26,200	W	173,000	W	37,400	237,000
2018	20,640	W	173,100	W	31,640	225,600
2019	16,930	W	151,600	W	55,250	200,400
2020[1]	19,560	W	139,636	W	28,058	187,309

[1] Preliminary. W = Withheld proprietary data, included in "Other States." [2] Includes Arizona, California, Colorado, Idaho, Montana, New Mexico, South Dakota, Utah, and Washington. *Source: U.S. Geological Survey (USGS)*

U.S. Exports of Gold, Total In Kilograms

Year	Australia	Canada	China	Germany	Hong Kong	India	Mexico	South Africa	Switzer-land	Thailand	United Arab Emirates	United Kingdom	Total
2007	2,470	9,210	10	664	1,170	17,000	5,890	----	266,000	1,330	20,000	191,000	519,000
2008	12,300	11,800	219	305	4,280	18,800	4,660	5,270	296,000	8,510	20,700	181,000	568,000
2009	26,700	3,110	51	832	844	21,000	3,120	----	103,000	----	147	220,000	381,000
2010	14,200	8,750	558	1,390	18,400	30,900	2,270	9,510	113,000	5,000	3,080	170,000	383,000
2011	18,200	1,460	5,150	1,440	111,000	15,500	5,160	11,900	105,000	21,200	10,300	161,000	474,000
2012	5,140	18,400	1,200	2,230	133,000	66,900	7,040	8,260	280,000	9,280	64,200	137,000	692,000
2013	5,200	18,900	14,400	941	217,000	32,500	947	19,600	284,000	27,000	34,300	29,000	691,000
2014	6,430	3,300	12,600	232	147,000	27,300	434	----	173,000	13,800	20,300	80,000	500,000
2015	336	2,650	5,730	694	120,000	60,500	2,910	----	167,000	6,490	17,900	96,200	478,000
2016	952	5,390	4,500	1,430	69,900	41,400	1,880	----	150,000	2,030	17,000	94,900	393,000

Source: U.S. Geological Survey (USGS)

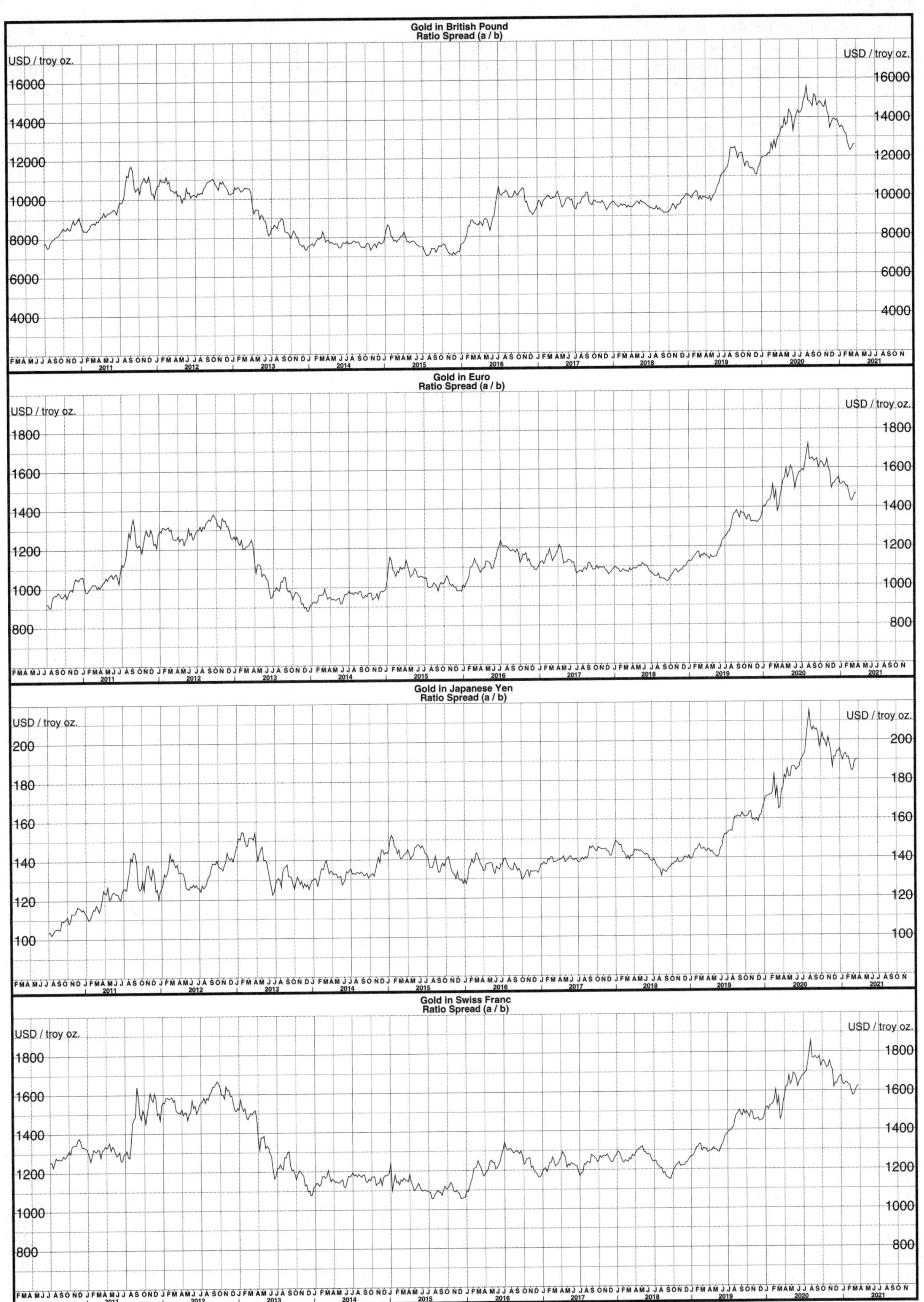
Gold in British Pound
Ratio Spread (a / b)
USD / troy oz.
16000
14000
12000
10000
8000
6000
4000
Gold in Euro
Ratio Spread (a / b)
USD / troy oz.
1800
1600
1400
1200
1000
800
Gold in Japanese Yen
Ratio Spread (a / b)
USD / troy oz.
200
180
160
140
120
100
Gold in Swiss Franc
Ratio Spread (a / b)
USD / troy oz.
1800
1600
1400
1200
1000
800
2011
2012
2013
2014
2015
2016
2017
2018
2019
2020
2021

Grain Sorghum

Grain sorghums include milo, kafir, durra, feterita, and kaoliang. Grain sorghums are tolerant of drought by going into dormancy during dry and hot conditions and then resuming growth as conditions improve. Grain sorghums are a staple food in China, India, and Africa, but in the U.S., they are mainly used as livestock feed. The two key U.S. producing states are Texas and Kansas, each with about one-third of total U.S. production. U.S. sorghum production has become more popular with the breeding of dwarf grain sorghum hybrids, which are only about 3 feet tall (versus up to 10 feet tall for wild sorghum) and are easier to harvest with a combine. The U.S. sorghum crop year begins September 1.

Prices – The monthly average price for sorghum grain received by U.S. farmers in the 2020/21 marketing year (Sep-Aug) rose by +36.1% yr/yr to $8.21 per hundred pounds (annualized through December 2020). The value of U.S. grain sorghum production in the 2019/20 marketing year fell by -2.5% to $1.152 billion.

Supply – World production of sorghum in the 2020/21 marketing year is expected to rise +6.3% to 61.623 million metric tons, but still below the 10-year high of 66.653 million metric tons posted in 2007/08. U.S. grain sorghum production in 2020/21 is expected to rise +0.2% yr/yr to 372.980 million bushels. Sorghum acreage harvested in 2020/21 is forecasted to rise +9.0% to 5.095 million acres. The harvested yield in 2020/21 is expected to rise +0.3% to 73.2 bushels per acre.

Demand – World utilization (consumption) of grain sorghum in the 2020/21 marketing year is expected to rise+4.2% to 61.159 million metric tons. The biggest consumers will be China utilizing 17.5% of the world supply and Nigeria utilizing 11.2%.

Trade – World exports of sorghum in the 2020/21 marketing year are expected to rise +44.8% to 9/310 million metric tons, but still well below the 2014/15 record high of 12.162 million metric tons. U.S. exports in 2020/21 are expected to rise +42.4% yr/yr to 7.355 million metric tons, accounting for 79.2% of total world exports. The other major exporters are Argentina with 1.0 million metric tons and Australia with 500,000 metric tons of exports expected. World imports of sorghum in 2020/21 are expected to rise +60.6% yr/yr to 8.985 million metric tons. Major world importers are China and Mexico.

World Production of Grain Sorghum In Thousands of Metric Tons

Crop Year	Argentina	Australia	Brazil	Burkina	China	Ethiopia	India	Mexico	Niger	Nigeria	Sudan	United States	World Total
2011-12	1,900	1,105	2,175	1,550	2,000	3,700	6,000	8,100	950	5,650	4,500	3,916	55,928
2012-13	2,300	1,080	2,300	1,850	2,500	3,700	5,150	8,100	1,200	5,794	2,650	4,796	56,111
2013-14	2,700	905	2,000	1,900	6,500	3,900	5,200	8,300	1,300	5,258	4,550	4,130	59,466
2014-15	2,800	505	2,000	1,700	12,700	4,100	5,100	6,600	1,450	6,833	6,000	2,459	65,887
2015-16	2,900	905	1,150	1,465	10,500	4,700	4,600	6,300	2,000	6,905	3,100	6,130	63,413
2016-17	2,900	675	1,700	1,640	7,400	4,700	4,500	5,300	2,000	7,350	5,950	6,283	62,478
2017-18	3,100	800	2,100	1,400	6,900	4,646	4,600	4,700	1,850	6,950	4,400	4,119	58,624
2018-19[1]	2,150	1,050	2,200	1,800	3,600	4,882	3,550	5,100	2,100	6,650	4,900	6,186	58,339
2019-20[2]	2,050	350	2,200	1,870	7,200	5,230	4,500	5,000	2,050	6,650	4,450	4,354	58,713
2020-21[3]	2,100	1,000	2,200	1,900	10,700	5,300	3,900	4,600	2,000	6,850	4,950	2,159	61,159

[1] Preliminary. [2] Estimate. [3] Forecast. *Source: Foreign Agricultural Service, U.S. Department of Agriculture (FAS-USDA)*

Salient Statistics of Grain Sorghum in the United States

Crop Year Beginning Sept. 1	Acreage Planted[4] for All Purposes	Acreage Harvested	For Grain: Production (1,000 Bushels)	For Grain: Yield Per Harvested Acre (Bushels)	For Grain: Price in Cents Per Bushel	For Grain: Value of Production (Million $)	For Silage: Acreage Harvested (1,000 Acres)	For Silage: Production (1,000 Tons)	For Silage: Yield Per Harvested Acre (Tons)	Sorghum Grain Stocks: Dec. 1 On Farms	Dec. 1 Off Farms	June 1 On Farms	June 1 Off Farms
	-- 1,000 Acres --									---- 1,000 Bushels ----			
2015-16	8,459	7,851	596,751	76.0	330.96	2,064.6	306	4,475	14.6	51,500	21,035	9,700	80,654
2016-17	6,690	6,163	480,261	77.9	278.88	1,352.4	298	4,171	14.0	43,000	265,149	8,620	76,088
2017-18	5,626	5,044	361,871	71.7	322	1,168.5	284	3,772	13.4	33,800	193,692	5,220	60,113
2018-19[1]	5,690	5,061	364,986	72.1	326	1,180.8	264	3,326	12.6	44,200	214,580	9,470	107,962
2019-20[2]	5,265	4,675	341,460	73.0	325	1,151.7	339	4,019	11.9	30,200	220,161	8,360	64,227
2020-21[3]	5,880	5,095	372,960	73.2	310								

[1] Preliminary. [2] Estimate. [3] Forecast. *Source: Foreign Agricultural Service, U.S. Department of Agriculture (FAS-USDA)*

Production of All Sorghum for Grain in the United States, by States In Thousands of Bushels

Year	Arkansas	Colorado	Illinois	Kansas	Louisiana	Mississippi	Missouri	Nebraska	New Mexico	Oklahoma	South Dakota	Texas	Total
2015	43,120	22,000	3,196	281,600	6,290	9,085	13,160	23,040	4,230	21,320	18,260	149,450	596,751
2016	3,212	20,750	1,488	268,450	4,692	979	5,130	17,850	3,485	20,350	15,800	115,500	480,261
2017	546	18,720	1,245	200,900	1,183	288	2,461	11,570	1,680	15,635	11,560	94,500	361,871
2018	770	17,225	1,776	233,200	504	270	2,100	15,980	1,786	12,000	16,000	62,100	364,986
2019	----	12,710	----	204,000	----	----	----	12,090	----	13,260	14,000	85,400	341,460
2020[1]	----	10,500	----	237,360	----	----	----	12,420	----	9,690	8,000	92,800	372,960

[1] Preliminary. *Source: National Agricultural Statistics Service, U.S. Department of Agriculture (NASS-USDA)*

Quarterly Supply and Disappearance of Grain Sorghum in the United States In Millions of Bushels

Crop Year Beginning Sept. 1	Supply: Beginning Stocks	Supply: Pro-duction	Supply: Imports[3]	Supply: Total Supply	Disapperance: Domestic Use: Food & Alcohol	Domestic Use: Seed	Domestic Use: Feed & Residual	Domestic Use: Total	Exports[3]	Total Disap-pearance	Ending Stocks
2017-18	33.5	361.9	2.0	397.3	59.7	.7	101.7	162.1	200.4	362.5	34.9
Sept.-Nov.	33.5	361.9	1.9	397.2	13.9	0	110.3	124.2	45.5	169.7	227.5
Dec.-Feb.	227.5	----	.1	227.5	10.2	0	3.4	13.6	73.7	87.3	140.3
Mar.-May	140.3	----	.0	140.3	15.4	.4	-7.2	8.6	66.3	74.9	65.3
June-Aug.	65.3	----	.0	65.4	20.1	.3	-4.8	15.7	14.8	30.5	34.9
2018-19	34.9	365.0	.0	399.9	105.0	.7	137.9	243.5	92.7	336.2	63.7
Sept.-Nov.	34.9	365.0	.0	399.8	25.6	0	99.1	124.7	16.4	141.1	258.8
Dec.-Feb.	258.8	----	.0	258.8	23.4	0	19.8	43.2	22.9	66.1	192.7
Mar.-May	192.7	----	.0	192.7	26.5	.2	26.4	53.1	22.2	75.3	117.4
June-Aug.	117.4	----	.0	117.5	29.5	.4	-7.4	22.5	31.3	53.8	63.7
2019-20[1]	63.7	341.5	.1	405.2	74.0	.7	96.7	171.4	203.6	375.1	30.1
Sept.-Nov.	63.7	341.5	.0	405.1	23.8	0	106.5	130.3	24.4	154.8	250.4
Dec.-Feb.	250.4	----	.0	250.4	29.0	0	18.2	47.1	38.3	85.4	164.9
Mar.-May	164.9	----	.0	165.0	16.9	.4	-8.1	9.2	83.2	92.4	72.6
June-Aug.	72.6	----	.0	72.6	4.3	.4	-19.9	-15.2	57.7	42.5	30.1
2020-21[2]	30.1	373.0	.1	403.1	14.4	.6	70.0	85.0	290.0	375.0	28.1
Sept.-Nov.	30.1	373.0	.0	403.1	3.0		118.2	121.2	62.8	183.9	219.1

[1] Preliminary. [2] Estimate. [3] Uncommitted inventory. [4] Includes quantity under loan and farmer-owned reserve. *Source: Economic Research Service, U.S. Department of Agriculture (ERS-USDA)*

Average Price of Sorghum Grain, No. 2, Yellow in Kansas City In Dollars Per Hundred Pounds (Cwt.)

Year	Sept.	Oct.	Nov.	Dec.	Jan.	Feb.	Mar.	Apr.	May	June	July	Aug.	Average
2013-14	8.15	7.57	7.40	7.52	7.62	8.08	8.64	8.89	8.74	7.98	6.79	6.05	7.79
2014-15	5.31	5.67	6.71	7.25	6.93	6.85	8.16	7.92	6.79	7.23	7.76	6.65	6.94
2015-16	6.09	6.31	6.22	6.53	----	----	5.91	5.92	6.00	6.34	5.05	4.90	5.93
2016-17	4.94	5.18	5.09	5.28	5.48	5.67	5.50	5.61	5.94	5.88	5.66	5.32	5.46
2017-18	5.39	5.49	5.51	5.85	6.12	5.81	6.13	6.17	6.22	6.07	5.62	5.73	5.84
2018-19	5.41	5.50	5.64	5.98	5.92	5.97	6.00	5.81	6.32	7.29	7.10	6.18	6.09
2019-20	5.90	6.39	6.14	6.22	6.36	6.25	6.24	6.00	5.90	6.30	6.37	6.00	6.17
2020-21[1]	7.82	8.97	9.75	10.24	11.78	12.39							10.16

[1] Preliminary. *Source: Economic Research Service, U.S. Department of Agriculture (ERS-USDA)*

Exports of Grain Sorghum, by Country of Destination from the United States In Metric Tons

Year	Canada	Ecuador	Eritrea (Ethiopia)	Israel	Japan	Jordan	Mexico	South Africa	Spain	Sudan	Turkey	World Total
2013-14	5,368	----	----	----	254,692	----	135,236	27,363	18,910	155,813	----	5,664,432
2014-15	6,053	----	----	----	86,137	----	12,515	10,000	----	179,450	----	9,243,031
2015-16	5,505	----	----	----	71,971	----	640,676	99,264	8,540	188,490	----	7,888,245
2016-17	4,937	----	----	----	220,243	----	530,086	68,936	----	121,825	----	5,982,920
2017-18	5,306	----	30,047	----	300,353	----	72,470	42,266	168,572	135,904	----	4,806,201
2018-19[1]	4,469	----	60,300	----	244,358	----	516,439	73,835	512,968	117,330	----	2,399,586
2019-20[2]	6,069	----	33,000	----	225,175	----	555,619	21,699	----	232,790	----	5,462,247

[1] Preliminary. [2] Estimate. *Source: Economic Research Service, U.S. Department of Agriculture (ERS-USDA)*

Grain Sorghum Price Support Program and Market Prices in the United States

Year	Price Support Operations: Price Support: Quantity (Million Cwt.)	Price Support: % of Pro-duction	Aquired by CCC (Million Cwt.)	Owned by CCC at Year End (Million Cwt.)	Basic Loan Rate (Dollars Per Bushel)	Target Price (Dollars Per Bushel)	Findley Loan Rate (Dollars Per Bushel)	Effective Base[3] (Million Acres)	Partici-pation Rate[4] % of Base	No. 2 Yellow ($ Per Cwt.): Kansas City	Texas High Plains	Los Angeles	Gulf Ports
2012-13	.2	.1	0	0	3.48	4.70	1.95	----	----	11.98	----	----	12.66
2013-14	.3	.1	0	0	3.48	4.70	1.95	----	----	7.79	----	----	9.53
2014-15	.4	.2	0	0	3.48	3.95	1.95	----	----	6.94	----	----	9.10
2015-16	1.4	.4	0	0	3.48	3.95	1.95	----	----	5.93	----	----	8.07
2016-17	1.9	.7	0	0	3.48	3.95	1.95	----	----	5.46	----	----	7.56
2017-18[1]	1.3	.6	0	0	3.48	3.95	1.95	----	----	5.84	----	----	----
2018-19[2]	1.2	.6	0	0	3.48	3.95	1.95	----	----	6.09	----	----	----

[1] Preliminary. [2] Estimate. [3] National effective crop acreage base as determined by ASCS. [4] Percentage of effective base acres enrolled in acreage reduction programs. 5/ Beginning with the 1996-7 marketing year, target prices are no longer applicable. *Source: Economic Research Service, U.S. Department of Agriculture (ERS-USDA)*

Hay

Hay is a catchall term for forage plants, typically grasses such as timothy and Sudan-grass, and legumes such as alfalfa and clover. Alfalfa and alfalfa mixtures account for nearly half of all hay production. Hay is generally used to make cured feed for livestock. Curing, which is the proper drying of hay, is necessary to prevent spoilage. Hay, when properly cured, contains about 20% moisture. If hay is dried excessively, however, there is a loss of protein, which makes it less effective as livestock feed. Hay is harvested in almost all the lower 48 states.

Prices – The average monthly price of hay received by U.S. farmers in the first eight months of the 2020/21 marketing year (May through April) was down -2.6% yr/yr at $159.00 per ton, and still below the record high of $189.67 per ton seen in 2012/13. The farm production value of hay produced in 2019/20 rose +5.0% to $18.151 million.

Supply – U.S. hay production in 2020/21 is expected to fall -0.9% yr/yr to 127.628 million tons. U.S. farmers are expected to harvest 53.283 million acres of hay in 2020/21, up +1.6%. The yield in 2020/21 is expected to fall -0.8% at 2.44 tons per acre, still below the 2004/05 record high of 2.55. U.S. carryover (May 1) in 2020/21 is expected to rise +37.0% to 20.426 million tons. The largest hay producing states in the U.S. for 2019 were Texas with 7.2% of U.S. hay production, Missouri with 5.7%, South Dakota with 5.4%, Nebraska with 4.7%, Oklahoma with 4.6%, and California with 4.5%.

Salient Statistics of All Hay in the United States

Crop Year Beginning May 1	Acres Harvested (1,000 Acres)	Yield Per Acre (Tons)	Production	Carry-over May 1	Disappearance	Supply	Disappearance	Animal Units Fed[3] (Millions)	Farm Price ($ Per Ton)	Farm Production Value Million $	Alfalfa (Certified)	Timothy	Red Clover	Sudan-grass
			Millions of Tons			Per Animal Unit In Tons					Retail Price Paid by Farmers for Seed, April 15 – Dollars Per Cwt.			
2015-16	54,447	2.47	134.7	24.5	133.9	2.29	1.93	69.0	145.3	16,549				
2016-17	53,185	2.52	134.1	25.1	135.5	2.24	1.90	71.0	129.8	15,477				
2017-18	52,777	2.43	128.2	24.4		2.15	1.93		142.9	16,109				
2018-19	52,839	2.34	123.6	15.3		1.95	1.74			17,288				
2019-20[1]	52,425	2.46	128.9	14.9		2.02	1.74			18,161				
2020-21[2]	53,283	2.44	127.7	20.4		2.08								

[1] Preliminary. [2] Estimate. [3] Roughage-consuming animal units fed annually. NA = Not available.
Source: Economic Research Service, U.S. Department of Agriculture (ERS-USDA)

Production of All Hay in the United States, by States In Thousands of Tons

Year	California	Idaho	Iowa	Minnesota	Missouri	New York	North Dakota	Ohio	Oklahoma	South Dakota	Texas	Wisconsin	Total
2014	7,513	4,881	3,675	4,486	7,100	6,028	5,460	2,710	6,121	6,665	11,746	4,866	140,119
2015	6,891	4,860	3,939	3,979	6,398	6,360	4,975	2,532	5,914	6,580	9,720	4,073	134,668
2016	6,790	5,126	3,210	4,440	6,066	5,717	4,285	2,471	5,611	5,425	11,714	3,926	134,082
2017	6,388	5,128	3,268	3,797	5,985	5,955	3,423	2,371	5,638	4,603	9,548	3,522	128,207
2018	5,682	5,019	2,998	3,077	5,408	6,985	4,419	2,356	5,121	5,788	8,374	2,953	123,600
2019[1]	5,795	5,111	3,116	2,966	7,367	6,085	4,116	2,137	5,935	7,003	9,216	2,784	128,864

[1] Preliminary. *Source: Agricultural Statistics Board, U.S. Department of Agriculture (ASB-USDA)*

Hay Production and Farm Stocks in the United States In Thousands of Short Tons

Year	Production: Alfalfa & Mixtures	All Others	All Hay	Corn for Silage[1]	Sorghum Silage[1]	Farm Stocks: May 1	Dec. 1
2015	59,060	75,608	134,668	127,311	4,475	24,517	94,993
2016	58,601	75,481	134,082	126,020	4,171	25,140	95,837
2017	55,812	72,395	128,207	127,434	3,772	24,400	84,422
2018	52,634	70,966	123,600	121,564	3,326	15,348	79,055
2019	54,875	73,989	128,864	132,807	4,019	14,906	84,488
2020[2]	52,625	75,053	127,678	137,729	3,125	20,426	84,020

[1] Not included in all tame hay. [2] Preliminary. *Source: Agricultural Statistics Board, U.S. Department of Agriculture (ASB-USDA)*

Mid-Month Price Received by Farmers for All Hay (Baled) in the United States In Dollars Per Ton

Year	May	June	July	Aug.	Sept.	Oct.	Nov.	Dec.	Jan.	Feb.	Mar.	Apr.	Average
2015-16	175.0	162.0	152.0	143.0	142.0	143.0	138.0	139.0	134.0	135.0	136.0	144.0	145.3
2016-17	140.0	134.0	128.0	130.0	128.0	129.0	126.0	123.0	122.0	124.0	131.0	143.0	129.8
2017-18	147.0	145.0	141.0	137.0	137.0	141.0	138.0	137.0	140.0	142.0	148.0	162.0	142.9
2018-19	167.0	160.0	161.0	163.0	164.0	163.0	162.0	166.0	167.0	170.0	173.0	184.0	166.7
2019-20	187.0	177.0	164.0	162.0	160.0	161.0	159.0	158.0	155.0	157.0	158.0	161.0	163.3
2020-21[1]	164.0	162.0	161.0	161.0	155.0	158.0	156.0	155.0	157.0				158.8

[1] Preliminary. [2] Marketing year average. *Source: Economic Research Service, U.S. Department of Agriculture (ERS-USDA)*

Heating Oil

Heating oil is a heavy fuel oil that is refined from crude oil. Heating oil is also known as No. 2 fuel oil and accounts for about 25% of the yield from a barrel of crude oil. That is the second-largest "cut" after gasoline. The price to consumers of home heating oil is generally comprised of 42% for crude oil, 12% for refining costs, and 46% for marketing and distribution costs (Source: EIA's Petroleum Marketing Monthly). Generally, a $1 increase in the price of crude oil translates into a 2.5-cent per gallon rise in heating oil. Because of this, heating oil prices are highly correlated with crude oil prices, although heating oil prices are also subject to swift supply and demand shifts due to weather changes or refinery shutdowns.

The primary use of heating oil is for residential heating. In the U.S., approximately 8.1 million households use heating oil as their main heating fuel. Most of the demand for heating oil occurs from October through March. The Northeast region, which includes the New England and the Central Atlantic States, is most reliant on heating oil. This region consumes approximately 70% of U.S. heating oil. However, demand for heating oil has been dropping as households switch to a more convenient heating source like natural gas. In fact, demand for heating oil is down by about 10 billion gallons/year from its peak use in 1976 (Source: American Petroleum Institute).

Refineries produce approximately 85% of U.S. heating oil as part of the "distillate fuel oil" product family, which includes heating oil and diesel fuel. The remainder of U.S. heating oil is imported from Canada, the Virgin Islands, and Venezuela.

Recently, a team of Purdue University researchers developed a way to make home heating oil from a mixture of soybean oil and conventional fuel oil. The oil blend is made by replacing 20% of the fuel oil with soybean oil, potentially saving 1.3 billion gallons of fuel oil per year. This soybean heating oil can be used in conventional furnaces without altering existing equipment. The soybean heating oil is relatively easy to produce and creates no sulfur emissions.

The "crack-spread" is the processing margin earned when refiners buy crude oil and refine it into heating oil and gasoline. The crack-spread ratio commonly used in the industry is the 3-2-1, which involves buying one heating oil contract and two gasoline futures contracts, and then selling three crude oil contracts. If the crack spread is positive, it is profitable for refiners to buy crude oil and refine it into products. The NYMEX has a crack-spread calculator on their web site at www.NYMEX.com.

Heating oil futures and options are traded at the CME Group. The CME's heating oil futures contract calls for the delivery of 1,000 barrels of fungible No. 2 heating oil in the New York harbor. Futures are also traded on ICE Futures Europe and the Multi Commodity Exchange of Index (MCX).

Prices – CME heating oil futures prices (Barchart.com symbol code HO) on the nearest-futures chart in 2020 opened at $2.0614 per gallon, moved sharply lower to post a 19-year low in May, and then moved higher the rest of the year to finally close the year down -23.2% at $1.5795 per gallon.

Supply – U.S. production of distillate fuel oil in 2020 fell – 7.7% yr/yr to 4.690 million barrels per day, down from the 2018 record high. Stocks of distillate fuel oil in December 2020 were up +14.6% yr/yr at 160.441 million barrels. U.S. production of residual fuel in 2020 fell by -47.1% yr/yr to an average of 191,771 barrels per day, which was less than about a quarter of the production level of over 1 million barrels per day produced in the 1970s. U.S. stocks of residual fuel oil as of December 2020 were down -2.2% to 30.234 million barrels, down from the 2015 record high of 42.189 million barrels.

Demand – U.S. usage of distillate fuel oil in 2020 fell -8.0% yr/yr to 3.759 million barrels per day, down from the 2007 record high of 4.198 million barrels a day.

Trade – U.S. imports of distillate fuel oil in 2019 rose +8.5% to an average of 214,627 barrels per day, down from the 2006 record high of 365,000 barrels per day. U.S. exports of distillate fuel oil in 2013 rose by +12.8% yr/yr to 1.134 million barrels per day. U.S. imports of residual fuel oil in 2019 fell by -30.3% yr/yr to 147.419 barrels per day, far less than the levels of over 1 million barrels per day seen back in the 1970s.

World Production of Distillate Fuel Oil In Thousands of Barrels Per Day

Year	Brazil	Canada	China	France	Germany	India	Italy	Japan	Korea, South	Russia	Saudi Arabia	United States	World Total
2008	793.0	557.0	2,767.5	991.2	1,104.4	1,054.0	642.0	908.7	388.3	640.0	577.8	3,945.4	25,428.5
2009	758.0	516.7	2,777.0	985.1	1,062.7	1,182.0	617.1	820.8	385.9	570.0	605.0	3,631.1	24,914.9
2010	855.0	569.6	3,011.3	983.7	1,096.5	1,226.0	614.5	825.8	399.4	583.0	618.9	3,800.3	25,366.6
2011	927.0	601.8	3,195.3	962.2	1,049.0	1,298.0	608.9	807.6	393.3	641.0	651.0	3,898.9	25,981.4
2012	992.0	582.7	3,461.4	962.9	1,076.1	1,420.0	569.5	811.3	405.2	582.0	704.8	3,741.4	26,602.0
2013	996.0	592.3	3,503.2	970.8	1,125.3	1,385.0	550.6	796.4	423.7	596.0	729.6	3,827.5	26,848.6
2014	1,023.0	580.8	3,513.6	949.2	1,079.8	1,417.7	568.2	772.8	432.2	577.1	753.3	4,037.2	27,209.9
2015[1]		571.5		965.1	1,100.8		558.0	770.1	472.6			3,995.2	
2016[2]		541.1		953.5	1,114.9		548.9	774.8	501.0				
2017[2]		533.1		890.3	1,046.5		505.0	696.4	462.5				

[1] Preliminary. [2] Estimate. *Source: Energy Information Administration, U.S. Department of Energy (EIA-DOE)*

World Imports of Distillate Fuel Oil   In Thousands of Barrels Per Day

Year	Australia	Belgium	France	Germany	Indonesia	Netherlands	Singapore	Spain	Turkey	United Kingdom	United States	Vietnam	World Total
2004	63.0	164.7	322.3	265.8	130.1	203.0	112.5	230.1	77.8	81.8	325.5	111.6	4,268.5
2005	81.7	198.1	380.7	277.6	170.2	196.2	78.9	263.4	84.7	98.6	328.8	120.4	4,499.6
2006	105.7	166.1	317.3	332.0	176.1	278.0	125.2	264.9	130.9	158.3	364.7	110.8	4,906.3
2007	105.2	148.9	271.6	187.8	229.7	188.4	127.0	286.6	162.3	159.0	304.1	132.5	5,090.9
2008	147.8	156.4	292.1	317.2	211.6	250.9	178.6	246.3	169.8	152.6	212.9	132.6	5,466.6
2009	144.0	124.6	380.2	297.0	146.7	333.5	155.0	234.1	186.2	127.5	225.1	132.9	5,485.7
2010	141.7	111.8	414.0	318.9	259.0	385.2	393.5	220.7	197.9	193.0	228.4	100.5	6,318.7
2011	176.6	161.7	408.0	278.9	244.3	375.1	383.0	174.1	207.5	191.4	178.7	108.5	6,444.8
2012[1]	202.0	128.3	469.9	276.1	290.2	384.2	279.2	136.4	226.1	218.6	126.2	113.6	6,523.9
2013[2]	226.8	246.5	478.1	322.7		378.6		95.2	245.5	217.2	154.7		

[1] Preliminary. [2] Estimate. *Source: Energy Information Administration, U.S. Department of Energy (EIA-DOE)*

World Exports of Distillate Fuel Oil   In Thousands of Barrels Per Day

Year	Belgium	Germany	India	Italy	Japan	Korea, South	Kuwait	Netherlands	Russia	Singapore	Taiwan	United States	World Total
2004	167.0	166.1	148.5	187.3	29.4	185.8	225.3	411.2	614.3	294.0	119.9	109.6	4,692.3
2005	182.3	204.4	173.0	179.8	64.1	234.3	221.2	430.4	649.2	300.0	149.2	138.4	5,038.9
2006	162.1	223.0	238.0	160.2	70.5	250.6	185.5	495.9	752.6	341.3	150.0	215.1	5,394.9
2007	177.9	250.6	292.4	183.5	137.2	281.9	194.0	420.4	751.9	359.3	176.5	267.7	5,268.0
2008	171.7	203.2	300.2	170.2	220.5	357.6	190.2	464.7	767.8	406.8	181.1	528.3	5,830.8
2009	140.2	181.8	377.3	168.2	215.7	343.6	152.8	562.3	812.9	346.3	206.6	587.4	6,153.4
2010	142.4	138.8	376.5	189.1	197.4	358.0	143.8	636.1	851.0	540.0	177.2	656.0	6,209.9
2011	156.2	132.2	430.5	153.6	160.0	436.8	143.8	631.1	807.8	553.7	157.5	854.1	6,404.8
2012[1]	160.7	128.9	459.1	178.8	120.2	481.8	153.0	608.5	840.9	469.8	191.7	1,007.2	6,781.3
2013[2]	226.4	135.0		142.8	167.6	446.6		604.1				1,133.9	

[1] Preliminary. [2] Estimate. *Source: Energy Information Administration, U.S. Department of Energy (EIA-DOE)*

Production of Distillate Fuel Oil in the United States   In Thousand Barrels per Day

Year	Jan.	Feb.	Mar.	Apr.	May	June	July	Aug.	Sept.	Oct.	Nov.	Dec.	Average
2011	4,303.3	4,033.2	4,326.0	4,188.8	4,283.3	4,470.8	4,656.4	4,667.7	4,576.5	4,538.7	4,902.4	4,918.8	4,488.8
2012	4,500.4	4,407.7	4,262.8	4,351.7	4,547.3	4,631.8	4,660.1	4,599.7	4,565.5	4,509.8	4,668.8	4,884.4	4,549.2
2013	4,479.8	4,280.5	4,283.8	4,416.4	4,767.1	4,791.5	4,933.8	4,930.0	4,888.4	4,814.8	5,049.7	5,121.6	4,729.8
2014	4,685.3	4,594.5	4,779.7	4,987.9	5,026.1	4,896.0	5,021.2	5,042.5	4,939.8	4,662.0	5,011.6	5,322.9	4,914.1
2015	4,835.2	4,752.4	4,893.7	4,991.4	4,982.8	5,031.8	5,101.2	5,106.6	5,060.8	4,816.5	5,169.0	5,042.1	4,982.0
2016	4,530.3	4,667.8	4,848.3	4,658.8	4,760.4	4,953.6	4,933.4	4,939.2	4,888.1	4,614.1	5,066.0	5,147.6	4,834.0
2017	4,785.5	4,656.6	4,792.5	5,018.9	5,215.5	5,283.8	5,161.9	5,044.1	4,559.7	4,972.0	5,362.1	5,407.9	5,021.7
2018	5,005.9	4,584.1	4,822.5	5,119.5	5,214.1	5,410.4	5,257.1	5,369.5	5,230.0	5,035.4	5,350.1	5,575.6	5,164.5
2019	5,252.2	4,901.7	4,968.0	5,053.8	5,212.6	5,349.2	5,243.4	5,266.3	5,034.9	4,792.7	5,232.2	5,309.1	5,134.7
2020[1]	5,084.9	4,811.6	4,951.2	5,100.5	4,821.2	4,579.6	4,842.5	4,822.6	4,493.2	4,212.6	4,521.8	4,656.0	4,741.5

[1] Preliminary. *Source: Energy Information Administration; U.S. Department of Energy (EIA-DOE)*

Stocks of Distillate Fuel in the United States, on First of Month   In Thousands of Barrels

Year	Jan.	Feb.	Mar.	Apr.	May	June	July	Aug.	Sept.	Oct.	Nov.	Dec.
2011	163,086	154,077	149,239	142,919	144,847	143,870	154,455	155,064	153,399	142,327	143,857	149,212
2012	147,210	139,289	133,697	124,665	121,445	119,890	126,454	127,309	127,384	118,653	117,993	134,809
2013	131,268	121,963	118,737	118,791	122,132	122,463	126,020	129,060	129,326	118,035	121,118	127,543
2014	114,534	112,897	115,337	116,827	121,757	121,674	125,559	128,132	131,289	120,093	126,085	136,065
2015	131,992	123,137	128,294	129,022	134,028	139,437	142,144	152,145	148,846	143,317	156,666	160,741
2016	160,583	162,696	160,620	154,692	154,389	149,239	155,969	159,534	160,378	153,884	160,173	165,456
2017	168,937	162,241	151,080	154,640	153,793	151,608	151,068	147,820	137,461	129,885	132,700	145,574
2018	141,129	138,578	130,391	120,591	115,199	120,379	127,081	132,037	137,060	124,183	126,356	140,006
2019	140,137	136,251	132,435	128,200	129,992	130,840	137,797	135,640	131,731	120,110	126,311	139,986
2020[1]	143,010	132,740	126,713	150,709	175,899	175,427	177,561	178,914	171,718	155,333	156,281	160,441

[1] Preliminary. *Source: Energy Information Administration; U.S. Department of Energy (EIA-DOE)*

Imports of Distillate Fuel Oil in the United States In Thousand of Barrels per Day

Year	Jan.	Feb.	Mar.	Apr.	May	June	July	Aug.	Sept.	Oct.	Nov.	Dec.	Average
2011	337	206	190	191	170	127	157	148	179	128	138	175	179
2012	157	142	137	98	113	87	117	112	86	88	188	190	126
2013	213	174	146	238	168	121	107	123	132	128	145	164	155
2014	283	337	324	181	198	121	129	143	126	120	136	245	195
2015	349	388	324	243	191	132	143	140	103	101	150	155	202
2016	172	231	150	177	123	88	123	164	150	75	145	167	147
2017	204	199	108	116	124	102	111	112	112	134	180	282	149
2018	290	284	157	91	122	90	144	175	172	161	227	190	175
2019	308	361	180	121	142	117	172	150	111	178	237	295	198
2020[1]	217	148	164	231	190	154	116	145	180	280	305	446	215

[1] Preliminary. *Source: Energy Information Administration, U.S. Department of Energy (EIA-DOE)*

Disposition of Distillate Fuel Oil, Total Product Supplied in the United States In Thousand of Barrels per Day

Year	Jan.	Feb.	Mar.	Apr.	May	June	July	Aug.	Sept.	Oct.	Nov.	Dec.	Average
2011	3,958.0	3,913.5	4,045.1	3,754.5	3,699.4	3,947.4	3,563.7	4,008.9	3,936.0	4,003.4	4,109.4	3,853.2	3,899.4
2012	3,860.9	3,922.9	3,714.8	3,718.9	3,756.3	3,732.5	3,556.6	3,743.0	3,674.3	3,852.4	3,847.6	3,528.8	3,742.4
2013	4,061.8	3,984.4	3,769.1	3,854.4	3,749.0	3,662.9	3,621.0	3,693.2	3,724.6	4,038.8	3,893.2	3,886.8	3,828.3
2014	4,340.0	4,160.3	4,066.2	3,989.8	3,951.6	3,901.6	3,866.5	3,874.8	3,933.4	4,266.3	3,917.2	4,178.2	4,037.1
2015	4,185.7	4,559.2	4,078.1	4,027.4	3,777.5	3,896.8	3,901.2	3,914.7	4,063.0	4,014.1	3,740.2	3,831.1	3,999.1
2016	3,850.3	3,996.1	3,947.0	3,798.9	3,732.0	3,852.7	3,597.4	3,880.4	3,912.0	3,986.3	3,938.4	4,043.1	3,877.9
2017	3,735.6	3,934.8	4,126.6	3,762.8	3,955.0	3,963.6	3,641.8	4,003.5	3,921.2	4,011.2	4,157.4	3,975.3	3,932.4
2018	4,491.0	3,979.3	4,196.5	4,139.0	4,208.8	3,959.4	3,962.6	4,195.7	4,022.2	4,347.8	4,203.8	4,019.4	4,143.8
2019	4,354.6	4,330.8	4,154.9	3,980.0	4,040.8	4,010.8	3,906.9	4,002.3	3,914.5	4,222.5	4,186.4	3,901.4	4,083.8
2020[1]	3,997.6	4,010.5	3,913.3	3,505.1	3,533.3	3,491.9	3,609.9	3,663.3	3,818.2	4,022.0	3,888.6	3,649.7	3,758.6

[1] Preliminary. *Source: Energy Information Administration, U.S. Department of Energy (EIA-DOE)*

World Production of Residual Fuel Oil In Thousands of Barrels Per Day

Year	Brazil	China	India	Iran	Italy	Japan	Korea, South	Mexico	Russia	Saudi Arabia	United States	Vene-zuela	World Total
2008	213.0	738.9	241.0	328.2	212.7	546.7	331.7	265.1	264.0	363.7	622.2	100.5	10,326.9
2009	160.0	684.5	295.0	359.9	180.1	411.4	320.5	246.0	324.0	275.5	511.1	105.0	10,106.0
2010	184.0	878.4	179.0	318.6	144.0	395.6	321.3	224.0	303.0	272.0	535.1	117.0	9,856.0
2011	161.0	609.1	185.0	379.2	115.9	446.6	277.7	242.6	423.0	316.9	461.1	123.1	9,534.6
2012	167.0	583.7	184.0	420.3	107.2	565.4	268.8	244.9	407.0	330.9	368.8	115.0	9,371.2
2013	114.0	580.3	155.0	357.6	82.6	475.1	256.8	226.9	350.0	370.2	318.6	109.1	9,044.0
2014	139.3	552.9	148.4	335.3	72.7	413.3	218.8	164.7	243.5	438.3	257.2	71.3	8,836.6
2015[1]					77.7	368.1	237.3	144.6			259.3		
2016[2]					64.4	340.2	277.0	133.0					
2017[2]					62.3	260.9	210.3	139.6					

[1] Preliminary. [2] Estimate. *Source: Energy Information Administration, U.S. Department of Energy (EIA-DOE)*

Supply and Disposition of Residual Fuel Oil in the United States

	Supply		Disposition				
Year	Total Production	Imports	Stock Change	Exports	Product Supplied	Ending Stocks (Million Barrels)	Average Sales to End Users[3] (USD per Gallon)
	In Thousands of Barrels Per Day						
2010	585	366	----	----	535	41	1.71
2011	537	328	----	----	461	34	2.40
2012	501	256	----	----	369	34	2.59
2013	467	225	----	----	319	38	2.48
2014	435	173	----	----	257	34	2.33
2015	417	192	----	----	259	42	1.29
2016	418	205	----	----	326	41	0.95
2017	427	189	----	----	342	29	1.29
2018	425	211	----	----	318	28	1.66
2019[1]	363	147	----	----	273	31	1.58

[1] Preliminary. [2] Less than +500 barrels per day and greater than -500 barrels per day. [3] Refiner price excluding taxes.
Source: Energy Information Administration, U.S. Department of Energy (EIA-DOE)

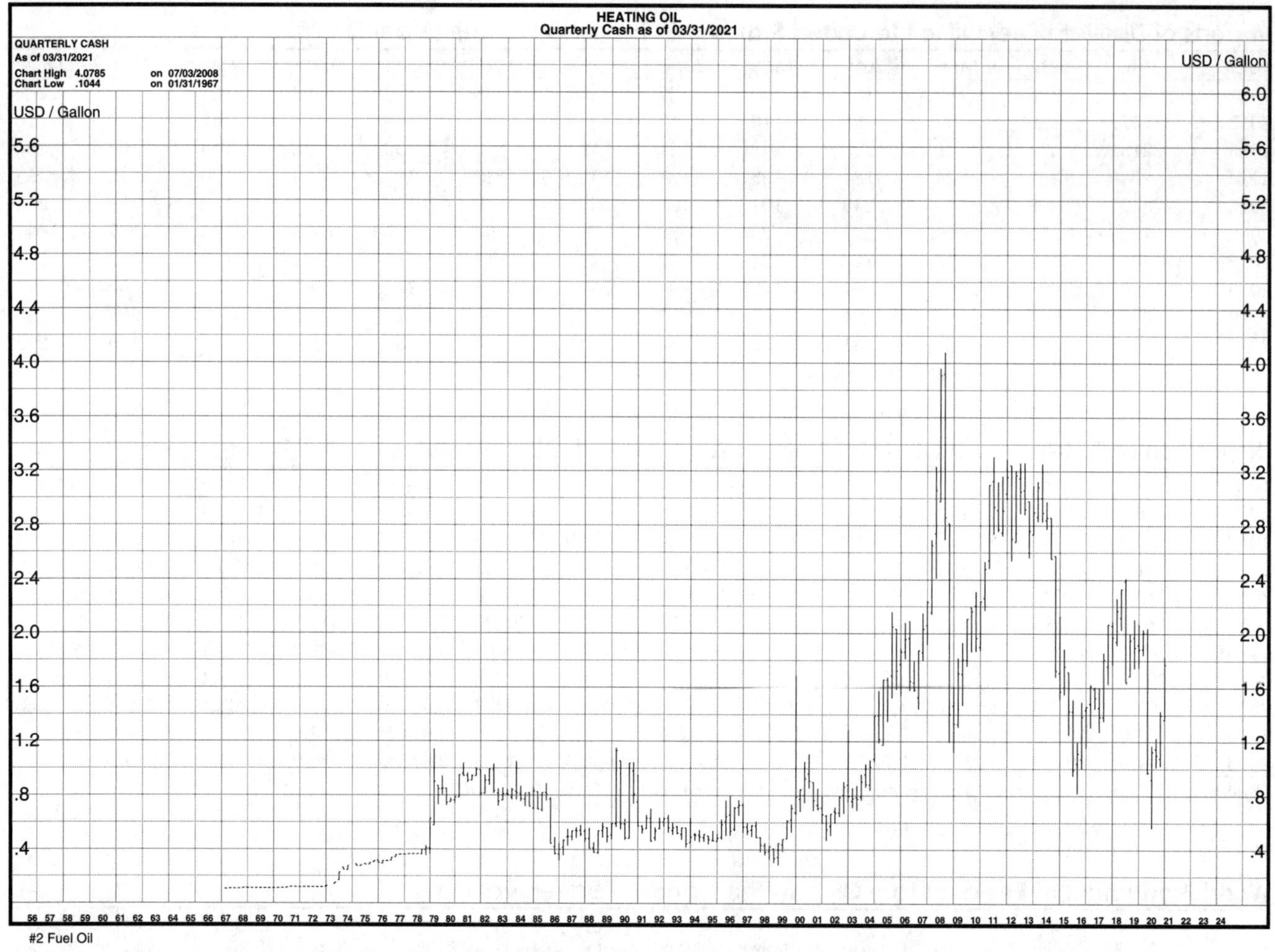

Production of Residual Fuel Oil in the United States In Thousands of Barrels per Day

Year	Jan.	Feb.	Mar.	Apr.	May	June	July	Aug.	Sept.	Oct.	Nov.	Dec.	Average
2011	552.5	529.4	525.7	534.3	538.2	553.5	562.6	604.0	516.1	529.8	515.7	485.9	537.3
2012	499.8	547.8	577.3	524.9	508.6	538.2	486.0	495.1	507.7	480.5	457.5	387.7	500.9
2013	395.4	504.1	569.4	508.2	488.1	469.0	481.4	416.9	433.8	420.3	466.2	454.8	467.3
2014	476.3	427.5	460.8	420.4	454.3	454.7	402.1	438.7	409.8	415.6	462.0	401.2	435.3
2015	376.7	419.5	478.3	466.8	435.5	413.3	426.1	403.7	414.1	419.3	376.5	376.4	417.2
2016	395.0	403.4	399.9	435.0	427.0	389.4	400.6	419.8	436.0	454.8	450.1	400.9	417.7
2017	485.2	482.5	405.7	416.6	407.7	406.3	390.5	452.5	459.2	442.2	407.8	372.5	427.4
2018	467.4	461.5	403.2	450.4	414.8	347.6	444.2	391.3	429.4	397.2	449.8	440.3	424.8
2019	397.7	306.0	357.3	388.0	363.5	429.8	389.9	409.5	382.8	339.9	318.5	264.4	362.3
2020[1]	229.2	229.3	232.5	144.9	167.2	239.0	225.4	192.4	165.1	162.8	153.3	160.2	191.8

[1] Preliminary. *Source: Energy Information Administration, U.S. Department of Energy (EIA-DOE)*

Average Price of Heating Oil #2 In Dollars Per Gallon

Year	Jan.	Feb.	Mar.	Apr.	May	June	July	Aug.	Sept.	Oct.	Nov.	Dec.	Average
2011	2.6035	2.7638	3.0339	3.1956	2.9514	2.9651	3.0692	2.9427	2.9199	2.9500	3.0524	2.8875	2.9446
2012	3.0452	3.1941	3.2146	3.1472	2.9123	2.6201	2.8200	3.0459	3.1295	3.1383	3.0107	2.9591	3.0198
2013	3.0720	3.1669	2.9468	2.7278	2.6882	2.7424	2.8863	2.9581	2.9613	2.9422	2.9228	3.0325	2.9206
2014	3.0633	3.0656	2.9124	2.8878	2.8603	2.8822	2.7758	2.7535	2.6332	2.4237	2.2493	1.8555	2.6969
2015	1.6163	1.8727	1.6315	1.7404	1.8317	1.7680	1.5505	1.3875	1.4311	1.4042	1.3198	1.0392	1.5494
2016	0.9396	0.9721	1.1289	1.1877	1.3527	1.4162	1.2850	1.3251	1.3521	1.4877	1.3872	1.5521	1.2822
2017	1.5474	1.5622	1.4925	1.5202	1.4521	1.3320	1.4248	1.5412	1.7915	1.7111	1.8216	1.8619	1.5882
2018	2.0315	1.8541	1.8698	2.0372	2.1880	2.1132	2.1067	2.1246	2.2260	2.3158	2.0360	1.7877	2.0576
2019	1.8310	1.9278	1.9668	2.0359	2.0086	1.8197	1.8894	1.7950	1.9247	1.9204	1.9146	1.9638	1.9165
2020	1.8290	1.5891	1.1564	0.8580	0.8425	1.0732	1.1874	1.1799	1.0694	1.0992	1.1673	1.3366	1.1990

Source: Energy Information Administration, U.S. Department of Energy (EIA-DOE)

Nearby Futures through Last Trading Day.

Volume of Trading of Heating Oil #2 Futures in New York In Thousands of Contracts

Year	Jan.	Feb.	Mar.	Apr.	May	June	July	Aug.	Sept.	Oct.	Nov.	Dec.	Total
2011	2,545.9	2,600.7	2,805.0	2,206.5	2,645.6	2,624.9	2,022.6	2,843.7	2,889.1	2,964.2	3,071.0	2,619.4	31,838.6
2012	3,149.6	3,203.3	2,953.3	2,693.2	2,913.9	3,172.8	2,875.1	3,071.6	2,812.8	3,887.9	2,913.4	2,440.8	36,087.7
2013	3,122.0	2,801.6	2,900.0	3,057.7	2,852.8	2,540.0	2,700.0	2,490.4	2,384.5	2,932.3	2,608.5	2,359.7	32,749.6
2014	3,400.6	2,893.3	2,533.8	2,209.6	2,253.3	2,483.3	2,857.3	2,719.9	2,875.9	3,409.5	3,126.2	3,183.6	33,946.4
2015	3,247.1	3,451.1	3,022.4	2,733.6	2,616.5	2,981.7	3,024.6	3,254.2	2,906.7	3,473.0	2,765.9	3,470.1	36,947.0
2016	3,341.1	3,201.8	2,861.8	3,286.1	3,452.2	3,431.1	3,052.5	3,455.0	3,288.4	3,183.1	3,518.7	3,317.7	39,389.3
2017	3,322.5	3,332.7	3,497.4	3,091.7	3,867.4	3,642.3	3,601.1	4,759.9	3,577.9	3,849.6	3,549.3	3,504.4	43,596.2
2018	4,542.6	3,826.2	3,715.8	4,066.3	4,334.6	3,738.0	3,326.2	3,566.0	3,440.1	3,966.1	4,516.8	3,239.0	46,277.9
2019	3,428.3	3,043.1	3,382.3	2,999.0	4,011.8	3,370.8	3,082.3	3,379.1	3,916.7	5,096.9	3,973.8	3,716.7	43,400.8
2020	5,655.2	4,206.4	5,101.5	3,880.6	3,347.1	2,772.6	2,454.6	2,927.0	3,547.1	3,714.6	3,420.4	2,975.9	44,003.2

Contract size = 42,000 US gallons. *Source: CME Group; New York Mercantile Exchange (NYMEX)*

Average Open Interest of Heating Oil #2 Futures in New York In Contracts

Year	Jan.	Feb.	Mar.	Apr.	May	June	July	Aug.	Sept.	Oct.	Nov.	Dec.
2011	306,262	312,145	305,872	310,288	310,053	316,026	306,360	307,607	323,485	303,460	291,931	274,679
2012	273,761	299,758	286,319	296,190	314,645	323,256	313,376	320,011	332,853	316,594	303,742	280,933
2013	297,517	316,763	297,280	304,306	307,574	291,583	287,422	290,885	284,372	280,863	298,480	292,422
2014	281,102	294,144	280,719	263,461	269,766	285,931	313,266	353,133	373,004	390,505	391,923	355,367
2015	375,870	384,974	375,278	361,933	360,017	362,447	388,442	425,342	399,488	382,414	367,273	348,763
2016	349,641	365,010	367,707	389,364	399,419	404,855	370,778	396,411	391,168	408,496	395,976	431,825
2017	422,678	424,439	413,555	428,260	418,050	405,141	411,503	404,442	444,276	442,998	445,430	443,590
2018	469,402	433,230	401,046	436,876	438,501	403,757	403,666	390,752	420,964	422,927	376,499	369,267
2019	367,498	415,805	401,238	397,296	399,818	407,129	412,377	439,510	415,640	443,137	436,588	427,092
2020	415,494	408,798	378,779	365,527	382,637	378,457	358,653	376,359	424,716	425,509	398,259	374,290

Contract size = 42,000 US gallons. *Source: CME Group; New York Mercantile Exchange (NYMEX)*

Hides and Leather

Hides and leather have been used since ancient times for boots, clothing, shields, armor, tents, bottles, buckets, and cups. Leather is produced through the tanning of hides, pelts, and skins of animals. The remains of leather have been found in the Middle East dating back at least 7,000 years.

Today, most leather is made of cowhide, but it is also made from the hides of lamb, deer, ostrich, snakes, crocodiles, and even stingray. Cattle hides are the most valuable byproduct of the meat-packing industry. U.S. exports of cowhides bring more than $1 billion in foreign trade, and U.S. finished leather production is worth about $4 billion.

Prices – The average monthly price of wholesale cattle hides (packer heavy native steers FOB Chicago) in 2020 fell -18.8% yr/yr to 32.30 cents per pound, well below the 2014 record high of 110.19 cents per pound.

Supply – World production of cattle and buffalo hides in 2019 rose 1.6% yr/yr to 9.366 million metric tons a new record high. The world's largest producers of cattle and buffalo hides in 2019 were the U.S. with 12.1% of world production, Brazil with 10.7%, and Argentina with 5.4%.

U.S. new supply of cattle hides from domestic slaughter in 2009 had fallen 3.0% yr/yr to 33.338 million hides, which is far below the record high of 43.582 million hides posted in 1976. U.S. production of leather footwear has been dropping sharply in recent years due to the movement of production offshore to lower-cost producers. For example, U.S. production of leather footwear in 2003 fell -46.0% yr/yr to 22.3 million pairs and was a mere 4% of the 562.3 million pairs produced in 1970.

Demand – World consumption of cowhides and skins in 2000, the last reporting year for the series, rose +1.4% to 4,774 metric tons, which was a record high for the data series, which goes back to 1984. The world's largest consumers of cowhides and skins in 2000 were the U.S., with 13.0% of world consumption, Italy (10.6%), Brazil (8.9%), Mexico, (6.0%), Argentina (6.0%), and South Korea (5.9%).

Trade – The total value of U.S. leather exports in 2004 was $1.344 billion. U.S. net exports of cattle hides in 2020 rose +28.2% to 20.078 million. hides. The largest destinations for U.S. exports in 2020 were China (which took 64.8% of U.S. exports), Mexico (21.3%), and South Korea (7.2%).

World Production of Cattle and Buffalo Hides In Metric Tons

Year	Argentina	Australia	Brazil	Canada	Colombia	France	Germany	Italy	Mexico	Russia	United Kingdom	United States	World Total
2010	425,303	246,917	911,500	104,213	92,304	147,140	143,236	139,075	216,477	206,065	84,074	1,078,220	8,579,140
2011	404,086	246,966	903,000	92,904	98,853	150,654	139,120	130,942	223,821	193,916	86,667	1,091,996	8,528,515
2012	419,749	249,636	930,700	86,186	102,856	143,641	136,253	127,686	225,883	195,830	81,944	1,087,080	8,595,976
2013	456,260	273,651	967,500	86,016	103,097	134,647	132,717	110,719	224,172	194,845	78,426	1,075,452	8,734,503
2014	432,391	301,037	972,300	89,762	100,828	135,659	135,819	92,177	226,702	197,335	81,204	1,067,197	8,779,305
2015	440,962	308,750	942,500	85,474	102,866	139,222	134,599	102,425	228,946	196,767	81,944	983,220	8,752,368
2016	427,540	268,655	928,400	93,407	95,910	140,971	137,350	105,260	233,099	189,537	84,722	1,046,441	8,791,798
2017	459,963	239,959	955,000	98,086	91,676	137,767	135,154	98,315	239,078	187,211	83,796	1,086,274	9,012,613
2018[1]	495,794	259,570	990,000	103,434	92,874	138,111	133,542	105,362	245,772	191,848	85,370	1,114,734	9,235,109
2019[2]	507,083	272,808	1,020,000	116,645	92,709				251,577	193,879	84,630	1,126,553	9,366,295

[1] Preliminary. [2] Forecast. *Source: Food and Agricultural Organization of the United Nations (FAO-UN)*

Imports of Bovine Hides and Skins in the United States In Thousands of Hides

Year	Australia	Belgium-Luxembourg	Brazil	Canada	China	Colombia	Italy	Mexico	New Zealand	Pakistan	Thailand	Turkey	World Total
2011	0.3	10.0	4.7	931.9	16.5	6.2	18.9	196.3	16.6	24.7	6.9	48.5	1,305.7
2012	7.2	10.0	36.9	1,209.4	36.9	10.3	3.9	240.8	7.5	2.6	6.8	17.3	1,609.7
2013	2.6	11.4	15.2	1,007.6	80.6	0.9	12.2	432.9	4.4	2.5	5.3	22.0	1,623.0
2014	72.2	24.4	7.1	1,181.0	92.9	0.6	5.0	638.2	6.8	0.5	6.9	0.8	2,077.4
2015	97.2	43.8	1.0	1,218.8	5.2	33.7	5.9	375.8	1.0	0.1	8.8	0.8	2,193.2
2016	0.0	139.4	8.2	794.2	8.5	107.1	11.9	69.4	1.9	1.1	20.3	0.7	2,336.2
2017	5.2	203.7	18.5	625.1	0.2	27.1	10.2	16.6	4.1	0.8	5.7	0.0	1,449.7
2018	3.4	196.5	19.6	653.7	4.9	13.7	10.6	9.2	16.5	1.2	4.7	0.0	1,404.5
2019	8.1	118.8	14.6	347.1	0.2	2.0	6.9	31.8	3.9		7.9	5.8	912.4
2020[1]	1.4	30.2	45.3	267.2	1.2	6.8	21.1	333.4	4.6		15.9	0.9	785.8

[1] Preliminary. *Source: Foreign Agricultural Service, U.S. Department of Agriculture (FAS-USDA)*

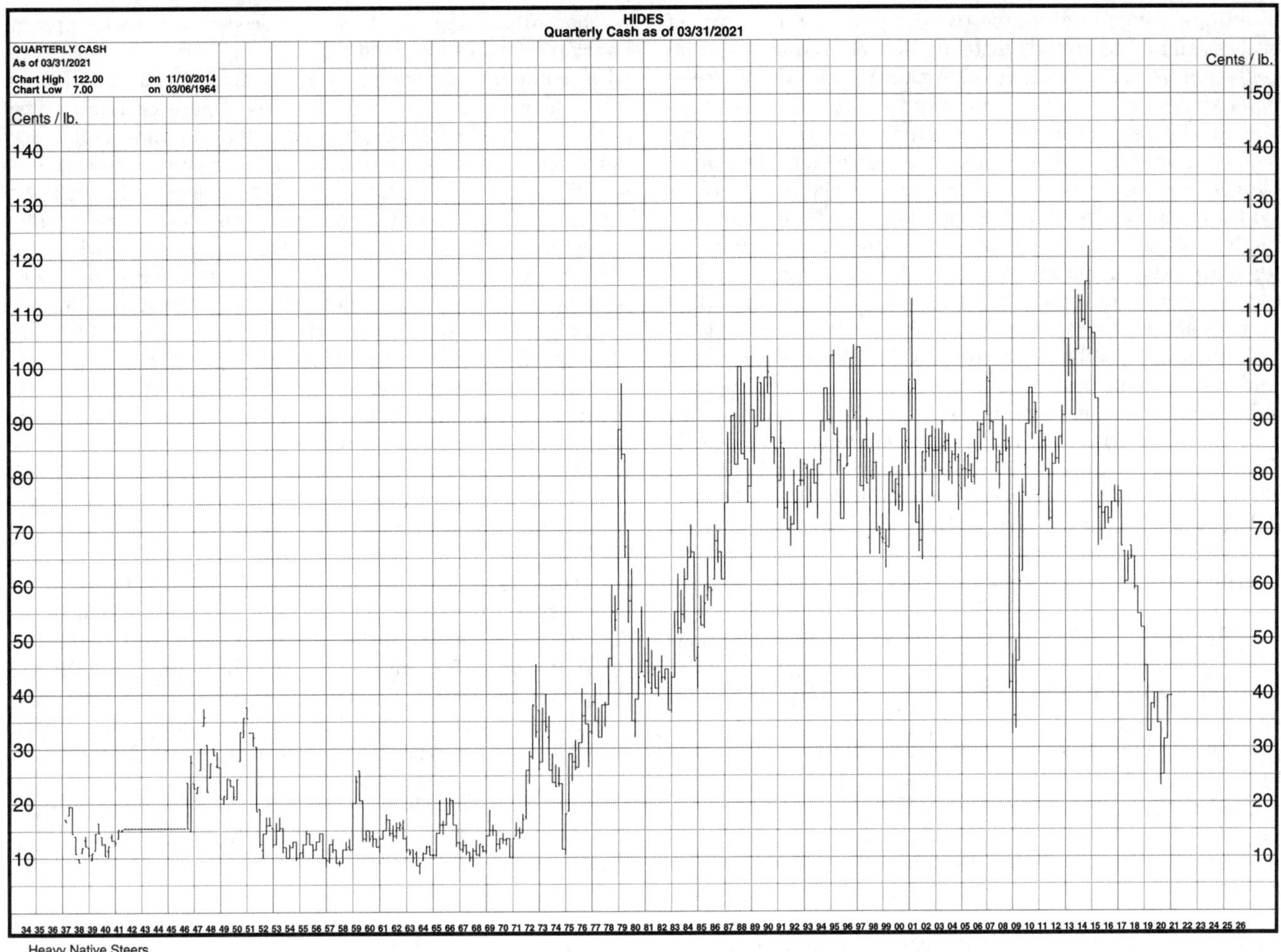

Exports of Bovine Hides and Skins from the United States In Thousands of Hides

Year	Canada	China	Hong Kong	Italy	Japan	Korea, South	Mexico	Nether-lands	Taiwan	Thailand	Turkey	Vietnam	World Total
2011	179	8,245	1,141	1,703	347	3,002	1,062	84	1,194	382	241	895	18,814
2012	97	10,761	399	547	211	3,473	1,264	13	983	400	182	597	19,200
2013	62	9,319	348	228	97	2,426	1,075	15	865	173	53	257	15,173
2014	33	10,881	227	174	180	2,282	1,277	127	1,232	221	37	53	16,882
2015	57	9,835	36	172	153	2,307	1,275	163	620	281	65	147	15,260
2016	79	9,856	39	292	164	2,538	1,906	69	481	292	65	115	16,180
2017		10,540	29	192	152	2,540	1,541	33	557	881	101	51	17,095
2018		8,882	12	183	175	2,474	1,670	64	374	1,497	114	30	16,047
2019		8,809	14	60	182	2,685	2,023	72	385	923	42	63	15,664
2020[1]		13,004	31	45	42	1,442	4,285	10	249	370	98	86	20,078

[1] Preliminary. *Source: Foreign Agricultural Service, U.S. Department of Agriculture (FAS-USDA)*

Wholesale Price of Hides (Packer Heavy Native Steers) F.O.B. Chicago In Cents Per Pound

Year	Jan.	Feb.	Mar.	Apr.	May	June	July	Aug.	Sept.	Oct.	Nov.	Dec.	Average
2011	78.24	81.78	85.20	88.18	84.12	86.26	85.60	85.66	82.40	79.54	76.76	72.10	82.15
2012	72.19	78.90	83.55	84.32	85.95	83.71	84.10	85.89	83.66	86.48	88.52	91.10	84.03
2013	91.45	97.00	96.81	103.14	99.66	98.93	99.32	95.39	91.50	94.39	106.00	105.38	98.25
2014	104.76	107.00	110.62	112.00	108.90	108.14	108.59	112.00	114.43	114.37	114.29	107.16	110.19
2015	104.20	103.24	103.68	98.57	95.90	94.00	73.86	71.86	75.90	73.64	68.95	71.64	86.29
2016	72.37	70.85	73.18	72.93	71.86	72.77	73.80	73.70	73.81	75.43	77.33	75.45	73.62
2017	75.15	75.61	77.04	74.79	68.50	67.64	63.90	61.74	61.17	60.80	61.19	64.15	67.64
2018	66.17	66.24	65.89	63.86	61.36	59.98	57.52	55.63	54.92	54.17	52.10	52.00	59.15
2019	47.71	43.42	45.00	45.00	38.86	34.00	33.00	36.86	38.00	38.74	38.90	37.95	39.79
2020	40.00	40.00	36.75	29.50	24.62	24.50	25.05	27.14	30.07	34.64	36.10	39.25	32.30

Source: National Agricultural Statistics Service, U.S. Department of Agriculture (NASS-USDA)

Hogs

Hogs are generally bred twice a year in a continuous cycle designed to provide a steady flow of production. The gestation period for hogs is 3-1/2 months, and the average litter size is nine pigs. The pigs are weaned at 3-4 weeks of age. The pigs are then fed to maximize weight gain. The feed consists primarily of grains such as corn, barley, milo, oats, and wheat. Protein is added from oilseed meals. Hogs typically gain 3.1 pounds per pound of feed. The time from birth to slaughter is typically six months. Hogs are ready for slaughter at about 254 pounds, producing a dressed carcass weight of around 190 pounds and an average 88.6 pounds of lean meat. The lean meat consists of 21% ham, 20% loin, 14% belly, 3% spareribs, 7% Boston butt roast and blade steaks, and 10% picnic, with the remaining 25% going into jowl, lean trim, fat, miscellaneous cuts, and trimmings. Futures on lean hogs are traded at the CME Group. The futures contract is settled in cash based on the CME Lean Hog Index price, meaning that no physical delivery of hogs occurs. The CME Lean Hog Index is based on the 2-day average net price of slaughtered hogs at the average lean percentage level.

Prices – CME lean hog futures prices (Barchart.com electronic symbol HE) moved sideways in Q1-2020 and then plunged to an 18-year low in April of 37.000 cents per pound. The spread of the Covid pandemic prompted lockdowns that closed restaurants and schools and decimated domestic pork demand. As a result, pork supply surged, and the Q1 USDA Hogs & Pigs Inventory report showed the U.S. hog herd on March 1 climbed to a record 77.6 million hogs. Hog prices recovered in May after 25% of U.S. pork production capacity was shut down as hog processing plants were forced to close when plant workers became infected with Covid. Also, the spread of the pandemic sparked a run-on retail meat supplies as consumers cleaned out retail stores of pork products. The USDA May Cold Storage report showed that U.S. pork supplies in cold storage sank -24% yr/yr to a 9-year low of 467 million lbs. Hog prices fell back into July as the pandemic forced slaughterhouses to close, forcing hog producers to hold their hogs since they had nowhere to sell them. However, hog prices then trended higher into October and posted the high for 2020 of 78.425 cents per pound. Global pork production concerns sparked a rally in hogs after Germany, Europe's biggest hog producer, reported its first case of African swine fever. That prompted China, Japan, and South Korea to suspend pork imports from Germany, giving a boost to U.S. hog exports. U.S. 2020 pork exports rose +16.6% yr/yr to a record 7.282 billion lbs. Hog futures prices ended 2020 down -1.6% yr/yr at 70.275 cents per pound.

Supply – The number of hogs on world farms as of January 1, 2021, rose by +4.1% to 682.300 million head. The number of hogs in the U.S. as of January 1, 2021, fell by -0.9% to 77.502 million head. The countries with the largest number of hogs as of January 1, 2021, were China with 49.8% of the world's hogs, the European Union with 24.61%, the U.S. with 11.4%, and Brazil with 5.5%.

Demand – The federally-inspected hog slaughter in the U.S. in 2020 rose by +1.2% yr/yr to 130.782 million head, a new record high.

Salient Statistics of Pigs and Hogs in the United States

	Pig Crop						Value of Hogs on Farms, Dec. 1					Hogs Slaughtered, Thousand Head				
	Spring[3]			Fall[4]								Commercial				
	Sows Farrowed	Pig Crop	Pigs Per Litter	Sows Farrowed	Pig Crop	Pigs Per Litter	$ Per	Total	Hog Marketings (1,000	Quantity Produced (Live Wt.)	Value of Production	Federally		U.S.		U.S.
Year	1,000 Head	1,000 Head		1,000 Head	1,000 Head		Head	Million $	Head)	(Mil. Lbs.)	(Million$)	Inspected	Other	Total	Farm	Total
2011	5,760	57,118	9.92	5,857	58,720	10.03	123.0	8,145	145,665	31,066	20,176	109,956	904	110,860	96	110,956
2012	5,759	57,749	10.03	5,810	58,906	10.14	116.0	7,683	151,353	31,961	20,224	112,265	898	113,163	83	113,247
2013	5,595	57,020	10.19	5,670	58,115	10.25	138.0	8,920	154,923	32,620	21,666	111,248	829	112,077	84	112,161
2014	5,573	53,821	9.66	5,985	61,035	10.20	144.0	9,732	149,097	32,126	24,184	106,123	753	106,876	82	106,958
2015	5,749	59,219	10.30	5,946	62,191	10.46	96.0	6,636	159,725	34,739	18,814	114,616	811	115,427	87	115,514
2016	5,896	61,236	10.39	6,103	64,703	10.60	92.0	6,578	165,539	35,899	17,363	117,388	831	118,219	84	118,303
2017	6,007	63,025	10.49	6,209	66,402	10.69	99.0	7,207	171,320	36,963	19,159	120,517	801	121,317	73	121,390
2018	6,041	64,053	10.60	6,377	68,515	10.74	98.0	7,299	180,251	38,498	18,770	123,696	738	124,435	76	124,511
2019[1]	6,231	67,617	10.85	6,471	71,829	11.10			187,648	41,570	19,827	129,211	702	129,913	76	129,989
2020[2]	6,217	68,389	11.00	6,424	71,030	11.06						130,782	765	131,547		131,547

[1] Preliminary. [2] Estimate. [3] December-May. [4] June-November. *Source: Economic Research Service, U.S. Department of Agriculture (ERS-USDA)*

World Hog Numbers in Specified Countries as of January 1 In Thousands of Head

Year	Australia	Belarus	Brazil	Canada	China	European Union	Japan	Korea, South	Mexico	Russia	Ukraine	United States	World Total
2012	2,285	3,989	38,336	12,770	470,748	149,809	9,735	8,171	9,276	17,263	7,373	66,259	796,014
2013	2,138	4,243	38,577	12,745	480,302	146,982	9,685	9,916	9,510	18,785	7,577	66,224	806,684
2014	2,098	3,267	38,844	12,835	478,931	146,172	9,537	9,912	9,775	19,010	7,922	64,775	803,078
2015	2,308	2,925	39,395	13,180	471,602	148,341	9,440	10,090	9,788	19,308	7,492	67,626	801,495
2016	2,272	3,205	39,422	13,630	458,029	148,716	9,313	10,187	10,043	21,239	7,240	69,019	792,315
2017	----	3,145	39,215	13,935	442,092	147,188	9,346	11,487	10,229	21,782	6,816	71,345	776,580
2018	----	3,156	38,829	14,170	441,589	150,257	9,280	11,273	10,410	22,945	6,236	73,145	781,290
2019	----	2,841	38,427	13,980	428,070	148,167	9,156	11,333	10,700	23,600	6,150	75,070	767,494
2020[1]	----	2,882	37,850	13,930	310,410	147,848	9,090	11,280	11,050	25,048	5,844	78,228	653,460
2021[2]	----	2,925	37,350	13,715	340,000	147,500	9,088	11,360	11,500	25,710	5,650	77,502	682,300

[1] Preliminary. [2] Forecast. *Source: Foreign Agricultural Service, U.S. Department of Agriculture (FAS-USDA)*

Hogs and Pigs on Farms in the United States on December 1 In Thousands of Head

Year	Georgia	Illinois	Indiana	Iowa	Kansas	Minne-sota	Missouri	Neb-raska	North Carolina	Ohio	South Dakota	Wis-consin	U.S. Total
2011	155	4,650	3,800	20,000	1,890	7,800	2,750	3,150	8,900	2,200	1,400	340	66,361
2012	155	4,600	3,800	20,600	1,900	7,650	2,750	3,000	9,000	2,050	1,200	320	66,374
2013	141	4,550	3,650	20,200	1,750	7,800	2,750	3,050	8,500	2,200	1,200	295	64,775
2014	155	4,700	3,700	21,300	1,840	8,100	2,850	3,200	8,800	2,230	1,270	310	67,776
2015	160	5,100	3,850	20,900	1,940	8,100	3,050	3,300	8,900	2,500	1,360	320	68,919
2016	65	5,100	4,100	22,200	1,910	8,500	3,100	3,400	9,300	2,700	1,450	335	71,545
2017	80	5,400	4,000	22,800	2,110	8,500	3,400	3,600	9,000	2,700	1,560	305	73,145
2018	72	5,400	4,250	23,600	2,050	9,100	3,650	3,550	9,200	2,550	1,750	320	75,070
2019	62	5,350	4,300	24,800	2,140	9,200	3,250	3,750	9,200	2,800	1,990	365	77,338
2020[1]													

[1] Preliminary. *Source: National Agricultural Statistics Service, U.S. Department of Agriculture (NASS-USDA)*

Cold Storage Holdings of Frozen Pork[2] in the United States, on First of Month In Thousands of Pounds

Year	Jan.	Feb.	Mar.	Apr.	May	June	July	Aug.	Sept.	Oct.	Nov.	Dec.
2011	475,829	538,754	574,236	574,398	549,279	548,322	495,064	454,337	442,903	491,910	488,721	495,117
2012	484,497	585,307	622,673	610,318	659,726	636,017	592,880	549,621	585,796	630,446	603,502	558,688
2013	551,510	606,425	633,399	647,784	700,977	658,947	565,063	543,668	548,975	567,827	565,020	546,238
2014	554,328	618,746	654,712	575,539	583,891	575,818	537,447	533,259	543,666	550,622	533,076	492,752
2015	503,792	595,673	686,063	672,431	701,083	655,301	634,525	633,214	653,760	655,930	603,454	560,915
2016	545,696	625,246	628,948	613,803	637,320	616,124	586,479	598,592	608,955	642,303	599,010	518,813
2017	475,387	524,215	567,855	545,463	590,324	588,216	559,010	554,854	575,698	618,563	598,374	502,324
2018	490,047	580,714	609,813	611,013	634,722	623,725	561,879	552,029	581,513	589,403	570,917	507,688
2019	505,287	562,733	615,674	608,379	621,456	628,956	619,454	611,692	606,784	598,750	611,916	574,840
2020[1]	580,464	625,588	648,975	616,734	611,222	467,927	460,173	460,635	465,465	465,619	447,115	419,753

[1] Preliminary. [2] Excludes lard. *Source: Economic Research Service, U.S. Department of Agriculture (ERS-USDA)*

Cold Storage Holdings of Frozen Pork Belly in the United States, on First of Month In Thousands of Pounds

Year	Jan.	Feb.	Mar.	Apr.	May	June	July	Aug.	Sept.	Oct.	Nov.	Dec.
2011	50,677	51,326	50,900	52,487	53,185	57,123	48,645	29,503	15,162	9,297	8,734	26,599
2012	41,469	53,685	61,577	66,031	74,927	65,648	49,034	27,962	14,210	15,668	18,720	23,837
2013	36,037	36,425	42,976	51,473	56,352	54,829	42,033	28,177	19,335	23,491	26,674	48,298
2014	80,367	87,171	87,675	79,721	83,579	85,888	83,936	64,644	45,562	34,311	29,006	35,894
2015	47,455	53,507	67,794	68,297	70,412	64,805	44,432	23,634	13,738	10,872	17,853	41,160
2016	53,392	60,698	61,433	65,028	72,592	77,683	62,921	50,733	32,053	25,084	20,386	18,526
2017	17,986	13,995	16,153	20,570	33,536	31,589	22,291	17,602	19,213	20,897	32,268	35,164
2018	39,620	43,810	49,012	59,202	64,563	61,234	53,279	38,556	34,805	30,354	26,690	36,859
2019	42,251	53,736	53,771	58,783	61,110	64,124	56,468	52,647	45,723	40,543	45,414	54,416
2020[1]	66,647	70,872	74,270	78,157	80,728	60,322	53,840	42,374	31,046	24,846	19,025	23,292

[1] Preliminary. *Source: National Agricultural Statistics Service, U.S. Department of Agriculture (NASS-USDA)*

Hog-Corn Price Ratio[2] in the United States In Bushels

Year	Jan.	Feb.	Mar.	Apr.	May	June	July	Aug.	Sept.	Oct.	Nov.	Dec.	Average
2011	11.3	10.9	11.4	10.7	10.9	10.9	11.3	11.0	10.5	12.0	11.0	10.8	11.1
2012	10.5	10.4	10.3	9.9	9.9	11.0	10.1	8.8	8.1	9.1	8.7	9.1	9.7
2013	9.2	9.2	8.3	8.9	9.8	10.7	11.2	11.9	13.1	14.8	14.6	13.9	11.3
2014	13.8	15.1	18.1	18.9	17.6	18.8	23.0	22.9	21.7	21.6	18.5	17.0	18.9
2015	15.0	13.3	13.2	13.1	16.2	16.7	15.4	16.0	14.8	15.1	12.8	11.7	14.4
2016	11.9	13.9	14.0	14.3	15.5	15.9	16.5	16.4	14.8	12.7	12.0	13.0	14.2
2017	14.1	15.8	15.2	14.1	15.5	18.1	19.3	18.8	15.0	14.5	15.9	15.0	15.9
2018	16.0	16.2	14.2	12.7	14.0	16.5	16.9	13.2	12.7	14.7	13.5	12.3	14.4
2019	12.5	12.1	12.9	16.8	17.2	14.9	13.6	14.9	12.6	12.8	13.0	12.7	13.8
2020[1]	12.6	12.0	13.0	12.9	15.9	13.1	12.4	13.8	14.6	15.6	13.7	12.4	13.5

[1] Preliminary. [2] Bushels of corn equal in value to 100 pounds of hog, live weight. *Source: Economic Research Service, U.S. Department of Agriculture (ERS-USDA)*

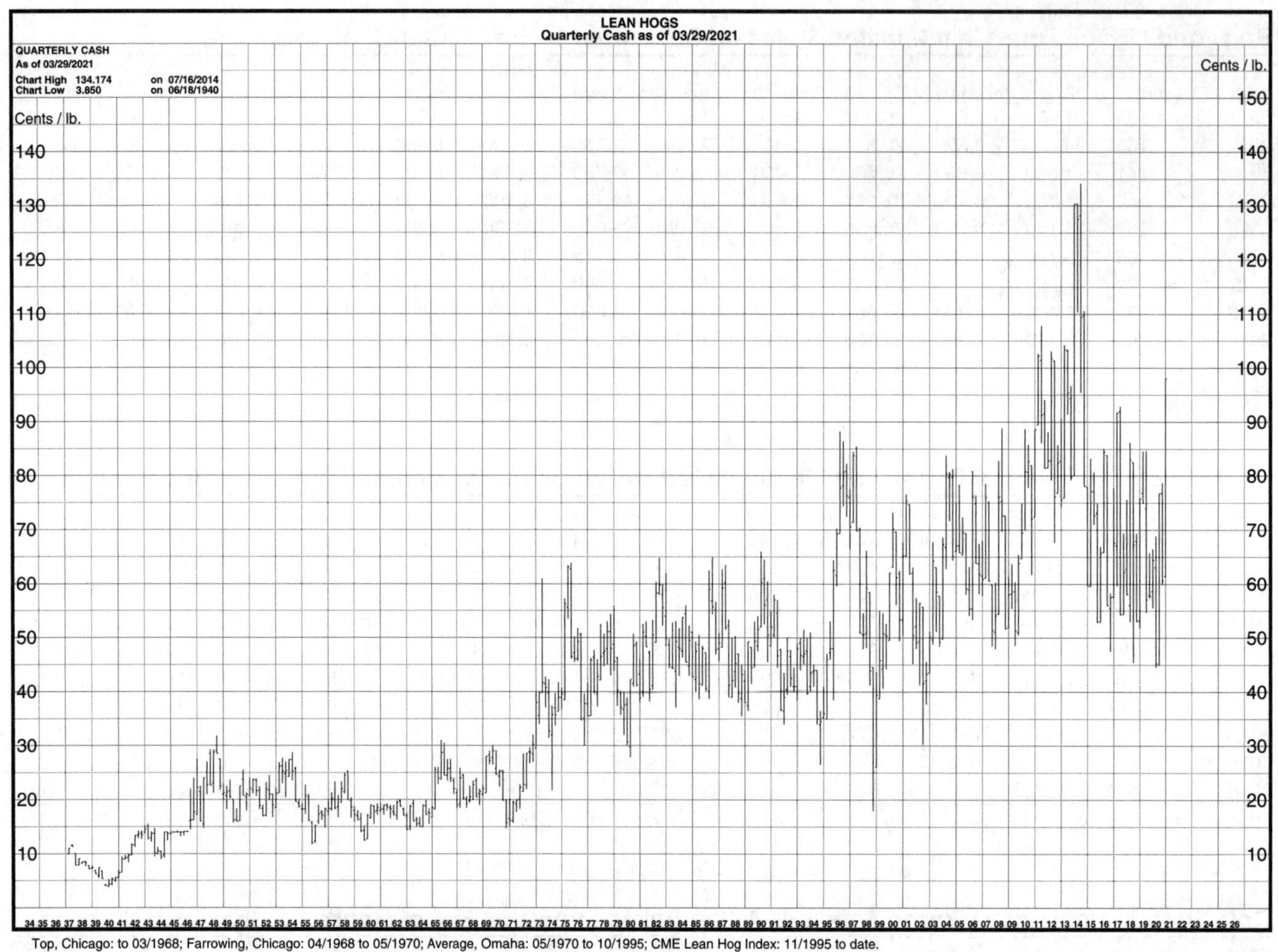

Top, Chicago: to 03/1968; Farrowing, Chicago: 04/1968 to 05/1970; Average, Omaha: 05/1970 to 10/1995; CME Lean Hog Index: 11/1995 to date.

Average Price of Hogs, National Base 51-52% lean In Dollars Per Hundred Pounds (Cwt.)

Year	Jan.	Feb.	Mar.	Apr.	May	June	July	Aug.	Sept.	Oct.	Nov.	Dec.	Average
2011	55.56	61.62	62.63	68.10	68.41	69.88	71.65	76.09	65.45	68.44	63.40	62.14	66.11
2012	62.18	63.94	61.86	58.99	58.51	67.87	69.93	63.51	50.85	59.06	57.67	59.16	61.13
2013	61.22	61.59	54.28	57.71	66.03	72.65	72.88	71.03	67.84	64.95	60.21	58.16	64.05
2014	58.36	63.88	83.82	89.09	81.76	85.35	95.17	80.39	74.36	75.24	63.76	61.24	76.03
2015	54.05	45.75	45.61	45.13	57.23	57.25	56.21	55.91	51.64	52.68	42.01	39.30	50.23
2016	40.34	46.61	46.95	47.96	54.75	58.42	56.28	48.12	43.36	37.07	34.45	39.45	46.15
2017	45.60	53.02	50.56	44.04	50.46	60.61	65.15	57.99	43.64	43.75	46.46	44.23	50.46
2018	50.40	51.49	45.46	39.88	46.86	56.99	55.38	37.88	38.43	47.54	42.19	38.58	45.92
2019	40.50	39.03	42.46	57.69	59.61	56.58	53.05	55.45	41.74	44.74	42.33	42.27	47.95
2020[1]	43.43	40.56	43.56	36.09	46.53	34.25	34.20	38.87	48.41	55.92	50.34	46.00	43.18

[1] Preliminary. *Source: Economic Research Service, U.S. Department of Agriculture (ERS-USDA)*

Average Price Received by Farmers for Hogs in the United States In Cents Per Pound

Year	Jan.	Feb.	Mar.	Apr.	May	June	July	Aug.	Sept.	Oct.	Nov.	Dec.	Average
2011	55.8	61.4	62.9	67.8	68.6	69.7	71.7	75.8	67.1	68.7	64.4	63.5	66.5
2012	63.5	65.5	65.2	62.8	62.8	70.2	72.1	66.9	55.7	62.0	61.1	62.4	64.2
2013	63.8	64.5	59.2	61.8	68.6	74.4	75.8	74.2	70.7	68.5	63.6	61.5	67.2
2014	61.2	65.5	81.9	88.8	82.8	84.8	93.3	83.2	75.7	77.0	66.7	64.3	77.1
2015	57.4	50.4	50.3	49.0	58.9	59.9	58.7	59.0	54.5	55.5	45.9	42.8	53.5
2016	43.6	49.6	50.0	51.0	57.2	60.6	59.4	52.6	47.8	41.7	39.0	43.1	49.6
2017	48.1	54.4	53.0	48.4	53.6	62.1	67.3	61.5	48.9	47.3	50.0	48.6	53.6
2018	52.5	54.6	50.0	45.3	51.5	59.1	58.6	44.3	43.2	50.3	46.2	43.4	49.9
2019	44.6	43.4	46.5	59.4	62.3	59.5	56.6	58.5	47.7	49.1	48.0	47.3	51.9
2020[1]	47.8	45.5	47.7	42.3	51.0	41.3	39.9	42.9	49.7	56.3	51.9	49.1	47.1

[1] Preliminary. *Source: Economic Research Service, U.S. Department of Agriculture (ERS-USDA)*

Quarterly Hogs and Pigs Report in the United States, 10 States In Thousands of Head

Year[2]	Inventory[3]	Breeding[3]	Market[3]	Farrowings	Pig Crop	Year[2]	Inventory[3]	Breeding[3]	Market[3]	Farrowings	Pig Crop
2011	64,625	5,778	59,147	11,616	115,838	2016	68,919	6,002	62,917	11,998	125,939
I	64,625	5,778	59,147	2,843	27,866	I	68,919	6,002	62,917	2,927	30,139
II	63,684	5,788	57,896	2,917	29,252	II	68,124	5,980	62,144	2,968	31,097
III	65,320	5,803	59,517	2,927	29,355	III	69,281	5,979	63,302	3,057	32,331
IV	67,234	5,806	61,428	2,929	29,365	IV	71,786	6,016	65,770	3,046	32,372
2012	66,361	5,803	60,558	11,567	116,655	2017	71,545	6,110	65,435	12,217	129,429
I	66,361	5,803	60,558	2,813	28,037	I	71,545	6,110	65,435	2,990	31,187
II	64,787	5,820	58,967	2,945	29,712	II	70,916	6,098	64,818	3,018	31,839
III	66,609	5,862	60,747	2,921	29,587	III	71,210	6,109	65,101	3,106	33,075
IV	68,172	5,788	62,384	2,888	29,319	IV	73,309	6,117	67,192	3,103	33,328
2013	66,374	5,819	60,555	11,264	115,135	2018	73,145	6,179	66,966	12,418	132,568
I	66,374	5,819	60,555	2,788	28,099	I	73,145	6,179	66,966	2,977	31,497
II	65,071	5,834	59,237	2,806	28,921	II	72,055	6,210	65,845	3,064	32,556
III	65,188	5,884	59,304	2,890	29,862	III	72,231	6,320	65,911	3,172	34,019
IV	66,906	5,816	61,090	2,780	28,253	IV	74,556	6,330	68,226	3,205	34,496
2014	64,775	5,757	59,018	11,558	114,856	2019	75,070	6,326	68,745	12,701	139,448
I	64,775	5,757	59,018	2,763	26,326	I	75,070	6,326	68,745	3,098	33,164
II	61,494	5,851	55,643	2,810	27,495	II	74,661	6,349	68,313	3,132	34,455
III	61,568	5,855	55,713	2,991	30,402	III	75,725	6,410	69,316	3,274	36,370
IV	65,979	5,920	60,059	2,994	30,633	IV	78,583	6,431	72,153	3,197	35,459
2015	67,776	5,939	61,838	11,695	121,411	2020[1]	78,228	6,471	72,577	12,641	139,418
I	67,776	5,939	61,838	2,895	29,627	I	78,228	6,471	72,577	3,068	33,745
II	67,399	5,982	61,418	2,854	29,593	II	76,179	6,375	71,254	3,149	34,644
III	67,165	5,926	61,240	3,017	31,343	III	77,364	6,326	73,308	3,260	36,056
IV	69,185	5,986	63,200	2,929	30,848	IV	78,434	6,333	72,101	3,164	34,973

[1] Preliminary. [2] Quarters are Dec. preceding year-Feb.(I), Mar.-May(II), June-Aug.(III) and Sept.-Nov.(IV).
[3] Beginning of period. *Source: National Agricultural Statistics Service, U.S. Department of Agriculture (NASS-USDA)*

Federally Inspected Hog Slaughter in the United States In Thousands of Head

Year	Jan.	Feb.	Mar.	Apr.	May	June	July	Aug.	Sept.	Oct.	Nov.	Dec.	Total
2011	9,036	8,440	9,795	8,559	8,470	8,866	8,089	9,440	9,603	9,822	9,968	9,868	109,956
2012	9,467	8,975	9,454	8,757	9,212	8,481	8,493	9,858	9,376	10,770	10,030	9,393	112,265
2013	9,885	8,526	9,252	9,292	9,147	8,132	9,003	9,474	8,952	10,341	9,579	9,665	111,248
2014	9,726	8,609	8,614	8,794	8,561	8,040	8,394	8,199	8,762	9,880	8,754	9,788	106,123
2015	9,698	9,018	9,818	9,612	8,686	9,364	9,332	9,272	9,652	10,173	9,700	10,292	114,616
2016	9,682	9,364	10,015	9,303	9,114	9,505	8,696	10,308	10,096	10,369	10,539	10,398	117,388
2017	10,059	9,310	10,611	9,282	9,886	9,809	8,953	10,583	10,213	10,922	10,487	10,400	120,517
2018	10,653	9,578	10,661	9,939	10,163	9,553	9,532	11,081	9,583	11,571	10,982	10,403	123,696
2019	10,984	10,051	10,667	10,526	10,301	9,939	10,516	10,798	10,581	12,233	11,279	11,336	129,211
2020[1]	11,760	10,670	11,883	9,353	8,524	11,104	11,155	11,047	10,957	11,949	10,961	11,419	130,782

[1] Preliminary. *Source: National Agricultural Statistics Service, U.S. Department of Agriculture (NASS-USDA)*

Average Live Weight of all Hogs Slaughtered Under Federal Inspection In Pounds Per Head

Year	Jan.	Feb.	Mar.	Apr.	May	June	July	Aug.	Sept.	Oct.	Nov.	Dec.	Average
2011	278	278	278	277	276	273	268	266	271	276	279	278	275
2012	279	278	279	279	277	274	269	269	271	274	276	276	275
2013	277	277	277	277	276	274	271	271	273	279	283	283	277
2014	284	283	285	287	287	285	284	283	283	286	287	287	285
2015	287	285	285	285	284	282	280	278	280	284	286	285	283
2016	286	284	284	285	283	281	278	276	280	282	283	283	282
2017	285	284	284	285	282	279	277	278	282	283	286	286	283
2018	286	286	287	287	285	280	277	278	280	283	286	286	283
2019	288	287	287	287	287	285	280	279	282	285	288	288	285
2020[1]	290	288	288	290	294	288	283	283	285	291	294	294	289

[1] Preliminary. *Source: National Agricultural Statistics Service, U.S. Department of Agriculture (NASS-USDA)*

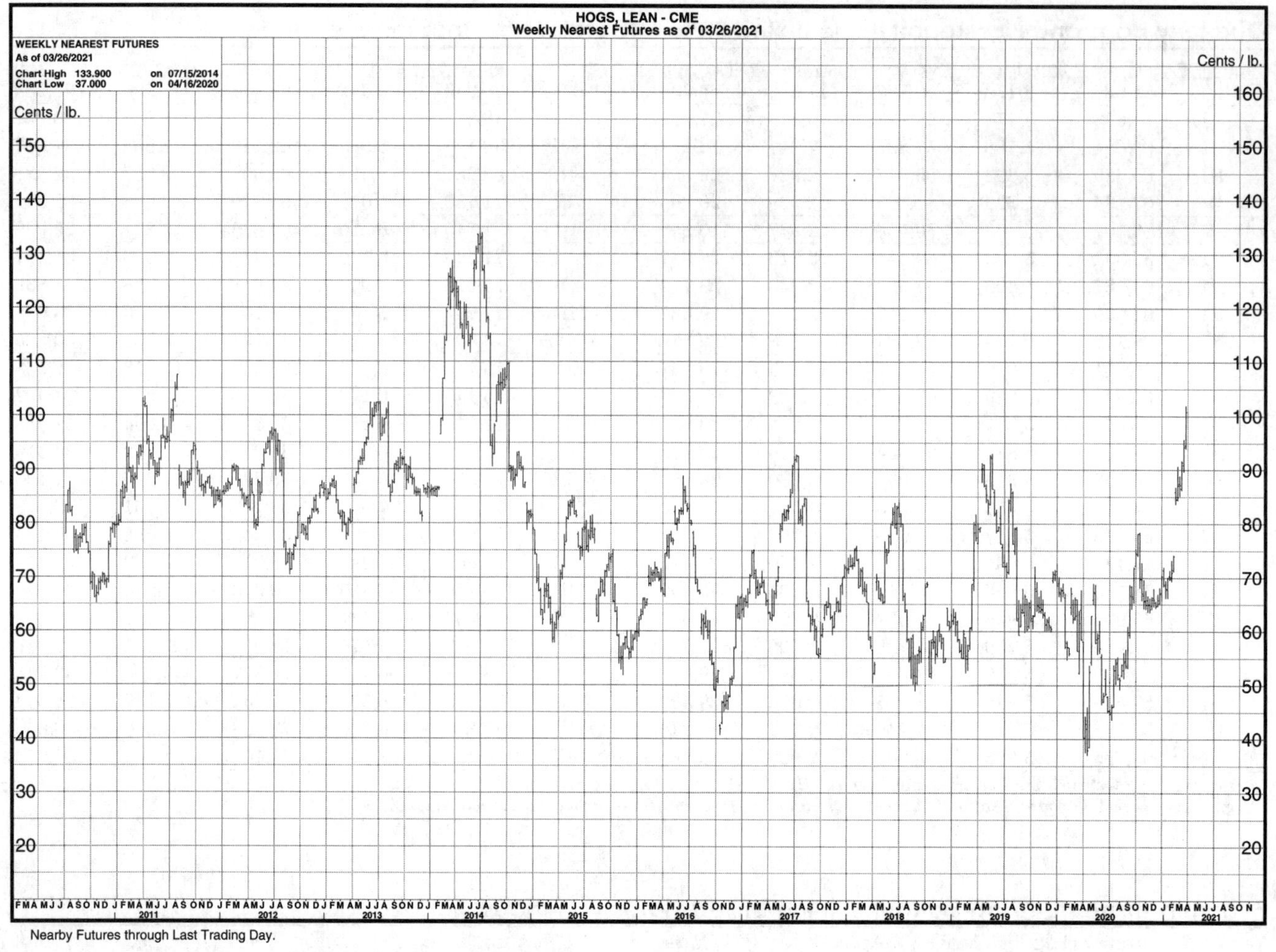

Nearby Futures through Last Trading Day.

Volume of Trading of Lean Hog Futures in Chicago In Contracts

Year	Jan.	Feb.	Mar.	Apr.	May	June	July	Aug.	Sept.	Oct.	Nov.	Dec.	Total (1,000)
2011	879,859	660,332	925,083	660,983	881,184	991,400	900,953	770,608	1,047,769	785,722	857,709	608,359	9,970.0
2012	908,368	715,081	1,093,713	882,705	1,312,891	1,189,274	1,082,496	819,332	979,379	869,169	949,221	660,263	11,461.9
2013	999,025	807,974	1,017,485	832,949	1,100,627	1,151,018	1,076,200	778,067	1,155,621	861,514	833,759	662,790	11,277.0
2014	940,059	880,082	1,402,273	760,629	892,977	937,458	1,046,618	818,841	1,000,387	674,141	707,984	595,495	10,656.9
2015	883,049	743,293	961,823	716,421	830,092	962,100	971,169	640,789	745,310	717,480	836,679	567,677	9,575.9
2016	665,222	645,429	797,006	589,363	726,478	937,796	826,532	645,478	849,779	762,690	915,391	833,836	9,195.0
2017	847,298	742,428	963,173	690,533	1,012,116	1,120,066	981,241	976,007	1,124,085	955,604	1,098,220	731,250	11,242.0
2018	992,415	936,449	1,149,911	962,589	1,236,082	1,312,538	1,250,892	1,308,397	1,241,177	1,140,731	1,267,228	753,302	13,551.7
2019	1,112,391	982,779	1,716,059	1,353,304	1,435,164	1,417,134	1,570,486	1,216,746	1,456,363	1,240,075	1,234,991	886,352	15,621.8
2020	1,351,172	977,394	1,381,558	1,197,240	995,647	1,046,866	1,049,972	750,534	1,236,230	872,973	854,016	682,807	12,396.4

Contract size = 40,000 lbs. *Source: Chicago Mercantile Exchange (CME)*

Average Open Interest of Lean Hog Futures in Chicago In Contracts

Year	Jan.	Feb.	Mar.	Apr.	May	June	July	Aug.	Sept.	Oct.	Nov.	Dec.
2011	218,818	243,878	226,344	233,168	222,193	221,633	242,921	253,224	247,476	273,568	257,632	246,758
2012	243,120	256,724	262,970	259,367	268,655	258,585	231,982	224,131	237,138	219,733	230,592	242,093
2013	244,228	226,691	235,834	229,097	247,125	279,932	297,930	306,652	326,192	302,314	282,782	263,509
2014	266,366	282,321	288,484	265,981	256,474	248,869	248,878	234,967	237,877	236,417	230,578	216,735
2015	208,643	192,716	208,128	216,998	219,669	221,626	210,767	196,682	196,033	198,965	204,049	173,053
2016	168,096	191,458	218,393	224,392	233,337	255,818	234,949	212,182	215,947	227,447	225,542	199,554
2017	210,582	227,286	214,122	207,945	223,068	251,117	272,856	258,984	256,269	253,357	260,573	239,469
2018	246,345	232,492	230,504	241,846	244,654	231,674	233,594	230,352	222,734	225,483	227,359	207,286
2019	211,589	236,596	270,420	296,832	311,184	303,772	284,851	265,214	264,332	277,164	293,006	287,240
2020	294,780	291,757	257,704	222,412	208,909	218,716	225,379	219,996	223,259	223,208	206,542	189,728

Contract size = 40,000 lbs. *Source: Chicago Mercantile Exchange (CME)*

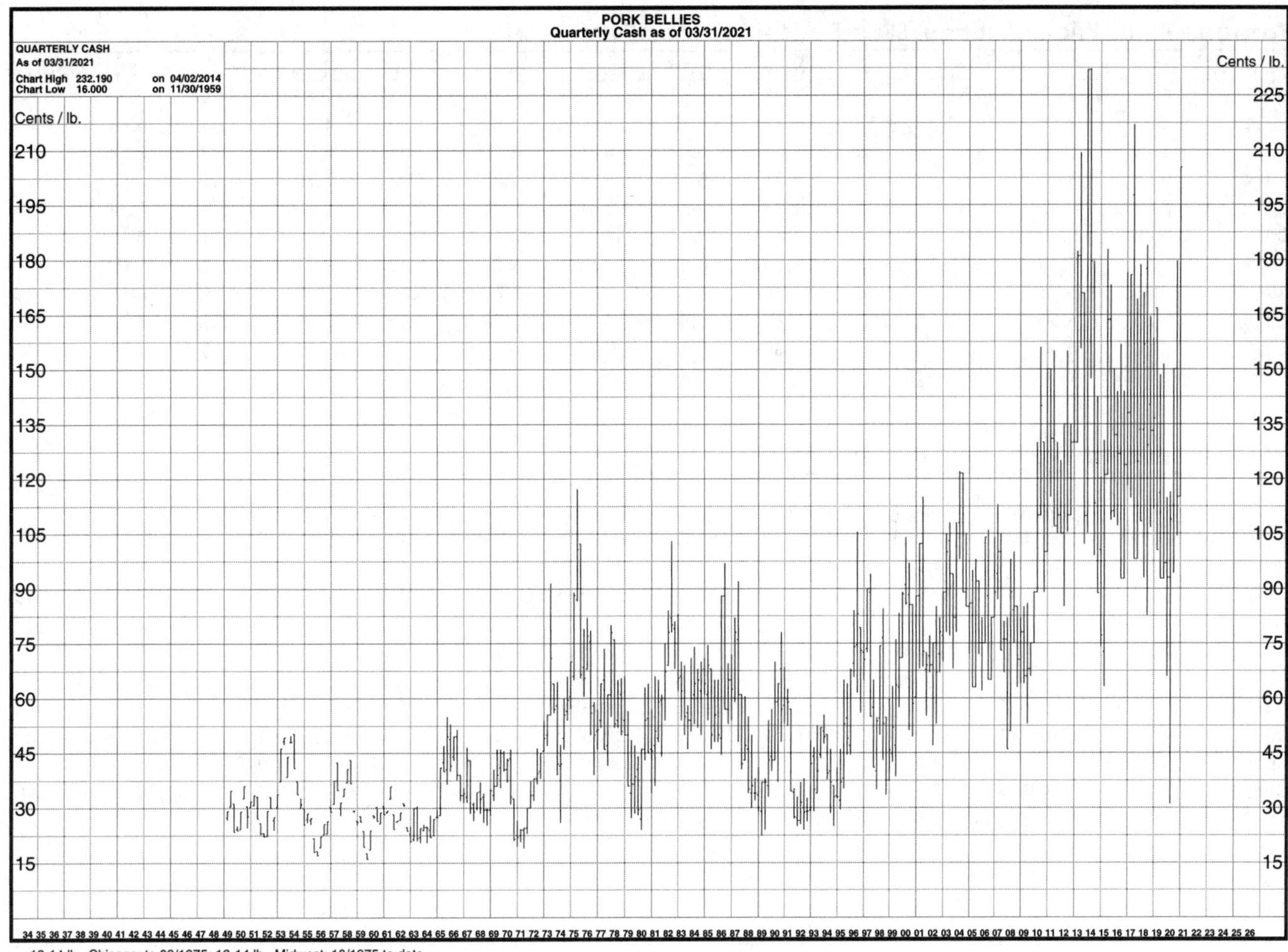

12-14 lb., Chicago: to 09/1975; 12-14 lb., Midwest: 10/1975 to date.

Average Price of Pork Bellies (12-14 lbs.), Central, U.S. In Cents Per Pound

Year	Jan.	Feb.	Mar.	Apr.	May	June	July	Aug.	Sept.	Oct.	Nov.	Dec.	Average
2011	NA	NA	NA	144.17	NA	NA	121.00	135.09	NA	111.00	91.33	NA	120.52
2012	96.50	NA	90.00	80.00	NA	NA	NA	NA	NA	NA	NA	NA	88.83
2013	NA	NA	NA	151.44	161.60	175.55	163.12	177.24	149.62	134.99	128.41	127.35	152.15
2014	124.07	137.58	176.77	191.73	156.63	173.03	174.29	139.46	120.57	127.81	111.33	105.57	144.90
2015	122.30	102.97	81.14	75.33	82.51	108.15	NA	184.67	166.82	165.54	127.35	114.96	121.07
2016	128.18	NA	NA	134.91	119.13	130.09	146.67	115.14	96.21	127.29	120.69	121.10	123.94
2017	136.39	NA	158.66	136.79	139.18	176.76	216.28	170.18	116.74	107.75	135.04	142.64	148.76
2018	137.69	157.64	133.63	111.96	110.14	157.22	NA	106.71	109.96	NA	181.14	131.26	133.73
2019	146.10	121.61	142.66	160.07	138.55	123.36	122.41	NA	113.37	140.82	131.25	110.06	131.84
2020[1]	108.16	88.40	91.46	51.13	101.79	104.92	107.72	113.28	NA	NA	NA	NA	95.86

[1] Preliminary. *Source: Economic Research Service, U.S. Department of Agriculture (ERS-USDA)*

Average Price of Pork Loins (12-14 lbs.)[2], Central, U.S. In Cents Per Pound

Year	Jan.	Feb.	Mar.	Apr.	May	June	July	Aug.	Sept.	Oct.	Nov.	Dec.	Average
2011	119.02	119.98	123.08	131.20	138.84	136.21	139.57	149.33	131.78	131.07	116.40	117.61	129.51
2012	116.21	118.22	123.09	119.81	128.27	149.14	127.43	119.00	108.86	117.45	105.20	105.56	119.85
2013	107.12	111.73	108.86	106.77	120.28	138.64	129.84	128.96	116.92	115.78	107.25	106.24	116.53
2014	115.27	128.19	165.28	147.55	135.39	153.75	167.79	150.01	153.69	152.92	117.50	115.82	141.93
2015	108.25	99.88	100.25	101.55	124.08	112.35	111.13	107.61	102.46	103.50	88.44	85.76	103.77
2016	100.14	93.52	90.52	89.61	111.77	112.56	104.71	98.27	110.10	89.52	76.73	85.90	96.95
2017	91.73	90.66	99.36	88.58	106.12	118.21	118.69	100.58	94.97	89.85	85.62	82.96	97.28
2018	83.63	89.53	88.98	84.45	96.25	101.34	98.72	98.35	107.17	92.36	98.72	75.40	92.91
2019	79.70	75.19	82.42	88.03	101.05	103.19	98.04	92.14	85.29	88.61	86.24	86.68	88.88
2020[1]	85.62	85.04	112.98	129.14	192.07	88.83	74.05	82.25	81.48	100.89	80.43	77.82	99.22

[1] Preliminary. *Source: Economic Research Service, U.S. Department of Agriculture (ERS-USDA)*

Average Retail Price of Bacon, Sliced In U.S. Dollars Per Pound

Year	Jan.	Feb.	Mar.	Apr.	May	June	July	Aug.	Sept.	Oct.	Nov.	Dec.	Average
2011	4.25	4.37	4.54	4.66	4.77	4.84	4.76	4.77	4.82	4.59	4.64	4.55	4.63
2012	4.57	4.66	4.60	4.53	4.39	4.33	4.37	4.61	4.69	4.66	4.64	4.64	4.56
2013	4.72	4.83	4.91	4.89	5.09	5.33	5.49	5.62	5.68	5.71	5.62	5.54	5.29
2014	5.56	5.46	5.55	5.69	6.05	6.11	6.01	6.07	5.95	5.76	5.57	5.53	5.78
2015	5.59	5.47	5.37	5.21	4.94	5.06	5.18	5.41	5.73	5.90	5.85	5.73	5.45
2016	5.66	5.39	5.49	5.61	5.55	5.37	5.45	5.45	5.48	5.38	5.11	5.10	5.42
2017	5.18	5.33	5.75	5.78	5.70	5.67	5.82	6.24	6.37	6.07	5.71	5.63	5.77
2018	5.65	5.53	5.53	5.42	5.45	5.25	5.42	5.58	5.50	5.37	5.39	5.50	5.47
2019	5.52	5.50	5.61	5.55	5.81	5.88	5.70	5.58	5.58	5.65	5.51	5.47	5.61
2020[1]	5.51	5.50	5.26	5.35	5.35	5.77	5.78	5.56	5.62	5.72	5.75	5.83	5.58

[1] Preliminary. *Source: Economic Research Service, U.S. Department of Agriculture (ERS-USDA)*

World Production of Honey In Metric Tons

Year	Argentina	Australia	Brazil	Canada	China	Germany	Japan	Mexico	Russia	United States	World Total
2010	59,000	14,418	38,073	81,672	409,149	23,178	2,639	55,684	51,535	80,042	1,588,061
2011	72,000	10,000	41,793	79,824	446,089	25,831	2,684	57,783	60,010	67,294	1,657,628
2012	76,000	12,006	33,932	90,759	462,203	17,869	2,763	58,602	64,898	64,544	1,697,853
2013	67,500	13,864	35,365	76,468	461,431	18,953	2,766	56,907	68,446	67,812	1,736,479
2014	76,000	13,094	38,481	85,644	474,786	20,195	2,839	60,624	74,868	80,862	1,814,734
2015	52,600	12,281	37,859	92,011	484,726	23,398	2,865	61,881	67,736	71,008	1,877,235
2016	68,123	11,843	39,677	94,578	562,875	21,600	2,754	55,358	69,764	73,429	1,926,018
2017	76,379	11,460	41,696	96,012	548,813	20,364	2,827	51,066	65,167	67,596	1,926,289
2018	79,468	11,078	42,378	94,996	457,203	20,333	2,846	64,253	65,006	69,857	1,882,001
2019[1]	78,927	10,695	45,981	80,345	447,007		2,753	61,986	63,526	71,179	1,852,598

[1] Preliminary. *Source: Food and Agricultural Organization of the United Nations (FAO)*

United States Imports of Honey In Metric Tons

Year	Argentina	Brazil	Canada	India	Mexico	New Zealand	Taiwan	Thailand	Turkey	Ukraine	Uruguay	Vietnam	World Total
2010	17,414	10,036	11,053	18,462	3,325	1,048	1,755	1,699	37	440	852	20,738	113,930
2011	33,502	14,981	7,148	26,912	2,846	965	903	1,637	183	453	7,083	27,826	130,764
2012	42,482	11,303	15,971	21,454	6,179	966	1,324	258	1,073	1,302	10,877	20,700	141,016
2013	44,221	11,677	9,385	25,867	5,648	1,234	1,827	846	1,897	3,308	8,710	33,586	153,102
2014	36,888	19,249	5,612	20,290	7,254	1,625	2,523	3,458	2,581	8,876	5,362	47,107	165,777
2015	27,081	15,440	8,234	36,123	5,364	1,992	4,442	10,753	5,195	11,411	7,243	36,973	175,243
2016	34,708	19,062	13,510	29,364	4,557	1,840	1,580	4,238	1,852	11,086	1,767	38,494	166,442
2017	35,378	24,031	15,762	45,143	4,783	4,200	1,649	4,453	2,393	19,362	4,025	36,288	202,449
2018	36,219	23,604	15,222	44,201	3,315	1,673	1,680	4,639	2,248	8,324	1,326	39,156	196,600
2019[1]	36,466	23,858	7,870	49,691	3,321	1,661	1,651	1,583	826	8,713	1,362	36,980	188,602

[1] Preliminary. *Source: Foreign Agricultural Service, U.S. Department of Agriculture (FAS-USDA)*

Production of Honey in the United States In Thousands of Pounds

Year	California	Florida	Georgia	Idaho	Louisiana	Michigan	Minnesota	Montana	North Dakota	South Dakota	Texas	Wisconsin	U.S. Total
2011	17,760	10,980	2,795	3,132	2,772	4,736	6,360	13,340	32,660	16,500	4,524	3,591	148,357
2012	11,550	12,352	3,009	2,944	3,526	4,161	8,375	7,540	33,120	16,380	4,784	4,140	142,296
2013	10,890	13,420	3,350	2,656	4,900	4,675	7,540	14,946	33,120	14,840	6,254	3,540	149,499
2014	12,480	14,700	4,526	3,400	4,032	5,733	7,920	14,256	42,140	24,360	9,048	2,862	178,270
2015	8,250	11,880	2,760	2,848	4,356	5,220	8,296	12,118	36,260	19,140	8,316	3,484	156,544
2016	11,160	10,750	3,744	3,298	4,300	5,340	7,316	12,243	37,830	19,880	9,310	3,348	161,882
2017	13,735	8,815	3,168	4,180	3,483	3,915	7,812	10,440	33,670	14,535	7,920	2,968	148,980
2018	13,735	10,535	3,332	2,976	3,735	4,048	7,259	14,720	38,160	11,985	7,392	2,295	154,008
2019	16,080	9,225	3,366	2,944	3,888	4,700	6,962	14,878	33,800	19,440	7,560	2,162	156,922
2020[1]	13,760	8,832	3,434	3,745	2,277	4,465	5,940	8,910	38,610	14,945	8,949	2,250	147,594

[1] Preliminary. *Source: National Agricultural Statistics Service, U.S. Department of Agriculture (NASS-USDA)*

Honey

Honey is the thick, supersaturated sugar solution produced by bees to feed their larvae. It is composed of fructose, glucose, and water in varying proportions and also contains several enzymes and oils. The color of honey varies due to the source of nectar and the age of the honey. Light-colored honeys are usually of higher quality than darker honeys. The average honeybee colony can produce more than 700 pounds of honey per year, but only 10 percent is usually harvested by the beekeeper. The rest of the honey is consumed by the colony during the year. American per capita honey consumption is 1 pound per person per year. Honey is said to be humanity's oldest sweet and beeswax the first plastic.

Honey is used in many ways, including direct human consumption, baking, and medicine. Honey has several healing properties. Its high sugar content nourishes injured tissues, thus enhancing faster healing time. Honey's phytochemicals create a form of hydrogen peroxide that cleans out the wound, and the thick consistency protects the wound from contact with air. Honey has also proven superior to antibiotic ointments for reducing rates of infection in people with burns.

Prices – U.S. average domestic honey prices in 2019 fell by -10.9% to 197.0 cents per pound, farther down from the 2018 record high of 221.0 cents per pound. The value of U.S. honey production in 2019 fell by -9.2% to $309.136 million, down from the 2018 record high of $340.358 million.

Supply – World production of honey in 2019 fell -1.6% to 1.853 million metric tons, down from the 2017 record high of 1. 926.The major producers of honey in 2019 were China with 24.1% of the world's total, Argentina and Canada with 4.3%, the U.S. with 3.8%, and Russia with 3.4%.

U.S. production of honey in 2019 rose +1.9% to 156.922 million pounds, remaining well below the 20-year high of 220.339 million pounds posted in 2000. Stocks rose by +40.0% to 41.022 million pounds in 2018, which is still far below 2000's 20-year high of 85.328 million pounds. Yield per colony in 2019 rose by +2.4% to 55.8 pounds per colony. The number of colonies in 2019 fell by -0.6.5% to 2.803 million.

Trade – U.S. imports of honey in 2018 rose by +2.4% to 442.390 million pounds, a new record high U.S. exports of honey in 2018 fell -1.9% to 9.716 million pounds.

Salient Statistics of Honey in the United States In Millions of Pounds

Year	Number of Colonies (1,000)	Yield Per Colony (Pounds)	Stocks Jan. 1	Total U.S. Production	Imports for Consumption	Domestic Disappearance	Exports	Total Supply	Domestic Avg. Price All Honey (cents/lb.)	Value of Production ($1,000)	U.S. Production: Beeswax	Domestic Avg. Price: Beeswax (cents/lb.)
2011	2,491	59.6	36.8	148.4	288.3	----	11.9	473.4	176.5	261.9	----	----
2012	2,539	56.0	31.8	142.3	310.9	----	12.3	485.0	199.2	283.5	----	----
2013	2,640	56.6	38.2	149.5	337.5	----	12.0	525.2	214.1	320.1	----	----
2014	2,740	65.1	41.2	178.3	365.5	----	10.9	584.9	217.3	387.4	----	----
2015	2,660	58.9	42.2	156.5	386.3	----	11.3	585.1	208.3	326.1	----	----
2016	2,775	58.3	41.3	161.9	367.0	----	11.1	570.2	211.9	343.0	----	----
2017	2,683	55.5	30.7	149.0	432.1	----	9.9	611.7	219.9	334.2	----	----
2018	2,828	54.5	29.3	154.0	442.4	----	9.7	625.7	221.0	340.4	----	----
2019	2,812	55.8	40.9	156.9		----			199.0	312.3	----	----
2020[1]	2,702	54.5	39.7	147.6		----			203.0	299.6	----	----

[1] Preliminary. *Source: Economic Research Service, U.S. Department of Agriculture (ERS-USDA)*

Average Price of Honey, by Color Class in the United States In Cents Per Pound

	Co-op and Private					Retail					All				
Year	Water White, Extra White, White	Extra Light Amber	Light Amber, Amber, Dark Amber	All Other Honey, Area Specialties	All Honey	Water White, Extra White, White	Extra Light Amber	Light Amber, Amber, Dark Amber	All Other Honey, Area Specialties	All Honey	Water White, Extra White, White	Extra Light Amber	Light Amber, Amber, Dark Amber	All Other Honey, Area Specialties	All Honey
2011	170.1	164.4	165.7	182.6	167.7	274.1	307.1	315.4	461.0	314.7	172.9	171.1	183.4	225.2	176.5
2012	192.3	195.4	183.0	213.4	191.3	323.9	303.5	352.4	519.5	348.0	194.2	200.2	205.8	281.6	199.2
2013	210.9	204.0	197.3	222.4	205.8	340.9	330.6	405.1	492.5	382.4	212.9	209.0	219.2	248.9	214.1
2014	204.6	209.6	208.8	255.4	207.1	328.5	392.2	417.1	535.2	405.4	206.2	218.3	234.2	318.2	217.3
2015	188.6	202.5	200.4	284.9	195.0	305.4	411.8	412.1	656.6	409.9	190.6	213.2	234.7	351.5	208.3
2016	189.1	190.8	194.8	245.7	192.0	463.8	433.7	452.9	781.6	474.5	195.5	200.8	233.0	385.2	211.9
2017	204.7	206.0	202.8	287.2	205.1	314.3	487.3	497.0	627.9	445.0	206.3	217.3	241.1	383.4	219.9
2018	198.0	201.0	210.0	264.0	203.0	363.0	344.0	489.0	717.0	738.0	201.0	212.0	251.0	362.0	221.0
2019	163.0	170.0	195.0	316.0	173.0	470.0	363.0	530.0	662.0	482.0	170.0	190.0	257.0	399.0	199.0
2020[1]	169.0	176.0	187.0	236.0	178.0	494.0	464.0	526.0	762.0	522.0	177.0	188.0	235.0	287.0	203.0

[1] Preliminary. *Source: National Agricultural Statistics Service, U.S. Department of Agriculture (NASS-USDA)*

Interest Rates - U.S.

U.S. interest rates can be characterized in two main ways, by credit quality and by maturity. Credit quality refers to the level of risk associated with a particular borrower. U.S. Treasury securities, for example, carry the lowest risk. Maturity refers to the time at which the security matures and must be repaid. Treasury securities carry a full spectrum of maturities, from short-term cash management bills, to T-bills (4-weeks, 3-months, 6-months), T-notes (2-year, 3-year, 5-year, 7-year, and 10-year), and 30-year T-bonds. The most active futures markets are the 10-year T-note futures, 30-year T-bond futures, and Eurodollar futures, all of which are traded at the CME Group.

Prices – CME 10-year T-note futures prices (Barchart.com electronic symbol ZN) came into 2020 on a strong note after a sharp rally in 2019. T-note prices rallied in 2019 as the U.S. economy weakened due to trade tensions and the fading stimulative effects from the massive 2018 tax cut. T-notes in 2019 were also boosted by the Federal Reserve's three 25 basis point (bp) interest rate cuts made in the latter half of 2019, which left the federal funds rate target range at 1.50%/1.75% by the end of 2019.

T-note prices then soared in February 2020 when it became clear that a global Covid pandemic would cause massive economic disruptions. T-note prices also soared on flight-to-quality buying as the markets worried that there could be a systemic breakdown in the global financial system.

U.S. GDP plunged by -10% in the first half of 2020 because of the business shutdowns caused by the effort to slow the pandemic. The U.S. unemployment rate quickly soared to a record high of 14.7% as 22 million payroll jobs were lost during the two months of March and April.

However, the Fed quickly swung into action in March 2020 with a 1.50 percentage point cut in its funds rate target to 0.00%/0.25%. The Fed also announced a new quantitative easing (QE) program that by June was running at $120 billion per month. The Fed also activated a series of emergency lending programs that allowed the Fed to provide loans and funding directly to troubled financial sectors, private companies, and state and local governments.

The Fed's massive liquidity injections, along with targeted pandemic aid and fiscal stimulus from U.S. federal government, proved successful in keeping the economy and the financial system afloat long enough to curb the pandemic and allow some businesses to reopen. The U.S. economy during the summer and autumn 2020 was able to slowly recover. T-note prices traded mostly sideways from April 2020 through autumn 2020.

T-note prices then started to fall in late 2020 as vaccine trials were successful and it became clear that vaccines would eventually end the pandemic. T-note prices fell sharply in the first quarter of 2021 as the end of the pandemic came into sight and hopes grew for a full economic recovery. The horrendous level of U.S. Covid infections peaked in mid-January 2021 and then fell sharply through February due to (1) antibody immunity for those in the population that had recovered from a Covid infection, (2) the start of vaccinations in December, and (3) a likely seasonal improvement.

T-note prices also fell in early 2021 due to the massive pandemic aid packages that were signed into law in late December 2020 ($900 billion) and early-March 2021 ($1.9 trillion). The combination of monetary and fiscal stimulus caused concerns that the U.S. economy might run very hot by mid-2021, thus causing higher inflation and downward pressure on T-note prices.

U.S. Producer Price Index[2] for All Commodities 1982 = 100

Year	Jan.	Feb.	Mar.	Apr.	May	June	July	Aug.	Sept.	Oct.	Nov.	Dec.	Average
2011	192.7	195.8	199.2	203.1	204.1	203.9	204.6	203.2	203.7	201.1	201.4	199.8	201.1
2012	200.7	201.6	204.2	203.7	201.9	199.8	200.1	202.7	204.4	203.5	201.8	201.5	202.2
2013	202.5	204.3	204.0	203.5	204.1	204.3	204.4	204.2	203.9	202.5	201.2	202.0	203.4
2014	203.8	205.7	207.0	208.3	208.0	208.3	208.0	207.0	206.4	203.4	200.9	197.0	205.3
2015	192.0	191.1	191.5	190.9	193.4	194.8	193.9	191.9	189.1	187.5	185.7	183.5	190.4
2016	182.6	181.3	182.1	183.2	185.3	187.6	187.7	186.6	186.9	186.7	186.3	188.2	185.4
2017	190.7	191.6	191.5	193.0	192.8	193.6	193.5	193.8	194.8	194.9	195.9	196.3	193.5
2018	197.9	199.3	199.3	200.3	203.2	204.2	204.3	203.4	203.6	204.6	202.3	201.0	202.0
2019	199.1	199.2	200.8	202.1	201.7	200.3	200.7	199.2	198.4	198.6	199.0	199.0	199.8
2020[1]	199.3	196.7	193.1	185.5	188.6	191.2	193.0	194.3	195.5	196.5	198.2	200.6	194.4

[1] Preliminary. [2] Not seasonally adjusted. *Source: Bureau of Labor Statistics, U.S. Department of Commerce (BLS)*

U.S. Consumer Price Index[2] for All Urban Consumers 1982-84 = 100

Year	Jan.	Feb.	Mar.	Apr.	May	June	July	Aug.	Sept.	Oct.	Nov.	Dec.	Average
2011	220.2	221.3	223.5	224.9	226.0	225.7	225.9	226.5	226.9	226.4	226.2	225.7	224.9
2012	226.7	227.7	229.4	230.1	229.8	229.5	229.1	230.4	231.4	231.3	230.2	229.6	229.6
2013	230.3	232.2	232.8	232.5	232.9	233.5	233.6	233.9	234.1	233.5	233.1	233.0	233.0
2014	233.9	234.8	236.3	237.1	237.9	238.3	238.3	237.9	238.0	237.4	236.2	234.8	236.7
2015	233.7	234.7	236.1	236.6	237.8	238.6	238.7	238.3	237.9	237.8	237.3	236.5	237.0
2016	236.9	237.1	238.1	239.3	240.2	241.0	240.6	240.8	241.4	241.7	241.4	241.4	240.0
2017	242.8	243.6	243.8	244.5	244.7	245.0	244.8	245.5	246.8	246.7	246.7	246.5	245.1
2018	247.9	249.0	249.6	250.5	251.6	252.0	252.0	252.1	252.4	252.9	252.0	251.2	251.1
2019	251.7	252.8	254.2	255.5	256.1	256.1	256.6	256.6	256.8	257.3	257.2	257.0	255.7
2020[1]	258.0	258.7	258.1	256.4	256.4	257.8	259.1	259.9	260.3	260.4	260.2	260.5	258.8

[1] Preliminary. [2] Not seasonally adjusted. *Source: Bureau of Labor Statistics, U.S. Department of Commerce (BLS)*

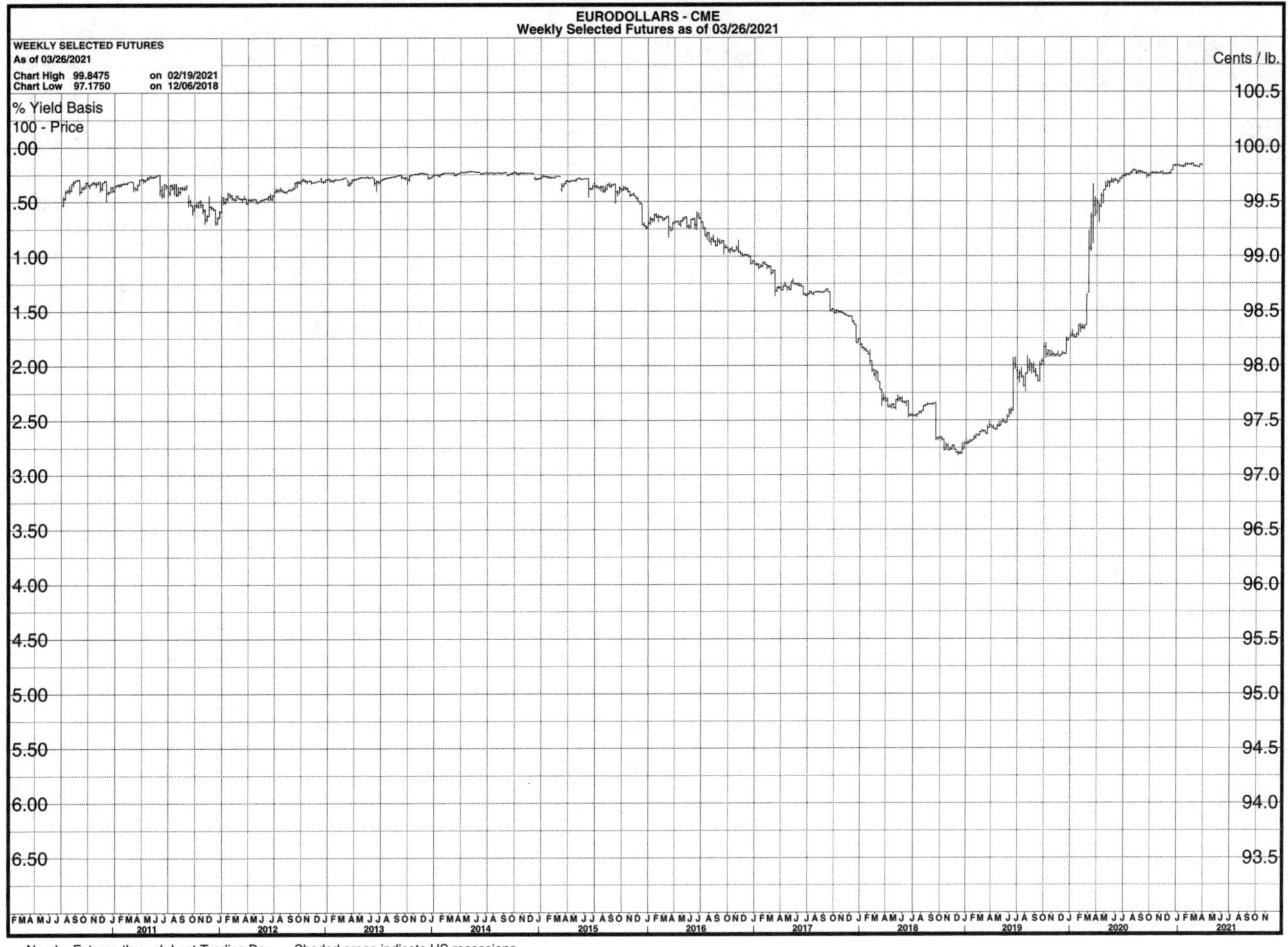

Nearby Futures through Last Trading Day. Shaded areas indicate US recessions.

Volume of Trading of 3-month Eurodollar Futures in Chicago In Thousands of Contracts

Year	Jan.	Feb.	Mar.	Apr.	May	June	July	Aug.	Sept.	Oct.	Nov.	Dec.	Total
2011	42,213.1	51,117.3	62,877.0	49,748.5	46,199.0	62,516.2	46,462.8	61,739.9	38,864.4	34,186.8	39,340.0	28,821.7	564,087
2012	41,620.4	38,145.0	46,496.1	32,895.5	40,756.4	38,105.8	28,199.5	34,119.2	37,238.4	35,652.7	26,998.6	26,210.8	426,438
2013	40,800.6	32,152.3	37,526.2	30,235.7	51,371.9	69,283.3	41,177.9	38,851.4	51,413.1	43,321.9	39,422.5	41,693.4	517,250
2014	54,761.3	38,750.1	57,945.4	46,118.3	54,063.9	55,196.8	57,448.5	47,862.5	67,835.8	86,823.2	34,561.1	63,066.5	664,433
2015	60,557.7	53,474.6	56,886.5	39,486.9	46,358.9	55,022.2	45,717.3	51,075.2	47,750.9	44,983.2	39,937.9	45,661.9	586,913
2016	60,730.2	58,698.8	53,857.5	41,209.6	46,085.8	56,564.7	49,539.9	49,707.1	49,586.2	42,365.9	84,793.1	61,808.7	654,947
2017	62,542.9	57,145.8	72,934.8	51,369.1	53,434.7	54,122.6	40,527.4	44,393.5	54,731.0	52,213.9	49,599.8	46,831.7	639,847
2018	69,710.4	90,635.0	87,329.3	54,086.4	68,834.0	53,227.4	38,782.1	43,758.4	55,084.0	72,841.9	58,947.3	71,972.4	765,209
2019	61,232.1	46,129.1	69,360.8	50,245.2	73,665.3	78,392.8	56,286.0	73,101.1	52,788.6	53,025.6	36,353.1	36,492.9	687,073
2020	43,767.3	70,530.7	109,077.1	40,101.1	34,866.2	34,777.6	22,937.0	28,911.5	27,773.7	26,825.1	39,452.2	30,893.0	509,913

Contract size = $1,000,000. *Source: CME Group; International Monetary Market (IOM), division of the Chicago Mercantile Exchange (CME)*

Average Open Interest of 3-month Eurodollar Futures in Chicago In Thousands of Contracts

Year	Jan.	Feb.	Mar.	Apr.	May	June	July	Aug.	Sept.	Oct.	Nov.	Dec.
2011	7,675.5	8,820.5	9,086.9	9,494.8	10,101.6	10,117.4	10,018.2	9,997.3	9,011.2	8,239.0	8,624.3	8,123.4
2012	7,787.5	8,387.6	8,508.1	8,593.1	8,776.6	8,213.4	7,889.8	7,858.5	8,210.5	8,269.0	8,508.1	8,292.0
2013	8,320.7	8,898.0	9,261.8	9,350.3	9,681.0	9,020.2	8,685.1	9,291.6	9,141.1	9,420.5	10,163.4	10,422.3
2014	10,142.7	10,022.8	10,453.9	10,875.2	11,635.9	11,593.8	12,101.1	12,734.0	13,139.9	11,819.9	11,685.4	10,902.1
2015	10,860.6	11,099.2	10,806.9	10,972.8	11,415.8	11,292.4	11,483.9	12,050.4	11,528.6	11,072.0	11,202.6	10,704.9
2016	10,869.1	10,865.4	10,132.9	10,143.2	10,621.0	10,281.7	10,434.1	10,977.1	11,138.0	11,410.5	12,131.6	12,064.2
2017	11,865.7	12,254.8	12,710.3	13,160.6	13,531.5	13,596.4	12,979.5	13,523.7	13,474.4	12,863.1	13,241.6	13,513.2
2018	14,034.4	15,871.7	17,114.1	16,815.8	16,141.1	14,660.5	14,124.0	14,084.0	14,114.7	14,373.2	14,151.3	13,543.0
2019	12,512.6	12,419.9	12,454.4	12,738.4	12,954.5	12,974.4	13,014.0	13,194.8	12,634.5	12,047.7	12,116.6	11,583.0
2020	11,060.8	11,742.0	11,096.0	10,613.3	10,799.8	10,252.2	9,703.1	9,768.4	9,420.7	9,336.8	9,801.5	9,439.9

Contract size = $1,000,000. *Source: CME Group; International Monetary Market (IOM), division of the Chicago Mercantile Exchange (CME)*

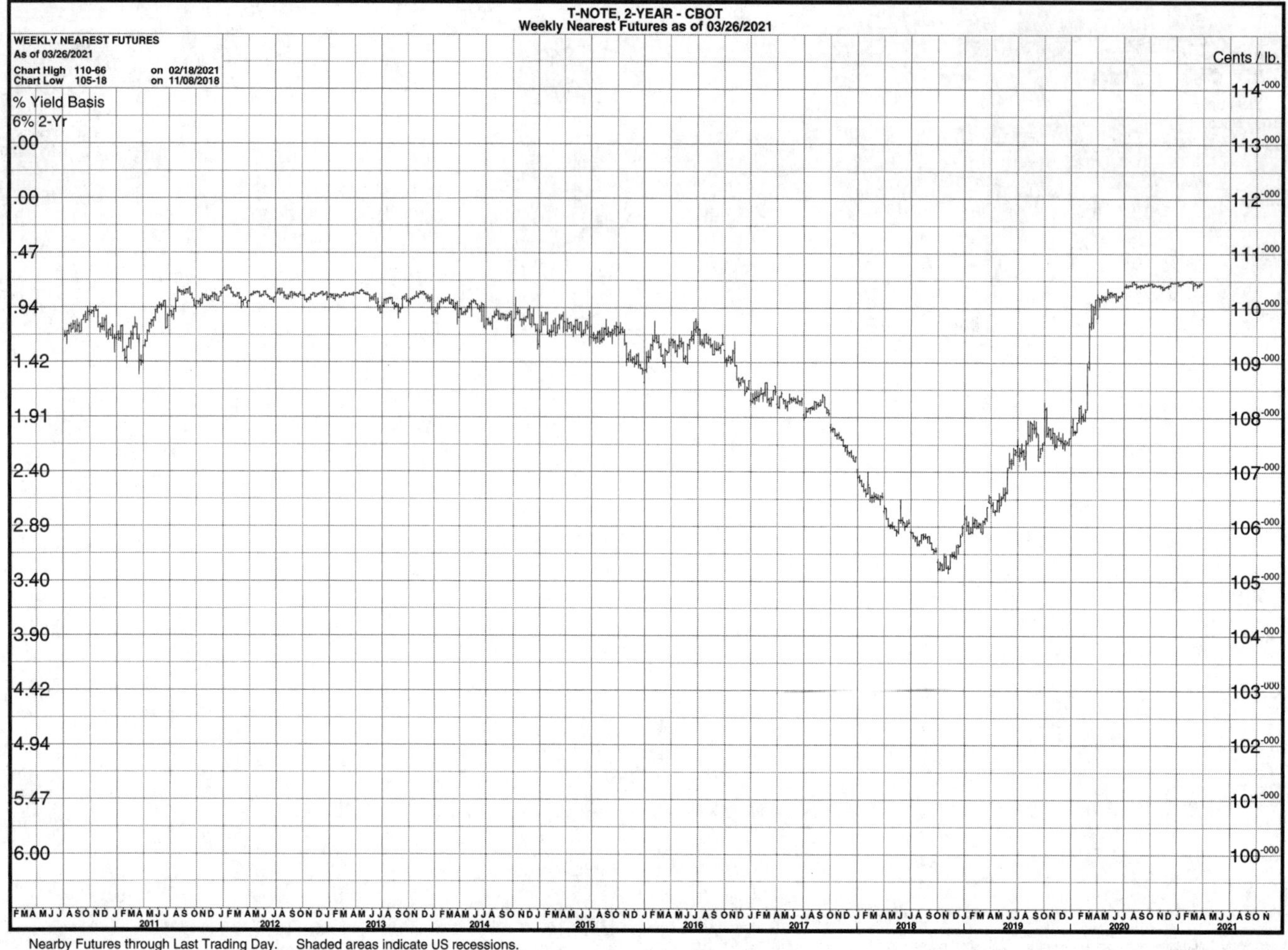

Nearby Futures through Last Trading Day. Shaded areas indicate US recessions.

Volume of Trading of 2-Year U.S. Treasury Note Futures in Chicago In Thousands of Contracts

Year	Jan.	Feb.	Mar.	Apr.	May	June	July	Aug.	Sept.	Oct.	Nov.	Dec.	Total
2011	4,172.3	9,276.8	7,161.9	5,363.7	8,520.4	6,814.1	5,166.5	9,198.7	3,990.7	3,743.3	6,105.9	2,664.6	72,179
2012	3,162.6	6,083.1	4,858.3	3,568.9	6,748.6	3,626.2	3,831.4	6,593.6	3,575.3	3,318.0	6,615.1	3,127.6	55,109
2013	4,249.9	7,408.8	3,786.5	3,169.7	8,812.1	4,703.0	3,008.5	6,380.5	4,134.8	3,133.0	5,982.2	3,046.9	57,816
2014	4,004.9	4,637.1	4,670.2	4,402.3	8,206.8	4,404.6	3,913.5	9,120.7	6,155.0	6,801.9	8,643.1	5,054.2	70,014
2015	5,113.2	11,269.7	6,108.6	4,349.9	10,776.5	6,555.7	4,983.7	10,933.2	5,556.6	4,681.9	7,946.4	4,765.3	83,041
2016	5,229.6	9,923.0	5,521.3	4,421.2	8,907.1	6,095.0	5,000.2	8,969.9	5,775.0	5,733.4	11,524.6	4,773.8	81,874
2017	5,753.0	10,850.4	6,893.6	5,031.7	11,816.4	6,878.7	4,794.3	11,174.2	6,379.3	6,749.4	14,716.4	6,212.1	97,249
2018	8,227.0	19,349.2	9,652.2	7,441.3	17,938.9	6,815.9	5,398.5	14,407.6	6,704.9	10,226.4	20,088.5	9,248.8	135,499
2019	10,151.3	20,428.2	10,462.9	9,357.5	25,719.8	12,310.8	11,126.1	25,807.0	11,851.2	13,137.1	22,728.1	9,543.9	182,624
2020	11,002.4	26,537.8	19,825.0	7,580.4	14,444.6	6,637.1	4,419.0	12,570.6	5,110.8	4,401.1	11,777.0	4,544.2	128,850

Contract size = $200,000. *Source: CME Group; Chicago Board of Trade (CBT)*

Average Open Interest of 2-Year U.S. Treasury Note Futures in Chicago In Thousands ofContracts

Year	Jan.	Feb.	Mar.	Apr.	May	June	July	Aug.	Sept.	Oct.	Nov.	Dec.
2011	711.7	900.2	892.0	1,031.0	1,066.2	1,030.5	1,012.9	976.2	772.3	714.5	748.0	698.8
2012	781.4	904.4	842.3	835.7	975.7	928.1	953.8	1,012.6	963.5	942.0	1,030.2	1,015.8
2013	998.1	1,046.5	989.2	916.5	945.3	816.8	791.7	864.5	863.5	925.2	978.2	866.6
2014	858.0	934.8	942.0	1,077.5	1,153.4	1,051.2	1,164.8	1,400.5	1,546.2	1,425.6	1,432.8	1,292.8
2015	1,269.4	1,462.5	1,346.2	1,378.7	1,363.1	1,183.6	1,274.7	1,356.3	1,143.8	1,117.1	1,091.9	989.4
2016	1,048.4	1,164.5	961.0	1,021.2	1,117.2	1,004.6	1,053.3	1,124.5	1,008.8	1,225.0	1,202.6	1,140.2
2017	1,215.9	1,444.9	1,412.6	1,378.3	1,392.5	1,350.8	1,354.0	1,488.8	1,527.0	1,667.8	1,837.2	1,765.6
2018	1,900.4	2,030.6	1,896.1	1,973.5	2,138.0	1,828.2	1,930.1	4,255.5	2,164.6	2,268.6	2,682.1	2,636.3
2019	2,681.8	3,159.8	3,027.8	3,614.3	4,089.5	3,615.8	3,634.0	3,849.5	3,557.2	3,872.6	3,972.1	3,581.8
2020	3,643.6	3,813.2	3,203.0	2,607.4	2,389.1	2,130.8	2,110.2	2,129.6	2,006.4	1,982.9	2,001.6	1,883.6

Contract size = $200,000. *Source: CME Group; Chicago Board of Trade (CBT)*

Nearby Futures through Last Trading Day. Shaded areas indicate US recessions.

Volume of Trading of 5-Year U.S. Treasury Note Futures in Chicago In Thousands of Contracts

Year	Jan.	Feb.	Mar.	Apr.	May	June	July	Aug.	Sept.	Oct.	Nov.	Dec.	Total
2011	10,654.1	16,398.4	16,604.1	11,371.9	17,958.8	16,524.9	13,314.4	21,004.3	12,074.6	11,607.0	15,320.7	7,729.7	170,563
2012	9,260.0	14,543.1	12,251.9	8,980.8	14,647.3	10,565.4	7,291.7	13,493.4	10,510.3	9,281.0	13,968.6	8,549.0	133,342
2013	12,206.3	18,750.5	11,971.1	11,023.9	23,914.4	17,072.7	11,763.4	18,021.9	13,464.8	10,198.2	16,397.4	10,543.6	175,328
2014	13,081.6	18,022.0	16,060.6	14,088.2	20,473.5	13,605.3	14,182.4	20,546.3	16,596.0	20,858.3	15,933.0	12,982.0	196,429
2015	14,739.3	20,925.8	14,020.7	11,619.5	20,929.9	15,289.6	12,668.2	22,856.6	12,974.5	12,321.4	20,512.7	11,849.6	190,708
2016	13,618.7	24,294.8	13,229.2	11,144.4	22,079.7	15,245.5	11,120.9	23,442.5	12,453.2	11,484.3	30,046.2	13,745.4	201,905
2017	15,623.7	26,990.8	17,509.9	13,761.0	26,563.2	16,462.0	12,784.2	24,543.1	14,990.7	14,944.5	27,741.3	14,526.8	226,441
2018	18,302.4	35,388.6	19,974.6	16,208.0	36,454.5	17,379.4	14,187.0	30,353.9	15,664.4	25,561.2	36,989.9	20,757.0	287,221
2019	21,297.1	31,298.5	20,637.9	16,018.8	39,172.1	21,319.0	18,801.4	40,355.5	19,616.5	18,960.9	31,401.5	15,520.5	294,400
2020	17,703.1	39,907.6	33,449.4	13,308.2	26,063.5	14,361.0	9,499.5	25,390.4	11,492.4	13,501.2	26,265.6	13,900.9	244,843

Contract size = $100,000. *Source: CME Group; Chicago Board of Trade (CBT)*

Average Open Interest of 5-Year U.S. Treasury Note Futures in Chicago In Thousands of Contracts

Year	Jan.	Feb.	Mar.	Apr.	May	June	July	Aug.	Sept.	Oct.	Nov.	Dec.
2011	1,075.8	1,293.9	1,223.4	1,364.8	1,524.6	1,576.9	1,513.4	1,435.6	1,326.7	1,200.4	1,277.5	1,261.2
2012	1,398.3	1,444.8	1,390.1	1,306.6	1,384.1	1,144.6	1,145.8	1,236.3	1,330.2	1,399.5	1,461.6	1,506.2
2013	1,532.5	1,653.7	1,733.6	1,847.6	1,842.2	1,535.0	1,584.4	1,641.0	1,668.5	1,745.1	1,968.7	1,865.1
2014	1,939.7	2,002.5	1,959.1	2,036.7	2,126.3	2,070.6	2,130.6	2,190.1	2,130.5	1,992.7	1,993.5	1,844.4
2015	1,837.5	1,983.8	1,992.9	2,016.3	2,038.9	2,096.2	2,200.8	2,398.5	2,352.1	2,422.1	2,469.2	2,371.4
2016	2,497.2	2,734.3	2,476.6	2,477.3	2,575.0	2,632.8	2,676.0	2,866.4	2,799.2	2,756.9	2,961.3	2,924.3
2017	3,019.1	3,313.3	3,035.8	3,103.9	3,261.9	3,144.0	1,350.8	3,000.0	3,144.0	2,998.1	3,293.4	3,051.2
2018	3,236.9	3,538.2	3,376.7	3,519.0	3,813.1	3,742.6	3,892.1	4,255.5	4,380.4	4,536.9	4,922.3	4,702.5
2019	4,539.9	4,511.1	4,256.0	4,485.2	4,870.6	4,535.7	4,475.3	4,567.4	4,129.1	4,360.5	4,613.6	4,248.8
2020	4,334.7	4,699.7	4,280.2	3,683.9	3,658.0	3,471.2	3,481.9	3,455.3	3,261.6	3,126.7	3,204.8	3,184.9

Contract size = $100,000. *Source: CME Group; Chicago Board of Trade (CBT)*

Nearby Futures through Last Trading Day. Shaded areas indicate US recessions.

Volume of Trading of 10-year U.S. Treasury Note Futures in Chicago In Thousands of Contracts

Year	Jan.	Feb.	Mar.	Apr.	May	June	July	Aug.	Sept.	Oct.	Nov.	Dec.	Total
2010	16,865.3	23,588.6	19,582.2	22,070.6	35,156.5	24,198.2	22,294.5	30,744.0	26,070.6	22,947.9	29,360.3	20,840.2	293,719
2011	22,260.8	27,531.8	29,500.1	20,162.8	31,149.4	31,897.7	25,851.1	39,911.1	24,612.4	23,559.8	26,614.2	14,351.4	317,403
2012	19,336.4	26,546.0	24,188.9	20,706.8	32,255.6	24,036.4	16,688.1	25,178.8	18,527.4	18,740.5	23,319.0	15,473.1	264,997
2013	24,720.9	33,572.4	24,606.7	23,859.0	43,005.7	32,912.7	21,673.6	31,715.3	23,332.3	21,265.7	27,463.8	17,800.2	325,928
2014	23,218.1	29,772.2	27,675.3	25,202.1	34,569.3	24,098.5	23,402.1	34,087.3	28,122.5	39,126.2	28,205.8	23,005.8	340,485
2015	27,499.2	33,705.2	24,770.7	22,343.8	38,005.7	29,805.4	23,574.7	34,287.1	22,586.7	23,505.9	28,612.5	19,644.2	328,341
2016	27,310.1	41,327.8	24,480.8	22,290.2	32,571.1	28,364.5	23,198.0	34,699.7	24,140.8	22,878.3	46,296.5	23,204.4	350,762
2017	28,552.5	38,619.2	29,608.9	25,570.4	39,797.5	28,177.2	24,476.4	39,078.3	27,756.7	28,826.3	41,497.4	23,377.8	375,338
2018	32,939.1	51,555.5	33,837.1	27,450.9	53,075.1	31,980.5	25,504.3	44,233.8	27,721.0	48,099.0	49,321.5	32,001.5	457,719
2019	31,722.5	41,654.0	34,503.4	27,261.9	56,919.4	33,426.3	29,998.8	56,558.9	34,095.1	32,378.8	42,883.4	28,427.2	449,830

Contract size = $100,000. *Source: CME Group; Chicago Board of Trade (CBT)*

Average Open Interest of 10-year U.S. Treasury Note Futures in Chicago In Thousands of Contracts

Year	Jan.	Feb.	Mar.	Apr.	May	June	July	Aug.	Sept.	Oct.	Nov.	Dec.
2010	1,292.9	1,420.4	1,423.8	1,632.0	1,838.8	1,756.8	1,802.2	1,973.0	1,686.3	1,617.2	1,527.4	1,335.3
2011	1,360.1	1,521.3	1,563.5	1,643.4	1,854.0	1,834.0	1,843.5	1,937.7	1,627.4	1,504.3	1,505.7	1,460.6
2012	1,647.6	1,847.4	1,796.4	1,804.4	1,949.8	1,806.5	1,787.3	1,640.5	1,593.8	1,685.3	1,783.4	1,674.9
2013	1,815.9	2,089.8	2,125.6	2,230.3	2,331.8	2,132.2	2,199.4	2,308.6	2,031.6	2,079.2	2,341.3	2,261.2
2014	2,260.5	2,426.0	2,433.4	2,526.5	2,720.3	2,591.6	2,679.0	2,853.2	2,705.4	2,776.0	2,855.5	2,652.6
2015	2,684.1	2,610.3	2,690.8	2,822.7	2,884.8	2,730.7	2,751.9	2,941.1	2,729.8	2,776.5	2,680.6	2,594.4
2016	2,747.8	3,065.1	2,714.8	2,726.7	2,732.6	2,750.5	2,815.6	2,849.5	2,818.1	2,890.3	3,017.2	3,026.9
2017	3,130.7	3,343.9	3,139.4	3,137.3	3,365.2	3,179.9	3,162.4	3,384.4	3,277.1	3,132.4	3,399.8	3,271.5
2018	3,420.6	3,740.6	3,480.6	3,590.4	3,854.8	3,462.9	3,696.0	3,990.4	3,963.9	4,153.7	4,281.3	4,136.0
2019	4,067.1	4,130.2	3,880.5	3,966.4	4,183.5	3,887.9	3,816.5	3,989.9	3,589.1	3,683.7	3,935.0	3,663.1

Contract size = $100,000. *Source: CME Group; Chicago Board of Trade (CBT)*

Nearby Futures through Last Trading Day. Shaded areas indicate US recessions.

Volume of Trading of 30-year U.S. Treasury Bond Futures in Chicago In Thousands of Contracts

Year	Jan.	Feb.	Mar.	Apr.	May	June	July	Aug.	Sept.	Oct.	Nov.	Dec.	Total
2011	6,272.2	8,551.9	7,823.2	5,528.4	9,231.3	8,358.3	6,471.5	11,892.5	7,487.1	6,694.3	9,057.7	4,969.9	92,339
2012	6,143.3	8,623.0	7,335.2	5,890.8	11,326.7	9,060.1	6,493.7	8,685.7	6,680.1	6,866.2	8,530.8	6,109.6	91,745
2013	7,892.2	10,758.6	7,691.9	8,269.7	13,337.5	9,601.6	5,788.0	8,792.7	6,759.6	6,193.9	7,712.2	5,165.3	97,963
2014	5,871.1	8,211.2	6,867.7	6,259.9	9,648.8	7,044.9	6,719.0	9,948.4	7,678.1	10,370.2	7,827.0	6,742.1	93,188
2015	7,956.2	8,611.4	5,183.2	4,747.5	6,832.7	5,708.3	5,453.9	7,438.7	4,884.1	4,927.9	5,625.7	4,531.9	71,902
2016	5,569.8	8,184.8	5,000.5	4,428.4	6,276.8	5,736.6	4,734.9	6,655.2	5,245.9	5,042.9	8,707.2	4,620.4	70,203
2017	5,165.8	7,149.6	5,818.2	4,614.0	7,713.7	6,144.7	4,672.2	7,620.6	5,442.3	5,668.0	8,212.6	5,115.4	73,337
2018	6,648.4	10,573.9	6,380.0	5,517.2	10,025.2	6,048.6	5,244.4	8,677.5	5,961.9	10,301.0	10,299.4	6,984.4	92,662
2019	6,441.9	8,404.9	6,758.6	4,783.9	9,727.9	6,005.7	5,736.2	12,286.6	6,763.9	6,752.0	8,383.3	5,750.6	87,796
2020	7,429.5	12,839.9	10,085.2	4,285.4	7,990.3	5,747.3	5,080.8	10,012.5	6,187.7	7,678.1	11,469.9	6,877.9	95,685

Contract size = $100,000. *Source: CME Group; Chicago Board of Trade (CBT)*

Average Open Interest of 30-year U.S. Treasury Bond Futures in Chicago In Contracts

Year	Jan.	Feb.	Mar.	Apr.	May	June	July	Aug.	Sept.	Oct.	Nov.	Dec.
2011	552,937	613,356	609,003	573,206	702,197	668,848	628,174	661,826	647,168	618,884	634,941	597,183
2012	612,937	615,616	583,579	576,419	661,058	664,479	636,745	610,065	570,346	564,706	623,227	586,502
2013	551,333	632,060	630,148	681,045	667,210	568,046	574,724	626,392	630,549	644,843	696,333	656,867
2014	666,663	716,926	712,174	722,390	780,781	738,607	758,214	870,115	860,417	870,759	850,561	889,272
2015	829,094	640,877	414,934	437,101	478,017	484,216	500,019	533,913	505,812	501,845	491,806	519,574
2016	517,291	562,305	510,970	525,831	528,077	570,427	575,832	583,950	562,062	562,046	574,628	586,673
2017	616,403	637,810	646,801	644,707	706,590	737,002	729,176	873,263	730,878	740,311	798,709	772,841
2018	790,518	834,751	806,285	798,849	878,533	804,968	826,864	878,497	859,024	917,822	964,126	966,317
2019	954,146	1,007,000	967,026	947,620	1,001,286	958,051	929,612	994,150	974,482	987,321	1,022,854	1,010,372
2020	1,052,137	1,294,602	1,154,433	997,024	1,048,643	1,003,052	1,048,720	1,152,639	1,168,654	1,212,653	1,248,831	1,155,056

Contract size = $100,000. *Source: CME Group; Chicago Board of Trade (CBT)*

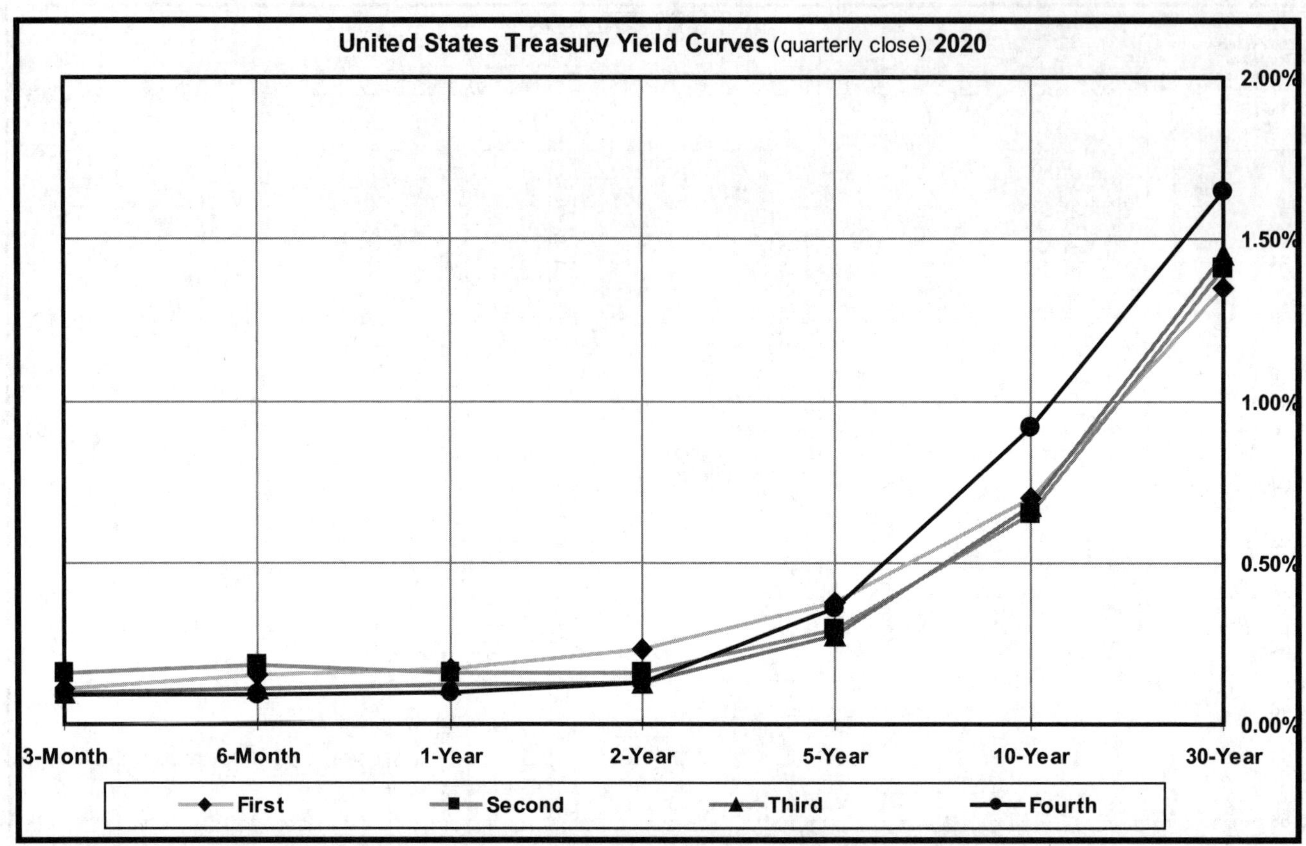

U.S. Federal Funds Rate In Percent

Year	Jan.	Feb.	Mar.	Apr.	May	June	July	Aug.	Sept.	Oct.	Nov.	Dec.	Average
2011	0.17	0.16	0.14	0.10	0.09	0.09	0.07	0.10	0.08	0.07	0.08	0.07	0.10
2012	0.08	0.10	0.13	0.14	0.16	0.16	0.16	0.13	0.14	0.16	0.16	0.16	0.14
2013	0.14	0.15	0.14	0.15	0.11	0.09	0.09	0.08	0.08	0.09	0.08	0.09	0.11
2014	0.07	0.07	0.08	0.09	0.09	0.10	0.09	0.09	0.09	0.09	0.09	0.12	0.09
2015	0.11	0.11	0.11	0.12	0.12	0.13	0.13	0.14	0.14	0.12	0.12	0.24	0.13
2016	0.34	0.38	0.36	0.37	0.37	0.38	0.39	0.40	0.40	0.40	0.41	0.54	0.40
2017	0.65	0.66	0.79	0.90	0.91	1.04	1.15	1.16	1.15	1.15	1.16	1.30	1.00
2018	1.41	1.42	1.51	1.69	1.70	1.82	1.91	1.91	1.95	2.19	2.20	2.27	1.83
2019	2.40	2.40	2.41	2.42	2.39	2.38	2.40	2.13	2.04	1.83	1.55	1.55	2.16
2020	1.55	1.58	0.65	0.05	0.05	0.08	0.09	0.10	0.09	0.09	0.09	0.09	0.38

Source: Bureau of Economic Analysis, U.S. Department of Commerce (BEA)

U.S. Municipal Bond Yield[1] In Percent

Year	Jan.	Feb.	Mar.	Apr.	May	June	July	Aug.	Sept.	Oct.	Nov.	Dec.	Average
2007	4.23	4.22	4.15	4.26	4.31	4.60	4.56	4.64	4.51	4.39	4.46	4.42	4.40
2008	4.27	4.64	4.93	4.70	4.58	4.69	4.68	4.69	4.86	5.50	5.23	5.56	4.86
2009	5.07	4.90	4.99	4.78	4.56	4.81	4.72	4.60	4.24	4.20	4.37	4.21	4.62
2010	4.33	4.36	4.36	4.41	4.29	4.36	4.32	4.03	3.87	3.87	4.40	4.92	4.29
2011	5.28	5.15	4.92	4.99	4.59	4.51	4.52	4.02	4.01	4.13	4.05	3.95	4.51
2012	3.68	3.66	3.91	3.95	3.77	3.94	3.78	3.74	3.73	3.65	3.46	3.48	3.73
2013	3.60	3.72	3.96	3.92	3.72	4.27	4.56	4.82	4.79	4.56	4.60	4.73	4.27
2014	4.59	4.44	4.46	4.35	4.29	4.35	4.33	4.23	4.13	3.96	3.96	3.70	4.23
2015	3.40	3.58	3.59	3.51	3.76	3.82	3.79	3.74	3.78	3.67	3.68	3.57	3.66
2016	3.41	3.30	3.38	3.30	3.29	3.13	2.83	2.85	2.93	3.20	Discontinued		3.16

[1] 20-bond average. *Source: Bureau of Economic Analysis, U.S. Department of Commerce (BEA)*

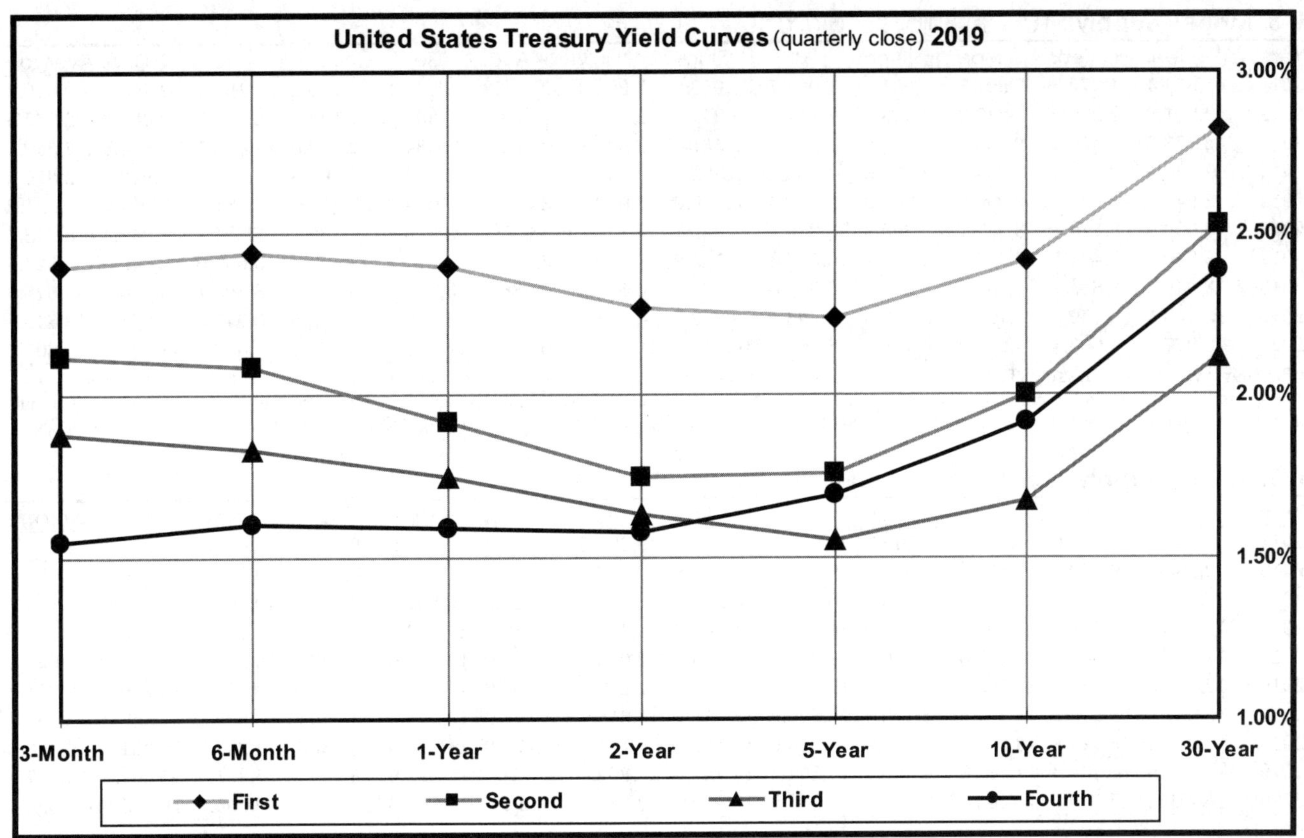

U.S. Industrial Production Index[1] 1997 = 100

Year	Jan.	Feb.	Mar.	Apr.	May	June	July	Aug.	Sept.	Oct.	Nov.	Dec.	Average
2011	95.9	95.5	96.5	96.1	96.3	96.6	97.1	97.7	97.6	98.3	98.2	98.8	94.1
2012	99.4	99.6	99.2	99.9	100.1	100.1	100.3	99.9	99.9	100.1	100.6	101.0	97.1
2013	100.8	101.4	101.8	101.6	101.7	102.0	101.5	102.2	102.7	102.5	102.8	103.2	100.0
2014	102.7	103.6	104.6	104.6	105.0	105.4	105.6	105.5	105.8	105.8	106.7	106.5	102.0
2015	106.0	105.4	105.1	104.5	104.1	103.7	104.3	104.2	103.8	103.4	102.7	102.1	105.2
2016	103.0	102.2	101.4	101.5	101.4	101.9	102.1	102.0	102.0	102.2	102.1	102.9	104.1
2017	103.0	102.6	103.3	104.3	104.4	104.6	104.5	104.0	104.1	105.6	106.2	106.5	102.1
2018	106.3	106.6	107.3	108.2	107.4	108.2	108.7	109.5	109.7	109.9	110.5	110.6	104.4
2019	110.1	109.6	109.7	109.0	109.2	109.3	109.1	109.9	109.5	109.0	110.0	109.7	108.6
2020[1]	109.2	109.3	104.5	91.3	92.1	97.8	101.9	102.9	102.8	103.9	104.9	106.2	109.5

[1] Total Index of the Federal Reserve Index of Quantity Output, seasonally adjusted. [2] Preliminary. *Source: Bureau of Economic Analysis, U.S. Department of Commerce (BEA)*

U.S. Gross National Product, National Income, and Personal Income In Billions of Constant Dollars[1]

	Gross Domestic Product					National Income					Personal Income				
Year	First Quarter	Second Quarter	Third Quarter	Fourth Quarter	Total	First Quarter	Second Quarter	Third Quarter	Fourth Quarter	Total	First Quarter	Second Quarter	Third Quarter	Fourth Quarter	Total
2011	15,286	15,496	15,592	15,796	15,543	13,091	13,256	13,455	13,607	13,352	13,078	13,195	13,347	13,398	13,255
2012	16,020	16,152	16,257	16,359	16,197	13,943	13,997	14,062	14,246	14,062	13,662	13,814	13,867	14,317	13,915
2013	16,570	16,638	16,849	17,083	16,785	14,276	14,382	14,479	14,642	14,445	13,904	14,017	14,135	14,238	14,074
2014	17,103	17,426	17,720	17,838	17,522	14,734	15,037	15,311	15,494	15,144	14,486	14,714	14,925	15,149	14,818
2015	17,970	18,221	18,331	18,354	18,219	15,553	15,720	15,785	15,901	15,740	15,301	15,516	15,626	15,769	15,553
2016	18,424	18,637	18,807	18,992	18,715	15,925	15,952	16,083	16,254	16,054	15,938	16,029	16,176	16,343	16,121
2017	19,190	19,357	19,612	19,919	19,519	16,475	16,612	16,753	16,995	16,709	16,604	16,750	16,930	17,231	16,879
2018	20,242	20,553	20,743	20,910	20,612	17,430	17,576	17,821	17,932	17,690	17,549	17,750	17,977	18,132	17,852
2019	21,115	21,330	21,540	21,747	21,433	18,033	18,214	18,302	18,528	18,269	18,367	18,481	18,598	18,761	18,552
2020[1]	21,561	19,520	21,170	21,488	20,935	18,406	16,151	17,442		17,333	18,951	20,457	19,854	19,504	19,692

[1] Seasonally adjusted at annual rates. [2] Preliminary. *Source: Bureau of Economic Analysis, U.S. Department of Commerce (BEA)*

U.S. Money Supply M1[2] In Billions of Dollars

Year	Jan.	Feb.	Mar.	Apr.	May	June	July	Aug.	Sept.	Oct.	Nov.	Dec.	Average
2011	1,853.4	1,872.5	1,891.3	1,901.4	1,938.7	1,956.2	2,001.9	2,113.8	2,128.1	2,140.2	2,164.1	2,163.5	2,010.4
2012	2,201.8	2,209.9	2,229.0	2,248.8	2,257.2	2,277.3	2,318.5	2,348.9	2,390.1	2,422.5	2,421.2	2,460.6	2,315.5
2013	2,473.3	2,472.4	2,480.4	2,515.8	2,530.7	2,531.4	2,545.8	2,552.1	2,584.5	2,623.0	2,623.1	2,664.4	2,549.7
2014	2,696.4	2,726.4	2,754.8	2,778.6	2,795.2	2,829.5	2,841.6	2,802.9	2,862.2	2,868.8	2,884.9	2,940.7	2,815.2
2015	2,941.0	3,007.1	2,999.6	3,000.9	2,986.6	3,020.0	3,039.7	3,028.5	3,044.2	3,018.6	3,081.7	3,094.9	3,021.9
2016	3,099.0	3,130.4	3,151.1	3,200.3	3,238.7	3,245.7	3,247.9	3,315.1	3,326.5	3,335.7	3,354.1	3,342.4	3,248.9
2017	3,390.9	3,404.7	3,445.5	3,454.2	3,517.3	3,525.9	3,550.9	3,580.7	3,574.2	3,606.7	3,630.6	3,612.0	3,524.5
2018	3,649.5	3,619.7	3,661.8	3,662.3	3,658.0	3,657.6	3,677.1	3,686.4	3,704.0	3,719.1	3,698.1	3,746.4	3,678.3
2019	3,740.4	3,759.6	3,729.8	3,780.9	3,792.4	3,832.8	3,858.1	3,853.2	3,903.0	3,922.8	3,947.4	3,976.9	3,841.4
2020[1]	3,977.3	4,003.8	4,257.0	4,799.1	16,268.1	16,599.5	16,803.2	16,921.5	17,194.0	17,368.4	17,643.9	17,776.2	12,801.0

[1] Preliminary. [2] *M1* -- The sum of currency held outside the vaults of depository institutions, Federal Reserve Banks, and the U.S. Treasury; travelers checks; and demand and other checkable deposits issued by financial institutions (except demand deposits due to the Treasury and depository institutions), minus cash items in process of collection and Federal Reserve float. Seasonally adjusted. *Source: Board of Governors of the Federal Reserve System*

U.S. Money Supply M2[2] In Billions of Dollars

Year	Jan.	Feb.	Mar.	Apr.	May	June	July	Aug.	Sept.	Oct.	Nov.	Dec.	Average
2011	8,826.2	8,871.6	8,916.0	8,978.2	9,029.5	9,113.7	9,301.6	9,515.3	9,539.9	9,571.5	9,612.5	9,651.3	9,243.9
2012	9,730.6	9,773.4	9,818.0	9,872.4	9,903.9	9,973.8	10,046.9	10,118.0	10,200.2	10,261.5	10,320.1	10,445.9	10,038.7
2013	10,471.7	10,468.5	10,540.0	10,575.3	10,611.5	10,666.0	10,721.9	10,780.3	10,832.7	10,945.6	10,953.3	11,015.9	10,715.2
2014	11,066.4	11,148.9	11,190.5	11,246.9	11,314.6	11,366.8	11,428.0	11,457.3	11,492.2	11,552.6	11,591.7	11,670.3	11,377.2
2015	11,733.4	11,852.6	11,869.0	11,916.4	11,947.8	11,993.3	12,045.5	12,097.0	12,154.0	12,187.9	12,277.7	12,336.1	12,034.2
2016	12,461.5	12,533.7	12,595.4	12,685.0	12,751.2	12,819.6	12,880.8	12,968.2	13,031.5	13,105.4	13,178.6	13,209.8	12,851.7
2017	13,282.5	13,340.2	13,405.5	13,470.3	13,520.9	13,550.8	13,616.1	13,671.0	13,716.9	13,779.0	13,809.5	13,852.0	13,584.6
2018	13,858.4	13,892.8	13,952.7	13,989.2	14,054.9	14,120.0	14,153.0	14,197.0	14,228.5	14,235.4	14,245.4	14,351.7	14,106.6
2019	14,434.6	14,464.3	14,511.8	14,558.7	14,654.3	14,782.6	14,862.1	14,933.3	15,022.9	15,149.9	15,251.2	15,307.1	14,827.7
2020[1]	15,416.4	15,459.7	16,002.4	17,033.8	17,883.2	18,179.0	18,328.8	18,392.4	18,618.0	18,754.6	19,005.5	19,088.8	17,680.2

[1] Preliminary. [2] *M2* -- M1 plus savings deposits (including money market deposit accounts) and small-denomination (less than $100,000) time deposits issued by financial institutions; and shares in retail money market mutual funds (funds with initial investments of less than $50,000), net of retirement accounts. Seasonally adjusted. *Source: Board of Governors of the Federal Reserve System*

U.S. Money Supply MZM[2] In Billions of Dollars

Year	Jan.	Feb.	Mar.	Apr.	May	June	July	Aug.	Sept.	Oct.	Nov.	Dec.	Average
2011	9,745.1	9,784.2	9,866.3	9,972.1	10,058.3	10,134.0	10,300.6	10,436.9	10,491.0	10,531.2	10,574.3	10,625.4	10,210.0
2012	10,708.1	10,752.8	10,818.0	10,878.0	10,918.3	10,989.7	11,073.0	11,164.1	11,258.3	11,319.5	11,383.2	11,530.3	11,066.1
2013	11,591.3	11,599.4	11,659.7	11,714.3	11,753.8	11,825.0	11,893.8	11,952.7	12,037.8	12,145.5	12,159.9	12,210.3	11,878.6
2014	12,274.0	12,359.2	12,395.3	12,439.2	12,509.1	12,557.7	12,623.4	12,641.8	12,695.2	12,779.8	12,838.9	12,940.7	12,587.9
2015	13,012.5	13,131.5	13,166.5	13,212.8	13,259.4	13,325.0	13,414.1	13,493.6	13,542.7	13,611.1	13,707.3	13,745.8	13,385.2
2016	13,795.8	13,886.7	13,988.5	14,084.8	14,162.4	14,245.4	14,314.8	14,415.7	14,457.0	14,489.1	14,568.4	14,599.0	14,250.6
2017	14,643.3	14,699.4	14,757.5	14,828.4	14,894.3	14,915.7	14,966.2	15,050.3	15,118.0	15,185.8	15,201.7	15,267.7	14,960.7
2018	15,277.6	15,311.7	15,374.6	15,417.1	15,466.5	15,528.3	15,542.1	15,562.0	15,586.7	15,571.9	15,574.1	15,680.7	15,491.1
2019	15,768.9	15,800.1	15,854.0	15,902.5	16,028.7	16,199.2	16,339.7	16,453.3	16,580.4	16,756.9	16,901.3	16,976.1	16,296.8
2020[1]	17,118.8	17,183.9	17,984.2	19,649.8	20,744.3	20,995.0	21,089.2	21,113.5	21,271.5	21,365.5	21,576.9	21,649.5	20,145.2

[1] Preliminary. [2] *MZM* (money, zero maturity): M2 minus small-denomination time deposits, plus institutional money market mutual funds (that is, those included in M3 but excluded from M2). The label MZM was coined by William Poole (1991); the aggregate itself was proposed earlier by Motley (1988). Seasonally adjusted. *Source: Board of Governors of the Federal Reserve System*

U.S. Money Supply M3[2] In Billions of Dollars

Year	Jan.	Feb.	Mar.	Apr.	May	June	July	Aug.	Sept.	Oct.	Nov.	Dec.	Average
1997	5,013.2	5,041.7	5,080.2	5,119.8	5,147.1	5,177.4	5,235.8	5,291.4	5,332.3	5,376.3	5,417.1	5,460.5	5,224.4
1998	5,508.8	5,541.3	5,611.5	5,647.3	5,686.9	5,728.4	5,750.0	5,815.0	5,882.0	5,953.7	6,010.1	6,051.9	5,765.6
1999	6,080.7	6,129.5	6,133.6	6,172.3	6,201.0	6,237.7	6,269.0	6,299.1	6,323.0	6,378.4	6,464.1	6,551.8	6,270.0
2000	6,605.5	6,642.2	6,704.0	6,767.3	6,776.9	6,823.6	6,875.2	6,945.0	7,003.5	7,027.0	7,038.3	7,117.6	6,860.5
2001	7,237.2	7,308.5	7,372.0	7,507.8	7,564.1	7,644.7	7,691.9	7,696.3	7,853.2	7,897.8	7,973.0	8,035.4	7,648.5
2002	8,063.9	8,109.3	8,117.3	8,142.6	8,175.1	8,190.8	8,244.2	8,298.1	8,331.5	8,368.9	8,498.8	8,568.0	8,259.0
2003	8,588.1	8,628.7	8,648.8	8,686.0	8,741.9	8,791.6	8,888.7	8,918.2	8,906.5	8,896.8	8,880.3	8,872.3	8,787.3
2004	8,930.2	9,000.3	9,080.7	9,149.6	9,243.8	9,275.7	9,282.7	9,314.4	9,351.8	9,359.4	9,395.1	9,433.0	9,234.7
2005	9,487.2	9,531.6	9,565.3	9,620.9	9,665.0	9,725.3	9,762.4	9,864.6	9,950.8	10,032.0	10,078.5	10,154.0	9,786.5
2006[1]	10,242.8	10,298.7	Discontinued										10,270.8

[1] Preliminary. [2] *M3* -- M2 plus large-denomination ($100,000 or more) time deposits; repurchase agreements issued by depository institutions; Eurodollar deposits, specifically, dollar-denominated deposits due to nonbank U.S. addresses held at foreign offices of U.S. banks worldwide and all banking offices in Canada and the United Kingdom; and institutional money market mutual funds (funds with initial investments of $50,000 or more). Seasonally adjusted. *Source: Board of Governors of the Federal Reserve System*

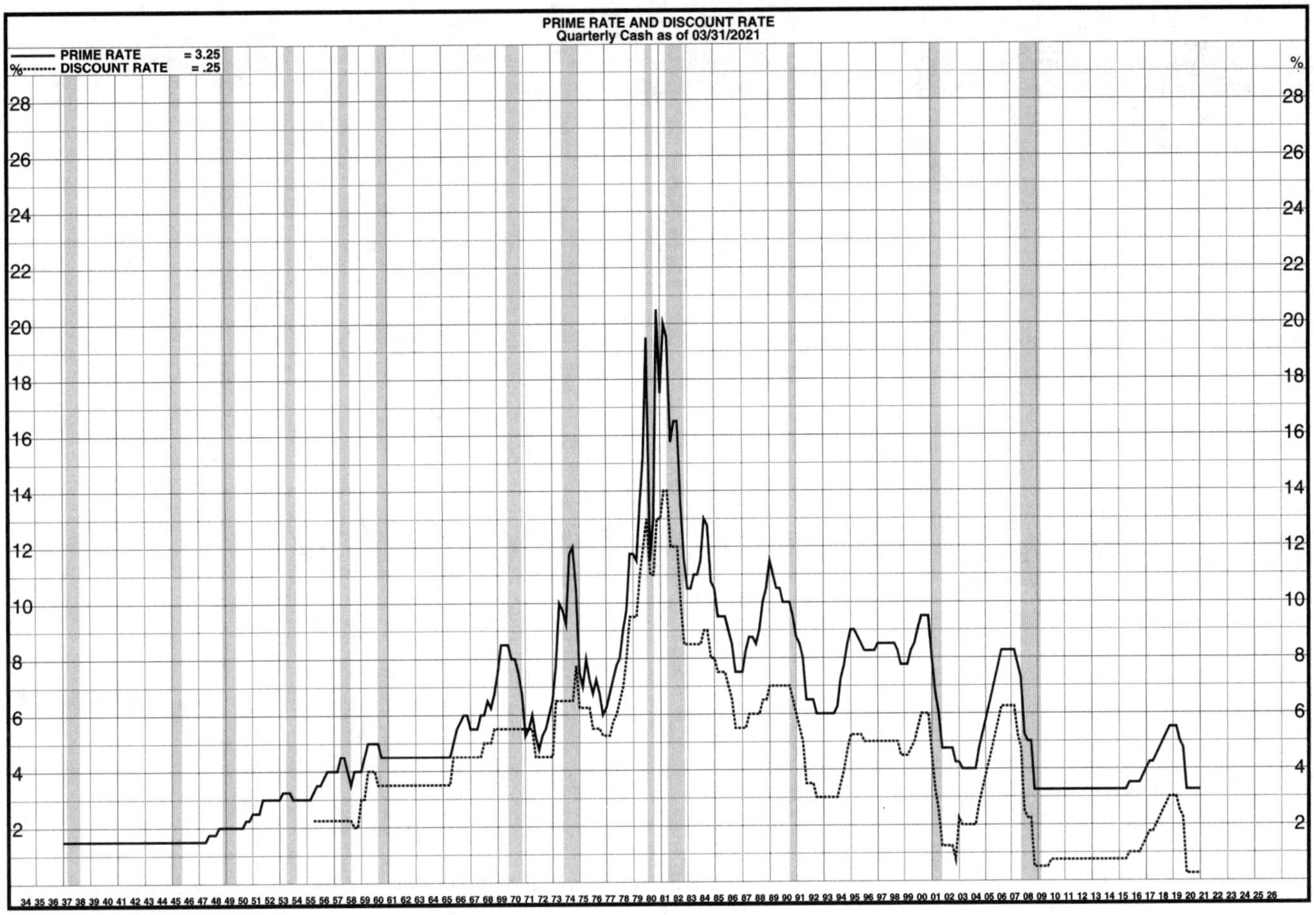
PRIME RATE AND DISCOUNT RATE
Quarterly Cash as of 03/31/2021
PRIME RATE = 3.25
DISCOUNT RATE = .25
%
28
26
24
22
20
18
16
14
12
10
8
6
4
2

Shaded areas indicate US recessions.

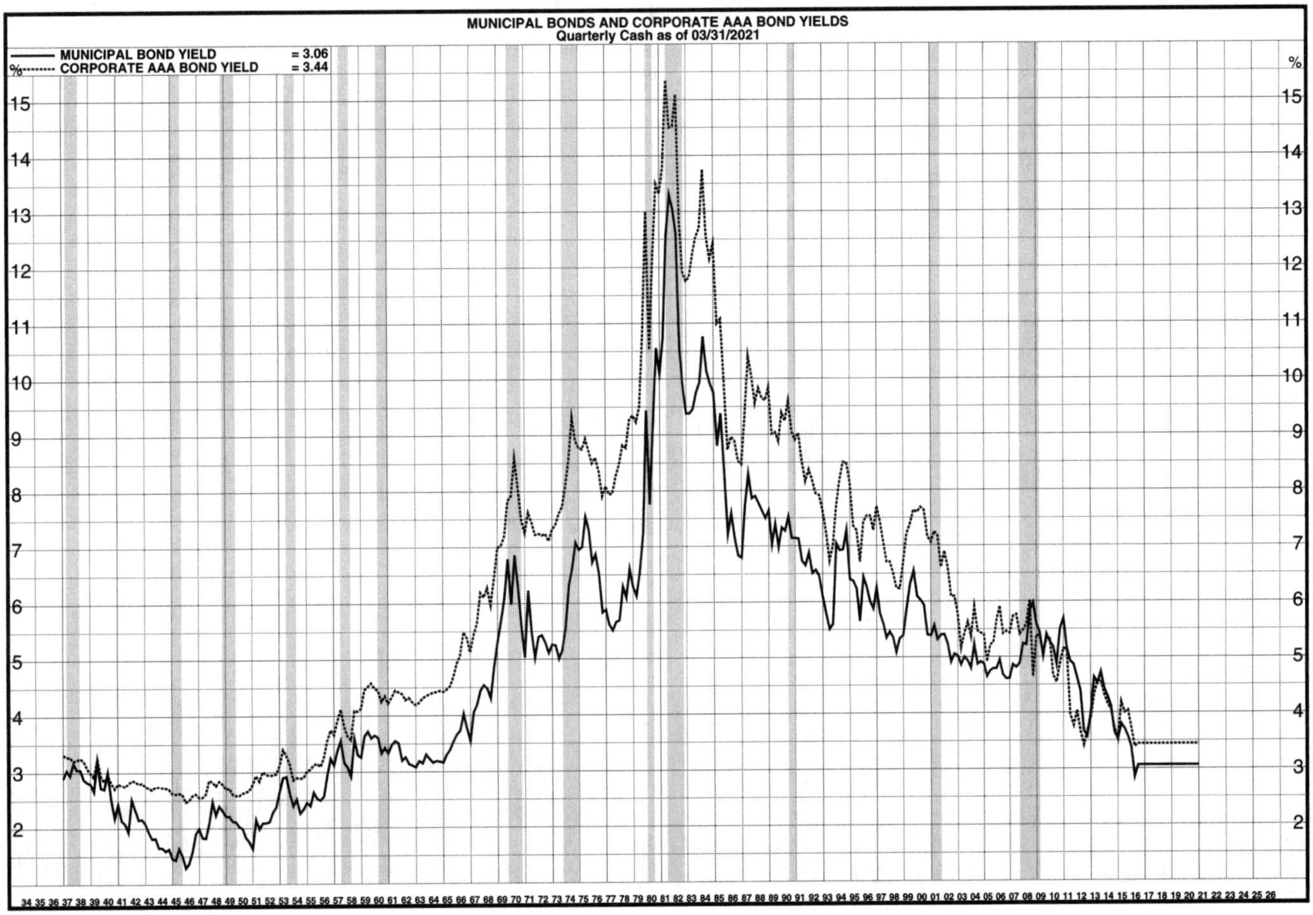
MUNICIPAL BONDS AND CORPORATE AAA BOND YIELDS
Quarterly Cash as of 03/31/2021
MUNICIPAL BOND YIELD = 3.06
CORPORATE AAA BOND YIELD = 3.44
%
15
14
13
12
11
10
9
8
7
6
5
4
3
2

Shaded areas indicate US recessions.

INTEREST RATES - U.S.

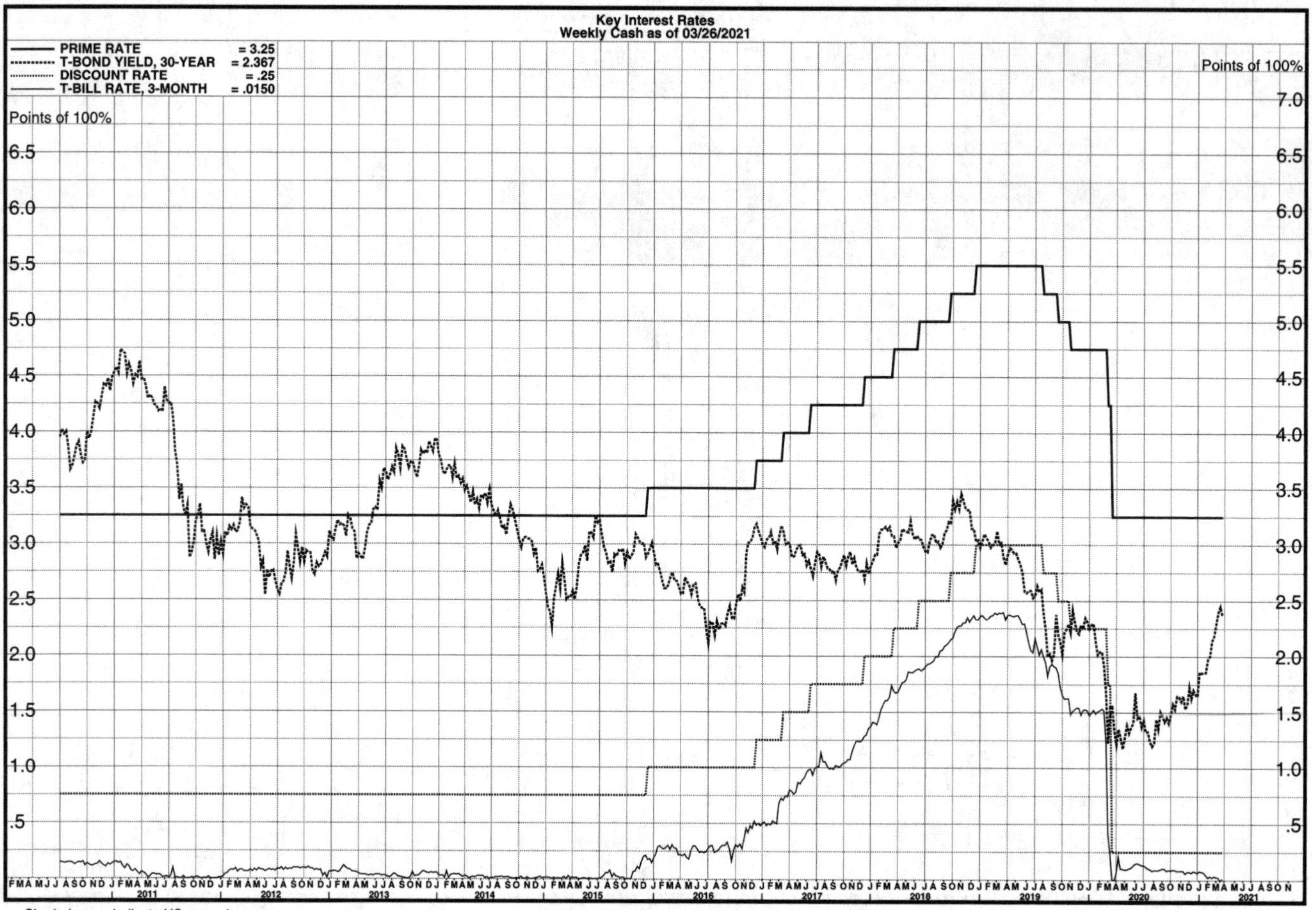

Key Interest Rates
Weekly Cash as of 03/26/2021
PRIME RATE = 3.25
T-BOND YIELD, 30-YEAR = 2.367
DISCOUNT RATE = .25
T-BILL RATE, 3-MONTH = .0150
Points of 100%

Shaded areas indicate US recessions.

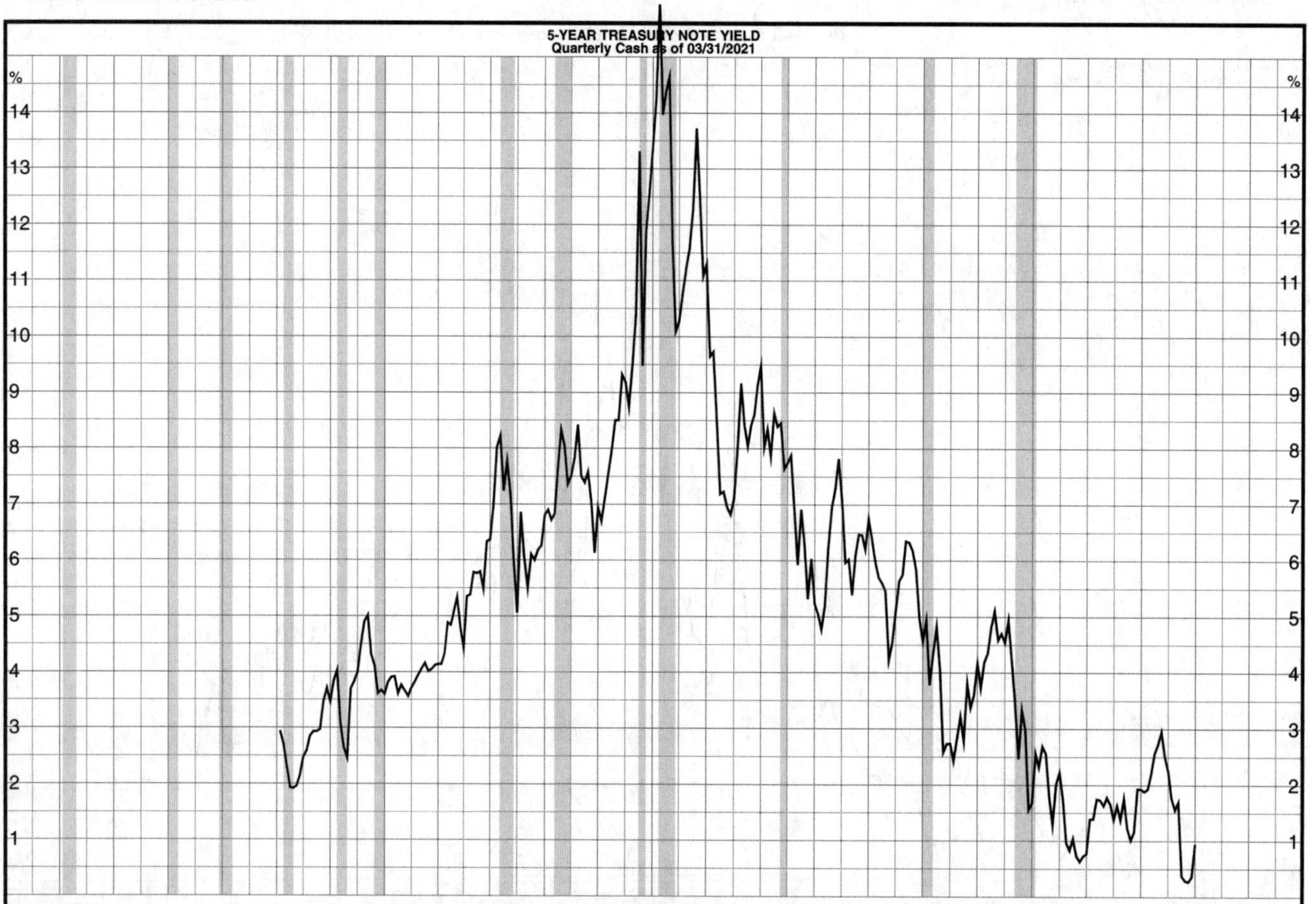

5-YEAR TREASURY NOTE YIELD
Quarterly Cash as of 03/31/2021
%

Shaded areas indicate US recessions.

Interest Rates - Worldwide

Interest rate futures contracts are widely traded throughout the world. The most popular futures contracts are generally 10-year government bonds and 3-month interest rate contracts. In Europe, futures on German interest rates are traded at the Eurex Exchange. Futures on UK interest rates are traded at the EuroNext-Liffe Exchange in London. Futures on Canadian interest rates are traded at the Montreal Exchange. Futures on Japanese interest rates are traded at the Singapore Exchange (SGX) and at the Tokyo Stock Exchange. A variety of other interest rate futures contracts are traded throughout the rest of the world (please see the front of this Yearbook for a complete list).

Euro-Zone – The Eurex German 10-year Euro Bund futures contract (Barchart.com symbol GG) rallied sharply during 2020 and closed the year up +15.96 points. The Eurex French 10-year OAT bond futures contract (Barchart.com symbol FN) also rallied sharply and closed the year up +17.06 points. The Eurex Italy Euro BTP 10-year bond futures contract (Barchart.com symbol II) also rallied sharply during 2020 and closed the year up +24.19 points.

European 10-year bond prices rallied sharply during 2020 due to the plunge in the Eurozone economy on the Covid pandemic and the ECB's aggressive monetary stimulus. Eurozone real GDP in 2020 fell sharply by -6.6% due to the pandemic shutdowns. The Eurozone's four biggest countries all showed major GDP declines in 2020, with Spain and Italy being hit the hardest: Germany -4.9%, France -8.1%, Italy -8.9%, and Spain -11.0%.

Eurozone bond prices during 2020 saw support from weak inflation and expectations that it could be a matter of years before Eurozone inflation rises on a sustained basis to the ECB's inflation target of just below +2.0%. The Eurozone core CPI fell sharply to -0.3% yr/yr by late 2020.

The ECB in 2020 kept its key interest rates unchanged despite the pandemic. The ECB did not cut its deposit rate any farther into negative territory for fear of putting banks under more stress. The ECB had already cut its deposit rate by -10 basis points to -0.50% in September 2019 and the ECB during 2020 left its deposit rate unchanged at -0.50%. The ECB during 2020 kept its main refinancing rate at zero percent, where it has been since 2016.

The ECB in 2020 ran two quantitative easing (QE) programs. During 2020, the ECB kept in place its Asset Purchase Program (APP) of 20 billion euros per month, which it began in November 2019 when the Eurozone was struggling. In March 2020, the ECB then announced a second QE program called the Pandemic Emergency Purchase Program (PEPP). The PEPP program started out at a total size of 750 billion euros, but the size of the program was raised by 600 billion euros in June 2020 and by another 500 billion in December 2020, for a total size by the end of 2020 of 1.85 trillion euros. The current schedule is for the program to last at least until March 2022.

UK – The Liffe UK 10-year gilt government bond futures contract (Barchart.com symbol G) rallied moderately during 2020 and closed the year up +4.16 points. Gilts rallied as UK GDP in 2020 plunged by -10%. The UK was hit particularly hard by the pandemic and forced into highly-restrictive lockdowns. However, the UK was relatively quick with vaccinations, and by March 2021, roughly half of the UK population had already been vaccinated. That raised hopes that the pandemic might soon end in the UK and allow restrictions to be relaxed, leading to improved GDP growth. The consensus is for GDP growth of +4.8% in 2021 and +5.6% in 2022. The Bank of England in March 2020 quickly moved into action on the pandemic and slashed its base rate by -65 basis points to 0.10%. The Bank of England also increased the size of its quantitative easing program, which was another bullish factor for gilts. The UK in late 2020 was able to reach a post-Brexit trade deal with the EU that allowed the UK to officially leave the EU at the end of 2020 in a relatively smooth manner.

Canada – The Montreal Exchange's Canadian 10-year government note futures contract (Barchart.com symbol CG) rallied sharply early in 2020 but then tailed off later in the year to close the year up +11.62 points. Canadian bond prices in 2020 were supported by the sharp -5.4% drop in Canada's GDP caused by the pandemic. The consensus is for Canada's GDP to grow by +5.3% in 2021, which would recover nearly all of 2020's decline. In response to the pandemic, the Bank of Canada in March 2020 slashed its overnight lending rate by -1.50 percentage points to 0.25%. The lending rate then stayed at 0.25% for the rest of the year. The Bank of Canada also started buying securities under a quantitative easing (QE) program. The Canadian economy took an extra hit during the first half of 2020 when oil prices plunged on the pandemic and the Saudi-Russian oil price war.

Japan – The SGX Japan 10-year Japanese government bond (JGB) futures contract (Barchart.com symbol JX) saw some strength in early 2020 on the pandemic but then fell back and closed the year little changed. The Bank of Japan (BOJ) has pursued a yield-curve control (YCC) policy since September 2016. Under that YCC policy, the BOJ enforces a steeper yield curve with the 10-year JGB yield targeted near zero, potentially allowing its 80-trillion-yen per year bond-purchase program to fluctuate in size to meet its yield target. The 10-year JGB yield has therefore been trading in a narrow range near zero, within the BOJ's target boundary of plus-or-minus 0.20%. The BOJ in March 2021 expanded that target boundary to 0.25% as JGB yields saw upward pressure from hopes for an end of the pandemic as vaccinations spread. The Bank of Japan already had its policy rate at -0.10% when the pandemic struck, and the BOJ did not cut it further into negative territory since that could further damage banks' health. Japan's GDP growth was already weak in 2019 at +0.3% due to the Japanese government's hike in Japan's national sales tax to 10% from 8% that took effect on October 1, 2019. Japan's real GDP then fell sharply by -4.9% in 2020 due to the pandemic. The consensus is for Japan's GDP to grow by only +2.8% in 2021, which would fall short of recovering 2020's decline.

GILT, LONG - ICE-LIFF
Weekly Nearest Futures as of 03/26/2021

WEEKLY NEAREST FUTURES
As of 03/26/2021
Chart High 140.32 on 03/09/2020
Chart Low 106.00 on 01/02/2014

% Yield Basis
6% 10-Yr
.96
1.30
1.65
2.01
2.38
2.77
3.18
3.60
4.04
4.50
4.98
5.48
6.00

Points of 100%
152
148
144
140
136
132
128
124
120
116
112
108
104
100

2011 2012 2013 2014 2015 2016 2017 2018 2019 2020 2021

Nearby Futures through Last Trading Day.

STERLING, 3-MONTH - ICE-LIFF
Weekly Selected Futures as of 03/26/2021

WEEKLY SELECTED FUTURES
As of 03/26/2021
Chart High 100.030 on 01/06/2021
Chart Low 98.830 on 11/18/2011

% Yield Basis
100 - Price
.00
.20
.40
.60
.80
1.00
1.20
1.40
1.60
1.80
2.00
2.20
2.40

USD / troy oz.
100.2
100.0
99.8
99.6
99.4
99.2
99.0
98.8
98.6
98.4
98.2
98.0
97.8
97.6

2011 2012 2013 2014 2015 2016 2017 2018 2019 2020 2021

Nearby Futures through Last Trading Day.

JAPANESE GOVT BOND, 10-YEAR - JPX
Weekly Nearest Futures as of 03/26/2021

Nearby Futures through Last Trading Day.

EUROYEN, 3-MONTH - TIFFE
Weekly Nearest Futures as of 03/26/2021

Nearby Futures through Last Trading Day.

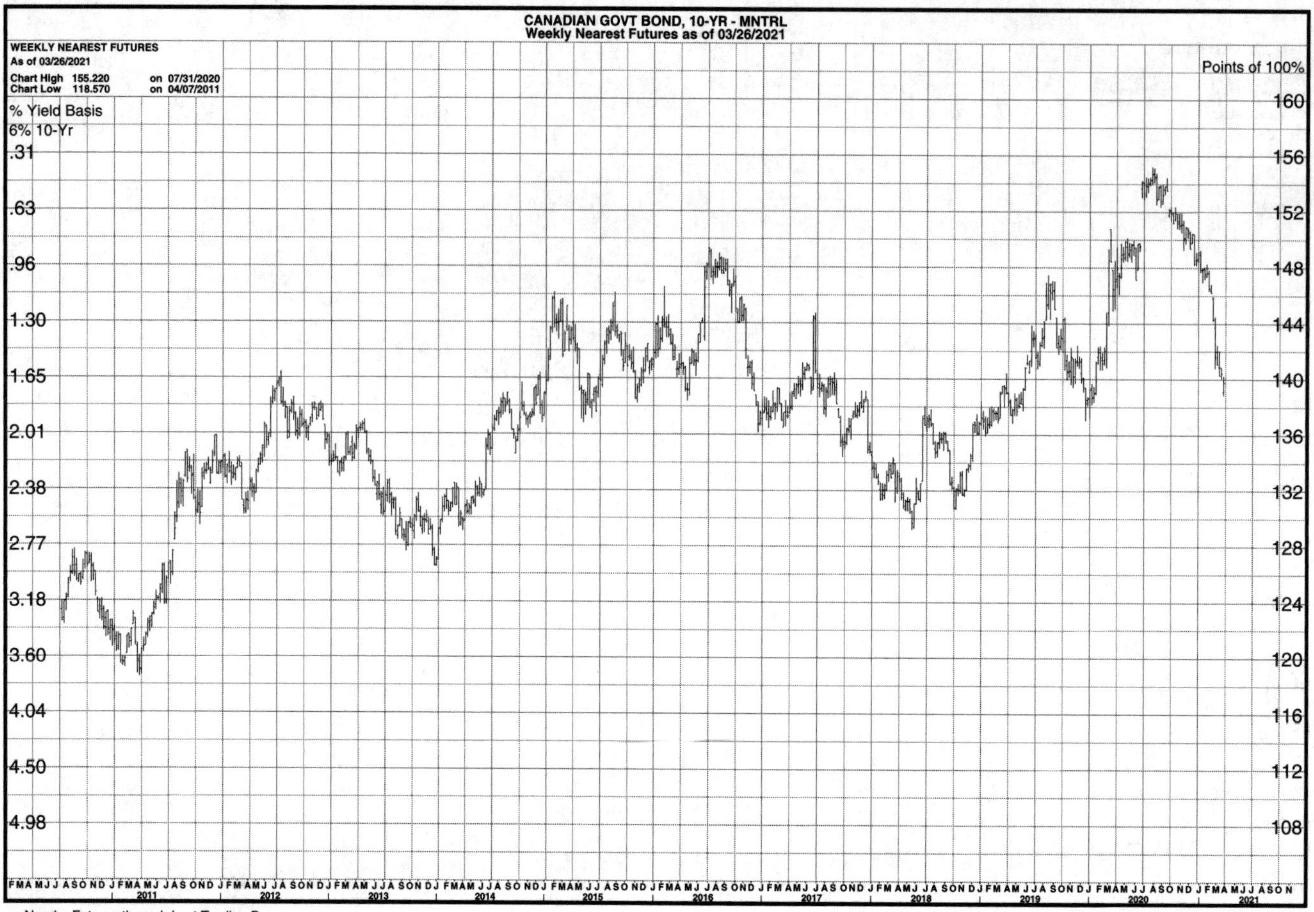

CANADIAN GOVT BOND, 10-YR - MNTRL
Weekly Nearest Futures as of 03/26/2021

WEEKLY NEAREST FUTURES
As of 03/26/2021
Chart High 155.220 on 07/31/2020
Chart Low 118.570 on 04/07/2011

% Yield Basis
6% 10-Yr

Points of 100%

Nearby Futures through Last Trading Day.

CAN. BANKERS' ACCEPTANCE, 3-MO - MNTRL
Weekly Selected Futures as of 03/26/2021

WEEKLY SELECTED FUTURES
As of 03/26/2021
Chart High 99.600 on 01/18/2021
Chart Low 97.620 on 10/31/2018

% Yield Basis
100 - Price

USD / troy oz.

Nearby Futures through Last Trading Day.

Australia -- Economic Statistics Percentage Change from Previous Period

Year	Real GDP	Nominal GDP	Real Private Consump-tion	Real Public Consump-tion	Grossed Fixed Invest-ment	Real Total Domestic Demand	Real Exports of Goods & Services	Real Imports of Goods & Services	Consumer Prices[3]	Unem-ployment Rate
2012	3.9	3.3	2.5	1.5	10.0	4.2	5.9	5.7	1.7	5.2
2013	2.2	3.5	1.9	1.9	-1.9	.4	5.8	-2.0	2.5	5.7
2014	2.5	2.9	2.5	.1	-2.3	.9	6.9	-1.4	2.5	6.1
2015	2.5	1.7	2.4	4.3	-3.4	1.3	6.3	1.7	1.5	6.1
2016	2.6	3.8	2.9	4.1	-2.2	1.9	6.8	.5	1.3	5.7
2017	2.2	5.8	2.7	3.7	3.4	3.0	3.7	7.8	1.9	5.6
2018	3.1	4.6	2.5	4.4	3.4	3.1	4.6	5.6	2.0	5.4
2019[1]	2.9	4.1	2.1	3.2	4.0	2.7	4.1	6.1	2.2	5.3
2020[2]	2.6	4.1	1.7	2.8	2.9	2.2	3.8	4.9		

[1] Estimate. [2] Projection. [3] National accounts implicit private consumption deflator. *Source: Organization for Economic Co-operation and Development (OECD)*

Canada -- Economic Statistics Percentage Change from Previous Period

Year	Real GDP	Nominal GDP	Real Private Consump-tion	Real Public Consump-tion	Grossed Fixed Invest-ment	Real Total Domestic Demand	Real Exports of Goods & Services	Real Imports of Goods & Services	Consumer Prices[3]	Unem-ployment Rate
2012	1.7	3.0	1.9	.7	4.9	2.1	2.6	3.6	1.5	7.3
2013	2.5	4.1	2.6	-.7	1.3	3.4	2.7	1.6	.9	7.1
2014	2.9	4.9	2.6	.5	2.4	1.8	5.9	2.3	1.9	6.9
2015	1.0	.2	2.2	1.6	-5.1	.1	3.5	.7	1.1	6.9
2016	1.4	2.0	2.3	2.2	-3.0	.8	1.0	-1.0	1.4	7.0
2017	3.0	5.4	3.4	2.3	2.8	3.8	1.1	3.6	1.5	6.4
2018	2.1	4.1	2.3	2.4	3.8	2.6	2.6	4.2	1.9	6.1
2019[1]	2.2	4.2	2.3	1.4	2.5	2.1	3.4	3.2	2.0	5.9
2020[2]	1.9	4.0	1.8	1.2	2.4	1.8	3.4	3.1		

[1] Estimate. [2] Projection. [3] National accounts implicit private consumption deflator. *Source: Organization for Economic Co-operation and Development (OECD)*

France -- Economic Statistics Percentage Change from Previous Period

Year	Real GDP	Nominal GDP	Real Private Consump-tion	Real Public Consump-tion	Grossed Fixed Invest-ment	Real Total Domestic Demand	Real Exports of Goods & Services	Real Imports of Goods & Services	Consumer Prices[3]	Unem-ployment Rate
2012	.4	1.6	-.4	1.6	.4	-.4	3.0	.4	2.2	9.8
2013	.6	1.4	.6	1.5	-.7	.7	2.1	2.5	1.0	10.3
2014	1.0	1.6	.8	1.3	.0	1.5	3.4	4.9	.6	10.3
2015	1.0	2.2	1.4	1.0	.9	1.5	4.4	5.7	.1	10.4
2016	1.1	1.3	1.9	1.4	2.7	1.6	1.5	3.1	.3	10.1
2017	2.3	3.0	1.2	1.4	4.7	2.2	4.7	4.1	1.1	9.4
2018	1.6	2.6	1.0	.9	2.9	1.1	3.3	1.5	1.1	9.2
2019[1]	1.6	3.0	1.6	.8	2.4	1.5	3.6	3.2	1.3	8.8
2020[2]	1.5	3.1	1.5	.4	2.4	1.4	3.4	3.3		

[1] Estimate. [2] Projection. [3] National accounts implicit private consumption deflator. *Source: Organization for Economic Co-operation and Development (OECD)*

Germany -- Economic Statistics Percentage Change from Previous Period

Year	Real GDP	Nominal GDP	Real Private Consump-tion	Real Public Consump-tion	Grossed Fixed Invest-ment	Real Total Domestic Demand	Real Exports of Goods & Services	Real Imports of Goods & Services	Consumer Prices[3]	Unem-ployment Rate
2012	.7	2.2	1.4	1.1	-.1	-.8	3.5	.4	2.1	5.4
2013	.6	2.6	.8	1.4	-1.2	1.0	1.9	3.1	1.6	5.2
2014	2.2	4.0	1.1	1.6	3.9	1.6	4.6	3.6	.8	5.0
2015	1.5	3.5	1.6	2.9	1.0	1.4	4.7	5.2	.1	4.6
2016	2.2	3.6	1.9	4.0	3.4	2.9	2.1	4.0	.4	4.2
2017	2.5	4.0	2.0	1.6	3.6	2.2	5.3	5.3	1.7	3.7
2018	1.6	3.5	1.2	1.2	3.0	2.0	2.5	3.6	1.8	3.5
2019[1]	1.6	3.9	1.8	2.5	2.5	2.2	2.9	4.4	2.0	3.4
2020[2]	1.4	3.7	1.7	1.8	2.2	1.8	3.2	4.4		

[1] Estimate. [2] Projection. [3] National accounts implicit private consumption deflator. *Source: Organization for Economic Co-operation and Development (OECD)*

Italy -- Economic Statistics Percentage Change from Previous Period

Year	Real GDP	Nominal GDP	Real Private Consump-tion	Real Public Consump-tion	Grossed Fixed Invest-ment	Real Total Domestic Demand	Real Exports of Goods & Services	Real Imports of Goods & Services	Consumer Prices[3]	Unem-ployment Rate
2012	-2.9	-1.5	-4.0	-1.4	-9.4	-5.7	2.0	-8.2	3.3	10.7
2013	-1.7	-.6	-2.4	-.3	-6.6	-2.7	.9	-2.3	1.2	12.1
2014	.2	1.1	.2	-.7	-2.2	.3	2.4	3.0	.2	12.6
2015	.8	1.8	1.9	-.6	1.9	1.4	4.2	6.6	.1	11.9
2016	1.0	1.8	1.4	.6	3.3	1.3	2.6	3.8	-.1	11.7
2017	1.6	2.2	1.4	.1	3.9	1.3	6.0	5.7	1.4	11.2
2018	1.0	2.5	.8	.1	4.5	1.4	.2	1.6	1.2	10.5
2019[1]	.9	2.5	.7	.2	3.5	1.1	2.7	3.5	1.4	10.1
2020[2]	.9	2.3	.7	.1	2.9	1.0	2.8	3.1		

[1] Estimate. [2] Projection. [3] National accounts implicit private consumption deflator. *Source: Organization for Economic Co-operation and Development (OECD)*

Japan -- Economic Statistics Percentage Change from Previous Period

Year	Real GDP	Nominal GDP	Real Private Consump-tion	Real Public Consump-tion	Grossed Fixed Invest-ment	Real Total Domestic Demand	Real Exports of Goods & Services	Real Imports of Goods & Services	Consumer Prices[3]	Unem-ployment Rate
2012	1.5	.7	2.0	1.7	3.5	2.3	-.1	5.4	.0	4.4
2013	2.0	1.7	2.4	1.5	4.9	2.4	.8	3.3	.3	4.0
2014	.4	2.1	-.9	.5	3.1	.4	9.3	8.3	2.8	3.6
2015	1.4	3.5	.0	1.5	1.7	1.0	2.9	.8	.8	3.4
2016	1.0	1.2	.1	1.3	1.1	.4	1.7	-1.6	-.1	3.1
2017	1.7	1.5	1.0	.4	2.5	1.2	6.7	3.5	.4	2.8
2018	.9	.7	.4	.5	1.7	.8	2.8	2.6	1.0	2.8
2019[1]	1.0	1.2	.9	.6	1.5	1.0	1.4	1.4	1.7	2.8
2020[2]	.7	2.3	-.1	1.0	.8	.4	3.8	2.0		

[1] Estimate. [2] Projection. [3] National accounts implicit private consumption deflator. *Source: Organization for Economic Co-operation and Development (OECD)*

Switzerland -- Economic Statistics Percentage Change from Previous Period

Year	Real GDP	Nominal GDP	Real Private Consump-tion	Real Public Consump-tion	Grossed Fixed Invest-ment	Real Total Domestic Demand	Real Exports of Goods & Services	Real Imports of Goods & Services	Consumer Prices[3]	Unem-ployment Rate
2012	1.0	.8	2.3	1.5	3.4	-1.4	1.1	-2.5	-.7	4.5
2013	1.9	1.9	2.6	2.3	.6	-.7	15.2	13.6	-.2	4.7
2014	2.5	1.8	1.3	2.2	2.9	2.7	-6.1	-7.7	.0	4.8
2015	1.3	.6	1.7	1.1	2.3	2.2	2.5	4.3	-1.1	4.8
2016	1.6	1.0	1.5	1.2	3.4	.3	6.7	5.9	-.4	4.9
2017	1.7	1.2	1.2	.9	3.3	1.5	-.1	-.7	.6	4.8
2018	2.9	3.6	1.2	1.0	3.1	1.7	1.4	-.8	.6	4.5
2019[1]	1.6	2.7	1.5	1.0	2.9	2.6	1.9	3.8	.6	4.4
2020[2]	1.6	2.8	1.7	1.1	2.6	1.9	2.9	3.5		

[1] Estimate. [2] Projection. [3] National accounts implicit private consumption deflator. *Source: Organization for Economic Co-operation and Development (OECD)*

United Kingdom -- Economic Statistics Percentage Change from Previous Period

Year	Real GDP	Nominal GDP	Real Private Consump-tion	Real Public Consump-tion	Grossed Fixed Invest-ment	Real Total Domestic Demand	Real Exports of Goods & Services	Real Imports of Goods & Services	Consumer Prices[3]	Unem-ployment Rate
2012	1.4	3.0	1.5	1.2	2.1	1.9	1.4	3.0	2.8	8.0
2013	2.0	4.0	1.8	-.2	3.4	2.5	1.5	3.2	2.6	7.6
2014	2.9	4.7	2.0	2.2	7.2	3.4	2.3	3.8	1.5	6.2
2015	2.3	2.8	2.6	1.4	3.4	2.7	4.4	5.5	.1	5.4
2016	1.8	3.9	3.1	.8	2.3	2.5	1.0	3.3	.6	4.9
2017	1.7	3.8	1.8	-.1	3.3	1.2	5.7	3.2	2.7	4.4
2018	1.3	3.2	1.5	.8	.0	1.0	1.2	.2	2.6	4.4
2019[1]	1.4	3.2	1.1	1.9	.8	1.1	1.1	.1	2.2	4.6
2020[2]	1.1	2.9	.6	2.0	.4	.8	1.8	.7		

[1] Estimate. [2] Projection. [3] National accounts implicit private consumption deflator. *Source: Organization for Economic Co-operation and Development (OECD)*

Iron and Steel

Iron (atomic symbol Fe) is a soft, malleable, and ductile metallic element. Next to aluminum, iron is the most abundant of all metals. Pure iron melts at about 1535 degrees Celsius and boils at 2750 degrees Celsius. Archaeologists in Egypt discovered the earliest iron implements dating back to about 3000 BC, and iron ornaments were used even earlier.

Steel is an alloy of iron and carbon, often with an admixture of other elements. The physical properties of various types of steel and steel alloys depend primarily on the amount of carbon present and how it is distributed in the iron. Steel is marketed in a variety of sizes and shapes, such as rods, pipes, railroad rails, tees, channels, and I-beams. Steel mills roll and form heated ingots into the required shapes. The working of steel improves the quality of the steel by refining its crystalline structure and making the metal tougher. There are five classifications of steel: carbon steels, alloy steels, high-strength low-alloy steels, stainless steel, and tool steels.

Prices – In 2020, the average wholesale price for No. 1 heavy-melting steel scrap in Chicago fell -5.1% yr/yr to $235.05 per metric ton.

Supply – World production of iron ore in 2020 fell -2.0% yr/yr to 2.400 billion metric tons, down from the 2018 record high of 2.460. The world's largest producers of iron ore are Australia with 3752% of world production, Brazil with 16.7%, and China with 14.2%. The U.S. accounted for only 1.5% of world iron ore production.

World production of raw steel (ingots and castings) in 2020 fell -3.2 % yr/yr to 1.800 billion metric tons., down from the 2019 record high of 1.860. The largest producers were China with 56.6% of world production, Japan with 4.5%, and Russia with 3.8%. U.S. production of steel ingots in 2020 was down -18.2% yr/yr at 72.0 million metric tons, remaining up from the 2009 record low of 59.400 million metric tons.

U.S. production of pig iron (excluding ferro-alloys) in 2020 (annualized through December fell -18.9% yr/yr to 18.086 million short tons.

Demand – U.S. consumption of ferrous scrap and pig iron in 2017 fell -9.5% yr/yr to 72.590 million metric tons, which is a record low. The largest consumers of ferrous scrap and pig iron were the manufacturers of steel ingots and castings, with 87.8% of consumption. Iron foundries and miscellaneous users accounted for 6.6% of consumption, and manufacturers of steel castings (scrap) accounted for 0.6% of consumption.

Trade – The U.S. imported 5.100 million metric tons of iron ore in 2019, down -33.9% yr/yr. In 2017, the bulk of U.S. iron ore imports came from Brazil (54.5% with 2.040 million metric tons) and Canada (26.2% with 790,000 metric tons).

World Production of Raw Steel (Ingots and Castings) In Thousands of Metric Tons

Year	Brazil	Canada	China	France	Germany	Italy	Japan	Korea, South	Russia	Ukraine	United Kindom	United States	World Total
2011	35,220	12,891	701,968	15,780	44,284	28,735	107,601	68,519	68,852	35,332	9,478	86,400	1,540,000
2012	34,524	13,507	723,880	15,609	42,661	27,257	107,232	69,073	70,392	33,511	9,579	88,700	1,560,000
2013	34,163	12,417	779,040	15,685	42,645	23,093	110,595	66,061	68,861	32,771	11,858	86,900	1,610,000
2014	33,912	12,730	822,300	16,143	42,943	23,714	110,666	71,542	70,548	27,373	12,120	88,200	1,670,000
2015	33,300	12,473	803,820	14,984	42,676	22,018	105,134	69,670	69,421	22,935	10,907	78,800	1,620,000
2016	31,275	12,646	808,366	14,413	42,080	23,373	104,775	68,576	70,808	24,128	7,635	78,500	1,630,000
2017	34,000	14,000	832,000	16,000	43,000		105,000	71,000	70,000	21,000	8,000	82,000	1,690,000
2018	35,000	15,000	928,000	17,000	42,000		104,000	72,000	72,000	21,000		87,000	1,810,000
2019[1]	32,000		996,000		40,000		99,000	71,000	72,000	21,000		88,000	1,860,000
2020[2]	28,000		1,000,000		33,000		81,000	65,000	69,000	19,000		72,000	1,800,000

[1] Preliminary. [2] Estimate. *Source: U.S. Geological Survey (USGS)*

Average Wholesale Prices of Iron and Steel in the United States

	No. 1 Heavy Melting Steel Scrap		Pittsburg Prices								
			Sheet Bars								
Year	Pittsburg	Chicago	Hot Rolled	Hot Rolled	Cold Finished	Hot Rolled Strip	Carbon Steel Plates	Cold Rolled Strip	Galvanized Sheets	Rail Road Steel Scrap[2]	Used Steel Cans[3]
	$ Per Gross Ton		Cents Per Pound							$ Per Gross Ton	
2002	101.06	89.92	16.46	----	23.26	----	----	----	22.00	NA	66.71
2003	128.32	113.82	14.80	----	25.15	----	----	----	20.08	----	116.21
2004	221.05	220.13	30.84	----	38.67	----	----	----	36.69	----	192.80
2005	199.10	196.75	27.83	----	44.96	----	----	----	33.77	----	172.00
2006	222.39	225.21	29.78	----	44.02	----	----	----	38.09	----	212.63
2007	250.98	262.80	26.89	----	45.26	----	----	----	38.25	----	244.65
2008	365.62	357.88	44.56	----	61.67	----	----	----	54.91	----	314.63
2009	204.21	206.14	24.60	----	42.10	----	----	----	34.23	----	121.84
2010	339.54	334.48	31.65	----	50.82	----	----	----	41.72	----	296.91
2011[1]	408.64	417.00	38.02	----	63.63	----	----	----	48.45	----	391.50

[1] Preliminary. [2] Specialties scrap. [3] Consumer buying prices. NA = Not available. *Source: American Metal Market (AMM)*

Salient Statistics of Steel in the United States In Thousands of Short Tons

Year	Pig Iron Production	Producer Price Index for Steel Mill Products (1982=100)	Raw Steel Production: By Type of Furnace: Basic Oxygen	Open Hearth	Electric[2]	Stainless	Carbon	Alloy	Total	Net Shipments Steel Mill Products	Total Steel Products: Exports	Imports
2011	30,200	216.2	34,943	----	57,430	2,282	87,192	5,754	95,239	83,300	12,200	25,900
2012	30,100	208.0	36,817	----	57,761	2,183	90,278	5,258	97,774	87,000	12,500	30,400
2013	30,300	195.0		----		2,238	88,956	4,530	95,790	86,600	11,500	29,200
2014	29,400	200.2		----		2,634	89,727	4,872	97,223	89,100	10,900	40,200
2015	25,400	177.1		----		2,590	81,129	3,230	86,861	78,500	9,050	35,200
2016	22,300	167.8		----		2,734	80,688	3,108	86,531	78,500	8,450	30,000
2017	22,400	187.4		----								
2018	24,100	211.1		----								
2019	22,300	204.0		----								
2020[1]	18,000	180.2		----								

[1] Preliminary. [2] Includes crucible steels. *Sources: American Iron & Steel Institute (AISI); U.S. Geological Survey (USGS)*

Production of Steel Ingots, Rate of Capability Utilization[1] in the United States In Percent

Year	Jan.	Feb.	Mar.	Apr.	May	June	July	Aug.	Sept.	Oct.	Nov.	Dec.	Average
2011	73.2	75.4	75.0	74.2	72.7	76.2	75.0	75.7	76.1	71.9	73.0	75.2	74.5
2012	77.6	80.7	79.6	80.9	79.2	74.8	73.3	76.3	70.4	68.0	70.1	71.7	75.2
2013	76.5	78.3	76.2	76.7	76.5	76.1	77.3	77.6	78.3	76.5	76.2	74.0	76.7
2014	75.8	77.9	77.7	76.6	77.3	78.5	79.6	80.2	78.1	76.5	77.2	74.6	77.5
2015	76.4	72.1	67.7	69.8	72.1	74.4	73.2	72.2	70.5	68.1	62.7	62.1	70.1
2016	68.7	73.1	72.1	72.6	74.3	75.1	71.3	70.8	68.0	65.4	67.1	67.8	70.5
2017	73.3	75.9	73.6	73.6	73.7	74.9	74.3	75.8	73.4	73.2	73.3	71.9	73.9
2018	73.6	77.9	78.3	76.0	77.1	77.4	78.4	79.4	79.6	80.2	81.2	79.4	78.2
2019	80.4	82.4	82.2	81.3	80.8	80.1	79.4	79.1	77.4	78.0	78.8	78.5	79.9
2020[1]	81.7	81.3	75.3	55.4	54.6	56.8	60.3	65.9	68.6	70.1	73.3	72.9	68.0

[1] Based on tonnage capability to produce raw steel for a full order book. [2] Preliminary. *Sources: American Iron and Steel Institute (AISI); U.S. Geological Survey (USGS)*

World Production of Pig Iron (Excludes Ferro-Alloys) In Thousands of Metric Tons

Year	Belgium	Brazil	China	France	Germany	India	Italy	Japan	Russia	Ukraine	United Kingdom	United States	World Total
2011	5,815	33,319	640,510	9,698	27,563	43,624	9,838	81,028	48,117	28,876	6,625	30,200	1,170,000
2012	4,073	26,900	663,500	9,532	26,493	47,987	9,424	81,405	50,459	28,484	7,183	32,100	1,190,000
2013	4,343	26,200	708,970	10,276	26,678	51,359	6,933	83,849	49,945	29,089	9,471	30,300	1,240,000
2014	4,388	27,016	713,740	10,866	27,379	55,166	6,371	83,872	51,460	24,801	9,705	29,400	1,260,000
2015	4,248	27,803	691,410	10,095	27,842	58,393	5,051	81,011	52,411	21,863	8,774	25,400	1,230,000
2016	4,869	26,031	700,740	9,724	27,264	62,994	6,048	80,170	51,829	23,613	6,218	22,300	1,240,000
2017	4,900	28,400	710,800	10,700	28,400	66,000	51,010	78,300	51,600	20,100	6,000	22,400	1,250,000
2018		29,000	771,000	12,000	27,000	71,000	5,000	77,000	52,000	21,000		24,000	1,250,000
2019[1]		26,000	809,000		25,000	74,000	5,000	75,000	50,000	20,000		22,000	1,280,000
2020[2]		23,000	830,000		21,000	56,000	4,000	61,000	49,000	19,000		18,000	1,200,000

[1] Preliminary. [2] Estimate. *Source: U.S. Geological Survey (USGS)*

Production of Pig Iron (Excludes Ferro-Alloys) in the United States In Thousands of Short Tons

Year	Jan.	Feb.	Mar.	Apr.	May	June	July	Aug.	Sept.	Oct.	Nov.	Dec.	Total
2011	2,400	2,490	2,790	2,550	2,870	2,820	2,520	2,610	2,540	3,010	2,990	3,190	32,780
2012	3,080	3,050	3,430	2,920	3,320	2,970	2,930	2,860	2,440	2,260	2,820	2,900	34,980
2013	3,060	2,760	3,040	2,800	2,880	2,760	2,760	2,890	2,880	2,870	2,760	2,780	34,240
2014	2,430	2,450	2,820	2,580	2,710	2,760	2,930	2,920	2,740	2,690	2,740	2,860	32,630
2015	2,760	2,310	2,390	2,330	2,530	2,670	2,830	2,690	2,390	2,270	2,120	2,110	29,400
2016	2,200	2,260	2,380	2,150	1,910	2,280	2,220	1,860	1,770	1,610	1,660	1,810	24,110
2017	1,940	1,930	1,960	1,870	1,940	1,830	1,860	1,930	1,850	1,690	1,770	1,840	22,410
2018	1,920	1,790	1,970	1,930	2,070	2,060	2,100	2,030	2,010	2,060	2,030	2,100	24,070
2019	1,880	1,840	2,080	1,860	1,930	1,900	1,830	1,840	1,870	1,700	1,720	1,850	22,300
2020[1]	1,680	1,920	1,910	1,110	949	1,170	1,310	1,520	1,610	1,700	1,700	1,660	18,239

[1] Preliminary. *Source: American Iron and Steel Institute*

Salient Statistics of Ferrous Scrap and Pig Iron in the United States In Thousands of Metric Tons

	Consumption: Ferrous Scrap & Pig Iron Charged To												Stocks, Dec. 31 Ferrous Scrap & Pig Iron at Consumers		
	Mfg. of Pig Iron & Steel Ingots & Castings			Iron Foundries & Misc. Users			Mfg. of Steel Castings	All Uses							
Year	Scrap	Pig Iron	Total	Scrap	Pig Iron	Total	(Scrap)	Ferrous Scrap	Pig Iron	Grand Total	Imports of Scrap[2]	Exports of Scrap[3]			Total
2008	56,600	33,500	92,050	7,760	844	8,608	2,070	66,400	34,400	102,760	3,600	21,500	4,340	885	5,660
2009	47,600	28,300	77,240	838	17	859	838	53,100	30,200	84,660	2,990	22,400	3,070	506	3,810
2010	53,100	34,100	88,690	5,180	1,910	7,093	1,810	60,100	36,000	97,590	3,780	20,500	3,330	418	3,909
2011	56,400	34,900	92,920	5,960	1,970	7,933	756	63,100	36,900	101,620	4,010	24,300	3,980	423	4,529
2012	55,800	35,400	94,780	6,710	1,980	8,693	639	63,100	37,400	104,080	3,720	21,400	4,170	405	4,722
2013	52,100	31,800	88,390	5,660	2,260	7,923	1,180	59,000	34,100	97,590	3,930	18,500	3,970	427	4,504
2014	51,900	25,900	82,590	5,560	2,100	7,663	1,190	58,600	28,100	91,490	4,220	15,300	4,070	442	4,729
2015	46,100	22,200	72,430	4,420	632	5,055	1,970	52,500	22,900	79,530	3,510	12,800	4,200	672	5,088
2016	44,900	20,700	70,380	5,020	1,620	6,643	3,100	53,000	22,400	80,180	3,860	12,600	4,340	440	5,017
2017[1]	45,600	19,800	67,290	4,130	634	4,767	409	50,200	20,500	72,590	4,630	15,000	4,440	497	5,202

[1] Preliminary. [2] Includes tinplate and terneplate. [3] Excludes used rails for rerolling and other uses and ships, boats, and other vessels for scrapping.
Source: U.S. Geological Survey (USGS)

Consumption of Pig Iron in the United States, by Type of Furance or Equipment In Thousands of Metric Tons

Year	Open Hearth	Electric	Cupola	Basic Oxygen Process	Air & Other Furnace	Direct Casting	Total
2008	----	3,350	401	30,600	5	36	33,600
2009	----	4,140	148	25,900	----	36	30,200
2010	----	4,740	55	31,200	----	16	36,000
2011	----	5,410	76	31,300	12	36	36,900
2012	----	5,790	57	31,500	10	36	37,400
2013	----	4,150	345	29,600	----	----	34,100
2014	----	4,230	148	23,800	----	----	28,100
2015	----	2,350	152	20,300	----	----	22,900
2016	----	3,620	155	18,600	----	----	22,400
2017[1]	----	3,310	160	17,000	----	----	20,500

[1] Preliminary. W = Withheld. *Source: U.S. Geological Survey (USGS)*

Volume of Trading of Hot Rolled Steel Futures in New York In Contracts

Year	Jan.	Feb.	Mar.	Apr.	May	June	July	Aug.	Sept.	Oct.	Nov.	Dec.	Total
2011	1,727	1,036	1,549	684	2,128	1,320	4,588	3,197	3,098	5,021	5,205	2,185	31,738
2012	6,214	5,905	1,187	1,772	4,421	2,848	4,081	3,055	3,838	5,301	2,823	2,422	43,867
2013	4,567	6,619	6,814	6,972	3,415	3,700	2,874	2,572	1,728	8,033	3,869	2,630	53,793
2014	3,953	2,376	6,002	4,292	4,220	1,082	3,543	905	4,863	5,777	7,661	3,556	48,230
2015	3,096	2,344	4,705	6,489	4,084	3,083	6,478	6,156	7,222	6,559	5,405	3,196	58,817
2016	3,058	7,225	4,165	8,576	2,303	4,454	3,415	5,006	4,506	5,836	2,623	2,717	53,884
2017	5,501	2,870	2,897	1,182	7,188	4,905	6,639	7,316	7,495	7,107	4,598	5,531	63,229
2018	10,435	9,072	9,655	12,074	9,487	5,226	10,861	17,235	6,668	9,665	11,986	7,205	119,569
2019	21,700	15,281	13,165	19,031	28,415	14,031	13,715	5,113	9,200	14,616	10,396	9,093	173,756
2020	15,359	11,979	30,709	14,865	17,503	18,463	10,608	21,175	20,827	22,823	19,194	16,901	220,406

Contract size = 20 short tons. *Source: CME Group; New York Mercantile Exchange (CME-NYMEX)*

Average Open Interest of Hot Rolled Steel Futures in New York In Contracts

Year	Jan.	Feb.	Mar.	Apr.	May	June	July	Aug.	Sept.	Oct.	Nov.	Dec.
2011	7,951	7,919	8,287	8,459	8,827	9,592	10,330	11,253	9,604	9,774	11,324	10,568
2012	10,469	12,009	13,228	12,572	13,910	14,995	13,809	12,914	13,181	12,982	12,382	10,394
2013	9,679	10,033	12,210	14,098	14,810	14,668	14,328	14,565	14,114	13,517	13,613	11,741
2014	10,308	10,308	9,720	9,537	10,242	10,769	11,092	11,507	12,037	15,739	19,703	22,501
2015	21,609	20,954	18,637	18,859	19,351	19,356	20,474	20,783	21,273	22,758	23,472	24,299
2016	23,157	24,528	24,610	22,721	21,525	20,796	19,304	18,927	17,829	18,390	16,825	14,694
2017	13,068	12,862	13,145	12,646	12,815	13,952	13,369	14,007	14,493	14,065	13,384	13,600
2018	12,892	12,056	13,044	14,466	14,375	13,879	13,800	16,712	15,926	16,338	17,185	16,261
2019	17,430	20,320	19,221	17,425	18,040	18,600	17,519	16,597	15,791	14,393	15,249	15,535
2020	17,062	18,409	22,053	23,953	23,226	22,892	23,499	24,443	23,059	21,712	21,311	22,280

Contract size = 20 short tons. *Source: CME Group; New York Mercantile Exchange (CME-NYMEX)*

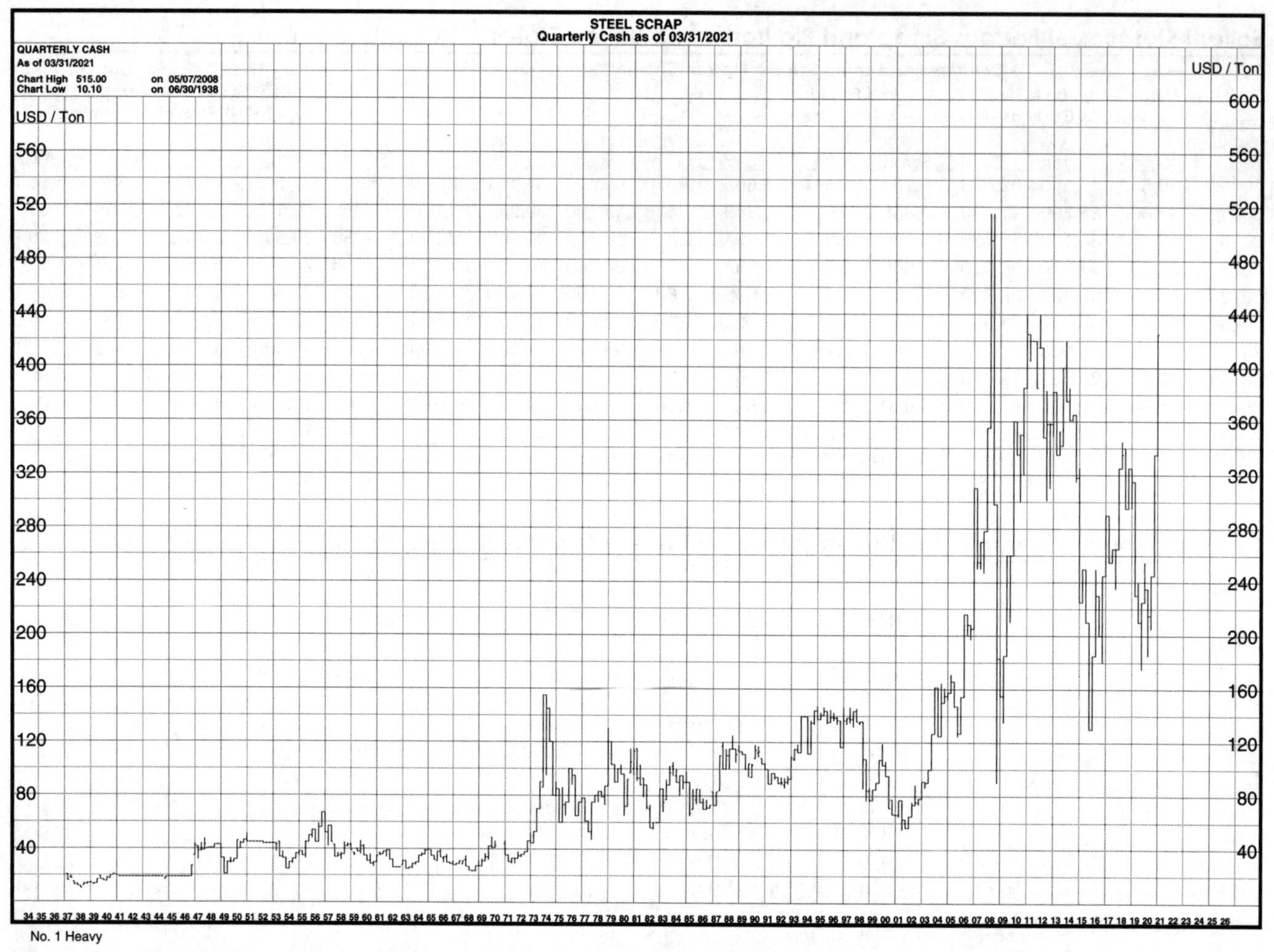

Wholesale Price of No. 1 Heavy Melting Steel Scrap in Chicago In Dollars Per Metric Ton

Year	Jan.	Feb.	Mar.	Apr.	May	June	July	Aug.	Sept.	Oct.	Nov.	Dec.	Average
2011	429.00	427.37	425.00	425.00	407.86	419.32	420.00	420.00	420.00	411.43	388.75	408.68	416.87
2012	436.25	417.50	415.00	406.43	405.00	358.86	310.05	372.30	361.95	320.43	349.20	358.17	375.93
2013	358.00	350.89	375.71	363.86	342.82	336.20	351.36	351.18	343.35	344.61	370.26	395.16	356.95
2014	414.29	396.00	378.10	383.64	373.67	362.90	362.55	363.00	364.71	350.13	322.11	317.43	365.71
2015	323.60	250.00	225.91	225.00	229.00	246.36	242.27	222.86	211.43	171.36	136.32	130.00	217.84
2016	146.84	150.00	180.43	221.43	246.19	233.64	222.00	220.00	204.76	183.81	198.75	235.48	203.61
2017	274.75	261.58	283.91	266.00	260.00	255.91	255.00	263.26	265.00	240.45	235.00	259.00	259.99
2018	289.29	295.00	319.55	341.19	336.82	335.00	340.00	321.74	300.26	303.26	324.00	325.00	319.26
2019	302.14	295.00	311.19	294.76	266.82	236.00	222.27	236.36	216.00	181.09	190.79	219.29	247.64
2020	249.29	239.21	235.00	201.67	210.50	215.00	207.27	205.00	239.29	245.00	252.89	320.45	235.05

Source: American Metal Market (AMM)

World Production of Iron Ore[3] In Thousands of Metric Tons (Gross Weight)

Year	Australia	Brazil	Canada	China	India	Mauritania	Russia	South Africa	Sweden	Ukraine	United States	Venezula	World Total
2011	488,000	398,131	35,705	442,179	168,582	11,400	103,607	58,057	26,100	65,807	56,200	17,037	2,030,000
2012	519,356	400,822	38,892	420,206	122,491	11,700	104,010	67,100	26,200	67,100	54,700	15,403	2,070,000
2013	609,730	386,270	42,063	417,287	140,416	11,975	102,157	71,645	25,300	70,400	52,800	11,198	2,190,000
2014	739,682	411,183	43,173	410,123	138,000	13,306	102,019	80,759	25,700	68,300	56,100	11,256	2,330,000
2015	809,882	430,836	46,220	374,838	142,399	11,607	100,985	72,806	24,500	66,900	46,100	11,716	2,310,000
2016	857,726	430,000	47,083	347,594	184,511	13,268	101,358	66,456	26,900	62,900	41,800	12,000	2,340,000
2017	880,000	440,000	47,000	340,000	190,000	13,300	100,000	68,000	27,000	63,000	46,000	12,000	2,430,000
2018	900,000	460,000	52,400	335,000	205,000		96,100	74,300	35,800	60,300	49,500		2,460,000
2019[1]	919,000	405,000	58,500	351,000	238,000		97,500	72,400	35,700	63,200	46,900		2,450,000
2020[2]	900,000	400,000	57,000	340,000	230,000		95,000	71,000	35,000	62,000	37,000		2,400,000

[1] Preliminary. [2] Estimate. [3] Iron ore, iron ore concentrates and iron ore agglomerates. *Source: U.S. Geological Survey (USGS)*

Salient Statistics of Iron Ore[3] in the United States In Thousands of Metric Tons

Year	Net Import Reliance As a % of Apparent Consump	Production Total	Production Lake Superior	Production Other Regions	Shipments	Value Million $ (at Mine)	Average Value $ at Mine Per Ton	Stock, Dec. 31 Mines	Stock, Dec. 31 Consuming Plants	Stock, Dec. 31 Lake Erie Docks	Imports	Exports	Consumption	Total
2011	E	54,700	----	----	55,600	5,850.0	99.45	3,260	----	----	5,300	11,100	49,100	841.0
2012	E	54,700	----	----	53,900	5,080.0	116.48	4,440	----	----	5,200	11,200	46,500	759.0
2013	E	52,800	----	----	53,400	4,610.0	87.42	2,350	----	----	3,200	11,000	47,100	426.0
2014	E	56,100	----	----	55,000	4,730.0	84.43	4,460	----	----	5,140	12,400	46,700	676.0
2015	E	46,100	----	----	43,500	3,750.0	81.19	4,760	----	----	4,550	7,500	42,100	455.0
2016	E	41,800	----	----	46,600	3,050.0	73.11	2,990	----	----	3,010	8,710	37,900	241.0
2017	E	47,900	----	----	46,900	3,760.0	78.54	3,930	----	----	3,710	10,600	40,100	355.0
2018	E	49,500	----	----	50,400		93.00	3,100	----	----	3,810	1,300	41,200	
2019[1]	E	48,000	----	----	50,000		112.15	2,700	----	----	5,100	13,000	41,000	
2020[2]	E		----	----					----	----				

[1] Preliminary. [2] Estimate. [3] Usable iron ore exclusive of ore containing 5% or more manganese and includes byproduct ore.
NA = Not available. *Source: U.S. Geological Survey (USGS)*

U.S. Imports (for Consumption) of Iron Ore[2] In Thousands of Metric Tons

Year	Australia	Brazil	Canada	Chile	Mauritania	Peru	Sweden	Venezuela	Total
2008	----	2,620	5,900	215	----	59	88	68	9,250
2009	----	188	3,140	203	----	34	31	21	3,870
2010	----	506	4,490	131	----	14	54	251	6,420
2011	----	562	3,910	165	----	14	81	279	5,270
2012	----	739	3,820	104	----	44	72	75	5,160
2013	----	630	2,090	152	----	12	49	----	3,250
2014	----	1,730	2,860	----	----	35	154	----	5,100
2015	----	2,050	2,040	1	----	22	85	25	4,550
2016	[3]	1,760	557	62	----	66	350	28	3,010
2017[1]	24	2,040	790	283	----	31	363	----	3,710

[1] Preliminary. [2] Including agglomerates. [3] Less than 1/2 unit. *Source: U.S. Geological Survey (USGS)*

Iron Ore Stocks in the United States, at End of Month In Thousands of Metric Tons

Year	Jan.	Feb.	Mar.	Apr.	May	June	July	Aug.	Sept.	Oct.	Nov.	Dec.
2011	4,250	7,470	9,750	9,250	8,970	8,200	7,060	6,380	5,140	4,660	4,250	3,390
2012	3,200	6,750	8,910	7,730	6,410	5,340	3,850	2,980	2,660	2,970	3,020	2,200
2013	3,290	6,580	8,960	7,830	6,350	5,390	4,130	3,320	2,770	2,110	2,470	3,690
2014	6,530	9,240	12,400	13,600	12,500	11,300	9,770	8,190	7,320	6,600	6,290	5,430
2015	6,640	10,600	14,500	14,800	13,100	11,500	9,740	8,040	7,460	7,070	7,550	7,490
2016	8,940	11,800	13,600	12,100	11,000	10,200	9,470	8,300	7,630	7,170	6,500	6,050
2017	6,730	9,970	12,400	12,200	11,200	10,100	9,080	7,670	6,470	6,210	6,300	6,120
2018	8,290	12,000	14,700	14,300	13,000	12,200	10,900	9,520	8,270	7,480	4,120	3,100
2019	4,390	7,490	9,910	9,330	9,150	8,020	6,850	5,550	4,460	3,800	3,230	2,720
2020[1]	4,790	8,100	10,700	9,430	6,900	4,980	3,760	4,410	4,470	4,070	3,690	4,060

[1] Preliminary. *Source: U.S. Geological Survey (USGS)*

Lard

Lard is the layer of fat found along the back and underneath the skin of a hog. The hog's fat is purified by washing it with water, melting it under constant heat, and straining it several times. Lard is an important byproduct of the meatpacking industry. It is valued highly as cooking oil because there is very little smoke when it is heated. However, demand for lard in cooking is declining because of the trend toward healthier eating. Lard is also used for medicinal purposes such as ointments, plasters, liniments, and occasionally as a laxative for children. Lard production is directly proportional to commercial hog production, meaning the largest producers of hogs are the largest producers of lard.

Prices – The average monthly wholesale price of lard in 2020 rose +15.2% to 37.50 cents per pound, far below the 2011 record high of 54.55 cents per pound.

Supply – World production of lard in the 2018/19 marketing year fell by -1.3% yr/yr to 8.772 million metric tons, which was down from the 2017/18 record high of 8.884. The world's largest lard producers were China with 39.4% of world production, the U.S with 8.0%, Russia with 7.1%, Germany with 6.3%, Brazil with 6.0%, Spain with 4.6%, and Poland with 3.1%. U.S. production of lard in 2018/19 rose +4.2% yr/yr to 1.549 billion pounds.

Demand – U.S. consumption of lard in 2011 rose +0.5% to 148.316 million pounds, down from 2008 record high of 490.602 million pounds. The current level of consumption is less than 10% of the consumption of 1.574 billion pounds in 1971.

Trade – U.S. exports of lard in 2018/19 rose by +33.8% to 49.6 million pounds and accounted for only 3.2% of U.S. production.

World Production of Lard In Thousands of Metric Tons

Year	Brazil	Canada	China	France	Germany	Italy	Japan	Poland	Romania	Spain	United States	Ex-USSR	World Total
2010-11	429.5	130.7	3,421.7	136.6	566.7	208.4	51.0	234.3	76.2	302.2	586.9	448.3	8,024.4
2011-12	443.0	132.8	3,546.2	133.2	561.5	208.4	51.4	222.7	75.4	309.3	599.7	466.2	8,185.7
2012-13	439.6	131.9	3,670.5	132.1	562.3	213.0	51.3	213.9	73.7	301.3	598.7	499.2	8,356.7
2013-14	443.5	131.3	3,745.1	132.1	558.0	186.3	51.0	231.5	70.5	310.7	594.3	514.5	8,434.5
2014-15	444.3	132.5	3,623.4	133.5	570.4	190.9	49.0	243.7	72.1	334.4	625.1	528.2	8,435.2
2015-16	470.8	136.9	3,640.9	135.6	566.1	198.4	51.0	252.6	71.9	356.0	639.9	556.8	8,593.0
2016-17[1]	488.1	137.7	3,684.7	143.2	565.6	193.7	50.5	253.9	70.9	366.0	657.6	577.3	8,727.8
2017-18[2]	504.4	136.9	3,715.0	148.9	547.1	193.4	51.2	267.2	75.5	392.6	674.3	598.7	8,883.6
2018-19[3]	522.2	138.7	3,459.2	149.9	553.9	195.0	51.6	272.2	76.0	407.8	702.8	621.5	8,772.0

[1] Preliminary. [2] Estimate. [3] Forecast. *Source: The Oil World*

Supply and Distribution of Lard in the United States In Millions of Pounds

	Supply			Disappearance						
Year	Production	Stocks Oct. 1	Total Supply	Domestic	Baking or Frying Fats	Margarine[3]	Exports	Total Disap-pearance	Direct Use	Per Capita (Lbs.)
2011-12	1,322.1	20.0	1,342.1	830.2	W	W	54.7	884.9	NA	NA
2012-13	1,319.9	20.0	1,339.9	819.8	W	W	61.5	881.2	NA	NA
2013-14	1,310.2	20.0	1,330.2	821.9	W	W	51.8	873.7	NA	NA
2014-15	1,378.1	20.0	1,398.1	881.1	W	W	46.6	927.7	NA	NA
2015-16	1,410.7	8.6	1,419.3	901.4	W	W	42.1	943.5	NA	NA
2016-17	1,449.7	8.0	1,457.7	934.7	W	W	38.0	972.8	NA	NA
2017-18	1,486.6	6.8	1,493.3	960.5	W	W	37.1	997.6	NA	NA
2018-19[1]	1,549.4	10.8	1,560.2	1,002.6	W	W	49.6	1,052.2	NA	NA
2019-20[2]		9.0		1,103.0	W	W	43.0	1,146.0	NA	NA

[1] Preliminary. [2] Forecast. [3] Includes edible tallow. W = Withheld.
Source: Economic Research Service, U.S. Department of Agriculture (ERS-USDA)

Consumption of Lard (Edible and Inedible) in the United States In Millions of Pounds

Year	Jan.	Feb.	Mar.	Apr.	May	June	July	Aug.	Sept.	Oct.	Nov.	Dec.	Total
2002	26.4	26.1	21.8	26.7	24.8	21.2	22.9	26.4	23.6	26.4	28.1	28.7	303.2
2003	22.6	22.3	23.4	21.4	23.3	24.0	23.0	21.4	22.5	24.3	20.2	21.0	269.5
2004	22.9	25.8	25.9	23.9	23.5	22.0	19.1	19.7	21.3	22.4	21.9	19.9	268.1
2005	19.0	15.4	21.4	18.7	19.9	20.4	18.9	19.5	20.1	19.7	22.2	17.9	233.1
2006	15.7	16.4	20.6	21.4	20.2	16.7	14.9	17.7	17.8	18.9	22.3	20.9	223.4
2007	21.6	16.2	22.2	19.7	20.5	20.8	22.8	23.9	22.8	31.1	29.7	31.4	282.8
2008	34.8	32.2	44.6	50.7	50.8	44.4	47.8	39.7	44.0	37.5	31.7	32.2	490.6
2009	23.4	17.3	26.8	26.0	26.3	25.8	21.3	20.5	25.4	32.4	29.9	27.0	302.3
2010	22.2	W	38.8	W	30.4	30.8	30.4	32.4	30.1	31.1	30.4	28.8	366.6
2011[1]	22.2	26.3	36.0	W	28.8	29.6	31.4	W	W	W	W	W	348.7

[1] Preliminary. *Source: Bureau of the Census, U.S. Department of Commerce*

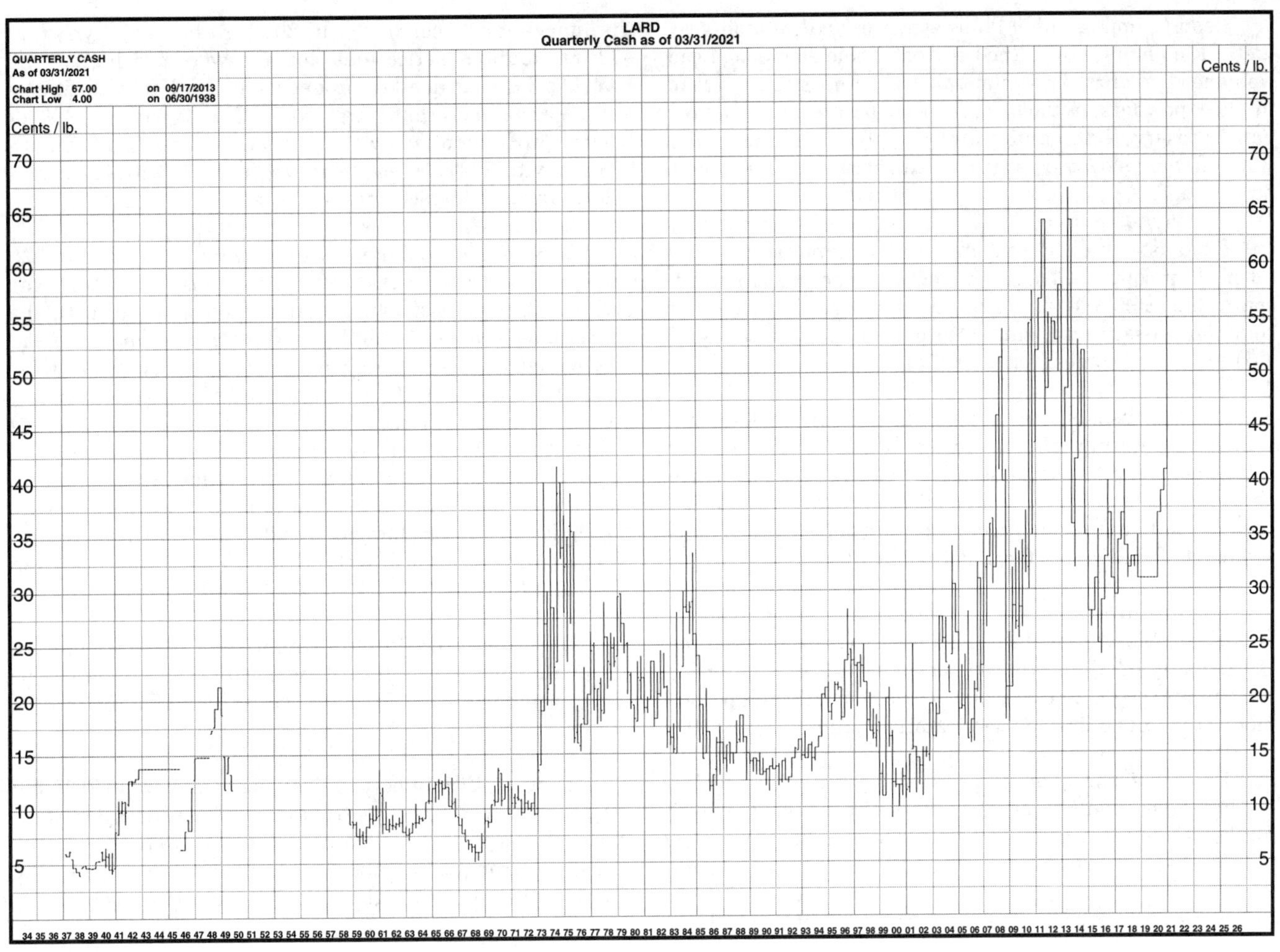

Average Wholesale Price of Lard--Loose, Tank Cars, in Chicago In Cents Per Pound

Year	Jan.	Feb.	Mar.	Apr.	May	June	July	Aug.	Sept.	Oct.	Nov.	Dec.	Average
2011	48.50	49.60	52.00	51.50	54.31	56.75	63.00	58.96	61.33	61.10	48.86	48.71	54.55
2012	NA	52.55	54.60	52.59	54.82	54.83	53.00	NA	NA	51.60	57.00	NA	53.87
2013	52.45	45.56	NA	43.50	44.50	48.50	53.25	56.89	64.78	43.00	48.00	41.50	49.27
2014	33.00	38.00	40.67	53.00	NA	45.00	NA	46.50	50.67	48.00	42.81	35.91	43.36
2015	29.50	28.00	NA	26.64	28.00	NA	31.00	31.00	NA	34.23	35.50	28.80	30.30
2016	24.00	NA	29.00	33.00	NA	NA	NA	36.53	36.75	34.00	NA	31.00	32.04
2017	30.10	NA	NA	NA	NA	34.50	NA	NA	35.75	36.00	38.17	37.00	35.25
2018	32.08	32.20	NA	NA	NA	32.50	NA	32.38	32.93	33.00	34.33	31.00	32.55
2019	NA	NA	NA	NA	NA	NA	NA	NA	NA	NA	NA	NA	NA
2020	NA	NA	NA	32.00	35.50	36.50	NA	39.00	NA	NA	41.00	41.00	37.50

Source: Economic Research Service, U.S. Department of Agriculture (ERS-USDA)

Cold Storage Holdings of all Lard[1] in the United States, on First of Month In Millions of Pounds

Year	Jan.	Feb.	Mar.	Apr.	May	June	July	Aug.	Sept.	Oct.	Nov.	Dec.
2002	13.2	18.0	16.4	16.5	20.3	22.4	18.9	18.3	12.0	10.5	14.6	11.3
2003	10.5	14.0	19.6	18.7	16.5	13.5	11.9	9.7	8.4	9.3	10.1	12.4
2004	13.3	19.8	18.6	20.3	20.5	15.0	12.9	10.8	10.3	11.8	11.4	13.2
2005	13.7	14.6	20.6	19.0	17.8	12.3	12.0	12.3	12.5	13.0	12.2	14.7
2006	9.6	11.5	13.7	13.6	9.3	9.9	13.0	12.4	13.0	11.5	16.1	16.0
2007	16.4	14.9	13.3	18.5	10.9	14.6	11.3	12.8	11.0	9.2	14.6	18.8
2008	14.0	22.4	20.4	22.9	23.0	19.5	22.7	13.6	18.0	17.8	16.1	20.4
2009	12.1	13.6	15.4	16.2	14.5	18.8	17.3	21.6	20.5	26.7	18.5	15.4
2010	13.9	14.5	21.0	22.9	26.1	15.7	19.4	17.9	14.1	13.8	15.6	15.5
2011[2]	17.5	20.5	25.3	20.9	26.2	19.9	23.4	23.9	NA	NA	NA	NA

[1] Stocks in factories and warehouses (except that in hands of retailers). [2] Preliminary. *Source: Bureau of the Census, U.S. Department of Commerce*

Lead

Lead (atomic symbol Pb) is a dense, toxic, bluish-gray metallic element, and is the heaviest stable element. Lead was one of the first known metals. The ancients used lead in face powders, rouges, mascaras, paints, condiments, wine preservatives, and water supply plumbing. The Romans were slowly poisoned by lead because of its diverse daily usage.

Lead is usually found in ore with zinc, silver, and most often copper. The most common lead ore is galena, containing 86.6% lead. Cerussite and angleside are other common varieties of lead. More than half of the lead currently used comes from recycling.

Lead is used in building construction, bullets and shot, tank and pipe lining, storage batteries, and electric cable sheathing. Lead is used extensively as a protective shielding for radioactive material (e.g., X-ray apparatus) because of its high density and nuclear properties. Lead is also part of solder, pewter, and fusible alloys.

Lead futures and options trade at the London Metal Exchange (LME). The LME lead futures contract calls for the delivery of 25 metric tons of at least 99.970% purity lead ingots (pigs). The contract is priced in U.S. dollars per metric ton. Lead first started trading on the LME in 1903.

Prices – The average price of pig lead among U.S. producers reached a record high of $1.25 per pound in 2007 but has since remained below that level. Pig lead prices in 2020 ended the year down -8.6% at 91.85 cents per pound.

Supply – World smelter production of lead (both primary and secondary) in 2016 rose +3.8% yr/yr to 11.000 million metric tons, for a new record high. The world's largest smelter producers of lead (both primary and secondary) that year were China with 42.4% of world production, followed by the U.S. with 10.1%, South Korea with 7.6%, India with 4.7%, the UK with 3.4%, and Germany and Mexico with 3.1 % each.

U.S. mine production of recoverable lead in 2020 rose +6.5% yr/yr to 284,182 metric tons. Missouri was responsible for 94% of U.S. production in 2009, with the remainder produced mainly by Idaho and Montana. Lead recovered from scrap in the U.S. (secondary production) fell -0.6% yr/yr in 2020 (annualized through November) to 1.149 million metric tons, down from the 2008 record high of 1.220 million metric tons. The amount of lead recovered from scrap is almost three times the amount of lead produced in the U.S. from mines. The value of U.S. secondary lead production in 2016 rose +4.7% yr/yr to $2.210 billion, but still well below the 2008 record high of $3.040 billion.

Demand – U.S. lead consumption in 2020 (annualized through November) fell -6.5% yr/yr to 1.524 million metric tons, still down from the 2017 record high of 1.760 million metric tons.

Trade – U.S. imports of lead pigs and bars in 2016 fell -0.2% yr/yr to 416,000 metric tons. U.S. lead exports that year were comprised of ore concentrate (341,000 metric tons), unwrought lead (36,400 metric tons), scrap (16,700 metric tons), and wrought lead (2,500 metric tons).

World Smelter (Primary and Secondary) Production of Lead In Thousands of Metric Tons

Year	Australia[3]	Belgium[4]	Canada[3]	China[2]	France	Germany	Italy	Japan	Mexico[3]	Spain	United Kingdom[3]	United States	World Total
2008	248.0	259.1	3,200.0	415.1	294.0	211.8	279.5	244.1	243.8	125.0	283.0	1,275	8,730
2009	229.0	258.9	3,710.0	390.6	332.0	149.0	192.4	326.9	239.4	138.0	279.0	1,213	8,850
2010	204.0	272.9	4,200.0	404.0	367.0	150.0	215.8	327.9	286.0	165.0	295.0	1,255	9,610
2011	213.0	282.6	4,600.0	429.0	419.0	149.5	218.0	416.9	317.7	177.0	269.0	1,248	10,300
2012	210.0	299.2	4,590.0	424.0	460.0	138.4	209.0	460.0	384.0	160.0	311.9	1,261	10,600
2013	232.5	281.8	4,940.0	400.0	463.0	180.0	208.1	427.7	371.0	157.0	329.2	1,274	10,900
2014	225.8	281.5	4,740.0	380.0	477.0	210.0	202.7	639.0	363.0	166.0	267.0	1,060	10,600
2015	222.3	268.9	4,700.0	378.0	501.0	210.0	194.4	641.0	343.9	172.0	267.0	1,050	10,600
2016[1]	223.8	274.2	4,666.0	339.0	519.0	187.0	199.1	831.0	341.0	170.0	374.6	1,110	11,000

[1] Preliminary. [2] Estimate. [3] Refinded & bullion. [4] Includes scrap. *Source: U.S. Geological Survey (USGS)*

Consumption of Lead in the United States, by Products In Metric Tons

Year	Ammunition: Shot and Bullets	Bearing Metals	Brass and Bronze	Cable Covering	Calking Lead	Casting Metals	Pipes, Traps & Bends[2]	Sheet Lead	Solder	Storage Batteries: Total	Other Metal Products[3]	Other Oxides[4]	Total U.S. Consumption
2008	67,400	1,250	2,460	W	W	20,100	1,190	26,400	6,610	1,290,000	7,670	10,700	1,440,000
2009	67,900	1,100	1,370	W	W	15,900	1,130	25,400	6,450	1,140,000	5,790	10,100	1,290,000
2010	65,700	1,230	1,410	W	W	16,400	990	23,400	6,420	1,280,000	8,800	9,760	1,430,000
2011	75,100	1,150	1,620	W	W	16,000	6,110	7,170	6,170	1,250,000	23,100	9,760	1,410,000
2012	73,900	1,090	1,120	W	W	16,700	6,240	7,390	6,280	1,190,000	18,500	9,740	1,350,000
2013	84,800	1,110	1,420	W	W	20,400	7,030	4,870	8,200	1,200,000	177	9,740	1,390,000
2014	85,300	1,150	2,990	W	W	19,100	6,900	6,090	7,380	1,320,000	33,000	9,740	1,510,000
2015	78,400	1,090	1,580	W	W	14,200	7,060	9,020	6,490	1,770,000	31,100	11,500	1,960,000
2016[1]	69,800	1,060	1,580	W	W	15,000	7,160	6,510	6,520	1,800,000	31,100	11,700	1,970,000

[1] Preliminary. [2] Including building. [3] Including terne metal, type metal, and lead consumed in foil, collapsible tubes, annealing, plating, galvanizing and fishing weights. [4] Includes paints, glass and ceramic products, and other pigments and chemicals. W = Withheld.
Source: U.S. Geological Survey (USGS)

Salient Statistics of Lead in the United States In Thousands of Metric Tons

Year	Net Import Reliance as a % of Apparent Consump	Production of Refined Lead From: Domestic Ores[3]	Foreighn Ores[3]	Total Primary	Total Value of Refined Million $	Secondary Lead Recovered: As Soft Lead	In Anti-monial Lead	In Other Alloys	Total	Total Value of Secondary Million USD	Stocks, Dec. 31: Primary	Con-sumer[4]	Average Price Cents Per Pound: New York	London
2011	19	118	W	118	----	966	167	----	1,130	3,040	W	48.3	121.70	108.92
2012	26	111	W	111	----	863	236	----	1,150	2,790	W	63.0	114.16	93.53
2013	26	114	W	114	----	860	282	----	1,160	2,910	W	61.1	----	97.15
2014	35	----	W	----	----	786	224	8.8	1,060	2,640	W	56.4	----	95.04
2015	31	----	W	----	----	827	214	4.8	1,050	2,110	W	60.1	----	81.02
2016	33	----	W	----	----	877	223	5.7	1,110	2,210	W	60.3	----	84.84
2017	36	----	W	----	----				1,140		W		----	105.10
2018	30	----	W	----	----				1,140		W		----	101.80
2019[1]	29	----	W	----	----				1,170		W		----	91.00
2020[2]	24	----	W	----	----				1,100		W		----	81.50

[1] Preliminary. [2] Estimate. [3] And base bullion. [4] Also at secondary smelters. W = Withheld. E = Net exporter.
Source: U.S. Geological Survey (USGS)

U.S. Foreign Trade of Lead In Thousands of Metric Tons

Year	Exports: Ore Con-centrate	Un-wrought Lead[3]	Wrought Lead[4]	Scrap	Ash & Re-sidues[5]	Imports for Consumption: Ores, Flue Dust or Fume & Mattes	Base Bullion	Pigs & Bars	Re-claimed Scrap, Etc.	Value Million $	General Import From: Ore, Flue, Dust & Matte: Aus-tralia	Can-ada	Peru	Pigs & Bars: Can-ada	Mexico	Peru
2007	300.0	51.8	4.6	129.0	----	----	2.0	263.0	2.4	591.4	----	----	----	208.0	35.6	16.5
2008	277.0	68.1	6.2	175.0	----	----	2.7	309.0	1.3	681.6	----	----	----	219.0	58.1	10.6
2009	287.0	77.6	4.3	140.0	----	----	0.8	251.0	1.3	418.8	----	----	----	205.0	41.1	1.0
2010	299.0	77.7	5.6	43.5	----	----	0.6	271.0	3.7	575.9	----	----	----	237.0	29.4	----
2011	223.0	40.1	7.0	31.1	----	----	0.4	313.0	2.4	718.4	----	----	----	250.0	56.0	0.1
2012	214.0	47.0	6.3	25.9	----	1.5	1.0	349.0	16.8	730.4	----	----	----	240.0	56.1	0.0
2013	215.0	41.6	6.6	34.9	----	0.0	1.9	500.0	15.6	1,060.4	----	----	----	257.0	111.0	39.6
2014	356.0	55.3	5.0	36.4	----	----	1.1	593.0	11.4	1,243.8	----	----	----	264.0	120.0	49.7
2015[1]	350.0	50.1	2.9	29.1	----	----	0.3	417.0	3.5	771.2	----	----	----	162.0	105.0	----
2016[2]	341.0	36.4	2.6	16.7	----	----	0.2	416.0	2.0	817.6	----	----	----	176.0	71.8	1.4

[1] Preliminary. [2] Estimate. [3] And lead alloys. [4] Blocks, pigs, etc. [5] Less than 1/2 unit. *Source: U.S. Geological Survey (USGS)*

Annual Mine Production of Recoverable Lead in the United States In Metric Tons

Year	Idaho	Missouri	Montana	Total
2011	W	W	W	334,000
2012	----	----	----	336,000
2013	----	----	----	331,000
2014	----	----	----	367,000
2015	----	----	----	360,000
2016	----	----	----	336,000
2017	----	----	----	311,000
2018	----	----	----	271,000
2019[1]	----	----	----	266,800
2020[2]	----	----	----	291,000

[1] Preliminary. [2] Estimate. W = Withheld, included in Total. *Source: U.S. Geological Survey (USGS)*

Mine Production of Recoverable Lead in the United States In Metric Tons

Year	Jan.	Feb.	Mar.	Apr.	May	June	July	Aug.	Sept.	Oct.	Nov.	Dec.	Total
2011	30,400	25,100	29,500	32,500	27,400	27,200	29,300	24,400	29,200	25,200	28,100	30,700	334,000
2012	28,700	27,900	27,600	27,300	27,600	28,100	27,500	29,700	27,000	27,500	27,700	29,100	336,000
2013	27,000	25,717	26,000	28,600	28,900	28,000	28,500	28,700	29,600	27,200	25,700	28,600	331,000
2014	30,300	26,600	28,800	31,300	32,800	29,600	30,500	30,389	31,200	32,000	32,700	34,500	367,000
2015	28,200	30,100	35,700	32,100	31,300	28,900	31,200	31,500	26,100	27,100	27,200	27,400	360,000
2016	29,100	26,000	27,900	30,100	27,000	28,400	24,800	30,400	28,400	28,000	22,000	20,000	336,000
2017	25,400	25,500	31,300	27,900	24,400	25,300	23,100	25,400	21,000	24,900	27,500	21,900	311,000
2018	21,700	17,400	20,700	22,200	23,000	23,400	24,000	W	W	W	W	W	271,000
2019	22,800	19,800	18,100	24,600	26,700	23,800	22,100	24,700	24,000	17,200	21,300	21,700	266,800
2020[1]	22,600	22,900	23,100	19,900	23,500	24,600	26,100	28,700	23,700	24,000	22,700	29,200	291,000

[1] Preliminary. W = Withheld to avoid disclosing company proprietary data. *Source: U.S. Geological Survey (USGS)*

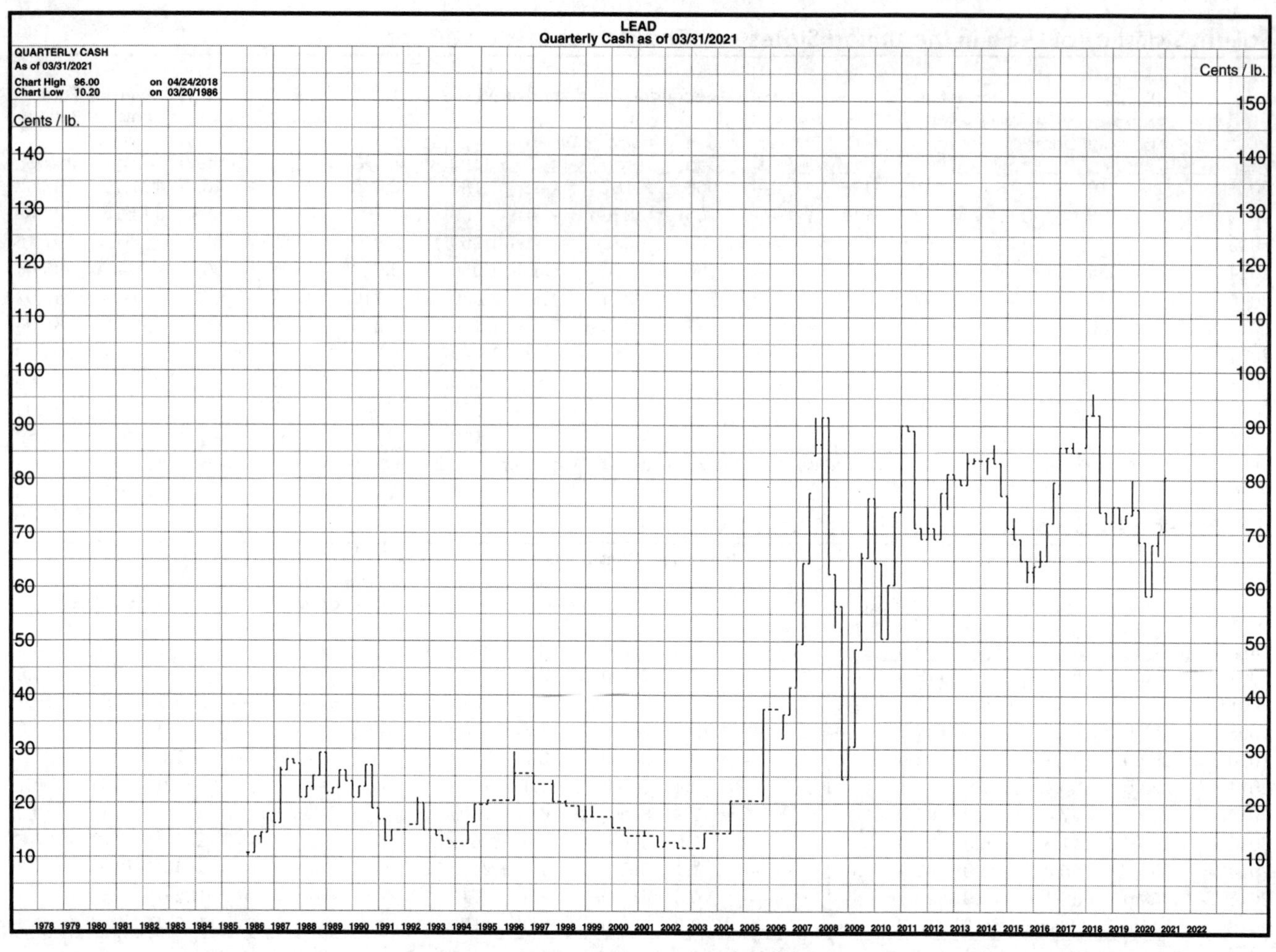

Average Price of Pig Lead, U.S. Primary Producers (Common Corroding)[1] In Cents Per Pound

Year	Jan.	Feb.	Mar.	Apr.	May	June	July	Aug.	Sept.	Oct.	Nov.	Dec.	Average
2011	123.37	122.83	124.67	130.68	117.43	121.38	129.14	116.63	111.36	95.84	97.61	100.19	115.93
2012	103.68	105.11	101.81	100.71	98.42	91.70	92.52	93.54	106.29	112.62	113.81	117.08	103.11
2013	120.19	121.68	112.79	106.17	105.82	109.38	106.18	111.56	107.53	108.72	107.97	109.40	110.62
2014	110.40	108.69	106.23	107.71	107.99	108.35	112.31	114.44	108.97	105.16	104.11	100.29	107.89
2015	95.45	94.25	93.41	102.60	103.12	94.25	92.01	93.72	91.66	88.54	84.72	89.21	93.58
2016	86.75	92.12	93.74	90.37	89.89	89.70	95.09	95.44	100.00	103.71	109.36	111.81	96.50
2017	111.53	114.71	112.58	110.76	106.56	106.67	112.97	116.68	117.90	123.74	121.73	123.64	114.96
2018	127.40	126.93	118.69	116.99	116.98	120.64	109.97	103.62	101.77	99.98	97.87	99.13	111.66
2019	100.38	103.54	103.14	98.27	92.49	95.74	99.68	102.70	103.98	108.61	102.06	95.79	100.53
2020	96.89	94.35	88.10	83.78	81.89	87.40	91.00	96.85	94.32	90.19	96.04	101.42	91.85

[1] New York Delivery. *Source: American Metal Market*

Refiners Production[1] of Lead in the United States In Metric Tons

Year	Jan.	Feb.	Mar.	Apr.	May	June	July	Aug.	Sept.	Oct.	Nov.	Dec.	Total
2001	NA	NA	NA	NA	NA	NA	NA	NA	NA	NA	NA	NA	290,000
2002	NA	NA	NA	NA	NA	NA	NA	NA	NA	NA	NA	NA	262,000
2003	NA	NA	NA	NA	NA	NA	NA	NA	NA	NA	NA	NA	245,000
2004	NA	NA	NA	NA	NA	NA	NA	NA	NA	NA	NA	NA	NA
2005	NA	NA	NA	NA	NA	NA	NA	NA	NA	NA	NA	NA	143,000
2006	NA	NA	NA	NA	NA	NA	NA	NA	NA	NA	NA	NA	143,000
2007	NA	NA	NA	NA	NA	NA	NA	NA	NA	NA	NA	NA	NA
2008	NA	NA	NA	NA	NA	NA	NA	NA	NA	NA	NA	NA	NA
2009	NA	NA	NA	NA	NA	NA	NA	NA	NA	NA	NA	NA	NA
2010[2]	NA	NA	NA	NA	NA	NA	NA	NA	NA	NA	NA	NA	NA

[1] Represents refined lead produced from domestic ores by primary smelters plus small amounts of secondary material passing through these smelters. Includes GSA metal purchased for remelt. [2] Preliminary. NA = Not available. *Source: U.S. Geological Survey (USGS)*

Total Stocks of Lead[1] in the United States at Refiners, at End of Month In Metric Tons

Year	Jan.	Feb.	Mar.	Apr.	May	June	July	Aug.	Sept.	Oct.	Nov.	Dec.
2010	60,200	60,200	55,700	50,700	55,500	57,200	57,600	59,100	59,800	58,700	67,700	67,400
2011	67,100	53,000	53,200	61,100	62,600	61,500	62,800	60,500	58,800	56,300	53,500	54,800
2012	58,700	63,300	54,800	54,000	51,800	56,600	62,600	65,700	63,400	63,800	56,000	57,500
2013	69,900	76,200	83,100	94,300	98,000	93,400	83,600	81,400	77,400	69,300	65,100	69,400
2014	68,100	63,600	65,400	65,700	64,000	66,600	62,500	62,080	63,300	63,100	66,300	66,300
2015	64,900	63,800	63,600	64,100	62,700	62,400	60,800	66,900	69,500	68,600	67,900	64,500
2016	97,300	63,800	63,200	65,500	70,000	67,100	66,900	85,300	84,600	74,800	79,800	101,000
2017[1]	111,000	103,000	113,000	106,000	126,000	128,000	131,000	132,000	115,000	116,000	139,000	161,000
2018[1]	----	----	----	----	----	----	----	----	----	----	----	----
2019[1]	----	----	----	----	----	----	----	----	----	----	----	----

[1] Preliminary. [2] Secondary smelters and consumers. *Source: U.S. Geological Survey (USGS)*

Total[2] Lead Consumption in the United States In Metric Tons

Year	Jan.	Feb.	Mar.	Apr.	May	June	July	Aug.	Sept.	Oct.	Nov.	Dec.	Total
2011	131,000	118,000	118,000	133,000	132,000	133,000	132,000	133,000	132,000	132,000	132,000	131,000	1,557,000
2012	122,000	130,000	135,000	123,000	121,000	122,000	120,000	122,000	121,000	122,000	122,000	123,000	1,483,000
2013	146,000	123,000	118,000	117,000	117,000	117,000	116,000	118,000	117,000	119,000	115,000	134,000	1,750,000
2014	159,000	159,000	148,000	153,000	148,000	146,000	131,000	155,309	128,000	134,000	131,000	138,000	1,670,000
2015	132,000	121,000	135,000	151,000	130,000	135,000	128,000	125,000	121,000	145,000	134,000	129,000	1,590,000
2016	97,300	120,000	136,000	133,000	128,000	133,000	134,000	125,000	119,000	129,000	149,000	153,000	1,490,000
2017	146,000	157,000	167,000	156,000	171,000	125,000	147,000	128,000	147,000	130,000	129,000	120,000	1,760,000
2018	131,000	154,000	161,000	139,000	129,000	144,000	127,000	128,000	144,000	121,000	126,000	128,000	1,630,000
2019	139,000	130,000	133,000	149,000	124,000	133,000	127,000	154,000	142,000	134,000	125,000	140,000	1,630,000
2020[1]	141,000	125,000	128,000	126,000	109,000	132,000	125,000	121,000	119,000	146,000	126,000	121,000	1,519,000

[1] Preliminary. [1] Represents total consumption of primary & secondary lead as metal, in chemicals, or in alloys. *Source: U.S. Geological Survey (USGS)*

Lead Recovered from Scrap in the United States In Metric Tons (Lead Content)

Year	Jan.	Feb.	Mar.	Apr.	May	June	July	Aug.	Sept.	Oct.	Nov.	Dec.	Total
2011	104,000	96,200	95,500	104,000	101,000	100,000	102,000	103,000	95,400	95,900	98,800	99,600	1,195,400
2012	102,000	101,000	97,800	98,000	99,400	102,000	100,000	98,000	97,300	100,000	100,000	99,200	1,194,700
2013	104,000	96,700	100,000	97,300	100,000	98,100	97,200	100,000	99,500	104,000	102,000	95,000	1,200,000
2014	92,700	91,100	97,300	96,300	94,500	94,500	96,900	93,796	94,800	94,400	88,600	94,800	1,130,000
2015	88,600	88,900	92,200	94,600	93,600	92,900	92,500	95,400	96,300	97,500	96,100	89,700	1,120,000
2016	94,300	90,800	92,300	93,500	91,900	86,500	83,900	92,600	86,700	106,000	102,000	102,000	1,000,000
2017	82,900	105,000	108,000	107,000	101,000	83,700	85,000	85,300	83,300	84,600	81,400	84,300	1,130,000
2018	95,100	90,300	96,300	97,300	91,400	92,400	97,000	96,600	92,900	94,600	93,600	96,000	1,140,000
2019	94,100	94,500	96,700	94,600	90,600	93,800	97,000	97,200	98,200	101,000	97,800	100,000	1,155,500
2020[1]	101,000	99,500	95,900	86,100	82,600	98,100	99,700	98,100	95,800	97,800	98,700	98,400	1,151,700

[1] Preliminary. *Source: U.S. Geological Survey (USGS)*

Salient Statistics of Recycling Lead in the United States

Year	Percent Recycled	New Scrap[1]	Old Scrap[2]	Recycled Metal[3]	Apparent Supply	New Scrap[1]	Old Scrap[2]	Recycled Metal[3]	Apparent Supply
		In Metric Tons				Value in Thousands of Dollars			
2008	74.5	20,100	1,120,000	1,140,000	1,540,000	53,300	2,980,000	3,040,000	4,080,000
2009	80.5	21,600	1,090,000	1,110,000	1,380,000	41,400	2,090,000	2,130,000	2,640,000
2010	81.0	24,100	1,120,000	1,140,000	1,380,000	57,900	2,680,000	2,740,000	3,310,000
2011	73.0	21,600	1,110,000	1,130,000	1,520,000	58,000	2,980,000	3,040,000	4,080,000
2012	74.0	19,200	1,090,000	1,110,000	1,490,000	48,200	2,740,000	2,790,000	3,760,000
2013	80.0	19,200	1,140,000	1,160,000	1,440,000	46,600	3,760,000	3,800,000	3,870,000
2014	72.0	16,900	1,010,000	1,020,000	1,470,000	39,500	2,350,000	2,390,000	3,650,000
2015	74.0	16,900	989,000	1,010,000	1,410,000	34,000	1,990,000	2,020,000	3,100,000
2016	75.0	17,600	1,060,000	1,070,000	1,490,000	36,700	2,200,000	2,230,000	3,100,000
2017	69.0	18,500	1,080,000	1,100,000	1,650,000	46,700	2,790,000	2,840,000	4,170,000

[1] Scrap that results from the manufacturing process. [2] Scrap that results from consumer products. [3] Metal recovered from new plus old scrap.
Source: U.S. Geological Survey (USGS)

Lumber and Plywood

Humans have utilized lumber for construction for thousands of years, but due to the heaviness of timber and the manual methods of harvesting, large-scale lumbering didn't occur until the mechanical advances of the Industrial Revolution. Lumber is produced from both hardwood and softwood. Hardwood lumber comes from deciduous trees that have broad leaves. Most hardwood lumber is used for miscellaneous industrial applications, primarily wood pallets, and includes oak, gum, maple, and ash. Hardwood species with beautiful colors and patterns are used for such high-grade products as furniture, flooring, paneling, and cabinets and include black walnut, black cherry, and red oak. Wood from cone-bearing trees is called softwood, regardless of its actual hardness. Most lumber from the U.S. is softwood. Softwoods, such as southern yellow pine, Douglas fir, ponderosa pine, and true firs, are primarily used as structural lumber such as 2x4s and 2x6s, poles, paper, and cardboard.

Plywood consists of several thin layers of veneer bonded together with adhesives. The veneer sheets are layered so that the grain of one sheet is perpendicular to that of the next, which makes plywood exceptionally strong for its weight. Most plywood has from three to nine layers of wood. Plywood manufacturers use both hard and soft woods, although hardwoods serve primarily for appearance and are not as strong as those made from softwoods. Plywood is primarily used in construction, particularly for floors, roofs, walls, and doors. Homebuilding and remodeling account for two-thirds of U.S. lumber consumption. The price of lumber and plywood is highly correlated with the strength of the U.S. home-building market.

The forest and wood products industry is dominated by Weyerhaeuser Company (ticker symbol WY), which has about $20 billion in annual sales. Weyerhaeuser is a forest products conglomerate that engages not only in growing and harvesting timber, but also in the production and distribution of forest products, real estate development, and construction of single-family homes. Forest products include wood products, pulp and paper, and containerboard. The timberland segment of the business manages 7.2 million acres of company-owned land and 800,000 acres of leased commercial forestlands in North America. The company's Canadian division has renewable, long-term licenses on about 35 million acres of forestland in five Canadian provinces. In order to maximize its long-term yield from its acreage, Weyerhaeuser engages in a number of forest management activities such as extensive planting, suppression of non-merchantable species, thinning, fertilization, and operational pruning.

Lumber futures and options are traded at the CME Group. The CME Group's lumber futures contract calls for the delivery of 111,000 board feet (one 73-foot rail car) of random length 8 to 12-foot 2 x 4s, the type used in construction. The contract is priced in terms of dollars per thousand board feet.

Prices – CME lumber futures prices (Barchart.com electronic symbol code LS) on the nearest-futures chart opened the year 2020 at about $427 per thousand board feet, rose briefly, fell to a 5-year low in April and then rallied the rest of the year to close +61.6% at $690 per thousand board feet which was then a new all-time high. The price rise continued into early 2021.

Supply – The U.S. still leads the world in the production of industrial round wood, but in 2019, production fell -1.2% yr/yr to 387.702 million cubic meters, followed by Russia down by -7.5% to 203.194 million cubic meters, and then Canada, down by -7.5% at 1443.194 cubic meters.

The U.S. also led the world in the production of plywood in 2019 with 9.925 million cubic meters of production (-1.8% yr/yr), followed by Russia with 4.061 million cubic meters (+1.2% yr/yr), and then Japan with 3.298 million cubic meters (unchanged y/yr)

Trade – World exports of plywood in 2019 fell by -11.4% yr/yr to 28.033 million cubic meters. The world's largest exporter of plywood is Russia, with a 10.4% share of world plywood exports in 2019, followed by Finland with 3.3%, Canada with 2.3%, and the Baltic States with 1.8%. In 2019 U.S. exports fell by -11.4% yr/yr to 556.000 million cubic meters.

World exports of industrial roundwood in 2019 by +0.4% yr/yr to 138.063 million cubic meters. Russia was the world's largest exporter of roundwood in 2019 with an 11.5% share of world exports, followed by the Czech Republic with a 10.2% share, the U.S. with 5.6%, and Canada with 5.5%. Russian exports of industrial roundwood in 2019 fell by 17.4% yr/yr to 15.857 million cubic meters. U.S. exports of industrial roundwood in 2019 fell by -36.4% yr/yr to 7.801 million cubic meters.

World Production of Industrial Roundwood by Selected Countries In Thousands of Cubic Meters

Year	Austria	Canada	Czech Republic	Finland	France	Germany	Poland	Romania	Russia	Spain	Sweden	Turkey	United States
2010	13,281	138,802	14,771	45,420	29,634	47,136	31,343	10,548	161,595	10,969	66,300	15,695	336,135
2011	13,631	146,735	13,467	45,526	28,387	49,878	32,200	10,344	175,625	11,528	66,000	16,423	354,704
2012	12,831	146,741	13,041	44,614	24,945	45,851	32,972	11,050	177,455	11,627	63,599	17,701	347,076
2013	12,433	147,751	13,149	49,331	24,451	44,700	33,795	10,091	180,378	12,124	63,700	16,762	354,937
2014	12,030	148,825	13,365	49,202	25,750	45,386	35,677	10,471	188,300	12,686	67,400	18,535	356,812
2015	12,570	151,358	13,827	51,446	24,998	45,654	35,878	10,235	190,507	12,905	67,300	20,008	354,678
2016	12,173	154,694	15,273	54,327	25,086	44,016	37,106	9,953	198,194	13,325	67,900	20,389	374,476
2017	12,738	155,183	17,011	55,330	25,361	43,328	40,064	9,578	197,612	14,642	67,580	19,462	372,321
2018[1]	13,949	155,629	21,443	60,530	25,721	52,874	41,353	10,436	219,569	15,457	68,300	22,466	392,510
2019[2]	13,325	143,994	26,664	55,951	25,655	53,425	38,853	10,186	203,194	15,859	68,500	22,700	387,702

[1] Preliminary. [2] Estimate. *Source: Food and Agriculture Organization of the United Nations (FAO)*

Imports of Industrial Roundwood by Selected Countries In Thousands of Cubic Meters

Year	Austria	Belgium	Canada	Finland	France	Germany	Italy	Norway	Poland	Portugal	Spain	Sweden	United States
2010	8,041	4,193	4,745	6,256	1,690	7,656	3,198	1,288	2,289	855	1,839	6,276	816
2011	7,427	4,326	4,275	5,736	1,454	7,005	3,328	1,355	3,419	1,717	2,135	6,724	959
2012	7,319	4,338	4,495	5,457	1,368	6,567	2,802	940	2,469	1,644	1,727	6,855	1,167
2013	8,214	4,507	4,872	6,694	1,244	8,442	2,691	661	2,270	2,320	2,047	7,532	926
2014	7,239	4,472	4,262	6,257	1,512	8,417	2,913	447	2,633	2,600	1,750	8,127	909
2015	7,849	4,021	4,616	5,709	1,349	8,745	2,665	378	2,535	2,014	751	6,941	1,191
2016	9,188	3,899	6,185	5,911	1,444	8,697	2,763	417	2,482	2,131	599	6,807	1,248
2017	8,825	3,373	4,293	4,830	1,222	8,783	2,846	513	1,682	2,042	584	6,673	1,154
2018[1]	10,113	4,133	5,133	6,935	1,143	8,910	3,860	455	1,071	2,010	638	9,479	1,778
2019[2]	10,505	3,889	4,710	6,234	1,263	7,271	3,212	402	1,155	2,274	667	8,791	1,804

[1] Preliminary. [2] Estimate. *Source: Food and Agricultural Organization of the United Nations (FAO)*

Exports of Industrial Roundwood by Selected Countries In Thousands of Cubic Meters

Year	Canada	Czech Republic	Estonia	France	Germany	Hungary	Latvia	Lithuania	Russia	Slovakia	Sweden	Switzer-land	United States
2010	4,019	1,743	2,250	6,665	3,726	873	4,158	1,329	20,983	2,434	1,217	796	11,583
2011	5,706	3,487	2,610	6,380	3,658	881	4,401	1,844	20,429	2,533	846	926	13,755
2012	6,094	3,912	2,392	4,571	3,398	858	4,107	1,464	17,652	2,085	794	801	12,227
2013	7,023	4,292	2,747	4,740	3,316	975	3,737	1,809	19,045	2,662	756	740	14,700
2014	6,696	4,931	2,758	4,398	3,387	871	3,836	1,716	20,909	2,932	630	764	13,962
2015	6,060	4,530	2,431	4,311	3,747	680	3,002	1,406	19,437	2,358	570	641	11,561
2016	8,172	5,225	2,548	4,000	3,947	683	2,871	1,473	20,046	2,157	573	559	12,047
2017	7,402	6,583	2,557	4,092	4,259	634	2,652	1,559	19,430	1,955	963	570	12,200
2018[1]	8,494	8,309	2,927	4,066	5,364	547	2,652	2,028	19,197	2,042	755	753	12,270
2019[2]	7,548	14,146	2,396	3,877	8,558	547	2,652	1,889	15,857	1,711	862	642	7,801

[1] Preliminary. [2] Estimate. *Source: Food and Agricultural Organization of the United Nations (FAO)*

U.S. Housing Starts: Seasonally Adjusted Annual Rate In Thousands

Year	Jan.	Feb.	Mar.	Apr.	May	June	July	Aug.	Sept.	Oct.	Nov.	Dec.	Average
2011	630	517	600	554	561	608	623	585	650	610	711	694	612
2012	723	704	695	753	708	757	740	754	847	915	833	976	784
2013	888	970	999	826	920	852	891	898	860	921	1,104	1,010	928
2014	902	948	973	1,038	987	928	1,085	984	999	1,094	994	1,081	1,001
2015	1,101	893	964	1,192	1,063	1,213	1,147	1,132	1,189	1,073	1,171	1,160	1,108
2016	1,123	1,209	1,128	1,164	1,119	1,190	1,223	1,164	1,062	1,328	1,149	1,268	1,177
2017	1,225	1,289	1,179	1,165	1,122	1,225	1,185	1,172	1,158	1,265	1,303	1,210	1,208
2018	1,335	1,295	1,332	1,267	1,332	1,180	1,184	1,279	1,236	1,211	1,202	1,142	1,250
2019	1,272	1,137	1,203	1,267	1,268	1,235	1,212	1,377	1,274	1,340	1,371	1,587	1,295
2020[1]	1,617	1,567	1,269	934	1,038	1,265	1,487	1,373	1,437	1,530	1,553	1,670	1,395

[1] Preliminary. Total Privately owned. *Source: Bureau of the Census, U.S. Department of Commerce*

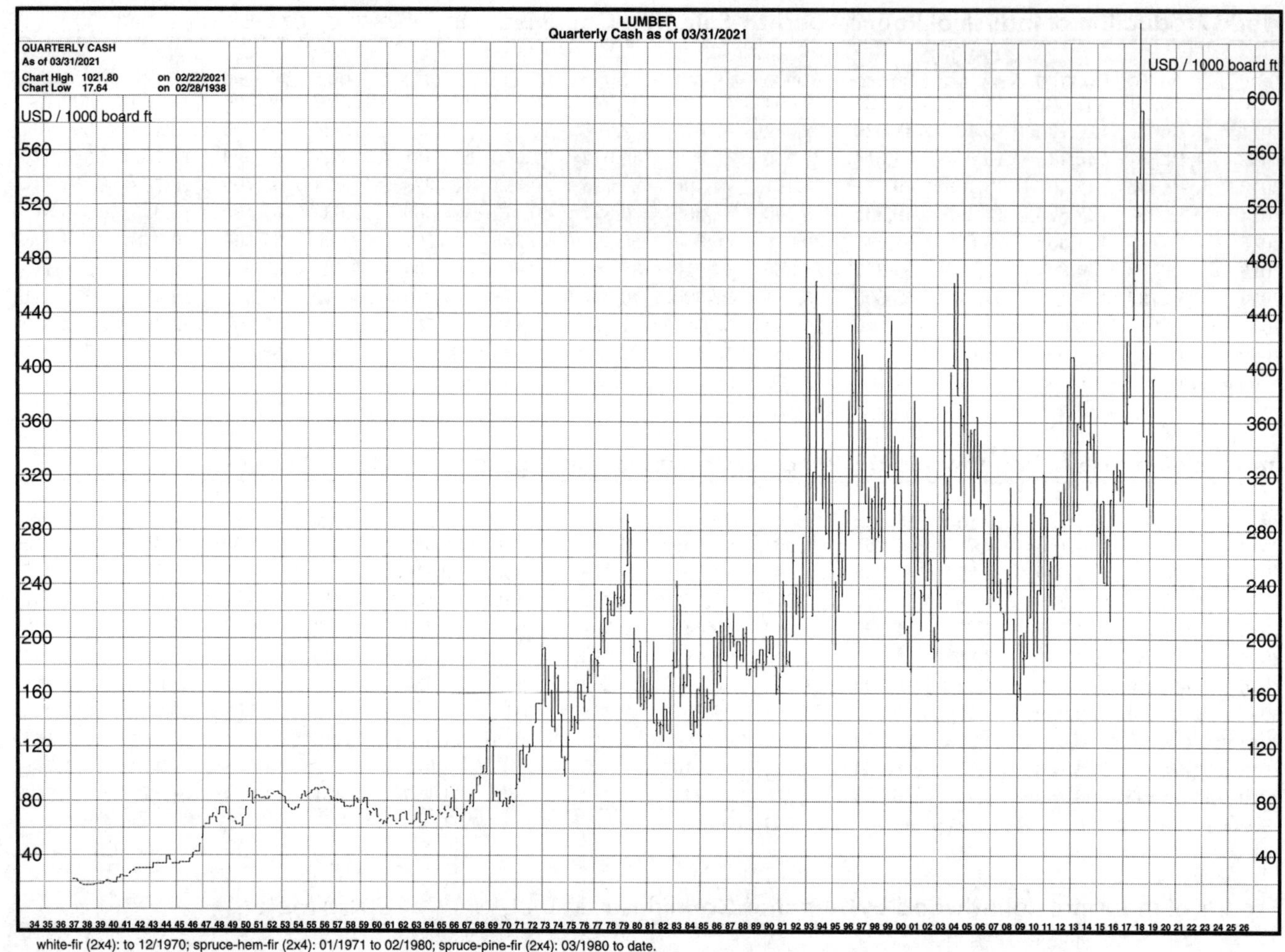

white-fir (2x4): to 12/1970; spruce-hem-fir (2x4): 01/1971 to 02/1980; spruce-pine-fir (2x4): 03/1980 to date.

Average Price of Lumber in the United States In Dollars per Thousand Board Feet

Year	Jan.	Feb.	Mar.	Apr.	May	June	July	Aug.	Sept.	Oct.	Nov.	Dec.	Average
2010	238.50	287.00	281.50	312.00	272.50	207.50	203.40	219.75	231.75	245.80	275.33	283.80	254.90
2011	307.25	286.25	294.25	269.50	227.25	222.75	254.50	231.75	250.80	236.50	230.25	248.00	254.92
2012	253.50	262.67	280.75	281.25	305.50	300.00	294.25	310.20	292.33	298.00	339.50	370.00	299.00
2013	382.25	377.33	401.50	386.60	325.50	298.40	312.25	326.00	346.75	360.25	381.80	364.25	355.24
2014	373.20	364.00	362.75	339.00	342.00	323.75	351.50	361.00	355.25	347.00	333.75	337.75	349.25
2015	326.00	313.50	283.75	261.50	256.40	292.25	294.25	267.75	246.00	259.20	259.75	267.25	277.30
2016	258.75	251.50	292.00	298.60	317.50	319.50	323.40	326.00	313.60	318.75	306.25	319.60	303.79
2017	309.50	374.75	359.20	405.33	387.75	368.40	403.25	394.50	413.80	446.25	485.00	461.40	400.76
2018	492.50	523.25	524.20	551.75	621.33	617.80	564.25	468.20	413.75	316.33	338.00	320.25	479.30
2019	334.50	405.75	370.80	326.00	312.00	359.75	356.00	330.00	----	----	----	----	349.35

Source: National Agricultural Statistics Service, U.S. Department of Agriculture (NASS-USDA)

Average Price of Plywood in the United States In Dollars per Thousand Board Feet

Year	Jan.	Feb.	Mar.	Apr.	May	June	July	Aug.	Sept.	Oct.	Nov.	Dec.	Average
2010	191.50	220.00	233.00	353.75	330.00	206.25	217.20	171.25	164.50	183.00	189.33	196.40	221.35
2011	210.75	196.75	189.25	178.25	167.25	180.25	171.25	192.25	188.60	190.75	185.00	192.00	186.86
2012	201.00	194.67	213.25	212.50	233.75	252.00	257.50	331.00	343.33	300.00	343.75	354.50	269.77
2013	401.50	412.67	430.00	410.00	354.33	279.25	256.25	254.40	244.75	263.00	244.00	227.75	314.83
2014	226.60	215.00	214.50	210.33	233.00	210.25	212.25	215.40	222.00	222.00	219.00	204.00	217.03
2015	200.80	194.25	183.50	177.50	194.00	207.25	194.00	200.50	218.33	239.20	257.00	233.50	208.32
2016	232.50	230.75	224.25	244.20	275.75	278.00	295.40	306.25	300.00	287.00	285.75	282.00	270.15
2017	278.50	291.25	307.00	327.00	329.75	330.40	378.00	412.00	432.20	454.25	396.25	304.00	353.38
2018	318.75	377.50	405.00	405.00	418.33	445.00	403.75	347.00	342.50	268.33	242.00	208.25	348.45
2019	209.50	214.50	212.00	188.75	189.00	184.25	211.75	218.00	----	----	----	----	203.47

Source: National Agricultural Statistics Service, U.S. Department of Agriculture (NASS-USDA)

Nearby Futures through Last Trading Day.

Volume of Trading of Random Lumber Futures in Chicago In Contracts

Year	Jan.	Feb.	Mar.	Apr.	May	June	July	Aug.	Sept.	Oct.	Nov.	Dec.	Total
2011	22,691	25,642	25,141	32,161	20,134	30,740	18,440	32,615	28,562	26,650	22,589	33,968	319,333
2012	20,678	33,593	25,208	30,526	24,563	26,638	23,663	32,211	19,595	31,797	24,513	31,538	324,523
2013	26,219	29,842	18,671	26,472	23,349	19,914	18,572	18,118	19,271	17,021	11,100	15,073	243,622
2014	13,001	14,025	12,632	14,563	13,365	17,276	10,119	14,977	11,766	16,481	8,959	13,333	160,497
2015	13,744	16,696	14,710	21,116	16,757	19,374	14,253	20,509	15,592	21,061	11,475	16,065	201,352
2016	13,340	14,415	16,933	15,931	12,953	16,806	10,911	19,397	13,373	16,510	13,574	12,839	176,982
2017	11,400	20,115	14,942	21,705	16,706	15,346	14,333	15,684	16,030	21,713	18,739	18,386	205,099
2018	15,690	21,225	15,354	22,545	22,211	23,128	15,731	19,983	14,424	20,532	14,222	11,541	216,586
2019	14,464	14,588	11,140	17,457	13,524	16,484	12,478	13,524	10,085	14,511	12,554	11,873	162,682
2020	11,487	20,021	14,549	9,142	7,448	11,808	15,612	24,128	10,932	9,071	7,691	14,136	156,025

Contract size = 110,000 board feet. *Source: CME Group; Chicago Mercantile Exchange (CME)*

Average Open Interest of Random Lumber Futures in Chicago In Contracts

Year	Jan.	Feb.	Mar.	Apr.	May	June	July	Aug.	Sept.	Oct.	Nov.	Dec.
2011	11,235	10,223	9,471	9,813	10,090	10,408	9,233	10,170	9,465	10,314	9,663	10,768
2012	9,261	10,228	10,192	9,962	9,226	7,885	7,666	9,259	8,153	8,275	10,713	10,624
2013	9,354	8,222	8,609	7,345	5,872	6,726	5,816	5,539	5,699	4,816	4,672	4,086
2014	3,945	4,602	4,618	5,020	4,422	5,013	4,080	4,419	3,751	3,698	4,610	4,289
2015	4,831	5,256	6,336	6,860	6,379	4,660	4,389	6,151	6,104	5,553	3,974	4,158
2016	4,619	5,292	4,478	4,561	5,050	4,782	4,692	5,167	3,479	4,323	3,818	4,005
2017	3,786	4,992	5,353	6,044	5,180	4,378	4,158	4,510	5,489	6,494	6,800	6,278
2018	6,775	7,290	6,406	6,964	6,827	6,550	5,649	4,714	3,986	4,078	4,120	3,984
2019	3,657	3,334	2,510	3,357	3,913	3,497	2,541	2,593	2,052	2,554	3,108	3,240
2020	3,302	4,078	2,990	2,761	2,602	2,509	3,672	4,520	3,642	3,300	2,829	3,026

Contract size = 110,000 board feet. *Source: CME Group; Chicago Mercantile Exchange (CME)*

Production of Plywood by Selected Countries In Thousands of Cubic Meters

Year	Austria	Canada	Finland	France	Germany	Italy	Japan	Poland	Romania	Russia	Spain	Sweden	United States
2010	322	2,005	980	271	232	310	2,645	402	266	2,689	267	60	9,397
2011	271	1,794	1,010	258	218	310	2,486	411	331	3,040	299	84	9,365
2012	241	1,824	1,020	324	178	280	2,549	388	472	3,150	255	54	9,493
2013	311	1,792	1,090	255	135	225	2,761	430	665	3,303	275	87	9,680
2014	306	1,810	1,160	245	148	266	2,813	406	623	3,540	284	82	11,151
2015	241	1,929	1,150	246	108	244	2,756	390	316	3,607	371	60	10,972
2016	291	2,205	1,140	250	114	280	3,063	462	285	3,759	379	60	11,239
2017	291	2,253	1,240	254	100	236	3,287	546	277	3,729	509	85	11,600
2018[1]	290	1,742	1,230	258	118	180	3,298	583	73	4,013	541	85	10,104
2019[2]	290	1,701	1,090	256	111	180	3,298	590	89	4,061	503	85	9,925

[1] Preliminary. [2] Estimate. *Source: Food and Agricultural Organization of the United Nations (FAO)*

Imports of Plywood by Selected Countries In Thousands of Cubic Meters

Year	Austria	Belgium	Canada	Denmark	France	Germany	Italy	Japan	Netherlands	Sweden	Switzerland	United Kingdom	United States
2010	155	544	1,909	219	544	1,288	485	3,255	495	152	68	1,264	2,551
2011	196	593	1,554	262	492	1,423	463	3,809	620	185	74	1,330	2,632
2012	209	533	1,621	270	374	1,336	420	3,645	476	173	86	1,285	3,113
2013	145	537	1,469	266	368	1,338	428	3,765	399	155	99	1,370	2,829
2014	160	554	1,587	266	429	1,369	453	3,597	468	163	184	1,399	2,872
2015	190	525	1,492	211	420	1,412	448	2,886	552	150	182	1,466	4,253
2016	181	575	1,228	242	478	1,458	458	2,771	536	175	192	1,479	4,877
2017	231	589	1,744	242	529	1,528	539	3,017	632	206	203	1,215	4,934
2018[1]	242	589	1,562	281	539	1,620	527	2,934	640	222	200	1,598	5,466
2019[2]	218	799	1,395	276	533	1,469	451	2,558	605	248	197	1,454	4,664

[1] Preliminary. [2] Estimate. *Source: Food and Agricultural Organization of the United Nations (FAO)*

Exports of Plywood by Selected Countries In Thousands of Cubic Meters

Year	Austria	Baltic States	Belgium	Canada	Finland	France	Germany	Italy	Netherlands	Poland	Russia	Spain	United States
2010	304	289	440	301	833	163	337	218	50	133	1,512	141	871
2011	353	302	437	359	863	127	355	228	63	141	1,600	165	837
2012	334	310	368	287	855	143	298	201	89	169	1,717	152	914
2013	339	312	369	426	920	141	297	192	71	181	1,758	166	888
2014	346	302	403	482	998	145	310	210	75	203	1,969	189	828
2015	298	345	381	647	981	156	334	215	68	250	2,206	224	643
2016	340	439	437	625	940	153	349	240	73	257	2,458	252	697
2017	348	454	404	670	1,039	171	381	279	83	307	2,483	274	936
2018[1]	307	474	395	733	1,012	174	393	211	102	336	2,696	291	700
2019[2]	311	504	499	657	918	160	372	213	84	414	2,909	326	556

[1] Preliminary. [2] Estimate. *Source: Food and Agricultural Organization of the United Nations (FAO)*

Magnesium

Magnesium (atomic symbol Mg) is a silvery-white, light, and fairly tough, metallic element and is relatively stable. Magnesium is one of the alkaline earth metals. Magnesium is the eighth-most abundant element in the earth's crust and the third most plentiful element found in seawater. Magnesium is ductile and malleable when heated, and except for beryllium, is the lightest metal that remains stable under ordinary conditions. First isolated by the British chemist Sir Humphrey Davy in 1808, magnesium today is obtained mainly by electrolysis of fused magnesium chloride.

Magnesium compounds, primarily magnesium oxide, are used in the refractory material that line the furnaces used to produce iron and steel, nonferrous metals, glass, and cement. Magnesium oxide and other compounds are also used in the chemical, agricultural, and construction industries. Magnesium's principal use is as an alloying addition for aluminum. These aluminum-magnesium alloys are used primarily in beverage cans. Due to their lightness and considerable tensile strength, the alloys are also used in structural components in airplanes and automobiles.

Prices – The average price of magnesium in 2018 (latest data) rose +6.5% yr/yr to $1.99 per pound, well below the 2008 record high of $3.38 per pound.

Supply – World primary production of magnesium in 2018 (latest data) fell -7.6% yr/yr to 970,000 metric tons. The current level of magnesium production is about four times what it was in the mid-1970s. Total U.S. consumption of primary magnesium in 2018 rose +7.7% yr/yr to 70,000 metric tons. The world's largest primary producer of magnesium in 2018 (latest data) was China with 800,000 metric tons, which is 82.5% of the world's total production. Russia produced 65,000 metric tons, and Israel produced 25,000 metric tons. The U.S. production amount is not available because it is considered proprietary data but is probably less than about 50,000 metric tons. China increased production from 70,500 metric tons in 1998 to a new record high of 930,000 metric tons in 2017.

Demand – Total U.S. consumption of magnesium for all structural products in 2017 (latest data) fell -7.4% yr/yr to 29,263 metric tons. For structural products, 97.4% of magnesium was used for castings, and the remaining 2.6% was used for wrought products. U.S. consumption of magnesium for aluminum alloys rose +17.7% yr/yr to 15.300 metric tons. The consumption of magnesium for other uses fell -11.3% yr/yr to 49.7 metric tons.

Trade – U.S. exports of magnesium in 2018 fell -14.3% yr/yr to 12,000 metric tons, but still well above the 2005 record low of 9,650 metric tons. U.S. imports of magnesium in 2018 rose 16.7% yr/yr to 49,000 metric tons.

World Production of Magnesium (Primary) In Metric Tons

Year	Brazil	Canada	China	Israel	Kazakhstan	Russia	Serbia	Ukraine	United States	Total
2015	15,000	859,000	19,307	8,100	----	60,000	200	7,700	W	970,000
2016	15,000	871,000	22,548	10,000	----	58,000	3,750	6,770	W	989,000
2017	15,000	930,000	23,000	9,000	----	40,000	14,000	8,000	W	1,040,000
2018	15,000	800,000	25,000	23,000	----	65,000	10,000	19,000	W	970,000
2019[1]	22,000	970,000	21,000	25,000	----	67,000	7,000	8,000	W	1,120,000
2020[2]	20,000	900,000	20,000	20,000	----	60,000	11,000	5,000	W	1,000,000

[1] Preliminary. [2] Estimate. W = Withheld. *Source: U.S. Geological Survey (USGS)*

Salient Statistics of Magnesium in the United States In Metric Tons

	Production								Domestic Consumption of Primary Magnesium					
		Secondary							Structural Products					
Year	Primary (Ingot)	New Scrap	Old Scrap	Total	Total Exports[3]	Imports for Consumption	Stocks Dec. 31[4]	Price $ Per Pound[5]	Castings	Wrought	Total	Aluminum Alloys	Other Uses	Total
2015	W	65,600	22,900	88,500	15,200	49,200	W	2.15	9,361	1,040	10,401	21,400	42,400	63,800
2016	W	72,700	29,400	102,000	19,300	45,500	W	2.15	29,739	1,870	31,609	13,000	56,000	69,000
2017	W	85,400	29,000	112,000	13,700	41,900	W	2.15	28,494	769	29,263	15,300	49,700	65,000
2018	W			109,000	12,000	47,000	W	2.17						51,000
2019[1]	W			101,000	10,000	59,000	W	2.45						55,000
2020[2]	W			90,000	12,000	61,000	W	2.50						50,000

[1] Preliminary. [2] Estimate. [3] Metal & alloys in crude form & scrap. [4] Estimate of Industry Stocks, metal. [5] Magnesium ingots (99.8%), f.o.b. Valasco, Texas. [6] Distributive or sacrificial purposes. W = Withheld proprietary data. *Source: U.S. Geological Survey (USGS)*

Average Price of Magnesium In Dollars Per Pound

Year	Jan.	Feb.	Mar.	Apr.	May	June	July	Aug.	Sept.	Oct.	Nov.	Dec.	Average
2015	1.96	1.92	1.90	1.90	1.92	1.92	1.92	1.92	1.92	1.92	1.87	1.74	1.90
2016	1.74	1.74	1.75	1.75	1.85	1.79	1.77	1.80	1.84	1.90	1.94	1.95	1.82
2017	1.91	1.81	1.84	1.87	1.87	1.87	1.84	1.86	1.87	1.87	1.87	1.90	1.87
2018	1.94	1.99	2.00	1.98	1.99	1.99	1.99	1.99	1.99	1.99	1.99	1.99	1.99
2019	----	----	----	----	----	----	----	----	----	----	----	----	----

Source: American Metal Market (AMM)

Manganese

Manganese (atomic symbol Mn) is a silvery-white, very brittle, metallic element used primarily in making alloys. Manganese was first distinguished as an element and isolated in 1774 by Johan Gottlieb Gahn. Manganese dissolves in acid and corrodes in moist air.

Manganese is found in the earth's crust in the form of ores such as rhodochrosite, franklinite, psilomelane, and manganite. Pyrolusite is the principal ore of manganese. Pure manganese is produced by igniting pyrolusite with aluminum powder or by electrolyzing manganese sulfate.

Manganese is used primarily in the steel industry for creating alloys, such as ferromanganese and spiegeleisen. In steel, manganese improves forging and rolling qualities, strength, toughness, stiffness, wear resistance, and hardness. Manganese is also used in plant fertilizers, animal feed, pigments, and dry cell batteries.

Prices – The average monthly price of ferromanganese (high carbon, FOB plant) in 2019 fell -8.9% yr/yr to $1,317.95 per gross ton, and still well below the 2008 record high of $2,953.84 per gross ton. The 2019 price, however, is still about three times the 25-year low price of $447.44 per gross ton posted in 2001.

Supply – World production of manganese ore in 2016 fell -5.4% yr/yr to 49,000 million metric tons. The world's largest producers of manganese ore in 2016 were China with 31.7% of world production, South Africa with 28.0%, Australia with 10.1%, and Gabon with 6.9%.

Demand – U.S. consumption of manganese ore in 2020 fell -10.8% yr/yr to 330,000 metric tons. U.S. consumption of ferromanganese in 2020 fell -10.7% yr/yr to 300,000 metric tons, still down from the 2012 record high of 382,000 metric tons. The current figures are about 25% of the U.S. consumption back in the early 1970s.

Trade – The U.S. still relies on imports for 100% of its manganese consumption, as it has since 1985. U.S. imports of manganese ore for consumption in 2020 fell -28.6% yr/yr to 310,000 metric tons, but still up from 2009's 20-year low of 69,000 metric tons. U.S. imports of ferromanganese for consumption in 2020 fell -24.7% yr/yr to 240,000 metric tons. U.S. imports of silico-manganese in 2020 fell -31.6% yr/yr to 240,000 metric tons, but still well above 2009's 27-year low of 130,000 metric tons.

World Production of Manganese Ore In Thousands of Metric Tons (Gross Weight)

Year	Australia[2] (37%-53%)	Brazil (37%)	China (20%-30%)	Gabon (45%-53%)	Ghana (32%-34%)	India (10%-54%)	Kazakh-stan (29%-30%)	Malaysia (32%-45%)	Mexico (27%-50%)	South Africa (30%-48%+)	Ukraine (30%-35%)	Other	World Total
2007	5,289	1,570	10,000	3,300	1,854	2,016	1,003	57	423	5,996	1,720	1,270	34,500
2008	4,812	3,200	11,000	3,248	914	2,293	1,117	537	472	6,807	1,447	1,700	37,900
2009	4,451	2,575	12,000	1,992	882	2,347	982	469	330	4,579	932	1,660	33,800
2010	6,474	3,125	13,000	3,201	1,530	2,858	1,094	900	485	7,172	1,589	1,450	44,000
2011	6,963	2,738	14,000	4,070	1,689	2,015	1,096	598	468	8,652	972	1,410	45,700
2012	7,208	2,796	21,930	3,337	1,467	1,196	1,071	1,100	511	8,931	1,234	1,340	52,900
2013	7,447	2,883	17,547	3,997	1,812	3,112	1,121	1,125	580	10,958	1,525	1,670	54,600
2014	7,670	2,723	19,671	3,787	1,497	2,200	1,092	835	652	14,051	1,526	1,670	58,000
2015	7,500	2,817	13,024	4,112	1,478	2,117	616	481	600	15,952	1,203	1,470	51,800
2016[1]	4,968	2,437	15,528	3,379	1,967	2,100	588	682	572	13,736	1,250		49,000

[1] Preliminary. [2] Metallurgical Ore. [3] Concentrate. [4] Ranges of percentage of manganese. *Source: U.S. Geological Survey (USGS)*

Salient Statistics of Manganese in the United States In Thousands of Metric Tons (Gross Weight)

Year	Net Import Reliance As a % of Apparent Consump	Manganese Ore (35% or More Manganese): Imports for Consumption	Exports	Consumption	Stocks Dec. 31[3]	Ferromanganese: Imports for Consumption	Exports	Consumption	Avg Price Mn. Metallurgical Ore $/Metric Ton Unit[4]	Silicomanganese: Exports	Imports
2011	100	552	1	532	250	348	5	303	6.67	8.5	348.0
2012	100	506	2	538	203	401	5	382	4.97	5.9	348.0
2013	100	558	1	523	217	335	2	368	4.61	6.0	329.0
2014	100	387	1	508	189	365	6	360	4.49	3.0	448.0
2015	100	441	1	451	187	292	5	344	3.53	1.0	301.0
2016	100	282	1	410	207	229	7	342	3.41	2.0	264.0
2017	100	297	1	378	148	331	9	345	6.43	8.0	351.0
2018	100	440	3	370	185	427	10	348	7.17	4.0	412.0
2019[1]	100	434	1	370	190	332	8	336	6.60	2.0	351.0
2020[2]	100	310	1	330	190	240	21	300		2.0	240.0

[1] Preliminary. [2] Estimate. [3] Including bonded warehouses; excludes Gov't stocks; also excludes small tonnages of dealers' stocks.
[4] 46-48% Mn, C.I.F. U.S. Ports. *Source: U.S. Geological Survey (USGS)*

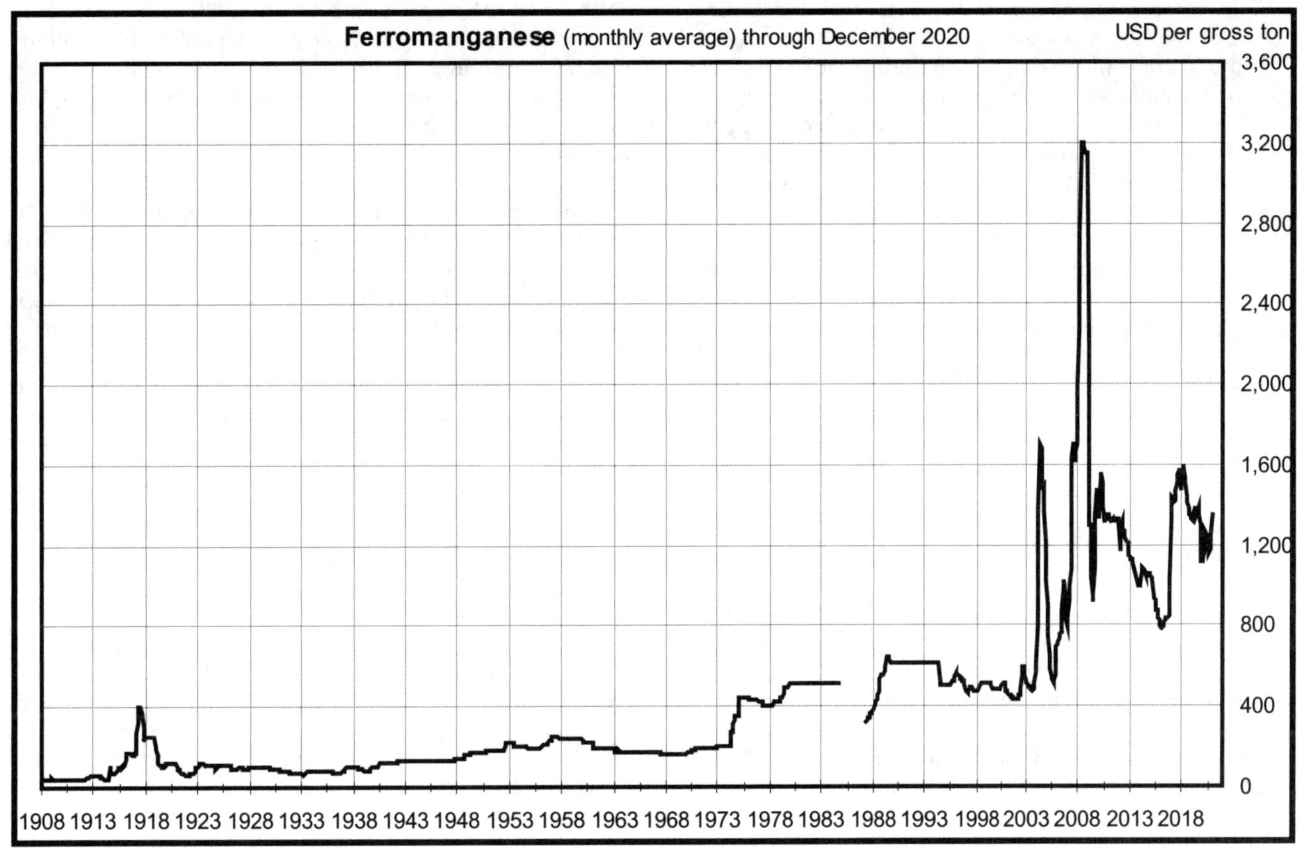

Imports[3] of Manganese Ore (20% or More Mn) in the United States In Metric Tons (Mn Content)

Year	Australia	Brazil	Gabon	Mexico	Morocco	South Africa	Total	Customs Value ($1,000)
2011	70,500	4,750	183,000	1,640	454	5,530	266,000	145,000
2012	15,000	3,970	152,000	2,200	2,670	46,400	226,000	101,000
2013	29,200	3,850	192,000	4,810	3,800	12,900	263,000	126,000
2014	17,500	1,690	143,000	3,440	954	17,200	186,000	88,300
2015	16,700	2,210	171,000	2,100	128	23,800	232,000	92,500
2016	3,510	290	106,530	8,820	87	14,968	135,200	40,700
2017	9,770	340	134,640	10,690	135	14,400	170,100	73,300
2018	6,430	3,890	141,130	15,290	66	38,170	204,800	122,000
2019[1]	----	9,070	187,000	21,400	165	22,540	241,000	126,000
2020[2]	----	----	----	30,000	762	31,482	185,700	86,700

[1] Preliminary. [2] Estimate. [3] Imports for consumption. *Source: U.S. Geological Survey (USGS)*

Average Price of Ferromanganese[1] In Dollars Per Gross Ton -- Carloads

Year	Jan.	Feb.	Mar.	Apr.	May	June	July	Aug.	Sept.	Oct.	Nov.	Dec.	Average
2011	1,336.25	1,320.00	1,320.00	1,327.62	1,321.43	1,315.00	1,315.00	1,327.39	1,330.00	1,330.00	1,330.00	1,303.95	1,323.05
2012	1,171.50	1,179.38	1,285.23	1,317.86	1,280.68	1,263.34	1,238.45	1,220.33	1,214.48	1,202.39	1,171.25	1,144.58	1,224.12
2013	1,140.00	1,128.16	1,128.81	1,121.14	1,076.94	1,071.25	1,037.50	1,037.50	1,031.88	1,000.00	1,000.00	1,000.00	1,064.43
2014	1,006.19	1,066.50	1,088.58	1,090.00	1,080.00	1,078.22	1,041.25	1,060.00	1,053.34	1,055.22	1,060.00	1,039.53	1,059.90
2015	1,042.00	1,036.06	1,029.09	944.66	939.75	929.77	876.82	875.00	841.67	836.36	825.00	797.73	914.49
2016	779.34	792.00	797.50	805.00	813.57	821.59	836.25	835.00	836.67	845.00	1,012.12	1,320.24	874.52
2017	1,410.00	1,438.42	1,430.87	1,406.50	1,418.64	1,470.68	1,509.00	1,547.39	1,568.50	1,552.84	1,540.00	1,473.12	1,480.50
2018	1,500.60	1,564.21	1,595.45	1,527.62	1,509.32	1,438.57	1,433.57	1,404.57	1,375.00	1,345.65	1,337.50	1,327.12	1,446.60
2019	1,321.90	1,324.34	1,346.67	1,379.76	1,374.55	1,374.00	1,358.18	1,386.36	1,344.50	1,296.09	1,193.42	1,115.63	1,317.95
2020	1,112.50	1,125.63	1,167.50	1,265.00	1,247.50	1,220.00	1,220.00	1,191.25	1,155.00	1,172.50	1,247.50	1,343.00	1,205.62

[1] Domestic standard, high carbon, FOB plant, carloads. *Source: American Metal Market (AMM)*

Meats

U.S. commercial red meat includes beef, veal, lamb, and pork. Red meat is a good source of iron, vitamin B12, and protein, and eliminating it from the diet can lead to iron and zinc deficiencies. Today, red meat is far leaner than it was 30 years ago due to newer breeds of livestock that carry less fat. The leanest cuts of beef include tenderloin, sirloin, and flank. The leanest cuts of pork include pork tenderloin, loin chops, and rib chops.

The USDA (United States Department of Agriculture) grades various cuts of meat. "Prime" is the highest USDA grade for beef, veal, and lamb. "Choice" is the grade designation below Prime for beef, veal, and lamb. "Commercial" and "Cutter" grades are two of the lower designations for beef, usually sold as ground meat, sausage, and canned meat. "Canner" is the lowest USDA grade designation for beef and is used primarily in canned meats not sold at retail.

Supply – World total meat production in 2020 fell -3.4% to 158.039 million metric tons (MMT), well below the record high of 173.611 MMT in 2018. China was the world's largest meat producer in 2020 with 44.550 MMT of production (down -9.5% yr/yr), accounting for 28.2% of world production. U.S. production of red meats in 2020 rose +2.2% yr/yr to 56.113 billion pounds, a new record high. U.S. production of beef in 2020 rose +0.9% yr/yr to 27.576 billion pounds, which is a record high. Beef accounted for 49.1% of all U.S. meat production in 2020. U.S. production of pork in 2020 rose +3.5% yr/yr to 28.299 billion pounds, a new record high. Pork accounted for 50.40% of U.S. meat production. Based on 2015 data, veal accounted for only 0.4% of U.S. meat production, and lamb and mutton account for only 0.1% of U.S. meat production.

Demand – U.S. per-capita meat consumption in 2020 rose 0.7% yr/yr to 111.9 pounds per person per year, well above the 2014 record low of 101.7 pounds per person. Meat consumption has fallen sharply from 192 pounds per person back in 1970, reflecting the trend towards eating more chicken and fish and the availability of meat substitutes. Per-capita beef consumption in 2020 was unchanged from 2019's 57.7 pounds, half the record high of 127.5 pounds seen in 1976. Per capita pork consumption in 2020 rose +1.5% yr/yr to 52.9 pounds per person per year and remains above the 2011 record low of 45.7 pounds. Based on 2015 data, per-capita consumption of veal is negligible at 0.2 pounds per person, and lamb/mutton consumption is also negligible at 1.0 pound per person.

Trade – World red meat exports in 2020 rose +8.0% to 21.842 million metric tons, a new record high. The world's largest red meat exporters in 2020 were the U.S. with 21.3% of world exports, the European Union with 21.5%, Brazil with 17.0%, Canada with 9.2%. India with 4.8%, and Australia with 3.9%.

World Total Meat Production[4] In Thousands of Metric Tons

Year	Argentina	Australia	Brazil	Canada	China[4]	European Union	India	Mexico	New Zealand	Russia	South Africa	United States	World Total
2011	2,831	2,473	12,257	2,958	57,423	31,067	3,308	2,862	651	3,436	1,075	22,309	159,953
2012	2,951	2,504	12,637	2,904	60,582	30,234	3,491	2,911	673	3,556	1,058	22,399	163,725
2013	3,266	2,719	13,010	2,879	62,314	29,747	3,800	2,937	667	3,761	1,119	22,276	166,839
2014	3,142	2,957	13,123	2,906	64,365	29,983	4,000	2,962	705	3,846	1,207	21,443	169,040
2015	3,204	2,921	12,944	2,946	62,623	30,933	4,080	3,014	734	3,953	1,271	21,938	169,266
2016	3,172	2,511	12,984	3,044	60,424	31,746	4,170	3,090	693	4,159	1,334	22,827	169,307
2017	3,405	2,557	13,275	3,159	60,864	31,529	4,230	3,192	700	4,284	1,278	23,554	171,238
2018	3,671	2,730	13,663	3,220	60,480	32,085	4,240	3,301	718	4,512	1,275	24,199	173,611
2019[1]	3,755	2,830	14,175	3,342	49,220	31,834	4,270	3,438	757	4,698	1,281	24,927	163,620
2020[2]	3,875	2,525	14,225	3,390	44,550	31,800	3,650	3,540	741	4,900	1,220	25,222	158,039

[1] Preliminary. [2] Forecast. [4] Predominately pork production. *Source: Foreign Agricultural Service, U.S. Department of Agriculture (FAS-USDA)*

Production and Consumption of Red Meats in The United States

	Beef			Veal			Lamb & Mutton			Pork (Excluding Lard)			All Meats		
	Commercial Production	Consumption Total	Consumption Per Capita	Commercial Production	Consumption Total	Consumption Per Capita	Commercial Production	Consumption Total	Consumption Per Capita	Commercial Production	Consumption Total	Consumption Per Capita	Commercial Production	Consumption Total	Consumption Per Capita
Year	Million Pounds	Million Pounds	Lbs.	Million Pounds	Million Pounds	Lbs.	Million Pounds	Million Pounds	Lbs.	Million Pounds	Million Pounds	Lbs.	Million Pounds	Million Pounds	Lbs.
2011	26,195	25,538	57.3	130	137	0.4	149	295	0.8	22,758	18,382	45.7	49,232	44,351	104.2
2012	25,913	25,755	57.3	118	123	0.3	156	299	0.8	23,253	18,607	45.9	49,439	44,784	104.4
2013	25,720	25,476	56.3	111	119	0.3	156	324	0.9	23,187	19,104	46.8	49,174	45,022	104.3
2014	24,250	24,687	54.2	94	97	0.3	156	340	0.9	22,843	19,071	45.8	47,345	44,195	101.7
2015	23,698	24,773	54.0	82	88	0.2	150	357	1.0	24,501	20,593	49.8	48,520	45,810	105.0
2016	25,288	25,673	55.6	----	----	----	----	----	----	24,956	20,891	50.1	50,480	47,018	106.9
2017	26,250	26,490	56.9	----	----	----	----	----	----	25,598	21,035	50.1	52,078	47,998	108.2
2018[1]	26,938	26,767	57.2	----	----	----	----	----	----	26,330	21,497	50.9	53,507	48,769	109.5
2019[2]	27,335	27,165	57.7	----	----	----	----	----	----	27,337	22,114	52.1	54,907	49,775	111.1
2020[3]	27,576	27,306	57.7	----	----	----	----	----	----	28,299	22,574	52.9	56,113	50,381	111.9

[1] Preliminary. [2] Estimate. [3] Forecast. *Source: Economic Research Service, U.S. Department of Agriculture (ERS-USDA)*

Total Red Meat Imports (Carcass Weight Equivalent) of Principal Countries In Thousands of Metric Tons

Year	Brazil	Canada	Egypt	European Union	Hong Kong	Japan	Korea, South	Mexico	Philip-pines	Russia	Taiwan	United States	World Total
2011	37	471	217	376	583	1,977	1,015	751	279	1,781	183	1,297	12,010
2012	59	524	250	360	651	1,974	821	797	268	1,945	144	1,371	12,500
2013	57	499	195	382	869	1,960	716	877	310	1,757	165	1,419	12,915
2014	80	485	270	377	989	2,049	823	879	357	1,375	196	1,796	13,186
2015	59	482	360	365	727	1,955	963	982	313	954	237	2,034	13,453
2016	65	456	340	371	851	2,058	1,065	1,024	350	809	226	1,861	14,793
2017	56	447	250	342	971	2,266	1,113	1,073	401	836	264	1,864	14,944
2018	48	464	300	377	932	2,320	1,268	1,166	470	533	279	1,833	15,697
2019[1]	45	446	340	357	687	2,346	1,244	1,174	407	508	291	1,816	17,270
2020[2]	52	540	275	323	925	2,240	1,120	1,045	325	370	245	1,945	19,893

[1] Preliminary. [2] Forecast. *Source: Foreign Agricultural Service, U.S. Department of Agriculture (FAS-USDA)*

Total Red Meat Exports (Carcass Weight Equivalent) of Principal Countries In Thousands of Metric Tons

Year	Argentina	Australia	Brazil	Canada	China	European Union	India	New Zealand	Russia	Ukraine	United States	Uruguay	World Total
2011	194	1,390	1,871	1,554	302	2,459	1,260	483	9	30	3,620	308	14,564
2012	162	1,380	2,119	1,511	282	2,353	1,409	495	12	45	3,552	345	14,928
2013	183	1,552	2,367	1,508	279	2,387	1,713	507	13	32	3,436	323	15,616
2014	193	1,795	2,398	1,528	312	2,375	2,022	552	14	35	3,477	331	16,423
2015	181	1,802	2,277	1,561	257	2,585	1,754	609	18	65	3,300	352	16,200
2016	211	1,445	2,472	1,684	217	3,333	1,709	560	33	44	3,536	396	17,147
2017	286	1,454	2,579	1,734	229	3,078	1,786	565	44	56	3,852	409	17,612
2018	509	1,623	2,743	1,755	223	3,133	1,511	603	53	53	4,099	437	18,352
2019[1]	772	1,771	3,175	1,809	156	3,878	1,494	624	85	51	4,240	436	20,227
2020[2]	862	1,490	3,717	2,020	117	4,700	1,050	623	135	46	4,649	400	21,842

[1] Preliminary. [2] Forecast. *Source: Foreign Agricultural Service, U.S. Department of Agriculture (FAS-USDA)*

Exports and Imports of Meats in the United States (Carcass Weight Equivalent)[3]

	Exports				Imports			
Year	Beef and Veal	Lamb and Mutton	Pork[3]	All Meat	Beef and Veal	Lamb and Mutton	Pork[3]	All Meat
2009	1,935	16	4,095	6,045	2,626	171	834	3,631
2010	2,300	16	4,223	6,539	2,298	166	859	3,322
2011	2,785	19	5,196	8,000	2,057	162	803	3,022
2012	2,452	11	5,379	7,842	2,220	154	802	3,176
2013	2,588	7	4,986	7,581	2,250	173	880	3,303
2014	2,574	7	5,092	7,673	2,947	195	1,011	4,153
2015	2,267	4	5,010	7,281	3,368	214	1,116	4,698
2016	2,557	5	5,239	7,801	3,012	216	1,091	4,319
2017[1]	2,860	6	5,632	8,498	2,993	252	1,116	4,361
2018[2]	3,156	6	5,870	9,032	2,998	273	1,042	4,313

[1] Preliminary. [2] Estimate. [3] Includes meat content of minor meats and of mixed products.
Source: Economic Research Service, U.S. Department of Agriculture (FAS-USDA)

Average Wholesale Prices of Meats in the United States In Cent Per Pound

Year	Composite Retail Price of Beef, Choice, Grade 3	Composite Retail Price of Pork[3]	Wholesale Value[4] Beef	Wholesale Value[4] Pork	Net Farm Value[5] of Pork	Cow Beef Canner & Cutter, Central US	Boxed Beef Cut-out, Choice1-3, Central US 550-700 Lb.	Pork Carcass Cut-out, U.S., No. 2	Lamb Carcass, Choice-Prime, E. Coast, 55-65 lbs.	Pork[6] Loins, Central US 14-18 lbs.	Skinned Ham, Central US 17-20 lbs.	Pork Bellies, Central US 12-14 lbs.
2011	480.73	343.35	275.82	158.89	113.93	----	181.29	93.69	364.95	129.51	82.19	120.52
2012	498.59	346.67	290.59	147.10	104.88	----	190.68	84.65	329.48	119.85	73.04	88.83
2013	528.93	364.39	298.48	157.58	110.07	----	195.64	91.69	281.52	116.53	79.12	152.15
2014	597.03	401.88	364.71	187.66	131.80	----	238.94	110.10	339.65	141.93	107.00	144.90
2015	628.89	385.25	362.78	145.72	87.39	----	237.48	78.96	343.07	103.77	65.11	121.07
2016	596.38	374.67	316.78	150.12	80.05	----	207.00	78.36	332.90	96.95	66.73	123.94
2017	590.86	378.42	321.47	155.37	87.41	----	209.74	84.02	339.16	97.28	64.63	148.76
2018	592.33	374.45	328.55	140.14	79.16	----	214.06	76.09	----	92.91	56.80	133.73
2019[1]	604.37	384.33	341.48	145.38	82.95	----	222.86	77.14	----	88.88	67.66	131.84
2020[2]	653.55	402.93	365.51	148.09	74.51	----	236.36	77.31	----	99.22	54.66	95.86

[1] Preliminary. [2] Estimate. [3] Sold as retail cuts (ham, bacon, loin, etc.). [4] Quantity equivalent to 1 pound of retail cuts.
[5] Portion of gross farm value minus farm by-product allowance. *Source: Economic Research Service, U.S. Department of Agriculture (ERS-USDA)*

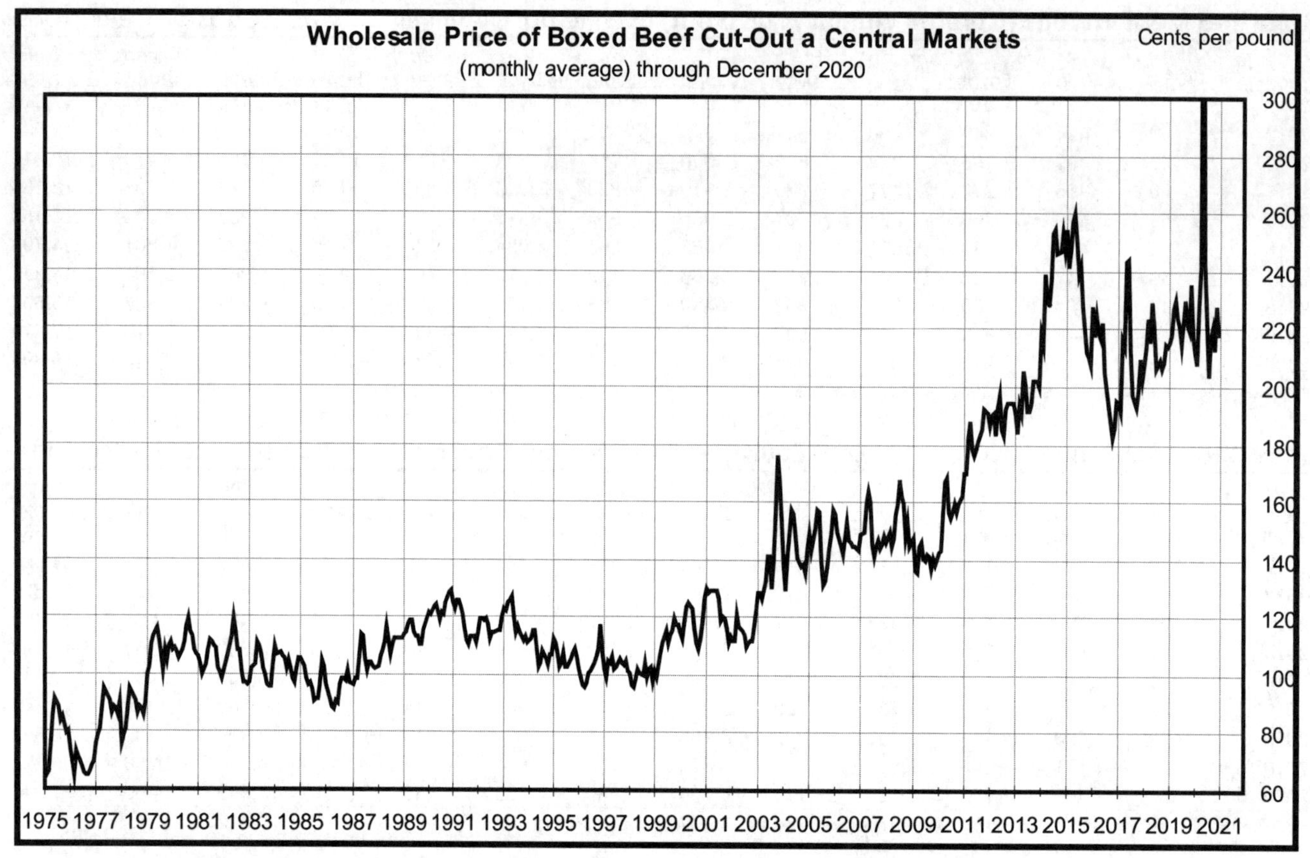

Average Wholesale Price of Boxed Beef Cut-Out[2], Choice 1-3, at Central US In Cents Per Pound

Year	Jan.	Feb.	Mar.	Apr.	May	June	July	Aug.	Sept.	Oct.	Nov.	Dec.	Average
2011	169.96	169.82	182.52	188.05	177.96	176.02	178.44	181.12	183.05	185.34	192.51	190.72	181.29
2012	186.77	190.46	190.54	183.43	192.84	197.24	185.25	186.82	192.09	194.19	194.22	194.25	190.68
2013	191.12	183.60	193.79	191.01	205.64	200.83	191.87	191.66	194.01	202.33	202.01	199.77	195.64
2014	218.00	214.43	239.03	229.14	228.96	236.60	252.87	254.83	246.14	246.80	253.18	247.35	238.94
2015	254.45	241.30	247.62	257.44	260.25	250.06	238.91	241.81	227.68	212.10	210.63	207.46	237.48
2016	227.76	217.46	224.61	218.88	216.91	222.59	204.88	199.30	187.77	182.29	186.27	195.23	207.00
2017	194.40	191.42	216.36	213.78	243.43	244.16	212.22	197.48	192.79	198.65	209.08	203.09	209.74
2018	207.94	213.66	223.50	215.29	229.34	221.03	206.32	209.15	206.07	208.18	214.59	213.60	214.06
2019	215.03	217.81	227.45	230.30	223.61	221.28	214.81	230.17	221.35	219.70	235.53	217.24	222.86
2020[1]	211.87	207.60	228.05	241.94	405.80	242.31	203.24	216.71	220.56	212.41	228.00	217.82	236.36

[1] Preliminary. [2] 600-900 pounds. *Source: Economic Research Service, U.S. Department of Agriculture (ERS-USDA)*

Production (Commercial) of All Red Meats in the United States In Millions of Pounds (Carcass Weight)

Year	Jan.	Feb.	Mar.	Apr.	May	June	July	Aug.	Sept.	Oct.	Nov.	Dec.	Total
2011	4,041.1	3,809.9	4,346.8	3,867.8	3,914.8	4,218.8	3,792.2	4,303.5	4,192.1	4,270.6	4,258.9	4,215.2	49,232
2012	4,122.9	3,914.0	4,171.4	3,855.3	4,182.7	4,022.5	3,945.3	4,391.0	3,948.0	4,580.1	4,309.3	3,996.9	49,439
2013	4,348.4	3,673.2	3,994.3	4,091.6	4,151.4	3,859.7	4,158.0	4,203.2	3,937.9	4,509.5	4,119.5	4,136.0	49,183
2014	4,248.9	3,653.1	3,814.8	3,976.9	3,952.8	3,824.0	3,906.9	3,795.3	3,958.8	4,319.3	3,759.3	4,136.2	47,346
2015	4,087.0	3,731.8	4,064.3	4,015.5	3,805.3	4,017.4	4,038.5	3,901.4	4,140.2	4,313.4	4,033.2	4,274.0	48,422
2016	4,055.6	3,904.2	4,261.8	3,982.9	3,997.1	4,225.9	3,866.0	4,432.2	4,323.1	4,426.5	4,498.4	4,402.2	50,376
2017	4,291.4	3,937.9	4,535.1	3,968.1	4,276.0	4,350.8	3,988.9	4,630.5	4,403.8	4,635.3	4,553.2	4,402.4	51,973
2018	4,588.4	4,059.5	4,520.5	4,278.2	4,501.5	4,327.7	4,235.3	4,765.9	4,187.8	4,901.4	4,682.7	4,367.8	53,417
2019	4,701.6	4,172.4	4,433.7	4,551.5	4,566.2	4,369.3	4,588.8	4,650.2	4,443.5	5,064.0	4,743.1	4,726.6	55,011
2020[1]	4,959.2	4,452.7	4,995.3	3,862.1	3,762.5	4,792.1	4,810.8	4,691.6	4,706.2	5,085.9	4,683.8	4,852.6	55,655

[1] Preliminary. *Source: Economic Research Service, U.S. Department of Agriculture (ERS-USDA)*

Production (Commercial) of Beef in the United States In Millions of Pounds (Carcass Weight)

Year	Jan.	Feb.	Mar.	Apr.	May	June	July	Aug.	Sept.	Oct.	Nov.	Dec.	Total
2011	2,122.9	2,020.4	2,266.2	2,052.5	2,131.9	2,375.0	2,134.1	2,386.9	2,215.2	2,215.1	2,148.8	2,126.3	26,195
2012	2,113.1	2,008.9	2,159.5	1,990.6	2,231.9	2,250.7	2,201.4	2,368.6	2,015.5	2,344.8	2,207.5	2,020.1	25,913
2013	2,260.0	1,873.7	2,038.6	2,127.3	2,228.0	2,161.4	2,293.5	2,241.6	2,073.6	2,316.5	2,057.3	2,046.5	25,718
2014	2,141.1	1,788.9	1,938.4	2,042.8	2,071.6	2,068.7	2,085.9	2,024.4	2,067.4	2,171.5	1,850.6	2,000.7	24,252
2015	1,963.8	1,768.7	1,931.6	1,928.5	1,924.9	2,001.2	2,046.1	1,934.1	2,085.7	2,125.3	1,934.1	2,045.9	23,690
2016	1,953.5	1,885.0	2,096.0	1,964.0	2,029.5	2,193.0	2,024.4	2,264.4	2,179.2	2,210.1	2,239.3	2,173.3	25,212
2017	2,118.3	1,933.7	2,247.7	1,962.7	2,162.1	2,279.1	2,107.5	2,401.2	2,222.3	2,300.7	2,289.6	2,148.0	26,173
2018	2,279.0	1,983.9	2,203.5	2,117.7	2,307.0	2,300.9	2,231.6	2,429.6	2,157.5	2,430.6	2,315.1	2,116.0	26,872
2019	2,308.9	1,987.6	2,117.7	2,261.5	2,327.9	2,224.6	2,359.9	2,373.5	2,189.3	2,438.1	2,297.0	2,265.0	27,151
2020[1]	2,387.6	2,130.7	2,410.8	1,815.4	1,865.1	2,373.6	2,421.2	2,334.6	2,354.5	2,471.5	2,262.9	2,324.8	27,153

[1] Preliminary. *Source: Economic Research Service, U.S. Department of Agriculture (ERS-USDA)*

Production (Commercial) of Pork in the United States In Millions of Pounds (Carcass Weight)

Year	Jan.	Feb.	Mar.	Apr.	May	June	July	Aug.	Sept.	Oct.	Nov.	Dec.	Total
2011	1,896.2	1,768.1	2,054.4	1,790.7	1,759.7	1,820.0	1,637.1	1,892.1	1,954.4	2,033.2	2,086.7	2,065.6	22,758
2012	1,987.3	1,883.0	1,987.7	1,841.9	1,926.8	1,750.5	1,721.9	1,998.1	1,911.2	2,210.7	2,079.2	1,954.2	23,253
2013	2,065.5	1,779.0	1,932.7	1,941.8	1,900.0	1,677.1	1,840.8	1,938.7	1,844.1	2,169.9	2,041.3	2,066.5	23,197
2014	2,086.1	1,844.4	1,854.5	1,910.5	1,859.5	1,734.3	1,799.3	1,752.1	1,871.9	2,126.7	1,890.7	2,114.5	22,845
2015	2,104.7	1,945.2	2,111.5	2,066.8	1,861.9	1,995.8	1,972.6	1,949.1	2,035.5	2,168.9	2,080.2	2,207.1	24,499
2016	2,084.2	2,000.6	2,145.1	2,000.1	1,948.6	2,013.3	1,824.6	2,149.1	2,125.7	2,198.1	2,240.3	2,209.0	24,939
2017	2,154.5	1,987.4	2,267.3	1,988.1	2,095.8	2,053.0	1,864.7	2,210.1	2,164.2	2,316.3	2,244.8	2,235.0	25,581
2018	2,290.1	2,058.1	2,296.8	2,141.9	2,174.4	2,008.6	1,985.5	2,316.3	2,012.9	2,450.5	2,348.0	2,232.1	26,315
2019	2,373.6	2,167.5	2,297.2	2,268.8	2,218.6	2,127.6	2,210.7	2,258.1	2,237.2	2,606.2	2,428.8	2,443.0	27,637
2020[1]	2,553.3	2,306.2	2,566.5	2,030.8	1,879.6	2,400.4	2,371.7	2,341.2	2,335.9	2,598.5	2,405.5	2,510.2	28,300

[1] Preliminary. *Source: Economic Research Service, U.S. Department of Agriculture (ERS-USDA)*

Cold Storage Holdings of All[2] Meats in the United States, on First of Month In Millions of Pounds

Year	Jan.	Feb.	Mar.	Apr.	May	June	July	Aug.	Sept.	Oct.	Nov.	Dec.
2011	939.9	1,017.4	1,050.6	1,036.6	1,009.5	1,014.9	949.4	894.2	896.7	944.9	929.3	961.1
2012	961.5	1,092.6	1,118.7	1,139.8	1,201.0	1,157.7	1,087.6	1,039.1	1,047.7	1,082.8	1,060.9	1,023.4
2013	1,043.8	1,114.8	1,148.1	1,182.4	1,238.0	1,166.3	1,071.3	1,035.5	1,005.0	1,041.0	1,033.0	1,021.9
2014	1,022.2	1,077.0	1,093.6	1,012.3	1,015.9	981.4	930.1	939.1	934.0	970.8	956.5	930.3
2015	988.5	1,131.2	1,224.3	1,196.3	1,229.0	1,172.9	1,147.6	1,136.2	1,170.0	1,202.1	1,159.5	1,122.8
2016	1,105.9	1,213.4	1,182.7	1,142.9	1,151.1	1,129.1	1,099.2	1,118.1	1,130.5	1,205.1	1,173.3	1,079.2
2017	1,083.8	1,101.3	1,112.9	1,051.4	1,092.7	1,042.4	1,012.8	1,029.8	1,100.0	1,159.7	1,149.4	1,032.3
2018	1,021.2	1,129.2	1,118.6	1,124.4	1,159.9	1,142.2	1,064.1	1,096.5	1,136.4	1,150.8	1,135.7	1,069.3
2019	1,045.6	1,119.9	1,134.5	1,095.9	1,098.1	1,077.8	1,069.4	1,113.9	1,128.7	1,115.1	1,121.6	1,092.6
2020[1]	1,101.5	1,157.3	1,185.8	1,161.7	1,136.9	936.2	938.3	950.9	961.3	968.6	981.7	966.2

[1] Preliminary. [2] Includes beef and veal, mutton and lamb, pork and products, rendered pork fat, and miscellaneous meats. Excludes lard.
Source: Economic Research Service, U.S. Department of Agriculture (ERS-USDA)

Cold Storage Holdings of Frozen Beef in the United States, on First of Month In Millions of Pounds

Year	Jan.	Feb.	Mar.	Apr.	May	June	July	Aug.	Sept.	Oct.	Nov.	Dec.
2011	445.0	461.7	459.8	445.5	443.2	447.6	432.8	415.2	428.6	427.6	417.0	443.8
2012	457.2	485.1	470.8	503.2	517.9	497.9	468.7	461.1	432.8	424.9	430.3	441.8
2013	465.7	484.6	490.0	511.2	510.1	482.6	481.2	462.6	430.2	445.2	440.1	450.8
2014	439.4	429.3	409.5	405.8	402.3	377.6	358.2	367.9	346.6	378.2	380.9	400.8
2015	444.4	492.0	491.9	481.5	484.3	474.6	474.3	460.1	470.3	498.3	509.1	510.6
2016	512.5	534.1	506.4	481.8	467.8	461.7	464.5	469.7	476.6	519.0	533.1	531.0
2017	567.9	538.2	502.4	464.0	458.4	411.5	415.3	431.8	476.6	496.0	507.0	485.2
2018	488.1	501.7	459.3	464.0	471.2	464.7	448.6	484.2	501.3	507.2	515.6	514.7
2019	495.6	510.2	474.0	451.9	430.2	405.2	405.6	454.5	469.9	469.0	466.3	478.3
2020[1]	480.1	488.2	494.6	502.3	479.5	417.4	428.2	440.2	449.4	463.0	500.2	511.5

[1] Preliminary. *Source: Economic Research Service, U.S. Department of Agriculture (ERS-USDA)*

Mercury

Mercury (atomic symbol Hg) was known to the ancient Hindus and Chinese and was also found in Egyptian tombs dating back to 1500 BC. The ancient Greeks used mercury in ointments, and the Romans used it in cosmetics. Alchemists thought mercury turned into gold when it hardened.

Mercury, also called quicksilver, is a heavy, silvery, toxic, transitional metal. Mercury is the only common metal that is liquid at room temperatures. When subjected to a pressure of 7,640 atmospheres (7.7 million millibars), mercury becomes a solid. Mercury dissolves in nitric or concentrated sulfuric acid but is resistant to alkalis. It is a poor conductor of heat. Mercury has superconductivity when cooled to sufficiently low temperatures. It has a freezing point of about –39 degrees Celsius and a boiling point of about 357 degrees Celsius.

Prices – The average monthly price of mercury in 2019 fell -8.2% yr/yr to $2,550.00 per flask (34.5 kilograms), still below the record high of $3,438.59 posted in 2013.

Supply – World mine production of mercury in 2020 fell -5.1% yr/yr at 3,700 metric tons, down from the 2018 record high of 4,060 metric tons. The record low of 1,150 metric tons was posted in 2006. The world's largest miners of mercury are China, with 91.9% of world production, and Tajikistan with 2.7%. China has posted a new record high most years since 2009. China's record low of 190 metric tons was posted in 2001.

Demand – The breakdown of domestic consumption of mercury by categories is no longer available. However, in 1997 records showed that chlorine and caustic soda accounted for 46% of U.S. mercury consumption, followed by wiring devices and switches (17%), dental equipment (12%), electrical lighting (8%), and measuring control instruments (7%). Substitutes for mercury include lithium and composite ceramic materials.

Trade – U.S. foreign trade in mercury has been relatively small, but U.S. imports of mercury in 2019 rose +50.0% yr/yr to 9.0 metric tons, but still far below the almost 3-decade high of 294 metric tons in 2010. By contrast, the U.S.'s record high imports were in 1974 at 1,799 metric tons. U.S. imports were mostly from Chile and Peru.

World Mine Production of Mercury In Metric Tons (1 tonne = 29.008216 flasks)

Year	Chile (byproduct)	China	Finland	Kyrgyzstan	Mexico (Exports)	Morocco	Peru (Exports)	Russia	Tajikistan	United States	World Total
2013	19	1,820	----	71	266	8	45	NA	30	NA	2,320
2014	18	2,260	----	48	301	8	40	NA	35	NA	2,770
2015	14	2,800	----	46	306	5	35	NA	30	NA	3,300
2016	2	3,250	----	40	262	5	40	----	30	----	3,670
2017	2	3,380	----	20	197	10	40	----	100	----	3,790
2018	----	3,600	----	20	234	----	40	----	100	----	4,060
2019[1]	----	3,600	----	15	63	----	40	----	100	----	3,900
2020[2]	----	3,400	----	15	60	----	40	----	100	----	3,700

[1] Preliminary. [2] Estimate. NA = Not available W = Withheld. *Source: U.S. Geological Survey (USGS)*

Salient Statistics of Mercury in the United States In Metric Tons

		Secondary Production						
Year	Producing Mines	Industrial	Government[3]	NDS[4] Shipments	Consumer & Dealer Stocks, Dec. 31	Industrial Demand	Exports	Imports
2013	NA	NA	----	----	NA	NA	0	38
2014	NA	NA	----	----	NA	NA	----	50
2015	NA	NA	----	----	NA	NA	0	26
2016	NA	NA	----	----	NA	NA	----	24
2017	NA	NA	----	----	NA	NA	----	20
2018	NA	NA	----	----	NA	NA	----	6
2019[1]	NA	NA	----	----	NA	NA	----	9
2020[2]	NA	NA	----	----	NA	NA	----	----

[1] Preliminary. [2] Estimate. [3] Secondary mercury shipped from the Department of Energy. [4] National Defense Stockpile. [5] Less than 1/2 unit. NA = Not available. *Source: U.S. Geological Survey (USGS)*

Average Price of Mercury in New York In Dollars Per Flask of 76 Pounds (34.5 Kilograms)

Year	Jan.	Feb.	Mar.	Apr.	May	June	July	Aug.	Sept.	Oct.	Nov.	Dec.	Average
2013	3,313.05	3,450.00	3,450.00	3,450.00	3,450.00	3,450.00	3,450.00	3,450.00	3,450.00	3,450.00	3,450.00	3,450.00	3,438.59
2014	3,269.57	3,175.00	2,991.67	2,850.00	2,563.64	2,550.00	2,550.00	2,550.00	2,550.00	2,550.00	2,550.00	2,550.00	2,724.99
2015	2,550.00	2,550.00	2,550.00	2,550.00	2,550.00	2,550.00	2,550.00	2,550.00	2,550.00	2,515.91	1,716.67	1,484.78	2,388.95
2016	1,450.00	1,450.00	1,406.52	1,350.00	1,350.00	1,304.55	1,155.24	1,110.00	1,095.68	1,095.00	1,107.27	1,162.50	1,253.06
2017	1,162.50	1,162.50	1,162.50	1,168.12	1,275.00	1,275.00	1,275.00	1,351.09	1,400.00	1,400.00	1,400.00	1,590.48	1,301.85
2018	1,971.74	2,603.00	2,901.82	3,030.95	2,875.00	2,875.00	2,915.91	2,925.00	2,925.00	2,925.00	2,822.73	2,550.00	2,776.76
2019	2,550.00	2,550.00	2,550.00	2,550.00	2,550.00	2,550.00	2,550.00	2,550.00	2,550.00	2,550.00	2,550.00	2,550.00	2,550.00
2020	2,550.00	2,550.00	2,550.00	2,550.00	2,550.00	2,550.00	2,550.00	2,550.00	2,550.00	2,550.00	2,550.00	2,550.00	2,550.00

Source: American Metal Market (AMM)

Milk

Evidence of human consumption of animal milk was discovered in a temple in the Euphrates Valley near Babylon, dating back to 3,000 BC. Humans drink the milk produced from a variety of domesticated mammals, including cows, goats, sheep, camels, reindeer, buffaloes, and llama. In India, half of all milk consumed is from water buffalo. Camels' milk spoils slower than other types of milk in the hot desert, but virtually all milk used for commercial production and consumption comes from cows.

Milk directly from a cow in its natural form is called raw milk. Raw milk is processed by spinning it in a centrifuge, homogenizing it to create a consistent texture (i.e., by forcing hot milk under high pressure through small nozzles), and then sterilizing it through pasteurization (i.e., heating to a high temperature for a specified length of time to destroy pathogenic bacteria). Condensed, powdered, and evaporated milk are produced by evaporating some or all of the water content. Whole milk contains 3.5% milk fat. Lower-fat milks include 2% low-fat milk, 1% low- fat milk, and skim milk, which has only 1/2 gram of milk fat per serving.

The CME Group has three different milk futures contracts: Milk Class III which is milk used in the manufacturing of cheese, Milk Class IV which is milk used in the production of butter and all dried milk products, and Nonfat Dry Milk which is used in commercial or consumer cooking or to reconstitute nonfat milk by the consumer. The Milk Class III contract has the largest volume and open interest.

Prices – The average monthly price received by farmers for all milk sold to plants in 2020 fell by -1.7% yr/yr to $18.32 per hundred pounds, but still well below the 2014 record high of $23.98.

Supply – World milk production in 2021 is expected to rise +1.5% to 651.823 million metric tons, a new record high. The biggest producers are expected to be India with 31.2% of world production, the European Union with 25.0%, and the U.S. with 15.7%. U.S. 2020 milk production rose +2.1% yr/yr to 223.055 billion pounds, setting a record high.

The number of dairy cows on U.S. farms has fallen sharply in the past three decades from the 12 million seen in 1970. In 2020, there were 9.382 million dairy cows on U.S. farms, virtually unchanged yr/yr. Dairy farmers have been able to increase milk production even with fewer cows because of a dramatic increase in milk yield per cow. In 2020, the average cow produced 23,774 pounds of milk per year, a +1.6% yr/yr increase, more than double the 9,751 pounds seen in 1970.

Demand – Per capita consumption of milk in the U.S. fell to a new record low of 204 pounds per year in 2008, down sharply by -26.0% from 277 pounds in 1977. The utilization breakdown for 2002 shows the largest manufacturing usage categories are cheese (64.504 billion pounds of milk) and creamery butter (30.250 billion pounds).

Trade – U.S. imports of milk in 2020 rose +1.5% yr/yr to 6.600 billion pounds, still well below the record high of 7.500 billion pounds posted in 2005-06.

World Fluid Milk Production (Cow's Milk) In Thousands of Metric Tons

Year	Argentina	Australia	Brazil	Canada	China	European Union	India	Mexico	New Zealand	Russia	Ukraine	United States	World Total
2013	11,519	9,309	24,259	8,443	31,458	144,850	137,686	11,451	20,200	29,865	11,488	91,290	548,478
2014	11,326	9,798	25,489	8,437	33,149	150,850	146,313	11,624	21,893	29,795	11,426	93,462	570,245
2015	11,552	10,091	25,650	8,773	33,298	154,550	155,481	11,900	21,587	29,688	10,864	94,579	585,047
2016	10,191	9,486	25,857	9,081	32,240	155,550	165,118	12,122	21,224	29,587	10,625	96,367	594,498
2017	10,090	9,462	26,766	9,675	31,886	158,000	176,061	12,288	21,530	29,972	10,520	97,762	611,142
2018	10,837	9,451	26,745	9,944	32,250	159,255	187,700	12,537	22,017	30,398	10,300	98,688	627,250
2019	10,640	8,832	27,292	9,903	33,000	159,900	191,000	12,820	21,896	31,154	9,866	99,056	632,580
2020[1]	11,350	9,100	26,505	9,950	34,100	162,210	194,800	12,921	22,000	31,650	9,190	101,015	642,466
2021[2]	11,575	9,400	26,970	9,980	35,700	162,820	199,000	13,070	22,200	31,800	8,780	102,648	651,823

[1] Preliminary. [2] Forecast. *Source: Foreign Agricultural Service, U.S. Department of Agriculture (FAS-USDA)*

Salient Statistics of Milk in the United States In Millions of Pounds

	Number of Milk Cows on Farms3 (Thousands)	Supply					Utilization				Average Farm Price Received Per Cwt.			Per Capita Consumption[6] (Fluid Milk in Lbs)
		Production						Domestic						
Year		Per Cow[4] (Pounds)	Total[4]	Beginning Stocks[5]	Imports	Total Supply	Exports[5]	Fed to Calves	Humans	Total Use	All Milk, Wholesale	Milk Eligible for Fluid Market	Milk, Manufacturing Grade	
2013	9,215	21,413	201,218	11,403	3,772	216,393	12,065	877	192,137	205,079	20.04	----	----	
2014	9,257	22,259	206,046	10,344	4,372	220,762	12,159	872	196,308	209,340	23.98	----	----	
2015	9,314	22,396	208,633	10,487	5,759	224,879	8,500	879	202,260	211,639	17.11	----	----	
2016	9,328	22,775	212,436	12,335	6,937	231,708	8,395	898	211,412	220,705	16.30	----	----	
2017	9,392	22,941	215,466	12,722	5,977	234,165	9,223	901	214,535	224,659	17.66	----	----	
2018	9,399	23,149	217,575	13,397	6,347	237,319	10,458	928	216,551	227,937	16.26	----	----	
2019[1]	9,336	23,391	218,382	13,790	6,500	238,672	10,700	932	217,362	228,994	18.63	----	----	
2020[2]	9,388	23,778	223,220	13,623	6,600	243,443	10,200				18.32	----	----	

[1] Preliminary. [2] Estimate. [3] Average number on farms during year including dry cows, excluding heifers not yet fresh. [4] Excludes milk sucked by calves. [5] Government and commercial. [6] Product pounds of commercial sales and on farm consumption.
Source: Economic Research Service, U.S. Department of Agriculture (ERS-USDA)

Milk-Feed Price Ratio[1] in the United States In Pounds

Year	Jan.	Feb.	Mar.	Apr.	May	June	July	Aug.	Sept.	Oct.	Nov.	Dec.	Average
2011	1.96	2.01	2.12	1.81	1.73	1.87	1.91	1.83	1.84	1.82	1.89	1.81	1.88
2012	1.72	1.56	1.48	1.41	1.34	1.38	1.34	1.37	1.59	1.74	1.74	1.65	1.53
2013	1.57	1.52	1.48	1.54	1.53	1.52	1.53	1.68	1.88	2.10	2.27	2.30	1.74
2014	2.46	2.59	2.54	2.42	2.24	2.20	2.36	2.63	2.96	2.92	2.75	2.40	2.54
2015	2.11	2.05	2.01	1.95	1.97	2.07	2.01	2.10	2.23	2.30	2.45	2.29	2.13
2016	2.18	2.18	2.12	1.99	1.89	1.91	2.16	2.44	2.49	2.38	2.59	2.73	2.26
2017	2.71	2.62	2.40	2.22	2.20	2.31	2.27	2.51	2.46	2.47	2.54	2.38	2.42
2018	2.18	2.03	1.99	1.89	1.90	1.98	1.93	2.06	2.13	2.22	2.21	2.07	2.05
2019	2.06	2.07	2.14	2.11	2.10	2.08	2.16	2.26	2.34	2.42	2.65	2.57	2.25
2020[1]	2.42	2.34	2.23	1.84	1.77	2.36	2.69	2.50	2.28	2.50	2.58	2.18	2.31

[1] Pounds of 16% protein mixed dairy feed equal in value to one pound of whole milk. [2] Preliminary. *Source: Economic Research Service, U.S. Department of Agriculture (ERS-USDA)*

Milk Production[2] in the United States In Millions of Pounds

Year	Jan.	Feb.	Mar.	Apr.	May	June	July	Aug.	Sept.	Oct.	Nov.	Dec.	Total
2011	16,393	15,077	16,989	16,652	17,278	16,518	16,479	16,422	15,783	16,278	15,820	16,556	196,245
2012	17,016	16,310	17,718	17,232	17,601	16,676	16,585	16,403	15,687	16,267	16,008	16,821	200,324
2013	17,109	15,759	17,677	17,249	17,813	16,935	16,788	16,789	15,831	16,475	16,003	16,790	201,218
2014	17,284	15,907	17,829	17,480	18,094	17,323	17,435	17,224	16,514	17,071	16,551	17,334	206,046
2015	17,685	16,166	18,085	17,788	18,428	17,504	17,665	17,403	16,617	17,130	16,689	17,473	208,633
2016	17,693	16,904	18,401	17,947	18,613	17,771	17,908	17,692	16,990	17,565	17,100	17,852	212,436
2017	18,128	16,694	18,740	18,332	18,952	18,060	18,268	18,049	17,156	17,769	17,260	18,058	215,466
2018	18,437	16,973	18,989	18,412	19,131	18,288	18,329	18,245	17,395	17,873	17,348	18,155	217,575
2019	18,612	16,966	18,845	18,433	19,058	18,225	18,375	18,267	17,595	18,135	17,506	18,365	218,382
2020[1]	18,877	17,895	19,402	18,684	18,972	18,414	18,756	18,632	18,031	18,603	18,103	18,851	223,220

[1] Preliminary. [2] Excludes milk sucked by calves. *Source: Economic Research Service, U.S. Department of Agriculture (ERS-USDA)*

Milk Cows[2] in the United States In Thousands of Head

Year	Jan.	Feb.	Mar.	Apr.	May	June	July	Aug.	Sept.	Oct.	Nov.	Dec.	Total
2011	9,160	9,163	9,180	9,182	9,194	9,196	9,198	9,200	9,201	9,212	9,213	9,223	9,194
2012	9,242	9,257	9,271	9,273	9,263	9,241	9,222	9,217	9,195	9,189	9,201	9,218	9,232
2013	9,222	9,223	NA	NA	NA	NA	9,235	9,229	9,208	9,203	9,198	9,202	9,215
2014	9,212	9,212	9,223	9,240	9,252	9,267	9,268	9,268	9,274	9,277	9,284	9,299	9,257
2015	9,308	9,308	9,311	9,316	9,324	9,323	9,314	9,315	9,317	9,320	9,322	9,320	9,314
2016	9,304	9,311	9,321	9,321	9,322	9,326	9,329	9,334	9,331	9,335	9,344	9,354	9,328
2017	9,359	9,365	9,383	9,392	9,401	9,404	9,404	9,404	9,399	9,395	9,398	9,400	9,392
2018	9,438	9,436	9,430	9,418	9,422	9,414	9,392	9,389	9,368	9,367	9,358	9,353	9,399
2019	9,354	9,352	9,333	9,332	9,333	9,327	9,315	9,318	9,333	9,347	9,345	9,343	9,336
2020[1]	9,365	9,377	9,391	9,377	9,360	9,355	9,372	9,374	9,395	9,414	9,432	9,442	9,388

[1] Preliminary. [2] Includes dry cows, excludes heifers not yet fresh. *Source: Economic Research Service, U.S. Department of Agriculture (ERS-USDA)*

Milk Per Cow[2] in the United States In Pounds

Year	Jan.	Feb.	Mar.	Apr.	May	June	July	Aug.	Sept.	Oct.	Nov.	Dec.	Total
2011	1,790	1,645	1,851	1,814	1,879	1,796	1,792	1,785	1,715	1,767	1,717	1,795	21,346
2012	1,841	1,762	1,911	1,858	1,900	1,805	1,798	1,780	1,706	1,770	1,740	1,825	21,696
2013	1,855	1,709	NA	NA	NA	NA	1,818	1,819	1,719	1,790	1,740	1,825	21,413
2014	1,876	1,727	1,933	1,892	1,956	1,869	1,881	1,858	1,781	1,840	1,783	1,864	22,259
2015	1,900	1,737	1,942	1,909	1,976	1,878	1,897	1,868	1,784	1,838	1,790	1,875	22,396
2016	1,902	1,815	1,974	1,925	1,997	1,906	1,920	1,895	1,821	1,882	1,830	1,908	22,775
2017	1,937	1,783	1,997	1,952	2,016	1,920	1,943	1,919	1,825	1,891	1,837	1,921	22,941
2018	1,953	1,799	2,014	1,955	2,030	1,943	1,952	1,943	1,857	1,908	1,854	1,941	23,149
2019	1,990	1,814	2,019	1,975	2,042	1,954	1,973	1,960	1,885	1,940	1,873	1,966	23,391
2020[1]	2,016	1,908	2,066	1,993	2,027	1,968	2,001	1,988	1,919	1,976	1,919	1,997	23,778

[1] Preliminary. [2] Excludes milk sucked by calves. *Source: Economic Research Service, U.S. Department of Agriculture (ERS-USDA)*

Average Price Received by Farmers for All Milk (Sold to Plants) In Dollars Per Hundred Pounds (Cwt.)

Year	Jan.	Feb.	Mar.	Apr.	May	June	July	Aug.	Sept.	Oct.	Nov.	Dec.	Average
2011	16.70	19.10	20.40	19.60	19.60	21.10	21.80	22.10	21.10	20.00	20.50	19.70	20.14
2012	19.00	17.70	17.20	16.80	16.20	16.30	16.90	18.20	18.90	21.60	22.10	20.80	18.48
2013	19.90	19.50	19.10	19.50	19.70	19.50	19.10	19.60	20.10	20.90	21.60	22.00	20.04
2014	23.50	24.90	25.10	25.30	24.20	23.20	23.30	24.20	25.70	24.90	23.00	20.40	23.98
2015	17.60	16.80	16.60	16.50	16.80	17.00	16.70	16.70	17.50	17.70	18.20	17.20	17.11
2016	16.10	15.70	15.30	15.10	14.50	14.80	16.10	17.20	17.40	16.70	17.80	18.90	16.30
2017	18.90	18.50	17.30	16.50	16.70	17.30	17.20	18.10	17.90	18.10	18.20	17.20	17.66
2018	16.10	15.30	15.70	15.70	16.20	16.30	15.50	16.10	16.90	17.50	17.20	16.60	16.26
2019	16.60	16.80	17.60	17.70	18.00	18.10	18.70	18.90	19.30	20.00	21.10	20.70	18.63
2020[1]	19.60	18.90	18.00	14.40	13.60	18.10	20.50	18.80	17.90	20.20	21.30	18.50	18.32

[1] Preliminary. *Source: Economic Research Service, U.S. Department of Agriculture (ERS-USDA)*

Production of Nonfat Dry Milk in the United States In Thousands of Pounds

Year	Jan.	Feb.	Mar.	Apr.	May	June	July	Aug.	Sept.	Oct.	Nov.	Dec.	Total
2011	114,896	106,785	124,065	145,323	147,290	145,125	131,502	113,299	103,115	99,751	119,686	148,640	1,499,477
2012	152,085	171,394	189,227	190,728	193,362	168,394	140,169	106,014	84,498	95,064	115,854	157,660	1,764,449
2013	142,799	137,674	146,576	160,117	150,531	130,901	116,616	106,039	74,026	85,830	101,185	125,570	1,477,864
2014	138,661	141,187	167,853	160,342	162,139	148,648	166,602	116,134	112,467	134,973	151,402	164,224	1,764,632
2015	167,705	150,960	180,878	180,771	180,013	165,441	155,265	123,892	119,974	118,360	127,939	151,150	1,822,348
2016	137,463	142,978	172,003	170,796	165,837	146,643	150,787	117,550	125,486	140,051	128,105	154,935	1,752,634
2017	153,868	143,252	160,931	172,840	167,912	162,827	151,831	136,767	134,587	145,008	141,440	164,014	1,835,277
2018	159,272	157,105	177,980	169,428	165,670	152,244	150,193	129,077	114,030	121,595	134,424	142,522	1,773,540
2019	172,690	153,806	161,829	167,758	173,666	157,948	172,329	132,525	117,806	132,716	138,880	164,869	1,846,822
2020[1]	176,259	159,128	172,389	195,159	158,591	147,134	163,198	144,216	125,980	138,720	159,182	204,534	1,944,490

[1] Preliminary. *Source: Economic Research Service, U.S. Department of Agriculture (ERS-USDA)*

Production of Dry Whey in the United States In Thousands of Pounds

Year	Jan.	Feb.	Mar.	Apr.	May	June	July	Aug.	Sept.	Oct.	Nov.	Dec.	Total
2011	90,192	82,035	94,304	92,037	91,293	83,740	81,752	79,759	76,800	77,517	77,614	83,074	1,010,117
2012	95,588	89,274	88,348	84,014	86,760	83,819	79,807	77,543	74,810	77,195	72,559	89,181	998,898
2013	86,558	77,097	83,248	81,653	75,535	75,425	76,416	73,122	68,692	71,883	74,718	108,633	952,980
2014	70,011	65,603	71,504	71,629	82,480	79,309	73,475	71,192	69,537	68,684	70,994	75,283	869,701
2015	75,342	76,630	86,409	76,512	80,778	85,506	81,225	83,585	78,823	75,576	82,959	94,223	977,568
2016	83,459	74,891	82,762	82,075	81,836	80,002	82,354	76,505	75,864	83,966	72,893	78,534	955,141
2017	82,255	77,548	87,602	85,218	83,545	87,886	99,652	94,248	90,561	79,749	81,237	85,913	1,035,414
2018	90,569	89,431	91,368	85,731	85,904	86,603	90,171	78,814	69,951	84,003	72,306	74,505	999,356
2019	81,202	74,948	77,378	74,998	79,090	82,976	82,906	84,897	90,627	90,843	75,111	79,821	974,797
2020[1]	84,272	76,490	82,100	77,844	86,534	84,795	84,826	78,818	74,758	74,751	69,359	81,651	956,198

[1] Preliminary. Excludes all modified dry whey products. *Source: Economic Research Service, U.S. Department of Agriculture (ERS-USDA)*

Production of Whey Protein Concentrate in the United States In Thousands of Pounds

Year	Jan.	Feb.	Mar.	Apr.	May	June	July	Aug.	Sept.	Oct.	Nov.	Dec.	Total
2011	34,871	32,701	36,809	34,668	36,669	36,292	34,683	35,248	35,571	37,323	36,818	39,285	430,938
2012	38,845	35,064	41,433	39,077	38,417	39,942	35,590	36,804	37,469	38,627	37,735	40,471	459,474
2013	39,262	36,941	41,742	40,396	43,391	41,501	40,265	39,461	39,386	45,542	43,194	46,567	497,648
2014	44,325	42,165	45,076	46,127	46,630	43,871	44,876	44,945	41,621	46,971	46,066	47,428	540,101
2015	44,061	38,365	42,234	42,375	43,812	39,307	41,736	39,380	37,474	41,302	40,137	42,766	492,949
2016	42,602	39,780	41,851	39,027	39,349	38,037	38,437	35,665	36,745	38,060	39,419	39,457	468,429
2017	40,714	36,457	42,736	42,469	41,993	40,669	41,587	38,737	39,109	41,203	40,935	42,313	488,922
2018	44,257	41,182	50,463	41,887	42,424	41,001	40,877	42,856	41,991	42,392	40,919	43,722	513,971
2019	43,170	39,295	42,026	40,639	41,911	38,840	39,802	39,903	40,068	40,672	40,696	43,106	490,128
2020[1]	41,935	35,600	39,800	38,650	38,509	39,785	39,600	39,512	39,400	38,689	40,053	43,205	474,738

[1] Preliminary. *Source: Economic Research Service, U.S. Department of Agriculture (ERS-USDA)*

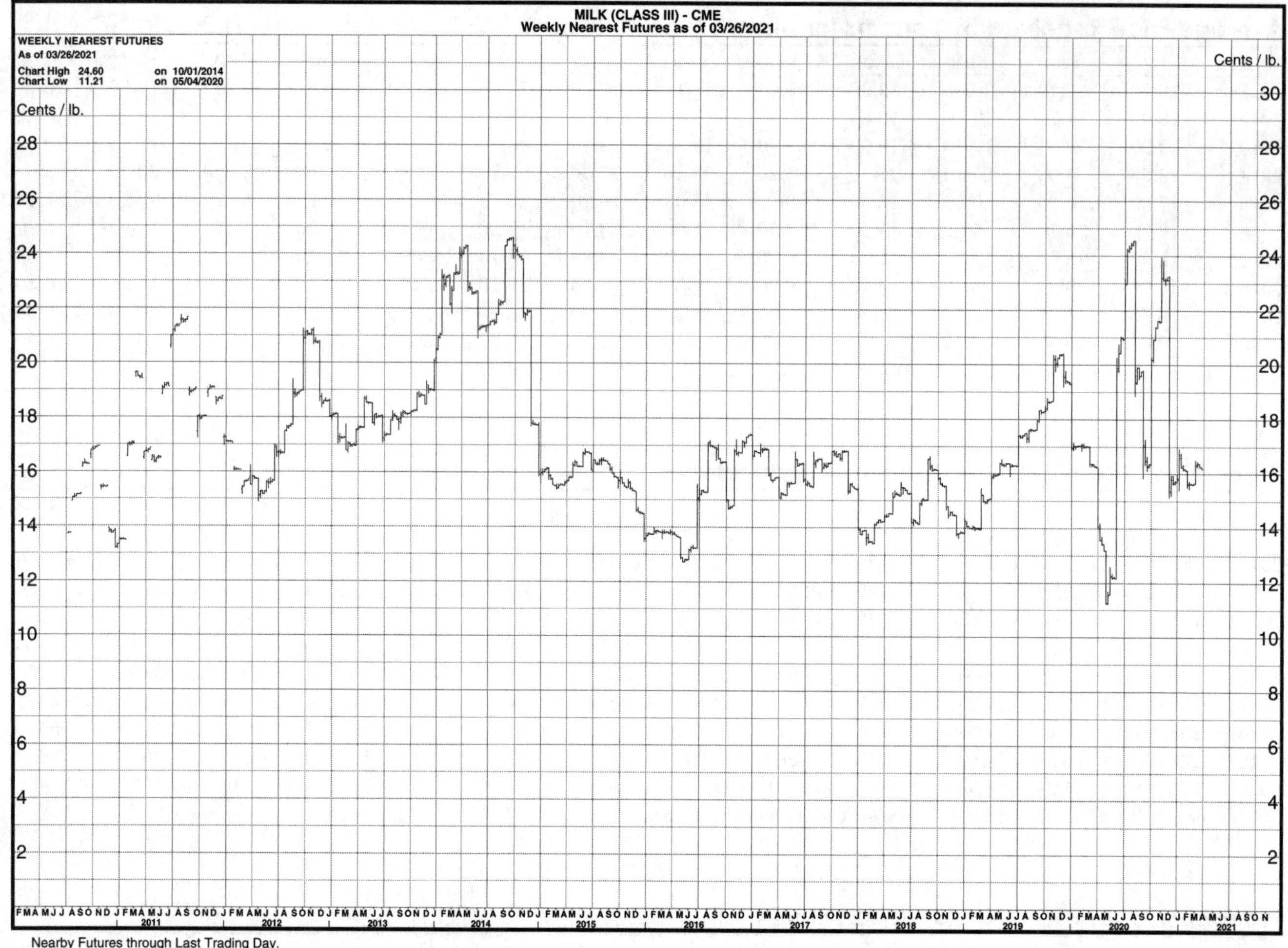

Nearby Futures through Last Trading Day.

Volume of Trading of Class III Milk Futures in Chicago In Contracts

Year	Jan.	Feb.	Mar.	Apr.	May	June	July	Aug.	Sept.	Oct.	Nov.	Dec.	Total
2011	48,169	40,246	37,892	16,713	24,145	30,885	27,495	37,989	29,503	25,880	25,522	24,175	368,614
2012	27,318	27,399	31,079	21,345	22,468	19,617	27,152	28,798	23,819	25,021	22,239	18,242	294,497
2013	22,182	20,654	25,964	29,668	24,403	22,482	23,762	28,680	19,519	24,806	21,210	30,611	293,941
2014	37,317	27,468	31,390	23,084	22,764	21,118	26,702	28,532	38,651	33,233	25,464	42,936	358,659
2015	30,448	29,457	23,844	22,999	21,087	21,649	23,920	16,422	19,958	18,049	22,488	25,218	275,539
2016	20,769	20,574	19,533	22,613	27,322	44,457	18,030	30,654	28,089	24,141	28,134	37,643	321,959
2017	27,439	28,001	33,774	20,263	30,371	25,574	25,564	31,494	22,438	22,205	27,303	25,402	319,828
2018	23,610	18,682	17,419	19,020	21,425	33,116	23,538	27,829	22,004	35,993	30,999	28,617	302,252
2019	27,638	25,049	23,083	26,149	24,669	22,034	26,154	24,635	35,003	36,380	31,377	33,676	335,847
2020	29,402	29,816	35,523	41,515	38,908	40,852	38,242	37,938	27,094	36,808	33,363	39,179	428,640

Contract size = 200,000 lbs. *Source: CME Group; Chicago Mercantile Exchange (CME)*

Average Open Interest of Class III Milk Futures in Chicago In Contracts

Year	Jan.	Feb.	Mar.	Apr.	May	June	July	Aug.	Sept.	Oct.	Nov.	Dec.
2011	33,741	38,813	38,723	34,509	33,021	35,150	35,730	36,553	33,284	31,322	33,127	33,472
2012	32,511	33,482	31,516	28,476	26,706	24,376	24,511	26,462	26,559	25,497	22,784	20,226
2013	19,320	20,206	21,408	23,180	22,062	21,456	21,802	23,267	23,463	22,153	22,480	24,287
2014	26,264	28,094	29,393	28,695	27,114	26,298	26,128	29,218	32,844	36,731	39,197	43,959
2015	46,134	44,918	42,292	37,710	34,509	31,725	28,890	28,792	26,554	25,839	27,821	29,784
2016	32,267	33,051	31,996	31,881	32,970	30,976	30,323	29,969	31,548	31,845	31,605	33,695
2017	31,058	31,194	34,015	34,006	31,200	28,498	28,226	25,863	25,933	23,510	24,940	25,949
2018	24,834	23,883	23,021	22,280	22,375	22,572	23,397	22,391	22,843	25,498	29,760	28,206
2019	26,355	25,593	23,301	21,497	22,591	22,221	20,718	19,169	20,918	21,182	22,763	20,166
2020	17,223	17,888	18,801	23,000	23,875	24,576	26,035	23,371	19,973	21,649	22,465	20,318

Contract size = 200,000 lbs. *Source: CME Group; Chicago Mercantile Exchange (CME)*

Molybdenum

Molybdenum (atomic symbol Mo) is a silvery-white, hard, malleable, metallic element. Molybdenum melts at about 2610 degrees Celsius and boils at about 4640 degrees Celsius. Swedish chemist Carl Wilhelm Scheele discovered molybdenum in 1778.

Molybdenum occurs in nature in the form of molybdenite and wulfenite. Contributing to the growth of plants, it is an important trace element in soils. Approximately 70% of the world supply of molybdenum is obtained as a by-product of copper mining. Molybdenum is chiefly used as an alloy to strengthen steel and resist corrosion. It is used for structural work, aircraft parts, and forged automobile parts because it withstands high temperatures and pressures and adds strength. Other uses include lubricants, a refractory metal in chemical applications, electron tubing, and as a catalyst.

Prices – The average monthly U.S. merchant price of molybdic oxide in 2020 fell -24.4% yr/yr to $8.74 per pound, well below the 2005 record high of $32.70 per pound.

Supply – World mine production of molybdenum in 2020 rose +2.0% yr/yr to 300,000 metric tons. The two-decade low of 122,000 metric tons was seen in 2002. The major producers were China with 40.0% of world production, Chile with 19.3%, and the U.S. with 16.3%. U.S. mine production of molybdenum in 2020 rose +12.4% yr/yr to 49,000 metric tons. U.S. net production of molybdenum metal powder is now being withheld as proprietary data, but in 2008 the figure was 1,640 metric tons.

Demand –U.S. consumption of molybdenum products in 2020 fell -15.2% yr/yr to 14,000 metric tons.

Trade – U.S. imports of molybdenum concentrate for consumption in 2018 fell by -5.8% yr/yr to 22,900 metric tons, still well above the 2-decade low of 4,710 metric tons posted in 2002.

World Mine Production of Molybdenum In Metric Tons (Contained Molybdenum)

Year	Armenia	Canada[3]	Chile	China	Iran	Kazakhstan	Mexico	Mongolia	Peru	Russia	United States	Uzbekisten	World Total
2014	7,162	9,358	48,770	129,000	3,494	----	14,370	1,999	17,018	3,114	68,200	450	306,000
2015	6,300	2,505	52,579	135,000	3,500	----	12,279	2,557	20,153	3,000	47,400	450	288,000
2016	6,300	2,708	55,647	129,000	3,500	----	11,896	2,444	25,757	3,000	36,200	450	278,000
2017	5,800	5,290	62,500	130,000	3,500	----	14,000	1,800	28,100	3,100	40,700	450	297,000
2018	5,000	4,680	60,200	133,000	3,500	----	15,100	1,800	28,000	2,800	41,400	200	297,000
2019[1]	5,000	3,900	56,000	130,000	3,500	----	16,600	1,800	30,400	2,800	43,600	200	294,000
2020[2]	7,000	2,700	58,000	120,000	3,500	----	17,000	1,800	30,000	2,800	49,000	200	300,000

[1] Preliminary. [2] Estimate. [3] Shipments. *Source: U.S. Geological Survey (USGS)*

Salient Statistics of Molybdenum in the United States In Metric Tons (Contained Molybdenum)

	Concentrate							Primary Products[4]							
		Shipments						Net Production				Shipments			
Year	Production	Total (Including Exports)	Value Million $	For Exports	Consumption	Imports For Consumption	Stocks Dec. 31[3]	Grand Total	Molybolic Oxide[5]	Molybdenum Metal Powder	Avg Price Value $ / Kg.[6]	Domestic Destinations	To Oxide for Exports, Gross Weight	Consumption	Producer Stocks, Dec. 31
2014	68,200	71,900	----	----	W	15,800	W	----	----	----	25.84	W	1,740	19,500	W
2015	47,400	50,500	----	----	W	12,900	W	----	----	----	15.01	W	1,300	17,600	W
2016	36,200	38,600	----	----	W	14,900	W	----	----	----	14.40	W	853	15,800	W
2017	40,700	40,400	----	----	W	24,300	W	----	----	----	18.06	W	534	17,400	W
2018	41,400	42,600	----	----	W	22,900	W	----	----	----	27.04	W	874	16,700	W
2019[1]	43,600		----	----	W		W	----	----	----	26.50	W		16,500	W
2020[2]	49,000		----	----	W		W	----	----	----	20.00	W		14,000	W

[1] Preliminary. [2] Estimate. [3] At mines & at plants making molybdenum products. [4] Comprises ferromolybdenum, molybdic oxide, & molybdenum salts & metal. [5] Includes molybdic oxide briquets, molybdic acid, molybdenum trioxide, all other. [6] U.S. producer price per kilogram of molybdenum oxide contained in technical-grade molybdic oxide. W = Withheld proprietary data. E = Net exporter. *Source: U.S. Geological Survey (USGS)*

US Merchant Price of Molybdic Oxide In Dollars Per Pound

Year	Jan.	Feb.	Mar.	Apr.	May	June	July	Aug.	Sept.	Oct.	Nov.	Dec.	Average
2014	9.92	10.26	10.29	11.60	14.05	14.72	13.55	13.25	12.84	10.59	9.78	9.59	11.70
2015	9.41	8.58	8.17	8.02	7.63	7.32	6.04	6.11	5.88	5.01	4.73	5.02	6.83
2016	5.32	5.45	5.45	5.55	6.87	7.95	6.91	7.11	7.13	6.88	6.82	6.71	6.51
2017	7.22	7.75	8.38	9.03	8.56	7.49	7.41	8.22	8.76	8.53	8.53	9.33	8.27
2018	11.42	12.33	12.96	12.48	11.95	11.43	11.28	12.15	12.16	12.06	12.01	12.22	12.04
2019	11.59	11.64	12.50	12.14	12.33	12.32	12.10	11.99	11.91	11.28	9.41	9.53	11.56
2020	9.89	10.34	9.14	8.31	8.66	8.18	7.27	7.73	8.35	8.55	9.20	9.31	8.74

Source: American Metal Market (AMM)

Nickel

Nickel (atomic symbol Ni) is a hard, malleable, ductile metal that has a silvery tinge that can take on a high polish. Nickel is somewhat ferromagnetic and is a fair conductor of heat and electricity. Nickel is primarily used in the production of stainless steel and other corrosion-resistant alloys. Nickel is used in coins to replace silver, in rechargeable batteries, and in electronic circuitry. Nickel plating techniques, like electro-less coating or single-slurry coating, are employed in such applications as turbine blades, helicopter rotors, extrusion dies, and rolled steel strip.

Nickel futures and options trade at the London Metal Exchange (LME). The nickel futures contract calls for the delivery of 6 metric tons of primary nickel with at least 99.80% purity in the form of full plate, cut cathodes, pellets or briquettes. The contract is priced in terms of U.S. dollars per metric ton.

Prices – Nickel prices posted a record high of $17.75 per pound in 2007 but have since remained well below that level. The average price of nickel in 2018 rose +26.9% yr/yr to $6.62 per pound.

Supply – World mine production of nickel in 2020 fell -4.2% yr/yr to 2.500 million metric tons, down from the 2019 record high of 2,610. The current levels are almost triple the production seen in 1970.

The world's largest mine producers of nickel in 2020 were Indonesia with 30.4% of world production, the Philippines with 12.8%, Russia with 11.2%, and New Caledonia with 8.0%.

U.S. secondary nickel production in 2016 fell -0.7% yr/yr to 89,990 metric tons, below the 2006 decade-high of 103,630 metric tons.

Demand – U.S. consumption of nickel in 2020 fell -7.8% yr/yr to 200,000 metric tons. In 2016, the primary U.S. nickel consumption use was for stainless and heat-resisting steels, which accounted for 53.6% of U.S. consumption. Other consumption uses in 2016 were super alloys at 10.7%, nickel alloys at 4.9%, electro-plating anodes at 3.1%, alloy steels at 1.5%, copper-base alloys at 1.0%, and chemicals at 0.7%.

Trade – The U.S. relied on imports for 50% of its nickel consumption in 2020. U.S. imports of primary and secondary nickel in 2020 fell -9.4% yr/yr to 142,000 metric tons, still well above the 2009 record low of 117,600 metric tons. U.S. exports of primary and secondary nickel in 2020 fell -29.6% yr/yr to 62,000 metric tons.

World Mine Production of Nickel In Metric Tons (Contained Nickel)

Year	Australia[3]	Botswana	Brazil	Canada	China	Dominican Republic	Greece	Indonesia	New Caledonia	Philippines	Russia	South Africa	Total
2014	266,181	14,958	102,000	228,867	101,100	----	21,405	177,100	175,174	443,909	283,150	54,956	2,170,000
2015	225,227	16,789	89,302	234,519	101,400	4,000	19,610	129,600	193,199	470,042	276,710	56,689	2,180,000
2016	204,356	16,878	77,000	235,707	98,000	19,900	19,431	198,900	204,207	347,423	252,520	48,994	2,040,000
2017	179,000	----	78,600	214,000	103,000	----	----	345,000	215,000	366,000	214,000	48,400	2,160,000
2018	170,000	----	74,400	176,000	110,000	----	----	606,000	216,000	345,000	272,000	44,000	2,400,000
2019[1]	159,000		60,600	181,000	120,000	56,900		853,000	208,000	323,000	279,000		2,610,000
2020[2]	170,000		73,000	150,000	120,000	47,000		760,000	200,000	320,000	280,000		2,500,000

[1] Preliminary. [2] Estimate. [3] Content of nickel sulfate and concentrates. *Source: U.S. Geological Survey (USGS)*

Salient Statistics of Nickel in the United States In Metric Tons (Contained Nickel)

	Net Import Reliance As a % of Apparent	- Production -		---- Nickel Consumed[1], By Uses ----									Stocks, ---- Dec. 31 ----		Primary & --- Secondary ---		Avg. Price
Year	Consumption	Plant[4]	Secondary[5]	Alloy Sheets	Cast Iron	Copper Base Alloys	Electro-plating Anodes	Nickel Alloys	Stainless & Heat Resisting Steels	Super Alloys	Chemicals	Apparent Consumption	At Consumer Plants	At Producer Plants	Exports	Imports	LME $/Lb.
2014	58	----	91,510	4,960	272	2,300	8,100	15,000	133,000	25,700	2,120	264,000	23,300	9,030	66,700	195,000	7.65
2015	50	----	90,600	3,330	205	2,240	7,490	W	127,000	26,900	252	234,000	19,200	10,300	61,510	157,100	5.37
2016	44	----	89,990	3,530	160	2,780	7,370	11,600	126,000	25,200	1,750	235,000	15,100	10,500	74,000	143,300	4.35
2017	51	----										273,000	14,600		62,500	188,100	4.72
2018	52	----										259,000	16,300		69,180	189,100	5.95
2019[1]	49	----										217,000	13,400		63,900	156,700	6.31
2020[2]	50	----										200,000	13,000		45,000	142,000	6.40

[1] Exclusive of scrap. [2] Preliminary. [3] Estimate. [4] Smelter & refinery. [5] From purchased scrap (ferrous & nonferrous).
W = Withheld proprietary data. NA = Not available. *Source: U.S. Geological Survey (USGS)*

Average Price of Nickel (Cash) in London In U.S. Dollars per Metric Ton

Year	Jan.	Feb.	Mar.	Apr.	May	June	July	Aug.	Sept.	Oct.	Nov.	Dec.	Average
2016	8,507.3	8,298.5	8,717.3	8,878.9	8,660.4	8,928.4	10,262.9	10,336.0	10,191.8	10,259.7	11,128.9	10,972.3	9,595.2
2017	9,971.5	10,643.3	10,204.7	9,609.3	9,155.1	8,931.8	9,491.4	10,890.0	11,215.8	11,335.8	11,972.1	11,499.4	10,410.0
2018	12,840.1	13,566.4	13,416.6	13,938.1	14,366.5	15,105.7	13,793.9	13,411.4	12,510.4	12,314.9	11,239.7	10,835.1	13,111.5
2019	11,523.1	12,685.2	13,026.3	12,772.8	12,016.3	11,943.9	13,546.3	15,748.6	17,656.9	17,046.2	15,171.8	13,829.4	13,913.9
2020	13,506.9	12,715.6	11,846.2	11,804.0	12,179.6	12,727.2	13,402.3	14,537.8	14,857.5	15,239.4	15,807.7	16,283.0	13,742.3

Contract Size = 6 Metric Tons *Source: London Metal Exchange (LME)*

Oats

Oats are seeds or grains of a genus of plants that thrive in cool, moist climates. There are about 25 species of oats that grow worldwide in the cooler temperate regions. The oldest known cultivated oats were found inside caves in Switzerland and are believed to be from the Bronze Age. Oats are usually sown in early spring and harvested in mid to late summer, but in southern regions of the northern hemisphere, they may be sown in the fall. Oats are used in many processed foods such as flour, livestock feed, and furfural, a chemical used as a solvent in various refining industries. The oat crop year begins in June and ends in May. Oat futures and options are traded at the CME Group.

Prices – CME oat futures prices (Barchart.com electronic symbol ZO) on the nearest-futures chart moved lower early in 2020, rallied into the summer, faded into the fall, but then rallied to finally close the year up +14.8% at $3.58 per bushel. Regarding cash prices, the average monthly price received by farmers for oats in the U.S. in the first seven months of the 2020/21 marketing year (June/May) fell -5.1% yr/yr to $2.80 per bushel.

Supply – World oat production in 2020/21 is expected to rise +10.6 % yr/yr to 25.457 million metric tons, above the record low of 19.625 million metric tons posted in 2010/11. World annual oat production in the past three decades has dropped very sharply from levels above 50 million metric tons in the early 1970s. The world's largest oat producers in 2020/21 are expected to be the European Union with 36.7% of world production, Canada with 17.7%, Russia with 16.1%, and Australia with 6.3%.

U.S. oat production in the 2020/21 marketing year is expected to rise +22.7% yr/yr to 65.365 million bushels. U.S. oat production has fallen sharply from levels mostly above 1 billion bushels seen from the early 1900s into the early 1960s. U.S. farmers are expected to harvest 1.004 million acres of oats in 2020/21, up +21.3% yr/yr. That is far below the almost 40 million acres harvested back in the 1950s. The oat yield in 2020/21 is expected to rise +1.2% to 65.1 bushels per acre. Oat stocks in the U.S. as of December 2019 were down -19.6% yr/yr to 54.966 million bushels. The largest U.S. oat-producing states in 2020 were the states of South Dakota with 16.5% of U.S. production, Minnesota with 16.2%, Wisconsin with 12.6%, and North Dakota with 12.5%.

Demand – U.S. usage of oats in 2020/21 is expected to rise +6.7% yr/yr to 154.000 million bushels, above the 2011-12 record low of 106.360 million bushels. U.S. usage of oats in 202/21 is expected to be 48.7% for feed and residual, 46.8% for food, alcohol and industrial, 4.5% for seed, and the rest for export.

Trade – U.S. exports of oats in 2020/21 are expected to fall -3.3% yr/yr to 2.000 million bushels. U.S. imports of oats in 2020/21 are expected to rise +2.1% yr/yr to 94.000 million bushels, but still below the 2007 record high of 123.29 million bushels.

World Production of Oats In Thousands of Metric Tons

Crop Year	Argentina	Australia	Belarus	Brazil	Canada	Chile	China	European Union	Kazakstan	Russia	Ukraine	United States	World Total
2011-12	345	1,262	448	354	3,158	451	295	7,927	258	5,332	506	728	21,953
2012-13	496	1,121	422	361	2,830	680	250	7,909	200	4,027	630	892	20,766
2013-14	445	1,255	352	380	3,928	610	235	8,380	305	4,932	467	938	23,174
2014-15	525	1,198	522	307	2,977	421	255	7,821	226	5,267	610	1,019	22,107
2015-16	553	1,300	492	351	3,425	533	350	7,524	244	4,527	498	1,298	22,119
2016-17	785	2,266	390	828	3,231	713	525	8,044	335	4,750	510	938	24,390
2017-18	492	1,227	460	634	3,733	573	550	8,058	285	5,448	481	720	23,655
2018-19[1]	572	1,135	342	795	3,436	385	575	7,790	336	4,715	423	815	22,249
2019-20[2]	600	860	368	879	4,227	477	625	8,079	267	4,420	427	773	23,007
2020-21[3]	650	1,600	370	910	4,503	638	625	9,340	300	4,100	450	949	25,457

[1] Preliminary. [2] Estimate. [3] Forecast. *Source: Foreign Agricultural Service, U.S. Department of Agriculture (FAS-USDA)*

Official Oats Crop Production Reports in the United States In Thousands of Bushels

Year	July 1	Aug. 1	Sept. 1	Oct. 1	Dec. 1	Final	Year	July 1	Aug. 1	Sept. 1	Oct. 1	Dec. 1	Final
2009	91,277	91,960	----	----	----	93,081	2015	83,640	85,456	----	----	----	89,535
2010	87,726	87,239	----	----	----	81,190	2016	76,609	76,854	----	----	----	64,770
2011	56,551	57,489	----	----	----	53,649	2017	53,674	53,719	----	----	----	49,585
2012	65,276	66,519	----	----	----	61,486	2018	66,384	65,668	----	----	----	56,130
2013	74,459	75,210	----	----	----	64,642	2019	61,628	60,385	----	----	----	53,258
2014	75,507	77,267	----	----	----	70,232	2020[1]	65,024	64,907	----	----	----	65,355

[1] Preliminary. *Source: National Agricultural Statistics Service, U.S. Department of Agriculture (NASS-USDA)*

Oat Stocks in the United States In Thousands of Bushels

Year	On Farms Mar. 1	June 1	Sept. 1	Dec. 1	Off Farms Mar. 1	June 1	Sept. 1	Dec. 1	Total Stocks Mar. 1	June 1	Sept. 1	Dec. 1
2011	26,950	14,580	31,000	24,900	59,361	53,049	47,391	54,235	86,311	67,629	78,391	79,135
2012	19,750	11,120	34,100	26,100	55,044	43,869	50,872	47,051	74,794	54,989	84,972	73,151
2013	18,900	11,380	37,150	25,650	33,726	24,957	26,339	22,394	52,626	36,337	63,489	48,044
2014	19,800	9,710	41,400	31,300	15,323	15,029	32,910	35,670	35,123	24,739	74,310	66,970
2015	20,810	15,120	47,800	36,750	38,609	38,625	46,066	45,981	59,419	53,745	93,866	82,731
2016	26,800	18,350	37,400	30,430	48,429	38,452	41,190	45,003	75,229	56,802	78,590	75,433
2017	22,320	13,540	33,950	23,300	40,885	36,790	38,039	43,166	63,205	50,330	71,989	66,466
2018	17,240	11,410	39,200	25,410	37,699	29,606	35,573	41,864	54,939	41,016	74,773	67,274
2019	18,050	10,500	37,900	24,770	32,232	27,314	22,153	29,139	50,282	37,814	60,053	53,909
2020[1]	16,970	10,070	39,850	28,830	30,722	26,693	27,017	28,848	47,692	36,763	66,867	57,678

[1] Preliminary. *Source: National Agricultural Statistics Service, U.S. Department of Agriculture (NASS-USDA)*

Supply and Utilization of Oats in the United States In Millions of Bushels

Crop Year Beginning June 1	Acreage Planted (1,000 Acres)	Harvested (1,000 Acres)	Yield Per Acre (Bushels)	Production	Imports	Total Supply	Feed & Residual	Food, Alcohol & Industrial	Seed	Exports	Total Use	Ending Stocks	Farm Price ($/Bu)	Findley Loan Rate	Target Price
2011-12	2,496	939	57.1	53.6	94.1	211.8	78.5	68.8	7.2	156.9	2.4	54.9	3.49	1.39	1.79
2012-13	2,700	1,005	61.2	61.5	92.9	209.3	95.7	68.1	7.8	172.9	1.4	36.3	3.89	1.39	1.79
2013-14	2,980	1,009	64.1	64.6	97.1	198.1	98.4	66.2	7.2	173.4	1.6	24.7	3.75	1.39	1.79
2014-15	2,753	1,035	67.9	70.2	108.9	203.8	71.2	69.0	8.0	148.2	1.8	53.7	3.21	1.39	2.40
2015-16	3,088	1,276	70.2	89.5	85.6	228.8	93.5	69.4	7.1	170.1	2.0	56.8	2.12	1.39	2.40
2016-17	2,829	981	66.0	64.8	90.2	211.7	81.6	69.9	6.4	157.9	3.4	50.3	2.06	1.39	2.40
2017-18	2,589	804	61.7	49.6	89.2	189.1	68.3	70.6	6.8	145.7	2.4	41.0	2.59	1.39	2.40
2018-19	2,746	865	64.9	56.1	86.5	183.6	66.2	70.9	7.0	144.1	1.7	37.8	2.66	1.39	2.40
2019-20[1]	2,830	828	64.3	53.3	92.1	183.1	63.3	74.0	7.0	144.3	2.1	36.8	2.95		
2020-21[2]	2,984	1,004	65.1	65.4	94.0	196.1	75.0	72.0	7.0	154.0	2.0	40.1			

[1] Preliminary. [2] Forecast. [3] Less than 500,000 bushels. NA = Not available.
Source: Economic Research Service, U.S. Department of Agiculture (ERS-USDA)

Production of Oats in the United States, by States In Thousands of Bushels

Year	Illinois	Iowa	Michigan	Minnesota	Nebraska	New York	North Dakota	Ohio	Pennsylvania	South Dakota	Texas	Wisconsin	Total
2011	1,360	3,250	1,920	5,940	1,300	1,700	4,420	2,052	2,760	4,130	2,100	7,130	53,649
2012	1,140	3,770	2,100	8,370	1,026	3,250	6,510	2,576	3,965	3,060	3,185	7,800	61,486
2013	1,725	3,960	1,860	5,985	1,625	3,082	8,370	1,575	3,100	9,240	1,840	6,825	64,642
2014	2,000	3,520	2,760	7,875	2,400	2,520	7,665	2,205	3,480	9,300	1,710	8,680	70,232
2015	1,925	4,161	3,350	12,480	2,680	2,320	10,360	2,520	3,575	12,615	2,640	14,040	89,535
2016	1,620	3,268	1,740	8,160	1,500	3,300	7,260	1,850	3,350	9,020	3,000	6,600	64,770
2017	1,580	3,234	2,160	7,125	1,715	1,925	4,640	1,400	2,320	4,200	2,700	5,015	49,585
2018	2,075	2,079	3,150	6,195	1,518	2,322	8,610	1,950	1,610	7,790	2,500	5,490	56,130
2019	650	4,002	1,425	6,200	1,134	2,340	9,890	1,150	2,650	6,150	2,000	6,480	53,258
2020[1]	870	5,694	1,650	10,560	1,827	1,696	8,190	900	2,750	10,780	2,700	8,253	65,355

[1] Preliminary. *Source: National Agricultural Statistics Service, U.S. Department of Agriculture (NASS-USDA)*

Average Cash Price of No. 2 Heavy White Oats in Toledo In U.S. Dollars Per Bushel

Year	Jan.	Feb.	Mar.	Apr.	May	June	July	Aug.	Sept.	Oct.	Nov.	Dec.	Average
1996-97	NQ	2.45	2.34	2.19	2.02	1.96	1.96	1.99	2.16	2.26	2.12	2.08	2.14
1997-98	2.12	1.79	1.84	1.80	1.77	NQ	NQ	NQ	NQ	NQ	NQ	NQ	1.86
1998-99	NQ	NQ	NQ	NQ	NQ	NQ	NQ	NQ	NQ	NQ	NQ	NQ	NQ
1999-00	NQ	NQ	NQ	NQ	NQ	NQ	NQ	NQ	NQ	NQ	NQ	NQ	NQ
2000-01	NQ	NQ	NQ	NQ	NQ	NQ	NQ	NQ	NQ	NQ	NQ	NQ	NQ
2001-02	NQ	NQ	NQ	NQ	NQ	NQ	NQ	NQ	NQ	NQ	NQ	NQ	NQ
2002-03	NQ	NQ	NQ	NQ	NQ	NQ	NQ	NQ	NQ	NQ	NQ	NQ	NQ
2003-04	NQ	NQ	NQ	NQ	NQ	NQ	NQ	NQ	NQ	NQ	NQ	NQ	NQ
2004-05	NQ	NQ	NQ	NQ	NQ	NQ	NQ	NQ	NQ	NQ	NQ	NQ	NQ
2005-06[1]	NQ	NQ	NQ										

[1] Preliminary. NQ = No quotes. *Source: Economic Research Service, U.S. Department of Agriculture (ERS-USDA)*

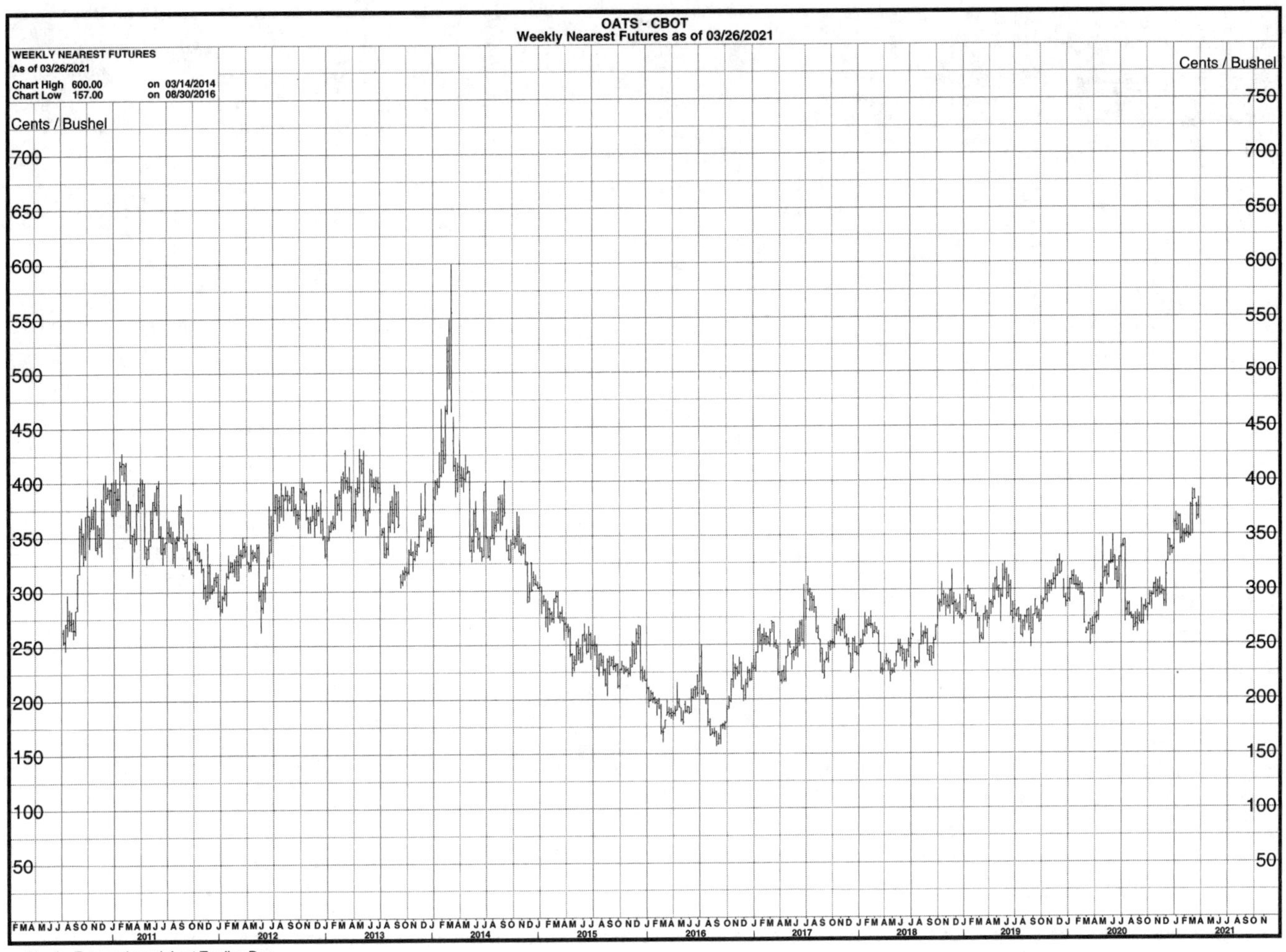

Nearby Futures through Last Trading Day.

Volume of Trading in Oats Futures in Chicago In Contracts

Year	Jan.	Feb.	Mar.	Apr.	May	June	July	Aug.	Sept.	Oct.	Nov.	Dec.	Total
2011	28,513	41,210	32,798	35,451	25,962	42,810	17,687	26,037	24,613	23,352	41,624	9,259	349,316
2012	19,267	27,361	29,511	22,787	28,013	31,967	16,898	20,154	15,311	22,011	28,859	17,431	279,570
2013	21,246	34,411	16,949	31,035	16,891	28,267	18,156	16,459	17,388	21,863	22,977	9,316	254,958
2014	18,860	30,902	18,786	18,113	11,938	19,491	11,446	13,556	11,300	16,754	21,903	7,482	200,531
2015	14,618	19,923	12,461	25,243	15,152	21,734	11,399	13,953	9,614	13,216	24,979	12,283	194,575
2016	15,634	25,543	14,663	26,235	14,762	34,447	11,971	19,094	9,399	21,957	21,435	10,090	225,230
2017	15,129	16,691	13,180	17,122	10,845	24,381	10,292	11,920	8,370	11,522	19,561	10,239	169,252
2018	15,633	14,913	14,719	21,901	10,995	16,616	7,060	16,254	9,029	17,965	20,659	7,195	172,939
2019	10,494	16,765	10,206	19,410	14,000	22,122	9,460	9,034	9,145	12,466	19,901	9,548	162,551
2020	10,088	17,749	13,193	9,646	10,702	18,060	6,579	9,703	10,037	10,124	15,829	8,962	140,672

Contract size = 5,000 bu. *Source: CME Group; Chicago Board of Trade (CBT)*

Average Open Interest of Oats in Chicago In Contracts

Year	Jan.	Feb.	Mar.	Apr.	May	June	July	Aug.	Sept.	Oct.	Nov.	Dec.
2011	13,104	14,297	13,191	13,677	12,577	12,457	12,287	13,127	14,082	15,902	16,557	12,802
2012	13,363	11,924	10,849	10,879	11,516	11,021	9,959	10,708	11,328	11,802	11,567	10,439
2013	10,568	11,022	10,619	9,356	8,634	10,207	8,659	9,000	9,941	10,805	9,767	8,937
2014	10,414	11,168	9,529	8,350	7,356	7,793	7,292	8,382	8,987	9,787	9,813	8,151
2015	7,684	8,794	8,965	8,729	8,375	8,570	7,926	8,408	8,902	10,129	10,793	8,789
2016	9,457	10,452	10,883	10,418	9,947	10,282	9,969	10,511	10,755	9,261	8,304	6,946
2017	7,314	7,952	6,597	6,656	6,104	6,764	6,687	6,369	5,902	6,674	7,795	6,561
2018	6,491	5,995	5,740	6,470	5,468	5,232	4,898	4,723	3,990	6,113	6,608	5,712
2019	5,686	5,322	4,562	5,973	6,623	6,305	4,809	4,560	5,178	6,016	6,991	5,585
2020	5,004	5,405	4,391	3,450	4,211	4,809	4,420	4,677	5,238	5,491	5,783	4,519

Contract size = 5,000 bu. *Source: CME Group; Chicago Board of Trade (CBT)*

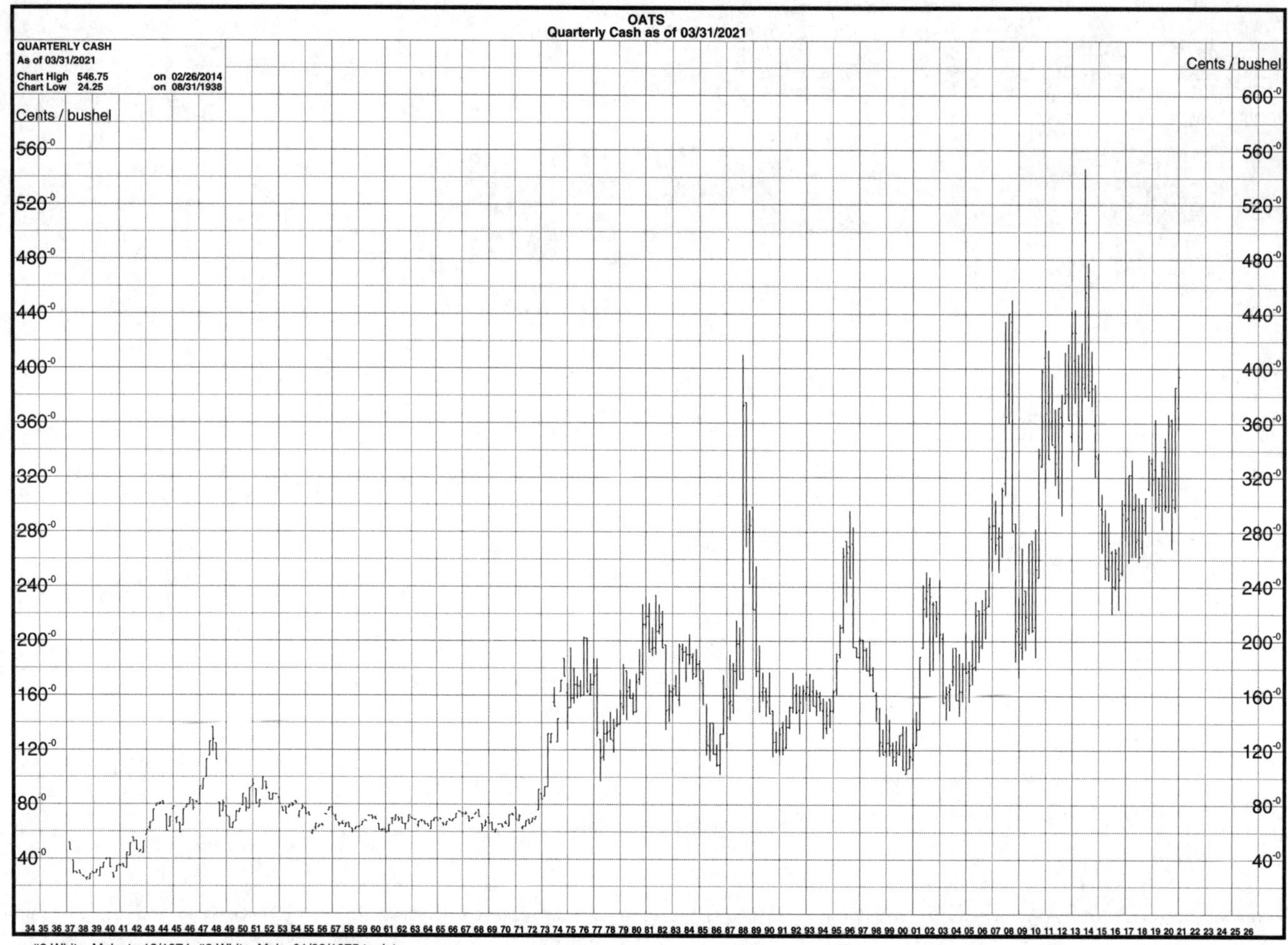

Average Cash Price of No. 2 Heavy White Oats in Minneapolis In U.S. Dollars Per Bushel

Year	June	July	Aug.	Sept.	Oct.	Nov.	Dec.	Jan.	Feb.	Mar.	Apr.	May	Average
2011-12	3.68	3.68	3.69	3.72	3.51	3.36	3.30	3.16	3.46	3.48	3.55	3.48	3.50
2012-13	3.37	3.95	3.99	3.89	3.98	3.85	3.94	3.79	4.07	4.26	4.13	3.99	3.93
2013-14	4.21	3.84	3.78	3.40	3.57	3.79	3.80	4.30	4.64	4.66	4.58	4.03	4.05
2014-15	3.88	3.85	3.83	3.86	3.68	3.53	3.49	3.26	3.11	3.14	2.94	2.75	3.44
2015-16	2.89	2.82	2.63	2.70	2.58	2.67	2.60	2.64	2.60	2.43	2.49	2.49	2.63
2016-17	2.58	2.61	2.34	2.29	2.67	2.84	2.97	2.92	3.07	2.90	2.86	2.88	2.74
2017-18	2.95	3.17	2.98	2.87	2.97	2.94	2.90	2.73	2.96	2.79	2.72	2.89	2.90
2018-19	2.88	2.84	2.91	2.91	3.18	3.22	3.28	3.31	3.23	3.18	3.25	3.25	3.12
2019-20	3.15	3.10	3.01	3.03	3.15	3.22	3.43	3.21	3.37	3.21	3.21	3.40	3.21
2020-21[1]	3.43	3.35	----	2.97	3.07	3.17	3.71	3.59	3.68				3.37

[1] Preliminary. *Source: Economic Research Service, U.S. Department of Agriculture (ERS-USDA)*

Average Price Received by Farmers for Oats in the United States In U.S. Dollars Per Bushel

Year	June	July	Aug.	Sept.	Oct.	Nov.	Dec.	Jan.	Feb.	Mar.	Apr.	May	Average
2011-12	3.43	3.35	3.20	3.67	3.69	3.38	3.57	3.56	3.47	3.77	3.84	4.12	3.59
2012-13	3.80	3.70	3.82	3.76	3.93	3.88	3.90	4.06	4.14	4.20	4.43	4.45	4.01
2013-14	3.93	3.88	3.67	3.57	3.49	3.63	3.59	3.70	3.75	4.13	3.96	3.98	3.77
2014-15	3.73	3.49	3.24	3.20	3.16	2.95	3.21	3.02	3.08	2.96	2.82	2.90	3.15
2015-16	2.83	2.33	2.07	2.04	2.20	2.11	2.12	1.93	2.21	2.20	1.97	2.26	2.19
2016-17	1.98	1.89	1.84	1.97	2.03	2.23	2.35	2.31	2.39	2.39	2.32	2.63	2.19
2017-18	2.74	2.33	2.32	2.56	2.55	2.68	2.94	3.29	2.63	2.80	2.93	3.14	2.74
2018-19	3.04	2.61	2.47	2.62	2.71	2.55	2.67	2.67	2.84	2.67	3.01	3.11	2.75
2019-20	3.31	3.09	2.72	2.67	2.83	2.95	3.02	2.84	2.73	2.96	3.10	3.10	2.94
2020-21[1]	3.16	2.97	2.54	2.49	2.73	3.02	2.69	2.95					2.82

[1] Preliminary. *Source: National Agricultural Statistics Service, U.S. Department of Agriculture (NASS-USDA)*

Olive Oil

Olive oil is derived from the fruit of the olive tree and originated in the Mediterranean area. Olives designated for oil are picked before ripening in the fall. Olive picking is usually done by hand. The olives are then weighed and washed in cold water. The olives, along with their oil-rich pits, are then crushed and kneaded until a homogeneous paste is formed. The paste is spread by hand onto metal plates, which are then stacked and pressed hydraulically to yield a liquid. The liquid is then centrifuged to separate the oil. It takes 1,300 to 2,000 olives to produce 1 quart of olive oil. The best olive oil is still produced from the first pressing, which is usually performed within 24 to 72 hours after harvest and is called extra virgin olive oil.

Supply – World production of olive oil (pressed oil) in the marketing year 2018/19 fell -0.7% to 3.469 million metric tons, below the 2011/12 record high of 3.629 million metric tons. The world's largest producers of olive oil in 2018/19 were Spain with 55.8% of world production, Italy and Turkey with 5.7%, Greece with 6.3%, Morocco with 6.3%, Tunisia with 4.4%, and Syria with 3.1%. Production levels in the various countries vary considerably from year-to-year depending on weather and crop conditions.

Demand – World consumption of olive oil in the 2018/19 marketing year rose +2.4% yr/yr to 3.262 million metric tons, not far below the 2011/12 record high of 3.356 million metric tons. The U.S. consumption of olive oil in the 2018/19 period rose +1.2% yr/yr to 331,000 metric tons, which is a new record high. That is 10.0% of world consumption.

Trade – World olive oil imports in 2018/19 fell -0.3% to 1.076 million metric tons. The U.S. was the world's largest importer in 2018/19 with 325,000 metric tons, representing 30.2% of world imports. World olive oil exports in 2018/19 fell -1.4% to 1.071million metric tons. The world's largest exporters were Spain with 34.8% of world exports, Italy with 19.6%, and Tunisia with 13.5%.

World Production of Olive Oil (Pressed Oil) In Thousands of Metric Tons

Crop Year	Algeria	Argentina	Greece	Italy	Jordan	Libya	Morocco	Portugal	Spain	Syria	Tunisia	Turkey	World Total
2010-11	67.0	20.0	334.0	551.8	28.0	15.0	137.0	67.9	1,512.9	196.0	140.0	174.0	3,384.4
2011-12	39.5	32.0	322.6	576.0	19.5	15.0	126.5	82.3	1,701.9	165.0	202.0	205.0	3,629.1
2012-13	66.0	17.0	393.9	440.5	21.5	15.0	107.0	64.6	709.6	155.0	240.0	209.0	2,573.0
2013-14	44.0	30.0	146.6	491.5	19.0	18.0	140.0	102.9	1,913.0	147.0	84.0	149.0	3,440.3
2014-15	69.5	15.0	333.0	235.3	23.0	15.5	132.0	69.0	959.3	113.0	374.0	174.0	2,685.0
2015-16	82.0	20.0	354.0	498.3	29.5	18.0	142.0	123.0	1,518.0	127.0	154.0	164.0	3,415.8
2016-17[1]	63.0	34.0	216.0	193.3	20.0	16.0	120.0	78.0	1,408.0	121.0	124.0	191.0	2,779.8
2017-18[2]	82.5	43.5	380.0	451.0	25.0	18.0	152.0	150.0	1,323.4	106.0	295.0	278.0	3,495.1
2018-19[3]	76.5	20.0	220.0	197.0	24.0	16.0	220.0	118.0	1,935.0	106.0	153.0	197.0	3,469.1

[1] Preliminary. [2] Estimate. [3] Forecast. *Source: The Oil World*

World Imports and Exports of Olive Oil (Pressed Oil) In Thousands of Metric Tons

	Imports							Exports					
Crop Year	Australia	Brazil	Italy	Japan	Spain	United States	World Total	Greece	Italy	Spain	Tunisia	Turkey	World Total
2010-11	32.0	65.0	57.5	37.7	16.5	292.0	802.0	14.4	243.3	229.2	109.0	12.9	808.1
2011-12	31.9	71.0	73.9	45.6	21.4	317.4	895.4	18.1	254.9	285.8	149.5	19.4	902.8
2012-13	28.8	74.9	79.8	54.0	61.5	298.2	950.0	20.1	235.3	223.5	178.3	80.7	940.1
2013-14	28.9	73.6	29.1	56.2	20.4	312.4	895.1	17.9	255.6	333.8	84.0	34.9	919.6
2014-15	22.8	67.8	98.2	61.9	119.8	312.1	1,047.3	18.8	220.5	282.5	313.1	16.9	1,056.1
2015-16	26.9	50.6	42.6	56.7	57.5	331.5	934.1	21.4	232.0	348.2	114.3	12.8	920.1
2016-17[1]	29.6	58.5	37.1	56.9	60.3	316.6	930.9	20.3	219.2	340.5	99.3	34.7	930.0
2017-18[2]	31.7	78.6	64.5	57.0	123.7	322.2	1,078.3	20.3	204.7	337.0	217.5	70.0	1,086.0
2018-19[3]	32.0	81.0	71.0	58.0	73.0	325.0	1,075.5	22.0	210.0	373.0	145.0	65.0	1,070.5

[1] Preliminary. [2] Estimate. [3] Forecast. *Source: The Oil World*

World Consumption and Ending Stocks of Olive Oil (Pressed Oil) In Thousands of Metric Tons

	Consumption							Ending Stocks					
Crop Year	Brazil	Morocco	Syria	Tunisia	Turkey	United States	World Total	European Union	Morocco	Syria	Tunisia	Turkey	World Total
2010-11	65.0	96.7	138.1	34.5	129.2	284.8	3,294.2	775.0	90.0	45.0	30.0	60.0	1,105.9
2011-12	71.0	113.3	136.6	37.8	155.7	298.7	3,356.0	959.9	95.0	50.0	45.0	90.0	1,371.6
2012-13	74.9	116.3	139.5	40.0	153.3	304.1	3,125.9	459.7	75.0	40.0	67.0	65.0	824.6
2013-14	73.6	120.1	144.7	43.5	149.2	309.3	3,237.5	690.7	90.0	20.0	26.0	30.0	1,002.9
2014-15	67.8	130.7	119.8	45.5	149.7	310.0	3,068.7	339.0	60.0	10.0	43.0	40.0	610.4
2015-16	50.6	132.5	111.2	46.0	157.7	321.0	3,164.3	585.1	55.0	15.0	42.0	35.0	875.9
2016-17[1]	58.5	130.9	103.9	46.2	161.3	322.9	3,099.7	343.2	28.0	----	24.0	30.0	556.9
2017-18[2]	78.6	134.6	83.7	45.6	183.1	327.1	3,186.8	575.4	27.0	----	59.0	55.0	857.5
2018-19[3]	81.0	137.0	80.0	45.0	177.0	331.0	3,262.2	827.5	73.0	----	26.0	30.0	1,069.4

[1] Preliminary. [2] Estimate. [3] Forecast. *Source: The Oil World*

Onions

Onions are the bulbs of plants in the lily family. Onions can be eaten raw, cooked, pickled, used as a flavoring or seasoning, or dehydrated. Onions rank in the top 10 vegetables produced in the U.S. in terms of dollar value. Since 1629, onions have been cultivated in the U.S., but are believed to be indigenous to Asia.

The two main types of onions produced in the U.S. are yellow and white onions. Yellow varieties comprise approximately 75% of all onions grown for bulb production in the U.S. Onions that are planted as a winter crop in warm areas are milder in taste and odor than onions planted during the summer in cooler regions.

Prices – Onion prices in 2020 averaged $222.55 per hundred pounds, up 54.5% yr/yr.

Supply – U.S. production in 2015 fell -17.9% to 6.503 billion pounds, far below the 2004 record high of 12.031 billion pounds. The farm value of the U.S. production crop in 2020 fell -12.46% to $877.816 million, well below the 2006 record high of $1.084 billion. In 2020 U.S. farmers harvested 132,900 acres, up +2.6% yr/yr . The yield in 2020 was up +4.93% at 556.1 pounds per acre but still below the record high of 566.5 pounds per acre in 2016.

Demand – U.S. per capita consumption of onions in 2017 rose +7.6% yr/yr to 22.4 pounds.

Trade – U.S. exports of fresh onions in 2017 totaled 679 million pounds, and imports totaled 1.154 billion pounds.

Salient Statistics of Onions in the United States

Crop Year	Harvested Acres	Yield Per Acre	Production 1,000 Cwt.	Price Per Cwt.	Farm Value $1,000	Jan. 1 Pack Frozen	Anual Pack Frozen	Imports Canned	Exports (Fresh)	Imports (Fresh)	Per Capita[3] Utilization -- Lbs., Farm Weight -- All	Fresh
						In Millions of Pounds						
2011	155,930	147,630	502	74,097	10.90	742,236	37.5	----	18.8	705.3	893.2	20.4 19.1
2012	154,950	146,870	487	71,495	14.20	942,340	73.7	----	21.1	651.6	876.8	20.8 19.5
2013	151,540	143,340	486	69,654	15.00	969,183	58.0	----		702.4	994.4	19.4 18.5
2014	145,500	139,150	523	72,806	13.60	933,630	49.8	----		657.1	1,134.7	19.8 18.3
2015	143,900	132,900	507	67,380	17.60	993,360	45.0	----		605.5	1,109.7	20.3 18.9
2016	154,000	147,900	567	83,791	13.70	1,059,318	45.0	----		671.6	1,190.6	20.8 19.0
2017	154,700	151,500	544	82,389	12.90	1,042,090	62.1	----		679.1	1,153.6	22.4 21.9
2018	134,800	129,600	559	72,438	12.50	886,941	69.8	----				
2019[1]	132,400	129,400	540	69,893	14.60	1,001,986	68.8	----				
2020[2]	134,700	132,800	566	75,214	11.90	877,816	65.9	----				

[1] Preliminary. [2] Forecast. [3] Includes fresh and processing. *Source: Economic Research Service, U.S. Department of Agriculture (ERS-USDA)*

Cold Storage Stocks of Frozen Onions in the United States, on First of Month In Thousands of Pounds

Year	Jan.	Feb.	Mar.	Apr.	May	June	July	Aug.	Sept.	Oct.	Nov.	Dec.
2011	37,504	33,942	34,401	43,066	49,076	58,596	53,773	56,913	68,638	74,735	58,288	68,902
2012	73,678	68,208	67,465	71,295	72,894	75,430	75,960	74,299	82,451	62,101	65,917	59,641
2013	58,030	53,882	55,947	52,566	52,835	51,059	50,557	53,048	50,048	50,252	49,506	52,770
2014	49,806	50,425	47,054	46,423	46,175	50,046	55,773	64,252	60,862	52,736	50,282	45,791
2015	45,001	43,865	48,055	48,960	52,702	56,379	56,673	53,467	53,428	48,106	48,935	46,921
2016	45,024	46,533	48,136	50,950	58,093	57,549	57,806	54,588	61,991	58,574	59,158	59,871
2017	62,106	61,514	63,908	66,174	72,770	76,063	71,368	68,219	73,667	70,900	64,044	67,319
2018	69,847	68,858	73,548	77,794	80,907	78,747	78,136	74,810	76,314	72,265	64,402	65,232
2019	68,823	69,721	71,636	75,066	82,588	89,921	87,458	77,280	78,543	76,481	67,368	68,541
2020[1]	65,942	67,871	74,223	84,038	92,375	87,078	87,703	77,129	80,877	78,285	73,373	73,617

[1] Preliminary. *Source: National Agricultural Statistics Service, U.S. Department of Agiculture (NASS-USDA)*

Average Price Received by Growers for Onions in the United States In Dollars Per Hundred Pounds (Cwt.)

Year	Jan.	Feb.	Mar.	Apr.	May	June	July	Aug.	Sept.	Oct.	Nov.	Dec.	Season Average
2011	12.40	9.97	8.04	10.80	15.10	22.40	19.00	9.46	8.59	7.82	9.35	9.48	10.90
2012	6.59	4.90	7.07	18.80	26.30	21.30	27.50	30.50	11.10	10.10	12.40	17.50	14.20
2013	32.30	28.80	21.10	NQ	NQ	NQ	NQ	NQ	NQ	NQ	NQ	NQ	15.00
2014	NQ	NQ	NQ	25.10	27.20	17.30	23.50	14.50	11.90	10.30	9.12	9.56	13.60
2015	8.39	7.67	7.89	18.90	19.30	30.20	31.90	15.60	11.80	12.50	12.00	12.20	17.60
2016	14.40	15.30	14.90	21.10	25.80	27.70	26.70	12.70	9.78	7.58	6.76	6.43	13.70
2017	11.10	8.82	7.77	14.00	14.00	20.90	22.30	13.60	16.40	16.30	15.60	17.00	12.90
2018	15.00	13.20	11.60	14.80	17.10	18.20	21.40	15.20	11.20	11.20	11.30	10.90	12.50
2019	14.20	12.30	17.90	23.60	24.30	32.40	39.80	30.30	11.90	13.70	10.90	11.20	14.60
2020[1]	14.10	19.30	20.60	24.80	27.90	30.40	30.80	23.30	19.40	20.00	20.50	19.50	

[1] Preliminary. NQ = Not quoted. *Source: Economic Research Service, U.S. Department of Agriculture (ERS-USDA)*

Oranges and Orange Juice

The orange tree is a semi-tropical, non-deciduous tree, and the fruit is technically a hesperidium, a kind of berry. The three major varieties of oranges include the sweet orange, the sour orange, and the mandarin orange (or tangerine). In the U.S., only sweet oranges are grown commercially. Those include Hamlin, Jaffa, navel, Pineapple, blood orange, and Valencia. Sour oranges are mainly used in marmalade and in liqueurs such as triple sec and curacao.

Frozen Concentrated Orange Juice (FCOJ) was developed in 1945, which led to oranges becoming the main fruit crop in the U.S. The world's largest producer of orange juice is Brazil, followed by Florida. Two to four medium-sized oranges will produce about 1 cup of juice, and modern mechanical extractors can remove the juice from 400 to 700 oranges per minute. Before juice extraction, orange oil is recovered from the peel. Approximately 50% of the orange weight is juice, with the remainder being peel, pulp, and seeds, which are dried to produce nutritious cattle feed.

The U.S. marketing year for oranges begins December 1 of the first year shown (e.g., the 2005-06 marketing year extends from December 1, 2005, to November 30, 2006). Orange juice futures prices are subject to upward spikes during the U.S. hurricane season (officially June 1 to November 30), and the Florida freeze season (late-November through March).

Frozen concentrate orange juice futures and options are traded at the Intercontinental Exchange (ICE). The ICE orange juice futures contract calls for the delivery of 15,000 pounds of orange solids and is priced in terms of cents per pound.

Prices – ICE frozen concentrate orange juice (FCOJ) futures prices (Barchart.com symbol OJ) in 2020 tumbled to a 1-1/2-year low in February of 91.20 cents. Prices retreated as weak demand boosted supplies after Brazil, the world's largest orange producer, reported that its 2019/20 orange juice stocks surged +42% yr/yr to a 6-year high of 853,778 MT in February. However, FCOJ prices recovered as the Covid pandemic spread sparked an increase in domestic FCOJ demand as consumers remain sheltered at home. Nielsen reported U.S. weekly orange juice sales surged +41% yr/yr to 10.808 million gallons in the four-week period ending March 14. FCOJ prices rallied into Q2 when they posted a 2-year high of 132.00 cents in June. The USDA, in its June WASDE report, cut its 2019/20 U.S. orange crop estimate to 67.65 million boxes, down -5.8% yr/yr and the lowest in 56 years. The USDA's Foreign Agricultural Service (FAS) projected that global 2019/20 orange juice production would fall -23% yr/yr to 1.6 MMT. FCOJ prices traded sideways into year-end and finished 2020 up sharply by +26.8% yr/yr at 123.25 cents.

Supply – World production of oranges in the 2020/21 marketing year are forecasted to rise +7.9% yr/yr to 49.361 million metric tons. The world's largest producers of oranges in 2020/21 marketing year are expected to be Brazil with 34.3% of world production, followed by China with 15.2%, European Union with 13.3%, the U.S. with 8.3%, and Mexico with 8.1%.

U.S. production of oranges in 2019/20 fell -3.6% yr/yr to 121.940 million boxes (1 box equals 90 lbs). Florida's production in 2019/20 fell -6.3% yr/yr to 67.300 million boxes, and California's production rose +2.1% yr/yr to 53.300 million boxes.

World Production of Oranges In Thousands of Metric Tons

Year	Argentina	Australia	Brazil	China	Egypt	European Union	Mexico	Morocco	South Africa	Turkey	United States	Vietnam	World Total
2011-12	565	415	20,482	6,900	2,350	6,023	3,666	850	1,466	1,650	8,166	531	53,866
2012-13	550	432	16,361	7,000	2,450	5,890	4,400	784	1,659	1,600	7,501	521	49,859
2013-14	800	467	17,870	7,600	2,570	6,550	4,533	1,001	1,723	1,700	6,140	590	52,291
2014-15	800	504	16,714	6,600	2,635	5,954	4,515	868	1,645	1,650	5,763	566	48,830
2015-16	800	506	14,414	6,900	2,930	6,038	4,603	925	1,275	1,800	5,523	637	47,111
2016-17	700	526	20,890	7,000	3,000	6,739	4,630	1,037	1,363	1,850	4,616	768	53,859
2017-18	750	528	15,953	7,300	3,120	6,270	4,737	1,021	1,586	1,905	3,515	770	48,191
2018-19[1]	800	515	19,298	7,200	3,600	6,796	4,716	1,183	1,590	1,900	4,923	770	53,992
2019-20[2]	650	485	14,908	7,400	3,200	6,205	2,530	806	1,650	1,700	4,733	770	45,732
2020-21[3]	700	535	16,932	7,500	3,400	6,556	4,010	1,100	1,700	1,360	4,113	770	49,361

[1] Preliminary. [2] Estimate. [3] Forecast. NA = Not available. *Source: Foreign Agricultural Service, U.S. Department of Agriculture (FAS-USDA)*

Salient Statistics of Oranges & Orange Juice in the United States

Year	Production[4]: California (Million Boxes)	Production[4]: Florida (Million Boxes)	Production[4]: Total U.S. (Million Boxes)	Farm Price $ Per Box	Farm Value Million $	Florida Crop Processed: Frozen Concentrates (Million Boxes)	Florida Crop Processed: Chilled Products (Million Boxes)	Florida Crop Processed: Total Processed (Million Boxes)	Florida Crop Processed: Yield Per Box Gallons[5]	Frozen Concentrated Orange Juice - Florida: Carry-in (In Millions of Gallons (42 Deg. Brix))	Pack	Total Supply	Total Season Movement
2010-11	62.5	140.5	204.9	10.90	2,230.4	51.8	82.6	135.2	1.6	95.0	82.1	177.1	148.5
2011-12	58.0	146.7	206.1	12.70	2,621.6	65.4	75.5	141.3	1.6	51.6	175.4	227.0	124.3
2012-13	54.5	133.6	189.9	10.85	2,073.6	48.0	79.2	127.6	1.6	61.1	127.9	189.0	108.4
2013-14	49.5	104.7	156.0	14.29	2,254.3	22.7	76.0	99.2	1.6	76.9	85.4	162.3	97.3
2014-15	48.2	97.0	146.6	13.29	1,963.4	19.2	71.9	92.0	1.5	66.0	72.6	138.5	86.2
2015-16	58.5	81.7	141.9	13.55	1,927.3	15.8	61.8	77.8	1.4	70.8	63.7	134.5	88.2
2016-17	48.3	68.9	118.5	16.30	1,943.7	12.6	53.2	66.0	1.4	52.7	55.9	108.6	87.5
2017-18[1]	44.2	45.1	91.1	19.82	1,830.4	7.7	34.4	42.3		46.2	38.4	84.7	73.1
2018-19[2]	52.2	71.9	126.6	14.43	1,765.3	15.2	53.8	69.1		58.5	51.1	109.6	76.3
2019-20[3]	53.3	67.3	121.9	14.06	1,714.7	14.1	49.8	64.1		76.5	47.9	124.3	76.0

[1] Preliminary. [2] Estimate. [3] Forecast. 4/ Fruit ripened on trees, but destroyed prior to picking not included. [5] 42 deg. Brix equivalent.
Source: Economic Research Service, U.S. Department of Agriculture (ERS-USDA); Florida Department of Citrus

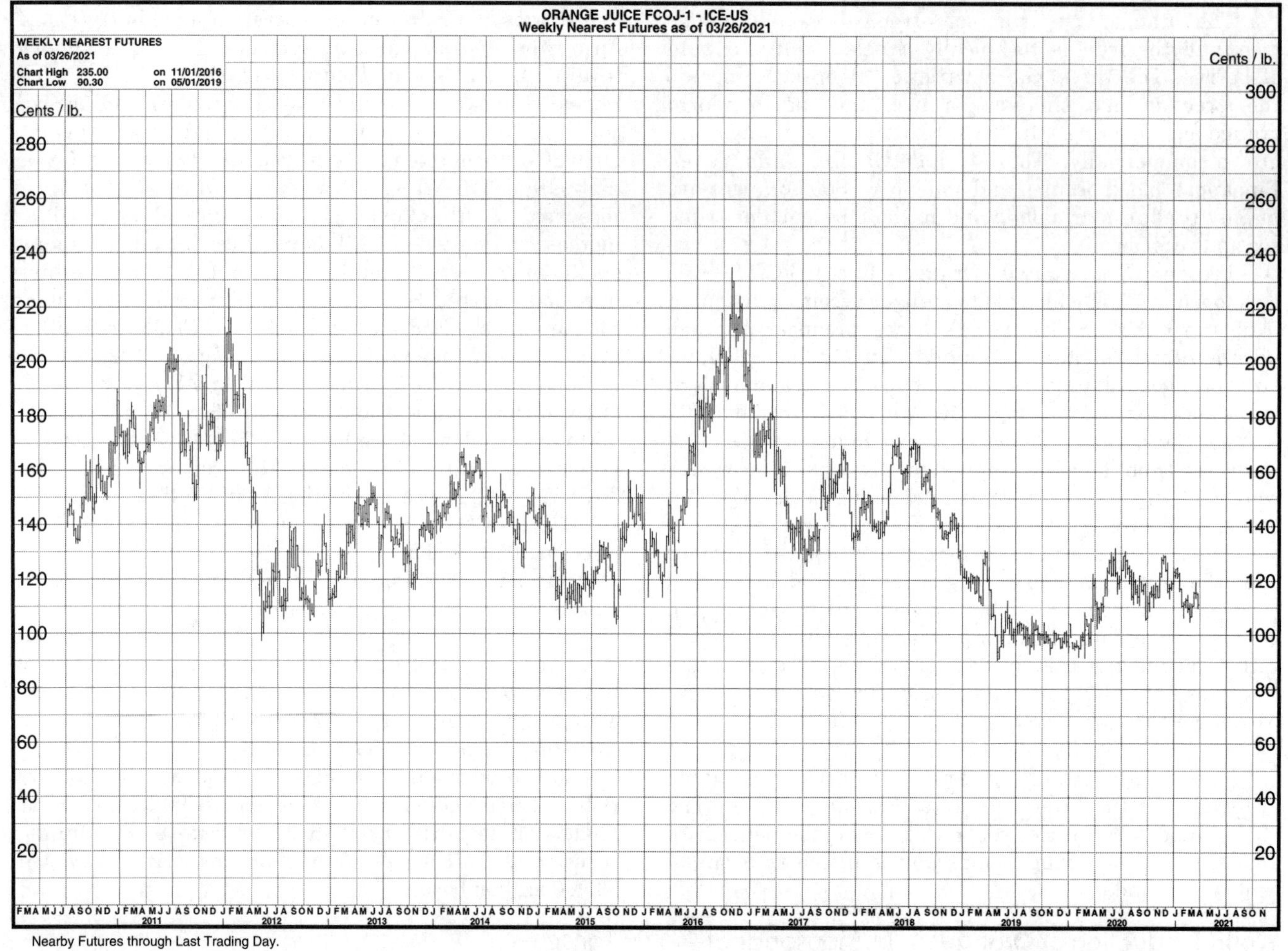

Nearby Futures through Last Trading Day.

Volume of Trading of Frozen Concentrated Orange Juice Futures in New York In Contracts

Year	Jan.	Feb.	Mar.	Apr.	May	June	July	Aug.	Sept.	Oct.	Nov.	Dec.	Total
2011	39,184	63,134	43,077	63,680	41,142	89,150	28,260	80,733	32,920	59,502	24,493	62,335	627,610
2012	59,578	68,746	29,672	58,405	42,001	56,218	28,654	57,465	31,796	51,993	36,729	65,518	586,775
2013	46,432	54,711	37,532	67,361	31,399	63,622	26,724	43,047	29,937	40,275	24,295	39,684	505,019
2014	27,695	39,560	29,605	51,337	24,033	51,811	21,141	36,438	18,068	35,974	27,182	35,685	398,529
2015	21,377	37,435	34,855	39,065	23,789	42,032	18,914	42,607	24,694	48,774	28,965	36,060	398,567
2016	28,008	34,218	25,553	40,101	20,743	50,207	24,414	47,704	24,848	49,991	22,202	45,915	413,904
2017	30,883	37,187	35,311	33,218	25,193	34,836	18,627	36,316	34,697	25,936	16,504	34,791	363,499
2018	23,671	29,581	16,795	36,685	27,571	36,726	16,771	40,982	18,075	46,573	25,131	38,293	356,854
2019	23,436	50,269	30,857	55,326	27,698	43,007	17,848	51,082	18,589	47,780	14,462	53,282	433,636
2020	21,096	55,057	43,596	23,691	18,093	29,550	16,520	27,567	21,867	28,658	20,472	28,289	334,456

Contract size = 15,000 lbs. *Source: ICE Futures U.S. (ICE)*

Average Open Interest of Frozen Concentrated Orange Juice Futures in New York In Contracts

Year	Jan.	Feb.	Mar.	Apr.	May	June	July	Aug.	Sept.	Oct.	Nov.	Dec.
2011	31,885	31,086	27,618	27,153	31,594	36,039	35,046	28,253	23,967	25,308	27,118	27,105
2012	26,892	23,743	21,892	20,278	22,652	25,461	21,779	23,214	23,078	23,687	22,412	24,458
2013	20,672	20,900	18,819	20,972	20,719	22,432	19,760	19,241	16,646	15,809	14,609	14,636
2014	15,542	15,905	16,793	18,372	18,487	17,605	13,552	13,068	12,175	13,385	13,798	12,089
2015	10,973	12,605	15,506	15,799	14,630	14,192	12,421	13,196	13,358	15,172	14,651	14,759
2016	12,887	12,224	12,408	13,452	13,239	17,154	18,182	16,433	16,312	15,940	16,285	14,857
2017	12,528	11,357	10,887	11,104	11,212	11,929	11,277	11,441	8,972	8,741	9,378	9,882
2018	10,670	10,703	12,349	13,460	14,934	15,644	15,041	14,133	13,370	16,227	17,994	16,807
2019	19,118	21,665	20,689	20,601	21,261	19,818	19,459	19,413	17,375	17,719	17,325	18,687
2020	18,961	19,374	15,961	11,510	10,593	11,095	10,244	9,590	9,214	10,873	10,713	10,877

Contract size = 15,000 lbs. *Source: ICE Futures U.S. (ICE)*

Cold Storage Stocks of Orange Juice Concentrate[2] in the U.S., on First of Month In Millions of Pounds

Year	Jan.	Feb.	Mar.	Apr.	May	June	July	Aug.	Sept.	Oct.	Nov.	Dec.
2011	809.7	834.7	869.2	842.0	835.2	864.5	797.3	732.0	641.5	588.9	522.3	479.6
2012	632.1	710.1	788.8	889.0	1,006.7	1,057.6	956.6	857.9	773.6	675.6	606.4	598.0
2013	695.4	781.6	875.4	946.8	1,021.3	1,042.3	996.2	915.0	864.6	795.8	785.9	732.6
2014	739.5	750.5	799.3	813.0	877.8	872.9	853.7	815.9	773.0	712.0	721.9	676.8
2015	734.8	720.7	728.4	832.3	857.5	947.9	943.8	868.1	807.8	757.1	695.9	641.7
2016	639.3	623.0	633.4	702.0	751.4	772.5	766.5	711.0	653.1	603.1	579.9	519.6
2017	516.6	503.4	506.3	517.1	542.2	575.4	544.4	505.5	471.5	495.6	493.5	468.1
2018	505.1	517.1	501.0	563.1	632.6	730.9	733.8	691.1	633.4	609.0	566.4	528.9
2019	547.9	604.7	633.5	704.4	795.4	884.2	859.8	822.3	808.0	809.6	757.8	725.6
2020[1]	766.2	772.9	784.9	802.4	838.5	852.7	830.4	777.8	723.9	677.1	653.1	620.3

[1] Preliminary. [2] Adjusted to 42.0 degrees Brix equivalent (9.896 pounds per gallon). Source: Agricultural Statistics Board, U.S. Department of Agriculture (ASB-USDA)

Producer Price Index of Frozen Orange Juice Concentrate 1982 = 100

Year	Jan.	Feb.	Mar.	Apr.	May	June	July	Aug.	Sept.	Oct.	Nov.	Dec.	Average
2011	2.461	2.434	2.459	2.499	2.631	2.634	2.734	2.730	2.720	2.749	2.788	2.755	2.633
2012	2.753	2.769	2.782	2.781	2.642	2.639	2.643	2.625	2.610	2.652	2.595	2.604	2.675
2013	2.511	2.487	2.484	2.555	2.606	2.512	2.540	2.539	2.518	2.540	2.443	2.431	2.514
2014	2.414	2.430	2.457	2.426	2.571	2.510	2.547	2.547	2.566	2.605	2.646	2.651	2.531
2015	2.732	2.734	2.678	2.662	2.709	2.680	2.658	2.739	2.732	2.753	2.715	2.733	2.710
2016	2.731	2.752	2.758	2.747	2.796	2.772	2.768	2.774	2.810	2.550	2.530	2.571	2.713
2017	2.608	2.653	2.661	2.645	2.579	2.582	2.827	2.868	2.619	2.619	2.573	2.615	2.654
2018	2.521	2.538	2.513	2.481	2.481	2.469	2.504	2.440	2.493	2.478	2.475	2.434	2.486
2019	2.407	2.427	2.450	2.448	2.454	2.486	2.404	2.416	2.414	2.369	2.264	2.336	2.406
2020[1]	2.321	2.319	2.277	2.398	2.375	2.360	2.339	2.339	2.257	2.307	2.285	2.333	2.326

[1] Preliminary. *Source: Bureau of Labor Statistics, U.S. Department of Labor (BLS)*

Average Price Received by Farmers for Oranges (Equivalent On-Tree) in the U.S. In Dollars Per Box

Year	Jan.	Feb.	Mar.	Apr.	May	June	July	Aug.	Sept.	Oct.	Nov.	Dec.	Average
2011	6.58	6.50	6.77	7.00	7.53	8.46	7.74	7.53	7.60	8.47	8.86	7.29	7.53
2012	7.65	8.25	8.52	9.53	10.35	12.49	9.60	7.81	9.08	9.57	8.92	6.64	9.03
2013	6.85	7.05	7.84	8.46	9.27	12.85	10.64	10.00	12.24	12.94	13.07	6.93	9.85
2014	8.24	10.71	10.90	9.68	10.27	11.12	14.60	14.78	15.84	13.82	16.26	9.43	12.14
2015	9.35	9.85	11.32	10.78	10.74	10.53	10.79	12.01	15.25	17.73	17.35	9.59	12.11
2016	8.96	9.78	9.30	9.08	9.47	8.21	8.19	8.62	8.66	10.11	16.57	9.64	9.72
2017	9.63	11.62	12.35	11.81	12.46	18.53	20.33	18.18	20.52	25.61	16.47	12.55	15.84
2018	15.06	21.28	15.05	13.93	16.32	23.08	20.29	17.73	20.17	19.60	15.61	10.46	17.38
2019	10.10	9.95	11.70	11.23	11.06	7.56	7.26	7.31	7.70	11.95	15.18	10.20	10.10
2020[1]	9.40	9.65	9.97	11.09	12.97	16.15	15.53	15.21	15.56	23.80	18.83	11.03	14.10

[1] Preliminary. *Source: Economic Research Service, U.S. Department of Agriculture (ERS-USDA)*

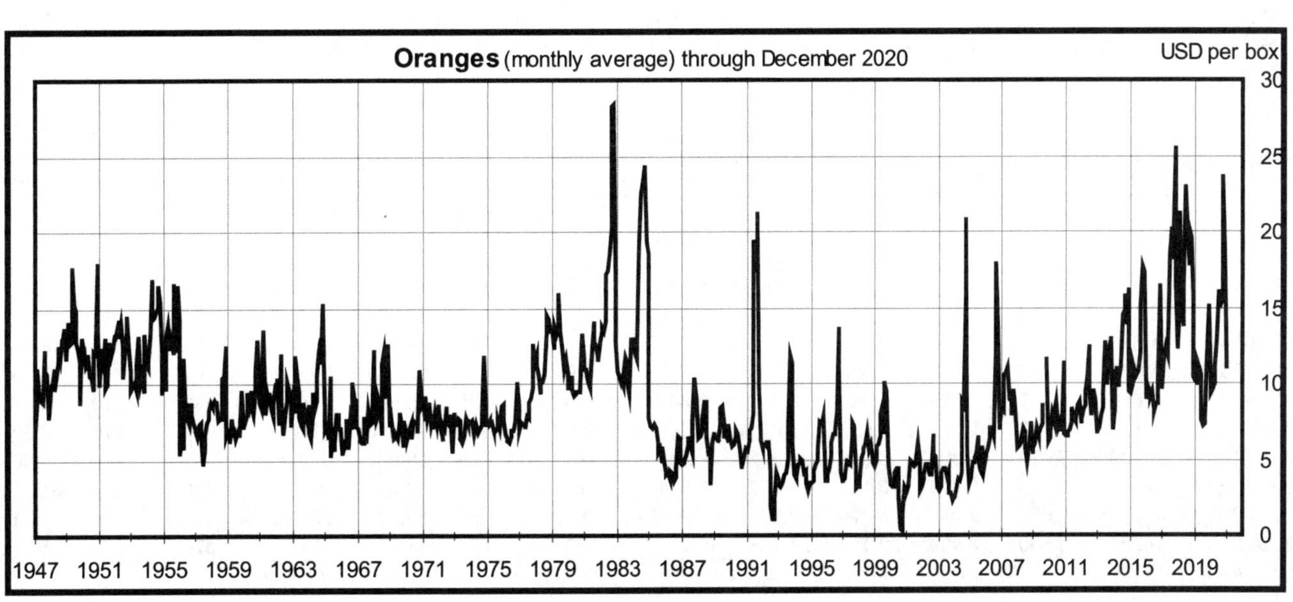

Palm Oil

Palm oil is an edible vegetable oil produced from the flesh of the fruit of the oil palm tree. The oil palm tree is a tropical palm tree that is a native of the west coast of Africa and is different from the coconut palm tree. The fruit of the oil palm tree is reddish, about the size of a large plum, and grows in large bunches. A single seed, the palm kernel, is contained in each fruit. Oil is extracted from both the pulp of the fruit (becoming palm oil) and the kernel (palm kernel oil). About one metric ton of palm kernel oil is obtained for every ten metric tons of palm oil.

Palm oil is commercially used in soap, ointments, cosmetics, detergents, and machinery lubricants. It is also used worldwide as cooking oil, shortening, and margarine. Palm kernel oil is a lighter oil and is used exclusively for food use. Crude palm oil and crude palm kernel oil are traded on the Kuala Lumpur Commodity Exchange.

Prices – The monthly average wholesale price of palm oil (CIF, bulk, U.S. ports) in 2019 fell by -5.2% yr/yr to 29.63 cents per pound, well below the 2011 record high of 55.98 cents per pound.

Supply – World production of palm oil in the 2017/18 marketing year rose by +7.6% to 69.774 million metric tons. World palm oil production has grown by more than thirty times the production level of 1.922 million metric tons seen back in 1970. Indonesia and Malaysia are the world's two major global producers of palm oil. Indonesian production in 2017/18 rose +6.9% yr/yr to a record high of 38.500 million metric tons, and Indonesian production will account for 55.2% of world production. Malaysian production in 2017/18 rose +8.7% to a record high of 20.500 million metric tons, and Malaysian production will account for 31.0% of world production. Other smaller global producers include Thailand with 3.9% of world production, Columbia with 2.3%, and Nigeria with 1.4%.

Demand – U.S. total disappearance of palm oil in 2017/18 rose +4.7% yr/yr to 1.629 million metric tons, which was a new record high.

Trade – World palm oil exports in 2017/18 rose +2.7% to 50.121 million metric tons, which is a new record high. The world's largest exporters were Indonesia, with a 56.9% share of world exports, and Malaysia, with a share of 34.5%. World palm oil imports in 2017/18 rose +2.8% to 47.177 million metric tons. The world's largest importers were India with a 22.5% share of world imports and the European Union with a 13.8% share.

World Production of Palm Oil   In Thousands of Metric Tons

Crop Year	Brazil	Colombia	Costa Rica	Cote d'Ivoire	Ecuador	Guatemala	Honduras	Indonesia	Malaysia	Nigeria	Papua New Guinea	Thailand	World Total
2011-12	310	945	242	371	473	291	395	26,200	18,202	970	580	1,892	52,524
2012-13	340	974	256	418	539	365	425	28,500	19,321	940	520	2,135	56,424
2013-14	370	1,041	300	415	499	434	460	30,500	20,161	880	500	2,000	59,268
2014-15	400	1,110	203	415	484	510	470	33,000	19,879	940	537	2,068	61,847
2015-16	415	1,275	188	415	535	625	490	32,000	17,700	955	560	1,804	58,838
2016-17	485	1,146	251	486	587	740	620	36,000	18,858	990	650	2,500	65,252
2017-18	500	1,627	235	483	570	852	580	39,500	19,683	1,025	680	2,780	70,537
2018-19[1]	525	1,631	250	514	557	862	580	41,500	20,800	1,130	705	3,000	74,135
2019-20[2]	540	1,529	247	515	455	862	580	42,500	19,255	1,220	555	2,800	73,201
2020-21[3]	540	1,559	244	515	540	865	580	43,500	19,600	1,280	561	3,100	75,093

[1] Preliminary. [2] Estimate. [3] Forecast. *Source: Foreign Agricultural Service, U.S. Department of Agriculture (FAS-USDA)*

World Trade of Palm Oil   In Thousands of Metric Tons

	Imports						Exports						
Crop Year	China	European Union	India	Pakistan	Other	World Total	Benin	European Union	Indonesia	Malaysia	Papua/ New Guinea	United Arab Emirates	World Total
2011-12	5,841	5,707	7,201	2,217	17,483	38,449	253	169	18,453	17,586	585	386	39,855
2012-13	6,589	6,812	8,364	2,245	18,038	42,048	430	135	20,373	18,524	564	217	43,066
2013-14	5,573	6,969	7,820	2,725	18,823	41,910	600	162	21,719	17,344	556	250	43,175
2014-15	5,696	6,935	9,139	2,826	20,169	44,765	500	116	25,964	17,403	607	250	47,392
2015-16	4,689	6,717	8,860	2,720	19,562	42,548	450	148	22,906	16,667	580	210	43,879
2016-17	4,881	7,217	9,341	3,075	21,676	46,190	500	134	27,633	16,313	664	270	48,891
2017-18	5,320	7,079	8,608	3,093	22,547	46,647	476	146	26,967	16,472	684	180	48,658
2018-19[1]	6,795	7,349	9,710	3,175	23,472	50,501	275	116	28,279	18,362	720	170	51,772
2019-20[2]	6,719	7,639	7,398	3,275	22,865	47,896	180	87	26,249	17,212	565	170	48,342
2020-21[3]	6,900	6,800	8,400	3,450	24,168	49,718	190	75	28,850	17,275	570	165	51,191

[1] Preliminary. [2] Estimate. [3] Forecast. *Source: Foreign Agricultural Service, U.S. Department of Agriculture (FAS-USDA)*

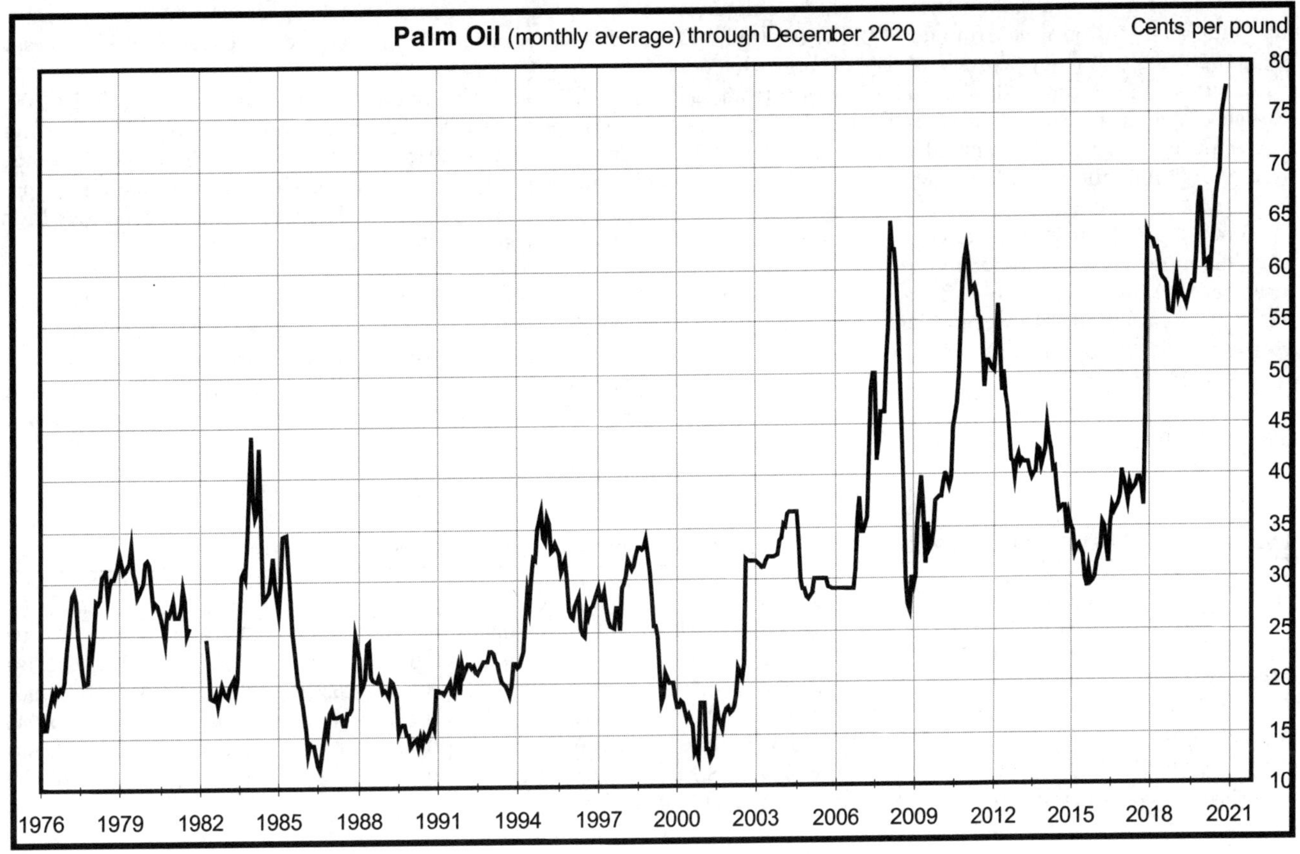

Supply and Distribution of Palm Oil in the United States In Thousands of Metric Tons

Crop Year Beginning Oct. 1	Stocks Oct. 1	Imports	Total Supply	Consumption: Edible Products	Consumption: Inedible Products	Consumption: Total End Products	Total Disap-pearance	Exports	Prices: U.S. Import Value[4]	Prices: Malaysia, F.O.B., RBD	Prices: Palm Kernel Oil, Malaysia, C.I.F Rotterdam
				In Millions of Pounds					U.S. $ Per Metric Ton		
2008-09	73.0	1,036.0	1,109.0	973.6	W	973.6	1,109.0	20.0	----	628	662
2009-10	130.0	994.0	1,124.0	1,140.8	W	1,140.8	1,124.0	16.0	----	807	972
2010-11	151.0	980.0	1,131.0	1,049.7	W	1,049.7	1,131.0	27.0	----	1146	1741
2011-12	147.0	1,032.0	1,179.0	NA	NA	NA	1,179.0	18.0	----	1053	1220
2012-13	118.0	1,293.0	1,411.0	----	----	----	1,411.0	37.0	----	835	836
2013-14	136.0	1,220.0	1,356.0	----	----	----	1,356.0	13.0	----	867	1146
2014-15	136.0	1,143.0	1,279.0	----	----	----	1,279.0	22.0	----	659	941
2015-16[1]	165.0	1,307.0	1,472.0	----	----	----	1,472.0	14.0	----	655	1126
2016-17[2]	189.0	1,367.0	1,556.0	----	----	----	1,556.0	17.0	----	751	1436
2017-18[3]	184.0	1,445.0	1,629.0	----	----	----	1,629.0	21.0	----		

[1] Preliminary. [2] Estimate. [3] Forecast. [4] Market value in the foreign country, excluding import duties, ocean freight and marine insurance.
W = Withheld. *Sources: The Oil World; Economic Research Service, U.S. Department of Agriculture (ERS-USDA)*

Average Wholesale Palm Oil Prices, CIF, Bulk, U.S. Ports In Cents Per Pound

Year	Jan.	Feb.	Mar.	Apr.	May	June	July	Aug.	Sept.	Oct.	Nov.	Dec.	Average
2011	60.88	62.06	60.44	57.80	58.44	57.56	55.40	55.25	53.25	48.63	51.00	51.05	55.98
2012	50.25	50.19	52.60	56.56	52.94	48.20	50.06	47.75	46.63	41.44	41.25	39.69	48.13
2013	41.38	42.06	41.00	41.38	41.35	41.31	40.19	39.70	40.00	40.19	42.65	42.38	41.13
2014	40.90	42.50	45.00	43.44	42.40	40.38	40.63	38.35	36.56	37.00	36.94	34.19	39.86
2015	36.05	34.88	34.50	32.38	33.05	33.19	32.15	29.88	29.25	30.75	29.50	29.60	32.10
2016	30.06	31.44	32.80	35.35	34.94	33.00	31.45	35.25	36.85	36.44	37.13	37.95	34.39
2017	37.75	37.38	35.90	34.06	36.31	35.05	35.19	35.06	36.44	36.19	35.44	33.25	35.67
2018	34.13	33.69	34.10	33.81	32.88	32.35	30.38	30.10	29.94	29.63	27.00	27.13	31.26
2019	28.94	30.00	28.40	28.63	28.00	27.75	27.19	28.90	28.63	28.94	32.95	37.25	29.63
2020	39.40	35.31	31.38	30.81	29.20	32.38	34.00	37.00	38.56	39.35	44.44	47.45	36.61

Source: Economic Research Service, U.S. Department of Agriculture (ERS-USDA)

Paper

The earliest known paper that is still in existence was made from cotton rags around 150 AD. Around 800 AD, paper made its appearance in Egypt but was not manufactured there until 900 AD. The Moors introduced the use of paper to Europe, and around 1150, the first papermaking mill was established in Spain, followed by England in 1495, and the U.S. in 1690.

During the 17th and 18th centuries, the increased usage of paper created a shortage of cotton rags, which were then the only source for papermaking. The solution to this problem led to the introduction of the ground-wood process of pulp-making in 1840 and the first chemical pulp process ten years later.

Today, the paper and paperboard industries, including newsprint, are sensitive to the economic cycle. As the economy strengthens, paper use increases, and vice versa.

Prices – The average monthly index price (1982 = 100) for paperboard in 2020 fell -4.3% yr/yr to 256.5, farther down from the 2018 record high of 273.5. The average monthly producer price index of standard newsprint paper in 2020 fell by –16.7 to 115.5, well below the 11-year high of 151.8 posted in 2006.

Supply – U.S. production of paper and paperboard in 2019 fell -3.9% yr/yr to 68.157 million metric tons. The U.S. is the world's largest producer of paper and paperboard by far with 16.9% of the world's supply, followed by Germany with 5.5%. Canada with 2.3%, and Finland and Sweden both with 2.4%.

Production of Paper and Paperboard by Selected Countries In Thousands of Metric Tons

Year	Austria	Canada	Finland	France	Germany	Italy	Nether-lands	Norway	Russia/3	Spain	Sweden	United Kingdom	United States
2014	4,865	10,775	10,408	8,096	22,540	8,648	2,767	1,023	8,023	6,036	10,419	4,397	73,093
2015	4,965	10,300	10,320	7,984	22,601	8,840	2,643	979	8,068	6,195	10,255	3,970	72,397
2016	4,995	9,911	10,140	7,984	22,629	8,888	2,671	1,099	8,547	6,219	10,102	3,677	71,902
2017	4,860	9,958	10,276	8,021	22,925	9,071	2,983	1,097	8,717	6,218	10,261	3,857	72,045
2018	5,055	10,142	10,540	7,864	22,682	9,081	2,980	1,134	9,048	6,157	10,141	3,895	70,891
2019[1]	4,985	9,473	9,710	7,325	22,073	8,901	2,895	1,155	9,106	5,800	9,616	3,852	68,157

[1] Preliminary. *Source: Food and Agriculture Organization of the United Nations (FAO)*

Production of Newsprint by Selected Countires (Monthly Average) In Thousands of Metric Tons

Year	Australia	Brazil	Canada	China	Finland	France	Germany	India	Japan	Korea, South	Russia	Sweden	United States
2013	----	----	----	305.4	----	----	176.4	----	268.2	124.1	132.1	127.4	----
2014	----	----	----	282.5	----	----	NA	----	261.1	118.1	136.3	104.0	----
2015	----	----	----	278.9	----	----	----	----	248.7	113.7	124.1	99.7	----
2016	----	----	----	244.5	----	----	----	----	242.1	117.9	122.5	84.7	----
2017[1]	----	----	----	212.9	----	----	----	----	231.6	100.0	119.9	84.2	----
2018[2]	----	----	----	158.0	----	----	----	----	224.5		124.4	80.4	----

[1] Preliminary. [2] Estimate. *Source: Food and Agriculture Organization of the United Nations (FAO)*

Index Price of Paperboard (1982 = 100)

Year	Jan.	Feb.	Mar.	Apr.	May	June	July	Aug.	Sept.	Oct.	Nov.	Dec.	Average
2013	235.7	235.8	236.8	236.8	241.1	246.4	247.7	249.3	249.0	249.0	248.8	248.3	243.7
2014	249.0	249.6	249.7	249.2	249.3	249.3	249.2	248.8	247.7	247.3	247.0	246.9	248.6
2015	246.9	245.2	244.5	242.6	243.6	242.6	241.9	241.4	242.2	242.1	242.2	242.0	243.1
2016	241.2	236.0	232.2	230.6	230.9	230.5	230.6	230.0	230.0	232.3	236.2	240.7	233.4
2017	244.7	244.1	244.2	249.3	252.5	262.7	264.0	264.5	265.5	266.3	266.1	266.6	257.5
2018	265.5	265.9	264.8	266.6	275.6	276.8	278.3	278.1	277.9	278.0	276.9	277.3	273.5
2019	276.9	274.6	273.9	273.1	272.9	270.4	264.8	262.3	262.2	262.4	261.9	260.9	268.0
2020[1]	259.0	256.5	256.0	255.0	255.7	254.7	256.1	256.3	255.4	256.2	256.3	260.9	256.5

[1] Preliminary. *Source: Bureau of Labor Statistics, U.S. Department of Commerce (BLS) (0914)*

Producer Price Index of Standard Newsprint (1982 = 100)

Year	Jan.	Feb.	Mar.	Apr.	May	June	July	Aug.	Sept.	Oct.	Nov.	Dec.	Average
2013	136.3	132.6	130.1	129.7	129.1	127.8	130.8	129.6	129.4	129.9	131.3	130.3	130.6
2014	130.7	130.5	130.2	129.2	128.3	129.2	129.1	129.0	128.7	128.4	128.1	127.2	129.1
2015	126.3	123.3	121.4	119.1	116.1	114.4	112.9	106.5	106.3	105.6	105.4	105.4	113.6
2016	106.7	109.6	111.9	112.3	113.3	114.9	116.4	117.8	118.3	118.4	118.1	118.3	114.7
2017	118.8	118.3	117.4	117.0	117.3	118.1	118.0	117.5	118.0	118.1	120.8	122.9	118.5
2018	124.8	127.0	128.1	130.4	136.0	141.2	143.5	146.0	146.3	146.2	146.0	146.2	138.5
2019	146.2	146.0	147.5	145.9	137.9	137.4	136.4	136.8	136.0	134.3	130.8	129.9	138.8
2020[1]	125.8	123.0	119.8	118.8	116.6	116.6	115.3	111.6	110.6	110.4	110.4	107.4	115.5

[1] Preliminary. *Source: Bureau of Labor Statistics, U.S. Department of Commerce (BLS) (0913-02)*

Peanuts and Peanut Oil

Peanuts are the edible seeds of a plant from the pea family. Although called a nut, the peanut is actually a legume. Ancient South American Inca Indians were the first to grind peanuts to make peanut butter. Peanuts originated in Brazil and were later brought to the U.S. via Africa. The first major use of peanuts was as feed for pigs. It wasn't until the Civil War that peanuts were used as human food when both Northern and Southern troops used the peanut as a food source during hard times. In 1903, Dr. George Washington Carver, a talented botanist who is considered the "father of commercial peanuts," introduced peanuts as a rotation crop in cotton-growing areas. Carver discovered over 300 uses for the peanut, including shaving cream, leather dye, coffee, ink, cheese, and shampoo.

Peanuts come in many varieties, but there are four basic types grown in the U.S.: Runner, Spanish, Valencia, and Virginia. Over half of Runner peanuts are used to make peanut butter. Spanish peanuts are primarily used to make candies and peanut oil. Valencia peanuts are the sweetest of the four types. Virginia peanuts are mainly roasted and sold in and out of the shell.

Peanut oil is extracted from shelled and crushed peanuts through hydraulic pressing, expelled pressing, or solvent extraction. Crude peanut oil is used as a flavoring agent, salad oil, and cooking oil. Refined, bleached and deodorized peanut oil is used for cooking and in margarines and shortenings. The by-product called press cake is used for cattle feed along with the tops of the plants after the pods are removed. The dry shells can be burned as fuel.

Prices – The average monthly price received by farmers for peanuts (in the shell) in the first five months of the 2020/21 marketing year (Aug/July) rose +1.7% to 20.7 cents per pound. The record high is 34.7 cents posted in 1990/91. The average monthly price of peanut oil in the first four months of the 2020/21 marketing year rose +37.3% yr/yr to 95.44 cents per pound, but still below the 2007/08 record high of 100.91 cents per pound.

Supply – World peanut production in 2020/21 is forecasted to rise +2.8% to 47.357 million metric tons, a new record high. The world's largest peanut producers are expected to be China with 37.0% of world production, India with 13.7%, Nigeria with 8.2%, and the U. S. with 5.9%.

U.S. peanut production in the 2020/221 marketing year is expected to rise by +21.5% yr/yr to 6.643 billion pounds, but still down from the 2017/18 record high of 7.115. U.S. farmers are expected to harvest 1.623 million acres of peanuts in 2020/21, up +16.8% yr/yr, but that is still below the 30-year high harvest of 2.015 million acres in 1992-93. U.S. peanut yield in 2020/21 is expected to rise +4.0% yr/yr to 4,093 pounds per acre, but still below the 2012/13 record high of 4,211 pounds per acre. The largest peanut-producing states in the U.S. in 2020 were Georgia with 54.2% of U.S. production, Alabama with 11.0%, Florida with 9.2%, Texas with 7.3%, North Carolina with 6.5%, and South Carolina with 4.7.0%. U.S. crude peanut oil production in 2019/20 rose +10.2% to 405.622 million pounds.

Demand – U.S. disposition of peanuts in 2020/21 is expected to rise +8.4% yr/yr to 6.375 billion pounds. Of that disposition, 52.1% of the peanuts will go for food, 23.5% for exports, 11.8% for seed, loss and residual, and 12.5% for crushing into peanut oil. The most popular type of peanut grown in the U.S. is the Runner peanut with 88.0% of U.S. production in 2018/19. The next most popular peanut is the Virginia peanut with 10.3% of production, and the Spanish peanut is far behind with only 1.7% of production. Peanut butter is a primary use for Runner and Virginia peanuts. Peanut butter accounts for 59.6% of Runner peanut usage and 51.1% of Virginia peanut usage. Lagging in third place, only about 5% of Spanish peanuts are used for peanut butter. Snack peanuts are also a key usage category and account for 34.3% of Virginia peanut usage, 28.7% of Runner peanut usage, and 20.0% of Spanish peanut usage. Candy accounts for 53.3% of Spanish peanut usage, 17.1% of Runner peanut usage, and 6.8% of Virginia peanut usage.

Trade – U.S. exports of peanuts in 2020/21 are expected to fall -6.7% yr/yr to 1.500 billion pounds. U.S. imports of peanuts are expected to rise by +0.9% yr/yr to 115 million pounds.

World Production of Peanuts (in the Shell) In Thousands of Metric Tons

Crop Year	Argen-tina	Burma	Came-roon	China	India	Indo-nesia	Nigeria	Senegal	Sudan	Tanzania	United States	Vietnam	World Total
2011-12	1,020	1,370	564	15,302	6,015	1,165	2,963	528	1,185	651	1,660	471	38,610
2012-13	1,016	1,372	634	15,792	4,334	1,145	3,314	693	1,032	810	3,064	468	40,274
2013-14	997	1,428	636	16,082	6,482	1,160	2,475	677	1,767	1,425	1,893	455	41,769
2014-15	1,188	1,465	579	15,901	4,855	1,150	3,399	669	1,871	1,635	2,354	452	41,790
2015-16	930	1,502	609	15,961	4,470	1,130	3,467	1,050	1,042	1,836	2,722	441	41,283
2016-17	1,288	1,518	748	16,361	6,924	1,120	3,582	991	1,826	1,100	2,532	462	45,155
2017-18	867	1,572	600	17,092	6,665	1,075	4,248	1,405	1,648	1,100	3,228	450	46,825
2018-19	1,419	1,583	600	17,333	4,685	1,025	4,422	1,502	2,884	1,100	2,493	439	46,807
2019-20[1]	1,300	1,375	600	17,520	6,255	990	3,500	1,420	1,800	1,100	2,480	434	46,076
2020-21[2]	1,400	1,550	600	17,500	6,500	970	3,900	1,400	1,800	1,100	2,782	447	47,357

[1] Preliminary. [2] Estimate. *Source: Foreign Agricultural Service, U.S. Department of Agriculture (FAS-USDA)*

PEANUTS AND PEANUT OIL

Salient Statistics of Peanuts in the United States

Crop Year Beginning Aug. 1	Acreage Planted	Acreage Harvested for Nuts	Average Yield Per Acre In Lbs.	Production (1,000 Lbs)	Season Farm Price (Cents Lb.)	Farm Value (Million Dollars)	Exports Unshelled	Exports Shelled	Imports Unshelled	Imports Shelled
	1,000 Acres						In Thousands of Pounds			
2011-12	1,140.6	1,080.6	3,386	3,658,590	31.8	1,168.6	546,000	352,994	253,897	163,852
2012-13	1,638.0	1,604.0	4,211	6,753,880	30.1	2,026.3	1,190,000	741,103	118,743	72,871
2013-14	1,067.0	1,043.0	4,001	4,173,170	24.9	1,055.1	1,096,000	708,141	88,000	60,738
2014-15	1,353.5	1,322.5	3,923	5,188,665	22.0	1,158.3	1,080,000	676,509	90,000	64,345
2015-16	1,625.0	1,560.9	3,845	6,001,357	19.3	1,160.6	1,544,000		94,000	
2016-17	1,671.0	1,536.0	3,634	5,581,570	19.7	1,088.2	1,328,000		162,000	
2017-18	1,871.6	1,775.6	4,007	7,115,410	22.9	1,634.0	1,271,000		171,000	
2018-19	1,425.5	1,373.5	4,001	5,461,600	21.5	1,170.0	1,200,000		117,000	
2019-20[1]	1,432.7	1,389.7	3,934	5,466,487	20.6	1,129.6	1,608,000		114,000	
2020-21[2]	1,665.2	1,623.2	4,093	6,643,320						

[1] Preliminary. [2] Estimate. *Source: Economic Research Service, U.S. Department of Agriculture (ERS-USDA)*

Supply and Disposition of Peanuts (Farmer's Stock Basis) in the United States

Crop Year Beginning Aug. 1	Supply: Production	Supply: Imports	Supply: Stocks Aug. 1	Supply: Total	Disposition: Exports	Disposition: Crushed for Oil	Disposition: Seed, Loss & Residual	Disposition: Food	Disposition: Total Disappearance
	In Millions of Pounds								
2012-13	6,754	119	1,003	7,876	1,190	656	524	2,735	5,105
2013-14	4,173	88	2,771	7,032	1,096	663	530	2,886	5,174
2014-15	5,189	90	1,858	7,136	1,080	675	298	2,982	5,035
2015-16	6,001	94	2,101	8,197	1,544	709	1,100	3,053	6,406
2016-17	5,582	162	1,791	7,534	1,328	880	799	3,086	6,093
2017-18	7,115	171	1,442	8,728	1,271	705	887	3,149	6,011
2018-19	5,462	117	2,717	8,330	1,200	648	962	3,099	5,909
2019-20[1]	5,466	114	2,421	8,001	1,608	774	287	3,214	5,883
2020-21[2]	6,643	115	2,118	8,367	1,500	800	752	3,323	6,375

[1] Preliminary. [2] Estimate. *Source: Economic Research Service, U.S. Department of Agriculture (ERS-USDA)*

Production of Peanuts (Harvested for Nuts) in the United States, by States In Thousands of Pounds

Crop Year	Alabama	Florida	Georgia	Mississippi	New Mexico	North Carolina	Oklahoma	South Carolina	Texas	Virgina	Total
2011	489,700	549,500	1,645,750	56,000	19,800	291,600	54,600	240,900	249,240	61,500	3,658,590
2012	876,000	760,500	3,343,400	215,600	26,000	427,180	80,300	417,300	525,600	82,000	6,753,880
2013	489,900	517,450	1,887,180	122,100	21,700	315,900	59,200	273,000	423,540	63,200	4,173,170
2014	544,950	668,000	2,435,515	124,000	15,750	401,760	44,000	410,400	459,740	84,550	5,188,665
2015	637,000	648,000	3,364,410	143,500	15,337	302,760	30,600	262,400	528,000	69,350	6,001,357
2016	619,200	554,800	2,753,400	152,000	22,400	349,470	44,400	339,200	559,650	76,650	5,581,570
2017	704,450	638,250	3,572,250	172,000	26,600	479,700	79,380	472,000	697,200	119,880	7,115,410
2018	571,550	564,850	2,875,450	93,600	15,675	379,260	46,050	272,000	464,000	100,800	5,461,600
2019	522,600	589,000	2,752,200	76,000	15,087	448,800	56,000	235,600	488,000	111,600	5,466,487
2020[1]	728,000	610,500	3,600,000	99,000	19,220	430,500	54,000	311,600	486,000	113,400	6,643,320

[1] Preliminary. *Source: Agricultural Statistics Board, U.S. Department of Agriculture (ASB-USDA)*

Supply and Reported Uses of Shelled Peanuts and Products in the United States In Thousands of Pounds

Crop Year Beginning Aug. 1	Shelled Peanuts Stocks, Aug. 1: Edible	Shelled Peanuts Stocks, Aug. 1: Oil Stock[2]	Shelled Peanuts Production: Edible	Shelled Peanuts Production: Oil Stock[2]	Edible Grades Used In: Candy[3]	Edible Grades Used In: Snack[4]	Edible Grades Used In: Butter[5]	Edible Grades Used In: Other Products	Edible Grades Used In: Total	Shelled Peanuts Crushed[6]	Crude Oil Production	Cake & Meal Production
					Reported Used (Shelled Peanuts - Raw Basis)							
2011-12	466,310	52,883	2,399,094	345,565	394,678	390,068	1,197,748	19,661	2,002,155	453,835	188,479	250,037
2012-13	547,965	33,883	3,125,786	351,284	381,914	400,429	1,227,859	20,664	2,030,866	493,205	210,702	270,328
2013-14	519,824	25,364	3,098,392	373,008	395,726	429,796	1,218,170	29,103	2,072,795	497,272	209,808	268,554
2014-15	431,674	31,012	2,997,078	391,728	375,856	428,477	1,303,755	53,179	2,161,267	506,677	214,041	278,380
2015-16	467,139	65,350	3,141,099	442,650	377,505	505,692	1,299,634	61,388	2,244,219	531,770	226,219	291,193
2016-17	482,010	26,372	2,944,760	448,377	407,701	470,292	1,338,195	56,769	2,272,957	659,966	283,689	357,751
2017-18	535,730	24,232	2,853,147	358,282	379,504	524,845	1,314,567	95,943	2,314,859	528,750	231,748	282,346
2018-19	540,802	23,498	2,932,229	368,168	380,936	467,676	1,342,437	112,651	2,303,700	486,398	219,334	255,683
2019-20[1]	510,369	29,092	2,908,778	405,622	395,647	481,430	1,410,264	91,567	2,378,908	580,628	254,109	304,718

[1] Preliminary. [2] Includes straight run oil stock peanuts. [3] Includes peanut butter made by manufacturers for own use in candy. [4] Formerly titled "Salted Peanuts." [5] Includes peanut butter made by manufacturers for own use in cookies and sandwiches, but excludes peanut butter used in candy. [6] All crushings regardless of grade. *Source: National Agricultural Statistics Service, U.S. Department of Agriculture (NASS-USDA)*

Shelled Peanuts (Raw Basis) Used in Primary Products, by Type In Thousands of Pounds

Crop Year Beginning Aug. 1	Virginia				Runner				Spanish			
	Candy[2]	Peanuts	Butter[3]	Total	Candy[2]	Peanuts	Butter[3]	Total	Candy[2]	Peanuts	Butter[3]	Total
2010-11	16,070	62,708	W	211,194	365,260	319,529	1,076,521	1,774,346	14,122	12,940	W	35,207
2011-12	17,856	78,333	W	203,958	360,797	303,631	1,091,541	1,770,809	16,025	8,104	W	27,390
2012-13	17,731	83,722	82,981	192,888	347,428	309,860	1,143,108	1,812,591	16,755	6,847	W	25,389
2013-14	17,109	85,298	86,759	202,536	W	337,934	1,128,206	1,844,490	15,996	6,564	W	W
2014-15	12,079	91,909	102,340	232,768	348,367	329,930	1,196,277	1,901,311	15,410	6,638	W	27,188
2015-16	14,319	89,766	108,156	238,494	346,831	408,726	1,186,810	1,977,495	16,355	7,200	W	28,225
2016-17	13,427	92,331	118,109	247,473	379,549	370,766	1,215,212	1,998,683	14,725	7,195	W	26,801
2017-18	15,455	84,479	129,823	258,754	346,985	434,139	1,179,186	2,027,253	17,064	6,227	W	28,851
2018-19	15,589	81,418	120,939	236,696	349,081	380,165	1,213,018	2,036,161	16,266	6,093	W	30,840
2019-20[1]	9,145	94,614	140,527	264,121	372,153	W	1,259,768	2,084,164	14,349	W	W	30,622

[1] Preliminary. [2] Includes peanut butter made by manufacturers for own use in candy. [3] Includes peanut butter made by manufacturers for own use in cookies and sandwiches, but excludes peanut butter used in candy.
Source: National Agricultural Statistics Service, U.S. Department of Agriculture (NASS-USDA)

Production, Consumption, Stocks and Foreign Trade of Peanut Oil in the United States In Millions of Pounds

Crop Year Beginning Aug. 1	Production		Consumption		Stocks, Dec. 31		Imports for Consumption	Exports
	Crude	Refined	In Refining	In End Products	Crude	Refined		
2002-03	267.7	166.3	W	277.6	52.9	3.5	----	----
2003-04	180.7	115.8	W	203.8	23.0	1.8	----	----
2004-05	135.7	91.0	W	181.9	40.3	2.4	----	----
2005-06	188.0	119.9	W	152.1	15.4	3.7	----	----
2006-07	173.8	115.1	W	W	35.5	5.6	----	----
2007-08	168.7	111.2	W	W	14.1	1.8	----	----
2008-09	150.8	99.9	W	W	17.6	3.0	----	----
2009-10[1]	146.3	96.6	W	W	18.1	2.1	----	----
2010-11[2]	196.9	132.0	W	W	----	----	----	----
2011-12[2]	NA	NA	NA	NA	NA	NA	----	----

[1] Preliminary. [2] Forecast. W = Withheld. *Source: Bureau of the Census, U.S. Department of Commerce*

Farmer Stock Equivalent Total[2/3] Stocks of Peanuts in the United States at End of Month In Million Pounds

Crop Year	Aug.	Sept.	Oct.	Nov.	Dec.	Jan.	Feb.	Mar.	Apr.	May.	June	July
2011-12	1,171.5	1,252.4	2,888.2	3,389.3	3,237.9	2,938.7	2,652.9	2,333.0	1,966.5	1,553.1	1,261.8	1,003.3
2012-13	669.6	1,623.1	5,050.1	5,758.2	5,570.7	5,184.7	4,792.2	4,382.6	3,953.0	3,559.0	3,202.7	2,770.7
2013-14	2,427.0	2,172.4	3,776.3	4,641.5	4,710.1	4,299.6	3,919.4	3,505.5	3,092.3	2,741.2	2,304.4	1,857.8
2014-15	1,426.7	1,330.5	4,246.1	4,717.3	4,573.2	4,297.1	3,893.3	3,487.2	3,105.8	2,717.9	2,401.4	2,101.0
2015-16	1,455.3	1,846.4	4,496.2	5,317.9	5,360.6	4,863.2	4,347.8	3,798.7	3,279.7	2,656.4	2,108.6	1,790.9
2016-17	1,239.1	1,509.3	4,156.1	4,701.6	4,389.9	3,992.8	3,550.0	3,087.8	2,668.3	2,241.0	1,806.7	1,441.6
2017-18	1,013.5	1,806.4	4,739.2	5,587.7	5,379.1	5,032.3	4,585.7	4,225.5	3,787.6	3,357.5	2,982.1	2,717.1
2018-19	2,309.8	2,594.7	4,195.3	5,002.8	5,056.8	4,727.8	4,326.0	3,976.9	3,490.6	3,075.9	2,765.4	27,421.1
2019-20	2,045.2	2,442.1	4,106.7	4,637.5	4,610.5	4,322.4	4,001.2	3,636.6	3,214.2	2,744.7	2,379.4	2,118.2
2020-21[1]	1,551.8	1,457.9	3,486.5	4,488.1	4,373.7	4,129.4						

[1] Preliminary. [2] Excludes stocks on farms. Includes stocks owned by or held for account of peanut producers and CCC in commercial storage facilities. Farmer stock on net weight basis. [3] Actual farmer stock, plus roasting stock, plus shelled peanuts. W = Withheld. *Source: Agricultural Marketing Service, U.S. Department of Agriculture (AMS-USDA)*

Farmer Stock Peanuts[2], Total All Types, in the United States at End of Month In Millions of Pounds

Crop Year	Aug.	Sept.	Oct.	Nov.	Dec.	Jan.	Feb.	Mar.	Apr.	May.	June	July
2011-12	472.0	613.8	2,300.1	2,780.8	2,581.2	2,239.4	1,888.5	1,514.2	1,145.2	772.3	507.9	272.8
2012-13	98.2	1,164.8	4,442.1	5,098.6	4,865.5	4,447.0	4,032.1	3,548.0	3,073.4	2,629.0	2,266.4	1,925.0
2013-14	1,527.6	1,296.5	2,909.0	3,790.8	3,876.1	3,472.0	3,045.7	2,615.1	2,195.8	1,819.1	1,423.3	1,059.5
2014-15	661.8	573.0	3,517.7	4,046.4	3,947.9	3,622.6	3,224.0	2,789.6	2,394.6	2,056.4	1,697.5	1,445.3
2015-16	874.6	1,305.6	3,883.8	4,690.3	4,733.5	4,207.8	3,621.4	3,058.7	2,584.2	1,948.7	1,413.6	1,051.1
2016-17	648.2	960.2	3,594.2	4,093.3	3,747.5	3,317.9	2,828.0	2,342.8	1,919.8	1,465.8	1,050.4	733.0
2017-18	373.9	1,252.0	4,131.7	4,977.2	4,679.2	4,283.4	3,831.6	3,351.3	2,906.0	2,508.7	2,192.0	1,916.8
2018-19	1,568.9	1,811.5	3,426.7	4,286.5	4,301.9	3,976.5	3,576.0	3,144.1	2,703.0	2,334.7	1,964.9	1,627.9
2019-20	1,312.9	1,702.2	3,350.0	3,905.2	3,865.2	3,577.5	3,247.9	2,951.6	2,442.2	2,048.5	1,685.8	1,363.4
2020-21[1]	839.0	792.9	2,878.8	3,858.8	3,713.5	3,418.6						

[1] Preliminary. [2] Excludes stocks on farms. Includes stocks owned by or held for account of peanut producers and CCC in commercial storage facilities. Farmer stock on net weight basis. *Source: Agricultural Marketing Service, U.S. Department of Agriculture (AMS-USDA)*

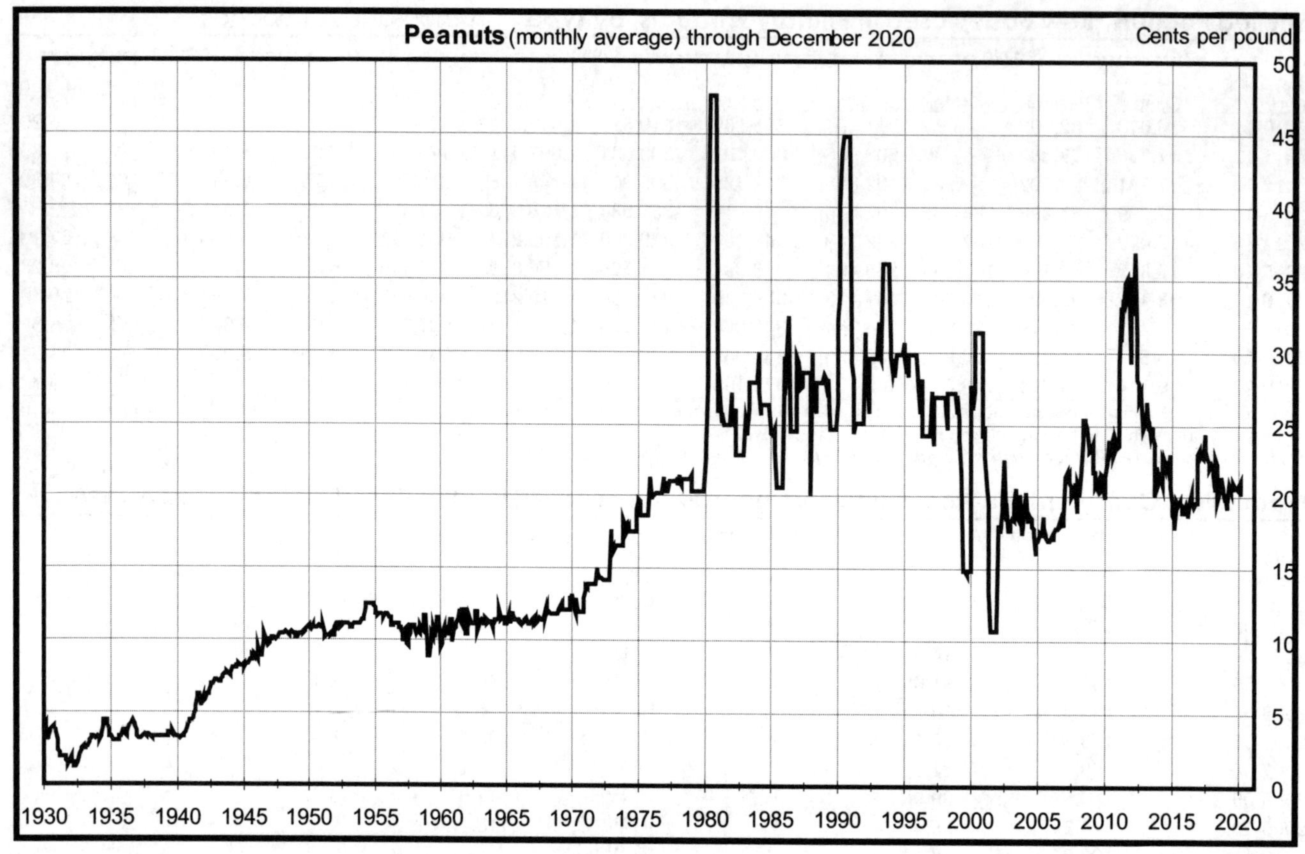

Average Price[2] Received by Farmers for Peanuts (in the Shell) in the United States In Cents Per Pound

Year	Aug.	Sept.	Oct.	Nov.	Dec.	Jan.	Feb.	Mar.	Apr.	May.	June	July	Average[1]
2011-12	23.4	23.5	28.9	33.2	30.8	33.7	32.9	34.8	35.1	33.8	34.4	34.5	31.6
2012-13	29.3	35.2	33.7	32.6	36.9	31.2	28.2	27.8	26.8	27.1	27.0	24.7	30.0
2013-14	25.1	25.3	26.0	26.6	24.6	25.4	24.3	25.0	24.2	23.7	20.0	21.7	24.3
2014-15	22.1	21.5	21.0	21.4	20.9	22.5	22.2	22.5	22.1	22.5	21.8	23.0	22.0
2015-16	20.7	19.6	18.8	18.5	17.8	19.3	19.8	19.5	19.8	19.6	19.5	19.0	19.3
2016-17	19.0	19.1	19.5	19.0	18.6	19.8	20.1	20.6	19.8	19.4	19.7	20.5	19.6
2017-18	19.7	23.0	23.2	22.7	23.0	22.9	22.7	24.4	23.3	22.7	22.7	22.4	22.7
2018-19	22.0	22.3	21.8	21.6	20.5	22.7	22.3	19.8	20.3	20.5	21.5	20.6	21.3
2019-20	20.5	19.8	20.4	19.2	19.6	20.9	20.5	20.6	20.6	21.1	20.7	20.7	20.4
2020-21[1]	20.6	20.5	20.9	21.2	20.4	20.5							20.7

[1] Preliminary. [2] Weighted average by sales. *Source: National Agricultural Statistics Service, U.S. Department of Agriculture (NASS-USDA)*

Average Price of Domestic Crude Peanut Oil (in Tanks) F.O.B. Southeast Mills In Cents Per Pound

Year	Oct.	Nov.	Dec.	Jan.	Feb.	Mar.	Apr.	May	June	July	Aug.	Sept.	Average
2011-12	97.00	98.75	96.10	95.81	95.00	96.60	102.38	106.13	111.00	110.00	110.00	104.50	101.94
2012-13	103.00	99.90	98.56	96.75	86.00	79.05	77.50	80.00	82.75	84.00	83.00	82.00	87.71
2013-14	81.00	78.70	75.38	65.70	62.06	59.06	57.75	57.20	58.25	58.63	62.80	61.75	64.86
2014-15	59.95	60.63	60.13	56.15	55.56	54.69	54.81	54.65	56.31	58.15	58.63	58.69	57.36
2015-16	57.70	58.06	58.50	56.19	55.00	55.55	56.20	61.38	61.10	62.10	61.00	61.60	58.70
2016-17	64.88	66.00	63.10	62.88	63.13	65.80	69.69	70.75	76.20	75.75	69.63	66.60	67.87
2017-18	65.44	65.00	65.20	66.13	66.63	67.00	66.88	66.50	67.70	68.00	68.00	67.63	66.68
2018-19	66.63	64.80	62.25	61.88	61.13	61.00	65.25	66.00	66.00	66.13	66.00	67.00	64.51
2019-20	61.50	63.10	60.13	59.00	59.00	59.75	59.50	62.10	84.75	85.00	90.00	90.00	69.49
2020-21[1]	93.00	98.75	100.00	90.00									95.44

[1] Preliminary. *Source: Agricultural Marketing Service, U.S. Department of Agriculture (AMS-USDA)*

Pepper

The pepper plant is a perennial climbing shrub that originated in India and Sri Lanka. Pepper is considered the world's most important spice and has been used to flavor foods for over 3,000 years. Pepper was once considered so valuable that it was used to ransom Rome from Attila the Hun. Black pepper alone accounts for nearly 35% of the world's spice trade. Unlike many other popular herbs and spices, pepper can only be cultivated in tropical climates. The pepper plant produces a berry called a peppercorn. Both black and white pepper are obtained from the same plant. The colors of pepper are determined by the maturity of the berry at harvest and by different processing methods.

Black pepper is picked when the berries are still green and immature. The peppercorns are then dried in the sun until they turn black. White pepper is picked when the berries are fully ripe and bright red. The red peppercorns are then soaked, washed to remove the skin of the berry, and dried to produce a white to yellowish-white peppercorn. Black pepper has a slightly hotter flavor and stronger aroma than white pepper. Piperine, an alkaloid of pyridine, is the active ingredient in pepper that makes it hot.

Black pepper oil is obtained from crushed berries using solvent extraction. Black pepper oil is used in the treatment of pain, chills, flu, muscular aches, and in some perfumes. It is also helpful in promoting digestion in the colon.

The world's key pepper varieties are known by their place of origin. Popular types of pepper include Lampong Black and Muntok White from Indonesia, Brazilian Black, and Malabar Black and Tellicherry from India.

Production – World production of pepper in 2019 rose by +6.1% yr/yr to 1.103 million metric tons. The world's largest pepper producer in 2019 was Vietnam with a 24.0% share of world production, followed by Brazil with 9.3%, Indonesia with an 8.1% share, and India with a 6.0% share. Pepper production in 2019 in Vietnam rose by +0.8% yr/yr to 264,854 metric tons, and in Brazil production rose by +7.7% yr/yr to 109,401 metric tons.

Trade – The world's largest exporters of pepper in 2019 were Vietnam with 46.0% at 252,921 metric tons of exports, Brazil with 14.8% at 84,676 metric tons, Indonesia with 13.2% at 76,571 metric tons, the European Union with 7.6% at 43,546 metric tons, India with 3.4% at 19,542 metric tons, and Germany with 2.4% at 13,964 metric tons.

World Production of Pepper In Metric Tons

Year	Brazil	Cambodia	China	India	Indonesia	Madagascar	Malaysia	Mexico	Philippines	Sri Lanka	Thailand	Vietnam	World Total
2012	43,345	2,400	31,200	41,000	87,841	4,824	26,000	3,025	3,248	24,950	2,241	120,276	817,339
2013	42,312	2,468	31,410	53,000	91,000	4,894	26,500	3,199	2,716	26,730	1,332	125,023	720,069
2014	42,339	2,505	32,940	51,000	87,400	4,465	27,500	3,309	2,563	27,847	1,174	151,761	661,715
2015	51,739	2,503	34,224	65,000	81,501	6,881	28,300	3,567	1,847	31,226	1,405	176,789	829,440
2016	54,430	2,493	34,729	55,000	86,334	6,183	29,245	5,206	1,436	32,145	1,409	216,432	971,021
2017	79,106	2,497	35,700	72,000	87,991	5,559	30,433	7,951	1,369	35,142	2,536	252,576	983,061
2018[1]	101,624	2,501	36,672	66,000	88,949	5,286	32,292	9,141	1,308	48,253	2,005	262,658	1,039,283
2019[2]	109,401	2,506	37,645	66,000	88,949	4,500	33,940	9,384	1,132	41,429	2,219	264,854	1,103,024

[1] Preliminary. [2] Estimate. *Source: Food and Agricultural Organization of the United Nations (FAO-UN)*

World Imports of Pepper In Metric Tons

Year	European Union	France	Germany	India	Japan	Netherlands	Pakistan	Russia	Singapore	United Arab Em.	United Kingdom	United States	World Total
2012	111,559	7,882	27,653	16,009	8,130	16,950	5,691	9,705	11,936	6,013	11,944	62,458	325,951
2013	116,507	8,690	30,706	15,919	8,514	15,077	6,602	9,797	20,254	18,467	12,946	71,741	364,291
2014	110,157	9,564	25,978	23,068	8,833	15,863	8,105	7,996	27,005	19,967	10,936	68,987	376,561
2015	112,961	10,203	29,239	21,460	9,068	13,630	7,119	6,922	20,177	18,363	12,038	80,357	393,341
2016	116,203	11,505	29,452	23,484	8,741	12,450	10,160	7,699	6,452	14,969	14,270	75,178	388,851
2017	119,495	10,814	32,630	30,431	8,193	13,063	8,932	8,204	5,583	19,361	12,963	78,287	422,341
2018[1]	120,409	11,372	30,765	26,009	9,485	14,219	8,239	8,047	5,782	17,257	11,771	74,923	407,600
2019[2]	128,865	11,264	33,955	29,357	9,714	15,215	11,187	10,306	2,753	27,003	12,722	84,312	469,537

[1] Preliminary. [2] Estimate. *Source: Food and Agricultural Organization of the United Nations (FAO-UN)*

World Exports of Pepper In Metric Tons

Year	Brazil	European Union	Germany	India	Indonesia	Malaysia	Mexico	Netherlands	Singapore	Sri Lanka	United States	Vietnam	World Total
2012	29,129	41,735	10,915	29,263	62,608	10,613	6,122	13,903	12,504	10,488	9,213	116,842	350,450
2013	30,605	39,714	13,310	38,576	47,908	12,099	7,434	10,526	18,603	21,330	9,730	132,763	384,632
2014	34,269	42,197	11,709	27,415	34,733	13,634	7,176	12,858	25,405	7,930	11,790	155,036	403,776
2015	38,034	42,158	14,067	34,801	58,075	13,910	8,216	10,115	19,088	16,657	15,933	131,544	421,011
2016	31,085	44,198	14,841	23,863	53,100	12,549	8,556	9,283	5,485	7,876	14,129	178,134	418,210
2017	59,501	46,488	15,482	18,269	45,430	12,184	6,478	9,916	3,859	13,312	12,947	215,049	483,922
2018[1]	72,580	44,233	15,304	16,726	47,614	11,777	8,414	8,582	4,807	12,691	9,292	97,180	371,770
2019[2]	84,676	43,546	13,964	19,642	75,571	9,860	3,525	8,500	2,023	7,830	7,891	262,921	571,492

[1] Preliminary. [2] Estimate. *Source: Food and Agricultural Organization of the United Nations (FAO-UN)*

Petroleum

Crude oil is petroleum that is acquired directly from the ground. Crude oil was formed millions of years ago from the remains of tiny aquatic plants and animals that lived in ancient seas. Ancient societies such as the Persians, 10th century Sumatrans, and pre-Columbian Indians believed that crude oil had medicinal benefits. Around 4,000 BC in Mesopotamia, bitumen, a tarry crude, was used as caulking for ships, as a setting for jewels and mosaics, and as an adhesive to secure weapon handles. The walls of Babylon and the famed pyramids were held together with bitumen, and Egyptians used it for embalming. During the 19th century in America, an oil find was often met with dismay. Pioneers, who dug wells to find water or brine, were disappointed when they struck oil. It wasn't until 1854, with the invention of the kerosene lamp, that the first large-scale demand for petroleum emerged. Crude oil is a relatively abundant commodity. The world has produced approximately 650 billion barrels of oil, but another trillion barrels of proved reserves have yet to be extracted. Crude oil was the world's first trillion-dollar industry and accounts for the single largest product in world trade.

Futures and options on crude oil trade at the CME Group and at the ICE Futures Europe exchange in London. The CME trades two main types of crude oil: light sweet crude oil and Brent crude oil. The light sweet futures contract calls for the delivery of 1,000 barrels of crude oil in Cushing, Oklahoma. Light sweet crude is preferred by refiners because of its low sulfur content and relatively high yield of high-value products such as gasoline, diesel fuel, heating oil, and jet fuel. The Brent blend crude is based on a light, sweet North Sea crude oil. Brent blend crude production is approximately 500,000 barrels per day and is shipped from Sullom Voe in the Shetland Islands.

Prices – CME West-Texas Intermediate (WTI) crude oil prices (Barchart.com symbol CL) in 2020 rallied to a 1-3/4 year high in January of $65.65 a barrel on ramped-up geopolitical tensions in the Middle East after the U.S. killed Iran's top military commander. Iran reportedly retaliated by encouraging missile attacks by Iranian-backed forces on U.S. bases in Iraq. However, the situation soon de-escalated, and crude prices retreated. Also, the spread of the Covid pandemic in Q1 caused lockdowns and travel restrictions that slashed crude oil consumption. Global crude oil demand plummeted by as much as -20% of global consumption by spring 2020. In April, crude prices collapsed to a record low of -$40.32 a barrel in April as the expiration of the May (K20) WTI crude oil contract forced holders of long positions to pay up to $40 a barrel to exit their long positions or be forced to take delivery of the crude. Prices recovered and traded near $40 a barrel into November. The pandemic undercut energy demand and boosted supplies as the EIA reported that U.S. crude inventories soared to a record 540.7 million bbl in June. Crude prices found support after OPEC+ in May agreed to cut its crude output by 9.7 million bpd through July in an attempt to shore up prices. Crude prices recovered more of their losses into year-end after OPEC+ in December agreed to add 500,000 bpd to the market starting in January 2021, well below than the 2.0 million bpd increase originally planned. Crude prices also garnered support after the U.S. stock market rallied to record highs in December as the rollout of Covid vaccines and expectations for additional U.S. pandemic stimulus bolstered optimism in the economy. Crude oil finished the year down -20.5% yr/yr at $48.52 a barrel.

Supply – World crude oil supply in 2019 fell by -0.1% yr/yr to 98.004 million bpd. U.S. crude oil production in 2020 fell by -7.7% yr/yr to 11.303 million barrels per day. Alaskan oil production in 2020 fell by -3.0% yr/yr to 451,750 barrels per day and was far below the peak level of 2.017 million barrels per day seen in 1988.

Demand – U.S. demand for crude oil in 2020 fell by -14.1% yr/yr to 14.221 million barrels per day. Most of that demand went for U.S. refinery production of products such as gasoline fuel, diesel fuel, aviation fuel, heating oil, kerosene, asphalt, and lubricants.

Trade – The U.S. is still dependent on imports of crude oil to meet its energy needs, but imports in 2020 fell by -13.8% yr/yr to 5.860 million barrels per day, down sharply from the 2005 record high of 10.126 million barrels. U.S. exports of crude oil in 2020 rose by +5.7% yr/yr to 3.153 million barrels per day.

World Production of Crude Petroleum In Thousands of Barrels Per Day

Year	Canada	China	Iran	Iraq	Kuwait	Mexico	Nigeria	Russia	Saudi Arabia	United Arab Em	United States	Vene-zuela	World Total
2010	3,364	4,351	4,248	2,412	2,450	2,954	2,458	10,278	10,900	2,804	8,630	2,585	86,233
2011	3,524	4,401	4,219	2,638	2,682	2,935	2,524	10,394	11,458	3,204	9,075	2,675	86,620
2012	3,783	4,477	3,523	2,995	2,787	2,911	2,507	10,580	11,832	3,389	10,083	2,675	88,683
2013	4,001	4,609	3,198	3,066	2,802	2,882	2,357	10,748	11,693	3,429	11,309	2,675	89,180
2014	4,322	4,737	3,384	3,380	2,794	2,789	2,402	10,836	11,615	3,531	13,077	2,675	91,715
2015	4,434	4,838	3,488	4,055	2,884	2,592	2,231	11,019	12,064	3,660	14,093	2,569	94,466
2016	4,516	4,569	4,367	4,459	2,995	2,459	1,934	11,230	12,379	3,753	13,732	2,322	94,928
2017	4,881	4,456	4,698	4,471	2,828	2,230	2,011	11,190	12,081	3,708	14,562	2,055	95,497
2018[1]	5,299	4,469	4,447	4,631	2,913	2,064	1,979	11,369	12,395	3,770	16,772	1,531	98,106
2019[2]	5,419	4,574	3,190	4,813	2,950	1,899	2,011	11,457	11,601	4,114	18,402	918	98,004

Includes lease condensate. [1] Preliminary. [2] Estimate. *Source: Energy Information Administration, U.S. Department of Energy (EIA-DOE)*

World Imports of Crude Petroleum In Thousands of Barrels Per Day

Year	China	France	Germany	India	Italy	Japan	Korea, South	Nether-lands	Singa-pore	Spain	United Kingdom	United States	World Total
2007	3,277	1,636	2,157	2,480	1,790	4,036	2,390	977	1,164	1,161	1,007	10,031	44,313
2008	3,583	1,666	2,122	2,516	1,662	3,841	2,342	998	1,165	1,178	1,036	9,783	43,831
2009	4,076	1,442	1,979	2,812	1,532	3,416	2,324	975	884	1,056	951	9,013	41,912
2010	4,773	1,294	1,883	3,040	1,540	3,467	2,401	1,033	953	1,059	959	9,213	42,852
2011	5,096	1,296	1,828	3,366	1,449	3,398	2,528	996	980	1,053	1,003	8,935	42,840
2012	5,428	1,139	1,881	3,746	1,377	3,429	2,583	1,008	974	1,184	1,083	8,527	43,498
2013	5,658	1,120	1,829	3,857	1,154	3,393	2,475	953	948	1,169	1,016	7,730	42,276
2014	6,193	1,082	1,805	3,785	1,059	3,205	2,525	959	954	1,192	940	7,344	42,019
2015[1]	6,737	1,146	1,843	3,927	1,230	3,203	2,802	1,055	993	1,305	862	7,363	43,879
2016[2]	7,621	1,092	1,837	4,255	1,217	3,147	2,946	1,090	1,057	1,292	798	7,850	45,166

Includes lease condensate. [1] Preliminary. [2] Estimate. *Source: Energy Information Administration, U.S. Department of Energy (EIA-DOE)*

World Exports of Crude Petroleum In Thousands of Barrels Per Day

Year	Angola	Canada	Iran	Iraq	Kuwait	Mexico	Nigeria	Norway	Russia	Saudi Arabia	United Arab Em	Vene-zuela	World Total
2007	1,591	1,486	2,492	1,637	1,613	1,808	2,152	1,989	5,179	6,909	2,358	1,835	42,990
2008	1,635	1,553	2,412	1,835	1,739	1,505	1,961	1,838	4,843	7,105	2,405	1,841	42,424
2009	1,770	1,515	2,235	1,902	1,348	1,312	2,071	1,776	4,997	5,977	2,051	1,697	40,638
2010	1,711	1,590	2,269	1,890	1,491	1,446	2,322	1,600	4,991	5,979	2,108	1,730	41,184
2011	1,585	1,808	2,328	2,163	1,816	1,421	2,222	1,455	4,943	7,077	2,487	1,785	41,858
2012	1,663	1,933	1,455	2,414	2,070	1,333	2,288	1,314	4,759	7,397	2,571	1,741	41,954
2013	1,677	2,218	1,086	2,363	2,058	1,270	2,028	1,226	4,700	7,553	2,654	1,857	41,186
2014	1,632	2,382	1,084	2,518	1,995	1,208	2,120	1,294	4,500	7,120	2,651	1,729	40,656
2015[1]	1,746	2,661	1,113	2,990	1,964	1,210	2,114	1,312	4,937	7,242	2,593	1,872	42,486
2016[2]	1,681	2,750	1,897	3,577	2,128	1,236	1,655	1,395	5,114	7,334	2,488	1,725	43,607

Includes lease condensate. [1] Preliminary. [2] Estimate. *Source: Energy Information Administration, U.S. Department of Energy (EIA-DOE)*

World Production of Petroleum Products In Thousands of Barrels Per Day

Year	Brazil	Canada	China	Germany	India	Italy	Japan	Korea, South	Russia	Saudi Arabia	United Kingdom	United States	World Total
2005	2,180	2,102	6,354	2,617	2,745	2,116	4,360	2,502	4,361	2,088	1,823	17,800	82,535
2006	2,167	2,069	6,495	2,580	2,896	2,050	4,262	2,559	4,548	2,289	1,757	17,975	82,611
2007	2,184	2,117	7,018	2,539	3,122	2,112	4,215	2,552	4,568	2,146	1,719	17,994	81,606
2008	2,007	2,029	7,069	2,484	3,226	1,971	4,136	2,535	4,803	2,103	1,678	18,146	81,772
2009	2,237	1,962	8,209	2,333	3,836	1,823	3,863	2,476	4,935	1,935	1,570	17,882	82,410
2010	2,467	2,015	8,737	2,197	4,220	1,886	3,857	2,537	5,299	1,935	1,532	18,453	84,163
2011	2,472	1,905	9,298	2,183	4,356	1,791	3,658	2,686	5,390	1,901	1,578	18,673	84,687
2012	2,555	1,926	9,880	2,207	4,506	1,693	3,645	2,789	5,516	1,971	1,436	18,564	85,182
2013[1]	2,810	1,893	10,345	2,151	4,776	1,506	3,689	2,697	5,770	1,884	1,380	19,106	86,426
2014[2]	2,899	1,877	10,852	2,126	4,793	1,418	3,536	2,772	6,174	2,221	1,301	19,654	87,766

Includes lease condensate. [1] Preliminary. [2] Estimate. *Source: Energy Information Administration, U.S. Department of Energy (EIA-DOE)*

Supply and Disposition of Crude Oil in the United States In Thousands of Barrels Per Day

	Supply						Stock Withdrawal[3]		Disposition		Ending Stocks		
	Field Production		Imports			Unaccounted for Crude Oil							
Year	Total Domestic	Alaskan	Total	SPR[2]	Other		SPR[2]	Other	Refinery Inputs	Exports	Total	SPR[2]	Other Primary
	In Thousands of Barrels Per Day										In Millions of Barrels		
2013	7,494	515	7,730	----	----	----	----	----	15,312	134	1,023	696	327
2014	8,789	496	7,344	----	----	----	----	----	15,848	351	1,052	691	361
2015	9,446	483	7,363	----	----	----	----	----	16,188	465	1,144	695	449
2016	8,852	490	7,850	----	----	----	----	----	16,187	591	1,180	695	485
2017	9,371	495	7,969	----	----	----	----	----	16,590	1,158	1,084	663	422
2018	10,964	479	7,768	----	----	----	----	----	16,969	2,048	1,092	649	443
2019	12,248	466	6,801	----	----	----	----	----	16,563	2,982	1,068	635	433
2020[1]	11,303	452	5,860	----	----	----	----	----	14,221	3,153	1,124	638	485

[1] Preliminary. [2] Strategic Petroleum Reserve. [3] A negative number indicates a decrease in stocks and a positive number indicates an increase.
Source: Energy Information Administration, U.S. Department of Energy (EIA-DOE)

Crude Petroleum Refinery Operations Ratio[2] in the United States In Percent of Capacity

Year	Jan.	Feb.	Mar.	Apr.	May	June	July	Aug.	Sept.	Oct.	Nov.	Dec.	Average
2011	84.8	80.0	84.4	82.9	85.3	89.0	90.2	90.3	88.7	84.9	87.0	86.5	86.2
2012	85.6	86.5	85.6	86.6	90.6	92.5	92.5	91.1	87.6	87.1	88.6	90.4	88.7
2013	83.8	81.7	84.0	85.8	88.2	91.7	92.6	91.5	90.7	86.9	90.6	92.0	88.3
2014	87.2	86.6	85.8	90.7	90.2	90.3	94.6	93.7	91.8	87.7	92.0	94.2	90.4
2015	88.4	87.6	88.7	92.0	92.5	94.0	95.1	93.9	90.5	86.6	91.8	92.6	91.1
2016	89.4	88.3	88.8	88.6	89.9	91.1	92.2	92.1	90.4	85.4	89.6	91.3	89.8
2017	88.4	85.0	88.0	92.7	94.3	94.3	95.0	92.8	85.3	88.3	92.5	94.7	90.9
2018	91.1	88.1	91.3	92.0	93.3	97.0	95.1	96.6	93.5	90.0	94.1	95.4	93.1
2019	91.1	85.8	86.1	88.8	90.6	94.2	94.1	94.9	89.0	85.8	90.7	92.5	90.3
2020[1]	88.8	86.7	83.1	70.2	72.0	76.3	79.6	78.8	76.9	75.3	79.3	79.1	78.8

[1] Preliminary. [2] Based on the ration of the daily average crude runs to stills to the rated capacity of refineries per day. *Source: Energy Information Administration, U.S. Department of Energy (EIA-DOE)*

Crude Oil Refinery Inputs in the United States In Thousands of Barrels Per Day

Year	Jan.	Feb.	Mar.	Apr.	May	June	July	Aug.	Sept.	Oct.	Nov.	Dec.	Average
2011	14,423	13,676	14,451	14,231	14,718	15,294	15,589	15,556	15,275	14,570	14,960	14,842	14,799
2012	14,374	14,615	14,476	14,609	15,097	15,637	15,665	15,325	14,910	14,843	15,085	15,330	14,997
2013	14,567	14,230	14,703	14,864	15,305	15,833	16,042	15,793	15,636	14,991	15,633	16,069	15,306
2014	15,311	15,128	15,116	15,864	15,946	15,817	16,534	16,460	16,074	15,361	16,043	16,469	15,844
2015	15,456	15,342	15,640	16,273	16,402	16,701	16,879	16,700	16,168	15,440	16,458	16,742	16,183
2016	15,951	15,843	16,082	15,920	16,237	16,433	16,621	16,593	16,340	15,454	16,235	16,516	16,186
2017	16,118	15,493	16,048	16,954	17,222	17,204	17,317	16,981	15,460	16,061	16,840	17,274	16,581
2018	16,599	15,936	16,665	16,766	16,969	17,666	17,357	17,623	16,991	16,412	17,162	17,409	16,963
2019	16,785	15,837	15,939	16,338	16,719	17,233	17,175	17,300	16,404	15,681	16,482	16,793	16,557
2020[1]	16,231	15,867	15,226	12,786	12,958	13,732	14,338	14,151	13,573	13,445	14,124	14,237	14,222

[1] Preliminary. *Source: Energy Information Administration, U.S. Department of Energy (EIA-DOE)*

Production of Major Refined Petroleum Products in Continental United States In Millions of Barrels

			Fuel Oil							Liquified Gasses		
Year	Asphalt	Aviation Gasoline	Distillate	Residual	Gasoline	Jet Fuel	Kero-sene	Natural Gas Plant Liquids	Lubri-cants	Total	at L.P.G.[2]	AT L.P.G.[3]
2011	129.6	5.4	1,405.1	175.3	3,189	520.2	4.4	825.0	45.3	915.5	689.1	226.4
2012	124.5	5.0	1,369.8	126.2	3,185	512.2	1.4	830.7	41.4	992.0	762.6	229.4
2013	117.0	4.2	1,727.0	170.4	3,347	547.8	4.0	809.0	59.8	1,162.2	933.1	229.1
2014	118.7	4.3	1,463.7	93.9	3,257	536.6	3.2	940.7	45.2	1,322.3	1,081.9	240.3
2015	125.4	4.2	1,451.1	94.7	3,344	561.6	2.4	1,038.1	49.4	1,418.1	1,194.6	223.4
2016	128.8	4.1	1,419.1	130.6	3,414	587.9	2.6	1,114.4	47.4	1,501.5	1,272.9	228.6
2017	128.7	4.1	1,437.3	130.9	3,401	613.8	1.6	1,363.7	39.7	1,593.1	1,363.7	229.4
2018	120.1	4.4	1,508.8	117.4	3,402	624.5	1.9	1,090.2	41.0	1,818.8	1,587.4	231.4
2019	116.7	4.5	1,875.0	131.8	3,685	655.7	3.7	1,145.7	60.9	1,982.1	1,760.9	221.1
2020[1]	117.5	3.7	1,734.9	69.8	3,199	372.6	4.4	1,170.0	55.6	2,088.8	1,889.0	199.8

[1] Preliminary. [2] Gas processing plants. [3] Refineries. *Source: Energy Information Administration, U.S. Department of Energy (EIA-DOE)*

Stocks of Petroleum and Products in the United States on January 1 In Millions of Barrels

			Refined Products											
						Fuel Oil							Motor Gasoline	
Year	Crude Petroleum	Strategic Reserve	Total	Asphalt	Aviation Gasoline	Distillate	Residual	Finished Gasoline	Jet Fuel	Kero-sene	Gases[2]	Lubri-cants	Total	Finished[3]
2011	1,038.6	726.5	357.4	19.9	1.1	164.3	41.3	63.4	43.2	2.4	121.3	8.2	219	63
2012	1,004.2	696.0	332.7	19.6	1.1	149.2	34.2	61.4	41.5	2.4	111.1	9.9	223	61
2013	1,033.1	695.3	313.6	22.1	1.0	134.8	34.0	56.8	39.6	1.7	140.9	9.6	231	57
2014	1,023.2	696.0	291.3	21.4	0.9	127.5	38.1	39.7	37.2	1.9	112.7	10.1	228	40
2015	1,051.8	691.0	286.9	21.2	1.1	136.3	33.7	30.6	38.3	2.1	154.8	11.2	240	31
2016	1,144.3	695.1	325.1	24.6	0.9	161.3	42.1	28.5	40.4	2.6	176.7	13.5	235	28
2017	1,179.7	695.1	329.7	22.9	1.0	166.1	41.5	28.6	43.0	2.3	178.4	12.4	239	29
2018	1,084.5	662.8	291.6	21.5	1.0	145.6	29.4	24.6	41.3	2.1	184.8	12.0	237	25
2019	1,091.6	649.1	294.3	27.0	1.0	140.0	28.3	25.7	41.6	2.6	188.5	14.0	221	26
2020[1]	1,065.7	635.0	291.9	23.1	1.1	140.0	30.9	26.0	40.5	2.9	217.7	12.7	247	26

[1] Preliminary. [2] Includes ethane & ethylene at plants and refineries. [3] Includes oxygenated.
Source: Energy Information Administration, U.S. Department of Energy (EIA-DOE)

Stocks of Crude Petroleum in the United States, on First of Month In Millions of Barrels

Year	Jan.	Feb.	Mar.	Apr.	May	June	July	Aug.	Sept.	Oct.	Nov.	Dec.
2011	1,071.6	1,075.0	1,086.8	1,093.1	1,094.9	1,082.3	1,064.6	1,043.2	1,026.1	1,032.9	1,032.8	1,026.6
2012	1,039.4	1,044.4	1,069.1	1,078.8	1,083.9	1,083.9	1,068.6	1,058.4	1,064.9	1,071.3	1,074.4	1,060.8
2013	1,073.5	1,080.9	1,088.1	1,091.8	1,088.2	1,071.7	1,062.5	1,059.5	1,067.1	1,079.8	1,072.5	1,053.6
2014	1,059.7	1,069.3	1,079.7	1,086.5	1,085.0	1,074.9	1,059.7	1,051.6	1,051.9	1,073.0	1,078.5	1,084.7
2015	1,112.4	1,139.0	1,165.8	1,174.3	1,171.7	1,163.4	1,150.6	1,152.9	1,155.9	1,181.8	1,182.5	1,176.5
2016	1,166.9	1,187.3	1,199.9	1,204.4	1,207.0	1,196.0	1,188.6	1,181.8	1,166.6	1,186.3	1,185.8	1,179.7
2017	1,201.9	1,220.2	1,230.1	1,213.1	1,201.3	1,180.7	1,162.3	1,138.8	1,143.2	1,128.7	1,114.3	1,084.5
2018	1,085.0	1,089.3	1,090.4	1,100.5	1,094.4	1,075.2	1,069.7	1,067.6	1,076.7	1,088.6	1,098.9	1,091.6
2019	1,097.9	1,100.9	1,108.4	1,117.4	1,125.0	1,108.8	1,086.9	1,075.6	1,071.3	1,085.4	1,081.9	1,067.9
2020[1]	1,077.8	1,089.2	1,117.4	1,167.0	1,169.3	1,187.9	1,175.4	1,151.5	1,139.5	1,132.1	1,138.5	1,123.5

[1] Preliminary. *Source: Energy Information Administration; U.S. Department of Energy*

Production of Crude Petroleum in the United States In Thousands of Barrels Per Day

Year	Jan.	Feb.	Mar.	Apr.	May	June	July	Aug.	Sept.	Oct.	Nov.	Dec.	Average
2011	5,492	5,399	5,612	5,552	5,613	5,578	5,430	5,651	5,583	5,886	6,001	6,032	5,652
2012	6,161	6,245	6,301	6,296	6,351	6,269	6,421	6,329	6,563	6,946	7,037	7,088	6,501
2013	7,025	7,144	7,208	7,355	7,316	7,268	7,483	7,531	7,784	7,699	7,873	7,899	7,465
2014	8,051	8,136	8,274	8,573	8,612	8,718	8,782	8,886	9,041	9,221	9,303	9,467	8,755
2015	9,385	9,511	9,578	9,650	9,464	9,344	9,430	9,400	9,460	9,388	9,318	9,251	9,431
2016	9,197	9,055	9,081	8,866	8,824	8,671	8,635	8,670	8,519	8,787	8,888	8,778	8,831
2017	8,861	9,101	9,162	9,100	9,183	9,108	9,235	9,248	9,512	9,653	10,071	9,973	9,351
2018	10,018	10,281	10,504	10,510	10,460	10,649	10,891	11,361	11,498	11,631	11,999	12,038	10,987
2019	11,865	11,679	11,937	12,135	12,163	12,088	11,819	12,425	12,495	12,673	12,860	12,802	12,245
2020[1]	12,755	12,746	12,737	12,010	10,019	10,442	10,973	10,584	10,870	10,432	11,124	11,010	11,308

[1] Preliminary. *Source: Energy Information Administration, U.S. Department of Energy (EIA-DOE)*

U.S. Foreign Trade of Petroleum and Products In Thousands of Barrels Per Day

	Exports		Imports				
Year	Total[2]	Petroleum Products	Crude	Petroleum Products	Distillate Fuel Oil	Residual Fuel Oil	Net Imports[3]
2011	2,986	2,939	8,935	1,994	179	328	8,450
2012	3,205	3,137	8,527	1,689	126	256	7,393
2013	3,621	3,487	7,730	1,749	155	225	6,237
2014	4,176	3,824	7,344	1,529	195	173	5,065
2015	4,738	4,273	7,363	1,694	200	192	4,711
2016	5,261	4,670	7,850	1,854	147	205	4,795
2017	6,376	5,166	7,969	1,836	151	189	3,768
2018	7,601		7,768	1,788	175	211	2,341
2019	8,471		6,801	1,989	202	149	670
2020[1]	8,459		5,860	1,592	215	168	-623

[1] Preliminary. [2] Includes crude oil. [3] Equals imports minus exports.
Source: Energy Information Administration, U.S. Department of Energy (EIA-DOE)

Domestic First Purchase Price of Crude Petroleum at Wells[2] In U.S. Dollars Per Barrel

Year	Jan.	Feb.	Mar.	Apr.	May	June	July	Aug.	Sept.	Oct.	Nov.	Dec.	Average
2011	85.66	86.69	99.19	108.80	102.46	97.30	97.82	89.00	90.22	92.28	100.18	98.71	95.69
2012	98.99	102.04	105.42	103.62	95.57	83.59	86.10	92.53	95.98	92.24	89.64	89.81	94.63
2013	95.00	95.01	95.54	94.41	94.75	93.82	101.41	102.96	102.32	96.18	88.70	91.85	96.00
2014	89.57	96.86	96.17	96.49	95.74	98.68	96.70	90.72	86.87	78.84	71.07	54.86	87.71
2015	43.06	44.35	42.66	49.30	54.38	55.88	47.70	39.98	41.60	42.33	38.19	32.26	44.31
2016	27.02	25.51	31.87	35.59	41.02	43.96	40.70	40.46	40.54	45.00	41.65	47.12	38.37
2017	48.19	49.41	46.39	47.23	45.19	42.19	43.42	44.96	47.17	49.13	55.19	56.98	47.95
2018	62.25	61.20	60.68	63.50	66.16	62.80	67.00	62.64	63.55	65.18	55.65	47.72	61.53
2019	47.85	52.51	57.47	63.01	59.68	54.22	56.47	53.63	55.07	53.14	54.96	58.41	55.54
2020[2]	56.86	50.03	31.80	15.99	18.09	33.53	37.55	39.42	36.89	36.46	38.23	43.96	36.57

[1] Preliminary. [2] Buyers posted prices. *Source: Energy Information Administration, U.S. Department of Energy (EIA-DOE)*

Refiner Sales Prices of Residual Fuel Oil In U.S. Dollars Per Gallon

Year	Jan.	Feb.	Mar.	Apr.	May	June	July	Aug.	Sept.	Oct.	Nov.	Dec.	Average
2013	2.530	2.571	2.479	2.354	2.316	2.285	2.282	2.331	2.359	2.338	2.296	2.315	2.371
2014	2.337	2.459	2.470	2.401	2.350	2.358	2.287	2.148	2.100	1.893	1.639	1.237	2.140
2015	0.936	1.150	1.093	1.124	1.198	1.175	1.080	0.797	0.819	0.812	0.766	0.552	0.959
2016	0.477	0.475	0.582	0.633	0.729	0.850	0.876	0.842	0.846	0.961	0.920	1.024	0.768
2017	1.099	1.174	1.103	1.038	0.986	0.937	1.026	1.042	1.150	1.153	1.302	1.254	1.105
2018	1.301	1.221	1.227	1.311	1.462	1.487	1.543	1.499	1.520	1.620	1.360	1.252	1.400
2019	1.626	1.808	W	W	W	W	1.455	1.331	W	1.535	1.681	1.758	1.599
2020[1]	1.788	1.673	1.188	0.796	0.792	1.018	1.153	1.189	1.098	1.078	1.164	1.350	1.191

Sulfur 1% or less, excluding taxes. [1] Preliminary. *Source: Energy Information Administration, U.S. Department of Energy (EIA-DOE)*

Refiner Sales Prices of No. 2 Fuel Oil In U.S. Dollars Per Gallon

Year	Jan.	Feb.	Mar.	Apr.	May	June	July	Aug.	Sept.	Oct.	Nov.	Dec.	Average
2013	3.069	3.168	2.977	2.793	2.708	2.741	2.894	2.954	2.973	2.955	2.910	3.011	2.966
2014	3.059	3.051	2.979	2.911	2.883	2.878	2.825	2.784	2.701	2.476	2.371	2.050	2.747
2015	1.669	1.850	1.847	1.740	1.852	1.813	1.654	1.461	1.438	1.411	1.356	1.126	1.601
2016	0.976	0.948	1.070	1.113	1.291	1.404	1.305	1.307	1.341	1.443	1.386	1.507	1.258
2017	1.560	1.553	1.495	1.499	1.447	1.375	1.392	1.522	1.668	1.695	1.781	1.841	1.569
2018	1.990	1.889	1.848	1.982	2.143	2.089	2.079	2.114	2.214	2.281	2.098	1.796	2.044
2019	1.813	1.907	1.958	1.993	1.989	1.824	1.847	1.795	1.901	1.926	1.884	1.919	1.896
2020[1]	1.863	1.627	1.238	0.872	0.795	1.002	1.152	1.179	1.091	1.089	1.156	1.341	1.200

Excluding taxes. [1] Preliminary. *Source: Energy Information Administration, U.S. Department of Energy (EIA-DOE)*

Refiner Sales Prices of No. 2 Diesel Fuel In U.S. Dollars Per Gallon

Year	Jan.	Feb.	Mar.	Apr.	May	June	July	Aug.	Sept.	Oct.	Nov.	Dec.	Average
2013	3.046	3.259	3.082	2.969	2.958	2.923	3.015	3.084	3.095	3.006	2.949	2.998	3.028
2014	2.981	3.091	3.031	3.027	2.987	2.973	2.921	2.900	2.806	2.639	2.558	1.980	2.825
2015	1.616	1.861	1.815	1.805	1.973	1.881	1.729	1.562	1.551	1.572	1.456	1.176	1.666
2016	1.015	1.043	1.189	1.251	1.432	1.531	1.426	1.440	1.471	1.592	1.469	1.606	1.372
2017	1.636	1.641	1.581	1.627	1.552	1.465	1.533	1.681	1.847	1.852	1.936	1.918	1.689
2018	2.042	1.972	1.952	2.099	2.258	2.203	2.192	2.203	2.282	2.379	2.130	1.794	2.126
2019	1.789	1.950	2.020	2.100	2.106	1.874	1.938	1.865	1.955	1.984	1.974	1.943	1.958
2020[1]	1.858	1.671	1.278	0.908	0.878	1.135	1.254	1.275	1.195	1.215	1.315	1.475	1.288

Excluding taxes. [1] Preliminary. *Source: Energy Information Administration, U.S. Department of Energy (EIA-DOE)*

Refiner Sales Prices of Kerosine-Type Jet Fuel In U.S. Dollars Per Gallon

Year	Jan.	Feb.	Mar.	Apr.	May	June	July	Aug.	Sept.	Oct.	Nov.	Dec.	Average
2013	3.093	3.250	3.036	2.884	2.763	2.784	2.899	2.995	3.017	2.928	2.868	2.978	2.953
2014	2.964	2.981	2.939	2.911	2.932	2.917	2.882	2.882	2.823	2.547	2.410	1.998	2.766
2015	1.612	1.722	1.731	1.709	1.933	1.813	1.655	1.479	1.443	1.451	1.400	1.207	1.596
2016	1.022	1.017	1.100	1.155	1.311	1.428	1.354	1.313	1.366	1.471	1.406	1.511	1.288
2017	1.561	1.592	1.520	1.545	1.459	1.378	1.436	1.587	1.771	1.704	1.795	1.846	1.600
2018	1.969	1.911	1.893	2.032	2.175	2.152	2.140	2.148	2.214	2.296	2.100	1.811	2.070
2019	1.822	1.925	1.960	2.022	2.061	1.879	1.938	1.864	1.898	1.931	1.922	1.932	1.930
2020[1]	1.891	1.613	1.189	0.703	0.690	1.002	1.144	1.162	1.076	1.107	1.180	1.353	1.176

Excluding taxes. [1] Preliminary. *Source: Energy Information Administration, U.S. Department of Energy (EIA-DOE)*

Refiner Sales Prices of Propane[2] In U.S. Dollars Per Gallon

Year	Jan.	Feb.	Mar.	Apr.	May	June	July	Aug.	Sept.	Oct.	Nov.	Dec.	Average
2013	0.928	0.953	0.952	0.949	0.932	0.861	0.903	1.059	1.114	1.154	1.219	1.342	1.048
2014	1.641	1.654	1.198	1.121	1.057	1.054	1.075	1.055	1.097	1.044	0.966	0.819	1.148
2015	0.713	0.748	0.689	0.566	0.475	0.404	0.405	0.402	0.469	0.524	0.505	0.499	0.533
2016	0.460	0.470	0.497	0.458	0.511	0.497	0.476	0.453	0.494	0.608	0.588	0.703	0.518
2017	0.788	0.792	0.671	0.641	0.631	0.585	0.634	0.742	0.864	0.942	0.997	0.991	0.773
2018	0.990	0.889	0.827	0.792	0.867	0.807	0.854	0.907	0.951	0.948	0.826	0.798	0.871
2019	0.775	0.772	0.754	0.660	0.595	0.493	0.478	0.458	0.477	0.544	0.655	0.632	0.608
2020[1]	0.557	0.530	0.410	0.378	0.454	0.514	0.507	0.536	0.516	0.597	0.630	0.725	0.530

[1] Preliminary. [2] Consumer Grade, Excluding taxes. *Source: Energy Information Administration, U.S. Department of Energy (EIA-DOE)*

Nearby Futures through Last Trading Day.

Volume of Trading of Crude Oil Futures in New York In Thousands of Contracts

Year	Jan.	Feb.	Mar.	Apr.	May	June	July	Aug.	Sept.	Oct.	Nov.	Dec.	Total
2011	17,948	17,757	15,675	12,089	15,126	15,815	11,571	17,178	13,488	14,785	13,609	9,994	175,036
2012	12,557	14,693	13,290	10,627	12,402	12,593	10,870	11,687	10,572	11,660	11,055	8,524	140,532
2013	12,028	11,540	10,515	13,354	13,825	13,111	15,384	12,849	11,139	13,792	10,569	9,586	147,691
2014	11,162	9,862	11,700	11,467	10,283	11,398	13,174	11,016	12,824	15,939	12,204	14,119	145,147
2015	16,514	20,263	17,884	17,638	13,553	13,995	14,863	19,197	16,605	17,484	16,145	18,064	202,202
2016	21,710	25,607	22,954	23,614	21,494	20,790	18,841	23,051	24,332	23,019	27,375	23,981	276,768
2017	22,430	20,528	26,417	21,225	27,527	29,141	27,618	34,725	27,571	25,031	27,636	20,205	310,053
2018	28,504	26,784	25,003	27,977	30,951	28,578	23,056	19,661	21,113	24,507	27,571	22,909	306,613
2019	25,965	22,698	23,824	27,629	28,524	23,436	22,825	27,902	26,970	23,298	19,066	19,327	291,465
2020	26,079	28,131	40,910	39,351	21,325	19,172	16,204	15,728	17,103	17,063	17,680	15,434	274,180

Contract size = 1,000 bbl. *Source: CME Group; New York Mercantile Exchange (NYMEX)*

Average Open Interest of Crude Oil Futures in New York In Thousands of Contracts

Year	Jan.	Feb.	Mar.	Apr.	May	June	July	Aug.	Sept.	Oct.	Nov.	Dec.
2011	1,494.0	1,540.7	1,551.4	1,565.5	1,591.3	1,531.0	1,517.1	1,521.8	1,433.7	1,406.6	1,332.6	1,321.5
2012	1,374.6	1,475.5	1,565.8	1,561.7	1,520.9	1,446.8	1,408.6	1,473.6	1,575.5	1,574.3	1,548.8	1,514.8
2013	1,504.5	1,636.4	1,690.3	1,751.8	1,753.7	1,813.5	1,835.7	1,872.0	1,896.1	1,821.8	1,682.1	1,631.0
2014	1,607.4	1,628.5	1,653.4	1,654.8	1,633.4	1,703.8	1,687.6	1,572.7	1,518.4	1,495.4	1,464.1	1,450.3
2015	1,699.2	1,713.6	1,725.0	1,734.5	1,683.7	1,648.2	1,693.9	1,702.7	1,661.4	1,652.0	1,666.0	1,674.5
2016	1,741.4	1,821.0	1,774.8	1,751.3	1,708.3	1,737.3	1,727.7	1,810.2	1,842.7	1,851.9	1,982.7	2,063.4
2017	2,143.1	2,148.1	2,181.9	2,190.6	2,241.2	2,168.4	2,158.7	2,259.7	2,379.9	2,446.4	2,550.6	2,513.1
2018	2,589.4	2,509.2	2,444.7	2,567.8	2,662.5	2,501.2	2,425.1	2,292.2	2,246.9	2,182.7	2,044.7	2,065.2
2019	2,082.0	2,044.0	2,000.5	2,077.4	2,121.6	2,039.0	2,049.8	2,033.4	2,071.4	2,094.0	2,141.0	2,170.0
2020	2,193.9	2,195.2	2,199.0	2,321.5	2,200.6	2,073.0	1,984.7	2,049.4	2,065.0	2,047.8	2,070.4	2,135.4

Contract size = 1,000 bbl. *Source: CME Group; New York Mercantile Exchange (NYMEX)*

Plastics

Plastics are moldable, chemically fabricated materials produced mostly from fossil fuels, such as oil, coal, or natural gas. The word plastic is derived from the Greek *plastikos*, meaning "to mold," and the Latin *plasticus*, meaning "capable of molding." Leo Baekeland created the first commercially successful thermosetting synthetic resin in 1909. More than 50 families of plastics have since been produced.

All plastics can be divided into either thermoplastics or thermosetting plastics. The difference is the way in which they respond to heat. Thermoplastics can be repeatedly softened by heat and hardened by cooling. Thermosetting plastics harden permanently after being heated once.

Prices – The average monthly producer price index (1982=100) of plastic resins and materials in the U.S. in 2020 fell -4.4% yr/yr to 215.7, remaining below the 2014 record high of 257.0. The average producer price index of thermoplastic resins in the U.S. in 2020 fell -4.6% yr/yr to 215.2, remaining below the 2014 record high of 262.1. The average monthly producer price index of thermosetting resins in the U.S. in 2020 fell -2.8% to 234.8, below the 2014 record high of 244.4.

Supply – Total U.S. plastics production in 2016 rose +1.6% yr/yr to 112.227 billion pounds, which was still below the 2007 record high of 115.793 billion pounds. U.S. plastics production has more than doubled in the past two decades. By sector, the thermoplastics sector is by far the largest, with 2016 production up +1.5 yr/yr to 95.721 billion pounds and accounting for 85.3% of total U.S. plastic production. Production in the thermosetting plastic sector (polyester unsaturated, phenolic, and epoxy) rose +2.0% yr/yr in 2016 to 16.506 billion pounds and accounted for 14.7% of total U.S. plastics production.

Average Producer Price Index of Plastic Resins and Materials (066) in the United States (1982 = 100)

Year	Jan.	Feb.	Mar.	Apr.	May	June	July	Aug.	Sept.	Oct.	Nov.	Dec.	Average
2011	213.2	218.8	223.2	229.1	239.5	238.4	236.7	233.8	235.3	229.2	231.5	227.2	229.7
2012	232.0	234.9	238.0	239.6	238.7	236.3	233.8	234.8	231.8	234.4	234.2	233.9	235.2
2013	239.7	244.1	247.1	245.9	244.6	245.4	244.4	245.1	245.5	245.8	247.9	247.7	245.3
2014	250.6	253.8	256.6	257.5	257.3	255.2	257.1	259.4	261.7	263.0	259.7	252.4	257.0
2015	243.2	237.3	230.2	229.4	230.3	231.5	230.5	227.7	221.3	218.9	217.7	218.1	228.0
2016	215.0	216.3	213.5	213.7	216.7	219.5	219.3	220.1	221.0	225.6	223.1	218.4	218.5
2017	220.5	225.2	232.3	235.8	234.3	232.8	230.4	230.3	232.9	237.7	239.7	240.2	232.7
2018	235.1	236.4	240.3	238.3	241.9	243.8	248.5	252.3	250.2	251.2	246.7	242.4	243.9
2019	235.9	230.8	226.6	225.0	227.4	223.9	223.9	224.7	224.2	224.6	222.0	217.3	225.5
2020[1]	216.8	220.9	220.1	207.9	201.5	202.4	206.3	212.1	219.3	226.2	224.6	230.3	215.7

[1] Preliminary. *Source: Bureau of Labor Statistics, U.S. Department of Commerce (BLS)*

Average Producer Price Index of Thermoplastic Resins (0662) in the United States (1982 = 100)

Year	Jan.	Feb.	Mar.	Apr.	May	June	July	Aug.	Sept.	Oct.	Nov.	Dec.	Average
2011	214.7	221.1	226.0	232.6	244.6	242.1	239.9	236.3	238.1	230.9	233.6	228.6	232.4
2012	234.3	237.6	241.1	242.9	241.7	238.8	235.6	236.8	233.2	236.2	236.1	235.4	237.5
2013	242.8	247.4	250.7	249.4	247.7	248.7	246.7	247.7	249.2	249.6	251.8	251.7	248.6
2014	254.9	258.5	261.7	262.8	262.1	260.0	262.3	265.0	267.2	269.0	265.3	255.9	262.1
2015	245.6	239.2	231.3	230.5	233.0	234.3	233.2	229.8	222.1	219.8	218.4	218.9	229.7
2016	215.7	217.1	214.0	214.7	218.1	221.2	221.2	222.0	223.0	227.7	224.6	219.0	219.9
2017	221.4	226.8	235.7	239.2	237.4	235.8	233.0	233.0	236.1	241.5	243.9	244.5	235.7
2018	238.5	238.5	243.2	240.4	244.7	246.9	252.3	257.5	254.9	255.5	250.1	244.8	247.3
2019	237.9	231.4	227.0	224.8	227.8	224.1	223.7	224.1	223.9	224.7	221.6	216.5	225.6
2020[1]	215.8	219.8	219.2	205.2	199.6	199.8	205.1	211.6	218.9	228.1	226.6	232.3	215.2

[1] Preliminary. *Source: Bureau of Labor Statistics, U.S. Department of Commerce (BLS)*

Average Producer Price Index of Thermosetting Resins (0663) in the United States (1982 = 100)

Year	Jan.	Feb.	Mar.	Apr.	May	June	July	Aug.	Sept.	Oct.	Nov.	Dec.	Average
2011	218.0	219.4	220.6	223.0	224.8	231.9	233.0	233.7	234.0	233.9	233.8	233.4	228.3
2012	233.2	234.0	235.1	235.9	236.4	236.6	238.1	237.6	238.6	238.6	238.1	239.3	236.8
2013	236.4	240.1	241.8	241.4	241.8	241.8	246.2	245.6	239.7	239.9	240.7	240.2	241.3
2014	241.5	242.6	243.4	243.7	245.9	244.3	243.5	244.2	246.3	245.7	244.6	247.6	244.4
2015	244.6	241.0	237.9	237.2	229.2	230.1	229.5	229.6	230.5	227.7	226.9	226.7	232.6
2016	224.4	224.9	223.4	221.6	222.4	222.9	221.8	222.7	223.3	228.0	228.4	228.0	224.3
2017	228.6	230.1	227.6	231.3	230.9	230.2	230.1	229.4	229.3	230.5	230.6	230.8	230.0
2018	230.9	240.1	239.9	242.3	242.1	242.0	242.8	238.3	238.6	242.6	243.8	245.3	240.7
2019	241.1	244.4	240.6	243.0	241.5	238.9	241.8	244.5	243.1	240.5	240.8	238.5	241.6
2020[1]	239.0	244.1	241.8	239.7	228.7	233.7	228.9	230.8	237.7	230.6	228.3	234.4	234.8

[1] Preliminary. *Source: Bureau of Labor Statistics, U.S. Department of Commerce (BLS)*

Platinum-Group Metals

Platinum (atomic symbol Pt) is a relatively rare, chemically inert metallic element that is more valuable than gold. Platinum is a grayish-white metal that has a high fusing point, is malleable and ductile, and has a high electrical resistance. Chemically, platinum is relatively inert and resists attack by air, water, single acids, and ordinary reagents. Platinum is the most important of the six-metal group, which also includes ruthenium, rhodium, palladium, osmium, and iridium. The word "platinum" is derived from the Spanish word *platina* meaning silver.

Platinum is one of the world's rarest metals with new mine production totaling only about 5 million troy ounces a year. All the platinum mined to date would fit in the average-size living room. Platinum is mined all over the world with supplies concentrated in South Africa. South Africa accounts for nearly 80% of world supply, followed by Russia, and North America.

Because platinum will never tarnish, lose its rich white luster, or even wear down after many years, it is prized by the jewelry industry. The international jewelry industry is the largest consumer sector for platinum, accounting for 51% of total platinum demand. In Europe and the U.S., the normal purity of platinum is 95%. Ten tons of ore must be mined, and a five-month process is needed, to produce one ounce of pure platinum.

The second major consumer sector for platinum is for auto catalysts, with 21% of total platinum demand. Catalysts in autos are used to convert most of vehicle emissions into less harmful carbon dioxide, nitrogen, and water vapor. Platinum is also used in the production of hard disk drive coatings, fiber optic cables, infra-red detectors, fertilizers, explosives, petrol additives, platinum-tipped spark plugs, glassmaking equipment, biodegradable elements for household detergents, dental restorations, and in anti-cancer drugs.

Palladium (atomic symbol Pd) is very similar to platinum and is part of the same general metals group. Palladium is mined with platinum, but it is somewhat more common because it is also a by-product of nickel mining. The primary use for palladium is in the use of automotive catalysts, with that sector accounting for about 63% of total palladium demand. Other uses for palladium include electronic equipment (21%), dental alloys (12%), and jewelry (4%).

Rhodium (atomic symbol Rh), another member of the platinum group, is also used in the automotive industry in pollution control devices. To some extent, palladium has replaced rhodium. Iridium (atomic symbol Ir) is used to process catalysts, and it has also found use in some auto catalysts. Iridium and ruthenium (atomic symbol Ru) are used in the production of polyvinyl chloride. As the prices of these metals change, there is some substitution. Therefore, strength of platinum prices relative to palladium should lead to the substitution of palladium for platinum in catalytic converters.

Platinum futures and options and palladium futures are traded at the CME Group. Platinum and palladium futures are traded on the Tokyo Commodity Exchange (TOCOM). The CME platinum futures contract calls for the delivery of 50 troy ounces of platinum (0.9995 fineness) and the contract trades in terms of dollars and cents per troy ounce. The CME palladium futures contract calls for the delivery of 50 troy ounces of palladium (0.9995 fineness), and the contract is priced in terms of dollars and cents per troy ounce.

Prices – CME platinum futures prices (Barchart.com symbol PL) on the nearest-futures chart in 2020 started the year at $1,024.80 per troy ounce, moved lower to an 18-year low of $729.90 in March, and then moved higher the rest of the year to finally close the year up by +4.5% at $1,071.30. CME palladium futures prices (Barchart.com symbol PA) on the nearest-futures chart in 2020 started the year at $2,072.90, fell to a 1-1/2 year low, and then moved higher the rest of the year to finally close the year up +14.1% at $2,365.01.

Supply – World mine production of platinum in 2020 fell -8.6% yr/yr to 170,000 kilograms and remained well below the 2006 record high of 218,000 kilograms. South Africa is the world's largest producer of platinum by far with 70.6% of world production in 2020, followed by Russia with 12.4%, Zimbabwe with 8.2%, the U.S. with 240%. World mine production of palladium in 2020 was down -7.5% at 210,000 kilograms, below the record high production level of 224,000 kg in 2007. The world's largest palladium producers were Russia with 43.3% of world production in 2020, South Africa with 33.3%, Canada with 9.5%, and the U.S. with 6.7%. World production of platinum group metals other than platinum and palladium in 2018 rose +8.4% yr/yr to 60,800 kilograms, below the 2005 record high of 77,700 kilograms.

U.S. mine production of platinum in 2020 fell -3.6% yr/yr to 4,000 kilograms, below the record high of 4,390 kilograms posted in 2002. U.S. mine production of palladium in 2020 fell -2.1 yr/yr to 14,000 kilograms, below the record high of 14,800 kilograms posted in 2002. U.S. refinery secondary production of scrap platinum and palladium in 2018 fell -21.9% yr/yr to 51,400 kilograms, down from the 2016 record.

Trade – U.S. imports of refined platinum and palladium in 2020 for consumption rose +44.4% yr/yr to 300,300 kilograms. U.S. exports of refined platinum and palladium in 2020 fell -11.2% yr/yr to 84,300 kilograms, far below the record high of 403,640 kilograms in 2013. The U.S. relied on imports for 79% of its platinum and palladium consumption in 2019.

World Mine Production of Platinum In Kilograms

Year	Australia	Canada	Colombia[3]	Finland	Japan	Russia	Serbia/ Montenegro	Africa	United States	Zimbabwe	World Total
2011	95	8,000	1,231	836	1,765	27,300	6	148,008	3,700	10,826	202,000
2012	160	7,870	1,460	429	1,735	26,500	3	128,590	3,670	10,500	181,000
2013	170	8,900	1,520	946	1,273	23,000	2	137,024	3,720	13,066	192,000
2014	170	7,200	1,142	1,060	1,124	23,000	3	93,991	3,660	12,483	145,000
2015	120	8,600	861	992	1,379	23,000	4	139,125	3,670	12,564	191,000
2016	170	8,400	917	1,178	1,485	22,000	4	133,241	3,890	15,110	188,000
2017	170	7,600	566	1,418	1,747	22,000	2	131,242	3,980	14,257	184,000
2018	120	7,400	269	1,576		22,000	2	137,053	4,000	15,000	190,000
2019[1]		7,800				24,000		133,000	4,150	13,500	186,000
2020[2]		7,800				21,000		120,000	4,000	14,000	170,000

[1] Preliminary. [2] Estimate. [3] Placer platinum. W = Withheld. *Source: U.S. Geological Survey (USGS)*

World Mine Production of Palladium and Other Group Metals In Kilograms

	Palladium										Other Group Metals		
Year	Australia	Canada	Finland	Japan	Russia	Serbia/ Montenegro	South Africa	United States	Zim- babwe	Total	Russia	South Africa	World Total
2011	350	17,400	1,058	7,534	84,100	4	82,731	12,407	8,241	216,000	12,000	58,111	72,700
2012	550	13,800	1,100	8,052	81,700	22	74,738	12,300	8,140	203,000	8,200	51,010	62,100
2013	610	16,000	766	6,239	80,247	25	76,008	12,600	10,153	205,000	7,400	51,156	62,100
2014	600	23,000	808	6,969	86,000	23	58,410	12,400	10,138	193,000	8,200	36,043	48,000
2015	420	24,000	784	7,073	85,000	31	82,691	12,500	10,055	218,000	7,600	53,699	65,100
2016	590	22,000	901	7,172	83,000	31	76,273	13,100	12,222	209,000	7,700	54,139	66,000
2017	600	19,000	1,021	7,715	88,000	38	80,132	14,000	12,000	216,000	3,415	48,890	56,090
2018	420	20,000	1,157		90,000	38	80,629	14,300	12,000	220,000	3,900	52,964	60,800
2019[1]		20,000			98,000		80,700	14,300	12,000	227,000			
2020[2]		20,000			91,000		70,000	14,000		210,000			

[1] Preliminary. [2] Estimate. *Source: U.S. Geological Survey (USGS)*

Salient Statistics of Platinum and Allied Metals[3] in the United States In Kilograms

	Net Import Reliance as a % of Apparent	Mine Production		Refinery Pro- duction (Secon-		Refiner, Importer & Dealer Stocks as of Dec. 31				Imports		Exports		Apparent Con-
Year	Consump	Platinum	Palladium	dary)	Total Refined	Platinum	Palladium	Other[4]	Total	Refined	Total	Refined	Total	sumptio
2011	89	3,700	12,400	33,000	33,000	261	----	18	279	257,138	----	45,820	----	----
2012	73	3,670	12,300	37,600	37,600	261	----	18	279	276,160	----	128,310	----	----
2013	67	3,720	12,600	74,500	74,500	261	----	18	279	227,217	----	403,540	----	----
2014	69	3,660	12,400	69,400	69,400	261	----	15	276	274,682	----	292,234	----	----
2015	66	3,670	12,500	65,100	65,100	261	----	15	276	270,848	----	284,940	----	----
2016	66	3,890	13,100	69,900	69,900	261	----	15	276	297,137	----	81,130	----	----
2017	71	4,000	14,000	65,800	65,800	261	----	15	276	521,576	----	107,544	----	----
2018	74	4,160	14,300	51,400	51,400	261	----	15	276	225,545	----	105,510	----	----
2019[1]	67	4,150	14,300				----			207,975	----	94,910	----	----
2020[2]	79	4,000	14,000				----			300,300	----	84,300	----	----

[1] Preliminary. [2] Estimate. [3] Includes platinum, palladium, iridium, osmium, rhodium, and ruthenium. [4] Includes iridium, osmium, rhodium, and ruthenium. W = Withheld. *Source: U.S. Geological Survey (USGS)*

Average Producer Price of Rhodium in the United States In Dollars Per Troy Ounce

Year	Jan.	Feb.	Mar.	Apr.	May	June	July	Aug.	Sept.	Oct.	Nov.	Dec.	Average
2011	2,436.9	2,475.0	2,396.7	2,340.0	2,120.2	2,067.1	1,982.5	1,876.1	1,817.9	1,625.0	1,660.0	1,475.0	2,022.7
2012	1,390.0	1,513.8	1,484.1	1,383.3	1,345.9	1,250.0	1,224.5	1,123.3	1,175.0	1,184.8	1,137.5	1,091.5	1,275.3
2013	1,123.6	1,226.0	1,254.0	1,184.3	1,128.0	1,037.0	988.6	1,000.2	1,000.0	987.8	958.5	916.4	1,067.0
2014	1,047.7	1,068.0	1,092.1	1,134.5	1,071.7	1,118.8	1,187.3	1,375.2	1,310.5	1,228.7	1,224.4	1,206.4	1,172.1
2015	1,196.0	1,184.5	1,166.6	1,146.9	1,105.8	976.1	857.1	847.9	772.4	768.0	741.9	678.7	953.5
2016	650.0	654.3	711.5	740.0	690.9	657.3	647.4	640.2	675.0	692.1	786.1	783.0	694.0
2017	833.4	874.1	959.6	1,023.5	955.7	982.1	1,023.8	1,052.8	1,160.2	1,401.1	1,443.9	1,607.6	1,109.8
2018	1,709.6	1,848.8	1,932.3	2,070.7	2,137.2	2,255.2	2,296.4	2,360.2	2,468.3	2,511.5	2,515.7	2,533.3	2,219.9
2019	2,473.3	2,624.8	3,152.6	2,992.3	2,896.1	3,173.8	3,493.5	3,960.7	5,008.6	5,364.1	5,744.1	6,048.0	3,911.0
2020	8,863.6	11,851.3	10,511.4	8,266.7	7,682.5	8,406.8	8,645.5	11,348.8	13,790.5	14,004.6	15,138.2	16,485.7	11,249.6

Source: American Metal Market (AMM)

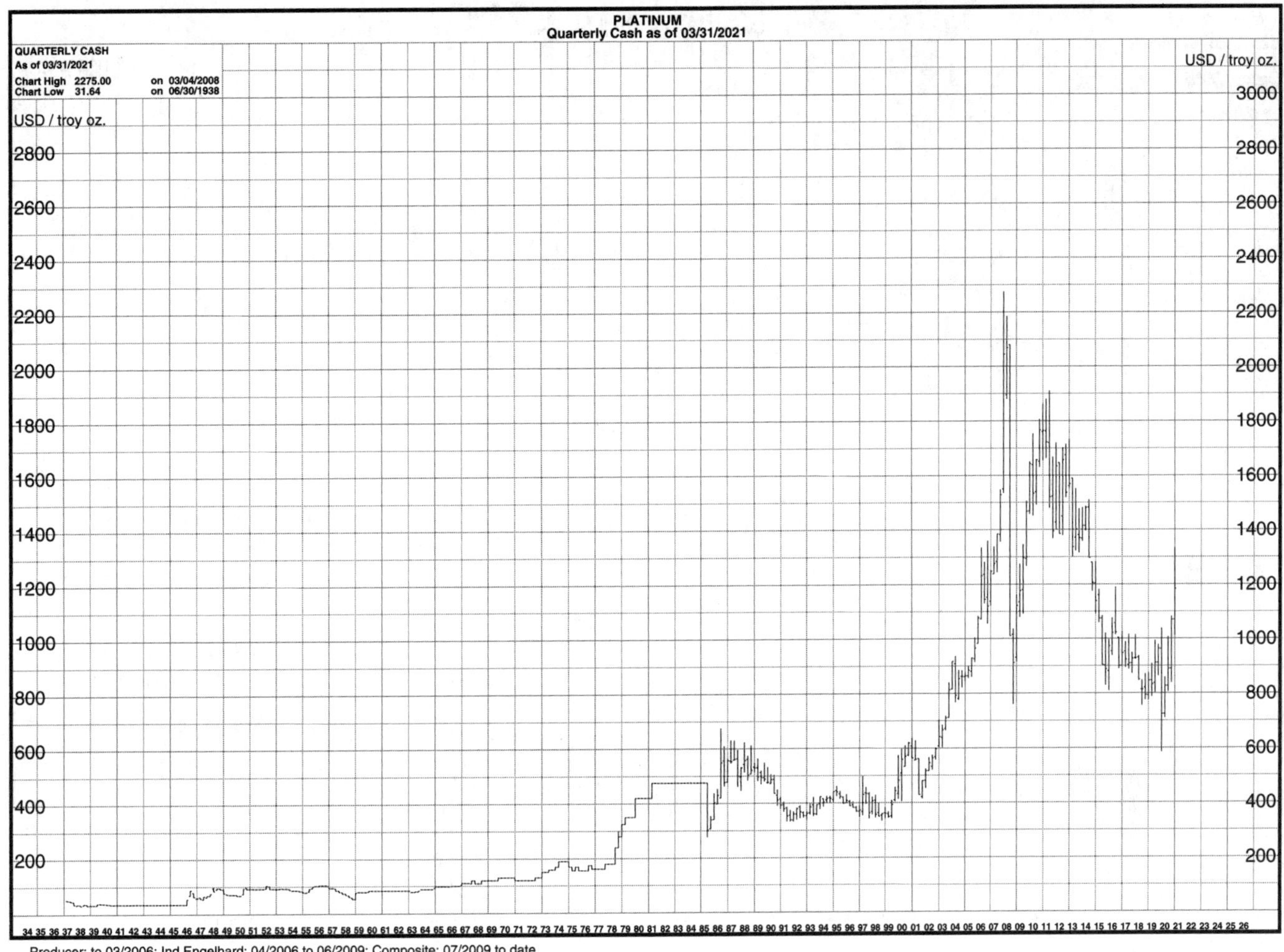

Producer: to 03/2006; Ind Engelhard: 04/2006 to 06/2009; Composite: 07/2009 to date.

Average Merchant's Price of Platinum in the United States In Dollars Per Troy Ounce

Year	Jan.	Feb.	Mar.	Apr.	May	June	July	Aug.	Sept.	Oct.	Nov.	Dec.	Average
2011	1,790.62	1,828.68	1,773.26	1,804.00	1,792.24	1,771.45	1,766.65	1,810.52	1,745.43	1,539.81	1,607.65	1,461.81	1,724.34
2012	1,510.85	1,664.50	1,660.05	1,590.85	1,474.45	1,450.05	1,425.86	1,455.70	1,629.89	1,639.26	1,578.85	1,583.00	1,555.28
2013	1,646.43	1,676.95	1,586.30	1,497.23	1,478.95	1,431.20	1,405.14	1,496.50	1,454.05	1,415.52	1,423.85	1,355.25	1,488.95
2014	1,423.73	1,411.30	1,457.52	1,435.38	1,461.07	1,457.81	1,497.05	1,449.90	1,362.10	1,263.61	1,213.00	1,222.48	1,387.91
2015	1,247.38	1,200.79	1,140.00	1,154.33	1,143.25	1,091.77	1,011.23	985.86	966.38	978.95	885.10	863.30	1,055.70
2016	857.19	924.14	971.78	997.19	1,036.73	986.50	1,087.29	1,123.91	1,047.36	961.10	955.91	919.27	989.03
2017	970.55	1,009.75	965.22	963.35	934.35	933.64	921.52	975.65	968.76	924.00	937.73	912.52	951.42
2018	991.35	991.20	956.82	927.05	907.78	887.90	835.27	807.91	807.20	833.57	849.45	793.62	882.43
2019	808.91	820.45	847.05	890.32	834.96	811.20	846.48	861.86	947.70	900.78	905.10	929.00	866.98
2020	990.41	963.79	764.18	756.86	795.35	823.77	867.64	943.57	911.95	879.95	912.58	1,032.81	886.91

Source: American Metal Market (AMM)

Average Dealer Price[1] of Palladium in the United States In Dollars Per Troy Ounce

Year	Jan.	Feb.	Mar.	Apr.	May	June	July	Aug.	Sept.	Oct.	Nov.	Dec.	Average
2011	797.48	823.47	766.48	777.30	743.38	774.55	794.80	766.57	710.14	620.45	637.70	650.57	738.57
2012	664.28	708.05	689.86	660.65	624.68	617.95	582.95	607.04	664.00	637.78	639.20	694.95	649.28
2013	716.62	755.68	761.20	710.27	723.91	716.70	725.18	746.23	711.75	727.61	737.20	721.45	729.48
2014	738.59	733.90	783.19	804.62	829.67	841.19	880.95	884.10	844.57	784.30	783.78	810.71	809.96
2015	788.29	789.95	789.55	771.86	787.00	729.77	643.64	598.24	612.76	693.82	575.57	555.96	694.70
2016	505.67	510.48	572.78	578.81	582.64	557.27	649.19	703.57	686.32	652.62	700.68	706.20	617.19
2017	749.09	780.35	780.65	803.90	797.04	867.68	859.29	917.26	937.52	963.91	1,005.45	1,028.48	874.22
2018	1,097.74	1,027.60	990.91	974.81	984.70	990.00	936.41	924.17	1,017.90	1,089.52	1,147.50	1,254.14	1,036.28
2019	1,333.96	1,448.70	1,541.14	1,396.95	1,336.96	1,449.65	1,551.39	1,460.73	1,611.00	1,735.22	1,771.14	1,910.85	1,545.64
2020	2,247.77	2,535.42	2,136.64	2,097.05	1,910.40	1,930.77	2,056.55	2,181.90	2,313.71	2,363.41	2,367.21	2,369.10	2,209.16

[1] Based on wholesale quantities, prompt delivery. Source: American Metal Market (AMM)

Volume of Trading of Platinum Futures in Chicago In Contracts

Year	Jan.	Feb.	Mar.	Apr.	May	June	July	Aug.	Sept.	Oct.	Nov.	Dec.	Total
2011	123,012	97,150	235,375	105,524	113,655	216,647	95,589	188,066	293,142	156,172	136,109	232,822	1,993,263
2012	150,111	172,872	252,464	136,954	181,216	283,780	138,326	217,759	371,411	211,656	183,154	322,051	2,621,754
2013	280,979	275,013	335,276	277,634	243,442	388,436	188,942	216,194	341,340	222,190	185,380	307,949	3,262,775
2014	217,465	194,296	389,315	182,628	239,397	379,860	210,163	179,938	399,265	271,921	211,151	360,542	3,235,941
2015	243,017	200,204	408,528	217,744	211,710	434,374	262,007	268,391	443,850	281,094	261,514	408,711	3,641,144
2016	284,203	262,873	413,082	248,758	249,861	435,018	279,689	278,246	456,092	302,621	360,457	423,172	3,994,072
2017	345,619	286,893	515,593	280,575	354,263	529,562	321,062	394,884	528,953	344,217	381,004	569,535	4,852,160
2018	444,074	346,507	562,720	423,705	392,326	652,863	393,517	412,710	580,643	383,720	372,849	498,165	5,463,799
2019	362,449	384,444	633,174	398,312	414,824	593,552	444,188	496,003	739,168	408,309	399,670	588,197	5,862,290
2020	468,298	473,531	738,101	218,691	242,913	350,424	316,024	301,382	453,351	271,140	277,596	466,080	4,577,531

Contract size = 50 oz. *Source: CME Group; New York Mercantile Exchange (NYMEX)*

Average Open Interest of Platinum Futures in Chicago In Contracts

Year	Jan.	Feb.	Mar.	Apr.	May	June	July	Aug.	Sept.	Oct.	Nov.	Dec.
2011	40,572	41,823	35,986	35,925	36,214	35,150	32,278	37,063	39,229	37,910	38,779	42,652
2012	43,893	44,519	43,028	40,337	45,372	50,530	50,160	53,902	57,555	63,289	60,641	62,626
2013	64,184	70,544	64,608	63,193	63,406	62,590	61,937	65,515	61,739	59,391	59,092	63,028
2014	59,980	63,324	69,278	65,308	68,150	68,004	71,271	64,416	64,103	59,701	61,768	65,647
2015	66,436	66,642	70,775	69,165	71,645	79,378	79,326	76,953	73,817	72,160	72,938	73,105
2016	68,301	65,306	62,884	59,152	64,862	63,825	72,441	80,327	74,296	70,022	66,480	65,869
2017	62,849	66,421	66,618	65,191	72,742	73,137	72,273	72,013	76,162	75,280	78,273	85,097
2018	86,391	87,064	78,963	76,759	80,900	86,235	81,652	83,049	86,436	74,712	72,385	81,227
2019	84,646	82,418	74,956	73,945	78,080	87,406	77,906	77,789	93,443	86,189	90,358	96,111
2020	104,485	99,383	69,178	62,027	50,911	49,719	50,513	57,638	59,353	52,240	53,169	62,949

Contract size = 50 oz. *Source: CME Group; New York Mercantile Exchange (NYMEX)*

Nearby Futures through Last Trading Day.

Volume of Trading of Palladium Futures in Chicago In Contracts

Year	Jan.	Feb.	Mar.	Apr.	May	June	July	Aug.	Sept.	Oct.	Nov.	Dec.	Total
2011	72,121	121,271	94,402	85,897	132,608	80,665	66,290	139,208	80,932	72,895	119,732	73,508	1,139,529
2012	74,977	125,721	75,910	61,833	136,033	67,710	59,308	123,731	85,209	84,730	145,835	77,483	1,118,480
2013	126,987	198,821	87,681	122,520	181,016	93,497	77,175	163,892	82,470	99,944	182,133	69,880	1,486,016
2014	87,502	158,760	136,126	111,648	195,880	101,610	97,809	208,474	126,132	115,708	161,947	72,376	1,573,972
2015	99,787	146,928	100,748	78,232	131,105	91,044	102,665	185,094	87,201	92,284	162,382	66,956	1,344,426
2016	90,129	151,159	96,917	93,887	142,585	94,937	104,219	169,852	88,440	113,977	198,537	91,224	1,435,863
2017	111,959	141,648	98,308	97,861	191,603	120,488	82,725	164,153	80,618	87,270	153,217	72,890	1,402,740
2018	98,800	164,476	101,277	145,138	127,272	93,661	98,611	176,108	89,368	116,003	148,110	74,888	1,433,712
2019	107,039	147,433	113,193	96,677	129,839	74,368	79,652	133,300	80,152	90,724	131,275	83,049	1,266,701
2020	148,896	127,560	76,650	23,544	39,796	23,542	41,067	51,521	29,227	34,644	59,389	34,951	690,787

Contract size = 100 oz. *Source: CME Group; New York Mercantile Exchange (NYMEX)*

Average Open Interest of Palladium Futures in Chicago In Contracts

Year	Jan.	Feb.	Mar.	Apr.	May	June	July	Aug.	Sept.	Oct.	Nov.	Dec.
2011	22,340	22,939	21,584	21,325	20,376	20,615	21,809	21,576	19,590	19,074	19,368	18,558
2012	18,051	21,035	20,978	21,174	22,931	21,951	22,676	23,304	19,987	20,172	22,005	25,798
2013	31,036	37,519	37,181	37,118	36,554	36,219	35,682	38,564	34,971	37,152	39,264	36,781
2014	39,059	40,226	41,494	42,071	43,466	39,964	43,791	44,286	38,776	33,587	34,170	32,060
2015	33,813	33,807	31,897	32,138	31,396	33,426	36,629	34,717	27,329	25,978	27,440	25,030
2016	26,200	27,339	22,964	23,573	23,912	23,048	24,043	28,475	25,272	23,968	24,431	26,124
2017	27,919	29,500	29,601	34,312	35,204	35,544	33,508	35,549	32,465	32,910	35,411	35,320
2018	38,468	29,987	24,894	23,645	23,008	23,045	21,676	22,511	19,056	26,129	27,046	26,158
2019	27,723	28,365	26,618	22,825	20,757	20,861	25,138	22,436	22,028	26,569	25,844	25,338
2020	25,122	19,937	10,294	7,754	7,209	6,698	8,719	9,970	9,523	10,030	10,608	9,322

Contract size = 100 oz. *Source: CME Group; New York Mercantile Exchange (NYMEX)*

Potatoes

The potato is a member of the nightshade family. The leaves of the potato plant are poisonous, and a potato will begin to turn green if left too long in the light. This green skin contains solanine, a substance that can cause the potato to taste bitter and even cause illness in humans.

In Peru, the Inca Indians were the first to cultivate potatoes around 200 BC. The Indians developed potato crops because their staple diet of corn would not grow above an altitude of 3,350 meters. In 1536, after conquering the Incas, the Spanish Conquistadors brought potatoes back to Europe. At first, Europeans did not accept the potato because it was not mentioned in the Bible and was therefore considered an "evil" food. But after Marie Antoinette wore a crown of potato flowers, it finally became a popular food. In 1897, during the Alaskan Klondike gold rush, potatoes were so valued for their vitamin C content that miners traded gold for potatoes. The potato became the first vegetable to be grown in outer space in October 1995.

The potato is a highly nutritious, fat-free, cholesterol-free, and sodium-free food. The potato is an important dietary staple in over 130 countries. A medium-sized potato contains only 100 calories. Potatoes are an excellent source of vitamin C and provide B vitamins as well as potassium, copper, magnesium, and iron. According to the U.S. Department of Agriculture, "a diet of whole milk and potatoes would supply almost all of the food elements necessary for the maintenance of the human body."

Potatoes are one of the largest vegetable crops grown in the U.S. and are grown in all fifty states. The U.S. ranks about 4th in world potato production. The top three types of potatoes grown extensively in the U.S. are white, red, and Russets (Russets account for about two-thirds the U.S. crop). Potatoes in the U.S. are harvested in all four seasons, but the vast majority of the crop is harvested in fall. Potatoes harvested in the winter, spring, and summer are used mainly to supplement fresh supplies of fall-harvested potatoes and are also important to the processing industries. The four principal categories for U.S. potato exports are frozen, potato chips, fresh, and dehydrated. Fries account for approximately 95% of U.S. frozen potato exports.

Prices – The average monthly price received for potatoes by U.S. farmers in 2020 rose +7.0% to $13.23 per hundred pounds, a new record high.

Supply –The total U.S. potato crop in 2020 fell -2.1% to 41.548 billion pounds, well below the record high of 50.936 billion pounds posted in 2000. The fall crop in 2018 rose by +1.9% to 41.450 billion pounds, and it accounted for 81.4% of the total crop. Stocks of the fall crop (as of Dec 1, 2018) were 28.360 billion pounds. In 2018, the spring crop fell -18.4% to 1.757 billion pounds, and the summer crop fell -20.6% to 1.776 billion pounds.

The largest producing states for the 2018 fall crop were Idaho with 34.2% of the crop, Washington with 24.3%, Wisconsin and Oregon with 6.5%, North Dakota with 5.7%, and Colorado with 5.2%. For the spring crop, the largest producing states were California, with 68.5% of the crop, and Florida with 31.1% of the crop. Farmers harvested 915.7 acres in 2020, down -2.3% yr/yr. The yield per harvested acre in 2020 was up 0.2% to 454 pounds per acre for a new record high.

Demand – Total utilization of potatoes in 2019 was down -5.7% yr/yr at 42.442 billion pounds, but still above the 2010 record low of 40.427 billion pounds. The breakdown shows that the largest consumption category for potatoes is frozen French fries with 38.3% of total consumption, followed closely by table stock with 23.1%, chips, shoestrings with 14.1%, and dehydration with 19.8%. U.S. per capita consumption of potatoes in 2019 rose +2.4% to 118.83 pounds, below the record high of 145.0 pounds per capita seen in 1996.

Trade – U.S. exports of potatoes in 2016 rose +18.7% to 1.074 billion pounds, a new record high.

Salient Statistics of Potatoes in the United States

Crop Year	Acreage: Planted (1,000 Acres)	Acreage: Harvested (1,000 Acres)	Yield Per Harvested Acre (Cwt.)	Total Production (In Thousands of Cwt.)	Farm Disposition – Used Where Grown: Seed & Feed (In Thousands of Cwt.)	Farm Disposition – Used Where Grown: Shrinkage & Loss (In Thousands of Cwt.)	Sold[2] (In Thousands of Cwt.)	Farm Price ($ Cwt.)	Value of Production[3] (Million $)	Value of Sales (Million $)	Stocks Jan. 1 (1,000 Cwt)	Foreign Trade[4]: Exports (Fresh) (Millions of Lbs.)	Foreign Trade[4]: Imports (Millions of Lbs.)	Consumption[4] Per Capita: Fresh (In Pounds)	Consumption[4] Per Capita: Total (In Pounds)
2011	1,099	1,077	399	429,647	4,142	27,755	397,750	9.37	4,041	3,743	NA	989,979	909,645	34.0	110.3
2012	1,155	1,139	408	464,970	4,869	28,356	429,541	8.63	4,017	3,728	NA	986,497		34.5	114.7
2013	1,064	1,051	414	434,652	4,323	26,211	404,118	9.75	4,237	3,943	NA	1,055,601		34.5	113.3
2014	1,063	1,051	421	442,170	4,192	26,762	411,216	8.88	3,928	3,658	NA	922,366		33.5	112.1
2015	1,066	1,054	418	441,205	4,631	26,509	410,065	8.76	3,866	3,597	NA	904,958		34.1	113.7
2016	1,057	1,038	434	450,324	4,437	26,883	419,004	9.08	4,091	3,812	NA	1,073,734		33.2	
2017	1,053	1,045	432	450,921	4,410	25,139	421,372	9.17	4,133	3,875					
2018	1,027	1,015	443	450,020	4,047	25,526	420,447	8.48	4,006	3,747					
2019	963	937	453	424,419	4,608	25,016	394,795		4,217	3,935					
2020[1]	923	916	454	415,481											

[1] Preliminary. [2] For all purposes, including food, seed processing & livestock feed. [3] Farm weight basis, excluding canned and frozen potatoes. [4] Calendar year. *Source: Economic Research Service, U.S. Department of Agriculture (ERS-USDA)*

Potato Crop Production Estimates, Stocks and Disappearance in the United States In Millions of Cwt.

	Crop Production Estimates			Total Storage Stocks[2]								Fall Crop (1,000 Cwt.)				
	Total Crop			Fall Crop			Following Year									
Year	Oct. 1	Nov. 1	Dec. 1	Oct. 1	Nov. 1	Dec. 1	Jan. 1	Feb. 1	Mar. 1	Apr. 1	May 1	Production	Disappearance (Sold)	Stocks Dec. 1	Average Price ($/Cwt.)	Value of Sales ($1,000)
2011	----	429.6	----	----	391.2	253.0	NA	187.5	NA	115.7	NA	382,318	360,620	253,000	8.87	3,197,096
2012	----	467.2	----	----	422.0	271.5	NA	204.6	NA	NA	NA	410,367	385,767	271,500	8.05	3,111,362
2013	----	439.7	----	----	401.5	NA	NA	NA	NA	119.5	NA	396,655	404,118	NA	9.05	3,320,712
2014	----	442.8	----	----	406.2	267.5	NA	206.6	NA	139.2	NA	406,080	411,216	265,700	8.35	3,113,990
2015	----	441.2	----	----	404.7	267.9	NA	205.9	NA	137.2	NA	409,281	410,667	262,700	8.27	3,094,832
2016	----	439.6	----	----	405.2	275.8	NA	213.0	NA	142.6	NA	412,688	382,471	272,900	8.46	3,231,305
2017	----	439.0	----	----	398.9	277.9	NA	210.6	NA	138.8	NA	406,800	377,994	274,900	8.28	3,135,521
2018	----	452.6	----	----	417.5	279.3	NA	212.8	NA	144.7	NA	414,499	385,794	283,600	8.48	3,269,884
2019	----	424.4	----	----	----	266.4	NA	203.0	NA	127.0	NA	----	----	----	----	----
2020[1]	----	415.5	----	----	----	270.7	NA	207.3	NA		NA	----	----	----	----	----

[1] Preliminary. [2] Held by growers and local dealers in the fall producing areas.
Source: Agricultural Statistics Board, U.S. Department of Agriculture (ASB-USDA)

Production of Potatoes in the United States In Thousands of Cwt.

Year	California	Colorado	Idaho	Maine	Michigan	Minnesota	Nebraska	New York	North Dakota	Oregon	Washington	Wisconsin	U.S. Total
2011	4,312	21,291	128,760	14,310	15,180	16,685	7,800	4,050	18,865	23,342	97,600	25,938	382,318
2012	3,901	19,980	141,820	16,088	16,100	18,800	10,369	5,130	25,200	22,935	95,940	30,360	410,367
2013	3,504	20,304	131,131	15,660	15,840	17,325	8,418	4,959	22,620	21,582	96,000	26,040	396,655
2014	3,901	23,196	132,880	14,645	15,725	16,400	7,943	4,345	23,870	22,562	101,475	26,240	406,080
2015	3,528	22,575	130,400	16,160	17,550	16,200	6,885	4,144	27,600	21,784	100,300	27,813	409,281
2016	3,516	22,236	139,320	15,113	17,390	17,200	7,380	3,552	21,600	22,951	105,625	27,840	412,688
2017	3,321	21,220	134,850	15,200	18,315	18,428	9,025	4,032	24,420	25,245	99,220	29,750	406,800
2018	3,212	21,722	141,750	15,035	18,240	18,705	9,264	3,886	23,725	27,000	100,800	27,135	414,499
2019	16,842	19,666	130,900	16,738	20,370	17,845	9,595	----	19,430	25,311	104,960	28,700	424,419
2020[1]	13,694	22,865	136,500	13,383	17,390	17,430	9,163	----	22,913	27,900	96,250	28,290	415,481

[1] Preliminary. *Source: Agricultural Statistics Board, U.S. Department of Agriculture (ASB-USDA)*

Utilization of Potatoes in the United States In Thousands of Cwt.

	Sales											Non-Sales			
		For Processing							Other Sales						
Crop Year	Table Stock	Chips, Shoestrings	Dehydration	Frozen French Fries	Other Frozen Products	Canned Potatoes	Other Canned Products[2]	Starch & Flour	Livestock Feed	Seed	Total Sales	Used on Farms Where Grown	Shrinkage & Loss	Total Non-Sales	Total
2010	107,407	54,508	34,164	135,703	13,374	1,659	700	6,334	593	20,621	375,063	3,002	24,990	29,210	404,273
2011	102,655	58,703	45,511	144,626	15,188	1,650	716	6,013	825	21,863	397,750	3,012	27,755	31,897	429,647
2012	118,535	59,304	49,894	142,993	20,635	1,741	734	7,919	4,080	23,706	429,541	3,286	28,356	33,225	462,766
2013	106,930	60,485	47,411	134,966	18,451	188	1,089	8,579	1,251	22,431	404,118	3,215	26,211	30,534	434,652
2014	107,344	73,960	48,707	152,832	9,208	435	886	6,907	768	22,774	411,216	3,343	26,762	30,954	442,170
2015	110,960	56,807	48,016	152,329	13,573	985	730	6,420	919	25,648	410,065	3,765	26,509	31,140	441,205
2016	114,227	60,266	48,015	156,985	12,695	1,234	698	6,000	1,150	26,811	419,004	3,758	26,883	31,320	450,324
2017	109,824	58,751	45,761	155,798	13,803	1,152	703	6,160	1,913	25,224	421,372	3,526	25,139	29,549	450,921
2018	106,462	62,700	49,066	163,140	15,956	1,113	758	5,550	697	24,079	420,447	3,491	25,526	29,573	450,020
2019[1]	97,856	59,639	41,621	162,394	11,848	898	836	6,031	1,528	19,677	394,795	3,995	25,016	29,624	424,419

[1] Preliminary. [2] Hash, stews and soups. *Source: Agricultural Statistics Board, U.S. Department of Agriculture (ASB-USDA)*

Cold Storage Stocks of All Frozen Potatoes in the United States, on First of Month In Millions of Pounds

Year	Jan.	Feb.	Mar.	Apr.	May	June	July	Aug.	Sept.	Oct.	Nov.	Dec.
2011	1,018.9	1,095.0	1,102.9	1,086.1	1,070.3	1,073.8	1,073.8	1,073.8	1,073.8	1,073.8	1,073.8	1,073.8
2012	999.9	1,072.0	1,111.7	1,129.0	1,138.7	1,091.6	1,161.5	1,065.7	1,019.8	1,123.4	1,184.7	1,144.2
2013	1,110.4	1,175.1	1,232.7	1,226.8	1,222.4	1,181.3	1,270.3	1,138.4	1,091.3	1,137.6	1,175.3	1,150.8
2014	1,095.3	1,104.8	1,124.1	1,044.3	1,009.2	983.4	1,012.8	924.2	936.6	1,039.7	1,099.5	1,105.6
2015	1,030.4	1,091.7	1,132.9	1,146.4	1,127.2	1,135.6	1,151.7	1,065.4	1,047.0	1,058.0	1,093.0	1,055.6
2016	1,006.9	1,021.7	1,046.0	1,072.2	1,095.0	1,122.2	1,175.8	1,149.0	1,160.5	1,217.2	1,253.5	1,180.5
2017	1,124.6	1,195.7	1,210.6	1,212.3	1,219.7	1,209.3	1,230.6	1,201.7	1,190.2	1,237.0	1,273.5	1,274.1
2018	1,183.0	1,258.3	1,265.2	1,225.8	1,192.8	1,156.7	1,212.0	1,096.7	1,140.8	1,185.0	1,250.2	1,198.4
2019	1,174.6	1,265.2	1,299.0	1,291.8	1,211.2	1,172.9	1,184.5	1,134.3	1,162.3	1,160.7	1,170.7	1,180.9
2020[1]	1,155.9	1,201.2	1,249.5	1,309.5	1,192.8	1,099.4	1,085.1	1,087.7	1,139.5	1,175.4	1,241.4	1,176.5

[1] Preliminary. *Source: Agricultural Statistics Board, U.S. Department of Agriculture (ASB-USDA)*

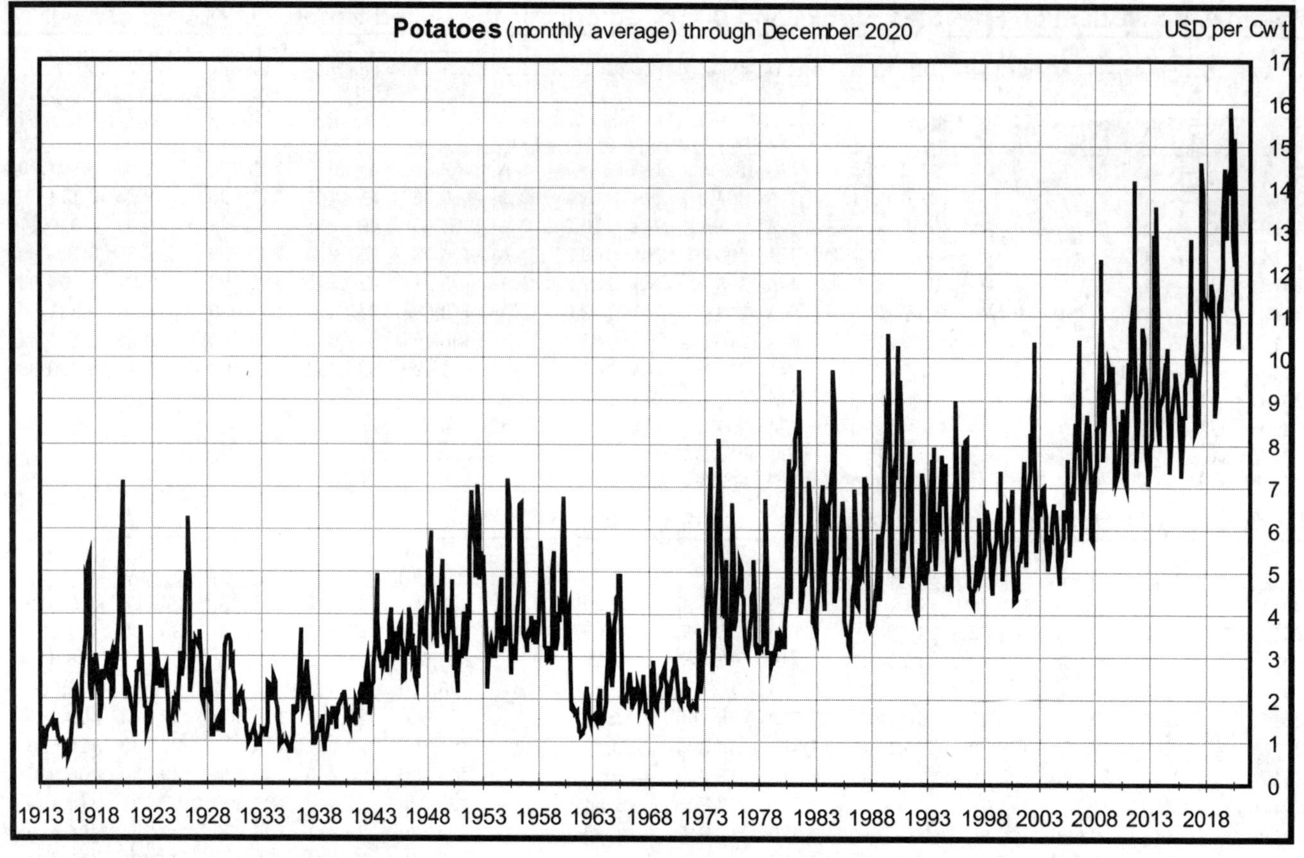

Average Price Received by Farmers for Potatoes in the U.S. In Dollars Per Hundred Pounds (Cwt.)

Year	Jan.	Feb.	Mar.	Apr.	May	June	July	Aug.	Sept.	Oct.	Nov.	Dec.	Season Average
2011	9.08	9.26	10.74	11.17	11.17	11.59	14.19	10.47	8.05	7.46	8.58	9.06	9.37
2012	9.23	9.31	9.98	10.75	10.44	9.93	9.29	7.80	7.31	7.02	7.39	7.74	8.63
2013	7.87	8.12	8.72	9.63	12.89	12.57	13.56	11.15	8.48	7.96	8.87	9.02	9.75
2014	9.02	9.22	9.47	9.92	9.53	10.28	9.72	8.88	7.76	7.30	8.19	8.63	8.88
2015	9.12	9.14	9.38	9.69	9.26	9.27	8.62	8.45	7.58	7.24	8.23	8.38	8.76
2016	8.63	8.64	9.41	9.61	9.98	10.52	9.58	12.80	10.48	9.59	9.91	9.59	9.08
2017	8.27	8.42	8.65	8.40	9.40	10.25	10.79	14.61	13.86	11.33	11.22	11.39	9.17
2018	11.30	11.20	11.10	11.20	11.40	11.80	11.50	11.20	9.44	8.65	9.22	9.37	8.48
2019	9.88	10.70	11.30	11.50	11.10	12.10	13.30	14.50	13.30	12.80	13.90	13.90	12.36
2020[1]	14.30	14.50	15.90	14.60	12.80	12.20	14.80	15.20	12.00	11.20	10.90	10.30	13.23

[1] Preliminary. *Source: Agricultural Statistics Board, U.S. Department of Agriculture (ASB-USDA)*

Per Capita Utilization of Potatoes in the United States In Pounds (Farm Weight)

			Processing				
Year	Total	Fresh	Freezing	Chips & Shoe-string	Dehy-drating	Canning	Total Processing
2010	114.0	36.9	50.1	15.0	11.2	0.7	77.1
2011	110.5	34.1	48.3	16.8	10.6	0.7	76.4
2012	114.9	34.6	48.1	17.6	13.9	0.8	80.3
2013	113.6	34.6	47.7	17.8	12.9	0.6	79.0
2014	113.1	33.6	47.1	20.0	12.1	0.3	79.5
2015	115.4	34.2	49.7	19.6	11.6	0.4	81.3
2016	110.2	33.7	47.4	16.6	12.0	0.4	76.5
2017	117.8	34.9	51.9	17.8	12.9	0.5	82.9
2018[1]	116.0	33.0	51.7	17.8	12.8	0.4	83.0
2019[2]	118.8	34.1					84.7

[1] Preliminary. [2] Forecast. *Source: Agricultural Statistics Board, U.S. Department of Agriculture (ASB-USDA)*

Potatoes Processed[1] in the United States, Eight States In Thousands of Cwt.

States	Storage Season	to Dec. 1	to Jan. 1	to Feb. 1	to Mar. 1	to Apr. 1	to May 1	to June 1	Entire Season
Idaho and Oregon-Malheur Co.	2012-13	27,900	34,740	41,890	49,980	57,750	65,430	73,430	89,780
	2013-14	25,770	32,060	39,090	46,320	53,755	61,780	70,425	85,280
	2014-15	27,685	33,995	40,850	47,985	54,665	63,025	70,600	86,870
	2015-16	26,850	33,115	39,655	46,455	53,710	61,050	68,435	86,250
	2016-17	25,720	32,650	39,475	46,880	54,625	61,950	70,110	92,760
	2017-18	24,840	31,920	38,950	46,610	54,060	61,285	69,840	87,379
	2018-19	25,325	32,020	39,495	47,395	55,250	63,225	71,340	95,974
	2019-20	26,655	33,170	39,840	47,980	55,775	61,640	69,395	86,863
	2020-21	27,195	34,360	41,695					
Maine[2]	2012-13	1,890	2,380	3,005	3,600	4,290	5,075	5,740	7,720
	2013-14	1,570	1,990	2,510	3,060	3,680	4,240	4,800	6,315
	2014-15	1,410	1,845	2,415	2,930	3,475	3,980	4,445	5,622
	2015-16	1,170	1,590	2,050	2,490	2,980	3,495	4,065	5,724
	2016-17	1,260	1,665	2,175	2,660	3,080	3,470	3,825	5,059
	2017-18	1,510	1,880	2,370	2,880	3,460	4,010	4,560	4,829
	2018-19	1,470	1,890	2,400	2,870	3,450	3,870	4,290	5,050
	2019-20	1,585	2,050	2,610	2,875	3,285	3,590	4,040	5,050
	2020-21	1,475	1,750	2,095					
Washington & Oregon-Other	2012-13	31,295	37,730	43,820	51,765	57,915	64,500	70,470	80,400
	2013-14	31,575	37,990	45,420	52,690	59,025	64,905	72,325	80,655
	2014-15	31,870	37,190	42,715	50,380	57,340	64,525	72,365	88,615
	2015-16	33,955	39,970	46,320	54,455	60,985	67,560	74,285	91,720
	2016-17	36,700	42,180	47,835	55,365	62,125	68,705	76,635	90,785
	2017-18	32,885	39,925	46,515	54,355	61,780	68,555	76,495	91,160
	2018-19	36,405	43,420	50,400	57,720	65,095	71,405	79,130	97,176
	2019-20	34,755	42,045	49,685	59,535	67,325	71,280	78,895	94,700
	2020-21	31,930	38,235	45,085					
Other States[3]	2012-13	14,270	16,765	19,785	22,520	25,170	28,320	31,100	40,395
	2013-14	11,365	14,280	17,470	20,475	23,695	26,990	30,195	37,425
	2014-15	13,705	17,295	20,865	24,685	28,550	32,080	35,415	40,456
	2015-16	8,995	12,515	16,380	20,720	24,550	28,665	33,020	38,742
	2016-17	10,035	13,570	17,140	21,005	25,085	28,505	32,385	38,631
	2017-18	10,030	14,181	18,075	22,740	26,535	30,425	34,740	42,856
	2018-19	10,643	15,048	18,836	23,479	27,079	30,423	34,392	40,470
	2019-20	13,315	17,485	21,170	24,940	28,430	31,263	34,565	39,346
	2020-21	11,380	14,854	18,134					
Total	2012-13	75,355	91,615	108,500	127,865	145,125	163,325	180,740	218,295
	2013-14	70,280	86,320	104,490	122,545	140,155	157,915	177,745	209,675
	2014-15	74,670	90,325	106,845	125,980	144,030	163,610	182,825	221,563
	2015-16	70,970	87,190	104,405	124,120	142,225	160,770	179,805	222,436
	2016-17	73,715	90,065	106,625	125,910	144,915	162,630	182,955	227,235
	2017-18	69,265	87,906	105,910	126,585	145,835	164,275	185,635	226,224
	2018-19	73,843	92,378	111,131	131,464	150,874	168,923	189,152	238,670
	2019-20	76,310	94,750	113,305	135,330	154,815	167,773	186,895	225,959
	2020-21	71,980	89,199	107,009					
Dehydrated[4]	2012-13	13,965	17,640	22,000	26,105	30,135	34,610	38,945	47,305
	2013-14	12,065	15,875	19,835	23,380	27,140	31,095	34,895	44,385
	2014-15	13,045	16,325	19,965	23,645	26,345	31,515	35,490	46,340
	2015-16	12,155	15,885	19,620	23,560	27,605	31,585	35,645	45,735
	2016-17	11,560	15,305	19,085	22,675	26,565	30,545	34,890	46,317
	2017-18	10,595	14,304	18,085	21,680	25,775	29,800	34,410	44,263
	2018-19	13,810	17,065	20,775	24,420	28,315	32,620	36,660	47,648
	2019-20	11,850	15,075	18,620	21,865	25,510	28,780	32,080	40,285
	2020-21	13,140	16,435	19,715					

[1] Total quantity received and used for processing regardless of the State in which the potatoes were produced. Amount excludes quantities used for potato chips in Maine, Michigan and Wisconsin. [2] Includes Maine grown potatoes only. [3] Colorado, Minnesota, , Nevada, North Dakota and Wisconsin.
[4] Dehydrated products except starch and flour. Included in above totals. Includes CO, ID, NV, ND, OR, WA, and WI.
Source: National Agricultural Statistics Service, U.S. Department of Agriculture (NASS-USDA)

Rice

Rice is a grain that is cultivated on every continent except Antarctica and is the primary food for half the people in the world. Rice cultivation probably originated as early as 10,000 BC in Asia. Rice is grown at varying altitudes (sea level to about 3,000 meters), in varying climates (tropical to temperate), and on dry to flooded land. The growth duration of rice plants is 3-6 months, depending on variety and growing conditions. Rice is harvested by hand in developing countries or by combines in industrialized countries. Asian countries produce about 90% of rice grown worldwide. Rough rice futures and options are traded at the CME Group.

Prices – CME rough rice futures price (Barchart.com electronic symbol ZR) on the monthly nearest-futures chart opened the year 2020 around $13.333 per hundred weight (cwt), moved sharply higher to about around $17.000 in May, dropped to around $12.540 on June 1st, and then drifted sideways to finally close the year down -0.67% at $12.660.

Supply – World rice production in the 2020/21 marketing year is expected to rise +1.4% to 750.924 million metric tons, for a new record high. The world's largest rice producers are expected to be China with 28.2% of world production in 2020/21, India with 24.0%, Indonesia with 7.3%, Bangladesh with 7.1%, Vietnam with 5.8%, and Thailand with 3.8%. U.S. production of rice in 2020/21 is expected to rise +22.4% yr/yr to 226.121 million cwt (hundred pounds).

Demand – World consumption of rice in 2020/21 is expected to rise +1.0% to a record high of 499.562 million metric tons. U.S. rice consumption in 2020/21is expected to rise +10.8% yr/yr to a record high of 160.000 million cwt (hundred pounds).

Trade – World exports of rice in 2020/21 is expected to rise +6.2% yr/yr to 45.377 million metric tons, which is a record high. The world's largest rice exporters will be India with 30.4% of world exports, Thailand with 15.45%, Vietnam with 13.9%, Pakistan with 8.8%, the U.S. with 6.5%, and Burma with 4.8%. U.S. rice imports in 2020/21are expected to fall -2.9% yr/yr to 36.200 million cwt (hundred pounds), down from the 2019/20 record of 37.300. U.S. rice exports in 2020/21 are expected to fall -1.3% yr/yr to 93.000 million cwt.

World Production of Rough Rice In Thousands of Metric Tons

Year	Bangladesh	Brazil	Burma	China	India	Indonesia	Japan	Pakistan	Philippines	Thailand	United States	Vietnam	World Total
2014-15	51,755	12,449	19,688	209,609	158,239	56,000	11,098	10,506	18,911	28,409	10,079	45,066	720,024
2015-16	51,755	10,603	19,000	212,141	156,628	57,008	10,819	10,204	17,473	23,939	8,759	44,134	711,522
2016-17	51,872	12,328	19,766	211,094	164,563	58,505	10,891	10,275	18,549	29,091	10,167	43,840	734,149
2017-18	48,980	12,065	20,625	212,676	169,157	58,268	10,696	11,251	19,421	31,177	8,084	44,251	737,950
2018-19[1]	52,369	10,500	20,625	212,129	174,737	53,858	10,518	10,951	18,622	30,818	10,153	43,750	742,150
2019-20[2]	53,780	11,179	19,844	209,614	177,657	53,543	10,455	10,801	18,932	26,750	8,396	43,360	740,911
2020-21[3]	52,955	11,000	20,156	211,857	180,018	54,961	10,467	11,401	19,048	28,182	10,323	43,360	750,924

[1] Preliminary. [2] Estimate. [3] Forecast. *Source: Foreign Agricultural Service, U.S. Department of Agriculture (FAS-USDA)*

World Imports of Rice (Milled Basis) In Thousands of Metric Tons

Year	China	Cote d'Ivoire	European Union	Indonesia	Iran	Iraq	Malaysia	Nigeria	Philippines	Saudi Arabia	Senegal	South Africa	World Total
2014-15	4,700	1,300	1,706	1,350	1,350	1,205	1,051	2,600	1,800	1,601	1,200	980	41,736
2015-16	4,800	1,250	1,804	1,050	1,100	912	823	2,100	1,600	1,260	1,020	950	38,775
2016-17	5,300	1,300	1,837	350	1,400	1,191	900	2,500	1,100	1,195	1,100	1,006	41,443
2017-18	5,500	1,370	2,007	2,350	1,200	1,170	800	2,000	1,300	1,290	1,100	1,074	47,233
2018-19[1]	3,200	1,350	2,150	600	1,300	1,209	1,000	1,900	3,600	1,425	1,100	1,010	44,037
2019-20[2]	2,600	1,050	2,441	550	1,200	1,154	1,150	1,300	2,450	1,500	1,150	960	42,249
2020-21[3]	2,200	1,200	2,400	500	1,200	1,150	1,100	1,500	2,300	1,500	1,175	1,050	42,970

[1] Preliminary. [2] Estimate. [3] Forecast. *Source: Foreign Agricultural Service, U.S. Department of Agriculture (FAS-USDA)*

World Exports of Rice (Milled Basis) In Thousands of Metric Tons

Year	Argentina	Brazil	Burma	Cambodia	Guyana	India	Pakistan	Paraguay	Thailand	United States	Uruguay	Vietnam	World Total
2014-15	312	931	1,735	1,150	446	12,238	3,800	371	9,779	3,078	766	6,606	43,868
2015-16	526	547	1,300	1,050	486	10,357	4,200	556	9,867	3,384	972	5,088	40,685
2016-17	343	830	3,350	1,150	431	11,710	3,548	538	11,615	3,645	947	6,488	47,537
2017-18	426	1,152	2,750	1,300	455	12,041	4,011	653	11,056	2,763	773	6,590	47,420
2018-19[1]	348	878	2,700	1,350	414	10,420	4,493	689	7,562	2,971	846	6,581	43,900
2019-20[2]	330	1,200	2,300	1,350	496	12,487	3,800	800	5,500	2,990	840	6,100	42,710
2020-21[3]	280	1,000	2,200	1,450	520	13,800	4,000	620	7,000	2,985	800	6,300	45,377

[1] Preliminary. [2] Estimate. [3] Forecast. *Source: Foreign Agricultural Service, U.S. Department of Agriculture (FAS-USDA)*

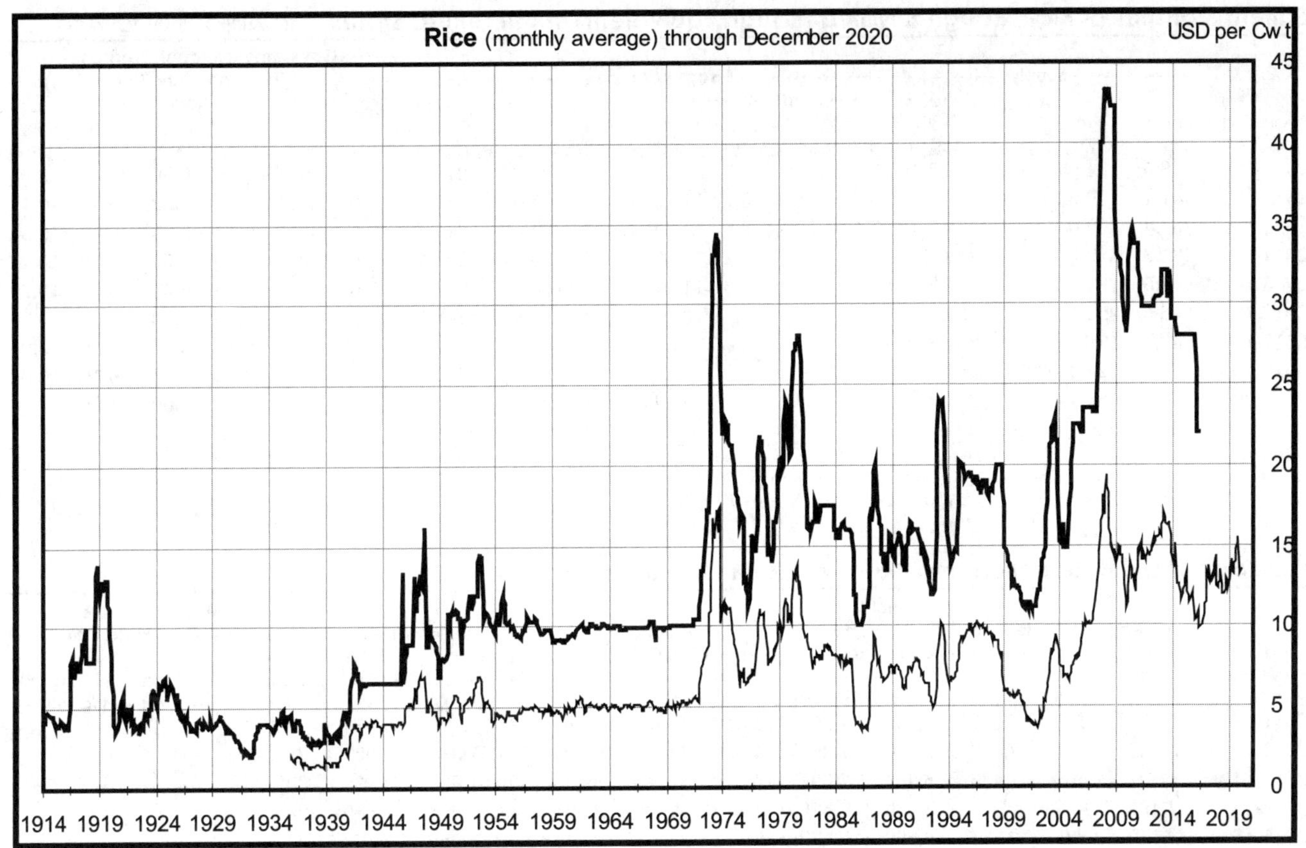

Average Wholesale Price of Rice No. 2 (Medium)[2] Southwest Louisiana In Dollars Per Cwt. Bagged

Year	Aug.	Sept.	Oct.	Nov.	Dec.	Jan.	Feb.	Mar.	Apr.	May	June	July	Average
2010-11	28.35	28.16	29.69	32.70	33.75	34.15	34.75	34.75	34.00	33.75	33.75	33.75	32.63
2011-12	33.75	33.75	32.55	32.06	31.50	30.70	30.31	29.75	29.75	29.75	29.75	29.75	31.11
2012-13	29.75	29.75	29.75	29.75	29.75	29.75	30.19	30.38	30.38	30.38	30.38	30.38	30.05
2013-14	30.44	30.50	32.00	32.00	32.00	32.00	32.00	32.00	32.00	30.25	32.00	32.00	31.60
2014-15	30.50	29.00	29.00	29.00	29.00	28.75	28.00	28.00	28.00	28.00	28.00	28.00	28.60
2015-16	28.00	28.00	28.00	28.00	28.00	28.00	28.00	28.00	28.00	28.00	28.00	28.00	28.00
2016-17	28.00	28.00	28.00	26.00	22.00	22.00	22.00	22.00	22.00	22.00	22.00	22.20	23.85
2017-18	23.00	23.60	24.50	24.50	24.50	25.63	28.00	28.00	28.00	29.50	30.00	30.00	26.60
2018-19	30.00	30.00	31.13	31.50	31.50	31.50	31.50	31.50	31.50	31.50	31.50	31.50	31.22
2019-20[1]	31.50	31.50	31.50	31.50	31.50	31.50	31.50						31.50

[1] Preliminary. [2] U.S. No. 2 -- broken not to exceed 4%. *Source: Economic Research Service, U.S. Department of Agriculture (ERS-USDA)*

Average Price Received by Farmers for Rice (Rough) in the United States In Dollars Per Hundred Pounds (Cwt.)

Year	Aug.	Sept.	Oct.	Nov.	Dec.	Jan.	Feb.	Mar.	Apr.	May	June	July	Average[2]
2011-12	13.60	14.40	14.70	15.00	14.70	15.20	14.10	14.10	14.40	14.10	14.20	14.40	14.41
2012-13	14.60	14.30	14.40	14.60	14.80	15.30	15.00	15.20	15.40	15.50	15.50	15.60	15.02
2013-14	15.80	15.60	15.80	16.20	16.50	17.10	16.70	16.40	16.20	16.20	16.30	16.10	16.24
2014-15	15.60	14.40	14.00	14.30	13.60	15.10	12.80	12.60	12.60	12.50	12.00	11.60	13.43
2015-16	12.00	11.90	12.20	12.50	12.80	13.30	12.10	11.80	11.50	11.70	11.70	12.10	12.13
2016-17	11.80	10.60	10.30	10.40	10.50	10.90	10.10	10.10	10.10	10.20	10.20	10.70	10.49
2017-18	11.30	11.50	12.20	13.30	12.90	13.70	12.70	12.70	13.10	12.80	13.10	13.70	12.75
2018-19	14.30	12.40	12.30	12.60	12.70	13.50	12.40	11.90	12.00	11.90	12.20	12.90	12.59
2019-20	12.70	12.30	12.80	13.60	12.80	14.10	13.30	13.20	13.80	14.00	14.70	15.10	13.53
2020-21[1]	15.40	13.50	13.20	13.40	13.50	13.40							13.73

[1] Preliminary. [2] Weighted average by sales. *Source: Economic Research Service, U.S. Department of Agriculture (ERS-USDA)*

Salient Statistics of Rice, Rough & Milled (Rough Equivalent) in the United States In Millions of Cwt.

Crop Year Beginning Aug. 1	Supply: Stocks Aug. 1	Supply: Production	Supply: Imports	Supply: Total Supply	Disappearance: Domestic: Food	Brewers	Seed	Total	Residual	Exports	Total Disappearance	Government Support Program: CCC Stocks July 31	Put Under Price Support	Loan Rate ($ Per Cwt.): Rough[3]: Long	Medium	All Classes	Milled Long
2011-12	48.5	184.9	19.4	252.8	107.5	[4]	3.3	110.8	[4]	100.9	211.7	0	65.8	6.50	6.50	6.50	9.93
2012-13	41.1	199.9	21.1	262.1	116.0	[4]	3.1	119.0	[4]	106.6	225.7	0	65.9	6.50	6.50	6.50	10.13
2013-14	36.4	190.0	23.1	249.5	120.7	[4]	3.6	124.4	[4]	93.3	217.7	0	36.0	6.50	6.50	6.50	10.34
2014-15	31.8	222.2	24.7	278.7	131.2	[4]	3.2	133.9	[4]	96.3	230.2	0	42.3	6.50	6.50	6.50	10.25
2015-16	48.5	193.1	24.1	264.9	107.7	[4]	3.9	112.7	[4]	106.6	219.3	0		6.50	6.50	6.50	10.22
2016-17	46.5	224.1	23.5	294.1	NA	[4]	NA	133.2	[4]	114.8	248.0	0		6.50	6.50	6.50	9.98
2017-18	46.0	178.2	26.9	251.8	----	[4]	----	135.4	[4]	87.1	222.4			6.50	6.50	6.50	10.01
2018-19	29.4	224.2	29.0	282.2	----	[4]	----	143.8	[4]	93.6	237.3			6.50	6.50	6.50	10.08
2019-20[1]	44.9	184.7	37.3	267.3	----	[4]	----	144.4	[4]	94.2	238.6			7.00	7.00	7.00	
2020-21[2]	28.7	226.1	36.2	292.4	----	[4]	----	160.0	[4]	93.0	253.0						

[1] Preliminary. [2] Forecast. [3] Loan rate for each class of rice is the sum of the whole kernels' loan rate weighted by its milling yield (average 56%) and the broken kernels' loan rate weighted by its milling yield (average 12%). [4] Included in Food.
Source: Economic Research Service, U.S. Department of Agriculture (ERS-USDA)

Acreage, Yield, Production and Prices of Rice in the United States

Crop Year Beginning Aug. 1	Acreage Harvested (1,000 Acres): Southern States	California	United States	Yield Per Harvested Acre (In Lbs.): California	United States	Production (1,000 Cwt.): Southern States	California	United States	Value of Production ($1,000)	Wholesale Prices ($ Per Cwt.): Arkansas[2]	Houston[3]	Milled Rice, Average C.I.F. Rotterdam ($ Per Metric Ton): U.S. No. 2[4]	Thai "A"[5]	Thai "B"[5]
2011-12	2,037	580	2,617	8,350	7,067	136,539	48,402	184,941	2,737,423	30.64	28.47	----	----	----
2012-13	2,122	557	2,679	8,150	7,463	154,526	45,413	199,939	3,067,365	28.27	28.46	----	----	----
2013-14	1,907	562	2,469	8,480	7,694	142,312	47,641	189,953	3,181,993	30.39	30.17	----	----	----
2014-15	2,491	442	2,933	8,580	7,576	184,279	37,936	222,215	3,075,618	29.87	26.52	----	----	----
2015-16	2,159	426	2,585	8,890	7,472	155,271	37,877	193,148	2,421,955	24.23	24.72	----	----	----
2016-17	2,561	536	3,097	8,840	7,237	176,751	47,394	224,145	2,384,690	22.51	22.51	----	----	----
2017-18	1,931	443	2,374	8,410	7,507	140,951	37,277	178,228	2,360,439	27.86	25.31	----	----	----
2018-19	2,411	504	2,915	8,620	7,692	180,786	43,425	224,211	2,903,041	30.69	26.56	----	----	----
2019-20	1,976	496	2,472	8,450	7,471	142,742	41,933	184,675	2,459,035			----	----	----
2020-21[1]	2,481	510	2,991	8,800	7,560	181,241	44,880	226,121				----	----	----

[1] Preliminary. [2] F.O.B. mills, Arkansas, medium. [3] Houston, Texas (long grain). [4] Milled, 4%, container, FAS.
[5] SWR, 100%, bulk. NA = Not available. *Source: Economic Research Service, U.S. Department of Agriculture (ERS-USDA)*

U.S. Exports of Milled Rice, by Country of Destination In Thousands of Metric Tons

Trade Year Beginning October	Canada	Haiti	Iran	Ivory Coast	Jamaica	Mexico	Netherlands	Peru	Saudi Arabia	South Africa	Switzerland	United Kingdom	Total
2010-11	229.1	324.1	----	1.9	23.3	942.0	5.1	1.5	120.3	1.7	.6	47.4	3,920
2011-12	219.9	287.3	3.1	.3	9.1	804.2	5.6	.7	133.4	2.1	.3	36.2	3,578
2012-13	231.6	365.0	125.7	14.9	2.7	885.8	4.6	.3	126.2	2.6	.6	21.4	3,848
2013-14	242.6	346.0	.2	13.5	2.3	741.2	5.4	6.8	106.1	2.3	.6	23.6	3,355
2014-15	219.2	392.1	----	.1	2.6	837.4	5.3	9.0	111.9	1.6	.6	30.6	3,971
2015-16	207.1	413.5	61.4	16.0	2.5	769.6	6.7	6.6	115.7	.9	.7	28.0	3,789
2016-17	212.6	478.0	----	17.2	3.1	962.0	6.0	8.7	130.1	.8	.6	34.0	3,986
2017-18	211.3	450.0	----	19.0	3.8	730.5	7.4	.2	88.5	.3	.5	22.3	3,052
2018-19	238.0	459.0	----	1.2	4.0	861.4	5.8	.2	110.4	.6	.6	18.6	3,599
2019-20[1]	237.9	399.0	----	38.2	5.2	609.9	5.3	.1	119.8	.3	.6	28.5	3,118

[1] Preliminary. *Source: Economic Research Service, U.S. Department of Agriculture (ERS-USDA)*

Production of Rice (Rough) in the United States, by Type and Variety In Thousands of Cwt.

Year	Long Grain	Medium Grain	Short Grain	Total	Year	Long Grain	Medium Grain	Short Grain	Total
2011	116,352	65,562	3,027	184,941	2016	166,465	54,533	3,147	224,145
2012	144,280	51,819	3,840	199,939	2017	127,850	47,867	2,511	178,228
2013	131,896	54,915	3,142	189,953	2018	163,956	57,339	2,916	224,211
2014	162,665	57,222	2,328	222,215	2019	125,610	56,669	2,396	184,675
2015	133,401	57,041	2,706	193,148	2020[1]	169,800	53,615	2,706	226,121

[1] Preliminary. *Source: National Agricultural Statistics Service, U.S. Department of Agriculture (NASS-USDA)*

Rubber

Rubber is a natural or synthetic substance characterized by elasticity, water repellence, and electrical resistance. Pre-Columbian Native South Americans discovered many uses for rubber such as containers, balls, shoes, and waterproofing for fabrics such as coats and capes. The Spaniards tried to duplicate these products for many years but were unsuccessful. The first commercial application of rubber began in 1791 when Samuel Peal patented a method of waterproofing cloth by treating it with a solution of rubber and turpentine. In 1839, Charles Goodyear revolutionized the rubber industry with his discovery of a process called vulcanization, which involves combining rubber and sulfur and heating the mixture.

Natural rubber is obtained from latex, a milky white fluid, from the Hevea Brasiliensis tree. The latex is gathered by cutting a chevron shape through the bark of the rubber tree. The latex is collected in a small cup, with approximately one fluid ounce per cutting. The cuttings are usually done every other day until the cuttings reach the ground. The tree is then allowed to renew itself before a new tapping is started. The collected latex is strained, diluted with water, and treated with acid to bind the rubber particles together. The rubber is then pressed between rollers to consolidate the rubber into slabs or thin sheets and is air-dried or smoke-dried for shipment.

During World War II, natural rubber supplies from the Far East were cut off, and the rubber shortage accelerated the development of synthetic rubber in the U.S. Synthetic rubber is produced by chemical reactions, condensation or polymerization, of certain unsaturated hydrocarbons. Synthetic rubber is made of raw material derived from petroleum, coal, oil, natural gas, and acetylene and is almost identical to natural rubber in chemical and physical properties.

Natural rubber and Rubber Index futures are traded on the Osaka Mercantile Exchange (OME). The OME's natural rubber contract is based on the RSS3 ribbed smoked sheet No. 3. The OME's Rubber Index Futures Contract is based on a composite of 8 component grades from 6 rubber markets in the world. Rubber futures are also traded on the Shanghai Futures Exchange (SHFE), the Singapore Exchange (SGX), and the Tokyo Commodity Exchange (TOCOM).

Prices – Singapore SGX Rubber futures prices (Barchart.com symbol U6K) on the nearest-futures chart in 2020 rose to a 3-year high in November and then moved lower to finally close the year up +37.3% at $222.40 per metric ton.

Supply – World production of natural rubber in 2019 fell -0.4% to 14.616 million metric tons, down from the 2018 record high of 14.676. The world's largest producers of natural rubber in 2019 were Thailand with 33.1% of world production, Indonesia with 23.6%, Vietnam with 8.1%, India with 6.9%, China with 5.7%, and Malaysia with 4.4%.

Trade – World exports of natural rubber in 2019 fell -1.8% yr/yr to 1.672 million metric tons. The world's largest exporter of natural rubber in 2019 was Thailand with 64.2% of world exports. U.S. imports of natural dry rubber in 2019 rose by +1.4% yr/yr to 962.455 metric tons.

World Production of Natural Rubber   In Thousands of Metric Tons

Year	Brazil	China	Côte d'Ivoire	India	Indonesia	Liberia	Malaysia	Nigeria	Philippines	Sri Lanka	Thailand	Vietnam	Total
2010	134.0	690.8	235.0	862.0	2,734.9	62.1	939.2	144.9	395.2	153.0	3,051.8	751.7	10,846.1
2011	164.5	750.9	238.7	800.0	2,990.2	62.7	996.3	144.9	425.7	158.2	3,348.9	789.6	11,630.7
2012	177.1	802.3	256.6	900.0	3,012.3	78.3	923.0	148.1	443.0	150.6	4,139.4	877.1	12,715.9
2013	185.7	864.8	289.6	900.0	3,107.5	74.6	826.4	150.1	444.8	130.4	4,305.1	946.9	13,084.3
2014	192.4	840.2	316.1	940.0	3,153.2	47.5	668.6	148.9	453.1	109.2	4,566.3	961.1	13,326.6
2015	191.5	816.1	350.0	944.5	3,145.4	46.3	722.1	146.9	398.1	91.0	4,466.1	1,012.8	13,283.8
2016	189.8	815.9	453.0	967.2	3,307.1	47.2	673.5	147.7	362.6	79.1	4,519.0	1,035.3	13,554.1
2017	190.5	817.4	580.0	975.3	3,680.4	48.6	740.1	148.3	407.0	83.1	4,503.1	1,094.5	14,304.9
2018[1]	199.7	824.1	624.2	988.4	3,630.4	54.9	603.3	149.0	423.4	82.6	4,813.5	1,137.7	14,675.8
2019[2]	217.4	839.9	664.7	1,001.4	3,448.8	42.0	639.8	149.7	431.7	74.8	4,840.0	1,185.2	14,616.6

[1] Preliminary. [2] Estimate. *Source: Food and Agricultural Organization of the United Nations (FAO-UN)*

World Imports of Natural Rubber   In Metric Tons

Year	Brazil	Canada	China	European Union	Germany	Italy	Korea, South	Malaysia	Mexico	Pakistan	United Kingdom	United States	Total
2010	17,180	22,241	262,089	155,548	40,107	24,604	21,316	348,487	20,323	17,218	19,031	53,222	1,027,962
2011	17,752	23,058	280,663	141,970	31,817	24,123	19,252	306,561	19,433	14,819	20,376	49,264	975,316
2012	17,397	23,315	327,683	137,333	29,621	20,253	19,306	330,910	19,963	14,021	20,337	44,887	1,032,232
2013	17,849	22,309	345,330	164,192	32,169	20,894	20,130	344,581	19,318	14,023	28,656	45,939	1,094,304
2014	29,603	18,870	375,537	218,819	26,123	21,480	33,718	315,711	21,531	20,086	45,644	49,914	1,268,089
2015	28,048	18,802	386,157	145,988	18,092	21,065	34,398	318,300	21,795	14,223	38,546	50,278	1,194,948
2016	27,825	3,088	432,273	129,249	21,089	22,518	34,302	318,419	22,967	6,722	19,313	48,619	1,171,475
2017	28,546	2,593	501,350	134,852	18,580	21,556	32,686	323,121	24,000	10,095	14,388	54,721	1,268,655
2018[1]	29,674	2,204	597,641	142,200	17,086	21,600	26,268	333,427	25,605	10,542	14,332	47,793	1,360,356
2019[2]	30,088	1,292	560,346	132,490	14,837	20,008	24,172	312,006	30,203	8,755	13,341	47,384	1,306,139

[1] Preliminary. [2] Estimate. *Source: Food and Agricultural Organization of the United Nations (FAO-UN)*

World Exports of Natural Rubber In Metric Tons

Year	Belgium	Cameroon	Hong Kong	Germany	Guatemala	India	Indonesia	Malaysia	Myanmar	Netherlands	Thailand	United States	Total
2010	14,255	8,160	3,224	6,039	20,603	7,407	12,929	47,773	1,886	694	898,454	5,369	1,056,340
2011	26,934	6,627	2,031	6,273	22,742	9,943	9,502	41,586	1,378	3,127	876,382	7,279	1,037,161
2012	37,031	4,826	1,675	7,332	23,301	4,499	7,620	31,748	50	2,288	949,103	7,909	1,151,861
2013	54,754	9,866	1,414	8,209	24,068	4,635	5,907	33,538	80	3,328	1,038,421	5,398	1,253,098
2014	80,932	7,169	1,802	5,980	42,899	815	5,410	32,370	----	12,967	1,057,520	6,470	1,348,074
2015	19,980	5,596	2,346	5,136	41,910	653	6,410	31,904	18	17,834	1,072,710	7,119	1,301,858
2016	37,911	6,241	1,692	6,070	40,242	2,148	6,067	30,375	410	20,240	1,240,189	6,045	1,510,522
2017	24,628	6,918	1,888	9,598	51,286	15,580	8,388	32,920	2,798	30,436	1,185,942	5,753	1,536,033
2018[1]	20,076	10,071	1,970	11,030	52,390	535	5,154	27,019	12,859	30,667	1,298,800	5,176	1,702,984
2019[2]	27,710	12,712	768	8,726	54,842	1,093	4,797	23,188	16,586	19,035	1,073,727	3,327	1,671,596

[1] Preliminary. [2] Estimate. *Source: Food and Agricultural Organization of the United Nations (FAO-UN)*

World Imports of Natural Dry Rubber In Metric Tons

Year	Brazil	Canada	China	European Union	France	Germany	Italy	Japan	Korea, South	Malaysia	Spain	United States	Total
2010	232,161	128,087	1,724,502	1,393,603	171,252	367,791	103,302	731,498	366,255	329,683	177,182	891,688	6,512,249
2011	205,351	124,911	1,935,738	1,663,523	192,644	392,475	117,765	770,804	382,908	360,872	171,838	999,373	7,179,882
2012	163,742	120,209	1,962,901	1,468,217	162,806	338,306	93,204	685,966	378,016	541,519	141,411	923,981	7,126,938
2013	205,903	109,375	2,241,937	1,440,785	159,935	342,548	97,455	711,490	376,217	660,136	143,491	881,396	7,494,686
2014	211,843	110,737	2,352,994	1,534,474	154,532	361,112	107,043	678,942	383,051	589,328	164,149	897,012	7,873,472
2015	191,039	113,698	2,460,397	1,588,333	161,966	353,750	115,196	677,834	367,806	639,001	169,108	899,721	8,163,897
2016	206,383	118,204	2,178,575	1,619,848	160,774	315,651	116,682	655,335	361,975	611,916	162,042	897,493	7,870,584
2017	196,052	125,100	2,409,916	1,663,255	167,182	292,603	122,666	477,278	364,758	789,885	183,887	917,584	8,256,906
2018[1]	195,665	139,483	2,105,366	1,711,502	168,438	282,150	119,539	705,767	352,674	681,357	175,553	949,535	8,306,711
2019[2]	195,287	141,174	1,998,757	1,672,740	156,892	247,256	115,854	727,556	341,110	770,694	183,639	962,455	8,256,856

[1] Preliminary. [2] Estimate. *Source: Food and Agricultural Organization of the United Nations (FAO-UN)*

World Exports of Natural Dry Rubber In Metric Tons

Year	Côte d'Ivoire	Germany	Guatemala	India	Indonesia	Liberia	Malaysia	Nigeria	Philippines	Sri Lanka	Thailand	Vietnam	Total
2010	238,701	96,979	55,695	8,601	2,338,986	70,620	853,108	42,435	36,355	46,924	1,834,828	782,213	6,824,352
2011	259,459	130,568	65,351	28,154	2,546,237	70,339	904,494	58,088	42,209	41,052	2,120,597	817,502	7,499,757
2012	267,368	112,745	64,267	8,893	2,436,819	70,606	739,426	56,847	38,614	35,313	2,049,683	799,489	7,055,019
2013	259,860	110,488	64,182	22,134	2,696,087	58,946	813,714	51,332	66,930	23,007	2,398,556	674,342	7,648,372
2014	352,543	148,976	65,355	2,171	2,618,061	67,688	689,352	38,760	87,162	15,415	2,351,795	918,574	7,930,459
2015	409,815	142,222	60,862	4,685	2,623,903	55,819	674,589	37,115	78,604	12,050	2,579,309	709,029	8,070,623
2016	492,322	98,908	57,302	5,882	2,572,097	66,393	611,588	33,292	68,788	15,529	2,356,971	585,250	7,651,714
2017	644,446	60,326	64,269	9,584	3,283,140	65,025	583,120	42,738	133,745	13,290	2,482,824	473,634	8,662,622
2018[1]	557,764	53,822	66,110	5,516	2,806,801	76,148	611,896	40,773	111,178	15,981	2,226,029	559,463	7,955,102
2019[2]	691,056	44,444	62,079	8,872	2,574,449	89,078	608,116	42,311	122,946	17,356	2,043,688	590,749	7,838,814

[1] Preliminary. [2] Estimate. *Source: Food and Agricultural Organization of the United Nations (FAO-UN)*

U.S. Imports of Natural Rubber (Includes Latex & Guayule) In Metric Tons

Year	Jan.	Feb.	Mar.	Apr.	May	June	July	Aug.	Sept.	Oct.	Nov.	Dec.	Total
2011	82,559	83,695	100,449	94,540	104,094	82,569	92,187	95,040	68,872	90,280	79,167	75,984	1,049,435
2012	80,134	87,794	93,327	95,541	75,109	62,804	68,098	83,118	88,059	75,963	80,187	78,828	968,960
2013	75,848	66,517	84,667	80,380	72,054	82,234	77,067	72,617	76,176	76,111	88,195	76,234	928,100
2014	80,647	75,094	87,363	95,293	70,447	72,062	79,663	82,402	71,885	77,073	74,484	80,532	946,946
2015	84,504	57,323	86,017	81,059	102,381	78,643	83,734	79,336	83,083	77,489	73,360	65,115	952,042
2016	77,751	72,275	77,523	85,225	88,091	79,224	86,991	80,035	70,754	83,342	72,110	72,826	946,147
2017	78,217	71,901	88,085	85,883	64,955	97,920	82,746	79,584	82,898	80,086	71,825	88,396	972,495
2018	82,600	75,326	96,446	75,441	101,791	86,553	65,733	84,977	87,418	97,657	73,051	70,410	997,403
2019	103,581	64,889	102,213	91,161	84,602	88,177	64,568	93,991	78,237	72,177	96,745	69,546	1,009,887
2020[1]	70,468	80,501	83,060	94,526	87,448	45,332	43,862	51,601	58,419	48,980	66,297		796,900

[1] Preliminary. *Source: Economic Research Service, U.S. Department of Agriculture (ERS-USDA)*

Rye

Rye is a cereal grain and a member of the grass family. Hardy varieties of rye have been developed for winter planting. Rye is most widely grown in northern Europe and Asia. In the U.S., rye is used as an animal feed and as an ingredient in bread and some whiskeys. Bread using rye was developed in northern Europe in the Middle Ages, where bakers developed dark, hearty bread consisting of rye, oat, and barley flours. Those were crops that grew more readily in the wet and damp climate of northern Europe, as opposed to wheat, which fares better in the warmer and drier climates in central Europe. Modern rye bread is made with a mixture of white and rye flours. Coarsely ground rye flour is also used in pumpernickel bread and helps provide the dark color and coarse texture, along with molasses. The major producing states are North and South Dakota, Oklahoma, and Georgia. The crop year runs from June to May.

Supply – World rye production in 2020/21 marketing year is forecasted to rise +16.2% yr/yr to 14.194 million metric tons.

The world's largest producers of rye are the European Union with 64.6% of world production followed by Russia with 16.7%, Belarus with 6.3%, and Ukraine with 2.8%. U.S. production of rye accounted for only 2.1% of world production.

U.S. production of rye in 2020 rose +8.6% to 11.532 million bushels, far below the production levels of over 20 million bushels seen from the late 1800s through the 1960s. U.S. production of rye fell off in the 2010s and fell to a record low of 6.051million bushels in 2011. U.S. acreage harvested with rye in 2020/21 is expected to rise +6.5% yr/yr to 330,000 acres. U.S. farmers in the late 1800s through the 1960s typically harvested more than 1 million acres of rye, showing how domestic planting of rye has dropped off sharply in the past several decades. Rye yield in 2019/20 is expected to rise +11.0% to 34.3 bushels per acre, which is a new record high.

Demand – Total U.S. domestic usage of rye in 2020/21 rose +5.8% yr/yr to 22.890 million bushels. The breakdown of 2020/21 domestic usage shows that 40.1% of rye was used for feed and residual, 27.1% for industry, 17.2% for seed, and 15.7% for food.

Trade – World exports of rye in the 2020/21 marketing year are expected to rise +10.3% yr/yr to 480,000 metric tons, above the record low of 225,000 metric tons in 2008/09. The largest exporters will be Canada, with 41.7% of the world total at 200,000 metric tons, and the European Union with 33.1% at 150,000 metric tons. World imports of rye in 2020/21 are expected to fall -17.6% to 385,000 metric tons. U.S. imports of rye in 2020/21 are expected to fall -7.6% yr/yr to 279,000 metric tons.

World Production of Rye In Thousands of Metric Tons

Crop Year	Argen-tina	Australia	Belarus	Canada	Chile	European Union	Kazak-hstan	Norway	Russia	Turkey	Ukraine	United States	World Total
2011-12	45	40	801	241	1	6,900	28	16	2,967	366	579	154	12,191
2012-13	40	40	1,082	337	4	8,763	50	5	2,132	370	676	166	13,713
2013-14	52	31	648	223	4	10,151	43	13	3,360	365	638	194	15,772
2014-15	97	30	867	218	5	8,864	61	38	3,279	300	475	183	14,469
2015-16	61	30	753	226	5	7,833	37	66	2,084	330	394	295	12,162
2016-17	79	29	651	436	5	7,440	41	23	2,538	300	394	339	12,332
2017-18	86	30	670	341	5	7,401	39	50	2,540	320	510	260	12,304
2018-19[1]	87	30	503	236	5	6,208	23	9	1,914	320	396	214	9,999
2019-20[2]	220	30	756	333	5	8,392	23	50	1,424	320	339	270	12,216
2020-21[3]	140	30	900	431	5	9,175	20	50	2,375	320	400	293	14,194

[1] Preliminary. [2] Estimate. [3] Forecast. *Source: Foreign Agricultural Service, U.S. Department of Agriculture (FAS-USDA)*

World Imports and Exports of Rye In Thousands of Metric Tons

	Imports							Exports					
Year	European Union	Japan	Korea, South	Norway	Russia	United States	World Total	Belarus	Canada	European Union	Russia	United States	World Total
2011-12	291	46	11	16	----	152	538	11	166	57	238	4	490
2012-13	98	27	12	19	25	228	454	----	189	113	133	8	462
2013-14	77	37	8	22	5	234	425	----	118	169	74	7	420
2014-15	102	22	4	8	5	237	409	----	86	184	114	6	413
2015-16	51	16	5	1	8	222	335	20	98	161	48	5	353
2016-17	16	24	4	3	4	167	229	11	142	76	9	4	254
2017-18	61	21	3	4	----	224	354	----	193	81	71	4	388
2018-19[1]	298	23	3	18	----	304	691	----	144	195	283	4	715
2019-20[2]	3	19	4	9	90	302	443	----	163	258	1	5	435
2020-21[3]	25	20	5	5	----	279	365	----	200	150	75	5	480

[1] Preliminary. [2] Estimate. [3] Forecast. *Source: Foreign Agricultural Service, U.S. Department of Agriculture (FAS-USDA)*

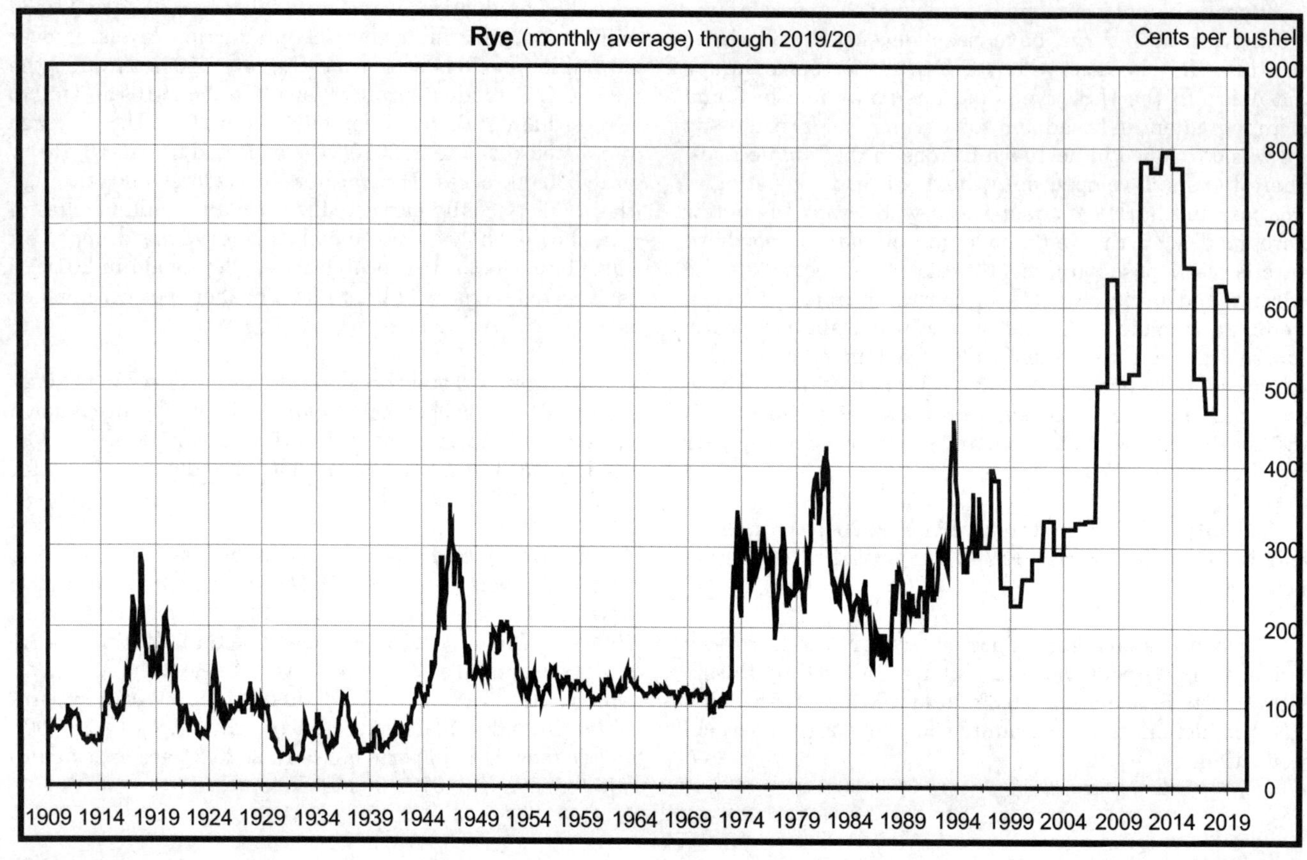

Production of Rye in the United States In Thousands of Bushels

Year	Georgia	Minnesota	North Dakota	Oklahoma	Pennsylvania	Other States[2]	Total
2011	945	----	----	825	----	4,556	6,051
2012	575	----	----	1,680	----	4,287	6,542
2013	1,080	----	----	1,600	----	4,946	7,626
2014	540	----	----	495	----	6,154	7,189
2015	420	----	----	2,040	----	9,156	11,616
2016	630	----	----	1,875	----	10,832	13,337
2017	475	W	W	1,080	W	8,697	10,252
2018	390	W	W	1,100	W	6,942	8,432
2019	W	702	2,565	1,485	364	4,826	10,622
2020[1]	W	570	2,200	728	1,872	5,362	11,532

[1] Preliminary. [2] Includes IL, KS, ME, MD, MI, MN, NE, NJ, NY, NC, ND, PA, SC, SD, TX, VA, and WI. *Source: Agricultural Statistics Board, U.S. Department of Agriculture (ASB-USDA)*

Salient Statistics of Rye in the United States In Thousands of Bushels

Crop Year Beginning June 1	Supply: Stocks June 1	Supply: Pro-duction	Supply: Imports	Supply: Total Supply	Disappearance: Domestic Use: Food	Domestic Use: Industry	Domestic Use: Seed	Domestic Use: Feed & Residual	Domestic Use: Total	Exports	Total Disap-pearance	Acreage: Planted (1,000 Acres)	Acreage: Harvested for Grain (1,000 Acres)	Yield Per Harvested Acre (Bushels)
2011-12	801	6,051	5,994	12,846	3,380	2,531	2,610	3,716	12,237	157	12,394	1,266	242	26.1
2012-13	452	6,542	8,966	15,960	3,400	2,786	2,990	6,073	15,249	310	15,559	1,300	248	28.0
2013-14	401	7,626	9,213	17,240	3,430	3,399	2,970	6,888	16,687	268	16,955	1,451	278	27.4
2014-15	285	7,189	9,319	16,793	3,450	3,173	3,200	6,141	15,964	240	16,204	1,434	258	27.9
2015-16	589	11,616	8,757	20,962	3,480	5,321	3,840	7,685	20,326	181	20,507	1,584	365	31.8
2016-17	455	13,337	6,586	20,378	3,500	5,727	4,110	6,168	19,505	175	19,680	1,891	411	32.5
2017-18	698	10,252	8,825	19,775	3,530	5,800	4,250	5,445	19,025	157	19,182	1,961	300	34.2
2018-19[1]	593	8,432	11,964	20,989	3,550	6,000	3,890	6,982	20,422	148	20,570	2,011	273	30.9
2019-20[2]	419	10,622	11,899	22,940	3,570	6,100	4,680	7,285	21,635	205	21,840	1,855	310	34.3
2020-21[3]	1,100	11,532	11,000	23,632	3,590	6,200	3,930	9,170	22,890	200	23,090	1,955	330	34.9

[1] Preliminary. [2] Estimate. [3] Forecast *Source: Economic Research Service, U.S. Department of Agriculture (ERS-USDA)*

Salt

Salt, also known as sodium chloride, is a chemical compound that is an essential element in the diet of humans, animals, and even many plants. Since prehistoric times, salt has been used to preserve foods and was commonly used in the religious rites of the Greeks, Romans, Hebrews, and Christians. Salt, in the form of salt cakes, served as money in ancient Ethiopia and Tibet. As long ago as 1450 BC, Egyptian art shows records of salt production.

The simplest method of obtaining salt is through the evaporation of saltwater from areas near oceans or seas. In most regions, rock salt is obtained from underground mining or by wells sunk into deposits. Salt is soluble in water, is slightly soluble in alcohol, but is insoluble in concentrated hydrochloric acid. In its crystalline form, salt is transparent and colorless, shining with an ice-like luster.

Prices – The price of salt in 2020 (FOB mine, vacuum and open pan) was unchanged from 2019 at $215.00 per metric ton, down from 2018's record high.

Supply – World production of salt in 2020 fell -4.6% yr/yr to 270.000 million metric tons. The world's largest salt producers were China with 25.0% and the U.S. with 16.7% of world production. U.S. salt production in 2020 fell -7.1% yr/yr to 38.000 million metric tons.

Demand – U.S. consumption of salt in 2020 fell -8.6% at 53.000 million metric tons, down from the 2014 record high of 65.300 million.

Trade – U.S. imports of salt for consumption in 2020 fell -14.0% yr/yr to 16.000 million metric tons, down from the 2015 record high of 21.600. The U.S. relied on imports for 32% of its salt consumption in 2020. U.S. exports of salt in 2020 rose by 17.6% to 1.2 million metric tons, with the bulk of those exports going to Canada.

World Production of All Salt   In Thousands of Metric Tons

Year	Australia	Canada	China	France	Germany	India	Italy	Mexico	Poland	Spain	United Kingdom	United States	World Total
2013	12,900	12,244	73,676	5,890	17,396	26,888	3,037	9,461	4,743	4,278	6,930	39,955	296,000
2014	13,000	14,473	70,497	5,810	13,338	23,017	3,288	10,251	4,127	4,300	4,690	45,385	292,000
2015	11,000	14,343	66,655	6,000	12,480	24,241	3,336	9,088	4,119	4,300	5,000	45,125	292,000
2016	12,000	14,000	67,000	6,000	12,890	25,000	3,035	9,000	4,170	4,300	5,100	41,795	284,000
2017	11,000	12,000	67,000	4,500	13,000	28,000	3,047	9,000	4,450	4,500	5,100	40,000	286,000
2018	12,000	12,000	58,000	5,700	14,000	29,000	3,000	9,000	4,400	4,200	5,100	41,000	286,000
2019[1]	13,000	11,000	59,000	5,600	14,300	29,000	4,200	9,000	4,480	4,200	4,100	42,000	283,000
2020[2]	12,000	10,000	60,000	5,500	14,000	28,000	4,000	9,000	4,000	4,000	4,000	39,000	270,000

[1] Preliminary. [2] Estimate. *Source: U.S. Geological Survey (USGS)*

Salient Statistics of the Salt Industry in the United States   In Thousands of Metric Tons

	Net Import Reliance As a % of Apparent Con-	Average Value FOB Mine Vacuum & Open Pan	Production					Sold or Used, Producers					Imports for Con-	Exports		Ap- parent Con-
Year	sumption	($ Per Ton)	Total	Open & Vacuum Pan	Solar	Rock	Brine	Open & Vacuum Pan	Rock	Brine	Total Salt	Value[3] Million $	sump- tion	Total	To Can- ada	sump- tion
2013	22	172.09	39,900	4,130	3,580	14,800	17,400	4,090	18,300	17,400	43,100	1,980.0	11,900	525	434	54,500
2014	29	180.61	45,300	4,140	3,900	20,000	17,300	4,080	20,800	17,500	46,000	2,180.0	20,200	935	809	65,300
2015	33	188.87	45,100	4,190	3,590	20,400	16,900	4,220	18,200	17,000	42,800	2,360.0	21,600	830	699	63,600
2016	22	197.78	41,700	4,050	2,900	17,900	16,900	4,040	16,100	16,400	39,900	2,190.0	12,100	729	594	51,300
2017	23	211.71	39,600	4,120	3,340	16,500	15,600	4,130	15,500	15,500	38,200	2,330.0	12,600	1,120	956	49,700
2018	29	220.00	42,000								41,000		17,900	986		58,000
2019[1]	30	215.00	42,000								41,000		18,600	1,020		58,000
2020[2]	27	215.00	39,000								38,000		16,000	1,200		53,000

[1] Preliminary. [2] Estimate. [3] Values are f.o.b. mine or refinery & do not include cost of cooperage or containers. *Source: U.S. Geological Survey* (USGS)

Salt Sold or Used by Producers in the U.S. by Classes & Consumers or Uses   In Thousands of Metric Tons

Year	Chem- ical[2]	Tanning Leather	Textile & Dyeing	Meat Packers[3]	Can- ning	Baking	Agri- cultural Distri- bution	Feed Dealers	Feed Manu- facturers	Rubber	Oil	Paper & Pulp	Metal Pro- cessing	Water Treat- ment	Grocery Stores	Water Condi- tioning Distrib.	Ice Control and/or Stabili- zation
2010	20,190	39	59	275	258	364	359	1,330	425	5	325	59	26	913	761	461	18,640
2011	18,530	42	49	260	195	162	375	1,170	438	5	322	67	44	312	706	493	19,560
2012	16,824	36	41	248	182	160	253	1,010	392	7	441	61	53	446	591	472	11,100
2013	17,990	38	39	258	179	162	351	913	516	5	409	66	42	472	665	627	20,340
2014	20,360	39	38	240	171	158	389	939	514	6	400	71	56	603	708	504	24,490
2015	19,430	38	39	275	175	181	306	849	336	3	302	69	46	723	707	440	22,760
2016	18,350	36	64	283	181	171	428	660	377	4	316	63	41	469	669	437	20,300
2017[1]	17,050	33	30	257	177	177	470	708	458	3	275	62	34	471	537	447	19,520

[1] Preliminary. [2] Chloralkali producers and other chemical. *Source: U.S. Geological Survey (USGS)*

Sheep and Lambs

Sheep and lambs are raised for both their wool and meat. In countries that have high wool production, there is also demand for sheep and lamb meat due to the easy availability. Production levels have declined in New Zealand and Australia, but that has been counteracted by a substantial increase in China.

Prices – The average monthly wholesale price of slaughter lambs (choice) at San Angelo, Texas in 2020 rose +7.6% at 161.04 cents per pound, which is a new record high.

Supply – World sheep and goat numbers in 2019 rose +2.4% to 2.233 billion head, a new record high. The world's largest producers of sheep and goats are China with 12.9% of world production in 2019, India with 9.6%, Australia with 3.0%, Turkey with 2.0%, and the United Kingdom with 1.4%.

The number of sheep and lambs on U.S. farms in 2020 (Jan 1) was down -0.6% yr/yr to 5.200 million head. U.S. states with the most sheep and lambs are Texas with 14.1% of the U.S. total, California with 11.0%, Colorado with 8.2%, Wyoming with 6.5%, and Utah with 5.5%.

World Sheep and Goat Numbers in Specified Countries on January 1 In Thousands of Head

Year	Argentina	Australia	China	India	Kazakhstan	New Zealand	Romania	Russia	South Africa	Spain	Turkey	United Kingdom	World Total
2010	19,062	71,585	287,509	205,065	17,370	32,658	10,059	21,986	30,776	21,455	26,923	31,177	2,016,857
2011	19,011	76,599	286,847	202,766	17,988	31,218	9,658	21,820	30,468	19,696	29,383	31,728	2,050,911
2012	19,047	78,272	285,319	200,242	18,092	31,353	9,770	22,858	30,533	18,977	32,310	32,313	2,085,088
2013	18,950	79,098	289,520	197,800	17,633	30,867	10,100	24,180	30,556	18,729	35,783	32,954	2,127,838
2014	18,934	76,182	289,507	196,000	17,561	29,901	10,449	24,337	30,094	18,136	38,510	33,843	2,136,209
2015	19,580	74,510	304,072	205,085	18,016	29,196	10,935	24,683	29,810	19,533	41,485	33,438	2,188,038
2016	19,576	71,193	311,900	208,879	18,184	27,696	11,250	24,606	28,906	19,051	41,924	34,047	2,228,411
2017	19,610	75,725	302,464	212,348	18,329	27,625	11,359	24,717	28,164	19,023	41,329	34,936	2,256,340
2018[1]	18,907	73,709	297,281	216,013	18,699	27,389	11,716	24,389	27,905	18,617	44,312	33,885	2,278,491
2019[2]	19,413	69,653	300,857	223,145	19,156	26,915	11,958	23,129	27,336	18,138	46,117	33,684	2,332,788

[1] Preliminary. [2] Forecast. *Source: Food and Agricultural Organization of the United Nations (FAO-UN)*

Salient Statistics of Sheep & Lambs in the United States (Average Live Weight) In Thousands of Head

	- Inventory, Jan. 1 -				--- Marketings[3] ---		--------- Slaughter ---------							------ Farm Value Jan. 1 ------
Year	Without New Crop Lambs	With New Crop Lambs	Lamb Crop	Total Supply	Sheep	Lambs	Farm	Commercial	Total[4]	Net Exports	Total Disappearance	Production (Live Weight) (Mil. Lbs.)		Total
2011	5,470	5,579	3,490	9,069	----	----	93	2,164	2,258	----	----	----	938.4	170.0
2012	5,375	5,484	3,445	8,929	----	----	93	2,183	2,275	----	----	----	----	----
2013	5,360	5,467	3,370	8,837	----	----	94	2,319	2,412	----	----	----	----	----
2014	5,245	5,356	3,440	8,796	----	----	95	2,310	2,404	----	----	----	----	----
2015	5,280	5,385	3,290	8,675	----	----	95	2,224	2,319	----	----	----	----	----
2016	5,300	5,405	3,265	8,670	----	----	95	2,238	2,333	----	----	----	----	----
2017	5,250	5,356	3,230	8,586	----	----	96	2,178	2,274	----	----	----	----	----
2018	5,265	5,372	3,235	8,607	----	----	92	2,261	2,353	----	----	----	----	----
2019[1]	5,230	5,338	3,230	8,568	----	----	92	2,322	2,413	----	----	----	----	----
2020[2]	5,200	5,308	3,210	8,518	----	----	93	2,219	2,312	----	----	----	----	----

[1] Preliminary. [2] Estimate. [3] Excludes interfarm sales. [4] Includes all commercial and farm.
Source: Economic Research Service, U.S. Department of Agriculture (ERS-USDA)

Sheep and Lambs[3] on Farms in the United States on January 1 In Thousands of Head

Year	California	Colorado	Idaho	Iowa	Minnesota	Montana	New Mexico	Ohio	Dakota	Texas	Utah	Wyoming	Total
2013	570	435	235	175	135	235	100	121	275	700	295	375	5,360
2014	590	365	250	155	135	220	81	117	270	730	280	355	5,245
2015	600	420	260	175	130	215	90	121	255	720	290	345	5,280
2016	575	435	255	175	125	230	90	120	265	725	285	355	5,300
2017	600	420	250	175	130	230	97	117	250	710	275	360	5,250
2018	570	445	235	165	130	225	96	119	250	750	275	345	5,265
2019	550	420	220	153	125	215	100	121	255	750	290	350	5,230
2020	570	425	230	151	115	200	95	126	250	735	285	340	5,200
2021[1]	555	445	230	160	113	200	85	126	245	730	285	340	5,170

[1] Preliminary. [2] Includes sheep & lambs on feed for market and stock sheep & lambs. *Source: Economic Research Service, U.S. Department of Agriculture (ERS-USDA)*

Average Wholesale Price of Slaughter Lambs (Choice[2]) at San Angelo Texas In Dollars Per Hundred Pounds (Cwt.)

Year	Jan.	Feb.	Mar.	Apr.	May	June	July	Aug.	Sept.	Oct.	Nov.	Dec.	Average
2012	147.40	148.13	141.94	136.75	128.50	116.00	103.64	83.32	80.88	96.20	84.67	88.67	113.01
2013	114.25	109.57	98.76	88.90	92.50	93.76	91.90	86.50	104.38	146.50	143.09	163.33	111.12
2014	165.00	168.38	154.88	150.97	135.17	160.83	150.23	152.94	164.90	159.25	162.00	166.83	157.62
2015	155.25	148.75	137.75	137.38	147.25	147.88	140.50	148.00	150.20	139.00	148.67	139.88	145.04
2016	139.00	134.07	127.45	136.56	136.40	135.50	130.66	139.90	142.00	130.50	126.13	139.00	134.76
2017	138.10	139.25	139.38	140.50	159.00	160.88	146.00	147.00	138.88	127.50	130.17	136.00	141.89
2018	130.88	133.75	135.50	149.05	155.63	159.91	157.29	145.58	140.98	136.58	134.35	131.98	142.62
2019	132.45	134.63	141.61	152.39	156.15	159.93	160.22	153.47	151.10	150.12	151.64	151.69	149.62
2020[1]	153.52	161.27	163.15	----	----	----	----	----	----	----	167.50	159.78	161.04

[1] Preliminary. *Source: Economic Research Service, U.S. Department of Agriculture (ERS-USDA)*

Federally Inspected Slaughter of Sheep & Lambs in the United States In Thousands of Head

Year	Jan.	Feb.	Mar.	Apr.	May	June	July	Aug.	Sept.	Oct.	Nov.	Dec.	Total
2012	153.8	154.6	180.0	165.8	164.4	154.8	164.5	185.5	160.6	189.5	165.5	173.3	2,012.1
2013	164.7	150.3	184.0	174.9	188.4	167.7	192.9	189.5	167.2	186.5	169.5	184.6	2,120.1
2014	166.9	155.4	176.5	204.0	176.5	175.3	188.9	161.4	172.7	186.8	157.1	182.8	2,104.6
2015	153.0	149.9	190.0	179.1	152.7	172.8	166.8	155.5	167.4	166.3	162.6	182.3	1,998.4
2016	144.4	159.9	187.5	169.7	166.7	174.0	152.4	173.3	170.1	163.0	169.6	178.9	2,009.5
2017	161.6	144.8	177.3	156.1	157.1	165.5	146.3	171.9	153.9	165.1	167.3	170.1	1,937.0
2018	161.9	146.0	185.2	163.3	177.8	158.8	158.0	174.1	148.1	176.1	174.1	176.2	1,999.6
2019	165.7	146.1	170.3	204.5	182.0	151.6	162.6	171.3	154.7	179.8	158.9	172.9	2,020.4
2020[1]	161.3	142.6	165.0	154.1	166.6	166.7	163.9	148.6	154.4	151.0	152.2	168.5	1,894.9

[1] Preliminary. *Source: Economic Research Service, U.S. Department of Agriculture (ERS-USDA)*

Average Live Weight of Sheep & Lambs Slaughtered in the United States In Pounds per Head

Year	Jan.	Feb.	Mar.	Apr.	May	June	July	Aug.	Sept.	Oct.	Nov.	Dec.	Average
2012	151	153	152	147	157	152	144	145	148	140	140	138	147
2013	143	145	142	143	142	142	136	134	128	127	130	133	137
2014	140	140	142	140	147	141	135	131	130	132	135	137	138
2015	144	144	142	142	145	142	141	137	132	131	134	135	139
2016	142	145	141	138	144	138	138	132	128	130	133	135	137
2017	141	144	143	133	134	136	135	134	131	131	136	138	136
2018	144	148	142	141	140	141	138	136	137	134	136	134	139
2019	138	138	142	134	132	135	131	129	125	127	128	127	132
2020[1]	134	136	136	128	135	135	129	127	121	121	122	126	129

[1] Preliminary. *Source: Economic Research Service, U.S. Department of Agriculture (ERS-USDA)*

Federally Inspected Slaughter of Goats in the United States In Thousands of Head

Year	Jan.	Feb.	Mar.	Apr.	May	June	July	Aug.	Sept.	Oct.	Nov.	Dec.	Total
2012	43.3	38.4	44.1	45.9	45.5	44.6	52.0	54.3	44.4	52.5	44.6	48.3	557.9
2013	39.8	34.0	44.8	42.0	44.7	40.7	53.3	48.6	43.7	49.5	41.6	45.3	528.0
2014	35.4	31.5	36.4	41.6	39.8	44.3	45.3	40.9	42.7	43.9	37.2	47.4	486.5
2015	34.9	28.3	38.2	35.5	33.8	40.1	38.5	37.2	40.4	36.5	36.2	41.7	441.3
2016	31.1	32.5	38.1	32.0	35.5	39.9	35.4	41.8	40.8	38.1	38.8	44.9	448.9
2017	36.9	32.2	36.8	38.1	45.1	42.9	38.9	43.9	41.7	43.2	42.4	46.7	488.8
2018	39.4	35.3	42.4	38.6	45.8	42.6	43.0	47.7	36.8	46.0	46.4	50.1	514.1
2019	42.9	36.6	41.0	48.1	49.3	40.0	47.7	48.2	44.4	48.9	46.3	52.2	545.6
2020[1]	43.2	37.6	44.4	36.1	39.9	43.4	44.9	41.7	44.3	46.0	45.2	51.1	517.8

[1] Preliminary. *Source: Economic Research Service, U.S. Department of Agriculture (ERS-USDA)*

Cold Storage Holdings of Lamb and Mutton in the United States, on First of Month In Thousands of Pounds

Year	Jan.	Feb.	Mar.	Apr.	May	June	July	Aug.	Sept.	Oct.	Nov.	Dec.
2012	16,857	19,275	20,851	21,846	19,711	19,680	22,460	24,291	24,233	23,453	23,210	18,978
2013	21,379	18,768	19,833	17,624	21,463	19,793	19,307	23,324	21,988	23,444	23,967	21,697
2014	24,508	25,658	26,191	28,076	26,536	25,208	31,119	33,968	40,157	39,693	38,686	31,366
2015	33,942	35,206	36,771	34,250	37,004	38,360	35,470	39,064	41,883	41,921	40,742	44,693
2016	41,452	47,111	40,051	40,648	39,787	44,816	39,518	40,979	36,563	32,736	29,439	21,876
2017	26,140	20,361	25,694	25,792	28,603	29,859	26,177	26,770	32,383	31,415	31,594	28,977
2018	26,714	26,790	28,280	28,615	33,992	35,591	38,678	42,129	39,386	40,466	39,321	37,859
2019	36,454	38,376	35,503	31,026	40,949	38,484	40,025	43,052	46,642	41,648	37,805	34,022
2020[1]	34,752	36,856	37,379	37,575	40,790	48,023	46,524	44,712	39,466	30,668	25,731	25,917

[1] Preliminary. *Source: Economic Research Service, U.S. Department of Agriculture (ERS-USDA)*

Silk

Silk is a fine, tough, elastic fiber produced by caterpillars, commonly called silkworms. Silk is one of the oldest known textile fibers. Chinese tradition credits Lady Hsi-Ling-Shih, wife of the Emperor Huang Ti, with the discovery of the silkworm and the invention of the first silk reel. A group of ribbons, threads, and woven silk fragments were found in China dating back to 3000 BC. Also found, along the lower Yangzi River, were 7,000-year-old spinning tools, silk thread, and fabric fragments.

Silk filament was first woven into cloth in Ancient China. The Chinese successfully guarded this secret until 300AD, when Japan, and later India, learned the secret. In 550 AD, two Nestorian monks were sent to China to steal mulberry seeds and silkworm eggs, which they hid in their walking staffs, and then brought them back to Rome. By the 17th century, France was the silk center of the West. Unfortunately, the silkworm did not flourish in the English climate, nor has it ever flourished in the U.S.

Sericulture is the term for the raising of silkworms. The blind, flightless moth, Bombyx mori, lays more than 500 tiny eggs. After hatching, the tiny worms eat chopped mulberry leaves continuously until they are ready to spin their cocoons. After gathering the complete cocoons, the first step in silk manufacturing is to kill the insects inside the cocoons with heat. The cocoons are then placed in boiling water to loosen the gummy substance, sericin, holding the filament together. The filament is unwound, and then rewound in a process called reeling. Each cocoon's silk filament is between 600 and 900 meters long. Four different types of silk thread may be produced: organzine, crepe, tram, and thrown singles. During the last 30 years, despite the use of man-made fibers, world silk production has doubled.

Raw silk is traded on the Kansai Agricultural Commodities Exchange (KANEX) in Japan. Dried cocoons are traded on the Chuba Commodity Exchange (CCE). Raw silk and dried cocoons are traded on the Yokohama Commodity Exchange.

Supply – World production of raw silk in 2018, rose + 0.7% yr/y to 175.337 metric tons, just below the 2015 record high of 178.213 metric tons. China is the world's largest silk producer by far, with a 78.2% share of world production in 2018. Another key producer is India, with 17.1% of world production.

Trade – In 2019, the world's largest exporter of silk was China, with 59.5 % of world exports. Others were not available. In 2017, the world's largest importers of silk were India with 40.1% of world imports, Italy with 11.2%, and Japan with 3.6%.

World Production of Raw Silk In Metric Tons

Year	Brazil	China	India	Iran	Japan	Korea, North	Korea, South	Kyrgyzstan	Thailand	Turkmenistan	Uzbekistan	Vietnam	World Total
2009	793	127,631	18,370	919	71	400	3	50	1,600	4,500	1,665	1,105	155,152
2010	584	125,831	19,690	908	58	400	3	50	1,600	4,500	1,637	1,066	154,372
2011	515	122,392	20,410	911	47	400	3	50	1,600	4,500	1,715	1,059	151,651
2012	437	125,800	23,060	902	44	400	3	50	1,600	4,500	1,740	1,128	157,709
2013	433	129,190	23,679	902	37	400	3	50	1,600	4,500	1,841	954	161,634
2014	429	126,001	23,679	900	33	----	3	50	1,600	4,500	1,200	6,761	163,602
2015	481	135,233	28,708	901	30	----	3	50	1,600	----	1,721	6,543	178,213
2016	457	134,366	28,523	914	29	----	3	50	1,600	----	1,845	1,040	171,761
2017[1]	486	135,696	30,348	920	28	----	3	50	1,600	----	874	1,103	174,043
2018[2]	489	137,027	30,000	900	24	----	3	50	1,600	----	1,254	1,050	175,337

[1] Preliminary. [2] Estimate. NA = Not avaliable. *Source: Food and Agricultural Organization of the United Nations (FAO-UN)*

World Trade of Silk by Selected Countries In Metric Tons

	Imports							Exports					
Year	France	Hong Kong	India	Italy	Japan	Korea, South	World Total	Brazil	China	Hong Kong	Japan	Korea, South	World Total
2010	109	34	4,525	698	737	645	9,992	6	8,543	34	36	57	10,406
2011	110	9	5,597	711	563	533	16,803	----	7,122	----	35	59	8,608
2012	135	----	5,235	692	607	503	21,161	----	7,676	2	25	245	9,158
2013	248	----	3,609	676	570	410	24,917	----	6,690	----	18	118	8,454
2014	230	----	3,403	785	497	346	8,264	----	6,359	----	1	73	8,647
2015	185	----	3,454	733	391	313	8,906	----	6,695	----	----	17	8,921
2016	156	----	3,757	710	395	310	9,650	----	6,927	----	----	97	9,206
2017	185	----	4,003	607	456	271	8,881	----	5,936	----	----	----	9,503
2018	236	----	2,728	660	303	184	7,505	----	4,581	----	----	----	6,704
2019[1]	131	----	3,264	911	292	138	8,144	----	4,305	----	----	----	7,237

[1] Preliminary. *Source: Food and Agricultural Organization of the United Nations (FAO-UN)*

Silver

Silver is a white, lustrous metallic element that conducts heat and electricity better than any other metal. In ancient times, many silver deposits were near the earth's surface. Before 2,500 BC, silver mines were worked in Asia Minor. Around 700 BC, ancient Greeks stamped a turtle on their first silver coins. Silver assumed a key role in the U.S. monetary system in 1792 when Congress based the currency on the silver dollar. However, the U.S. discontinued the use of silver in coinage in 1965. Today Mexico is the only country that uses silver in its circulating coinage.

Silver is the most malleable and ductile of all metals, apart from gold. Silver melts at about 962 degrees Celsius and boils at about 2212 degrees Celsius. Silver is not very chemically active, although tarnishing occurs when sulfur and sulfides attack silver, forming silver sulfide on the surface of the metal. Because silver is too soft in its pure form, a hardening agent, usually copper, is mixed into the silver. Copper is usually used as the hardening agent because it does not discolor the silver. The term "sterling silver" refers to silver that contains at least 925 parts of silver per thousand (92.5%) to 75 parts of copper (7.5%).

Silver is usually found combined with other elements in minerals and ores. In the U.S., silver is mined in conjunction with lead, copper, and zinc. In the U.S., Nevada, Idaho, Alaska, and Arizona are the leading silver-producing states. For industrial purposes, silver is used for photography, electrical appliances, glass, and as an antibacterial agent for the health industry.

Silver futures and options are traded at the CME Group and the London Metal Exchange (LME). Silver futures are traded on the Tokyo Commodity Exchange (TOCOM). The CME silver futures contract calls for the delivery of 5,000 troy ounces of silver (0.999 fineness) and is priced in terms of dollars and cents per troy ounce.

Prices – CME silver futures prices (Barchart.com symbol SI) traded sideways in Q1-2020 but then plunged to a 12-year low in March 2020 of $11.740 per troy ounce. A rally in the dollar index to a 4-year high in March undercut silver prices, as did the spread of the Covid pandemic, which forced lockdowns around the world that decimated industrial metals demand and silver prices. Silver prices snapped back and trended higher into August when they posted an 8-year high of $29.92 per troy ounce. Silver garnered safe-haven support from the pandemic along with a disruption in supplies as silver mining operations around the world were shut down as workers became infected with Covid. Record stimulus measures from global central banks to offset the pandemic's negative economic effects also spurred demand for silver and precious metals as a store of value. The dollar retreated to a 2-1/2-year low in December, which underpinned silver prices the rest of the year. Silver prices finished 2020 up sharply by +47% yr/yr at $26.41 per troy ounce.

Supply – World mine production of silver in 2020 fell by -5.7 yr/yr to 25,000 metric tons, down from the 2016 record high of 27,900. The world's largest mine producers in 2020 were Mexico with 22.4% of world production, Peru with 13.6%, China with 12.8%, Russia with 7.2%, and Poland, Chili, and Australia each with 5.2%. U.S. production of refined silver in 2020 (annualized through October) rose by +42.2% yr/yr to 6,773 metric tons, a new record high.

Trade – U.S. imports of silver bullion in 2020 (through October annualized) rose +50.7% yr/yr to 5,708 metric tons. The bulk of U.S. silver imports come from Mexico and Canada.

World Mine Production of Silver In Thousands of Kilograms (Metric Ton)

Year	Australia	Bolivia	Canada[3]	Chile	China	Kazak-hstan	Mexico	Peru	Poland	Russia	Sweden	United States	World Total[2]
2011	1,725	1,214	582	1,291	3,192	547	4,778	3,473	1,270	1,198	283	1,120	23,600
2012	1,727	1,207	657	1,195	3,639	545	5,353	3,481	1,284	1,384	309	1,060	24,900
2013	1,735	1,287	640	1,174	3,673	584	5,821	3,674	1,393	2,176	341	1,050	26,700
2014	1,888	1,398	495	1,572	3,568	475	5,766	3,768	1,384	2,360	383	1,180	27,800
2015	1,506	1,306	384	1,504	3,393	370	5,592	4,102	1,407	2,297	480	1,090	27,400
2016	1,434	1,353	405	1,497	3,496	414	5,409	4,375	1,482	2,200	499	1,150	27,900
2017	1,200	1,243	395	1,260	3,502	441	6,109	4,304	1,290	2,030	468	1,030	27,800
2018	1,220	1,190		1,370	3,570		6,120	4,160	1,470	2,100		934	26,900
2019[1]	1,330	1,160		1,350	3,440		5,920	3,860	1,470	2,000		977	26,500
2020[2]	1,300	1,100		1,300	3,200		5,600	3,400	1,300	1,800		1,000	25,000

[1] Preliminary. [2] Estimate. [3] Shipments. *Source: U.S. Geological Survey (USGS)*

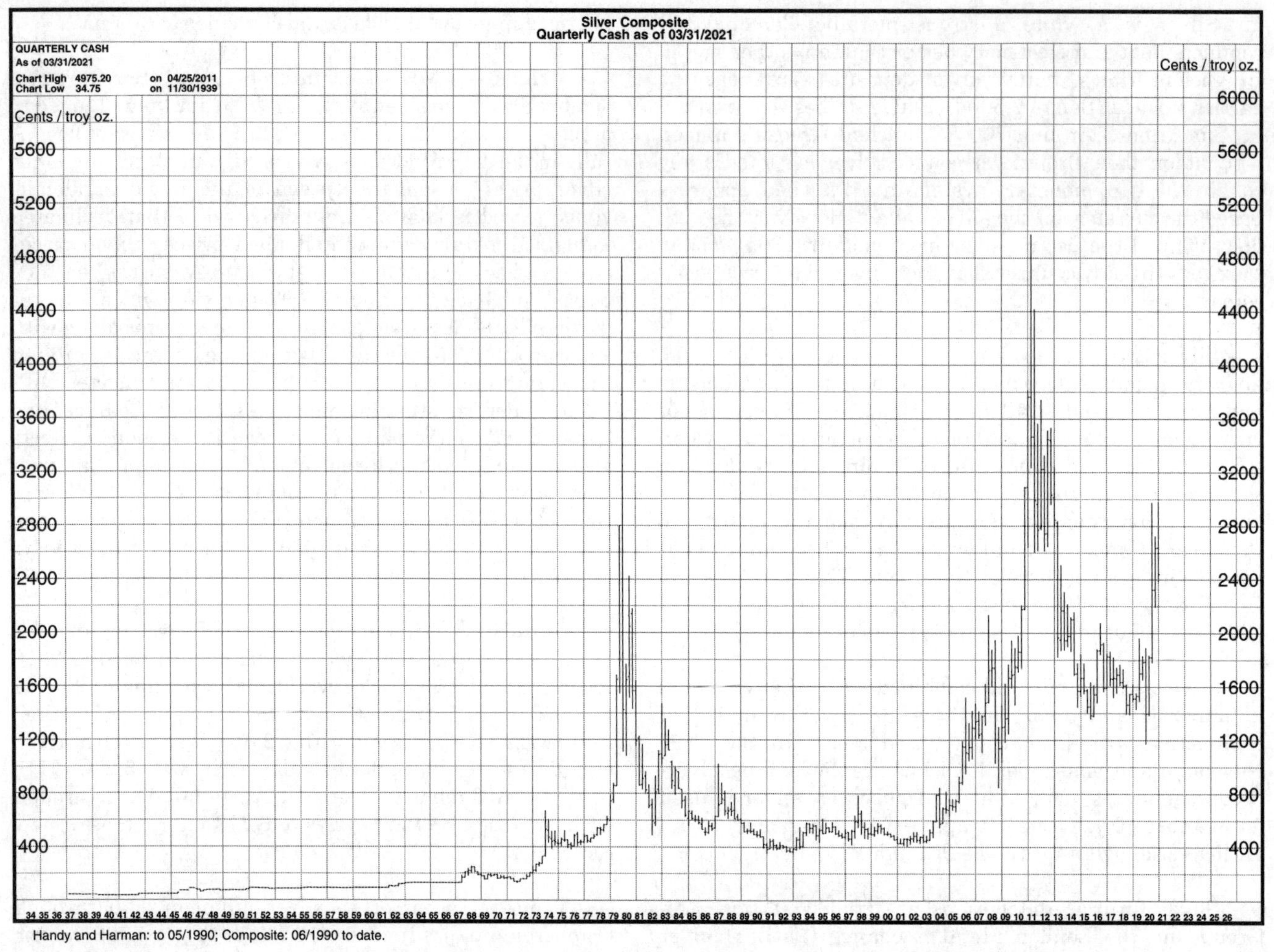

Handy and Harman: to 05/1990; Composite: 06/1990 to date.

Average Price of Silver in New York (Handy & Harman) In Cents Per Troy Ounce (.999 Fine)

Year	Jan.	Feb.	Mar.	Apr.	May	June	July	Aug.	Sept.	Oct.	Nov.	Dec.	Average
2011	2,855.15	3,085.61	3,594.61	4,264.45	3,702.67	3,584.09	3,832.95	4,035.17	3,802.10	3,206.33	3,336.08	3,028.07	3,527.27
2012	3,095.25	3,421.95	3,296.32	3,154.65	2,882.00	2,810.29	2,739.74	2,891.35	3,379.18	3,328.57	3,271.00	3,177.13	3,120.62
2013	3,112.05	3,027.53	2,878.90	2,525.25	2,301.95	2,111.53	1,968.66	2,208.02	2,249.40	2,201.43	2,072.35	1,962.29	2,384.95
2014	1,987.52	2,086.53	2,071.60	1,973.64	1,934.19	1,989.24	2,092.25	1,973.56	1,837.10	1,716.33	1,596.61	1,629.48	1,907.34
2015	1,723.55	1,678.71	1,624.00	1,634.00	1,683.28	1,607.45	1,505.32	1,494.12	1,475.02	1,581.25	1,445.22	1,408.55	1,571.71
2016	1,411.18	1,516.72	1,546.45	1,636.02	1,694.71	1,728.61	1,999.18	1,958.74	1,932.98	1,764.07	1,740.74	1,644.62	1,714.50
2017	1,690.20	1,793.32	1,761.96	1,803.34	1,674.48	1,693.11	1,615.20	1,695.17	1,743.15	1,694.14	1,697.71	1,616.50	1,706.52
2018	1,712.71	1,658.24	1,647.30	1,664.84	1,648.99	1,654.14	1,572.30	1,498.70	1,427.17	1,459.67	1,435.34	1,477.24	1,571.39
2019	1,562.42	1,581.46	1,530.03	1,505.51	1,466.25	1,503.71	1,579.11	1,722.40	1,815.96	1,764.53	1,716.41	1,714.00	1,621.82
2020	1,797.00	1,788.00	1,489.00	1,506.00	1,630.00	1,771.00	2,065.00	2,700.00	2,574.00	2,423.00	2,408.00	2,497.00	2,054.00

Source: American Metal Market (AMM)

Average Price of Silver in London (Spot Fix) In Pence Per Troy Ounce (.999 Fine)

Year	Jan.	Feb.	Mar.	Apr.	May	June	July	Aug.	Sept.	Oct.	Nov.	Dec.	Average
2011	1,808.34	1,912.09	2,224.65	2,602.69	2,266.24	2,209.81	2,373.37	2,466.59	2,410.10	2,032.85	2,111.63	1,942.66	2,196.75
2012	1,994.05	2,164.96	2,082.42	1,970.51	1,811.54	1,806.56	1,756.42	1,839.55	2,097.22	2,070.91	2,049.00	1,967.97	1,967.59
2013	1,949.80	1,957.31	1,908.68	1,649.50	1,505.82	1,362.47	1,296.54	1,424.04	1,416.94	1,368.26	1,286.22	1,197.73	1,526.94
2014	1,206.90	1,259.53	1,246.67	1,178.50	1,148.47	1,175.94	1,225.31	1,181.77	1,126.82	1,067.60	1,012.22	1,042.49	1,156.02
2015	1,138.45	1,094.75	1,084.93	1,092.25	1,089.22	1,031.34	967.53	958.94	961.93	1,031.14	951.23	940.07	1,028.48
2016	980.88	1,060.00	1,084.79	1,142.90	1,166.93	1,216.44	1,520.83	1,494.89	1,470.13	1,430.05	1,399.15	1,318.71	1,273.81
2017	1,368.47	1,436.17	1,426.87	1,426.35	1,295.78	1,321.55	1,242.52	1,308.41	1,309.00	1,283.21	1,283.06	1,205.93	1,325.61
2018	1,238.59	1,187.71	1,178.66	1,183.28	1,224.89	1,245.10	1,193.92	1,163.69	1,093.05	1,121.87	1,113.01	1,166.61	1,175.87
2019	1,210.50	1,215.42	1,161.38	1,155.60	1,142.05	1,186.50	1,267.14	1,417.60	1,470.10	1,394.21	1,332.48	1,308.15	1,271.76
2020	1,374.49	1,380.56	1,205.21	1,213.03	1,326.14	1,413.94	1,628.04	2,055.69	1,987.14	1,867.73	1,822.36	1,857.07	1,594.28

Source: American Metal Market (AMM)

Nearby Futures through Last Trading Day.

Volume of Trading of Silver Futures in Chicago In Thousands of Contracts

Year	Jan.	Feb.	Mar.	Apr.	May	June	July	Aug.	Sept.	Oct.	Nov.	Dec.	Total
2011	1,429.7	1,674.7	1,685.7	3,014.6	2,461.1	1,768.9	1,325.0	1,982.8	1,220.4	952.6	1,327.4	765.6	19,608.6
2012	826.9	1,478.7	1,120.1	1,224.1	1,028.2	1,416.8	804.5	1,231.9	1,068.8	874.2	1,437.3	804.2	13,315.7
2013	1,021.7	1,346.4	780.3	1,980.5	1,172.0	1,555.4	932.3	1,652.5	958.1	948.4	1,270.3	857.7	14,475.6
2014	915.0	1,498.8	973.7	1,388.9	883.1	1,459.4	957.2	1,216.7	990.8	1,013.7	1,435.1	964.7	13,697.2
2015	979.5	1,196.0	875.8	1,431.4	886.3	1,499.6	988.4	1,511.0	822.3	1,107.5	1,291.7	864.9	13,454.4
2016	960.5	1,694.2	1,212.5	1,974.1	1,183.6	1,828.3	1,458.7	1,939.3	1,290.1	1,327.6	2,214.4	1,135.5	18,218.7
2017	1,414.0	1,809.3	1,495.9	2,120.9	1,904.5	2,371.5	1,829.7	2,604.7	1,730.4	1,826.4	2,539.5	1,388.1	23,035.0
2018	2,186.6	2,155.7	1,842.3	2,625.8	1,702.2	2,486.3	1,582.4	2,364.1	1,648.3	1,793.5	2,299.1	1,300.6	23,987.1
2019	1,526.3	1,783.6	1,418.5	1,920.3	1,476.3	2,651.2	2,087.0	3,018.6	2,579.9	1,810.5	2,334.3	1,542.7	24,149.1
2020	2,012.7	2,515.3	2,275.1	1,357.8	1,210.9	1,846.7	2,623.6	4,633.8	2,183.5	1,645.6	2,139.7	1,682.0	26,126.8

Contract size = 5,000 oz. *Source: CME Group; Commodity Exchange (COMEX)*

Average Open Interest of Silver Futures in Chicago In Contracts

Year	Jan.	Feb.	Mar.	Apr.	May	June	July	Aug.	Sept.	Oct.	Nov.	Dec.
2011	133,030	138,901	135,793	143,245	124,278	118,740	115,246	117,217	109,908	103,939	107,600	100,220
2012	103,766	108,478	110,777	117,254	113,514	122,240	122,555	124,907	125,957	140,254	145,146	141,906
2013	143,032	141,751	149,900	156,813	145,964	147,042	133,417	130,278	113,116	116,266	130,050	133,668
2014	137,682	145,743	141,847	157,064	152,154	161,079	161,447	161,613	168,883	172,012	169,706	148,854
2015	158,200	167,554	171,411	177,026	176,403	190,678	190,121	173,457	155,598	164,457	167,660	164,215
2016	161,725	167,337	170,875	190,935	203,017	203,311	217,206	207,634	197,360	192,183	177,922	161,707
2017	172,215	198,811	194,560	220,791	202,476	203,230	207,098	192,201	187,569	190,554	198,941	199,229
2018	197,597	198,883	207,295	218,714	199,496	220,429	212,471	233,201	206,398	201,730	211,615	175,572
2019	189,481	213,207	191,157	210,647	206,496	226,614	227,668	234,590	215,936	214,545	220,824	211,176
2020	233,640	228,860	169,311	140,127	145,645	175,076	179,905	192,625	159,633	157,366	157,744	161,855

Contract size = 5,000 oz. *Source: CME Group; Commodity Exchange (COMEX)*

Mine Production of Recoverable Silver in the United States In Metric Tons

Year	Arizona	Idaho	Montana	Nevada	New Mexico	Other States	U.S. Total
2011	W	W	W	209	W	913	1,120
2012	W	W	W	250	W	805	1,060
2013	W	W	W	255	W	791	1,050
2014	W	W	W	326	W	858	1,180
2015	W	W	W	296	W	777	1,070
2016	W	W	W	276	W	871	1,150
2017	W	W	W	265	W	766	1,030
2018	W	W	W	247	W	687	934
2019	W	W	W	188	W	787	975
2020[1]	W	W	W	149	W	837	986

[1] Preliminary. W = Withheld proprietary data; included in "Other States". *Source: U.S. Geological Survey (USGS)*

Production[2] of Refined Silver in the United States, from All Sources In Metric Tons

Year	Jan.	Feb.	Mar.	Apr.	May	June	July	Aug.	Sept.	Oct.	Nov.	Dec.	U.S. Total
2011	626	512	748	477	485	462	493	491	499	522	426	634	6,375
2012	559	443	443	419	457	426	423	375	344	385	407	393	5,073
2013	505	438	421	486	376	337	415	365	364	450	292	431	4,880
2014	431	334	348	399	450	418	458	386	506	456	430	474	5,080
2015	515	507	473	505	434	479	467	498	453	480	390	547	5,750
2016	496	476	581	507	496	429	455	575	545	503	475	481	6,020
2017	507	497	398	461	390	426	485	348	326	374	425	345	4,980
2018	480	380	317	357	458	304	395	424	383	392	382	412	4,684
2019	415	356	419	426	375	301	377	488	425	417	375	390	4,764
2020[1]	398	322	380	470	444	606	1,076	543	746	577	643	590	6,796

[1] Preliminary. [2] Includes U.S. mine production of recoverable silver plus imports of refined silver. *Source: U.S. Geological Survey (USGS)*

Mine Production of Recoverable Silver in the United States In Metric Tons

Year	Jan.	Feb.	Mar.	Apr.	May	June	July	Aug.	Sept.	Oct.	Nov.	Dec.	U.S. Total
2011	98.1	85.2	103.0	95.2	99.3	92.6	91.5	91.0	88.4	84.7	90.2	103.0	1,122.2
2012	83.0	78.7	85.5	80.9	84.0	88.5	85.4	91.0	84.5	85.0	94.3	101.0	1,041.8
2013	88.8	84.2	88.5	90.2	89.6	91.5	90.3	86.2	83.9	86.4	79.0	88.3	1,046.9
2014	95.5	86.2	95.5	94.2	102.0	90.8	106.0	101.0	103.0	103.0	105.0	110.0	1,180.0
2015	94.2	90.1	99.5	89.8	90.6	87.5	88.0	90.8	83.6	93.9	89.2	94.2	1,090.0
2016	94.0	95.4	98.0	92.2	93.8	90.6	91.0	104.0	98.5	100.0	94.6	96.1	1,150.0
2017	98.4	84.1	94.3	87.5	82.9	85.4	84.7	83.6	74.5	82.4	87.6	82.4	1,030.0
2018	75.1	67.6	69.7	73.7	76.5	79.4	73.6	80.1	78.7	87.2	80.0	88.3	934.0
2019	80.7	71.2	75.6	84.3	84.1	84.2	86.7	83.2	85.2	75.1	87.0	77.8	975.1
2020[1]	80.1	77.1	77.1	70.5	75.9	75.3	88.2	87.3	86.2	88.4	86.1	93.5	985.7

[1] Preliminary. *Source: U.S. Geological Survey (USGS)*

Mine Production of Recoverable Silver in Nevada In Metric Tons

Year	Jan.	Feb.	Mar.	Apr.	May	June	July	Aug.	Sept.	Oct.	Nov.	Dec.	U.S. Total
2011	18.8	16.8	19.9	18.0	17.9	19.6	16.8	17.2	14.0	14.8	17.6	17.6	209.0
2012	15.8	16.5	19.3	21.0	23.6	20.8	19.1	23.5	19.9	22.1	24.3	24.1	250.0
2013	21.1	18.4	20.6	23.6	21.0	22.0	17.7	23.1	20.9	23.0	19.5	24.2	255.1
2014	25.0	23.9	26.5	24.9	29.2	28.3	29.1	29.1	28.3	29.9	29.6	31.1	326.0
2015	25.1	23.7	25.6	26.0	26.2	25.3	24.8	24.2	22.5	22.8	21.5	22.9	290.0
2016	22.1	20.7	21.6	22.6	22.9	22.0	23.5	24.3	23.6	23.9	24.5	25.8	276.0
2017	23.1	22.1	22.1	22.2	22.8	23.1	20.7	19.4	19.2	21.5	22.6	23.2	265.0
2018	18.8	18.4	19.6	19.4	18.9	19.2	19.9	20.3	20.4	22.8	21.7	23.7	247.0
2019	16.2	14.6	15.7	14.9	16.0	15.9	16.2	16.1	15.8	15.5	15.8	15.7	188.4
2020[1]	12.2	12.4	12.5	12.3	12.5	12.8	12.2	12.3	12.5	12.0	12.6	12.7	149.0

[1] Preliminary. *Source: U.S. Geological Survey (USGS)*

U.S. Imports of Silver Bullion In Metric Tons

Year	Jan.	Feb.	Mar.	Apr.	May	June	July	Aug.	Sept.	Oct.	Nov.	Dec.	U.S. Total
2011	528.0	427.0	645.0	382.0	386.0	369.0	401.0	400.0	411.0	437.0	336.0	531.0	5,253.0
2012	476.0	364.0	357.0	338.0	373.0	337.0	338.0	284.0	259.0	300.0	313.0	292.0	4,031.0
2013	416.0	354.0	332.0	396.0	286.0	245.0	325.0	279.0	280.0	364.0	213.0	343.0	3,833.0
2014	335.0	248.0	252.0	305.0	348.0	327.0	352.0	285.0	403.0	353.0	325.0	364.0	3,900.0
2015	421.0	417.0	373.0	415.0	343.0	391.0	379.0	407.0	369.0	386.0	301.0	453.0	4,660.0
2016	402.0	381.0	483.0	415.0	402.0	338.0	364.0	471.0	446.0	403.0	380.0	385.0	4,870.0
2017	409.0	413.0	304.0	373.0	307.0	341.0	400.0	264.0	251.0	292.0	337.0	263.0	3,950.0
2018	405.0	312.0	247.0	283.0	381.0	225.0	321.0	344.0	304.0	305.0	302.0	324.0	3,750.0
2019	334.0	285.0	343.0	342.0	291.0	217.0	290.0	405.0	340.0	342.0	288.0	312.0	3,789.0
2020[1]	318.0	245.0	303.0	399.0	368.0	531.0	988.0	456.0	660.0	489.0	557.0	496.0	5,810.0

[1] Preliminary. *Source: U.S. Geological Survey (USGS)*

Commodity Exchange Warehouse of Stocks of Silver, on First of Month In Thousands of Troy Ounces

Year	Jan. 1	Feb. 1	Mar. 1	Apr. 1	May 1	June 1	July 1	Aug. 1	Sept. 1	Oct. 1	Nov. 1	Dec. 1
2011	104,548	103,594	102,549	105,495	102,014	100,968	101,720	104,176	104,085	106,012	107,096	110,415
2012	126,218	129,403	130,318	137,073	142,125	143,150	145,933	139,218	140,678	142,047	142,362	145,284
2013	148,205	154,577	162,830	164,163	166,050	165,749	166,746	164,711	163,771	165,329	169,012	169,985
2014	173,927	179,297	182,831	179,791	174,483	175,267	175,517	175,317	179,292	182,194	181,185	177,008
2015	174,359	178,053	177,163	176,650	176,310	179,287	182,384	175,671	170,562	165,009	162,813	158,954
2016	160,671	158,266	154,261	154,999	151,780	153,898	151,481	154,090	162,921	173,354	173,583	178,616
2017	183,006	180,805	186,606	190,223	196,524	201,367	208,937	215,512	217,741	218,121	225,904	235,906
2018	244,724	246,977	251,320	260,510	262,948	270,519	275,911	286,599	295,357	289,725	290,258	295,015
2019	293,901	298,005	298,844	305,542	306,750	304,961	305,683	310,364	311,900	313,603	315,503	314,008
2020	317,166	321,312	324,302	321,002	316,635	311,570	321,179	334,509	344,970	375,203	381,797	388,052

Source: CME Group; Commodity Exchange (COMEX)

U.S. Exports of Refined Silver In Kilograms

Year	Australia	Canada	Germany	Hong Kong	India	Italy	Japan	Mexico	Singa-pore	Switzer-land	United Arab Emirates	United Kingdom	Total
2008	37,300	123,000	38,500	----	106,000	328	65,800	1,360	----	750	----	25,100	413,000
2009	76,100	12,100	35,900	4,580	----	19	51	29,900	1,360	3,720	----	164	167,000
2010	97,300	104,000	33,000	4,320	----	43	38,600	218,000	8,590	2,070	----	12,100	523,000
2011	20,700	98,400	6,030	8,830	----	237	148,000	288,000	9,700	823	1,100	19,500	625,000
2012	27,800	79,200	16,900	5,670	19,100	115	86,200	250,000	4,010	12,100	270	320,000	837,000
2013	124,000	77,300	8,760	4,030	36,300	302	----	76,300	11,800	64	28	73	347,000
2014	55,300	200,000	1,190	1,330	1,180	3,410	----	62,400	9,820	1,090	198	1,550	346,000
2015	24,000	430,000	8,720	2,720	284,000	5,880	----	8,650	6,560	1,700	----	2,690	781,000
2016	18,800	136,000	10,400	1,050	39,300	1,460	----	7,330	6,120	3,300	----	1,590	237,000
2017[1]	7,620	55,700	5,380	136	2,000	2,750	36	3,470	4,630		28	1,070	91,800

[1] Preliminary. *Source: U.S. Geological Survey (USGS)*

U.S. Imports of Silver From Selected Countries In Kilograms

	Ores and Concentrates				Refined Bullion						
Year	Canada	Mexico	Other Countries	Total	Canada	Korea, South	Mexico	Peru	Poland	United Kingdom	Total
2008	----	----	----	32	781,000	----	2,610,000	645,000	----	274	4,440,000
2009	----	----	----	87	747,000	36,100	2,050,000	261,000	----	534	3,450,000
2010	3,230	----	----	3,230	1,590,000	----	2,580,000	801,000	311,000	454,000	5,370,000
2011	84,200	----	----	84,200	1,340,000	207,000	2,760,000	109,000	780,000	20,500	6,410,000
2012	73,800	7,770	----	82,700	1,420,000	55,600	3,080,000	142,000	36,700	973	5,140,000
2013	26	10,700	----	10,700	1,600,000	36,300	2,880,000	181,000	55,500	20,700	5,030,000
2014	----	----	59	59	1,120,000	333,000	2,920,000	196,000	77,000	41,100	4,960,000
2015	----	----	----	253	1,920,000	159,000	2,850,000	285,000	234,000	3,050	5,930,000
2016	4,430	203	[3]	4,630	1,740,000	188,000	2,770,000	407,000	265,000	22,200	6,160,000
2017[1]	5,940	803	90	6,840	1,180,000	126,000	2,480,000	313,000	175,000	55,400	5,050,000

[1] Preliminary. [3] Less than 1/2 unit.. *Source: U.S. Geological Survey (USGS)*

Soybean Meal

Soybean meal is produced through processing and separating soybeans into oil and meal components. If the soybeans are of particularly good quality, then the processor can get more meal weight by including more hulls in the meal while still meeting a 48% protein minimum. Soybean meal can be further processed into soy flour and isolated soy protein, but the bulk of soybean meal is used as animal feed for poultry, hogs, and cattle. Soybean meal accounts for about two-thirds of the world's high-protein animal feed, followed by cottonseed and rapeseed meal, which together account for less than 20%. Soybean meal consumption has been moving to record highs in recent years. The soybean meal marketing year begins in October and ends in September. Soybean meal futures and options are traded at the CME Group. The CME soybean meal futures contract calls for the delivery of 100 tons of soybean meal produced by conditioning ground soybeans and reducing the oil content of the conditioned product and having a minimum of 48.0% protein, minimum of 0.5% fat, maximum of 3.5% fiber, and maximum of 12.0% moisture.

Soybean crush – The term soybean "crush" refers to both to the physical processing of soybeans and to the dollar-value premium received for processing soybeans into their component products of meal and oil. The conventional model says that processing 60 pounds (one bushel) of soybeans produces 11 pounds of soybean oil, 44 pounds of 48% protein soybean meal, 3 pounds of hulls, and 1 pound of waste. The Gross Processing Margin (GPM) or crush equals (0.22 times Soybean Meal Prices in dollars per ton) + (11 times Soybean Oil prices in cents/pound) – Soybean prices in $/bushel. A higher crush value will occur when the price of the meal and oil products are strong relative to soybeans, e.g., because of supply disruptions or because of an increase in demand for the products. When the crush value is high, companies will have a strong incentive to buy raw soybeans and boost the output of the products. That supply increase should eventually bring the crush value back into line with the long-term equilibrium.

Prices – CME soybean meal futures prices (Barchart.com electronic symbol ZM) opened the year 2020 at about $309.5 per short ton, fell to a 4-year low of about $284 in May, and then moved steadily higher the rest of the year to close the year up +49.8% at about $463.2 per short ton. The price started to fall early in 2021.

Supply – World soybean meal production in 2020/21 is expected to rise +4.0% yr/yr to a new record high of 252.785 million metric tons. The world's largest soybean meal producers are expected to be China with 31.0% of world production in 2020/21, the U.S. with 18.6%, Brazil with 14.0%, and Argentina with 11.8%.

U.S. production of soybean meal in 2020/21 is expected to rise +1.7% yr/yr to 51.959 million short tons, a new record high. U.S. soybean meal ending stocks in 2020/21 are expected to rise +2.6% yr/yr to 350,000 short tons.

Demand – World consumption of soybean meal in 2020/21 is expected to rise +4.1% yr/yr to 250.957 million metric tons, a new record high. China is expected to account for 30.9% of that consumption, the U.S. for 13.8%, and the European Union for 12.4%. U.S. consumption of soybean meal in 2018/19 is expected to rise +1.5% yr/yr to 34.745 million metric tons, a new record high.

Trade – World exports of soybean meal in 2020/21 is expected to fall -1.6% to 65.970 million metric tons. Argentina is expected to account for 39.9% of total world exports, Brazil for 25.5%, and the U.S. for 19.6%. World imports of soybean meal in 2020/21 are expected to rise +0.1% yr/yr to 62.812 million metric tons, a record high. U.S. exports of soybean meal in 2020/21 are expected to rise +1.2% yr/yr to 14.250 million short tons, a record high. U.S. imports of soybean meal in 2020/21 are expected to fall -6.1% yr/yr to 600,000 short tons.

Supply and Distribution of Soybean Meal in the United States In Thousands of Short Tons

	Supply			Distribution			Dollars Per Metric Ton			
Crop Year Beginning Oct. 1	For Stocks Oct. 1	Production	Total Supply	Domestic	Exports	Total	Decatur 48% Protein Solvent	Decatur 44% Protein Solvent	Brazil FOB 45-46% Protein	Rotterdam CIF
2011-12	350	41,025	39,731	31,548	9,743	41,291	393.53	434	442	461
2012-13	300	39,875	41,591	29,031	11,114	40,145	468.11	516	489	538
2013-14	275	40,685	40,420	29,547	11,546	41,093	489.94	540	500	533
2014-15	250	45,062	41,343	32,277	13,108	45,384	368.49	406	376	403
2015-16	260	44,672	45,645	33,118	11,954	45,072	324.56	358	335	351
2016-17	264	44,787	45,336	33,420	11,580	45,000	316.88	349	322	336
2017-18	401	49,226	45,400	35,497	14,057	49,554	345.02	380	368	382
2018-19[1]	555	48,814	50,121	36,212	13,438	49,651	308.28	340	325	329
2019-20[2]	402	51,100	50,053	37,723	14,077	51,800	305.00	332	319	325
2020-21[3]	341	51,959	50,375	38,300	14,250	52,250				

[1] Preliminary. [2] Estimate. [3] Forecast. *Source: Economic Research Service, U.S. Department of Agriculture (ERS-USDA)*

World Production of Soybean Meal In Thousands of Metric Tons

Crop Year	Argentina	Bolivia	Brazil	China	European Union	India	Japan	Mexico	Para-guay	Russia	Taiwan	United States	World Total
2011-12	27,945	1,580	29,510	48,312	9,164	8,240	1,483	2,910	706	1,655	1,588	37,217	180,941
2012-13	26,089	1,700	27,310	51,480	10,033	8,640	1,447	2,890	2,315	1,734	1,510	36,174	182,296
2013-14	27,892	1,760	28,540	54,569	10,349	6,960	1,487	3,185	2,787	2,600	1,513	36,909	190,527
2014-15	30,928	1,915	31,300	59,004	11,416	6,160	1,627	3,300	2,905	2,837	1,555	40,880	208,412
2015-16	33,211	1,995	30,750	64,548	11,811	4,400	1,723	3,480	2,983	3,152	1,555	40,525	216,090
2016-17	33,280	1,995	31,280	69,696	11,376	7,200	1,805	3,635	2,940	3,467	1,606	40,630	225,723
2017-18	28,400	1,800	34,300	71,280	11,811	6,160	1,811	4,152	3,040	3,625	1,688	44,657	232,276
2018-19	31,200	1,995	32,960	67,320	12,324	7,680	1,863	4,860	2,800	3,664	1,767	44,283	233,618
2019-20[1]	29,800	1,955	34,350	72,468	12,917	6,720	1,855	4,900	2,675	3,664	1,850	46,358	243,076
2020-21[2]	29,950	1,975	35,275	78,408	13,311	7,600	1,900	5,060	2,940	3,703	1,890	47,136	252,785

Crop year beginning October 1. [1] Preliminary. [2] Forecast. *Source: Foreign Agricultural Service, U.S. Department of Agriculture (FAS-USDA)*

World Exports of Soybean Meal In Thousands of Metric Tons

Crop Year	Argen-tina	Bolivia	Brazil	Canada	China	European Union	India	Korea, South	Norway	Para-guay	Russia	United States	World Total
2011-12	26,043	1,208	14,678	173	966	884	4,877	38	165	505	10	8,845	58,705
2012-13	23,667	1,562	13,242	245	1,365	536	4,943	115	148	2,020	92	10,111	58,469
2013-14	24,972	1,608	13,948	241	2,017	296	3,252	179	153	2,428	526	10,504	60,867
2014-15	28,575	1,674	14,290	212	1,595	362	1,521	112	175	2,569	505	11,891	64,657
2015-16	30,333	1,726	15,407	335	1,909	304	409	76	198	2,561	480	10,843	65,903
2016-17	31,323	1,289	13,762	291	1,111	334	2,019	100	181	2,370	323	10,505	64,986
2017-18	26,265	1,653	16,032	357	1,198	395	1,863	41	182	2,628	384	12,717	65,327
2018-19	28,833	1,638	16,093	425	932	374	2,185	71	157	2,333	374	12,191	67,729
2019-20[1]	27,367	1,600	17,499	329	1,012	359	850	44	195	2,200	557	12,770	67,038
2020-21[2]	26,300	1,665	16,800	370	1,000	300	1,870	60	165	2,450	350	12,927	65,970

Crop year beginning October 1. [1] Preliminary. [2] Forecast. *Source: Foreign Agricultural Service, U.S. Department of Agriculture (FAS-USDA)*

World Imports of Soybean Meal In Thousands of Metric Tons

Crop Year	Algeria	European Union	Indo-nesia	Iran	Japan	Korea, South	Malaysia	Mexico	Peru	Philip-pines	Thailand	Vietnam	World Total
2011-12	861	20,872	3,278	2,192	2,282	1,571	1,078	1,548	1,113	1,879	2,936	2,276	57,014
2012-13	1,333	16,941	3,600	2,099	1,765	1,654	1,276	1,295	1,099	1,968	2,874	2,981	54,437
2013-14	1,441	18,140	3,806	2,683	1,976	1,825	1,397	1,410	1,173	2,335	2,665	3,344	58,198
2014-15	1,132	19,623	3,844	1,948	1,699	1,751	1,465	1,795	1,145	2,204	3,068	4,311	60,907
2015-16	1,488	19,213	4,203	1,420	1,721	2,118	1,291	2,367	1,277	2,617	2,433	5,094	62,655
2016-17	1,242	18,793	4,255	1,623	1,621	1,764	1,427	2,064	1,327	2,660	2,782	4,945	61,011
2017-18	1,513	18,367	4,486	1,544	1,728	1,846	1,609	1,875	1,353	2,886	3,191	4,969	62,414
2018-19	1,371	18,755	4,449	2,542	1,596	1,855	1,278	1,887	1,345	2,897	2,889	5,149	62,815
2019-20[1]	1,143	17,616	5,043	1,600	1,858	1,992	1,414	1,843	1,445	2,875	2,854	5,150	62,777
2020-21[2]	900	18,050	4,950	1,600	1,700	2,020	1,450	1,925	1,465	2,900	2,800	5,200	62,812

Crop year beginning October 1. [1] Preliminary. [2] Forecast. *Source: Foreign Agricultural Service, U.S. Department of Agriculture (FAS-USDA)*

U.S. Exports of Soybean Cake & Meal by Country of Destination In Thousands of Metric Tons

Year	Algeria	Australia	Canada	Dominican Republic	Italy	Japan	Mexico	Nether-lands	Philip-pines	Russia	Spain	Vene-zuela	Total
2011	17.4	0.5	1,048.5	358.4	33.7	338.6	1,423.7	0.4	869.5	22.6	0.2	636.1	7,821
2012	16.5	41.8	1,073.0	393.9	63.2	211.6	1,343.0	0.2	1,305.9	25.1	50.5	705.8	9,691
2013	17.3	69.0	895.1	331.6	229.6	180.2	1,269.5	0.9	1,120.1	0.1	198.4	755.1	10,133
2014	3.0	0.1	971.6	374.4	253.0	211.0	1,593.3	1.6	1,104.3	15.0	267.0	842.6	10,281
2015	30.6	0.2	805.4	472.8	75.2	174.4	2,001.4	10.3	1,509.2	----	315.5	540.9	11,394
2016	27.3	0.5	755.9	506.2	0.4	158.4	2,130.3	1.1	1,847.2	----	0.0	311.9	10,539
2017	15.1	0.7	894.6	489.4	2.0	250.0	1,598.3	2.5	2,041.1	----	114.3	301.8	10,585
2018	----	0.6	979.9	491.5	125.1	330.6	1,760.3	4.5	2,156.7	----	354.7	182.8	12,852
2019	----	0.4	961.3	543.4	106.1	336.1	1,758.5	4.4	2,136.0	----	70.0	150.3	12,106
2020[1]	----	30.5	1,120.4	481.0	----	226.3	1,771.0	3.0	2,429.5	----	224.3	244.4	12,938

[1] Preliminary. *Source: Foreign Agricultural Service, U.S. Department of Agriculture (FAS-USDA)*

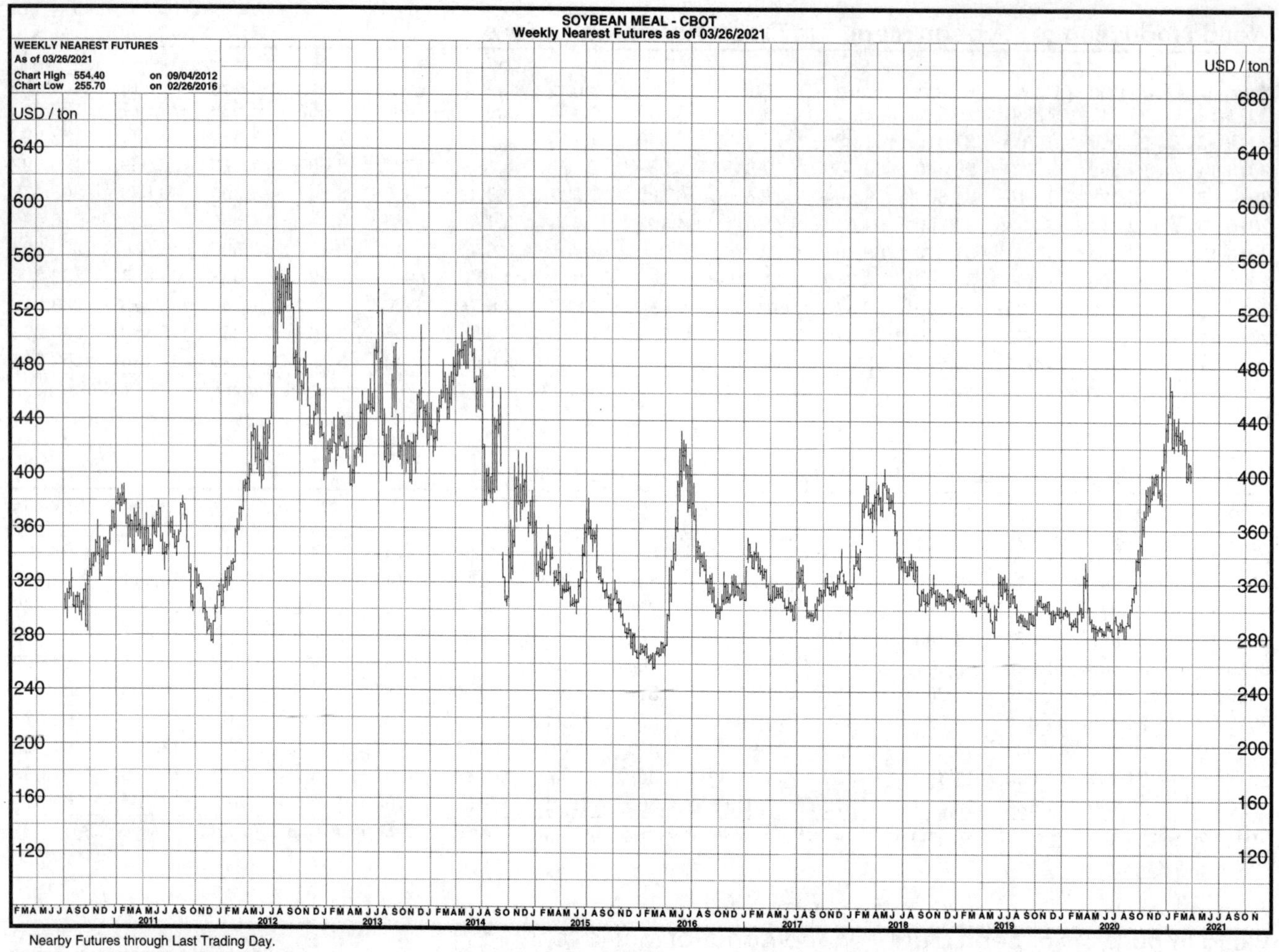

Volume of Trading of Soybean Meal Futures in Chicago In Thousands of Contracts

Year	Jan.	Feb.	Mar.	Apr.	May	June	July	Aug.	Sept.	Oct.	Nov.	Dec.	Total
2011	1,115.7	1,437.9	1,475.1	1,546.9	1,141.0	1,642.3	1,211.5	1,485.3	1,726.2	1,329.8	1,511.7	1,296.8	16,920.2
2012	1,182.2	1,484.7	1,545.3	1,914.5	1,481.2	1,812.1	1,848.1	1,594.8	1,389.8	1,263.9	1,436.3	1,234.5	18,187.4
2013	1,520.3	1,758.3	1,277.9	1,985.6	1,558.3	1,839.5	1,919.1	1,797.3	1,433.2	1,632.4	1,881.6	1,633.7	20,237.2
2014	1,519.1	1,918.1	1,409.7	1,711.2	1,138.3	1,811.9	1,703.3	1,664.5	1,613.9	2,456.8	2,070.8	1,619.9	20,637.4
2015	1,558.6	1,863.0	1,627.7	2,118.1	1,655.7	2,861.9	2,181.3	2,145.4	1,942.1	2,106.6	2,147.4	2,107.4	24,315.3
2016	1,547.6	2,055.5	1,696.5	3,289.2	2,564.1	2,971.6	2,027.7	1,880.0	1,738.5	1,967.8	2,156.9	2,058.7	25,953.9
2017	1,858.5	2,157.2	1,854.4	2,379.1	1,812.1	2,591.4	2,356.1	2,184.0	1,940.2	1,781.8	2,591.0	2,490.8	25,996.4
2018	2,482.4	3,466.9	2,294.9	3,361.6	2,275.4	3,268.2	2,417.4	2,725.2	2,329.5	2,641.3	2,470.2	2,105.7	31,838.9
2019	1,838.0	2,688.8	1,871.1	2,796.4	2,667.8	2,811.9	1,992.6	2,270.8	2,086.4	2,372.2	3,009.2	2,998.4	29,403.5
2020	2,241.9	3,323.9	2,982.5	2,240.4	1,489.6	2,759.8	2,252.5	2,244.2	2,847.2	2,570.3	2,454.8	2,507.8	29,914.8

Contract size = 100 tons. *Source: CME Group; Chicago Board of Trade (CBT)*

Average Open Interest of Soybean Meal Futures in Chicago In Contracts

Year	Jan.	Feb.	Mar.	Apr.	May	June	July	Aug.	Sept.	Oct.	Nov.	Dec.
2011	203,340	215,886	213,717	226,365	228,210	223,375	180,790	176,598	187,326	186,973	204,468	206,053
2012	193,344	187,100	226,979	261,896	251,386	253,037	263,064	255,541	235,650	211,525	217,752	222,206
2013	248,644	287,037	281,914	262,103	264,520	305,549	285,970	266,192	267,963	272,131	279,717	274,139
2014	272,424	307,186	312,283	321,497	310,358	320,237	309,536	319,263	340,910	362,209	382,227	353,605
2015	347,095	363,919	341,479	342,428	352,507	402,421	400,309	385,239	379,936	401,497	422,294	415,217
2016	411,932	416,103	376,318	369,967	367,597	389,845	373,020	359,333	362,886	375,331	373,239	350,214
2017	356,312	382,823	366,137	377,335	379,196	399,940	353,194	370,584	381,819	380,034	403,480	409,863
2018	401,624	465,945	454,202	506,093	522,647	510,772	518,013	507,407	524,092	525,893	503,197	448,462
2019	449,026	460,468	453,985	454,723	493,991	477,710	441,846	445,260	442,094	419,844	429,417	446,866
2020	467,470	500,452	426,318	406,124	435,722	451,089	430,972	445,888	453,829	443,089	440,686	425,125

Contract size = 100 tons. *Source: CME Group; Chicago Board of Trade (CBT)*

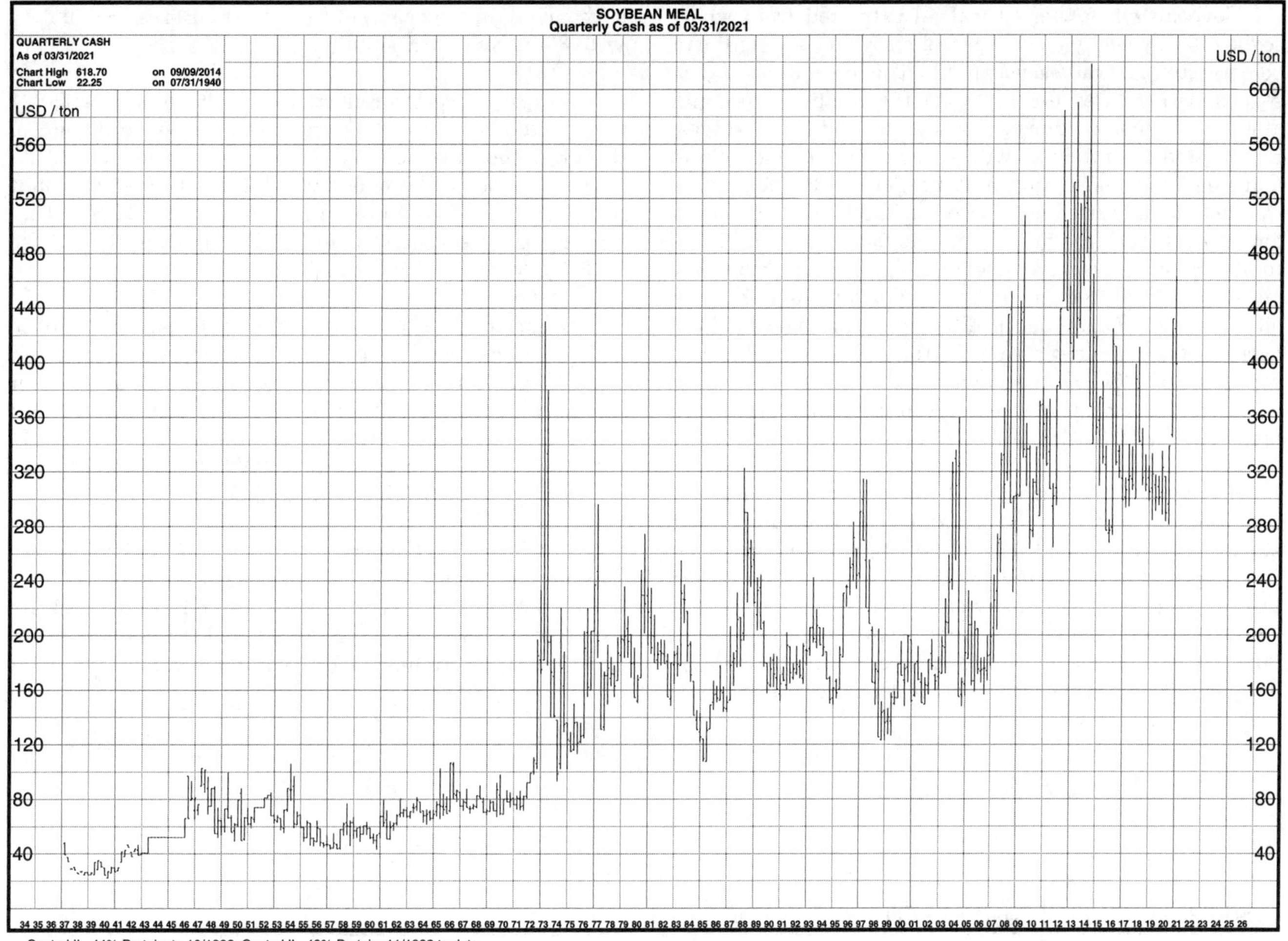

Central IL, 44% Protein: to 10/1992; Central IL, 48% Protein: 11/1992 to date.

Average Price of Soybean Meal (48% Solvent) in Decatur Illinois In Dollars Per Short Ton -- Bulk

Year	Oct.	Nov.	Dec.	Jan.	Feb.	Mar.	Apr.	May.	June	July	Aug.	Sept.	Average
2011-12	301.45	290.37	281.65	310.65	330.37	365.95	394.29	415.17	422.59	515.82	564.69	529.37	393.53
2012-13	488.46	465.64	459.40	431.39	440.66	437.33	422.07	465.72	496.78	544.59	464.90	500.39	468.11
2013-14	443.63	451.13	498.10	479.54	509.25	495.71	514.01	519.38	501.72	450.79	490.32	525.72	489.94
2014-15	381.50	441.39	431.73	380.03	370.38	357.83	336.61	320.23	335.03	375.71	357.85	333.62	368.49
2015-16	327.97	308.60	289.78	279.56	273.61	276.22	303.81	376.35	408.57	371.49	340.80	337.95	324.56
2016-17	323.37	322.41	321.02	332.34	334.42	320.34	305.67	307.63	300.72	326.04	301.05	307.70	316.89
2017-18	315.23	313.52	319.22	322.60	362.85	379.85	385.84	393.55	355.71	341.08	332.50	318.32	345.02
2018-19	319.15	310.62	311.70	314.92	306.83	306.38	304.26	297.52	324.75	310.77	296.92	295.57	308.28
2019-20	309.48	303.13	299.59	300.11	295.28	312.38	295.40	288.56	288.66	291.25	290.18	319.99	299.50
2020-21	366.62	387.83	396.68	439.24									397.59

Source: Economic Research Service, U.S. Department of Agriculture (ERS-USDA)

Average Price of Soybean Meal (44% Solvent) in Decatur Illinois In Dollars Per Short Ton -- Bulk

Year	Oct.	Nov.	Dec.	Jan.	Feb.	Mar.	Apr.	May.	June	July	Aug.	Sept.	Average
1992-93	168.6	170.9	176.4	175.6	167.5	172.4	175.6	181.7	181.3	217.6	206.9	186.5	181.8
1993-94	180.6	195.7	192.5	185.9	184.4	182.0	176.4	191.1	183.0	168.1	165.6	162.5	180.7
1994-95	156.4	150.9	145.4	145.1	149.4	145.7	151.0	148.1	149.1	160.1	157.5	171.8	152.5
1995-96	183.4	194.1	213.6	220.5	216.7	215.7	237.9	232.3	227.9	242.3	251.1	265.5	225.1
1996-97	238.0	242.7	240.9	240.7	253.6	270.4	277.7	296.0	275.9	261.5	261.6	265.7	260.4
1997-98	216.0	231.6	214.9	193.1	182.1	165.3	152.8	150.3	157.8	173.3	135.7	126.9	175.0
1998-99	129.4	139.3	139.6	131.0	124.4	127.2	128.6	127.0	131.7	125.7	135.9	144.1	132.0
1999-00	147.2	148.1	145.4	155.0	163.6	166.6	168.1	180.1	170.2	156.8	151.4	166.9	160.0
2000-01	166.0	173.7	187.9	175.6	158.3	149.1	149.7	155.6	163.1	183.9	170.6	163.5	166.4
2001-02	157.7	157.2	146.6	Discontinued									153.8

Source: Economic Research Service, U.S. Department of Agriculture (ERS-USDA)

Soybean Oil

Soybean oil is the natural oil extracted from whole soybeans. Typically, about 19% of a soybean's weight can be extracted as crude soybean oil. The oil content of U.S. soybeans correlates directly with the temperatures and amount of sunshine during the soybean pod-filling stages. Edible products produced with soybean oil include cooking and salad oils, shortening, and margarine. Soybean oil is the most widely used cooking oil in the U.S. It accounts for 80% of margarine production and for more than 75% of total U.S. consumer vegetable fat and oil consumption. Soy oil is cholesterol-free and high in polyunsaturated fat. Soy oil is also used to produce inedible products such as paints, varnish, resins, and plastics. Of the edible vegetable oils, soy oil is the world's largest at about 32%, followed by palm oil and rapeseed oil. Soybean oil futures and options are traded at the CME Group.

Prices – CME soybean oil futures prices (Barchart.com electronic symbol ZL) on the nearest-futures chart started the year of 2020 at about 35.08 cents per pound, fell to a 15-year low of about 25.64 in March, and then rallied the rest of the year to finally close the year up +24.3% at 43.59 cents per pound. The price continued to rise into 2021. Regarding cash prices for the year 2020/21 (through January 2021), the average monthly price of crude domestic soybean oil (in tank cars) in Decatur (FOB) rose +32.2% yr/yr to 39.22 cents per pound.

Supply – World production of soybean oil in 2020/21 is expected to rise +4.1% yr/yr to a new record high of 60.308 million metric tons. China will account for 29.4% of world soybean oil production, while the U.S. will account for 19.2%, Brazil for 14.5%, and Argentina for 12.8%. U.S. production of soybean oil in 2020/21 is expected to rise +2.5% yr/yr to 25.565 billion pounds.

Demand – World consumption of soybean oil in 2020/21 is expected to rise +5.1% yr/yr to a new record high of 59.558 million metric tons. China will account for 331.4% of world consumption, while the U.S. will account for 17.7%, Brazil for 12.9%, and India for 8.6%. U.S. consumption of soybean oil in 2020/21 is expected to rise +4.4% yr/yr to 23.300 billion pounds.

Trade – World exports of soybean oil in 2020/221 are expected to rise +0.6% yr/yr to 12.002 million metric tons, a record high. U.S. exports of soybean oil in 2020/221 are expected to fall -3.2% yr/yr to1.247 million pounds, below the 2009/10 record high of 1.524 million pounds.

World Production of Soybean Oil In Thousands of Metric Tons

Crop Year	Argentina	Bolivia	Brazil	China	European Union	India	Japan	Mexico	Paraguay	Russia	Taiwan	United States	World Total
2011-12	6,839	355	7,310	10,931	2,204	1,854	380	657	167	376	360	8,954	42,830
2012-13	6,364	400	6,760	11,648	2,413	1,944	379	653	553	394	345	8,990	43,363
2013-14	6,785	415	7,074	12,347	2,489	1,566	389	720	669	591	343	9,131	45,263
2014-15	7,687	450	7,759	13,350	2,746	1,386	414	745	700	645	352	9,706	49,276
2015-16	8,433	470	7,627	14,605	2,841	990	445	785	720	717	352	9,956	51,621
2016-17	8,395	479	7,755	15,770	2,736	1,620	466	820	711	788	364	10,035	53,812
2017-18	7,236	432	8,485	16,128	2,841	1,386	468	937	733	824	383	10,783	55,149
2018-19[1]	7,910	478	8,180	15,232	2,964	1,728	482	1,100	685	834	401	10,976	55,821
2019-20[2]	7,674	469	8,500	16,397	3,107	1,512	480	1,110	655	834	420	11,300	57,931
2020-21[3]	7,720	474	8,750	17,741	3,202	1,710	491	1,145	719	841	428	11,596	60,308

Crop year beginning October 1. [1] Preliminary. [2] Forecast. *Source: Foreign Agricultural Service, U.S. Department of Agriculture (FAS-USDA)*

World Consumption of Soybean Oil In Thousands of Metric Tons

Crop Year	Algeria	Argentina	Bangladesh	Brazil	China	Egypt	European Union	India	Iran	Korea, South	Mexico	United States	World Total
2011-12	490	3,020	483	5,390	12,050	462	2,050	2,900	600	445	845	8,396	42,454
2012-13	540	2,245	493	5,534	12,550	562	1,850	3,000	600	445	860	8,522	42,555
2013-14	590	2,844	551	5,705	13,650	587	1,990	3,350	600	440	905	8,577	45,423
2014-15	640	2,401	673	6,215	14,200	752	2,040	4,100	660	435	961	8,599	47,648
2015-16	690	2,840	785	6,288	15,350	960	2,285	5,250	660	440	1,050	9,145	52,106
2016-17	715	3,085	1,010	6,570	16,350	660	2,215	5,150	650	450	1,100	9,010	53,428
2017-18	740	2,981	1,085	6,940	16,500	760	2,225	4,670	635	470	1,160	9,698	54,483
2018-19[1]	770	2,624	1,170	7,165	15,885	910	2,455	4,750	650	505	1,235	10,376	55,125
2019-20[2]	800	2,176	1,250	7,390	17,093	960	2,540	5,100	580	547	1,265	10,124	56,676
2020-21[3]	825	2,104	1,330	7,700	18,691	1,010	2,640	5,150	510	579	1,300	10,523	59,558

Crop year beginning October 1. [1] Preliminary. [2] Forecast. *Source: Foreign Agricultural Service, U.S. Department of Agriculture (FAS-USDA)*

World Exports of Soybean Oil In Thousands of Metric Tons

Crop Year	Argentina	Bolivia	Brazil	Canada	European Union	Malaysia	Paraguay	Russia	South Africa	Ukraine	United States	Vietnam	World Total
2011-12	3,794	224	1,885	72	742	146	123	142	68	49	664	73	8,536
2012-13	4,244	285	1,251	102	1,011	127	537	129	76	70	981	44	9,375
2013-14	4,087	371	1,378	92	766	157	641	332	94	118	852	91	9,435
2014-15	5,094	392	1,510	118	1,010	170	703	423	71	136	914	104	11,152
2015-16	5,698	444	1,550	151	915	148	702	431	64	152	1,017	17	11,801
2016-17	5,387	338	1,241	175	819	137	680	529	63	177	1,159	35	11,328
2017-18	4,164	380	1,511	157	902	124	702	568	48	192	1,108	40	10,561
2018-19[1]	5,268	390	1,079	169	788	120	653	572	47	334	880	9	11,175
2019-20[2]	5,403	370	1,156	144	768	118	640	641	45	338	1,288	10	11,928
2020-21[3]	5,650	375	1,150	150	825	120	680	600	45	190	1,247	10	12,002

Crop year beginning October 1. [1] Preliminary. [2] Forecast. *Source: Foreign Agricultural Service, U.S. Department of Agriculture (FAS-USDA)*

World Imports of Soybean Oil In Thousands of Metric Tons

Crop Year	Algeria	Bangladesh	China	Colombia	Egypt	European Union	India	Iran	Korea, South	Peru	Morocco	Venezuela	World Total
2011-12	438	439	1,502	257	----	386	1,190	411	343	367	344	415	8,013
2012-13	575	400	1,409	216	324	322	1,081	543	300	364	363	374	8,522
2013-14	629	442	1,353	288	230	329	1,804	551	278	444	355	403	9,275
2014-15	631	508	773	304	498	253	2,815	421	257	432	395	365	10,051
2015-16	720	647	586	372	688	325	4,269	299	250	465	382	208	11,735
2016-17	674	830	711	352	246	285	3,534	257	306	497	449	289	10,980
2017-18	776	859	481	344	262	284	2,984	127	276	502	503	226	9,867
2018-19[1]	889	985	783	343	306	416	3,000	346	328	536	538	53	10,659
2019-20[2]	699	685	1,000	360	532	485	3,612	79	402	573	550	75	11,372
2020-21[3]	650	750	1,100	370	300	415	3,400	100	400	560	560	84	11,177

Crop year beginning October 1. [1] Preliminary. [2] Forecast. *Source: Foreign Agricultural Service, U.S. Department of Agriculture (FAS-USDA)*

Supply and Distribution of Soybean Oil in the United States In Millions of Pounds

Crop Year	Beginning Stocks Oct. 1	Production	Imports	Exports	Domestic Total	Biodiesel	Food & Other	Exports	Total Disappearance	Ending Stocks
2011-12	2,425	19,740	149	22,564	18,510	4,874	13,437	1,464	19,775	2,540
2012-13	2,540	19,820	196	22,606	18,787	4,689	13,997	2,164	20,851	1,705
2013-14	1,655	20,130	165	21,950	18,908	5,010	13,948	1,877	20,785	1,165
2014-15	1,165	21,399	264	22,828	18,959	5,039	13,922	2,014	20,973	1,855
2015-16	1,855	21,950	288	24,093	20,163	5,670	14,493	2,243	22,406	1,687
2016-17	1,687	22,123	319	24,129	19,862	6,200	13,662	2,556	22,418	1,711
2017-18	1,711	23,772	335	25,819	21,380	7,134	14,247	2,443	23,823	1,995
2018-19	1,995	24,197	398	26,590	22,873	7,863	15,010	1,941	24,814	1,775
2019-20[1]	1,775	24,912	319	27,006	22,319	7,858	14,461	2,839	25,158	1,849
2020-21[2]	1,849	25,565	350	27,764	23,300	8,300	15,000	2,750	26,050	1,714

Crop year beginning October 1. [1] Preliminary . [2] Forecast. *Source: Economic Research Service, U.S. Department of Agriculture (ERS-USDA)*

U.S. Exports of Soybean Oil[2], by Country of Destination In Metric Tons

Crop Year	Canada	Ecuador	Ethiopia	Haiti	India	Mexico	Morocco	Pakistan	Panama	Peru	Turkey	Venezuela	Total
2010-11	35,001	8,722	700	13,314	49	167,760	291,890	20,900	6,123	44,999	1,120	57,707	1,466,468
2011-12	25,417	15	890	3,156	12	151,224	159,917	----	2,307	7	1,092	22,942	664,111
2012-13	30,867	28	----	2,230	113,104	187,117	23,248	0	6,374	193	76	51,377	981,345
2013-14	31,755	13	390	1,576	22	189,759	29,702	0	4,139	42,121	----	18,988	852,074
2014-15	28,755	11	450	649	39	245,163	64,658	9,190	5,434	104,743	----	61,920	913,704
2015-16	15,647	6	----	2,687	51	235,554	50,521	11,165	6,054	75,355	----	50,055	1,017,200
2016-17	22,658	8	----	1,307	139	265,028	30,432	7,137	7,055	2	75	32,437	1,159,229
2017-18	21,213	9	----	----	105	166,657	11,798	----	7,723	93,051	17	48,345	1,108,143
2018-19	21,805	47	----	28	118	125,570	----	10,893	3,157	11,959	----	1,007	880,161
2019-20[1]	31,612	31	----	2,645	103	129,530	82,900	12,975	2,304	26,437	----	59,037	1,287,684

Crop year beginning October 1. [1] Preliminary. [2] Crude & Refined oil combined as such. *Source: Foreign Agricultural Service, U.S. Department of Agriculture (FAS-USDA)*

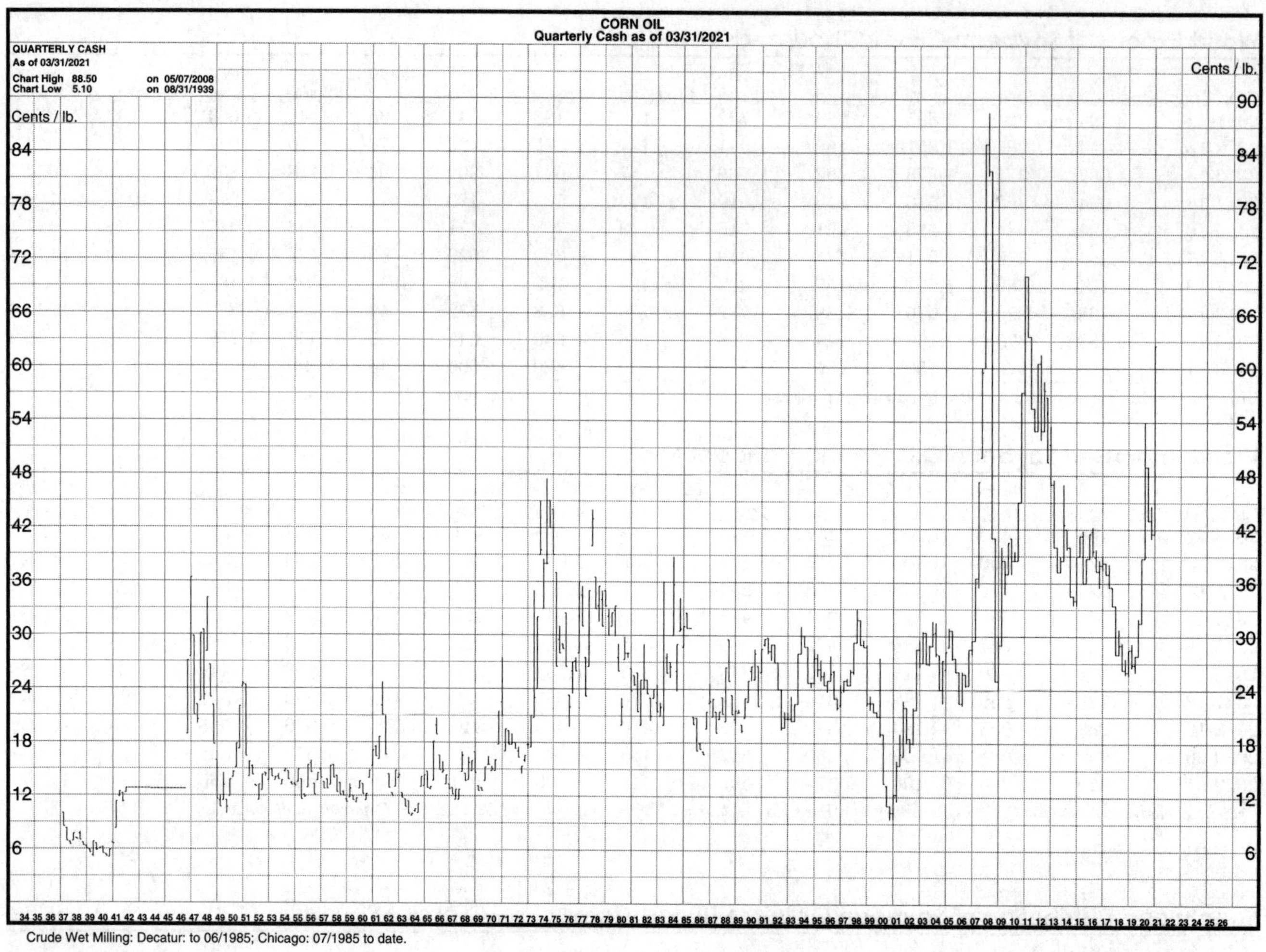

Crude Wet Milling: Decatur: to 06/1985; Chicago: 07/1985 to date.

Production of Soybean Oil in the United States In Millions of Pounds

Year	Oct.	Nov.	Dec.	Jan.	Feb.	Mar.	Apr.	May	June	July	Aug.	Sept.	Total
2011-12	----	----	----	----	----	----	----	----	----	----	----	----	19,740.0
2012-13	----	----	----	----	----	----	----	----	----	----	----	----	19,820.0
2013-14	----	----	----	----	----	----	----	----	----	----	----	----	20,130.0
2014-15	----	----	----	----	----	----	----	----	----	----	----	----	21,399.0
2015-16	1,962.9	1,901.9	1,929.0	1,864.9	1,795.9	1,943.5	1,840.3	1,876.2	1,787.2	1,789.4	1,642.5	1,616.6	21,950.0
2016-17	2,028.5	1,961.3	1,950.2	1,977.2	1,752.5	1,857.1	1,731.7	1,839.3	1,735.6	1,801.4	1,762.2	1,701.8	22,098.8
2017-18	2,016.9	1,977.0	2,015.3	1,995.6	1,889.8	2,079.1	1,964.9	1,966.5	1,936.9	2,043.3	1,945.0	1,936.9	23,767.2
2018-19	2,134.6	2,060.6	2,135.4	2,115.8	1,899.2	2,094.4	1,989.1	1,916.0	1,811.5	2,090.2	2,048.2	1,900.7	24,195.7
2019-20	2,150.0	1,999.6	2,110.9	2,154.4	1,999.5	2,201.1	2,099.5	2,057.6	2,035.3	2,123.2	2,012.8	1,967.6	24,911.5
2020-21[1]	2,282.5	2,206.8	2,231.7										26,884.0

[1] Preliminary. *Source: Economic Research Service, U.S. Department of Agriculture (ERS-USDA)*

U.S. Exports of Soybean Oil (Crude and Refined) In Millions of Pounds

Year	Jan.	Feb.	Mar.	Apr.	May	June	July	Aug.	Sept.	Oct.	Nov.	Dec.	Total
2011	466.3	301.2	330.1	188.6	91.7	129.7	120.0	114.6	223.6	78.0	107.8	59.6	2,211
2012	91.4	142.5	69.8	121.2	193.6	123.8	198.1	206.7	71.6	253.1	274.6	358.6	2,105
2013	258.9	339.7	136.7	135.9	79.3	75.1	70.7	92.8	87.9	71.4	135.9	320.2	1,805
2014	267.2	277.5	195.5	92.6	45.8	79.7	198.0	119.0	75.6	159.2	231.4	236.2	1,978
2015	256.7	220.5	233.5	125.7	72.5	157.4	64.6	154.6	101.9	179.6	233.0	320.7	2,121
2016	168.0	114.6	233.1	126.2	103.8	158.4	281.8	93.1	227.2	241.0	236.7	235.5	2,219
2017	259.4	238.7	294.5	258.3	161.2	138.2	199.4	163.1	130.2	212.8	132.0	173.0	2,361
2018	180.7	181.1	201.5	212.3	431.4	228.3	174.7	197.6	121.7	146.1	215.8	170.5	2,462
2019	221.1	91.7	271.8	148.2	205.7	95.4	174.3	165.6	48.5	252.5	247.4	184.3	2,106
2020[1]	125.1	396.2	320.8	230.2	357.8	167.7	164.6	201.7	180.1	184.0	177.2	235.0	2,740

[1] Preliminary. *Source: Bureau of the Census, U.S. Department of Commerce*

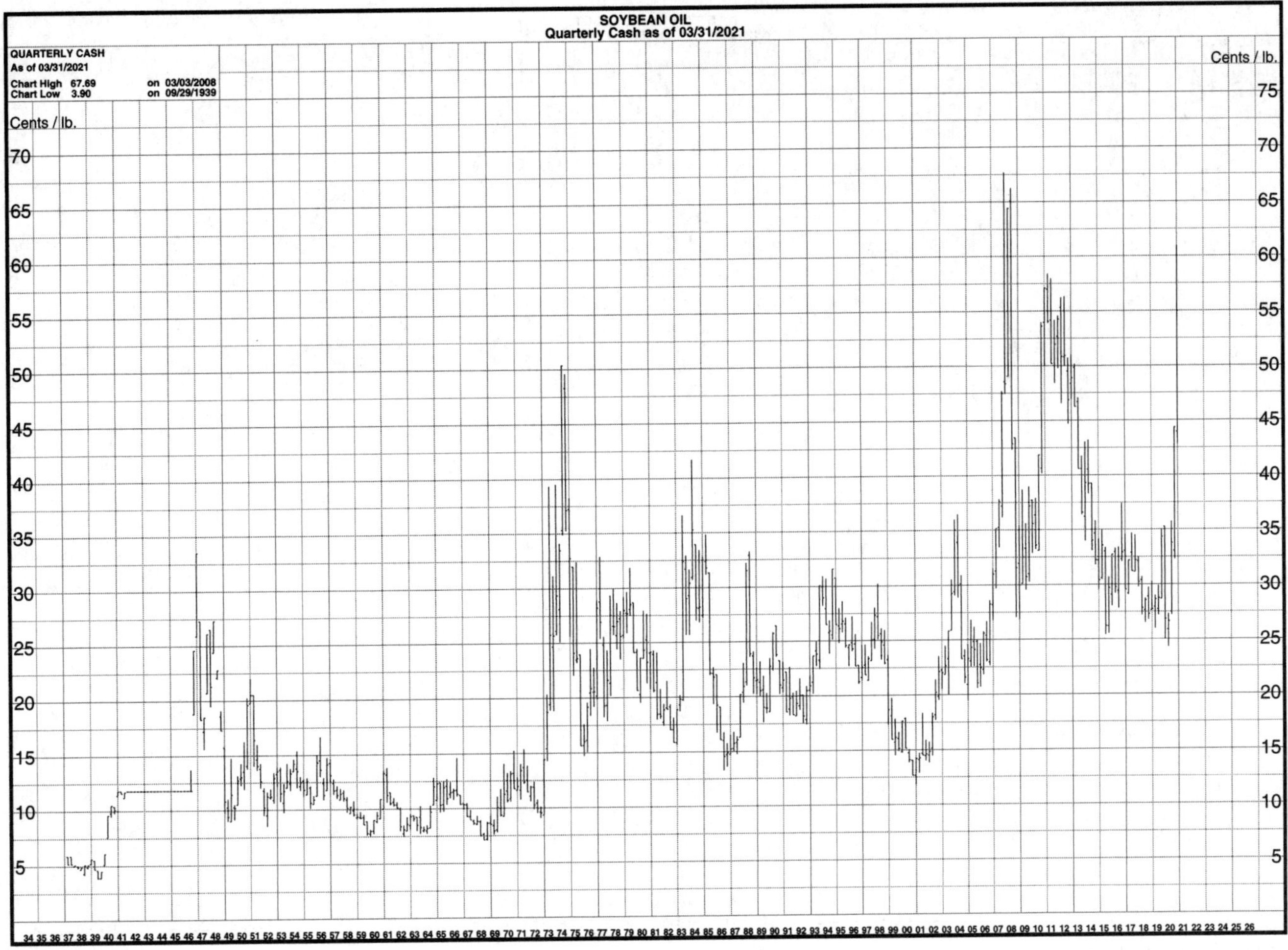

Central IL, Crude: to date.

Stocks of Soybean Oil (Crude and Refined) at Factories and Warehouses in the U.S. In Millions of Pounds

Year	Oct. 1	Nov. 1	Dec. 1	Jan. 1	Feb. 1	Mar. 1	Apr. 1	May 1	June 1	July 1	Aug. 1	Sept. 1
2011-12	2,425.0	----	----	----	----	----	----	----	----	----	----	----
2012-13	2,540.0	----	----	----	----	----	----	----	----	----	----	----
2013-14	1,655.0	----	----	----	----	----	----	----	----	----	----	----
2014-15	1,165.0	----	----	----	----	----	----	----	----	----	----	----
2015-16	1,854.8	1,940.4	1,965.9	1,972.5	2,110.8	2,280.2	2,324.9	2,420.0	2,466.1	2,424.1	2,214.3	1,985.7
2016-17	1,686.8	1,795.3	1,780.7	1,872.3	2,112.6	2,205.9	2,353.4	2,233.8	2,269.3	2,142.9	2,000.6	1,810.3
2017-18	1,711.0	1,626.2	1,690.6	1,950.7	2,239.8	2,425.4	2,444.5	2,688.8	2,374.1	2,304.8	2,383.6	2,214.8
2018-19	1,995.4	2,047.6	1,900.3	1,945.8	2,004.7	2,149.1	2,232.9	2,257.6	2,018.9	2,014.4	2,039.5	1,805.6
2019-20	1,775.3	1,821.0	1,880.4	2,134.1	2,351.8	2,377.4	2,327.6	2,602.0	2,447.2	2,270.7	2,123.1	1,942.0
2020-21[1]	1,848.5	1,963.9	2,117.7									

On First of Month. [1] Preliminary. *Source: Economic Research Service, U.S. Department of Agriculture (ERS-USDA)*

Average Price of Crude Domestic Soybean Oil (in Tank Cars) F.O.B. Decatur In Cents Per Pound

Year	Oct.	Nov.	Dec.	Jan.	Feb.	Mar.	Apr.	May	June	July	Aug.	Sept.	Average
2011-12	51.73	51.44	50.17	50.99	52.36	53.43	54.96	50.69	48.65	51.96	52.65	53.81	51.90
2012-13	49.31	46.27	47.16	48.85	49.33	48.62	49.28	49.31	47.84	45.19	42.33	42.12	47.13
2013-14	39.66	39.58	37.63	34.95	37.11	40.82	41.87	40.68	39.84	37.60	35.04	33.99	38.23
2014-15	34.10	33.45	32.56	32.33	31.57	30.89	31.13	32.65	33.73	31.54	28.87	26.43	31.60
2015-16	27.14	26.42	29.72	28.89	29.79	30.86	32.45	30.76	30.35	28.75	31.21	31.99	29.86
2016-17	33.86	34.52	35.57	33.58	32.00	30.86	29.57	30.60	30.74	32.82	33.17	33.28	32.55
2017-18	32.35	33.43	32.27	31.61	30.63	30.28	29.70	29.40	28.30	27.21	27.60	27.73	30.04
2018-19	28.89	27.49	28.14	28.44	29.58	28.62	27.86	26.93	28.24	27.68	28.41	28.81	28.26
2019-20	30.14	30.62	32.27	33.04	30.26	27.04	25.69	25.27	26.61	28.71	32.13	34.20	29.67
2020-21[1]	33.92	37.79	40.85	44.31									39.22

[1] Preliminary. *Source: Economic Research Service, U.S. Department of Agriculture (ERS-USDA)*

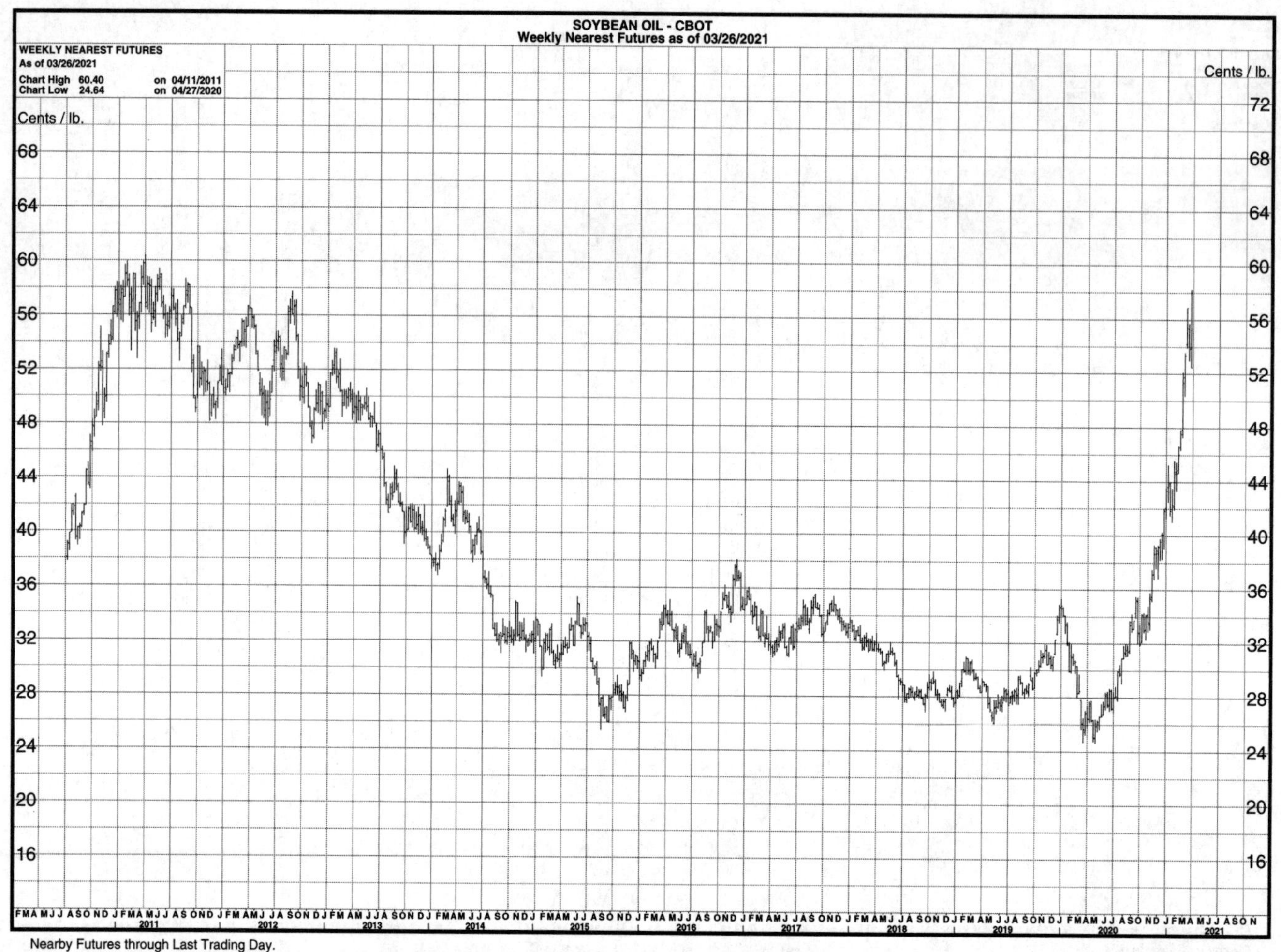

Nearby Futures through Last Trading Day.

Volume of Trading of Soybean Oil Futures in Chicago In Thousands of Contracts

Year	Jan.	Feb.	Mar.	Apr.	May	June	July	Aug.	Sept.	Oct.	Nov.	Dec.	Total
2011	1,660.1	2,427.9	2,153.7	2,276.7	1,613.1	2,427.4	1,616.1	1,924.0	2,027.5	1,866.4	2,296.1	1,867.6	24,157
2012	1,649.0	2,155.3	2,107.2	2,732.0	2,333.5	2,846.1	2,394.5	2,206.0	1,958.3	2,392.5	2,683.3	2,169.7	27,628
2013	2,043.6	2,403.6	1,465.9	2,453.7	1,831.6	2,213.7	1,918.7	1,850.1	1,560.5	1,908.5	2,263.2	1,892.7	23,806
2014	1,752.1	2,531.9	1,657.5	2,058.5	1,450.2	2,199.9	1,869.4	1,775.4	1,768.9	2,199.9	2,386.3	2,119.2	23,769
2015	1,985.3	2,348.9	1,683.5	2,527.2	2,042.6	3,236.5	2,358.9	2,412.7	2,190.7	2,519.5	2,667.4	2,924.0	28,897
2016	1,713.2	2,310.9	1,866.0	3,407.3	2,476.6	2,822.7	2,165.3	2,385.6	2,143.2	2,393.9	3,144.7	2,599.8	29,429
2017	2,001.6	2,737.6	2,421.6	2,639.6	1,882.5	2,952.5	2,467.6	2,721.7	2,451.3	2,125.4	3,128.1	2,702.9	30,232
2018	2,127.2	3,503.1	2,185.3	3,210.2	2,097.3	3,481.7	2,175.5	2,203.0	2,375.4	2,312.2	3,139.3	2,455.6	31,266
2019	1,975.0	2,890.1	2,023.1	3,012.6	2,405.6	2,762.6	2,231.8	2,651.3	2,527.4	2,759.0	3,242.7	3,213.2	31,694
2020	2,779.1	3,334.0	3,258.7	2,946.4	1,772.2	2,785.2	2,494.8	2,316.3	2,775.4	2,674.1	2,927.0	2,898.7	32,962

Contract size = 60,000 lbs. *Source: CME Group; Chicago Board of Trade (CBT)*

Average Open Interest of Soybean Oil Futures in Chicago In Contracts

Year	Jan.	Feb.	Mar.	Apr.	May	June	July	Aug.	Sept.	Oct.	Nov.	Dec.
2011	375,563	391,930	358,625	357,657	313,673	322,642	287,408	278,784	287,250	297,663	305,955	305,279
2012	296,889	314,752	340,827	380,916	386,924	377,817	329,673	332,182	314,359	322,262	347,898	310,982
2013	313,467	327,562	329,956	353,044	351,425	357,052	340,600	308,032	291,005	314,235	333,607	344,607
2014	364,056	339,211	302,398	326,545	313,757	333,690	325,337	347,395	373,086	391,486	395,330	365,382
2015	370,576	385,819	367,203	383,502	394,773	410,233	372,932	390,494	413,151	420,227	448,872	412,621
2016	404,388	411,898	415,026	457,557	404,143	389,896	361,443	378,813	399,625	443,699	446,001	407,110
2017	391,377	386,979	385,217	423,805	412,142	414,657	398,719	416,321	438,439	440,831	469,775	467,647
2018	480,781	499,421	496,026	519,883	514,763	505,702	512,638	534,033	575,527	539,882	556,831	497,905
2019	492,981	507,871	480,036	483,650	535,026	472,080	435,429	466,176	498,072	496,430	536,756	521,342
2020	537,082	509,621	460,552	460,731	468,485	464,880	440,128	448,159	473,386	469,071	484,466	482,763

Contract size = 60,000 lbs. *Source: CME Group; Chicago Board of Trade (CBT)*

Soybeans

Soybean is the common name for the annual leguminous plant and its seed. The soybean is a member of the oilseed family and is not considered a grain. The soybean seeds are contained in pods, and are nearly spherical. The seeds are usually light yellow. The seeds contain 20% oil and 40% protein. Soybeans were an ancient food crop in China, Japan, and Korea and were only introduced to the U.S. in the early 1800s. Today, soybeans are the second-largest crop produced in the U.S. behind corn. Soybean production in the U.S. is concentrated in the Midwest and the lower Mississippi Valley. Soybean crops in the U.S. are planted in May or June and are harvested in autumn. Soybean plants usually reach maturity 100-150 days after planting, depending on growing conditions.

Soybeans are used to produce a wide variety of food products. The key value of soybeans lies in the relatively high protein content, which makes it an excellent source of protein without many of the negative factors of animal meat. Popular soy-based food products include whole soybeans (roasted for snacks or used in sauces, stews and soups), soy oil for cooking and baking, soy flour, protein concentrates, isolated soy protein (which contains up to 92% protein), soy milk and baby formula (as an alternative to dairy products), soy yogurt, soy cheese, soy nut butter, soy sprouts, tofu and tofu products (soybean curd), soy sauce (which is produced by a fermentation process), and meat alternatives (hamburgers, breakfast sausage, etc.).

The primary market for soybean futures is at the CME Group. The CME's soybean contract calls for the delivery of 5,000 bushels of No. 2 yellow soybeans (at contract par), No. 1 yellow soybeans (at 6 cents per bushel above the contract price), or No. 3 yellow soybeans (at 6 cents under the contract price). Soybean futures are also traded at exchanges in Brazil, Argentina, China, and Tokyo.

Prices – CME soybean futures prices (Barchart.com electronic symbol ZS) drifted lower in early 2020 and then sank to a 1-3/4-year low of $8.08 per bushel in April. Soybean prices were under pressure in early 2020 on a strong dollar, as the dollar index climbed to a 4-year high in March. The stronger dollar prompted the USDA in April to cut its U.S. 2019/20 soybean export estimate to 48.2 MMT from a prior forecast of 49.7 and to hike its Brazil 2019/20 soybean export estimate to 78.5 MMT from 77 MMT, citing Brazil's competitive exchange rate. Also, a record soybean crop in Brazil, now the world's biggest soybean producer, undercut prices after Conab projected Brazil's 2019/20 soybean crop would climb +4% yr/yr to a record 124.8 MMT. The raging Covid pandemic in 2020 roiled commodity markets on concern that lockdowns and travel restrictions to slow the pandemic would undercut economic growth and demand for commodities. Soybean prices in May then trended higher for the remainder of the year. Robust demand for U.S. soybeans from China was one of the main bullish factors for soybean prices in 2020. The USDA reported that China bought 25.9 MMT of U.S. soybeans in 2020, up +53% y/y. China imported a record 100.3 MMT soybeans in 2020 to feed its pig herd that was being rebuilt after it was devastated by the African swine fever. The surge in Chinese demand reduced U.S. soybean stockpiles, with the USDA in its December WASDE report cutting its U.S. 2020/21 soybean ending stocks estimate to a 7-year low of 175 million bushels. The USDA also cut its global 2020/21 soybean ending stocks estimate to a 5-year low of 85.6 MMT, down -10% yr/yr. A surge in palm oil prices to a 10-year high in December also underpinned soybean oil and soybean prices. In December, soybean prices rallied to a 6-year high of $13.21 a bushel and finished 2020 up sharply by +39.4% yr/yr at $13.15 per bushel.

Supply – World soybean production during the 2020/21 marketing year (Sep-Aug) is expected to rise +7.3% yr/yr to 361.004 million metric tons. World soybean production has risen sharply from only 80 million metric tons back in the 1980s. The world's largest soybean producers in 2020/21 are expected to be Brazil with 36.8% of world production, the U.S. with 31.2%, Argentina with 13.3%, China with 5.4%, and India with 2.9%. Brazil's production has risen by almost eight-fold since 1980. China's soybean production has roughly doubled since 1980.

U.S. soybean production in 2020/21 is expected to rise by +15.8% yr/yr to 4.575 billion bushels, a new record high. U.S. farmers are expected to harvest 82,289 million acres of soybeans in 2020/21 rose by +9.8% yr/yr but still below the 2017/18 record high of 89.542 billion bushels. The average yield in 2020/21 is expected to rise +7.0% yr/yr to 50.7 bushels per acre, but still below the 2016/17 record high of 51.9 bushels per acre. U.S. ending stocks for the 2020/21 marketing year are expected to fall by -77.1% yr/yr to 120.0 million bushels.

Demand – Total U.S. distribution in 2020/21 is expected to rise +15.8% yr/yr to 4.575 billion bushels. The distribution tables for U.S. soybeans for the 2020/21 marketing year show that 48.1% of U.S. soybean usage will go for crush, 49.2% went for exports, and 2.7% for seed, feed, and residual. The quantity of U.S. soybeans that will go for crushing is expected to rise +1.6% yr/yr in 2020/21 to 2.200 billion bushels. The world soybean crush in 2020/21 is expected to rise +4.0% yr/yr to a new record high of 321.805 million metric tons, which is about triple the level seen in 1993/94.

Trade – World exports of soybeans in 2020/21 are expected to rise +2.7% at 169.098 million metric tons, a new record high. The world's largest soybean exporters in 2020/21 are expected to be Brazil with 50.3% of world exports, the U.S. with 35.9%, Argentina with 4.1%, Paraguay with 3.7%, and Canada with 2.5%. Brazil's soybean exports have more than doubled in the past decade, and Canada's exports have almost tripled. U.S. soybean exports in 2020/21 are expected to rise by +170.6% yr/yr to 4.551 billion bushels.

World soybean imports in 2020/21 are expected to rise +0.9% yr/yr to 166.842 million metric tons which is a new record high. The world's largest importers of soybeans in 2019/20 are expected to be China with 58.9% of world imports, the European Union with 9.23%, Mexico with 3.7%, and Egypt with 2.5%. China's imports in 2020/21 are expected to rise +1.5% yr/yr to 100.000 million metric tons.

World Production of Soybeans In Thousands of Metric Tons

Crop Year[4]	Argentina	Bolivia	Brazil	Canada	China	European Union	India	Paraguay	Russia	Ukraine	United States	Uruguay	World Total
2011-12	40,100	2,429	66,500	4,467	14,879	1,220	11,940	4,043	1,641	2,264	84,291	2,726	240,832
2012-13	49,300	2,646	82,000	5,086	13,436	948	12,186	8,202	1,683	2,410	82,791	3,650	268,957
2013-14	53,400	2,814	86,200	5,356	12,407	1,211	9,477	8,190	1,517	2,774	91,363	3,163	282,699
2014-15	61,450	3,106	97,100	6,045	12,686	1,832	8,711	8,154	2,362	3,900	106,905	3,109	320,489
2015-16	58,800	3,205	95,700	6,456	12,367	2,320	6,929	9,217	2,707	3,932	106,869	2,208	315,458
2016-17	55,000	2,671	114,900	6,597	13,596	2,410	10,992	10,336	3,134	4,286	116,931	3,212	349,771
2017-18	37,800	2,819	123,400	7,717	15,283	2,539	8,350	10,263	3,621	3,985	120,065	1,334	342,929
2018-19[1]	55,300	2,991	119,700	7,417	15,967	2,667	10,930	8,512	4,027	4,831	120,515	2,828	361,036
2019-20[2]	48,800	2,800	126,000	6,145	18,100	2,615	9,300	9,900	4,359	4,499	96,667	1,990	336,472
2020-21[3]	48,000	2,900	133,000	6,350	19,600	2,700	10,500	10,250	4,300	3,100	112,549	2,200	361,004

[1] Preliminary. [2] Estimate. [3] Forecast. [4] Spilt year includes Northern Hemisphere crops harvested in the late months of the first year shown combined with Southern Hemisphere crops harvested in the early months of the following year. *Sources: Foreign Agricultural Service, U.S. Department of Agriculture (FAS-USDA)*

World Crushings of Soybeans In Thousands of Metric Tons

Crop Year	Argentina	Bolivia	Brazil	China	European Union	India	Japan	Mexico	Paraguay	Russia	Taiwan	United States	World Total
2011-12	35,886	2,000	38,083	61,000	11,600	10,300	1,960	3,675	900	2,100	2,020	46,348	229,194
2012-13	33,611	2,175	35,235	65,000	12,700	10,800	1,915	3,650	2,950	2,200	1,920	45,967	231,873
2013-14	36,173	2,250	36,861	68,900	13,100	8,700	1,969	4,030	3,550	3,300	1,925	47,192	242,957
2014-15	40,235	2,450	40,435	74,500	14,450	7,700	2,150	4,175	3,700	3,600	1,980	50,975	264,704
2015-16	43,267	2,550	39,747	81,500	14,950	5,500	2,283	4,400	3,800	4,000	1,980	51,335	275,309
2016-17	43,309	2,550	40,411	88,000	14,400	9,000	2,392	4,600	3,750	4,400	2,045	51,742	287,601
2017-18	36,933	2,300	44,205	90,000	14,950	7,700	2,400	5,250	3,870	4,600	2,150	55,926	294,674
2018-19[1]	40,567	2,550	42,527	85,000	15,600	9,600	2,470	6,150	3,620	4,650	2,250	56,935	298,064
2019-20[2]	38,763	2,500	44,250	91,500	16,350	8,400	2,460	6,200	3,450	4,650	2,350	58,910	309,368
2020-21[3]	39,000	2,525	45,500	99,000	16,850	9,500	2,520	6,400	3,800	4,700	2,400	59,874	321,805

[1] Preliminary. [2] Estimate. [3] Forecast. *Sources: Foreign Agricultural Service, U.S. Department of Agriculture (FAS-USDA)*

World Exports of Soybeans In Thousands of Metric Tons

Crop Year	Argentina	Bolivia	Brazil	Canada	China	India	Paraguay	Russia	Serbia	Ukraine	United States	Uruguay	World Total
2011-12	7,368	322	36,257	2,933	275	39	3,162	90	17	1,338	37,186	2,607	91,774
2012-13	7,738	523	41,904	3,470	266	115	5,082	102	6	1,323	36,129	3,527	100,383
2013-14	7,842	141	46,829	3,469	215	183	4,844	24	23	1,261	44,594	3,150	112,777
2014-15	10,575	8	50,612	3,855	143	234	4,576	313	136	2,422	50,136	3,114	126,428
2015-16	9,922	91	54,383	4,236	114	134	5,381	456	68	2,369	52,869	2,124	132,695
2016-17	7,025	13	63,137	4,592	114	268	6,129	375	186	2,904	58,964	3,224	147,630
2017-18	2,132	8	76,136	4,925	134	217	6,029	892	28	2,757	58,071	1,250	153,139
2018-19[1]	9,104	13	74,887	5,258	116	165	4,901	796	143	2,531	47,676	2,750	148,826
2019-20[2]	9,973	15	92,126	3,907	90	110	6,200	1,305	252	2,633	45,777	1,920	164,725
2020-21[3]	7,000	20	85,000	4,200	100	175	6,300	800	175	2,050	60,691	2,125	169,098

[1] Preliminary. [2] Estimate. [3] Forecast. *Sources: Foreign Agricultural Service, U.S. Department of Agriculture (FAS-USDA)*

World Imports of Soybeans In Thousands of Metric Tons

Crop Year	China	Egypt	European Union	Indonesia	Japan	Korea, South	Mexico	Russia	Taiwan	Thailand	Turkey	Vietnam	World Total
2011-12	59,231	1,661	12,070	1,922	2,758	1,139	3,606	741	2,285	1,907	1,057	1,290	94,659
2012-13	59,865	1,725	12,538	1,795	2,830	1,115	3,409	717	2,286	1,867	1,244	1,291	97,201
2013-14	70,364	1,694	13,293	2,241	2,894	1,271	3,842	2,048	2,335	1,798	1,750	1,564	113,305
2014-15	78,350	1,947	13,914	2,006	3,004	1,246	3,819	1,986	2,520	2,411	2,256	1,707	124,299
2015-16	83,230	1,575	15,120	2,274	3,186	1,249	4,126	2,336	2,476	2,798	2,376	1,602	133,760
2016-17	93,495	2,114	13,441	2,649	3,175	1,286	4,126	2,221	2,566	3,078	2,273	1,646	144,601
2017-18	94,095	3,255	14,584	2,483	3,256	1,256	4,873	2,237	2,666	2,482	2,872	1,807	153,368
2018-19[1]	82,540	3,650	14,985	2,623	3,314	1,373	5,867	2,162	2,614	3,155	2,411	1,638	145,472
2019-20[2]	98,533	5,077	15,664	2,636	3,325	1,300	6,000	2,047	2,850	3,831	3,148	1,900	165,408
2020-21[3]	100,000	4,150	15,400	2,800	3,410	1,290	6,200	2,000	2,900	3,890	3,000	2,000	166,842

[1] Preliminary. [2] Estimate. [3] Forecast. *Sources: Foreign Agricultural Service, U.S. Department of Agriculture (FAS-USDA)*

World Ending Stocks of Soybeans In Thousands of Metric Tons

Crop Year	Argentina	Bolivia	Brazil	Canada	China	European Union	India	Japan	Paraguay	Turkey	Ukraine	United States	World Total
2011-12	14,338	326	16,899	231	16,076	1,482	1,235	154	383	338	----	4,610	57,449
2012-13	17,291	24	19,605	158	12,411	1,076	1,210	221	540	196	99	3,825	58,070
2013-14	21,677	139	20,120	246	13,967	1,253	600	256	298	379	265	2,504	63,408
2014-15	27,069	433	23,828	466	17,060	843	200	212	133	401	166	5,188	78,137
2015-16	27,156	635	23,158	301	16,643	1,559	338	259	75	328	113	5,354	78,390
2016-17	26,996	383	32,112	277	20,120	1,150	880	217	344	314	151	8,208	94,065
2017-18	23,734	497	32,696	651	23,064	1,397	339	205	514	515	76	11,923	98,908
2018-19[1]	28,890	528	32,472	700	19,455	1,610	432	182	318	155	223	24,740	112,795
2019-20[2]	26,800	440	20,400	721	26,798	1,644	472	179	288	328	112	14,276	95,387
2020-21[3]	25,600	421	20,700	475	28,598	934	347	174	143	313	65	3,798	84,313

[1] Preliminary. [2] Estimate. [3] Forecast. *Sources: Foreign Agricultural Service, U.S. Department of Agriculture (FAS-USDA)*

Supply and Distribution of Soybeans in the United States In Millions of Bushels

Crop Year Beginning Sept. 1	Supply: Stocks, Sept. 1: Farms	Mills, Elevators[3]	Total Stocks	Production	Imports	Total Supply	Distribution: Crushings	Seed, Feed & Residual Use	Exports	Total Distribution	Ending Stocks
2011-12	48.5	166.5	215.0	3,094	16	3,328	1,703	91	1,365	3,159	169
2012-13	38.3	131.1	169.4	3,042	41	3,252	1,689	95	1,328	3,111	141
2013-14	39.6	101.0	140.6	3,358	72	3,570	1,734	107	1,638	3,478	92
2014-15	21.3	70.7	92.0	3,927	33	4,052	1,873	146	1,842	3,862	191
2015-16	49.7	140.9	190.6	3,926	24	4,140	1,886	115	1,942	3,944	197
2016-17	41.6	155.2	196.7	4,296	22	4,515	1,901	146	2,166	4,214	302
2017-18	87.9	213.7	301.6	4,412	22	4,735	2,055	108	2,134	4,297	438
2018-19	101.0	337.1	438.1	4,428	14	4,880	2,092	127	1,752	3,971	909
2019-20[1]	265.0	644.1	909.1	3,552	15	4,476	2,165	105	1,682	3,952	525
2020-21[2]	141.2	383.3	524.5	4,170	35	4,695	2,200	125	2,250	4,575	120

[1] Preliminary. [2] Estimate. [3] Also warehouses. *Source: Economic Research Service, U.S. Department of Agriculture (ERS-USDA)*

Salient Statistics & Official Crop Production Reports of Soybeans in the United States In Millions of Bushels

Year	Planted (1,000 Acres)	Acreage Harvested (1,000 Acres)	Yield Per Acre (Bu.)	Farm Price ($/Bu.)	Farm Value (Million Dollars)	Yield of Oil (Lbs. Per Bushel Crushed)	Yield of Meal (Lbs. Per Bushel Crushed)	Crop Production Reports (In Thousands of Bushels): Aug. 1	Sept. 1	Oct. 1	Nov. 1	Dec. 1	Final
2011-12	75,046	73,776	41.9	13.13	38,498	----	----	3,055,882	3,085,340	3,059,987	3,045,558	----	3,093,524
2012-13	77,198	76,144	40.0	14.53	43,723	----	----	2,692,014	2,634,310	2,860,290	2,971,022	----	3,042,044
2013-14	76,840	76,253	44.0	13.32	43,583	----	----	3,255,444	3,149,166	NA	3,257,746	----	3,357,984
2014-15	83,276	82,591	47.5	10.00	39,475	----	----	3,815,679	3,913,079	3,926,812	3,958,272	----	3,927,090
2015-16	82,650	81,732	48.0	9.18	35,192	----	----	3,916,448	3,935,277	3,887,721	3,981,337	----	3,926,339
2016-17	83,453	82,706	51.9	9.46	40,695	----	----	4,060,188	4,200,985	4,268,884	4,361,023	----	4,296,496
2017-18	90,162	89,542	49.3	9.38	41,309	----	----	4,381,053	4,431,043	4,430,621	4,425,279	----	4,411,633
2018-19	89,167	87,594	50.6	8.43	36,819	----	----	4,585,916	4,693,135	4,689,628	4,599,530	----	4,428,150
2019-20[1]	76,100	74,939	47.4	8.52	31,203	----	----	3,680,217	3,632,651	3,550,281	3,549,977	----	3,551,908
2020-21[2]	83,105	82,289	50.7	10.11		----	----	4,424,800	4,312,819	4,267,890	4,170,262	----	4,170,262

[1] Preliminary. [2] Forecast. NA = Not available. *Source: National Agricultural Statistics Service, U.S. Department of Agriculture (NASS-USDA)*

Stocks of Soybeans in the United States In Thousands of Bushels

Year	On Farms: Mar. 1	June 1	Sept. 1	Dec. 1	Off Farms: Mar. 1	June 1	Sept. 1	Dec. 1	Total Stocks: Mar. 1	June 1	Sept. 1	Dec. 1
2011	505,000	217,700	48,500	1,139,000	743,800	401,583	166,513	1,230,885	1,248,800	619,283	215,013	2,369,885
2012	555,000	179,000	38,250	910,000	819,488	488,465	131,120	1,056,161	1,374,488	667,465	169,370	1,966,161
2013	456,700	171,100	39,550	955,000	541,320	263,564	101,007	1,198,621	998,020	434,664	140,557	2,153,621
2014	381,900	109,100	21,325	1,218,000	611,928	295,945	70,666	1,309,744	993,828	405,045	91,991	2,527,744
2015	609,200	246,300	49,700	1,308,500	717,399	380,768	140,910	1,405,577	1,326,599	627,068	190,610	2,714,077
2016	727,500	281,300	41,560	1,335,000	803,406	590,481	155,169	1,563,379	1,530,906	871,781	196,729	2,898,379
2017	668,500	332,500	87,900	1,485,000	1,070,433	633,356	213,695	1,675,679	1,738,933	965,856	301,595	3,160,679
2018	855,000	377,000	101,000	1,935,000	1,254,303	842,329	337,105	1,810,824	2,109,303	1,219,329	438,105	3,745,824
2019	1,270,000	730,000	265,000	1,519,500	1,457,069	1,053,080	644,052	1,732,988	2,727,069	1,783,080	909,052	3,252,488
2020[1]	1,011,500	633,000	141,200	1,308,500	1,243,382	748,394	383,341	1,624,822	2,254,882	1,381,394	524,541	2,933,322

[1] Preliminary. *Source: National Agricultural Statistics Service, U.S. Department of Agriculture (NASS-USDA)*

Commercial Stocks of Soybeans in the United States, on First of Month In Millions of Bushels

Year	Jan.	Feb.	Mar.	Apr.	May	June	July	Aug.	Sept.	Oct.	Nov.	Dec.
2005	26.5	21.5	19.5	16.0	14.8	12.1	11.5	8.8	5.4	17.0	36.7	36.1
2006	36.8	30.2	26.1	25.7	17.6	20.5	14.6	14.5	14.5	19.0	40.1	43.7
2007	42.0	36.5	37.3	34.3	29.7	27.4	26.6	24.6	25.5	32.0	54.0	61.3
2008	51.1	45.5	41.8	36.3	28.2	25.6	19.2	14.8	11.4	19.6	40.5	46.1
2009	44.6	36.8	27.0	15.6	13.9	11.8	10.0	5.8	5.9	24.7	40.5	44.3
2010	30.0	28.5	20.1	22.3	10.8	8.0	8.2	4.5	3.3	19.2	45.0	32.0
2011	32.6	23.2	16.0	11.3	10.2	5.9	6.2	5.7	4.6	9.8	49.4	50.7
2012	42.7	34.8	29.9	28.5	27.1	23.8	16.6	10.4	5.2	18.8	41.6	33.8
2013	25.2	20.3	16.1	10.0	6.4	6.6	4.1	2.9	2.1	27.2	36.9	35.5
2014	30.7	20.4	15.5	12.2	7.0	5.1	5.2	2.3	----	----	----	----

This report was discontinued as of August 26, 2014. *Source: Livestock Division, U.S. Department of Agriculture (LD-USDA)*

Production of Soybeans for Beans in the United States, by State In Millions of Bushels

Year	Arkansas	Illinois	Indiana	Iowa	Kentucky	Michigan	Minnesota	Mississippi	Missouri	Nebraska	Ohio	Tennessee	Total
2011-12	126.3	423.2	240.7	475.3	57.7	85.4	274.6	70.2	190.2	261.4	217.9	40.3	3,093.5
2012-13	137.0	384.0	225.3	419.0	58.8	85.6	304.5	87.8	158.1	207.1	206.6	46.7	3,042.0
2013-14	140.9	474.0	267.3	420.9	83.0	85.4	278.0	91.5	202.0	255.2	222.3	72.1	3,358.0
2014-15	158.4	547.1	301.9	498.3	83.1	86.7	301.7	113.9	259.9	287.8	246.2	74.1	3,927.1
2015-16	155.3	544.3	275.0	553.7	88.7	99.0	377.5	104.4	181.0	305.7	237.0	79.1	3,926.3
2016-17	145.2	593.0	323.7	566.4	89.0	104.0	389.5	97.0	271.5	314.2	263.8	73.4	4,296.5
2017-18	178.5	611.9	320.8	566.6	102.8	96.5	384.3	115.0	292.5	326.0	252.0	83.0	4,411.6
2018-19	162.1	666.8	342.7	550.5	98.4	109.7	374.9	118.3	257.2	324.2	281.1	76.0	4,428.2
2019-20	127.9	532.4	273.4	501.6	77.7	69.7	297.9	81.5	230.5	283.1	209.2	64.4	3,551.9
2020-21[1]	139.0	594.5	329.4	503.3	101.2	105.1	373.8	111.2	283.2	298.7	263.5	79.4	4,170.3

[1] Preliminary. *Source: Agricultural Statistics Board, U.S. Department of Agriculture (ASB-USDA)*

U. S. Exports of Soybeans In Millions of Bushels

Year	Sept.	Oct.	Nov.	Dec.	Jan.	Feb.	Mar.	Apr.	May	June	July	Aug.	Total
2011-12	47.6	193.3	184.2	151.2	175.0	153.5	116.0	74.8	67.5	53.9	73.8	76.5	1,367.1
2012-13	96.8	274.3	255.4	186.4	194.5	141.6	72.1	34.6	22.1	19.5	13.7	17.4	1,328.3
2013-14	55.3	290.1	331.5	255.0	259.0	198.7	117.0	42.9	32.2	22.2	19.2	16.4	1,639.5
2014-15	77.9	329.9	405.3	301.7	257.5	166.6	94.1	49.7	44.0	34.4	39.7	42.6	1,843.5
2015-16	86.4	369.0	336.3	250.1	218.1	207.5	95.8	52.3	33.8	36.8	98.5	152.6	1,937.1
2016-17	138.5	415.9	378.6	291.2	272.9	162.4	114.7	89.4	53.3	66.0	83.2	113.1	2,179.3
2017-18	170.6	347.1	332.1	237.2	211.9	154.9	119.1	79.7	110.0	119.7	126.0	123.8	2,131.9
2018-19	119.0	205.2	186.3	150.9	177.5	168.3	136.3	88.2	94.1	117.4	135.3	181.3	1,759.8
2019-20	143.0	218.6	257.5	204.8	195.6	101.4	94.5	79.5	72.3	66.1	81.5	167.3	1,682.1
2020-21[1]	286.0	425.5	408.0	397.7									4,551.5

[1] Preliminary. *Source: Economic Research Service, U.S. Department of Agriculture (ERS-USDA)*

Soybean Crushed (Factory Consumption) in the United States In Millions of Bushels

Year	Sept.	Oct.	Nov.	Dec.	Jan.	Feb.	Mar.	Apr.	May	June	July	Aug.	Total
2011-12	----	516.6	----	----	524.0	----	----	453.9	----	----	299.0	----	1,703.0
2012-13	----	631.2	----	----	453.5	----	----	442.3	----	----	267.3	----	1,688.9
2013-14	----	675.8	----	----	457.0	----	----	422.0	----	----	285.6	----	1,733.9
2014-15	----	687.3	----	----	480.2	----	----	522.7	----	151.6	155.8	144.6	1,873.5
2015-16	134.6	170.1	165.8	167.0	160.5	154.6	166.4	158.2	160.9	154.1	153.5	140.6	1,886.3
2016-17	138.3	175.9	170.7	169.0	170.4	151.0	160.0	149.8	158.0	148.2	155.6	151.6	1,898.5
2017-18	145.4	175.9	173.3	176.3	174.7	165.0	182.2	171.6	172.5	169.6	178.9	169.9	2,055.3
2018-19	169.3	183.6	178.1	183.8	183.1	162.8	179.4	171.5	165.4	157.6	179.5	177.3	2,091.4
2019-20	162.3	187.2	174.6	184.7	188.8	175.3	192.2	183.4	179.6	177.3	184.5	174.7	2,164.6
2020-21[1]	171.1	196.6	191.0	193.8									2,257.5

[1] Preliminary. *Source: Economic Research Service, U.S. Department of Agriculture (ERS-USDA)*

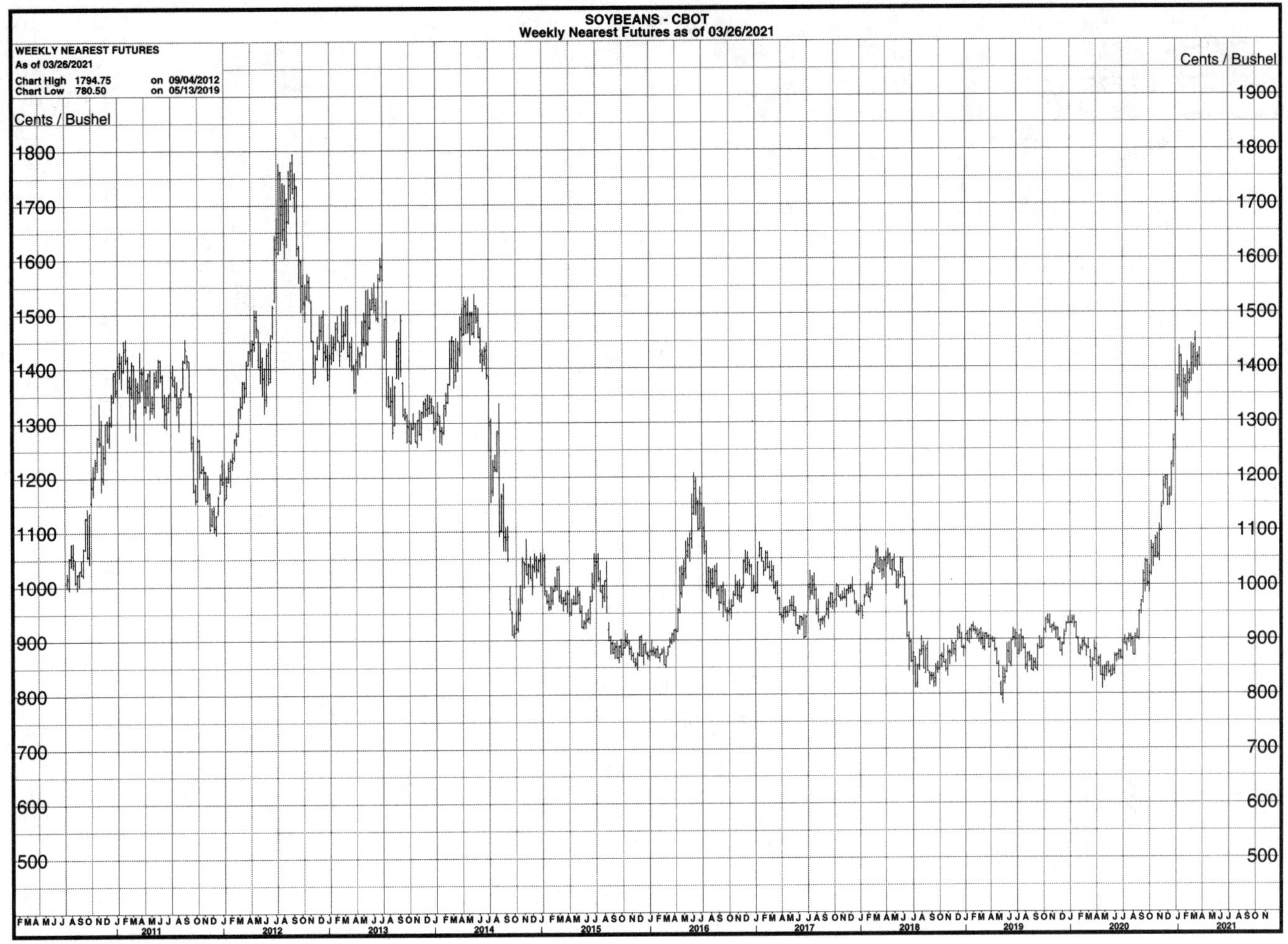

Nearby Futures through Last Trading Day.

Volume of Trading of Soybean Futures in Chicago In Thousands of Contracts

Year	Jan.	Feb.	Mar.	Apr.	May	June	July	Aug.	Sept.	Oct.	Nov.	Dec.	Total
2011	3,572.5	4,577.6	3,906.0	4,143.1	2,790.6	3,822.9	2,708.7	3,332.7	4,053.1	5,309.5	3,004.7	3,922.4	45,144
2012	3,342.4	4,370.8	4,388.0	5,314.9	4,556.2	4,887.6	5,195.8	3,879.3	3,925.5	5,272.1	3,027.3	3,881.7	52,042
2013	3,628.0	4,568.4	3,193.0	4,516.5	3,522.9	3,644.1	3,328.3	4,132.9	3,442.2	5,288.6	3,401.3	4,054.9	46,721
2014	3,692.7	5,090.5	3,613.9	4,191.9	2,914.6	3,929.4	3,765.7	2,967.5	3,672.1	7,261.6	3,661.2	4,408.2	49,169
2015	3,570.3	4,867.3	4,011.2	5,029.8	3,422.5	6,284.1	4,425.8	4,256.8	3,693.6	6,251.6	3,314.6	4,967.4	54,095
2016	3,846.1	5,203.8	4,455.3	8,380.0	6,211.8	7,135.0	4,779.8	3,432.5	3,373.1	5,936.7	4,085.1	4,891.6	61,731
2017	3,760.7	5,197.1	3,837.0	4,612.5	3,781.0	5,251.6	5,287.5	4,132.3	3,629.0	6,075.2	3,726.4	5,213.9	54,504
2018	4,066.9	6,799.5	5,116.2	6,789.1	4,592.8	6,603.2	3,794.3	4,088.9	3,151.9	5,831.5	3,439.6	4,264.6	58,539
2019	3,245.1	4,692.8	3,351.5	4,801.5	5,096.2	5,784.5	3,820.6	3,771.8	3,445.3	6,913.2	3,416.5	4,994.4	53,333
2020	3,719.9	5,513.0	5,500.2	4,709.2	3,341.8	5,562.8	4,115.7	4,432.9	5,669.6	7,545.1	4,910.5	6,102.4	61,123

Contract size = 5,000 bu. *Source: CME Group; Chicago Board of Trade (CBT)*

Average Open Interest of Soybean Futures in Chicago In Contracts

Year	Jan.	Feb.	Mar.	Apr.	May	June	July	Aug.	Sept.	Oct.	Nov.	Dec.
2011	643,422	673,796	618,157	624,350	559,493	582,529	529,949	524,547	590,297	567,081	521,277	525,510
2012	474,050	532,738	623,973	793,781	787,884	769,806	805,353	748,382	732,388	704,191	609,007	588,185
2013	549,767	615,897	589,572	565,212	565,761	596,479	517,022	535,645	615,389	626,484	582,859	625,222
2014	589,906	675,981	649,898	645,604	601,103	616,406	622,020	642,043	724,924	766,218	664,485	668,492
2015	644,320	698,627	708,314	746,322	698,151	722,449	663,522	653,707	675,762	701,419	673,127	681,902
2016	674,273	721,934	723,375	824,649	840,893	859,598	747,309	668,100	636,957	657,062	642,826	709,587
2017	681,161	736,942	691,919	729,828	654,509	695,963	648,861	645,305	666,063	723,614	712,476	747,181
2018	762,139	781,574	846,901	923,139	879,489	893,661	838,433	797,279	846,361	839,514	743,667	723,335
2019	683,830	706,877	693,239	767,901	763,593	734,373	658,702	636,025	675,040	736,987	753,829	807,431
2020	767,124	846,942	790,798	826,659	849,949	865,514	830,455	839,763	938,439	1,010,657	928,015	935,198

Contract size = 5,000 bu. *Source: CME Group; Chicago Board of Trade (CBT)*

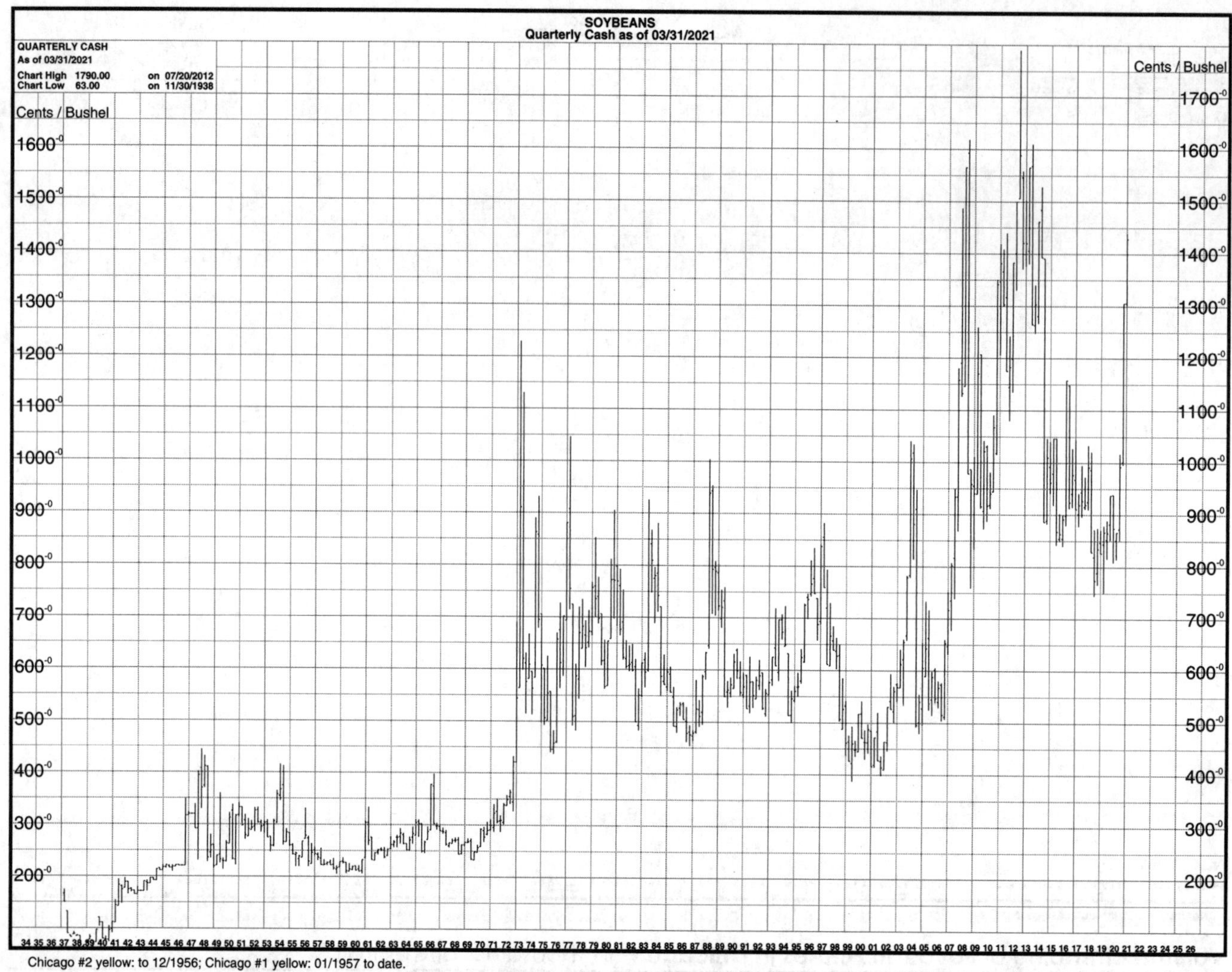

Chicago #2 yellow: to 12/1956; Chicago #1 yellow: 01/1957 to date.

Average Price Received by Farmers for Soybeans in the United States In Dollars Per Bushel

Year	Sept.	Oct.	Nov.	Dec.	Jan.	Feb.	Mar.	Apr.	May	June	July	Aug.	Average
2011-12	12.20	11.80	11.70	11.50	11.90	12.20	13.00	13.80	14.00	13.90	15.40	16.20	13.13
2012-13	14.30	14.20	14.30	14.30	14.30	14.60	14.60	14.40	14.90	15.10	15.30	14.10	14.53
2013-14	13.30	12.50	12.70	13.00	12.90	13.20	13.70	14.30	14.40	14.30	13.10	12.40	13.32
2014-15	10.90	9.97	10.20	10.30	10.30	9.91	9.85	9.69	9.58	9.58	9.95	9.71	10.00
2015-16	9.05	8.81	8.68	8.76	8.71	8.51	8.56	9.01	9.76	10.20	10.20	9.93	9.18
2016-17	9.41	9.30	9.47	9.64	9.71	9.86	9.69	9.33	9.29	9.10	9.42	9.24	9.46
2017-18	9.35	9.18	9.22	9.30	9.30	9.50	9.81	9.85	9.84	9.55	9.08	8.59	9.38
2018-19	8.78	8.59	8.36	8.56	8.64	8.52	8.52	8.28	8.02	8.31	8.38	8.22	8.43
2019-20	8.35	8.60	8.59	8.70	8.84	8.59	8.46	8.35	8.28	8.34	8.50	8.66	8.52
2020-21[1]	9.24	9.63	10.30	10.50	10.90								10.11

[1] Preliminary. *Source: Economic Research Service, U.S. Department of Agriculture (ERS-USDA)*

Average Cash Price of No. 1 Yellow Soybeans at Illinois Processor In Cents Per Bushel

Year	Sept.	Oct.	Nov.	Dec.	Jan.	Feb.	Mar.	Apr.	May	June	July	Aug.	Average
2001-02	469	430	441	438	437	440	464	471	492	519	575	567	479
2002-03	579	541	575	566	570	590	580	611	640	635	601	589	590
2003-04	639	729	763	772	823	872	975	992	958	890	809	641	822
2004-05	562	519	534	545	539	544	628	622	644	701	703	639	598
2005-06	565	553	574	592	576	575	569	562	581	576	577	542	570
2006-07	535	580	661	657	683	735	730	718	749	792	801	804	704
2007-08	907	944	1,032	1,123	1,216	1,335	1,312	1,292	1,324	1,499	1,516	1,288	1,232
2008-09	1,140	903	893	868	991	938	917	1,025	1,166	1,237	1,096	1,136	1,026
2009-10	1,012	978	1,009	1,033	984	944	949	975	955	955	1,030	1,066	991
2010-11[1]	1,065	1,148	1,252	1,311	1,378	1,386	1,350	1,364	1,368	1,382	1,384	1,381	1,314

[1] Preliminary. *Source: Economic Research Service, U.S. Department of Agriculture (ERS-USDA)*

Stock Index Futures - U.S.

A stock index simply represents a basket of underlying stocks. Indexes can be either price-weighted or capitalization-weighted. In a price-weighted index, such as the Dow Jones Industrial Average, the individual stock prices are simply added up and then divided by a divisor, meaning that stocks with higher prices have a higher weighting in the index value. In a capitalization-weighted index, such as the Standard and Poor's 500 index, the weighting of each stock corresponds to the size of the company as determined by its capitalization (i.e., the total dollar value of its stock). Stock indexes cover a variety of different sectors. For example, the Dow Jones Industrial Average contains 30 blue-chip stocks that represent the industrial sector. The S&P 500 index includes 500 of the largest blue-chip U.S. companies. The NYSE index includes all the stocks that are traded at the New York Stock Exchange. The Nasdaq 100 includes the largest 100 companies that are traded on the Nasdaq Exchange. The most popular U.S. stock index futures contract is the E-mini S&P 500 futures contract, which is traded at the CME Group.

Prices – The S&P 500 index (Barchart.com symbol $SPX) in early 2020 initially rallied to a new record high and extended the +29% rally seen in 2019. However, U.S. stocks then plunged starting in late February 2020 when it became clear that the Covid pandemic would spread globally.

The U.S. economy was partially shut down starting in March when the Covid infection rates in the U.S. started to soar. Lockdowns became necessary to slow the spread of Covid and prevent the U.S. hospital system from being overwhelmed. The lockdowns sent the U.S. economy over a cliff, with a plunge of -10% in U.S. GDP in the first half of 2020.

The S&P 500 index, in the space of just a few weeks in late February and early March 2020, plunged by a terrifying -35% from the early-February then-record high. However, U.S. stock prices quickly bottomed out in late March as the Fed took extremely aggressive action to provide liquidity to the financial system, financial institutions, private companies, and state and local governments. Also, the U.S. federal government in March 2020 approved pandemic relief with the massive $2.2 trillion Cares Act that pumped cash into the U.S. economy.

The S&P 500 index continued to rally through the remainder of 2020, producing an annual gain of +16.3%. From the 4-year low posted in March 2020, the S&P 500 index rallied by a total of +71% through the end of 2020.

Stocks rallied in the latter part of 2020 as the Fed promised to continue pumping a huge amount of liquidity into the financial system. Also, the U.S. economy started to recover fairly quickly in the second half of 2020 as Americans learned to live with the pandemic and as many businesses reopened. U.S. GDP in the second half of 2020 rose by +8.6%, recovering a large portion of the -10.1% loss seen in the first half.

Earnings growth for the S&P 500 companies plunged by -30% yr/yr in Q2-2020 due to the pandemic lockdowns and remained weak at -6.5% yr/yr in Q3-2020. However, earnings growth turned positive in Q4-2020 by +4.1% yr/yr. On a calendar year basis, the consensus is for S&P 500 earnings to grow by +24% in 2021, more than reversing the -12% decline seen in 2020.

U.S. stocks continued to rally in early 2021 due to expectations for the economy to strengthen during mid-2021 after the U.S. government approved a $900 billion pandemic aid package in late December 2020 and a $1.9 trillion pandemic aid package in March 2021. Also, the pandemic infection rates plunged starting in mid-January 2021 as vaccines started to become available, leading to market hopes for a full economic recovery by 2022.

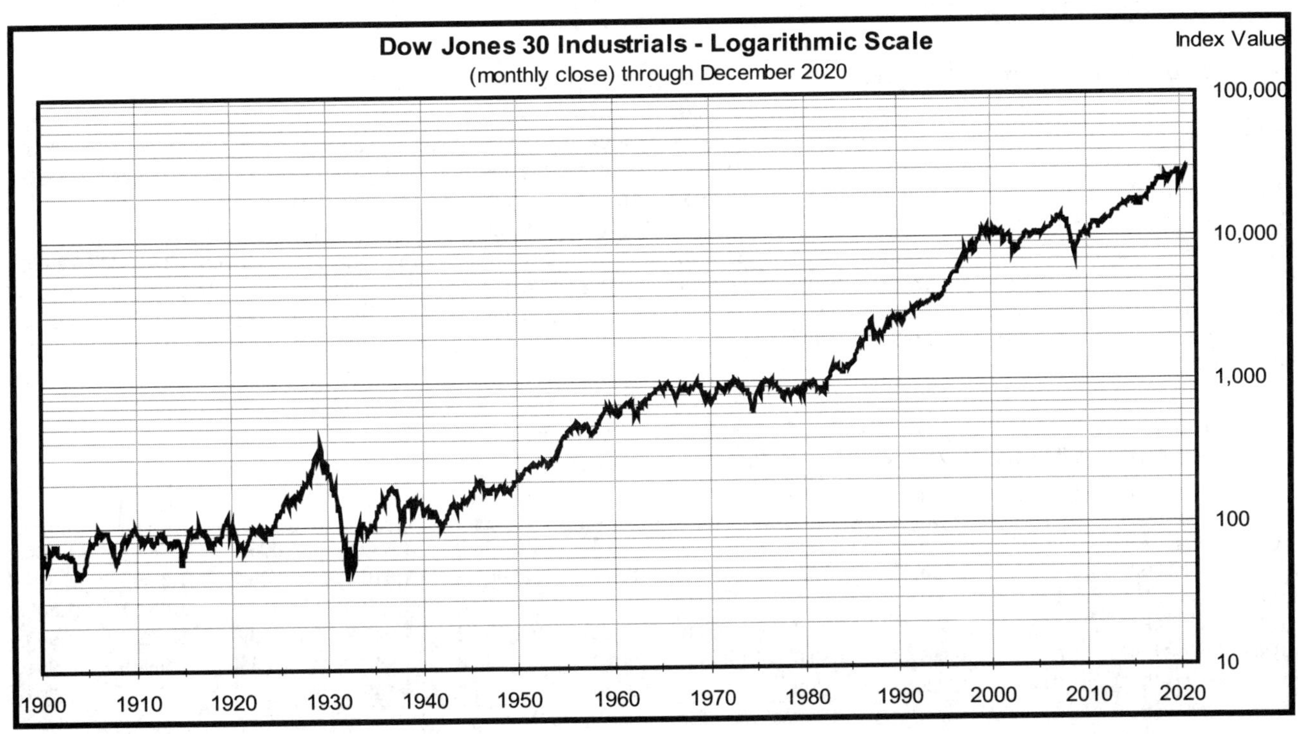

Composite Index of Leading Indicators (1992 = 100)

Year	Jan.	Feb.	Mar.	Apr.	May	June	July	Aug.	Sept.	Oct.	Nov.	Dec.	Average
2006	104.7	104.4	104.6	104.4	103.7	103.9	103.7	103.3	103.7	103.9	103.8	104.4	104.0
2007	104.0	103.7	104.1	103.9	104.0	103.9	104.6	103.6	103.7	103.2	102.8	102.6	103.7
2008	102.1	101.9	101.9	102.0	101.9	101.9	101.2	100.3	100.3	99.4	99.0	98.8	100.9
2009	98.8	98.3	98.1	99.2	100.6	101.3	102.5	103.1	104.2	104.7	105.8	106.2	101.9
2010	106.7	107.2	108.6	108.6	109.0	108.8	109.0	109.1	109.9	110.1	111.4	112.3	109.2
2011	91.8	92.7	93.7	93.7	94.2	94.2	94.4	93.7	93.2	93.8	94.1	92.2	93.5
2012	92.2	92.9	93.1	92.9	93.3	92.7	93.1	92.7	93.2	93.4	93.4	94.3	93.1
2013	94.8	95.3	95.1	95.8	96.0	96.1	96.5	97.2	98.2	98.5	99.4	113.8	98.1
2014	113.7	114.3	115.4	115.8	116.5	117.2	118.4	118.5	119.2	119.9	120.5	121.0	117.5
2015[1]	121.2	120.9	121.2	121.9	122.9	123.6	Discontinued						122.0

[1] Preliminary. *Source: The Conference Board*

Consumer Confidence, The Conference Board (2004 = 100)

Year	Jan.	Feb.	Mar.	Apr.	May	June	July	Aug.	Sept.	Oct.	Nov.	Dec.	Average
2006	106.8	102.7	107.5	109.8	104.7	105.4	107.0	100.2	105.9	105.1	105.3	110.0	105.9
2007	110.2	111.2	108.2	106.3	108.5	105.3	111.9	105.6	99.5	95.2	87.8	90.6	103.4
2008	87.3	76.4	65.9	62.8	58.1	51.0	51.9	58.5	61.4	38.8	44.7	38.6	58.0
2009	37.4	25.3	26.9	40.8	54.8	49.3	47.4	54.5	53.4	48.7	50.6	53.6	45.2
2010	56.5	46.4	52.3	57.7	62.7	54.3	51.0	53.2	48.6	49.9	57.8	63.4	54.5
2011	64.8	72.0	63.8	66.0	61.7	57.6	59.2	45.2	46.4	40.9	55.2	64.8	58.1
2012	61.5	71.6	69.5	68.7	64.4	62.7	65.4	61.3	68.4	73.1	71.5	66.7	67.1
2013	58.4	68.0	61.9	69.0	74.3	82.1	81.0	81.8	80.2	72.4	72.0	77.5	73.2
2014	79.4	78.3	83.9	81.7	82.2	86.4	90.3	93.4	89.0	94.1	91.0	93.1	86.9
2015[1]	103.8	98.8	101.4	94.3	94.6	101.4	Discontinued						99.1

[1] Preliminary. *Source: The Conference Board (TCB) Copyrighted.*

Capacity Utilization Rates (Total Industry) In Percent

Year	Jan.	Feb.	Mar.	Apr.	May	June	July	Aug.	Sept.	Oct.	Nov.	Dec.	Average
2011	75.6	75.3	76.0	75.7	75.8	76.0	76.3	76.6	76.5	76.9	76.7	77.0	76.2
2012	77.4	77.4	76.9	77.4	77.4	77.2	77.3	76.9	76.8	76.8	77.1	77.2	77.2
2013	77.1	77.4	77.6	77.5	77.4	77.5	77.1	77.6	77.9	77.7	77.9	78.1	77.6
2014	77.6	78.2	78.9	78.9	79.1	79.2	79.2	79.1	79.2	79.1	79.6	79.4	79.0
2015	78.8	78.4	78.1	77.7	77.3	76.9	77.3	77.2	76.9	76.6	76.1	75.7	77.3
2016	75.9	75.3	74.7	74.7	74.6	74.9	75.1	75.0	74.9	75.0	74.9	75.5	75.0
2017	75.5	75.2	75.7	76.4	76.5	76.6	76.5	76.2	76.1	77.3	77.6	77.9	76.5
2018	77.6	77.8	78.2	78.8	78.1	78.6	78.8	79.3	79.3	79.3	79.6	79.5	78.7
2019	79.0	78.5	78.4	77.8	77.8	77.7	77.4	77.8	77.4	77.0	77.6	77.2	77.8
2020[1]	76.9	76.9	73.6	64.2	64.8	68.9	71.8	72.5	72.5	73.2	73.9	74.6	72.0

[1] Preliminary. *Source: Bureau of Economic Analysis, U.S. Department of Commerce (BEA)*

Manufacturers New Orders, Durable Goods In Millions of Constant Dollars

Year	Jan.	Feb.	Mar.	Apr.	May	June	July	Aug.	Sept.	Oct.	Nov.	Dec.	Average
2011	204,128	194,899	210,464	201,736	205,946	200,008	208,990	215,074	208,403	209,201	216,898	226,410	208,513
2012	224,677	224,092	220,496	218,897	217,012	218,729	224,611	202,598	216,919	218,153	218,345	230,294	219,569
2013	216,919	229,202	211,757	220,286	231,193	240,895	215,452	221,749	231,395	224,605	238,295	230,735	226,040
2014	221,898	229,822	233,750	236,290	232,665	238,124	290,709	238,736	235,647	230,525	228,416	223,741	236,694
2015	226,806	219,304	230,337	226,960	220,679	233,102	231,512	227,210	221,142	227,110	225,927	220,920	225,917
2016	226,398	217,882	216,926	225,797	220,851	208,990	216,738	220,654	219,736	231,303	219,574	224,108	220,746
2017	223,049	222,023	228,253	228,086	227,201	243,829	224,989	229,906	242,818	235,856	238,976	245,755	232,562
2018	236,368	248,330	251,696	248,509	250,389	250,063	247,899	258,372	262,205	250,552	251,931	254,801	250,926
2019	250,492	242,267	252,004	240,268	236,720	236,884	242,842	244,018	241,713	241,557	235,237	241,852	242,155
2020[1]	241,417	246,195	205,020	167,502	192,605	207,474	231,914	232,933	237,786	242,098	245,247	248,307	224,875

[1] Preliminary. *Source: Bureau of Economic Analysis, U.S. Department of Commerce (BEA)*

Corporate Profits After Tax -- Quarterly In Billions of Dollars

Year	First Quarter	Second Quarter	Third Quarter	Fourth Quarter	Total	Year	First Quarter	Second Quarter	Third Quarter	Fourth Quarter	Total
2009	1,082.8	1,088.2	1,249.9	1,309.6	1,182.6	2015	1,706.9	1,689.2	1,675.6	1,585.2	1,664.2
2010	1,386.2	1,378.5	1,523.6	1,537.5	1,456.5	2016	1,661.4	1,616.8	1,636.7	1,675.4	1,647.6
2011	1,385.2	1,506.6	1,562.1	1,662.1	1,529.0	2017	1,750.8	1,783.3	1,813.9	1,864.7	1,803.2
2012	1,705.7	1,672.7	1,643.7	1,629.2	1,662.8	2018	1,950.2	1,947.9	1,969.8	1,972.4	1,960.1
2013	1,622.8	1,643.1	1,646.4	1,680.0	1,648.1	2019	1,886.6	1,958.2	1,963.4	1,998.9	1,951.8
2014	1,563.7	1,712.5	1,793.1	1,783.3	1,713.1	2020[1]	1,779.5	1,589.4	2,018.5		1,795.8

[1] Preliminary. *Source: Bureau of Economic Analysis, U.S. Department of Commerce (BEA)*

Change in Manufacturing and Trade Inventories In Billions of Dollars

Year	Jan.	Feb.	Mar.	Apr.	May	June	July	Aug.	Sept.	Oct.	Nov.	Dec.	Average
2006	85.9	-49.7	129.5	82.7	169.3	169.3	92.2	93.2	65.9	22.9	28.3	4.2	85.2
2007	37.8	43.6	-17.0	59.5	68.1	55.0	75.6	62.7	87.7	23.8	53.3	96.3	53.4
2008	169.4	78.5	35.6	81.4	66.2	133.3	202.6	34.8	-64.9	-99.6		-250.0	35.2
2009	-170.2	-188.5	-232.1	-197.4	-196.7	-218.1	-159.1	-232.5	-46.8	59.8	75.6	-14.9	-126.7
2010	27.9	104.4	95.5	95.3	54.9	136.3	173.2	139.3	179.6	190.5	63.3	173.4	119.5
2011	167.1	129.1	226.8	154.7	184.1	50.0	75.1	114.0	-26.5	158.7	69.4	79.7	115.2
2012	139.9	118.4	47.8	46.5	56.8	27.0	128.1	85.0	118.2	60.8	37.4	33.6	75.0
2013	205.4	30.2	-18.8	66.4	-1.8	17.5	62.3	71.5	117.8	137.2	95.7	82.0	72.1
2014	65.6	74.8	82.9	124.5	104.5	64.6	70.8	32.9	54.1	52.7	20.9	15.3	63.6
2015[1]	-29.5	57.0	25.4	83.8	59.8	Discontinued							39.3

[1] Preliminary. *Source: Bureau of Economic Analysis, U.S. Department of Commerce (BEA)*

Productivity: Index of Output per Hour, All Persons, Nonfarm Business -- Quarterly (1992 = 100)

Year	First Quarter	Second Quarter	Third Quarter	Fourth Quarter	Total	Year	First Quarter	Second Quarter	Third Quarter	Fourth Quarter	Total
2009	93.4	95.3	96.8	98.1	95.9	2015	102.7	103.1	103.3	102.8	103.0
2010	98.6	98.9	99.4	99.7	99.2	2016	103.0	103.0	103.3	103.9	103.3
2011	99.0	99.2	98.9	99.5	99.2	2017	104.2	104.2	104.8	105.2	104.6
2012	99.9	100.3	100.1	99.7	100.0	2018	105.8	106.1	106.2	106.4	106.1
2013	100.3	100.0	100.5	101.2	100.5	2019	107.4	107.9	108.0	108.4	107.9
2014	100.2	101.2	102.2	101.7	101.4	2020[1]	108.3	111.1	112.3		110.6

[1] Preliminary. *Source: Bureau of Economic Analysis, U.S. Department of Commerce (BEA)*

Civilian Unemployment Rate - U3

Year	Jan.	Feb.	Mar.	Apr.	May	June	July	Aug.	Sept.	Oct.	Nov.	Dec.	Average
2011	9.1	9.0	9.0	9.1	9.0	9.1	9.0	9.0	9.0	8.8	8.6	8.5	8.9
2012	8.2	8.3	8.2	8.2	8.2	8.2	8.2	8.1	7.8	7.8	7.8	7.9	8.1
2013	7.9	7.7	7.5	7.5	7.5	7.5	7.3	7.2	7.2	7.2	7.0	6.7	7.4
2014	6.6	6.7	6.6	6.2	6.3	6.1	6.2	6.1	5.9	5.7	5.8	5.6	6.2
2015	5.7	5.5	5.4	5.4	5.5	5.3	5.2	5.1	5.0	5.0	5.0	5.0	5.3
2016	4.9	4.9	5.0	5.0	4.7	4.9	4.9	4.9	4.9	4.8	4.6	4.7	4.9
2017	4.8	4.7	4.5	4.4	4.3	4.4	4.3	4.4	4.2	4.1	4.1	4.1	4.4
2018	4.1	4.1	4.1	3.9	3.8	4.0	3.9	3.8	3.7	3.8	3.7	3.9	3.9
2019	4.0	3.8	3.8	3.6	3.6	3.7	3.7	3.7	3.5	3.6	3.5	3.5	3.7
2020[1]	3.5	3.6	4.4	14.7	13.3	11.1	10.2	8.4	7.9	6.9	6.7	6.7	8.1

[1] Preliminary. *Source: Bureau of Economic Analysis, U.S. Department of Commerce (BEA)*

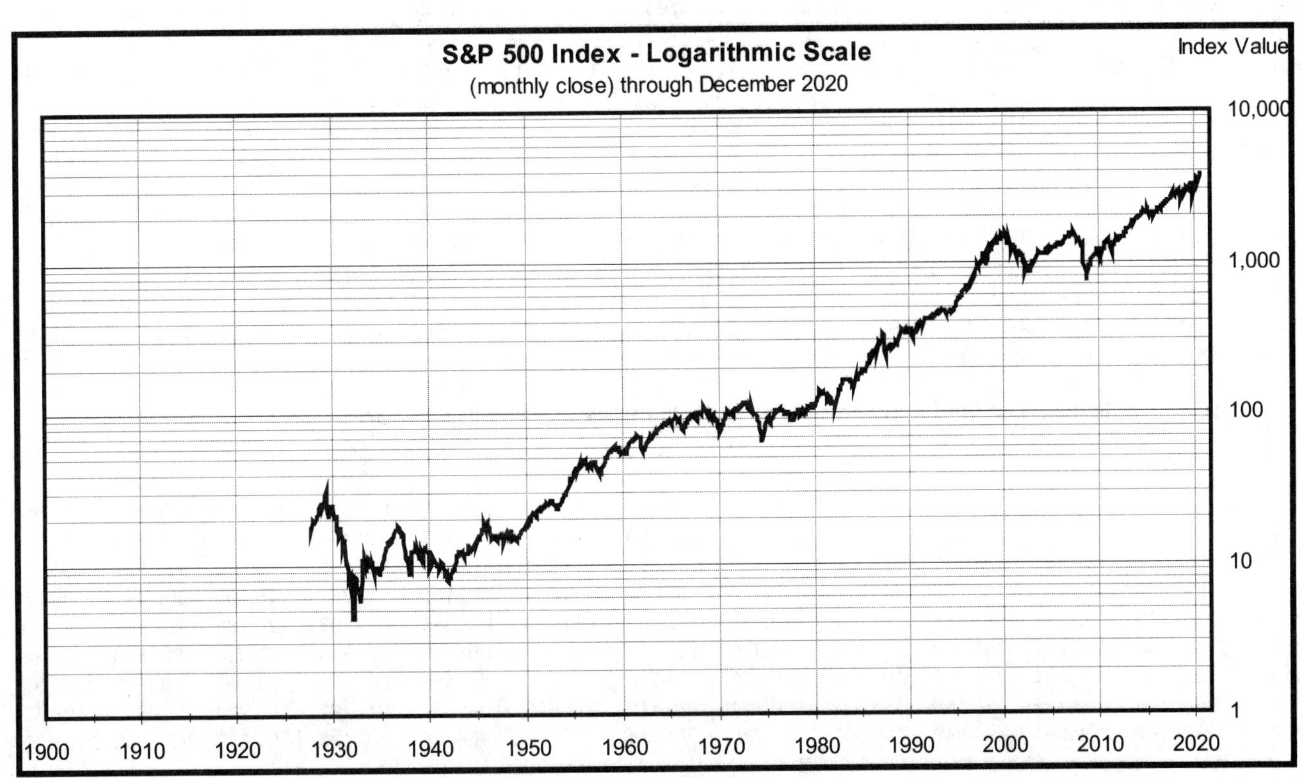

"Dow Jones", "The Dow", "Dow Jones Industrial Average" and "DJIA" are service marks of Dow Jones & Company, Inc. Shaded areas indicate US recessions.

Average Value of Dow Jones Industrials Index (30 Stocks)

Year	Jan.	Feb.	Mar.	Apr.	May	June	July	Aug.	Sept.	Oct.	Nov.	Dec.	Average
2011	11,802.4	12,190.0	12,081.5	12,434.9	12,580.0	12,097.3	12,512.3	11,326.6	11,175.5	11,515.9	11,804.2	12,075.7	11,966.4
2012	12,550.9	12,889.1	13,079.5	13,030.8	12,721.1	12,544.9	12,814.1	13,134.9	13,418.5	13,380.7	12,896.4	13,144.2	12,967.1
2013	13,615.3	13,967.3	14,418.3	14,675.9	15,172.2	15,035.8	15,390.2	15,195.3	15,269.8	15,289.8	15,870.8	16,095.8	14,999.7
2014	16,243.6	15,958.4	16,308.6	16,399.5	16,567.3	16,843.8	16,988.3	16,775.2	17,098.1	16,701.9	17,649.0	17,754.2	16,774.0
2015	17,542.3	17,945.4	17,931.7	17,970.5	18,124.7	17,927.2	17,795.0	17,061.6	16,340.0	17,182.3	17,723.8	17,542.9	17,590.6
2016	16,305.3	16,299.9	17,302.1	17,844.4	17,692.3	17,754.9	18,341.2	18,495.2	18,267.4	18,184.6	18,697.3	19,712.4	17,908.1
2017	19,908.2	20,424.1	20,823.1	20,684.7	20,936.8	21,317.8	21,581.3	21,914.1	22,173.4	23,036.2	23,557.9	24,545.4	21,741.9
2018	25,804.0	24,981.5	24,582.2	24,304.2	24,572.5	24,790.1	24,978.2	25,630.0	26,232.7	25,609.3	25,258.7	23,805.5	25,045.8
2019	24,157.8	25,605.5	25,722.6	26,401.6	25,744.8	26,160.1	27,089.2	26,057.8	26,900.2	26,736.8	27,797.1	28,167.0	26,378.4
2020	28,880.0	28,519.7	22,637.4	23,293.9	24,271.0	26,062.3	26,385.8	27,821.4	27,733.4	28,005.1	29,124.0	30,148.6	26,906.9

Source: New York Stock Exchange (NYSE)

Volume of Trading of Mini Dow Jones Industrials Index Futures in Chicago In Thousands of Contracts

Year	Jan.	Feb.	Mar.	Apr.	May	June	July	Aug.	Sept.	Oct.	Nov.	Dec.	Total
2011	2,086.5	2,020.2	3,177.6	1,830.8	2,475.5	2,990.4	2,367.0	4,344.6	3,249.6	2,790.5	2,769.2	2,395.0	32,496.9
2012	1,873.4	2,057.1	2,582.9	2,398.8	3,488.5	3,359.7	2,570.8	2,236.0	2,406.3	2,623.1	2,745.3	2,560.3	30,902.0
2013	2,143.3	2,525.2	3,044.9	3,417.8	3,212.1	4,386.6	2,492.1	2,820.5	2,934.8	3,480.8	2,494.0	2,496.7	35,448.8
2014	3,180.8	3,115.6	3,965.0	3,351.6	2,637.7	2,641.1	3,028.9	2,683.7	3,476.0	5,444.0	1,954.8	3,574.5	39,053.7
2015	4,146.7	2,343.8	3,126.0	2,988.1	2,558.3	3,546.6	3,063.7	4,651.2	4,649.7	3,226.2	2,566.1	3,734.5	40,601.1
2016	5,169.8	4,307.1	3,300.6	3,164.9	3,083.4	4,152.0	2,600.0	2,641.6	4,047.4	3,274.0	3,887.6	2,927.5	42,555.9
2017	2,515.6	2,343.6	3,891.9	2,722.0	2,564.0	3,465.6	2,132.3	2,858.2	2,672.1	2,144.2	2,707.7	2,849.1	32,866.3
2018	3,623.3	6,592.1	6,939.8	5,479.4	4,405.7	4,558.5	3,310.8	2,989.4	3,521.3	7,088.2	4,886.0	6,929.7	60,324.2
2019	4,900.8	3,651.9	4,927.9	3,353.4	5,889.6	4,224.5	3,566.3	5,763.7	3,868.9	3,924.5	2,713.2	3,593.0	50,377.7
2020	5,015.6	6,334.8	8,432.1	4,349.6	4,357.1	6,025.1	4,459.1	3,451.9	5,188.2	4,656.0	3,681.5	3,420.6	59,371.7

Contract value = $5. *Source: Chicago Board of Trade (CBT)*

Average Open Interest of Mini Dow Jones Industrials Index Futures in Chicago In Contracts

Year	Jan.	Feb.	Mar.	Apr.	May	June	July	Aug.	Sept.	Oct.	Nov.	Dec.
2011	89,055	94,278	97,112	117,217	113,517	94,274	113,353	86,802	77,776	77,465	86,666	106,153
2012	102,192	109,321	116,358	102,473	103,582	100,349	87,422	109,011	128,525	115,960	99,172	105,089
2013	104,630	122,311	131,290	114,419	118,633	113,230	113,658	115,707	119,479	106,434	131,168	134,255
2014	127,534	114,491	134,383	119,028	127,150	131,818	124,601	115,822	140,265	119,716	139,521	135,980
2015	106,993	111,350	109,677	104,565	112,992	110,880	92,351	93,151	77,209	75,595	100,777	98,535
2016	65,416	62,194	83,643	117,857	119,596	122,482	120,095	144,885	135,208	120,288	127,896	140,802
2017	131,853	130,492	145,630	130,214	121,956	129,328	131,569	149,149	159,249	157,990	155,973	154,854
2018	153,793	126,347	118,343	100,414	102,356	96,326	87,601	100,558	112,896	95,850	80,908	80,929
2019	77,165	83,432	85,168	80,534	79,824	80,412	91,970	90,051	100,267	105,282	112,609	108,479
2020	102,791	102,595	75,348	60,895	71,735	79,524	78,506	90,866	76,430	91,547	94,005	94,361

Contract value = $5. *Source: Chicago Board of Trade (CBT)*

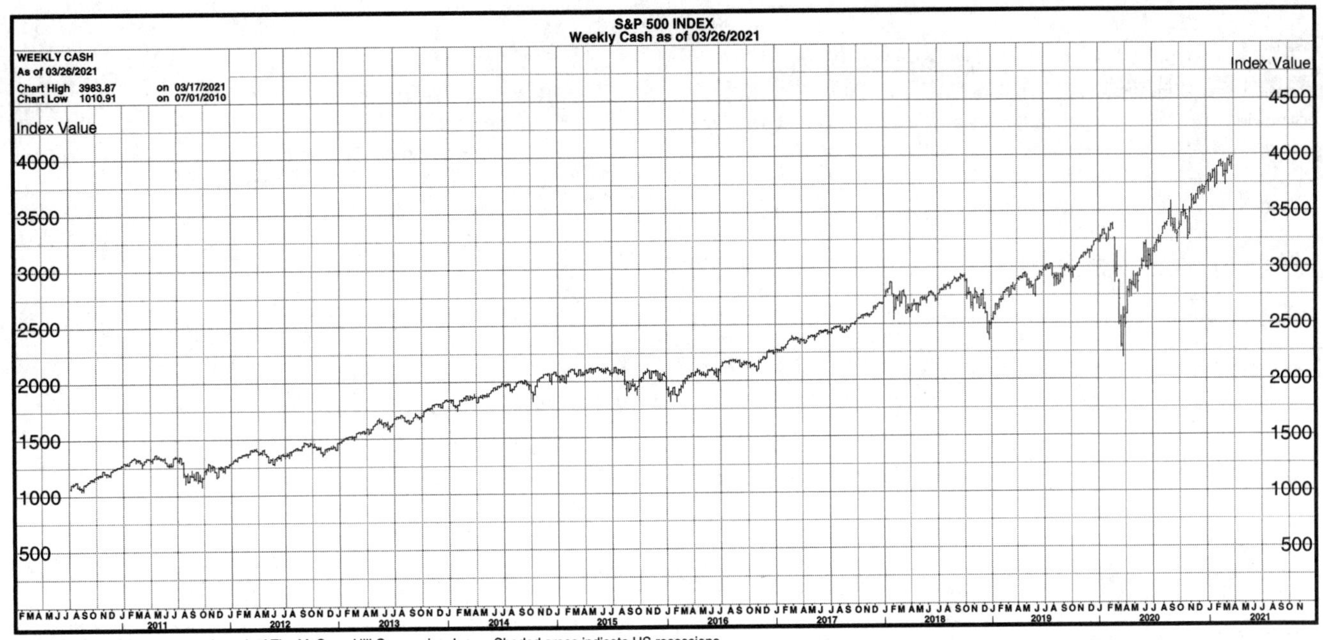

The S&P 500® Index is a trademark of The McGraw-Hill Companies, Inc. Shaded areas indicate US recessions.

Average Value of Standard & Poor's 500 Index

Year	Jan.	Feb.	Mar.	Apr.	May	June	July	Aug.	Sept.	Oct.	Nov.	Dec.	Average
2011	1,282.6	1,321.1	1,304.5	1,331.5	1,338.3	1,287.3	1,325.2	1,185.3	1,173.9	1,207.2	1,226.4	1,243.3	1,268.9
2012	1,300.6	1,352.5	1,389.2	1,386.4	1,341.3	1,323.5	1,359.8	1,403.5	1,443.4	1,437.8	1,394.5	1,422.3	1,379.6
2013	1,480.4	1,512.3	1,550.8	1,570.7	1,639.8	1,618.8	1,668.7	1,670.1	1,687.2	1,720.1	1,783.5	1,807.8	1,642.5
2014	1,822.4	1,817.0	1,863.5	1,864.3	1,889.8	1,947.1	1,973.1	1,961.5	1,993.2	1,937.3	2,044.6	2,054.3	1,930.7
2015	2,028.2	2,082.2	2,080.0	2,094.9	2,111.9	2,099.3	2,094.1	2,039.9	1,944.4	2,024.8	2,080.6	2,054.1	2,061.2
2016	1,918.6	1,904.4	2,022.0	2,075.5	2,065.6	2,083.9	2,148.9	2,177.5	2,157.7	2,143.0	2,165.0	2,246.6	2,092.4
2017	2,275.1	2,329.9	2,366.8	2,359.3	2,395.4	2,434.0	2,454.1	2,456.2	2,492.8	2,557.0	2,593.6	2,664.3	2,448.2
2018	2,789.8	2,705.2	2,702.8	2,653.6	2,701.5	2,754.4	2,793.6	2,857.8	2,901.5	2,785.5	2,723.2	2,567.3	2,744.7
2019	2,607.4	2,754.9	2,804.0	2,903.8	2,854.7	2,890.2	2,996.1	2,897.5	2,982.2	2,977.7	3,104.9	3,176.8	2,912.5
2020	3,278.2	3,277.3	2,652.4	2,762.0	2,919.6	3,104.7	3,207.6	3,391.7	3,365.5	3,418.7	3,549.0	3,695.3	3,218.5

Source: Index and Option Market (IOM), division of the Chicago Mercantile Exchange (CME)

Volume of Trading of E-mini S&P 500 Stock Index Futures in Chicago In Thousands of Contracts

Year	Jan.	Feb.	Mar.	Apr.	May	June	July	Aug.	Sept.	Oct.	Nov.	Dec.	Total
2011	38,684	36,326	60,446	32,705	43,114	59,186	43,083	82,693	71,646	55,044	51,593	45,850	620,369
2012	34,720	32,505	44,161	35,956	47,447	54,942	38,614	33,377	38,685	36,912	39,528	37,433	474,279
2013	30,743	35,953	43,787	41,242	41,901	52,896	29,323	34,906	39,752	39,069	28,689	34,028	452,291
2014	33,770	33,265	43,038	34,460	27,653	33,330	33,263	28,020	40,843	54,465	22,223	40,690	425,020
2015	38,362	25,643	38,949	26,801	24,516	39,037	32,990	46,325	48,962	36,264	28,643	43,312	429,803
2016	47,987	42,532	44,628	34,639	33,049	48,583	31,172	33,429	49,729	32,532	38,250	36,148	472,679
2017	28,663	26,871	43,248	27,397	28,105	40,315	22,213	32,605	33,473	24,444	27,662	30,604	365,602
2018	29,153	42,946	47,450	35,694	28,915	35,955	23,295	25,086	33,325	53,156	37,153	53,071	445,199
2019	33,983	25,491	38,615	23,894	41,914	36,451	25,475	44,708	35,370	31,055	23,059	35,129	395,144
2020	37,026	46,041	78,873	38,201	35,313	52,930	35,600	26,785	50,101	36,020	31,134	34,203	502,227

Contract value = $50. *Source: Index and Option Market (IOM), division of the Chicago Mercantile Exchange (CME)*

Average Open Interest of E-mini S&P 500 Stock Index Futures in Chicago In Thousands of Contracts

Year	Jan.	Feb.	Mar.	Apr.	May	June	July	Aug.	Sept.	Oct.	Nov.	Dec.
2011	2,581.7	2,829.5	2,960.3	2,704.1	2,762.3	2,887.0	2,578.6	3,318.6	3,424.6	3,008.7	2,955.1	2,903.6
2012	2,651.8	2,769.8	2,904.4	2,797.2	2,949.5	2,964.8	2,799.8	2,945.7	3,182.3	2,951.7	3,088.0	3,116.6
2013	2,872.7	3,117.0	3,199.6	3,038.9	3,279.6	3,245.5	2,778.0	2,910.8	2,954.2	2,717.7	2,848.0	2,973.0
2014	2,865.8	3,123.2	3,283.5	2,800.4	2,949.6	3,160.0	2,946.3	2,985.7	3,153.2	2,821.8	2,990.2	3,025.6
2015	2,724.4	2,820.5	3,000.4	2,707.2	2,776.2	2,863.5	2,672.8	2,893.6	3,179.8	2,921.9	2,889.2	2,801.6
2016	2,792.2	3,072.3	3,109.5	2,863.7	2,884.5	3,056.9	2,971.7	2,971.2	3,115.3	2,960.2	2,985.0	2,989.9
2017	2,833.2	2,991.5	3,112.3	2,905.0	3,049.8	3,062.1	2,924.0	3,192.3	3,279.6	3,104.8	3,293.9	3,348.8
2018	3,310.8	3,366.2	3,200.3	3,017.3	3,081.8	2,985.4	2,745.8	2,833.8	2,950.5	2,887.7	2,993.6	3,024.4
2019	2,669.4	2,643.7	2,620.1	2,604.3	2,667.3	2,721.3	2,617.6	2,585.9	2,677.3	2,532.7	2,772.7	2,940.4
2020	2,737.3	2,820.8	3,584.9	3,415.4	3,232.2	3,077.7	2,637.2	2,720.0	2,664.9	2,452.8	2,492.2	2,666.4

Contract value = $50. *Source: Index and Option Market (IOM), division of the Chicago Mercantile Exchange (CME)*

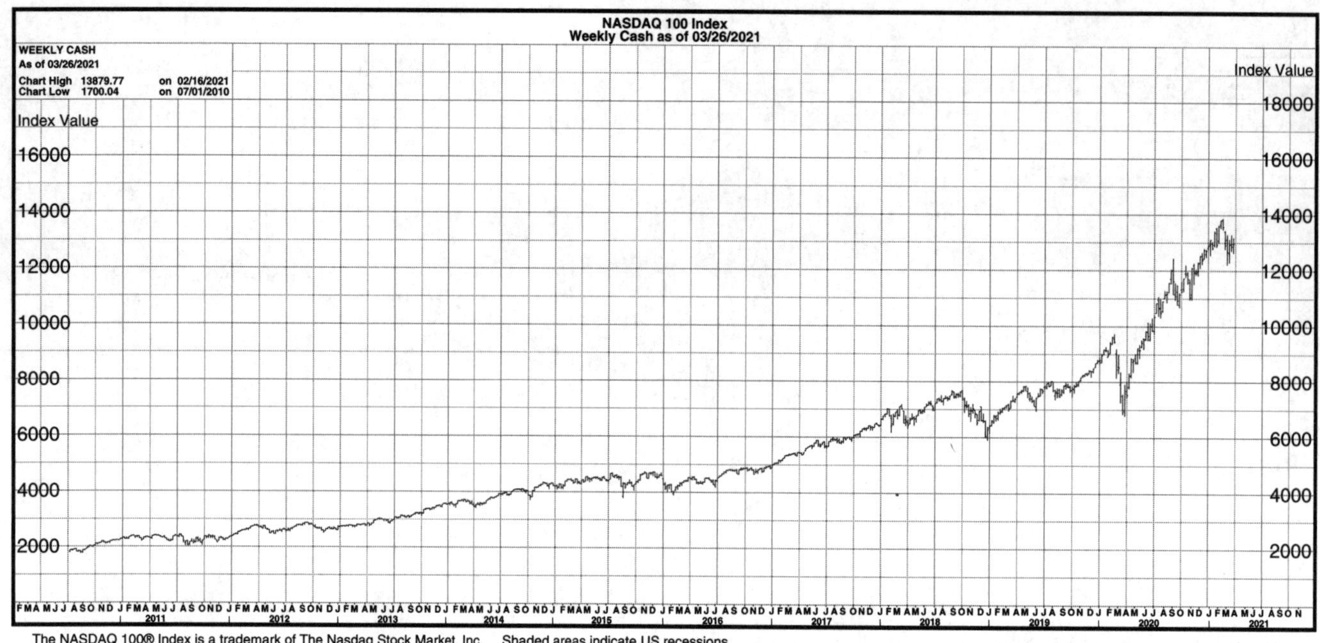

The NASDAQ 100® Index is a trademark of The Nasdaq Stock Market, Inc. Shaded areas indicate US recessions.

Average Value of NASDAQ 100 Index

Year	Jan.	Feb.	Mar.	Apr.	May	June	July	Aug.	Sept.	Oct.	Nov.	Dec.	Average
2011	2,291.2	2,353.4	2,298.7	2,344.1	2,364.6	2,255.1	2,379.5	2,173.8	2,224.5	2,298.7	2,291.8	2,279.2	2,296.2
2012	2,404.3	2,567.0	2,699.0	2,716.1	2,589.0	2,549.9	2,605.7	2,739.1	2,820.9	2,735.9	2,616.6	2,658.8	2,641.9
2013	2,736.9	2,748.2	2,795.3	2,818.6	2,981.2	2,937.3	3,033.0	3,105.5	3,187.5	3,292.0	3,399.5	3,513.8	3,045.7
2014	3,557.9	3,615.0	3,661.1	3,554.5	3,621.1	3,792.1	3,926.7	3,979.4	4,070.3	3,964.6	4,221.1	4,260.8	3,852.0
2015	4,182.6	4,343.5	4,389.2	4,418.9	4,476.4	4,481.7	4,528.3	4,422.3	4,261.6	4,445.5	4,653.2	4,628.0	4,435.9
2016	4,259.3	4,129.6	4,377.1	4,491.9	4,379.4	4,427.0	4,592.6	4,785.7	4,813.3	4,845.3	4,791.8	4,886.3	4,564.9
2017	5,056.8	5,261.2	5,386.2	5,447.9	5,687.4	5,767.0	5,816.1	5,874.4	5,954.9	6,088.5	6,328.2	6,398.0	5,755.5
2018	6,790.5	6,704.4	6,844.9	6,606.9	6,875.9	7,159.6	7,296.6	7,453.1	7,528.0	7,171.6	6,855.0	6,498.0	6,982.0
2019	6,619.8	7,021.1	7,254.2	7,660.6	7,481.0	7,505.2	7,897.8	7,619.8	7,814.0	7,859.7	8,284.4	8,527.4	7,628.7
2020	9,031.2	9,297.5	7,835.4	8,437.0	9,208.0	9,898.7	10,658.3	11,406.5	11,330.8	11,605.0	11,893.3	12,622.1	10,268.6

Source: Index and Option Market (IOM), division of the Chicago Mercantile Exchange (CME)

Volume of Trading of E-mini NASDAQ 100 Index Futures in Chicago In Thousands of Contracts

Year	Jan.	Feb.	Mar.	Apr.	May	June	July	Aug.	Sept.	Oct.	Nov.	Dec.	Total
2011	4,986.1	4,764.0	8,138.5	4,912.7	5,944.0	6,778.1	5,276.4	8,884.3	8,034.8	6,813.7	5,807.2	4,825.6	75,165.3
2012	3,623.4	4,274.5	6,068.6	5,655.0	6,428.6	6,100.5	4,852.6	4,448.9	5,148.7	5,578.6	5,845.3	5,506.0	63,530.8
2013	4,420.0	4,365.7	4,911.6	5,226.0	4,549.5	6,411.2	4,222.9	4,686.9	5,210.9	6,077.2	4,280.9	5,030.3	59,393.1
2014	5,641.0	5,236.1	7,514.0	7,765.8	5,541.1	5,252.7	5,305.9	4,774.4	7,103.7	10,105.5	4,013.9	7,229.6	75,483.7
2015	6,833.3	3,985.2	6,094.0	4,617.1	3,880.7	5,542.4	5,100.7	7,432.1	7,310.1	5,782.1	4,431.2	6,301.3	67,310.3
2016	8,223.6	6,818.4	5,768.6	5,007.9	4,813.8	6,045.0	3,857.8	4,059.2	6,567.4	4,716.0	5,396.7	4,476.2	65,750.5
2017	3,626.6	3,403.0	5,698.7	4,376.9	5,129.1	9,012.5	5,528.7	7,491.5	6,785.4	5,498.9	6,481.7	6,526.1	69,559.1
2018	7,000.4	10,100.0	12,243.8	10,030.7	7,692.8	8,400.0	7,283.8	7,592.7	9,416.3	16,684.0	13,094.0	14,657.0	124,195.5
2019	10,846.1	7,708.1	10,799.4	8,157.1	12,812.9	9,468.0	7,921.1	13,397.1	9,556.8	9,475.4	6,734.3	8,204.2	115,080.5
2020	12,102.9	15,474.5	17,447.9	9,248.0	9,155.6	11,842.5	12,107.8	9,570.3	16,216.4	13,214.9	10,349.1	9,987.2	146,717.1

Contract value = $20. *Source: Index and Option Market (IOM), division of the Chicago Mercantile Exchange (CME)*

Average Open Interest of E-mini NASDAQ 100 Index Futures in Chicago In Contracts

Year	Jan.	Feb.	Mar.	Apr.	May	June	July	Aug.	Sept.	Oct.	Nov.	Dec.
2011	367,204	361,772	350,534	351,601	370,994	321,623	346,518	350,282	369,902	321,427	325,938	308,063
2012	335,164	435,422	484,224	435,734	402,222	376,770	354,698	422,296	480,174	390,199	382,542	380,507
2013	313,000	337,571	376,894	365,878	419,450	381,375	361,111	391,874	393,462	380,763	406,143	439,961
2014	427,403	428,404	452,936	352,802	355,239	383,300	365,320	359,978	399,636	349,013	357,410	376,694
2015	314,070	325,766	352,413	335,425	322,640	342,629	327,815	337,292	287,155	285,539	348,170	334,859
2016	287,540	269,926	244,045	227,743	227,844	237,463	242,541	295,495	301,601	303,400	269,558	247,601
2017	224,988	233,695	249,237	256,682	273,541	324,978	286,106	295,726	292,471	278,159	286,310	306,756
2018	264,915	239,065	250,925	242,489	243,195	251,523	243,189	244,958	268,030	250,113	245,902	240,458
2019	212,112	217,827	217,867	206,137	217,691	222,946	218,856	200,522	213,935	214,090	228,363	224,543
2020	213,795	208,540	226,372	181,126	199,383	206,398	220,553	233,772	300,472	238,614	235,732	237,238

Contract value = $20. *Source: Index and Option Market (IOM), division of the Chicago Mercantile Exchange (CME)*

Average Value of Dow Jones Transportation Index (20 Stocks)

Year	Jan.	Feb.	Mar.	Apr.	May	June	July	Aug.	Sept.	Oct.	Nov.	Dec.	Average
2011	5,135.4	5,130.2	5,110.7	5,319.1	5,431.5	5,212.9	5,395.0	4,569.8	4,420.8	4,628.8	4,820.8	4,943.3	5,009.8
2012	5,206.5	5,245.1	5,225.4	5,239.7	5,121.6	5,050.9	5,117.2	5,088.7	5,038.1	5,041.0	5,056.3	5,218.7	5,137.4
2013	5,665.7	5,908.1	6,167.2	6,073.4	6,370.3	6,225.1	6,420.2	6,438.7	6,555.1	6,767.9	7,131.0	7,220.9	6,412.0
2014	7,361.9	7,235.3	7,512.0	7,587.8	7,854.6	8,135.4	8,308.7	8,272.8	8,534.2	8,308.9	9,033.8	9,025.7	8,097.6
2015	8,853.6	9,005.2	8,942.9	8,725.1	8,592.8	8,361.0	8,214.8	8,134.2	7,929.8	8,117.2	8,174.0	7,658.2	8,392.4
2016	6,871.7	7,133.1	7,771.2	7,919.7	7,700.9	7,615.7	7,817.1	7,845.3	7,913.3	8,054.3	8,622.5	9,207.6	7,872.7
2017	9,192.9	9,368.9	9,184.5	9,096.5	9,058.9	9,382.3	9,542.7	9,208.8	9,573.3	9,901.8	9,665.7	10,463.4	9,470.0
2018	11,106.0	10,471.7	10,477.7	10,427.8	10,631.9	10,795.0	10,663.5	11,220.3	11,443.3	10,604.3	10,507.1	9,544.1	10,657.7
2019	9,657.2	10,426.4	10,262.2	10,816.6	10,427.1	10,222.2	10,581.9	10,053.4	10,474.0	10,376.8	10,907.5	10,779.3	10,415.4
2020	10,994.0	10,617.1	7,941.0	8,002.8	8,307.7	9,249.4	9,600.0	10,829.0	11,292.7	11,603.4	12,095.7	12,568.9	10,258.5

Source: New York Stock Exchange (NYSE)

Average Value of Dow Jones Utilities Index (15 Stocks)

Year	Jan.	Feb.	Mar.	Apr.	May	June	July	Aug.	Sept.	Oct.	Nov.	Dec.	Average
2011	410.1	411.9	409.9	416.5	434.8	427.0	435.3	419.9	431.7	439.9	443.0	451.5	427.6
2012	451.0	451.3	454.8	459.4	467.9	475.6	485.0	479.3	471.5	479.2	449.7	453.9	464.9
2013	463.6	474.7	493.1	522.2	511.0	481.1	496.7	490.3	480.7	492.3	499.5	485.4	490.9
2014	491.9	513.0	519.8	540.7	540.0	556.0	557.5	547.2	555.3	569.2	596.5	609.7	549.7
2015	634.5	610.4	582.6	589.7	584.5	564.1	570.8	587.1	558.1	588.0	566.9	567.7	583.7
2016	585.1	621.9	649.2	655.4	657.7	682.6	712.9	686.2	676.4	654.6	642.6	650.1	656.2
2017	658.2	674.0	696.8	703.8	705.4	726.4	712.0	738.2	736.9	740.9	760.2	742.3	716.3
2018	694.2	671.0	679.0	693.4	687.0	683.9	719.6	729.3	729.1	734.2	730.9	734.5	707.2
2019	708.6	741.2	773.2	776.7	784.7	810.1	820.1	829.5	859.4	867.4	848.0	863.5	806.9
2020	901.5	929.8	776.3	784.2	764.6	796.7	806.9	820.2	804.7	870.5	888.6	856.6	833.4

Source: New York Stock Exchange (NYSE)

Average Value of Standard & Poor's MidCap 400 Index

Year	Jan.	Feb.	Mar.	Apr.	May	June	July	Aug.	Sept.	Oct.	Nov.	Dec.	Average
2011	921.6	959.0	959.6	991.0	990.7	950.8	980.4	843.9	829.1	841.9	867.8	872.2	917.3
2012	917.3	975.0	988.8	978.7	949.4	915.3	939.9	962.7	1,001.1	986.0	979.7	1,010.8	967.1
2013	1,070.4	1,104.0	1,132.3	1,133.9	1,188.1	1,163.1	1,214.3	1,221.6	1,230.2	1,270.6	1,297.6	1,311.4	1,194.8
2014	1,333.5	1,333.4	1,373.9	1,355.0	1,361.6	1,410.5	1,413.6	1,402.5	1,415.2	1,351.5	1,435.2	1,438.2	1,385.3
2015	1,440.1	1,493.5	1,509.4	1,527.7	1,525.0	1,528.8	1,499.9	1,463.3	1,399.8	1,427.8	1,449.2	1,413.6	1,473.2
2016	1,299.3	1,296.5	1,408.0	1,456.5	1,458.3	1,489.2	1,534.0	1,559.7	1,546.7	1,526.0	1,571.6	1,668.8	1,484.5
2017	1,684.1	1,720.7	1,715.5	1,715.7	1,724.7	1,749.1	1,763.1	1,722.3	1,754.8	1,822.3	1,845.6	1,892.9	1,759.2
2018	1,959.7	1,876.7	1,902.7	1,886.0	1,930.2	1,981.1	1,988.5	2,016.0	2,032.4	1,892.6	1,859.1	1,715.6	1,920.0
2019	1,765.3	1,892.3	1,888.8	1,951.4	1,898.0	1,902.8	1,956.5	1,876.9	1,935.3	1,923.8	1,997.6	2,035.0	1,918.6
2020	2,062.5	2,034.1	1,520.6	1,523.4	1,656.9	1,804.9	1,820.0	1,931.5	1,867.7	1,963.4	2,108.2	2,265.3	1,879.9

Source: Index and Option Market (IOM), division of the Chicago Mercantile Exchange (CME)

Civilian Unemployment Rate - U6

Year	Jan.	Feb.	Mar.	Apr.	May	June	July	Aug.	Sept.	Oct.	Nov.	Dec.	Average
2011	16.1	15.9	15.7	15.9	15.8	16.2	16.1	16.2	16.5	16.2	15.6	15.2	16.0
2012	15.1	15.0	14.5	14.5	14.8	14.8	14.9	14.7	14.7	14.5	14.4	14.4	14.7
2013	14.4	14.3	13.8	13.9	13.8	14.3	14.0	13.6	13.6	13.7	13.1	13.1	13.8
2014	12.7	12.6	12.7	12.3	12.2	12.1	12.2	12.0	11.7	11.5	11.4	11.2	12.1
2015	11.3	11.0	10.9	10.8	10.8	10.5	10.4	10.3	10.0	9.8	9.9	9.9	10.5
2016	9.9	9.7	9.8	9.7	9.7	9.6	9.7	9.7	9.7	9.5	9.3	9.2	9.6
2017	9.4	9.2	8.9	8.6	8.4	8.6	8.6	8.6	8.3	7.9	8.0	8.1	8.6
2018	8.2	8.2	8.0	7.8	7.6	7.8	7.5	7.4	7.5	7.4	7.6	7.6	7.7
2019	8.1	7.3	7.3	7.3	7.1	7.2	7.0	7.2	6.9	7.0	6.9	6.7	7.2
2020[1]	6.9	7.0	8.7	22.8	21.2	18.0	16.5	14.2	12.8	12.1	12.0		13.8

The U6 unemployment rate counts not only people without work seeking full-time employment (the more familiar U-3 rate), but also counts "marginally attached workers and those working part-time for economic reasons." Note that some of these part-time workers counted as employed by U-3 could be working as little as an hour a week. And the "marginally attached workers" include those who have gotten discouraged and stopped looking, but still want to work. The age considered for this calculation is 16 years and over.

[1] Preliminary. *Source: Bureau of Economic Analysis, U.S. Department of Commerce (BEA)*

STOCK INDEX FUTURES - U.S.

Volume of Trading of S&P 500 Index Futures in Chicago In Contracts

Year	Jan.	Feb.	Mar.	Apr.	May	June	July	Aug.	Sept.	Oct.	Nov.	Dec.	Total
2011	321,230	330,793	1,161,950	306,622	309,799	1,027,261	283,409	713,632	1,124,309	389,089	394,757	857,769	7,220,620
2012	228,210	222,899	812,486	232,960	301,759	818,852	243,463	247,857	729,728	192,426	257,122	744,888	5,032,650
2013	263,398	248,841	699,646	203,842	232,649	693,771	151,373	190,394	584,401	186,798	136,416	564,970	4,156,499
2014	200,461	192,965	525,447	137,151	145,735	500,052	135,986	118,435	518,784	229,310	152,715	530,699	3,387,740
2015	200,265	109,971	521,653	132,407	134,537	455,419	131,114	218,785	465,263	145,559	134,391	382,196	3,031,560
2016	177,856	168,307	332,830	116,852	98,936	336,958	100,807	94,459	311,370	101,081	111,981	286,440	2,237,877
2017	110,481	99,344	255,028	77,484	97,315	207,957	52,266	80,197	190,828	65,559	78,261	194,543	1,509,263
2018	93,762	173,394	235,765	136,742	108,631	157,986	98,813	62,472	217,043	127,769	98,505	143,941	1,654,823
2019	113,377	75,344	173,885	79,311	65,384	124,123	55,726	98,733	84,416	35,082	32,755	93,127	1,031,263
2020	101,545	135,188	349,049	129,807	95,692	210,395	45,550	28,017	57,443	52,498	51,407	47,806	1,304,397

Contract value = $250. *Source: Index and Option Market (IOM), division of the Chicago Mercantile Exchange (CME)*

Average Open Interest of S&P 500 Index Futures in Chicago In Contracts

Year	Jan.	Feb.	Mar.	Apr.	May	June	July	Aug.	Sept.	Oct.	Nov.	Dec.
2011	295,221	328,406	351,308	312,007	326,135	314,542	277,586	351,944	367,322	292,018	295,609	285,435
2012	247,547	249,536	248,980	234,595	260,383	266,290	236,315	235,725	225,849	199,981	217,709	215,589
2013	193,514	217,014	202,882	169,581	189,144	203,898	162,175	170,134	196,824	159,233	167,647	168,253
2014	150,125	197,844	198,079	126,277	142,806	163,129	144,257	161,528	165,415	142,572	149,630	146,618
2015	130,204	146,778	154,302	112,920	126,006	132,006	106,046	127,294	149,564	104,817	103,028	97,764
2016	104,123	134,488	109,898	73,227	77,419	84,363	93,313	95,738	84,687	77,392	87,557	76,983
2017	63,927	74,879	72,959	58,118	74,418	59,727	49,623	63,689	57,097	54,499	70,733	68,740
2018	62,941	79,712	64,362	75,398	101,975	84,641	60,976	66,560	57,264	47,401	57,130	56,018
2019	53,522	62,624	34,269	33,873	40,974	35,071	27,773	31,565	29,411	20,721	25,607	25,272
2020	30,732	42,900	72,675	91,158	104,663	67,579	15,026	28,201	22,582	14,168	24,278	21,636

Contract value = $250. *Source: Index and Option Market (IOM), division of the Chicago Mercantile Exchange (CME)*

Volume of Trading of E-mini S&P 400 Index Futures in Chicago In Contracts

Year	Jan.	Feb.	Mar.	Apr.	May	June	July	Aug.	Sept.	Oct.	Nov.	Dec.	Total
2011	421,293	362,478	797,744	427,817	519,082	768,346	407,619	937,031	976,312	687,489	628,695	755,400	7,689,306
2012	408,514	411,301	751,336	513,459	613,049	820,825	494,705	410,688	615,845	453,404	431,072	612,709	6,536,907
2013	309,335	334,867	582,358	434,406	403,614	726,068	369,807	400,705	622,836	478,458	338,633	600,460	5,601,547
2014	369,537	360,548	604,474	385,135	334,222	500,963	343,309	283,606	618,774	648,830	242,848	593,469	5,285,715
2015	414,909	332,866	599,168	325,498	293,658	554,697	369,498	498,662	649,465	402,087	332,728	607,797	5,381,033
2016	529,519	442,219	633,841	325,445	347,829	654,024	305,479	313,218	626,528	336,632	352,772	538,251	5,405,757
2017	356,153	255,217	592,956	327,303	308,302	537,053	246,470	308,005	431,674	229,221	282,517	457,169	4,332,040
2018	316,880	430,453	590,759	332,663	294,698	498,591	268,791	227,276	481,588	531,815	363,033	614,553	4,951,100
2019	300,487	282,789	506,895	226,763	307,568	431,823	276,230	328,178	448,052	278,563	214,891	505,898	4,108,137
2020	331,980	370,629	776,538	235,431	224,250	549,761	278,221	239,926	497,873	286,787	252,149	488,901	4,532,446

Contract value = $20. *Source: Index and Option Market (IOM), division of the Chicago Mercantile Exchange (CME)*

Stock Index Futures - WorldWide

World stocks – World stock markets in 2020 closed mostly higher. The MSCI World Index, a benchmark for large companies based in 23 developed countries, closed +14.1% higher in 2020, adding to the +25.2% gain seen in 2019. Despite the severe economic damage from the pandemic, world stocks rallied in 2020 due to the aggressive monetary and fiscal policies launched by governments worldwide to address the pandemic.

Small-Capitalization Stocks – The MSCI World Small-Cap Index, which tracks companies with market caps between $200 million and $1.5 billion, rose by +14.4% in 2020, adding to the +24.1% gain in 2019. The +14.4% rise in the MSCI World Small-Cap Index in 2020 was slightly better than the +14.1% gain in the large-cap MSCI World Index. Small caps in 2020 slightly out-performed the large-caps in 2020 after two years of under-performance in 2018 and 2019.

World Industry Groups – Eight of the ten MSCI industry groups showed gains in 2020, while two groups showed losses. The Information Technology sector was the strongest group with a +42.7% gain, adding to 2019's gain of +46.0%. Seven other sectors showed annual gains with ranked returns as follows: Consumer Discretionary (+35.4%), Telecom (+21.5%), Materials (+17.1%), Health Care (+11.9%), Industrials (+10.1%), Consumer Staples (+5.4%), and Utilities (+2.1%). Groups that showed losses on the year included Financials (-5.0%) and Energy (-34.4%).

Emerging markets – The MSCI Emerging Markets Free Index, which tracks companies based in 26 emerging countries, rose by +15.8% in 2020, adding to the +15.4% gain seen in 2019. The +15.8% gain in emerging market stocks seen in 2020 was slightly better than the +14.1% gain seen in the MSCI World Index.

G7 – The G7 stock markets in 2020 were mixed. The leader was the U.S. S&P 500 index with a +16.3% annual gain, with Japan's Nikkei index following close behind at +16.0%. G7 countries that showed small gains included Germany's Dax index (+3.5%) and Canada's Toronto Composite (+2.2%). G7 stock markets that lost ground during 2020 included Italy's MIB index (-5.4%), France's CAC-40 index (-7.1%), and the UK's FTSE 100 index (-14.3%).

North America – In North America, the U.S. S&P 500 index in 2020 showed the largest gain of +16.3%. Canada's Toronto Composite index showed a small increase of +2.2%, while Mexico's Bolsa index rose by +1.2%.

Latin America – The Latin American stock markets in 2020 closed mixed. The ranked returns in 2020 were as follows: Argentina's Merval Index +22.9%, Brazil's Bovespa Index +2.9%, Peru's Lima General Index +1.4%, Ecuador's Guayaqui Bolsa Index -2.9%, Chile's Stock Market Select Index -10.5%, Colombia's General Index -13.5%, and Jamaica's Stock Exchange Index -22.4%.

Europe – European stocks in 2020 showed weakness as Europe was hard-hit by the pandemic. The Euro Stoxx 50 index in 2020 fell by -8.7%, giving back some of the +23.3% gain seen in 2019. The ranked European returns in 2020 were as follows: German Dax index +3.5%, Italian MIB index -5.4%, French CAC-40 index -7.1%, UK FTSE 100 index -14.3%, and Spanish IBEX 35 index -15.5%.

Asia – The Asian-Pacific stock markets in 2020 closed mixed. The MSCI Far East Index in 2020 rose by +12.8%, adding to the +18.6% gain seen in 2019. The ranked returns for the Asian-Pacific stock markets in 2020 were as follows: South Korea's Composite Index +30.8%, Taiwan's TAIEX Index +22.8%, Japan's Nikkei 225 Index +16.0%, India's Mumbai Sensex 30 index +15.8%, Vietnam's Stock Index +14.9%, New Zealand's Exchange 50 Index +13.9%, China's Shanghai Composite Index +13.9%, Pakistan's 100 Index +7.4%, Malaysia's Kuala Lumpur Composite index +2.4%, Australia's All-Ordinaries Index +0.7%, Hong Kong's Hang Seng -3.4%, Indonesia's Jakarta Composite Index -5.1%, Philippines' Composite index -8.6%, Thailand's Stock Exchange index -8.3%, and Singapore's Straights Times Index -11.8%.

Comparison of International Indices (2010=100)

Year	Jan.	Feb.	Mar.	Apr.	May	June	July	Aug.	Sept.	Oct.	Nov.	Dec.	Average
United States													
2013	137.6	141.1	145.7	148.3	153.3	151.9	155.5	153.5	154.3	154.5	160.4	162.6	151.6
2014	164.1	161.2	164.8	165.7	167.4	170.2	171.7	169.5	172.8	168.8	178.3	179.4	169.5
2015	177.3	181.3	181.2	181.6	183.1	181.1	179.8	172.4	165.1	173.6	179.1	177.3	177.7
2016	164.8	164.7	174.8	180.3	178.8	179.4	185.3	186.9	184.6	183.7	188.9	199.2	180.9
2017	201.2	206.4	210.4	209.0	211.6	215.4	218.1	221.4	224.0	232.8	238.0	248.0	219.7
2018	260.7	252.4	248.4	245.6	248.3	250.5	252.4	259.0	265.1	258.8	255.2	240.5	253.1
2019	244.1	258.7	259.9	266.8	260.1	264.3	273.7	263.3	271.8	270.2	280.9	284.6	266.5
2020	291.8	288.2	228.7	235.4	245.2	263.3	266.6	281.1	280.2	283.0	294.3	304.6	271.9
Canada													
2013	104.9	105.5	105.8	101.9	104.3	101.2	103.4	104.6	106.2	108.2	111.0	110.5	105.6
2014	113.7	115.7	118.3	119.6	121.2	123.9	126.5	127.5	127.2	119.8	122.8	118.7	121.2
2015	119.8	125.5	123.6	126.7	125.3	122.9	119.6	116.1	111.6	113.9	111.2	108.6	118.7
2016	102.4	104.6	110.9	113.1	114.7	116.3	119.7	121.6	121.2	121.9	122.8	126.4	116.3
2017	128.3	129.6	128.5	129.6	128.3	126.8	125.5	125.2	126.6	131.1	132.8	133.3	128.8
2018	134.8	127.8	128.3	127.4	132.2	134.6	136.1	135.3	133.6	127.9	125.4	120.5	130.3
2019	124.5	131.0	133.5	136.4	135.2	135.2	136.8	134.6	138.2	135.9	140.2	141.0	135.2
2020	144.0	145.3	114.0	116.6	123.5	128.2	132.1	137.4	134.5	134.4	138.7	145.1	132.8
France													
2013	99.6	98.2	101.0	99.7	105.9	101.2	103.4	108.0	109.9	112.8	114.2	111.0	105.4
2014	113.4	114.8	115.8	118.4	119.7	120.7	116.4	113.4	118.1	110.2	113.7	113.7	115.7
2015	117.0	127.2	133.4	138.0	135.0	131.5	132.2	130.4	120.8	125.8	131.0	124.5	128.9
2016	115.8	111.7	118.1	118.6	116.7	114.6	115.2	118.1	118.7	120.0	120.2	127.1	117.9
2017	129.8	129.3	133.6	137.0	142.8	140.5	138.1	136.7	139.0	143.8	144.0	143.4	138.2
2018	146.3	140.3	138.8	142.6	147.8	144.3	144.3	145.1	143.6	138.0	134.3	128.0	141.1
2019	128.7	136.6	141.8	147.1	143.0	144.6	148.9	142.8	135.2	150.1	157.2	157.8	144.5
2020	160.1	158.0	119.6	118.1	119.9	132.3	133.4	132.4	131.7	129.2	142.4	148.0	135.4
Germany													
2013	125.2	123.9	127.9	124.8	134.4	130.7	131.9	134.7	137.3	142.2	148.2	149.3	134.2
2014	153.8	153.7	151.0	153.4	156.9	160.5	157.6	149.9	155.8	145.0	153.4	158.6	154.1
2015	163.8	177.4	190.5	193.2	187.5	181.6	182.4	174.8	160.9	165.2	177.6	172.5	177.3
2016	158.8	150.2	159.4	162.0	161.8	159.3	161.0	170.2	169.8	171.7	171.2	181.3	164.7
2017	187.8	189.8	194.7	197.7	204.6	205.4	200.4	196.4	201.7	210.3	212.7	211.4	201.1
2018	214.5	201.4	196.6	200.6	208.7	204.7	203.3	201.4	196.9	188.4	183.6	175.1	197.9
2019	177.3	182.3	186.6	195.0	195.2	196.6	200.5	189.4	198.6	202.6	213.4	213.2	195.9
2020	216.1	215.5	162.2	167.7	177.7	199.0	205.9	208.2	209.5	203.7	209.5	217.0	199.3
Italy													
2013	82.6	77.9	75.1	75.3	81.8	76.1	75.5	80.8	83.1	89.4	89.9	86.9	81.2
2014	92.8	95.1	98.9	102.8	100.4	103.9	99.4	94.4	99.1	91.7	92.1	91.2	96.8
2015	92.0	101.1	107.9	111.5	110.8	109.1	109.2	108.3	102.2	105.3	105.6	10.2	97.8
2016	91.9	81.1	87.3	85.9	84.8	80.4	78.0	79.0	79.0	79.8	78.7	88.2	82.8
2017	92.0	89.7	94.3	95.9	101.0	99.1	101.1	103.1	105.4	106.8	106.7	105.8	100.1
2018	110.5	107.4	106.6	111.2	111.0	103.7	103.6	99.6	99.7	92.5	90.5	89.1	102.1
2019	91.6	95.0	99.5	103.3	98.4	98.5	103.7	98.4	103.9	105.0	111.1	110.8	101.6
2020	113.0	115.0	83.5	81.2	82.6	92.2	94.8	94.3	92.2	----	----	----	94.3
Japan													
2013	107.4	113.2	122.4	132.1	144.8	130.9	143.0	137.1	143.6	143.2	149.2	156.4	135.3
2014	155.6	146.0	146.8	144.6	143.3	151.2	153.6	153.4	159.3	153.8	171.6	175.2	154.6
2015	172.6	180.4	191.8	197.5	199.5	203.8	203.5	199.0	179.3	183.6	195.6	191.8	191.5
2016	172.9	163.3	168.8	165.3	166.0	160.5	161.5	165.7	167.2	170.3	176.7	190.5	169.1
2017	191.8	191.7	193.2	187.2	197.1	200.3	200.3	196.5	199.1	212.5	225.0	227.5	201.8
2018	236.9	219.7	213.7	218.5	225.7	225.4	222.9	224.7	231.4	226.7	219.5	210.1	222.9
2019	204.4	211.0	213.9	219.4	212.0	210.4	215.7	206.1	215.6	221.8	232.6	236.4	216.6
2020	236.2	231.6	189.6	191.9	205.2	224.7	225.1	228.8	232.8	234.4	253.6	267.5	226.8

Not Seasonally Adjusted. *Source: Economic and Statistics Administration, U.S. Department of Commerce (ESA)*

DAX® is Deutsche Börse's blue chip index for the German stock market. It comprises the 30 largest and most actively traded German companies. Shaded areas indicate German recessions.

Average Value of Deutscher Aktienindex (DAX)

Year	Jan.	Feb.	Mar.	Apr.	May	June	July	Aug.	Sept.	Oct.	Nov.	Dec.	Average
2011	7,039.7	7,294.2	6,952.0	7,227.1	7,330.6	7,158.7	7,292.8	5,923.8	5,402.3	5,871.8	5,826.5	5,867.8	6,598.9
2012	6,278.3	6,789.6	6,966.5	6,731.9	6,424.8	6,184.0	6,549.6	6,949.8	7,274.4	7,288.2	7,238.6	7,576.2	6,854.3
2013	7,747.6	7,666.7	7,913.9	7,723.1	8,317.4	8,089.2	8,161.8	8,332.5	8,497.8	8,800.5	9,170.6	9,235.0	8,304.7
2014	9,516.8	9,509.5	9,339.9	9,490.0	9,709.5	9,927.4	9,751.8	9,273.1	9,638.7	8,971.9	9,490.3	9,812.3	9,535.9
2015	10,133.6	10,977.1	11,784.9	11,956.3	11,599.1	11,236.3	11,288.1	10,818.0	9,953.3	10,222.3	10,986.3	10,673.0	10,969.0
2016	9,827.1	9,291.4	9,859.9	10,023.2	10,010.6	9,859.2	9,960.5	10,530.3	10,504.5	10,624.2	10,595.5	11,214.9	10,191.8
2017	11,620.1	11,745.4	12,047.6	12,232.6	12,661.1	12,710.6	12,397.5	12,153.8	12,479.5	13,012.1	13,159.4	13,079.9	12,441.6
2018	13,270.7	12,459.4	12,165.9	12,411.6	12,911.2	12,667.6	12,581.7	12,458.9	12,185.2	11,659.1	11,359.6	10,834.5	12,247.1
2019	10,968.9	11,280.8	11,542.6	12,068.0	12,079.6	12,164.2	12,406.9	11,719.8	12,285.3	12,538.2	13,200.8	13,193.3	12,120.7
2020	13,370.5	13,330.6	10,034.3	10,374.5	10,993.7	12,313.7	12,741.0	12,882.4	12,960.9	12,603.1	12,960.7	13,426.0	12,332.6

Source: EUREX

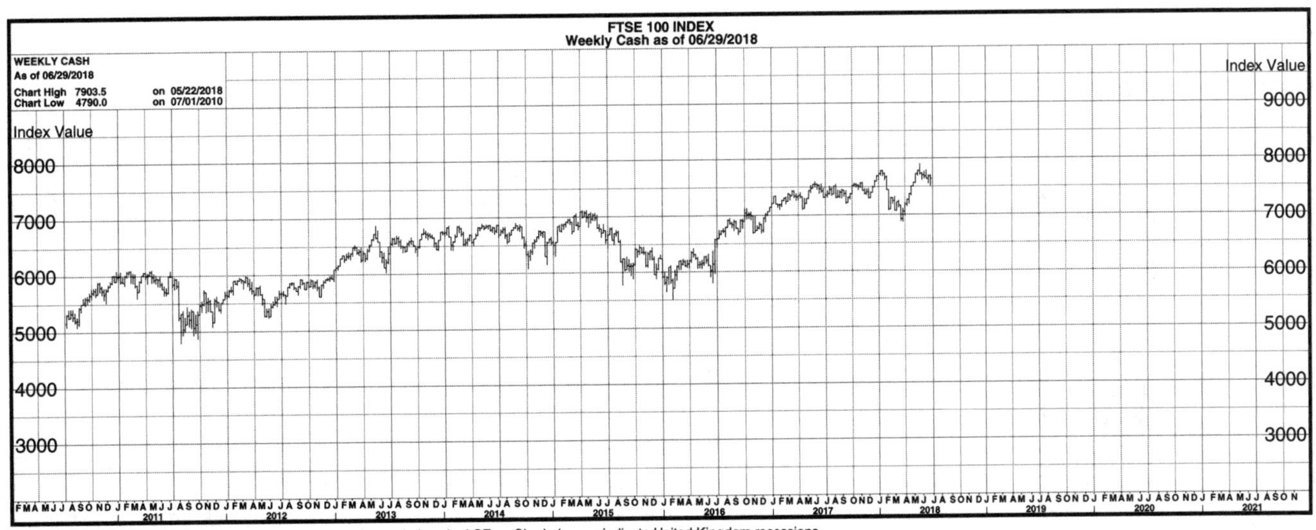

The FTSE 100 Index covers 100 of the largest companies traded on the LSE. Shaded areas indicate United Kingdom recessions.

Average Value of FTSE 100 Stock Index

Year	Jan.	Feb.	Mar.	Apr.	May	June	July	Aug.	Sept.	Oct.	Nov.	Dec.	Average
2009	4,281.85	4,074.38	3,760.23	4,046.33	4,393.78	4,349.25	4,374.50	4,755.63	5,033.13	5,161.18	5,242.29	5,309.54	4,565.17
2010	5,411.65	5,231.92	5,621.03	5,720.73	5,238.81	5,139.26	5,158.39	5,276.00	5,514.67	5,687.17	5,735.84	5,874.87	5,467.53
2011	5,971.31	6,021.12	5,858.24	6,007.85	5,937.95	5,792.18	5,909.81	5,271.31	5,228.50	5,408.62	5,402.52	5,480.08	5,690.79
2012	5,694.45	5,893.35	5,875.40	5,725.58	5,461.45	5,480.44	5,636.47	5,796.96	5,805.45	5,831.81	5,787.52	5,922.72	5,742.63
2013	6,161.87	6,316.35	6,435.58	6,361.01	6,647.35	6,299.43	6,517.86	6,521.48	6,552.36	6,571.95	6,694.32	6,572.98	6,471.05
2014	6,714.51	6,690.79	6,631.69	6,651.96	6,834.80	6,804.31	6,772.02	6,712.21	6,777.75	6,408.63	6,644.12	6,542.62	6,682.12
2015	6,612.63	6,878.54	6,884.51	7,012.39	6,981.68	6,783.17	6,646.60	6,455.96	6,087.34	6,340.81	6,306.91	6,162.31	6,596.07
2016	5,922.67	5,881.74	6,155.24	6,271.90	6,164.88	6,175.30	6,655.88	6,821.69	6,813.75	7,011.20	6,803.33	6,961.04	6,469.89
2017	7,211.36	7,240.42	7,359.53	7,263.60	7,422.66	7,463.97	7,395.85	7,409.18	7,334.65	7,508.18	7,441.23	7,481.74	7,377.70
2018	7,695.65	7,255.90	7,090.09	7,288.22	7,690.22	7,656.93	Discontinued		----	----	----	----	7,446.17

Source: Euronext LIFFE

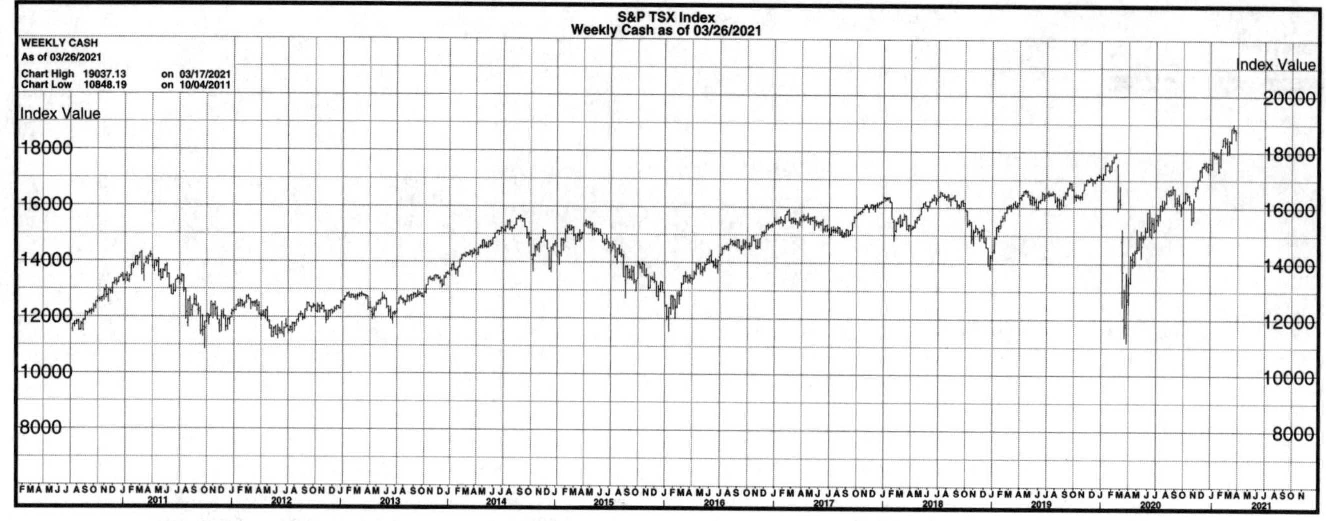

Average Value of S&P TSX Index

Year	Jan.	Feb.	Mar.	Apr.	May	June	July	Aug.	Sept.	Oct.	Nov.	Dec.	Average
2011	13,392.8	13,908.2	13,932.9	13,962.4	13,621.2	13,126.1	13,294.7	12,380.7	12,130.8	11,922.8	12,038.1	11,860.7	12,964.3
2012	12,331.8	12,552.7	12,464.0	12,135.4	11,644.1	11,495.7	11,626.9	11,921.0	12,285.6	12,337.7	12,163.2	12,290.3	12,104.0
2013	12,668.8	12,737.0	12,777.3	12,299.2	12,585.1	12,221.4	12,479.7	12,622.7	12,818.9	13,057.7	13,396.1	13,339.2	12,750.3
2014	13,728.1	13,964.5	14,281.4	14,440.5	14,635.7	14,960.5	15,268.3	15,389.4	15,353.5	14,460.8	14,824.8	14,330.5	14,636.5
2015	14,460.9	15,155.0	14,921.6	15,299.3	15,127.2	14,835.9	14,436.4	14,010.4	13,477.6	13,751.9	13,424.2	13,115.1	14,334.6
2016	12,361.0	12,632.4	13,382.1	13,650.4	13,851.9	14,042.4	14,445.8	14,680.8	14,634.0	14,718.2	14,821.9	15,254.5	14,039.6
2017	15,486.6	15,639.7	15,515.3	15,642.3	15,486.8	15,308.8	15,153.5	15,108.9	15,284.5	15,826.0	16,032.6	16,092.8	15,548.2
2018	16,272.5	15,430.6	15,490.4	15,380.4	15,964.4	16,253.3	16,432.6	16,332.4	16,125.6	15,441.2	15,144.0	14,546.8	15,734.5
2019	15,031.9	15,811.2	16,119.6	16,470.4	16,316.8	16,322.6	16,515.0	16,243.1	16,683.3	16,403.2	16,926.0	17,020.0	16,321.9
2020	17,382.0	17,542.7	13,757.1	14,071.5	14,903.8	15,480.9	15,942.5	16,584.3	16,234.7	16,226.7	16,743.6	17,521.0	16,032.6

Source: Toronto Stock Exchange

The CAC 40® is a free float market capitalization weighted index that reflects the performance of the 40 largest and most actively traded shares listed on Euronext Paris, and is the most widely used indicator of the Paris stock market. Shaded areas indicate French recessions.

Average Value of CAC 40 Index

Year	Jan.	Feb.	Mar.	Apr.	May	June	July	Aug.	Sept.	Oct.	Nov.	Dec.	Average
2011	3,960.7	4,086.4	3,941.7	4,020.3	3,998.6	3,853.3	3,818.0	3,201.9	2,983.1	3,148.4	3,033.0	3,091.9	3,594.8
2012	3,250.6	3,420.4	3,490.0	3,248.8	3,084.4	3,055.9	3,199.6	3,427.4	3,490.9	3,435.7	3,461.5	3,631.8	3,349.7
2013	3,734.0	3,679.4	3,786.4	3,735.1	3,968.7	3,792.5	3,876.6	4,046.3	4,117.7	4,228.0	4,279.9	4,161.4	3,950.5
2014	4,248.4	4,301.1	4,338.1	4,437.3	4,484.8	4,522.0	4,362.0	4,249.6	4,425.3	4,129.8	4,261.0	4,262.2	4,335.1
2015	4,384.2	4,768.5	5,000.7	5,173.4	5,058.2	4,927.9	4,956.2	4,887.1	4,526.6	4,715.6	4,910.3	4,665.7	4,831.2
2016	4,340.1	4,184.8	4,427.5	4,445.2	4,373.5	4,293.9	4,317.6	4,425.4	4,448.6	4,497.6	4,504.3	4,764.5	4,418.6
2017	4,863.6	4,846.7	5,008.4	5,134.6	5,352.0	5,263.8	5,175.0	5,122.7	5,208.8	5,389.8	5,398.0	5,373.0	5,178.0
2018	5,483.0	5,257.8	5,200.6	5,345.3	5,537.6	5,408.3	5,409.4	5,438.3	5,381.7	5,170.1	5,035.1	4,798.2	5,288.8
2019	4,822.7	5,118.2	5,315.3	5,511.4	5,360.8	5,420.3	5,578.7	5,351.9	5,067.5	5,623.6	5,892.8	5,915.3	5,414.9
2020	6,001.1	5,923.3	4,481.8	4,425.2	4,492.5	4,958.3	4,999.9	4,962.6	4,937.4	4,843.4	5,335.7	5,546.8	5,075.7

Source: Euronext Paris

The Hang Seng Index is a freefloat-adjusted market capitalization-weighted stock market index in Hong Kong. The Index was created by Hong Kong banker Stanley Kwan in 1969.

Average Value of Hang Seng Index

Year	Jan.	Feb.	Mar.	Apr.	May	June	July	Aug.	Sept.	Oct.	Nov.	Dec.	Average
2011	23,864.8	23,196.7	23,110.2	24,009.1	23,133.3	22,342.4	22,280.3	20,333.7	19,007.3	18,352.1	18,865.3	18,585.7	21,423.4
2012	19,455.8	21,128.5	21,013.0	20,665.8	19,615.2	18,940.3	19,372.3	19,946.2	20,226.8	21,293.3	21,650.2	22,406.2	20,476.1
2013	23,470.7	23,148.3	22,518.0	22,054.3	22,933.1	21,063.9	21,298.5	22,009.5	22,932.7	23,102.2	23,304.5	23,370.8	22,600.5
2014	22,725.2	22,188.3	21,980.8	22,598.5	22,584.9	23,144.9	23,760.0	24,812.1	24,341.8	23,301.2	23,779.1	23,386.2	23,216.9
2015	24,209.9	24,670.4	24,306.8	27,451.5	27,656.2	27,009.0	25,032.2	23,223.2	21,365.1	22,649.3	22,509.5	21,910.2	24,332.8
2016	19,733.6	19,134.5	20,299.8	20,986.5	20,174.0	20,646.4	21,497.8	22,663.9	23,543.0	23,406.1	22,618.9	22,229.6	21,411.2
2017	22,814.5	23,725.3	24,029.6	24,262.7	25,189.4	25,828.2	26,326.0	27,532.4	27,790.9	28,394.4	29,213.7	29,109.6	26,184.7
2018	31,831.9	30,969.3	30,898.1	30,376.0	30,698.7	30,070.3	28,466.1	27,925.8	27,275.6	25,705.4	26,081.0	26,075.6	28,864.5
2019	26,711.6	28,392.4	28,900.0	29,882.0	28,132.3	27,718.0	28,465.3	25,987.1	26,474.3	26,458.2	26,979.0	27,264.3	27,613.7
2020	28,214.4	27,214.7	24,107.0	24,008.8	23,807.6	24,478.4	25,316.2	25,100.2	24,253.2	24,440.4	26,119.8	26,524.8	25,298.8

Source: Hong Kong Futures Exchange

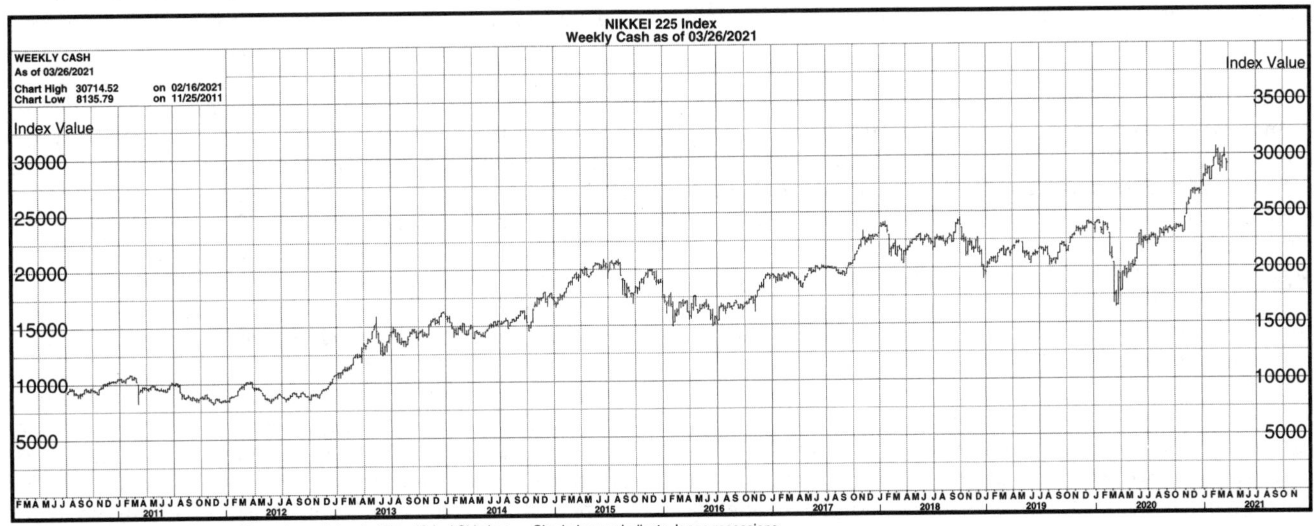

The Nikkei Stock Average is owned by and proprietary to Nihon Keisai Shimbun. Shaded areas indicate Japan recessions.

Average Value of Nikkei 225 Index

Year	Jan.	Feb.	Mar.	Apr.	May	June	July	Aug.	Sept.	Oct.	Nov.	Dec.	Average
2011	10,449.5	10,622.3	9,852.5	9,644.6	9,650.8	9,541.5	9,996.7	9,072.9	8,695.4	8,733.6	8,506.1	8,506.0	9,439.3
2012	8,616.7	9,242.3	9,962.4	9,627.4	8,842.5	8,638.1	8,760.7	8,949.9	8,948.6	8,827.4	9,059.9	9,814.4	9,107.5
2013	10,750.9	11,327.3	12,254.7	13,224.1	14,494.3	13,106.6	14,317.5	13,726.7	14,372.1	14,329.0	14,931.7	15,655.2	13,540.8
2014	15,578.3	14,617.6	14,694.8	14,475.3	14,343.2	15,131.8	15,379.3	15,358.7	15,948.5	15,394.1	17,179.0	17,541.7	15,470.2
2015	17,274.4	18,053.2	19,197.6	19,767.9	19,974.2	20,403.8	20,372.6	19,919.1	17,944.2	18,374.1	19,581.8	19,202.6	19,172.1
2016	17,302.3	16,347.0	16,897.3	16,543.5	16,612.7	16,068.8	16,168.3	16,586.1	16,737.0	17,044.5	17,689.5	19,066.0	16,921.9
2017	19,194.1	19,188.7	19,340.2	18,736.4	19,726.8	20,045.6	20,044.9	19,670.2	19,924.4	21,267.5	22,525.2	22,769.9	20,202.8
2018	23,712.2	21,991.7	21,395.5	21,868.8	22,590.1	22,562.9	22,309.1	22,494.1	23,159.3	22,690.8	21,967.9	21,032.4	22,314.6
2019	20,460.5	21,123.6	21,414.9	21,964.9	21,218.4	21,060.2	21,593.7	20,629.7	21,585.5	22,197.5	23,278.1	23,660.4	21,682.3
2020	23,642.9	23,181.9	18,974.0	19,208.4	20,543.3	22,486.9	22,529.5	22,901.5	23,307.0	23,464.1	25,384.9	26,773.0	22,699.8

Source: Singapore Exchange

Sugar

The white crystalline substance called "sugar" is the organic chemical compound sucrose, one of several related compounds, all known as sugars. These include glucose, dextrose, fructose, and lactose. All sugars are members of the larger group of compounds called carbohydrates and are characterized by a sweet taste. Sucrose is considered a double sugar because it is composed of one molecule of glucose and one molecule of fructose. While sucrose is common in many plants, it occurs in the highest concentration in sugarcane (Saccharum officinarum) and sugar beets (Beta vulgaris). Sugarcane is about 7 to 18 percent sugar by weight, while sugar beets are 8 to 22 percent.

Sugarcane is a member of the grass family and is a perennial. Sugarcane is cultivated in tropical and subtropical regions around the world roughly between the Tropics of Cancer and Capricorn. It grows best in hot, wet climates where there is heavy rainfall followed by a dry season. The largest cane producers are Florida, Louisiana, Texas, and Hawaii. On a commercial basis, sugarcane is not grown from seeds but from cuttings or pieces of the stalk.

Sugar beets, which are produced in temperate or colder climates, are annuals grown from seeds. Sugar beets do best with moderate temperatures and evenly distributed rainfall. The beets are planted in the spring and harvested in the fall. The sugar is contained in the root of the beet, but the sugars from beets and cane are identical. Sugar beet production takes place mostly in Europe, the U.S., China, and Japan. The largest sugar beet producing states are Minnesota, Idaho, North Dakota, and Michigan. Sugar beets are refined to yield white sugar, and very little raw sugar is produced.

Sugar beets and sugarcane are produced in over 100 countries around the world. Of all the sugar produced, about 25% is processed from sugar beets, and the remaining 75% is from sugar cane. The trend has been that the production of sugar from cane is increasing relative to that produced from beets. The significance of this in that sugarcane is a perennial plant while the sugar beet is an annual, and due to the longer production cycle, sugarcane production and the sugar processed from that cane, may not be quite as responsive to changes in price.

Sugar futures are traded at the ICE Futures U.S. exchange , the Bolsa de Mercadorias & Futuros (BM&F), Kansai Commodities Exchange (KANEX), the Tokyo Grain Exchange (TGE), and the ICE Futures Europe exchange.

Raw sugar is traded on the ICE Futures U.S. exchange, while white sugar is traded on the ICE Futures Europe exchange. The most actively traded contract is the No. 11 (World) sugar contract at the ICE exchange. The No. 11 contract calls for the delivery of 112,000 pounds (50 long tons) of raw cane centrifugal sugar from any of 28 foreign countries of origin and the United States. The ICE exchange also trades the No. 14 sugar contract (Domestic), which calls for the delivery of raw centrifugal cane sugar in the United States. Futures on white sugar are traded on the London International Financial Futures Exchange and call for the delivery of 50 metric tons of white beet sugar, cane crystal sugar, or refined sugar of any origin from the crop current at the time of delivery.

Prices – ICE World No. 11 sugar futures prices (Barchart.com symbol SB) in early 2020 raced higher and posted a 3-1/2 year high of 15.90 cents per pound in February. Concern about a global sugar shortage propelled prices higher. The worst drought in 40 years in Thailand, the world's second-largest sugar exporter, ravaged its sugar crop as Thailand's 2019/20 sugar production plunged -40% yr/yr to a 10-year low of 8.3 MMT. However, the rally in sugar was short-lived as prices sank to a 13-year low of 9.05 cents per pound in April. The Covid pandemic's spread prompted governments to impose lockdowns and travel restrictions that curbed energy demand and sent crude oil prices plummeting. Weaker crude oil prices undercut ethanol prices and prompted Brazil's sugar mills to divert more sugarcane crushing toward sugar production rather than ethanol production, thus boosting sugar supplies. In addition, a plunge in the Brazilian real to a record low against the dollar in May weighed on sugar prices. A weaker real encourages export selling by Brazil's sugar producers, which boosts supplies. The International Sugar Organization (ISO) in September cut its global 2019/20 sugar deficit estimate to -140,000 MT from a prior estimate of a -9.3 MMT deficit due to higher Brazil sugar production and lower consumption due to the pandemic. However, after sinking to a 13-year low in April, sugar prices trended higher the remainder of the year. A recovery in crude prices underpinned sugar prices, as did tighter global sugar supplies. The ISO in November raised its global 2020/21 sugar deficit estimate to -3.5 MMT from an August estimate of -700,000 MT. Sugar prices finished 2020 up +15.4% yr/yr at 15.49 cents per pound.

Supply – World production of centrifugal (raw) sugar in the 2020/21 marketing year (Oct 1 to Sep 30) is expected to rise +9.9% yr/yr to 181.866 million metric tons. The world's largest sugar producers in 2020.21 are expected to be Brazil with 23.1% of world production, India with 18.6%, and the European Union with 8.8%. U.S. sugar production in 2020/21 is expected to rise 1+10.5% yr/yr to 8.166 million metric tons. U.S. production of cane sugar in 2020/21 is expected to rise +14.3% to 5.046 million short tons, and beet sugar production is expected to rise +12.3% yr/yr to 4.265 million short tons. World ending stocks in 2019/20 fell -13.1% yr/yr to 46.253 million metric tons, down from the 2018/19 record high of 53.232.

Demand – World domestic consumption of centrifugal (raw) sugar in 2020/21 is expected to rise +2.1% yr/yr to a new record high of 174.476 million metric tons. U.S. domestic disappearance (consumption) of sugar in 2020/21 is expected to be down -1.7% yr/yr at 12.340 million short tons.

Trade – World exports of centrifugal sugar in 2020/21 are expected to rise +22.6% yr/yr to 65.333 million metric tons, a new record high. The world's largest sugar exporters are Brazil at 49.0% of total world exports, Thailand at 11.2%, and India at 9.2%.

U.S. sugar exports in 2020/21 are expected to be down -42.6% yr/yr at 35,000 short tons, which is far down from the 3-decade high of 422,000 seen in 2006/07. U.S. sugar imports in 2020/21 are expected to fall -25.9% yr/yr to 2.745 million metric tons.

World Production, Supply & Stocks/Consumption Ratio of Sugar In 1000's of Metric Tons (Raw Value)

Marketing Year	Beginning Stocks	Production	Imports	Total Supply	Exports	Domestic Consumption	Ending Stocks	Stocks As a % of Consumption
2011-12	29,491	172,349	48,563	250,403	54,996	160,217	35,190	22.0
2012-13	35,190	177,833	51,444	264,467	55,742	166,437	42,288	25.4
2013-14	42,288	175,971	51,450	269,709	57,951	166,960	44,798	26.8
2014-15	44,798	177,582	50,248	272,648	55,033	168,839	48,756	28.9
2015-16	48,756	164,972	54,645	268,310	53,857	170,034	44,482	26.2
2016-17	44,482	174,050	54,445	272,643	59,039	171,388	42,550	24.8
2017-18	42,550	194,259	54,217	291,026	65,097	173,813	52,116	30.0
2018-19[1]	52,116	179,347	52,030	283,493	57,090	173,171	53,232	30.7
2019-20[2]	53,232	165,496	51,657	270,385	53,273	170,869	46,243	27.1
2020-21[3]	46,243	181,866	54,507	282,616	65,333	174,476		

[1] Preliminary. [2] Estimate. [3] Forecast. *Source: Foreign Agricultural Service, U.S. Department of Agriculture (FAS-USDA)*

World Production of Sugar (Centrifugal Sugar-Raw Value) In Thousands of Metric Tons

Year	Australia	Brazil	China	Cuba	European Union	India	Indo-nesia	Mexico	Pakistan	Thailand	United States	Ukraine	World Total
2011-12	3,683	36,150	12,341	1,400	18,320	28,620	1,830	5,351	4,520	10,235	2,300	7,700	172,349
2012-13	4,250	38,600	14,001	1,600	16,655	27,337	2,300	7,393	5,000	10,024	2,400	8,148	177,833
2013-14	4,380	37,800	14,263	1,650	16,020	26,605	2,300	6,382	5,630	11,333	1,196	7,676	175,971
2014-15	4,700	35,950	11,000	1,850	18,449	30,460	2,100	6,344	5,164	10,793	1,728	7,853	177,582
2015-16	4,900	34,650	9,050	1,625	14,283	27,385	2,025	6,484	5,265	9,743	1,638	8,155	164,972
2016-17	5,100	39,150	9,300	1,800	18,314	22,200	2,050	6,314	6,825	10,033	2,156	8,137	174,050
2017-18	4,480	38,870	10,300	1,100	20,938	34,309	2,100	6,371	7,225	14,710	2,180	8,430	194,259
2018-19[1]	4,725	29,500	10,760	1,300	17,982	34,300	2,200	6,812	5,270	14,581	1,753	8,164	179,347
2019-20[2]	4,285	29,925	10,400	1,200	17,003	28,900	2,250	5,596	5,260	8,294	1,609	7,393	165,496
2020-21[3]	4,300	42,060	10,500	1,280	16,050	33,760	2,200	6,307	5,990	7,850	1,559	8,166	181,866

[1] Preliminary. [2] Estimate. [3] Forecast. *Source: Foreign Agricultural Service, U.S. Department of Agriculture (FAS-USDA)*

World Stocks of Centrifugal Sugar at Beginning of Marketing Year In Thousands of Metric Tons (Raw Value)

Year	Australia	Brazil	China	Cuba	European Union	India	Indo-nesia	Iran	Mexico	Philip-pines	Russia	United States	World Total
2011-12	193	260	1,621	59	1,974	6,299	602	650	806	934	350	1,250	29,491
2012-13	64	260	4,140	109	3,303	7,163	409	640	1,024	932	390	1,795	35,190
2013-14	83	10	6,793	170	3,836	9,373	879	700	1,548	942	395	1,958	42,288
2014-15	111	350	9,977	140	3,066	8,227	1,299	700	881	1,032	370	1,642	44,798
2015-16	140	950	10,390	180	4,151	10,607	949	400	860	997	100	1,647	48,756
2016-17	230	750	9,591	115	1,241	9,294	1,098	460	1,099	1,168	150	1,863	44,482
2017-18	220	850	7,811	125	2,238	6,570	1,743	535	1,062	1,167	360	1,702	42,550
2018-19[1]	130	920	6,567	110	1,997	14,214	1,793	480	1,479	1,067	440	1,822	52,116
2019-20[2]	137	220	5,408	145	1,417	17,614	2,300	495	1,239	1,234	450	1,618	53,232
2020-21[3]	38	215	4,543	130	1,020	14,614	1,952	440	910	1,289	732	1,472	46,243

[1] Preliminary. [2] Estimate. [3] Forecast. *Source: Foreign Agricultural Service, U.S. Department of Agriculture (FAS-USDA)*

Centrifugal Sugar (Raw Value) Imported into Selected Countries In Thousands of Metric Tons

Year	Algeria	Canada	China	European Union	Indo-nesia	Iran	Japan	Korea, South	Malaysia	Nigeria	Russia	United States	World Total
2011-12	1,594	1,103	4,430	3,552	3,027	1,079	1,301	1,668	1,721	1,399	510	3,294	48,563
2012-13	2,014	1,156	3,802	3,790	3,570	1,553	1,244	1,806	1,966	1,450	735	2,925	51,444
2013-14	1,854	1,007	4,275	3,262	3,570	1,629	1,360	1,909	1,897	1,470	1,020	3,395	51,450
2014-15	1,844	1,184	5,058	2,918	2,950	266	1,360	1,882	2,063	1,465	1,100	3,223	50,248
2015-16	1,921	1,229	6,116	3,055	3,724	822	1,275	1,900	2,009	1,470	750	3,031	54,645
2016-17	2,135	1,139	4,600	2,942	4,781	962	1,232	1,757	1,893	1,820	379	2,943	54,445
2017-18	2,261	1,239	4,350	1,341	4,325	203	1,240	1,864	2,002	1,870	274	2,972	54,217
2018-19[1]	2,328	1,269	4,086	1,987	5,362	932	1,187	1,999	2,139	1,870	353	2,785	52,030
2019-20[2]	2,470	1,273	4,350	2,100	4,758	981	1,142	1,926	1,966	1,890	207	3,705	51,657
2020-21[3]	2,305	1,335	4,400	3,000	5,650	981	1,107	2,000	2,075	1,880	315	2,745	54,507

[1] Preliminary. [2] Estimate. [3] Forecast. *Source: Foreign Agricultural Service, U.S. Department of Agriculture (FAS-USDA)*

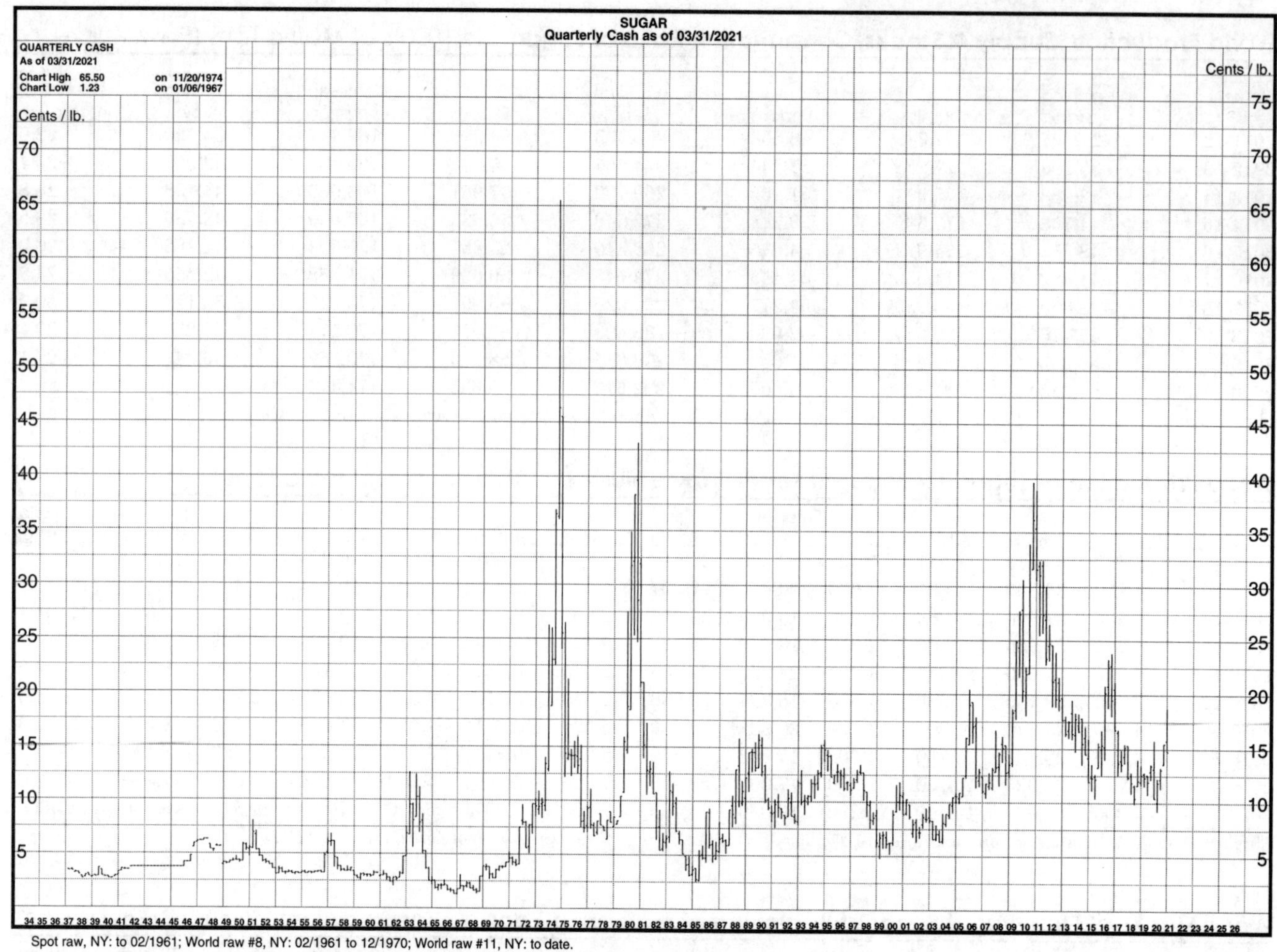

Centrifugal Sugar (Raw Value) Exported From Selected Countries In Thousands of Metric Tons

Year	Australia	Brazil	Colombia	Cuba	Dominican Republic	European Union	Guatemala	India	Mauritius	South Africa	Swaziland	Thailand	World Total
2011-12	2,800	24,650	876	830	211	315	2,343	1,619	3,764	370	271	7,898	54,996
2012-13	3,100	27,650	542	775	165	353	1,662	1,911	1,261	384	356	6,693	55,742
2013-14	3,242	26,200	900	957	208	412	1,552	2,100	2,806	416	868	7,200	57,951
2014-15	3,561	23,950	835	915	186	641	1,582	2,340	2,580	457	772	8,252	55,033
2015-16	3,700	24,350	584	1,112	186	665	1,548	2,029	3,800	463	305	7,055	53,857
2016-17	4,000	28,500	695	1,166	185	587	1,509	1,978	2,125	474	218	7,016	59,039
2017-18	3,600	28,200	732	571	184	519	3,920	1,881	2,236	390	768	10,907	65,097
2018-19[1]	3,735	19,600	801	588	185	582	1,949	2,125	4,700	347	1,041	10,612	57,090
2019-20[2]	3,600	19,280	750	550	222	660	1,200	1,947	5,800	395	1,451	7,000	53,273
2020-21[3]	3,400	32,020	750	550	190	650	1,000	1,970	6,000	410	1,240	7,300	65,333

[1] Preliminary. [2] Estimate. [3] Forecast. *Source: Foreign Agricultural Service, U.S. Department of Agriculture (FAS-USDA)*

Average Wholesale Price of Refined Beet Sugar[2]--Midwest Market In Cents Per Pound

Year	Jan.	Feb.	Mar.	Apr.	May	June	July	Aug.	Sept.	Oct.	Nov.	Dec.	Average
2011	54.50	54.00	56.50	56.80	54.00	55.00	55.40	57.00	58.60	59.00	58.75	55.10	56.22
2012	51.75	51.00	51.00	50.25	47.81	45.00	42.00	41.20	38.25	36.00	34.60	31.75	43.38
2013	30.50	28.50	27.60	26.63	26.30	26.50	26.00	25.50	26.25	27.38	28.00	27.50	47.22
2014	26.50	26.25	26.50	29.75	31.60	35.00	36.00	36.60	37.50	36.60	36.00	36.00	32.86
2015	36.00	35.25	35.13	35.50	34.30	34.00	33.80	33.13	33.00	32.40	32.00	32.00	33.88
2016	32.00	31.00	31.00	30.50	30.00	29.75	29.00	28.50	28.50	28.50	28.50	28.50	29.65
2017	28.50	28.63	29.10	29.50	29.50	30.70	31.88	32.13	32.90	33.50	34.63	35.00	31.33
2018	35.25	36.00	36.00	36.00	36.00	36.00	36.00	36.00	36.00	33.38	34.90	35.00	35.54
2019	35.00	35.00	35.00	35.00	35.00	35.00	35.00	35.00	35.00	35.00	40.40	43.25	36.14
2020[1]	44.00	44.00	44.00	44.00	44.00	44.00	44.00	44.00	44.00	36.50	36.50	36.50	42.13

[1] Preliminary. [2] These are f.o.b. basis prices in bulk, not delivered prices. *Source: Economic Research Service, U.S. Department of Agriculture (ERS)*

Average Price of World Raw Sugar[1] In Cents Per Pound

Year	Jan.	Feb.	Mar.	Apr.	May	June	July	Aug.	Sept.	Oct.	Nov.	Dec.	Average
2011	36.11	35.01	33.22	29.35	26.64	29.75	30.51	28.87	27.71	26.30	24.52	23.42	29.28
2012	24.05	25.81	24.73	22.98	20.25	20.44	22.76	20.53	19.47	20.39	19.31	19.50	21.69
2013	18.37	18.28	18.33	17.71	17.08	16.79	16.38	16.44	17.33	18.81	17.58	16.41	17.46
2014	15.42	16.28	17.58	17.01	17.50	17.22	17.18	15.89	14.60	16.48	15.89	14.99	16.34
2015	15.06	14.52	12.84	12.93	12.70	11.75	11.88	10.67	11.32	14.14	14.89	15.00	13.14
2016	14.29	13.31	15.43	15.00	16.68	19.34	19.69	20.01	21.30	22.92	20.81	18.83	18.13
2017	20.54	20.40	18.06	16.32	15.66	13.53	14.11	13.80	13.92	14.23	14.66	14.43	15.81
2018	13.99	13.56	12.83	11.82	11.85	12.06	11.17	10.46	10.78	13.18	12.78	12.55	12.25
2019	12.70	12.94	12.47	12.55	11.82	12.44	12.15	11.56	11.16	12.46	12.69	13.34	12.36
2020[1]	14.18	15.07	11.81	10.07	10.65	11.83	11.92	12.81	12.42	14.29	14.93	14.67	12.89

[1] Contract No. 11, f.o.b. stowed Caribbean port, including Brazil, bulk spot price. [2] Preliminary. *Source: Economic Research Service, U.S. Department of Agriculture (ERS-USDA)*

Average Price of Raw Sugar in New York (C.I.F., Duty/Free Paid, Contract #12 & #14) In Cents Per Pound

Year	Jan.	Feb.	Mar.	Apr.	May	June	July	Aug.	Sept.	Oct.	Nov.	Dec.	Average
2011	38.46	39.69	39.65	38.32	35.04	35.65	37.93	40.16	40.15	38.19	37.92	36.32	38.12
2012	34.69	33.57	34.94	31.87	30.20	28.89	28.68	28.84	26.27	23.89	22.52	22.41	28.90
2013	21.20	20.72	20.82	20.38	19.51	19.31	19.22	20.97	21.05	21.82	20.61	19.95	20.46
2014	20.27	21.65	22.03	24.33	24.66	25.65	24.78	25.64	25.36	26.41	24.26	24.81	24.15
2015	25.24	24.62	24.07	24.39	24.61	24.76	24.67	24.50	24.21	25.04	26.63	25.83	24.88
2016	25.76	25.50	26.32	27.90	27.26	27.68	28.15	28.54	28.16	28.57	28.76	29.24	27.65
2017	29.44	30.59	29.95	28.72	28.41	27.83	26.77	25.11	26.90	27.09	27.28	26.93	27.92
2018	26.60	25.83	24.73	24.92	24.59	25.72	25.56	25.60	25.40	25.21	25.04	25.23	25.37
2019	25.57	25.90	26.23	26.95	26.33	26.49	25.66	25.80	25.65	26.07	27.21	26.01	26.16
2020[1]	25.90	26.71	27.09	26.02	25.85	25.95	26.59	27.39	26.85	27.55	29.33	28.42	26.97

[1] Preliminary. *Source: Economic Research Service, U.S. Department of Agriculture (ERS-USDA)*

Supply and Utilization of Sugar (Cane and Beet) in the United States In Thousands of Short Tons (Raw Value)

	Supply								Utilization						
	Production			Offshore Receipts									Domestic Disappearance		
Year	Cane	Beet	Total	Foreign	Territories	Total	Beginning Stocks	Total Supply	Total Use	Exports	Net Changes in Invisible Stocks	Refining Loss Adjustment	In Polyhydric Alcohol[4]	Total	Per Capita Pounds
2011-12	3,588	4,900	8,488	3,632	0	3,632	1,378	13,498	11,519	269	-64	0	33	11,141	66.0
2012-13	3,905	5,076	8,981	3,224	0	3,224	1,979	14,185	12,027	274	-23	0	185	11,511	66.7
2013-14	3,667	4,794	8,462	3,742	0	3,742	2,158	14,362	12,552	306	0	0	346	11,819	68.1
2014-15	3,763	4,893	8,656	3,553	0	3,553	1,810	14,019	12,204	185	0	0	28	11,888	68.2
2015-16	3,870	5,119	8,989	3,341	0	3,341	1,815	14,145	12,091	74	-33	0	22	11,881	69.3
2016-17	3,867	5,103	8,970	3,244	0	3,244	2,054	14,267	12,391	95	38	0	29	12,102	69.8
2017-18	4,014	5,279	9,293	3,277	0	3,277	1,876	14,445	12,438	170	82	0	28	12,048	69.3
2018-19[1]	4,060	4,939	8,999	3,070	0	3,070	2,008	14,077	12,294	35	28	0	27	12,106	68.7
2019-20[2]	3,798	4,351	8,149	4,235	0	4,235	1,783	14,166	12,549	61	74	0	20	12,316	68.5
2020-21[3]	4,265	5,046	9,312	3,404	0	3,404	1,618	14,333	12,340	35	0	0	25	12,200	

[1] Preliminary. [2] Estimate. [3] Forecast. [4] Includes feed use. *Source: Economic Research Service, U.S. Department of Agriculture (ERS-USDA)*

Sugarcane for Sugar & Seed and Production of Cane Sugar and Molasses in the United States

			Production					Farm Value		Sugar Production				
										Raw Value			Molasses Made	
Year	Acreage Harvested (1,000 Acres)	Yield of Cane Per Havested Acre Net Tons	for Sugar (1,000 Tons)	for Seed (1,000 Tons)	Total (1,000 Tons)	Sugar Yield Per Acre (Short Tons)	Farm Price ($ Per Ton)	of Cane Used for Sugar (1,000 Dollars)	of Cane Used for Sugar & Seed (1,000 Dollars)	Total (1,000 Tons)	Per Ton of Cane (In Lbs.)	Refined Basis (1,000 Tons)	Edible (1,000 Gallons)	Total[3] (1,000 Gallons)
2011	872.6	33.5	27,738	1,486	29,224	4.35	47.2	1,308,951	1,379,498	3,599	----	----	----	----
2012	902.4	35.7	30,500	1,727	32,227	4.57	41.9	1,276,631	1,348,361	3,905	----	----	----	----
2013	910.8	33.8	29,023	1,738	30,761	4.27	31.4	910,377	962,807	3,667	----	----	----	----
2014	868.5	35.0	28,895	1,529	30,424	4.57	34.7	1,002,138	1,054,657	3,763	----	----	----	----
2015	874.7	36.7	30,555	1,567	32,122	4.66	31.2	953,328	1,000,620	3,870	----	----	----	----
2016	903.1	35.6	30,371	1,747	32,118	4.53	32.6	990,209	1,043,953	3,869	----	----	----	----
2017	904.1	36.8	31,182	2,056	33,238		31.0	1,025,524			----	----	----	----
2018	899.7	38.4	32,934	1,608	34,542		33.4	1,154,907			----	----	----	----
2019[1]	913.2	35.0	30,287	1,650	31,937						----	----	----	----
2020[2]	948.8	37.9	34,232	1,753	34,944						----	----	----	----

[1] Preliminary. [2] Estimate. [3] Excludes edible molasses. *Source: Economic Research Service, U.S. Department of Agriculture (ERS-USDA)*

U.S. Sugar Beets, Beet Sugar, Pulp & Molasses Produced from Sugar Beets and Raw Sugar Spot Prices

Year of Harvest	Acreage: Planted (1,000 Acres)	Acreage: Harvested (1,000 Acres)	Yield Per Harvested Acre (Sh. Tons)	Production (1,000 Tons)	Sugar Yield Per Acre (Sh. Tons)	Price[3] (Dollars)	Farm Value (1,000 $)	Sugar Production: Equivalent Raw Value[4] (1,000 Short Tons)	Sugar Production: Refined Basis (1,000 Short Tons)	Raw Sugar Prices: World[5] Refined #5 (In Cents Per Pound)	Raw Sugar Prices: CSCE #11 World (In Cents Per Pound)	Raw Sugar Prices: CSCE N.Y. Duty Paid (In Cents Per Pound)	Wholesale List Price HFCS (42%) Midwest
2011	1,233	1,213	23.8	28,896	4.04	69.40	2,004,116	4,900	----	31.68	29.28	38.12	30.11
2012	1,230	1,204	29.3	35,224	4.22	66.40	2,338,789	5,076	----	26.50	21.69	28.90	32.92
2013	1,198	1,154	28.4	32,789	4.15	46.90	1,536,422	4,794	----	22.17	17.46	20.46	35.86
2014	1,163	1,146	27.3	31,285	4.27	46.00	1,440,068	4,893	----	20.05	16.34	24.15	29.96
2015	1,160	1,145	30.9	35,359	4.47	47.20	1,669,310	5,119	----	16.94	13.14	24.88	32.75
2016	1,163	1,126	32.8	36,920	4.53	35.70	1,318,267	5,106	----	22.63	18.13	27.65	37.68
2017	1,132	1,114	31.7	35,317		41.20	1,456,165		----	19.62	15.81	27.92	39.79
2018	1,113	1,095	30.3	33,145		35.50	1,177,992		----	15.56	12.25	25.37	----
2019[1]	1,132	979	29.2	28,600					----	15.18	12.36	26.16	----
2020[2]	1,162	1,142	29.4	33,958					----				

[1] Preliminary. [2] Estimate. [3] Includes support payments, but excludes Gov't. sugar beet payments. [4] Refined sugar multiplied by factor of 1.07. [5] F.O.B. Europe. *Source: Economic Research Service, U.S. Department of Agriculture (ERS-USDA)*

Sugar Deliveries and Stocks in the United States In Thousands of Short Tons (Raw Value)

Year	Quota Allocation	Actual Imports	Deliveries by Primary Distributors: Cane Sugar Refineries Deliveries	Beet Sugar Factories Deliveries	Importers of Direct Consumption Sugar	Mainland Cane Sugar Mills[3]	Total Deliveries	Total Domestic Consumption	Stocks, Jan. 1: Cane Sugar Refineries[4]	Beet Sugar Factories	CCC	Refiners' Raw	Mainland Cane Mills	Total
2011	----	----	5,572	4,552	995	----	11,118	11,370	466	1,691	0	257	1,455	3,869
2012	----	----	5,648	4,633	977	----	11,257	11,405	315	1,597	0	498	1,370	3,780
2013	----	----	5,849	4,777	949	----	11,575	12,124	388	2,013	0	574	1,646	4,621
2014	----	----	6,069	4,875	760	----	11,704	11,831	572	1,603	0	592	1,714	4,481
2015	----	----	6,285	4,614	1,034	----	11,933	12,067	351	1,589	0	556	1,634	4,130
2016	----	----	6,386	4,809	921	----	12,115	12,287	413	1,889	0	322	1,336	3,960
2017	----	----	5,976	5,425	682	----	12,083	12,232	325	2,041	0	362	1,623	4,351
2018	----	----	6,219	5,121	705	----	12,045	12,184	316	1,716	0	538	1,529	4,099
2019[1]	----	----	6,317	5,099	645	----	12,062	12,185	288	1,889	0	528	1,673	4,378
2020[2]	----	----	6,593	4,387	1,277	----	12,258	12,352	326	1,454	0	565	1,510	3,855

[1] Preliminary. [2] Estimate. [3] Sugar for direct consumption only. [4] Refined. *Source: Economic Research Service, U.S. Department of Agriculture (ERS-USDA)*

Sugar, Refined--Deliveries to End User in the United States In Thousands of Short Tons

Year	Bakery & Cereal Products	Beverages	Confectionery[2]	Hotels, Restar. & Institutions	Ice Cream & Dairy Products	Canned, Bottled & Frozen Foods	All Other Food Uses	Retail Grocers[3]	Wholesale Grocers[4]	Non-food Uses	Non-Industrial Uses	Industrial Uses	Total Deliveries
2011	2,324	404	1,048	120	622	411	625	1,239	2,511	128	4,104	5,562	9,665
2012	2,330	486	1,044	130	674	412	687	1,172	2,374	123	3,959	5,755	9,715
2013	2,296	547	1,149	112	678	399	760	1,109	2,427	117	4,040	5,947	9,987
2014	2,435	598	1,142	118	756	434	853	1,193	2,151	118	3,965	6,336	10,300
2015	2,391	755	1,172	103	764	473	791	1,230	2,086	162	3,832	6,509	10,341
2016	2,517	695	1,156	92	764	433	880	1,303	2,248	179	4,094	6,625	10,719
2017	2,519	680	1,171	105	753	420	1,048	1,250	2,206	137	4,055	6,729	10,784
2018	2,468	725	1,222	91	812	375	1,147	1,224	2,175	138	3,836	6,877	10,713
2019	2,526	725	1,189	83	760	409	1,160	1,237	2,264	127	3,876	6,896	10,771
2020[1]	2,421	620	993	90	766	430	1,016	1,311	2,244	143	3,951	6,389	10,340

[1] Preliminary. [2] And related products. [3] Chain stores, supermarkets. [4] Jobbers, sugar dealers.
Source: Economic Research Service, U.S. Department of Agriculture (ERS-USDA)

Deliveries[1] of All Sugar by Primary Distributors in the United States, by Quarters In Thousands of Short Tons

Year	First Quarter	Second Quarter	Third Quarter	Fourth Quarter	Total	Year	First Quarter	Second Quarter	Third Quarter	Fourth Quarter	Total
2009	2,431	2,649	2,823	2,754	10,657	2015	2,861	3,070	3,274	2,862	12,067
2010	2,565	2,759	3,074	2,833	11,231	2016	2,992	2,946	3,250	3,098	12,287
2011	2,649	2,809	3,131	2,781	11,370	2017	2,869	3,130	3,161	3,073	12,232
2012	2,663	2,915	2,954	2,873	11,405	2018	2,926	2,964	3,223	3,071	12,184
2013	2,720	2,954	3,222	3,229	12,124	2019	2,935	3,059	3,166	3,030	12,190
2014	2,742	3,053	3,189	2,847	11,831	2020[2]	3,119	2,964	3,307	2,962	12,352

[1] Includes for domestic consumption and for export. [2] Preliminary. *Source: Economic Research Service, U.S. Department of Agriculture (ERS-USDA)*

Nearby Futures through Last Trading Day using selected contract months: March, May, July and October.

Volume of Trading of World Sugar #11 Futures in New York In Thousands of Contracts

Year	Jan.	Feb.	Mar.	Apr.	May	June	July	Aug.	Sept.	Oct.	Nov.	Dec.	Total
2011	2,180.8	3,341.9	1,774.8	2,338.8	1,832.4	3,266.1	1,702.0	1,986.6	2,555.9	1,258.7	1,286.7	1,104.7	24,629
2012	1,999.3	2,765.1	2,316.0	2,765.4	1,941.5	3,460.7	2,251.7	2,049.8	2,736.2	1,781.4	1,633.1	1,426.4	27,127
2013	2,368.0	3,038.0	2,039.9	3,086.2	1,908.9	3,974.1	2,037.0	2,117.1	3,791.9	2,279.9	1,559.9	1,612.7	29,814
2014	2,461.6	4,157.3	2,477.4	2,857.3	1,906.5	3,370.3	1,981.4	1,853.3	3,657.9	1,651.3	1,574.3	1,448.0	29,397
2015	2,547.7	3,635.6	2,790.0	3,850.9	2,274.2	3,789.2	2,260.8	2,315.0	4,329.7	2,600.5	2,303.8	1,697.0	34,394
2016	3,182.7	3,772.8	2,652.9	3,517.9	2,596.7	4,210.0	1,738.1	2,008.6	3,963.5	1,721.8	1,964.4	1,786.0	33,115
2017	2,494.1	3,269.3	2,773.6	3,294.8	2,484.6	3,515.7	1,859.0	2,291.5	3,359.1	1,665.9	2,055.1	1,898.4	30,961
2018	3,212.7	3,692.3	2,839.4	4,157.9	3,195.2	3,984.1	2,003.6	2,836.6	4,144.2	3,216.5	2,129.3	1,599.2	37,011
2019	3,371.9	3,497.8	3,015.9	4,319.7	3,170.8	4,020.9	2,198.2	2,495.6	4,812.1	2,059.5	2,308.6	2,417.1	37,688
2020	4,764.5	5,033.4	4,650.2	3,940.6	2,903.6	3,812.2	2,238.7	2,418.5	3,936.7	2,522.3	2,033.8	1,694.8	39,949

Contract size = 112,000 lbs. *Source: ICE Futures U.S. (ICE)*

Average Open Interest of World Sugar #11 Futures in New York In Contracts

Year	Jan.	Feb.	Mar.	Apr.	May	June	July	Aug.	Sept.	Oct.	Nov.	Dec.
2011	619,904	648,027	597,384	613,301	583,047	627,566	630,027	598,737	544,893	489,135	495,699	533,588
2012	612,932	699,780	729,307	728,645	728,515	744,254	669,730	688,099	705,221	697,064	726,541	756,324
2013	796,708	824,203	804,682	852,113	846,873	901,021	848,276	878,813	870,124	818,823	803,346	810,753
2014	834,655	838,471	787,473	792,420	809,219	870,191	842,551	885,193	851,724	766,320	811,959	828,791
2015	824,778	848,192	862,965	876,247	853,458	885,602	805,457	837,922	790,609	766,704	838,992	861,944
2016	870,944	830,246	795,043	820,305	841,639	894,893	837,385	880,629	885,571	841,889	837,131	818,873
2017	828,436	824,169	778,676	791,551	790,116	833,483	768,669	812,524	773,437	700,720	709,575	752,794
2018	844,185	891,797	915,120	1,003,293	1,012,957	977,622	973,446	1,041,981	871,673	774,976	791,152	840,548
2019	905,607	889,863	889,788	890,306	997,302	947,567	903,584	1,036,573	1,012,939	913,104	968,649	1,002,550
2020	1,084,021	1,222,255	1,073,698	991,547	960,551	970,496	942,507	1,026,601	1,009,797	992,075	1,065,231	1,059,590

Contract size = 112,000 lbs. *Source: ICE Futures U.S. (ICE)*

Sulfur

Sulfur (atomic symbol S) is an odorless, tasteless, light yellow, nonmetallic element. As early as 2000 BC, Egyptians used sulfur compounds to bleach fabric. The Chinese used sulfur as an essential component when they developed gunpowder in the 13th century.

Sulfur is widely found in both its free and combined states. Free sulfur is found mixed with gypsum and pumice stone in volcanic regions. Sulfur dioxide is an air pollutant that is released by the burning of fossil fuels. The most important use of sulfur is for the production of sulfur compounds. Sulfur is used in skin ointments, matches, dyes, gunpowder, and phosphoric acid.

Supply – World production of all forms of sulfur in 2020 was down -2.5% yr/yr at 78.000 million metric tons, which is down from the 2017 record high of 80.200. The world's largest producers of sulfur are China with 21.8% of the world's production, the U.S. with 10.4%, Russia with 9.6%, Saudi Arabia with 8.3%, and Canada with 8.1%. U.S. production of sulfur in 2020 fell -7.0% yr/yr to 8.100 million metric tons, a record low.

Demand – U.S. consumption of all forms of sulfur in 2020 was up +6.1% at 9.800 million metric tons, up from the 2019 record low. U.S. consumption of elemental sulfur in 2016 fell -4.9% yr/yr to 8.850 million metric tons. U.S. consumption of sulfuric acid in 2016 rose +19.5% yr/yr to 7,750 million metric tons.

Trade – U.S. exports of recovered sulfur in 2016 rose +10.3% yr/yr to 2.040 million metric tons, well above the 25-year low of 635,000 metric tons in 2006. U.S. imports of recovered sulfur in 2016 rose +10.3% yr/yr to 2.040 million metric tons, a new record high.

World Production of Sulfur (All Forms) In Thousands of Metric Tons

Year	Canada	China	France	Germany	Kazakh-stan	Japan	Mexico	Poland	Russia	Saudi Arabia	Spain	United States	World Total
2013	6,300	8,110	478	3,800	3,465	3,050	1,030	1,080	7,300	3,900	270	9,210	69,800
2014	5,840	8,840	478	3,800	3,503	3,070	993	1,160	6,860	4,400	270	9,630	71,300
2015	5,750	8,800	478	3,800	3,421	3,120	859	1,200	6,960	4,900	----	9,540	73,800
2016	5,320	8,800	478	3,800	3,420	3,120	673	1,210	6,960	4,900	----	9,740	73,500
2017	5,460	17,400	478	888	3,490	3,520	551	1,240	7,080	6,000	----	9,640	80,200
2018	5,320	17,400		868	3,400	3,510	550	1,230	7,080	6,500	----	9,680	79,400
2019[1]	6,940	17,500		670	3,400	3,500		1,190	7,560	6,500	----	8,710	80,000
2020[2]	6,300	17,000		670	3,400	3,500		1,200	7,500	6,500	----	8,100	78,000

[1] Preliminary. [2] Estimate. *Source: U.S. Geological Survey (USGS)*

Salient Statistics of Sulfur in the United States In Thousands of Metric Tons (Sulfur Content)

	Production of											Sales Value of Shipments		
	Elemental Sulfur											F.O.B. Mine/Plant		
	Native	Recovered												
Year	- Sulfur[3] - Frasch	Petroleum & Cole	Natural Gas	Total	Total Elemental Sulfur	By-product Sulfuric Acid[4]	Other Sulf. Acid Com-pounds	Imports Sulfuric Acid[4]	Exports Sulfuric Acid[4]	Producer Stocks, Dec. 31[5]	Apparent Con-sumption (All Forms)	Frasch	Recovered	Average Total
2013	----	7,580	1,020	8,590	616	----	9,210	2,980	165	160	11,300	----	----	68.71
2014	----	8,040	1,000	9,040	587	----	9,630	3,070	160	141	11,000	----	----	80.07
2015	----	7,910	984	8,890	646	----	9,540	3,540	177	138	11,000	----	----	87.62
2016	----	8,290	781	9,070	673	----	9,740	3,220	180	142	10,500	----	----	37.88
2017	----	8,410	662	9,070	560	----	9,630	2,920	254	124	10,100	----	----	46.39
2018	----	8,378	626	9,005	672	----	9,670			118	10,400	----	----	81.16
2019[1]	----	7,788	341	8,128	596	----	8,710			124	9,240	----	----	51.08
2020[2]	----	7,031	273	7,303	520	----	8,100			110	9,800	----	----	40.00

[1] Preliminary. [2] Estimate. [3] Or sulfur ore; Withheld included in natural gas. [4] Basis 100% H2SO4, sulfur equivalent. [5] Frasch & recovered.
W = Withheld proprietary data. Source: U.S. Geological Survey (USGS)

Sulfur Consumption & Foreign Trade of the United States In Thousands of Metric Tons (Sulfur Content)

	Consumption			Sulfuric Acid Sold or Used, by End Use[2]						Foreign Trade					
										Exports			Imports		
Year	Native Sulfur (Frasch)	Rec-overed Sulfur	Total Elemental Form	Pulpmills & Paper Products	Inorganic Chem-icals[3]	Synthetic Rubber & Plastic	Phosph-atic Fertilizers	Petro-leum Refining[4]	Frasch	Frasch	Re-covered	Value $1,000	Frasch	Re-covered	Value $1,000
2009	----	----	8,380	7,740	188	286	64	5,430	283	----	1,430	82,200	----	1,700	54,100
2010	----	----	9,870	6,980	79	31	6	5,700	368	----	1,450	171,000	----	2,950	214,000
2011	----	----	10,200	7,650	168	118	70	5,740	422	----	1,310	266,000	----	3,270	301,000
2012	----	----	9,520	7,410	168	107	70	5,420	423	----	1,860	366,000	----	2,930	238,000
2013	----	----	9,810	7,780	168	101	70	5,270	1,270	----	1,770	235,000	----	2,990	202,000
2014	----	----	9,450	6,410	129	74	6	4,810	410	----	2,010	315,000	----	2,370	134,000
2015	----	----	9,310	6,320	124	128	6	4,610	428	----	1,850	284,000	----	2,240	136,000
2016[1]	----	----	8,850	7,550	119	79	6	5,820	387	----	2,040	213,000	----	1,960	79,800

[1] Preliminary. [2] Sulfur equivalent. [3] Including inorganic pigments, paints & allied products, and other inorganic chemicals & products.
[4] Including other petroleum and coal products. W = Withheld proprietary data. NA = Not available. *Source: U.S. Geological Survey (USGS)*

Sunflowerseed, Meal and Oil

Sunflowers are native to South and North America but are now grown almost worldwide. Sunflower oil accounts for approximately 14% of the world's production of seed oils. Sunflower varieties that are commercially grown contain from 39% to 49% oil in the seed. Sunflower crops produce about 50 bushels of seed per acre on average, which yields approximately 50 gallons of oil.

Sunflower oil accounts for around 80% of the value of the sunflower crop. Refined sunflower oil is edible and used primarily as a salad and cooking oil and in margarine. Crude sunflower oil is used industrially for making soaps, candles, varnishes, and detergents. Sunflower oil contains 93% of the energy of U.S. No. 2 diesel fuel and is being explored as a potential alternate fuel source in diesel engines. Sunflower meal is used in livestock feed, and when fed to poultry, increases the yield of eggs. Sunflower seeds are also used for birdfeed and as a snack for humans.

Prices – The average monthly price received by U.S. farmers for sunflower seeds in the first four months of the 2020/21 marketing year (Sep/Aug) fell -0.3% to $20.23 per hundred pounds, well below the 2011/12 record high of $28.96 per hundred pounds.

Supply – World sunflower seed production in 2020/21 is expected to fall -9.0% yr/yr to 50.035 million metric tons. The world's largest sunflower seed producers will be Ukraine with 28.0% of world production, Russia with 27.0%, European Union with 18.4%, China with 6.6%, Argentina with 5.8%, Turkey with 3.1%, and the U.S. with 2.7%. U.S. production of sunflower seeds in 2020/21 is expected to rise by +52,5% yr/yr to 1.353 million metric tons, but still far below the record production level of 3.309 million metric tons posted in 1979-80. U.S. farmers are expected to harvest 1.622 million acres of sunflowers in 2020/21, up +29.4% yr/yr, but still well below the 10-year high of 2.610 million acres posted in 2005/06. U.S sunflower seed yield in 2020/21 is expected to be 17.30 hundred pounds per acre, down -0.4% yr/yr from the previous year's record high of 17.31 hundred pounds per acre.

Demand – Total U.S. disappearance of sunflower seeds in 2020/21 is expected to rise +31.1% yr/yr to 1.570 million metric tons, of which 47.1% will go to non-oil and seed use, 34.6& to exports, and 3.8% to crushing for oil and meal.

Trade – World sunflower seed exports in 2020/21 are expected to fall -21.0% yr/yr to 2.900 million metric tons. The world's largest exporters will be Moldova, which will account for 19.8% of world exports, Russia with 19.0%, China with 15.5%, the European Union with 12.1%, and Kazakhstan with 12.1%. World sunflower seed imports in 2020/21 are expected to fall -21.9% yr/yr to 2.548 million metric tons. The world's largest importers will be Turkey with 33.4% of world imports and the European Union with 24.3%.

World Production of Sunflowerseed In Thousands of Metric Tons

Crop Year	Argentina	China	European Union	India	Kazakhstan	Pakistan	Russia	Serbia	South Africa	Turkey	Ukraine	United States	World Total
2013-14	2,065	2,448	9,054	580	573	193	9,842	425	832	1,400	11,600	917	41,529
2014-15	3,160	2,582	8,974	383	513	169	8,374	525	661	1,200	10,200	1,004	39,238
2015-16	3,000	2,872	7,721	323	534	90	9,173	450	755	1,100	11,900	1,327	40,704
2016-17	3,547	3,201	8,651	318	755	75	10,858	650	874	1,320	15,200	1,203	48,225
2017-18	3,538	3,149	10,128	230	903	90	10,362	540	862	1,550	13,700	970	47,826
2018-19	3,825	2,494	9,505	172	848	144	12,710	680	678	1,800	15,000	956	50,557
2019-20[1]	3,235	3,250	9,643	140	918	145	15,305	660	785	1,750	16,500	887	54,963
2020-21[2]	2,900	3,300	9,200	185	750	160	13,500	675	640	1,560	14,000	1,353	50,035

[1] Preliminary. [2] Forecast. *Source: Economic Research Service, U.S. Department of Agriculture (ERS-USDA)*

World Exports of Sunflowerseed In Thousands of Metric Tons

Crop Year	Argentina	Canada	China	European Union	Israel	Kazakhstan	Moldova	Russia	Serbia	Turkey	Ukraine	United States	World Total
2013-14	74	49	202	712	3	146	322	135	106	57	70	120	2,010
2014-15	63	34	244	518		118	342	61	77	41	45	116	1,674
2015-16	308	29	286	424	2	168	316	107	134	109	83	99	2,077
2016-17	75	18	365	358	1	275	534	368	127	126	191	90	2,545
2017-18	55	17	480	639	1	321	613	98	112	148	39	79	2,619
2018-19	173	27	452	611	1	451	590	358	162	116	104	64	3,121
2019-20[1]	190	27	500	456	1	318	590	1,237	140	99	53	45	3,669
2020-21[2]	150	50	450	350	1	350	575	550	145	80	125	59	2,900

[1] Preliminary. [2] Forecast. *Source: Economic Research Service, U.S. Department of Agriculture (ERS-USDA)*

World Imports of Sunflowerseed In Thousands of Metric Tons

Crop Year	Belarus	Canada	Egypt	European Union	Iran	Mexico	Moldova	Morocco	Pakistan	Russia	Turkey	United States	World Total
2013-14	13	25	43	319	42	18	2	1	197	35	597	65	1,626
2014-15	19	30	57	266	69	18	3	38	178	88	462	75	1,555
2015-16	25	22	63	622	82	20	6	15	94	121	483	72	1,975
2016-17	53	30	62	694	160	27	5	8	40	107	656	80	2,264
2017-18	27	22	102	512	150	27	3	19	45	47	770	97	2,237
2018-19	56	24	90	545	100	25	3	2	4	52	1,116	115	2,608
2019-20[1]	58	30	76	968	120	27	3	11	5	56	1,178	181	3,264
2020-21[2]	50	27	90	620	115	25	1	50	10	50	850	129	2,548

[1] Preliminary. [2] Forecast. *Source: Economic Research Service, U.S. Department of Agriculture (ERS-USDA)*

World Production of Sunflowerseed Oil In Thousands of Metric Tons

Crop Year	Argentina	Burma	China	European Union	India	Pakistan	Russia	Serbia	South Africa	Turkey	Ukraine	United States	World Total
2013-14	934	112	466	3,196	179	148	3,785	123	347	774	4,759	195	15,616
2014-15	1,153	131	466	3,232	121	132	3,428	161	298	677	4,429	146	14,935
2015-16	1,170	131	502	3,042	105	68	3,552	153	335	587	5,010	205	15,407
2016-17	1,335	131	609	3,338	105	38	4,171	191	348	761	6,351	211	18,202
2017-18	1,385	131	645	3,760	75	44	4,192	212	352	881	5,913	197	18,501
2018-19	1,425	131	466	3,675	58	48	4,935	212	272	1,066	6,364	201	19,472
2019-20[1]	1,200	131	672	3,739	45	51	5,700	225	306	1,141	7,390	187	21,475
2020-21[2]	1,225	131	699	3,692	62	60	5,203	221	293	1,000	5,923	226	19,420

[1] Preliminary. [2] Forecast. *Source: Economic Research Service, U.S. Department of Agriculture (ERS-USDA)*

World Production of Sunflowerseed Meal In Thousands of Metric Tons

Crop Year	Argentina	Burma	China	European Union	India	Kazakhstan	Pakistan	Russia	South Africa	Turkey	Ukraine	United States	World Total
2013-14	963	110	709	4,108	238	144	155	3,571	356	990	4,646	240	16,809
2014-15	1,147	128	709	4,131	156	135	137	3,407	302	866	4,254	179	16,138
2015-16	1,180	128	763	3,888	135	135	71	3,530	340	743	4,811	252	16,538
2016-17	1,350	128	927	4,266	135	176	40	4,146	353	963	6,030	259	19,397
2017-18	1,400	128	981	4,806	97	217	46	4,167	357	1,114	5,679	242	19,944
2018-19	1,435	128	709	4,700	75	155	50	4,911	275	1,348	6,112	247	20,812
2019-20[1]	1,170	128	1,022	4,780	74	225	54	5,672	310	1,429	6,455	230	22,231
2020-21[2]	1,235	128	1,063	4,727	80	185	63	5,179	288	1,252	5,689	277	20,884

[1] Preliminary. [2] Forecast. *Source: Economic Research Service, U.S. Department of Agriculture (ERS-USDA)*

Sunflowerseed Statistics in the United States In Thousands of Metric Tons

Crop Year Beginning Sept. 1	Acres Harvested (1,000)	Harvested Yield Per CWT	Farm Price ($/Metric Ton)	Value of Production (Million $)	Supply: Stocks, Sept. 1	Supply: Production	Supply: Imports	Supply: Total Supply	Disappearance: Crush	Disappearance: Exports	Disappearance: Non-Oil Use & Seed	Disappearance: Total Disappearance
2013-14	1,465	13.80	472	443.3	154	917	65	1,136	120	463	462	1,136
2014-15	1,510	14.69	478	497.8	91	1,004	75	1,170	116	366	580	1,170
2015-16	1,799	16.25	432	574.2	108	1,327	72	1,507	99	495	726	1,507
2016-17	1,532	17.31	384	464.0	187	1,203	80	1,470	90	508	605	1,470
2017-18	1,334	16.03	379	375.1	267	970	97	1,334	79	475	605	1,334
2018-19	1,217	17.31	384	370.4	175	956	115	1,246	64	485	567	1,246
2019-20[1]	1,254	15.60	392	358.4	130	887	181	1,198	45	450	615	1,198
2020-21[2]	1,623	17.30			88	1,353	129	1,570	59	544	739	1,570

[1] Preliminary. [2] Forecast. *Source: Economic Research Service, U.S. Department of Agriculture (ERS-USDA)*

Sunflower Oil Statistics in the United States In Thousands of Metric Tons

Crop Year Beginning Sept. 1	Supply: Stocks, Oct. 1	Supply: Production	Supply: Imports	Supply: Total Supply	Disappearance: Exports	Disappearance: Domestic Use	Disappearance: Total Disappearance	Price $ Per Metric Ton (Crude Mpls.)
2013-14	23	195	35	253	37	193	230	1,305
2014-15	23	146	80	249	29	197	226	1,449
2015-16	23	205	42	270	39	197	236	1,309
2016-17	34	211	54	299	32	226	258	1,182
2017-18	41	197	73	311	40	238	278	1,205
2018-19	33	201	60	294	55	220	275	1,173
2019-20[1]	19	187	169	375	40	313	353	1,430
2020-21[2]	22	226	91	339	39	266	305	1,257

[1] Preliminary. [2] Forecast. *Source: Economic Research Service, U.S. Department of Agriculture (ERS-USDA)*

Sunflower Meal Statistics in the United States In Thousands of Metric Tons

Crop Year Beginning Sept. 1	Supply: Stocks, Oct. 1	Supply: Production	Supply: Imports	Supply: Total Supply	Disappearance: Exports	Disappearance: Domestic Use	Disappearance: Total Disappearance	Price USD Per Metric Ton 28% Protein
2013-14	5	240	11	256	8	243	256	270
2014-15	5	179	20	204	7	192	204	224
2015-16	5	252	21	278	12	261	278	175
2016-17	5	259	11	275	5	265	275	161
2017-18	5	242	1	248	6	237	248	190
2018-19	5	247	2	254	15	234	254	182
2019-20[1]	5	230	2	237	20	212	237	201
2020-21[2]	5	277	5	287	18	264	287	258

[1] Preliminary. [2] Forecast. *Source: Economic Research Service, U.S. Department of Agriculture (ERS-USDA)*

Average Price Received by Farmers for Sunflower[2] in the United States In Dollars Per Hundred Pounds (Cwt.)

Year	Sept.	Oct.	Nov.	Dec.	Jan.	Feb.	Mar.	Apr.	May	June	July	Aug.	Average
2013-14	22.60	23.00	20.70	18.80	19.60	22.80	21.60	22.30	24.10	22.80	22.10	22.40	21.90
2014-15	20.20	21.70	20.30	19.70	19.10	21.50	22.50	23.20	26.40	25.40	26.40	24.20	22.55
2015-16	25.20	18.40	18.30	19.30	20.10	20.40	21.10	20.90	19.50	20.10	19.00	19.60	20.16
2016-17	17.90	17.00	16.40	17.20	17.20	17.60	17.40	17.90	17.30	17.60	17.90	19.10	17.54
2017-18	17.40	16.80	16.60	17.00	17.60	17.70	17.30	18.00	17.90	17.70	17.40	16.90	17.36
2018-19	16.70	16.70	17.00	16.90	17.30	18.00	17.80	17.60	18.30	17.90	18.00	17.80	17.50
2019-20	18.50	17.50	17.70	17.80	19.50	20.20	20.60	20.20	20.40	21.70	23.70	25.90	20.31
2020-21[1]	23.70	19.10	18.90	19.20	19.60								20.10

[1] Preliminary. [2] KS, MN, ND and SD average. *Source: Economic Research Service, U.S. Department of Agriculture (ERS-USDA)*

Average Price of Crude Sunflower Oil at Minneapolis In Cents Per Pound

Year	Sept.	Oct.	Nov.	Dec.	Jan.	Feb.	Mar.	Apr.	May	June	July	Aug.	Average
2013-14	63.75	60.50	57.40	57.00	57.00	57.00	58.00	59.00	59.00	57.50	61.00	63.00	59.18
2014-15	63.00	63.00	61.75	58.00	63.00	65.63	65.56	65.50	65.00	69.75	73.40	75.00	65.72
2015-16	75.00	72.00	64.50	62.00	58.00	54.25	53.80	53.80	54.00	54.20	55.20	56.00	59.40
2016-17	56.00	56.00	56.00	56.00	56.00	55.00	52.00	51.00	50.50	50.80	51.25	52.75	53.61
2017-18	55.20	56.00	55.50	54.80	55.50	55.00	54.00	54.00	54.00	54.00	54.00	54.00	54.67
2018-19	54.00	54.00	52.80	53.50	53.50	53.00	53.20	54.00	53.40	51.00	52.50	53.40	53.19
2019-20	55.00	56.00	56.00	76.00	70.00	70.00	76.00	76.00	74.00	56.00	56.40	57.00	64.87
2020-21[1]	57.00	57.00	NA	NA	NA								57.00

[1] Preliminary. *Source: Economic Research Service, U.S. Department of Agriculture (ERS-USDA)*

Average Price of Sunflower Meal (26% protein) in the United States In Cents Per Pound

Year	Sept.	Oct.	Nov.	Dec.	Jan.	Feb.	Mar.	Apr.	May	June	July	Aug.	Average
2013-14	218.13	236.25	246.88	277.50	283.75	285.00	271.25	267.50	265.00	250.00	192.50	151.25	245.42
2014-15	139.50	162.50	208.13	245.00	247.50	225.63	202.50	202.50	192.50	180.50	214.38	222.50	203.60
2015-16	216.00	212.50	187.50	163.13	156.88	131.88	120.00	109.38	149.50	165.63	151.88	141.00	158.77
2016-17	148.75	148.75	140.50	145.00	159.00	161.88	155.00	147.50	144.00	140.00	130.63	134.50	146.29
2017-18	134.38	153.00	165.00	185.00	178.00	185.63	187.50	191.88	201.50	175.63	155.50	153.13	172.18
2018-19	150.63	164.00	171.25	187.50	190.50	187.50	189.38	166.50	141.25	143.13	142.00	144.38	164.84
2019-20	142.50	169.00	166.88	180.00	185.00	188.13	180.00	183.75	180.63	187.50	202.50	217.50	181.95
2020-21[1]	211.50	211.25	213.13	252.50	280.63								233.80

[1] Preliminary. *Source: Economic Research Service, U.S. Department of Agriculture (ERS-USDA)*

Production of Sunflower in the United States In Thousands of Pounds

Crop Year	California	Colorado	Kansas	Minnesota	Nebraska	North Dakota	Oklahoma	South Dakota	Texas	Total
2013	75,150	45,600	82,000	69,250	32,975	600,560	5,180	996,800	114,250	2,021,765
2014	61,925	95,700	91,540	87,870	47,375	847,420	3,200	876,620	137,400	2,219,050
2015	44,720	85,200	135,560	166,050	79,410	1,068,800	6,600	1,230,040	107,350	2,923,730
2016	61,875	90,500	82,660	113,550	58,150	1,137,450	----	1,057,050	50,400	2,651,635
2017	51,305	86,200	84,520	68,475	61,800	704,250	----	1,020,000	61,200	2,137,750
2018	76,500	61,950	74,250	113,835	47,380	739,400	----	966,150	27,580	2,107,045
2019	70,680	59,400	53,925	102,630	44,850	740,700	----	831,600	39,650	1,943,435
2020[1]	56,675	64,700	101,250	120,450	68,140	1,225,600	----	1,107,300	63,000	2,807,115

[1] Preliminary. *Source: Economic Research Service, U.S. Department of Agriculture (ERS-USDA)*

Production of Sunflower Oil in the United States In Thousands of Pounds

Crop Year	California	Colorado	Kansas	Minnesota	Nebraska	North Dakota	Oklahoma	South Dakota	Texas	Total
2012	65,075	40,120	74,750	70,300	20,650	1,283,500	4,180	761,600	39,600	2,359,775
2013	72,150	29,600	58,000	51,200	19,975	504,000	3,480	820,800	78,000	1,637,205
2014	57,200	44,800	57,540	65,250	29,000	683,400	2,100	668,000	56,800	1,664,090
2015	42,900	68,400	80,560	123,750	42,660	889,350	4,800	1,048,000	82,650	2,383,870
2016	60,075	68,400	57,540	96,000	37,800	1,055,300	----	960,300	33,600	2,369,015
2017	49,875	73,000	65,000	64,350	37,050	628,650	----	848,000	45,600	1,847,525
2018	74,100	53,900	61,500	99,000	34,080	665,000	----	878,400	21,280	1,887,260
2019[1]	68,600	44,000	44,800	94,350	33,800	645,000	----	782,000	33,800	1,746,350

[1] Preliminary. *Source: Economic Research Service, U.S. Department of Agriculture (ERS-USDA)*

Tallow and Greases

Tallow and grease are derived from processing (rendering) the fat of cattle. Tallow is used to produce both edible and inedible products. Edible tallow products include margarine, cooking oil, and baking products. Inedible tallow products include soap, candles, and lubricants. Production of tallow and greases is directly related to the number of cattle produced. Those countries that are the leading cattle producers are also the largest producers of tallow. The American Fats and Oils Association provides specifications for a variety of different types of tallow and grease, including edible tallow, lard (edible), top white tallow, all beef packer tallow, extra fancy tallow, fancy tallow, bleachable fancy tallow, prime tallow, choice white grease, and yellow grease. The specifications include such characteristics as the melting point, color, density, moisture content, insoluble impurities, and others.

Prices – The monthly average wholesale price of tallow (inedible, No. 1 Packers-Prime, delivered to Chicago) in 2020 rose +12.3% yr/yr to 31.05 cents per pound. The wholesale price of inedible tallow in 2015 fell -26.7% yr/yr to 26.87 cents per pound.

Supply – World production of tallow and greases (edible and inedible) in 2018 rose +3.3% yr/yr to 9.849 million metric tons, which is a new record high. The world's largest producer of tallow and greases by far is the U.S. with 47.0% of world production, followed by Brazil far behind with 7.0%, Australia with 5.7%, and Canada with 2.7%. U.S. production of edible tallow in 2018 rose +8.8% yr/yr to 2.233 billion pounds, a new record high. U.S. production of inedible tallow and greases in 2011 fell -37.9% yr/yr to 3.654 billion pounds, well below the record high of 7.156 billion pounds posted in 2002.

Demand – U.S. consumption of inedible tallow and greases in 2011 fell 0.9% yr/yr to 1.560 billion pounds, of which virtually all went for animal feed. U.S. consumption of edible tallow in 2019 rose +0.2% yr/yr to 2.014 billion pounds, a new record high. U.S. per capita consumption of edible tallow in 2010 rose from 0.7 pounds per person to 3.4 pounds per person yr/yr, down from the 2000 and 2004 record high of 4.0 pounds.

Trade – U.S. exports of inedible tallow and grease in 2011 fell -3.2% yr/yr to 752.990 million pounds and accounted for 48.3% of total U.S. supply. U.S. exports of edible tallow in 2019 rose by +3.0% yr/yr to 268 million pounds and accounted for 11.7% of U.S. supply.

World Production of Tallow and Greases (Edible and Inedible) In Thousands of Metric Tons

Year	Argentina	Australia	Brazil	Canada	France	Germany	Korea, South	Nether-lands	New Zealand	Russia	United Kingdom	United States	World Total
2009	204	483	547	252	188	131	16	123	168	195	134	3,655	8,304
2010	160	488	566	262	200	134	16	131	169	200	141	3,575	8,331
2011	153	493	551	255	209	134	15	121	167	198	144	4,529	9,186
2012	160	494	587	242	198	131	18	106	166	199	139	4,488	9,190
2013	175	548	654	241	191	130	21	103	169	207	138	4,457	9,319
2014	167	601	635	248	192	131	20	101	167	213	142	4,225	9,189
2015	171	605	600	238	196	132	20	105	176	219	145	4,205	9,191
2016	167	507	620	248	198	132	19	108	165	224	147	4,432	9,372
2017[1]	180	525	652	260	201	130	19	112	172	224	147	4,469	9,538
2018[2]	193	566	689	271	203	128	19	116	177	228	148	4,634	9,849

[1] Preliminary. [2] Forecast. *Source: Foreign Agricultural Service, U.S. Department of Agriculture (FAS-USDA)*

Salient Statistics of Tallow and Greases (Inedible) in the United States In Millions of Pounds

	Supply				Consumption			Wholesale Prices, Cents Per Lb.	
Year	Production	Stocks, Jan. 1	Total	Exports	Soap	Feed	Total	Edible, (Loose) Chicago	Inedible, Chicago No. 1
2006	6,460	309	6,769	730	W	2,585	2,585	18.6	16.9
2007	6,369	291	6,661	795	W	2,385	2,385	30.7	27.8
2008	6,224	350	6,573	703	W	2,095	2,095	38.0	34.2
2009	5,878	315	6,193	727	W	1,770	1,770	27.5	25.2
2010	5,887	286	6,174	778	W	1,574	1,574	35.1	33.3
2011	3,654	281	3,934	753	W	1,560	1,560	53.2	49.6
2012[1]	NA	NA	NA	NA	NA	NA	NA	47.8	43.8
2013[2]	NA	NA	NA	NA	NA	NA	NA	42.6	40.4
2014[2]	----	----	----	----	----	----	----	38.7	36.7
2015[2]	----	----	----	----	----	----	----	28.4	26.9

[1] Preliminary. [2] Forecast. *Source: Foreign Agricultural Service, U.S. Department of Agriculture (FAS-USDA)*

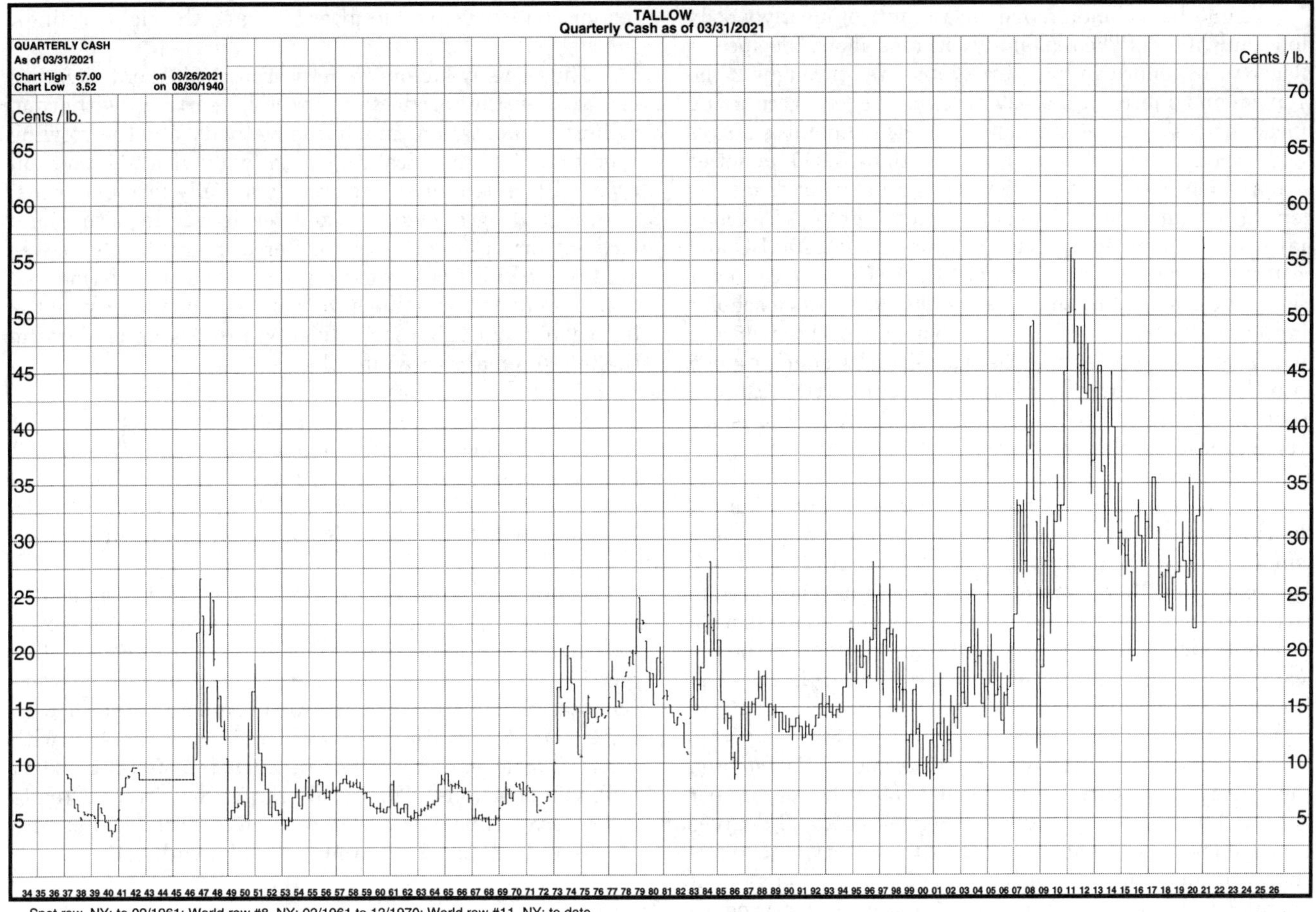

Spot raw, NY: to 02/1961; World raw #8, NY: 02/1961 to 12/1970; World raw #11, NY: to date.

Supply and Disappearance of Edible Tallow in the United States In Millions of Pounds, Rendered Basis

	Supply			Disappearance					
Year	Stocks, Jan. 1	Production	Total Supply	Domestic Disap-pearance	Exports	Total Disap-pearance	Direct Use	Baking or Frying Fats	Per Capita (Lbs.)
2011	38	2,050	2,116	1,954	132	2,086	NA	NA	NA
2012	30	2,055	2,137	1,940	166	2,107	NA	NA	NA
2013	30	2,043	2,122	1,935	157	2,092	----	----	----
2014	30	1,922	2,004	1,884	90	1,974	----	----	----
2015	30	1,928	2,003	1,830	143	1,973	----	----	----
2016	30	2,143	2,235	1,929	265	2,194	----	----	----
2017	41	2,053	2,159	1,945	181	2,126	----	----	----
2018	33	2,233	2,302	2,010	260	2,270	----	----	----
2019[1]	31	2,252	2,298	2,012	268	2,280	----	----	----
2020[2]	18	1,970	2,020	1,813	207	2,020	----	----	----

[1] Preliminary. [2] Forecast. W = Withheld. *Sources: Economic Research Service, U.S. Department of Agriculture (ERS-USDA); Bureau of the Census, U.S. Department of Commerce*

Average Wholesale Price of Tallow, Inedible, No. 1 Packers (Prime), Delivered, Chicago In Cents Per Pound

Year	Jan.	Feb.	Mar.	Apr.	May	June	July	Aug.	Sept.	Oct.	Nov.	Dec.	Average
2011	47.83	47.61	49.49	51.59	52.33	54.52	53.69	49.36	50.02	47.36	44.35	47.21	49.61
2012	44.17	45.67	48.16	47.33	48.98	45.39	45.38	44.59	45.72	40.07	34.05	36.20	43.81
2013	40.00	40.00	42.42	43.06	41.67	45.00	45.39	42.74	40.53	33.37	35.14	35.14	40.37
2014	31.95	31.61	38.52	42.60	44.57	42.04	39.96	39.85	34.90	29.51	32.47	32.09	36.67
2015	28.77	28.84	30.42	28.22	28.64	29.72	28.50	29.21	28.71	22.41	19.48	19.50	26.87
2016	23.14	26.50	29.64	32.93	32.67	31.34	29.04	27.50	27.50	27.90	31.49	31.64	29.27
2017	31.35	31.11	30.11	30.33	33.49	35.40	35.50	35.37	33.96	27.83	26.36	26.50	31.44
2018	26.38	25.00	25.59	24.61	24.20	26.35	28.05	27.88	25.20	23.76	25.85	26.50	25.78
2019	26.50	26.50	26.52	28.14	28.69	29.63	30.65	31.32	28.26	26.29	23.77	25.56	27.65
2020[1]	30.57	34.67	31.57	30.95	33.94	25.14	23.50	30.33	31.58	32.10	32.50	35.80	31.05

[1] Preliminary. *Sources: Economic Research Service, U.S. Department of Agriculture (ERS-USDA)*

Tea

Tea is the common name for a family of mostly woody flowering plants. The tea family contains about 600 species placed in 28 genera and they are distributed throughout the tropical and subtropical areas, with most species occurring in eastern Asia and South America. The tea plant is native to Southeast Asia. There are more than 3,000 varieties of tea, each with its own distinct character, and each is generally named for the area in which it is grown. Tea may have been consumed in China as long ago as 2700 BC and certainly since 1000 BC. In 2737 BC, the Chinese Emperor Shen Nung, according to Chinese mythology, was a scholar and herbalist. While his servant boiled drinking water, a leaf from the wild tea tree he was sitting under dropped into the water, and Shen Nung decided to try the brew. Today, half the world's population drinks tea. Tea is the world's most popular beverage next to water.

Tea is a healthful drink and contains antioxidants, fluoride, niacin, folic acid, and as much vitamin C as a lemon. The average 5 ounce cup of brewed tea contains approximately 40 to 60 milligrams of caffeine (compared to 80 to 115 mg in brewed coffee). Decaffeinated tea has been available since the 1980s. Herbal tea contains no true tea leaves but is actually brewed from a collection of herbs and spices.

Tea grows mainly between the tropic of Cancer and the tropic of Capricorn, requiring 40 to 50 inches of rain per year and a temperature ideally between 50 to 86 degrees Fahrenheit. The bushes must be pruned every four to five years to rejuvenate the bush and keep it at a convenient height for the pickers to access. A tea bush can produce tea for 50 to 70 years, but after 50 years, the yield declines.

The two key factors in determining different varieties of tea are the production process (sorting, withering, rolling, fermentation, and drying methods) and the growing conditions (geographical region, growing altitude, and soil type). Black tea, often referred to as fully fermented tea, is produced by allowing picked tea leaves to wither and ferment for up to 24 hours. After fermenting, the leaves are fired, which stops oxidation. Green tea, or unfermented tea, is produced by immediately and completely drying the leaves and omitting the oxidization process, thus allowing the tea to remain green in color.

Supply – World production of tea in 2019 rose +2.7% to 6.497 million metric tons, a new record high. The world's largest producers of tea in 2019 were China with 43,0% of world production, India with 21.4%, Kenya with 7.1%, Sri Lanka with 4.6%, Turkey with 4.0%, and Iran with 1.4%.

Trade – U.S. tea imports in 2020 fell -3.4% to 194,847 metric tons, below the 2013 record high of 216,864 metric tons. World tea imports in 2019 fell -1.7% to 1.873 million metric tons. The world's largest tea importers were Pakistan with 11.0% of total world imports, Russia with 8.0%, thc United Kingdom with 6.6%, and the U.S with 6.3%. World exports of tea in 2019 fell -0.2% to 2.011 million metric tons. The world's largest exporters of tea in 2019 were Kenya with 23.7% of world exports, China with 19.2%, India with 12.8%, and Sri Lanka with 8.4%.

World Tea Production, in Major Producing Countries In Metric Tons

Year	Argentina	Bangladesh	China	India	Indonesia	Iran	Japan	Kenya	Malawi	Sri Lanka	Turkey	Ex-USSR[2]	World Total
2013	80,423	66,259	1,939,175	1,208,780	145,855	97,475	84,800	432,400	46,460	340,230	212,400	3,958	5,309,841
2014	82,632	63,780	2,110,770	1,207,310	154,369	72,277	83,600	445,105	45,480	338,032	226,800	2,496	5,493,989
2015	82,492	66,101	2,291,405	1,233,140	132,615	196,957	79,500	399,100	47,877	317,967	239,028	2,925	5,761,926
2016	85,015	64,500	2,326,018	1,250,490	144,015	124,870	80,200	473,000	48,723	292,574	243,000	4,465	5,802,728
2017	81,476	81,850	2,473,843	1,325,050	146,251	100,580	82,000	439,857	48,717	307,720	234,000	3,629	5,994,682
2018	81,981	78,150	2,625,138	1,338,630	140,236	99,245	86,300	492,990	49,128	303,840	270,000	3,073	6,326,897
2019[1]	85,730	90,685	2,791,837	1,390,080	137,803	90,832	81,700	458,850	49,586	300,120	261,000	3,227	6,497,443

[1] Preliminary. [2] Mostly Georgia and Azerbaijan. *Sources: Foreign Agricultural Service, U.S. Department of Agriculture (FAS-USDA); Food and Agriculture Organization of the United Nations (FAO-UN)*

World Exports of Tea from Producing Countries In Metric Tons

Year	Argentina	Bangladesh	Brazil	China	India	Indonesia	Kenya	Malawi	Papua New Guinea	Sri Lanka	Vietnam	Zimbabwe	Total
2013	77,291	665	623	332,172	254,841	70,842	448,809	43,245	2,943	317,710	90,296	11,863	2,051,373
2014	76,892	2,475	447	307,480	212,606	66,399	296,112	40,000	1,933	325,141	132,252	12,790	1,924,260
2015	76,029	574	399	331,751	235,132	61,915	298,540	38,785	1,303	304,835	125,185	13,959	1,848,890
2016	78,177	721	367	336,618	230,456	51,317	302,532	43,656	896	286,760	136,361	11,083	1,861,120
2017	74,921	2,149	297	367,585	261,419	52,824	467,024	41,273	938	286,863	146,440	13,396	2,135,891
2018[1]	72,619	949	227	380,992	262,421	49,030	500,591	42,166	711	164,709	77,234	14,229	2,014,631
2019[2]	75,322	852	306	385,783	258,048	40,484	475,997	46,944	345	169,515	134,937	14,534	2,010,960

[1] Preliminary. [2] Estimate. *Source: Food and Agriculture Organization of the United Nations (FAO-UN)*

Imports of Tea in the United States In Metric Tons

Year	Jan.	Feb.	Mar.	Apr.	May	June	July	Aug.	Sept.	Oct.	Nov.	Dec.	Total
2015	13,344	13,018	19,870	18,794	19,750	20,863	19,625	20,091	23,682	15,621	15,734	13,692	214,084
2016	14,278	14,512	20,720	20,168	21,535	22,102	19,136	20,903	18,424	13,513	13,264	13,260	211,815
2017	14,923	12,784	16,132	18,980	21,458	19,263	20,082	19,684	18,930	12,874	13,657	13,349	202,116
2018	15,231	11,716	11,611	17,712	20,164	18,202	17,370	18,866	17,850	13,205	13,993	12,314	188,234
2019	14,523	14,128	16,810	18,058	19,626	17,829	20,574	18,243	15,784	15,231	15,738	14,250	200,796
2020[1]	16,085	11,457	17,037	17,600	18,745	16,861	15,970	17,250	17,458	15,650	15,075	14,861	194,048

[1] Preliminary. *Source: Foreign Agricultural Service, U.S. Department of Agriculture (FAS-USDA)*

Tin

Tin (atomic symbol Sn) is a silvery-white, lustrous gray metallic element. Tin is soft, pliable and has a highly crystalline structure. When a tin bar is bent or broken, a crackling sound called a "tin cry" is produced due to the breaking of the tin crystals. People have been using tin for at least 5,500 years. Tin has been found in the tombs of ancient Egyptians. In ancient times, tin and lead were considered different forms of the same metal. Tin was exported to Europe in large quantities from Cornwall, England, during the Roman period, from approximately 2100 BC to 1500 BC. Cornwall was one of the world's leading sources of tin for much of its known history and into the late 1800s.

The principal ore of tin is the mineral cassiterite, which is found in Malaya, Bolivia, Indonesia, Thailand, and Nigeria. About 80% of the world's tin deposits occur in unconsolidated placer deposits in riverbeds and valleys, or on the seafloor, with only about 20% occurring as primary hard-rock lodes. Tin deposits are generally small and are usually allied with granite. Tin is also recovered as a by-product of mining tungsten, tantalum, and lead. After extraction, tin ore is ground and washed to remove impurities, roasted to oxidize the sulfides of iron and copper, washed a second time, and then reduced by carbon in a reverberatory furnace. Electrolysis may also be used to purify tin.

Pure tin, rarely used by itself, was used as currency in the form of tin blocks and was considered legal tender for taxes in Phuket, Thailand, until 1932. Tin is used in the manufacture of coatings for steel containers used to preserve food and beverages. Tin is also used in solder alloys, electroplating, ceramics, and in plastic. The world's major tin research and development laboratory, ITRI Ltd, is funded by companies that produce and consume tin. The research efforts have focused on possible new uses for tin that would take advantage of tin's relative non-toxicity to replace other metals in various products. Some of the replacements could be lead-free solders, antimony-free flame-retardant chemicals, and lead-free shotgun pellets. No tin is currently mined in the U.S.

Tin futures and options trade on the London Metal Exchange (LME). Tin has traded on the LME since 1877, and the standard tin contract began in 1912. The futures contract calls for the delivery of 5 metric tons of tin ingots of at least 99.85% purity. The contract trades in terms of U.S. dollars per metric ton.

Prices – The average monthly price of tin (straights) in New York in 2020 fell -8.2% yr/yr to $10.62 per pound, well below the 2011 record high of $15.87 per pound. The price was far above the 3-decade low of $2.83 per pound seen in 2002. The average monthly price of ex-dock tin in New York in 2020 fell -8.1% yr/yr to $8.01 per pound.

Supply – World mine production of tin in 2020 fell -8.8% yr/yr to 270,000 metric tons, down from the 2018 record high of 318,000 metric tons. The world's largest mine producers of tin are China with 30.0% of world production in 2020, Indonesia with 24.4%, Burma with 12.2%, Peru with 6.7%, and Bolivia with 5.6% each. World smelter production of tin in 2016 fell -3.7% yr/yr to 341,000 metric tons. The world's largest producers of smelted tin are China, with 46.7% of world production in 2016, Indonesia with 13.2%, and Malaysia with 7.9%. The U.S. does not mine tin, and therefore its supply consists only of scrap and imports. U.S. tin recovery in 2020 rose +18.3% yr/yr to 5,550 metric tons, up from the 2019 record low.

Demand – U.S. consumption of tin (pig) in 2020 rose +3.3% yr/yr to 20,750 metric tons, up from the 2019 record low. The breakdown of U.S. consumption of tin by finished products in 2017 shows that the largest consuming industry of tin is chemicals and tinplate, each with 20.4% of consumption, followed by solder with 16.4%, and bronze and brass with 7.0%.

Trade – The U.S. relied on imports for 75% of its tin consumption in 2020. U.S. imports of unwrought tin metal in 2020 fell -7.3% yr/yr to 31,600 metric tons, for a new record low. The largest sources of U.S. imports in 2016 were Indonesia with 26.6%, Malaysia with 23.5%, and Bolivia with 18.6%. U.S. exports of tin in 2020 fell -60.1% yr/yr to 519 metric tons.

World Mine Production of Tin In Metric Tons (Contained Tin)

Year	Australia	Bolivia	Brazil	Burma	China	Congo	Indonesia	Malaysia	Nigeria	Peru	Rwanda	Vietnam	World Total
2011	14,014	20,373	10,725	11,000	120,000	5,600	89,600	3,340	270	28,882	4,400	5,400	315,000
2012	6,158	19,702	13,667	10,600	110,000	4,800	44,202	3,725	340	26,105	2,900	5,400	249,000
2013	6,472	19,282	16,830	17,000	97,000	4,500	59,412	3,697	2,600	23,668	3,100	5,400	260,000
2014	6,900	19,802	25,534	30,000	104,000	6,500	51,801	3,777	2,800	23,105	4,200	5,400	285,000
2015	7,000	20,000	25,000	34,271	110,156	6,400	52,000	3,800	2,500	19,511	2,000	5,400	289,000
2016	6,640	17,000	25,000	54,000	92,000	5,500	52,000	4,000	2,290	18,800	2,200	5,500	288,000
2017	7,200	18,500	18,000	47,000	93,000	9,500	83,000	3,810	5,960	17,800	2,860	4,560	313,000
2018	6,870	16,900	17,100	54,600	90,000	7,400	85,000	4,300	7,800	18,600	2,400	4,560	318,000
2019[1]	7,740	17,000	14,000	42,000	84,500	12,200	77,500	3,610	5,800	19,900	2,300	5,500	296,000
2020[2]	6,800	15,000	13,000	33,000	81,000	17,000	66,000	3,300	6,000	18,000	1,200	4,900	270,000

[1] Preliminary. [2] Estimate. *Source: U.S. Geological Survey (USGS)*

World Smelter Production of Primary Tin In Metric Tons

Year	Australia	Belgium	Bolivia	Brazil	China	Indo-nesia	Japan	Malaysia	Peru	Russia	Thailand	United States	World Total
2007	518	5,000	12,251	9,634	149,000	64,127	879	25,263	36,004	4,200	23,104	12,200	346,000
2008	570	5,000	12,667	11,300	140,000	53,417	956	31,691	38,865	1,730	21,860	11,700	334,000
2009	400	8,700	14,995	8,561	140,000	51,418	757	36,407	34,388	1,430	19,423	11,100	331,000
2010	400	9,900	15,003	9,348	150,000	51,418	841	38,771	36,451	1,381	20,000	11,100	348,000
2011	400	10,000	14,295	9,632	156,000	43,832	947	40,281	32,290	726	20,000	11,000	344,000
2012	400	11,400	14,626	12,205	148,000	51,400	1,133	37,823	24,811	700	19,996	11,200	342,000
2013	400	12,000	14,862	14,971	159,000	48,800	1,786	32,633	24,181	550	19,088	10,600	346,000
2014	400	9,810	15,439	25,784	187,000	58,233	1,746	35,018	24,462	550	16,929	10,100	394,000
2015	400	8,860	15,700	26,250	166,900	48,000	1,700	30,260	20,396	550	16,500	10,100	354,000
2016[1]	400	8,540	16,800	26,000	166,000	45,000	1,620	26,849	19,390	----	11,088	10,100	341,000

[1] Preliminary. *Source: U.S. Geological Survey (USGS)*

United States Foreign Trade of Tin In Metric Tons

		Imports for Consumption											
		Concentrates[2] (Ore)			Unwrought Tin Metal								
Year	Exports (Metal)	Total All Ore	Bolivia	Peru	Total All Metal	Bolivia	Brazil	China	Indo-nesia	Malaysia	Singa-pore	Thailand	United Kingdom
2011	5,450	----	----	----	34,200	5,680	676	1,490	4,930	3,980	645	2,310	18
2012	5,560	----	----	----	36,900	5,100	2,930	174	6,180	4,590	424	1,750	[1]
2013	5,870	----	----	----	34,900	6,510	3,100	1,610	5,560	4,190	101	2,380	----
2014	5,700	----	----	----	35,600	4,570	3,030	3,470	8,140	6,050	375	291	----
2015	3,350	----	----	----	33,600	6,260	2,950	1,230	5,210	9,990	225	20	2
2016	1,150	----	----	----	32,200	6,170	2,120	229	8,580	7,560	176	392	----
2017	1,560	----	----	----	32,400								
2018	962	----	----	----	36,800								
2019[1]	1,300	----	----	----	34,100								
2020[1]	519	----	----	----	31,600								

[1] Preliminary. [2] Tin content. [4] Less than 1/2 unit. *Source: U.S. Geological Survey (USGS)*

Consumption (Total) of Tin (Pig) in the United States In Metric Tons

Year	Jan.	Feb.	Mar.	Apr.	May	June	July	Aug.	Sept.	Oct.	Nov.	Dec.	Total
2011	2,782	2,769	2,833	2,831	2,862	2,983	2,961	2,823	3,064	3,061	2,973	2,750	34,692
2012	2,718	2,748	2,868	2,829	2,908	2,775	2,735	2,745	2,696	2,724	2,684	2,725	33,155
2013	2,959	2,970	3,009	2,989	2,970	2,949	2,099	2,140	2,079	2,069	2,026	2,047	30,306
2014	1,819	1,818	1,878	1,938	2,164	2,212	2,202	2,202	2,212	2,182	2,193	2,143	24,963
2015	2,183	2,181	2,211	2,241	2,211	2,271	2,251	2,261	2,261	2,231	2,161	2,191	26,590
2016	2,239	2,239	2,179	2,179	2,189	2,209	2,189	2,239	2,209	2,197	2,165	2,127	26,360
2017	2,137	2,127	2,155	2,165	2,194	2,176	2,166	2,195	2,158	2,187	2,061	1,804	25,525
2018	1,870	1,832	1,835	1,874	1,856	1,843	1,823	1,859	1,838	1,809	1,827	1,949	22,215
2019	1,874	1,884	1,857	1,834	1,875	1,947	1,854	1,908	1,826	1,875	1,855	1,805	22,394
2020[1]	1,880	1,910	1,937	1,951	1,925	1,921	1,913	1,932	1,920	1,972	1,924	1,904	23,089

[1] Preliminary. *Source: U.S. Geological Survey (USGS)*

Tin Stocks (Pig-Industrial) in the United States, on First of Month In Metric Tons

Year	Jan.	Feb.	Mar.	Apr.	May	June	July	Aug.	Sept.	Oct.	Nov.	Dec.
2011	6,920	6,660	6,710	6,740	6,750	6,820	6,860	6,880	6,860	6,860	6,800	6,700
2012	5,230	6,810	6,860	6,780	6,710	6,750	6,790	7,290	7,280	7,340	7,310	6,360
2013	6,470	6,670	6,640	6,590	6,640	7,110	6,660	6,670	6,680	6,580	6,570	6,480
2014	6,520	6,540	6,560	6,570	6,490	6,800	6,800	6,770	6,740	7,360	7,060	6,970
2015	7,010	6,860	6,910	6,960	6,910	6,910	7,360	6,970	6,900	7,510	6,930	6,940
2016	6,420	6,420	6,400	6,350	6,380	6,310	6,220	6,220	6,210	6,320	6,480	6,510
2017	6,490	6,550	6,570	6,580	6,480	6,540	6,520	6,580	6,590	6,560	6,550	6,570
2018	6,300	6,330	6,300	6,430	6,280	6,360	6,400	6,310	6,400	5,180	5,610	5,610
2019	5,140	5,350	4,700	5,880	5,540	5,390	5,350	4,790	5,910	4,840	4,820	5,940
2020[1]	6,540	6,560	5,110	5,110	5,090	5,080	5,070	5,090	5,100	5,060	5,100	5,150

[1] Preliminary. *Source: U.S. Geological Survey (USGS)*

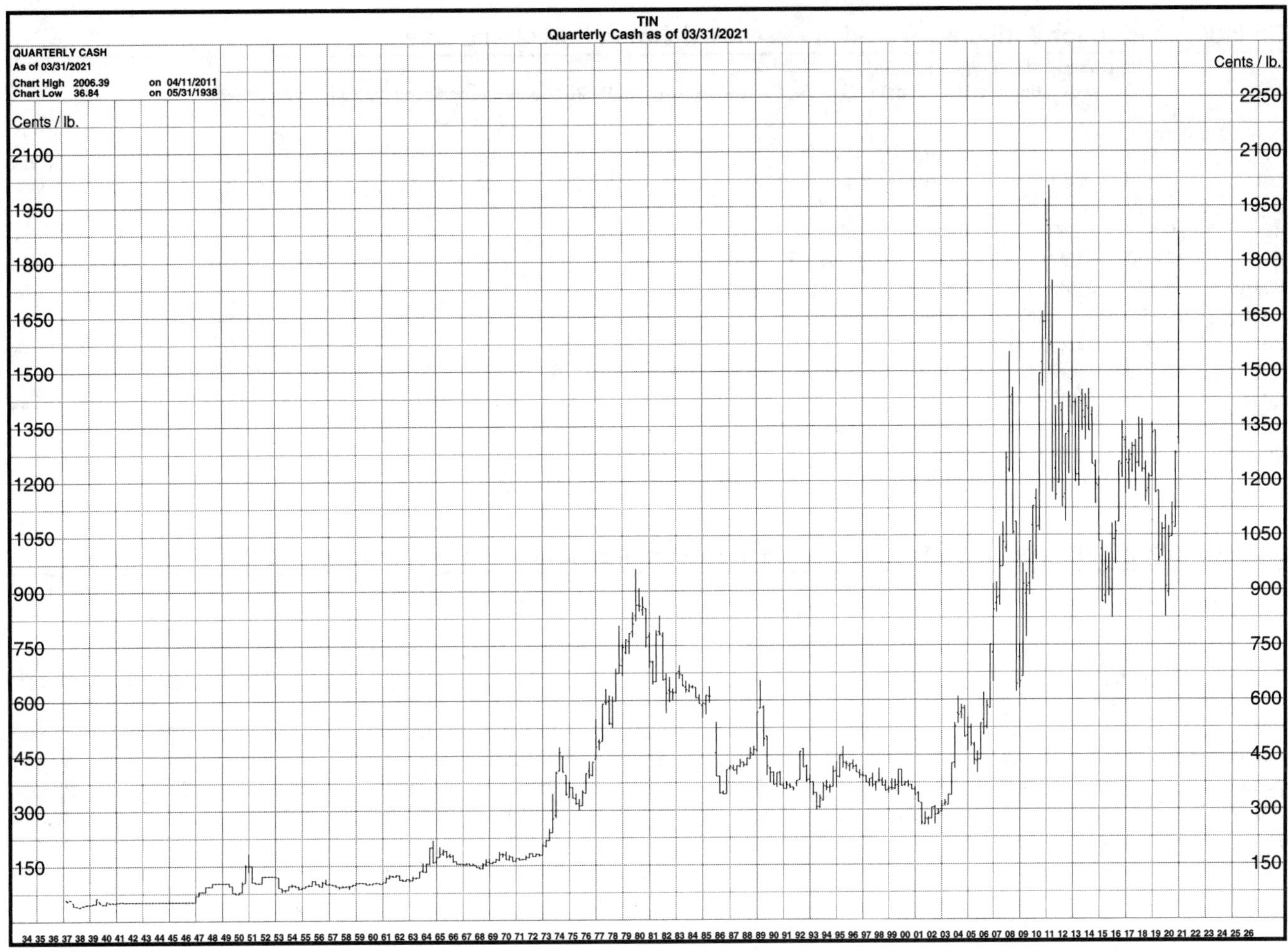

Straights, Composite: to date.

Average Price of Ex-Dock Tin in New York[1] In Cents Per Pound

Year	Jan.	Feb.	Mar.	Apr.	May	June	July	Aug.	Sept.	Oct.	Nov.	Dec.	Average
2011	1,274.29	1,456.60	1,422.69	1,501.64	1,339.50	1,188.91	1,271.42	1,137.37	1,055.80	1,019.31	998.78	913.27	1,214.96
2012	1,005.52	1,136.74	1,074.53	1,034.47	958.73	905.04	874.07	879.88	972.20	998.11	969.71	1,065.21	989.52
2013	1,147.61	1,132.62	1,088.32	1,016.82	968.64	946.60	914.64	1,008.50	1,062.18	1,076.08	1,064.68	1,061.89	1,040.71
2014	1,026.81	1,061.00	1,074.64	1,088.65	1,083.18	1,059.89	1,041.12	1,037.98	983.57	929.95	931.02	925.65	1,020.29
2015	910.45	857.51	818.81	754.37	745.34	721.70	NQ	NQ	NQ	733.84	694.41	693.59	770.00
2016	653.01	737.23	797.61	798.88	786.39	796.12	834.14	861.60	913.95	940.57	987.73	990.44	841.47
2017	965.02	907.96	925.11	931.47	943.03	920.97	946.70	959.93	971.40	953.69	913.47	907.11	937.15
2018	965.23	1,009.51	987.72	993.12	974.52	962.92	918.93	900.01	887.62	891.53	893.21	898.89	940.27
2019	955.87	993.47	1,001.46	964.84	910.96	893.74	838.94	773.46	786.32	777.06	767.10	799.46	871.89
2020	795.91	769.10	719.07	709.11	724.63	785.65	815.13	824.32	836.15	846.26	864.00	923.79	801.09

Source: American Metal Market (AMM)

Average Price of Tin (Straights) in New York In Cents Per Pound

Year	Jan.	Feb.	Mar.	Apr.	May	June	July	Aug.	Sept.	Oct.	Nov.	Dec.	Average
2011	1,661.33	1,906.31	1,857.97	1,958.08	1,750.23	1,555.57	1,663.54	1,486.24	1,378.26	1,330.78	1,298.42	1,191.48	1,586.52
2012	1,312.08	1,481.62	1,404.14	1,351.56	1,251.34	1,180.70	1,142.08	1,148.33	1,269.91	1,300.73	1,264.64	1,393.41	1,291.71
2013	1,502.64	1,480.17	1,422.82	1,328.61	1,265.73	1,252.58	1,200.86	1,321.68	1,391.23	1,413.19	1,392.13	1,391.85	1,363.62
2014	1,345.40	1,388.75	1,406.24	1,423.40	1,416.15	1,388.17	1,365.31	1,362.21	1,289.78	1,219.57	1,223.03	1,211.06	1,336.59
2015	1,193.00	1,125.26	1,076.19	989.76	978.73	930.77	924.68	933.28	945.21	973.65	908.21	909.01	990.65
2016	854.30	965.15	1,050.78	1,056.03	1,037.46	1,051.94	1,105.23	1,143.75	1,208.97	1,246.19	1,309.82	1,314.74	1,112.03
2017	1,282.89	1,205.68	1,232.26	1,233.41	1,251.83	1,218.85	1,253.86	1,272.12	1,289.49	1,263.32	1,212.57	1,207.57	1,243.65
2018	1,282.77	1,342.47	1,316.42	1,321.32	1,294.62	1,280.95	1,223.25	1,191.67	1,175.96	1,185.53	1,182.02	1,194.59	1,249.30
2019	1,268.38	1,318.36	1,326.39	1,276.72	1,210.19	1,189.98	1,114.63	1,027.78	1,043.50	1,029.41	1,012.80	1,062.75	1,156.74
2020	1,055.81	1,021.78	948.04	927.43	954.67	1,043.95	1,083.14	1,094.94	1,112.98	1,126.95	1,148.39	1,225.20	1,061.94

Source: U.S. Geological Survey (USGS)

Tin Plate Production & Tin Recovered in the United States In Metric Tons

	Tin Content of Tinplate Produced				Tin Recovered from Scrap by Form of Recovery								
	Tinplate Waste	Tinplate (All Forms)	Tin Content (Met. Ton)	Tin per Tonne of Plate (Kilograms)	Tin Metal	Bronze & Brass	Solder	Type Metal	Babbitt	Anti-monial Lead	Chemical Com-pounds	Misc.[2]	Grand Total
Year	Gross Weight												
2011	21,500	1,230,000	6,330	5.2	----	----	----	----	----	----	----	----	----
2012	16,300	1,160,000	6,090	5.2	----	----	----	----	----	----	----	----	----
2013	20,800	1,090,000	6,030	5.5	----	----	----	----	----	----	----	----	----
2014	32,900	1,030,000	5,680	5.5	----	----	----	----	----	----	----	----	----
2015	43,800	812,000	4,650	5.7	----	----	----	----	----	----	----	----	----
2016	29,800	623,000	7,840	12.6	----	----	----	----	----	----	----	----	----
2017	27,700	496,000	5,340	10.8	----	----	----	----	----	----	----	----	----
2018		487,000	4,600	9.3	----	----	----	----	----	----	----	----	----
2019		437,000	4,690	10.7	----	----	----	----	----	----	----	----	----
2020[1]		518,000	5,550	10.8	----	----	----	----	----	----	----	----	----

[1] Preliminary. [2] Includes foil, terne metal, cable lead, and items indicated by symbol "W". W = Withheld. NA = Not available.
Source: U.S. Geological Survey (USGS)

Consumption of Primary and Secondary Tin in the United States In Metric Tons

			Net Receipts							
Year	Net Import Reliance as a % of Apparent Consump	Stocks, Jan. 1[2]	Primary	Secondary	Scrap	Total	Available Supply	Stocks, Dec. 31 (Total Available Less Total Processed)	Total Pro-cessed	Consumed in Manu-facturing Products
2011	73	5,830	25,200	2,840	916	29,000	34,800	5,880	28,900	28,500
2012	72	5,800	24,900	2,810	892	28,600	34,400	6,200	28,200	27,800
2013	75	7,110	25,600	2,620	1,970	30,100	37,300	6,820	30,400	30,400
2014	76	5,530	24,000	1,250	2,450	27,700	33,200	5,350	27,800	27,500
2015	76	5,330	24,200	1,180	2,140	27,500	32,800	5,700	27,100	26,800
2016	76	7,090	22,600	1,140	2,040	25,800	31,200	5,480	25,700	25,400
2017	76	6,370	23,100	1,230	2,210	26,500	32,100	5,320	27,100	26,700
2018	77	6,660								
2019[1]	77	10,100								
2020[1]	75	10,200								

[1] Preliminary. [2] Includes tin in transit in the U.S. NA = Not available. *Source: U.S. Geological Survey (USGS)*

Consumption of Tin in the United States, by Finished Products In Metric Tons (Contained Tin)

Year	Tin-plate[2]	Solder	Babbitt	Bronze & Brass	Tinning	Chem-icals[3]	Tin Powder	Bar Tin & Anodes	White Metal	Other	Total
2008	6,840	5,110	604	2,460	395	5,440	227	767	W	5,370	29,200
2009	6,130	5,110	322	2,200	340	9,290	193	245	W	7,000	32,600
2010	6,920	7,340	288	2,460	387	9,470	192	W	W	811	30,100
2011	6,230	4,100	315	3,810	552	9,990	W	W	W	757	28,500
2012	6,090	4,930	281	2,460	467	9,860	W	W	W	726	27,800
2013	6,030	5,940	820	2,380	511	6,790	W	W	W	807	30,400
2014	5,940	4,860	282	1,720	514	5,420	W	W	W	4,780	27,500
2015	5,880	4,400	312	1,750	463	5,410	W	W	W	6,090	26,800
2016	4,660	4,220	289	1,720	405	5,320	W	W	W	6,190	25,400
2017[1]	5,440	4,410	332	1,880	337	5,450	W	W	W	6,190	26,700

[1] Preliminary. [2] Includes small quantity of secondary pig tin and tin acquired in chemicals. [3] Including tin oxide.
W = Withheld proprietary data. *Source: U.S. Geological Survey (USGS)*

Salient Statistics of Recycling Tin in the United States

	In Metric Tons					Value in Thousands of Dollars			
Year	New Scrap[1]	Old Scrap[2]	Recycled Metal[3]	Apparent Supply	Percent Recycled	New Scrap[1]	Old Scrap[2]	Recycled Metal[3]	Apparent Supply
2010	2,680	11,100	13,800	44,100	31.0	73,400	303,000	376,000	1,200,000
2011	2,530	11,000	13,600	42,800	32.0	87,900	383,000	470,000	1,490,000
2012	2,380	11,200	13,500	46,900	31.0	67,300	316,000	383,000	1,220,000
2013	2,150	10,600	12,700	45,100	28.0	49,300	243,000	292,000	1,050,000
2014	2,060	10,600	12,600	44,900	27.0	46,400	238,000	285,000	1,040,000
2015	1,120	10,100	11,200	43,800	26.0	18,700	168,000	186,000	722,000
2016	1,080	10,300	11,400	41,400	27.0	20,000	190,000	210,000	766,000
2017	1,400	10,000	11,400	43,900	26.0	29,000	207,000	236,000	907,000

[1] Scrap that results from the manufacturing process. [2] Scrap that results from consumer products. [3] Metal recovered from new plus old scrap.
Source: U.S. Geological Survey (USGS)

Titanium

Titanium (atomic symbol Ti) is a silver-white, metallic element used primarily to make light, strong alloys. It ranks ninth in abundance among the elements in the crust of the earth, but it is never found in its pure state. It occurs as an oxide in various minerals. It was first discovered in 1791 by Rev. William Gregor and was first isolated as a basic element in 1910. Titanium was named after the mythological Greek god Titan for its strength.

Titanium is extremely brittle when cold but is malleable and ductile at low heat, making it easy to fabricate. Due to its strength, low weight, and resistance to corrosion, titanium is used in metallic alloys and as a substitute for aluminum. It is used extensively in the aerospace industry, in desalinization plants, construction, medical implants, paints, pigments, and lacquers.

Supply – World production of titanium ilmenite concentrates in 2020 fell -1.3% yr/yr to 7.600 million metric tons, still down from the 2013 record high of 8.270 million metric tons. The world's largest producers of titanium ilmenite concentrates are China with 30.3% of world production in 2020, Australia with 10.5%, Ukraine with 6.2%, and Norway with 5.3%. World production of titanium rutile concentrates in 2020 fell -3.7% yr/yr to 630,000 metric tons. The world's largest producers are Australia, with 31.7% of world production in 2020, followed by Sierra Leone with 19.0%, South Africa with 15.9%, and Ukraine with 14.9%.

Demand – U.S. consumption of titanium dioxide pigment in 2019 rose +0.8% yr/yr to 900,000 metric tons, remaining below 2004's record high of 1.170 million metric tons. U.S. consumption of ilmenite in 2005 (lastest data) fell –12.8% yr/yr to 1.290 million metric tons, down from 2004's 8-year high of 1.480 million metric tons. U.S. consumption of rutile in 2005 fell 4.7% yr/yr to a 7-year low of 424,000 metric tons.

Trade – U.S. imports of titanium dioxide pigment in 2019 fell -110.8% yr/yr to 240,000 metric tons, still below the 2005 record high of 341,000 metric tons. U.S. imports of ilmenite in 2017 rose +28.4% yr/yr to 760,000 metric tons.

World Produciton of Titanium Ilmenite Concentrates In Thousands of Metric Tons

Year	Australia[2]	Brazil	China	Egypt	India	Malaysia	Norway	Ukraine	United States	Vietnam	World Total	-- Titaniferous Slag[4] --- Canada	Africa
2011	1,501	115	1,420	----	550	29	869	261	400	841	7,330	878	1,367
2012	1,570	115	1,330	----	340	22	831	247	300	978	7,250	900	1,300
2013	1,560	130	1,700	20	436	16	826	670	300	1,030	8,270	900	1,170
2014	1,250	135	1,860	----	320	8	864	450	200	558	7,640	900	1,030
2015	1,160	133	1,780	----	300	6	430	350	300	282	6,980	700	950
2016	1,300	130	1,400	----	300	30	439	350	100	400	7,000	900	830
2017	730	50	840	----	300		220	230	100	200	5,540	880	550
2018	720	66	2,100	----	319		236	373	100	105	6,870	850	500
2019	840	25	2,300	----	162		400	490	100	160	7,700	680	1,100
2020[1]	800	25	2,300	----	160		400	470	100	160	7,600	680	1,000

[1] Preliminary. [2] Includes leucoxene. [3] Approximately 10% of total production is ilmenite. Beginning in 1988, 25% of Norway's ilmenite production was used to produce slag containing 75% TiO2. NA = Not available. *Source: U.S. Geological Survey (USGS)*

Salient Statistics of Titanium in the United States In Metric Tons

	--- Titanium Dioxide Pigment ---			------ Ilmenite ------		-- Titanium Slag ---		------- Rutile[4] --------		------ Exports of Titamium Products ------			
Year	Production	Imports[3]	Apparent Consumption	Imports[3]	Consumption	Imports[3]	Consumption	Imports[3]	Consumption	Ores & Concentrates	Scrap	Dioxide & Pigments	Ingots, Billets, Etc.
2010	1,320,000	204,000	767,000	377,000	----	475,000	----	351,000	----	18,900	3,480	717,000	8,450
2011	1,290,000	200,000	706,000	377,000	----	513,000	----	381,000	----	26,600	5,150	741,000	15,600
2012	1,140,000	203,000	722,000	374,000	----	618,000	----	389,000	----	43,000	8,760	587,000	13,800
2013	1,280,000	213,000	826,000	389,000	----	681,000	----	406,000	----	11,500	4,700	624,000	12,500
2014	1,260,000	224,000	802,000	355,000	----	678,000	----	342,500	----	2,240	4,610	685,000	11,500
2015	1,220,000	221,000	792,000	649,000	----	399,000	----	394,000	----	2,040	6,860	649,000	10,400
2016	1,240,000	247,000	840,000	592,000	----	402,000	----	349,700	----	7,330	9,720	651,000	10,100
2017	1,260,000	239,000	870,000	760,000	----	479,000	----	334,200	----	8,940	9,480	634,000	10,900
2018[1]	1,150,000	269,000	893,000		----		----		----			529,000	
2019[2]	1,100,000	240,000	900,000		----		----		----			400,000	

[1] Preliminary. [2] Estimate. [3] For consumption. [4] Natural and synthetic. W = Withheld. *Source: U.S. Geological Survey (USGS)*

World Production of Titanium Rutile Concentrates In Metric Tons

Year	Australia	Brazil	India	Madagascar	Malaysia	Mozambique	Sierra Leone	South Africa	Sri Lanka	Ukraine	United States	World Total
2013	232,000	2,246	14,500	11,000	5,983	4,000	120,349	70,000	1,590	162,000	W	629,000
2014	212,000	2,038	18,600	6,900	3,069	6,100	114,163	120,000	1,749	110,000	W	660,000
2015	320,000	2,222	22,200	4,800	198	5,981	126,022	100,000	1,808	90,000	W	762,000
2016	400,000	2,000	16,400	4,800	200	7,781	143,000	110,000	2,000	100,000	W	886,000
2017	300,000	2,000	10,000	5,000	200	9,100	168,000	100,000	2,000	100,000	W	803,000
2018	141,000		15,000	8,000		6,000	114,000	103,000		94,000	W	594,000
2019	200,000		11,000	8,000		6,000	129,000	110,000		94,000	W	654,000
2020[1]	200,000		11,000			6,000	120,000	100,000		94,000	W	630,000

[1] Preliminary. *Source: U.S. Geological Survey (USGS)*

World Production of Titanium Sponge Metal & U.S. Consumption of Titanium Concentrates

	Production of Titanium (In Metric Tons) --- Sponge Metal[2]						--- U.S. Consumption of Titanium Concentrates, by Products (In Metric Tons) --- Ilmenite (TiO_2 Content)			Rutile (TiO_2 Content)			
Year	China	Japan	Russia	United Kingdom	United States	Total	Pigments	Misc.	Total	Welding Rod Coatings	Pigments	Misc.	Total
2013	105,000	42,000	44,000	----	W	209,000	NA	NA	1,460,000	----	----	----	----
2014	110,000	25,000	42,000	----	W	194,000	NA	NA	1,430,000	----	----	----	----
2015	62,000	42,000	40,000	----	W	160,000	NA	NA	1,390,000	----	----	----	----
2016	60,000	54,000	38,000	----	W	170,000	NA	NA	1,390,000	----	----	----	----
2017	72,000	51,000	40,000	----	W	181,000				----	----	----	----
2018	70,000	52,000	40,000	----	W	180,000				----	----	----	----
2019	85,000	49,000	44,000	----	W	200,000				----	----	----	----
2020[1]	110,000	50,000	33,000	----	W	210,000				----	----	----	----

[1] Preliminary. [2] Unconsolidated metal in various forms. [4] Included in Pigments. NA = Not available. W = Withheld.
Source: U.S. Geological Survey (USGS)

Average Prices of Titanium in the United States

Year	Ilmenite FOB Australian Ports[2]	Slag, 85% TiO2 FOB Richards Bay, South Africa	Rutile Large Lots Bulk, FOB U.S. East Coast[3]	Rutile Bagged FOB Australian Ports	Avg. Price of Grade A Titanium Sponge, FOB Shipping Point	Titanium Metal Sponge	Titanium Dioxide Pigments FOB US Plants Anatase	Titanium Dioxide Pigments FOB US Plants Rutile
	Dollars Per Metric Ton				Dollars Per Pound			
2010	$65 - $85	$367 - $433	$530 - $550	$760 - $805	----	$3.50 - $6.24	----	----
2011	$140 - $250	$468 - $494	$1,300-$1,400	$1,348-$1,600	----	$3.27 - $6.74	----	----
2012	$250 - $350	$512 - $763	$2,050-$2,400	$2,500-$2,800	----	$3.53 - $6.95	----	----
2013	$230 - $300	$405 - $455	$1,100-$1,400	$1,200-$1,500	----	$3.20 - $6.23	----	----
2014	$150 - $165	$690 - $835	$820 - $950	$840 - $1,000	----	$4.07 - $5.96	----	----
2015	$100 - $120	$630 - $751	$790 - $890	$800 - $840	----	$3.32 - $5.36	----	----
2016	$100 - $110	$674 - $676	$710 - $770	$770 - $850	----	$5.03 - $5.42	----	----
2017[1]	$160 - $185	$590 - $689	$710 - $770	$770 - $850	----	$5.03 - $5.42	----	----

[1] Preliminary. NA = Not available. *Source: U.S. Geological Survey (USGS)*

Average Price of Titanium[1] in United States In Dollars Per Pound

Year	Jan.	Feb.	Mar.	Apr.	May	June	July	Aug.	Sept.	Oct.	Nov.	Dec.	Average
2015	8.50	8.50	8.50	8.38	8.38	8.38	8.56	8.62	8.62	8.62	8.62	8.62	8.53
2016	8.62	8.62	8.62	8.62	8.48	8.38	8.38	8.38	8.38	8.38	8.12	8.12	8.43
2017	8.16	8.25	8.25	8.25	8.25	8.25	8.25	8.25	8.25	8.09	8.02	8.02	8.19
2018	8.02	8.02	8.02	8.10	8.12	8.12	8.12	8.12	8.12	8.30	8.38	8.38	8.15
2019	9.11	9.40	9.40	9.38	9.38	9.38	9.92	10.12	10.12	10.12	10.13	10.13	9.72
2020	10.13	10.13	10.13	10.13	10.13	9.53	9.25	9.25	9.25	9.25	9.25	9.25	9.64

[1] Ingot, 6Al - 4V. *Source: American Metal Market (AMM)*

Average Price of Titanium[1] in United States In Dollars Per Pound

Year	Jan.	Feb.	Mar.	Apr.	May	June	July	Aug.	Sept.	Oct.	Nov.	Dec.	Average
2015	25.50	25.50	25.50	25.50	25.50	25.50	25.50	25.50	25.50	25.50	25.50	25.50	25.50
2016	25.50	25.50	25.50	25.50	25.50	25.50	25.50	25.50	25.50	25.50	25.50	25.50	25.50
2017	26.40	28.50	28.50	28.02	28.00	28.00	28.80	29.00	29.00	29.00	29.00	29.00	28.44
2018	29.00	29.00	29.00	30.43	31.00	31.00	29.48	29.00	29.00	29.70	30.00	30.00	29.72
2019	32.50	33.50	33.50	33.50	33.50	33.50	33.50	33.50	33.50	32.80	32.50	32.50	33.19
2020	32.50	32.50	32.50	32.50	32.50	29.09	27.50	27.50	27.50	27.50	27.50	27.50	29.72

[1] Plate, Alloy. *Source: American Metal Market (AMM)*

Tobacco

Tobacco is a member of the nightshade family. It is commercially grown for its leaves and stems, which are rolled into cigars, shredded for use in cigarettes and pipes, processed for chewing, or ground into snuff. Christopher Columbus introduced tobacco cultivation and use to Spain after observing natives from the Americas smoking loosely rolled tobacco-stuffed tobacco leaves.

Tobacco is cured, or dried, after harvesting and then aged to improve its flavor. The four common methods of curing are: air cured, fire cured, sun cured, and flue cured. Flue curing is the fastest method of curing and requires only about a week compared with up to 10 weeks for other methods. Cured tobacco is tied into small bundles of about 20 leaves and aged one to three years.

Virginia tobacco is by far the most popular type used in pipe tobacco since it is the mildest of all blending tobaccos. Approximately 60% of the U.S. tobacco crop is Virginia-type tobacco. Burley tobacco is the next most popular tobacco. It is air-cured, burns slowly and provides a relatively cool smoke. Other tobacco varieties include Perique, Kentucky, Oriental, and Latakia.

Prices – U.S. tobacco farm prices in 2019 fell -1.4% to 202.2 cents per pound, below the 2013 record high of 217.7 cents per pound.

Supply – World production of leaf tobacco in 2019 rose +7.2% yr/yr to 6.686 million metric tons, but still down from the 2013 record high of 7.607 million metric tons. The world's largest producers of tobacco are China, with 39.1% of world production, followed at a distance by India with 12.0%, Brazil with 11.5%, and the U.S. with 3.2%.

U.S. production in 2019 fell -12.2% yr/yr to 212.250 metric tons, where it was down by almost three-quarters from the 2-decade high of 810,750 metric tons posted in 1997. Tobacco in the U.S. is grown primarily in the mid-Atlantic States. Specifically, in 2020 the largest tobacco-producing states in the U.S. were North Carolina with 47.5% of U.S. production, Kentucky with 27.9%, Tennessee with 7,8%, Virginia with 6.8%, Georgia with 4.3%, and South Carolina with 3.0%.

U.S. production of flue-cured tobacco (type 11-14), the most popular tobacco type grown in the U.S, fell by -20.9% yr/yr to 234.960 million pounds in 2020. The second most popular type is Class A light air-cured (type 31-32), which saw U.S. production in 2020 fall -14.2% yr/yr to 79.675 million pounds. Total U.S. production of tobacco in 2020 fell -17.2% yr/yr to 387.585 million pounds, which is less than one-third of the 2-decade high of 1.787 billion pounds posted in 1997. U.S. farmers have sharply reduced the planting acreage for tobacco. In 2020, harvested tobacco acreage fell -13.9% yr/yr to 195.450 acres, which was far below the 25-year high of 836,230 posted in 1997. Yield in 2020 fell -3.7% to 1,983 pounds per acre, still well below the 15-year high of 2,323 pounds per acre posted in 2009. The farm value of the U.S. tobacco crop in 2019 fell -13.5% yr/yr to $946.252 million.

Trade – U.S. tobacco exports in 2020 fell -7.2% yr/yr to 206.4 million pounds, which is a new record low.

World Production of Leaf Tobacco In Metric Tons

Year	Brazil	Canada	China	Greece	India	Indo-nesia	Italy	Japan	Pakistan	Turkey	United States	Zim-babwe	World Total
2010	787,817	34,904	3,005,928	29,948	690,000	135,700	89,112	29,300	119,323	53,018	325,764	109,737	6,983,628
2011	951,933	32,780	3,158,737	32,043	830,000	214,600	70,130	23,600	102,834	45,435	271,361	125,056	7,518,469
2012	810,550	30,723	3,408,142	34,250	820,000	260,800	50,620	19,700	97,878	73,285	345,957	139,179	7,593,914
2013	850,673	28,620	3,375,400	40,613	765,154	260,200	49,770	19,800	108,307	93,158	328,208	147,068	7,606,700
2014	862,396	27,175	2,997,050	40,940	719,420	196,300	53,925	20,000	129,878	74,696	397,533	184,003	7,294,672
2015	867,355	26,382	2,678,604	37,031	738,029	193,790	51,406	18,700	120,022	75,000	326,210	171,083	6,826,519
2016	677,472	24,411	2,575,371	37,865	759,594	126,728	48,470	17,900	115,574	74,238	285,180	168,974	6,388,495
2017	865,620	22,753	2,392,335	32,712	773,158	181,142	56,398	19,000	100,015	93,666	322,120	110,816	6,442,917
2018[1]	756,232	21,041	2,242,070	22,730	788,301	195,482	49,530	16,998	106,727	75,276	241,870	239,906	6,238,723
2019[2]	769,801	19,359	2,611,610	22,530	804,454	197,250	41,860	16,798	104,355	70,000	212,260	257,764	6,685,611

[1] Preliminary. [2] Estimate. *Source: Food and Agriculture Organization of the United Nations (FAO-UN)*

Production and Consumption of Tobacco Products in the United States

			--- Chewing Tobacco ---						---- Consumption[5] of Per Capita[6] ----						
Year	Cigarettes	Cigars[3]	Plug	Twist	Loose-leaf	Total	Smoking Tobacco	Snuff[4]	Cigarettes	Cigars[3]	Cigarettes	Cigars[3]	Smoking Tobacco	Chewing Tobacco	Total Products
	- Billions -	- Millions -	---- In Millions of Pounds ----						---- Number ----		---- In Pounds ----				
2000	593.2	2,825	2.6	0.8	46.0	49.4	13.6	69.5	2,049	38.0	3.40	.62	.13	.48	4.10
2001	562.8	3,741	2.4	0.8	43.9	47.1	12.8	70.9	2,051	41.2	3.50	.68	.15	.47	4.30
2002	484.3	3,816	2.2	0.8	41.5	44.5	15.5	72.7	1,982	41.8	3.40	.68	.16	.43	4.16
2003	499.4	4,017	1.7	0.7	39.2	41.6	17.8	73.8	1,890	44.5	3.20	.73	.16	.40	3.97
2004	492.7	4,342	1.7	0.7	37.0	39.3	16.1	79.3	1,814	47.9	3.10	.79	.15	.37	3.87
2005	498.7	3,674	1.4	0.6	37.2	39.2	17.4	86.7	1,716	46.9	2.90	.77	.16	.36	3.69
2006	483.7	4,256	1.3	0.6	36.4	38.3	16.5	81.8	1,691	47.8	2.90	.78	.15	.37	3.69
2007	449.7	4,797	1.2	0.5	35.1	36.8	NA	NA	NA	NA	NA	NA	NA	NA	NA
2008[1]	396.1	4,984	1.1	0.5	30.9	32.5	----	----	----	----	----	----	----	----	----
2009[2]	338.1	8,232	0.9	0.5	28.0	29.3	----	----	----	----	----	----	----	----	----

[1] Preliminary. [2] Estimate. [3] Large cigars and cigarillos. [4] Includes loose-leaf. [5] Consumption of tax-paid tobacco products. Unstemmed rocessing weight. [6] 18 years and older. NA = Not available. *Source: Economic Research Service, U.S. Department of Agriculture (ERS-USDA)*

Production of Tobacco in the United States, by States In Thousands of Pounds

Year	Georgia	Kentucky	North Carolina	Ohio	Pennsylvania	South Carolina	Tennessee	Virginia	Total
2011	26,775	172,140	251,565	3,360	20,655	26,350	45,363	48,125	598,252
2012	22,500	195,800	381,190	3,990	22,985	25,200	53,000	53,599	762,709
2013	22,400	187,240	362,660	4,620	21,260	24,650	44,570	52,613	723,579
2014	34,500	214,280	453,860	4,300	22,250	33,180	52,155	57,651	876,415
2015	32,400	149,830	380,250	3,610	18,090	26,000	48,770	55,655	719,171
2016	28,350	136,280	331,800	----	20,460	24,700	35,690	51,440	628,720
2017	26,250	183,300	360,040	----	18,990	25,200	43,000	53,381	710,161
2018	23,750	134,370	251,925	----	17,400	22,140	39,610	44,046	533,241
2019	18,900	123,390	234,700	----	14,300	15,770	30,490	30,406	467,956
2020[1]	16,560	108,210	184,095	----	12,650	9,600	30,180	26,290	387,585

[1] Preliminary. *Source: Agricultural Statistics Board, U.S. Department of Agriculture (ASB-USDA)*

Salient Statistics of Tobacco in the United States

						---- Tobacco ---- (June - July)		---- U. S. Exports of ----				---- Stocks of Tobacco[5] Various Types ----			
Year	Acres Harvested 1,000 Acres	Yield Per Acre Pounds	Production Million Pounds	Farm Price cents Lb.	Farm Value Million $	Exports[2]	Imports[3]	Cigarettes	Cigars & Cheroots	All Tobacco	Smoking Tobacco[4]	All Tobacco	Fire Cured[6]	Cigar Filler[7]	Maryland
						- Million Pounds -		---- In Millions ----		---- In Millions of Pounds ----					
2011	325.0	1,841	598	184.7	1,105	----	----	----	-----	----	----	----	----	----	----
2012	336.2	2,268	763	207.2	1,580	----	----	----	-----	----	----	----	----	----	----
2013	355.7	2,034	724	217.7	1,575	----	----	----	-----	----	----	----	----	----	----
2014	378.4	2,316	876	209.4	1,835	----	----	----	-----	----	----	----	----	----	----
2015	328.7	2,188	719	200.3	1,441	----	----	----	-----	----	----	----	----	----	----
2016	319.7	1,967	629	200.7	1,262	----	----	----	-----	----	----	----	----	----	----
2017	321.5	2,209	710	205.8	1,462	----	----	----	-----	----	----	----	----	----	----
2018	291.4	1,830	533	205.1	1,093	----	----	----	-----	----	----	----	----	----	----
2019	227.1	2,060	468	202.2	946	----	----	----	-----	----	----	----	----	----	----
2020[1]	195.5	1,983	388			----	----	----	-----	----	----	----	----	----	----

[1] Preliminary. [2] Domestic. [3] For consumption. [4] In bulk. [5] Flue-cured and cigar wrapper, year beginning July 1; for all other types, October 1. [6] Kentucky-Tennessee types 22-23. [7] Types 41-46. *Source: Economic Research Service, U.S. Department of Agriculture (ERS-USDA)*

Tobacco Production in the United States, by Types In Thousands of Pounds (Farm-Sale Weight)

Year	Class 1, Flue-cured (11-14)	Class 2, Fire-cured (21-23)	Class 3A, Light air-cured (31-32)	Class 3B, Dark air-cured (35-37)	Total Cigar types (41-61)	US Total
2011	344,610	51,721	178,265	16,082	7,574	598,252
2012	472,900	53,764	211,550	15,250	9,245	762,709
2013	454,350	50,388	197,165	13,790	7,886	723,579
2014	572,880	59,146	217,860	17,490	9,039	876,415
2015	489,475	56,125	148,195	17,050	8,326	719,171
2016	431,450	39,520	143,890	10,020	3,840	628,720
2017	460,650	59,531	165,460	20,200	4,320	710,161
2018	338,690	58,926	103,515	26,590	5,520	533,241
2019	297,170	45,766	92,830	24,390	5,500	467,956
2020[1]	234,960	41,550	79,675	24,690	5,750	387,585

[1] Preliminary. *Source: Agricultural Statistics Board, U.S. Department of Agriculture (ASB-USDA)*

U.S. Exports of Unmanufactured Tobacco In Millions of Pounds (Declared Weight)

Year	Australia	Belgium-Luxem.	Denmark	France	Germany	Italy	Japan	Netherlands	Sweden	Switzerland	Thailand	United Kingdom	Total U.S. Exports
2011	.8	10.0	.7	8.9	25.9	.8	.0	27.2	.5	65.6	3.7	6.0	406.5
2012	.7	10.3	.8	11.8	20.2	.5	.2	29.6	.2	46.2	3.6	2.9	353.4
2013	.3	3.8	.7	6.5	20.1	1.5	.0	25.0	.5	62.2	2.7	1.4	349.9
2014	.1	9.8	1.2	9.8	14.4	.5	.0	14.3	.4	63.5	3.2	3.2	330.2
2015	.1	10.9	1.1	5.2	15.2	.6	.0	7.9	.4	89.7	1.8	1.0	343.0
2016	.0	20.5	.9	2.0	11.9	6.3	.2	8.5	.3	79.5	.6	1.1	362.2
2017		14.6	.9	1.2	6.6	7.2	.3	7.5	.4	76.6		1.0	317.8
2018		13.8	.9	2.9	5.5	8.6	.2	9.4	.1	70.4		1.2	326.9
2019	.1	12.2	.7	.9	2.2	12.2	.1	2.6	.1	58.2		1.4	222.5
2020[1]	.0	11.2	.7	1.3	2.6	4.6	.1	3.9	.3	34.2			206.4

[1] Preliminary. *Source: Economic Research Service, U.S. Department of Agriculture (ERS-USDA)*

U.S. Salient Statistics for Flue-Cured Tobacco (Types 11-14) in the United States In Millions of Pounds

Year	Acres Harvested 1,000	Yield Per Acre Pounds	Marketings	Stocks Oct. 1	Total Supply	Exports	Domestic Disappearance	Total Disappearance	Farm Price cents/Lb.	Placed Under Gov't Loan (Mil. Lb.)	Price Support Level (cents/) Lb.	Loan Stocks Nov. 30	Loan Stocks Uncommitted
2011-12	206.9	1,666	----	----	----	----	----	----	----	----	----	----	----
2012-13	206.0	2,296	----	----	----	----	----	----	----	----	----	----	----
2013-14	228.8	1,986	----	----	----	----	----	----	----	----	----	----	----
2014-15	245.3	2,335	----	----	----	----	----	----	----	----	----	----	----
2015-16	220.0	2,225	----	----	----	----	----	----	----	----	----	----	----
2016-17	213.5	2,021	----	----	----	----	----	----	----	----	----	----	----
2017-18	209.5	2,199	----	----	----	----	----	----	----	----	----	----	----
2018-19	197.8	1,712	----	----	----	----	----	----	----	----	----	----	----
2019-20[1]	149.3	1,990	----	----	----	----	----	----	----	----	----	----	----
2020-21[2]	127.2	1,847	----	----	----	----	----	----	----	----	----	----	----

[1] Preliminary. [2] Estimate. NA = Not available. *Source: Economic Research Service, U.S. Department of Agriculture (ERS-USDA)*

Salient Statistics for Burley Tobacco (Type 31) in the United States In Millions of Pounds

Year	Acres Harvested 1,000	Yield Per Acre Pounds	Marketings	Stocks Oct. 1	Total Supply	Exports	Domestic Disappearance	Total Disappearance	Farm Price cents/Lb.	Gross Sales[3]	Price Support Level cents/Lb.	Loan Stocks Nov. 30	Loan Stocks Uncommitted
2011-12	88.9	1,938	----	----	----	----	----	----	----	----	----	----	----
2012-13	101.4	2,021	----	----	----	----	----	----	----	----	----	----	----
2013-14	99.0	1,944	----	----	----	----	----	----	----	----	----	----	----
2014-15	101.5	2,100	----	----	----	----	----	----	----	----	----	----	----
2015-16	78.9	1,834	----	----	----	----	----	----	----	----	----	----	----
2016-17	80.0	1,747	----	----	----	----	----	----	----	----	----	----	----
2017-18	81.5	1,977	----	----	----	----	----	----	----	----	----	----	----
2018-19	61.1	1,645	----	----	----	----	----	----	----	----	----	----	----
2019-20[1]	48.6	1,910	----	----	----	----	----	----	----	----	----	----	----
2020-21[2]	41.7	1,911	----	----	----	----	----	----	----	----	----	----	----

[1] Preliminary. [2] Estimate. [3] Before Christmas holidays. NA = Not available.
Source: Economic Research Service, U.S. Department of Agriculture (ERS-USDA)

Exports of Tobacco from the United States (Quantity and Value) In Metric Tons

	Unmanufactured							
Year	Flue-Cured	Value 1,000 USD	Burley	Value 1,000 USD	Total	Value 1,000 USD	Manufactured	Value 1,000 USD
2011	88,876	643,946	33,385	256,006	184,369	1,148,991	7,472	489,454
2012	77,073	607,725	32,051	243,411	160,308	1,101,214	18,405	482,614
2013	78,079	650,887	32,124	265,809	158,728	1,137,947	21,930	485,412
2014	76,239	645,462	25,441	217,329	149,758	1,085,958	18,111	426,981
2015	77,942	657,188	26,100	226,807	155,578	1,108,756	21,880	423,179
2016	88,283	707,889	20,202	166,246	164,276	1,085,439	18,620	408,341
2017	77,830	643,791	16,335	139,327	144,136	1,010,325	16,321	197,428
2018	81,873	670,927	19,888	165,051	148,259	1,049,085	14,540	184,761
2019[1]	52,250	427,691	10,098	85,776	100,924	732,495	12,711	210,483
2020[2]	36,848	290,318	9,614	78,289	93,626	665,914	14,229	212,966

[1] Preliminary. [2] Forecast. *Source: Foreign Agricultural Service, U.S. Department of Agriculture (FAS-USDA)*

Tungsten

Tungsten (atomic symbol W) is a grayish-white, lustrous, metallic element. The atomic symbol for tungsten is W because of its former name of Wolfram. Tungsten has the highest melting point of any metal at about 3410 degrees Celsius and boils at about 5660 degrees Celsius. In 1781, the Swedish chemist Carl Wilhelm Scheele discovered tungsten.

Tungsten is never found in nature but is instead found in the minerals wolframite, scheelite, huebnertite, and ferberite. Tungsten has excellent corrosion resistance qualities and is resistant to most mineral acids. Tungsten is used as filaments in incandescent lamps, electron and television tubes, alloys of steel, spark plugs, electrical contact points, cutting tools, and in the chemical and tanning industries.

Prices – The average monthly price of tungsten at U.S. ports in 2020 fell -8.3% yr/yr to $226.38 per short ton, below the 2012 record high of $375.16.

Supply – World concentrate production of tungsten in 2020 rose +0.2% yr/yr to 84,000 metric tons. The world's largest producer of tungsten by far is China, with 69,000 metric tons of production in 2020, which was 82.1% of total world production. Russia is the next largest producer at 2.6%, with a small production level of 2,200 metric tons.

Trade – The U.S. in 2020 relied on imports for somewhat over 50% of its tungsten consumption., which is down from 95% in 1994. U.S. imports for consumption in 2020 fell -27.5% yr/yr to 2,000 metric tons. U.S. exports in 2020 fell -48.6% yr/yr to 300 metric tons.

World Concentrate Production of Tungsten In Metric Tons (Contained Tungsten[3])

Year	Austria	Bolivia	Brazil	Burma	Canada	China	Korea, North	Mongolia	Portugal	Russia	Rwanda	Thailand	Total
2013	850	1,253	494	235	2,128	65,000	65	274	692	4,191	1,100	140	79,400
2014	819	1,252	510	247	2,344	65,000	70	557	671	3,775	1,000	99	82,600
2015	861	1,460	432	144	1,600	67,000	70	351	474	3,262	850	35	83,800
2016	954	1,110	200	157	----	64,000	50	753	549	2,672	820	33	79,600
2017	975	994	200	212	----	67,000	310	150	724	2,094	720	49	82,100
2018	936	1,370				65,000	1,410		715	1,500	920		81,100
2019[1]	892	1,060				69,000	1,130	1,900	518	2,200	900		83,800
2020[2]	890	1,400				69,000	500	1,900	680	2,200	1,000		84,000

[1] Preliminary. [2] Estimate. [3] Conversion Factors: WO_3 to W, multiply by 0.7931; 60% WO_3 to W, multiply by 0.4758.
Source: U.S. Geological Survey (USGS)

Salient Statistics of Tungsten in the United States In Metric Tons (Contained Tungsten)

			Consumption of Tungsten Products by End Uses										Stocks, Dec. 31 -- Concentrates --	
			Steel											
Year	Net Import Reliance as a % Apparent Consump	Total Consumption	Tool	Stainless & Heat Assisting	Alloy Steel[3]	Superalloys	Cutting & Wear Resistant Materials	Products Made From Metal Powder	Miscellaneous	Chemical and Ceramic	Exports	Imports for Consumption	Consumers	Producers
2013	41	W	W	86	W	W	6,260	W	----	88	1,050	3,690	W	W
2014	>25	W	W	82	W	W	6,880	W	----	88	1,230	4,080	W	W
2015	>25	W	W	205	W	W	6,310	W	----	88	398	3,970	W	W
2016	>25	W	W	94	W	W	5,760	W	----	88	183	3,580	W	W
2017	>50	W	W	87	W	W	6,550	W	----	88	532	3,920	W	W
2018	>50	W	W		W	W		W	----		284	4,050	W	W
2019[1]	>50	W	W		W	W		W	----		584	2,760	W	W
2020[2]	>50	W	W		W	W		W	----		300	2,000	W	W

[1] Preliminary. [2] Estimate. [3] Other than tool. [4] Included with stainless & heat assisting. W = Withheld.
Source: U.S. Geological Survey (USGS)

Average Price of Tungsten at U.S. Ports (Including Duty) In Dollars Per Short Ton

Year	Jan.	Feb.	Mar.	Apr.	May	June	July	Aug.	Sept.	Oct.	Nov.	Dec.	Average
2013	297.74	329.45	351.29	351.50	356.73	382.55	406.86	417.28	407.13	392.50	387.29	378.50	371.57
2014	374.39	368.18	367.12	363.64	368.81	376.00	369.60	363.57	353.81	345.00	329.31	309.19	357.39
2015	293.18	281.80	272.64	254.20	243.45	228.50	222.95	207.90	188.81	184.77	173.33	176.28	227.32
2016	171.79	167.74	175.43	189.52	217.82	212.75	188.69	191.74	190.00	192.45	198.89	191.39	190.68
2017	194.33	200.30	211.83	211.18	217.80	221.68	222.76	252.28	310.60	286.02	280.68	296.79	242.19
2018	311.96	321.62	327.93	327.55	338.02	349.36	341.50	307.52	282.50	283.48	285.00	281.31	313.15
2019	268.80	266.25	276.14	275.95	273.00	257.50	222.13	205.50	202.50	228.75	235.00	239.38	245.91
2020	240.00	242.50	242.50	236.88	219.00	215.00	208.50	208.75	220.88	219.90	222.50	228.13	225.38

U.S. Spot Quotations, 65% WO_3, Basis C.I.F. *Source: U.S. Geological Survey (USGS)*

Turkeys

During the past three decades, the turkey industry has experienced tremendous growth in the U.S. Turkey production has more than tripled since 1970, with a current value of over $7 billion. Turkey was not a popular dish in Europe until a roast turkey was eaten on June 27, 1570, at the wedding feast of Charles XI of France and Elizabeth of Austria. The King was so impressed with the birds that the turkey subsequently became a popular dish at banquets held by French nobility.

The most popular turkey product continues to be the whole bird, with strong demand at Thanksgiving and Christmas. The primary breeders maintain and develop the quality stock, concentrating on growth and conformation in males and fecundity in females, as well as characteristics important to general health and welfare. Turkey producers include large companies that produce turkeys all year round, and relatively small companies and farmers who produce turkeys primarily for the seasonal Thanksgiving market.

Prices – The average monthly price received by farmers for turkeys in the U.S. in 2020 rose +22.6% yr/yr to 70.9 cents per pound, but still below the 2016 record high of 82.5 cents per pound. The monthly average retail price of turkeys (whole frozen) in the U.S. in 2020 rose +5.9% yr/yr to 1610 cents per pound, below the 2013 record high of 164.9 cents per pound.

Supply – World production of turkeys in 2018 rose 0.4% yr/yr to 5.901 million metric tons. World production of turkeys has grown by more than 2.5 times since 1980, when production was 2.090 million metric tons.

The U.S. is the world's largest producer of turkeys by far, with 2.666 million metric tons of production in 2018, accounting for a hefty 45.2% of world production. The value of U.S. turkey production in the U.S. in 2018 was $3.875 billion.

Demand – World consumption of turkeys in 2014 fell -2.5% yr/yr to 4.937 million metric tons. U.S. turkey consumption was 2.253 million metric tons in 2014, which accounts for 45.6% of world consumption. U.S. per-capita consumption of turkeys in 2021 is expected to fall -1.3% yr/yr to 15.8 pounds per person per year.

U.S. per-capita consumption of turkeys has been in the range of 16-18 pounds since 1990, but the USDA is projecting that per-capita consumption will drop somewhat, which appears to be happening.

Production of Turkey Meat, by Selected Countries In Thousands of Metric Tons (RTC)

	Production							Consumption						
Year	Brazil	Canada	European Union	Mexico	Russia	United States	World Total	Brazil	Canada	European Union	Mexico	Russia	United States	World Total
2009	466	166	1,745	21	31	2,569	5,389	302	151	1,802	155	72	2,363	4,911
2010	485	158	1,862	21	70	2,560	5,519	327	143	1,913	163	105	2,306	5,023
2011	489	159	1,882	21	90	2,627	5,614	348	150	1,886	164	117	2,273	5,010
2012	510	161	1,972	21	100	2,707	5,839	340	142	1,953	173	120	2,282	5,105
2013	520	168	1,861	17	100	2,633	5,653	359	150	1,893	166	112	2,291	5,063
2014	470	168	1,898	19	105	2,611	5,640	350	152	1,848	158	115	2,253	4,937
2015	480	172	1,925	19	----	2,552	5,656	----	----	----	----	----	----	----
2016	536	183	2,029	17	----	2,713	5,995	----	----	----	----	----	----	----
2017[1]	553	171	1,943	16	----	2,713	5,876	----	----	----	----	----	----	----
2018[2]	576	169	1,955	17	----	2,666	5,901	----	----	----	----	----	----	----

[1] Preliminary. [2] Forecast. *Source: Foreign Agricultural Service, U.S. Department of Agriculture (FAS-USDA)*

Salient Statistics of Turkeys in the United States

			Liveweight			Ready-to-Cook Basis			Consumption		Production Costs (Liveweight Basis)		Wholesale Ready-to-Cook	
Year	Poults Placed[3] (In Thousands)	Number Raised[4] (In Thousands)	Produced Mil Lbs	Price cents Per Lb.	Value of Production Million $	Production (In Millions of Pounds)	Beginning Stocks (In Millions of Pounds)	Exports (In Millions of Pounds)	Total (In Millions of Pounds)	Per Capita Lbs.	Feed	Total	Production Costs	3-Region Weighted Avg Price[5]
2011	277,931	248,500	7,313.2	68.0	4,987.6	5,791	191,560	703	5,013	16.1	----	----	----	----
2012	283,550	253,500	7,561.9	71.9	5,452.1	5,967	210,787	797	5,028	16.0	----	----	----	----
2013	260,571	240,000	7,277.5	66.4	4,839.6	5,806	296,479	741	5,068	16.0	----	----	----	----
2014	267,153	237,500	7,217.0	73.2	5,304.5	5,756	237,407	775	5,052	15.8	----	----	----	----
2015	257,999	233,100	7,038.1	81.1	5,707.9	5,627	193,429	529	5,136	16.0	----	----	----	----
2016	270,711	241,418	7,487.0	82.5	6,184.2	5,981	201,011	569	5,386	16.6	----	----	----	----
2017	270,561	245,200	7,544.4	64.5	4,873.7	5,979	278,741	621		16.4	----	----	----	----
2018	267,489	244,750	7,359.1	51.0	3,875.1	5,970	309,625	645		16.2	----	----	----	----
2019[1]	261,185	240,000	7,287.5	57.9			302,763			16.0	----	----	----	----
2020[2]	252,115			70.9			232,652			15.7	----	----	----	----

[1] Preliminary. [2] Estimate. [3] Poults placed for slaughter by hatcheries. [4] Turkeys place August 1-July 31. [5] Regions include central, eastern and western. Central region receives twice the weight of the other regions in calculating the average.
Source: Economic Research Service, U.S. Department of Agriculture (ERS-USDA)

Turkey-Feed Price Ratio in the United States In Pounds[2]

Year	Jan.	Feb.	Mar.	Apr.	May	June	July	Aug.	Sept.	Oct.	Nov.	Dec.	Average
2011	4.6	4.2	4.4	4.5	4.6	4.8	4.7	4.7	5.2	5.8	5.9	5.4	4.9
2012	4.8	4.7	4.8	5.0	5.0	5.1	4.4	4.3	4.8	4.9	4.7	4.3	4.7
2013	4.0	3.9	4.1	4.2	4.1	4.1	4.3	4.6	5.0	5.8	5.3	5.5	4.6
2014	5.2	5.4	5.3	5.1	5.4	5.6	6.2	6.8	7.6	8.3	8.1	7.1	6.3
2015	6.3	6.6	6.8	7.1	7.9	8.4	8.5	9.4	10.0	10.6	10.2	9.8	8.5
2016	8.7	9.0	9.0	9.2	8.8	8.9	9.3	9.5	10.3	9.9	9.3	8.4	9.2
2017	7.6	7.3	7.5	7.5	7.7	7.4	7.3	7.2	6.9	7.1	6.5	6.0	7.2
2018	5.7	5.5	5.2	5.2	5.1	5.3	5.7	5.8	5.9	5.7	6.0	5.5	5.6
2019	5.6	5.8	5.3	6.3	6.1	6.1	6.2	6.6	7.0	7.0	7.5	6.9	6.4
2020[1]	6.7	4.2	7.4	7.9	8.3	8.5	8.7	8.7	8.6	8.2	7.3	6.9	7.6

[1] Preliminary. [2] Pounds of feed equal in value to one pound of turkey, liveweight. *Source: Economic Research Service, U.S. Department of Agriculture (ERS-USDA)*

Average Price Received by Farmers for Turkeys in the United States (Liveweight) In Cents Per Pound

Year	Jan.	Feb.	Mar.	Apr.	May	June	July	Aug.	Sept.	Oct.	Nov.	Dec.	Average
2011	56.4	57.8	59.9	65.7	67.9	69.5	67.5	70.7	73.1	77.3	78.1	71.5	68.0
2012	65.7	65.0	69.0	73.7	72.7	73.9	72.9	74.4	76.2	76.9	75.1	67.4	71.9
2013	62.9	62.7	65.0	66.2	64.9	65.7	67.7	67.4	67.9	72.4	65.6	68.7	66.4
2014	64.5	66.4	68.3	68.7	72.6	72.8	74.0	75.6	77.5	82.2	82.1	73.4	73.2
2015	66.2	66.9	68.3	70.2	75.9	81.2	84.8	89.7	92.5	97.2	92.2	88.6	81.1
2016	78.9	79.4	78.9	83.2	83.1	86.5	86.6	84.3	87.8	85.2	81.5	74.4	82.5
2017	68.9	67.2	69.0	66.6	68.6	65.8	67.8	64.7	62.3	62.7	57.7	52.9	64.5
2018	50.8	50.6	49.9	50.0	49.8	50.8	51.9	51.7	53.1	51.1	53.0	49.8	51.0
2019	50.9	52.8	53.2	55.6	53.3	56.1	57.6	59.2	62.2	63.9	67.1	62.4	57.9
2020[1]	62.5	64.4	66.4	67.7	70.1	71.4	73.7	73.5	77.6	78.4	73.4	72.1	70.9

[1] Preliminary. *Source: Economic Research Service, U.S. Department of Agriculture (ERS-USDA)*

Average Wholesale Price of Turkeys[1] (Hens, 8-16 Lbs.) in New York In Cents Per Pound

Year	Jan.	Feb.	Mar.	Apr.	May	June	July	Aug.	Sept.	Oct.	Nov.	Dec.	Average
2011	88.14	89.97	92.38	96.68	99.75	103.14	104.00	105.39	109.79	114.83	113.57	106.54	102.02
2012	98.35	100.15	103.70	106.89	107.77	106.00	106.43	108.53	110.54	110.27	108.86	99.08	105.55
2013	96.27	95.00	96.58	97.30	97.59	98.18	99.09	99.28	101.22	106.75	105.64	103.83	99.73
2014	99.78	99.88	102.34	103.52	106.15	107.18	108.56	109.15	112.79	116.20	118.78	106.79	107.59
2015	99.12	99.12	100.57	104.06	108.82	112.53	120.86	126.62	131.65	135.68	130.63	123.96	116.14
2016	114.71	114.77	114.73	116.17	116.00	117.21	119.45	118.95	123.57	121.84	122.54	105.33	117.11
2017	99.81	100.56	100.90	99.25	99.44	98.54	97.61	96.38	96.59	94.97	88.76	80.16	96.08
2018	79.10	79.64	79.31	79.50	79.31	79.98	79.11	80.03	82.09	82.00	82.24	79.85	80.18
2019	80.96	83.50	83.90	84.31	84.74	87.38	88.26	90.43	93.76	96.88	99.24	97.17	89.21
2020[1]	95.45	97.25	99.63	101.78	103.92	105.39	109.56	110.90	113.48	115.74	112.97	112.20	106.52

[1] Ready-to-cook. [2] Preliminary. *Source: Economic Research Service, U.S. Department of Agriculture (ERS-USDA)*

Certified Federally Inspected Turkey Slaughter in the U.S. (Ready-to-Cook Weights) In Thousands of Pounds

Year	Jan.	Feb.	Mar.	Apr.	May	June	July	Aug.	Sept.	Oct.	Nov.	Dec.	Total
2011	460,910	432,774	500,414	453,806	494,571	516,341	445,675	499,115	470,843	521,508	509,314	456,916	5,762,187
2012	474,530	464,839	499,864	475,184	516,910	504,083	494,852	526,318	450,670	576,265	512,931	438,521	5,934,967
2013	522,128	458,794	470,052	502,276	505,780	471,529	512,059	482,373	438,111	514,181	477,015	420,380	5,774,678
2014	451,344	419,636	454,990	468,525	469,331	484,245	497,961	480,569	490,385	558,196	478,421	472,065	5,725,668
2015	489,634	431,503	498,992	493,905	432,442	455,913	446,207	447,301	450,088	522,359	466,917	458,298	5,593,559
2016	472,415	451,760	500,407	482,346	496,204	532,226	476,204	535,290	492,914	514,928	511,897	475,553	5,942,144
2017	495,763	454,965	526,631	433,274	520,061	519,205	581,127	673,714	581,261	686,143	642,370	573,273	6,687,787
2018	633,654	571,596	598,038	597,493	633,247	603,743	604,483	644,881	531,593	710,416	619,092	558,969	7,307,205
2019	637,240	570,119	596,483	601,863	611,273	590,011	610,283	622,416	573,499	681,966	583,138	557,236	7,235,527
2020[1]	641,354	556,414	631,105	548,888	531,730	622,960	630,187	590,712	587,725	647,572	569,190	584,091	7,141,928

[1] Preliminary. *Source: Economic Research Service, U.S. Department of Agriculture (ERS-USDA)*

Per Capita Consumption of Turkeys in the United States In Pounds

Year	First Quarter	Second Quarter	Third Quarter	Fourth Quarter	Total	Year	First Quarter	Second Quarter	Third Quarter	Fourth Quarter	Total
2010	3.5	3.6	4.1	5.2	16.4	2016	3.6	3.9	4.2	4.9	16.6
2011	3.5	3.5	4.0	5.0	16.1	2017	3.7	3.7	4.0	5.0	16.4
2012	3.5	3.6	4.1	4.9	16.0	2018	3.5	3.8	3.9	4.9	16.2
2013	3.7	3.6	4.0	4.8	16.0	2019	3.5	3.7	4.0	4.9	16.0
2014	3.4	3.5	3.9	5.0	15.8	2020[1]	3.6	3.5	3.9	4.6	15.7
2015	3.5	3.6	3.9	4.9	16.0	2021[2]	3.4	3.6	3.9	4.6	15.5

[1] Preliminary. [2] Estimate. *Source: Economic Research Service, U.S. Department of Agriculture (ERS-USDA)*

Storage Stocks of Turkeys (Frozen) in the United States on First of Month In Thousands of Pounds

Year	Jan.	Feb.	Mar.	Apr.	May	June	July	Aug.	Sept.	Oct.	Nov.	Dec.
2011	191,560	253,527	288,976	325,688	364,503	447,895	508,657	524,846	528,396	509,650	406,864	194,227
2012	210,787	297,736	349,577	375,268	438,384	498,419	547,091	547,465	547,766	521,810	453,378	255,191
2013	296,479	360,018	394,755	401,246	457,575	521,556	566,475	581,357	580,069	541,183	434,493	221,221
2014	237,407	275,787	310,756	336,383	375,013	422,502	462,586	489,758	494,786	484,547	390,654	187,563
2015	193,429	280,400	321,337	345,578	394,415	441,388	462,020	494,037	477,579	449,622	351,828	190,268
2016	201,011	289,746	341,094	368,073	398,719	454,147	504,385	530,278	532,579	511,199	400,355	236,862
2017	278,741	339,493	378,370	428,752	471,484	529,904	565,123	595,623	600,013	569,963	460,856	288,536
2018	309,625	375,188	427,618	462,985	493,844	536,026	561,858	594,927	606,359	564,746	445,059	274,166
2019	302,763	390,972	452,174	470,335	471,592	494,439	538,714	557,031	563,076	528,394	393,008	221,996
2020[1]	232,652	301,623	340,709	387,503	417,981	420,129	474,786	522,325	533,285	501,131	376,347	192,554

[1] Preliminary. Source: Economic Research Service, U.S. Department of Agriculture (ERS-USDA)

Average Retail Price of Turkeys (Whole frozen) in the United States In U.S. Dollars Per Pound

Year	Jan.	Feb.	Mar.	Apr.	May	June	July	Aug.	Sept.	Oct.	Nov.	Dec.	Average
2011	1.459	1.526	1.572	1.562	1.596	1.581	1.603	1.641	1.676	1.673	1.541	1.574	1.584
2012	1.671	1.671	1.812	1.791	1.608	1.557	1.561	1.586	1.621	1.661	1.488	1.433	1.622
2013	1.579	1.591	1.593	1.649	1.654	1.595	1.624	1.663	1.819	NA	1.721	1.650	1.649
2014	1.713	1.699	1.733	1.610	1.602	1.606	1.641	1.604	1.584	1.667	1.425	1.331	1.601
2015	1.445	1.480	1.503	1.487	1.527	1.541	1.568	1.546	1.538	1.558	1.424	1.448	1.505
2016	1.528	1.494	1.509	1.488	1.527	1.515	1.586	1.622	1.649	1.692	1.527	1.495	1.553
2017	1.581	1.570	1.585	1.567	1.532	1.576	1.622	1.615	1.623	1.656	1.556	1.502	1.582
2018	1.399	1.435	1.512	1.483	1.526	1.529	1.585	1.567	1.578	1.582	1.400	1.413	1.501
2019	1.455	1.488	1.521	1.543	1.560	1.574	1.531	1.562	1.604	1.601	1.412	1.389	1.520
2020[1]	1.580	1.639	----	----	----	----	----	----	----	----	----	----	1.610

[1] Preliminary. *Source: Economic Research Service, U.S. Department of Agriculture (ERS-USDA)*

Average Retail-to-Consumer Price Spread of Turkeys (Whole) in the United States In Cents Per Pound

Year	Jan.	Feb.	Mar.	Apr.	May	June	July	Aug.	Sept.	Oct.	Nov.	Dec.	Average
2008	38.0	37.5	23.7	21.6	27.3	23.4	25.1	23.0	23.4	18.0	33.9	48.8	28.6
2009	NA	NA	NA	NA	NA	51.0	53.9	56.0	56.2	56.3	39.4	43.7	50.9
2010	55.6	50.6	51.9	55.5	52.2	NA	NA	42.8	42.9	49.3	22.7	28.8	45.2
2011	48.8	NA	NA	NA	NA	NA	NA	49.7	48.8	43.5	31.5	41.9	44.0
2012	59.8	58.0	68.5	63.2	44.0	40.7	40.7	41.1	42.6	46.8	30.9	35.2	47.6
2013	52.6	55.1	53.7	58.6	58.8	52.3	54.3	58.0	71.7	NA	57.5	52.2	56.8
2014	62.5	61.0	62.0	48.5	45.1	44.4	46.5	42.3	36.6	41.5	14.7	17.3	43.5
2015	36.4	39.9	40.7	35.6	34.9	32.6	26.9	19.0	NA	NA	2.8	11.8	28.1
2016	29.1	25.6	27.2	23.6	27.7	25.3	30.2	34.3	32.3	38.4	21.2	35.2	29.2
2017[1]	49.3	47.4	48.6	48.5	44.8	Discontinued		----	----	----	----	----	47.7

[1] Preliminary. *Source: Economic Research Service, U.S. Department of Agriculture (ERS-USDA)*

Uranium

Uranium (atomic symbol U) is a chemically reactive, radioactive, steel-gray, metallic element and is the main fuel used in nuclear reactors. Uranium is the heaviest of all the natural elements. Traces of uranium have been found in archeological artifacts dating back to 79 AD. Uranium was discovered in pitchblende by German chemist Martin Heinrich Klaproth in 1789. Klaproth named it uranium after the recently discovered planet Uranus. French physicist Antoine Henri Becquerel discovered the radioactive properties of uranium in 1896 when he produced an image on a photographic plate covered with a light-absorbing substance. Following Becquerel's experiments, investigations of radioactivity led to the discovery of radium (atomic symbol Ra) and to new concepts of atomic organization.

Uranium is mainly used as fuel in nuclear power plants. Demand for uranium concentrates is directly linked to the level of electricity generated by nuclear power plants. Uranium ores are widely distributed throughout the world and are primarily found in Canada, DRC (formerly Zaire), and the U.S. Uranium is obtained from primary mine production and secondary sources. Two Canadian companies, Cameco and Cogema Resources, are the primary producers of uranium from deposits in the Athabasca Basin of northern Saskatchewan. Secondary sources of uranium include excess inventories from utilities and other fuel cycle participants, used reactor fuel, and dismantled Russian nuclear weapons.

Prices – CME uranium swap futures prices (Barchart.com symbol UX) during 2020 started the year at $25.05 per pound, moved sharply higher in April to a 5-year high of $36.35, and then traded lower the rest of the year to finally end the year up +25.1% at $30.70 per pound. Uranium prices have fallen sharply from levels above $100 per pound seen around 2007.

Supply – World production of uranium oxide (U308) concentrate in 2017 fell -4.7% yr/yr to 57,083 metric tons, down from the previous year's record high. The world's largest uranium producers in 2017 were Kazakhstan with 41.0% of world production, Canada with 23.0%, Australia with 10.3%, Namibia with 7.4%, and Niger with 6.0%.

Trade – U.S. imports of uranium in 2018 fell -23.3% yr/yr to 41.500 million pounds. The record high of 66.100 million pounds was posted in 2004. The U.S. has generally been forced to import more uranium as domestic production steadily declined. U.S. exports of uranium in 2018 fell -6.1% yr/yr to 13.900 million pounds, which is below the record high of 23.500 million pounds posted in 2009.

Uranium Industry Statistics in the United States In Millions of Pounds U_3O_8

	Production			Employment - Person Years									
Year	Mine	Concentrate	Concentrate Shipments	Exploration	Mining	Milling	Processing	Total[1]	Deliveries to U.S. Utilities[2]	Avg Price Delivered Uranium $/lb U_3O_8	Imports	Avg Price Delivered Uranium Imports $/lb U_3O_8	Exports
2010	4.2	4.228	5.137	211	400	W	W	1,073	46.6	49.29	55.3	47.01	23.1
2011	4.1	3.991	4.000	208	462	W	W	1,191	54.8	55.64	54.4	54.00	16.7
2012	4.3	4.146	3.911	161	462	W	W	1,196	57.5	54.99	56.2	51.44	18.0
2013	4.6	4.659	4.655	149	392	W	W	1,156	57.4	51.99	57.4	48.27	18.9
2014	4.9	4.891	4.593	86	246	W	W	787	53.3	46.16	56.5	44.03	20.0
2015	3.7	3.343	4.023	58	251	W	W	625	56.5	44.13	64.2	42.95	25.7
2016	2.5	2.917	3.018	38	255	W	W	560	50.6	42.43	50.7	40.45	17.2
2017	1.2	2.443	2.277	50	136	W	W	424	43.0	38.80	42.1	37.09	14.0
2018	.7	1.466	1.489	27	110	W	W	372	40.3	38.81	41.5	35.73	13.9
2019	.2	0.174	0.190	40	48	W	W	265					

[1] From suppliers under domestic purchases. *Source: Energy Information Administration, U.S. Department of Energy (EIA-DOE)*

Commercial and U.S. Government Stocks of Uranium, End of Year In Millions of Pounds U_3O_8 Equivalent

	Utility		Domestic Supplier			DOE Owned & USEC Held	
Year	Natural Uranium	Enriched Uranium[1]	Natural Uranium	Enriched Uranium[1]	Total Commercial Stocks	Natural Uranium	Enriched Uranium[1]
2010	48.8	37.7	W	24.7	111.3	W	W
2011	50.6	39.2	W	22.3	112.1	W	W
2012	45.0	52.6	W	23.3	120.9	W	W
2013	56.5	56.6	W	21.3	134.4	W	W
2014	59.9	54.2	W	18.7	132.7	W	W
2015	68.8	52.4	W	14.3	135.5	W	W
2016	74.4	53.6	W	16.7	144.6	W	W
2017	71.2	52.6	W	17.8	141.7	W	W
2018	62.6	48.6	W	19.3	130.5	W	W
2019	64.6	48.2	W	14.3	127.1	W	W

[1] Includes amount reported as UF_6 at enrichment suppliers. DOE = Department of Energy USEC = U.S. Energy Commission
Source: Energy Information Administration, U.S. Department of Energy (EIA-DOE)

World Production of Uranium Oxide (U3O8) Concentrate In Metric Tons (Uranium Content)

Year	Australia	Canada	China	Czech Republic	Kazakh-stan	Namibia	Niger	Russia	South Africa	United States	Ukraine	Uzbeki-stan	World Total
2010	5,900	9,775	1,350	254	17,803	4,503	4,199	3,562	582	837	1,630	2,874	51,806
2011	5,967	9,145	1,400	229	19,450	3,954	4,264	2,993	556	873	1,582	2,500	52,266
2012	7,009	8,998	1,450	228	21,240	5,026	4,773	2,862	467	1,012	1,667	2,400	56,816
2013	6,350	9,000	1,450	215	22,500	5,627	4,277	3,133	540	1,075	1,792	2,400	58,103
2014	5,001	9,134	1,500	193	23,127	3,255	4,156	2,990	393	926	1,919	2,400	54,282
2015	5,654	11,709	1,616	155	23,800	2,993	4,116	3,055	322	1,200	1,256	2,385	56,452
2016[1]	6,315	14,039	1,616	138	24,575	3,654	3,479	3,004	490	1,005	1,125	2,404	59,887
2017[2]	5,882	13,116	1,885		23,391	4,224	3,449	2,917	308	550	940	2,404	57,083

[1] Preliminary. [2] Estimate. *Source: Food and Agriculture Organization of the United Nations (FAO-UN)*

Total Production of Uranium Concentrate in the United States, by Quarters In Pounds U_3O_8

Year	First Quarter	Second Quarter	Third Quarter	Fourth Quarter	Total	Year	First Quarter	Second Quarter	Third Quarter	Fourth Quarter	Total
2009	880,036	982,760	956,657	888,905	3,708,358	2015	1,154,408	789,980	774,541	624,278	3,343,207
2010	876,084	1,055,102	1,150,725	1,153,104	4,235,015	2016	626,522	745,306	818,783	725,947	2,916,558
2011	1,063,047	1,189,083	846,624	892,013	3,990,767	2017	450,215	726,375	643,212	622,987	2,442,789
2012	1,078,404	1,061,289	1,048,018	957,936	4,145,647	2018	226,780	365,421	528,870	345,425	1,466,496
2013	1,147,031	1,394,232	1,171,278	946,301	4,658,842	2019[1]	58,481	44,569	32,211	38,614	173,875
2014	1,242,179	1,095,011	1,468,608	1,085,534	4,891,332	2020[2]	8,098	W	W	W	8,098

[1] Preliminary. [2] Estimate. *Source: Energy Information Administration, U.S. Department of Energy (EIA-DOE)*

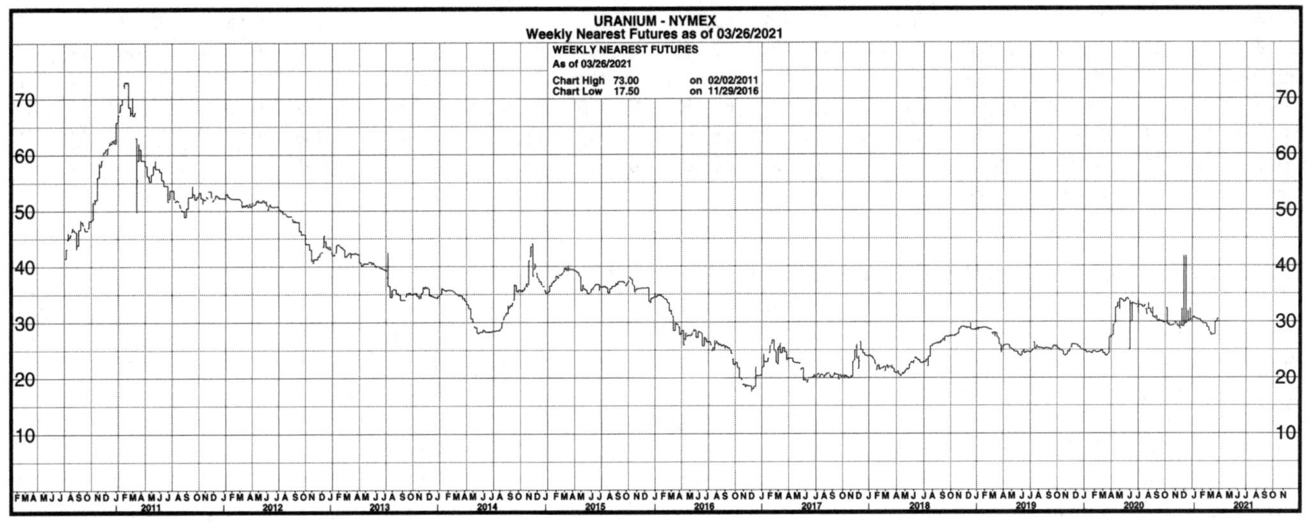

Nearby Futures through Last Trading Day.

Volume of Trading of Uranium Futures In Contracts

Year	Jan.	Feb.	Mar.	Apr.	May	June	July	Aug.	Sept.	Oct.	Nov.	Dec.	Total
2014	564	7	181	77	----	200	825	----	224	821	186	368	3,453
2015	186	706	300	----	1	1,154	----	1	600	402	----	1,198	4,548
2016	400	400	3,119	1,120	1,054	400	----	----	200	600	2	288	7,583
2017	370	1,180	744	200	915	530	286	232	17	----	978	941	6,393
2018	650	35	200	27	100	431	521	190	1,298	827	2,169	714	7,162
2019	1,558	1,000	3,117	1,000	1,175	1,234	300	----	1,217	----	----	20	10,621
2020	9	1,200	621	5	1	18	----	----	----	1	----	----	1,855

Contract size = 250 pounds of U_3O_8. *Source: CME Group; New York Mercantile Exchange (NYMEX)*

Average Open Interest of Uranium Futures In Contracts

Year	Jan.	Feb.	Mar.	Apr.	May	June	July	Aug.	Sept.	Oct.	Nov.	Dec.
2014	6,733	6,477	6,456	6,540	6,215	6,237	5,973	6,452	6,233	5,994	5,318	4,870
2015	4,202	4,368	4,614	4,529	4,439	4,816	4,605	4,549	4,492	4,537	4,242	4,193
2016	4,238	17,036	5,899	7,102	6,882	6,195	5,376	4,851	4,837	4,980	4,708	4,323
2017	4,100	4,447	4,768	4,348	4,565	4,808	4,447	4,288	4,236	4,191	3,785	3,810
2018	3,707	2,952	2,926	2,764	2,719	2,628	2,499	3,026	3,420	4,636	4,619	4,097
2019	3,854	3,322	3,218	3,611	3,003	2,688	2,699	2,718	2,406	2,406	2,403	2,343
2020	1,809	1,702	1,281	344	333	320	318	310	302	303	303	302

Contract size = 250 pounds of U_3O_8. *Source: CME Group; New York Mercantile Exchange (NYMEX)*

Uranium Industry Statistics in the United States   In Millions of Pounds U_3O_8

Year	Total Operable Units[2/3] Number	Net Summer Capacity of Operable Units[3/4] Million Kilowatts	Nuclear Electricity Net Generation Million Kilowatthours	Nuclear Share of Electricity Net Gen. Percent	Capacity Factor Percent
2007	104.0	100.3	806,425	19.4	91.8
2008	104.0	100.8	806,208	19.6	91.1
2009	104.0	101.0	798,855	20.2	90.3
2010	104.0	101.2	806,968	19.6	91.1
2011	104.0	101.4	790,204	19.3	89.1
2012	104.0	101.9	769,331	19.0	86.1
2013	100.0	99.2	789,016	19.4	89.9
2014	99.0	99.1	797,167	19.5	91.7
2015	99.0	98.6	797,177	19.6	92.3
2016	99.0	99.5	805,325	19.9	92.3
2017	99.0	99.6	804,950	20.0	92.2
2018	98.0	99.5	807,078	19.4	92.5
2019	96.0	98.8	809,412	19.7	93.5
2020[1]		97.3	789,943	19.8	92.4

[1] Preliminary. [2] Total of nuclear generating units holding full-power licenses, or equivalent permission to operate, at end of period. [3] At end of period. [4] Beginning in 2011, monthly capacity values are estimated in two steps: 1) uprates and derates reported on Form EIA-860M are added to specific months; and 2) the difference between the resulting year-end capacity and final capacity is allocated to the month of January. purchases. *Source: Energy Information Administration, U.S. Department of Energy (EIA-DOE)*

Nuclear Electricity Net Generation   In Million Kilowatthours

Year	Jan.	Feb.	Mar.	Apr.	May	June	July	Aug.	Sept.	Oct.	Nov.	Dec.	Total
2011	72,743	64,789	65,662	54,547	57,013	65,270	72,345	71,339	66,849	63,337	64,474	71,837	790,204
2012	72,381	63,847	61,729	55,871	62,081	65,140	69,129	69,602	64,511	59,743	56,713	68,584	769,331
2013	71,406	61,483	62,947	56,767	62,848	66,430	70,539	71,344	65,799	63,184	64,975	71,294	789,016
2014	73,163	62,639	62,397	56,385	62,947	68,138	71,940	71,129	67,535	62,391	65,140	73,363	797,167
2015	74,270	63,462	64,547	59,757	65,833	68,546	71,412	72,415	66,466	60,571	60,264	69,634	797,177
2016	72,525	65,638	66,149	62,365	66,576	67,175	70,349	71,526	65,448	60,733	65,179	71,662	805,325
2017	73,121	63,560	65,093	56,743	61,313	67,011	71,314	72,384	68,098	65,995	66,618	73,700	804,950
2018	74,649	64,790	67,033	59,133	67,320	69,688	72,456	72,282	64,725	59,397	63,948	71,657	807,078
2019	73,701	64,715	65,080	60,581	67,124	68,805	72,199	71,911	66,064	62,033	64,125	73,074	809,412
2020[1]	74,170	65,950	63,997	59,170	64,338	67,205	69,385	68,982	65,727	59,362			789,943

[1] Preliminary. Source: Energy Information Administration, U.S. Department of Energy (EIA-DOE)

Nuclear Share of Electricity Net Generation   In Percent

Year	Jan.	Feb.	Mar.	Apr.	May	June	July	Aug.	Sept.	Oct.	Nov.	Dec.	Average
2011	20.0	20.7	20.6	18.0	17.6	17.7	17.3	17.5	19.8	20.5	21.2	21.4	19.3
2012	21.3	20.6	20.0	18.9	18.4	18.1	16.7	17.6	19.3	19.2	18.5	20.5	19.0
2013	20.5	19.9	19.3	19.0	19.5	18.6	17.9	18.5	19.3	20.1	20.7	20.2	19.4
2014	19.4	19.3	18.8	18.9	19.4	19.0	18.6	18.5	19.9	19.8	20.5	21.7	19.5
2015	20.6	19.0	19.9	20.3	20.4	18.9	17.8	18.5	19.0	19.4	20.0	21.5	19.6
2016	20.6	20.9	21.7	21.3	21.0	18.2	17.1	17.4	18.6	19.4	21.9	20.8	19.9
2017	21.3	21.9	20.5	19.3	19.0	18.7	17.6	18.8	20.3	20.6	21.5	20.9	20.0
2018	19.9	21.2	20.9	19.6	19.8	18.7	17.6	17.7	18.1	18.2	19.8	21.2	19.4
2019	20.6	20.6	20.1	20.6	20.4	19.6	17.5	17.9	18.4	19.3	20.2	21.7	19.7
2020[1]	21.8	20.7	20.9	21.5	21.2	19.0	16.7	17.3	19.7	18.9			19.8

[1] Preliminary. Source: Energy Information Administration, U.S. Department of Energy (EIA-DOE)

Capacity Factor   In Percent

Year	Jan.	Feb.	Mar.	Apr.	May	June	July	Aug.	Sept.	Oct.	Nov.	Dec.	Average
2011	96.6	95.3	87.2	74.9	75.7	89.5	96.0	94.6	91.6	84.0	88.4	95.2	89.1
2012	95.8	90.3	81.7	76.4	82.1	89.0	91.3	91.8	88.0	78.8	77.3	90.5	86.1
2013	93.9	90.3	83.4	77.6	83.3	93.1	95.6	96.7	92.2	85.7	91.0	96.6	89.9
2014	99.1	94.0	84.5	78.8	85.2	95.4	97.5	96.4	94.6	84.5	91.3	99.6	91.7
2015	101.3	95.8	88.0	84.3	89.8	96.4	97.3	98.6	93.6	82.5	84.8	94.9	92.3
2016	98.5	95.3	89.9	88.1	90.5	94.2	94.5	96.1	90.9	81.7	90.9	96.7	92.3
2017	98.7	94.9	87.8	79.1	82.7	93.4	96.2	97.6	94.9	89.0	92.9	99.4	92.2
2018	100.7	96.7	90.4	82.4	90.8	97.1	97.7	97.5	90.4	80.5	89.4	96.9	92.5
2019	99.7	96.9	88.0	84.5	90.9	96.7	98.1	97.8	93.1	85.0	90.8	100.1	93.5
2020[1]	101.6	96.6	87.7	83.8	89.0	96.1	96.0	95.5	94.6	82.6			92.4

[1] Preliminary. [2] Beginning in 2008, capacity factor data are calculated using a new methodology. Source: Energy Information Administration, U.S. Department of Energy (EIA-DOE)

Vanadium

Vanadium (atomic symbol V) is a silvery-white, soft, ductile, metallic element. Discovered in 1801, but mistaken for chromium, vanadium was rediscovered in 1830 by Swedish chemist Nils Sefstrom, who named the element in honor of the Scandinavian goddess Vanadis.

Never found in the pure state, vanadium is found in about 65 different minerals such as carnotite, roscoelite, vanadinite, and patronite, as well as in phosphate rock, certain iron ores, some crude oils, and meteorites. Vanadium is one of the hardest of all metals. It melts at about 1890 degrees Celsius and boils at about 3380 degrees Celsius.

Vanadium has good structural strength and is used as an alloying agent with iron, steel, and titanium. It is used in aerospace applications, transmission gears, photography as a reducing agent, and as a drying agent in various paints.

Prices – The price of vanadium in 2020 fell -45.1% yr/yr to $6.70 per pound, remaining well below the record high of $16.28 per pound in 2005.

Supply – Virtually all (99%) vanadium is produced from ores, concentrates, and slag, with the remainder coming from petroleum residues, ash, and spent catalysts. World production in 2020 from ore, concentrates, and slag fell -0.9% yr/yr to 86,000 metric tons. The world's largest producer of vanadium from ores, concentrates, and slag was China, with 53,000 metric tons of production, which was 61.6% of total world production. The two other major producers were Russia with 18,000 metric tons of production, with 20.9% of world production, and South Africa with 8,200 metric tons of production, which was 9.5% of world production.

Production in Russia and South Africa has been relatively stable in recent years, while China's production grew sharply in the late 1990s. China's production level of 53,000 metric tons in 2020 was a new record high and more than four times the levels seen in the early 1990s.

Trade – U.S. exports of vanadium in 2020 were in the forms of vanadium pent-oxide and anhydride at 80 metric tons (down -81.1% yr/yr), ferro-vanadium at 200 metric tons (down -32.2% yr/yr), and oxides and hydroxides at 80 metric tons (down -89.3% yr/yr). U.S. imports of vanadium in 2018 were in the forms of ferro-vanadium at 3,000 metric tons (+6.8% yr/yr), vanadium pent-oxide at 4,700 metric tons (+38.2% yr/yr), ore, slag, and residues at 4,800 metric tons (unchanged yr/yr), and oxides and hydroxides at 160 metric tons (+8.1% yr/yr).

World Production of Vanadium In Metric Tons (Contained Vanadium)

	From Ores, Concentrates and Slag						From Petroleum Residues Ash, Spent Catalysts			
Year	Australia	China[3]	Kazak-hstan	Russia	South Africa	Total[4]	Japan[5]	United States[6]	Total	World Total
2015	3,250	45,000	16,000	17,788	----	82,000	600	----	600	79,400
2016	4,460	41,000	16,000	8,160	----	69,600	----	----	----	----
2017	5,210	40,000	18,000	7,960	----	71,200	----	----	----	----
2018	5,500	40,000	18,000	7,700	----	71,200	----	----	----	----
2019[1]	5,940	54,000	18,400	8,030	460	86,800	----	----	----	----
2020[2]	6,600	53,000	18,000	8,200	170	86,000	----	----	----	----

[1] Preliminary. [2] Estimate. [3] In vanadiferous slag product. [4] Excludes U.S. production. [5] In vanadium pentoxide product.
[6] In vanadium pentoxide and ferrovanadium products. Source: U.S. Geological Survey (USGS)

Salient Statistics of Vanadium in the United States In Metric Tons (Contained Vanadium)

		Vanadium Consumption by Uses in the U.S.									Exports			Imports			
Year	Con-sumer & Producer Stocks, Dec. 31	Tool Steel	Cast Irons	High Strength, Low Alloy	Stainless & Heat Resisting	Super-alloys	Carbon	Full Alloy	Total	Average $ Per Lb. V_2O_5	Vanadium Pent-oxide, Anhydride	Oxides & Hydr-oxides	Ferro-Vana-dium	Ores, Slag, Residues	Vanadium Pent-oxide, Anhydride	Oxides & Hydr-oxides	Ferro-Vana-dium
2015	W	W	W	W	61	9	743	1,460	3,930	4.16	303	66	122	8,210	2,870	94	1,980
2016	W	W	W	W	61	10	718	1,460	3,830	3.38	5	81	394	5,030	2,460	660	1,590
2017	W	W	W	W	62	9	755	1,470	3,880	7.61	126	148	229	4,800	3,400	148	2,810
2018[1]									3,800	16.40	563	53	575		4,600	98	3,000
2019[2]										12.20	423	750	295		3,660	105	
2020[2]										6.70	80	80	200		2,800	140	

[1] Preliminary. [2] Estimate. W = Withheld. *Source: U.S. Geological Survey (USGS)*

Average Price of Vanadium Pentoxide In Dollars Per Pound

Year	Jan.	Feb.	Mar.	Apr.	May	June	July	Aug.	Sept.	Oct.	Nov.	Dec.	Average
2015	4.97	4.55	3.94	3.80	3.97	4.25	3.83	3.44	3.09	2.72	2.51	2.38	3.62
2016	2.73	3.10	2.88	3.20	3.62	3.49	3.09	3.50	3.85	3.87	4.71	4.97	3.58
2017	5.13	5.16	5.10	5.76	5.98	5.54	5.98	9.28	10.67	7.76	7.30	9.26	6.91
2018	11.42	13.46	14.89	15.59	14.63	15.86	18.85	18.85	20.36	24.19	28.26	21.95	18.19
2019	16.18	17.22	16.08	10.87	8.15	7.48	6.80	7.18	7.61	5.88	5.08	5.33	9.49
2020	5.71	6.94	5.67	6.45	6.28	5.65	5.30	5.35	5.35	5.35	5.21	5.29	5.71

Source: American Metal Market (AMM)

Vegetables

Vegetables are the edible products of herbaceous plants, which are plants with soft stems. Vegetables are grouped according to the edible part of each plant, including leaves (e.g., lettuce), stalks (celery), roots (carrot), tubers (potato), bulbs (onion), fruits (tomato), seeds (pea), and flowers (broccoli). Each of these groups contributes to the human diet in its own way. Fleshy roots are high in energy value and good sources of the vitamin B group, seeds are relatively high in carbohydrates and proteins, while leaves, stalks, and fruits are excellent sources of minerals, vitamins, water, and roughage. Vegetables are an important food for the maintenance of health and prevention of disease. Higher intakes of vegetables have been shown to lower the risks of cancer and coronary heart disease.

Vegetables are best consumed fresh in their raw state to derive the maximum benefits from their nutrients. While canned and frozen vegetables are often thought to be inferior to fresh vegetables, they are sometimes nutritionally superior to fresh produce because they are usually processed immediately after harvest when nutrient content is at its peak. When cooking vegetables, aluminum utensils should not be used, because aluminum is a soft metal that is affected by food acids and alkalis. Scientific evidence shows that tiny particles of aluminum from foods cooked in aluminum utensils enter the stomach and can injure the sensitive lining of the stomach.

Prices – The monthly average index of fresh vegetable prices received by growers in the U.S. in 2020 rose +2.3% yr/yr to 266.5, a new record high.

Demand – The leading vegetable in terms of U.S. per capita consumption in 2019 was the potato with 118.8 pounds of consumption, tomatoes with 88.3 pounds, lettuce with 25.0 pounds, onions with 22.1 pounds, and sweet corn with 18.9 pounds. Total U.S. per capita vegetable consumption in 2019 was 409.2 pounds.

Index of Prices Received by Growers for Fresh Vegetables in the United States (1990-92=100)

Year	Jan.	Feb.	Mar.	Apr.	May	June	July	Aug.	Sept.	Oct.	Nov.	Dec.	Average
2011	211.2	341.1	267.7	184.7	156.9	174.2	148.7	146.6	174.1	171.4	199.1	169.7	195.5
2012	146.9	129.5	150.2	133.7	144.2	156.2	147.1	159.4	163.7	143.2	164.7	154.0	149.4
2013	240.8	182.0	236.8	201.0	211.6	195.8	175.1	229.1	188.8	222.2	218.5	177.0	206.6
2014	197.0	193.3	197.1	200.2	195.9	214.6	197.3	184.7	191.0	219.6	249.1	229.0	205.7
2015	253.2	197.1	200.5	211.0	230.2	213.5	209.9	206.2	235.1	229.4	228.3	284.0	224.9
2016	343.7	266.3	222.6	209.1	240.2	226.3	225.4	184.8	217.0	205.8	179.7	182.3	225.3
2017	185.1	223.6	244.6	332.3	266.8	228.1	211.8	185.4	209.9	262.3	268.3	239.8	238.2
2018	252.3	160.8	247.0	183.7	235.5	189.5	173.9	197.7	190.2	221.6	317.8	432.9	233.6
2019	295.9	238.4	289.4	242.7	262.1	272.2	277.6	205.5	191.6	287.8	296.1	265.2	260.4
2020[1]	350.0	208.0	203.3	200.8	220.9	256.9	220.3	213.4	276.9	381.3	342.6	323.2	266.5

[1] Preliminary. Not seasonally adjusted. *Source: National Agricultural Statistics Service, U.S. Department of Agriculture (NASS-USDA)*

Producer Price Index of Canned[2] Processed Vegetables in the United States (1982 = 100)

Year	Jan.	Feb.	Mar.	Apr.	May	June	July	Aug.	Sept.	Oct.	Nov.	Dec.	Average
2011	162.2	162.0	162.7	164.4	164.4	164.9	166.9	168.1	169.8	169.7	170.3	170.3	166.3
2012	171.3	171.1	171.7	171.5	170.7	172.9	172.4	175.6	175.0	175.3	174.2	174.3	173.0
2013	173.9	174.1	173.9	174.6	174.0	173.7	173.9	174.1	174.0	173.9	173.6	173.6	173.9
2014	173.2	173.4	173.0	172.4	172.3	172.9	173.0	173.7	174.2	174.6	174.7	174.8	173.5
2015	175.7	176.3	179.4	175.0	174.9	177.0	176.2	172.6	172.1	172.3	172.6	168.8	174.4
2016	166.7	168.4	165.4	166.6	167.3	166.0	165.9	166.2	165.9	165.4	165.4	165.5	166.2
2017	164.2	164.6	163.6	165.4	166.4	165.7	165.6	166.4	165.5	165.8	167.6	167.4	165.7
2018	167.4	170.2	168.8	169.1	168.6	169.5	168.5	170.8	171.5	173.4	175.7	177.4	170.9
2019	176.5	176.5	176.8	176.0	175.2	175.7	175.9	177.2	178.0	178.8	180.4	181.8	177.4
2020[1]	183.3	182.7	183.3	184.4	185.0	183.8	183.3	182.0	185.3	185.9	186.2	185.6	184.2

[1] Preliminary. [2] Includes canned vegetables and juices, including hominy and mushrooms. Not seasonally adjusted. *Source: Bureau of Labor Statistics, U.S. Department of Labor (BLS)*

Producer Price Index of Frozen Processed Vegetables in the United States (1982 = 100)

Year	Jan.	Feb.	Mar.	Apr.	May	June	July	Aug.	Sept.	Oct.	Nov.	Dec.	Average
2011	174.8	175.2	175.3	176.0	176.1	177.7	183.9	185.1	186.0	186.5	191.4	193.3	181.8
2012	193.8	193.7	193.7	194.1	194.1	194.5	194.5	194.1	193.6	193.6	193.9	193.9	194.0
2013	194.0	194.5	194.4	194.4	194.6	194.6	194.6	192.4	192.5	192.3	192.4	192.3	193.6
2014	192.2	192.3	192.3	192.4	192.4	192.3	192.3	192.9	193.2	193.5	193.5	193.5	192.7
2015	193.8	193.1	193.2	193.3	193.5	193.3	193.3	193.1	195.9	195.8	195.3	195.3	194.1
2016	195.2	195.2	195.2	195.2	195.3	195.4	195.5	195.3	195.3	195.6	196.0	196.0	195.4
2017	198.6	199.5	199.6	199.5	199.6	199.6	202.7	202.7	204.3	205.7	205.7	206.8	202.0
2018	208.0	208.1	209.3	209.5	209.6	210.3	211.5	211.5	213.6	213.9	213.5	211.5	210.9
2019	211.6	211.9	212.1	212.1	212.1	212.2	212.2	214.7	214.4	215.2	215.2	215.9	213.3
2020[1]	216.4	216.1	216.2	216.4	216.3	216.3	216.4	216.8	217.6	217.1	217.1	221.0	217.0

[1] Preliminary. Not seasonally adjusted. *Source: Bureau of Labor Statistics, U.S. Department of Labor (BLS)*

Per Capita Use of Selected Commercially Produced Fresh and Processing Vegetables and Melons in the United States In Pounds, farm weight basis

Crop	2010	2011	2012	2013	2014	2015	2016	2017	2018[10]	2019[11]
Asparagus, All	1.6	1.6	1.7	1.6	1.8	1.6	1.8	1.8	1.9	1.9
Fresh	1.4	1.4	1.4	1.4	1.7	1.5	1.6	1.6	1.8	1.8
Canning	0.1	0.1	0.1	0.1	0.1	0.1	0.1	0.1	0.1	0.1
Freezing	0.1	0.1	0.1	0.1	0.1	0.1	0.2	0.1	0.1	0.1
Snap beans, All	7.5	6.4	6.5	6.6	6.0	6.4	6.9	6.6	6.3	6.6
Fresh	1.9	1.7	1.6	1.6	1.5	1.6	1.7	1.6	1.6	1.8
Canning	3.7	3.2	2.9	2.9	2.8	3.0	3.2	3.1	2.9	2.9
Freezing	2.0	1.5	1.9	2.1	1.8	1.9	2.0	1.9	1.8	1.9
Broccoli, All [1]	8.4	8.6	8.9	9.4	9.2	10.0	10.1	9.5	8.4	8.8
Fresh	6.0	6.0	6.3	6.9	6.7	7.4	7.5	7.1	5.9	6.1
Freezing	2.5	2.7	2.6	2.5	2.6	2.6	2.6	2.4	2.5	2.6
Cabbage, All	8.5	7.6	7.4	7.9	7.6	7.2	7.0	7.5	6.4	7.1
Fresh	7.5	6.6	6.3	6.9	6.7	6.3	5.9	6.2	5.7	6.5
Canning (kraut)	1.0	1.0	1.2	1.0	0.9	0.9	1.0	1.3	0.8	0.7
Carrots, All [2]	10.0	9.9	9.9	10.5	10.4	10.9	10.8	10.9	15.6	16.6
Fresh	7.8	7.5	8.0	8.0	8.5	8.8	7.8	7.4	12.2	13.6
Canning	0.8	0.8	0.8	0.8	0.7	0.7	1.1	1.1	1.0	1.2
Freezing	1.5	1.6	1.2	1.7	1.2	1.4	1.9	2.4	2.4	1.8
Cauliflower, All [1]	1.7	1.7	1.5	1.7	1.6	1.9	2.1	2.9	3.1	3.7
Fresh	1.3	1.2	1.2	1.3	1.3	1.6	1.7	2.4	2.5	3.0
Freezing	0.4	0.4	0.3	0.3	0.4	0.3	0.4	0.5	0.6	0.7
Celery	6.1	6.0	6.0	5.5	5.5	5.1	5.0	4.7	4.9	5.3
Sweet Corn, All [3]	24.7	23.8	24.3	21.7	21.1	22.0	19.6	20.3	19.9	18.9
Fresh	9.3	8.2	8.7	8.9	7.7	8.6	7.1	7.2	6.8	6.8
Canning	6.9	5.8	5.9	5.8	5.8	5.3	5.0	5.1	5.2	5.3
Freezing	8.6	9.8	9.8	7.0	7.7	8.0	7.5	8.1	7.9	6.9
Cucumbers, All	10.5	9.2	10.1	10.6	11.3	11.0	11.1	11.1	11.3	11.4
Fresh	6.7	6.4	7.1	7.3	7.4	7.6	8.1	7.4	8.0	8.0
Pickling	3.7	2.8	3.0	3.2	3.9	3.4	3.0	3.7	3.3	3.4
Melons	26.4	25.5	----	----	----	----	----	----	----	----
Watermelon	15.7	14.8	----	----	----	----	----	----	----	----
Cantaloupe	8.6	8.7	----	----	----	----	----	----	----	----
Honeydew	1.5	1.5	----	----	----	----	----	----	----	----
Other	0.6	0.5	----	----	----	----	----	----	----	----
Lettuce, All	27.9	27.6	27.9	25.5	25.3	25.5	31.4	30.4	24.5	25.0
Head lettuce	15.9	15.8	16.0	14.1	14.5	13.6	16.9	15.3	12.3	12.7
Romaine & Leaf	12.0	11.7	11.9	11.4	10.8	11.9	14.5	15.1	12.1	12.3
Onions, All	20.9	20.4	20.7	19.6	19.4	19.7	24.5	26.5	21.1	22.1
Fresh	19.6	19.1	19.3	18.5	18.4	18.3	22.8	25.1	20.5	20.4
Dehydrating	1.3	1.2	1.4	1.1	1.1	1.4	1.7	1.4	0.6	1.7
Green Peas, All [4]	2.6	2.4	2.7	2.4	2.3	2.3	1.8	2.0	1.9	1.9
Canning	1.1	0.8	0.8	0.9	0.7	0.8	0.8	0.7	0.6	0.7
Freezing	1.5	1.6	1.9	1.5	1.6	1.5	1.0	1.3	1.3	1.3
Peppers, All	11.2	11.4	11.7	10.9	11.6	11.6	12.0	12.2	12.0	12.2
Bell Peppers, All	10.3	10.6	10.8	10.0	10.7	10.7	11.1	11.3	11.2	11.3
Chile Peppers, All	0.8	0.8	0.9	0.9	0.9	0.9	1.0	0.9	0.9	0.9
Tomatoes, All	91.3	86.8	87.4	86.3	88.0	76.9	81.5	78.0	85.9	88.3
Fresh	20.6	21.0	20.8	20.3	20.6	20.6	20.3	20.1	20.3	20.3
Canning	70.8	65.8	66.6	66.0	67.4	56.3	61.2	57.9	65.6	68.0
Other, Fresh [5]	18.3	18.8	19.3	18.8	20.5	18.3	23.9	24.5	23.4	23.4
Other, Canning [6]	2.5	2.6	2.7	2.7	2.6	2.9	3.0	3.0	3.3	3.2
Other, Freezing [7]	4.5	4.3	4.5	4.3	4.6	4.7	4.6	4.7	6.1	6.4
Subtotal, All [8]	262.7	253.8	258.2	251.1	254.5	242.9	262.0	261.8	261.4	267.6
Fresh	144.7	142.2	144.8	141.2	142.6	141.9	155.9	157.1	149.2	153.3
Canning	97.1	89.6	91.1	90.3	92.1	80.6	86.0	83.3	89.6	92.6
Freezing	20.9	22.0	22.3	19.6	19.9	20.5	20.2	21.4	22.6	21.6
Potatoes, All	113.8	110.5	114.9	113.6	113.1	115.4	110.2	117.8	116.0	118.8
Fresh	36.8	34.1	34.6	34.6	33.6	34.2	33.7	34.9	33.0	34.1
Processing	77.0	76.4	80.3	79.0	79.5	81.2	76.5	82.9	83.0	84.7
Sweet Potatoes	6.3	7.1	6.9	6.3	7.5	7.6	7.2	8.0	5.6	7.9
Mushrooms	3.7	3.8	4.0	3.8	3.8	3.9	4.0	4.0	3.9	3.8
Dry Peas & Lentils [9]	1.6	1.1	0.9	1.0	0.8	1.2	4.0	3.4	4.8	4.2
Dry Edible Beans	6.7	5.1	5.9	5.5	5.6	7.2	6.7	7.7	8.9	6.9
Total, All Items	394.9	381.4	390.8	381.3	385.3	378.2	394.1	402.7	400.6	409.2

[1] All production for processing broccoli and cauliflower is for freezing. [2] Industry allocation suggests that 27 percent of processing carrot production is for canning and 73 percent is for freezing. [3] On-cob basis. [4] In-shell basis. [5] Includes artichokes, brussels sprouts, eggplant, endive/escarole, garlic, radishes, green limas, squash, and spinach. In 2000, okra, pumpkins, kale, collards, turnip greens and mustard greens added. [6] Includes beets, green limas (1992-2003), spinach, and miscellaneous imports (1990-2001). [7] Includes green limas, spinach, and miscellaneous freezing vegetables. [8] Fresh, canning, and freezing data do not sum to the total because onions for dehydrating are included in the total. [9] Production from new areas in upper midwest added in 1998. A portion of this is likely for feed use. [10] Preliminary. [11] Forecast. NA = Not available. *Source: Economic Research Service, U.S. Department of Agriculture (ERS-USDA)*

Average Price Received by Growers for Broccoli in the United States In Dollars Per Cwt

Year	Jan.	Feb.	Mar.	Apr.	May	June	July	Aug.	Sept.	Oct.	Nov.	Dec.	Season Average
2013	80.40	38.10	30.60	NA	NA	NA	NA	NA	NA	NA	NA	NA	43.20
2014	NA	NA	NA	40.10	48.00	49.60	31.80	47.10	53.40	34.60	45.00	33.10	40.70
2015	67.30	29.90	47.80	50.60	54.50	34.70	38.20	49.90	57.10	58.10	65.10	84.70	49.10
2016	50.80	26.80	30.90	39.30	48.10	49.30	41.60	28.00	36.60	37.70	35.90	34.80	37.70
2017	55.70	54.10	70.90	95.60	82.60	50.50	51.00	62.10	82.10	66.60	54.80	40.30	45.40
2018	45.00	28.50	46.80	39.70	56.90	46.80	37.60	53.90	51.40	56.50	70.70	85.50	42.80
2019	56.20	50.60	62.40	50.00	77.90	51.10	40.20	43.60	71.60	77.40	57.50	38.10	56.38
2020[1]	99.00	41.00	79.60	53.80	46.00	118.00	54.20	48.10	102.00	64.50	106.00	71.60	73.65

[1]Preliminary. NA = Not available. *Source: National Agricultural Statistics Service, U.S. Department of Agriculture (NASS-USDA)*

Average Price Received by Growers for Carrots in the United States In Dollars Per Cwt

Year	Jan.	Feb.	Mar.	Apr.	May	June	July	Aug.	Sept.	Oct.	Nov.	Dec.	Season Average
2013	28.20	28.50	30.80	NA	NA	NA	NA	NA	NA	NA	NA	NA	28.60
2014	NA	NA	NA	28.20	27.20	25.50	25.10	23.00	21.50	26.90	28.00	33.40	27.10
2015	33.80	33.00	32.20	31.80	31.40	30.60	29.90	30.20	30.40	31.30	31.00	32.90	30.50
2016	34.40	35.80	34.90	38.60	39.30	31.80	29.90	29.30	28.90	28.90	28.90	27.90	24.80
2017	28.60	28.40	28.00	27.80	27.80	25.70	25.90	28.90	30.80	24.20	31.30	31.30	22.50
2018	31.40	31.00	27.90	27.30	27.70	26.70	27.10	25.80	26.30	26.60	26.50	26.40	22.20
2019	26.50	26.30	29.00	28.10	28.10	28.20	28.60	28.50	28.80	29.30	29.70	29.90	28.42
2020[1]	50.90	49.70	57.50	47.50	47.00	48.30	49.30	48.30	46.10	45.10	42.30	42.60	47.88

[1]Preliminary. NA = Not available. *Source: National Agricultural Statistics Service, U.S. Department of Agriculture (NASS-USDA)*

Average Price Received by Growers for Cauliflower in the United States In Dollars Per Cwt

Year	Jan.	Feb.	Mar.	Apr.	May	June	July	Aug.	Sept.	Oct.	Nov.	Dec.	Season Average
2013	69.90	43.30	46.00	NA	NA	NA	NA	NA	NA	NA	NA	NA	44.50
2014	NA	NA	NA	65.80	79.10	66.30	43.10	31.80	64.70	43.20	67.60	84.80	50.10
2015	58.40	40.10	85.10	87.80	108.00	49.60	31.10	42.80	55.50	68.60	121.00	184.00	61.50
2016	59.10	45.30	39.80	53.70	82.00	62.20	41.00	39.10	42.70	42.80	42.40	81.10	55.70
2017	56.70	65.00	134.00	136.00	70.60	55.60	44.90	35.60	49.90	56.00	73.20	90.10	45.90
2018	47.80	42.90	87.60	60.80	78.60	35.50	38.40	39.80	45.30	46.40	95.50	74.80	45.80
2019	79.00	105.00	99.70	67.00	112.00	47.50	65.40	57.70	65.20	111.00	92.20	41.90	78.63
2020[1]	97.00	70.40	102.00	72.00	43.30	79.90	40.90	32.00	40.30	45.80	95.90	101.00	68.38

[1]Preliminary. NA = Not available. *Source: National Agricultural Statistics Service, U.S. Department of Agriculture (NASS-USDA)*

Average Price Received by Growers for Celery in the United States In Dollars Per Cwt

Year	Jan.	Feb.	Mar.	Apr.	May	June	July	Aug.	Sept.	Oct.	Nov.	Dec.	Season Average
2013	39.70	47.00	29.20	NA	NA	NA	NA	NA	NA	NA	NA	NA	25.40
2014	NA	NA	NA	15.50	15.80	14.50	20.60	18.70	17.90	16.90	26.60	28.70	17.10
2015	19.40	14.60	14.00	18.60	26.80	17.60	17.10	23.50	22.70	28.00	40.60	59.80	24.80
2016	67.20	29.90	18.80	20.00	26.20	18.80	17.70	16.40	15.80	18.60	26.60	17.30	18.10
2017	17.50	15.60	24.50	39.30	79.90	42.40	27.70	17.70	17.30	19.20	29.60	23.60	20.10
2018	20.80	19.20	25.20	30.70	27.10	24.70	21.10	16.80	18.60	20.20	30.50	46.60	25.00
2019	52.10	70.90	96.00	113.00	109.00	88.80	26.60	23.30	26.30	29.90	35.60	27.40	58.24
2020[1]	45.90	33.90	55.70	49.60	45.10	46.80	58.70	40.50	35.00	36.90	49.80	55.10	46.08

[1]Preliminary. NA = Not available. *Source: National Agricultural Statistics Service, U.S. Department of Agriculture (NASS-USDA)*

Average Price Received by Growers for Sweet Corn in the United States In Dollars Per Cwt

Year	Jan.	Feb.	Mar.	Apr.	May	June	July	Aug.	Sept.	Oct.	Nov.	Dec.	Season Average
2013	30.40	36.70	33.30	NA	NA	NA	NA	NA	NA	NA	NA	NA	24.10
2014	NA	NA	NA	26.00	25.40	32.00	37.70	29.00	23.10	42.20	40.70	41.40	23.90
2015	39.80	40.00	31.70	29.60	26.80	27.70	33.70	29.50	32.30	47.90	24.40	26.00	21.80
2016	43.80	58.70	67.50	34.30	26.20	25.40	29.50	23.60	28.20	33.60	37.40	37.50	20.70
2017	30.90	35.70	26.20	30.80	29.80	34.30	30.70	26.80	21.30	32.50	54.70	34.10	29.10
2018	35.40	24.70	26.90	32.60	28.30	27.10	26.20	24.40	30.50	30.50	45.80	31.70	30.34
2019	35.70	47.90	26.60	34.80	30.50	31.20	35.90	51.80	NA	NA	34.30	30.50	35.92
2020[1]	52.70	38.20	28.60	28.20	33.20	75.90	54.30	33.30	49.60	61.20	35.60	72.90	46.98

[1]Preliminary. NA = Not available. *Source: National Agricultural Statistics Service, U.S. Department of Agriculture (NASS-USDA)*

Average Price Received by Growers for Head Lettuce in the United States In Dollars Per Cwt

Year	Jan.	Feb.	Mar.	Apr.	May	June	July	Aug.	Sept.	Oct.	Nov.	Dec.	Season Average
2011	27.20	54.40	35.20	17.80	26.40	17.10	19.40	14.70	14.80	17.00	30.50	17.40	23.00
2012	13.40	12.60	12.00	17.90	19.00	19.00	19.10	19.20	20.50	17.70	20.10	12.80	17.70
2013	44.80	31.70	46.90	NA	NA	NA	NA	NA	NA	NA	NA	NA	26.70
2014	NA	NA	NA	18.20	26.10	35.30	29.00	29.60	32.90	33.40	49.10	15.90	24.40
2015	38.20	15.20	19.10	23.10	25.10	30.30	18.80	35.70	48.90	34.40	60.10	51.90	29.10
2016	42.00	20.90	15.40	20.80	32.50	25.90	26.00	20.70	20.80	20.60	26.60	30.20	26.70
2017	29.10	51.40	49.60	82.50	26.10	22.80	25.60	24.70	31.70	42.20	23.00	30.50	35.90
2018	26.00	27.00	46.70	25.50	28.90	25.90	20.90	27.80	25.90	28.60	76.70	74.80	30.10
2019	33.80	37.60	52.40	28.10	19.70	41.00	41.50	22.70	22.90	39.20	65.30	49.00	37.77
2020[1]	80.50	20.60	27.40	22.30	20.80	24.50	25.00	18.60	38.60	48.60	58.30	21.20	33.87

[1]Preliminary. NA = Not available. *Source: National Agricultural Statistics Service, U.S. Department of Agriculture (NASS-USDA)*

Average Price Received by Growers for Tomatoes in the United States In Dollars Per Cwt

Year	Jan.	Feb.	Mar.	Apr.	May	June	July	Aug.	Sept.	Oct.	Nov.	Dec.	Season Average
2011	51.90	108.00	98.70	67.60	49.10	44.60	33.10	30.30	35.50	26.60	42.40	26.50	36.10
2012	28.90	30.60	36.60	26.70	34.10	45.10	24.70	23.70	26.20	20.90	45.30	49.40	30.50
2013	34.10	37.70	53.50	NA	NA	NA	NA	NA	NA	NA	NA	NA	44.60
2014	NA	NA	NA	45.20	39.10	57.60	27.00	33.20	34.70	54.60	71.80	66.70	41.50
2015	34.80	49.40	44.20	45.20	24.00	33.50	41.30	36.30	35.80	41.80	39.30	42.50	46.30
2016	108.00	88.30	70.90	38.60	30.40	32.00	30.40	28.10	34.50	37.50	42.80	29.40	42.50
2017	28.40	28.50	30.20	32.90	62.80	43.90	28.20	30.10	37.20	42.40	62.40	80.20	37.30
2018	47.90	34.40	40.00	25.70	35.40	28.30	15.30	29.90	29.00	39.60	55.50	57.20	36.52
2019	53.30	45.40	52.20	43.40	36.20	36.10	32.10	34.20	33.00	40.90	54.40	112.00	47.77
2020[1]	130.00	84.70	57.60	65.00	87.00	57.10	47.70	44.60	48.00	86.50	82.60	73.50	72.03

[1]Preliminary. NA = Not available. *Source: National Agricultural Statistics Service, U.S. Department of Agriculture (NASS-USDA)*

Frozen Vegetables: January 1 and July 1 Cold Storage Holdings in the United States In Thousands of Pounds

Crop	2016 July 1	2017 Jan. 1	July 1	2018 Jan. 1	July 1	2019 Jan. 1	July 1	2020 Jan. 1	July 1	2021[1] Jan. 1
Asparagus	14,490	11,395	11,137	10,188	10,855	8,106	7,220	6,002	8,393	5,293
Lima Beans	40,193	55,895	36,817	54,024	33,421	38,647	14,441	33,509	14,576	21,497
Green Beans, Reg. Cut	121,414	209,496	115,498	191,291	81,164	152,495	82,556	155,713	68,409	204,173
Green Beans, Fr. Style	9,912	14,482	8,923	15,187	11,184	13,747	9,879	14,887	9,697	13,061
Broccoli, Spears	27,650	21,870	30,877	23,877	45,339	26,691	43,927	41,991	47,273	34,491
Broccoli, Chopped & Cut	37,574	42,915	31,521	32,738	34,532	37,761	32,061	34,048	31,362	36,427
Brussels sprouts	13,061	22,021	16,253	21,878	17,361	15,680	12,774	13,254	9,613	8,016
Carrots, Diced	99,573	161,641	97,296	142,941	84,708	125,994	100,442	173,673	100,000	152,684
Carrots, Other	119,697	191,102	112,691	164,466	94,449	110,822	64,844	98,720	59,108	112,189
Cauliflower	22,634	27,325	28,013	34,083	25,340	29,760	18,926	24,382	27,252	30,408
Corn, Cut	287,223	522,396	220,012	479,654	240,908	475,712	240,636	567,306	270,432	597,036
Corn, Cob	91,313	207,064	73,922	257,185	79,134	269,689	137,539	275,612	106,869	272,573
Mixed vegetables	60,593	62,424	69,734	57,762	56,417	53,845	47,214	41,323	45,371	50,758
Okra	27,167	33,964	24,246	27,190	30,181	44,156	28,658	48,906	33,460	33,817
Onion Rings	16,005	13,769	12,810	12,375	17,976	17,160	15,146	14,918	14,144	14,203
Onions, Other	41,801	48,337	58,558	57,472	60,160	51,663	72,312	51,024	73,559	60,448
Blackeye Peas	1,377	1,600	1,804	1,484	1,293	1,479	1,413	1,227	2,168	1,779
Green Peas	360,749	323,820	322,460	277,206	284,008	207,808	233,194	212,684	232,490	243,072
Peas and Carrots Mixed	8,348	6,884	8,989	7,914	6,754	7,262	9,098	9,058	8,779	7,809
Spinach	57,913	54,850	68,427	50,731	57,896	30,994	41,009	33,492	58,434	53,278
Squash, Summer/Zucchini	42,122	64,176	48,617	66,948	44,881	60,482	40,456	56,884	37,204	56,841
Southern greens	19,105	18,899	18,600	12,803	10,996	12,174	12,907	10,908	11,380	15,577
Other Vegetables	327,268	453,978	397,044	626,616	377,555	582,039	355,236	435,111	373,489	460,079
Total	1,847,182	2,570,303	1,814,249	2,626,013	1,706,512	2,374,166	1,621,888	2,354,632	1,643,462	2,485,509
Potatoes, French Fries	889,492	893,453	954,888	940,958	941,336	944,230	945,264	948,850	868,583	917,398
Potatoes, Other Frozen	287,996	231,118	275,721	242,085	270,621	230,329	239,233	207,080	216,545	204,660
Potatoes, Total	1,177,488	1,124,571	1,230,609	1,183,043	1,211,957	1,174,559	1,184,497	1,155,930	1,085,128	1,122,058
Grand Total	3,024,670	3,694,874	3,044,858	3,809,056	2,918,469	3,548,725	2,806,385	3,510,562	2,728,590	3,607,567

Cold Storage Stocks of Frozen Green Beans[2] in the United States, on First of Month

In Thousands of Pounds

Year	Jan.	Feb.	Mar.	Apr.	May	June	July	Aug.	Sept.	Oct.	Nov.	Dec.
2015	182,136	161,510	153,916	135,211	123,221	119,151	113,449	155,410	226,850	255,661	243,986	225,001
2016	199,994	180,082	158,534	142,228	136,727	131,014	122,127	169,238	242,529	265,200	263,320	233,980
2017	209,496	190,073	174,009	159,278	144,992	132,483	115,498	138,593	196,016	238,830	230,850	216,052
2018	191,291	172,503	155,853	128,304	109,337	93,324	81,164	115,005	173,836	202,123	190,921	173,687
2019	152,495	143,960	130,780	117,427	110,140	87,598	82,556	125,225	163,225	203,481	185,412	173,403
2020[1]	155,713	142,537	126,346	107,604	91,905	76,783	68,409	125,541	197,229	252,835	240,075	219,751

[1] Preliminary. [2] Regular cut. *Source: Economic Research Service, U.S. Department of Agriculture (ERS-USDA)*

Cold Storage Stocks of Frozen Sweet Corn[2] in the United States, on First of Month

In Thousands of Pounds

Year	Jan.	Feb.	Mar.	Apr.	May	June	July	Aug.	Sept.	Oct.	Nov.	Dec.
2015	529,586	464,026	431,593	395,330	348,564	313,388	262,028	287,729	446,215	621,237	640,668	582,672
2016	520,804	488,940	479,571	412,766	381,312	339,900	289,897	301,633	464,716	587,865	600,062	552,697
2017	522,396	463,549	414,754	371,774	316,608	275,307	220,012	216,938	377,400	519,847	568,117	521,589
2018	479,654	446,194	403,945	356,223	312,151	276,599	240,908	257,797	443,885	558,378	592,617	530,696
2019	475,712	433,018	394,400	351,796	295,948	259,917	240,636	250,720	461,516	662,567	674,400	637,174
2020[1]	567,306	510,508	451,650	418,608	372,483	316,418	270,432	261,628	428,748	648,159	694,618	644,835

[1] Preliminary. [2] Cut. *Source: Economic Research Service, U.S. Department of Agriculture (ERS-USDA)*

Cold Storage Stocks of Frozen Sweet Corn[2] in the United States, on First of Month

In Thousands of Pounds

Year	Jan.	Feb.	Mar.	Apr.	May	June	July	Aug.	Sept.	Oct.	Nov.	Dec.
2015	223,053	206,000	175,910	156,425	132,387	110,912	88,817	112,873	165,657	239,922	244,687	229,113
2016	220,295	216,834	198,513	164,351	135,956	112,977	91,597	97,354	177,551	223,337	250,261	227,305
2017	207,064	197,123	177,461	150,107	128,032	101,904	73,922	74,754	181,921	278,137	297,466	286,139
2018	257,185	231,840	207,582	176,477	142,645	107,713	79,134	105,145	208,224	276,776	307,075	288,300
2019	269,689	242,621	226,032	202,924	169,151	149,776	137,539	137,583	246,139	332,852	345,723	307,982
2020[1]	275,612	246,556	216,990	191,158	177,364	133,697	106,869	128,561	207,409	290,645	317,958	306,616

[1] Preliminary . [2] Cob. *Source: Economic Research Service, U.S. Department of Agriculture (ERS-USDA)*

Cold Storage Stocks of Frozen Green Peas in the United States, on First of Month

In Thousands of Pounds

Year	Jan.	Feb.	Mar.	Apr.	May	June	July	Aug.	Sept.	Oct.	Nov.	Dec.
2015	243,251	205,887	189,997	154,385	127,621	127,985	314,155	414,632	397,020	372,987	335,536	308,934
2016	274,778	251,096	225,590	195,128	166,005	173,146	360,749	455,262	437,827	401,126	361,786	343,397
2017	323,820	294,248	267,497	238,263	205,494	191,203	322,460	428,002	410,645	381,666	342,202	305,457
2018	277,206	247,040	223,679	198,966	190,125	177,152	284,008	341,193	319,549	303,905	268,892	244,288
2019	207,808	188,769	174,792	147,662	132,510	121,763	233,194	385,001	352,447	309,511	277,596	250,797
2020[1]	212,684	185,946	154,812	135,690	112,569	90,073	232,490	341,429	342,402	309,867	279,854	259,484

[1] Preliminary. *Source: Economic Research Service, U.S. Department of Agriculture (ERS-USDA)*

Cold Storage Stocks of Other Frozen Vegetables in the United States, on First of Month

In Thousands of lbs

Year	Jan.	Feb.	Mar.	Apr.	May	June	July	Aug.	Sept.	Oct.	Nov.	Dec.
2015	381,070	357,718	335,823	327,915	319,475	307,475	302,891	321,753	364,047	397,496	407,400	391,876
2016	391,886	368,774	346,407	326,102	322,249	328,465	331,768	340,474	405,041	441,482	476,689	463,852
2017	453,978	447,244	447,065	451,698	416,977	385,932	397,044	418,221	518,807	618,682	660,094	646,967
2018	626,616	563,016	504,878	461,985	406,018	376,945	377,555	422,205	502,853	569,778	623,597	603,165
2019	582,039	535,862	510,354	476,131	440,646	377,702	355,236	354,953	384,582	423,955	458,115	455,499
2020[1]	435,111	406,680	402,718	386,470	381,515	366,163	373,489	363,933	686,604	449,473	499,333	477,272

[1] Preliminary. *Source: Economic Research Service, U.S. Department of Agriculture (ERS-USDA)*

Cold Storage Stocks of Total Frozen Vegetables in the United States, on First of Month

In Millions of Pounds

Year	Jan.	Feb.	Mar.	Apr.	May	June	July	Aug.	Sept.	Oct.	Nov.	Dec.
2015	2,359.3	2,144.9	1,995.5	1,850.1	1,714.1	1,620.7	1,697.1	1,889.1	2,222.9	2,570.1	2,688.7	2,580.2
2016	2,423.8	2,302.3	2,169.7	1,973.7	1,861.4	1,769.2	1,855.6	2,028.6	2,413.9	2,626.6	2,757.7	2,695.1
2017	2,570.3	2,407.5	2,256.6	2,125.7	1,954.2	1,803.6	1,814.2	1,938.1	2,366.1	2,731.8	2,866.1	2,788.6
2018	2,626.0	2,412.9	2,221.9	2,018.1	1,838.3	1,682.5	1,706.5	1,867.7	2,276.2	2,544.6	2,669.9	2,548.1
2019	2,374.2	2,193.7	2,064.7	1,902.1	1,738.6	1,575.7	1,621.9	1,821.9	2,191.6	2,530.1	2,615.7	2,555.2
2020[1]	2,354.6	2,184.6	2,018.9	1,869.7	1,759.6	1,598.3	1,643.5	1,781.1	2,122.8	2,531.8	2,693.7	2,616.6

[1] Preliminary. *Source: Economic Research Service, U.S. Department of Agriculture (ERS-USDA)*

Wheat

Wheat is a cereal grass. Wheat was a wild grass before humans started to cultivate it for larger-scale food production. It has been grown in temperate regions and cultivated for food since prehistoric times. Wheat is believed to have originated in southwestern Asia. Archeological research indicates that wheat was grown as a crop in the Nile Valley about 5,000 BC. Wheat is not native to the U.S. and was first grown here in 1602 near the Massachusetts coast. The common types of wheat grown in the U.S. are spring and winter wheat. Wheat planted in the spring for summer or autumn harvest is mostly red wheat. Wheat planted in the fall or winter for spring harvest is mostly white wheat. Winter wheat accounts for nearly three-fourths of total U.S. production. Wheat is used mainly for human consumption and supplies about 20% of the food calories for the world's population. The primary use for wheat is flour, but it is also used for brewing and distilling, and for making oil, gluten, straw for livestock bedding, livestock feed, hay or silage, newsprint, and other products.

Wheat futures and options are traded at the CME Group, the Mercado a Termino de Buenos Aires (MAT), Sydney Futures Exchange (SFE), London International Financial Futures and Options Exchange (LIFFE), Marche a Terme International de France (MATIF), Budapest Commodity Exchange (BCE), the Kansas City Board of Trade (KCBT), and the Minneapolis Grain Exchange (MGE). The CME's wheat futures contract calls for the delivery of soft red wheat (No. 1 and 2), hard red winter wheat (No. 1 and 2), dark northern spring wheat (No. 1 and 2), No.1 northern spring at 3 cents/bushel premium, or No. 2 northern spring at par.

Prices – CME wheat futures prices (Barchart.com electronic symbol ZW) climbed to a 2-1/2 year high of $5.9250 per bushel in January 2020. Concern about global wheat supplies boosted wheat prices after Russia, the world's largest wheat exporter, proposed to limit wheat export limits through June of 2020 to ensure adequate domestic wheat supplies. Also, the USDA's Foreign Agricultural Service (FAS) in January projected the 2019/20 wheat crop in Australia, the world's fifth-largest wheat exporter, would fall -13% yr/yr to a 12-year low of 15 MMT due to a multi-year drought. Wheat prices then zigzagged lower into Q2-2020 and posted a 1-1/2-year low of $4.6825 per bushel in June. A surge in the dollar to a 4-year high in March weighed on wheat prices as that made U.S. wheat more expensive and less competitive in the global market. The spread of the Covid pandemic in early 2020 forced governments to impose lockdowns that closed restaurants, which undercut wheat demand and weighed on wheat prices. The weak demand boosted wheat inventories, with the USDA in its June WASDE report projecting that global 2020/21 wheat ending stocks would climb +6.0% yr/yr to a record 316.1 MMT. Wheat prices soon recovered after the USDA in June unexpectedly cut its 2020 U.S. wheat acreage estimate to 44.2 million acres, down -2.0% yr/yr. Also, the pandemic prompted countries to boost their wheat imports to secure grain in case there were any Covid-related supply or transportation disruptions. The dollar retreated into year-end and fell to a 2-3/4-year low in December, which bolstered U.S. wheat export prospects. In its December WASDE report, the USDA raised its China 2020/21 wheat import estimate for the fourth consecutive month to 8.5 MMT, the most in more than 25 years. Wheat prices rallied to a 6-year high in December at $6.4450 per bushel and finished 2020 up +14.6% yr/yr at $6.4050 per bushel.

Supply – World wheat production in the 2019/20 marketing year is forecasted to rise +1.1% yr/yr to 772.642 million metric tons, a new record high The world's largest wheat producers in 2020/21 are expected to be the European Union with 17.6% of world production, China with 17.4%, India with 13.9%, Russia with 11.0%, and the U.S. with 6.4%. China's wheat production in 2020/21 is expected to rise +0.5% yr/yr to 134.250 million metric tons, but still a little down from the 2017/18 record high of 134.334. India's wheat production in 2020/21 is expected to rise by +3.9% yr/yr to a record high of 107.592 million metric tons. The world land area harvested with wheat in 2020/21 is expected to rise +2.5% yr/yr to 222.3 million hectares (1 hectare equals 10,000 square meters or 2.471 acres). World wheat yield in 2020/21 is expected to fall -1.6% yr/yr to 3.47 million metric tons, down from the 2019/29 record high of 3.52.

U.S. wheat production in 2020/21 is expected to fall by -4.3% yr/yr to 1.837 billion bushels, which would be below the record crop of 2.785 billion bushels seen in 1981/82. The U.S. winter wheat crop in 2020 fell -11.1% yr/yr to 1.171 billion bushels, which was well below the record winter wheat crop of 2.097 billion bushels seen in 1981. U.S. production of durum wheat in 2020 rose by +27.5% yr/yr to 68.808 million bushels. U.S. production of other spring wheat in 2020 rose +4.4% yr/yr to 585.990 million bushels. The largest U.S. producing states of winter wheat in 2020 were Kansas with 25.1% of U.S. production, Washington with 10.4%, Oklahoma with 9.7%, Montana with 6.4%, and Texas with 5.4%. U.S. farmers planted 45.158 million acres of wheat in 2020, which was down -2.0% yr/yr. U.S. wheat yield in 2020/21 is expected to be down by -3.9% yr/yr to 49.7 bushels per acre, remaining below the 2016/17 record high of 52.7 bushels per acre.

Demand – World wheat utilization in 2020/21 is forecasted to rise +0.4% yr/yr to 750.9 million metric tons, a new record high. U.S. consumption of wheat in 2019/20 is expected to rise +1.4% yr/yr to 1.111 billion bushels, which would be below the 2012/13 record high of 1.389 billion bushels. The wheat usage breakdown in 2020/21 is expected to be 86.4% for food, 9.2% for feed and residuals, and 5.5% for seed.

Trade – World trade in wheat in 2020/21 is expected to fall by -1.0% yr/yr to 189.4 million metric tons. U.S. exports of wheat in 2020/21 are expected to rise by +1.0% yr/yr to 975.0 million bushels but remain below the record high of 1.771 billion bushels seen in 1981/82. U.S. imports of wheat in 2020/21 are expected to rise +23.8% yr/yr at 130.0 million bushels and remain below the 2013/14 record high of 172.5 million bushels.

World Production of Wheat In Thousands of Metric Tons

Crop Year	Australia	Canada	China	European Union	India	Iran	Kazakhstan	Pakistan	Russia	Turkey	Ukraine	United States	World Total
2011-12	29,905	25,288	118,625	138,182	86,874	12,400	22,732	25,214	56,240	18,800	22,324	54,244	698,721
2012-13	22,856	27,246	122,540	133,949	94,882	13,800	9,841	23,473	37,720	16,000	15,761	61,298	660,556
2013-14	25,303	37,589	123,710	144,583	93,506	14,000	13,941	24,211	52,091	18,750	22,278	58,105	716,590
2014-15	23,743	29,442	128,321	156,912	95,850	13,000	12,996	25,979	59,080	15,250	24,750	55,147	730,420
2015-16	22,275	27,647	132,639	160,480	86,527	14,500	13,748	25,086	61,044	19,500	27,274	56,117	738,220
2016-17	31,819	32,140	133,271	145,369	87,000	14,500	14,985	25,633	72,529	17,250	26,791	62,832	756,502
2017-18	20,941	30,377	134,334	151,125	98,510	14,000	14,802	26,600	85,167	21,000	26,981	47,380	762,792
2018-19[1]	17,598	32,352	131,430	136,579	99,870	14,500	13,947	25,100	71,685	19,000	25,057	51,306	730,899
2019-20[2]	15,200	32,670	133,590	154,510	103,600	16,800	11,452	24,300	73,610	17,500	29,171	52,581	763,905
2020-21[3]	30,000	35,183	134,250	135,800	107,592	16,750	12,500	25,700	85,300	18,250	25,500	49,691	772,642

[1] Preliminary. [2] Estimate. [3] Forecast. *Source: Foreign Agricultural Service, U.S. Department of Agriculture (FAS-USDA)*

World Supply and Demand of Wheat In Millions of Metric Tons/Hectares

Year	Area Harvested	Yield	Production	World Trade	Utilization Total	Ending Stocks	Stocks as a % of Utilization
2011-12	221.2	3.16	698.7	157.6	690.8	201.6	29.2
2012-13	216.2	3.06	660.6	138.1	679.4	182.6	26.9
2013-14	220.0	3.26	716.6	165.9	697.4	201.7	28.9
2014-15	221.3	3.30	730.4	164.2	705.4	226.8	32.2
2015-16	224.0	3.30	738.1	172.6	715.9	249.0	34.8
2016-17	222.4	3.40	756.3	183.5	738.2	267.1	36.2
2017-18	218.6	3.49	763.0	182.6	741.8	288.3	38.9
2018-19[1]	215.4	3.39	731.0	173.6	735.3	284.0	38.6
2019-20[2]	216.9	3.52	764.0	191.4	748.2	299.8	40.1
2020-21[3]	222.3	3.47	770.5	189.4	750.9	319.4	42.5

[1] Preliminary. [2] Estimate. [3] Forecast. *Source: Foreign Agricultural Service, U.S. Department of Agriculture (FAS-USDA)*

Salient Statistics of Wheat in the United States

Year	Planting Intentions	Acreage Harvested: Winter	Acreage Harvested: Spring	Acreage Harvested: All	Average All Yield Per Acre in Bushels	Value of Production $1,000	Foreign Trade[5]: Domestic Exports[2]	Foreign Trade[5]: Imports[3]	Per Capita[4] Consumption: Flour	Per Capita[4] Consumption: Cereal
	1,000 Acres						In Millions of Bushels		In Pounds	
2011-12	54,409	32,314	13,391	45,705	43.7	14,322,909	1,051.1	113.1	133.0	----
2012-13	55,294	34,609	14,149	48,758	46.2	17,383,149	1,012.1	124.3	134.0	----
2013-14	56,236	32,650	12,672	45,332	47.1	14,604,442	1,176.2	172.5	135.0	----
2014-15	56,841	32,299	14,086	46,385	43.7	11,914,954	864.3	151.2	----	----
2015-16	54,999	32,346	14,972	47,318	43.6	10,018,323	777.8	112.8	----	----
2016-17	50,116	20,235	13,613	43,848	52.7	9,179,190	1,050.9	118.0	----	----
2017-18	46,052	25,301	12,254	37,555	46.3	8,255,119	905.9	158.0	----	----
2018-19	47,815	24,742	14,870	39,612	47.6	9,661,916	936.1	135.0	----	----
2019-20	45,158	24,592	12,802	37,394	51.7	8,882,766	965.0	105.0	----	----
2020-21[1]	44,250	23,024	13,722	36,746	49.7		975.0	130.0	----	----

[1] Preliminary. [2] Includes flour milled from imported wheat. [3] Total wheat, flour & other products. [4] Civilian only. [5] Year beginning June.
Source: Economic Research Service, U.S. Department of Agriculture (ERS-USDA)

Supply and Distribution of Wheat in the United States In Millions of Bushels

Crop Year Beginning June 1	Supply: Stocks, June 1: On Farms	Supply: Stocks, June 1: Mills, Elevators[3]	Supply: Stocks, June 1: Total Stocks	Supply: Production	Supply: Imports[4]	Supply: Total Supply	Domestic Disappearance: Food	Domestic Disappearance: Seed	Domestic Disappearance: Feed & Residual[5]	Domestic Disappearance: Total	Exports[4]	Total Disappearance
2011-12	130.9	731.3	862.2	1,999.3	113.1	2,969.2	941.4	75.6	158.5	1,175.5	1,051.1	2,226.6
2012-13	112.0	630.6	742.6	2,252.3	124.3	3,119.2	950.8	73.1	365.3	1,389.3	1,012.1	2,401.4
2013-14	120.2	597.7	717.9	2,135.0	172.5	3,025.3	955.1	75.6	228.2	1,258.8	1,176.2	2,435.1
2014-15	97.0	493.3	590.3	2,026.3	151.2	2,767.8	958.3	79.4	113.4	1,151.1	864.3	2,015.4
2015-16	155.2	597.2	752.4	2,061.9	112.8	2,927.1	957.2	67.2	149.4	1,173.8	777.8	1,951.5
2016-17	197.2	778.4	975.6	2,308.7	118.0	3,402.3	948.9	61.3	160.7	1,170.8	1,050.9	2,221.7
2017-18	191.8	988.8	1,180.6	1,739.6	158.0	3,079.5	964.2	63.4	47.2	1,074.7	905.9	1,980.7
2018-19	130.5	968.4	1,098.9	1,885.2	135.0	3,119.1	954.6	58.8	89.8	1,103.2	936.1	2,039.3
2019-20[1]	206.5	873.2	1,079.8	1,920.1	105.0	3,104.9	962.0	60.0	135.0	1,096.0	965.0	2,061.0
2020-21[2]	228.6	799.7	1,028.3	1,837.6	130.0	3,011.0	960.0	61.0	100.0	1,111.0	975.0	2,086.0

[1] Preliminary. [2] Estimate. [3] Also warehouses and all off-farm storage not otherwise designated, including flour mills. [4] Imports & exports are for wheat, including flour & other products in terms of wheat. [5] Mostly feed use.
Source: Economic Research Service, U.S. Department of Agriculture (ERS-USDA)

Stocks, Production and Exports of Wheat in the United States, by Class In Millions of Bushels

Year	Hard Spring Stocks June 1	Hard Spring Production	Hard Spring Exports[3]	Durum[2] Stocks June 1	Durum[2] Production	Durum[2] Exports[3]	Hard Winter Stocks June 1	Hard Winter Production	Hard Winter Exports[3]	Soft Red Winter Stocks June 1	Soft Red Winter Production	Soft Red Winter Exports[3]	White Stocks June 1	White Production	White Exports[3]
2011-12	185	396	243	35	47	27	387	783	397	171	453	165	85	314	219
2012-13	151	503	233	25	82	29	317	998	382	185	413	194	64	257	175
2013-14	165	491	246	23	58	32	343	747	446	124	568	283	63	271	170
2014-15	169	556	274	22	54	37	237	739	272	113	455	134	50	224	147
2015-16	212	568	254	26	84	29	294	830	227	154	359	120	67	221	147
2016-17	272	491	319	28	104	25	446	1,082	453	157	345	91	74	286	163
2017-18	235	384	229	36	55	18	589	750	373	215	293	91	105	259	194
2018-19	191	587	259	35	78	22	581	662	331	205	286	128	87	272	197
2019-20	263	522	268	55	54	42	516	833	376	158	239	92	88	272	187
2020-21[1]	280	530	270	43	62	30	521	695	410	280	530	85	95	274	180

[1] Preliminary. [2] Includes "Red Durum." [3] Includes four made from U.S. wheat & shipments to territories.
Source: Economic Research Service, U.S. Department of Agriculture (ERS-USDA)

Seeded Acreage, Yield and Production of all Wheat in the United States

Year	Seed Acreage - 1,000 Acres: Winter	Other Spring	Durum	All	Yield Per Harvested Acre (Bushels): Winter	Other Spring	Durum	All	Production (Million Bushels): Winter	Other Spring	Durum	All
2011	40,646	12,394	1,369	54,409	46.2	37.7	38.5	43.7	1,493.7	455.2	50.5	1,999.3
2012	40,897	12,259	2,138	55,294	47.1	44.9	38.4	46.2	1,630.4	540.4	81.5	2,252.3
2013	43,230	11,606	1,400	56,236	47.3	47.1	43.3	47.1	1,542.9	534.1	58.0	2,135.0
2014	42,409	13,025	1,407	56,841	42.6	46.7	40.2	43.7	1,377.2	595.0	54.1	2,026.3
2015	39,681	13,367	1,951	54,999	42.5	46.3	43.5	43.6	1,374.7	603.2	84.0	2,061.9
2016	36,149	11,555	2,412	50,116	55.3	47.3	44.0	52.7	1,672.6	532.2	103.9	2,308.7
2017	32,726	11,019	2,307	46,052	50.2	41.0	26.0	46.3	1,270.3	415.9	54.8	1,739.6
2018	32,542	13,200	2,073	47,815	47.9	48.3	39.5	47.6	1,183.9	623.2	78.0	1,885.2
2019	31,159	12,660	1,339	45,158	53.6	48.2	45.7	51.7	1,317.0	561.1	54.0	1,920.1
2020[1]	30,550	12,200	1,500	44,250	51.1	49.0	42.8	50.1	1,171.0	586.0	68.8	1,837.6

[1] Preliminary. *Source: Economic Research Service, U.S. Department of Agriculture (ERS-USDA)*

Production of Winter Wheat in the United States, by State In Thousands of Bushels

Year	Colorado	Idaho	Illinois	Kansas	Missouri	Montana	Nebraska	Ohio	Oklahoma	Oregon	Texas	Washington	US Total
2011	78,000	63,140	46,665	276,500	34,000	89,790	65,250	49,300	70,400	63,525	49,400	129,750	1,493,677
2012	68,200	59,200	40,960	382,200	39,440	84,630	53,300	30,600	154,800	51,810	95,700	116,900	1,630,387
2013	40,750	63,640	56,280	321,100	56,145	81,700	39,900	44,800	105,400	48,360	68,150	115,230	1,542,902
2014	89,300	58,400	44,890	246,400	42,920	91,840	71,050	40,330	47,600	40,700	67,500	85,280	1,377,216
2015	81,030	58,220	33,800	321,900	32,330	91,020	45,980	32,160	98,800	34,545	106,500	89,040	1,374,690
2016	105,120	66,740	34,780	467,400	39,900	105,350	70,740	44,800	136,500	35,500	89,600	130,260	1,672,582
2017	86,860	53,600	35,720	333,600	36,720	66,780	46,920	34,040	98,600	43,470	68,150	120,450	1,270,282
2018	70,200	61,200	36,960	277,400	30,680	78,500	49,490	33,750	70,000	46,565	56,000	125,400	1,183,939
2019	98,000	59,160	36,850	338,000	24,570	95,000	55,290	21,560	110,000	49,640	69,700	119,000	1,316,963
2020[1]	46,500	61,640	34,000	294,400	24,570	75,400	36,550	34,080	113,400	43,070	63,000	122,100	1,171,022

[1] Preliminary. *Source: Crop Reporting Board, U.S. Department of Agriculture (CRB-USDA)*

Official Winter Wheat Crop Production Reports in the United States In Thousands of Bushels

Crop Year	May 1	June 1	July 1	August 1	September 1	Current December	Final
2011-12	1,424,357	1,450,115	1,491,739	1,497,429	----	----	1,493,677
2012-13	1,693,710	1,683,667	1,670,346	1,682,726	----	----	1,630,387
2013-14	1,485,757	1,509,142	1,543,095	1,542,605	----	----	1,542,902
2014-15	1,402,505	1,381,060	1,367,432	1,396,742	----	----	1,377,216
2015-16	1,471,802	1,505,072	1,455,516	1,438,278	----	----	1,374,690
2016-17	1,427,084	1,506,626	1,627,664	1,657,440	----	----	1,672,582
2017-18	1,246,392	1,250,192	1,279,363	1,287,133	----	----	1,270,282
2018-19	1,191,542	1,197,716	1,192,585	1,189,199	----	----	1,183,939
2019-20	1,268,461	1,274,451	1,290,626	1,326,223	----	----	1,316,963
2020-21[1]	1,254,600	1,265,700	1,217,784	1,198,362	----	----	1,171,022

[1] Preliminary. *Source: Crop Reporting Board, U.S. Department of Agriculture (CRB-USDA)*

Production of All Spring Wheat in the United States, by State In Thousands of Bushels

	Durum Wheat						Other Spring Wheat							
Year	Arizona	California	Montana	North Dakota	South Dakota	Total	Idaho	Minnesota	Montana	North Dakota	Oregon	South Dakota	Washington	Total
2011	7,979	12,535	10,780	18,233	196	50,482	52,080	69,000	74,400	167,750	10,990	37,820	38,130	455,188
2012	9,880	12,720	15,260	42,720	115	81,501	37,240	74,670	95,700	256,500	5,766	41,410	27,775	540,419
2013	7,548	4,900	15,225	29,453	168	57,976	39,270	66,120	104,710	235,290	5,544	51,260	30,300	534,101
2014	8,436	3,150	13,330	28,223	180	54,056	34,580	64,900	104,300	291,650	3,744	71,680	23,180	595,038
2015	15,150	6,695	18,755	42,463	246	84,009	30,450	85,800	78,740	319,200	4,650	60,480	22,860	603,240
2016	9,408	4,042	31,365	58,118	231	103,914	34,365	74,340	75,960	269,100	4,437	47,250	27,030	532,227
2017	8,989	2,484	12,560	28,920	108	54,777	35,275	75,710	48,090	270,050	4,599	20,770	22,050	415,851
2018	7,738	3,515	23,250	42,463	84	77,985	42,275	92,630	95,880	318,010	5,025	40,530	27,810	623,232
2019	3,432	2,244	22,145	25,500	----	53,959	39,160	79,800	102,120	291,550	----	26,015	23,735	561,095
2020/1	5,720	1,980	22,420	30,800	----	68,808	41,820	73,080	114,000	280,800	----	36,675	31,110	585,990

[1] Preliminary. *Source: Crop Reporting Board, U.S. Department of Agriculture (CRB-USDA)*

Stocks of All Wheat in the United States In Thousands of Bushels

	On Farms				Off Farms				Total Stocks			
Year	Mar. 1	June 1	Sept. 1	Dec. 1	Mar. 1	June 1	Sept. 1	Dec. 1	Mar. 1	June 1	Sept. 1	Dec. 1
2011	288,010	130,915	633,000	405,400	1,137,292	731,331	1,513,669	1,257,318	1,425,302	862,246	2,146,669	1,662,718
2012	217,100	112,030	572,900	399,500	982,245	630,590	1,531,837	1,271,079	1,199,345	742,620	2,104,737	1,670,579
2013	236,970	120,150	555,000	398,400	997,860	597,739	1,314,637	1,076,451	1,234,830	717,889	1,869,637	1,474,851
2014	237,530	96,995	713,450	472,800	819,435	493,288	1,193,770	1,056,830	1,056,965	590,283	1,907,220	1,529,630
2015	278,710	155,170	650,200	503,450	861,697	597,224	1,446,889	1,242,457	1,140,407	752,394	2,097,089	1,745,907
2016	319,800	197,210	728,200	571,280	1,051,862	778,393	1,816,830	1,506,042	1,371,662	975,603	2,545,030	2,077,322
2017	349,500	191,755	491,800	394,080	1,309,175	988,847	1,774,275	1,479,335	1,658,675	1,180,602	2,266,075	1,873,415
2018	259,310	130,475	632,700	504,280	1,236,131	968,414	1,757,071	1,505,205	1,495,441	1,098,889	2,389,771	2,009,485
2019	367,870	206,545	734,500	519,470	1,225,201	873,216	1,611,025	1,321,305	1,593,071	1,079,761	2,345,525	1,840,775
2020[1]	338,690	228,585	705,050	483,470	1,076,724	799,699	1,452,775	1,190,125	1,415,414	1,028,284	2,157,825	1,673,595

[1] Preliminary. *Source: National Agricultural Statistics Service, U.S. Department of Agriculture (NASS-USDA)*

Stocks of Durum Wheat in the United States In Thousands of Bushels

	On Farms				Off Farms				Total Stocks			
Year	Mar. 1	June 1	Sept. 1	Dec. 1	Mar. 1	June 1	Sept. 1	Dec. 1	Mar. 1	June 1	Sept. 1	Dec. 1
2011	35,700	22,100	34,900	24,500	20,720	13,366	28,828	24,006	56,420	35,466	63,728	48,506
2012	17,900	15,200	43,600	36,700	17,899	10,270	24,842	24,306	35,799	25,470	68,442	61,006
2013	21,400	13,600	42,900	32,800	21,088	9,450	23,465	21,175	42,488	23,050	66,365	53,975
2014	20,700	12,800	38,700	23,900	17,430	8,724	19,121	20,147	38,130	21,524	57,821	44,047
2015	16,200	10,250	44,900	35,700	21,454	15,406	29,146	24,787	37,654	25,656	74,046	60,487
2016	17,700	12,190	65,500	49,200	24,785	15,609	26,386	23,696	42,485	27,799	91,886	72,896
2017	32,400	18,350	33,400	30,700	20,584	17,953	32,756	25,351	52,984	36,303	66,156	56,051
2018	25,800	14,950	51,800	46,700	23,740	19,996	38,260	36,830	49,540	34,946	90,060	83,530
2019	40,600	26,050	49,600	33,200	33,789	28,920	38,773	31,187	74,389	54,970	88,373	64,387
2020[1]	23,500	17,700	43,500	39,000	27,898	24,230	27,517	22,250	51,398	41,930	71,017	61,250

[1] Preliminary. *Source: National Agricultural Statistics Service, U.S. Department of Agriculture (NASS-USDA)*

Wheat Supply and Distribution in Canada, Australia and Argentina In Millions of Metric Tons

	Canada (Year Beginning Aug. 1)					Australia (Year Beginning Oct. 1)					Argentina (Year Beginning Dec. 1)				
	Supply			Disappearance		Supply			Disappearance		Supply			Disappearance	
Crop Year	Stocks Aug. 1	New Crop	Total Supply	Domestic	Exports[3]	Stocks Oct. 1	New Crop	Total Supply	Domestic	Exports[3]	Stocks Dec. 1	New Crop	Total Supply	Domestic	Exports[3]
2010-11	7.7	23.3	31.0	7.5	16.6	5.1	27.4	32.5	5.8	18.6	2.3	17.2	19.5	6.0	9.5
2011-12	7.4	25.3	32.6	9.8	17.4	8.2	29.9	38.1	6.5	24.7	4.1	15.5	19.6	6.0	12.9
2012-13	5.9	27.2	33.2	9.6	19.0	7.1	22.9	29.9	6.7	18.6	0.7	9.3	10.0	6.2	3.6
2013-14	5.1	37.6	42.7	9.5	23.3	4.7	25.3	30.0	7.0	18.6	0.3	10.5	10.8	6.1	2.3
2014-15	10.4	29.4	39.8	9.1	24.2	4.6	23.7	28.3	7.2	16.6	2.5	13.9	16.4	6.4	5.3
2015-16	7.1	27.6	34.7	8.0	22.1	4.7	22.3	26.9	7.1	16.1	4.8	11.3	16.1	5.7	9.6
2016-17	5.2	32.1	37.3	10.7	20.2	3.9	31.8	35.7	7.5	22.6	0.8	18.4	19.2	5.2	13.8
2017-18	6.9	30.4	37.3	9.0	22.0	5.7	20.9	26.7	7.5	13.8	0.2	18.5	18.7	5.6	12.7
2018-19[1]	6.7	32.2	38.9	9.0	24.4	5.5	17.3	22.8	9.2	9.0	0.5	19.5	20.0	6.1	12.2
2019-20[2]	6.0	32.4	38.4	9.9	23.0	5.0	15.2	20.2	8.7	8.0	1.7	19.5	21.2	6.2	13.5

[1] Preliminary. [2] Forecast. [3] Including flour. *Source: Foreign Agricultural Service, U.S. Department of Agriculture (FAS-USDA)*

Quarterly Supply and Disappearance of Wheat in the United States In Millions of Bushels

Crop Year Beginning June 1	Supply				Disappearance: Domestic Use						Ending Stocks		
	Beginning Stocks	Production	Imports[3]	Total Supply	Food	Seed	Feed & Residual	Total	Exports[3]	Total Disappearance	Gov't Owned[4]	Privately Owned[5]	Total Stocks
2010-11	976.0	2,207.0	96.0	3,279.0	930.0	80.0	170.0	1,180.0	1,288.0	2,468.0	----	----	862.0
June-Aug.	976.0	2,207.0	27.0	3,212.0	235.0	2.0	262.0	499.0	266.0	765.0	----	----	2,450.0
Sept.-Nov.	2,450.0	----	24.0	2,473.0	242.0	52.0	-63.0	231.0	310.0	541.0	----	----	1,933.0
Dec.-Feb.	1,933.0	----	23.0	1,956.0	221.0	1.0	-2.0	220.0	311.0	531.0	----	----	1,425.0
Mar.-May	1,425.0	----	22.0	1,448.0	233.0	73.0	-65.0	241.0	401.0	642.0	----	----	862.0
2011-12	862.0	1,993.1	112.1	2,968.2	941.4	75.6	157.4	1,174.4	1,051.2	2,225.6	----	----	742.6
June-Aug.	862.0	1,993.1	20.8	2,876.9	230.0	4.7	200.8	435.5	294.8	730.3	----	----	2,146.7
Sept.-Nov.	2,146.7	----	32.3	2,178.9	244.0	51.0	-16.4	278.5	237.9	516.4	----	----	1,662.5
Dec.-Feb.	1,662.5	----	30.1	1,692.6	230.9	1.4	43.5	275.9	217.4	493.3	----	----	1,199.3
Mar.-May	1,199.3	----	28.9	1,228.2	236.5	18.5	-70.5	184.5	301.1	485.6	----	----	742.6
2012-13	742.6	2,252.3	124.3	3,119.2	950.8	73.1	365.3	1,389.3	1,012.1	2,401.4	----	----	717.9
June-Aug.	742.6	2,252.3	25.5	3,020.4	237.6	1.4	402.7	641.7	263.7	905.3	----	----	2,115.1
Sept.-Nov.	2,115.1	----	32.9	2,148.0	246.6	55.4	-22.4	279.6	197.9	477.5	----	----	1,670.6
Dec.-Feb.	1,670.6	----	34.7	1,705.3	229.0	1.4	4.9	235.3	235.2	470.4	----	----	1,234.8
Mar.-May	1,234.8	----	31.2	1,266.0	237.6	15.0	-19.9	232.8	315.4	548.1	----	----	717.9
2013-14	717.9	2,135.0	172.5	3,025.3	955.1	75.6	228.2	1,258.8	1,176.2	2,435.1	----	----	590.3
June-Aug.	717.9	2,135.0	35.7	2,888.5	234.8	4.1	422.4	661.4	357.5	1,018.9	----	----	1,869.6
Sept.-Nov.	1,869.6	----	48.0	1,917.7	249.3	52.7	-168.0	134.0	308.8	442.8	----	----	1,474.9
Dec.-Feb.	1,474.9	----	42.0	1,516.9	231.1	1.9	-0.8	232.2	227.7	459.9	----	----	1,057.0
Mar.-May	1,057.0	----	46.7	1,103.7	239.9	16.8	-25.4	231.3	282.1	513.4	----	----	590.3
2014-15	590.3	2,026.3	151.2	2,767.8	958.3	79.4	113.4	1,151.1	864.3	2,015.4	----	----	752.4
June-Aug.	590.3	2,026.3	44.2	2,660.8	238.9	6.4	255.7	501.0	252.5	753.5	----	----	1,907.2
Sept.-Nov.	1,907.2	----	34.6	1,941.8	248.2	48.8	-92.6	204.4	207.7	412.1	----	----	1,529.6
Dec.-Feb.	1,529.6	----	36.7	1,566.4	230.8	2.1	7.9	240.9	185.1	426.0	----	----	1,140.4
Mar.-May	1,140.4	----	35.8	1,176.2	240.3	22.1	-57.6	204.8	219.0	423.8	----	----	752.4
2015-16	752.4	2,061.9	112.8	2,927.1	957.1	67.2	149.5	1,173.8	777.8	1,951.5	----	----	975.6
June-Aug.	752.4	2,061.9	26.5	2,840.9	240.2	1.0	297.8	539.0	204.8	743.8	----	----	2,097.1
Sept.-Nov.	2,097.1	----	27.0	2,124.1	248.7	44.2	-107.2	185.8	192.4	378.2	----	----	1,745.9
Dec.-Feb.	1,745.9	----	34.4	1,780.3	229.5	1.7	2.2	233.5	175.2	408.6	----	----	1,371.7
Mar.-May	1,371.7	----	24.9	1,396.5	238.6	20.3	-43.4	215.5	205.5	420.9	----	----	975.6
2016-17	975.6	2,308.7	118.0	3,402.3	948.9	61.3	160.7	1,170.8	1,050.9	2,221.7	----	----	1,180.6
June-Aug.	975.6	2,308.7	32.6	3,316.9	237.6	0.6	265.7	504.0	267.9	771.9	----	----	2,545.0
Sept.-Nov.	2,545.0	----	29.5	2,574.5	245.5	40.6	-30.2	255.8	239.3	495.2	----	----	2,079.4
Dec.-Feb.	2,079.4	----	24.6	2,104.0	227.9	1.3	-13.0	216.2	229.1	445.3	----	----	1,658.7
Mar.-May	1,658.7	----	31.3	1,689.9	237.9	18.7	-61.8	194.8	314.5	509.3	----	----	1,180.6
2017-18	1,180.6	1,740.9	158.0	3,079.5	964.2	63.4	47.2	1,074.7	905.9	1,980.7	----	----	1,098.9
June-Aug.	1,180.6	1,740.9	42.0	2,963.6	238.8	0.9	164.8	404.4	292.4	696.8	----	----	2,266.8
Sept.-Nov.	2,266.8	----	35.9	2,302.7	250.6	40.1	-54.7	235.9	193.3	429.2	----	----	1,873.5
Dec.-Feb.	1,873.5	----	37.8	1,911.3	232.9	1.8	-19.5	215.1	200.8	415.9	----	----	1,495.4
Mar.-May	1,495.4	----	42.2	1,537.7	242.0	20.6	-43.3	219.3	219.5	438.8	----	----	1,098.9
2018-19	1,098.9	1,885.2	134.6	3,118.7	954.5	59.5	87.9	1,101.9	937.0	2,038.9	----	----	1,079.8
June-Aug.	1,098.9	1,885.2	40.9	3,024.9	239.3	2.1	189.2	430.5	204.6	635.2	----	----	2,389.8
Sept.-Nov.	2,389.8	----	31.3	2,421.0	246.5	37.6	-75.1	209.0	202.5	411.6	----	----	2,009.5
Dec.-Feb.	2,009.5	----	32.1	2,041.6	229.2	2.8	-27.4	204.6	243.9	448.5	----	----	1,593.1
Mar.-May	1,593.1	----	30.4	1,623.5	239.5	17.0	1.2	257.7	286.0	543.7	----	----	1,079.8
2019-20[1]	1,079.8	1,932.0	105.0	3,116.8	961.9	60.0	101.2	1,123.0	965.5	2,088.5	----	----	1,028.3
June-Aug.	1,079.8	1,932.0	23.3	3,035.0	238.3	3.6	195.8	437.6	251.9	689.5	----	----	2,345.5
Sept.-Nov.	2,345.5	----	22.9	2,368.4	247.0	37.3	10.2	294.5	233.1	527.6	----	----	1,840.8
Dec.-Feb.	1,840.8	----	28.4	1,869.2	236.2	2.0	-19.1	219.1	234.7	453.8	----	----	1,415.4
Mar.-May	1,415.4	----	30.5	1,445.9	240.4	17.1	-85.7	171.9	245.7	417.6	----	----	1,028.3
2020-21[2]	1,028.3	1,825.8	120.0	2,974.1	965.0	63.0	125.0	1,153.0	985.0	2,138.0	----	----	836.1
June-Aug.	1,028.3	1,825.8	30.2	2,884.3	238.9	1.6	216.1	456.6	270.0	726.5	----	----	2,157.8
Sept.-Nov.	2,157.8	----	28.0	2,185.9	244.1	40.1	-9.1	275.1	237.2	512.3	----	----	1,673.6

[1] Preliminary. [2] Forecast. [3] Imports & exports include flour and other products expressed in wheat equivalent. [4] Uncommitted, Government only. [5] Includes total loans. [6] Includes alcoholic beverages. *Source: Economic Research Service, U.S. Department of Agriculture (ERS-USDA)*

Exports of Wheat (Only)[2] from the United States   In Thousands of Bushels

Year	June	July	Aug.	Sept.	Oct.	Nov.	Dec.	Jan.	Feb.	Mar.	Apr.	May	Total
2011-12	105,733	83,453	100,102	99,523	72,101	61,287	71,503	72,751	69,020	86,759	103,778	104,449	1,030,459
2012-13	88,538	70,378	97,627	92,901	52,669	46,420	61,495	77,006	91,861	103,441	111,234	95,236	988,805
2013-14	94,904	114,879	142,197	151,935	87,681	64,108	73,735	80,725	68,543	77,859	102,988	95,876	1,155,431
2014-15	77,912	73,314	95,989	97,967	58,258	45,692	59,967	51,471	68,363	74,564	74,102	64,539	842,136
2015-16	59,531	60,229	79,422	90,351	44,850	50,968	62,994	51,899	54,281	70,087	65,495	63,676	753,784
2016-17	83,009	75,485	103,642	103,742	63,389	65,452	80,095	60,537	82,555	98,116	98,509	112,397	1,026,928
2017-18	109,687	87,501	89,362	86,496	48,308	54,448	72,945	64,994	58,101	76,469	72,031	66,140	886,482
2018-19	57,363	65,546	76,856	66,047	70,998	60,225	84,023	72,254	82,437	74,980	101,249	104,930	916,907
2019-20	83,330	68,853	94,836	79,886	83,518	64,494	80,655	68,888	80,477	67,209	86,786	86,327	945,258
2020-21[1]	83,890	86,837	93,902	98,665	63,967	69,540							993,604

[1] Preliminary. [2] Grains. *Source: Economic Research Service, U.S. Department of Agriculture (ERS-USDA)*

Wheat Government Loan Program Data in the United States   Loan Rates--Cents Per Bushel

Crop Year Beginning June 1	National Average[3]	Target Rate[4]	Farm Loan Prices: Corn Belt (Soft Red Winter)	Central & Southern Plains (Hard Winter)	Northern Plains (Spring & Durum)	Pacific Northwest (White)	Placed Under Loan	% of Production	Acquired by CCC Under Program	Stocks, May 31: Total Stocks May 31	Total CCC Stocks May 31	Outstanding: CCC Loans	Farmer-Owned Reserve	"Free"
							In Millions of Bushels							
2009-10	275	392	----	----	----	----	103	4.6	0	976	0	----	----	----
2010-11	294	417	----	----	----	----	67	3.0	0	862	0	----	----	----
2011-12	294	417	----	----	----	----	36	1.8	0	743	0	----	----	----
2012-13	294	417	----	----	----	----	28	1.2	0	718	0	----	----	----
2013-14	294	417	----	----	----	----	25	1.2	0	590	0	----	----	----
2014-15	294	550	----	----	----	----	43	2.1	0	752	0	----	----	----
2015-16	294	550	----	----	----	----	81	3.9	0	976	0	----	----	----
2016-17	294	550	----	----	----	----	151	6.5	0.25	1,181	0	----	----	----
2017-18[1]	294	550	----	----	----	----	45	2.6	0	1,099	0	----	----	----
2018-19[2]	294	550	----	----	----	----	65	5.9	0	1,080	0	----	----	----

[1] Preliminary. [2] Estimate. [3] The national average loan rate at the farm as a percentage of the parity-priced wheat at the beginning of the marketing year. [4] 1996-97 through 2001-02 marketing year, target prices not applicable. NA = Not avaliable.
Source: Agricultural Marketing Service, U.S. Department of Agriculture (AMS-USDA)

United States Wheat and Wheat Flour Imports and Exports   In Thousands of Bushels

Crop Year Beginning June 1	Imports: Wheat: Suitable for Milling	Wheat Unfit for Human Consump.	Grain	Flour & Products[2]	Total	Exports: P.L. 480	Foreign Donations Sec. 416	Aid[3]	Total con-cessional	CCC Export Credit	Export Enhance-ment Program	Total U.S. Wheat
			-- Wheat Equivalent --			In Thousands of Metric Tons						
2012-13	96,103	----	96,103	28,214	124,317	----	----	----	----	----	----	----
2013-14	141,665	----	141,665	30,802	172,467	----	----	----	----	----	----	----
2014-15	116,973	----	116,973	34,276	151,246	----	----	----	----	----	----	----
2015-16	76,433	----	76,433	36,381	112,815	----	----	----	----	----	----	----
2016-17	83,777	----	83,777	34,248	118,025	----	----	----	----	----	----	----
2017-18	120,781	----	120,781	37,245	158,027	----	----	----	----	----	----	----
2018-19[1]	98,004	----	98,004	37,006	135,010	----	----	----	----	----	----	----

[1] Preliminary. [2] Includes macaroni, semolina & similar products. [3] Shipment mostly under the Commodity Import Program, financed with foreign aid funds. NA = Not available. *Source: Economic Research Service, U.S. Department of Agriculture (ERS-USDA)*

Comparative Average Cash Wheat Prices   In Dollars Per Bushel

Crop Year June to May	Received by U.S. Farmers	No. 2 Soft Red Winter, Chicago	No 1 Hard Red Ordinary Protein, Kansas City	No 2 Soft Red Winter, St. Louis	Minneapolis: No 1 Dark Northern Spring 14%	Minneapolis: No 1 Hard Amber Durum	No 1 Soft White, Portland, Oregon	No 2 Western White Pacific Northwest	No 2 Soft White, Toledo	Export Prices2 (U.S. $ Per Metric Ton): Australian Standard White	Canada Vancouver No 1 CWRS 13 1/2 %	Argentina F.O.B. B.A.	U.S. Gulf No. 2 Hard Winter	Rotterdam C.I.F. U.S. No 2 Hard Winter
2013-14	6.87	6.52	8.34	6.71	8.82	----	7.26	----	6.38	281	331	327	309	----
2014-15	5.99	5.31	7.04	5.32	8.08	----	6.65	----	5.13	253	285	270	252	----
2015-16	4.89	4.90	5.58	4.60	6.34	----	5.38	----	4.99	218	232	209	187	----
2016-17	3.89	4.06	4.60	4.14	6.28	----	4.79	----	4.09	195	216	191	157	----
2017-18	4.72	4.46	5.58	4.58	7.62	----	5.35	----	4.49	227	260	198	188	----
2018-19	5.16	4.90	6.10	5.12	6.79	----	6.09	----	4.96	275	254	235	212	----
2019-20	4.58	5.28	5.66	5.46	6.39	----	5.99	----	5.34	238	242	232	205	----
2020-21[1]	4.50	5.52	5.89	5.74	6.50	----	5.90	----	5.45	229	251	252	198	----

[1] Preliminary. [2] Calendar year. NA = Not available. *Source: Economic Research Service, U.S. Department of Agriculture (ERS-USDA)*

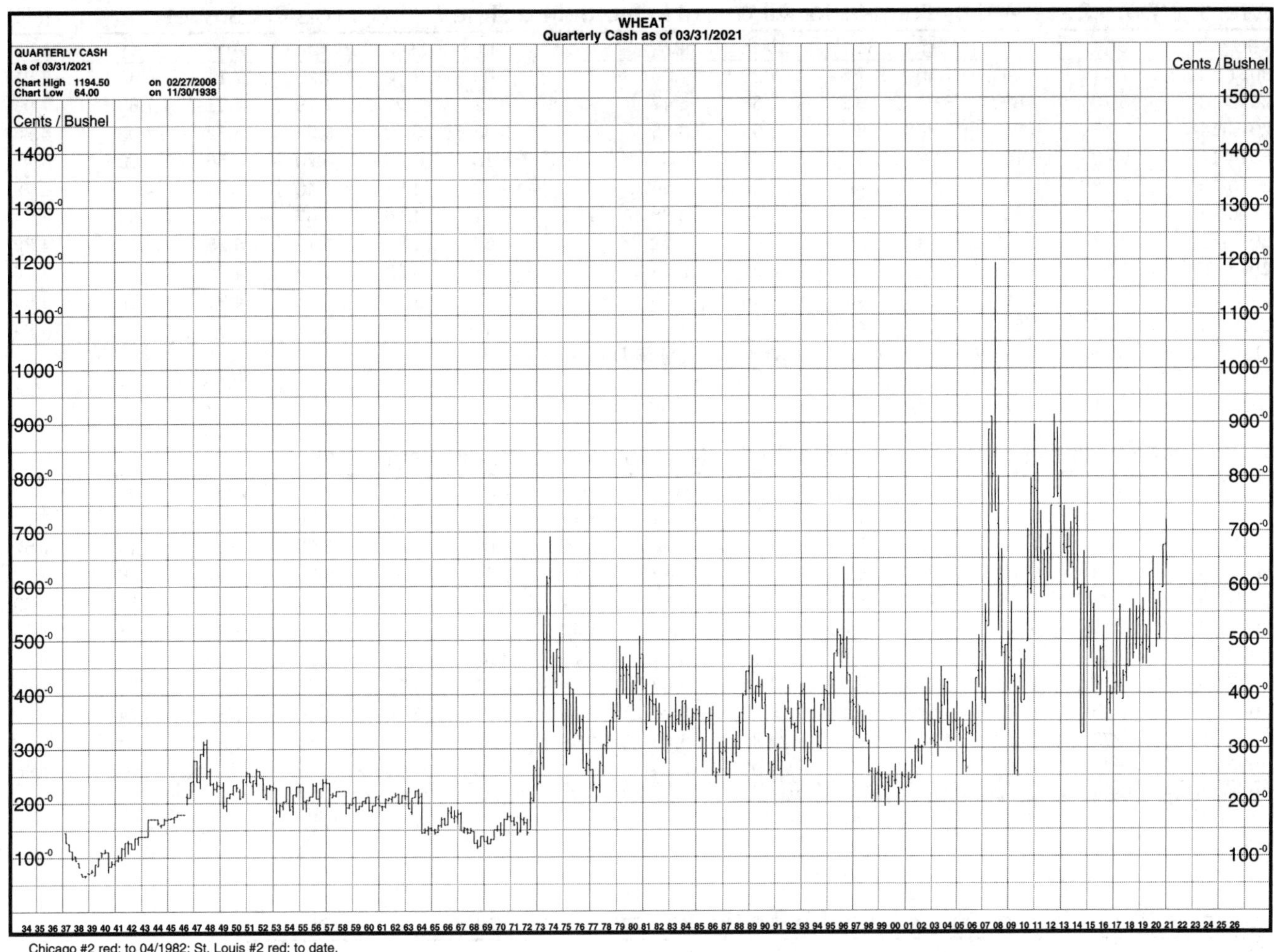

Chicago #2 red: to 04/1982; St. Louis #2 red: to date.

Average Price of No. 2 Soft Red Winter (30 Days) Wheat in Chicago In Dollars Per Bushel

Year	June	July	Aug.	Sept.	Oct.	Nov.	Dec.	Jan.	Feb.	Mar.	Apr.	May	Average
2011-12	6.71	6.54	7.03	6.40	5.96	6.09	5.94	6.23	6.44	6.44	6.24	6.29	6.36
2012-13	6.56	8.57	8.70	8.62	8.49	8.58	8.03	7.69	7.40	7.18	6.97	7.01	7.82
2013-14	6.94	6.60	6.26	6.41	6.77	6.46	6.23	5.86	6.08	6.91	6.91	6.86	6.52
2014-15	5.87	5.30	5.34	4.82	5.04	5.43	6.21	5.56	5.19	5.07	5.02	4.87	5.31
2015-16	5.17	5.40	5.00	4.86	5.02	4.98	4.83	4.75	4.69	4.70	4.71	4.65	4.90
2016-17	4.70	4.12	3.99	3.76	3.82	3.88	3.94	4.16	4.26	4.06	3.93	4.08	4.06
2017-18	4.41	4.96	4.12	4.23	4.22	4.13	4.12	4.27	4.55	4.69	4.74	5.08	4.46
2018-19	4.92	4.98	5.32	4.81	4.88	5.01	5.24	5.20	4.97	4.46	4.43	4.57	4.90
2019-20	5.27	5.12	4.78	4.76	5.05	5.15	5.42	5.86	5.76	5.47	5.51	5.22	5.28
2020-21[1]	5.08	5.25	5.12	5.37	5.94	5.94	5.93						5.52

[1] Preliminary. *Source: Economic Research Service, U.S. Department of Agriculture (ERS-USDA)*

Average Price of No. 1 Hard Red Winter (Ordinary Protein) Wheat in Kansas City In Dollars Per Bushel

Year	June	July	Aug.	Sept.	Oct.	Nov.	Dec.	Jan.	Feb.	Mar.	Apr.	May	Average
2011-12	8.61	8.03	8.63	8.30	7.77	7.74	7.46	7.69	7.59	7.52	7.11	7.24	7.81
2012-13	7.61	9.13	9.43	9.56	9.62	9.73	9.36	9.09	8.70	8.35	8.30	8.53	8.95
2013-14	8.32	8.14	8.12	8.00	8.70	8.44	8.03	7.56	8.04	8.87	8.81	9.01	8.34
2014-15	8.23	7.61	7.33	7.11	7.35	7.20	7.54	6.75	6.44	6.46	6.22	6.18	7.04
2015-16	6.40	6.27	5.70	5.44	5.62	5.55	5.60	5.46	5.28	5.34	5.22	5.08	5.58
2016-17	5.04	4.24	4.15	4.24	4.40	4.64	4.56	4.91	5.04	4.80	4.37	4.80	4.60
2017-18	5.24	5.65	4.80	5.07	5.11	5.30	5.38	5.73	5.93	6.05	6.09	6.56	5.58
2018-19	6.35	6.20	6.61	6.03	6.11	6.18	6.36	6.26	6.02	5.94	5.61	5.50	6.10
2019-20	6.06	5.56	5.11	5.00	5.24	5.54	5.72	5.92	6.59	5.74	5.83	5.63	5.66
2020-21[1]	5.44	5.45	5.24	5.70	6.34	6.48	6.61						5.89

[1] Preliminary. *Source: Economic Research Service, U.S. Department of Agriculture (ERS-USDA)*

Average Price Received by Farmers for All Wheat in the United States In Dollars Per Bushel

Year	June	July	Aug.	Sept.	Oct.	Nov.	Dec.	Jan.	Feb.	Mar.	Apr.	May	Average
2011-12	7.41	7.10	7.59	7.54	7.27	7.30	7.20	7.05	7.10	7.20	7.11	6.67	7.21
2012-13	6.70	7.89	8.04	8.27	8.38	8.47	8.30	8.12	7.97	7.79	7.71	7.68	7.94
2013-14	7.37	6.95	6.88	6.80	6.94	6.85	6.73	6.65	6.50	6.74	6.82	7.08	6.86
2014-15	6.49	6.15	5.97	5.71	5.71	6.04	6.14	6.15	5.89	5.70	5.56	5.33	5.90
2015-16	5.42	5.23	4.84	4.72	4.86	4.86	4.75	4.82	4.61	4.40	4.46	4.45	4.79
2016-17	4.20	3.75	3.68	3.48	3.68	3.88	3.90	4.01	4.16	4.37	4.16	4.05	3.94
2017-18	4.37	4.77	4.84	4.65	4.64	4.72	4.50	4.65	4.92	5.10	5.28	5.39	4.82
2018-19	5.17	5.00	5.31	5.15	5.22	5.23	5.28	5.28	5.33	5.19	4.93	4.78	5.16
2019-20	4.81	4.52	4.34	4.26	4.45	4.39	4.64	4.88	4.88	4.86	4.84	4.76	4.64
2020-21[1]	4.56	4.54	4.55	4.73	4.98	5.24	5.43	5.48					4.94

[1] Preliminary. *Source: Economic Research Service, U.S. Department of Agriculture (ERS-USDA)*

Average Farm Prices of Winter Wheat in the United States In Dollars Per Bushel

Year	June	July	Aug.	Sept.	Oct.	Nov.	Dec.	Jan.	Feb.	Mar.	Apr.	May	Average
2011-12	7.13	6.77	7.27	7.00	6.53	6.44	6.41	6.57	6.68	6.70	6.47	6.42	6.70
2012-13	6.55	7.76	7.92	8.25	8.33	8.38	8.15	8.01	7.85	7.63	7.52	7.49	7.82
2013-14	7.18	6.85	6.81	6.80	7.07	6.96	6.84	6.72	6.58	6.92	7.07	7.26	6.92
2014-15	6.34	5.99	5.90	5.69	5.65	5.87	6.14	6.02	5.70	5.55	5.50	5.19	5.80
2015-16	5.20	5.15	4.80	4.64	4.76	4.66	4.57	4.63	4.47	4.28	4.31	4.28	4.65
2016-17	3.97	3.56	3.41	3.25	3.37	3.41	3.40	3.53	3.77	3.82	3.70	3.77	3.58
2017-18	4.11	4.56	4.27	4.11	4.17	4.07	3.89	4.15	4.63	4.73	4.90	5.05	4.39
2018-19	5.05	4.92	5.24	5.14	5.22	5.20	5.24	5.25	5.40	5.16	4.86	4.74	5.12
2019-20	4.77	4.48	4.28	4.19	4.35	4.35	4.58	4.86	4.98	4.84	4.88	4.84	4.62
2020-21[1]	4.44	4.53	4.51	4.68	4.97	5.34	5.57	5.55					4.95

[1] Preliminary. *Source: Economic Research Service, U.S. Department of Agriculture (ERS-USDA)*

Average Farm Prices of Durum Wheat in the United States In Dollars Per Bushel

Year	June	July	Aug.	Sept.	Oct.	Nov.	Dec.	Jan.	Feb.	Mar.	Apr.	May	Average
2011-12	9.18	10.20	10.20	10.80	9.60	10.30	10.30	8.84	8.98	8.39	9.22	8.95	9.58
2012-13	8.31	8.67	7.76	7.77	7.61	8.11	8.31	8.24	8.19	8.12	8.01	8.06	8.10
2013-14	8.51	8.32	7.73	7.84	7.03	6.72	6.90	7.01	6.43	6.69	6.80	7.21	7.27
2014-15	7.96	8.13	8.03	8.25	8.48	11.00	10.70	9.89	10.10	9.50	7.79	8.02	8.99
2015-16	9.16	8.74	7.28	6.36	6.57	6.97	6.93	6.60	6.08	6.03	6.24	6.57	6.96
2016-17	6.50	6.47	5.66	5.61	5.51	6.00	6.07	5.90	5.71	5.72	5.90	5.82	5.91
2017-18	6.69	6.30	6.89	6.31	6.41	6.55	6.25	6.05	6.19	5.66	5.41	6.02	6.23
2018-19	6.33	5.79	5.05	5.00	4.99	4.72	4.83	4.86	4.72	5.05	4.85	4.92	5.09
2019-20	5.58	5.53	4.67	4.64	4.54	4.17	4.44	4.72	4.96	5.46	5.26	5.27	4.94
2020-21[1]	6.52	6.13	5.59	5.65	5.65	5.82	5.87	5.88					5.89

[1] Preliminary. *Source: Economic Research Service, U.S. Department of Agriculture (ERS-USDA)*

Average Farm Prices of Other Spring Wheat in the United States In Dollars Per Bushel

Year	June	July	Aug.	Sept.	Oct.	Nov.	Dec.	Jan.	Feb.	Mar.	Apr.	May	Average
2011-12	9.26	8.45	8.28	8.09	8.19	8.43	8.25	8.09	8.01	8.04	7.96	7.93	8.25
2012-13	7.78	8.39	8.27	8.38	8.56	8.65	8.48	8.34	8.11	7.95	7.90	7.84	8.22
2013-14	7.72	7.30	6.97	6.71	6.66	6.70	6.55	6.48	6.40	6.56	6.61	6.85	6.79
2014-15	6.60	6.23	5.93	5.51	5.57	5.73	5.80	5.84	5.55	5.53	5.51	5.29	5.76
2015-16	5.20	5.15	4.71	4.68	4.78	4.91	4.80	4.81	4.56	4.47	4.55	4.64	4.77
2016-17	4.61	4.48	4.26	4.22	4.38	4.48	4.66	4.74	4.83	4.86	4.83	4.81	4.60
2017-18	5.35	6.09	5.86	5.62	5.56	5.78	5.62	5.72	5.66	5.74	5.78	5.84	5.72
2018-19	5.66	5.41	5.41	5.16	5.26	5.33	5.36	5.37	5.30	5.23	5.03	4.86	5.28
2019-20	4.79	4.64	4.43	4.35	4.70	4.53	4.79	4.92	4.73	4.82	4.68	4.50	4.66
2020-21[1]	4.47	4.35	4.51	4.73	4.90	5.02	5.18	5.33					4.81

[1] Preliminary. *Source: Economic Research Service, U.S. Department of Agriculture (ERS-USDA)*

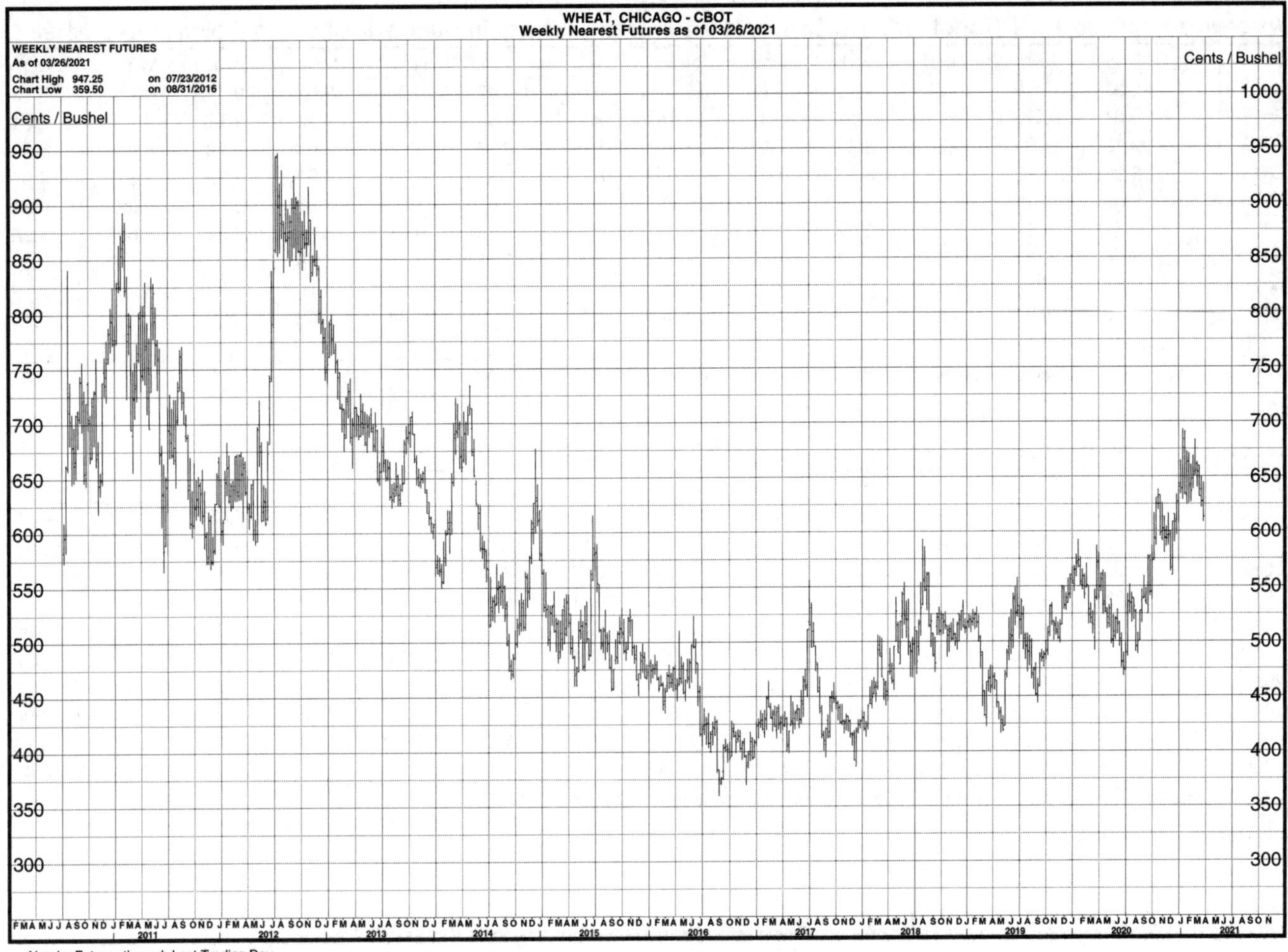

Volume of Trading of Wheat Futures in Chicago In Thousands of Contracts

Year	Jan.	Feb.	Mar.	Apr.	May	June	July	Aug.	Sept.	Oct.	Nov.	Dec.	Total
2011	1,651.7	2,601.4	2,131.8	2,475.9	2,095.9	2,857.2	1,699.9	2,301.0	1,470.5	1,594.4	2,217.0	1,186.8	24,283.3
2012	2,014.0	2,433.7	2,088.5	2,563.3	2,670.7	3,244.9	2,404.1	2,433.4	1,541.6	1,776.4	2,769.4	1,439.5	27,379.4
2013	2,006.5	2,679.0	1,937.3	2,888.9	1,872.7	2,488.8	1,872.6	2,487.0	1,323.5	1,741.4	2,312.0	1,235.7	24,845.5
2014	1,888.8	2,681.9	2,375.1	2,605.2	2,389.1	3,028.9	2,210.8	3,064.6	1,804.6	1,793.2	2,387.5	1,962.5	28,192.3
2015	1,787.2	2,612.3	2,394.8	3,074.8	2,433.3	4,087.8	2,753.5	2,961.6	1,919.4	2,322.0	3,144.4	1,611.0	31,102.0
2016	1,820.7	3,224.7	2,084.5	3,611.5	2,355.1	3,693.2	2,353.2	3,410.3	1,457.6	2,200.7	3,270.0	1,578.1	31,059.7
2017	2,384.5	3,190.9	2,293.9	3,293.2	2,515.3	4,132.5	3,121.2	3,381.6	1,891.5	2,200.8	3,692.9	1,619.4	33,717.8
2018	2,699.7	3,731.2	3,045.3	3,473.5	3,416.5	4,219.7	2,990.5	4,177.6	2,082.6	2,407.8	3,073.7	1,486.9	36,805.2
2019	1,924.5	3,438.2	2,584.2	3,062.6	2,879.6	3,497.9	2,271.6	2,877.3	1,539.8	1,952.4	2,614.6	1,764.3	30,407.1
2020	2,524.0	3,404.0	3,342.7	2,699.6	1,870.2	3,369.4	2,600.7	3,292.5	2,253.8	2,749.4	3,199.5	2,059.6	33,365.3

Contract size = 5,000 bu. *Source: CME Group; Chicago Board of Trade (CBT)*

Average Open Interest of Wheat Futures in Chicago In Contracts

Year	Jan.	Feb.	Mar.	Apr.	May	June	July	Aug.	Sept.	Oct.	Nov.	Dec.
2011	515,137	538,874	482,060	482,702	457,289	451,965	428,043	427,516	411,468	426,188	411,485	376,671
2012	435,379	458,289	446,242	462,078	431,133	425,379	450,423	456,537	450,653	462,690	478,767	444,929
2013	463,359	470,154	457,785	436,052	410,871	414,728	404,821	399,943	358,054	366,743	394,264	396,016
2014	429,507	413,808	350,290	371,767	371,689	389,610	407,989	417,932	400,815	419,886	403,348	372,284
2015	382,618	415,559	426,147	453,404	444,906	432,352	402,961	406,381	372,538	377,775	381,822	351,546
2016	396,301	436,358	430,193	437,750	404,026	411,893	457,192	456,866	460,023	483,899	494,269	445,295
2017	473,794	458,494	463,099	508,045	445,294	441,396	430,971	452,301	433,612	486,843	551,386	521,674
2018	546,304	499,112	481,428	477,365	489,652	514,394	472,514	483,532	460,995	500,521	493,664	435,278
2019	450,353	467,963	494,051	479,684	469,294	412,885	371,636	380,149	358,914	396,981	392,793	385,505
2020	476,950	499,412	397,950	364,502	368,140	405,629	387,116	380,385	380,499	430,462	434,387	388,969

Contract size = 5,000 bu. *Source: CME Group; Chicago Board of Trade (CBT)*

Average Price of No. 1 Dark Northern Spring (14% Protein) Wheat in Minneapolis In Dollars Per Bushel

Year	June	July	Aug.	Sept.	Oct.	Nov.	Dec.	Jan.	Feb.	Mar.	Apr.	May	Average
2011-12	12.97	11.16	10.21	9.80	9.80	10.61	9.69	9.43	9.53	9.62	9.63	9.11	10.13
2012-13	9.31	10.12	9.71	9.82	10.17	10.15	9.83	9.43	9.33	9.17	9.11	9.15	9.61
2013-14	9.18	8.57	8.36	8.22	8.78	8.40	8.64	9.32	9.03	9.64	8.72	8.95	8.82
2014-15	9.00	8.66	8.18	8.48	8.12	8.50	8.22	7.37	7.51	7.91	7.39	7.62	8.08
2015-16	7.56	7.12	6.16	6.15	6.44	6.49	6.25	6.05	5.93	5.84	6.11	6.02	6.34
2016-17	6.11	5.74	5.87	5.62	6.48	6.32	6.64	6.75	6.58	6.33	6.34	6.60	6.28
2017-18	7.66	8.64	7.64	7.18	7.36	7.66	7.40	7.41	7.68	7.58	7.57	7.66	7.62
2018-19	7.14	6.86	6.72	6.48	6.76	7.02	6.77	6.79	7.17	7.19	6.33	6.23	6.79
2019-20	6.59	6.22	5.90	6.24	6.54	6.98	6.76	5.82	6.54	6.58	6.22	6.32	6.39
2020-21[1]	6.66	6.16	6.14	6.73	6.82								6.50

[1] Preliminary. *Source: Economic Research Service, U.S. Department of Agriculture (ERS-USDA)*

Average Price of No. 2 Soft Red Winter Wheat in Toledo, OH In Dollars Per Bushel

Year	June	July	Aug.	Sept.	Oct.	Nov.	Dec.	Jan.	Feb.	Mar.	Apr.	May	Average
2011-12	6.75	6.73	7.28	6.61	6.09	6.07	6.04	6.45	6.69	6.58	6.38	6.30	6.50
2012-13	6.62	8.70	8.69	8.59	8.40	8.38	7.91	7.40	7.10	7.00	6.87	6.91	7.71
2013-14	6.75	6.50	6.32	6.32	6.61	6.29	6.01	5.60	5.91	6.73	6.78	6.74	6.38
2014-15	5.89	5.41	4.65	3.65	5.13	5.44	6.19	5.54	4.45	5.17	5.08	4.92	5.13
2015-16	5.22	5.58	5.20	5.04	5.25	5.16	4.97	4.93	4.69	4.61	4.63	4.61	4.99
2016-17	4.69	4.22	4.03	3.72	3.90	3.92	3.80	4.09	4.28	4.14	4.08	4.19	4.09
2017-18	4.44	4.94	4.20	4.27	4.24	4.18	4.04	4.22	4.54	4.75	4.85	5.24	4.49
2018-19	5.15	5.20	5.48	5.04	5.04	5.00	5.14	5.12	4.95	4.48	4.43	4.50	4.96
2019-20	5.42	5.28	4.99	4.99	5.26	5.31	5.54	5.78	5.62	5.41	5.35	5.07	5.34
2020-21[1]	4.95	5.28	5.14	5.43	5.93	5.74	5.67						5.45

[1] Preliminary. *Source: Economic Research Service, U.S. Department of Agriculture (ERS-USDA)*

Average Price of No. 1 Soft White Wheat in Portland, OR In Dollars Per Bushel

Year	June	July	Aug.	Sept.	Oct.	Nov.	Dec.	Jan.	Feb.	Mar.	Apr.	May	Average
2011-12	7.45	6.75	6.92	6.75	6.25	6.05	5.93	6.27	6.98	7.07	7.03	6.87	6.69
2012-13	6.97	8.53	8.69	8.77	8.75	8.87	8.56	8.53	8.59	8.16	7.93	7.71	8.34
2013-14	----	7.23	7.32	7.17	7.27	7.04	6.97	6.78	7.20	7.55	7.65	7.65	7.26
2014-15	6.99	6.69	6.88	6.75	6.79	7.00	7.19	6.52	6.49	6.36	6.23	5.94	6.65
2015-16	----	----	5.55	5.38	5.49	5.37	----	5.31	5.30	----	5.33	5.34	5.38
2016-17	5.46	5.07	4.89	4.77	4.65	4.64	4.57	4.63	4.74	4.70	4.61	4.77	4.79
2017-18	4.91	5.40	5.13	5.19	5.30	5.26	5.22	5.30	5.39	5.64	5.63	5.79	5.35
2018-19	5.92	5.88	6.18	5.98	6.11	6.25	6.23	6.29	6.36	6.10	5.94	5.83	6.09
2019-20	5.94	5.96	5.76	5.83	5.99	5.96	5.96	6.22	6.24	6.02	6.06	5.94	5.99
2020-21[1]	5.86	5.78	5.42	5.73	----	6.20	6.42						5.90

[1] Preliminary. *Source: Economic Research Service, U.S. Department of Agriculture (ERS-USDA)*

Average Producer Price Index of Wheat Flour (Spring[2]) June 1983 = 100

Year	Jan.	Feb.	Mar.	Apr.	May	June	July	Aug.	Sept.	Oct.	Nov.	Dec.	Average
2011	212.0	228.4	211.8	226.5	225.2	219.5	217.0	224.1	224.8	216.1	216.5	207.8	219.1
2012	206.8	216.4	219.2	219.7	214.3	214.4	231.2	226.5	232.0	232.4	236.4	233.8	223.6
2013	231.0	223.5	219.6	220.6	229.1	230.2	226.0	219.8	218.4	225.5	220.1	218.4	223.5
2014	223.3	224.9	235.6	229.5	234.8	225.5	225.7	218.8	231.5	225.3	225.6	230.5	227.6
2015	213.4	214.5	214.5	210.5	212.2	216.1	214.3	193.5	189.1	192.6	191.2	196.3	204.9
2016	194.3	192.1	193.5	193.4	195.2	195.1	186.3	183.8	183.8	187.9	186.4	186.2	189.8
2017	188.9	189.2	184.5	181.1	187.4	194.5	215.4	197.9	194.0	193.1	197.1	193.1	193.0
2018	194.8	193.0	196.0	196.4	197.0	197.9	193.3	196.5	191.8	193.1	193.8	193.5	194.8
2019	192.4	193.5	191.8	190.4	188.1	194.3	192.4	185.2	182.9	191.0	192.1	192.3	190.5
2020[1]	195.6	193.3	192.7	193.4	191.3	192.4	192.2	189.5	190.2	191.1	194.2	196.3	192.7

[1] Preliminary. [2] Standard patent. *Source: Bureau of Labor Statistics, U.S. Department of Commerce (BLS) (0212-0301)*

World Wheat Flour Production (Monthly Average) In Thousands of Metric Tons

Year	Australia	France	Germany	Hungary	India	Japan	Kazak-hstan	Korea, South	Mexico	Poland	Russia	Turkey	United Kingdom
2009	----	449.5	429.1	59.2	195.1	379.9	255.0	150.7	249.3	143.2	774.1	349.7	----
2010	----	461.9	458.0	NA	212.5	401.0	NA	160.5	257.5	122.6	746.7	371.4	----
2011	----	443.8	446.7	----	215.0	408.9	----	159.9	266.8	118.3	753.5	399.1	----
2012	----	NA	453.5	----	NA	404.8	----	161.9	266.5	124.5	735.1	374.6	----
2013	----	----	465.3	----	----	403.1	----	156.9	277.2	125.4	759.4	407.5	----
2014	----	----	487.3	----	----	403.0	290.6	163.6	277.6	125.4	738.0	455.6	----
2015	----	----	498.1	----	----	404.7	287.8	167.0	260.6	129.7	758.1	552.2	----
2016	----	----	510.4	----	----	403.0	308.3	170.3	254.7	134.3	745.4	544.2	----
2017[1]	----	----	508.7	----	----	406.1	309.1	171.0	270.2	147.2	704.0	596.2	----
2018[2]	----	----	503.7	----	----	399.3	339.1		283.6	146.3	684.8	429.8	----

[1] Preliminary. [2] Estimate. NA = Not available. *Source: United Nations (UN)*

United States Wheat Flour Exports (Grain Equivalent[2]) In Thousands of Bushels

Year	June	July	Aug.	Sept.	Oct.	Nov.	Dec.	Jan.	Feb.	Mar.	Apr.	May	Total
2011-12	1,099	863	1,771	1,104	1,021	1,182	736	766	727	1,115	817	1,529	12,731
2012-13	1,264	1,885	1,619	1,790	1,241	1,027	987	1,080	1,147	928	781	1,505	15,252
2013-14	1,626	975	836	1,005	1,218	986	1,173	955	807	954	1,141	1,140	12,816
2014-15	955	1,214	1,067	1,301	1,182	1,430	1,096	1,057	1,283	1,524	1,062	1,315	14,486
2015-16	1,222	1,225	1,208	1,431	1,466	1,491	1,521	1,457	1,085	1,685	1,303	1,467	16,562
2016-17	1,711	1,338	1,399	1,672	1,872	1,774	1,469	1,624	1,430	1,288	1,191	1,574	18,344
2017-18	1,463	1,438	1,664	915	716	873	1,072	935	1,136	1,162	1,094	1,367	13,833
2018-19	1,371	945	1,097	1,016	1,624	1,191	1,250	1,282	1,267	1,172	1,167	1,105	14,485
2019-20	1,057	1,198	1,284	1,227	1,327	1,141	993	1,142	1,163	1,265	1,291	1,168	14,255
2020-21[1]	1,211	1,163	1,250	1,074	1,086	1,228	1,086	983					13,624

[1] Preliminary. [2] Includes meal, groats and durum. *Source: Economic Research Service, U.S. Department of Agriculture (ERS-USDA)*

Supply and Distribution of Wheat Flour in the United States

Year	Wheat Ground	Milfeed Production	Flour Production[3]	Flour & Product Imports[2]	Total Supply	Exports: Flour	Exports: Products	Domestic Disap-pearance	Total Population July 1	Per Capita Disap-pearance
	1,000 Bu.	1,000 Tons	In 1,000 Cwt.						Millions	Pounds
2010	901,843	6,480	417,396	11,206	428,602	7,004	3,930	417,667	309.8	134.8
2011	895,255	6,402	411,745	11,698	423,443	6,309	3,615	413,519	312.2	132.5
2012	921,853	6,637	420,365	11,991	432,356	5,997	3,894	422,465	314.5	134.3
2013	919,830	6,367	424,550	12,281	436,831	5,274	3,755	427,803	316.8	135.0
2014	921,264	6,423	424,949	13,859	438,808	5,303	3,664	429,841	319.2	134.7
2015	923,641	6,641	424,910	14,753	439,663	6,376	3,567	429,720	323.0	133.0
2016	914,635	6,559	423,846	15,038	438,884	7,368	2,973	428,543	323.1	132.6
2017	917,816	6,447	426,399	14,843	441,242	6,212	2,777	432,253	325.1	132.9
2018	918,373	6,458	426,871	15,569	442,440	5,693	2,723	434,024	326.9	132.8
2019[1]	912,609	6,485	422,277	15,718	437,995	5,864	2,601	429,530	328.6	130.7

[1] Preliminary. [2] Commercial production of wheat flour, whole wheat, industrial and durum flour and farina reported by Bureau of Census.
Source: Economic Research Service, U.S. Department of Agriculture (ERS-USDA)

Wheat and Flour Price Relationships at Milling Centers in the United States In Dollars

	At Kansas City					At Minneapolis				
		Wholesale Price of		Total Products			Wholesale Price of		Total Products	
Year	Cost of Wheat to Produce 100 lb. Flour[1]	Bakery Flour 100 lb. Flour[2]	By-Products Obtained 100 lb. Flour[3]	Actual	Over Cost of Wheat	Cost of Wheat to Produce 100 lb. Flour[1]	Bakery Flour 100 lb. Flour[2]	By-Products Obtained 100 lb. Flour[3]	Actual	Over Cost of Wheat
2012-13	21.29	19.92	3.62	23.53	2.25	21.91	19.46	4.06	23.52	1.61
2013-14	19.20	19.23	2.70	21.93	2.73	20.17	19.17	2.79	21.96	1.78
2014-15	16.16	17.24	1.91	19.15	2.99	19.35	18.75	1.86	20.61	1.37
2015-16	13.16	14.00	1.61	15.61	2.45	14.00	14.34	1.28	15.62	1.17
2016-17	12.74	13.14	1.35	14.49	1.75	14.32	14.51	.65	15.16	.84
2017-18	15.33	15.51	1.79	17.31	1.97	17.38	17.24	.73	17.96	.59
2018-19	14.41	15.40	1.96	17.37	2.96	15.57	15.28	.79	16.06	.48
2019-20	14.11	14.31	2.07	16.38	2.26	14.58	14.63	.91	15.55	.96
June-Aug.	13.82	14.85	1.58	16.43	2.61	14.21	14.47	.79	15.26	1.05
Sept.-Nov.	14.02	13.62	2.22	15.84	1.82	15.01	14.38	.99	15.38	.36

[1] Based on 73% extraction rate, cost of 2.28 bushels: At Kansas City, No. 1 hard winter 13% protein; and at Minneapolis, No. 1 dark northern spring, 14% protein. [2] quoted as mid-month bakers' standard patent at Kansas City and spring standard patent at Minneapolis, bulk basis. [3] Assumed 50-50 millfeed distribution between bran and shorts or middlings, bulk basis. *Source: Agricultural Marketing Service, U.S. Department of Agriculture*

Wool

Wool is light, warm, absorbs moisture, and is resistant to fire. Wool is also used for insulation in houses, for carpets and furnishing, and for bedding. Sheep are sheared once a year and produce about 4.3 kg of "greasy" wool per year.

Greasy wool is wool that has not been washed or cleaned. Wool fineness is determined by fiber diameter, which is measured in microns (one-millionth of a meter). Fine wool is softer, lightweight, and produces fine clothing. Merino sheep produce the finest wool.

Wool futures and options are traded on the Sydney Futures Exchange (SFE), where there are futures and options contracts on greasy wool, and futures on fine wool and broad wool. All three futures contracts call for the delivery of merino combing wool. Wool yarn futures are traded on the Chubu Commodity Exchange (CCE), the Osaka Mercantile Exchange (OME), and the Tokyo Commodity Exchange (TOCOM).

Prices – Average monthly wool prices at U.S. mills in 2020 fell by -46.3% yr/yr to $3.09 per pound, down from the 2018 record high of $6.04 per pound. The value of U.S. wool production in 2019 rose +6.1% yr/yr to $45.364 million, but still below the 2011 record high of $48.925 million.

Supply – World production of wool has been falling in the past decade due to the increased use of polyester fabrics. Greasy wool world production in 2019 fell -4.7% yr/yr to 1.720 million metric tons. The world's largest producers of greasy wool in 2019 were China with 19.8% of world production, followed by Australia with 19.1%, and New Zealand with 7.1%. U.S. wool production of 10.580 metric tons in 2019 accounted for only 0.6% of world production.

Trade – U.S. exports of domestic wool in 2018 rose +11.3% yr/yr to 12.250 million pounds. U.S. imports in 2018 fell -10.2% to 3.050 million pounds.

World Production of Wool, Greasy In Metric Tons

Year	Argentina	Australia	China	Kazakhstan	New Zealand	Pakistan	Romania	Russia	South Africa	United Kingdom	United States	Uruguay	World Total
2010	54,000	349,788	386,768	37,635	176,300	42,000	20,457	53,521	43,489	65,468	13,776	34,700	2,019,653
2011	48,000	368,992	443,981	38,455	163,700	42,500	19,026	52,575	41,365	67,500	13,286	34,700	2,089,996
2012	42,000	351,919	437,119	38,437	165,000	43,000	19,713	55,253	39,904	68,000	12,428	36,000	2,022,468
2013	44,000	358,854	471,111	37,638	159,548	43,600	----	54,651	43,902	67,571	12,247	36,224	2,055,757
2014	45,483	350,546	459,564	37,779	152,543	44,100	----	56,409	45,200	67,232	12,111	35,604	2,033,475
2015	46,000	363,824	413,134	38,025	147,803	44,600	----	55,644	49,788	67,854	12,270	32,778	1,992,794
2016	42,700	354,991	411,642	38,518	140,518	45,100	----	56,006	54,187	68,762	11,816	32,845	1,967,523
2017	42,400	376,967	410,523	38,980	134,267	45,700	----	56,733	41,602	69,318	11,204	32,133	1,965,244
2018[1]	40,424	385,945	356,607	39,166	128,248	45,843	----	55,471	42,203	69,887	11,068	31,420	1,804,938
2019[2]	42,000	328,608	341,120	39,492	122,227	45,444	----	50,211	41,899	70,467	10,891	30,707	1,719,876

[1] Preliminary. [2] Estimate. NA = Not avaliable. *Source: Food and Agriculture Organization of the United Nations (FAO-UN)*

Average Wool Prices[1] of Australian 64's, Type 62, Duty Paid at U.S. Mills In Dollars Per Pound

Year	Jan.	Feb.	Mar.	Apr.	May	June	July	Aug.	Sept.	Oct.	Nov.	Dec.	Average
2011	5.17	5.44	5.86	6.37	6.43	7.42	7.13	6.49	6.10	5.62	4.50	6.24	6.06
2012	6.35	6.67	6.68	6.35	6.07	5.76	5.78	5.36	5.17	5.33	5.42	5.89	5.90
2013	5.87	5.95	5.84	5.38	5.17	5.09	4.71	4.67	4.79	5.45	5.37	4.89	5.27
2014	5.18	5.06	4.86	4.92	5.04	4.98	5.02	4.86	4.79	4.71	4.68	4.56	4.89
2015	4.34	4.27	4.21	4.34	4.90	5.17	4.64	4.62	4.30	4.28	4.43	4.55	4.50
2016	4.53	4.65	4.72	4.89	4.80	4.86	5.17	5.23	5.06	4.99	4.90	4.94	4.90
2017	5.14	5.16	5.28	5.10	5.23	5.40	5.48	5.97	5.77	5.70	5.81	5.96	5.50
2018	6.60	6.86	6.85	6.92	7.26	7.95	7.67	7.70	7.47	7.23	7.08	7.17	7.23
2019	7.38	7.72	7.54	7.45	7.11	6.82	6.60	5.34	5.36	5.44	5.53	5.50	6.48
2020	5.66	5.88	4.88	4.32	4.00	4.06	3.98	3.52	3.30	3.74	4.10	4.19	4.30

[1] Raw, clean basis. *Source: Economic Research Service, U.S. Department of Agriculture (ERS-USDA)*

United States Imports[2] of Unmanufactured Wool (Clean Yield) In Thousands of Pounds

Year	Jan.	Feb.	Mar.	Apr.	May	June	July	Aug.	Sept.	Oct.	Nov.	Dec.	Total
2011	857.1	451.2	564.5	681.2	698.5	503.3	1,046.5	1,306.0	1,590.9	1,168.2	635.5	404.2	9,907.1
2012	711.7	968.1	1,018.9	880.7	919.9	944.7	715.9	536.0	779.2	693.8	610.2	416.4	9,195.5
2013	457.3	251.4	358.7	819.7	909.1	891.0	796.5	889.8	437.1	919.6	458.2	430.8	7,619.2
2014	597.6	379.1	348.3	583.8	868.5	553.2	707.7	718.8	544.0	967.5	403.5	420.5	7,092.5
2015	504.8	800.1	420.0	657.0	765.2	585.8	681.5	619.8	404.9	664.2	527.1	655.5	7,285.9
2016	564.6	321.8	600.5	942.4	514.6	746.8	419.2	229.9	330.1	300.3	488.1	568.8	6,027.1
2017	488.1	490.8	747.9	706.3	427.9	552.7	341.0	627.6	486.6	357.7	283.0	171.7	5,681.3
2018	279.8	281.0	485.3	624.8	416.8	383.4	629.0	591.4	550.5	443.1	449.3	328.9	5,463.3
2019	271.8	784.0	1,158.3	787.8	1,241.1	590.6	380.1	497.4	254.9	622.1	667.5	248.0	7,503.6
2020[1]	623.4	299.1	933.0	650.5	281.2	291.1	296.1	368.7	963.7	483.9	397.0	348.8	5,936.5

[1] Preliminary. [2] Data are imports for consumption. *Source: Economic Research Service, U.S. Department of Agriculture (ERS-USDA)*

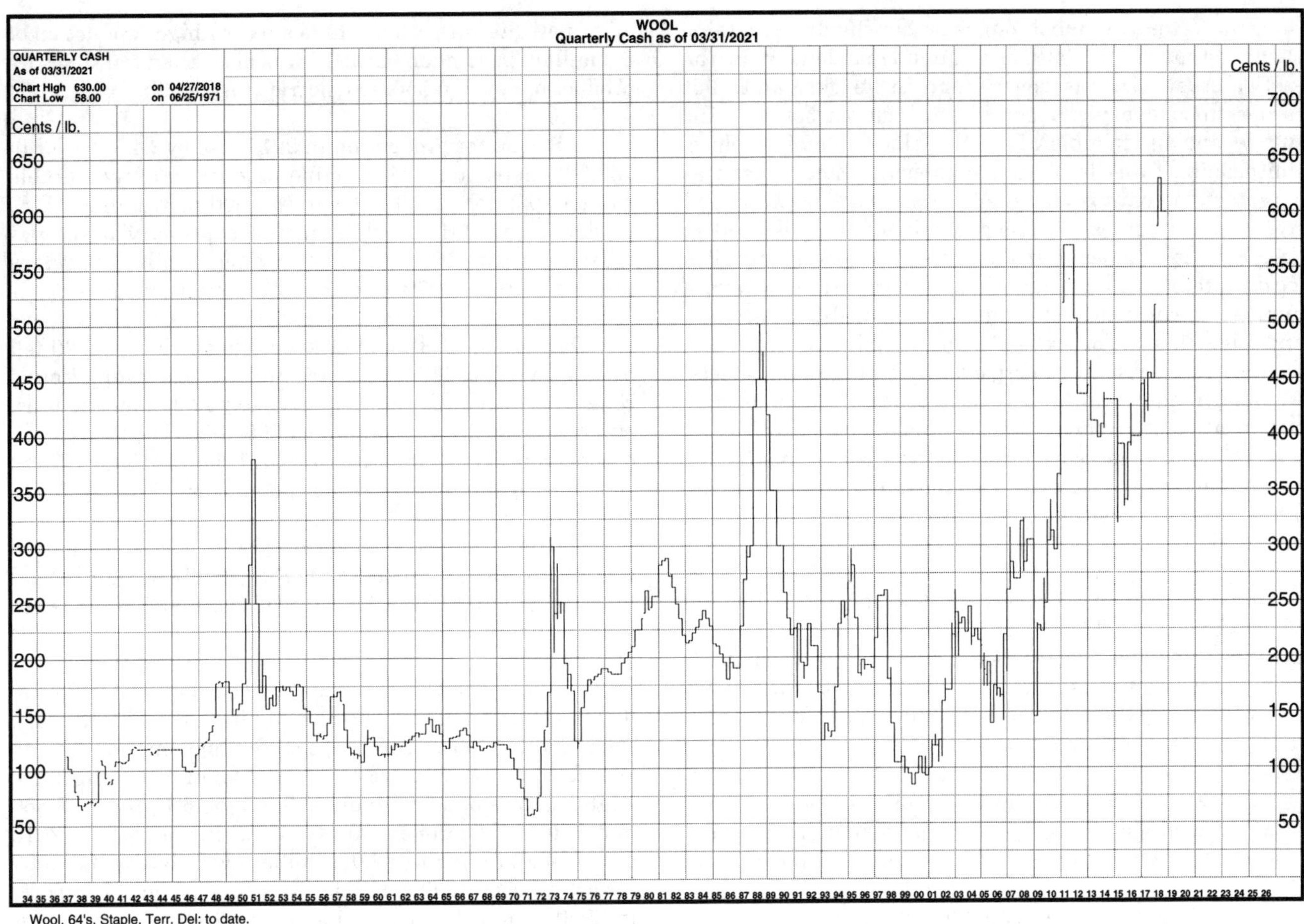

Wool, 64's, Staple, Terr. Del: to date.

Salient Statistics of Wool in the United States

Year	Sheep & Lambs Shorn[4] (1,000's)	Weight per Fleece (In Lbs.)	Shorn Wool Production (1,000 Lbs.)	Price per Lb.	Value of Production ($1,000)	Shorn Wool Support (Cents Per Lb.)	Shorn Payment Rate (Cents Per Lb.)	Raw Wool (Clean Content): Total Wool Production	Domestic Production	Domestic Wool Exports	Dutiable Imports for Consumption[3] (48's & Finer)	Total New Supply[2]	Duty Free Raw Imports (Not Finer than 46's)	Mill Consumption: Apparel	Mill Consumption: Carpet
								In Thousands of Pounds							
2012	3,750	7.30	27,400	152.0	41,595	115	40.0	27,630	14,467	7,741	4,564	15,841	4,551	----	----
2013	3,700	7.30	26,990	145.0	39,209	115	40.0	26,990	14,256	9,998	3,858	11,857	3,746	----	----
2014	3,680	7.30	26,680	146.0	38,909	115	40.0	26,680	14,200	7,918	3,917	13,247	3,363	----	----
2015	3,675	7.40	27,015	145.0	39,205	115	40.0	27,015	14,300	7,847	3,980	13,718	3,321	----	----
2016	3,585	7.30	26,050	145.0	37,721	115	40.0	26,050	13,800	7,826	3,909	12,015	2,178	----	----
2017	3,435	7.20	24,810	148.0	36,774	115	40.0	24,700	13,100	11,000	3,396	7,779	2,285	----	----
2018	3,372	7.20	24,400	175.0	42,772				13,000	12,000				----	----
2019[1]	3,320	7.20	24,010	189.0	45,364									----	----

[1] Preliminary. [2] Production minus exports plus imports; stocks not taken into consideration. [3] Apparel wool includes all dutiable wool; carpet wool includes all duty-free wool. [4] Includes sheep shorn at commercial feeding yards.
Source: Economic Research Service, U.S. Department of Agriculture (ERS-USDA)

Shorn Wool Prices In Dollars Per Pound

Year	US Farm Price Shorn Wool Greasy Basis[1] (cents/Lb)	Australian Offering Price, Clean[2]: Grade 70's type 61	Grade 64's type 63	Grade 62's type 64	Grade 60/62's type 64A	Grade 58's-56's 433-34	Market Indicator[3] (Cents/Kg.)	Graded Territory Shorn Wool, Clean Basis[4]: 62's Staple 3"& up	60's Staple 3"& up	58's Staple 3 1/4"& up	56's Staple 3 1/4"& up	54's Staple 3 1/2"& up
		In Dollars Per Pound						In Dollars Per Pound				
2012	152.0	5.77	5.90	5.98	5.78	5.66	NA	2.81	1.65	3.46	NA	NA
2013	145.0	5.59	5.34	5.39	5.24	3.69	1,073	4.23	3.36	3.01	2.17	NA
2014	146.0	5.03	4.89	4.91	4.80	3.39	1,046	4.17	3.44	3.00	2.47	2.21
2015	145.0	4.71	4.50	4.54	4.38	3.58	1,198	3.58	3.15	3.04	2.63	2.39
2016	145.0	5.19	4.89	4.98	4.79	3.69	1,293	3.94	3.22	3.21	2.43	2.36
2017	148.0	6.67	5.50	5.84	5.13	3.80	1,540	4.36	3.57	3.24	2.36	NA
2018	175.0	7.70	7.23	7.37	7.04	4.62	1,908	6.04	4.85	4.43	4.18	NA
2019	189.0	6.60	6.50	6.47	6.53	4.29	1,740	5.75	5.04	3.90	3.54	NA

[1] Annual weighted average. [2] F.O.B. Australian Wool Corporation South Carolina warehouse in bond. [3] Index of prices of all wool sold in Australia for the crop year July-June. [4] Wool principally produced in Texas and the Rocky Mountain States.
Source: Economic Research Service, U.S. Department of Agriculture (ERS-USDA)

Zinc

Zinc (atomic symbol Zn) is a bluish-white metallic element that is the 24th most abundant element in the earth's crust. Zinc is never found in its pure state but rather in zinc oxide, zinc silicate, zinc carbonate, zinc sulfide, and also in minerals such as zincite, hemimorphite, smithsonite, franklinite, and sphalerite. Zinc is used as a protective coating for other metals, such as iron and steel, in a process known as galvanizing. Zinc is used as an alloy with copper to make brass, and also as an alloy with aluminum and magnesium. There are, however, a number of substitutes for zinc in chemicals, electronics, and pigments. For example, for aluminum, steel and plastics can substitute for galvanized aluminum sheets. Aluminum alloys can also replace brass. Zinc is used as the negative electrode in dry cell (flashlight) batteries and also in the zinc-mercuric-oxide battery cell, which is the round, flat battery typically used in watches, cameras, and other electronic devices. Zinc is also used in medicine as an antiseptic ointment.

Zinc futures and options are traded on the London Metals Exchange (LME). The LME zinc futures contract calls for the delivery of 25 metric tons of at least 99.995% purity zinc ingots (slabs and plates). The contract trades in terms of U.S. dollars per metric ton. Zinc first started trading on the LME in 1915.

Prices – Zinc prices in 2020 fell -10.7% yr/yr to a monthly average of 111.05 cents per pound, remaining below the 2006 record high of 158.44 cents per pound.

Supply – World smelter production of zinc in 2017 was unchanged at 13.800 million metric tons, at the previous year's record high. The world's largest producer of zinc is China, with 44.5% of world smelter production, followed by Canada with 4.4%, Japan with 3.8%, Spain with 3.7%, and Australia with 3.3%. China's record-high production of 6.3 million metric tons in 2016 was more than ten times its production level of 550,000 metric tons seen in 1990.

U.S. smelter production in 2017 rose by +4.8% yr/yr to 132,000 metric tons. U.S. mine production of recoverable zinc in 2020 fell -7.7% yr/yr to 691,900 metric tons. U.S. production in 2017 of slab zinc on a primary basis was unchanged at 135,000 metric tons, while secondary production rose +2.7% yr/yr to 30,100 metric tons.

Demand – U.S. consumption of slab zinc in 2020 fell by -8.4% yr/yr to 860,000 metric tons. U.S. consumption of refined zinc in 2020 fell -9.3 yr/yr to 847,300 metric tons, still below the 2014 record high of 965,000. The breakdown of consumption by industries for 2017 showed that 87.5% of slab zinc consumption was for galvanizers, 5.8% for brass products, and the rest for other miscellaneous industries. The consumption breakdown by grades for 2017 showed that 49.2% was for re-melt and other, 29.4% was for special high grade, 16.9% was for high grade, and 3.8% was for prime western.

Trade – The U.S. in 2020 relied on imports for 83% of its consumption of zinc, up sharply from the 35% average seen in the 1990s. U.S. imports for consumption of slab zinc fell by -14.5% yr/yr to 710,000 metric tons in 2020, while imports of zinc ore in 2013 fell -58.5% yr/yr to 2,550 metric tons. The dollar value of U.S. zinc imports in 2015 fell by -8.0% yr/yr to $2.072 billion, well below the 2007 record high of $3.091 billion. The breakdown of imports in 2020 shows that most zinc is imported as blocks; pigs and slabs (700,400 metric tons); ores (120.000 metric tons); dust, powder, and flakes (272 metric tons); dross, ashes, and fume (20,600 metric tons); and sheets, plates, other (4,200 metric tons).

Salient Statistics of Zinc in the United States In Metric Tons

	Slab Zinc Production			Imports for Consumption		Exports		Consumption				
Year	Primary	Secondary	Mine Production Recovered	Slab Zinc	Ore (Zinc Content)	Slab Zinc	Ore (Zinc Content)	Slab Zinc	Consumed as Ore	All Classes[3]	Net Import Reliance As a % of Apparent Consump	High-Grade, Price -Cents/Lb.-
2011	110,000	138,000	769,000	716,000	26,700	18,400	653,000	939,000	----	----	74	106.24
2012	114,000	147,000	738,000	655,000	6,140	14,200	591,000	902,000	----	----	71	95.80
2013	106,000	127,000	784,000	713,000	2,550	11,500	669,000	935,000	----	----	75	95.60
2014	110,000	70,000	831,000	805,000	2	19,800	644,000	965,000	----	----	81	107.10
2015	145,000	52,800	825,000	771,000	----	13,000	708,000	931,000	----	----	81	95.50
2016	135,000	29,300	805,000	713,000	----	47,000	597,000	792,000	----	----	84	101.40
2017	135,000	30,100	774,000	729,000	----	33,000	682,000	829,000	----	----	84	139.30
2018			824,000	775,000	----	23,000	806,000	868,000	----	----	87	141.00
2019[1]			753,000	830,000	----	5,000	796,000	939,000	----	----	88	124.10
2020[2]			670,000	710,000	----	2,000	560,000	860,000	----	----	83	109.00

[1] Preliminary. [2] Estimate. [3] Based on apparent consumption of slab zinc plus zinc content of ores and concentrates and secondary materials used to make zinc dust and chemicals. *Source: U.S. Geological Survey (USGS)*

World Smelter Production of Zinc[3] In Thousands of Metric Tons

Year	Australia	Belgium	Canada	China	France	Germany	Italy	Japan	Kazak-hstan	Mexico	Spain	United States	World Total
2008	505.0	239.0	764.3	4,000.0	117.9	292.3	100.0	615.5	365.6	305.4	456.1	286.0	11,700
2009	531.0	14.0	685.5	4,290.0	161.0	153.0	100.0	540.6	327.9	385.4	515.0	203.0	11,400
2010	499.0	260.0	691.2	5,210.0	163.0	165.0	105.0	574.0	318.9	327.7	480.1	249.0	12,900
2011	507.3	282.0	662.2	5,212.2	164.0	170.0	100.0	544.7	319.8	322.1	489.1	248.0	13,100
2012	498.3	250.0	648.6	4,890.0	161.0	169.4	100.0	571.0	319.8	323.6	489.5	261.0	12,600
2013	498.3	252.0	651.6	5,310.0	152.0	166.0	267.6	587.3	320.2	322.8	490.5	233.0	13,200
2014	481.6	262.0	649.2	5,780.0	171.0	168.0	155.0	583.0	324.9	320.9	491.3	180.0	13,500
2015	489.0	260.0	683.1	5,886.0	169.0	173.0	158.2	566.6	323.8	326.6	493.8	172.0	13,700
2016[1]	464.2	236.0	691.4	6,270.0	149.0	168.0	186.0	533.8	301.3	321.2	495.0	126.0	13,800
2017[2]	459.1	249.0	608.4	6,144.0	166.0	175.0	190.0	524.9	329.2	327.0	510.0	132.0	13,800

[1] Preliminary. [2] Estimate. [3] Secondary metal included. *Source: U.S. Geological Survey (USGS)*

Consumption (Reported) of Slab Zinc in the United States, by Industries and Grades In Metric Tons

		By Industries					By Grades			
Year	Total	Galvanizers	Brass Products	Zinc-Base Alloy[3]	Zinc Oxide	Other	Special High Grade	High Grade	Remelt and Other	Prime Western
2008	433,000	262,000	107,000	23,200	[4]	40,600	195,000	60,400	75,800	102,000
2009	306,000	226,000	45,500	17,900	[4]	17,200	170,000	46,600	55,000	34,600
2010	475,000	369,000	45,800	35,000	----	25,100	205,000	91,900	121,684	56,500
2011	604,000	496,000	40,400	40,400	----	27,600	177,000	111,000	237,233	78,000
2012	806,000	685,000	49,700	44,700	----	26,500	255,000	138,000	357,455	55,300
2013	428,000	369,000	24,900	24,200	----	9,660	105,000	85,200	208,038	30,300
2014	403,000	340,000	25,600	33,000	----	4,460	101,000	97,900	182,185	21,200
2015	433,000	367,000	27,400	34,300	----	4,710	126,000	78,200	210,260	18,800
2016[1]	462,000	397,000	26,900	34,000	----	4,190	136,000	78,200	227,337	21,100
2017[2]	536,000	469,000	29,000	33,900	----	4,540	189,000	89,200		20,200

[1] Preliminary. [2] Estimated. [3] Die casters. [4] Included in other. W = Withheld. NA = Not applicable. *Source: U.S. Geological Survey (USGS)*

United States Foreign Trade of Zinc In Metric Tons

	Imports for Consumption							Zinc Ore & Manufactures Exported						
								Blocks, Pigs, Anodes, etc.	Wrought & Alloys					
Year	Ores[3]	Blocks, Pigs, Slabs	Sheets, Plates, Other	Waste & Scrap	Dross, Ashes, Fume	Dust, Powder & Flakes	Total Value $1,000	Un-wrought	Un-wrought Alloys	Sheets, Plates & Strips	Angles, Bars, Rods, etc.	Waste & Scrap	Dust (Blue Powder)	Zinc Ore & Con-centrates
2011	26,600	716,000	3,650	18,500	14,400	30,100	2,023,910	19,000	13,500	8,730	25,700	85,600	15,600	660,000
2012	6,140	655,000	2,920	20,000	23,200	28,200	1,684,190	14,100	17,900	6,040	17,700	90,500	14,200	592,000
2013	2,550	713,000	3,570	21,000	13,000	24,500	1,787,320	11,500	23,200	6,500	8,580	87,500	10,700	670,000
2014	2	805,000	4,090	24,900	8,590	31,700	2,252,374	19,800	27,100	6,710	10,000	71,400	10,400	644,000
2015	22	771,000	3,680	18,000	5,610	29,100	2,072,026	12,700	19,700	8,010	15,400	55,200	12,300	708,000
2016	60	713,000	3,650	11,300	3,770	27,800		49,792	16,194	6,960	8,101	30,091	12,753	604,000
2017	6,780	730,000	3,690	11,100	6,350	27,100		32,700	14,500	7,670	9,110	33,600	12,800	688,000
2018	31,000	774,700	5,410	12,900	4,300	26,600		23,300	21,800	7,170	10,600	40,400	13,500	789,790
2019[1]	120,000	829,500	19	272	1,250	12,900		21,800	10,600	8,300	7,170	179	40,400	868,500
2020[2]		700,400	4,300	115,000	26,600	272		10,600	7,170	23,900	8,300	60,200	179	548,190

[1] Preliminary. [2] Estimate. [3] Zinc content. *Source: U.S. Geological Survey (USGS)*

Mine Production of Recoverable Zinc in the United States In Thousands of Metric Tons

Year	Jan.	Feb.	Mar.	Apr.	May	June	July	Aug.	Sept.	Oct.	Nov.	Dec.	Total
2011	69.5	54.9	62.1	59.3	66.2	57.9	70.0	63.6	60.0	55.4	58.5	67.8	743.0
2012	58.0	57.5	58.4	60.4	60.2	54.7	58.4	56.8	60.2	55.8	65.1	68.2	713.0
2013	64.1	54.5	56.0	63.2	65.8	61.3	61.7	67.2	66.7	68.0	68.8	68.7	761.0
2014	67.9	67.8	70.6	69.5	63.3	61.2	64.6	65.6	66.4	63.2	71.3	75.0	803.0
2015	67.3	63.6	72.4	68.5	74.5	70.4	62.5	65.9	58.4	58.9	59.6	56.9	781.0
2016	54.3	55.9	68.6	66.8	67.1	68.9	59.0	67.1	66.0	68.6	54.2	52.6	777.0
2017	58.2	50.5	60.0	62.3	53.7	53.4	64.9	71.3	62.9	73.7	72.2	62.5	748.0
2018	63.9	55.5	51.9	65.7	69.5	74.9	74.7	68.3	70.5	79.1	56.5	77.0	807.5
2019	71.6	43.3	46.1	73.2	67.7	70.3	70.4	65.1	66.1	57.8	50.3	57.2	739.1
2020[1]	56.0	58.8	60.1	38.2	47.0	47.6	57.9	75.0	59.9	59.9	59.5	62.0	681.9

[1] Preliminary. *Source: U.S. Geological Survey (USGS)*

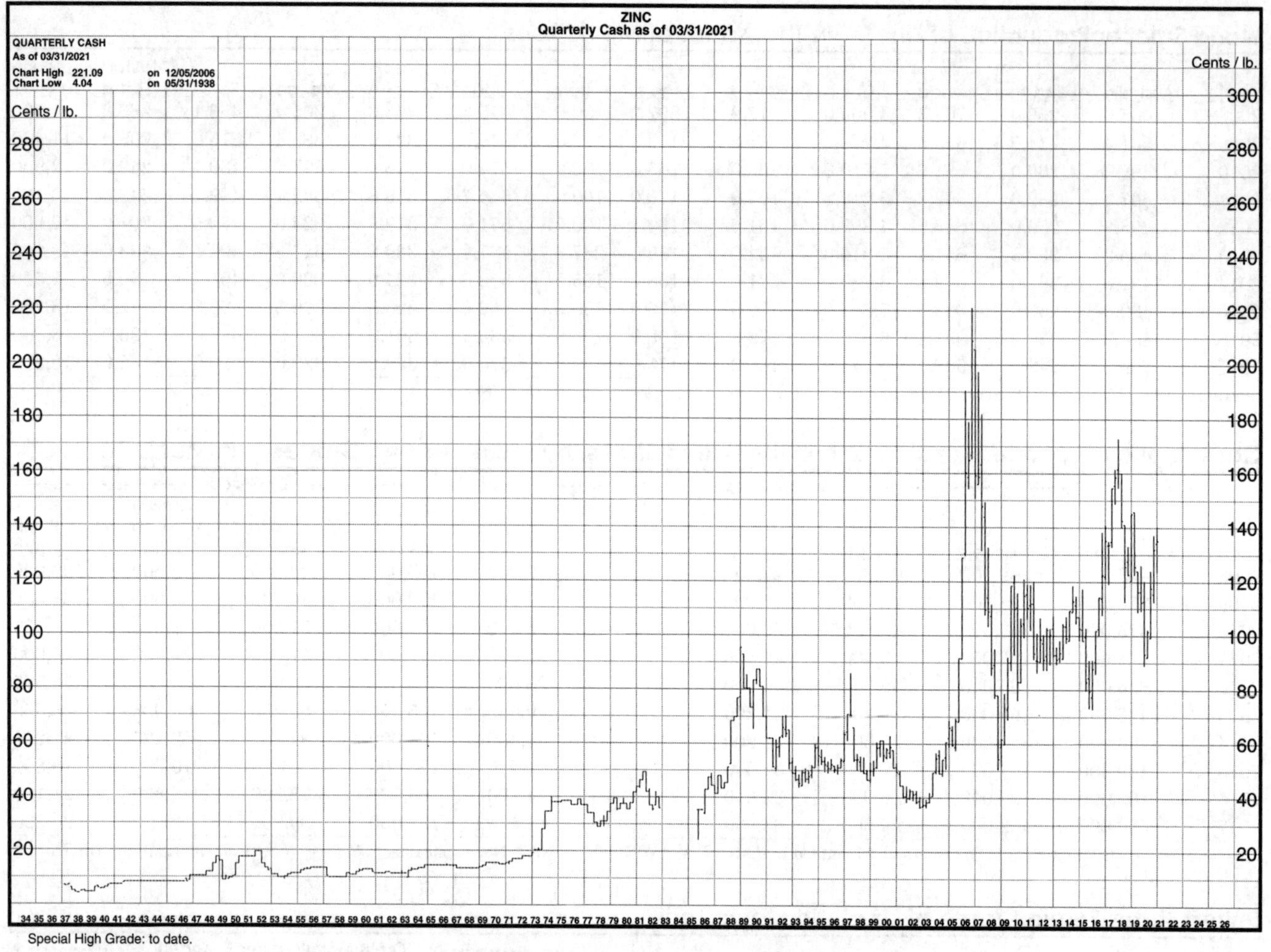

Average Price of Zinc, Prime Western Slab (Delivered U.S. Basis) In Cents Per Pound

Year	Jan.	Feb.	Mar.	Apr.	May	June	July	Aug.	Sept.	Oct.	Nov.	Dec.	Average
2011	112.47	116.61	111.76	112.83	104.86	108.12	115.41	107.26	101.03	91.28	94.18	94.73	105.88
2012	97.62	101.31	99.99	98.01	95.19	91.62	91.32	89.77	98.67	94.43	94.32	100.33	96.05
2013	100.21	104.53	95.62	92.04	91.25	91.88	92.18	95.47	93.11	93.86	93.40	98.17	95.14
2014	101.35	101.41	100.58	101.54	102.75	105.78	113.91	114.56	112.82	112.02	111.17	107.09	107.08
2015	104.08	103.48	100.33	108.09	112.42	102.59	98.49	89.77	85.54	86.07	79.26	76.02	95.51
2016	75.65	84.61	88.64	90.59	91.48	98.21	105.64	110.08	110.30	111.42	122.23	127.26	101.34
2017	129.14	135.58	134.68	128.04	126.96	125.45	135.06	144.21	150.02	157.19	155.18	153.34	139.57
2018	164.74	169.02	157.64	153.85	147.33	149.04	129.11	122.68	119.08	129.99	126.18	127.68	141.36
2019	124.85	131.63	138.27	142.02	133.68	126.46	119.18	111.66	113.84	119.36	119.36	111.58	124.32
2020	115.12	104.53	94.90	94.38	97.53	99.89	106.60	117.67	119.37	118.98	129.02	134.63	111.05

Source: American Metal Market (AMM)

Consumption of Refined Zinc in the United States In Thousands of Metric Tons

Year	Jan.	Feb.	Mar.	Apr.	May	June	July	Aug.	Sept.	Oct.	Nov.	Dec.	Total
2011	76.3	67.1	83.2	72.1	67.4	87.2	61.8	74.2	73.4	95.0	69.0	87.2	939.0
2012	73.1	71.4	72.9	77.0	77.4	85.2	71.7	74.6	71.7	77.1	71.5	78.6	904.0
2013	77.6	77.1	77.3	98.4	78.9	76.7	75.2	138.0	85.1	78.9	68.5	80.7	934.0
2014	106.0	62.4	69.2	86.7	116.0	69.3	70.6	92.3	72.2	62.4	79.3	79.2	965.0
2015	73.2	60.9	73.8	73.9	116.0	92.5	66.2	98.2	69.5	66.3	70.4	68.5	931.0
2016	----	41.2	63.2	56.7	95.5	60.3	69.8	67.4	72.7	68.9	73.5	64.8	789.0
2017	106.0	57.8	96.1	76.7	64.3	65.3	52.1	56.7	57.6	66.5	50.5	74.8	829.0
2018	66.9	62.9	78.0	90.5	71.8	68.9	68.3	76.1	71.6	86.0	65.1	65.6	871.7
2019	81.5	67.9	77.5	74.7	76.4	75.8	79.8	72.8	91.1	77.8	70.7	88.0	934.0
2020[1]	79.0	60.6	82.9	74.4	71.6	58.7	79.7	70.3	61.6	73.7	69.1	65.7	847.3

[1] Preliminary. *Source: U.S. Geological Survey (USGS)*